The Law of Disability Discrimination Handbook

Fifth Edition

Ruth Colker
Heck-Faust Memorial Chair of Constitutional Law
The Ohio State University College of Law

Adam A. Milani
Associate Professor of Law
Mercer University School of Law

LexisNexis™

ISBN#: 0820564141

Editorial Offices
744 Broad Street, Newark, NJ 07102 (973) 820-2000
201 Mission St., San Francisco, CA 94105-1831 (415) 908-3200
701 East Water Street, Charlottesville, VA 22902-7587 (804) 972-7600

(Pub.3554)

SUMMARY OF CONTENTS

TABLE OF CONTENTS

ADA GENERAL PROVISIONS

ADA TITLE I

ADA TITLE II

PUBLIC SERVICES

PROHIBITION AGAINST DISCRIMINATION AND OTHER GENERALLY APPLICABLE PROVISIONS

42 U.S.C. §

ACTIONS APPLICABLE TO PUBLIC TRANSPORTATION PROVIDED BY PUBLIC ENTITIES CONSIDERED DISCRIMINATORY

Public Transportation Other Than by Aircraft or Certain Rail Operations

ADA TITLE III

ADA TITLE IV

ADA TITLE V

MISCELLANEOUS PROVISIONS

REHABILITATION ACT

GENERAL PROVISIONS

29 C.F.R §

Subpart A—General Provisions

Subpart B—Employment Practices and
Employment Related Training Program Participation

Subpart C—Program Accessibility

FAIR HOUSING

42 U.S.C. §

DAMAGES

INDIVIDUALS WITH DISABILITIES EDUCATION ACT

Part D—National Activities to Improve Education of Children with Disabilities

Subpart 1—State Personnel Development Grants

Subpart 2— Personnel Preparation, Technical Assistance, Model Demonstration Projects and Dissemination of Information

Subpart 3—Supports to Improve Results for Children with Disabilities

Subpart 4—General Provisions

PREFACE

This Handbook includes reference material relevant to interpreting federal law prohibiting discrimination on the basis of disability.

Part I includes reference material relevant to interpreting the Americans with Disabilities Act of 1990 ("the ADA"). The ADA was codified under five Titles. Title I governs employment discrimination. Title II governs the provision of programs and services by state and local government entities. Title III governs the provision of goods and services by public accommodations and commercial facilities. Title IV governs telecommunication relay services for individuals with hearing and/or speech-impairments, as well as closed-captioning of public service announcements. Title V contains various miscellaneous provisions, including special rules for insurance providers.

This Handbook includes the statutory language of each of the five Titles of the ADA. In addition, with respect to ADA Titles I, II, and III, we have included the regulations, interpretive guidance and the technical assistance manuals promulgated by the Equal Employment Opportunity Commission ("EEOC") and the United States Department of Justice ("DOJ"). We have also included EEOC "Guidance" statements on various important topics relating to ADA Title I, such as the definition of "disability" and rules relating to employer-provided health insurance. The reader should note, however, that these sources are frequently updated. Current material can be found at the EEOC's web site at: **www.eeoc.gov**. Although we will try to keep this Handbook up-to-date by publishing future supplements, we encourage the reader to check these web sites for current regulatory developments under the ADA. The included material is the most current material available as of April 15, 2005.

This Handbook also includes reference material relevant to interpreting Section 504 of the Rehabilitation Act of 1973. In addition to the statutory language, we have included the EEOC's employment regulations promulgated under Section 504.

Also included is reference material relevant to interpreting the Fair Housing Act Amendments of 1988 ("FHAA"). In addition to the statutory language, we have included the regulations promulgated by the Department of Housing and Urban Development under the FHAA.

We also include excerpts from the Civil Rights Act of 1991 which pertains to the relief available under ADA Title I and Section 501 of the Rehabilitation Act.

Finally, this Handbook contains the Individuals with Disabilities Education Act, including the amendments made as part of the reauthorization in late 2004.

Space constraints preclude us from including all of the statutory language, rules, and regulations relating to all of the federal laws prohibiting discrimination on the basis of disability. Nonetheless, this Handbook should provide the reader with one of the best tools available for engaging in disability discrimination research.

A disk version of this volume will be made available upon request to individuals with disabilities who are unable to utilize the written version.

Ruth Colker
Adam A. Milani
April 2005

ACKNOWLEDGMENTS

The Second Edition of this Handbook was made possible, in part, by generous research assistance support at both Ohio State University College of Law and Arizona State University College of Law. Ruth Colker would like to thank Michele Whetzel-Newton for her work in helping type the manuscript. Bonnie Poitras Tucker would like to thank Robin Praytor for her assistance in helping us locate the documents collected in this Handbook.

The Fifth Edition of this Handbook reflects modest corrections in some statutes and the publication of the 2004 Amendments to the IDEA. Adam Milani would like to thank Debra Boney for her work in formatting the text of the IDEA. The authors would like to thank LexisNexis for keeping this Handbook current, and we hope this Handbook will become a standard research tool for lawyers, faculty and students who work in the field of disability discrimination.

ACKNOWLEDGMENTS

ADA GENERAL PROVISIONS

ADA GENERAL PROVISIONS

§ 12101. Findings and purposes

(a) Findings

The Congress finds that—

(1) some 43,000,000 Americans have one or more physical or mental disabilities, and this number is increasing as the population as a whole is growing older;

(2) historically, society has tended to isolate and segregate individuals with disabilities, and, despite some improvements, such forms of discrimination against individuals with disabilities continue to be a serious and pervasive social problem;

(3) discrimination against individuals with disabilities persists in such critical areas as employment, housing, public accommodations, education, transportation, communication, recreation, institutionalization, health services, voting, and access to public services;

(4) unlike individuals who have experienced discrimination on the basis of race, color, sex, national origin, religion, or age, individuals who have experienced discrimination on the basis of disability have often had no legal recourse to redress such discrimination;

(5) individuals with disabilities continually encounter various forms of discrimination, including outright intentional exclusion, the discriminatory effects of architectural, transportation, and communication barriers, overprotective rules and policies, failure to make modifications to existing facilities and practices, exclusionary qualification standards and criteria, segregation, and relegation to lesser services, programs, activities, benefits, jobs, or other opportunities;

(6) census data, national polls, and other studies have documented that people with disabilities, as a group, occupy an inferior status in our society, and are severely disadvantaged socially, vocationally, economically, and educationally;

(7) individuals with disabilities are a discrete and insular minority who have been faced with restrictions and limitations, subjected to a history of purposeful unequal treatment, and relegated to a position of political powerlessness in our society, based on characteristics that are beyond the control of such individuals and resulting from stereotypic assumptions not truly indicative of the individual ability of such individuals to participate in, and contribute to, society;

(8) the Nation's proper goals regarding individuals with disabilities are to assure equality of opportunity, full participation, independent living, and economic self-sufficiency for such individuals; and

(9) the continuing existence of unfair and unnecessary discrimination and prejudice denies people with disabilities the opportunity to compete on an equal basis and to pursue those opportunities for which our free society is justifiably famous, and costs the United States billions of dollars in unnecessary expenses resulting from dependency and nonproductivity.

(b) Purpose

It is the purpose of this chapter—

(1) to provide a clear and comprehensive national mandate for the elimination of discrimination against individuals with disabilities;

(2) to provide clear, strong, consistent, enforceable standards addressing discrimination against individuals with disabilities;

(3) to ensure that the Federal Government plays a central role in enforcing the standards established in this chapter on behalf of individuals with disabilities; and

(4) to invoke the sweep of congressional authority, including the power to enforce the fourteenth amendment and to regulate commerce, in order to address the major areas of discrimination faced day-to-day by people with disabilities.

§ 12102. Definitions

As used in this chapter:

(1) Auxiliary aids and services

The term "auxiliary aids and services" includes—

(A) qualified interpreters or other effective methods of making aurally delivered materials available to individuals with hearing impairments;

(B) qualified readers, taped texts, or other effective methods of making visually delivered materials available to individuals with visual impairments;

(C) acquisition or modification of equipment or devices; and

(D) other similar services and actions.

(2) Disability

The term "disability" means, with respect to an individual—

(A) a physical or mental impairment that substantially limits one or more of the major life activities of such individual;

(B) a record of such an impairment; or

(C) being regarded as having such an impairment.

(3) State

The term "State" means each of the several States, the District of Columbia, the Commonwealth of Puerto Rico, Guam, American Samoa, the Virgin Islands, the Trust Territory of the Pacific Islands, and the Commonwealth of the Northern Mariana Islands.

ADA TITLE I EMPLOYMENT

ADA TITLE I EMPLOYMENT

§ 12111. Definitions

As used in this subchapter:

(1) Commission

The term "Commission" means the Equal Employment Opportunity Commission established by section 2000e-4 of this title.

(2) Covered entity

The term "covered entity" means an employer, employment agency, labor organization, or joint labor-management committee.

(3) Direct threat

The term "direct threat" means a significant risk to the health or safety of others that cannot be eliminated by reasonable accommodation.

(4) Employee

The term "employee" means an individual employed by an employer. With respect to employment in a foreign country, such term includes an individual who is a citizen of the United States.

(5) Employer

(A) In general

The term "employer" means a person engaged in an industry affecting commerce who has 15 or more employees for each working day in each of 20 or more calendar weeks in the current or preceding calendar year, and any agent of such person, except that, for two years following the effective date of this subchapter, an employer means a person engaged in an industry affecting commerce who has 25 or more employees for each working day in each of 20 or more calendar weeks in the current or preceding year, and any agent of such person.

(B) Exceptions

The term "employer" does not include—

(i) the United States, a corporation wholly owned by the government of the United States, or an Indian tribe; or

(ii) a bona fide private membership club (other than a labor organization) that is exempt from taxation under section 501(c) of Title 26.

(6) Illegal use of drugs

(A) In general

The term "illegal use of drugs" means the use of drugs, the possession or distribution of which is unlawful under the Controlled Substances Act (21 U.S.C. 812). Such term does not include the use of a drug taken under supervision by a licensed health care professional, or other uses authorized by the Controlled Substances Act [21 U.S.C.A. § 801 et seq.] or other provisions of Federal law.

(B) Drugs

The term "drug" means a controlled substance, as defined in schedules I through V of section 202 of the Controlled Substances Act [21 U.S.C.A. § 812].

(7) Person, etc.

The terms "person", "labor organization", "employment agency", "commerce", and "industry affecting commerce", shall have the same meaning given such terms in section 2000e of this title.

(8) Qualified individual with a disability

The term "qualified individual with a disability" means an individual with a disability who, with or without reasonable accommodation, can perform the essential functions of the employment position that such individual holds or desires. For the purposes of this subchapter, consideration shall be given to the employer's judgment as to what functions of a job are essential, and if an employer has prepared a written description before advertising or interviewing applicants for the job, this description shall be considered evidence of the essential functions of the job.

(9) Reasonable accommodation

The term "reasonable accommodation" may include—

(A) making existing facilities used by employees readily accessible to and usable by individuals with disabilities; and

(B) job restructuring, part-time or modified work schedules, reassignment to a vacant position, acquisition or modification of equipment or devices, appropriate adjustment or modifications of examinations, training materials or policies, the provision of qualified readers or interpreters, and other similar accommodations for individuals with disabilities.

(10) Undue hardship

(A) In general

The term "undue hardship" means an action requiring significant difficulty or expense, when considered in light of the factors set forth in subparagraph (B).

(B) Factors to be considered

In determining whether an accommodation would impose an undue hardship on a covered entity, factors to be considered include—

(i) the nature and cost of the accommodation needed under this chapter;

(ii) the overall financial resources of the facility or facilities involved in the provision of the reasonable accommodation; the number of persons employed at such facility; the effect on expenses and resources, or the impact otherwise of such accommodation upon the operation of the facility;

(iii) the overall financial resources of the covered entity; the overall size of the business of a covered entity with respect to the number of its employees; the number, type, and location of its facilities; and

(iv) the type of operation or operations of the covered entity, including the composition, structure, and functions of the work force of such entity; the geographic separateness, administrative, or fiscal relationship of the facility or facilities in question to the covered entity.

§ 12112. Discrimination

(a) General rule

No covered entity shall discriminate against a qualified individual with a disability because of the disability of such individual in regard to job application procedures, the hiring, advancement, or discharge of employees, employee compensation, job training, and other terms, conditions, and privileges of employment.

(b) Construction

As used in subsection (a) of this section, the term "discriminate" includes—

(1) limiting, segregating, or classifying a job applicant or employee in a way that adversely affects the opportunities or status of such applicant or employee because of the disability of such applicant or employee;

(2) participating in a contractual or other arrangement or relationship that has the effect of subjecting a covered entity's qualified applicant or employee with a disability to the discrimination prohibited by this subchapter (such relationship includes a relationship with an employment or referral agency, labor union, an organization providing fringe benefits to an employee of the covered entity, or an organization providing training and apprenticeship programs);

(3) utilizing standards, criteria, or methods of administration—

(A) that have the effect of discrimination on the basis of disability; or

(B) that perpetuate the discrimination of others who are subject to common administrative control;

(4) excluding or otherwise denying equal jobs or benefits to a qualified individual because of the known disability of an individual with whom the qualified individual is known to have a relationship or association;

(5) (A) not making reasonable accommodations to the known physical or mental limitations of an otherwise qualified individual with a disability who is an applicant or employee, unless such covered entity can demonstrate that the accommodation would impose an undue hardship on the operation of the business of such covered entity; or

(B) denying employment opportunities to a job applicant or employee who is an otherwise qualified individual with a disability, if such denial is based on the need of such covered entity to make reasonable accommodation to the physical or mental impairments of the employee or applicant;

(6) using qualification standards, employment tests or other selection criteria that screen out or tend to screen out an individual with a disability or a class of individuals with disabilities unless the standard, test or other selection criteria, as used by the covered entity, is shown to be job-related for the position in question and is consistent with business necessity; and

(7) failing to select and administer tests concerning employment in the most effective manner to ensure that, when such test is administered to a job applicant or employee who has a disability that impairs sensory, manual, or speaking skills, such test results accurately reflect the skills, aptitude, or whatever other factor of such applicant or employee that such test purports to measure, rather than reflecting the impaired sensory, manual, or speaking skills of such employee or applicant (except where such skills are the factors that the test purports to measure).

(c) Covered entities in foreign countries

(1) In general

It shall not be unlawful under this section for a covered entity to take any action that constitutes discrimination under this section with respect to an employee in a workplace in a foreign country if compliance with this section would cause such covered entity to violate the law of the foreign country in which such workplace is located.

(2) Control of corporation

(A) Presumption

If an employer controls a corporation whose place of incorporation is a foreign country, any practice that constitutes discrimination under this section and is engaged in by such corporation shall be presumed to be engaged in by such employer.

(B) Exception

This section shall not apply with respect to the foreign operations of an employer that is a foreign person not controlled by an American employer.

(C) Determination

For purposes of this paragraph, the determination of whether an employer controls a corporation shall be based on—

(i) the interrelation of operations;

(ii) the common management;

(iii) the centralized control of labor relations; and

(iv) the common ownership or financial control, of the employer and the corporation.

(d) Medical examinations and inquiries

(1) In general

The prohibition against discrimination as referred to in subsection (a) of this section shall include medical examinations and inquiries.

(2) Pre-employment

(A) Prohibited examination or inquiry

Except as provided in paragraph (3), a covered entity shall not conduct a medical examination or make inquiries of a job applicant as to whether such applicant is an individual with a disability or as to the nature or severity of such disability.

(B) Acceptable inquiry

A covered entity may make pre-employment inquiries into the ability of an applicant to perform job-related functions.

(3) Employment entrance examination

A covered entity may require a medical examination after an offer of employment has been made to a job applicant and prior to the commencement of the employment duties of such applicant, and may condition an offer of employment on the results of such examination, if—

(A) all entering employees are subjected to such an examination regardless of disability;

(B) information obtained regarding the medical condition or history of the applicant is collected and maintained on separate forms and in separate medical files and is treated as a confidential medical record, except that—

(i) supervisors and managers may be informed regarding necessary restrictions on the work or duties of the employee and necessary accommodations;

(ii) first aid and safety personnel may be informed, when appropriate, if the disability might require emergency treatment; and

(iii) government officials investigating compliance with this chapter shall be provided relevant information on request; and

(C) the results of such examination are used only in accordance with this subchapter.

(4) Examination and inquiry

(A) Prohibited examinations and inquiries

A covered entity shall not require a medical examination and shall not make inquiries of an employee as to whether such employee is an individual with a disability or as to the nature or severity of the disability, unless such examination or inquiry is shown to be job-related and consistent with business necessity.

(B) Acceptable examinations and inquiries

A covered entity may conduct voluntary medical examinations, including voluntary medical histories, which are part of an employee health program available to employees at that work site. A covered entity may make inquiries into the ability of an employee to perform job-related functions.

(C) Requirement

Information obtained under subparagraph (B) regarding the medical condition or history of any employee are subject to the requirements of subparagraphs (B) and (C) of paragraph (3).

§ 12113. Defenses

(a) In general

It may be a defense to a charge of discrimination under this chapter that an alleged application of qualification standards, tests, or selection criteria that screen out or tend to screen out or otherwise deny a job or benefit to an individual with a disability has been shown to be job-related and consistent with business necessity, and such performance cannot be accomplished by reasonable accommodation, as required under this subchapter.

(b) Qualification standards

The term "qualification standards" may include a requirement that an individual shall not pose a direct threat to the health or safety of other individuals in the workplace.

(c) Religious entities

(1) In general

This subchapter shall not prohibit a religious corporation, association, educational institution, or society from giving preference in employment to individuals of a particular religion to perform work connected with the carrying on by such corporation, association, educational institution, or society of its activities.

(2) Religious tenets requirement

Under this subchapter, a religious organization may require that all applicants and employees conform to the religious tenets of such organization.

(d) List of infectious and communicable diseases

(1) In general

The Secretary of Health and Human Services, not later than 6 months after July 26, 1990, shall—

(A) review all infectious and communicable diseases which may be transmitted through handling the food supply;

(B) publish a list of infectious and communicable diseases which are transmitted through handling the food supply;

(C) publish the methods by which such diseases are transmitted; and

(D) widely disseminate such information regarding the list of diseases and their modes of transmissibility to the general public.

Such list shall be updated annually.

(2) Applications

In any case in which an individual has an infectious or communicable disease that is transmitted to others through the handling of food, that is included on the list developed by the Secretary of Health and Human Services under paragraph (1), and which cannot be eliminated by reasonable accommodation, a covered entity may refuse to assign or continue to assign such individual to a job involving food handling.

(3) Construction

Nothing in this chapter shall be construed to preempt, modify, or amend any State, county, or local law, ordinance, or regulation applicable to food handling which is designed to protect the public health from individuals who pose a significant risk to the health or safety of others, which cannot be eliminated by reasonable accommodation, pursuant to the list of infectious or communicable diseases and the modes of transmissibility published by the Secretary of Health and Human Services.

§ 12114. Illegal use of drugs and alcohol

(a) Qualified individual with a disability

For purposes of this subchapter, the term "qualified individual with a disability" shall not include any employee or applicant who is currently engaging in the illegal use of drugs, when the covered entity acts on the basis of such use.

(b) Rules of construction

Nothing in subsection (a) of this section shall be construed to exclude as a qualified individual with a disability an individual who—

(1) has successfully completed a supervised drug rehabilitation program and is no longer engaging in the illegal use of drugs, or has otherwise been rehabilitated successfully and is no longer engaging in such use;

(2) is participating in a supervised rehabilitation program and is no longer engaging in such use; or

(3) is erroneously regarded as engaging in such use, but is not engaging in such use;

except that it shall not be a violation of this chapter for a covered entity to adopt or administer reasonable policies or procedures, including but not limited to drug testing, designed to ensure that an individual described in paragraph (1) or (2) is no longer engaging in the illegal use of drugs.

(c) Authority of covered entity

A covered entity—

(1) may prohibit the illegal use of drugs and the use of alcohol at the workplace by all employees;

(2) may require that employees shall not be under the influence of alcohol or be engaging in the illegal use of drugs at the workplace;

(3) may require that employees behave in conformance with the requirements established under the Drug-Free Workplace Act of 1988 (41 U.S.C. 701 et seq.);

(4) may hold an employee who engages in the illegal use of drugs or who is an alcoholic to the same qualification standards for employment or job performance and behavior that such entity holds other employees, even if any unsatisfactory performance or behavior is related to the drug use or alcoholism of such employee; and

(5) may, with respect to Federal regulations regarding alcohol and the illegal use of drugs, require that—

(A) employees comply with the standards established in such regulations of the Department of Defense, if the employees of the covered entity are employed in an industry subject to such regulations, including complying with regulations (if any) that apply to employment in sensitive positions in such an industry, in the case of employees of the covered entity who are employed in such positions (as defined in the regulations of the Department of Defense);

(B) employees comply with the standards established in such regulations of the Nuclear Regulatory Commission, if the employees of the covered entity are employed in an industry subject to such regulations, including complying with regulations (if any) that apply to employment in sensitive positions in such an industry, in the case of employees of the covered entity who are employed in such positions (as defined in the regulations of the Nuclear Regulatory Commission); and

(C) employees comply with the standards established in such regulations of the Department of Transportation, if the employees of the covered entity are employed in a transportation industry subject to such regulations, including complying with such regulations (if any) that apply to employment in sensitive positions in such an industry, in the case of employees of the covered entity who are employed in such positions (as defined in the regulations of the Department of Transportation).

(d) Drug testing

(1) In general

For purposes of this subchapter, a test to determine the illegal use of drugs shall not be considered a medical examination.

(2) Construction

Nothing in this subchapter shall be construed to encourage, prohibit, or authorize the conducting of drug testing for the illegal use of drugs by job applicants or employees or making employment decisions based on such test results.

(e) Transportation employees

Nothing in this subchapter shall be construed to encourage, prohibit, restrict, or authorize the otherwise lawful exercise by entities subject to the jurisdiction of the Department of Transportation of authority to—

(1) test employees of such entities in, and applicants for, positions involving safety-sensitive duties for the illegal use of drugs and for on-duty impairment by alcohol; and

(2) remove such persons who test positive for illegal use of drugs and on-duty impairment by alcohol pursuant to paragraph (1) from safety-sensitive duties in implementing subsection (c) of this section.

§ 12115. Posting notices

Every employer, employment agency, labor organization, or joint labor-management committee covered under this title shall post notices in an accessible format to applicants, employees, and members describing the applicable provisions of this Act, in the manner prescribed by section 711 of the Civil Rights Act of 1964 (42 U.S.C. 2000e-10).

§ 12116. Regulations

Not later than 1 year after the date of enactment of this Act [enacted July 26, 1990], the Commission shall issue regulations in an accessible format to carry out this title in accordance with subchapter II of chapter 5 of title 5, United States Code [5 USCS §§ 551 et seq.].

§ 12117. Enforcement

(a) Powers, remedies, and procedures

The powers, remedies, and procedures set forth in sections 2000e-4, 2000e-5, 2000e-6, 2000e-8, and 2000e-9 of this title shall be the powers, remedies, and procedures this subchapter provides to the Commission, to the Attorney General, or to any person alleging discrimination on the basis of disability in violation of any provision of this chapter, or regulations promulgated under section 12116 of this title, concerning employment.

(b) Coordination

The agencies with enforcement authority for actions which allege employment discrimination under this subchapter and under the Rehabilitation Act of 1973 [29 U.S.C.A. § 701 et seq.] shall develop procedures to ensure that administrative complaints filed under this subchapter and under the Rehabilitation Act of 1973 [29 U.S.C.A. § 701 et seq.] are dealt with in a manner that avoids duplication of effort and prevents imposition of inconsistent or conflicting standards for the same requirements under this subchapter and the Rehabilitation Act of 1973 [29 U.S.C.A. § 701 et seq.]. The Commission, the Attorney General, and the Office of Federal Contract Compliance Programs shall establish such coordinating mechanisms (similar to provisions contained in the joint regulations promulgated by the Commission and the Attorney General at part 42 of title 28 and part 1691 of title 29, Code of Federal Regulations, and the Memorandum of Understanding between the Commission and the Office of Federal Contract Compliance Programs dated January 16, 1981 (46 Fed. Reg. 7435, January 23, 1981)) in regulations implementing this subchapter and Rehabilitation Act of 1973 [29 U.S.C.A. § 701 et seq.] not later than 18 months after July 26, 1990.

ADA TITLE I
EEOC REGULATIONS

ADA TITLE I
EEOC REGULATIONS

§ 1630.1 Purpose, applicability, and construction.

(a) Purpose. The purpose of this part is to implement title I of the Americans with Disabilities Act (42 U.S.C. 12101, et seq.) (ADA), requiring equal employment opportunities for qualified individuals with disabilities, and sections 3(2), 3(3), 501, 503, 506(e), 508, 510, and 511 of the ADA as those sections pertain to the employment of qualified individuals with disabilities.

(b) Applicability. This part applies to "covered entities" as defined at § 1630.2(b).

(c) Construction—

(1) In general. Except as otherwise provided in this part, this part does not apply a lesser standard than the standards applied under title V of the Rehabilitation Act of 1973 (29 U.S.C. 790-794a), or the regulations issued by Federal agencies pursuant to that title.

(2) Relationship to other laws. This part does not invalidate or limit the remedies, rights, and procedures of any Federal law or law of any State or political subdivision of any State or jurisdiction that provides greater or equal protection for the rights of individuals with disabilities than are afforded by this part.

§ 1630.2 Definitions.

(a) Commission means the Equal Employment Opportunity Commission established by section 705 of the Civil Rights Act of 1964 (42 U.S.C. 2000e-4).

(b) Covered Entity means an employer, employment agency, labor organization, or joint labor management committee.

(c) Person, labor organization, employment agency, commerce and industry affecting commerce shall have the same meaning given those terms in section 701 of the Civil Rights Act of 1964 (42 U.S.C. 2000e).

(d) State means each of the several States, the District of Columbia, the Commonwealth of Puerto Rico, Guam, American Samoa, the Virgin Islands, the Trust Territory of the Pacific Islands, and the Commonwealth of the Northern Mariana Islands.

(e) Employer—

(1) In general. The term employer means a person engaged in an industry affecting commerce who has 15 or more employees for each working day in each of 20 or more calendar weeks in the current or preceding calendar year, and any agent of such person, except that, from July 26, 1992 through July 25, 1994, an employer means a person engaged in an industry affecting commerce who has 25 or more employees for each working day in each of 20 or more calendar weeks in the current or preceding year and any agent of such person.

(2) Exceptions. The term employer does not include—

(i) The United States, a corporation wholly owned by the government of the United States, or an Indian tribe; or

(ii) A bona fide private membership club (other than a labor organization) that is exempt from taxation under section 501(c) of the Internal Revenue Code of 1986.

(f) Employee means an individual employed by an employer.

(g) Disability means, with respect to an individual—

(1) A physical or mental impairment that substantially limits one or more of the major life activities of such individual;

(2) A record of such an impairment; or

(3) being regarded as having such an impairment.

(See § 1630.3 for exceptions to this definition).

(h) Physical or mental impairment means:

(1) Any physiological disorder, or condition, cosmetic disfigurement, or anatomical loss affecting one or more of the following body systems: neurological, musculoskeletal, special sense organs, respiratory (including speech organs), cardiovascular, reproductive, digestive, genito-urinary, hemic and lymphatic, skin, and endocrine; or

(2) Any mental or psychological disorder, such as mental retardation, organic brain syndrome, emotional or mental illness, and specific learning disabilities.

(i) Major Life Activities means functions such as caring for oneself, performing manual tasks, walking, seeing, hearing, speaking, breathing, learning, and working.

(j) Substantially limits—

(1) The term substantially limits means:

(i) Unable to perform a major life activity that the average person in the general population can perform; or

(ii) Significantly restricted as to the condition, manner or duration under which an individual can perform a particular major life activity as compared to the condition, manner, or duration under which the average person in the general population can perform that same major life activity.

(2) The following factors should be considered in determining whether an individual is substantially limited in a major life activity:

(i) The nature and severity of the impairment;

(ii) The duration or expected duration of the impairment; and

(iii) The permanent or long term impact, or the expected permanent or long term impact of or resulting from the impairment.

(3) With respect to the major life activity of working—

(i) The term substantially limits means significantly restricted in the ability to perform either a class of jobs or a broad range of jobs in various classes as compared to the average person having comparable training, skills and abilities. The inability to perform a single, particular job does not constitute a substantial limitation in the major life activity of working.

(ii) In addition to the factors listed in paragraph (j)(2) of this section, the following factors may be considered in determining whether an individual is substantially limited in the major life activity of "working":

(A) The geographical area to which the individual has reasonable access;

(B) The job from which the individual has been disqualified because of an impairment, and the number and types of jobs utilizing similar training, knowledge, skills or abilities, within that geographical area, from which the individual is also disqualified because of the impairment (class of jobs); and/or

(C) The job from which the individual has been disqualified because of an impairment, and the number and types of other jobs not utilizing similar training, knowledge, skills or abilities, within that geographical area, from which the individual is also disqualified because of the impairment (broad range of jobs in various classes).

(k) Has a record of such impairment means has a history of, or has been misclassified as having, a mental or physical impairment that substantially limits one or more major life activities.

(l) Is regarded as having such an impairment means:

(1) Has a physical or mental impairment that does not substantially limit major life activities but is treated by a covered entity as constituting such limitation;

(2) Has a physical or mental impairment that substantially limits major life activities only as a result of the attitudes of others toward such impairment; or

(3) Has none of the impairments defined in paragraphs (h) (1) or (2) of this section but is treated by a covered entity as having a substantially limiting impairment.

(m) Qualified individual with a disability means an individual with a disability who satisfies the requisite skill, experience, education and other job-related requirements of the employment position such individual holds or desires, and who, with or without reasonable accommodation, can perform the essential functions of such position. (See § 1630.3 for exceptions to this definition).

(n) Essential functions.—

(1) In general. The term essential functions means the fundamental job duties of the employment position the individual with a disability holds or desires. The term "essential functions" does not include the marginal functions of the position.

(2) A job function may be considered essential for any of several reasons, including but not limited to the following:

(i) The function may be essential because the reason the position exists is to perform that function;

(ii) The function may be essential because of the limited number of employees available among whom the performance of that job function can be distributed; and/or

(iii) The function may be highly specialized so that the incumbent in the position is hired for his or her expertise or ability to perform the particular function.

(3) Evidence of whether a particular function is essential includes, but is not limited to:

(i) The employer's judgment as to which functions are essential;

(ii) Written job descriptions prepared before advertising or interviewing applicants for the job;

(iii) The amount of time spent on the job performing the function;

(iv) The consequences of not requiring the incumbent to perform the function;

(v) The terms of a collective bargaining agreement;

(vi) The work experience of past incumbents in the job; and/or

(vii) The current work experience of incumbents in similar jobs.

(o) Reasonable accommodation.

(1) The term reasonable accommodation means:

(i) Modifications or adjustments to a job application process that enable a qualified applicant with a disability to be considered for the position such qualified applicant desires; or

(ii) Modifications or adjustments to the work environment, or to the manner or circumstances under which the position held or desired is customarily performed, that enable a qualified individual with a disability to perform the essential functions of that position; or

(iii) Modifications or adjustments that enable a covered entity's employee with a disability to enjoy equal benefits and privileges of employment as are enjoyed by its other similarly situated employees without disabilities.

(2) Reasonable accommodation may include but is not limited to:

(i) Making existing facilities used by employees readily accessible to and usable by individuals with disabilities; and

(ii) Job restructuring; part-time or modified work schedules; reassignment to a vacant position; acquisition or modifications of equipment or devices; appropriate adjustment or modifications of examinations, training materials, or policies; the provision of qualified readers or interpreters; and other similar accommodations for individuals with disabilities.

(3) To determine the appropriate reasonable accommodation it may be necessary for the covered entity to initiate an informal, interactive process with the qualified individual with a disability in need of the accommodation. This process should identify the precise limitations resulting from the disability and potential reasonable accommodations that could overcome those limitations.

(p) Undue hardship—

(1) In general. Undue hardship means, with respect to the provision of an accommodation, significant difficulty or expense incurred by a covered entity, when considered in light of the factors set forth in paragraph (p)(2) of this section.

(2) Factors to be considered. In determining whether an accommodation would impose an undue hardship on a covered entity, factors to be considered include:

(i) The nature and net cost of the accommodation needed under this part, taking into consideration the availability of tax credits and deductions, and/or outside funding;

(ii) The overall financial resources of the facility or facilities involved in the provision of the reasonable accommodation, the number of persons employed at such facility, and the effect on expenses and resources;

(iii) The overall financial resources of the covered entity, the overall size of the business of the covered entity with respect to the number of its employees, and the number, type and location of its facilities;

(iv) The type of operation or operations of the covered entity, including the composition, structure and functions of the work force of such entity, and the geographic separateness and administrative or fiscal relationship of the facility or facilities in question to the covered entity; and

(v) The impact of the accommodation upon the operation of the facility, including the impact on the ability of other employees to perform their duties and the impact on the facility's ability to conduct business.

(q) Qualification standards means the personal and professional attributes including the skill, experience, education, physical, medical, safety and other requirements established by a covered entity as requirements which an individual must meet in order to be eligible for the position held or desired.

(r) Direct Threat means a significant risk of substantial harm to the health or safety of the individual or others that cannot be eliminated or reduced by reasonable accommodation. The determination that an individual poses a "direct threat" shall be based on an individualized assessment of the individual's present ability to safely perform the essential functions of the job. This assessment shall be based on a reasonable medical judgment that relies on the most current medical knowledge and/or on the best available objective evidence. In determining whether an individual would pose a direct threat, the factors to be considered include:

(1) The duration of the risk;

(2) The nature and severity of the potential harm;

(3) The likelihood that the potential harm will occur; and

(4) The imminence of the potential harm.

§ 1630.3 Exceptions to the definitions of "Disability" and "Qualified Individual with a Disability."

(a) The terms disability and qualified individual with a disability do not include individuals currently engaging in the illegal use of drugs, when the covered entity acts on the basis of such use.

(1) Drug means a controlled substance, as defined in schedules I through V of Section 202 of the Controlled Substances Act (21 U.S.C. 812)

(2) Illegal use of drugs means the use of drugs the possession or distribution of which is unlawful under the Controlled Substances Act, as periodically updated by the Food and Drug Administration. This term does not include the use of a drug taken under the supervision of a licensed health care professional, or other uses authorized by the Controlled Substances Act or other provisions of Federal law.

(b) However, the terms disability and qualified individual with a disability may not exclude an individual who:

(1) Has successfully completed a supervised drug rehabilitation program and is no longer engaging in the illegal use of drugs, or has otherwise been rehabilitated successfully and is no longer engaging in the illegal use of drugs; or

(2) Is participating in a supervised rehabilitation program and is no longer engaging in such use; or

(3) Is erroneously regarded as engaging in such use, but is not engaging in such use.

(c) It shall not be a violation of this part for a covered entity to adopt or administer reasonable policies or procedures, including but not limited to drug testing, designed to ensure that an individual described in paragraph (b) (1) or (2) of this section is no longer engaging in the illegal use of drugs. (See § 1630.16(c) Drug testing).

(d) Disability does not include:

(1) Transvestism, transsexualism, pedophilia, exhibitionism, voyeurism, gender identity disorders not resulting from physical impairments, or other sexual behavior disorders;

(2) Compulsive gambling, kleptomania, or pyromania; or

(3) Psychoactive substance use disorders resulting from current illegal use of drugs.

(e) Homosexuality and bisexuality are not impairments and so are not disabilities as defined in this part.

§ 1630.4 Discrimination prohibited.

It is unlawful for a covered entity to discriminate on the basis of disability against a qualified individual with a disability in regard to:

(a) Recruitment, advertising, and job application procedures;

(b) Hiring, upgrading, promotion, award of tenure, demotion, transfer, layoff, termination, right of return from layoff, and rehiring;

(c) Rates of pay or any other form of compensation and changes in compensation;

(d) Job assignments, job classifications, organizational structures, position descriptions, lines of progression, and seniority lists;

(e) Leaves of absence, sick leave, or any other leave;

(f) Fringe benefits available by virtue of employment, whether or not administered by the covered entity;

(g) Selection and financial support for training, including: apprenticeships, professional meetings, conferences and other related activities, and selection for leaves of absence to pursue training;

(h) Activities sponsored by a covered entity including social and recreational programs; and

(i) Any other term, condition, or privilege of employment.

The term discrimination includes, but is not limited to, the acts described in §§ 1630.5 through 1630.13 of this part.

§ 1630.5 Limiting segregating, and classifying.

It is unlawful for a covered entity to limit, segregate, or classify a job applicant or employee in a way that adversely affects his or her employment opportunities or status on the basis of disability.

§ 1630.6 Contractual or other arrangements.

(a) In general. It is unlawful for a covered entity to participate in a contractual or other arrangement or relationship that has the effect of subjecting the covered entity's own qualified applicant or employee with a disability to the discrimination prohibited by this part.

(b) Contractual or other arrangement defined. The

phrase contractual or other arrangement or relationship includes, but is not limited to, a relationship with an employment or referral agency; labor union, including collective bargaining agreements; an organization providing fringe benefits to an employee of the covered entity; or an organization providing training and apprenticeship programs.

(c) Application. This section applies to a covered entity, with respect to its own applicants or employees, whether the entity offered the contract or initiated the relationship, or whether the entity accepted the contract or acceded to the relationship. A covered entity is not liable for the actions of the other party or parties to the contract which only affect that other party's employees or applicants.

§ 1630.7 Standards, criteria, or methods of administration.

It is unlawful for a covered entity to use standards, criteria, or methods of administration, which are not job-related and consistent with business necessity, and:

(a) That have the effect of discriminating on the basis of disability; or

(b) That perpetuate the discrimination of others who are subject to common administrative control.

§ 1630.8 Relationship or association with an individual with a disability.

It is unlawful for a covered entity to exclude or deny equal jobs or benefits to, or otherwise discriminate against, a qualified individual because of the known disability of an individual with whom the qualified individual is known to have a family, business, social or other relationship or association.

§ 1630.9 Not making reasonable accommodation.

(a) It is unlawful for a covered entity not to make reasonable accommodation to the known physical or mental limitations of an otherwise qualified applicant or employee with a disability, unless such covered entity can demonstrate that the accommodation would impose an undue hardship on the operation of its business.

(b) It is unlawful for a covered entity to deny employment opportunities to an otherwise qualified job applicant or employee with a disability based on the need of such covered entity to make reasonable accommodation to such individual's physical or mental impairments.

(c) A covered entity shall not be excused from the requirements of this part because of any failure to receive technical assistance authorized by section 506 of the ADA, including any failure in the development or dissemination of any technical assistance manual authorized by that Act.

(d) A qualified individual with a disability is not required to accept an accommodation, aid, service, opportunity or benefit which such qualified individual chooses not to accept. However, if such individual rejects a reasonable accommodation, aid, service, opportunity or benefit that is necessary to enable the individual to perform the essential functions of the position held or desired, and cannot, as a result of that rejection, perform the essential functions of the position, the individual will not be considered a qualified individual with a disability.

§ 1630.10 Qualification standards, tests, and other selection criteria.

It is unlawful for a covered entity to use qualification standards, employment tests or other selection criteria that screen out or tend to screen out an individual with a disability or a class of individuals with disabilities, on the basis of disability, unless the standard, test or other selection criteria, as used by the covered entity, is shown to be job-related for the position in question and is consistent with business necessity.

§ 1630.11 Administration of tests.

It is unlawful for a covered entity to fail to select and administer tests concerning employment in the most effective manner to ensure that, when a test is administered to a job applicant or employee who has a disability that impairs sensory, manual or speaking skills, the test results accurately reflect the skills, aptitude, or whatever other factor of the applicant or employee that the test purports to measure, rather than reflecting the impaired sensory, manual, or speaking skills of such employee or applicant (except where such skills are the factors that the test purports to measure).

§ 1630.12 Retaliation and coercion.

(a) Retaliation. It is unlawful to discriminate against any individual because that individual has opposed any act or practice made unlawful by this part or because that individual made a charge, testified, assisted, or participated in any manner in an investigation, proceeding, or hearing to enforce any provision contained in this part.

(b) Coercion, interference or intimidation. It is unlawful to coerce, intimidate, threaten, harass or interfere with any individual in the exercise or enjoyment of, or because that individual aided or encouraged any other individual in the exercise of, any right granted or protected by this part.

§ 1630.13 Prohibited medical examinations and inquiries.

(a) Pre-employment examination or inquiry. Except as permitted by § 1630.14, it is unlawful for a covered entity to conduct a medical examination of an applicant or to make inquiries as to whether an applicant is an individual with a disability or as to the nature or severity of such disability.

(b) Examination or inquiry of employees. Except as permitted by § 1630.14, it is unlawful for a covered entity to require a medical examination of an employee or to make inquiries as to whether an employee is an individual with a disability or as to the nature or severity of such disability.

§ 1630.14 Medical examinations and inquiries specifically permitted.

(a) Acceptable pre-employment inquiry. A covered entity may make pre-employment inquiries into the ability of an applicant to perform job-related functions, and/or may ask an applicant to describe or to demonstrate how, with or without reasonable accommodation, the applicant will be able to perform job-related functions.

(b) Employment entrance examination. A covered entity may require a medical examination (and/or inquiry) after making an offer of employment to a job applicant and before the applicant begins his or her employment duties, and may condition an offer of employment on the results of such examination (and/or inquiry), if all entering employees in the same job category are subjected to such an examination (and/or inquiry) regardless of disability.

(1) Information obtained under paragraph (b) of this section regarding the medical condition or history of the applicant shall be collected and maintained on separate forms and in separate medical files and be treated as a confidential medical record, except that:

(i) Supervisors and managers may be informed regarding necessary restrictions on the work or duties of the employee and necessary accommodations;

(ii) First aid and safety personnel may be informed, when appropriate, if the disability might require emergency treatment; and

(iii) Government officials investigating compliance with this part shall be provided relevant information on request.

(2) The results of such examination shall not be used for any purpose inconsistent with this part.

(3) Medical examinations conducted in accordance with this section do not have to be job-related and consistent with business necessity. However, if certain criteria are used to screen out an employee or employees with disabilities as a result of such an examination or inquiry, the exclusionary criteria must be job-related and consistent with business necessity, and performance of the essential job functions cannot be accomplished with reasonable accommodation as required in this part. (See § 1630.15(b) Defenses to charges of discriminatory application of selection criteria.)

(c) Examination of employees. A covered entity may require a medical examination (and/or inquiry) of an employee that is job-related and consistent with business necessity. A covered entity may make inquiries into the ability of an employee to perform job-related functions.

(1) Information obtained under paragraph (c) of this section regarding the medical condition or history of any employee shall be collected and maintained on separate forms and in separate medical files and be treated as a confidential medical record, except that:

(i) Supervisors and managers may be informed regarding necessary restrictions on the work or duties of the employee and necessary accommodations;

(ii) First aid and safety personnel may be informed, when appropriate, if the disability might require emergency treatment; and

(iii) Government officials investigating compliance with this part shall be provided relevant information on request.

(2) Information obtained under paragraph (c) of this section regarding the medical condition or history of any employee shall not be used for any purpose inconsistent with this part.

(d) Other acceptable examinations and inquiries. A covered entity may conduct voluntary medical examinations and activities, including voluntary medical histories, which are part of an employee health program available to employees at the work site.

(1) Information obtained under paragraph (d) of this section regarding the medical condition or history of any employee shall be collected and maintained on separate forms and in separate medical files and be treated as a confidential medical record, except that:

(i) Supervisors and managers may be informed regarding necessary restrictions on the work or duties of the employee and necessary accommodations;

(ii) First aid and safety personnel may be informed, when appropriate, if the disability might require emergency treatment; and

(iii) Government officials investigating compliance with this part shall be provided relevant information on request.

(2) Information obtained under paragraph (d) of this section regarding the medical condition or history of any employee shall not be used for any purpose inconsistent with this part.

§ 1630.15 Defenses.

Defenses to an allegation of discrimination under this part may include, but are not limited to, the following:

(a) Disparate treatment charges. It may be a defense to a charge of disparate treatment brought under §§ 1630.4 through 1630.8 and 1630.11 through 1630.12 that the challenged action is justified by a legitimate, nondiscriminatory reason.

(b) Charges of discriminatory application of selection criteria—

(1) In general. It may be a defense to a charge of discrimination, as described in § 1630.10, that an alleged application of qualification standards, tests, or selection criteria that screens out or tends to screen out or otherwise denies a job or benefit to an individual with a disability has been shown to be job-related and consistent with business necessity, and such performance cannot be accomplished with reasonable accommodation, as required in this part.

(2) Direct threat as a qualification standard. The term "qualification standard" may include a requirement that an individual shall not pose a direct threat to the health or safety of the individual or others in the workplace. (See § 1630.2(r) defining direct threat.)

(c) Other disparate impact charges. It may be a defense to a charge of discrimination brought under this part that a uniformly applied standard, criterion, or policy has a disparate impact on an individual with a disability or a class of individuals with disabilities that the challenged standard, criterion or policy has been shown to be job-related and consistent with business necessity, and such performance cannot be accomplished with reasonable accommodation, as required in this part.

(d) Charges of not making reasonable accommodation. It may be a defense to a charge of discrimination, as described in § 1630.9, that a requested or necessary accommodation would impose an undue hardship on the operation of the covered entity's business.

(e) Conflict with other federal laws. It may be a defense to a charge of discrimination under this part that a challenged action is required or necessitated by another Federal law or regulation, or that another Federal law or regulation prohibits an action (including the provision of a particular reasonable accommodation) that would otherwise be required by this part.

(f) Additional defenses. It may be a defense to a charge of discrimination under this part that the alleged discriminatory action is specifically permitted by §§ 1630.14 or 1630.16.

§ 1630.16 Specific activities permitted.

(a) Religious entities. A religious corporation, association, educational institution, or society is permitted to give preference in employment to individuals of a particular religion to perform work connected with the carrying on by that corporation, association, educational institution, or society of its activities. A religious entity may require that all applicants and employees conform to the religious tenets of such organization. However, a religious entity may not discriminate against a qualified individual, who satisfies the permitted religious criteria, because of his or her disability.

(b) Regulation of alcohol and drugs. A covered entity:

(1) May prohibit the illegal use of drugs and the use of alcohol at the workplace by all employees;

(2) May require that employees not be under the influence of alcohol or be engaging in the illegal use of drugs at the workplace;

(3) May require that all employees behave in conformance with the requirements established under the Drug-Free Workplace Act of 1988 (41 U.S.C. 701 et seq.);

(4) May hold an employee who engages in the illegal use of drugs or who is an alcoholic to the same qualification standards for employment or job performance and behavior to which the entity holds its other employees, even if any unsatisfactory performance or behavior is related to the employee's drug use or alcoholism;

(5) May require that its employees employed in an industry subject to such regulations comply with the standards established in the regulations (if any) of the Departments of Defense and Transportation, and of the Nuclear Regulatory Commission, regarding alcohol and the illegal use of drugs; and

(6) May require that employees employed in sensitive positions comply with the regulations (if any) of the Departments of Defense and Transportation and of the Nuclear Regulatory Commission that apply to employment in sensitive positions subject to such regulations.

(c) Drug testing—

(1) General policy. For purposes of this part, a test to determine the illegal use of drugs is not consid-

ered a medical examination. Thus, the administration of such drug tests by a covered entity to its job applicants or employees is not a violation of § 1630.13 of this part. However, this part does not encourage, prohibit, or authorize a covered entity to conduct drug tests of job applicants or employees to determine the illegal use of drugs or to make employment decisions based on such test results.

(2) Transportation Employees. This part does not encourage, prohibit, or authorize the otherwise lawful exercise by entities subject to the jurisdiction of the Department of Transportation of authority to:

(i) Test employees of entities in, and applicants for, positions involving safety sensitive duties for the illegal use of drugs or for on-duty impairment by alcohol; and

(ii) Remove from safety-sensitive positions persons who test positive for illegal use of drugs or on-duty impairment by alcohol pursuant to paragraph (c)(2)(i) of this section.

(3) Confidentiality. Any information regarding the medical condition or history of any employee or applicant obtained from a test to determine the illegal use of drugs, except information regarding the illegal use of drugs, is subject to the requirements of § 1630.14(b) (2) and (3) of this part.

(d) Regulation of smoking. A covered entity may prohibit or impose restrictions on smoking in places of employment. Such restrictions do not violate any provision of this part.

(e) Infectious and communicable diseases; food handling jobs—

(1) In general. Under title I of the ADA, section 103(d)(1), the Secretary of Health and Human Services is to prepare a list, to be updated annually, of infectious and communicable diseases which are transmitted through the handling of food. (Copies may be obtained from Center for Infectious Diseases, Centers for Disease Control, 1600 Clifton Road, NE., Mailstop C09, Atlanta, GA 30333.) If an individual with a disability is disabled by one of the infectious or communicable diseases included on this list, and if the risk of transmitting the disease associated with the handling of food cannot be eliminated by reasonable accommodation, a covered entity may refuse to assign or continue to assign such individual to a job involving food handling. However, if the individual with a disability is a current employee, the employer must consider whether he or she can be accommodated by reassignment to a vacant position not involving food handling.

(2) Effect on state or other laws. This part does not preempt, modify, or amend any State, county, or local law, ordinance or regulation applicable to food handling which:

(i) Is in accordance with the list, referred to in paragraph (e)(1) of this section, of infectious or communicable diseases and the modes of transmissibility published by the Secretary of Health and Human Services; and

(ii) Is designed to protect the public health from individuals who pose a significant risk to the health or safety of others, where that risk cannot be eliminated by reasonable accommodation.

(f) Health insurance, life insurance, and other benefit plans—

(1) An insurer, hospital, or medical service company, health maintenance organization, or any agent or entity that administers benefit plans, or similar organizations may underwrite risks, classify risks, or administer such risks that are based on or not inconsistent with State law.

(2) A covered entity may establish, sponsor, observe or administer the terms of a bona fide benefit plan that are based on underwriting risks, classifying risks, or administering such risks that are based on or not inconsistent with State law.

(3) A covered entity may establish, sponsor, observe, or administer the terms of a bona fide benefit plan that is not subject to State laws that regulate insurance.

(4) The activities described in paragraphs (f)(1), (2), and (3) of this section are permitted unless these activities are being used as a subterfuge to evade the purposes of this part.

ADA TITLE I EEOC INTERPRETIVE GUIDANCE

ADA TITLE I EEOC INTERPRETIVE GUIDANCE

Background

The ADA is a federal anti-discrimination statute de-signed to remove barriers which prevent qualified individuals with disabilities from enjoying the same employment opportunities that are available to persons without disabilities.

Like the Civil Rights Act of 1964 that prohibits discrimination on the bases of race, color, religion, national origin, and sex, the ADA seeks to ensure access to equal employment opportunities based on merit. It does not guarantee equal results, establish quotas, or require preferences favoring individuals with disabilities over those without disabilities.

However, while the Civil Rights Act of 1964 prohibits any consideration of personal characteristics such as race or national origin, the ADA necessarily takes a different approach. When an individual's disability creates a barrier to employment opportunities, the ADA requires employers to consider whether reasonable accommodation could remove the barrier.

The ADA thus establishes a process in which the employer must assess a disabled individual's ability to perform the essential functions of the specific job held or desired. While the ADA focuses on eradicating barriers, the ADA does not relieve a disabled employee or applicant from the obligation to perform the essential functions of the job. To the contrary, the ADA is intended to enable disabled persons to compete in the workplace based on the same performance standards and requirements that employers expect of persons who are not disabled.

However, where that individual's functional limitation impedes such job performance, an employer must take steps to reasonably accommodate, and thus help overcome the particular impediment, unless to do so would impose an undue hardship. Such accommodations usually take the form of adjustments to the way a job customarily is performed, or to the work environment itself.

This process of identifying whether, and to what extent, a reasonable accommodation is required should be flexible and involve both the employer and the individual with a disability. Of course, the determination of whether an individual is qualified for a particular position must necessarily be made on a case-by-case basis. No specific form of accommodation is guaranteed for all individuals with a particular disability. Rather, an accommodation must be tailored to match the needs of the disabled individual with the needs of the job's essential functions.

This case-by-case approach is essential if qualified individuals of varying abilities are to receive equal opportunities to compete for an infinitely diverse range of jobs. For this reason, neither the ADA nor this part can supply the "correct" answer in advance for each employment decision concerning an individual with a disability. Instead, the ADA simply establishes parameters to guide employers in how to consider, and take into account, the disabling condition involved.

Introduction

The Equal Employment Opportunity Commission (the Commission or EEOC) is responsible for enforcement of title I of the Americans with Disabilities Act (ADA), 42 U.S.C. 12101 et seq. (1990), which prohibits employment discrimination on the basis of disability. The Commission believes that it is essential to issue interpretive guidance concurrently with the issuance of this part in order to ensure that qualified individuals with disabilities understand their rights under this part and to facilitate and encourage compliance by covered entities. This appendix represents the Commission's interpretation of the issues discussed, and the Commission will be guided by it when resolving charges of employment discrimination. The appendix addresses the major provisions of this part and explains the major concepts of disability rights.

The terms "employer" or "employer or other covered entity" are used interchangeably throughout the appendix to refer to all covered entities subject to the employment provisions of the ADA.

Section 1630.1
Purpose, Applicability and Construction

Section 1630.1(a)
Purpose

The Americans with Disabilities Act was signed into law on July 26, 1990. It is an anti-discrimination statute that requires that individuals with disabilities be given the same consideration for employment that individuals without disabilities are given. An individual who is qualified for an employment opportunity cannot be denied that opportunity because of the fact that the individual is disabled. The purpose of title I and this part is to ensure that qualified individuals with disabilities are protected from discrimination on the basis of disability.

The ADA uses the term "disabilities" rather than the term "handicaps" used in the Rehabilitation Act of 1973, 29 U.S.C. 701-796. Substantively, these terms are equivalent. As noted by the House Committee on the Judiciary, "[t]he use of the term 'disabilities' instead of the term 'handicaps' reflects the desire of the Committee to use the most current terminology. It reflects the preference of persons with disabilities to use that term rather than 'handicapped' as used in previous laws, such as the Rehabilitation Act of 1973 * * *." H.R. Rep. No. 485 part 3, 101st Cong., 2d Sess. 26-27 (1990) (hereinafter House Judiciary Report); see also S. Rep. No. 116, 101st Cong., 1st Sess. 21 (1989) (hereinafter Senate Report); H.R. Rep. No. 485 part 2, 101st Cong., 2d Sess. 50-51 (1990) [hereinafter House Labor Report].

The use of the term "Americans" in the title of the ADA is not intended to imply that the Act only applies to United States citizens. Rather, the ADA protects all qualified individuals with disabilities, regardless of their citizenship status or nationality.

Section 1630.1(b) and (c)
Applicability and Construction

Unless expressly stated otherwise, the standards applied in the ADA are not intended to be lesser than the standards applied under the Rehabilitation Act of 1973.

The ADA does not preempt any Federal law, or any state or local law, that grants to individuals with disabilities protection greater than or equivalent to that provided by the ADA. This means that the existence of a lesser standard of protection to individuals with disabilities under the ADA will not provide a defense to failing to meet a higher standard under another law. Thus, for example, title I of the ADA would not be a defense to failing to collect information required to satisfy the affirmative action requirements of section 503 of the Rehabilitation Act. On the other hand, the existence of a lesser standard under another law will not provide a defense to failing to meet a higher standard under the ADA. See House Labor Report at 135; House Judiciary Report at 69-70.

This also means that an individual with a disability could choose to pursue claims under a state discrimination or tort law that does not confer greater substantive rights, or even confers fewer substantive rights, if the potential available remedies would be greater than those available under the ADA and this part. The ADA does not restrict an individual with a disability from pursuing such claims in addition to charges brought under this part. House Judiciary at 69-70.

The ADA does not automatically preempt medical standards or safety requirements established by Federal law or regulations. It does not preempt State, county, or local laws, ordinances or regulations that are consistent with this part, and are designed to protect the public health from individuals who pose a direct threat, that cannot be eliminated or reduced by reasonable accommodation, to the health or safety of others. However, the ADA does preempt inconsistent requirements established by state or local law for safety or security sensitive positions. See Senate Report at 27; House Labor Report at 57.

An employer allegedly in violation of this part cannot successfully defend its actions by relying on the obligation to comply with the requirements of any state or local law that imposes prohibitions or limitations on the eligibility of qualified individuals with disabilities to practice any occupation or profession. For example, suppose a municipality has an ordinance that prohibits individuals with tuberculosis from teaching school children. If an individual with dormant tuberculosis challenges a private school's refusal to hire him or her because of the tuberculosis, the private school would not be able to rely on the city ordinance as a defense under the ADA.

Section 1630.2(a)-(f)
Commission, Covered Entity, etc.

The definitions section of part 1630 includes several terms that are identical, or almost identical, to the terms found in title VII of the Civil Rights Act of 1964. Among these terms are "Commission," "Person," "State," and "Employer." These terms are to be given the same meaning under the ADA that they are given under title VII.

In general, the term "employee" has the same meaning that it is given under title VII. However, the ADA's definition of "employee" does not contain an exception, as does title VII, for elected officials and their personal staffs. It should be further noted that all state and local governments are covered by title II of the ADA whether or not they are also covered by this part. Title II, which is enforced by the Department of Justice, becomes effective on January 26, 1992. See 28 CFR part 35.

The term "covered entity" is not found in title VII. However, the title VII definitions of the entities included in the term "covered entity" (e.g., employer, employment agency, etc.) are applicable to the ADA.

Section 1630.2(g) Disability

In addition to the term "covered entity," there are several other terms that are unique to the ADA. The first of these is the term "disability." Congress adopted the definition of this term from the Rehabilitation Act definition of the term "individual with handicaps." By so doing, Congress intended that the relevant caselaw developed under the Rehabilitation Act be generally applicable to the term "disability" as used in the ADA. Senate Report at 21; House Labor Report at 50; House Judiciary Report at 27.

The definition of the term "disability" is divided into three parts. An individual must satisfy at least one of these parts in order to be considered an individual with a disability for purposes of this part. An individual is considered to have a "disability" if that individual either (1) has a physical or mental impairment which substantially limits one or more of that person's major life activities, (2) has a record of such an impairment, or, (3) is regarded by the covered entity as having such an impairment. To understand the meaning of the term "disability," it is necessary to understand, as a preliminary matter, what is meant by the terms "physical or mental impairment," "major life activity," and "substantially limits." Each of these terms is discussed below.

Section 1630.2(h)
Physical or Mental Impairment

This term adopts the definition of the term "physical or mental impairment" found in the regulations implementing section 504 of the Rehabilitation Act at 34 CFR part 104. It defines physical or mental impairment as any physiological disorder or condition, cosmetic disfigurement, or anatomical loss affecting one or more of several body systems, or any mental or psychological disorder.

Section 1630.2(i) Major Life Activities

This term adopts the definition of the term "major life activities" found in the regulations implementing section 504 of the Rehabilitation Act at 34 CFR part 104. "Major life activities" are those basic activities that the average person in the general population can perform with little or no difficulty. Major life activities include caring for oneself, performing manual tasks, walking, seeing, hearing, speaking, breathing, learning, and working. This list is not exhaustive. For example, other major life activities include, but are not limited to, sitting, standing, lifting, reaching. See Senate Report at 22; House Labor Report at 52; House

Judiciary Report at 28.

Section 1630.2(j) Substantially Limits

Determining whether a physical or mental impairment exists is only the first step in determining whether or not an individual is disabled. Many impairments do not impact an individual's life to the degree that they constitute disabling impairments. An impairment rises to the level of disability if the impairment substantially limits one or more of the individual's major life activities. Multiple impairments that combine to substantially limit one or more of an individual's major life activities also constitute a disability.

The ADA and this part, like the Rehabilitation Act of 1973, do not attempt a "laundry list" of impairments that are "disabilities." The determination of whether an individual has a disability is not necessarily based on the name or diagnosis of the impairment the person has, but rather on the effect of that impairment on the life of the individual. Some impairments may be disabling for particular individuals but not for others, depending on the stage of the disease or disorder, the presence of other impairments that combine to make the impairment disabling or any number of other factors.

Other impairments, however, such as HIV infection, are inherently substantially limiting.

On the other hand, temporary, non-chronic impairments of short duration, with little or no long term or permanent impact, are usually not disabilities. Such impairments may include, but are not limited to, broken limbs, sprained joints, concussions, appendicitis, and influenza. Similarly, except in rare circumstances, obesity is not considered a disabling impairment.

An impairment that prevents an individual from performing a major life activity substantially limits that major life activity. For example, an individual whose legs are paralyzed is substantially limited in the major life activity of walking because he or she is unable, due to the impairment, to perform that major life activity.

Alternatively, an impairment is substantially limiting if it significantly restricts the duration, manner or condition under which an individual can perform a particular major life activity as compared to the average person in the general population's ability to perform that same major life activity. Thus, for example, an individual who, because of an impairment, can only walk for very brief periods of time would be substantially limited in the major life activity of walking. It should be noted that the term "average person" is not intended to imply a precise mathematical "average."

Part 1630 notes several factors that should be considered in making the determination of whether an impairment is substantially limiting. These factors are (1) the nature and severity of the impairment, (2) the duration or expected duration of the impairment, and (3) the permanent or long term impact, or the expected permanent or long term impact of, or resulting from, the impairment. The term "duration," as used in this context, refers to the length of time an impairment persists, while the term "impact" refers to the residual effects of an impairment. Thus, for example, a broken leg that takes eight weeks to heal is an impairment of fairly brief duration. However, if the broken leg heals improperly, the "impact" of the impairment would be the resulting permanent limp. Likewise, the effect on cognitive functions resulting from traumatic head injury would be the "impact" of that impairment.

The determination of whether an individual is substantially limited in a major life activity must be made on a case by case basis. An individual is not substantially limited in a major life activity if the limitation, when viewed in light of the factors noted above, does not amount to a significant restriction when compared with the abilities of the average person. For example, an individual who had once been able to walk at an extraordinary speed would not be substantially limited in the major life activity of walking if, as a result of a physical impairment, he or she were only able to walk at an average speed, or even at moderately below average speed.

It is important to remember that the restriction on the performance of the major life activity must be the result of a condition that is an impairment. As noted earlier, advanced age, physical or personality characteristics, and environmental, cultural, and economic disadvantages are not impairments. Consequently, even if such factors substantially limit an individual's ability to perform a major life activity, this limitation will not constitute a disability. For example, an individual who is unable to read because he or she was never taught to read would not be an individual with a disability because lack of education is not an impairment. However, an individual who is unable to read because of dyslexia would be an individual with a disability because dyslexia, a learning disability, is an impairment.

If an individual is not substantially limited with respect to any other major life activity, the individual's ability to perform the major life activity of working should be considered. If an individual is substantially limited in any other major life activity, no determination should be made as to whether the individual is substantially limited in working. For example, if an individual is blind, i.e., substantially limited in the major life activity of seeing, there is no need to determine whether the individual is also substantially limited in the major life activity of working. The determination of whether an individual is substantially limited in working must also be made on a case by case basis.

This part lists specific factors that may be used in making the determination of whether the limitation in working is "substantial." These factors are:

(1) The geographical area to which the individual has reasonable access;

(2) The job from which the individual has been disqualified because of an impairment, and the number and types of jobs utilizing similar training, knowledge, skills or abilities, within that geographical area, from which the individual is also disqualified because of the impairment (class of jobs); and/or

(3) The job from which the individual has been disqualified because of an impairment, and the number and types of other jobs not utilizing similar training, knowledge, skills or abilities, within that geographical area, from which the individual is also disqualified because of the impairment (broad range of jobs in various classes).

Thus, an individual is not substantially limited in working just because he or she is unable to perform a particular job for one employer, or because he or she is unable to perform a specialized job or profession requiring extraordinary skill, prowess or talent. For example, an individual who cannot be a commercial airline pilot because of a minor vision impairment, but who can be a commercial airline co-pilot or a pilot for a courier service, would not be substantially limited in the major life activity of working. Nor would a professional baseball pitcher who develops a bad elbow and can no longer throw a baseball be considered substantially limited in the major life activity of working. In both of these examples, the individuals are not substantially limited in the ability to perform any other major life activity and, with regard to the major life activity of working, are only unable to perform either a particular specialized job or a narrow range of jobs. See *Forrisi v. Bowen*, 794 F.2d 931 (4th Cir. 1986); *Jasany v. U.S. Postal Service*, 755 F.2d 1244 (6th Cir. 1985); *E.E. Black, Ltd. v. Marshall*, 497 F. Supp. 1088 (D. Hawaii 1980).

On the other hand, an individual does not have to be totally unable to work in order to be considered substantially limited in the major life activity of working. An individual is substantially limited in working if the individual is significantly restricted in the ability to perform a class of jobs or a broad range of jobs in various classes, when compared with the ability of the average person with comparable qualifications to perform those same jobs. For example, an individual who has a back condition that prevents the individual from performing any heavy labor job would be substantially limited in the major life activity of working because the individual's impairment eliminates his or her ability to perform a class of jobs. This would be so even if the individual were able to perform jobs in another class, e.g., the class of semi-skilled jobs. Similarly, suppose an individual has an allergy to a substance found in most high rise office buildings, but seldom found elsewhere, that makes breathing extremely difficult. Since this individual would be substantially limited in the ability to perform the broad range of jobs in various classes that are conducted in high rise office buildings within the geographical area to which he or she has reasonable access, he or she would be substantially limited in working.

The terms "number and types of jobs" and "number and types of other jobs," as used in the factors discussed above, are not intended to require an onerous evidentiary showing. Rather, the terms only require the presentation of evidence of general employment demographics and/or of recognized occupational classifications that indicate the approximate number of jobs (e.g., "few," "many," "most") from which an individual would be excluded because of an impairment.

If an individual has a "mental or physical impairment" that "substantially limits" his or her ability to perform one or more "major life activities," that individual will satisfy the first part of the regulatory definition of "disability" and will be considered an individual with a disability. An individual who satisfies this first part of the definition of the term "disability" is not required to demonstrate that he or she satisfies either of the other parts of the definition. However, if an individual is unable to satisfy this part of the definition, he or she may be able to satisfy one of the other parts of the definition.

Section 1630.2(k)
Record of a Substantially Limiting Condition

The second part of the definition provides that an individual with a record of an impairment that substantially limits a major life activity is an individual with a disability. The intent of this provision, in part, is to ensure that people are not discriminated against because of a history of disability. For example, this provision protects former cancer patients from discrimination based on their prior medical history. This provision also ensures that individuals are not discriminated against because they have been misclassified as disabled. For example, individuals misclassified as learning disabled are protected from discrimination on the basis of that erroneous classification. Senate Report at 23; House Labor Report at 52-53; House Judiciary Report at 29.

This part of the definition is satisfied if a record relied on by an employer indicates that the individual has or has had a substantially limiting impairment. The impairment indicated in the record must be an impairment that would substantially limit one or more of the individual's major life activities. There are many types of records that could potentially contain this information, including but not limited to, education, medical, or employment records.

The fact that an individual has a record of being a disabled veteran, or of disability retirement, or is classified as disabled for other purposes does not guarantee that the individual will satisfy the definition of "disability" under part 1630. Other statutes, regulations and programs may have a definition of "disability" that is not the same as the definition set forth in the ADA and contained in part 1630. Accordingly, in order for an individual who has been classified in a record as "disabled" for some other purpose to be considered disabled for purposes of part 1630, the impairment indicated in the record must be a physical or mental impairment that substantially limits one or more of the individual's major life activities.

Section 1630.2(l)
Regarded as Substantially Limited in a Major Life Activity

If an individual cannot satisfy either the first part of the definition of "disability" or the second "record of" part of the definition, he or she may be able to satisfy the third part of the definition. The third part of the definition provides that an individual who is regarded by an employer or other covered entity as having an impairment that substantially limits a major life activity is an individual with a disability.

There are three different ways in which an individual may satisfy the definition of "being regarded as having a disability":

(1) The individual may have an impairment which is not substantially limiting but is perceived by the employer or other covered entity as constituting a substantially limiting impairment;

(2) The individual may have an impairment which is only substantially limiting because of the attitudes of others toward the impairment; or

(3) The individual may have no impairment at all but is regarded by the employer or other covered entity as having a substantially limiting impairment.

Senate Report at 23; House Labor Report at 53; House Judiciary Report at 29.

An individual satisfies the first part of this definition if the individual has an impairment that is not substantially limiting, but the covered entity perceives the impairment as being substantially limiting. For example, suppose an employee has controlled high blood pressure that is not substantially limiting. If an employer reassigns the individual to less strenuous work because of unsubstantiated fears that the individual will suffer a heart attack if he or she continues to perform strenuous work, the employer would be regarding the individual as disabled.

An individual satisfies the second part of the "regarded as" definition if the individual has an impairment that is only substantially limiting because of the attitudes of others toward the condition. For example, an individual may have a prominent facial scar or disfigurement, or may have a condition that periodically causes an involuntary jerk of the head but does not limit the individual's major life activities. If an employer discriminates against such an individual because of the negative reactions of customers, the employer would be regarding the individual as disabled and acting on the basis of that perceived disability. See Senate Report at 24; House Labor Report at 53; House Judiciary Report at 30-31.

An individual satisfies the third part of the "regarded as" definition of "disability" if the employer or other covered entity erroneously believes the individual has a substantially limiting impairment that the individual actually does not have. This situation could occur, for example, if an employer discharged an employee in response to a rumor that the employee is infected with Human Immunodeficiency Virus (HIV). Even though the rumor is totally unfounded and the individual has no impairment at all, the individual is considered an individual with a disability because the employer perceived of this individual as being disabled. Thus, in this example, the employer, by discharging this employee, is discriminating on the basis of disability.

The rationale for the "regarded as" part of the definition of disability was articulated by the Supreme Court in the context of the Rehabilitation Act of 1973 in *School Board of Nassau County v. Arline*, 480 U.S. 273 (1987). The Court noted that, although an individual may have an impairment that does not in fact substantially limit a major life activity, the reaction of others may prove just as disabling. "Such an impairment might not diminish a person's physical or mental capabilities, but could nevertheless substantially limit that person's ability to work as a result of the negative reactions of others to the impairment." 480 U.S. at 283. The Court concluded that by including "regarded as" in the Rehabilitation Act's definition, "Congress acknowledged that society's accumulated myths and fears about disability and diseases are as handicapping as are the physical limitations that flow from actual impairment." 480 U.S. at 284.

An individual rejected from a job because of the "myths, fears and stereotypes" associated with disabilities would be covered under this part of the definition of disability, whether or not the employer's or other covered entity's perception were shared by others in the field and whether or not the individual's actual physical or mental condition would be considered a disability under the first or second part of this definition. As the legislative history notes, sociologists have identified common attitudinal barriers that frequently result in employers excluding individuals with disabilities. These include concerns regarding productivity, safety, insurance, liability, attendance, cost of accommodation and accessibility, workers' compensation costs, and acceptance by coworkers and customers.

Therefore, if an individual can show that an employer or other covered entity made an employment decision because of a perception of disability based on "myth, fear or stereotype," the individual will satisfy the "regarded as" part of the definition of disability. If the employer cannot articulate a non-discriminatory reason for the employment action, an inference that the employer is acting on the basis of "myth, fear or stereotype" can be drawn.

Section 1630.2(m) Qualified Individual With a Disability

The ADA prohibits discrimination on the basis of disability against qualified individuals with disabilities. The determination of whether an individual with a disability is "qualified" should be made in two steps. The first step is to determine if the individual satisfies the prerequisites for the position, such as possessing the appropriate educational background, employment experience, skills, licenses, etc. For example, the first step in determining whether an accountant who is paraplegic is qualified for a certified public accountant (CPA) position is to examine the individual's credentials to determine whether the individual is a licensed CPA. This is sometimes referred to in the Rehabilitation Act caselaw as determining whether the individual is "otherwise qualified" for the position. See Senate Report at 33; House Labor Report at 64-65. (See § 1630.9 Not Making Reasonable Accommodation).

The second step is to determine whether or not the individual can perform the essential functions of the position held or desired, with or without reasonable accommodation. The purpose of this second step is to ensure that individuals with disabilities who can perform the essential functions of the position held or desired are not denied employment opportunities because they are not able to perform marginal functions of the position. House Labor Report at 55.

The determination of whether an individual with a disability is qualified is to be made at the time of the employment decision. This determination should be based on the capabilities of the individual with a disability at the time of the employment decision, and should not be based on speculation that the employee may become unable in the future or may cause increased health insurance premiums or workers compensation costs.

Section 1630.2(n) Essential Functions

The determination of which functions are essential may be critical to the determination of whether or not the individual with a disability is qualified. The essential functions are those functions that the individual who holds the position must be able to perform unaided or with the assistance of a reasonable accommodation.

The inquiry into whether a particular function is essential initially focuses on whether the employer actually requires employees in the position to perform the functions that the employer asserts are essential. For example, an employer may state that typing is an essential function of a position. If, in fact, the employer has never required any employee in that particular position to type, this will be evidence that typing is not actually an essential function of the position.

If the individual who holds the position is actually required to perform the function the employer asserts is an essential function, the inquiry will then center around whether removing the function would fundamentally alter that position. This determination of whether or not a particular function is essential will generally include one or more of the following factors listed in part 1630.

The first factor is whether the position exists to perform a particular function. For example, an individual may be hired to proofread documents. The ability to proofread the documents would then be an essential function, since this is the only reason the position exists.

The second factor in determining whether a function is essential is the number of other employees available to perform that job function or among whom the performance of that job function can be distributed. This may be a factor either because the total number of available employees is low, or because of the fluctuating demands of the business operation. For example, if an employer has a relatively small number of available employees for the volume of work to be performed, it may be necessary that each employee perform a multitude of different functions. Therefore, the performance of those functions by each employee becomes more critical and the options for reorganizing the work become more limited. In such a situation, functions that might not be essential if there were a larger staff may become essential because the staff size is small compared to the volume of work that has to be done. See *Treadwell v. Alexander*, 707 F.2d 473 (11th Cir. 1983).

A similar situation might occur in a larger work force if the work flow follows a cycle of heavy demand for labor intensive work followed by low demand periods. This type of workflow might also make the performance of each function during the peak periods more critical and might limit the employer's flexibility in reorganizing operating procedures. See *Dexler v. Tisch*, 660 F. Supp. 1418 (D. Conn. 1987).

The third factor is the degree of expertise or skill required to perform the function. In certain professions and highly skilled positions the employee is hired for his or her expertise or ability to perform the particular function. In such a situation, the performance of that specialized task would be an essential function.

Whether a particular function is essential is a factual determination that must be made on a case by case basis. In determining whether or not a particular function is essential, all relevant evidence should be considered. Part 1630 lists various types of evidence, such as an established job description, that should be considered in determining whether a particular function is essential. Since the list is not exhaustive, other relevant evidence may also be presented. Greater weight will not be granted to the types of evidence included on the list than to the types of evidence not listed.

Although part 1630 does not require employers to develop or maintain job descriptions, written job descriptions prepared before advertising or interviewing applicants for the job, as well as the employer's judgment as to what functions are essential are among the relevant evidence to be considered in determining whether a particular function is essential. The terms of a collective bargaining agreement are also relevant to the determination of whether a particular function is essential. The work experience of past employees in the job or of current employees in similar jobs is likewise relevant to the determination of whether a particular function is essential. See H.R. Conf. Rep. No. 101-596, 101st Cong., 2d Sess. 58 (1990) [hereinafter Conference Report]; House Judiciary Report at 33-34. See also *Hall v. U.S. Postal Service*, 857 F.2d 1073 (6th Cir. 1988). The time spent performing the particular function may also be an indicator of whether that function is essential. For example, if an employee spends the vast majority of his or her time working at a cash register, this would be evidence that operating the cash register is an essential function. The consequences of failing to require the employee to perform the function may be another indicator of whether a particular function is essential. For example, although a firefighter may not regularly have to carry an unconscious adult out of a burning building, the consequence of failing to require the firefighter to be able to perform this function would be serious.

It is important to note that the inquiry into essential functions is not intended to second guess an employer's business judgment with regard to production standards, whether qualitative or quantitative, nor to require employers to lower such standards. (See § 1630.10 Qualification Standards, Tests and Other Selection Criteria). If an employer requires its typists to be able to accurately type 75 words per minute, it will not be called upon to explain why an inaccurate work product, or a typing speed of 65 words per minute, would not be adequate. Similarly, if a hotel requires its service workers to thoroughly clean 16 rooms per day, it will not have to explain why it requires thorough cleaning, or why it chose a 16 room rather than a 10 room requirement. However, if an employer does require accurate 75 word per minute typing or the thorough cleaning of 16 rooms, it will have to show that it actually imposes such requirements on its employees in fact, and not simply on paper. It should also be noted that, if it is alleged that the employer intentionally selected the particular level of production to exclude individuals with disabilities, the employer may have to offer a legitimate, nondiscriminatory reason for its selection.

Section 1630.2(o) Reasonable Accommodation

An individual is considered a "qualified individual with a disability" if the individual can perform the essential functions of the position held or desired with or without reasonable accommodation. In general, an accommodation is any change in the work environment or in the way things are customarily done that enables an individual with a disability to enjoy equal employment opportunities. There are three categories of reasonable accommodation. These are (1) accommodations that are required to ensure equal opportunity in the application process; (2) accommodations that enable the employer's employees with disabilities to perform the essential functions of the position held or desired; and (3) accommodations that enable the employer's employees with disabilities to enjoy equal benefits and privileges of employment as are enjoyed by employees without disabilities. It should be noted that nothing in this part prohibits employers or other covered entities from providing accommodations beyond those required by this part.

Part 1630 lists the examples, specified in title I of the ADA, of the most common types of accommodation that an employer or other covered entity may be required to provide. There are any number of other specific accommodations that may be appropriate for particular situations but are not specifically mentioned in this listing. This listing is not intended to be exhaustive of accommodation possibilities. For example, other accommodations could include permitting the use of accrued paid leave or providing additional unpaid leave for necessary treatment, making employer provided transportation accessible, and providing reserved parking spaces. Providing personal assistants, such as a page turner for an employee with no hands or a travel attendant to act as a sighted guide to assist a blind employee on occasional business trips, may also be a reasonable accommodation. Senate Report at 31; House Labor Report at 62; House Judiciary Report at 39.

It may also be a reasonable accommodation to permit an individual with a disability the opportunity to provide and utilize equipment, aids or services that an employer is not required to provide as a reasonable accommodation. For example, it would be a reasonable accommodation for an employer to permit an individual who is blind to use a guide dog at work, even though the employer would not be required to provide a guide dog for the employee.

The accommodations included on the list of reasonable accommodations are generally self explanatory. However, there are a few that require further explanation. One of these is the accommodation of making existing facilities used by employees readily accessible to, and usable by, individuals with disabilities. This accommodation includes both those areas that must be accessible for the employee to perform essential job functions, as well as non-work areas used by the employer's employees for other purposes. For example, accessible break rooms, lunch rooms, training rooms, restrooms etc., may be required as reasonable accommodations.

Another of the potential accommodations listed is "job restructuring." An employer or other covered entity may restructure a job by reallocating or redistributing nonessential, marginal job functions. For example, an employer may have two jobs, each of which entails the performance of a number of marginal functions. The employer hires a qualified individual with a disability who is able to perform some of the marginal functions of each job but not all of the marginal functions of either job. As an accommodation, the employer may redistribute the marginal functions so that all of the marginal functions that the qualified individual with a disability can perform are made a part of the position to be filled by the qualified individual with a disability. The remaining marginal functions that the individual with a disability cannot perform would then be transferred to the other position. See Senate Report at 31; House Labor Report at 62.

An employer or other covered entity is not required to reallocate essential functions. The essential functions are by definition those that the individual who holds the job would have to perform, with or without reasonable accommodation, in order to be considered qualified for the position. For example, suppose a security guard position requires the individual who holds the job to inspect identification cards. An employer would not have to provide an individual who is legally blind with an assistant to look at the identification cards for the legally blind employee. In this situation the assistant would be performing the job for the individual with a disability rather than assisting the individual to perform the job. See *Coleman v. Darden*, 595 F.2d 533 (10th Cir. 1979).

An employer or other covered entity may also restructure a job by altering when and/or how an essential function is performed. For example, an essential function customarily performed in the early morning hours may be rescheduled until later in the day as a reasonable accommodation to a disability that precludes performance of the function at the customary hour. Likewise, as a reasonable accommodation, an employee with a disability that inhibits the ability to write, may be permitted to computerize records that were customarily maintained manually.

Reassignment to a vacant position is also listed as a potential reasonable accommodation. In general, reassignment should be considered only when accommodation within the individual's current position would pose an undue hardship. Reassignment is not available to applicants. An applicant for a position must be qualified for, and be able to perform the essential functions of, the position sought with or without reasonable accommodation.

Reassignment may not be used to limit, segregate, or otherwise discriminate against employees with disabilities by forcing reassignments to undesirable positions or to designated offices or facilities. Employers should reassign the individual to an equivalent position, in terms of pay, status, etc., if the individual is qualified, and if the position is vacant within a reasonable amount of time. A "reasonable amount of time" should be determined in light of the totality of the circumstances. As an example, suppose there is no vacant position available at the time that an individual with a disability requests reassignment as a reasonable accommodation. The employer, however, knows that an equivalent position for which the individual is qualified, will become vacant next week. Under these circumstances, the employer should reassign the individual to the position when it becomes available.

An employer may reassign an individual to a lower graded position if there are no accommodations that would enable the employee to remain in the current position and there are no vacant equivalent positions for which the individual is qualified with or without reasonable accommodation. An employer, however, is not required to maintain the reassigned individual with a disability at the salary of the higher graded position if it does not so maintain reassigned employees who are not disabled. It should also be noted that an employer is not required to promote an individual with a disability as an accommodation. See Senate Report at 31-32; House Labor Report at 63.

The determination of which accommodation is appropriate in a particular situation involves a process in which the employer and employee identify the precise limitations imposed by the disability and explore potential accommodations that would overcome those limitations. This process is discussed more fully in § 1630.9 Not Making Reasonable Accommodation.

Section 1630.2(p) Undue Hardship

An employer or other covered entity is not required to provide an accommodation that will impose an undue hardship on the operation of the employer's or other covered entity's business. The term "undue hardship" means significant difficulty or expense in, or resulting from, the provision of the accommodation. The "undue hardship" provision takes into account the financial realities of the particular employer or other covered entity. However, the concept of undue hardship is not limited to financial difficulty. "Undue hardship" refers to any accommodation that would be unduly costly, extensive, substantial, or disruptive, or that would fundamentally alter the nature or operation of the business. See Senate Report at 35; House Labor Report at 67.

For example, suppose an individual with a disabling visual impairment that makes it extremely difficult to see in dim lighting applies for a position as a waiter in a nightclub and requests that the club be brightly lit as a reasonable accommodation. Although the individual may be able to perform the job in bright lighting, the nightclub will probably be able to demonstrate that that particular accommodation, though inexpensive, would impose an undue hardship if the bright lighting would destroy the ambience of the nightclub and/or make it difficult for the customers to see the stage show. The fact that that particular accommodation poses an undue hardship, however, only means that the employer is not required to provide that accommodation. If there is another accommodation that will not create an undue hardship, the employer would be required to provide the alternative accommodation.

An employer's claim that the cost of a particular accommodation will impose an undue hardship will be analyzed in light of the factors outlined in part 1630. In part, this analysis requires a determination of whose financial resources should be considered in deciding whether the accommodation is unduly costly. In some cases the financial resources of the employer or other covered entity in its entirety should be considered in determining whether the cost of an accommodation poses an undue hardship. In other cases, consideration of the financial resources of the employer or other covered entity as a whole may be inappropriate because it may not give an accurate picture of the financial resources available to the particular facility that will actually be required to provide the accommodation. See House Labor Report at 68-69; House Judiciary Report at 40-41; see also Conference Report at 56-57.

If the employer or other covered entity asserts that only the financial resources of the facility where the individual will be employed should be considered, part 1630 requires a factual determination of the relationship between the employer or other covered entity and the facility that will provide the accommodation. As an example, suppose that an independently owned fast food franchise that receives no money from the franchisor refuses to hire an individual with a hearing impairment because it asserts that it would be an undue hardship to provide an interpreter to enable the individual to participate in monthly staff meetings. Since the financial relationship between the franchisor and the franchise is limited to payment of an annual franchise fee, only the financial resources of the franchise would be considered in determining whether or not providing the accommodation would be an undue hardship. See House Labor Report at 68; House Judiciary Report at 40.

If the employer or other covered entity can show that the cost of the accommodation would impose an undue hardship, it would still be required to provide the accommodation if the funding is available from another source, e.g., a State vocational rehabilitation agency, or if Federal, State or local tax deductions or tax credits are available to offset the cost of the accommodation. If the employer or other covered entity receives, or is eligible to receive, monies from an external source that would pay the entire cost of the accommodation, it cannot claim cost as an undue hardship. In the absence of such funding, the individual with a disability requesting the accommodation should be given the option of providing the accommodation or of paying that portion of the cost which constitutes the undue hardship on the operation of the business. To the extent that such monies pay or would pay for only part of the cost of the accommodation, only that portion of the cost of the accommodation that could not be recovered—the final net cost to the entity—may be considered in determining undue hardship. (See § 1630.9 Not Making Reasonable Accommodation). See Senate Report at 36; House Labor Report at 69.

Section 1630.2(r) Direct Threat

An employer may require, as a qualification standard, that an individual not pose a direct threat to the health or safety of himself/herself or others. Like any other qualification standard, such a standard must apply to all applicants or employees and not just to individuals with disabilities. If, however, an individual poses a direct threat as a result of a disability, the employer must determine whether a reasonable accommodation would either eliminate the risk or reduce it to an acceptable level. If no accommodation exists that would either eliminate or reduce the risk, the employer may refuse to hire an applicant or may discharge an employee who poses a direct threat.

An employer, however, is not permitted to deny an employment opportunity to an individual with a disability merely because of a slightly increased risk. The risk can only be considered when it poses a significant risk, i.e., high probability, of substantial harm; a speculative or remote risk is insufficient. See Senate Report at 27; House Report Labor Report at 56-57; House Judiciary Report at 45.

Determining whether an individual poses a significant risk of substantial harm to others must be made on a case by case basis. The employer should identify the specific risk posed by the individual. For individuals with mental or emotional disabilities, the employer must identify the specific behavior on the part of the individual that would pose the direct threat. For individuals with physical disabilities, the employer must identify the aspect of the disability that would pose the direct threat. The employer should then consider the four factors listed in part 1630:

(1) The duration of the risk;

(2) The nature and severity of the potential harm;

(3) The likelihood that the potential harm will occur; and

(4) The imminence of the potential harm.

Such consideration must rely on objective, factual evidence—not on subjective perceptions, irrational fears, patronizing attitudes, or stereotypes—about the nature or effect of a particular disability, or of disability generally. See Senate Report at 27; House Labor Report at 56-57; House Judiciary Report at 45-46. See also *Strathie v. Department of Transportation*, 716 F.2d 227 (3d Cir. 1983). Relevant evidence may include input from the individual with a disability, the experience of the individual with a disability in previous similar positions, and opinions of medical doctors, rehabilitation counselors, or physical therapists who have expertise in the disability involved and/or direct knowledge of the individual with the disability.

An employer is also permitted to require that an individual not pose a direct threat of harm to his or her own safety or health. If performing the particular functions of a job would result in a high probability of substantial harm to the individual, the employer could reject or discharge the individual unless a reasonable accommodation that would not cause an undue hardship would avert the harm. For example, an employer would not be required to hire an individual, disabled by narcolepsy, who frequently and unexpectedly loses consciousness for a carpentry job the essential functions of which require the use of power saws and other dangerous equipment, where no accommodation exists that will reduce or eliminate the risk.

The assessment that there exists a high probability of substantial harm to the individual, like the assessment that there exists a high probability of substantial harm to others, must be strictly based on valid medical analyses and/or on other objective evidence. This determination must be based on individualized factual data, using the factors discussed above, rather than on stereotypic or patronizing assumptions and must consider potential reasonable accommodations. Generalized fears about risks from the employment environment, such as exacerbation of the disability caused by stress, cannot be used by an employer to disqualify an individual with a disability. For example, a law firm could not reject an applicant with a history of disabling mental illness based on a generalized fear that the stress of trying to make partner might trigger a relapse of the individual's mental illness. Nor can generalized fears about risks to individuals with disabilities in the event of an evacuation or other emergency be used by an employer to disqualify an individual with a disability. See Senate Report at 56; House Labor Report at 73-74; House Judiciary Report at 45. See also *Mantolete v. Bolger*, 767 F.2d 1416 (9th Cir. 1985); *Bentivegna v. U.S. Department of Labor*, 694 F.2d 619 (9th Cir. 1982).

1630.3 Exceptions to the Definitions of "Disability" and "Qualified Individual with a Disability"
Section 1630.3 (a) through (c) Illegal Use of Drugs

Part 1630 provides that an individual currently engaging in the illegal use of drugs is not an individual with a disability for purposes of this part when the employer or other covered entity acts on the basis of such use. Illegal use of drugs refers both to the use of unlawful drugs, such as cocaine, and to the unlawful use of prescription drugs.

Employers, for example, may discharge or deny employment to persons who illegally use drugs, on the basis of such use, without fear of being held liable for discrimination. The term "currently engaging" is not intended to be limited to the use of drugs on the day of, or within a matter of days or weeks before, the employment action in question. Rather, the provision is intended to apply to the illegal use of drugs that has occurred recently enough to indicate that the individual is actively engaged in such conduct. See Conference Report at 64.

Individuals who are erroneously perceived as engaging in the illegal use of drugs, but are not in fact illegally using drugs are not excluded from the definitions of the terms "disability" and "qualified individual with a disability." Individuals who are no longer illegally using drugs and who have either been rehabilitated successfully or are in the process of completing a rehabilitation program are, likewise, not excluded from the definitions of those terms. The term "rehabilitation program" refers to both in-patient and out-patient programs, as well as to appropriate employee assistance programs, professionally recognized self-help programs, such as Narcotics Anonymous, or other programs that provide professional (not necessarily medical) assistance and counseling for individuals who illegally use drugs. See Conference Report at 64; see also House Labor Report at 77; House Judiciary Report at 47.

It should be noted that this provision simply provides that certain individuals are not excluded from the definitions of "disability" and "qualified individual with a disability." Consequently, such individuals are still required to establish that they satisfy the requirements of these definitions in order to be protected by the ADA and this part. An individual erroneously regarded as illegally using drugs, for example, would have to show that he or she was regarded as a drug addict in order to demonstrate that he or she meets the definition of "disability" as defined in this part.

Employers are entitled to seek reasonable assurances that no illegal use of drugs is occurring or has occurred recently enough so that continuing use is a real and ongoing problem. The reasonable assurances that employers may ask applicants or employees to provide include evidence that the individual is participating in a drug treatment program and/or evidence, such as drug test results, to show that the individual is not currently engaging in the illegal use of drugs. An employer, such as a law enforcement agency, may also be able to impose a qualification standard that excludes individuals with a history of illegal use of drugs if it can show that the standard is job-related and consistent with business necessity. (See § 1630.10 Qualification Standards, Tests and Other Selection Criteria) See Conference Report at 64.

Section 1630.4 Discrimination Prohibited

This provision prohibits discrimination against a qualified individual with a disability in all aspects of the employment relationship. The range of employment decisions covered by this nondiscrimination mandate is to be construed in a manner consistent with the regulations implementing section 504 of the Rehabilitation Act of 1973.

Part 1630 is not intended to limit the ability of covered entities to choose and maintain a qualified work force. Employers can continue to use job-related criteria to select qualified employees, and can continue to hire employees who can perform the essential functions of the job.

Section 1630.5
Limiting, Segregating and Classifying

This provision and the several provisions that follow describe various specific forms of discrimination that are included within the general prohibition of § 1630.4. Covered entities are prohibited from restricting the employment opportunities of qualified individuals with disabilities on the basis of stereotypes and myths about the individual's disability. Rather, the capabilities of qualified individuals with disabilities must be determined on an individualized, case by case basis. Covered entities are also prohibited from segregating qualified employees with disabilities into separate work areas or into separate lines of advancement.

Thus, for example, it would be a violation of this part for an employer to limit the duties of an employee with a disability based on a presumption of what is best for an individual with such a disability, or on a presumption about the abilities of an individual with such a disability. It would be a violation of this part for an employer to adopt a separate track of job promotion or progression for employees with disabilities based on a presumption that employees with disabilities are uninterested in, or incapable of, performing particular jobs. Similarly, it would be a violation for an employer to assign or reassign (as a reasonable accommodation) employees with disabilities to one particular office or installation, or to require that employees with disabilities only use particular employer provided non-work facilities such as segregated break-rooms, lunch rooms, or lounges. It would also be a violation of this part to deny employment to an applicant or employee with a disability based on generalized fears about the safety of an individual with such a disability, or based on generalized assumptions about the absenteeism rate of an individual with such a disability.

In addition, it should also be noted that this part is intended to require that employees with disabilities be accorded equal access to whatever health insurance coverage the employer provides to other employees. This part does not, however, affect pre-existing condition clauses included in health insurance policies offered by employers. Consequently, employers may continue to offer policies that contain such clauses, even if they adversely affect individuals with disabilities, so long as the clauses are not used as a subterfuge to evade the purposes of this part.

So, for example, it would be permissible for an employer to offer an insurance policy that limits coverage for certain procedures or treatments to a specified number per year. Thus, if a health insurance plan provided coverage for five blood transfusions a year to all covered employees, it would not be discriminatory to offer this plan simply because a hemophiliac employee may require more than five blood transfusions annually. However, it would not be permissible to limit or deny the hemophiliac employee coverage for other procedures, such as heart surgery or the setting of a broken leg, even though the plan would not have to provide coverage for the additional blood transfusions that may be involved in these procedures. Likewise, limits may be placed on reimbursements for certain procedures or on the types of drugs or procedures covered (e.g., limits on the number of permitted X-rays or non-coverage of experimental drugs or procedures), but that limitation must be applied equally to individuals with and without disabilities. See Senate Report at 28-29; House Labor Report at 58-59; House Judiciary Report at 36.

Leave policies or benefit plans that are uniformly applied do not violate this part simply because they do not address the special needs of every individual with a disability. Thus, for example, an employer that reduces the number of paid sick leave days that it will provide to all employees, or reduces the amount of medical insurance coverage that it will provide to all employees, is not in violation of this part, even if the benefits reduction has an impact on employees with disabilities in need of greater sick leave and medical coverage. Benefits reductions adopted for discriminatory reasons are in violation of this part. See *Alexander v. Choate,* 469 U.S. 287 (1985). See Senate Report at 85; House Labor Report at 137. (See also, the discussion at § 1630.16(f) Health Insurance, Life Insurance, and Other Benefit Plans).

Section 1630.6
Contractual or Other Arrangements

An employer or other covered entity may not do through a contractual or other relationship what it is prohibited from doing directly. This provision does not affect the determination of whether or not one is a "covered entity" or "employer" as defined in § 1630.2.

This provision only applies to situations where an employer or other covered entity has entered into a contractual relationship that has the effect of discriminating against its own employees or applicants with disabilities. Accordingly, it would be a violation for an employer to participate in a contractual relationship that results in discrimination against the employer's employees with disabilities in hiring, training, promotion, or in any other aspect of the employment relationship. This provision applies whether or not the employer or other covered entity intended for the contractual relationship to have the discriminatory effect.

Part 1630 notes that this provision applies to parties on either side of the contractual or other relationship. This is intended to highlight that an employer whose employees provide services to others, like an employer whose employees receive services, must ensure that those employees are not discriminated against on the basis of disability. For example, a copier company whose service representative is a dwarf could be required to provide a step stool, as a reasonable accommodation, to enable him to perform the necessary repairs. However, the employer would not be required, as a reasonable accommodation, to make structural changes to its customer's inaccessible premises.

The existence of the contractual relationship adds no new obligations under part 1630. The employer, therefore, is not liable through the contractual arrangement for any discrimination by the contractor against the contractors own employees or applicants, although the contractor, as an employer, may be liable for such discrimination.

An employer or other covered entity, on the other hand, cannot evade the obligations imposed by this part by engaging in a contractual or other relationship. For example, an employer cannot avoid its responsibility to make reasonable accommodation subject to the undue hardship limitation through a contractual arrangement. See Conference Report at 59; House Labor Report at 59-61; House Judiciary Report at 36-37.

To illustrate, assume that an employer is seeking to contract with a company to provide training for its employees. Any responsibilities of reasonable accommodation applicable to the employer in providing the training remain with that employer even if it contracts with another company for this service. Thus, if the training company were planning to conduct the training at an inaccessible location, thereby making it impossible for an employee who uses a wheelchair to attend, the employer would have a duty to make reasonable accommodation unless to do so would impose an undue hardship. Under these circumstances, appropriate accommodations might include (1) having the training company identify accessible training sites and relocate the training program; (2) having the training company make the training site accessible; (3) directly making the training site accessible or providing the training company with the means by which to make the site accessible; (4) identifying and contracting with another training company that uses accessible sites; or (5) any other accommodation that would result in making the training available to the employee.

As another illustration, assume that instead of contracting with a training company, the employer contracts with a hotel to host a conference for its employees. The employer will have a duty to ascertain and ensure the accessibility of the hotel and its conference facilities. To fulfill this obligation the employer could, for example, inspect the hotel first-hand or ask a local disability group to inspect the hotel. Alternatively, the employer could ensure that the contract with the hotel specifies it will provide accessible guest rooms for those who need them and that all rooms to be used for the conference, including exhibit and meeting rooms, are accessible. If the hotel breaches this accessibility provision, the hotel may be liable to the employer, under a non-ADA breach of contract theory, for the cost of any accommodation needed to provide access to the hotel and conference, and for any other costs accrued by the employer. (In addition, the hotel may also be independently liable under title III of the ADA). However, this would not relieve the employer of its responsibility under this part nor shield it from charges of discrimination by its own employees. See House Labor Report at 40; House Judiciary Report at 37.

Section 1630.8
Relationship or Association With an Individual With a Disability

This provision is intended to protect any qualified individual, whether or not that individual has a disability, from discrimination because that person is known to have an association or relationship with an individual who has a known disability. This protection is not limited to those who have a familial relationship with an individual with a disability.

To illustrate the scope of this provision, assume that a qualified applicant without a disability applies for a job and discloses to the employer that his or her spouse has a disability. The employer thereupon declines to hire the applicant because the employer believes that the applicant would have to miss work or frequently leave work early in order to care for the spouse. Such a refusal to hire would be prohibited by this provision. Similarly, this provision would prohibit an employer from discharging an employee because the employee does volunteer work with people who have AIDS, and the employer fears that the employee may contract the disease.

This provision also applies to other benefits and privileges of employment. For example, an employer that provides health insurance benefits to its employees for their dependents may not reduce the level of those benefits to an employee simply because that employee has a dependent with a disability. This is true even if the provision of such benefits would result in increased health insurance costs for the employer.

It should be noted, however, that an employer need not provide the applicant or employee without a disability with a reasonable accommodation because that duty only applies to qualified applicants or employees with disabilities. Thus, for example, an employee would not be entitled to a modified work schedule as an accommodation to enable the employee to care for a spouse with a disability. See Senate Report at 30; House Labor Report at 61-62; House Judiciary Report at 38-39.

Section 1630.9
Not Making Reasonable Accommodation

The obligation to make reasonable accommodation is a form of non-discrimination. It applies to all employment decisions and to the job application process. This obligation does not extend to the provision of adjustments or modifications that are primarily for the personal benefit of the individual with a disability. Thus, if an adjustment or modification is job-related, e.g., specifically assists the individual in performing the duties of a particular job, it will be considered a type of reasonable accommodation. On the other hand, if an adjustment or modification assists the individual throughout his or her daily activities, on and off the job, it will be considered a personal item that the employer is not required to provide. Accordingly, an employer would generally not be required to provide an employee with a disability with a prosthetic limb, wheelchair, or eyeglasses. Nor would an employer have to provide as an accommodation any amenity or convenience that is not job-related, such as a private hot plate, hot pot or refrigerator that is not provided to employees without disabilities. See Senate Report at 31; House Labor Report at 62.

It should be noted, however, that the provision of such items may be required as a reasonable accommodation where such items are specifically designed or required to meet job-related rather than personal needs. An employer, for example, may have to provide an individual with a disabling visual impairment with eyeglasses specifically designed to enable the individual to use the office computer monitors, but that are not otherwise needed by the individual outside of the office.

The term "supported employment," which has been applied to a wide variety of programs to assist individuals with severe disabilities in both competitive and non-competitive employment, is not synonymous with reasonable accommodation. Examples of supported employment include modified training materials, restructuring essential functions to enable an individual to perform a job, or hiring an outside professional ("job coach") to assist in job training. Whether a particular form of assistance would be required as a reasonable accommodation must be determined on an individualized, case by case basis without regard to whether that assistance is referred to as "supported employment." For example, an employer, under certain circumstances, may be required to provide modified training materials or a temporary "job coach" to assist in the training of a qualified individual with a disability as a reasonable accommodation. However, an employer would not be required to restructure the essential functions of a position to fit the skills of an individual with a disability who is not otherwise qualified to perform the position, as is done in certain supported employment programs. See 34 CFR part 363. It should be noted that it would not be a violation of this part for an employer to provide any of these personal modifications or adjustments, or to engage in supported employment or similar rehabilitative programs.

The obligation to make reasonable accommodation applies to all services and programs provided in connection with employment, and to all non-work facilities provided or maintained by an employer for use by its employees. Accordingly, the obligation to accommodate is applicable to employer sponsored placement or counseling services, and to employer provided cafeterias, lounges, gymnasiums, auditoriums, transportation and the like.

The reasonable accommodation requirement is best understood as a means by which barriers to the equal employment opportunity of an individual with a disability are removed or alleviated. These barriers may, for example, be physical or structural obstacles that inhibit or prevent the access of an individual with a disability to job sites, facilities or equipment. Or they may be rigid work schedules that permit no flexibility as to when work is performed or when breaks may be taken, or inflexible job procedures that unduly limit the modes of communication that are used on the job, or the way in which particular tasks are accomplished.

The term "otherwise qualified" is intended to make clear that the obligation to make reasonable accommodation is owed only to an individual with a disability who is qualified within the meaning of § 1630.2(m) in that he or she satisfies all the skill, experience, education and other job-related selection criteria. An individual with a disability is "otherwise qualified," in other words, if he or she is qualified for a job, except that, because of the disability, he or she needs a reasonable accommodation to be able to perform the job's essential functions.

For example, if a law firm requires that all incoming lawyers have graduated from an accredited law school and have passed the bar examination, the law firm need not provide an accommodation to an individual with a visual impairment who has not met these selection criteria. That individual is not entitled to a reasonable accommodation because the individual is not "otherwise qualified" for the position.

On the other hand, if the individual has graduated from an accredited law school and passed the bar examination, the individual would be "otherwise qualified." The law firm would thus be required to provide a reasonable accommodation, such as a machine that magnifies print, to enable the individual to perform the essential functions of the attorney position, unless the necessary accommodation would impose an undue hardship on the law firm. See Senate Report at 33-34; House Labor Report at 64-65.

The reasonable accommodation that is required by this part should provide the qualified individual with a disability with an equal employment opportunity. Equal employment opportunity means an opportunity to attain the same level of performance, or to enjoy the same level of benefits and privileges of employment as are available to the average similarly situated employee without a disability. Thus, for example, an accommodation made to assist an employee with a disability in the performance of his or her job must be adequate to enable the individual to perform the essential functions of the relevant position. The accommodation, however, does not have to be the "best" accommodation possible, so long as it is sufficient to meet the job-related needs of the individual being accommodated. Accordingly, an employer would not have to provide an employee disabled by a back impairment with a state-of-the art mechanical lifting device if it provided the employee with a less expensive or more readily available device that enabled the employee to perform the essential functions of the job. See Senate Report at 35; House Labor Report at 66; see also *Carter v. Bennett*, 840 F.2d 63 (D.C. Cir. 1988). Employers are obligated to make reasonable accommodation only to the physical or mental limitations resulting from the disability of a qualified individual with a disability that is known to the employer. Thus, an employer would not be expected to accommodate disabilities of which it is unaware. If an employee with a known disability is having difficulty performing his or her job, an employer may inquire whether the employee is in need of a reasonable accommodation. In general, however, it is the responsibility of the individual with a disability to inform the employer that an accommodation is needed. When the need for an accommodation is not obvious, an employer, before providing a reasonable accommodation, may require that the individual with a disability provide documentation of the need for accommodation.

See Senate Report at 34; House Labor Report at 65.

Process of Determining the Appropriate Reasonable Accommodation

Once a qualified individual with a disability has requested provision of a reasonable accommodation, the employer must make a reasonable effort to determine the appropriate accommodation. The appropriate reasonable accommodation is best determined through a flexible, interactive process that involves both the employer and the qualified individual with a disability. Although this process is described below in terms of accommodations that enable the individual with a disability to perform the essential functions of the position held or desired, it is equally applicable to accommodations involving the job application process, and to accommodations that enable the individual with a disability to enjoy equal benefits and privileges of employment. See Senate Report at 34-35; House Labor Report at 65-67.

When a qualified individual with a disability has requested a reasonable accommodation to assist in the performance of a job, the employer, using a problem solving approach, should:

(1) Analyze the particular job involved and determine its purpose and essential functions;

(2) Consult with the individual with a disability to ascertain the precise job-related limitations imposed by the individual's disability and how those limitations could be overcome with a reasonable accommodation;

(3) In consultation with the individual to be accommodated, identify potential accommodations and assess the effectiveness each would have in enabling the individual to perform the essential functions of the position; and

(4) Consider the preference of the individual to be accommodated and select and implement the accommodation that is most appropriate for both the employee and the employer.

In many instances, the appropriate reasonable accommodation may be so obvious to either or both the employer and the qualified individual with a disability that it may not be necessary to proceed in this step-by-step fashion. For example, if an employee who uses a wheelchair requests that his or her desk be placed on blocks to elevate the desktop above the arms of the wheelchair and the employer complies, an appropriate accommodation has been requested, identified, and provided without either the employee or employer being aware of having engaged in any sort of "reasonable accommodation process."

However, in some instances neither the individual requesting the accommodation nor the employer can readily identify the appropriate accommodation. For example, the individual needing the accommodation may not know enough about the equipment used by the employer or the exact nature of the work site to suggest an appropriate accommodation. Likewise, the employer may not know enough about the individual's disability or the limitations that disability would impose on the performance of the job to suggest an appropriate accommodation. Under such circumstances, it may be necessary for the employer to initiate a more defined problem solving process, such as the step-by-step process described above, as part of its reasonable effort to identify the appropriate reasonable accommodation.

This process requires the individual assessment of both the particular job at issue, and the specific physical or mental limitations of the particular individual in need of reasonable accommodation. With regard to assessment of the job, "individual assessment" means analyzing the actual job duties and determining the true purpose or object of the job. Such an assessment is necessary to ascertain which job functions are the essential functions that an accommodation must enable an individual with a disability to perform.

After assessing the relevant job, the employer, in consultation with the individual requesting the accommodation, should make an assessment of the specific limitations imposed by the disability on the individual's performance of the job's essential functions. This assessment will make it possible to ascertain the precise barrier to the employment opportunity which, in turn, will make it possible to determine the accommodation(s) that could alleviate or remove that barrier. If consultation with the individual in need of the accommodation still does not reveal potential appropriate accommodations, then the employer, as part of this process, may find that technical assistance is helpful in determining how to accommodate the particular individual in the specific situation. Such assistance could be sought from the Commission, from state or local rehabilitation agencies, or from disability constituent organizations. It should be noted, however, that, as provided in § 1630.9(c) of this part, the failure to obtain or receive technical assistance from the federal agencies that administer the ADA will not excuse the employer from its reasonable accommodation obligation.

Once potential accommodations have been identified, the employer should assess the effectiveness of each potential accommodation in assisting the individual in need of the accommodation in the performance of the essential functions of the position. If more than one of these accommodations will enable the individual to perform the essential functions or if the individual would prefer to provide his or her own accommodation, the preference of the individual with a disability should be given primary consideration. However, the employer providing the accommodation has the ultimate discretion to choose between effective accommodations, and may choose the less expensive accommodation or the accommodation that is easier for it to provide. It should also be noted that the individual's willingness to provide his or her own accommodation does not relieve the employer of the duty to provide the accommodation should the individual for any reason be unable or unwilling to continue to provide the accommodation.

Reasonable Accommodation Process Illustrated

The following example illustrates the informal reasonable accommodation process. Suppose a Sack Handler position requires that the employee pick up fifty pound sacks and carry them from the company loading dock to the storage room, and that a sack handler who is disabled by a back impairment requests a reasonable accommodation. Upon receiving the request, the employer analyzes the Sack Handler job and determines that the essential function and purpose of the job is not the requirement that the job holder physically lift and carry the sacks, but the requirement that the job holder cause the sack to move from the loading dock to the storage room.

The employer then meets with the sack handler to ascertain precisely the barrier posed by the individual's specific disability to the performance of the job's essential function of relocating the sacks. At this meeting the employer learns that the individual can, in fact, lift the sacks to waist level, but is prevented by his or her disability from carrying the sacks from the loading dock to the storage room. The employer and the individual agree that any of a number of potential accommodations, such as the provision of a dolly, hand truck, or cart, could enable the individual to transport the sacks that he or she has lifted.

Upon further consideration, however, it is determined that the provision of a cart is not a feasible effective option. No carts are currently available at the company, and those that can be purchased by the company are the wrong shape to hold many of the bulky and irregularly shaped sacks that must be moved. Both the dolly and the hand truck, on the other hand, appear to be effective options. Both are readily available to the company, and either will enable the individual to relocate the sacks that he or she has lifted. The sack handler indicates his or her preference for the dolly. In consideration of this expressed preference, and because the employer feels that the dolly will allow the individual to move more sacks at a time and so be more efficient than would a hand truck, the employer ultimately provides the sack handler with a dolly in fulfillment of the obligation to make reasonable accommodation.

Section 1630.9(b)

This provision states that an employer or other covered entity cannot prefer or select a qualified individual without a disability over an equally qualified individual with a disability merely because the individual with a disability will require a reasonable accommodation. In other words, an individual's need for an accommodation cannot enter into the employer's or other covered entity's decision regarding hiring, discharge, promotion, or other similar employment decisions, unless the accommodation would impose an undue hardship on the employer. See House Labor Report at 70.

Section 1630.9(d)

The purpose of this provision is to clarify that an employer or other covered entity may not compel a qualified individual with a disability to accept an accommodation, where that accommodation is neither requested nor needed by the individual. However, if a necessary reasonable accommodation is refused, the individual may not be considered qualified. For example, an individual with a visual impairment that restricts his or her field of vision but who is able to read unaided would not be required to accept a reader as an accommodation. However, if the individual were not able to read unaided and reading was an essential function of the job, the individual would not be qualified for the job if he or she refused a reasonable accommodation that would enable him or her to read. See Senate Report at 34; House Labor Report at 65; House Judiciary Report at 71-72.

Section 1630.10
Qualification Standards, Tests, and
Other Selection Criteria

The purpose of this provision is to ensure that individuals with disabilities are not excluded from job opportunities unless they are actually unable to do the job. It is to ensure that there is a fit between job criteria and an applicant's (or employee's) actual ability to do the job. Accordingly, job criteria that even unintentionally screen out, or tend to screen out, an individual with a disability or a class of individuals with disabilities because of their disability may not be used unless the employer demonstrates that that criteria, as used by the employer, are job-related to the position to which they are being applied and are consistent with business necessity. The concept of "business necessity" has the same meaning as the concept of "business necessity" under section 504 of the Rehabilitation Act of 1973.

Selection criteria that exclude, or tend to exclude, an individual with a disability or a class of individuals with disabilities because of their disability but do not concern an essential function of the job would not be consistent with business necessity.

The use of selection criteria that are related to an essential function of the job may be consistent with business necessity. However, selection criteria that are related to an essential function of the job may not be used to exclude an individual with a disability if that individual could satisfy the criteria with the provision of a reasonable accommodation. Experience under a similar provision of the regulations implementing section 504 of the Rehabilitation Act indicates that challenges to selection criteria are, in fact, most often resolved by reasonable accommodation. It is therefore anticipated that challenges to selection criteria brought under this part will generally be resolved in a like manner.

This provision is applicable to all types of selection criteria, including safety requirements, vision or hearing requirements, walking requirements, lifting requirements, and employment tests. See Senate Report at 37-39; House Labor Report at 70-72; House Judiciary Report at 42. As previously noted, however, it is not the intent of this part to second guess an employer's business judgment with regard to production standards. (See section 1630.2(n) Essential Functions). Consequently, production standards will generally not be subject to a challenge under this provision.

The Uniform Guidelines on Employee Selection Procedures (UGESP) 29 CFR part 1607 do not apply to the Rehabilitation Act and are similarly inapplicable to this part.

Section 1630.11 Administration of Tests

The intent of this provision is to further emphasize that individuals with disabilities are not to be excluded from jobs that they can actually perform merely because a disability prevents them from taking a test, or negatively influences the results of a test, that is a prerequisite to the job. Read together with the reasonable accommodation requirement of section 1630.9, this provision requires that employment tests be administered to eligible applicants or employees with disabilities that impair sensory, manual, or speaking skills in formats that do not require the use of the impaired skill.

The employer or other covered entity is, generally, only required to provide such reasonable accommodation if it knows, prior to the administration of the test, that the individual is disabled and that the disability impairs sensory, manual or speaking skills. Thus, for example, it would be unlawful to administer a written employment test to an individual who has informed the employer, prior to the administration of the test, that he is disabled with dyslexia and unable to read. In such a case, as a reasonable accommodation and in accordance with this provision, an alternative oral test should be administered to that individual. By the same token, a written test may need to be substituted for an oral test if the applicant taking the test is an individual with a disability that impairs speaking skills or impairs the processing of auditory information.

Occasionally, an individual with a disability may not realize, prior to the administration of a test, that he or she will need an accommodation to take that particular test. In such a situation, the individual with a disability, upon becoming aware of the need for an accommodation, must so inform the employer or other covered entity. For example, suppose an individual with a disabling visual impairment does not request an accommodation for a written examination because he or she is usually able to take written tests with the aid of his or her own specially designed lens. When the test is distributed, the individual with a disability discovers that the lens is insufficient to distinguish the words of the test because of the unusually low color contrast between the paper and the ink, the individual would be entitled, at that point, to request an accommodation. The employer or other covered entity would, thereupon, have to provide a test with higher contrast, schedule a retest, or provide any other effective accommodation unless to do so would impose an undue hardship.

Other alternative or accessible test modes or formats include the administration of tests in large print or braille, or via a reader or sign interpreter. Where it is not possible to test in an alternative format, the employer may be required, as a reasonable accommodation, to evaluate the skill to be tested in another manner (e.g., through an interview, or through education license, or work experience requirements). An employer may also be required, as a reasonable accommodation, to allow more time to complete the test. In addition, the employer's obligation to make reasonable accommodation extends to ensuring that the test site is accessible. (See § 1630.9 Not Making Reasonable Accommodation) See Senate Report at 37-38; House Labor Report at 70-72; House Judiciary Report at 42; see also *Stutts v. Freeman*, 694 F.2d 666 (11th Cir. 1983); *Crane v. Dole*, 617 F. Supp. 156 (D.D.C. 1985).

This provision does not require that an employer offer every applicant his or her choice of test format. Rather, this provision only requires that an employer provide, upon advance request, alternative, accessible tests to individuals with disabilities that impair sensory, manual, or speaking skills needed to take the test.

This provision does not apply to employment tests that require the use of sensory, manual, or speaking skills where the tests are intended to measure those skills. Thus, an employer could require that an applicant with dyslexia take a written test for a particular position if the ability to read is the skill the test is designed to measure. Similarly, an employer could require that an applicant complete a test within established time frames if speed were one of the skills for which the applicant was being tested. However, the results of such a test could not be used to exclude an individual with a disability unless the skill was necessary to perform an essential function of the position and no reasonable accommodation was available to enable the individual to perform that function, or the necessary accommodation would impose an undue hardship.

Section 1630.13 Prohibited Medical Examinations and Inquiries

Section 1630.13(a) Pre-employment Examination or Inquiry

This provision makes clear that an employer cannot inquire as to whether an individual has a disability at the pre-offer stage of the selection process. Nor can an employer inquire at the pre-offer stage about an applicant's workers' compensation history.

Employers may ask questions that relate to the applicant's ability to perform job-related functions. However, these questions should not be phrased in terms of disability. An employer, for example, may ask whether the applicant has a driver's license, if driving is a job function, but may not ask whether the applicant has a visual disability. Employers may ask about an applicant's ability to perform both essential and marginal job functions. Employers, though, may not refuse to hire an applicant with a disability because the applicant's disability prevents him or her from performing marginal functions. See Senate Report at 39; House Labor Report at 72-73; House Judiciary Report at 42-43.

Section 1630.13(b) Examination or Inquiry of Employees

The purpose of this provision is to prevent the administration to employees of medical tests or inquiries that do not serve a legitimate business purpose. For example, if an employee suddenly starts to use increased amounts of sick leave or starts to appear sickly, an employer could not require that employee to be tested for AIDS, HIV infection, or cancer unless the employer can demonstrate that such testing is job-related and consistent with business necessity. See Senate Report at 39; House Labor Report at 75; House Judiciary Report at 44.

Section 1630.14 Medical Examinations and Inquiries Specifically Permitted

Section 1630.14(a) Pre-employment Inquiry

Employers are permitted to make pre-employment inquiries into the ability of an applicant to perform job-related functions. This inquiry must be narrowly tailored. The employer may describe or demonstrate the job function and inquire whether or not the applicant can perform that function with or without reasonable accommodation. For example, an employer may explain that the job requires assembling small parts and ask if the individual will be able to perform that function, with or without reasonable accommodation. See Senate Report at 39; House Labor Report at 73; House Judiciary Report at 43.

An employer may also ask an applicant to describe or to demonstrate how, with or without reasonable accommodation, the applicant will be able to perform job-related functions. Such a request may be made of all applicants in the same job category regardless of disability. Such a request may also be made of an applicant whose known disability may interfere with or prevent the performance of a job-related function, whether or not the employer routinely makes such a request of all applicants in the job category. For example, an employer may ask an individual with one leg who applies for a position as a home washing machine repairman to demonstrate or to explain how, with or without reasonable accommodation, he would be able to transport himself and his tools down basement stairs. However, the employer may not inquire as to the nature or severity of the disability. Therefore, for example, the employer cannot ask how the individual lost the leg or whether the loss of the leg is indicative of an underlying impairment.

On the other hand, if the known disability of an applicant will not interfere with or prevent the performance of a job-related function, the employer may only request a description or demonstration by the applicant if it routinely makes such a request of all applicants in the same job category. So, for example, it would not be permitted for an employer to request that an applicant with one leg demonstrate his ability to assemble small parts while seated at a table, if the employer does not routinely request that all applicants provide such a demonstration.

An employer that requires an applicant with a disability to demonstrate how he or she will perform a job-related function must either provide the reasonable accommodation the applicant needs to perform the function or permit the applicant to explain how, with the accommodation, he or she will perform the function. If the job-related function is not an essential function, the employer may not exclude the applicant with a disability because of the applicant's inability to perform that function. Rather, the employer must, as a reasonable accommodation, either provide an accommodation that will enable the individual to perform the function, transfer the function to another position, or exchange the function for one the applicant is able to perform.

An employer may not use an application form that lists a number of potentially disabling impairments and ask the applicant to check any of the impairments he or she may have. In addition, as noted above, an employer may not ask how a particular individual became disabled or the prognosis of the individual's disability. The employer is also prohibited from asking how often the individual will require leave for treatment or use leave as a result of incapacitation because of the disability. However, the employer may state the attendance requirements of the job and inquire whether the applicant can meet them.

An employer is permitted to ask, on a test announcement or application form, that individuals with disabilities who will require a reasonable accommodation in order to take the test so inform the employer within a reasonable established time period prior to the administration of the test. The employer may also request that documentation of the need for the accommodation accompany the request. Requested accommodations may include accessible testing sites, modified testing conditions and accessible test formats. (See § 1630.11 Administration of Tests).

Physical agility tests are not medical examinations and so may be given at any point in the application or employment process. Such tests must be given to all similarly situated applicants or employees regardless of disability. If such tests screen out or tend to screen out an individual with a disability or a class of individuals with disabilities, the employer would have to demonstrate that the test is job-related and consistent with business necessity and that performance cannot be achieved with reasonable accommodation. (See § 1630.9 Not Making Reasonable Accommodation: Process of Determining the Appropriate Reasonable Accommodation).

As previously noted, collecting information and inviting individuals to identify themselves as individuals with disabilities as required to satisfy the affirmative action requirements of Section 503 of the Rehabilitation Act is not restricted by this part. (See § 1630.1 (b) and (c) Applicability and Construction).

Section 1630.14(b)
Employment Entrance Examination

An employer is permitted to require post-offer medical examinations before the employee actually starts working. The employer may condition the offer of employment on the results of the examination, provided that all entering employees in the same job category are subjected to such an examination, regardless of disability, and that the confidentiality requirements specified in this part are met.

This provision recognizes that in many industries, such as air transportation or construction, applicants for certain positions are chosen on the basis of many factors including physical and psychological criteria, some of which may be identified as a result of post-offer medical examinations given prior to entry on duty. Only those employees who meet the employer's physical and psychological criteria for the job, with or without reasonable accommodation, will be qualified to receive confirmed offers of employment and begin working.

Medical examinations permitted by this section are not required to be job-related and consistent with business necessity. However, if an employer withdraws an offer of employment because the medical examination reveals that the employee does not satisfy certain employment criteria, either the exclusionary criteria must not screen out or tend to screen out an individual with a disability or a class of individuals with disabilities, or they must be job-related and consistent with business necessity. As part of the showing that an exclusionary criteria is job-related and consistent with business necessity, the employer must also demonstrate that there is no reasonable accommodation that will enable the individual with a disability to perform the essential functions of the job. See Conference Report at 59-60; Senate Report at 39; House Labor Report at 73-74; House Judiciary Report at 43.

As an example, suppose an employer makes a conditional offer of employment to an applicant, and it is an essential function of the job that the incumbent be available to work every day for the next three months. An employment entrance examination then reveals that the applicant has a disabling impairment that, according to reasonable medical judgment that relies on the most current medical knowledge, will require treatment that will render the applicant unable to work for a portion of the three month period. Under these circumstances, the employer would be able to withdraw the employment offer without violating this part.

The information obtained in the course of a permitted entrance examination or inquiry is to be treated as a confidential medical record and may only be used in a manner not inconsistent with this part. State workers' compensation laws are not preempted by the ADA or this part. These laws require the collection of information from individuals for state administrative purposes that do not conflict with the ADA or this part. Consequently, employers or other covered entities may submit information to state workers' compensation offices or second injury funds in accordance with state workers' compensation laws without violating this part.

Consistent with this section and with § 1630.16(f) of this part, information obtained in the course of a permitted entrance examination or inquiry may be used for insurance purposes described in § 1630.16(f).

Section 1630.14(c)
Examination of Employees

This provision permits employers to make inquiries or require medical examinations (fitness for duty exams) when there is a need to determine whether an employee is still able to perform the essential functions of his or her job. The provision permits employers or other covered entities to make inquiries or require medical examinations necessary to the reasonable accommodation process described in this part. This provision also permits periodic physicals to determine fitness for duty or other medical monitoring if such physicals or monitoring are required by medical standards or requirements established by Federal, state, or local law that are consistent with the ADA and this part (or in the case of a federal standard, with section 504 of the Rehabilitation Act) in that they are job-related and consistent with business necessity.

Such standards may include federal safety regulations that regulate bus and truck driver qualifications, as well as laws establishing medical requirements for pilots or other air transportation personnel. These standards also include health standards promulgated pursuant to the Occupational Safety and Health Act of 1970, the Federal Coal Mine Health and Safety Act of 1969, or other similar statutes that require that employees exposed to certain toxic and hazardous substances be medically monitored at specific intervals. See House Labor Report at 74-75.

The information obtained in the course of such examination or inquiries is to be treated as a confidential medical record and may only be used in a manner not inconsistent with this part.

Section 1630.14(d) Other
Acceptable Examinations and Inquiries

Part 1630 permits voluntary medical examinations, including voluntary medical histories, as part of employee health programs. These programs often include, for example, medical screening for high blood pressure, weight control counseling, and cancer detection. Voluntary activities, such as blood pressure monitoring and the administering of prescription drugs, such as insulin, are also permitted. It should be noted, however, that the medical records developed in the course of such activities must be maintained in the confidential manner required by this part and must not be used for any purpose in violation of this part, such as limiting health insurance eligibility. House Labor Report at 75; House Judiciary Report at 43-44.

Section 1630.15 Defenses

The section on defenses in part 1630 is not intended to be exhaustive. However, it is intended to inform employers of some of the potential defenses available to a charge of discrimination under the ADA and this part.

Section 1630.15(a)
Disparate Treatment Defenses

The "traditional" defense to a charge of disparate treatment under title VII, as expressed in *McDonnell Douglas Corp. v. Green*, 411 U.S. 792 (1973), *Texas Department of Community Affairs v. Burdine*, 450 U.S. 248 (1981), and their progeny, may be applicable to charges of disparate treatment brought under the ADA. See *Prewitt v. U.S. Postal Service*, 662 F.2d 292 (5th Cir. 1981). Disparate treatment means, with respect to title I of the ADA, that an individual was treated differently on the basis of his or her disability. For example, disparate treatment has occurred where an employer excludes an employee with a severe facial disfigurement from staff meetings because the employer does not like to look at the employee. The individual is being treated differently because of the employer's attitude towards his or her perceived disability. Disparate treatment has also occurred where an employer has a policy of not hiring individuals with AIDS regardless of the individuals' qualifications.

The crux of the defense to this type of charge is that the individual was treated differently not because of his or her disability but for a legitimate nondiscriminatory reason such as poor performance unrelated to the individual's disability. The fact that the individual's disability is not covered by the employer's current insurance plan or would cause the employer's insurance premiums or workers' compensation costs to increase, would not be a legitimate nondiscriminatory reason justifying disparate treatment of an individual with a disability. Senate Report at 85; House Labor Report at 136 and House Judiciary Report at 70. The defense of a legitimate nondiscriminatory reason is rebutted if the alleged nondiscriminatory reason is shown to be pretextual.

Section 1630.15 (b) and (c)
Disparate Impact Defenses

Disparate impact means, with respect to title I of the ADA and this part, that uniformly applied criteria have an adverse impact on an individual with a disability or a disproportionately negative impact on a class of individuals with disabilities. Section 1630.15(b) clarifies that an employer may use selection criteria that have such a disparate impact, i.e., that screen out or tend to screen out an individual with a disability or a class of individuals with disabilities only when they are job-related and consistent with business necessity.

For example, an employer interviews two candidates for a position, one of whom is blind. Both are equally qualified. The employer decides that while it is not essential to the job it would be convenient to have an employee who has a driver's license and so could occasionally be asked to run errands by car. The employer hires the individual who is sighted because this individual has a driver's license. This is an example of a uniformly applied criterion, having a driver's permit, that screens out an individual who has a disability that makes it impossible to obtain a driver's permit. The employer would, thus, have to show that this criterion is job-related and consistent with business necessity. See House Labor Report at 55.

However, even if the criterion is job-related and consistent with business necessity, an employer could not exclude an individual with a disability if the criterion could be met or job performance accomplished with a reasonable accommodation. For example, suppose an employer requires, as part of its application process, an interview that is job-related and consistent with business necessity. The employer would not be able to refuse to hire a hearing impaired applicant because he or she could not be interviewed. This is so because an interpreter could be provided as a reasonable accommodation that would allow the individual to be interviewed, and thus satisfy the selection criterion.

With regard to safety requirements that screen out or tend to screen out an individual with a disability or a class of individuals with disabilities, an employer must demonstrate that the requirement, as applied to the individual, satisfies the "direct threat" standard in § 1630.2(r) in order to show that the requirement is job-related and consistent with business necessity.

Section 1630.15(c) clarifies that there may be uniformly applied standards, criteria and policies not relating to selection that may also screen out or tend to screen out an individual with a disability or a class of individuals with disabilities. Like selection criteria that have a disparate impact, non-selection criteria having such an impact may also have to be job-related and consistent with business necessity, subject to consideration of reasonable accommodation.

It should be noted, however, that some uniformly applied employment policies or practices, such as leave policies, are not subject to challenge under the adverse impact theory. "No-leave" policies (e.g., no leave during the first six months of employment) are likewise not subject to challenge under the adverse impact theory. However, an employer, in spite of its "no-leave" policy, may, in appropriate circumstances, have to consider the provision of leave to an employee with a disability as a reasonable accommodation, unless the provision of leave would impose an undue hardship. See discussion at § 1630.5 Limiting, Segregating and Classifying, and § 1630.10 Qualification Standards, Tests, and Other Selection Criteria.

Section 1630.15(d) Defense to Not Making Reasonable Accommodation

An employer or other covered entity alleged to have discriminated because it did not make a reasonable accommodation, as required by this part, may offer as a defense that it would have been an undue hardship to make the accommodation.

It should be noted, however, that an employer cannot simply assert that a needed accommodation will cause it undue hardship, as defined in § 1630.2(p), and thereupon be relieved of the duty to provide accommodation. Rather, an employer will have to present evidence and demonstrate that the accommodation will, in fact, cause it undue hardship. Whether a particular accommodation will impose an undue hardship for a particular employer is determined on a case by case basis. Consequently, an accommodation that poses an undue hardship for one employer at a particular time may not pose an undue hardship for another employer, or even for the same employer at another time. Likewise, an accommodation that poses an undue hardship for one employer in a particular job setting, such as a temporary construction work site, may not pose an undue hardship for another employer, or even for the same employer at a permanent worksite. See House Judiciary Report at 42.

The concept of undue hardship that has evolved under Section 504 of the Rehabilitation Act and is embodied in this part is unlike the "undue hardship" defense associated with the provision of religious accommodation under title VII of the Civil Rights Act of 1964. To demonstrate undue hardship pursuant to the ADA and this part, an employer must show substantially more difficulty or expense than would be needed to satisfy the "de minimis" title VII standard of undue hardship. For example, to demonstrate that the cost of an accommodation poses an undue hardship, an employer would have to show that the cost is undue as compared to the employer's budget. Simply comparing the cost of the accommodation to the salary of the individual with a disability in need of the accommodation will not suffice. Moreover, even if it is determined that the cost of an accommodation would unduly burden an employer, the employer cannot avoid making the accommodation if the individual with a disability can arrange to cover that portion of the cost that rises to the undue hardship level, or can otherwise arrange to provide the accommodation. Under such circumstances, the necessary accommodation would no longer pose an undue hardship. See Senate Report at 36; House Labor Report at 68-69; House Judiciary Report at 40-41. Excessive cost is only one of several possible bases upon which an employer might be able to demonstrate undue hardship. Alternatively, for example, an employer could demonstrate that the provision of a particular accommodation would be unduly disruptive to its other employees or to the functioning of its business. The terms of a collective bargaining agreement may be relevant to this determination. By way of illustration, an employer would likely be able to show undue hardship if the employer could show that the requested accommodation of the upward adjustment of the business' thermostat would result in it becoming unduly hot for its other employees, or for its patrons or customers. The employer would thus not have to provide this accommodation. However, if there were an alternate accommodation that would not result in undue hardship, the employer would have to provide that accommodation.

It should be noted, moreover, that the employer would not be able to show undue hardship if the disruption to its employees were the result of those employees fears or prejudices toward the individual's disability and not the result of the provision of the accommodation. Nor would the employer be able to demonstrate undue hardship by showing that the provision of the accommodation has a negative impact on the morale of its other employees but not on the ability of these employees to perform their jobs.

Section 1630.15(e) Defense—Conflicting Federal Laws and Regulations

There are several Federal laws and regulations that address medical standards and safety requirements. If the alleged discriminatory action was taken in compliance with another Federal law or regulation, the employer may offer its obligation to comply with the conflicting standard as a defense. The employer's defense of a conflicting Federal requirement or regulation may be rebutted by a showing of pretext, or by showing that the Federal standard did not require the discriminatory action, or that there was a non-exclusionary means to comply with the standard that would not conflict with this part. See House Labor Report at 74.

Section 1630.16 Specific Activities Permitted

Section 1630.16(a) Religious Entities

Religious organizations are not exempt from title I of the ADA or this part. A religious corporation, association, educational institution, or society may give a preference in employment to individuals of the particular religion, and may require that applicants and employees conform to the religious tenets of the organization. However, a religious organization may not discriminate against an individual who satisfies the permitted religious criteria because that individual is disabled. The religious entity, in other words, is required to consider qualified individuals with disabilities who satisfy the permitted religious criteria on an equal basis with qualified individuals without disabilities who similarly satisfy the religious criteria. See Senate Report at 42; House Labor Report at 76-77; House Judiciary Report at 46.

Section 1630.16(b) Regulation of Alcohol and Drugs

This provision permits employers to establish or comply with certain standards regulating the use of drugs and alcohol in the workplace. It also allows employers to hold alcoholics and persons who engage in the illegal use of drugs to the same performance and conduct standards to which it holds all of its other employees. Individuals disabled by alcoholism are entitled to the same protections accorded other individuals with disabilities under this part. As noted above, individuals currently engaging in the illegal use of drugs are not individuals with disabilities for purposes of part 1630 when the employer acts on the basis of such use.

Section 1630.16(c) Drug Testing

This provision reflects title I's neutrality toward testing for the illegal use of drugs. Such drug tests are neither encouraged, authorized nor prohibited. The results of such drug tests may be used as a basis for disciplinary action. Tests for the illegal use of drugs are not considered medical examinations for purposes of this part. If the results reveal information about an individual's medical condition beyond whether the individual is currently engaging in the illegal use of drugs, this additional information is to be treated as a confidential medical record. For example, if a test for the illegal use of drugs reveals the presence of a controlled substance that has been lawfully prescribed for a particular medical condition, this information is to be treated as a confidential medical record. See House Labor Report at 79; House Judiciary Report at 47.

1630.16(e) Infectious and Communicable Diseases; Food Handling Jobs

This provision addressing food handling jobs applies the "direct threat" analysis to the particular situation of accommodating individuals with infectious or communicable diseases that are transmitted through the handling of food. The Department of Health and Human Services is to prepare a list of infectious and communicable diseases that are transmitted through the handling of food. If an individual with a disability has one of the listed diseases and works in or applies for a position in food handling, the employer must determine whether there is a reasonable accommodation that will eliminate the risk of transmitting the disease through the handling of food. If there is an accommodation that will not pose an undue hardship, and that an individual is an applicant for a food handling position the employer is not required to hire the individual. However, if the individual is a current employee, the employer would be required to consider the accommodation of reassignment to a vacant position not involving food handling for which the individual is qualified. Conference Report at 61-63. (See § 1630.2(r) Direct Threat).

1630.16(f) Health Insurance, Life Insurance, and Other Benefit Plans

This provision is a limited exemption that is only applicable to those who establish, sponsor, observe or administer benefit plans, such as health and life insurance plans. It does not apply to those who establish, sponsor, observe or administer plans not involving benefits, such as liability insurance plans.

The purpose of this provision is to permit the development and administration of benefit plans in accordance with accepted principles of risk assessment. This provision is not intended to disrupt the current regulatory structure for self-insured employers. These employers may establish, sponsor, observe, or administer the terms of a bona fide benefit plan not subject to state laws that regulate insurance. This provision is also not intended to disrupt the current nature of insurance underwriting, or current insurance industry practices in sales, underwriting, pricing, administrative and other services, claims and similar insurance related activities based on classification of risks as regulated by the States.

The activities permitted by this provision do not violate part 1630 even if they result in limitations on individuals with disabilities, provided that these activities are not used as a subterfuge to evade the purposes of this part. Whether or not these activities are being used as a subterfuge is to be determined without regard to the date the insurance plan or employee benefit plan was adopted.

However, an employer or other covered entity cannot deny a qualified individual with a disability equal access to insurance or subject a qualified individual with a disability to different terms or conditions of insurance based on disability alone, if the disability does not pose increased risks. Part 1630 requires that decisions not based on risk classification be made in conformity with non-discrimination requirements. See Senate Report at 84-86; House Labor Report at 136-138; House Judiciary Report at 70-71. See the discussion of § 1630.5 Limiting, Segregating and Classifying.

ADA TITLE I EEOC TECHNICAL ASSISTANCE MANUAL

TABLE OF CONTENTS

January 1992 EEOC-M-1A

I-I. TITLE I: An Overview of Legal Requirements

This chapter of the manual provides a brief overview of the basic requirements of Title I of the ADA. Following chapters look at these and other requirements in more detail and illustrate how they apply to specific employment practices.

Who Must Comply with Title I of the ADA?

Private employers, state and local governments, employment agencies, labor unions, and joint labor-management committees must comply with Title I of the ADA. The ADA calls these "covered entities." For simplicity, this manual generally refers to all covered entities as "employers," except where there is a specific reason to emphasize the responsibilities of a particular type of entity.

An employer cannot discriminate against qualified applicants and employees on the basis of disability. The ADA's requirements ultimately will apply to employers with 15 or more employees. To give smaller employers more time to prepare for compliance, coverage is phased in two steps as follows:

Number of employees	Coverage begins
25 or more	July 26, 1992
15 or more	July 26, 1994

Covered employers are those who have 25 or more employees (1992) or 15 or more employees (1994), including part-time employees, working for them for 20 or more calendar weeks in the current or preceding calendar year. The ADA's definition of "employee" includes U.S. citizens who work for American companies, their subsidiaries, or firms controlled by Americans outside the USA. However, the Act provides an exemption from coverage for any action in compliance with the ADA which would violate the law of the foreign country in which a workplace is located.

(Note that state and local governments, regardless of size, are covered by employment nondiscrimination requirements under Title II of the ADA as of January 26, 1992. See Coordination of Overlapping Federal Requirements below.)

The definition of "employer" includes persons who are "agents" of the employer, such as managers, supervisors, foremen, or others who act for the employer, such as agencies used to conduct background checks on candidates. Therefore, the employer is responsible for actions of such persons that may violate the law. These coverage requirements are similar to those of Title VII of the Civil Rights Act of 1964.

Special Situations

Religious organizations are covered by the ADA, but they may give employment preference to people of their own religion or religious organization.

For example: A church organization could require that its employees be members of its religion However, it could not discriminate in employment on the basis of disability against members of its religion.

The legislative branch of the U.S. Government is covered by the ADA, but is governed by different enforcement procedures established by the Congress for its employees.

Certain individuals appointed by elected officials of state and local governments also are covered by the special enforcement procedures established for Congressional employees.

Who Is Exempt?

Executive agencies of the U.S. Government are exempt from the ADA, but these agencies are covered by similar nondiscrimination requirements and additional affirmative employment requirements under Section 501 of the Rehabilitation Act of 1973. Also exempted from the ADA (as they are from Title VII of the Civil Rights Act) are corporations fully owned by the U.S. Government, Indian tribes, and bona fide private membership clubs that are not labor organizations and that are exempt from taxation under the Internal Revenue Code.

Who is Protected by Title I?

The ADA prohibits employment discrimination against "qualified individuals with disabilities." A qualified individual with a disability is:

an individual with a disability who meets the skill, experience, education, and other job-related requirements of a position held or desired, and who, with or without reasonable accommodation, can perform the essential functions of a job.

To understand who is and who is not protected by the ADA, it is first necessary to understand the Act's definition of an "individual with a disability" and then determine if the individual meets the Act's definition of a "qualified individual with a disability."

The ADA definition of individual with a disability is very specific. A person with a "disability" is an individual who:

- has a physical or mental impairment that substantially limits one or more of his/her major life activities;
- has a record of such an impairment; or
- is regarded as having such an impairment.

(See Chapter II.)

Individuals Specifically not Protected by the ADA

The ADA specifically states that certain individuals are not protected by its provisions:

Persons who currently use drugs illegally

Individuals who currently use drugs illegally are not individuals with disabilities protected under the Act when an employer takes action because of their continued use of drugs. This includes people who use prescription drugs illegally as well as those who use illegal drugs.

However, people who have been rehabilitated and do not currently use drugs illegally, or who are in the process of completing a rehabilitation program may be protected by the ADA. (See Chapter VIII.)

Other Specific Exclusions

The Act states that homosexuality and bisexuality are not impairments and therefore are not disabilities under the ADA. In addition, the Act specifically excludes a number of behavior disorders from the definition of "individual with a disability." (See Chapter II.)

Employment Practices Regulated by Title I of the ADA

Employers cannot discriminate against people with disabilities in regard to any employment practices or terms, conditions, and privileges of employment. This prohibition covers all aspects of the employment process, including:

- application
- testing
- hiring
- assignments
- evaluation
- disciplinary actions
- training
- promotion
- medical examinations
- layoff/recall
- termination
- compensation
- leave
- benefits

Actions which Constitute Discrimination

The ADA specifies types of actions that may constitute discrimination. These actions are discussed more fully in the following chapters, as indicated:

1) Limiting, segregating, or classifying a job applicant or employee in a way that adversely affects employment opportunities for the applicant or employee because of his or her disability. (See Chapter VII.)
2) Participating in a contractual or other arrangement or relationship that subjects an employer's qualified applicant or employee with a disability to discrimination. (See Chapter VII.)
3) Denying employment opportunities to a qualified individual because s/he has a relationship or association with a person with a disability. (See Chapter VII.)
4) Refusing to make reasonable accommodation to the known physical or mental limitations of a qualified applicant or employee with a disability, unless the accommodation would pose an undue hardship on the business. (See Chapters III. and VII.)
5) Using qualification standards, employment tests, or other selection criteria that screen out or tend to screen out an individual with a disability unless they are job-related and necessary for the business. (See Chapter IV.)
6) Failing to use employment tests in the most effective manner to measure actual abilities. Tests must accurately reflect the skills, aptitude, or other factors being measured, and not the impaired sensory, manual, or speaking skills of an employee or applicant with a disability (unless those are the skills the test is designed to measure). (See Chapter V.)
7) Denying an employment opportunity to a qualified individual because s/he has a relationship or association with an individual with a disability. (See Chapter VII.)
8) Discriminating against an individual because s/he has opposed an employment practice of the employer or filed a complaint, testified, assisted, or participated in an investigation, proceeding, or hearing to enforce provisions of the Act. (See Chapter X.)

Reasonable Accommodation and the Undue Hardship Limitation

Reasonable accommodation

Reasonable accommodation is a critical component of the ADA's assurance of nondiscrimination. Reasonable accommodation is any change in the work environment or in the way things are usually done that results in equal employment opportunity for an individual with a disability.

An employer must make a reasonable accommodation to the known physical or mental limitations of a qualified applicant or employee with a disability unless it can show that the accommodation would cause an undue hardship on the operation of its business.

Some examples of reasonable accommodation include:

- making existing facilities used by employees readily accessible to, and usable by, an individual with a disability;
- job restructuring;
- modifying work schedules;
- reassignment to a vacant position;
- acquiring or modifying equipment or devices;
- adjusting or modifying examinations, training materials, or policies;
- providing qualified readers or interpreters.

An employer is not required to lower quality or quantity standards to make an accommodation. Nor is an employer obligated to provide personal use items, such as glasses or hearing aids, as accommodations.

Undue hardship

An employer is not required to provide an accommodation if it will impose an undue hardship on the operation of its business. Undue hardship is defined by the ADA as an action that is:

> "excessively costly, extensive, substantial, or disruptive, or that would fundamentally alter the nature or operation of the business."

In determining undue hardship, factors to be considered include the nature and cost of the accommodation in relation to the size, the financial resources, the nature and structure of the employer's operation, as well as the impact of the accommodation on the specific facility providing the accommodation. (See Chapter III.)

Health or Safety Defense

An employer may require that an individual not pose a "direct threat" to the health or safety of himself/herself or others. A health or safety risk can only be considered if it is "a significant risk of substantial harm." Employers cannot deny an employment opportunity merely because of a slightly increased risk. An assessment of "direct threat" must be strictly based on valid medical analyses and/or other objective evidence, and not on speculation. Like any qualification standard, this requirement must apply to all applicants and employees, not just to people with disabilities.

If an individual appears to pose a direct threat because of a disability, the employer must first try to eliminate or reduce the risk to an acceptable level with reasonable accommodation. If an effective accommodation cannot be found, the employer may refuse to hire an applicant or discharge an employee who poses a direct threat. (See Chapter IV.)

Pre-Employment Inquiries and Medical Examinations

An employer may not ask a job applicant about the existence, nature, or severity of a disability. Applicants may be asked about their ability to perform specific job functions. An employer may not make medical inquiries or conduct a medical examination until after a job offer has been made. A job offer may be conditioned on the results of a medical examination or inquiry, but only if this is required for all entering employees in similar jobs. Medical examinations of employees must be job-related and consistent with the employer's business needs. (See Chapters V. and VI.)

Drug and Alcohol Use

It is not a violation of the ADA for employers to use drug tests to find out if applicants or employees are currently illegally using drugs. Tests for illegal use of drugs are not subject to the ADA's restrictions on medical examinations. Employers may hold illegal users of drugs and alcoholics to the same performance and conduct standards as other employees.. (See Chapter VIII.)

Enforcement and Remedies

The U.S. Equal Employment Opportunity Commission (EEOC) has responsibility for enforcing compliance with Title I of the ADA. An individual with a disability who believes that (s)he has been discriminated against in employment can file a charge with EEOC. The procedures for processing charges of discrimination under the ADA are the same as those under Title VII of the Civil Rights Act of 1964. (See Chapter X.)

Remedies that may be required of an employer who is found to have discriminated against an applicant or employee with a disability include compensatory and punitive damages, back pay, front pay, restored benefits, attorney's fees, reasonable accommodation, reinstatement, and job offers. (See Chapter X.)

Posting Notices

An employer must post notices concerning the provisions of the ADA. The notices must be accessible, as needed, to persons with visual or other reading disabilities. A new equal employment opportunity (EEO) poster, containing ADA provisions and other federal employment nondiscrimination provisions may be obtained by writing EEOC at 1801 L Street N.W., Washington, D.C., 20507, or calling 1-800-669-EEOC or 1-800-800-3302 (TDD).

Coordination of Overlapping Federal Requirements

Employers covered by Title I of the ADA also may be covered by other federal requirements that prohibit discrimination on the basis of disability. The ADA directs the agencies with enforcement authority for these legal requirements to coordinate their activities to prevent duplication and avoid conflicting standards. Overlapping requirements exist for both public and private employers.

Title II of the ADA, enforced by the U.S. Department of Justice, prohibits discrimination in all state and local government programs and activities, including employment, after January 26, 1992.

The Department of Justice regulations implementing Title II provide that EEOC's Title I regulations will constitute the employment nondiscrimination requirements for those state and local governments covered by Title I (governments with 25 or more employees after July 26, 1992; governments with 15 or more employees after July 26, 1994). If a government is not covered by Title I, or until it is covered, the Title II employment nondiscrimination requirements will be those in the Department of Justice coordination regulations applicable to federally assisted programs under Section 504 of the Rehabilitation Act of 1973, which prohibits discrimination on the basis of disability by recipients of federal financial assistance.

Section 504 employment requirements in most respects are the same as those of Title I, because the ADA was based on the Section 504 regulatory requirements. (Note that governments receiving federal financial assistance, as well as federally funded private entities, will continue to be covered by Section 504.)

In addition, some private employers are covered by Section 503 of the Rehabilitation Act. Section 503 requires nondiscrimination and affirmative action by federal contractors and subcontractors to employ and advance individuals with disabilities, and is enforced by the Office of Federal Contract Compliance Programs (OFCCP) in the U.S. Department of Labor.

The EEOC, the Department of Labor, the Department of Justice and the other agencies that enforce Section 504 (i.e., Federal agencies with programs of financial assistance) will coordinate their enforcement efforts under the ADA and the Rehabilitation Act, to assure consistent standards and to eliminate unnecessary duplication. (See Chapter X For further information see Resource Directory: "Federal Agencies that Enforce Other Laws Prohibiting Discrimination on the Basis of Disability.")

I-II. Who is Protected by the ADA?

I-2.1 Introduction.

The ADA protects qualified individuals with disabilities from employment discrimination. Under other laws that prohibit employment discrimination, it usually is a simple matter to know whether an individual is covered because of his or her race, color, sex, national origin or age. But to know whether a person is covered by the employment provisions of the ADA can be more complicated It is first necessary to understand the Act's very specific definitions of "disability" and "qualified individual with a disability." Like other determinations under the ADA, deciding who is a "qualified" individual is a case-by case process, depending on the circumstances of the particular employment situation.

I-2.2 Individual With a Disability.

The ADA has a three-part definition of "disability." This definition, based on the definition under the Rehabilitation Act, reflects the specific types of discrimination experienced by people with disabilities. Accordingly, it is not the same as the definition of disability in other laws, such as state workers' compensation laws or other federal or state laws that provide benefits for people with disabilities and disabled veterans.

Under the ADA, an individual with a disability is a person who has:

- a physical or mental impairment that substantially limits one or more major life activities;
- a record of such an impairment; or
- is regarded as having such an impairment.

I-2.2(a) An Impairment that Substantially Limits Major Life Activities.

The first part of this definition has three major subparts that further define who is and who is not protected by the ADA.

(i) A Physical or Mental Impairment

A physical impairment is defined by the ADA as:

"[a]ny physiological disorder, or condition, cosmetic disfigurement, or anatomical loss affecting one or more of the following body systems: neurological, musculoskeletal, special sense organs, respiratory (including speech organs), cardiovascular, reproductive, digestive, genito-urinary, hemic and lymphatic, skin, and endocrine."

A mental impairment is defined by the ADA as:

"[a]ny mental or psychological disorder, such as mental retardation, organic brain syndrome, emotional or mental illness, and specific learning disabilities."

Neither the statute nor EEOC regulations list all diseases or conditions that make up "physical or mental impairments," because it would be impossible to provide a comprehensive list, given the variety of possible impairments.

A person's impairment is determined without regard to any medication or assistive device that s/he may use.

For example: A person who has epilepsy and uses medication to control seizures, or a person who walks with an artificial leg would be considered to have an impairment, even if the medicine or prosthesis reduces the impact of that impairment.

An impairment under the ADA is a physiological or mental disorder; simple physical characteristics, therefore, such as eye or hair color, lefthandedness, or height or weight within a normal range, are not impairments. A physical condition that is not the result of a physiological disorder, such as pregnancy, or a predisposition to a certain disease would not be an impairment. Similarly, personality traits such as poor judgment, quick temper or irresponsible behavior, are not themselves impairments. Environmental, cultural, or economic disadvantages, such as lack of education or a prison record also are not impairments.

For example: A person who cannot read due to dyslexia is an individual with a disability because dyslexia, which is a learning disability, is an impairment. But a person who cannot read because she dropped out of school is not an individual with a disability, because lack of education is not an impairment.

"Stress" and "depression" are conditions that may or may not be considered impairments, depending on whether these conditions result from a documented physiological or mental disorder.

For example: A person suffering from general "stress" because of job or personal life pressures would not be considered to have an impairment. However, if this person is diagnosed by a psychiatrist as having an identifiable stress disorder, s/he would have an impairment that may be a disability.

A person who has a contagious disease has an impairment For example, infection with the Human Immunodeficiency Virus (HIV) is an impairment. The Supreme Court has ruled that an individual with tuberculosis which affected her respiratory system had an impairment under Section 504 of the Rehabilitation Act.[1] However, although a person who has a contagious disease may be covered by the ADA, an employer would not have to hire or retain a person whose contagious disease posed a direct threat to health or safety, if no reasonable accommodation could reduce or eliminate this threat. (See Health and Safety Standards, Chapter IV.)

(ii) Major Life Activities

To be a disability covered by the ADA, an impairment must substantially limit one or more major life activities. These are activities that an average person can perform with little or no difficulty. Examples are:

– walking	– seeing
– speaking	– hearing
– breathing	– learning
– performing manual	– caring for oneself
– tasks	– working

These are examples only. Other activities such as sitting, standing, lifting, or reading are also major life activities.

(iii) Substantially Limits

An impairment is only a "disability" under the ADA if it substantially limits one or more major life activities. An individual must be unable to perform, or be significantly limited in the ability to perform, an activity compared to an average person in the general population.

The regulations provide three factors to consider in determining whether a person's impairment substantially limits a major life activity.

- its nature and severity;
- how long it will last or is expected to last;
- its permanent or long term impact, or expected impact.

These factors must be considered because, generally, it is not the name of an impairment or a condition that determines whether a person is protected by the ADA, but rather the effect of an impairment or condition on the life of a particular person. Some impairments, such as blindness, deafness, HIV infection or AIDS, are by their nature substantially limiting, but many other impairments may be disabling for some individuals but not for others, depending on the impact on their activities.

For example: Although cerebral palsy frequently significantly restricts major life activities such as speaking, walking and performing manual tasks, an individual with very mild cerebral palsy that only slightly interferes with his ability to speak and has no significant impact on other major life activities is not an individual with a disability under this part of the definition.

The determination as to whether an individual is substantially limited must always be based on the effect of an impairment on that individual's life activities.

For example: An individual who had been employed as a receptionist-clerk sustained a back injury that resulted in considerable pain. The pain permanently restricted her ability to walk, sit, stand, drive, care for her home, and engage in recreational activities. Another individual who had been employed as a general laborer had sustained a back injury, but was able to continue an active life, including recreational sports, and had obtained a new position as a security guard. The first individual was found by a court to be an individual with a disability; the second individual was found not significantly restricted in any major life activity, and therefore not an individual with a disability.

Sometimes, an individual may have two or more impairments, neither of which by itself substantially limits a major life activity, but that together have this effect. In such a situation, the individual has a disability.

For example: A person has a mild form of arthritis in her wrists and hands and a mild form of osteoporosis. Neither impairment by itself substantially

[1] See *School Board of Nassau Cty. v. Arline*, 480 U.S. 273 (1987).

limits a major life activity. Together, however, these impairments significantly restrict her ability to lift and perform manual tasks. She has a disability under the ADA.

Temporary Impairments

Employers frequently ask whether "temporary disabilities" are covered by the ADA. How long an impairment lasts is a factor to be considered, but does not by itself determine whether a person has a disability under the ADA. The basic question is whether an impairment "substantially limits" one or more major life activities. This question is answered by looking at the extent, duration, and impact of the impairment. Temporary, non-chronic impairments that do not last for a long time and that have little or no long term impact usually are not disabilities.

For example: Broken limbs, sprains, concussions, appendicitis, common colds, or influenza generally would not be disabilities. A broken leg that heals normally within a few months, for example, would not be a disability under the ADA. However, if a broken leg took significantly longer than the normal healing period to heal, and during this period the individual could not walk, s/he would be considered to have a disability. Or, if the leg did not heal properly, and resulted in a permanent impairment that significantly restricted walking or other major life activities, s/he would be considered to have a disability.

Substantially Limited in Working

It is not necessary to consider if a person is substantially limited in the major life activity of "working" if the person is substantially limited in any other major life activity.

For example: If a person is substantially limited in seeing, hearing, or walking, there is no need to consider whether the person is also substantially limited in working.

In general, a person will not be considered to be substantially limited in working if s/he is substantially limited in performing only a particular job for one employer, or unable to perform a very specialized job in a particular field.

For example: A person who cannot qualify as a commercial airline pilot because of a minor vision impairment, but who could qualify as a co-pilot or a pilot for a courier service, would not be considered substantially limited in working just because he could not perform a particular job. Similarly, a baseball pitcher who develops a bad elbow and can no longer pitch would not be substantially limited in working because he could no longer perform the specialized job of pitching in baseball.

But a person need not be totally unable to work in order to be considered substantially limited in working. The person must be significantly restricted in the ability to perform either a class of jobs or a broad range of jobs in various classes, compared to an average person with similar training, skills, and abilities.

The regulations provide factors to help determine whether a person is substantially limited in working. These include:

- the type of job from which the individual has been disqualified because of the impairment;
- the geographical area in which the person may reasonably expect to find a job;
- the number and types of jobs using similar training, knowledge, skill, or abilities from which the individual is disqualified within the geographical area, and/or
- the number and types of other jobs in the area that do not involve similar training, knowledge, skill, or abilities from which the individual also is disqualified because of the impairment.

For example: A person would be considered significantly restricted in a "class of jobs" if a back condition prevents him from working in any heavy labor job. A person would be considered significantly limited in the ability to perform "a broad range of jobs in various classes" if she has an allergy to a substance found in most high-rise office buildings in the geographic area in which she could reasonably seek work, and the allergy caused extreme difficulty in breathing. In this case, she would be substantially limited in the ability to perform the many different kinds of jobs that are performed in high-rise buildings. By contrast, a person who has a severe allergy to a substance in the particular office in which she works, but who is able to work in many other offices that do not contain this substance, would not be significantly restricted in working.

For example: A computer programmer develops a vision impairment that does not substantially limit her ability to see, but because of poor contrast is unable to distinguish print on computer screens. Her impairment prevents her from working as a computer operator, programmer, instructor, or systems analyst. She is substantially limited in working, because her impairment prevents her from working in the class of jobs requiring use of a computer.

In assessing the "number" of jobs from which a person might be excluded by an impairment, the regulations make clear that it is only necessary to indicate an approximate number of jobs from which an individual would be excluded (such as "few," "many," "most"), compared to an average person with similar training, skills and abilities, to show that the individual would be significantly limited in working.

Specific Exclusions

A person who currently illegally uses drugs is not protected by the ADA, as an "individual with a disability", when an employer acts on the basis of such use. However, former drug addicts who have been successfully rehabilitated may be protected by the Act. (See Chapter VIII.) (See also discussion below of a person "regarded as" a drug addict.)

Homosexuality and bisexuality are not impairments and therefore are not disabilities covered by the ADA. The Act also states that the term "disability" does not include the following sexual and behavioral disorders:

- transvestism, transsexualism, pedophilia, exhibitionism, voyeurism, gender identity disorders not resulting from physical impairments, or other sexual behavior disorders;
- compulsive gambling, kleptomania, or pyromania; or
- psychoactive substance use disorders resulting from current illegal use of drugs.

The discussion so far has focused on the first part of the definition of an "individual with a disability," which protects people who currently have an impairment that substantially limits a major life activity. The second and third parts of the definition protect people who may or may not actually have such an impairment, but who may be subject to discrimination because they have a record of or are regarded as having such an impairment.

I-2.2(b) Record of a Substantially Limiting Condition.

This part of the definition protects people who have a history of a disability from discrimination, whether or not they currently are substantially limited in a major life activity.

For example: It protects people with a history of cancer, heart disease, or other debilitating illness, whose illnesses are either cured, controlled or in remission. It also protects people with a history of mental illness.

This part of the definition also protects people who may have been misclassified or misdiagnosed as having a disability.

For example: It protects a person who may at one time have been erroneously classified as having mental retardation or having a learning disability. These people have a record of disability. (If an employer relies on any record [such as an educational, medical or employment record] containing such information to make an adverse employment decision about a person who currently is qualified to perform a job, the action is subject to challenge as a discriminatory practice.)

Other examples of individuals who have a record of disability, and of potential violations of the ADA if an employer relies on such a record to make an adverse employment decision:

- A job applicant formerly was a patient at a state institution. When very young she was misdiagnosed as being psychopathic and this misdiagnosis was never removed from her records. If this person is otherwise qualified for a job, and an employer does not hire her based on this record, the employer has violated the ADA.
- A person who has a learning disability applies for a job as secretary/receptionist. The employer reviews records from a previous employer indicating that he was labeled as "mentally retarded." Even though the person's resume shows that he meets all requirements for the job, the employer does not interview him because he doesn't want to hire a person who has mental retardation. This employer has violated the ADA.
- A job applicant was hospitalized for treatment for cocaine addiction several years ago. He has been successfully rehabilitated and has not engaged in the illegal use of drugs since receiving treatment. This applicant has a record of an impairment that substantially limited his major life activities. If he is qualified to perform a job, it would be discriminatory to reject him based on the record of his former addiction.

In the last example above, the individual was protected by the ADA because his drug addiction was an impairment that substantially limited his major life activities. However, if an individual had a record of casual drug use, s/he would not be protected by the

ADA, because casual drug use, as opposed to addiction, does not substantially limit a major life activity.

To be protected by the ADA under this part of the definition, a person must have a record of a physical or mental impairment that substantially limits one or more major life activities. A person would not be protected, for example, merely because s/he has a record of being a "disabled veteran," or a record of "disability" under another Federal statute or program unless this person also met the ADA definition of an individual with a record of a disability.

I-2.2(c) Regarded as Substantially Limited.

This part of the definition protects people who are not substantially limited in a major life activity from discriminatory actions taken because they are perceived to have such a limitation. Such protection is necessary, because, as the Supreme Court has stated and the Congress has reiterated, "society's myths and fears about disability and disease are as handicapping as are the physical limitations that flow from actual impairments."

The legislative history of the ADA indicates that Congress intended this part of the definition to protect people from a range of discriminatory actions based on "myths, fears and stereotypes" about disability, which occur even when a person does not have a substantially limiting impairment.

An individual may be protected under this part of the definition in three circumstances:

(1) The individual may have an impairment which is not substantially limiting, but is treated by the employer as having such an impairment.

> For example: An employee has controlled high blood pressure which does not substantially limit his work activities. If an employer reassigns the individual to a less strenuous job because of unsubstantiated fear that the person would suffer a heart attack if he continues in the present job, the employer has "regarded" this person as disabled.

(2) The individual has an impairment that is substantially limiting because of attitudes of others toward the condition.

> For example: An experienced assistant manager of a convenience store who had a prominent facial scar was passed over for promotion to store manager. The owner promoted a less experienced part-time clerk, because he believed that customers and vendors would not want to look at this person. The employer discriminated against her on the basis of disability, because he perceived and treated her as a person with a substantial limitation.

(3) The individual may have no impairment at all, but is regarded by an employer as having a substantially limiting impairment.

> For example: An employer discharged an employee based on a rumor that the individual had HIV disease. This person did not have any impairment, but was treated as though she had a substantially limiting impairment.

This part of the definition protects people who are "perceived" as having disabilities from employment decisions based on stereotypes, fears, or misconceptions about disability. It applies to decisions based on unsubstantiated concerns about productivity, safety, insurance, liability, attendance, costs of accommodation, accessibility, workers' compensation costs or acceptance by co-workers and customers.

Accordingly, if an employer makes an adverse employment decision based on unsubstantiated beliefs or fears that a person's perceived disability will cause problems in areas such as those listed above, and cannot show a legitimate, nondiscriminatory reason for the action, that action would be discriminatory under this part of the definition.

I-2.3 Qualified Individual with a Disability.

To be protected by the ADA, a person must not only be an individual with a disability, but must be qualified. An employer is not required to hire or retain an individual who is not qualified to perform a job. The regulations define a qualified individual with a disability as a person with a disability who:

> "satisfies the requisite skill, experience, education and other job-related requirements of the employment position such individual holds or desires, and who, with or without reasonable accommodation, can perform the essential functions of such position."

There are two basic steps in determining whether an individual is "qualified" under the ADA:

(1) Determine if the individual meets necessary prerequisites for the job, such as:

- education;
- work experience;
- training;
- skills;
- licenses;
- certificates;

- other job-related requirements, such as good judgment or ability to work with other people.

For example: The first step in determining whether an accountant who has cerebral palsy is qualified for a certified public accountant job is to determine if the person is a licensed CPA. If not, s/he is not qualified. Or, if it is a company's policy that all its managers have at least three years' experience working with the company, an individual with a disability who has worked for two years for the company would not be qualified for a managerial position.

This first step is sometimes referred to as determining if an individual with a disability is "otherwise qualified." Note, however, that if an individual meets all job prerequisites except those that s/he cannot meet because of a disability, and alleges discrimination because s/he is "otherwise qualified" for a job, the employer would have to show that the requirement that screened out this person is "job related and consistent with business necessity." (See Chapter IV)

If the individual with a disability meets the necessary job prerequisites:

(2) Determine if the individual can perform the essential functions of the job, with or without reasonable accommodation.

This second step, a key aspect of nondiscrimination under the ADA, has two parts:

- Identifying "essential functions of the job"; and
- Considering whether the person with a disability can perform these functions, unaided or with a "reasonable accommodation."

The ADA requires an employer to focus on the essential functions of a job to determine whether a person with a disability is qualified. This is an important nondiscrimination requirement. Many people with disabilities who can perform essential job functions are denied employment because they cannot do things that are only marginal to the job.

For example: A file clerk position description may state that the person holding the job answers the telephone, but if in fact the basic functions of the job are to file and retrieve written materials, and telephones actually or usually are handled by other employees, a person whose hearing impairment prevents use of a telephone and who is qualified to do the basic file clerk functions should not be considered unqualified for this position.

I-2.3(a) Identifying the Essential Functions of a Job.

Sometimes it is necessary to identify the essential functions of a job in order to know whether an individual with a disability is "qualified" to do the job. The regulations provide guidance on identifying the essential functions of the job. The first consideration is whether employees in the position actually are required to perform the function.

For example: A job announcement or job description for a secretary or receptionist may state that typing is a function of the job. If, in fact, the employer has never or seldom required an employee in that position to type, this could not be considered an essential function.

If a person holding a job does perform a function, the next consideration is whether removing that function would fundamentally change the job.

The regulations list several reasons why a function could be considered essential:

(1) The position exists to perform the function.

For example:

- A person is hired to proofread documents. The ability to proofread accurately is an essential function, because this is the reason that this position exists.
- A company advertises a position for a "floating" supervisor to substitute when regular supervisors on the day, night, and graveyard shifts are absent. The only reason this position exists is to have someone who can work on any of the three shifts in place of an absent supervisor. Therefore, the ability to work at any time of day is an essential function of the job.

(2) There are a limited number of other employees available to perform the function, or among whom the function can be distributed.

This may be a factor because there are only a few other employees, or because of fluctuating demands of a business operation.

For example: It may be an essential function for a file clerk to answer the telephone if there are only three employees in a very busy office and each employee has to perform many different tasks. Or, a company with a large workforce may have periods of very heavy labor-intensive activity alternating with less active periods. The heavy work flow during peak periods may make performance of each function essential, and limit an employer's flexibility to reassign a particular function.

(3) A function is highly specialized, and the person in the position is hired for special expertise or ability to perform it.

For example: A company wishes to expand its business with Japan. For a new sales position, in addition to sales experience, it requires a person who can communicate fluently in the Japanese language. Fluent communication in the Japanese language is an essential function of the job.

The regulation also lists several types of evidence to be considered in determining whether a function is essential. This list is not all-inclusive, and factors not on the list may be equally important as evidence. Evidence to be considered includes:

(a) The employer's judgment

An employer's judgment as to which functions are essential is important evidence. However, the legislative history of the ADA indicates that Congress did not intend that this should be the only evidence, or that it should be the prevailing evidence. Rather, the employer's judgment is a factor to be considered along with other relevant evidence.

However, the consideration of various kinds of evidence to determine which functions are essential does not mean that an employer will be second-guessed on production standards, setting the quality or quantity of work that must be performed by a person holding a job, or be required to set lower standards for the job.

For example: If an employer requires its typists to be able to accurately type 75 words per minute, the employer is not required to show that such speed and accuracy are "essential" to a job or that less accuracy or speed would not be adequate. Similarly, if a hotel requires its housekeepers to thoroughly clean 16 rooms per day, it does not have to justify this standard as "essential." However, in each case, if a person with a disability is disqualified by such a standard, the employer should be prepared to show that it does in fact require employees to perform at this level, that these are not merely paper requirements and that the standard was not established for a discriminatory reason.

(b) A written job description prepared before advertising or interviewing applicants for a job

The ADA does not require an employer to develop or maintain job descriptions. A written job description that is prepared before advertising or interviewing applicants for a job will be considered as evidence along with other relevant factors. However, the job description will not be given greater weight than other relevant evidence.

A written job description may state that an employee performs a certain essential function. The job description will be evidence that the function is essential, but if individuals currently performing the job do not in fact perform this function, or perform it very infrequently, a review of the actual work performed will be more relevant evidence than the job description.

If an employer uses written job descriptions, the ADA does not require that they be limited to a description of essential functions or that "essential functions" be identified. However, if an employer wishes to use a job description as evidence of essential functions, it should in some way identify those functions that the employer believes to be important in accomplishing the purpose of the job.

If an employer uses written job descriptions, they should be reviewed to be sure that they accurately reflect the actual functions of the current job. Job descriptions written years ago frequently are inaccurate.

For example: A written job description may state that an employee reads temperature and pressure gauges and adjusts machine controls to reflect these readings. The job description will be evidence that these functions are essential. However, if this job description is not up-to-date, and in fact temperature and pressure are now determined automatically, the machine is controlled by a computer and the current employee does not perform the stated functions or does so very infrequently, a review of actual work performed will be more relevant evidence of what the job requires.

In identifying an essential function to determine if an individual with a disability is qualified, the employer should focus on the purpose of the function and the result to be accomplished, rather than the manner in which the function presently is performed. An individual with a disability may be qualified to perform the function if an accommodation would enable this person to perform the job in a different way, and the accommodation does not impose an undue hardship. Although it may be essential that a function be performed, frequently it is not essential that it be performed in a particular way.

For example: In a job requiring use of a computer, the essential function is the ability to access, input, and retrieve information from the computer. It is not "essential" that a person in this job enter information manually, or visually read the information on the computer screen. Adaptive devices or computer software can enable a person without arms or a person with impaired vision to perform the essential functions of the job.

Similarly, an essential function of a job on a loading dock may be to move heavy packages from the dock to a storage room, rather than to lift and carry packages from the dock to the storage room.

(See also discussion of Job Analysis and Essential Functions of a Job, below).

If the employer intends to use a job description as evidence of essential functions, the job description must be prepared before advertising or interviewing for a job; a job description prepared after an alleged discriminatory action will not be considered as evidence.

(c) The amount of time spent performing the function

For example: If an employee spends most of the time or a majority of the time operating one machine, this would be evidence that operating this machine was an essential function.

(d) The consequences of not requiring a person in this job to perform a function

Sometimes a function that is performed infrequently may be essential because there will be serious consequences if it is not performed.

For example:

- An airline pilot spends only a few minutes of a flight landing a plane, but landing the plane is an essential function because of the very serious consequences if the pilot could not perform this function.
- A firefighter may only occasionally have to carry a heavy person from a burning building, but being able to perform this function would be essential to the firefighter's job.
- A clerical worker may spend only a few minutes a day answering the telephones, but this could be an essential function if no one else is available to answer the phones at that time, and business calls would go unanswered.

(e) The terms of a collective bargaining agreement

Where a collective bargaining agreement lists duties to be performed in particular jobs, the terms of the agreement may provide evidence of essential functions. However, like a position description, the agreement would be considered along with other evidence, such as the actual duties performed by people in these jobs.

(f) Work experience of people who have performed a job in the past and work experience of people who currently perform similar jobs

The work experience of previous employees in a job and the experience of current employees in similar jobs provide pragmatic evidence of actual duties performed. The employer should consult such employees and observe their work operations to identify essential job functions, since the tasks actually performed provide significant evidence of these functions.

(g) Other relevant factors

The nature of the work operation and the employer's organizational structure may be factors in determining whether a function is essential.

For example:

- A particular manufacturing facility receives large orders for its product intermittently. These orders must be filled under very tight deadlines. To meet these deadlines, it is necessary that each production worker be able to perform a variety of different tasks with different requirements. All of these tasks are essential functions for a production worker at that facility. However, another facility that receives orders on a continuous basis finds it most efficient to organize an assembly line process, in which each production worker repeatedly performs one major task. At this facility, this single task may be the only essential function of the production worker's job.
- An employer may structure production operations to be carried out by a "team" of workers. Each worker performs a different function, but every worker is required, on a rotating basis, to perform each different function. In this situation, all the functions may be considered to be essential for the job, rather than the function that any one worker performs at a particular time.

Changing Essential Job Functions

The ADA does not limit an employer's ability to establish or change the content, nature, or functions of a job. It is the employer's province to establish what a job is and what functions are required to perform it. The ADA simply requires that an individual with a disability's qualifications for a job are evaluated in relation to its essential functions.

For example: A grocery store may have two different jobs at the checkout stand, one titled, "checkout clerk" and the other "bagger." The essential functions of the checkout clerk are entering the price for each item into a cash register, receiving money, making change, and passing items to the bagger. The essential functions of the bagging job are putting items into bags, giving the bags to the customer directly or placing them in grocery carts.

For legitimate business reasons, the store management decides to combine the two jobs in a new job called "checker-bagger." In the new job, each employee will have to perform the essential functions of both former jobs. Each employee now must enter prices in a new, faster computer-scanner, put the items in bags, give the bags to the customer or place them in carts. The employee holding this job would have to perform all of these functions. There may be some aspects of each function, however, that are not "essential" to the job, or some possible modification in the way these functions are performed, that would enable a person employed as a "checker" whose disability prevented performance of all the bagging operations to do the new job.

For example: If the checker's disability made it impossible to lift any item over one pound, s/he might not be qualified to perform the essential bagging functions of the new job. But if the disability only precluded lifting items of more than 20 pounds, it might be possible for this person to perform the bagging functions, except for the relatively few instances when items or loaded bags weigh more than 20 pounds. If other employees are available who could help this individual with the few heavy items, perhaps in exchange for some incidental functions that they perform, or if this employee could keep filled bags loads under 20 pounds, then bagging loads over 20 pounds would not be an essential function of the new job.

I-2.3(b) Job Analysis and the "Essential Functions" of a Job.

The ADA does not require that an employer conduct a job analysis or any particular form of job analysis to identify the essential functions of a job. The information provided by a job analysis may or may not be helpful in properly identifying essential job functions, depending on how it is conducted.

The term "job analysis" generally is used to describe a formal process in which information about a specific job or occupation is collected and analyzed. Formal job analysis may be conducted by a number of different methods. These methods obtain different kinds of information that is used for different purposes. Some of these methods will not provide information sufficient to determine if an individual with a disability is qualified to perform "essential" job functions.

For example: One kind of formal job analysis looks at specific job tasks and classifies jobs according to how these tasks deal with data, people, and objects. This type of job analysis is used to set wage rates for various jobs; however, it may not be adequate to identify the essential functions of a particular job, as required by the ADA. Another kind of job analysis looks at the kinds of knowledge, skills, and abilities that are necessary to perform a job. This type of job analysis is used to develop selection criteria for various jobs. The information from this type of analysis sometimes helps to measure the importance of certain skills, knowledge and abilities, but it does not take into account the fact that people with disabilities often can perform essential functions using other skills and abilities.

Some job analysis methods ask current employees and their supervisors to rate the importance of general characteristics necessary to perform a job, such as "strength," "endurance," or "intelligence," without linking these characteristics to specific job functions or specific tasks that are part of a function. Such general information may not identify, for example, whether upper body or lower body "strength" is required, or whether muscular endurance or cardiovascular "endurance" is needed to perform a particular job function. Such information, by itself, would not be sufficient to determine whether an individual who has particular limitations can perform an essential function with or without an accommodation.

As already stated, the ADA does not require a formal job analysis or any particular method of analysis to identify the essential functions of a job. A small employer may wish to conduct an informal analysis by observing and consulting with people who perform the job or have previously performed it and their supervisors. If possible, it is advisable to observe and consult with several workers under a range of conditions, to get a better idea of all job functions and the different ways they may be performed. Production records and workloads also may be relevant factors to consider.

To identify essential job functions under the ADA,

a job analysis should focus on the purpose of the job and the importance of actual job functions in achieving this purpose. Evaluating "importance" may include consideration of the frequency with which a function is performed, the amount of time spent on the function, and the consequences if the function is not performed. The analysis may include information on the work environment (such as unusual heat, cold, humidity, dust, toxic substances or stress factors). The job analysis may contain information on the manner in which a job currently is performed, but should not conclude that ability to perform the job in that manner is an essential function, unless there is no other way to perform the function without causing undue hardship. A job analysis will be most helpful for purposes of the ADA if it focuses on the results or outcome of a function, not solely on the way it customarily is performed.

For example:

- An essential function of a computer programmer job might be described as "ability to develop programs that accomplish necessary objectives," rather than "ability to manually write programs." Although a person currently performing the job may write these programs by hand, that is not the essential function, because programs can be developed directly on the computer.
- If a job requires mastery of information contained in technical manuals, this essential function would be "ability to learn technical material," rather than "ability to read technical manuals." People with visual and other reading impairments could perform this function using other means, such as audiotapes.
- A job that requires objects to be moved from one place to another should state this essential function. The analysis may note that the person in the job "lifts 50 pound cartons to a height of 3 or 4 feet and loads them into truck-trailers 5 hours daily," but should not identify the "ability to manually lift and load 50 pound cartons" as an essential function unless this is the only method by which the function can be performed without causing an undue hardship.

A job analysis that is focused on outcomes or results also will be helpful in establishing appropriate qualification standards, developing job descriptions, conducting interviews, and selecting people in accordance with ADA requirements. It will be particularly useful in helping to identify accommodations that will enable an individual with specific functional abilities and limitations to perform the job. (See Chapter III.)

I-2.3(c) Perform Essential Functions "With or Without Reasonable Accommodation".

Many individuals with disabilities are qualified to perform the essential functions of jobs without need of any accommodation. However, if an individual with a disability who is otherwise qualified cannot perform one or more essential job functions because of his or her disability, the employer, in assessing whether the person is qualified to do the job, must consider whether there are modifications or adjustments that would enable the person to perform these functions. Such modifications or adjustments are called "reasonable accommodations."

Reasonable accommodation is a key nondiscrimination requirement under the ADA. An employer must first consider reasonable accommodation in determining whether an individual with a disability is qualified; reasonable accommodation also must be considered when making many other employment decisions regarding people with disabilities. The following chapter discusses the employer's obligation to provide reasonable accommodation and the limits to that obligation. The chapter also provides examples of reasonable accommodations.

I-III. The Reasonable Accommodation Obligation.

I-3.1 Overview of Legal Obligations.

- An employer must provide a reasonable accommodation to the known physical or mental limitations of a qualified applicant or employee with a disability unless it can show that the accommodation would impose an undue hardship on the business.
- Reasonable accommodation is any modification or adjustment to a job, an employment practice, or the work environment that makes it possible for an individual with a disability to enjoy an equal employment opportunity.
- The obligation to provide a reasonable accommodation applies to all aspects of employment. This duty is ongoing and may arise any time that a person's disability or job changes.
- An employer cannot deny an employment opportunity to a qualified applicant or employee because of the need to provide reasonable accommodation, unless it would cause an undue hardship.
- An employer does not have to make an accommodation for an individual who is not otherwise qualified for a position.

- Generally, it is the obligation of an individual with a disability to request a reasonable accommodation.
- A qualified individual with a disability has the right to refuse an accommodation. However, if the individual cannot perform the essential functions of the job without the accommodation, s/he may not be qualified for the job.
- If the cost of an accommodation would impose an undue hardship on the employer, the individual with a disability should be given the option of providing the accommodation or paying that portion of the cost which would constitute an undue hardship.

I-3.2 Why Is a Reasonable Accommodation Necessary?

Reasonable accommodation is a key nondiscrimination requirement of the ADA because of the special nature of discrimination faced by people with disabilities. Many people with disabilities can perform jobs without any need for accommodations. But many others are excluded from jobs that they are qualified to perform because of unnecessary barriers in the workplace and the work environment. The ADA recognizes that such barriers may discriminate against qualified people with disabilities just as much as overt exclusionary practices. For this reason, the ADA requires reasonable accommodation as a means of overcoming unnecessary barriers that prevent or restrict employment opportunities for otherwise qualified individuals with disabilities.

People with disabilities are restricted in employment opportunities by many different kinds of barriers. Some face physical barriers that make it difficult to get into and around a work site or to use necessary work equipment. Some are excluded or limited by the way people communicate with each other. Others are excluded because of rigid work schedules that allow no flexibility for people with special needs caused by disability. Many are excluded only by barriers in other people's minds; these include unfounded fears, stereotypes, presumptions, and misconceptions about job performance, safety, absenteeism, costs, or acceptance by co-workers and customers.

Under the ADA, when an individual with a disability is qualified to perform the essential functions of a job except for functions that cannot be performed because of related limitations and existing job barriers, an employer must try to find a reasonable accommodation that would enable this person to perform these functions. The reasonable accommodation should reduce or eliminate unnecessary barriers between the individual's abilities and the requirements for performing the essential job functions.

I-3.3 What Is a Reasonable Accommodation?

Reasonable accommodation is a modification or adjustment to a job, the work environment, or the way things usually are done that enables a qualified individual with a disability to enjoy an equal employment opportunity. An equal employment opportunity means an opportunity to attain the same level of performance or to enjoy equal benefits and privileges of employment as are available to an average similarly-situated employee without a disability. The ADA requires reasonable accommodation in three aspects of employment:

- to ensure equal opportunity in the application process;
- to enable a qualified individual with a disability to perform the essential functions of a job; and
- to enable an employee with a disability to enjoy equal benefits and privileges of employment.

Reasonable Accommodation in the Application Process

Reasonable accommodation must be provided in the job application process to enable a qualified applicant to have an equal opportunity to be considered for a job.

For example: A person who uses a wheelchair may need an accommodation if an employment office or interview site is not accessible. A person with a visual disability or a person who lacks manual dexterity may need assistance in filling out an application form. Without such accommodations, these individuals may have no opportunity to be considered for a job.

(See Chapter V. for further discussion of accommodations in the application process).

Accommodations to Perform the Essential Functions of a Job

Reasonable accommodation must be provided to enable a qualified applicant to perform the essential functions of the job s/he is seeking, and to enable a qualified employee with a disability to perform the essential functions of a job currently held. Modifications or adjustments may be required in the work environment, in the manner or circumstances in which the job customarily is performed, or in employment policies. Many accommodations of this nature are discussed later in this chapter.

Accommodations to Ensure Equal Benefits of Employment

Reasonable accommodations must be provided to enable an employee with a disability to enjoy benefits and privileges of employment equal to those enjoyed by similarly situated nondisabled employees.

For example: Employees with disabilities must have equal access to lunchrooms, employee lounges, rest rooms, meeting rooms, and other employer-provided or sponsored services such as health programs, transportation, and social events. (See Chapter VII for further discussion of this requirement).

I-3.4 Some Basic Principles of Reasonable Accommodation.

A modification or adjustment must be "reasonable" and "effective." It must provide an opportunity for a person with a disability to achieve the same level of performance or to enjoy benefits or privileges equal to those of an average similarly-situated nondisabled person. However, the accommodation does not have to ensure equal results or provide exactly the same benefits or privileges.

For example: An employer provides an employee lunchroom with food and beverages on the second floor of a building that has no elevator. If it would be an undue hardship to install an elevator for an employee who uses a wheelchair, the employer must provide a comparable facility on the first floor. The facility does not have to be exactly the same as that on the second floor, but must provide food, beverages and space for the disabled employee to eat with co-workers. It would not be a reasonable accomodation merely to provide a place for this employee to eat by himself. Nor would it be a reasonable accommodation to provide a separate facility for the employee if access to the common facility could be provided without undue hardship. For example, if the lunchroom was only several steps up, a portable ramp could provide access.

The reasonable accommodation obligation applies only to accommodations that reduce barriers to employment related to a person's disability; it does not apply to accommodations that a disabled person may request for some other reason.

For example: Reassignment is one type of accommodation that may be required under the ADA. If an employee whose job requires driving loses her sight, reassignment to a vacant position that does not require driving would be a reasonable accommodation, if the employee is qualified for that position with or without an accommodation However, if a blind computer operator working at an employer's Michigan facility requested reassignment to a facility in Florida because he prefers to work in a warmer climate, this would not be a reasonable accommodation required by the ADA In the second case, the accommodation is not needed because of the employee's disability.

A reasonable accommodation need not be the best accommodation available, as long as it is effective for the purpose; that is, it gives the person with a disability an equal opportunity to be considered for a job, to perform the essential functions of the job, or to enjoy equal benefits and privileges of the job.

For example: An employer would not have to hire a full-time reader for a blind employee if a coworker is available as a part-time reader when needed, and this will enable the blind employee to perform his job duties effectively.

An employer is not required to provide an accommodation that is primarily for personal use. Reasonable accommodation applies to modifications that specifically assist an individual in performing the duties of a particular job. Equipment or devices that assist a person in daily activities on and off the job are considered personal items that an employer is not required to provide. However, in some cases, equipment that otherwise would be considered "personal" may be required as an accommodation if it is specifically designed or required to meet job-related rather than personal needs.

For example: An employer generally would not be required to provide personal items such as eyeglasses, a wheelchair, or an artificial limb. However, the employer might be required to provide a person who has a visual impairment with glasses that are specifically needed to use a computer monitor. Or, if deep pile carpeting in a work area makes it impossible for an individual to use a manual wheelchair, the employer may need to replace the carpet, place a usable surface over the carpet in areas used by the employee, or provide a motorized wheelchair.

The ADA's requirements for certain types of

adjustments and modifications to meet the reasonable accommodation obligation do not prevent an employer from providing accommodations beyond those required by the ADA.

For example: "Supported employment" programs may provide free job coaches and other assistance to enable certain individuals with severe disabilities to learn and/or to progress in jobs. These programs typically require a range of modifications and adjustments to customary employment practices. Some of these modifications may also be required by the ADA as reasonable accommodations. However, supported employment programs may require modifications beyond those required under the ADA, such as restructuring of essential job functions. Many employers have found that supported employment programs are an excellent source of reliable productive new employees. Participation in these programs advances the underlying goal of the ADA—to increase employment opportunities for people with disabilities. Making modifications for supported employment beyond those required by the ADA in no way violates the ADA.

I-3.5 Some Examples of Reasonable Accommodation.

The statute and EEOC's regulations provide examples of common types of reasonable accommodation that an employer may be required to provide, but many other accommodations may be appropriate for particular situations. Accommodations may include:

- making facilities readily accessible to and usable by an individual with a disability;
- restructuring a job by reallocating or redistributing marginal job functions;
- altering when or how an essential job function is performed;
- part-time or modified work schedules;
- obtaining or modifying equipment or devices;
- modifying examinations, training materials or policies;
- providing qualified readers and interpreters;
- reassignment to a vacant position;
- permitting use of accrued paid leave or unpaid leave for necessary treatment;
- providing reserved parking for a person with a mobility impairment;
- allowing an employee to provide equipment or devices that an employer is not required to provide.

These and other types of reasonable accommodation are discussed in the pages that follow. However, the examples in this Manual cannot cover the range of potential accommodations, because every reasonable accommodation must be determined on an individual basis. A reasonable accommodation always must take into consideration two unique factors:

- the specific abilities and functional limitations of a particular applicant or employee with a disability; and
- the specific functional requirements of a particular job.

In considering an accommodation, the focus should be on the abilities and limitations of the individual, not on the name of a disability or a particular physical or mental condition. This is necessary because people who have any particular disability may have very different abilities and limitations. Conversely, people with different kinds of disabilities may have similar functional limitations.

For example: If it is an essential function of a job to press a foot pedal a certain number of times a minute and an individual with a disability applying for the job has some limitation that makes this difficult or impossible, the accommodation process should focus on ways that this person might be able to do the job function, not on the nature of her disability or on how persons with this kind of disability generally might be able to perform the job.

I-3.6 Who Is Entitled to a Reasonable Accommodation?

As detailed in Chapter II, an individual is entitled to a reasonable accommodation if s/he:

meets the ADA definition of "a qualified individual with a disability" (meets all prerequisities for preforming the essential functions of a job [being considered for a job or enjoying equal benefits and privileges of a job] except ant that cannot be met because of a disablility).

If there is a reasonable accommodation that will enable this person to perform the essential functions of a job (be considered, or receive equal benefits, etc.), the employer is obligated to provide it, unless it would impose an undue hardship on the operation of the business.

When is an Employer Obligated to Make a Reasonable Accommodation?

An employer is obligated to make an accommodation only to the known limitations of an otherwise qualified individual with a disability. In general, it is the responsibility of the applicant or employee with a disability to inform the employer that an accommodation is needed to participate in the application process, to perform essential job functions or to receive equal benefits and privileges of employment. An employer is not required to provide an accommodation if unaware of the need.

However, the employer is responsible for notifying job applicants and employees of its obligation to provide accommodations for otherwise qualified individuals with disabilities.

The ADA requires an employer to post notices containing the provisions of the ADA, including the reasonable accommodation obligation, in conspicuous places on its premises. Such notices should be posted in employment offices and other places where applicants and employees can readily see them EEOC provides posters for this purpose. (See Chapter I for additional information on the required notice.)

Information about the reasonable accommodation obligation also can be included in job application forms, job vacancy notices, and in personnel manuals, and may be communicated orally.

An applicant or employee does not have to specifically request a "reasonable accommodation," but must only let the employer know that some adjustment or change is needed to do a job because of the limitations caused by a disability.

If a job applicant or employee has a "hidden" disability—one that is not obvious—it is up to that individual to make the need for an accommodation known. If an applicant has a known disability, such as a visible disability, that appears to limit, interfere with, or prevent the individual from performing job-related functions, the employer may ask the applicant to describe or demonstrate how s/he would perform the function with or without a reasonable accommodation. Chapter V provides guidance on how to make such an inquiry without violating the ADA prohibition against pre-employment inquiries in the application and interview process.

If an employee with a known disability is not performing well or is having difficulty in performing a job, the employer should assess whether this is due to a disability. The employer may inquire at any time whether the employee needs an accommodation.

Documentation of Need for Accommodation

If an applicant or employee requests an accommodation and the need for the accommodation is not obvious, or if the employer does not believe that the accommodation is needed, the employer may request documentation of the individual's functional limitations to support the request.

> For example: An employer may ask for written documentation from a doctor, psychologist, rehabilitation counselor, occupational or physical therapist, independent living specialist, or other professional with knowledge of the person's functional limitations. Such documentation might indicate, for example, that this person cannot lift more than 15 pounds without assistance.

I-3.7 How Does an Employer Determine What Is a Reasonable Accommodation?

When a qualified individual with a disability requests an accommodation, the employer must make a reasonable effort to provide an accommodation that is effective for the individual (gives the individual an equally effective opportunity to apply for a job, perform essential job functions, or enjoy equal benefits and privileges).

In many cases, an appropriate accommodation will be obvious and can be made without difficulty and at little or no cost. Frequently, the individual with a disability can suggest a simple change or adjustment, based on his or her life or work experience.

An employer should always consult the person with the disability as the first step in considering an accommodation. Often this person can suggest must simpler and less costly accommodations than the employer might have believed necessary.

> For example: A small employer believed it necessary to install a special lower drinking fountain for an employee using a wheelchair, but the employee indicated that he could use the existing fountain if paper cups were provided in a holder next to the fountain.

However, in some cases, the appropriate accommodation may not be so easy to identify. The individual requesting the accommodation may not know enough about the equipment being used or the exact nature of the worksite to suggest an accommodation, or the employer may not know enough about the individual's functional limitations in relation to specific job tasks.

In such cases, the employer and the individual with a disability should work together to identify the appropriate accommodation. EEOC regulations require, when necessary, an informal, interactive process to find an effective accommodation. The process is described below in relation to an accommodation that will enable an individual with a disability to perform the essential functions of a job. However, the same approach can be used to identify accommodations for job applicants and accommodations to provide equal benefits and privileges of employment.

I-3.8 A Process for Identifying a Reasonable Accommodation.

(1) Look at the particular job involved. Determine its purpose and its essential functions.

Chapter II recommended that the essential functions of the job be identified before advertising or interviewing for a job. However, it is useful to reexamine the specific job at this point to determine or confirm its essential functions and requirements.

(2) Consult with the individual with a disability to find out his or her specific physical or mental abilities and limitations as they relate to the essential job functions.

Identify the barriers to job performance and assess how these barriers could be overcome with an accommodation.

(3) In consultation with the individual, identify potential accommodations and assess how effective each would be in enabling the individual to perform essential job functions.

If this consultation does not identify an appropriate accommodation, technical assistance is available from a number of sources, many without cost. There are also financial resources to help with accommodation costs. (See Financial and Technical Assistance for Accommodations, 4.1 below).

(4) If there are several effective accommodations that would provide an equal employment opportunity, consider the preference of the individual with a disability and select the accommodation that best serves the needs of the individual and the employer.

If more than one accommodation would be effective for the individual with a disability, or if the individual would prefer to provide his or her own accommodation, the individual's preference should be given first consideration. However, the employer is free to choose among effective accommodations, and may choose one that is less expensive or easier to provide.

The fact that an individual is willing to provide his or her own accommodation does not relieve the employer of the duty to provide this or another reasonable accommodation should this individual for any reason be unable or unwilling to continue to provide the accommodation.

Examples of the Reasonable Accommodation Process:

- A "sack-handler" position requires that the employee in this job pick up 50 pound sacks from a loading dock and carry them to the storage room An employee who is disabled by a back impairment requests an accommodation. The employer analyzes the job and finds that its real purpose and essential function is to move the sacks from the loading dock to the store room. The person in the job does not necessarily have to lift and carry the sacks. The employer consults with the employee to determine his exact physical abilities and limitations. With medical documentation, it is determined that this person can lift 50 pound sacks to waist level, but cannot carry them to the storage room. A number of potential accommodations are identified: use of a dolly, a hand-truck or a cart. The employee prefers the dolly. After considering the relative cost, efficiency, and availability of the alternative accommodations, and after considering the preference of the employee, the employer provides the dolly as an accommodation. In this case, the employer found the dolly to be the most cost-effective accommodation, as well as the one preferred by the employee. If the employer had found a hand-truck to be as efficient, it could have provided the hand-truck as a reasonable accommodation.
- A company has an opening for a warehouse foreman. Among other functions, the job requires checking stock for inventory, completing bills of lading and other reports, and using numbers. To perform these functions, the foreman must have good math skills. An individual with diabetes who has good experience performing similar warehouse supervisory functions applies for the job. Part of the application process is a computerized test for math skills, but the job itself does not require use of a computer. The applicant tells the employer that although he has no problem reading print, his disability causes some visual impairment which makes it difficult to read a computer screen. He says he can take the test if it is printed out by the computer. However, this accommodation won't work, because the computer test is interactive, and the questions change based on the applicant's replies to each previous question. Instead, the

employer offers a reader as an accommodation; this provides an effective equivalent method to test the applicant's math skills.

An individual with a disability is not required to accept an accommodation if the individual has not requested an accommodation and does not believe that one is needed. However, if the individual refuses an accommodation necessary to perform essential job functions, and as a result cannot perform those functions, the individual may not be considered qualified.

For example: An individual with a visual impairment that restricts her field of vision but who is able to read would not be required to accept a reader as an accommodation. However, if this person could not read accurately unaided, and reading is an essential function of the job, she would not be qualified for the job if she refused an accommodation that would enable her to read accurately.

I-3.9 The Undue Hardship Limitation.

An employer is not required to make a reasonable accommodation if it would impose an undue hardship on the operation of the business. However, if a particular accommodation would impose an undue hardship, the employer must consider whether there are alternative accommodations that would not impose such hardship.

An undue hardship is an action that requires "significant difficulty or expense" in relation to the size of the employer, the resources available, and the nature of the operation.

Accordingly, whether a particular accommodation will impose an undue hardship must always be determined on a case-by-case basis. An accommodation that poses an undue hardship for one employer at a particular time may not pose an undue hardship for another employer, or even for the same employer at another time. In general, a larger employer would be expected to make accommodations requiring greater effort or expense than would be required of a smaller employer. The concept of undue hardship includes any action that is:

- unduly costly;
- extensive;
- substantial;
- disruptive; or
- that would fundamentally alter the nature or operation of the business.

The statute and regulations provide factors to be considered in determining whether an accommodation would impose an undue hardship on a particular business:

(1) The nature and net cost of the accommodation needed.

The cost of an accommodation that is considered in determining undue hardship will be the actual cost to the employer. Specific Federal tax credits and tax deductions are available to employers for making accommodations required by the ADA, and there are also sources of funding to help pay for some accommodations. If an employer can receive tax credits or tax deductions or partial funding for an accommodation, only the net cost to the employer will be considered in a determination of undue hardship. (See Financial and Technical Assistance for Accommodations, 4.1 below);

(2) The financial resources of the facility making the accommodation, the number of employees at this facility, and the effect on expenses and resources of the facility.

If an employer has only one facility, the cost and impact of the accommodation will be considered in relation to the effect on expenses and resources of that facility. However, if the facility is part of a larger entity that is covered by the ADA, factors 3. and 4. below also will be considered in determinations of undue hardship.

(3) The overall financial resources, size, number of employees, and type and location of facilities of the entity covered by the ADA (if the facility involved in the accommodation is part of a larger entity).

(4) The type of operation of the covered entity, including the structure and functions of the workforce, the geographic separateness, and the administrative or fiscal relationship of the facility involved in making the accommodation to the larger entity.

Factor 4. may include consideration of special types of employment operations, on a case-by-case basis, where providing a particular accommodation might be an undue hardship.

For example: It might "fundamentally alter" the nature of a temporary construction site or be unduly costly to make it physically accessible to an employee using a wheelchair, if the terrain and structures are constantly changing as construction progresses.

Factor 4. will be considered, along with factors 2. and 3., where a covered entity operates more than one facility, in order to assess the financial resources actually available to the facility making the accommodation, in light of the interrelationship between the facility and the covered entity. In some cases, consideration of the resources of the larger covered entity may not be justified, because the particular facility making the accommodation may not have access to those resources.

For example: A local, independently owned fast food franchise of a national company that receives no funding from that company may assert that it would be an undue hardship to provide an interpreter to enable a deaf applicant for store manager to participate in weekly staff meetings, because its own resources are inadequate and it has no access to resources of the national company. If the financial relationship between the national company and the local company is limited to payment of an annual franchise fee, only the resources of the local franchise would be considered in determining whether this accommodation would be an undue hardship. However, if the facility was part of a national company with financial and administrative control over all of its facilities, the resources of the company as a whole would be considered in making this determination.

(5) The impact of the accommodation on the operation of the facility that is making the accommodation.

This may include the impact on the ability of other employees to perform their duties and the impact on the facility's ability to conduct business.

An employer may be able to show that providing a particular accommodation would be unduly disruptive to its other employees or to its ability to conduct business.

For example: If an employee with a disability requested that the thermostat in the workplace be raised to a certain level to accommodate her disability, and this level would make it uncomfortably hot for other employees or customers, the employer would not have to provide this accommodation. However, if there was an alternative accommodation that would not be an undue hardship, such as providing a space heater or placing the employee in a room with a separate thermostat, the employer would have to provide that accommodation.

For example: A person with a visual impairment who requires bright light to see well applies for a waitress position at an expensive nightclub. The club maintains dim lighting to create an intimate setting, and lowers its lights further during the floor show. If the job applicant requested bright lighting as an accommodation so that she could see to take orders, the employer could assert that this would be an undue hardship, because it would seriously affect the nature of its operation.

In determining whether an accommodation would cause an undue hardship, an employer may consider the impact of an accommodation on the ability of other employees to do their jobs. However, an employer may not claim undue hardship solely because providing an accommodation has a negative impact on the morale of other employees. Nor can an employer claim undue hardship because of "disruption" due to employees' fears about, or prejudices toward, a person's disability.

For example: If restructuring a job to accommodate an individual with a disability creates a heavier workload for other employees, this may constitute an undue hardship. But if other employees complain because an individual with a disability is allowed to take additional unpaid leave or to have a special flexible work schedule as a reasonable accommodation, such complaints or other negative reactions would not constitute an undue hardship.

For example: If an employee objects to working with an individual who has a disability because the employee feels uncomfortable or dislikes being near this person, this would not constitute an undue hardship. In this case, the problem is caused by the employee's fear or prejudice toward the individual's disability, not by an accommodation.

Problems of employee morale and employee negative attitudes should be addressed by the employer through appropriate consultations with supervisors and, where relevant, with union representatives. Employers also may wish to provide supervisors, managers and employees with "awareness" training, to help overcome fears and misconceptions about disabilities, and to inform them of the employer's obligations under the ADA.

Other Cost Issues

An employer may not claim undue hardship simply because the cost of an accommodation is high in relation to an employee's wage or salary. When enacting the ADA "factors" for determining undue hardship, Congress rejected a proposed amendment that would have established an undue hardship if an accommodation exceeded 10% of an individual's salary. This approach was rejected because it would unjustifiably harm lower-paid workers who need accommodations. Instead, Congress clearly established that the focus for determining undue hardship should be the resources available to the employer.

If an employer finds that the cost of an accommodation would impose an undue hardship and no funding is available from another source, an applicant or employee with a disability should be offered the option of paying for the portion of the cost that constitutes an undue hardship, or of providing the accommodation.

For example: If the cost of an assistive device is $2000, and an employer believes that it can demonstrate that spending more than $1500 would be an undue hardship, the individual with a disability should be offered the option of paying the additional $500. Or, if it would be an undue hardship for an employer to purchase brailling equipment for a blind applicant, the applicant should be offered the option of providing his own equipment (if there is no other effective accommodation that would not impose an undue hardship).

The terms of a collective bargaining agreement may be relevant in determining whether an accommodation would impose an undue hardship.

However, since both the employer and the union are covered by the ADA's requirements, including the duty to provide a reasonable accommodation, the employer should consult with the union and try to work out an acceptable accommodation.

To avoid continuing conflicts between a collective bargaining agreement and the duty to provide reasonable accommodation, employers may find it helpful to seek a provision in agreements negotiated after the effective date of the ADA permitting the employer to take all actions necessary to comply with this law. (See Chapter VII.)

I-3.10 Examples of Reasonable Accommodations.

(1) Making Facilities Accessible and Usable

The ADA establishes different requirements for accessibility under different sections of the Act. A private employer's obligation to make its facilities accessible to its job applicants and employees under Title I of the ADA differs from the obligation of a place of public accommodation to provide access in existing facilities to its customers and clients, and from the obligations of public accommodations and commercial facilities to provide accessibility in renovated or newly constructed buildings under Title III of the Act. The obligation of a state and local government to provide access for applicants and employees under Title I also differs from its obligation to provide accessibility under Title II of the ADA.

The employer's obligation under Title I is to provide access for an individual applicant to participate in the job application process, and for an individual employee with a disability to perform the essential functions of his/her job, including access to a building, to the work site, to needed equipment, and to all facilities used by employees. The employer must provide such access unless it would cause an undue hardship.

Under Title I, an employer is not required to make its existing facilities accessible until a particular applicant or employee with a particular disability needs an accommodation, and then the modifications should meet that individual's work needs. The employer does not have to make changes to provide access in places or facilities that will not be used by that individual for employment related activities or benefits.

In contrast, Title III of the ADA requires that places of public accommodation (such as banks, retail stores, theaters, hotels and restaurants) make their goods and services accessible generally, to all people with disabilities. Under Title III, existing buildings and facilities of a public accommodation must be made accessible by removing architectural barriers or communications barriers that are structural in nature, if this is "readily achievable." If this is not "readily achievable," services must be provided to people with disabilities in some alternative manner if this is "readily achievable."

The obligation for state and local governments to provide "program accessibility" in existing facilities under Title II also differs from their obligation to provide access as employers under Title I. Title II requires that these governments operate each service, program or activity in existing facilities so that, when viewed in its entirety, it is readily accessible to and useable by persons with disabilities, unless this would cause a "fundamental alteration" in the nature of the program or service, or would result in "undue financial and administrative burdens."

In addition, private employers that occupy commercial facilities or operate places of public accommodation and state and local governments must conform to more extensive accessibility requirements under Title III and Title II when making alterations to existing facilities or undertaking new construction. (See Requirements for Renovation and New Construction below.)

The accessibility requirements under Title II and III are established in Department of Justice regulations. Employers may contact the Justice Department's Office on the Americans with Disabilities Act for information on these requirements and for copies of the regulations with applicable accessibility guidelines (see Resource Directory).

When making changes to meet an individual's needs under Title I, an employer will find it helpful to consult the applicable Department of Justice accessibility guidelines as a starting point. It is advisable to make changes that conform to these guidelines, if they meet the individual's needs and do not impose an undue hardship, since such changes will be useful in the future for accommodating others. However, even if a modification meets the standards required under Title II or III, further adaptations may be needed to meet the needs of a particular individual.

For example: A restroom may be modified to meet standard accessibility requirements (including wider door and stalls, and grab bars in specified locations) but it may be necessary to install a lower grab bar for a very short person in a wheelchair so that this person can transfer from the chair to the toilet.

Although the requirement for accessibility in employment is triggered by the needs of a particular individual, employers should consider initiating changes that will provide general accessibility, particularly for job applicants, since it is likely that people with disabilities will apply for jobs in the future.

For example: Employment offices and interview facilities should be accessible to people using wheelchairs and others with mobility impairments. Plans also should be in place for making job information accessible and for communicating with people who have visual or hearing impairments. (See Chapter V. for additional guidance on accommodation in the application process.)

Accessibility to Perform the Essential Functions of the Job

The obligation to provide accessibility for a qualified individual with a disability includes accessibility of the job site itself and all work-related facilities.

Examples of accommodations that may be needed to make facilities accessible and usable include:

- installing a ramp at the entrance to a building;
- removing raised thresholds;
- reserving parking spaces close to the work site that are wide enough to allow people using wheelchairs to get in and out of vehicles;
- making restrooms accessible, including toilet stalls, sinks, soap, and towels;
- rearranging office furniture and equipment;
- making a drinking fountain accessible (for example, by installing a paper cup dispenser);
- making accessible, and providing an accessible "path of travel" to, equipment and facilities used by an employee, such as copying machines, meeting and training rooms, lunchrooms and lounges;
- removing obstacles that might be potential hazards in the path of people without vision;
- adding flashing lights when alarm bells are normally used, to alert an employee with a hearing impairment to emergencies.

Requirements for Renovation or New Construction

While an employer's requirements for accessibility under Title I relate to accommodation of an individual, as described above, employers will have more extensive accessibility requirements under Title II or III of the ADA if they make renovations to their facilities or undertake new construction.

Title III of the ADA requires that any alterations to, or new construction of "commercial facilities," as well as places of public accommodation, made after January 26, 1992, must conform to the "ADA Accessibility Guidelines" (incorporated in Department of Justice Title III regulations). "Commercial facilities" are defined as any nonresidential facility whose operations affect commerce, including office buildings, factories and warehouses; therefore, the facilities of most employers will be subject to this requirement An alteration is any change that affects the "usability" of a facility; it does not include normal maintenance, such as painting, roofing or changes to mechanical or electrical systems, unless the changes affect the "usability" of the facility.

For example: If, during remodeling or renovation, a doorway is relocated, the new doorway must be wide enough to meet the requirements of the ADA Accessibility Guidelines.

Under Title III, all newly constructed public accommodations and commercial facilities for which the last building permit is certified after January 26, 1992, and which are occupied after January 26, 1993, must be accessible in accordance with the standards of the ADA Accessibility Guidelines. However, Title III does not require elevators in facilities under 3 stories or with less than 3000 square feet per floor, unless the building is a shopping center, mall, professional office of a health provider, or public transportation station.

Under Title II, any alterations to, or new construction of, State or local government facilities made after January 26, 1992, must conform either with the ADA Accessibility Guidelines (however, the exception regarding elevators does not apply to State or local governments) or with the Uniform Federal Accessibility Standards. Facilities under design on January 26, 1992 must comply with this requirement if bids were invited after that date.

Providing accessibility in remodeled and new buildings usually can be accomplished at minimal additional cost. Over time, fully accessible new and remodeled buildings will reduce the need for many types of individualized reasonable accommodations Employers planning alterations to their facilities or new construction should contact the Office on the Americans with Disabilities Act in the U.S. Department of Justice for information on accessibility requirements, including the ADA Accessibility Guidelines and the Uniform Federal Accessibility Guidelines. Employers may get specific technical information and guidance on accessibility by calling, toll-free, the Architectural and Transportation Barriers Compliance Board, at 1-800-USA-ABLE. (See Resource Directory.)

(2) Job Restructuring

Job restructuring or job modification is a form of reasonable accommodation which enables many qualified individuals with disabilities to perform jobs effectively. Job restructuring as a reasonable accommodation may involve reallocating or redistributing the marginal functions of a job. However, an employer is not required to reallocate essential functions of a job as a reasonable accommodation. Essential functions, by definition, are those that a qualified individual must perform, with or without an accommodation.

For example: Inspection of identification cards is generally an essential function of the job of a security job. If a person with a visual impairment could not verify the identification of an individual using the photo and other information on the card, the employer would not be required to transfer this function to another employee.

Job restructuring frequently is accomplished by exchanging marginal functions of a job that cannot be performed by a person with a disability for marginal job functions performed by one or more other employees.

For example: An employer may have two jobs, each containing essential functions and a number of marginal functions. The employer may hire an individual with a disability who can perform the essential functions of one job and some, but not all, of the marginal functions of both jobs. As an accommodation, the employer may redistribute the marginal functions so that all of the functions that can be performed by the person with a disability are in this person's job and the remaining marginal functions are transferred to the other job.

Although an employer is not required to reallocate essential job functions, it may be a reasonable accommodation to modify the essential functions of a job by changing when or how they are done.

For example:

- An essential function that is usually performed in the early morning might be rescheduled to be performed later in the day, if an individual has a disability that makes it impossible to perform this function in the morning, and this would not cause an undue hardship.
- A person who has a disability that makes it difficult to write might be allowed to computerize records that have been maintained manually.
- A person with mental retardation who can perform job tasks but has difficulty remembering the order in which to do the tasks might be provided with a list to check off each task; the checklist could be reviewed by a supervisor at the end of the day.

Technical assistance in restructuring or modifying jobs for individuals with specific limitations can be obtained from state vocational rehabilitation agencies and other organizations with expertise in job analysis and job restructuring for people with various disabilities. (See Job Restructuring and Job Modification in Resource Directory Index.)

(3) Modified Work Schedules

An employer should consider modification of a regular work schedule as a reasonable accommodation unless this would cause an undue hardship. Modified work schedules may include flexibility in work hours or the work week, or part-time work, where this will not be an undue hardship.

Many people with disabilities are fully qualified to perform jobs with the accommodation of a modified work schedule. Some people are unable to work a standard 9-5 work day, or a standard Monday to Friday work week; others need some adjustment to regular schedules.

Some examples of modified work schedules as a reasonable accommodation:

- An accountant with a mental disability required two hours off, twice weekly, for sessions with a psychiatrist. He was permitted to take longer lunch breaks and to make up the time by working later on those days.
- A machinist has diabetes and must follow a strict schedule to keep blood sugar levels stable. She must eat on a regular schedule and take insulin at set times each day. This means that she cannot work the normal shift rotations for machinists. As an accommodation, she is assigned to one shift on a permanent basis.
- An employee who needs kidney dialysis treatment is unable to work on two days because his treatment is only available during work hours on weekdays. Depending on the nature of his work and the nature of the employer's operation, it may be possible, without causing an undue hardship, for him to work Saturday and Sunday in place of the two weekdays, to perform work assignments at home on the weekend, or to work three days a week as part-time employee.

People whose disabilities may need modified work schedules include those who require special medical treatment for their disability (such as cancer patients, people who have AIDS, or people with mental illness); people who need rest periods (including some people who have multiple sclerosis, cancer, diabetes, respiratory conditions, or mental illness); people whose disabilities (such as diabetes) are affected by eating or sleeping schedules; and people with mobility and other impairments who find it difficult to use public transportation during peak hours, or who must depend upon special para-transit schedules.

(4) Flexible Leave Policies

Flexible leave policies should be considered as a reasonable accommodation when people with disabilities require time off from work because of their disability. An employer is not required to provide additional paid leave as an accommodation, but should consider allowing use of accrued leave, advanced leave, or leave without pay, where this will not cause an undue hardship.

People with disabilities may require special leave for a number of reasons related to their disability, such as:

- medical treatment related to the disability;
- repair of a prosthesis or equipment;
- temporary adverse conditions in the work environment (for example, an air-conditioning breakdown causing temperature above 85 degrees could seriously harm the condition of a person with multiple sclerosis);
- training in the use of an assistive device or a dog guide. (However, if an assistive device is used at work and provided as a reasonable accommodation, and if other employees receive training during work hours, the disabled employee should receive training on this device during work hours, without need to take leave.)

(5) Reassignment to a Vacant Position

In general, the accommodation of reassignment should be considered only when an accommodation is not possible in an employee's present job, or when an accommodation in the employee's present job would cause an undue hardship. Reassignment also may be a reasonable accommodation if both employer and employee agree that this is more appropriate than accommodation in the present job.

Consideration of reassignment is only required for employees. An employer is not required to consider a different position for a job applicant if s/he is not able to perform the essential functions of the position s/he is applying for, with or without reasonable accommodation.

Reassignment may be an appropriate accommodation when an employee becomes disabled, when a disability becomes more severe, or when changes or technological developments in equipment affect the job performance of an employee with a disability. If there is no accommodation that will enable the person to perform the present job, or if it would be an undue hardship for the employer to provide such accommodation, reassignment should be considered.

Reassignment may not be used to limit, segregate, or otherwise discriminate against an employee with a disability. An employer may not reassign people with disabilities only to certain undesirable positions, or only to certain offices or facilities.

Reassignment should be made to a position equivalent to the one presently held in terms of pay and other job status, if the individual is qualified for the position and if such a position is vacant or will be vacant within a reasonable amount of time. A "reasonable amount of time" should be determined on a case-by-case basis, considering relevant factors such as the types of jobs for which the employee with a disability would be qualified; the frequency with which such jobs become available; the employer's general policies regarding reassignments of employees; and any specific policies regarding sick or injured employees.

For example: If there is no vacant position available at the time that an individual with a disability requires a reassignment, but the employer knows that an equivalent position for which this person is qualified will become vacant within one or two weeks, the employer should reassign the individual to the position when it becomes available.

An employer may reassign an individual to a lower graded position if there are no accommodations that would enable the employee to remain in the current position and there are no positions vacant or soon to be vacant for which the employee is qualified (with or without an accommodation). In such a situation, the employer does not have to maintain the individual's salary at the level of the higher graded position, unless it does so for other employees who are reassigned to lower graded positions.

An employer is not required to create a new job or to bump another employee from a job in order to provide reassignment as a reasonable accommodation. Nor is an employer required to promote an individual with a disability to make such an accommodation.

Generally, it will be "unreasonable" for an employer to violate a seniority system in order to provide a reassignment. However, there may be "special circumstances" that undermine employee expectations about the uniform application of the seniority system, and thus it may be a "reasonable accommodation," absent undue hardship, to reassign an employee despite the existence of a seniority system. There is not an exhaustive list of what constitutes "special circumstances," but examples may include where a seniority system contains exceptions such that one more is unlikely to matter, or where an employer retains the right to alter unilaterally the seniority system and has done so fairly frequently.

(6) Acquisition or Modification of Equipment and Devices

Purchase of equipment or modifications to existing equipment may be effective accommodations for people with many types of disabilities.

There are many devices that make it possible for people to overcome existing barriers to performing functions of a job. These devices range from very simple solutions, such as an elastic band that can enable a person with cerebral palsy to hold a pencil and write, to "high-tech" electronic equipment that can be operated with eye or head movements by people who cannot use their hands.

There are also many ways to modify standard equipment so as to enable people with different functional limitations to perform jobs effectively and safely.

Many of these assistive devices and modifications are inexpensive. Frequently, applicants and employees with disabilities can suggest effective low cost devices or equipment. They have had a great deal of experience in accommodating their disabilities, and many are informed about new and available equipment. Where the job requires special adaptations of equipment, the employer and the applicant or employee should use the process described earlier (see 3.8) to identify the exact functional abilities and limitations of the individual in relation to functional job needs, and to determine what type of assistance may be needed.

There are many sources of technical assistance to help identify and locate devices and equipment for specific job applications. An employer may be able to get information needed simply by telephoning the Job Accommodation Network, a free consulting service on accommodations, or other sources listed under "Accommodations" in the Resource Directory. Employers who need further assistance may use resources such as vocational rehabilitation specialists, occupational therapists and Independent Living Centers who will come on site to conduct a job analysis and recommend appropriate equipment or job modifications.

As indicated above (see 3.4), an employer is only obligated to provide equipment that is needed to perform a job; there is no obligation to provide equipment that the individual uses regularly in daily life, such as glasses, a hearing aid or a wheelchair. However, as previously stated, the employer may be obligated to provide items of this nature if special adaptations are required to perform a job.

For example: It may be a reasonable accommodation to provide an employee with a motorized wheelchair if her job requires movement between buildings that are widely separated, and her disability prevents her operation of a wheelchair manually for that distance, or if heavy, deep-pile carpeting prevents operation of a manual wheelchair.

In some cases, it may be a reasonable accommodation to allow an applicant or employee to provide and use equipment that an employer would not be obligated to provide.

For example: It would be a reasonable accommodation to allow an individual with a visual disability to provide his own guide dog.

Some examples of equipment and devices that may be reasonable accommodations:

- TDDs (Telecommunication Devices for the Deaf) make it possible for people with hearing and/or speech impairments to communicate over the telephone;
- telephone amplifiers are useful for people with hearing impairments;
- special software for standard computers and other equipment can enlarge print or convert print documents to spoken words for people with vision and/or reading disabilities;
- tactile markings on equipment in brailled or raised print are helpful to people with visual impairments;
- telephone headsets and adaptive light switches can be used by people with cerebral palsy or other manual disabilities;
- talking calculators can be used by people with visual or reading disabilities;
- speaker phones may be effective for people who are amputees or have other mobility impairments.

Some examples of effective low cost assistive devices as reported by the Job Accommodation Network and other sources:

- a timer with an indicator light allowed a medical technician who was deaf to perform laboratory tests. Cost $27.00;
- a clerk with limited use of her hands was provided a "lazy susan" file holder that enabled her to reach all materials needed for her job. Cost $85.00;
- A groundskeeper who had limited use of one arm was provided a detachable extension arm for a rake. This enabled him to grasp the handle on the extension with the impaired hand and control the rake with the functional arm. Cost $20.00;
- A desk layout was changed from the right to left side to enable a data entry operator who is visually impaired to perform her job. Cost $0;
- A telephone amplifier designed to work with a hearing aid allowed a plant worker to retain his job and avoid transfer to a lower paid job. Cost $24.00;
- A blind receptionist was provided a light probe which allowed her to determine which lines on the switchboard were ringing, on hold, or in use. (A light-probe gives an audible signal when held over an illuminated source.) Cost $50.00 to $100.00;
- A person who had use of only one hand, working in a food service position could perform all tasks except opening cans. She was provided with a one-handed can opener. Cost $35.00;
- Purchase of a light weight mop and a smaller broom enabled an employee with Downs syndrome and congenital heart problems to do his job with minimal strain. Cost under $40;
- A truck driver had carpal tunnel syndrome which limited his wrist movement and caused extreme discomfort in cold weather. A special wrist splint used with a glove designed for skin divers made it possible for him to drive even in extreme weather conditions. Cost $55.00;
- A phone headset allowed an insurance salesman with cerebral palsy to write while talking to clients. Rental cost $6.00 per month;
- A simple cardboard form, called a "jig" made it possible for a person with mental retardation to properly fold jeans as a stock clerk in a retail store. Cost $0.

Many recent technological innovations make it possible for people with severe disabilities to be very productive employees. Although some of this equipment is expensive, Federal tax credits, tax deductions, and other sources of financing are available to help pay for higher cost equipment.

For example: A company hired a person who was legally blind as a computer operator. The State Commission for the Blind paid half of the cost of a braille terminal. Since all programmers were provided with computers, the cost of the accommodation to this employer was only one-half of the difference in cost between the braille terminal and a regular computer. A smaller company also would be eligible for a tax credit for such cost. (See Tax Credit for Small Business, 4.1a below)

For sources of information and technical assistance to help employers develop or locate "assistive devices and equipment," see this listing in the Index to the Resource Directory.

(7) Adjusting and Modifying Examinations, Training Materials, and Policies

An employer may be required to modify, adjust, or make other reasonable accommodations in the ways that tests and training are administered in order to provide equal employment opportunities for qualified individuals with disabilities. Revisions to other employment policies and practices also may be required as reasonable accommodations.

(a) Tests and Examinations

Accommodations may be needed to assure that tests or examinations measure the actual ability of an individual to perform job functions, rather than reflecting limitations caused by the disability. The ADA requires that tests be given to people who have sensory, speaking, or manual impairments in a format that does not require the use of the impaired skill, unless that is the job-related skill the test is designed to measure.

For example: An applicant who has dyslexia, which causes difficulty in reading, should be given an oral rather than a written test, unless reading is an essential function of the job. Or, an individual with a visual disability or a learning disability might be allowed more time to take a test, unless the test is designed to measure speed required on a job.

The employer is only required to provide a reasonable accommodation for a test if the individual with a disability requests such an accommodation. But the employer has an obligation to inform job applicants in advance that a test will be given, so that an individual who needs an accommodation can make such a request. (See Chapter V. for further guidance on accommodations in testing.)

(b) Training

Reasonable accommodation should be provided, when needed, to give employees with disabilities equal opportunity for training to perform their jobs effectively and to progress in employment. Needed accommodations may include:

- providing accessible training sites;
- providing training materials in alternate formats to accommodate a disability.

For example: An individual with a visual disability may need training materials on tape, in large print, or on a computer diskette. A person with mental retardation may need materials in simplified language or may need help in understanding test instructions;

- modifying the manner in which training is provided.

For example: It may be a reasonable accommodation to allow more time for training or to provide extra assistance to people with learning disabilities or people with mental impairments.

Additional guidance on accommodations in training is provided in Chapter VII.

(c) Other Policies

Adjustments to various existing policies may be necessary to provide reasonable accommodation. As discussed above (see 3.10.3 and 3.10.4), modifications to existing leave policies and regular work hours may be required as accommodations. Or, for example, a company may need to modify a policy prohibiting animals in the work place, so that a visually impaired person can use a guide dog. Policies on providing information to employees may need adjustment to assure that all information is available in accessible formats for employees with disabilities. Policies on emergency evacuations should be adjusted to provide effective accommodations for people with different disabilities. (See Chapter VII).

(8) Providing Qualified Readers

It may be a reasonable accommodation to provide a reader for a qualified individual with a disability, if this would not impose an undue hardship.

For example: A court has held under the Rehabilitation Act that it was not an undue hardship for a large state agency to provide full-time readers for three blind employees, in view of its very substantial budget. However, it may be an undue hardship for a smaller agency or business to provide such an accommodation.

In some job situations a reader may be the most effective and efficient accommodation, but in other situations alternative accommodations may enable an individual with a visual disability to perform job tasks just as effectively.

When an applicant or employee has a visual disability, the employer and the individual should use the "process" outlined in 3.8 above to identify specific limitations of the individual in relation to specific needs of the job and to assess possible accommodations.

For example: People with visual impairments perform many jobs that do not require reading. Where reading is an essential job function, depending on the nature of a visual impairment and the nature of job tasks, print magnification equipment or a talking computer may be more effective for the individual and less costly for an employer than providing another employee as a reader. Where an individual has to read lengthy documents, a reader who transcribes documents onto tapes may be a more effective accommodation.

Providing a reader does not mean that it is necessary to hire a full-time employee for this service. Few jobs require an individual to spend all day reading. A reader may be a part-time employee or full-time employee who performs other duties. However, the person who reads to a visually impaired employee must read well enough to enable the individual to perform his or her job effectively. It would not be a reasonable accommodation to provide a reader whose poor skills hinder the job performance of the individual with a disability.

(9) Providing Qualified Interpreters

Providing an interpreter on an "as-needed" basis may be a reasonable accommodation for a person who is deaf in some employment situations, if this does not impose an undue hardship.

If an individual with a disability is otherwise qualified to perform essential job functions, the employer's basic obligation is to provide an accommodation that will enable this person to perform the job effectively. A person who is deaf or hearing-impaired should be able to communicate effectively with others as required by the duties of the job. Identifying the needs of the individual in relation to specific job tasks will determine whether or when an interpreter may be needed. The resources available to the employer would be considered in determining whether it would be an undue hardship to provide such an accommodation.

> For example: It may be necessary to obtain a qualified interpreter for a job interview, because for many jobs the applicant and interviewer must communicate fully and effectively to evaluate whether the applicant is qualified to do the job. Once hired, however, if the individual is doing clerical work, research, computer applications, or other job tasks that do not require much verbal communication, an interpreter may only be needed occasionally. Interpretation may be necessary for training situations, staff meetings or an employee party, so that this person can fully participate in these functions. Communication on the job may be handled through different means, depending on the situation, such as written notes, "signing" by other employees who have received basic sign language training, or by typing on a computer or typewriter.

People with hearing impairments have different communication needs and use different modes of communication. Some use signing in American Sign Language, but others use sign language that has different manual codes. Some people rely on an oral interpreter who silently mouths words spoken by others to make them easier to lip read. Many hearing-impaired people use their voices to communicate, and some combine talking and signing. The individual should be consulted to determine the most effective means of communication.

Communication between a person who is deaf and others through a supervisor and/or co-worker with basic sign language training may be sufficient in many job situations. However, where extensive discussions or complex subject matter is involved, a trained interpreter may be needed to provide effective communication. Experienced interpreters usually have received special training and may be certified by a professional interpreting organization or state or local Commission serving people who are deaf. (See Resource Directory Index listing of "Interpreters" for information about interpreters and how to obtain them.)

(10) Other Accommodations

There are many other accommodations that may be effective for people with different disabilities in different jobs. The examples of accommodations in EEOC regulations and the examples in this Manual are not the only types of accommodations that may be required. Some other accommodations that may be appropriate include:

- making transportation provided by the employer accessible;
- providing a personal assistant for certain job-related functions, such as a page turner for a person who has no hands, or a travel attendant to act as a sighted guide to assist a blind employee on occasional business trips.
- use of a job coach for people with mental retardation and other disabilities who benefit from individualized on-the job training and services provided at no cost by vocational rehabilitation agencies in "supported employment" programs. (See Resource Directory Index for "Supported Employment.")

I-3.11 Financial and Technical Assistance for Accommodations.

(a) Financial Assistance

There are several sources of financial assistance to help employers make accommodations and comply with ADA requirements.

(1) Tax Credit for Small Business (Section 44 of the Internal Revenue Code)

In 1990, Congress established a special tax credit to help smaller employers make accommodations required by the ADA. An eligible small business may take a tax credit of up to $5000 per year for accommodations made to comply with the ADA. The credit is available for one-half the cost of "eligible access expenditures" that are more than $250 but less than $10,250.

For example: If an accommodation cost $10,250, an employer could get a tax credit of $5000 ($10,250 minus $250, divided by 2). If the accommodation cost $7000, a tax credit of $3375 would be available.

An eligible small business is one with gross receipts of $1 million or less for the taxable year, or 30 or fewer full time employees.

"Eligible access expenditures" for which the tax credit may be taken include the types of accommodations required under Title I of the ADA as well as accessibility requirements for commercial facilities and places of public accommodation under Title III. "Eligible access expenditures" include:

- removal of architectural, communication, physical, or transportation barriers to make the business accessible to, or usable by, people with disabilities.
- providing qualified interpreters or other methods to make communication accessible to people with hearing disabilities;
- providing qualified readers, taped texts, or other methods to make information accessible to people with visual disabilities; and/or
- acquiring or modifying equipment or devices for people with disabilities.

To be eligible for the tax credit, changes made to remove barriers or to provide services, materials or equipment must meet technical standards of the ADA Accessibility Guidelines, where applicable.

(2) Tax Deduction for Architectural and Transportation Barrier Removal (Section 190 of the Internal Revenue Code)

Any business may take a full tax deduction, up to $15,000 per year, for expenses of removing specified architectural or transportation barriers. Expenses covered include costs of removing barriers created by steps, narrow doors, inaccessible parking spaces, toilet facilities, and transportation vehicles. Both the tax credit and the tax deduction are available to eligible small businesses.

For example: If a small business makes a qualified expenditure of $24,000, it may take the $5000 tax credit for the initial $10,250 and, if the remaining $13,750 qualifies under Section 190, may deduct that amount from its taxable income. However, a business may not receive a double benefit for the same expense: for example, it may not take both the tax credit and the tax deduction for $10,000 spent to renovate bathrooms.

Information on the Section 44 tax credit and the Section 190 tax deduction can be obtained from a local IRS office, or by contacting the Office of Chief Counsel, Internal Revenue Service. (See Resource Directory.)

(3) Targeted Jobs Tax Credit

Tax credits also are available under the Targeted Jobs Tax Credit Program (TJTCP) for employers who hire individuals with disabilities referred by state or local vocational rehabilitation agencies, State Commissions on the Blind and the U.S. Department of Veterans Affairs and certified by a State Employment Service. This program promotes hiring of several "disadvantaged" groups, including people with disabilities.

Under the TJTCP, a tax credit may be taken for 40% of the first $6000 of an employee's first-year salary. This program must be reauthorized each year by Congress, and currently has been extended through June 30, 1992. Information about this program can be obtained from the State Employment Services or from State Governor's Committees on the Employment of People with Disabilities. (See State listings in Resource Directory.)

(4) Other Funding Sources

State or local vocational rehabilitation agencies and State Commissions for the Blind can provide financial assistance for equipment and accommodations for their clients. The U.S. Department of Veterans Affairs also provides financial assistance to disabled veterans for equipment needed to help perform jobs. Some organizations that serve people with particular types of disabilities also provide financial assistance for needed accommodations. Other types of assistance may be available in the community. For example, some Independent Living Centers provide transportation service to the workplace for people with disabilities. For further information, see "Financial Assistance for Accommodations" in Resource Directory Index.

(b) Technical Assistance

There are many sources of technical assistance to help employers make effective accommodations for people with different disabilities in various job situations. Many of these resources are available without cost. Major resources for information, assistance, and referral to local specialized resources are 10 new ADA Regional Business and Disability Technical Assistance Centers that have been funded by Congress specifically to help implement the ADA. These Centers have been established to provide information, training and technical assistance to employers and all other entities covered by the ADA and to people with disabilities. The Centers also can refer employers to local technical assistance sources. (See ADA Regional Business and Disability Technical Assistance Centers in Resource Director.) Other resources include:

- State and local vocational rehabilitation agencies
- Independent Living Centers in some 400 communities around the country provide technical assistance to employers and people with disabilities on accessibility and other accommodations and make referrals to specialized sources of assistance.
- The Job Accommodation Network (JAN) a free national consultant service, available through a toll-free number, helps employers make individualized accommodations.
- ABLEDATA, a computerized database of disability-related products and services, conducts customized information searches on worksite modifications, assistive devices and other accommodations.
- The President's Committee on Employment of People with Disabilities provides technical information, including publications with practical guidance on job analysis and accommodations.
- Governors' Committees on Employment of People with Disabilities in each State, allied with the President's Committee, are local resources of information and technical assistance.

These and many other sources of specialized technical assistance are listed in the Resource Directory. The Index to the Directory will be helpful in locating specific types of assistance.

I-IV. Establishing Nondiscriminatory Qualification Standards and Selection Criteria.

I-4.1 Introduction.

The ADA does not prohibit an employer from establishing job-related qualification standards, including education, skills, work experience, and physical and mental standards necessary for job performance, health and safety.

The Act does not interfere with an employer's authority to establish appropriate job qualifications to hire people who can perform jobs effectively and safely, and to hire the best qualified person for a job. ADA requirements are designed to assure that people with disabilities are not excluded from jobs that they can perform.

ADA requirements apply to all selection standards and procedures, including, but not limited to:

- education and work experience requirements;
- physical and mental requirements;
- safety requirements;
- paper and pencil tests;
- physical or psychological tests;
- interview questions; and
- rating systems;

I-4.2 Overview of Legal Obligations.

- Qualification standards or selection criteria that screen out or tend to screen out an individual with a disability on the basis of disability must be job-related and consistent with business necessity.
- Even if a standard is job-related and consistent with business necessity, if it screens out an individual with a disability on the basis of disability, the employer must consider if the individual could meet the standard with a reasonable accommodation.
- An employer is not required to lower existing production standards applicable to the quality or quantity of work for a given job in considering qualifications of an individual with a disability, if these standards are uniformly applied to all applicants and employees in that job.
- If an individual with a disability cannot perform a marginal function of a job because of a disability, an employer may base a hiring decision only on the individual's ability to perform the essential functions of the job, with or without a reasonable accommodation.

I-4.3 What is Meant by "Job-Related" and "Consistent with Business Necessity"?

(1) Job-Related

If a qualification standard, test or other selection

criterion operates to screen out an individual with a disability, or a class of such individuals on the basis of disability, it must be a legitimate measure or qualification for the specific job it is being used for. It is not enough that it measures qualifications for a general class of jobs.

For example: A qualification standard for a secretarial job of "ability to take shorthand dictation" is not job-related if the person in the particular secretarial job actually transcribes taped dictation.

The ADA does not require that a qualification standard or selection criterion apply only to the "essential functions" of a job. A "job-related" standard or selection criterion may evaluate or measure all functions of a job and employers may continue to select and hire people who can perform all of these functions. It is only when an individual's disability prevents or impedes performance of marginal job functions that the ADA requires the employer to evaluate this individual's qualifications solely on his/her ability to perform the essential functions of the job, with or without an accommodation.

For example: An employer has a job opening for an administrative assistant. The essential functions of the job are administrative and organizational. Some occasional typing has been part of the job, but other clerical staff are available who can perform this marginal job function. There are two job applicants. One has a disability that makes typing very difficult, the other has no disability and can type. The employer may not refuse to hire the first applicant because of her inability to type, but must base a job decision on the relative ability of each applicant to perform the essential administrative and organizational job functions, with or without accommodation. The employer may not screen out the applicant with a disability because of the need to make an accommodation to perform the essential job functions. However, if the first applicant could not type for a reason not related to her disability (for example, if she had never learned to type) the employer would be free to select the applicant who could best perform all of the job functions.

(2) Business Necessity

"Business necessity" will be interpreted under the ADA as it has been interpreted by the courts under Section 504 of the Rehabilitation Act.

Under the ADA, as under the Rehabilitation Act:

If a test or other selection criterion excludes an individual with a disability because of the disability and does not relate to the essential functions of a job, it is not consistent with business necessity.

This standard is similar to the legal standard under Title VII of the Civil Rights Act which provides that a selection procedure which screens out a disproportionate number of persons of a particular race, sex or national origin "class" must be justified as a "business necessity." However, under the ADA the standard may be applied to an individual who is screened out by a selection procedure because of disability, as well as to a class of persons. It is not necessary to make statistical comparisons between a group of people with disabilities and people who are not disabled to show that a person with a disability is screened out by a selection standard.

Disabilities vary so much that it is difficult, if not impossible, to make general determinations about the effect of various standards, criteria and procedures on "people with disabilities." Often, there may be little or no statistical data to measure the impact of a procedure on any "class" of people with a particular disability compared to people without disabilities. As with other determinations under the ADA, the exclusionary effect of a selection procedure usually must be looked at in relation to a particular individual who has particular limitations caused by a disability.

Because of these differences, the federal Uniform Guidelines on Employee Selection Procedures that apply to selection procedures on the basis of race, sex, and national origin under Title VII of the Civil Rights Act and other Federal authorities do not apply under the ADA to selection procedures affecting people with disabilities.

A standard may be job-related but not justified by business necessity, because it does not concern an essential function of a job.

For example: An employer may ask candidates for a clerical job if they have a driver's license, because it would be desirable to have a person in the job who could occasionally run errands or take packages to the post office in an emergency. This requirement is "job-related," but it relates to an incidental, not an essential, job function. If it disqualifies a person who could not obtain a driver's license because of a disability, it would not be justified as a "business necessity" for purposes of the ADA.

Further, the ADA requires that even if a qualification standard or selection criterion is job-related and consistent with business necessity, it may not be used to exclude an individual with a disability if this individual could satisfy the legitimate standard or selection criterion with a reasonable accommodation.

For example: It may be job-related and necessary for a business to require that a secretary produce letters and other documents on a word processor. But it would be discriminatory to reject a person whose disability prevented manual keyboard operation, but who could meet the qualification standard using a computer assistive device, if providing this device would not impose an undue hardship.

I-4.4 Establishing Job-Related Qualification Standards.

The ADA does not restrict an employer's authority to establish needed job qualifications, including requirements related to:

- education;
- skills;
- work experience;
- licenses or certification;
- physical and mental abilities;
- health and safety; or
- other job-related requirements, such as judgment, ability to work under pressure or interpersonal skills.

Physical and Mental Qualification Standards

An employer may establish physical or mental qualifications that are necessary to perform specific jobs (for example, jobs in the transportation and construction industries; police and fire fighter jobs; security guard jobs) or to protect health and safety.

However, as with other job qualification standards, if a physical or mental qualification standard screens out an individual with a disability or a class of individuals with disabilities, the employer must be prepared to show that the standard is:

- job-related and
- consistent with business necessity.

Even if a physical or mental qualification standard is job-related and necessary for a business, if it is applied to exclude an otherwise qualified individual with a disability, the employer must consider whether there is a reasonable accommodation that would enable this person to meet the standard. The employer does not have to consider such accommodations in establishing a standard, but only when an otherwise qualified person with a disability requests an accommodation.

For example: An employer has a forklift operator job. The essential function of the job is mechanical operation of the forklift machinery. The job has a physical requirement of ability to lift a 70 pound weight, because the operator must be able to remove and replace the 70 pound battery which powers the forklift. This standard is job-related. However, it would be a reasonable accommodation to eliminate this standard for an otherwise qualified forklift operator who could not lift a 70 pound weight because of a disability, if other operators or employees are available to help this person remove and replace the battery.

Evaluating Physical and Mental Qualification Standards Under the ADA

Employers generally have two kinds of physical or mental standards:

(1) Standards that may exclude an entire class of individuals with disabilities.

For example: No person who has epilepsy, diabetes, or a heart or back condition is eligible for a job.

(2) Standards that measure a physical or mental ability needed to perform a job.

For example: The person in the job must be able to lift x pounds for x hours daily, or run x miles in x minutes.

Standards that exclude an entire class of individuals with disabilities

"Blanket" exclusions of this kind usually have been established because employers believed them to be necessary for health or safety reasons. Such standards also may be used to screen out people who an employer fears, or assumes, may cause higher medical insurance or workers' compensation costs, or may have a higher rate of absenteeism.

Employers who have such standards should review them carefully. In most cases, they will not meet ADA requirements.

The ADA recognizes legitimate employer concerns and the requirements of other laws for health and safety in the workplace. An employer is not required to hire or retain an individual who would pose a "direct threat" to health or safety (see below). But the ADA requires an objective assessment of a particular individual's current ability to perform a job safely and effectively. Generalized "blanket" exclusions of an entire group of people with a certain disability prevent such an individual consideration. Such class-wide exclusions that do not reflect up-to-date medical knowledge and technology, or that are based on fears about future medical or workers' compensation costs, are unlikely to survive a legal challenge under the ADA. (However, the ADA recognizes employers' obligations to comply with Federal laws that mandate such exclusions in certain occupations. [See Health and Safety Requirements of Other Federal or State Laws below.])

The ADA requires that:

- any determination of a direct threat to health or safety must be based on an individualized assessment of objective and specific evidence about a particular individual's present ability to perform essential job functions, not on general assumptions or speculations about a disability. (See Standards Necessary for Health and Safety: A "Direct Threat" below.)

For example: An employer who excludes all persons who have epilepsy from jobs that require use of dangerous machinery will be required to look at the life experience and work history of an individual who has epilepsy. The individual evaluation should take into account the type of job, the degree of seizure control, the type(s) of seizures (if any), whether the person has an "aura" (warning of seizure), the person's reliability in taking prescribed anti-convulsant medication, and any side effects of such medication. Individuals who have no seizures because they regularly take prescribed medication, or who have sufficient advance warning of a seizure so that they can stop hazardous activity, would not pose a "direct threat" to safety.

Standards that measure needed physical or mental ability to perform a job

Specific physical or mental abilities may be needed to perform certain types of jobs.

For example: Candidates for jobs such as airline pilots, policemen and firefighters may be required to meet certain physical and psychological qualifications.

In establishing physical or mental standards for such jobs, an employer does not have to show that these standards are "job related," justified by "business necessity" or that they relate only to "essential" functions of the job. However, if such a standard screens out an otherwise qualified individual with a disability, the employer must be prepared to show that the standard, as applied, is job-related and consistent with business necessity under the ADA. And, even if this can be shown, the employer must consider whether this individual could meet the standard with a reasonable accommodation.

For example: A police department that requires all its officers to be able to make forcible arrests and to perform all job functions in the department might be able to justify stringent physical requirements for all officers, if in fact they are all required to be available for any duty in an emergency.

However, if a position in a mailroom required as a qualification standard that the person in the job be able to reach high enough to place and retrieve packages from 6-foot high shelves, an employer would have to consider whether there was an accommodation that would enable a person with a disability that prevented reaching that high to perform these essential functions. Possible accommodations might include lowering the shelf-height, providing a step stool or other assistive device.

Physical agility tests

An employer may give a physical agility test to determine physical qualifications necessary for certain jobs prior to making a job offer if it is simply an agility test and not a medical examination. Such a test would not be subject to the prohibition against pre-employment medical examinations if given to all similarly situated applicants or employees, regardless of disability. However, if an agility test screens out or tends to screen out an individual with a disability or a class of such individuals because of disability, the employer must be prepared to show that the test is job-related and consistent with business necessity and that the test or the job cannot be performed with a reasonable accommodation.

It is important to understand the distinction between physical agility tests and prohibited pre-employment medical inquiries and examinations. One difference is that agility tests do not involve medical examinations or diagnoses by a physician, while medical examinations may involve a doctor.

For example: At the pre-offer stage, a police department may conduct an agility test to measure a candidate's ability to walk, run, jump, or lift in relation to specific job duties, but it cannot require the applicant to have a medical screening before taking the agility test. Nor can it administer a medical examination before making a conditional job offer to this person.

Some employers currently may require a medical

screening before administering a physical agility test to assure that the test will not harm the applicant. There are two ways that an employer can handle this problem under the ADA:

- the employer can request the applicant's physician to respond to a very restricted inquiry which describes the specific agility test and asks: "Can this person safely perform this test?"
- the employer may administer the physical agility test after making a conditional job offer, and in this way may obtain any necessary medical information, as permitted under the ADA. (See Chapter VI.) The employer may find it more cost-efficient to administer such tests only to those candidates who have met other job qualifications.

I-4.5 Standards Necessary for Health and Safety: A "Direct Threat".

An employer may require as a qualification standard that an individual not pose a "direct threat" to the health or safety of the individual or others, if this standard is applied to all applicants for a particular job. However, an employer must meet very specific and stringent requirements under the ADA to establish that such a "direct threat" exists.

The employer must be prepared to show that there is:

- significant risk of substantial harm;
- the specific risk must be identified;
- it must be a current risk, not one that is speculative or remote;
- the assessment of risk must be based on objective medical or other factual evidence regarding a particular individual; and
- even if a genuine significant risk of substantial harm exists, the employer must consider whether the risk can be eliminated or reduced below the level of a "direct threat" by reasonable accommodation.

Looking at each of these requirements more closely:

(1) Significant risk of substantial harm

An employer cannot deny an employment opportunity to an individual with a disability merely because of a slightly increased risk. The employer must be prepared to show that there is a significant risk, that is, a high probability of substantial harm, if the person were employed.

The assessment of risk cannot be based on mere speculation unrelated to the individual in question.

For example: An employer cannot assume that a person with cerebral palsy who has restricted manual dexterity cannot work in a laboratory because s/he will pose a risk of breaking vessels with dangerous contents. The abilities or limitations of a particular individual with cerebral palsy must be evaluated.

(2) The specific risk must be identified

If an individual has a disability, the employer must identify the aspect of the disability that would pose a direct threat, considering the following factors:

- the duration of the risk.

For example: An elementary school teacher who has tuberculosis may pose a risk to the health of children in her classroom. However, with proper medication, this person's disease would be contagious for only a two-week period. With an accommodation of two-weeks absence from the classroom, this teacher would not pose a "direct threat."

- the nature and severity of the potential harm.

For example: A person with epilepsy, who has lost consciousness during seizures within the past year, might seriously endanger her own life and the lives of others if employed as a bus driver. But this person would not pose a severe threat of harm if employed in a clerical job.

- the likelihood that the potential harm will occur.

For example: An employer may believe that there is a risk of employing an individual with HIV disease as a teacher. However, it is medically established that this disease can only be transmitted through sexual contact, use of infected needles, or other entry into a person's blood stream. There is little or no likelihood that employing this person as a teacher would pose a risk of transmitting this disease.

and

- the imminence of the potential harm.

For example: A physician's evaluation of an applicant for a heavy labor job that indicated the individual had a disc condition that might worsen in 8 or 10 years would not be sufficient indication of imminent potential harm.

If the perceived risk to health or safety arises from

the behavior of an individual with a mental or emotional disability, the employer must identify the specific behavior that would pose the "direct threat".

(3) The risk must be current, not one that is speculative or remote

The employer must show that there is a current risk —"a high probability of substantial harm"—to health or safety based on the individual's present ability to perform the essential functions of the job. A determination that an individual would pose a "direct threat" cannot be based on speculation about future risk. This includes speculation that an individual's disability may become more severe. An assessment of risk cannot be based on speculation that the individual will become unable to perform a job in the future, or that this individual may cause increased health insurance or workers compensation costs, or will have excessive absenteeism. (See Insurance, Chapter VII., and Workers' Compensation, Chapter IX.)

(4) The assessment of risk must be based on objective medical or other evidence related to a particular individual

The determination that an individual applicant or employee with a disability poses a "direct threat" to health or safety must be based on objective, factual evidence related to that individual's present ability to safely perform the essential functions of a job. It cannot be based on unfounded assumptions, fears, or stereotypes about the nature or effect of a disability or of disability generally. Nor can such a determination be based on patronizing assumptions that an individual with a disability may endanger himself or herself by performing a particular job.

For example: An employer may not exclude a person with a vision impairment from a job that requires a great deal of reading because of concern that the strain of heavy reading may further impair her sight.

The determination of a "direct threat" to health or safety must be based on a reasonable medical judgement that relies on the most current medical knowledge and/or the best available objective evidence. This may include:

- input from the individual with a disability;
- the experience of this individual in previous jobs;
- documentation from medical doctors, psychologists, rehabilitation counselors, physical or occupational therapists, or others who have expertise in the disability involved and/or direct knowledge of the individual with a disability.

Where the psychological behavior of an employee suggests a threat to safety, factual evidence of this behavior also may constitute evidence of a "direct threat." An employee's violent, aggressive, destructive or threatening behavior may provide such evidence.

Employers should be careful to assure that assessments of "direct threat" to health or safety are based on current medical knowledge and other kinds of evidence listed above, rather than relying on generalized and frequently out-of-date assumptions about risk associated with certain disabilities. They should be aware that Federal contractors who have had similar disability nondiscrimination requirements under the Rehabilitation Act have had to make substantial back-pay and other financial payments because they excluded individuals with disabilities who were qualified to perform their jobs, based on generalized assumptions that were not supported by evidence about the individual concerned.

Examples of Contractor Cases:

- A highly qualified experienced worker was rejected for a sheet metal job because of a company's general medical policy excluding anyone with epilepsy from this job. The company asserted that this person posed a danger to himself and to others because of the possibility that he might have a seizure on the job. However, this individual had been seizure-free for 6 years and co-workers on a previous job testified that he carefully followed his prescribed medication schedule. The company was found to have discriminated against this individual and was required to hire him, incurring large back pay and other costs.
- An applicant who was deaf in one ear was rejected for an aircraft mechanic job because the company feared that his impairment might cause a future workers' compensation claim. His previous work record gave ample evidence of his ability to perform the aircraft mechanic job. The company was found to have discriminated because it provided no evidence that this person would have been a danger to himself or to others on the job.
- An experienced carpenter was not hired because a blood pressure reading by the company doctor at the end of a physical exam was above the company's general medical standard. However,

his own doctor provided evidence of much lower readings, based on measurements of his blood pressure at several times during a physical exam. This doctor testified that the individual could safely perform the carpenter's job because he had only mild hypertension. Other expert medical evidence confirmed that a single blood pressure reading was not sufficient to determine if a person has hypertension, that such a reading clearly was not sufficient to determine if a person could perform a particular job, and that hypertension has very different effects on different people. In this case, it was found that there was merely a slightly elevated risk, and that a remote possibility of future injury was not sufficient to disqualify an otherwise qualified person. (Note that while it is possible that a person with mild hypertension does not have an impairment that "substantially limits a major life activity," in this case the person was excluded because he was "regarded as" having such an impairment. The employer was still required to show that this person posed a "direct threat" to safety.)

"Direct Threat" to Self

An employer may require that an individual not pose a direct threat of harm to his or her own safety or health, as well as to the health or safety of others. However, as emphasized above, such determinations must be strictly based on valid medical analyses or other objective evidence related to this individual, using the factors set out above. A determination that a person might cause harm to himself or herself cannot be based on stereotypes, patronizing assumptions about a person with a disability, or generalized fears about risks that might occur if an individual with a disability is placed in a certain job. Any such determination must be based on evidence of specific risk to a particular individual.

For example: An employer would not be required to hire an individual disabled by narcolepsy who frequently and unexpectedly loses consciousness to operate a power saw or other dangerous equipment, if there is no accommodation that would reduce or eliminate the risk of harm. But an advertising agency could not reject an applicant for a copywriter job who has a history of mental illness, based on a generalized fear that working in this high stress job might trigger a relapse of the individual's mental illness. Nor could an employer reject an applicant with a visual or mobility disability because of a generalized fear of risks to this person in the event of a fire or other emergency.

(5) If there is a significant risk, reasonable accommodation must be considered

Where there is a significant risk of substantial harm to health or safety, an employer still must consider whether there is a reasonable accommodation that would eliminate this risk or reduce the risk so that it is below the level of a "direct threat."

For example: A deaf bus mechanic was denied employment because the transit authority feared that he had a high probability of being injured by buses moving in and out of the garage. It was not clear that there was, in fact, a "high probability" of harm in this case, but the mechanic suggested an effective accommodation that enabled him to perform his job with little or no risk. He worked in a corner of the garage, facing outward, so that he could see moving buses. A co-worker was designated to alert him with a tap on the shoulder if any dangerous situation should arise.

"Direct Threat" and Accommodation in Food Handling Jobs

The ADA includes a specific application of the "direct threat" standard and the obligation for reasonable accommodation in regard to individuals who have infectious or communicable diseases that may be transmitted through the handling of food.

The law provides that the U.S. Department of Health and Human Services (HHS) must prepare and update annually a list of contagious diseases that are transmitted through the handling of food and the methods by which these diseases are transmitted.

When an individual who has one of the listed diseases applies for work or works in a job involving food handling, the employer must consider whether there is a reasonable accommodation that will eliminate the risk of transmitting the disease through handling of food. If there is such an accommodation, and it would not impose an undue hardship, the employer must provide the accommodation.

An employer would not be required to hire a job applicant in such a situation if no reasonable accommodation is possible. However, an employer would be required to consider accommodating an employee by reassignment to a position that does not require handling of food, if such a position is available, the employee is qualified for it, and it would not pose an undue hardship.

In August 1991, the Centers for Disease Control

(CDC) of the Public Health Service in HHS issued a list of infectious and communicable diseases that are transmitted through handling of food, together with information about how these diseases are transmitted. The list of diseases is brief. In conformance with established medical opinion, it does not include AIDS or the HIV virus. In issuing the list, the CDC emphasized that the greatest danger of food-transmitted illness comes from contamination of infected food-producing animals and contamination in food processing, rather than from handling of food by persons with infectious or communicable diseases. The CDC also emphasized that proper personal hygiene and sanitation in food-handling jobs were the most important measures to prevent transmission of disease.

The CDC list of diseases that are transmitted through food handling and recommendations for preventing such transmission appears in Appendix C.

I-4.6 Health and Safety Requirements of Other Federal or State Laws.

The ADA recognizes employers' obligations to comply with requirements of other laws that establish health and safety standards. However, the Act gives greater weight to Federal than to state or local law.

(1) Federal Laws and Regulations

The ADA does not override health and safety requirements established under other Federal laws. If a standard is required by another Federal law, an employer must comply with it and does not have to show that the standard is job related and consistent with business necessity.

> For example: An employee who is being hired to drive a vehicle in interstate commerce must meet safety requirements established by the U.S. Department of Transportation. Employers also must conform to health and safety requirements of the U.S. Occupational Safety and Health Administration (OSHA).

However, an employer still has the obligation under the ADA to consider whether there is a reasonable accommodation, consistent with the standards of other Federal laws, that will prevent exclusion of qualified individuals with disabilities who can perform jobs without violating the standards of those laws.

> For example: In hiring a person to drive a vehicle in interstate commerce, an employer must conform to existing Department of Transportation regulations that exclude any person with epilepsy, diabetes, and certain other conditions from such a job.
>
> But, for example, if DOT regulations require that a truck have 3 grab bars in specified places, and an otherwise qualified individual with a disability could perform essential job functions with the assistance of 2 additional grab bars, it would be a reasonable accommodation to add these bars, unless this would be an undue hardship.

The Department of Transportation, as directed by Congress, currently is reviewing several motor vehicle standards that require "blanket" exclusions of individuals with diabetes, epilepsy and certain other disabilities.

(2) State and Local Laws

The ADA does not override state or local laws designed to protect public health and safety, except where such laws conflict with ADA requirements. This means that if there is a state or local law that would exclude an individual with a disability for a particular job or profession because of a health or safety risk, the employer still must assess whether a particular individual would pose a "direct threat" to health or safety under the ADA standard. If there is such a "direct threat," the employer also must consider whether it could be eliminated or reduced below the level of a "direct threat" by reasonable accommodation. An employer may not rely on the existence of a state or local law that conflicts with ADA requirements as a defense to a charge of discrimination.

> For example: A state law that required a schoolbus driver to have a high level of hearing in both ears without use of a hearing aid was found by a court to violate Section 504 of the Rehabilitation Act, and would violate the ADA. The court found that the driver could perform his job with a hearing aid without a risk to safety.

(See further guidance on Medical Examinations and Inquiries in Chapter VI.)

I-V. Nondiscrimination in the Hiring Process: Recruitment; Applications.

I-5.1 Overview of Legal Obligations.

- An employer must provide an equal opportunity for an individual with a disability to participate in the job application process and to be considered for a job.
- An employer may not make any pre-employment inquiries regarding disability, but may ask

questions about the ability to perform specific job functions and may, with certain limitations, ask an individual with a disability to describe or demonstrate how s/he would perform these functions.

- An employer may not require pre-employment medical examinations or medical histories, but may condition a job offer on the results of a post-offer medical examination, if all entering employees in the same job category are required to take this examination.
- Tests for illegal drugs are not medical examinations under the ADA and may be given at any time.
- A test that screens out or tends to screen out a person with a disability on the basis of disability must be job-related and consistent with business necessity.
- Tests must reflect the skills and aptitudes of an individual rather than impaired sensory, manual, or speaking skills, unless those are job-related skills the test is designed to measure.

A careful review of all procedures used in recruiting and selecting employees is advisable to assure nondiscrimination in the hiring process. Reasonable accommodation must be provided as needed, to assure that individuals with disabilities have equal opportunities to participate in this process.

I-5.2 Job Advertisements and Notices.

It is advisable that job announcements, advertisements, and other recruitment notices include information on the essential functions of the job. Specific information about essential functions will attract applicants, including individuals with disabilities, who have appropriate qualifications.

Employers may wish to indicate in job advertisements and notices that they do not discriminate on the basis of disability or other legally prohibited bases. An employer may wish to include a statement such as: "We are an Equal Opportunity Employer. We do not discriminate on the basis of race, religion, color, sex, age, national origin or disability."

Accessibility of Job Information

Information about job openings should be accessible to people with different disabilities. An employer is not obligated to provide written information in various formats in advance, but should make it available in an accessible format on request.

> For example: Job information should be available in a location that is accessible to people with mobility impairments. If a job advertisement provides only a telephone number to call for information, a TDD (telecommunication device for the deaf) number should be included, unless a telephone relay service has been established.[2] Printed job information in an employment office or on employee bulletin boards should be made available, as needed, to persons with visual or other reading impairments. Preparing information in large print will help make it available to some people with visual impairments. Information can be recorded on a cassette or read to applicants with more severe vision impairments and those who have other disabilities which limit reading ability.

I-5.3 Employment Agencies.

Employment agencies are "covered entities" under the ADA, and must comply with all ADA requirements that are applicable to their activities.

The definition of an "employment agency" under the ADA is the same as that under Title VII of the Civil Rights Act. It includes private and public employment agencies and other organizations, such as college placement services, that regularly procure employees for an employer.

When an employer uses an employment agency to recruit, screen, and refer potential employees, both the employer and the employment agency may be liable if there is any violation of ADA requirements.

> For example: An employer uses an employment agency to recruit and the agency places a newspaper advertisement with a telephone number that all interested persons must call, because no address is given. However, there is no TDD number. If there is no telephone relay service, and a deaf person is unable to obtain information about a job for which she is qualified and files a discrimination charge, both the employer and the agency may be liable.

An employer should inform an employment agency used to recruit or screen applicants of the mutual

---

[2] Title IV of the ADA requires all telephone carriers to establish relay services by July 1993, that will enable people who use TDDs to speak directly to anyone through use of a relay operator. Many states already have such services. See Resource Directory for Telecommunications Relay Services.

obligation to comply with ADA requirements. In particular, these agencies should be informed about requirements regarding qualification standards, pre-employment inquiries, and reasonable accommodation.

If an employer has a contract with an employment agency, the employer may wish to include a provision stating that the agency will conduct its activities in compliance with ADA and other legal nondiscrimination requirements.

I-5.4 Recruitment.

The ADA is a nondiscrimination law. It does not require employers to undertake special activities to recruit people with disabilities. However, it is consistent with the purpose of the ADA for employers to expand their "outreach" to sources of qualified candidates with disabilities. (See Locating Qualified Individuals with Disabilities below.)

Recruitment activities that have the effect of screening out potential applicants with disabilities may violate the ADA.

> For example: If an employer conducts recruitment activity at a college campus, job fair, or other location that is physically inaccessible, or does not make its recruitment activity accessible at such locations to people with visual, hearing or other disabilities, it may be liable if a charge of discrimination is filed.

Locating Qualified Individuals with Disabilities

There are many resources for locating individuals with disabilities who are qualified for different types of jobs. People with disabilities represent a large, underutilized human resource pool. Employers who have actively recruited and hired people with disabilities have found valuable sources of employees for jobs of every kind.

Many of the organizations listed in the Resource Directory are excellent sources for recruiting qualified individuals with disabilities as well as sources of technical assistance for any accommodations needed. For example, many colleges and universities have coordinators of services for students with disabilities who can be helpful in recruitment and in making accommodations. The Association on Handicapped Student Service Programs in Postsecondary Education can provide information on these resources Local Independent Living Centers, state and local vocational rehabilitation agencies, organizations such as Goodwill Industries, and many organizations representing people who have specific disabilities are among other recruitment sources. (See "Recruitment Sources" in Resource Directory Index.)

I-5.5 Pre-Employment Inquiries.

The ADA Prohibits Any Pre-Employment Inquiries About a Disability.

This prohibition is necessary to assure that qualified candidates are not screened out because of their disability before their actual ability to do a job is evaluated. Such protection is particularly important for people with hidden disabilities who frequently are excluded, with no real opportunity to present their qualifications, because of information requested in application forms, medical history forms, job interviews, and pre-employment medical examinations.

The prohibition on pre-employment inquiries about disability does not prevent an employer from obtaining necessary information regarding an applicant's qualifications, including medical information necessary to assess qualifications and assure health and safety on the job.

The ADA requires only that such inquiries be made in two separate stages of the hiring process.

(1) Before making a job offer.

At this stage, an employer:

- may ask questions about an applicant's ability to perform specific job functions;
- may not make an inquiry about a disability;
- may make a job offer that is conditioned on satisfactory results of a post-offer medical examination or inquiry.

(2) After making a conditional job offer and before an individual starts work

At this stage, an employer may conduct a medical examination or ask health-related questions, providing that all candidates who receive a conditional job offer in the same job category are required to take the same examination and/or respond to the same inquiries.

Inquiries that may and may not be made at the pre-offer stage are discussed in the section that follows. Guidance on obtaining and using information from post-offer medical and inquiries and examinations is provided in Chapter VI.

I-5.5(a) Basic Requirements Regarding Pre-Offer Inquiries.

- An employer may not make any pre-employment inquiry about a disability, or about the nature or severity of a disability:
    - on application forms
    - in job interviews
    - in background or reference checks.
- An employer may not make any medical inquiry or conduct any medical examination prior to making a conditional offer of employment.
- An employer may ask a job applicant questions about ability to perform specific job functions, tasks, or duties, as long as these questions are not phrased in terms of a disability. Questions need not be limited to the "essential" functions of the job.
- An employer may ask all applicants to describe or demonstrate how they will perform a job, with or without an accommodation.
- If an individual has a known disability that might interfere with or prevent performance of job functions, s/he may be asked to describe or demonstrate how these functions will be performed, with or without an accommodation, even if other applicants are not asked to do so; however,
- If a known disability would not interfere with performance of job functions, an individual may only be required to describe or demonstrate how s/he will perform a job if this is required of all applicants for the position.
- An employer may condition a job offer on the results of a medical examination or on the responses to medical inquiries if such an examination or inquiry is required of all entering employees in the same job category, regardless of disability; information obtained from such inquiries or examinations must be handled according to the strict confidentiality requirements of the ADA. (See Chapter VI.)

I-5.5(b) The Job Application Form.

A review of job application forms should be a priority before the ADA's effective date, to eliminate any questions related to disability.

Some Examples of Questions that May Not be Asked on Application Forms or in Job Interviews:

- Have you ever had or been treated for any of the following conditions or diseases? (Followed by a checklist of various conditions and diseases.)
- Please list any conditions or diseases for which you have been treated in the past 3 years.
- Have you ever been hospitalized? If so, for what condition?
- Have you ever been treated by a psychiatrist or psychologist? If so, for what condition?
- Have you ever been treated for any mental condition?
- Is there any health-related reason you may not be able to perform the job for which you are applying?
- Have you had a major illness in the last 5 years?
- How many days were you absent from work because of illness last year?

(Pre-employment questions about illness may not be asked, because they may reveal the existence of a disability. However, an employer may provide information on its attendance requirements and ask if an applicant will be able to meet these requirements [See also The Job Interview below.])

- Do you have any physical defects which preclude you from performing certain kinds of work? If yes, describe such defects and specific work limitations.
- Do you have any disabilities or impairments which may affect your performance in the position for which you are applying?

(This question should not be asked even if the applicant is requested in a follow-up question to identify accommodations that would enable job performance. Inquiries should not focus on an applicant's disabilities. The applicant may be asked about ability to perform specific job functions, with or without a reasonable accommodation. [See Information That May be Asked, below.])

- Are you taking any prescribed drugs?

(Questions about use of prescription drugs are not permitted before a conditional job offer, because the answers to such questions might reveal the existence of certain disabilities which require prescribed medication.)

- Have you ever been treated for drug addiction or alcoholism?

(Information may not be requested regarding treatment for drug or alcohol addiction, because the ADA protects people addicted to drugs who have been successfully rehabilitated, or who are undergoing rehabilitation, from discrimination based on drug addiction. [See Chapter VI. for discussion of post-offer inquiries and Chapter VIII. for drug and alcohol issues.])

- Have you ever filed for workers' compensation insurance?

(An employer may not ask about an applicant's workers' compensation history at the pre-offer stage, but may obtain such information after making a conditional job offer. Such questions are prohibited because they are likely to reveal the existence of a disability. In addition, it is discriminatory under the ADA not to hire an individual with a disability because of speculation that the individual will cause increased workers' compensation costs. (See Chapter IV, 4.5(3), and Chapter IX.)

Information about an applicant's ability to perform job tasks, with or without accommodation, can be obtained through the application form and job interview, as explained below. Other needed information may be obtained through medical inquiries or examinations conducted after a conditional offer of employment, as described in Chapter VI.

I-5.5(c) Exception for Federal Contractors Covered by Section 503 of the Rehabilitation Act and Other Federal Programs Requiring Identification of Disability.

Federal contractors and subcontractors who are covered by the affirmative action requirements of Section 503 of the Rehabilitation Act may invite individuals with disabilities to identify themselves on a job application form or by other pre-employment inquiry, to satisfy the affirmative action requirements of Section 503 of the Rehabilitation Act. Employers who request such information must observe Section 503 requirements regarding the manner in which such information is requested and used, and the procedures for maintaining such information as a separate, confidential record, apart from regular personnel records. (For further information, see Office of Federal Contract Compliance Programs listing in Resource Directory.)

A pre-employment inquiry about a disability also is permissible if it is required or necessitated by another Federal law or regulation. For example, a number of programs administered or funded by the U.S. Department of Labor target benefits to individuals with disabilities, such as, disabled veterans, veterans of the Vietnam era, individuals eligible for Targeted Job Tax Credits, and individuals eligible for Job Training Partnership Act assistance. Pre-employment inquiries about disabilities may be necessary under these laws to identify disabled applicants or clients in order to provide the required special services for such persons. These inquiries would not violate the ADA.

I-5.5(d) Information that May Be Requested on Application Forms or in Interviews.

An employer may ask questions to determine whether an applicant can perform specific job functions. The questions should focus on the applicant's ability to perform the job, not on a disability.

For example: An employer could attach a job description to the application form with information about specific job functions. Or the employer may describe the functions. This will make it possible to ask whether the applicant can perform these functions. It also will give an applicant with a disability needed information to request any accommodation required to perform a task. The applicant could be asked:

- **Are you able to perform these tasks with or without an accommodation?**

If the applicant indicates that s/he can perform the tasks with an accommodation, s/he may be asked:

- **How would you perform the tasks, and with what accommodation(s)?**

However, the employer must keep in mind that it cannot refuse to hire a qualified individual with a disability because of this person's need for an accommodation that would be required by the ADA.

An employer may inform applicants on an application form that they may request any needed accommodation to participate in the application process. For example: accommodation for a test, a job interview, or a job demonstration.

The employer may wish to provide information on the application form and in the employment office about specific aspects of the job application process, so that applicants may request any needed accommodation. The employer is not required to provide such information, but without it the applicant may have no advance notice of the need to request an accommodation. Since the individual with a disability has the responsibility to request an accommodation and the employer has the responsibility to provide the accommodation (unless it would cause an undue hardship), providing advance information on various application procedures may help avoid last minute problems in making necessary accommodations. This information can be communicated orally or on tape for people who are visually impaired. (See also Testing, 5.6 below.)

I-5.5(e) Making Job Applications Accessible.

Employers have an obligation to make reasonable accommodations to enable an applicant with a disability to apply for a job. Some of the kinds of accommodations that may be needed have been suggested in the section on Accessibility of Job Information, 5.2 above. Individuals with visual or learning disabilities or other mental disabilities also may require assistance in filling out application forms.

I-5.5(f) The Job Interview.

The basic requirements regarding pre-employment inquiries and the types of questions that are prohibited on job application forms apply to the job interview as well. (See 5.5(a) and (b) above.) An interviewer may not ask questions about a disability, but may obtain more specific information about the ability to perform job tasks and about any needed accommodation, as set out below.

To assure that an interview is conducted in a nondiscriminatory manner, interviewers should be well-informed about the ADA's requirements. The employer may wish to provide written guidelines to people who conduct job interviews.

Most employment discrimination against people with disabilities is not intentional. Discrimination most frequently occurs because interviewers and others involved in hiring lack knowledge about the differing capabilities of individuals with disabilities and make decisions based on stereotypes, misconceptions, or unfounded fears. To avoid discrimination in the hiring process, employers may wish to provide "awareness" training for interviewers and others involved in the hiring process. Such training provides factual information about disability and the qualifications of people with disabilities, emphasizes the importance of individualized assessments, and helps interviewers feel more at ease in talking with people who have different disabilities.

Sources that provide "awareness training," some at little or no cost, may be found under this heading in the Resource Directory Index.

The job interview should focus on the ability of an applicant to perform the job, not on disability.

For example: If a person has only one arm and an essential function of a job is to drive a car, the interviewer should not ask if or how the disability would affect this person's driving. The person may be asked if s/he has a valid driver's license, and whether s/he can perform any special aspect of driving that is required, such as frequent long-distance trips, with or without an accommodation.

The interviewer also could obtain needed information about an applicant's ability and experience in relation to specific job requirements through statements and questions such as: "Eighty-percent of the time of this sales job must be spent on the road covering a three-state territory. What is your outside selling experience? Do you have a valid driver's license? What is your accident record?"

Where an applicant has a visible disability (for example, uses a wheelchair or a guide dog, or has a missing limb) or has volunteered information about a disability, the interviewer may not ask questions about:

- the nature of the disability;
- the severity of the disability;
- the condition causing the disability;
- any prognosis or expectation regarding the condition or disability; or
- whether the individual will need treatment or special leave because of the disability.

The interviewer may describe or demonstrate the specific functions and tasks of the job and ask whether an applicant can perform these functions with or without a reasonable accommodation.

For example: An interviewer could say: "The person in this mailroom clerk position is responsible for receiving incoming mail and packages, sorting the mail, and taking it in a cart to many offices in two buildings, one block apart. The mailclerk also must receive incoming boxes of supplies up to 50 pounds in weight, and place them on storage shelves up to 6 feet in height. Can you perform these tasks? Can you perform them with or without a reasonable accommodation?"

As suggested above, (see 5.5(d)), the interviewer also may give the applicant a copy of a detailed position description and ask whether s/he can perform the functions described in the position, with or without a reasonable accommodation.

Questions may be asked regarding ability to perform all job functions, not merely those that are essential to the job.

For example: A secretarial job may involve the following functions:

(1) transcribing dictation and written drafts from the supervisor and other staff into final written documents;
(2) proof-reading documents for accuracy;
(3) developing and maintaining files;
(4) scheduling and making arrangements for meetings and conferences;
(5) logging documents and correspondence in and out;
(6) placing, answering, and referring telephone calls;
(7) distributing documents to appropriate staff members;
(8) reproducing documents on copying machines; and
(9) occasional travel to perform clerical tasks at out of town conferences.

Taking into account the specific activities of the particular office in which this secretary will work, and availability of other staff, the employer has identified functions 1-6 as essential, and functions 7-9 as marginal to this secretary's job. The interviewer may ask questions related to all 9 functions; however, an applicant with limited mobility should not be screened out because of inability to perform the last 3 functions due to her disability. S/he should be evaluated on ability to perform the first 6 functions, with or without accommodation.

Inquiries Related to Ability to Perform Job Functions and Accommodations

An interviewer may obtain information about an applicant's ability to perform essential job functions and about any need for accommodation in several ways, depending on the particular job applicant and the requirements of a particular job:

- The applicant may be asked to describe or demonstrate how s/he will perform specific job functions, if this is required of everyone applying for a job in this job category, regardless of disability.

For example: An employer might require all applicants for a telemarketing job to demonstrate selling ability by taking a simulated telephone sales test, but could not require that a person using a wheelchair take this test if other applicants are not required to take it.

- If an applicant has a known disability that would appear to interfere with or prevent performance of a job-related function, s/he may be asked to describe or demonstrate how this function would be performed, even if other applicants do not have to do so.

For example: If an applicant has one arm and the job requires placing bulky items on shelves up to six feet high, the interviewer could ask the applicant to demonstrate how s/he would perform this function, with or without an accommodation If the applicant states that s/he can perform this function with a reasonable accommodation, for example, with a step stool fitted with a device to assist lifting, the employer either must provide this accommodation so that the applicant can show that s/he can shelve the items, or let the applicant describe how s/he would do this task.

- However, if an applicant has a known disability that would not interfere with or prevent performance of a job related function, the employer can only ask the applicant to demonstrate how s/he would perform the function if all applicants in the job category are required to do so, regardless of disability.

For example: If an applicant with one leg applies for a job that involves sorting small parts while seated, s/he may not be required to demonstrate the ability to do this job unless all applicants are required to do so.

If an applicant indicates that s/he cannot perform an essential job function even with an accommodation, the applicant would not be qualified for the job in question.

Inquiries About Attendance

An interviewer may not ask whether an applicant will need or request leave for medical treatment or for other reasons related to a disability.

The interviewer may provide information on the employer's regular work hours, leave policies, and any special attendance needs of the job, and ask if the applicant can meet these requirements (provided that the requirements actually are applied to employees in a particular job).

For example: "Our regular work hours are 9 to 5, five days weekly, but we expect employees in this job to work overtime, evenings, and weekends for 6 weeks during the Christmas season and on certain other holidays New employees get 1 week of vacation, 7 sick leave days and may take no more than

5 days of unpaid leave per year. Can you meet these requirements?"

Information about previous work attendance records may be obtained on the application form, in the interview or in reference checks, but the questions should not refer to illness or disability.

If an applicant has had a poor attendance record on a previous job, s/he may wish to provide an explanation that includes information related to a disability, but the employer should not ask whether a poor attendance record was due to illness, accident or disability. For example, an applicant might wish to disclose voluntarily that the previous absence record was due to surgery for a medical condition that is now corrected, treatment for cancer that is now in remission or to adjust medication for epilepsy, but that s/he is now fully able to meet all job requirements.

Accommodations for Interviews

The employer must provide an accommodation, if needed, to enable an applicant to have equal opportunity in the interview process. As suggested earlier, the employer may find it helpful to state in an initial job notice, and/or on the job application form, that applicants who need accommodation for an interview should request this in advance.

Needed accommodations for interviews may include:

- an accessible location for people with mobility impairments;
- a sign interpreter for a deaf person;
- a reader for a blind person.

Conducting an Interview

The purpose of a job interview is to obtain appropriate information about the background qualifications and other personal qualities of an applicant in relation to the requirements of a specific job.

This chapter has discussed ways to obtain this information by focusing on the abilities rather than the disability of a disabled applicant. However, there are other aspects of an interview that may create barriers to an accurate and objective assessment of an applicant's job qualifications. The interviewer may not know how to communicate effectively with people who have particular disabilities, or may make negative, incorrect assumptions about the abilities of a person with a disability because s/he misinterprets some external manifestation of the disability.

For example: An interviewer may assume that a person who displays certain characteristics of cerebral palsy, such as indistinct speech, lisping, and involuntary or halting movements, is limited in intelligence. In fact, cerebral palsy does not affect intelligence at all.

If an applicant who is known to have a disability was referred by a rehabilitation agency or other source familiar with the person, it may be helpful to contact the agency to learn more about this individual's ability to perform specific job functions; however, questions should not be asked about the nature or extent of the person's disability. General information on different disabilities may be obtained from many organizations listed in the Resource Directory. See Index under the specific disability.

I-5.5(g) Background and Reference Checks.

Before making a conditional job offer, an employer may not request any information about a job applicant from a previous employer, family member, or other source that it may not itself request of the job applicant.

If an employer uses an outside firm to conduct background checks, the employer should assure that this firm complies with the ADA's prohibitions on pre-employment inquiries. Such a firm is an agent of the employer. The employer is responsible for actions of its agents and may not do anything through a contractual relationship that it may not itself do directly.

Before making a conditional offer of employment, an employer may not ask previous employers or other sources about an applicant's:

- disability;
- illness;
- workers' compensation history;
- or any other questions that the employer itself may not ask of the applicant.

A previous employer may be asked about:

- job functions and tasks performed by the applicant;
- the quality and quantity of work performed;
- how job functions were performed;
- attendance record;
- other job-related issues that do not relate to disability.

If an applicant has a known disability and has indicated that s/he could perform a job with a reasonable accommodation, a previous employer may be asked about accommodations made by that employer.

I-5.6 Testing.

Employers may use any kind of test to determine job qualifications. The ADA has two major requirements in relation to tests:

(1) If a test screens out or tends to screen out an individual with a disability or a class of such individuals on the basis of disability, it must be job-related and consistent with business necessity.

- This requirement applies to all kinds of tests, including, but not limited to: aptitude tests, tests of knowledge and skill, intelligence tests, agility tests, and job demonstrations.

A test will most likely be an accurate predictor of the job performance of a person with a disability when it most directly or closely measures actual skills and ability needed to do a job.

For example: a typing test, a sales demonstration test, or other job performance test would indicate what the individual actually could do in performing a job, whereas a test that measured general qualities believed to be desirable in a job may screen out people on the basis of disability who could do the job.

For example, a standardized test used for a job as a heavy equipment operator might screen out a person with dyslexia or other learning disability who was able to perform all functions of the job itself.

An employer is only required to show that a test is job-related and consistent with business necessity if it screens out a person with a disability because of the disability. If a person was screened out for a reason unrelated to disability, ADA requirements do not apply.

For example: If a person with paraplegia who uses a wheelchair is screened out because s/he does not have sufficient speed or accuracy on a typing test, this person probably was not screened out because of his or her disability. The employer has no obligation to consider this person for a job which requires fast, accurate typing.

Even if a test is job-related and justified by business necessity, the employer has an obligation to provide a specific reasonable accommodation, if needed. For example, upon request, test sites must be accessible to people who have mobility disabilities. The ADA also has a very specific requirement for accommodation in testing, described below.

(2) Accommodation in testing

The ADA requires that tests be given to people who have impaired sensory, speaking or manual skills in a format and manner that does not require use of the impaired skill, unless the test is designed to measure that skill. (Sensory skills include the abilities to hear, see and to process information.)

The purpose of this requirement is to assure that tests accurately reflect a person's job skills, aptitudes, or whatever else the test is supposed to measure, rather than the person's impaired skills. This requirement applies the reasonable accommodation obligation to testing. It protects people with disabilities from being excluded from jobs that they actually can do because a disability prevents them from taking a test or negatively influences a test result. However, an employer does not have to provide an alternative test format for a person with an impaired skill if the purpose of the test is to measure that skill.

For example:

- A person with dyslexia should be given an opportunity to take a written test orally, if the dyslexia seriously impairs the individual's ability to read. But if ability to read is a job-related function that the test is designed to measure, the employer could require that a person with dyslexia take the written test. However, even in this situation, reasonable accommodation should be considered. The person with dyslexia might be accommodated with a reader, unless the ability to read unaided is an essential job function, unless such an accommodation would not be possible on the job for which s/he is being tested, or would be an undue hardship. For example, the ability to read without help would be essential for a proofreader's job. Or, a dyslexic firefighter applicant might be disqualified if he could not quickly read necessary instructions for dealing with specific toxic substances at the site of a fire when no reader would be available.
- Providing extra time to take a test may be a reasonable accommodation for people with certain disabilities, such as visual impairments, learning disabilities, or mental retardation. On the other hand, an employer could require that an applicant complete a test within an established time frame if speed is one of the skills that the test is designed to measure. However, the results of a timed test should not be used to exclude a person with a disability, unless the

test measures a particular speed necessary to perform an essential function of the job, and there is no reasonable accommodation that would enable this person to perform that function within prescribed time frames, or the accommodation would cause an undue hardship.

Generally, an employer is only required to provide such an accommodation if it knows, before administering a test, that an accommodation will be needed. Usually, it is the responsibility of the individual with a disability to request any required accommodation for a test. It has been suggested that the employer inform applicants, in advance, of any tests that will be administered as part of the application process so that they may request an accommodation, if needed. (See 5.5(d) above.) The employer may require that an individual with a disability request an accommodation within a specific time period before administration of the test. The employer also may require that documentation of the need for accommodation accompany such a request.

Occasionally, however, an individual with a disability may not realize in advance that s/he will need an accommodation to take a particular test.

For example: A person with a visual impairment who knows that there will be a written test may not request an accommodation because she has her own specially designed lens that usually is effective for reading printed material. However, when the test is distributed, she finds that her lens is not sufficient, because of unusually low color contrast between the paper and the ink. Under these circumstances, she might request an accommodation and the employer would be obligated to provide one. The employer might provide the test in a higher contrast format at that time, reschedule the test, or make any other effective accommodation that would not impose an undue hardship.

An employer is not required to offer an applicant the specific accommodation requested. This request should be given primary consideration, but the employer is only obligated to provide an effective accommodation. (See Chapter III.) The employer is only required to provide, upon request, an "accessible" test format for individuals whose disabilities impair sensory, manual, or speaking skills needed to take the test, unless the test is designed to measure these skills.

Some Examples of Alternative Test Formats and Accommodations:

- Substituting a written test for an oral test (or written instructions for oral instructions) for people with impaired speaking or hearing skills;
- Administering a test in large print, in Braille, by a reader, or on a computer for people with visual or other reading disabilities;
- Allowing people with visual or learning disabilities or who have limited use of their hands to record test answers by tape recorder, dictation or computer;
- Providing extra time to complete a test for people with certain learning disabilities or impaired writing skills;
- Simplifying test language for people who have limited language skills because of a disability;
- Scheduling rest breaks for people with mental and other disabilities that require such relief;
- Assuring that a test site is accessible to a person with a mobility disability;
- Allowing a person with a mental disability who cannot perform well if there are distractions to take a test in a separate room, if a group test setting is not relevant to the job itself;
- Where it is not possible to test an individual with a disability in an alternative format, an employer may be required, as a reasonable accommodation, to evaluate the skill or ability being tested through some other means, such as an interview, education, work experience, licenses or certification, or a job demonstration for a trial period.

There are a number of technical assistance resources for effective alternative methods of testing people with different disabilities. (See "Alternative Testing Formats" in Resource Directory Index).

I-VI. Medical Examination and Inquiries

I-6.1 Overview of Legal Obligations.

Pre-Employment, Pre-Offer

- An employer may not require a job applicant to take a medical examination, to respond to medical inquiries or to provide information about workers' compensation claims before the employer makes a job offer.

Pre-Employment, Post-Offer

- An employer may condition a job offer on the satisfactory result of a post-offer medical examination or medical inquiry if this is required of all entering employees in the same job category.

A post-offer examination or inquiry does not have to be "job-related" and "consistent with business necessity." Questions also may be asked about previous injuries and workers' compensation claims.

- If an individual is not hired because a post-offer medical examination or inquiry reveals a disability, the reason(s) for not hiring must be job-related and necessary for the business. The employer also must show that no reasonable accommodation was available that would enable this individual to perform the essential job functions, or that accommodation would impose an undue hardship.
- A post-offer medical examination may disqualify an individual who would pose a "direct threat" to health or safety. Such a disqualification is job- related and consistent with business necessity.
- A post-offer medical examination may not disqualify an individual with a disability who is currently able to perform essential job functions because of speculation that the disability may cause a risk of future injury.

Employee Medical Examinations and Inquiries

- After a person starts work, a medical examination or inquiry of an employee must be job related and necessary for the business.
- Employers may conduct employee medical examinations where there is evidence of a job performance or safety problem, examinations required by other Federal laws, examinations to determine current "fitness" to perform a particular job and voluntary examinations that are part of employee health programs.

Confidentiality

- Information from all medical examinations and inquiries must be kept apart from general personnel files as a separate, confidential medical record, available only under limited conditions specified in the ADA. (See 6.5 below.)

Drug Testing

- Tests for illegal use of drugs are not medical examinations under the ADA and are not subject to the restrictions on such examinations. (See Chapter VIII.)

I-6.2 Basic Requirements.

The ADA does not prevent employers from obtaining medical and related information necessary to evaluate the ability of applicants and employees to perform essential job functions, or to promote health and safety on the job. However, to protect individuals with disabilities from actions based on such information that are not job-related and consistent with business necessity, including protection of health and safety, the ADA imposes specific and differing obligations on the employer at three stages of the employment process:

1. Before making a job offer, an employer may not make any medical inquiry or conduct any medical examination.
2. After making a conditional job offer, before a person starts work, an employer may make unrestricted medical inquiries, but may not refuse to hire an individual with a disability based on results of such inquiries, unless the reason for rejection is job-related and justified by business necessity.
3. After employment, any medical examination or inquiry required of an employee must be job-related and justified by business necessity. Exceptions are voluntary examinations conducted as part of employee health programs and examinations required by other federal laws.

Under the ADA, "medical" documentation concerning the qualifications of an individual with a disability, or whether this individual constitutes a "direct threat" to health and safety, does not mean only information from medical doctors. It may be necessary to obtain information from other sources, such as rehabilitation experts, occupational or physical therapists, psychologists, and others knowledgeable about the individual and the disability concerned. It also may be more relevant to look at the individual's previous work history in making such determinations than to rely on an examination or tests by a physician.

The basic requirements regarding actions based on medical information and inquiries have been set out in Chapter IV. As emphasized there, such actions taken because of a disability must be job-related and consistent with business necessity. When an individual is rejected as a "direct threat" to health and safety:

- the employer must be prepared to show a significant current risk of substantial harm (not a speculative or remote risk);
- the specific risk must be identified;
- the risk must be documented by objective medical or other factual evidence regarding the particular individual;
- even if a genuine significant risk of substantial

harm exists, the employer must consider whether it can be eliminated or reduced below the level of a "direct threat" by reasonable accommodation.

This chapter discusses in more detail the content and manner of medical examinations and inquiries that may be made, and the documentation that may be required (1) before employment and (2) after employment.

I-6.3 Examinations and Inquiries Before Employment.

No Pre-Offer Medical Examination or Inquiry

The ADA prohibits medical inquiries or medical examinations before making a conditional job offer to an applicant. This prohibition is necessary because the results of such inquiries and examinations frequently are used to exclude people with disabilities from jobs they are able to perform.

Some employers have medical policies or rely on doctors' medical assessments that overestimate the impact of a particular condition on a particular individual, and/or underestimate the ability of an individual to cope with his or her condition. Medical policies that focus on disability, rather than the ability of a particular person, frequently will be discriminatory under the ADA.

For example: A policy that prohibits employment of any individual who has epilepsy, diabetes or a heart condition from a certain type of job, and which does not consider the ability of a particular individual, in most cases would violate the ADA. (See Chapter IV.)

Many employers currently use a pre-employment medical questionnaire, a medical history, or a pre-employment medical examination as one step in a several-step selection process. Where this is so, an individual who has a "hidden" disability such as diabetes, epilepsy, heart disease, cancer, or mental illness, and who is rejected for a job, frequently does not know whether the reason for rejection was information revealed by the medical exam or inquiry (which may not have any relation to this person's ability to do the job), or whether the rejection was based on some other aspect of the selection process.

A history of such rejections has discouraged many people with disabilities from applying for jobs, because of fear that they will automatically be rejected when their disability is revealed by a medical examination. The ADA is designed to remove this barrier to employment.

I-6.4 Post-Offer Examinations and Inquiries Permitted.

The ADA recognizes that employers may need to conduct medical examinations to determine if an applicant can perform certain jobs effectively and safely. The ADA requires only that such examinations be conducted as a separate, second step of the selection process, after an individual has met all other job prerequisites. The employer may make a job offer to such an individual, conditioned on the satisfactory outcome of a medical examination or inquiry, providing that the employer requires such examination or inquiry for all entering employees in a particular job category, not merely individuals with known disabilities, or those whom the employer believes may have a disability.

A post-offer medical examination does not have to be given to all entering employees in all jobs, only to those in the same job category.

For example: An examination might be given to all entering employees in physical labor jobs, but not to employees entering clerical jobs.

The ADA does not require an employer to justify its requirement of a post-offer medical examination. An employer may wish to conduct a post-offer medical exam or make post-offer medical inquiries for purposes such as:

To determine if an individual currently has the physical or mental qualifications necessary to perform certain jobs:

For example: If a job requires continuous heavy physical exertion, a medical examination may be useful to determine whether an applicant's physical condition will permit him/her to perform the job.

To determine that a person can perform a job without posing a "direct threat" to the health or safety of self or others.

For example:

- A medical examination and evaluation might be required to ensure that prospective construction crane operators do not have disabilities such as uncontrolled seizures that would pose a significant risk to other workers.
- Workers in certain health care jobs may need to

be examined to assure that they do not have a current contagious disease or infection that would pose a significant risk of transmission to others, and that could not be accommodated (for example, by giving the individual a delayed starting date until the period of contagion is over).

Compliance with medical requirements of other Federal laws.

Employers may comply with medical and safety requirements established under other Federal laws without violating the ADA.

For example: Federal Highway Administration regulations require medical examinations and evaluations of interstate truck drivers, and the Federal Aviation Administration requires examinations for pilots and air controllers.

However, an employer still has an obligation to consider whether there is a reasonable accommodation, consistent with the requirements of other Federal laws, that would not exclude individuals who can perform jobs safely.

Employers also may conduct post-offer medical examinations that are required by state laws, but, as explained in Chapter IV, may not take actions based on such examinations if the state law is inconsistent with ADA requirements. (See Health and Safety Requirements of Other Federal or State Laws, 4.6.)

Information That May Be Requested in Post-Offer Examinations or Inquiries

After making a conditional job offer, an employer may make inquiries or conduct examinations to get any information that it believes to be relevant to a person's ability to perform a job. For example, the employer may require a full physical examination. An employer may ask questions that are prohibited as pre-employment inquiries about previous illnesses, diseases or medications. (See Chapter V.)

If a post-offer medical examination is given, it must be administered to all persons entering a job category. If a response to an initial medical inquiry (such as a medical history questionnaire) reveals that an applicant has had a previous injury, illness, or medical condition, the employer cannot require the applicant to undergo a medical examination unless all applicants in the job category are required to have such examination. However, the ADA does not require that the scope of medical examinations must be identical. An employer may give follow-up tests or examinations where an examination indicates that further information is needed.

For example: All potential employees in a job category must be given a blood test, but if a person's initial test indicates a problem that may affect job performance, further tests may be given to that person only, in order to get necessary information.

A post-offer medical examination or inquiry, made before an individual starts work, need not focus on ability to perform job functions. Such inquiries and examinations themselves, unlike examinations/inquiries of employees, do not have to be "job related" and "consistent with business necessity." However, if a conditional job offer is withdrawn because of the results of such examination or inquiry, an employer must be able to show that:

- the reasons for the exclusion are job-related and consistent with business necessity, or the person is being excluded to avoid a "direct threat" to health or safety; and that
- no reasonable accommodation was available that would enable this person to perform the essential job functions without a significant risk to health or safety, or that such an accommodation would cause undue hardship.

Some examples of post-offer decisions that might be job-related and justified by business necessity, and/or where no reasonable accommodation was possible:

- a medical history reveals that the individual has suffered serious multiple re-injuries to his back doing similar work, which have progressively worsened the back condition. Employing this person in this job would incur significant risk that he would further re-injure himself.
- a workers' compensation history indicates multiple claims in recent years which have been denied. An employer might have a legitimate business reason to believe that the person has submitted fraudulent claims. Withdrawing a job offer for this reason would not violate the ADA, because the decision is not based on disability.
- a medical examination reveals an impairment that would require the individual's frequent lengthy absence from work for medical treatment, and the job requires daily availability for the next 3 months. In this situation, the individual is not available to perform the essential functions of the job, and no accommodation is possible.

Examples of discriminatory use of examination results that are not job related and justified by business necessity:

- A landscape firm sent an applicant for a laborer's job (who had been doing this kind of work for 20 years) for a physical exam. An x-ray showed that he had a curvature of the spine. The doctor advised the firm not to hire him because there was a risk that he might injure his back at some time in the future. The doctor provided no specific medical documentation that this would happen or was likely to happen. The company provided no description of the job to the doctor. The job actually involved riding a mechanical mower. This unlawful exclusion was based on speculation about future risk of injury, and was not job-related.
- An individual is rejected from a job because he cannot lift more than 50 pounds. The job requires lifting such a weight only occasionally. The employer has not considered possible accommodations, such as sharing the occasional heavy weight lifting with another employee or providing a device to assist lifting.

Risk Cannot be Speculative or Remote

The results of a medical examination may not disqualify persons currently able to perform essential job functions because of unsubstantiated speculation about future risk.

The results of a medical inquiry or examination may not be used to disqualify persons who are currently able to perform the essential functions of a job, either with or without an accommodation, because of fear or speculation that a disability may indicate a greater risk of future injury, or absenteeism, or may cause future workers' compensation or insurance costs. An employer may use such information to exclude an individual with a disability where there is specific medical documentation, reflecting current medical knowledge, that this individual would pose a significant, current risk of substantial harm to health or safety. (See Standards for Health and Safety: "Direct Threat" Chapter IV.)

For example:

- An individual who has an abnormal back X-ray may not be disqualified from a job that requires heavy lifting because of fear that she will be more likely to injure her back or cause higher workers' compensation or health insurance costs. However, where there is documentation that this individual has injured and re-injured her back in similar jobs, and the back condition has been aggravated further by injury, and if there is no reasonable accommodation that would eliminate the risk of reinjury or reduce it to an acceptable level, an employer would be justified in rejecting her for this position.
- If a medical examination reveals that an individual has epilepsy and is seizure-free or has adequate warning of a seizure, it would be unlawful to disqualify this person from a job operating a machine because of fear or speculation that he might pose a risk to himself or others. But if the examination and other medical inquiries reveal that an individual with epilepsy has seizures resulting in loss of consciousness, there could be evidence of significant risk in employing this person as a machine operator. However, even where the person might endanger himself by operating a machine, an accommodation, such as placing a shield over the machine to protect him, should be considered.

The Doctor's Role

A doctor who conducts medical examinations for an employer should not be responsible for making employment decisions or deciding whether or not it is possible to make a reasonable accommodation for a person with a disability. That responsibility lies with the employer.

The doctor's role should be limited to advising the employer about an individual's functional abilities and limitations in relation to job functions, and about whether the individual meets the employer's health and safety requirements.

Accordingly, employers should provide doctors who conduct such examinations with specific information about the job, including the type of information indicated in the discussions of "job descriptions" and "job analysis" in Chapter II. (See 2.3.)

Often, particularly when an employer uses an outside doctor who is not familiar with actual demands of the job, a doctor may make incorrect assumptions about the nature of the job functions and specific tasks, or about the ability of an individual with a disability to perform these tasks with a reasonable accommodation. It may be useful for the doctor to visit the job site to see how the job is done.

The employer should inform the doctor that any recommendations or conclusions related to hiring or placement of an individual should focus on only two concerns:

(1) Whether this person currently is able to perform this specific job, with or without an accommodation.

This evaluation should look at the individual's specific abilities and limitations in regard to specific job demands.

For example: The evaluation may indicate that a person can lift up to 30 pounds and can reach only 2 feet above the shoulder; the job as usually performed (without accommodation) requires lifting 50 pound crates to shelves that are 6 feet high.

(2) Whether this person can perform this job without posing a "direct threat" to the health or safety of the person or others.

The doctor should be informed that the employer must be able to show that an exclusion of an individual with a disability because of a risk to health or safety meets the "direct threat" standard of the ADA, based on "the most current medical knowledge and/or the best available objective evidence about this individual." (See Chapter IV., Standards Necessary for Health and Safety, and 6.2 above.)

For example: If a post-offer medical questionnaire indicates that a person has a history of repetitive motion injuries but has had successful surgery with no further problems indicated, and a doctor recommends that the employer reject this candidate because this medical history indicates that she would pose a higher risk of future injury, the employer would violate the ADA if it acted on the doctor's recommendation based only on the history of injuries. In this case, the doctor would not have considered this person's actual current condition as a result of surgery.

A doctor's evaluation of any future risk must be supported by valid medical analyses indicating a high probability of substantial harm if this individual performed the particular functions of the particular job in question. Conclusions of general medical studies about work restrictions for people with certain disabilities will not be sufficient evidence, because they do not relate to a particular individual and do not consider reasonable accommodation.

The employer should not rely only on a doctor's opinion, but on the best available objective evidence. This may include the experience of the individual with a disability in previous similar jobs, occupations, or non-work activities, the opinions of other doctors with expertise on the particular disability, and the advice of rehabilitation counselors, occupational or physical therapists, and others with direct knowledge of the disability and/or the individual concerned. Organizations such as Independent Living Centers, public and private rehabilitation agencies, and organizations serving people with specific disabilities such as the Epilepsy Foundation, United Cerebral Palsy Associations, National Head Injury Foundation, and many others can provide such assistance. (See Resource Directory.)

Where the doctor's report indicates that an individual has a disability that may prevent performance of essential job functions, or that may pose a "direct threat" to health or safety, the employer also may seek his/her advice on possible accommodations that would overcome these disqualifications.

I-6.5 Confidentiality and Limitations on Use of Medical Information.

Although the ADA does not limit the nature or extent of post-offer medical examinations and inquiries, it imposes very strict limitations on the use of information obtained from such examinations and inquiries. These limitations also apply to information obtained from examinations or inquiries of employees.

- All information obtained from post-offer medical examinations and inquiries must be collected and maintained on separate forms, in separate medical files and must be treated as a confidential medical record. Therefore, an employer should not place any medical-related material in an employee's personnel file. The employer should take steps to guarantee the security of the employee's medical information, including:
    - keeping the information in a medical file in a separate, locked cabinet, apart from the location of personnel files; and
    - designating a specific person or persons to have access to the medical file.
- All medical-related information must be kept confidential, with the following exceptions:
    - Supervisors and managers may be informed about necessary restrictions on the work or duties of an employee and necessary accommodations.
    - First aid and safety personnel may be informed, when appropriate, if the disability might require emergency treatment or if any specific procedures are needed in the case of fire or other evacuations.
    - Government officials investigating compli-

ance with the ADA and other Federal and state laws prohibiting discrimination on the basis of disability or handicap should be provided relevant information on request. (Other Federal laws and regulations also may require disclosure of relevant medical information.)

- Relevant information may be provided to state workers' compensation offices or "second injury" funds, in accordance with state workers' compensation laws. (See Chapter IX., Workers' Compensation and Work-Related Injury.)
- Relevant information may be provided to insurance companies where the company requires a medical examination to provide health or life insurance for employees. (See Health Insurance and Other Benefit Plans, Chapter VII.)

I-6.6 Employee Medical Examinations and Inquiries.

The ADA's requirements concerning medical examinations and inquiries of employees are more stringent than those affecting applicants who are being evaluated for employment after a conditional job offer. In order for a medical examination or inquiry to be made of an employee, it must be job related and consistent with business necessity. The need for the examination may be triggered by some evidence of problems related to job performance or safety, or an examination may be necessary to determine whether individuals in physically demanding jobs continue to be fit for duty. In either case, the scope of the examination also must be job-related.

For example:

- An attorney could not be required to submit to a medical examination or inquiry just because her leg had been amputated. The essential functions of an attorney's job do not require use of both legs; therefore such an inquiry would not be job related.
- An employer may require a warehouse laborer, whose back impairment affects the ability to lift, to be examined by an orthopedist, but may not require this employee to submit to an HIV test where the test is not related to either the essential functions of his job or to his impairment.

Medical examinations or inquiries may be job related and necessary under several circumstances:

- **When an employee is having difficulty performing his or her job effectively.**

In such cases, a medical examination may be necessary to determine if s/he can perform essential job functions with or without an accommodation.

For example: If an employee falls asleep on the job, has excessive absenteeism, or exhibits other performance problems, an examination may be needed to determine if the problem is caused by an underlying medical condition, and whether medical treatment is needed. If the examination reveals an impairment that is a disability under the ADA, the employer must consider possible reasonable accommodations. If the impairment is not a disability, the employer is not required to make an accommodation.

For example: An employee may complain of headaches caused by noise at the worksite. A medical examination may indicate that there is no medically discernible mental or physiological disorder causing the headaches. This employee would not be "an individual with a disability" under the ADA, and the employer would have no obligation to provide an accommodation. The employer may voluntarily take steps to improve the noise situation, particularly if other employees also suffer from noise, but would have no obligation to do so under the ADA.

- **When An Employee Becomes Disabled**

An employee who is injured on or off the job, who becomes ill, or suffers any other condition that meets the ADA definition of "disability," is protected by the Act if s/he can perform the essential functions of the job with or without reasonable accommodation.

Employers are accustomed to dealing with injured workers through the workers' compensation process and disability management programs, but they have different, although not necessarily conflicting obligations under the ADA. The relationship between ADA, workers' compensation requirements and medical examinations and inquiries is discussed in Chapter IX.

Under the ADA, medical information or medical examinations may be required when an employee suffers an injury on the job. Such an examination or inquiry also may be required when an employee wishes to return to work after an injury or illness, if it is job-related and consistent with business necessity:

- to determine if the individual meets the

ADA definition of "individual with a disability," if an accommodation has been requested.

- to determine if the person can perform essential functions of the job currently held, (or held before the injury or illness), with or without reasonable accommodation, and without posing a "direct threat" to health or safety that cannot be reduced or eliminated by reasonable accommodation.
- to identify an effective accommodation that would enable the person to perform essential job functions in the current (previous) job, or in a vacant job for which the person is qualified (with or without accommodation). (See Chapter IX.)

- **Examination Necessary for Reasonable Accommodation**

A medical examination may be required if an employee requests an accommodation on the basis of disability An accommodation may be needed in an employee's existing job, or if the employee is being transferred or promoted to a different job. Medical information may be needed to determine if the employee has a disability covered by the ADA and is entitled to an accommodation, and if so, to help identify an effective accommodation.

Medical inquiries related to an employee's disability and functional limitations may include consultations with knowledgeable professional sources, such as occupational and physical therapists, rehabilitation specialists, and organizations with expertise in adaptations for specific disabilities.

- **Medical examinations, screening and monitoring required by other laws.**

Employers may conduct periodic examinations and other medical screening and monitoring required by federal, state or local laws. As indicated in Chapter IV, the ADA recognizes that an action taken to comply with another Federal law is job-related and consistent with business necessity; however, requirements of state and local laws do not necessarily meet this standard unless they are consistent with the ADA.

For example: Employers may conduct medical examinations and medical monitoring required by:

- The U.S. Department of Transportation for interstate bus and truck drivers, railroad engineers, airline pilots and air controllers;
- The Occupational Safety and Health Act:
- The Federal Mine Health and Safety Act;
- Other statutes that require employees exposed to toxic or hazardous substances to be medically monitored at specific intervals.

However, if a state or local law required that employees in a particular job be periodically tested for AIDS or the HIV virus, the ADA would prohibit such an examination unless an employer can show that it is job-related and consistent with business necessity, or required to avoid a direct threat to health or safety. (See Chapter IV.)

- **Voluntary "Wellness" and Health Screening Programs**

An employer may conduct voluntary medical examinations and inquiries as part of an employee health program (such as medical screening for high blood pressure, weight control, and cancer detection), providing that:

- participation in the program is voluntary;
- information obtained is maintained according to the confidentiality requirements of the ADA (see 6.5); and
- this information is not used to discriminate against an employee.

Information from Medical Inquiries May Not be Used to Discriminate

An employer may not use information obtained from an employee medical examination or inquiry to discriminate against the employee in any employment practice. (See Chapter VII.)

Confidentiality

All information obtained from employee medical examinations and inquiries must be maintained and used in accordance with ADA confidentiality requirements. (See 6.5 above.)

I-VII. Nondiscrimination in Other Employment Practices

I-7.1 Introduction.

The nondiscrimination requirements of the ADA apply to all employment practices and activities. The preceding chapters have explained these requirements as they apply to job qualification and selection standards, the hiring process, and medical examinations and inquiries. This chapter discusses the application of nondiscrimination requirements to other employment practices and activities.

In most cases, an employer need only apply the basic nondiscrimination principles already emphasized; however, there are also some special requirements applicable to certain employment activities This chapter discusses:

- the ADA's prohibition of discrimination on the basis of a relationship or association with an individual with a disability;
- nondiscrimination requirements affecting:
  - promotion, assignment, training, evaluation, discipline, advancement opportunity and discharge;
  - compensation, insurance, leave, and other benefits and privileges of employment; and
  - contractual relationships.

I-7.2 Overview of Legal Obligations.

- An employer may not discriminate against a qualified individual with a disability because of the disability, in any employment practice, or any term, condition or benefit of employment.
- An employer may not deny an employment opportunity because an individual, with or without a disability, has a relationship or association with an individual who has a disability.
- An employer may not participate in a contractual or other arrangement that subjects the employer's qualified applicant or employee with a disability to discrimination.
- An employer may not discriminate or retaliate against any individual, whether or not the individual is disabled, because the individual has opposed a discriminatory practice, filed a discrimination charge, or participated in any way in enforcing the ADA.

I-7.3 Nondiscrimination in all Employment Practices.

The ADA prohibits discrimination against a qualified individual with a disability on the basis of disability in the following employment practices:

- Recruitment, advertising, and job application procedures;
- Hiring, upgrading, promotion, award of tenure, demotion, transfer, layoff, termination, right of return from layoff, and rehiring;
- Rates of pay or any other form of compensation, and changes in compensation;
- Job assignments, job classifications, organizational structures, position descriptions, lines of progression, and seniority lists;
- Leaves of absence, sick leave, or any other leave;
- Fringe benefits available by virtue of employment, whether or not administered by the covered entity;
- Selection and financial support for training, including: apprenticeships, professional meetings, conferences, and other related activities, and selection for leaves of absence to pursue training;
- Activities sponsored by a covered entity including social and recreational programs; and
- Any other term, condition, or privilege of employment.

Nondiscrimination, as applied to all employment practices, means that:

- an individual with a disability should have equal access to any employment opportunity available to a similarly situated individual who is not disabled;
- employment decisions concerning an employee or applicant should be based on objective factual evidence about the particular individual, not on assumptions or stereotypes about the individual's disability;
- the qualifications of an individual with a disability may be evaluated on ability to perform all job-related functions, with or without reasonable accommodation. However, an individual may not be excluded from a job because a disability prevents performance of marginal job functions;
- an employer must provide a reasonable accommodation that will enable an individual with a disability to have an equal opportunity in every aspect of employment, unless a particular accommodation would impose an undue hardship;
- an employer may not use an employment practice or policy that screens out or tends to screen out an individual with a disability or a class of individuals with disabilities, unless the practice or policy is job related and consistent with business necessity and the individual cannot be accommodated without undue hardship;
- an employer may not limit, segregate, or classify an individual with a disability in any way that negatively affects the individual in terms of job opportunity and advancement;

- an individual with a disability should not because of a disability be treated differently than a similarly situated individual in any aspect of employment, except when a reasonable accommodation is needed to provide an equal employment opportunity, or when another Federal law or regulation requires different treatment.

These requirements are discussed in this chapter as they apply to various employment practices. The prohibition against retaliation is discussed in Chapter X.

I-7.4 Nondiscrimination and Relationship or Association with an Individual with a Disability.

The ADA specifically provides that an employer or other covered entity may not deny an employment opportunity or benefit to an individual, whether or not that individual is disabled, because that individual has a known relationship or association with an individual who has a disability. Nor may an employer discriminate in any other way against an individual, whether or not disabled, because that individual has such a relationship or association.

The term "relationship or association" refers to family relationships and any other social or business relationship or association. Therefore, this provision of the law prohibits employers from making employment decisions based on concerns about the disability of a family member of an applicant or employee, or anyone else with whom this person has a relationship or association.

For example: An employer may not:

- refuse to hire or fire an individual because the individual has a spouse, child, or other dependent who has a disability. The employer may not assume that the individual will be unreliable, have to use leave time, or be away from work in order to care for the family member with a disability;
- refuse to hire or fire an individual because s/he has a spouse, child or other dependent who has a disability that is either not covered by the employer's current health insurance plan or that may cause future increased health care costs;
- refuse to insure, or subject an individual to different terms or conditions of insurance, solely because the individual has a spouse, child, or other dependent who has a disability;
- refuse to hire or fire an individual because the individual has a relationship or association with a person or persons who have disabilities.

For example: an employer cannot fire an employee because s/he does volunteer work with people who have AIDS.

This provision of the law prohibits discrimination in employment decisions concerning an individual, whether the individual is or is not disabled, because of a known relationship or association with an individual with a disability. However, an employer is not obligated to provide a reasonable accommodation to a nondisabled individual, because this person has a relationship or association with a disabled individual. The obligation to make a reasonable accommodation applies only to qualified individuals with disabilities.

For example: The ADA does not require that an employer provide an employee who is not disabled with a modified work schedule as an accommodation, to enable the employee to care for a spouse or child with a disability.

I-7.5 Nondiscrimination and Opportunity for Advancement.

The nondiscrimination requirements that apply to initial selection apply to all aspects of employment, including opportunities for advancement. For example, an employer may not discriminate in promotion, job classification, evaluation, disciplinary action, opportunities for training, or participation in meetings and conferences. In particular, an employer:

- should not assume that an individual is not interested in, or not qualified for, advancement because of disability;
- should not deny a promotion because of the need to make an accommodation, unless the accommodation would cause an undue hardship;
- should not place individuals with disabilities in separate lines of progression or in segregated units or locations that limit opportunity for advancement;
- should assure that supervisors and managers who make decisions regarding promotion and advancement are aware of ADA nondiscrimination requirements.

I-7.6 Training.

Employees with disabilities must be provided equal opportunities to participate in training to improve job performance and provide opportunity for advancement. Training opportunities cannot be denied because of the need to make a reasonable accommodation, unless the accommodation would be an undue hardship. Accommodations that may be necessary, depending on the needs of particular individuals, may include:

- accessible locations and facilities for people with mobility disabilities;
- interpreters and note-takers for employees who are deaf;
- materials in accessible formats and/or readers for people who are visually impaired, for people with learning disabilities, and for people with mental retardation;
- if audiovisual materials are used, captions for people who are deaf, and voice-overs for people who are visually impaired;
- good lighting on an interpreter, and good general illumination for people with visual impairments and other disabilities;
- clarification of concepts presented in training for people who have reading or other disabilities;
- individualized instruction for people with mental retardation and certain other disabilities.

If an employer contracts for training with a training company, or contracts for training facilities such as hotels or conference centers, the employer is responsible for assuring accessibility and other needed accommodations.

It is advisable that any contract with a company or facility used for training include a provision requiring the other party to provide needed accommodations. However, if the contractor does not do so, the employer remains responsible for providing the accommodation, unless it would cause an undue hardship.

For example: Suppose a company with which an employer has contracted proposes to conduct training at an inaccessible location. The employer is responsible for providing an accommodation that would enable an employee who uses a wheelchair to obtain this training. The employer might do this by: requiring the training company to relocate the program to an accessible site; requiring the company to make the site (including all facilities used by trainees) accessible; making the site accessible or providing resources that enable the training company to do so; contracting with another training company that uses accessible sites; or providing any other accommodation (such as temporary ramps) that would not impose an undue hardship. If it is impossible to make an accommodation because the need is only discovered when an employee arrives at the training site, the employer may have to provide accessible training at a later date.

Or, for example: An employer contracts with a hotel to hold a conference for its employees. The employer must assure physical and communications accessibility for employees with disabilities, including accessibility of guest rooms and all meeting and other rooms used by attendees. The employer may assure accessibility by inspecting the site, or may ask a local disability group with accessibility expertise (such as an Independent Living Center) to do so. The employer remains responsible for assuring accessibility. However, if the hotel breaches a contract provision requiring accessibility, the hotel may be liable to the employer under regular (non-ADA) breach of contract law. The hotel also may be liable under Title III of the ADA, which requires accessibility in public accommodations.

I-7.7 Evaluations, Discipline and Discharge.

- An employer can hold employees with disabilities to the same standards of production/performance as other similarly situated employees without disabilities for performing essential job functions (with or without reasonable accommodation).
- An employer also can hold employees with disabilities to the same standards of production/performance as other employees regarding marginal job functions, unless the disability affects the ability to perform these marginal functions. If the ability to perform marginal functions is affected by the disability, the employer must provide some type of reasonable accommodation such as job restructuring (unless to do so would be an undue hardship).
- A disabled employee who needs an accommodation (that is not an undue hardship for an employer) in order to perform a job function should not be evaluated on his/her ability to perform the function without the accommodation, and should not be downgraded because such an accommodation is needed to perform the function.
- An employer should not give employees with disabilities "special treatment." They should not be evaluated on a lower standard or disci-

plined less severely than any other employee. This is not equal employment opportunity.

- An employer must provide an employee with a disability with reasonable accommodation necessary to enable the employee to participate in the evaluation process (for example, counseling or an interpreter).
- If an employee with a disability is not performing well, an employer may require medical and other professional inquiries that are job-related and consistent with business necessity to discover whether the disability is causing the poor performance, and whether any reasonable accommodation or additional accommodation is needed. (See Chapter VI.)
- An employer may take the same disciplinary action against employees with disabilities as it takes against other similarly situated employees, if the illegal use of drugs or alcohol use affects job performance and/or attendance. (See Chapter VIII.)
- An employer may not discipline or terminate an employee with a disability if the employer has refused to provide a requested reasonable accommodation that did not constitute an undue hardship, and the reason for unsatisfactory performance was the lack of accommodation.

I-7.8 Compensation.

- An employer cannot reduce pay to an employee with a disability because of the elimination of a marginal job function or because it has provided a reasonable accommodation, such as specialized or modified equipment. The employer can give the employee with a disability other marginal functions that s/he can perform.
- An employee who is reassigned to a lower paying job or provided a part-time job as an accommodation may be paid the lower amount that would apply to such positions, consistent with the employer's regular compensation practices.

I-7.9 Health Insurance and Other Employee Benefit Plans.

As discussed above, an employer or other covered entity may not limit, segregate or classify an individual with a disability, on the basis of disability, in a manner that adversely affects the individual's employment. This prohibition applies to the provision and administration of health insurance and other benefit plans, such as life insurance and pension plans.

This means that:

- If an employer provides insurance or other benefit plans to its employees, it must provide the same coverage to its employees with disabilities. Employees with disabilities must be given equal access to whatever insurance or benefit plans the employer provides.
- An employer cannot deny insurance to an individual with a disability or subject an individual with a disability to different terms or conditions of insurance, based on disability alone, if the disability does not pose increased insurance risks. Nor may the employer enter into any contract or agreement with an insurance company or other entity that has such effect.
- An employer cannot fire or refuse to hire an individual with a disability because the employer's current health insurance plan does not cover the individual's disability, or because the individual may increase the employer's future health care costs.
- An employer cannot fire or refuse to hire an individual (whether or not that individual has a disability) because the individual has a family member or dependent with a disability that is not covered by the employer's current health insurance plan, or that may increase the employer's future health care costs.

While establishing these protections for employees with disabilities, the ADA permits employers to provide insurance plans that comply with existing Federal and state insurance requirements, even if provisions of these plans have an adverse affect on people with disabilities, provided that the provisions are not used as a subterfuge to evade the purpose of the ADA.

Specifically, the ADA provides that:

- Where an employer provides health insurance through an insurance carrier that is regulated by state law, it may provide coverage in accordance with accepted principles of risk assessment and/or risk classification, as required or permitted by such law, even if this causes limitations in coverage for individuals with disabilities.
- Similarly, self-insured plans which are not subject to state law may provide coverage in a manner that is consistent with basic accepted principles of insurance risk classification, even if this results in limitations in coverage to individuals with disabilities.

In each case, such activity is permitted only if it is not being used as a subterfuge to evade the intent of the ADA. Whether or not an activity is being used as a subterfuge will be determined regardless of the date that the insurance plan or employee benefit plan was adopted.
This means that:

- An employer may continue to offer health insurance plans that contain pre-existing condition exclusions, even if this adversely affects individuals with disabilities, unless these exclusions are being used as a subterfuge to evade the purpose of the ADA.
- An employer may continue to offer health insurance plans that limit coverage for certain procedures, and/or limit particular treatments to a specified number per year, even if these restrictions adversely affect individuals with disabilities, as long as the restrictions are uniformly applied to all insured individuals, regardless of the disability.

For example, an employer can offer a health insurance plan that limits coverage of blood transfusions to five transfusions per year for all employees, even though an employee with hemophilia may require more than five transfusions per year. However, the employer could not deny this employee coverage for another, otherwise covered procedure, because the plan will not pay for the additional blood transfusions that the procedure would require.

- An employer may continue to offer health insurance plans that limit reimbursements for certain types of drugs or procedures, even if these restrictions adversely affect individuals with disabilities, as long as the restrictions are uniformly applied without regard to disability.

For example, an employer can offer a health insurance plan that does not cover experimental drugs or procedures, as long as this restriction is applied to all insured individuals.

I-7.10 Leave.

- An employer may establish attendance and leave policies that are uniformly applied to all employees, regardless of disability, but may not refuse leave needed by an employee with a disability if other employees get such leave.
- An employer may be required to make adjustments in leave policy as a reasonable accommodation. The employer is not obligated to provide additional paid leave, but accommodations may include leave flexibility and unpaid leave. (See Chapter III.)
- A uniformly applied leave policy does not violate the ADA because it has a more severe effect on an individual because of his/her disability. However, if an individual with a disability requests a modification of such a policy as a reasonable accommodation, an employer may be required to provide it, unless it would impose an undue hardship.

For example: If an employer has a policy providing 2 weeks paid leave for all employees, with no other provision for sick leave and a "no leave" policy for the first 6 months of employment, an employee with a disability who cannot get leave for needed medical treatment could not successfully charge that the employer's policy is discriminatory on its face. However, this individual could request leave without pay or advance leave as a reasonable accommodation. Such leave should be provided, unless the employer can show undue hardship: For example, an employer might be able to show that it is necessary for the operation of the business that this employee be available for the time period when leave is requested.

- An employer is not required to give leave as a reasonable accommodation to an employee who has a relationship with an individual with a disability to enable the employee to care for that individual. (See p. 8 above.)

I-7.11 Contractual or Other Relationships.

An employer may not do anything through a contractual relationship that it cannot do directly. This applies to any contracts, including contracts with:

- training organizations (see above);
- insurers (see above);
- employment agencies and agencies used for background checks (see Chapter V);
- labor unions (see below).

I-7.11(a) Collective Bargaining Agreements.

Labor unions are covered by the ADA and have the same obligation as the employer to comply with its requirements. An employer also is prohibited by the

ADA from taking any action through a labor union contract that it may not take itself.

For example: If a union contract contained physical requirements for a particular job that screened out people with disabilities who were qualified to perform the job, and these requirements are not job-related and consistent with business necessity, they could be challenged as discriminatory by a qualified individual with a disability.

The terms of a collective bargaining agreement may be relevant in determining whether a particular accommodation would cause an employer undue hardship.

Where a collective bargaining agreement identifies functions that must be performed in a particular job, the agreement, like a job description, may be considered as evidence of what the employer and union consider to be a job's essential functions. However, just because a function is listed in a union agreement does not mean that it is an essential function. The agreement, like the job description, will be considered along with other types of evidence. (See Chapter II.)

The Congressional Committee Reports accompanying the ADA advised employers and unions that they could carry out their responsibilities under the Act, and avoid conflicts between the bargaining agreement and the employer's duty to provide reasonable accommodation, by adding a provision to agreements negotiated after the effective date of the ADA, permitting the employer to take all actions necessary to comply with the Act.

I-7.12 Nondiscrimination in Other Benefits and Privileges of Employment.

Nondiscrimination requirements, including the obligation to make reasonable accommodation, apply to all social or recreational activities provided or conducted by an employer, to any transportation provided by an employer for its employees or applicants, and to all other benefits and privileges of employment.
This means that:

- Employees with disabilities must have an equal opportunity to attend and participate in any social functions conducted or sponsored by an employer. Functions such as parties, picnics, shows, and award ceremonies should be held in accessible locations, and interpreters or other accommodation should be provided when necessary.
- Employees with disabilities must have equal access to break rooms, lounges, cafeterias, and any other non-work facilities that are provided by an employer for use by its employees.
- Employees with disabilities must have equal access to an exercise room, gymnasium, or health club provided by an employer for use by its employees. However, an employer would not have to eliminate facilities provided for employees because a disabled employee cannot use certain equipment or amenities because of his/her disability. For example, an employer would not have to remove certain exercise machines simply because an employee who is a paraplegic could not use them.
- Employees with disabilities must be given an equal opportunity to participate in employer-sponsored sports teams, leagues, or recreational activities such as hiking or biking clubs. However, the employer does not have to discontinue such activities because a disabled employee cannot fully participate due to his/her disability. For example, an employer would not have to discontinue the company biking club simply because a blind employee is unable to ride a bicycle.
- Any transportation provided by an employer for use by its employees must be accessible to employees with a disability. This includes transportation between employer facilities, transportation to or from mass transit and transportation provided on a occasional basis to employer-sponsored events.

I-VIII. Drug and Alcohol Abuse

I-8.1 Introduction.

The ADA specifically permits employers to ensure that the workplace is free from the illegal use of drugs and the use of alcohol, and to comply with other Federal laws and regulations regarding alcohol and drug use. At the same time, the ADA provides limited protection from discrimination for recovering drug addicts and for alcoholics.

I-8.2 Overview of Legal Obligations.

- An individual who is currently engaging in the illegal use of drugs is not an "individual with a disability" when the employer acts on the basis of such use.

- An employer may prohibit the illegal use of drugs and the use of alcohol at the workplace.
- It is not a violation of the ADA for an employer to give tests for the illegal use of drugs.
- An employer may discharge or deny employment to persons who currently engage in the illegal use of drugs.
- An employer may not discriminate against a drug addict who is not currently using drugs and who has been rehabilitated, because of a history of drug addiction.
- A person who is an alcoholic is an "individual with a disability" under the ADA.
- An employer may discipline, discharge or deny employment to an alcoholic whose use of alcohol impairs job performance or conduct to the extent that s/he is not a "qualified individual with a disability."
- Employees who use drugs or alcohol may be required to meet the same standards of performance and conduct that are set for other employees.
- Employees may be required to follow the Drug-Free Workplace Act of 1988 and rules set by Federal agencies pertaining to drug and alcohol use in the workplace.

I-8.3 Illegal Use of Drugs.

An employer may discharge or deny employment to current illegal users of drugs, on the basis of such drug use, without fear of being held liable for disability discrimination. Current illegal users of drugs are not "individuals with disabilities" under the ADA.

The illegal use of drugs includes the use, possession, or distribution of drugs which are unlawful under the Controlled Substances Act. It includes the use of illegal drugs and the illegal use of prescription drugs that are "controlled substances".

For example: Amphetamines can be legally prescribed drugs. However, amphetamines, by law, are "controlled substances" because of their abuse and potential for abuse. If a person takes amphetamines without a prescription, that person is using drugs illegally, even though they could be prescribed by a physician.

The illegal use of drugs does not include drugs taken under supervision of a licensed health care professional, including experimental drugs for people with AIDS, epilepsy, or mental illness.

For example: A person who takes morphine for the control of pain caused by cancer is not using a drug illegally if it is taken under the supervision of a licensed physician. Similarly, a participant in a methadone maintenance treatment program cannot be discriminated against by an employer based upon the individual's lawful use of methadone.

An individual who illegally uses drugs but also has a disability, such as epilepsy, is only protected by the ADA from discrimination on the basis of the disability (epilepsy). An employer can discharge or deny employment to such an individual on the basis of his/her illegal use of drugs.

What does "current" drug use mean?

If an individual tests positive on a test for the illegal use of drugs, the individual will be considered a current drug user under the ADA where the test correctly indicates that the individual is engaging in the illegal use of a controlled substance.

"Current" drug use means that the illegal use of drugs occurred recently enough to justify an employer's reasonable belief that involvement with drugs is an on-going problem. It is not limited to the day of use, or recent weeks or days, in terms of an employment action. It is determined on a case-by-case basis.

For example: An applicant or employee who tests positive for an illegal drug cannot immediately enter a drug rehabilitation program and seek to avoid the possibility of discipline or termination by claiming that s/he now is in rehabilitation and is no longer using drugs illegally. A person who tests positive for illegal use of drugs is not entitled to the protection that may be available to former users who have been or are in rehabilitation (see below).

I-8.4 Alcoholism.

While a current illegal user of drugs has no protection under the ADA if the employer acts on the basis of such use, a person who currently uses alcohol is not automatically denied protection simply because of the alcohol use. An alcoholic is a person with a disability under the ADA and may be entitled to consideration of accommodation, if s/he is qualified to perform the essential functions of a job. However, an employer may discipline, discharge or deny employment to an alcoholic whose use of alcohol adversely affects job performance or conduct to the extent that s/he is not "qualified."

For example: If an individual who has alcoholism often is late to work or is unable to perform the responsibilities of his/her job, an employer can take disciplinary action on the basis of the poor job performance and conduct. However, an employer may not discipline an alcoholic employee more severely than it does other employees for the same performance or conduct.

I-8.5 Recovering Drug Addicts.

Persons addicted to drugs, but who are no longer using drugs illegally and are receiving treatment for drug addiction or who have been rehabilitated successfully, are protected by the ADA from discrimination on the basis of past drug addiction.

For example: An addict who is currently in a drug rehabilitation program and has not used drugs illegally for some time is not excluded from the protection of the ADA. This person will be protected by the ADA because s/he has a history of addiction, or if s/he is "regarded as" being addicted. Similarly, an addict who is rehabilitated or who has successfully completed a supervised rehabilitation program and is no longer illegally using drugs is not excluded from the ADA.

However, a person who casually used drugs illegally in the past, but did not become addicted is not an individual with a disability based on the past drug use. In order for a person to be "substantially limited" because of drug use, s/he must be addicted to the drug.

To ensure that drug use is not recurring, an employer may request evidence that an individual is participating in a drug rehabilitation program or may request the results of a drug test (see below).

A "rehabilitation program" may include in-patient, out-patient, or employee assistance programs, or recognized self-help programs such as Narcotics Anonymous.

I-8.6 Persons "Regarded As" Addicts and Illegal Drug Users.

Individuals who are not illegally using drugs, but who are erroneously perceived as being addicts and as currently using drugs illegally, are protected by the ADA.

For example: If an employer perceived someone to be addicted to illegal drugs based upon rumor and the groggy appearance of the individual, but the rumor was false and the appearance was a side-effect of a lawfully prescribed medication, this individual would be "regarded as" an individual with a disability (a drug addict) and would be protected from discrimination based upon that false assumption. If an employer did not regard the individual as an addict, but simply as a social user of illegal drugs, the individual would not be "regarded as" an individual with a disability and would not be protected by the ADA.

As with other disabilities, an individual who claims that s/he was discriminated against because of past or perceived illegal drug addiction, may be asked to prove that s/he has a record of, or is regarded as having, an addiction to drugs.

I-8.7 Efforts to Prohibit Drug and Alcohol Use in the Workplace.

The ADA does not prevent efforts to combat the use of drugs and alcohol in the workplace

The ADA does not interfere with employers' programs to combat the use of drugs and alcohol in the workplace. The Act specifically provides that an employer may:

- prohibit the use of drugs and alcohol in the workplace.
- require that employees not be under the influence of alcohol or drugs in the workplace.

For example: An employer can require that employees not come to work or return from lunch under the influence of alcohol, or drugs used illegally.

- Require that employees who illegally use drugs or alcohol meet the same qualification and performance standards applied to other employees. Unsatisfactory behavior such as absenteeism, tardiness, poor job performance, or accidents caused by alcohol or illegal drug use need not be accepted nor accommodated.

For example: If an employee is often late or does not show up for work because of alcoholism, an employer can take direct action based on the conduct. However, an employer would violate the ADA if it imposed greater sanctions on such an alcoholic employee than it did on other employees for the same misconduct.

While the ADA permits an employer to discipline or discharge an employee for illegal use of drugs or where alcoholism results in poor performance or misconduct, the Act does not require this. Many employers have established employee assistance programs for employees who abuse drugs or alcohol that are helpful to both employee and employer. However, the ADA does not require an employer to provide an opportunity for rehabilitation in place of discipline or discharge to such employees. The ADA may, however, require consideration of reasonable accommodation for a drug addict who is rehabilitated and not using drugs or an alcoholic who remains a "qualified individual with a disability." For example, a modified work schedule, to permit the individual to attend an ongoing self-help program, might be a reasonable accommodation for such an employee.

An employer can fire or refuse to hire a person with a past history of illegal drug use, even if the person no longer uses drugs, in specific occupations, such as law enforcement, when an employer can show that this policy is job-related and consistent with business necessity.

> For example: A law enforcement agency might be able to show that excluding an individual with a history of illegal drug use from a police officer position was necessary, because such illegal conduct would undermine the credibility of the officer as a witness for the prosecution in a criminal case.

However, even in this case, exclusion of a person with a history of illegal drug use might not be justified automatically as a business necessity, if an applicant with such a history could demonstrate an extensive period of successful performance as a police officer since the time of drug use.

An employer also may fire or refuse to hire an individual with a history of alcoholism or illegal drug use if it can demonstrate that the individual poses a "direct threat" to health or safety because of the high probability that s/he would return to the illegal drug use or alcohol abuse. The employer must be able to demonstrate that such use would result in a high probability of substantial harm to the individual or others which could not be reduced or eliminated with a reasonable accommodation. Examples of accommodations in such cases might be to require periodic drug or alcohol tests, to modify job duties or to provide increased supervision.

An employer cannot prove a "high probability" of substantial harm simply by referring to statistics indicating the likelihood that addicts or alcoholics in general have a specific probability of suffering a relapse. A showing of "significant risk of substantial harm" must be based upon an assessment of the particular individual and his/her history of substance abuse and the specific nature of the job to be performed.

> For example: An employer could justify excluding an individual who is an alcoholic with a history of returning to alcohol abuse from a job as a ship captain.

I-8.8 Pre-Employment Inquiries About Drug and Alcohol Use.

An employer may make certain pre-employment, pre-offer inquiries regarding use of alcohol or the illegal use of drugs. An employer may ask whether an applicant drinks alcohol or whether he or she is currently using drugs illegally. However, an employer may not ask whether an applicant is a drug addict or alcoholic, nor inquire whether s/he has ever been in a drug or alcohol rehabilitation program. (See also Pre-Employment Inquiries, Chapter V.)

After a conditional offer of employment, an employer may ask any questions concerning past or present drug or alcohol use. However, the employer may not use such information to exclude an individual with a disability, on the basis of a disability, unless it can show that the reason for exclusion is job-related and consistent with business necessity, and that legitimate job criteria cannot be met with a reasonable accommodation. (For more information on pre-employment medical inquiries, see Chapter VI.)

I-8.9 Drug Testing.

An employer may conduct tests to detect illegal use of drugs. The ADA does not prohibit, require, or encourage drug tests. Drug tests are not considered medical examinations, and an applicant can be required to take a drug test before a conditional offer of employment has been made. An employee also can be required to take a drug test, whether or not such a test is job-related and necessary for the business. (On the other hand, a test to determine an individual's blood alcohol level would be a "medical examination" and only could be required by an employer in conformity with the ADA.)

An employer may refuse to hire an applicant or discharge or discipline an employee based upon a test result that indicates the illegal use of drugs. The employer may take these actions even if an applicant or employee claims that s/he recently stopped illegally using drugs.

Employers may comply with applicable Federal, State, or local laws regulating when and how drug tests may be used, what drug tests may be used, and confidentiality. Drug tests must be conducted to detect illegal use of drugs. However, tests for illegal use of drugs also may reveal the presence of lawfully-used drugs. If a person is excluded from a job because the employer erroneously "regarded" him/her to be an addict currently using drugs illegally when a drug test revealed the presence of a lawfully prescribed drug, the employer would be liable under the ADA. To avoid such potential liability, the employer would have to determine whether the individual was using a legally prescribed drug. Because the employer may not ask what prescription drugs an individual is taking before making a conditional job offer, one way to avoid liability is to conduct drug tests after making an offer, even though such tests may be given at anytime under the ADA. Since applicants who test positive for illegal drugs are not covered by the ADA, an employer can withdraw an offer of employment on the basis of illegal drug use.

If the results of a drug test indicate the presence of a lawfully prescribed drug, such information must be kept confidential, in the same way as any medical record. If the results reveal information about a disability in addition to information about drug use, the disability-related information is to be treated as a confidential medical record. (See confidentiality requirements regarding medical inquiries and examinations in Chapter VI.)

For example: If drug test results indicate that an individual is HIV positive, or that a person has epilepsy or diabetes because use of a related prescribed medicine is revealed, this information must remain confidential.

I-8.10 Laws and Regulations Concerning Drugs and Alcohol.

An employer may comply with other Federal laws and regulations concerning the use of drugs and alcohol, including the Drug-Free Workplace Act of 1988; regulations applicable to particular types of employment, such as law enforcement positions; regulations of the Department of Transportation for airline employees, interstate motor carrier drivers and railroad engineers; and regulations for safety sensitive positions established by the Department of Defense and the Nuclear Regulatory Commission. Employers may continue to require that their applicants and employees comply with such Federal laws and regulations.

For example: A trucking company can take appropriate action if an applicant or employee tests positive on a drug test required by Department of Transportation regulations or refuses to take such a drug test.

I-IX. Workers' Compensation and Work-Related Injury

I-9.1 Overview of Legal Obligations.

- An employer may not inquire into an applicant's workers' compensation history before making a conditional offer of employment.
- After making a conditional job offer, an employer may ask about a person's workers' compensation history in a medical inquiry or examination that is required of all applicants in the same job category.
- An employer may not base an employment decision on the speculation that an applicant may cause increased workers' compensation costs in the future. However, an employer may refuse to hire, or may discharge an individual who is not currently able to perform a job without posing a significant risk of substantial harm to the health or safety of the individual or others, if the risk cannot be eliminated or reduced by reasonable accommodation. (See Standards Necessary for Health and Safety: A "Direct Threat", Chapter IV.)
- An employer may submit medical information and records concerning employees and applicants (obtained after a conditional job offer) to state workers' compensation offices and "second injury" funds without violating ADA confidentiality requirements.
- Only injured workers who meet the ADA's definition of an "individual with a disability" will be considered disabled under the ADA, regardless of whether they satisfy criteria for receiving benefits under workers' compensation or other disability laws. A worker also must be "qualified" (with or without reasonable accommodation) to be protected by the ADA.

I-9.2 Is a Worker Injured on the Job Protected by the ADA?

Whether an injured worker is protected by the ADA will depend on whether or not the person meets the ADA definitions of an "individual with a disability" and "qualified individual with a disability." (See

Chapter II.) The person must have an impairment that "substantially limits a major life activity," have a "record of" or be "regarded as" having such an impairment. S/he also must be able to perform the essential functions of a job currently held or desired, with or without an accommodation.

Clearly, not every employee injured on the job will meet the ADA definition. Work-related injuries do not always cause physical or mental impairments severe enough to "substantially limit" a major life activity. Also, many on-the-job injuries cause non-chronic impairments which heal within a short period of time with little or no long-term or permanent impact. Such injuries, in most circumstances, are not considered disabilities under the ADA.

The fact that an employee is awarded workers' compensation benefits, or is assigned a high workers' compensation disability rating, does not automatically establish that this person is protected by the ADA. In most cases, the definition of disability under state workers' compensation laws differs from that under the ADA, because the state laws serve a different purpose. Workers' compensation laws are designed to provide needed assistance to workers who suffer many kinds of injuries, whereas the ADA's purpose is to protect people from discrimination on the basis of disability.

Thus, many injured workers who qualify for benefits under workers' compensation or other disability benefits laws may not be protected by the ADA. An employer must consider work-related injuries on a case-by-case basis to know if a worker is protected by the ADA. Many job injuries are not "disabling" under the ADA, but it also is possible that an impairment which is not "substantially limiting" in one circumstance could result in, or lead to, disability in other circumstances.

> For example: Suppose a construction worker falls from a ladder and breaks a leg and the leg heals normally within a few months. Although this worker may be awarded workers' compensation benefits for the injury, he would not be considered a person with a disability under the ADA. The impairment suffered from the injury did not "substantially limit" a major life activity, since the injury healed within a short period and had little or no long-term impact. However, if the worker's leg took significantly longer to heal than the usual healing period for this type of injury, and during this period the worker could not walk, s/he would be considered to have a disability. Or, if the injury caused a permanent limp, the worker might be considered disabled under the ADA if the limp substantially limited his walking, as compared to the average person in the general population.

An employee who was seriously injured while working for a former employer, and was unable to work for a year because of the injury, would have a "record of" a substantially limiting impairment. If an employer refused to hire or promote this person on the basis of that record, even if s/he had recovered in whole or in part from the injury, this would be a violation of the ADA.

If an impairment or condition caused by an on-the-job injury does not substantially limit an employee's ability to work, but the employer regards the individual as having an impairment that makes him/her unable to perform a class of jobs, such as "heavy labor," this individual would be "regarded" by the employer as having a disability. An employer who refused to hire or discharged an individual because of this perception would violate the ADA.

Of course, in each of the examples above, the employer would only be liable for discrimination if the individual was qualified for the position held or desired, with or without an accommodation.

I-9.3 What Can an Employer Do to Avoid Increased Workers' Compensation Costs and Comply With the ADA?

The ADA allows an employer to take reasonable steps to avoid increased workers' compensation liability while protecting persons with disabilities against exclusion from jobs they can safely perform.

Steps the Employer May Take

After making a conditional job offer, an employer may inquire about a person's workers' compensation history in a medical inquiry or examination that is required of all applicants in the same job category. However, an employer may not require an applicant to have a medical examination because a response to a medical inquiry (as opposed to results from a medical examination) discloses a previous on-the-job injury, unless all applicants in the same job category are required to have the examination. (See Chapter V.)

The employer may use information from medical inquiries and examinations for various purposes, such as:

- to verify employment history;
- to screen out applicants with a history of fraudulent workers' compensation claims;
- to provide information to state officials as

required by state laws regulating workers' compensation and "second injury" funds;

- to screen out individuals who would pose a "direct threat" to health or safety of themselves or others, which could not be reduced to an acceptable level or eliminated by a reasonable accommodation. (See Chapter IV.)

I-9.4 What Can an Employer Do When a Worker is Injured on the Job?

Medical Examinations

An employer may only make medical examinations or inquiries of an employee regarding disability if such examinations are job-related and consistent with business necessity. If a worker has an on-the-job injury which appears to affect his/her ability to do essential job functions, a medical examination or inquiry is job-related and consistent with business necessity. A medical examination or inquiry also may be necessary to provide reasonable accommodation. (See Chapter VI.)

When a worker wishes to return to work after absence due to accident or illness, s/he can only be required to have a "job-related" medical examination, not a full physical exam, as a condition of returning to work.

The ADA prohibits an employer from discriminating against a person with a disability who is "qualified" for a desired job. The employer cannot refuse to let an individual with a disability return to work because the worker is not fully recovered from injury, unless s/he: (1) cannot perform the essential functions of the job s/he holds or desires with or without an accommodation; or (2) would pose a significant risk of substantial harm that could not be reduced to an acceptable level with reasonable accommodation. (See Chapter IV.) Since reasonable accommodation may include reassignment to a vacant position, an employer may be required to consider an employee's qualifications to perform other vacant jobs for which s/he is qualified, as well as the job held when injured.

"Light Duty" Jobs

Many employers have established "light duty" positions to respond to medical restrictions on workers recovering from job-related injuries, in order to reduce workers' compensation liability. Such positions usually place few physical demands on an employee and may include tasks such as answering the telephone and simple administrative work. An employee's placement in such a position is often limited by the employer to a specific period of time.

The ADA does not require an employer to create a "light duty" position unless the "heavy duty" tasks an injured worker can no longer perform are marginal job functions which may be reallocated to co-workers as part of the reasonable accommodation of job-restructuring. In most cases however, "light duty" positions involve a totally different job from the job that a worker performed before the injury. Creating such positions by job restructuring is not required by the ADA. However, if an employer already has a vacant light duty position for which an injured worker is qualified, it might be a reasonable accommodation to reassign the worker to that position. If the position was created as a temporary job, a reassignment to that position need only be for a temporary period.

When an employer places an injured worker in a temporary "light duty" position, that worker is "otherwise qualified" for that position for the term of that position; a worker's qualifications must be gauged in relation to the position occupied, not in relation to the job held prior to the injury. It may be necessary to provide additional reasonable accommodation to enable an injured worker in a light duty position to perform the essential functions of that position.

> For example: Suppose a telephone line repair worker broke both legs and fractured her knee joints in a fall. The treating physician states that the worker will not be able to walk, even with crutches, for at least nine months. She therefore has a "disability." Currently using a wheelchair, and unable to do her previous job, she is placed in a "light duty" position to process paperwork associated with line repairs. However, the office to which she is assigned is not wheelchair accessible. It would be a reasonable accommodation to place the employee in an office that is accessible. Or, the office could be made accessible by widening the office door, if this would not be an undue hardship. The employer also might have to modify the employee's work schedule so that she could attend weekly physical therapy sessions.

Medical information may be very useful to an employer who must decide whether an injured worker can come back to work, in what job, and, if necessary, with what accommodations. A physician may provide an employer with relevant information about an employee's functional abilities, limitations, and work restrictions. This information will be useful in determining how to return the employee to productive work, but the employer bears the ultimate responsibility for deciding whether the individual is qualified, with or without a reasonable accommodation.

Therefore, an employer cannot avoid liability if it relies on a physician's advice which is not consistent with ADA requirements.

I-9.5 Do the ADA's Pre-Employment Inquiry and Confidentiality Restrictions Prevent an Employer from Filing Second Injury Fund Claims?

Most states have established "second injury" funds designed to remove financial disincentives in hiring employees with a disability. Without a second injury fund, if a worker suffered increased disability from a work-related injury because of a pre-existing condition, the employer would have to pay the full cost. The second injury fund provisions limit the amount the employer must pay in these circumstances, and provide for the balance to be paid out of a common fund.

Many second injury funds require an employer to certify that it knew at the time of hire that the employee had a pre-existing injury. The ADA does not prohibit employers from obtaining information about pre-existing injuries and providing needed information to second injury funds. As discussed in Chapter VI., an employer may make such medical inquiries and require a medical examination after a conditional offer of employment, and before a person starts work, so long as the examination or inquiry is made of all applicants in the same job category. Although the ADA generally requires that medical information obtained from such examinations or inquiries be kept confidential, information may be submitted to second injury funds or state workers' compensation authorities as required by state workers' compensation laws.

I-9.6 Compliance with State and Federal Workers' Compensation Laws.

a Federal Laws

It may be a defense to a charge of discrimination under the ADA that a challenged action is required by another Federal law or regulation, or that another Federal law prohibits an action that otherwise would be required by the ADA. This defense is not valid, however, if the Federal standard does not require the discriminatory action, or if there is a way that an employer can comply with both legal requirements.

b State Laws

ADA requirements supersede any conflicting state workers' compensation laws.

For example: Some state workers' compensation statutes make an employer liable for paying additional benefits if an injury occurs because the employer assigned a person to a position likely to jeopardize the person's health or safety, or exacerbate an earlier workers' compensation injury. Some of these laws may permit or require an employer to exclude a disabled individual from employment in cases where the ADA would not permit such exclusion. In these cases, the ADA takes precedence over the state law. An employer could not assert, as a valid defense to a charge of discrimination, that it failed to hire or return to work an individual with a disability because doing so would violate a state workers' compensation law that required exclusion of this individual.

I-9.7 Does Filing a Workers' Compensation Claim Prevent an Injured Worker from Filing a Charge Under the ADA?

Filing a workers' compensation claim does not prevent an injured worker from filing a charge under the ADA. "Exclusivity" clauses in state workers' compensation laws bar all other civil remedies related to an injury that has been compensated by a workers' compensation system. However, these clauses do not prohibit a qualified individual with a disability from filing a discrimination charge with EEOC, or filing a suit under the ADA, if issued a "right to sue" letter by EEOC. (See Chapter X.)

I-9.8 What if an Employee Provides False Information About his/her Health or Physical Condition?

An employer may refuse to hire or may fire a person who knowingly provides a false answer to a lawful post-offer inquiry about his/her condition or workers' compensation history.

Some state workers' compensation laws release an employer from its obligation to pay benefits if a worker falsely represents his/her health or physical condition at the time of hire and is later injured as a result. The ADA does not prevent use of this defense to a workers' compensation claim. The ADA requires only that information requests about health or workers compensation history are made as part of a post-offer medical examination or inquiry. (See Chapter VI.)

I-X. Enforcement Provisions

I-10.1 Introduction.

Title I of the ADA is enforced by the Equal Employment Opportunity Commission (EEOC) under the same procedures used to enforce Title VII of the Civil Rights Acts of 1964. The Commission receives and investigates charges of discrimination and seeks through conciliation to resolve any discrimination found and obtain full relief for the affected individual. If conciliation is not successful, the EEOC may file a suit or issue a "right to sue" letter to the person who filed the charge. Throughout the enforcement process, EEOC makes every effort to resolve issues through conciliation and to avoid litigation.

The Commission also recognizes that differences and disputes about the ADA requirements may arise between employers and people with disabilities as a result of misunderstandings. Such disputes frequently can be resolved more effectively through informal negotiation or mediation procedures, rather than through the formal enforcement process of the ADA. Accordingly, EEOC will encourage efforts to settle such differences through alternative dispute resolution, provided that such efforts do not deprive any individual of legal rights granted by the statute. (See "Alternative Dispute Resolution" in Resource Directory Index.)

I-10.2 Overview of Enforcement Provisions.

- A job applicant or employee who believes s/he has been discriminated against on the basis of disability in employment by a private, state, or local government employer, labor union, employment agency, or joint labor management committee can file a charge with EEOC.
- An individual, whether disabled or not, also may file a charge if s/he believes that s/he has been discriminated against because of an association with a person with a known disability, or believes that s/he has suffered retaliation because of filing a charge or assisting in opposing a discriminatory practice. (See Retaliation below). Another person or organization also may file a charge on behalf of such applicant or employee.
- The entity charged with violating the ADA should receive written notification of the charge within 10 days after it is filed.
- EEOC will investigate charges of discrimination If EEOC believes that discrimination occurred, it will attempt to resolve the charge through conciliation and obtain full relief for the aggrieved individual consistent with EEOC's standards for remedies.
- If conciliation fails, EEOC will file suit or issue a "right to sue" letter to the person who filed the charge. (If the charge involves a state or local government agency, EEOC will refer the case to the Department of Justice for consideration of litigation or issuance of a "right to sue" letter.)
- Remedies for violations of Title I of the ADA include hiring, reinstatement, promotion, back pay, front pay, restored benefits, reasonable accommodation, attorneys' fees, expert witness fees, and court costs. Compensatory and punitive damages also may be available in cases of intentional discrimination or where an employer fails to make a good faith effort to provide a reasonable accommodation.
- Employers may not retaliate against any applicant or employee who files a charge, participates in an EEOC investigation or opposes an unlawful employment practice.

I-10.3 Questions and Answers on the ADA Enforcement Process.

When do the ADA's employment enforcement provisions become effective?

Charges of discrimination can be filed against employers with 25 or more employees and other covered entities beginning July 26, 1992. The alleged discriminatory act(s) must have occurred on or after July 26, 1992.

Charges can be filed against employers with 15 or more employees beginning July 26, 1994. The alleged discriminatory act(s) must have occurred on or after July 26, 1994, if the charge is against an employer with 15 to 24 employees.

Who can file charges of discrimination?

An applicant or employee who feels that s/he has been discriminated against in employment on the basis of disability can file a charge with EEOC. An individual, group or organization also can file a charge on behalf of another person. An individual, group or organization that files a charge is called the "charging party."

How are charges of discrimination filed?

A person who feels s/he has been discriminated

against, or other potential "charging party" should contact the nearest EEOC office. (See Resource Directory listing.) If there is no EEOC office nearby, call, toll free 1-800-669-4000 (voice) or 1-800-800-3302 (TDD).

What are the time limits for filing charges of discrimination?

A charge of discrimination on the basis of disability must be filed with EEOC within 180 days of the alleged discriminatory act.

If there is a state or local fair employment practices agency that enforces a law prohibiting the same alleged discriminatory practice, it is possible that charges may be filed with EEOC up to 300 days after the alleged discriminatory act. However, to protect legal rights, it is recommended that EEOC be contacted promptly when discrimination is believed to have occurred.

How is a charge of discrimination filed?

A charge can be filed in person, by telephone, or by mail. If an individual does not live near an EEOC office, the charge can be filed by telephone and verified by mail. The type of information that will be requested from a charging party may include:

- the charging party's name, address, and telephone number (if a charge is filed on behalf of another individual, his/her identity may be kept confidential, unless required for a court action);
- the employer's name, address, telephone number, and number of employees;
- the basis or bases of the discrimination claimed by the individual (e.g., disability, race, color, religion, sex, national origin, age, retaliation);
- the issue or issues involved in the alleged discriminatory act(s) (e.g., hiring, promotion, wages, terms and conditions of employment, discharge);
- identification of the charging party's alleged disability (e.g., the physical or mental impairment and how it affects major life activities, the record of disability the employer relied upon, or how the employer regarded the individual as disabled);
- the date of the alleged discriminatory act(s);
- details of what allegedly happened; and
- identity of witnesses who have knowledge of the alleged discriminatory act(s).

Charging parties also may submit additional oral or written evidence on their behalf.

EEOC has work-sharing agreements with many state and local fair employment agencies. Depending on the agreement, some charges may be sent to a state or local agency for investigation; others may be investigated directly by EEOC. (See also Coordination Procedures to Avoid Duplicate Complaint Processing under the ADA and the Rehabilitation Act, below.)

Can a charging party file a charge on more than one basis?

EEOC also enforces other laws that bar employment discrimination based on race, color, religion, sex, national origin, and age (persons 40 years of age and older). An individual with a disability can file a charge of discrimination on more than one basis.

> For example: A cashier who is a paraplegic may claim that she was discriminated against by an employer based on both her sex and her disability. She can file a single charge claiming both disability and sex discrimination.

Can an individual file a lawsuit against an employer?

An individual can file a lawsuit against an employer, but s/he must first file the charge with EEOC. The charging party can request a "right to sue" letter from the EEOC 180 days after the charge was first filed with the Commission. A charging party will then have 90 days to file suit after receiving the notice of right to sue. If the charging party files suit, EEOC will ordinarily dismiss the original charges filed with the Commission. "Right to sue" letters also are issued when EEOC does not believe discrimination occurred or when conciliation attempts fail and EEOC decides not to sue on the charging party's behalf (see below).

Are charging parties protected from retaliation?

It is unlawful for an employer or other covered entity to retaliate against someone who files a charge of discrimination, participates in an investigation, or opposes discriminatory practices. Individuals who believe that they have been retaliated against should contact EEOC immediately. Even if an individual has already filed a charge of discrimination, s/he can file a new charge based on retaliation.

How does EEOC process charges of discrimination?

- A charge of employment discrimination may be filed with EEOC against a private employer, state or local government, employment agency, labor union or joint labor management committee. When a charge has been filed, EEOC calls these covered entities "respondents."

- Within 10 days after receipt of a charge, EEOC sends written notification of receipt to the respondent and the charging party.
- EEOC begins its investigation by reviewing information received from the charging party and requesting information from the respondent. Information requested from the respondent initially, and in the course of the investigation, may include:
  - specific information on the issues raised in the charge;
  - the identity of witnesses who can provide evidence about issues in the charge;
  - information about the business operation, employment process, and workplace; and
  - personnel and payroll records.

(Note: All or part of the data-gathering portion of an investigation may be conducted on-site, depending on the circumstances.)

- A respondent also may submit additional oral or written evidence on its own behalf.
- EEOC also will interview witnesses who have knowledge of the alleged discriminatory act(s).
- EEOC may dismiss a charge during the course of the investigation for various reasons. For example, it may find that the respondent is not covered by the ADA, or that the charge is not timely filed.
- EEOC may request additional information from the respondent and the charging party. They may be asked to participate in a fact-finding conference to review the allegations, obtain additional evidence, and, if appropriate, seek to resolve the charge through a negotiated settlement.
- The charging party and respondent will be informed of the preliminary findings of the investigation—that is, whether there is cause to believe that discrimination has occurred and the type of relief that may be necessary. Both parties will be provided opportunity to submit further information.
- After reviewing all information, the Commission sends an official "Letter of Determination" to the charging party and the respondent, stating whether it has or has not found "reasonable cause" to believe that discrimination occurred.

What if the EEOC concludes that no discrimination occurred?

If the investigation finds no cause to believe discrimination occurred, EEOC will take no further action EEOC will issue a "right to sue" letter to the charging party, who may initiate a private suit.

What if the EEOC concludes that discrimination occurred?

If the investigation shows that there is reasonable cause to believe that discrimination occurred, EEOC will attempt to resolve the issue through conciliation and to obtain full relief consistent with EEOC's standards for remedies for the charging party. (See Relief Available to Charging Party, below). EEOC also can request an employer to post a notice in the workplace stating that the discrimination has been corrected and that it has stopped the discriminatory practice.

What happens if conciliation fails?

At all stages of the enforcement process, EEOC will try to resolve a charge without a costly lawsuit.

If EEOC has found cause to believe that discrimination occurred, but cannot resolve the issue through conciliation, the case will be considered for litigation. If EEOC decides to litigate, a lawsuit will be filed in federal district court. If the Commission decides not to litigate, it will send the charging party a "right-to-sue" letter. The charging party may then initiate a private civil suit within 90 days, if desired. If conciliation fails on a charge against a state or local government, EEOC will refer the case to the Department of Justice for consideration of litigation or issuance of a "right to sue" letter.

I-10.4 Coordination Procedures to Avoid Duplicative Complaint Processing Under the ADA and the Rehabilitation Act.

The ADA requires EEOC and the federal agencies responsible for Section 503 and Section 504 of the Rehabilitation Act of 1973 to establish coordination procedures to avoid duplication and to assure consistent standards in processing complaints that fall within the overlapping jurisdiction of both laws EEOC and the Office of Federal Contract Compliance in the Department of Labor (OFCCP) have issued a joint regulation establishing such procedures for complaints against employers covered by the ADA who are also federal contractors or subcontractors (Published in the Federal Register of January 24, 1992.) EEOC and the

Department of Justice also will issue a joint regulation establishing procedures for complaints against employers covered by the ADA who are recipients of federal financial assistance.

Joint EEOC-OFCCP rule provides that a complaint of discrimination on the basis of disability filed with OFCCP under Section 503 will be considered a charge filed simultaneously under the ADA if the complaint falls within the ADA's jurisdiction. This will ensure that an individual's ADA rights are preserved OFCCP will process such complaints/charges for EEOC, with certain exceptions specified in the regulation, where OFCCP will refer the charge to EEOC. OFCCP also will refer to EEOC for litigation review any complaint/charge where a violation has been found, conciliation fails, and OFCCP decides not to pursue administrative enforcement.

EEOC will refer to OFCCP ADA charges that fall under Section 503 jurisdiction when the Commission finds cause to believe that discrimination has occurred but decides not to litigate, for any administrative action that OFCCP finds appropriate. Where a charge involves both allegations of discrimination and violation of OFCCP's affirmative action requirements, EEOC generally will refer the charge to OFCCP for processing and resolution.

(Note: Procedures established in an EEOC-Department of Justice joint rule on processing complaints that are within ADA and Section 504 jurisdiction will be summarized in a future supplement to this Manual, when a final regulation has been issued.)

I-10.5 Remedies.

The "relief" or remedies available for employment discrimination, whether caused by intentional acts or by practices that have a discriminatory effect, may include hiring, reinstatement, promotion, back pay, front pay, reasonable accommodation, or other actions that will make an individual "whole" (in the condition s/he would have been but for the discrimination) Remedies also may include payment of attorneys' fees, expert witness fees and court costs.

Compensatory and punitive damages also may be available where intentional discrimination is found. Damages may be available to compensate for actual monetary losses, for future monetary losses, for mental anguish and inconvenience. Punitive damages also may be available if an employer acted with malice or reckless indifference. The total amount of punitive damages and compensatory damages for future monetary loss and emotional injury for each individual is limited, based upon the size of the employer, using the following schedule:

Number of employees	Damages will not exceed
15-100	$ 50,000
101-200	100,000
201-500	200,000
500 and more	300,000

Punitive damages are not available against state or local governments.

In cases concerning reasonable accommodation, compensatory or punitive damages may not be awarded to the charging party if an employer can demonstrate that "good faith" efforts were made to provide reasonable accommodation.

What are EEOC's obligations to make the charge process accessible to and usable by individuals with disabilities?

EEOC is required by Section 504 of the Rehabilitation Act of 1973, as amended, to make all of its programs and activities accessible to and usable by individuals with disabilities. EEOC has an obligation to provide services or devices necessary to enable an individual with a disability to participate in the charge filing process. For example, upon request, EEOC will provide an interpreter when necessary for a charging party who is hearing impaired. People with visual or manual disabilities can request on-site assistance in filling out a "charge of discrimination" form and affidavits. EEOC will provide access to the charge process as needed by each individual with a disability, on a case-by-case basis.

ADA TITLE I INTERIM ENFORCEMENT GUIDANCE

SECTION 902

DEFINITION OF THE TERM "DISABILITY"

Table of Contents

SECTION 902

DEFINITION OF THE TERM "DISABILITY"

902.1 Introduction and Summary

(a) General—Title I of the Americans with Disabilities Act, 42 U.S.C. §§ 12101-17 (Supp. IV 1992) [hereinafter ADA or Act], prohibits employment discrimination on the basis of disability.[1] The ADA protects a qualified individual with a "disability" from discrimination in job application procedures; hiring; advancement; discharge; compensation; job training; and other terms, conditions, and privileges of employment. 42 U.S.C. § 12112(a). To be protected by the ADA, a person must meet the definition of the term "qualified individual with a disability" as defined by the Act and implementing regulations.[2] This

[1] The ADA uses the terms "disability" and "individual with a disability" rather than the terms "handicap" and "handicapped person" or "individual with handicaps." The use of these terms "represents an effort by [Congress] to make use of up-to-date, currently accepted terminology." The change in phraseology does not reflect a change in definition or substance. S. Rep. No. 116, 101st Cong., 1st Sess. 21 (1989) [hereinafter Senate Report]; H.R. Rep. No. 485 pt. 2, 101st Cong., 2d Sess. 50-51 (1990) [hereinafter House Education and Labor Report].

[2] The ADA also protects individuals from discrimination on the basis of their relationship or association with a person with a disability. 42 U.S.C. § 12112(b)(4); 29 C.F.R. § 1630.8; see also Senate Report at 30; House Education and Labor Report at 61-62; H.R. Rep. No. 485 pt. 3, 101st Cong., 2d Sess. 38-39 (1990) [hereinafter House Judiciary Report]. Further, the Act

Compliance Manual section discusses the ADA definition of the term "disability."[3] The definition of the term "qualified individual with a disability" and the appropriate analysis for determining whether a person meets that definition will be discussed in a separate forthcoming Compliance Manual section.

A major part of the inquiry in an ADA charge often will be the determination of whether the charging party is protected by the Act. This determination frequently requires more extensive analysis than does the determination of whether a person is protected by other nondiscrimination statutes. For example, it is generally clear whether a person is of a particular race, national origin, age, or sex that is alleged to be the basis of discrimination. By contrast, it often is less clear whether a person's physical or mental condition constitutes an impairment of sufficient degree to establish that the person meets the statutory definition of an individual with a "disability."

The definition of "disability" under the ADA reflects the intent of Congress to prohibit the specific forms of discrimination that persons with disabilities face. While individuals with disabilities may experience the types of discrimination that confront other groups, they also may encounter unique forms of discrimination because of the nature of their disabilities and the effect that their present, past, or perceived conditions have on other persons. The purpose of the ADA is to eliminate discrimination that confronts individuals with disabilities.

Since the definition of the term "disability" under the ADA is tailored to the purpose of eliminating discrimination prohibited by the ADA, it may differ from the definition of "disability" in other laws drafted for other purposes. For example, the definition of a "disabled veteran" is not the same as the definition of an individual with a disability under the ADA.[4] Similarly, an individual might be eligible for disability retirement but not be an individual with a disability under the ADA. Conversely, a person who meets the ADA definition of "disability" might not meet the requirements for disability retirement.

(b) Statutory Definition—With respect to an individual, the term "disability" means

(A) a physical or mental impairment that substantially limits one or more of the major life activities of such individual;
(B) a record of such an impairment; or
(C) being regarded as having such an impairment.
42 U.S.C. § 12102(2); see also 29 C.F.R. § 1630.2(g). A person must meet the requirements of at least one of these three criteria to be an individual with a disability under the Act.

The first part of the definition covers persons who actually have physical or mental impairments that substantially limit one or more major life activities. The focus under the first part is on the individual, to determine if (s)he has a substantially limiting impairment. To fall under the first part of the definition, a person must establish three elements:

(1) that (s)he has a physical or mental impairment
(2) that substantially limits
(3) one or more major life activities.

The second and third parts of the definition cover persons who may not have an impairment that substantially limits a major life activity but who have a history of, or have been misclassified as having, such a substantially limiting impairment, or who are perceived as having such a substantially limiting impairment. The focus under the second and third parts is on the reactions of other persons to a history of an impairment or to a perceived impairment. A history or perception of an impairment that substantially limits a

---

prohibits retaliation or coercion against individuals because they have opposed any act that the ADA makes unlawful, have participated in the enforcement process, or have encouraged others to exercise their rights secured by the ADA. 42 U.S.C. § 12203; 29 C.F.R. § 1630.12; see also Senate Report at 86; House Education and Labor Report at 138; House Judiciary Report at 72.

[3] The Rehabilitation Act Amendments of 1992 amended the Rehabilitation Act of 1973, 29 U.S.C. §§ 701-97 (1988 & Supp. IV 1992), to apply the substantive standards of Title I of the ADA to sections 501, 503, and 504 of the Rehabilitation Act for non-affirmative action employment discrimination cases. Pub. L. No. 102-569, 106 Stat. 4344 at 4424, 4428 (1992) (codified at 29 U.S.C. §§ 791(g), 793(d), 794(d) (Supp. IV 1992)). (Sections 501, 503, and 504 of the Rehabilitation Act prohibit federal agencies, federal contractors, and programs receiving federal financial assistance from discriminating on the basis of disability.) The ADA definition of the term "disability," therefore, also applies to those sections of the Rehabilitation Act.

[4] The Vietnam Era Veterans Readjustment Assistance Act of 1974 defines a disabled veteran as

> (A) a veteran who is entitled to compensation (or who but for the receipt of military retired pay would be entitled to compensation) under laws administered by the Secretary, or (B) a person who was discharged or released from active duty because of a service-connected disability.

38 U.S.C. § 4211(3) (Supp. III 1991).

major life activity is a "disability." These parts of the definition reflect a recognition by Congress that stereotyped assumptions about what constitutes a disability and unfounded concerns about the limitations of individuals with disabilities form major discriminatory barriers, not only to those persons presently disabled, but also to those persons either previously disabled, misclassified as previously disabled, or mistakenly perceived to be disabled. To combat the effects of these prevalent misperceptions, the definition of an individual with a disability precludes discrimination against persons who are treated as if they have a substantially limiting impairment, even if in fact they have no such current incapacity.

(c) Summary—To determine whether a charging party is protected by the ADA, the EEOC investigator initially should determine why the charging party believes that the respondent has discriminated against him/her on the basis of disability. The charging party's response usually will provide the investigator with a starting point for analysis by identifying the type of condition at issue. For example, if the charging party replies that the respondent refused to hire him/her because it learned that the charging party had received psychiatric treatment, then the investigator will know to investigate whether the charging party has, has a record of, or is regarded as having a psychiatric disability. (Of course, further investigation may reveal other disabilities that may constitute the reason for the challenged employment action.)

The investigator then should determine whether the charging party meets the first part of the definition of "disability"; that is, the investigator should determine whether the charging party actually has a physical or mental impairment that substantially limits a major life activity. In that regard, the investigator should determine whether the charging party's condition is an impairment. See § 902.2, infra. If the condition is an impairment, then the investigator should determine whether the charging party's impairment substantially limits a major life activity other than working. See § 902.4(c)(1), infra. If the impairment does not, then the investigator should determine whether the charging party is substantially limited in the ability to work. See § 902.4(c)(2), infra.

If the charging party does not meet the first part of the definition of "disability," or if the investigator after attempting an analysis is unsure whether the charging party meets the first part, then the investigator should determine whether the charging party meets the second or third part of the definition. See §§ 902.7, .8 infra. With respect to the second part, the investigator should determine whether the charging party has a history of, see § 902.7(b), infra, or has been misclassified as having, see § 902.7(c), infra, an impairment that substantially limited a major life activity. With respect to the third part, the investigator should determine whether the charging party is regarded as having an impairment that substantially limits a major life activity. In that regard, the investigator should determine whether the charging party (1) has an impairment that does not substantially limit a major life activity but that is regarded as being substantially limiting, see § 902.8(c), infra, (2) has an impairment that is substantially limiting only as a result of the attitudes of others, see § 902.8(d), infra, or (3) has no impairment but is regarded as having a substantially limiting impairment, see § 902.8(e), infra.

902.2 Impairment

(a) General—The person claiming to be an individual with a disability as defined by the first part of the definition must have an actual impairment. If the person does not have an impairment, (s)he does not meet the requirements of the first part of the definition of disability. Under the second and third parts of the definition, the person must have a record of a substantially limiting impairment or be regarded as having a substantially limiting impairment.[5]

A person has a disability only if his/her limitations are, were, or are regarded as being the result of an impairment. It is essential, therefore, to distinguish between conditions that are impairments and those that are not impairments. Not everything that restricts a person's major life activities is an impairment. For example, a person may be having financial problems that significantly restrict what that person does in life. Financial problems or other economic disadvantages,

---

5 This section frequently refers to the term "impairment" in the present tense. These references are not meant to imply that the determination of whether a condition is an impairment is relevant only to whether an individual meets the first part of the definition of "disability," i.e., actually has a physical or mental impairment that substantially limits a major life activity. This determination also is relevant to whether an individual has a record of such an impairment or is regarded as having such an impairment.

The determination of whether a condition constitutes an impairment should be made without regard to mitigating measures. See § 902.5, infra.

however, are not impairments under the ADA. Accordingly, the person in that situation does not have a "disability" as that term is defined by the ADA. On the other hand, an individual may be unable to cope with everyday stress because (s)he has bipolar disorder. Bipolar disorder is an impairment. In that situation, the analysis proceeds to whether the individual's impairment substantially limits a major life activity.

(b) Regulatory Definition—A physical or mental impairment means

> (1) [a]ny physiological disorder, or condition, cosmetic disfigurement, or anatomical loss affecting one or more of the following body systems: neurological, musculoskeletal, special sense organs, respiratory (including speech organs), cardiovascular, reproductive, digestive, genito-urinary, hemic and lymphatic, skin, and endocrine; or
> (2) [a]ny mental or psychological disorder, such as mental retardation, organic brain syndrome, emotional or mental illness, and specific learning disabilities.

29 C.F.R. § 1630.2(h); see also S. Rep. No. 116, 101st Cong., 1st Sess. 22 (1989) [hereinafter Senate Report]; H.R. Rep. No. 485 pt. 2, 101st Cong., 2d Sess. 51 (1990) [hereinafter House Education and Labor Report]; H.R. Rep. No. 485 pt. 3, 101st Cong., 2d Sess. 28 (1990) [hereinafter House Judiciary Report].

This regulatory definition does not set forth an exclusive list oÏf specific impairments covered by the ADA. Instead, the definition describes the type of condition that constitutes an impairment.

The first step in investigating whether a charging party has a disability is investigating whether (s)he has an impairment, has a record of an impairment, or is regarded as having an impairment. In many cases, it is obvious that a condition is an impairment. In other cases, however, it is not obvious. When it is unclear whether a charging party has an impairment, the investigator should ask the charging party for medical documentation that describes his/her condition. Medical documentation that describes the charging party's condition or that contains a diagnosis of the condition will help to determine if the charging party has an impairment.[6] In addition, the investigator should ask the respondent to provide copies of relevant medical documentation concerning the charging party's condition that the respondent has in his/her possession. Such documentation should include the results of any medical examination conducted or ordered by the respondent as well as copies of medical documentation that the charging party provided to the respondent. If the investigator requests the information directly from a third party, rather than from the charging party or the respondent, then the investigator first should obtain a signed medical release from the charging party and should submit the release with the request. Other information, such as the charging party's description of his/her condition or statements from the charging party's friends, family, or co-workers, also may be relevant to determining whether the charging party has an impairment.

(c) Conditions That Are Not Impairments

(1) *Statutory and Legislative History Exceptions*—The statute and the legislative history specifically state that certain conditions are not impairments under the ADA.[7] The term "impairment" does not include homosexuality and bisexuality. 42 U.S.C. § 12211(a); see also 29 C.F.R. § 1630.3(e); H.R. Rep. No. 596, 101st Cong., 2d Sess. 88 (1990) [hereinafter Conference Report]; House Education and Labor Report at 142; House Judiciary Report at 75. Further, environmental, cultural, and economic disadvantages such as a prison record or a lack of education are not impairments. Senate Report at 22; House Education and Labor Report at 51-52; House Judiciary Report at 28. In addition, age, by itself, is not an impairment. See Senate Report at 22; House Education and Labor Report at 52; House Judiciary Report at 28. A person who has a medical condition (such as hearing loss, osteoporosis[8], or arthritis) often associated with age

---

6 A diagnosis is relevant to determining whether a charging party has an impairment. It is important to remember, however, that a diagnosis may be insufficient to determine if the charging party has a disability. An impairment rises to the level of a disability when it substantially limits one or more major life activities. The investigator, therefore, also should obtain available medical or other documentation that describes the extent to which the impairment limits the charging party's major life activities. See §§ 902.3, 902.4, infra.

7 The statute also specifies that certain conditions, even though they may be impairments, are not disabilities covered by the ADA. See § 902.6, infra.

8 Osteoporosis is a "[r]eduction in the quantity of bone or atrophy of skeletal tissue." Stedman's Medical Dictionary 1110 (25th ed. 1990).

has an impairment on the basis of the medical condition. A person does not have an impairment, however, simply because (s)he is advanced in years. 29 C.F.R. pt. 1630 app. § 1630.2(h).

Example 1—CP has been unemployed for two years. Although she has actively sought work, CP has not been able to find a job. CP asserts that employers will not hire her because she is a convicted felon who served three years in prison for armed robbery. CP argues that her prison record is a disability because it prevents her from getting a job. CP, however, does not have a disability because she does not have a physical or mental impairment as defined by the ADA. A prison record is not an impairment for ADA purposes.

Example 2—CP applies for a job as a cashier at his neighborhood supermarket. The store manager speaks with CP briefly and then asks CP to fill out a written job application form. CP does not complete the form because he cannot read it. CP, who has the equivalent of a second-grade education, was never taught to read. CP does not have a physical or mental impairment as defined by the ADA. A lack of education is not an impairment for ADA purposes.

Example 3—Same as Example 2, above, except CP cannot read because he has a severe form of dyslexia. CP has an impairment as defined by the ADA. Dyslexia, a learning disability, is an impairment for ADA purposes.

Example 4—CP, who is sixty-three, has osteoporosis. The osteoporosis, a reduction in bone quantity, is an impairment as defined by the ADA. CP's age, sixty-three, is not a physical or mental impairment as defined by the ADA.

(2) *Physical Characteristics*—Simple physical characteristics are not impairments under the ADA. For example, a person cannot claim to be impaired because of blue eyes or black hair. Senate Report at 22; House Education and Labor Report at 51; House Judiciary Report at 28. Similarly, a person does not have an impairment simply because (s)he is left-handed. *de la Torres v. Bolger*, 781 F.2d 1134, 39 EPD Par. 35,883, 1 AD Cas. (BNA) 852 (5th Cir. 1986).[9]

Further, a characteristic predisposition to illness or disease is not an impairment. 29 C.F.R. pt. 1630 app. § 1630.2(h). A person may be predisposed to developing an illness or a disease because of factors such as environmental, economic, cultural, or social conditions. This predisposition does not amount to an impairment.

(3) *Pregnancy*—Because pregnancy is not the result of a physiological disorder, it is not an impairment. 29 C.F.R. pt. 1630 app. § 1630.2(h); see also Byerly v. Herr Foods, Inc., 61 EPD Par. 42,226, 2 AD Cas. (BNA) 666 (E.D. Pa. 1993). Complications resulting from pregnancy, however, are impairments.[10]

Example 1—CP is in the third trimester of her pregnancy. Her pregnancy has proceeded well, and she has developed no complications. CP does not have an impairment. Pregnancy, by itself, is not an impairment.

Example 2—Same as Example 1, above, except CP has developed hypertension. CP has an impairment, hypertension. (Remember that the mere presence of an impairment does not automatically mean that CP has a disability. Whether the hypertension rises to the level of a disability will turn on whether the impairment substantially limits, or is regarded as substantially limiting, a major life activity.)

(4) *Common Personality Traits*-Like physical characteristics, common personality traits also are not impairments. In *Daley v. Koch*, 892 F.2d 212, 214, 52 EPD Par. 39,534 at 60,471, 1 AD Cas. (BNA) 1549, 1550 (2d Cir. 1989), a psychological profile of an applicant for a police officer position determined that the applicant "showed 'poor judgment, irresponsible behavior and poor impulse control'" but did not have "any particular psychological disease or disorder." The court ruled that the applicant's personality traits did not constitute an impairment. 892 F.2d at 215, 52 EPD at 60,473, 1 AD Cas. at 1551.

---

9 The ADA definition of "disability" is similar to the definition of "individual with a disability" that has been applied to Title V of the Rehabilitation Act of 1973, 29 U.S.C. § 706(8)(B), (C) (Supp. IV 1992). See Senate Report at 21; House Education and Labor Report at 50; House Judiciary Report at 27. Since both Acts use the same three-part definition, this manual section draws on case law applying the Rehabilitation Act where appropriate.

10 Although other statutes may use the term "disability" when referring to pregnancy, pregnancy is not a "disability" for purposes of the ADA. Note, however, that allegations of employment discrimination based on pregnancy are covered by Title VII of the Civil Rights Act of 1964, 42 U.S.C. § 2000e. The appropriate analysis for assessing a charge of pregnancy-based employment discrimination is discussed in a separate Compliance Manual section. See § 626, supra.

Example 1—CP is a lawyer who is impatient with her co-workers and her boss. She often loses her temper, frequently shouts at her subordinates, and publicly questions her boss's directions. Her colleagues think that she is rude and arrogant, and they find it difficult to get along with her. CP does not have an impairment. Personality traits, such as impatience, a quick temper, and arrogance, in and of themselves are not impairments.

Example 2—Same as Example 1, above, except CP's behavior results from bipolar disorder. CP has an impairment, bipolar disorder.[11]

Example 3—CP is an account manager who is in charge of developing a major advertising campaign for his firm's biggest client. Although he used to be easygoing and relaxed in the office, CP has become very irritable at work. He has twice lost his temper with his assistant, and he recently engaged in a shouting match with one of his superiors. CP has consulted a psychiatrist, who diagnosed a recurrence of the post-traumatic stress disorder for which CP was treated several years ago. CP has an impairment. CP's post-traumatic stress disorder, a mental disorder, is a mental impairment.[12]

(5) *Normal Deviations in Height, Weight, or Strength*—Similarly, normal deviations in height, weight, or strength that are not the result of a physiological disorder are not impairments.[13] 29 C.F.R. pt. 1630 app. § 1630.2(h); see also *Jasany v. United States Postal Service*, 755 F.2d 1244, 1249, 36 EPD Par. 35,070 at 36,835, 1 AD Cas. (BNA) 706, 709 (6th Cir. 1985). At extremes, however, such deviations may constitute impairments. Further, some individuals may have underlying physical disorders that affect their height, weight, or strength.

(i) For example, a four foot, ten inch tall woman who was denied employment as an automotive production worker because the employer thought she was too small to do the work does not have an impairment. See *American Motors Corp. v. Wisconsin Labor and Industry Review Commission*, 119 Wis. 2d 706, 350 N.W.2d 120, 36 EPD Par. 34,936, 1 AD Cas. (BNA) 611 (1984) (interpreting state law). The woman's height was below the norm, but her small stature was not so extreme as to constitute an impairment and was not the result of a defect, disorder, or other physical abnormality. On the other hand, a four feet, five inches tall man with achondroplastic dwarfism[14] does have an impairment. See *Dexler v. Tisch*, 660 F. Supp. 1418, 1425, 43 EPD Par. 37,280 at 48,207, 1 AD Cas. (BNA) 1086, 1092 (D. Conn. 1987). The man's stature was the result of an underlying disorder, achondroplastic dwarfism, which is an impairment.

(ii) Being overweight, in and of itself, generally is not an impairment. See 29 C.F.R. pt. 1630 app. § 1630.2(h) (noting that weight that is "within 'normal' range and not the result of a physiological disorder" is not an impairment); see also id. § 1630.2(j) (noting that, "except in rare circumstances, obesity is not considered a disabling

---

[11] Note, however, that CP's employer does not have to excuse CP's misconduct, even if the misconduct results from an impairment that rises to the level of a disability, if it does not excuse similar misconduct from its other employees. See 56 Fed. Reg. 35,733 (1990) (referring to revisions that "clarify that employers may hold all employees, disabled (including those disabled by alcoholism or drug addiction) and nondisabled, to the same performance and conduct standards").

[12] As in Example 2, CP's employer does not have to excuse CP's misconduct, even if the misconduct results from an impairment that rises to the level of a disability, if it does not excuse similar misconduct from its other employees. See 56 Fed. Reg. 35,733 (1990) (referring to revisions that "clarify that employers may hold all employees, disabled (including those disabled by alcoholism or drug addiction) and nondisabled, to the same performance and conduct standards").

[13] Note, however, that persons who have normal deviations in height or weight may allege that height or weight standards violate Title VII of the Civil Rights Act of 1964, 42 U.S.C. § 2000e. See *Dothard v. Rawlinson*, 433 U.S. 321, 14 EPD Par. 7,632 (1977) (minimum height/weight requirement for correctional counselor position had adverse impact on women and was not job related and consistent with business necessity); *Gerdom v. Continental Airlines*, 692 F.2d 602, 30 EPD Par. 33,156 (9th Cir. 1982) (en banc), *cert. dismissed*, 460 U.S. 1074 (1983) (maximum weight standards that were applied to exclusively female position of flight hostess constituted disparate treatment based on sex where no such weight policy was applied to similar but exclusively male position of director of passenger service).

[14] Achondroplastic dwarfism is a growth disorder that affects all four extremities and results in short limbs and short stature." *Dexler v. Tisch*, 660 F. Supp. 1418, 1419, 43 EPD Par. 37,280 at 48,202, 1 AD Cas. (BNA) at 1086 (D. Conn. 1987).

impairment"). Thus, for example, a flight attendant who, because of avid body building (which resulted in a low percentage of body fat and a high percentage of muscle), exceeds the airline's weight guidelines does not have an impairment. See *Tudyman v. United Airlines*, 608 F. Supp. 739, 746, 38 EPD Par. 35,674 at 40,015, 1 AD Cas. (BNA) 664, 669 (C.D. Cal. 1984). Similarly, a mildly overweight flight attendant who has not been clinically diagnosed as having any medical anomaly does not have an impairment. *Underwood v. Trans World Airlines*, 710 F. Supp. 78, 83-84, 51 EPD Par. 39,297 at 59,106-07 (S.D.N.Y. 1989) (plaintiff's state action preempted by federal law where plaintiff failed to establish that being mildly overweight brought her within class protected by state human rights law with broad definition of disability).

On the other hand, severe obesity,[15] which has been defined as body weight more than 100% over the norm, see The Merck Manual of Diagnosis and Therapy 981 (Robert Berkow ed., 16th ed. 1992), is clearly an impairment. See *Cook v. Rhode Island Dep't of Mental Health, Retardation and Hosp.,* 10 F.3d 17, 63 EPD Par. 42,673, 2 AD Cas. (BNA) 1476 (1st Cir. 1993). In addition, a person with obesity may have an underlying or resultant physiological disorder, such as hypertension or a thyroid disorder. A physiological disorder is an impairment. See 29 C.F.R. § 1630.2(h).[16]

(6) *Persons with One of These Conditions and an Impairment*—A person who has one or more of these characteristics or traits also may have other conditions that are physical or mental impairments. See Senate Report at 22; House Education and Labor Report at 52; House Judiciary Report at 28. Thus, a left-handed individual who has a heart condition has an impairment. Although left-handedness is not an impairment, heart disease is an impairment.

(d) **Contagion**—A contagious disease is an impairment.[17] The contagious nature of the disease does not, by itself, remove that condition from the protection of the ADA. In *School Bd. of Nassau County v. Arline*, 480 U.S. 273, 42 EPD Par. 36,791, 1 AD Cas. (BNA) 1026 (1987), the United States Supreme Court considered the case of an elementary school teacher who had been discharged because she had experienced a recurrence of tuberculosis. The Supreme Court found that the tuberculosis, which had affected the teacher's respiratory system, constituted an impairment. 480 U.S. at 281, 42 EPD at 45,635, 1 AD Cas. at 1029. In so doing, the Court rejected the argument that the contagious effects of a condition (i.e., the effects of the condition on others) could be distinguished from the effects of the condition on the carrier. 480 U.S. at 282, 42 EPD at 45,636, 1 AD Cas. at 1029-30.

The legislative history to the ADA expressly provides that infection with the Human Immunodeficiency Virus (HIV) is an impairment under the Act. Senate Report at 22; House Education and Labor Report at 51; House Judiciary Report at 28. Thus, for the purposes of the ADA, an individual with HIV infection has an impairment.[18]

---

[15] Investigators should be aware that medical experts sometimes use the term "morbid obesity" or "gross obesity" to mean the same thing as "severe obesity," i.e., body weight more than 100% over the norm.

The term "obesity" has been defined as "[t]he excessive accumulation of body fat. Except for heavily muscled persons, a body weight 20% over that in standard height-weight tables is arbitrarily considered obesity." The Merck Manual of Diagnosis and Therapy 981 (Robert Berkow ed., 16th ed. 1992).

[16] The mere presence of an impairment does not automatically mean that an individual has a disability. Whether severe obesity rises to the level of a disability will turn on whether the obesity substantially limits, has substantially limited, or is regarded as substantially limiting, a major life activity. "[E]xcept in rare circumstances, obesity is not considered a disabling impairment." 29 C.F.R. pt. 1630 app. § 1630.2(j).

[17] The fact that a contagious disease is an impairment does not automatically mean that it is a disability. To be a disability, an impairment must substantially limit (or have substantially limited or be regarded as substantially limiting) one or more major life activities. See 29 U.S.C. § 12102(2); see also 29 C.F.R. § 1630.2(g).

[18] An individual who has HIV infection, including asymptomatic HIV infection, has a disability covered under the ADA. See § 902.4(c)(1), infra; see also *Doe v. Kohn Nast & Graf*, 862 F. Supp. 1310, 1321, 3 AD Cas. (BNA) 879, 885 (E.D. Pa. 1994); *Doe v. District of Columbia*, 796 F. Supp. 559, 59 EPD Par. 41,656, 2 AD Cas. (BNA) 197 (D.D.C. 1992); Senate Report at 22; House Education and Labor Report at 52; House Judiciary Report at 28 n.18; Memorandum from Douglas W. Kmiec, Acting Assistant Attorney General, to Arthur B. Culvahouse, Jr., Counsel to President Reagan, 8 Fair Empl. Prac. Manual (BNA) No. 641, at 405:1 (Sept. 27, 1988); Federal Contract Compliance Manual App. 6D, 8 Fair Empl. Prac. Manual (BNA) No. 694, at 405:352 (Dec. 23, 1988).

(e) Voluntariness—Voluntariness is irrelevant when determining whether a condition constitutes an impairment. For example, an individual who develops lung cancer as a result of smoking has an impairment, notwithstanding the fact that some apparently volitional act of the individual may have caused the impairment. The cause of a condition has no effect on whether that condition is an impairment. See House Judiciary Report at 29 (noting that "[t]he cause of a disability is always irrelevant to the determination of disability"); see also *Cook v. Rhode Island Dep't of Mental Health, Retardation and Hosp.*, 10 F.3d 17, 63 EPD Par. 42,673, 2 AD Cas. (BNA) 1476 (1st Cir. 1993). Further, the voluntary use of a prosthetic device or other mitigating measure to correct or to lessen the effects of a condition also has no bearing on whether that condition is an impairment. See § 902.5, infra.

902.3 Major Life Activities

(a) General—For an impairment to rise to the level of a disability, it must substantially limit, have previously substantially limited, or be perceived as substantially limiting, one or more of a person's major life activities. There has been little controversy about what constitutes a major life activity. In most cases, courts have simply stated that an impaired activity is a major life activity. In general, major life activities "are those basic activities that the average person in the general population can perform with little or no difficulty." 29 C.F.R. pt. 1630 app. § 1630.2(i).

(b) Regulatory Definition—Commission regulations define the term "major life activities" to mean "functions such as caring for oneself, performing manual tasks, walking, seeing, hearing, speaking, breathing, learning, and working." 29 C.F.R. § 1630.2(i); see also Senate Report at 22; House Education and Labor Report at 52; House Judiciary Report at 28.

This list is not an exhaustive list of all major life activities. Instead, it is representative of the types of activities that are major life activities. Specific activities that are similar to the listed activities in terms of their impact on an individual's functioning, as compared to the average person, also may be major life activities. Thus, as the interpretive appendix to the regulations notes, "other major life activities include, but are not limited to, sitting, standing, lifting, [and] reaching." 29 C.F.R. pt. 1630 app. § 1630.2(i). Mental and emotional processes such as thinking, concentrating, and interacting with others are other examples of major life activities.[19]

(c) Judicial Interpretations—Courts interpreting the Rehabilitation Act of 1973 also have found that other activities constitute major life activities. Such major life activities include sitting and standing, *Oesterling v. Walters*, 760 F.2d 859, 861, 36 EPD Par. 35,201 at 37,485, 1 AD Cas. (BNA) 722, 723 (8th Cir. 1985); and reading, *Pridemore v. Rural Legal Aid Society*, 625 F. Supp. 1180, 1183-84, 40 EPD Par. 36,184 at 42,659, 2 AD Cas. (BNA) 382, 384 (S.D. Ohio 1985) (mild cerebral palsy affected, but did not substantially limit, plaintiff's ability to read); see also *DiPompo v. West Point Military Academy*, 708 F. Supp. 540, 549, 50 EPD Par. 39,182 at 58,435 (S.D.N.Y. 1989).

902.4 Substantially Limits

(a) General—Unlike the term "major life activities," the term "substantially limits" frequently requires extensive analysis. The term "substantially limits" is a comparative term that implies a degree of severity and duration. The primary focus here is on the extent to which an impairment restricts one or more of an individual's major life activities. A secondary factor that may affect the analysis is the duration of the impairment.[20]

When analyzing the degree of limitation, one must remember that the determination of whether an impairment substantially limits a major life activity can be made only with reference to a specific individual. The issue is whether an impairment substantially limits any of the major life activities of the person in question,

---

[19] Note, however, that an individual is not substantially limited in a major life activity unless (s)he is unable to perform the activity or is significantly restricted in performing the activity as compared to the average person in the general population. See 29 C.F.R. § 1630.2(j); see also § 902.4, infra.

[20] This section frequently refers to the term "substantially limits" in the present tense. These references are not meant to imply that the determination of whether an impairment is substantially limiting is relevant only to whether an individual meets the first part of the definition of "disability," i.e., actually has a physical or mental impairment that substantially limits a major life activity. This determination also is relevant to whether an individual has a record of such an impairment or is regarded as having such an impairment. The determination of whether an impairment is substantially limiting should be made without regard to mitigating measures. See § 902.5, infra.

not whether the impairment is substantially limiting in general. Thus, one must consider the extent to which an impairment restricts a specific individual's activities and the duration of that individual's impairment.

(b) Regulatory Definition—Commission regulations define the term "substantially limits" and outline factors to consider when determining whether an impairment substantially limits any of an individual's major life activities. In that respect, the regulations state,

> (1) The term "substantially limits" means:
>
> (i) Unable to perform a major life activity that the average person in the general population can perform; or
> (ii) Significantly restricted as to the condition, manner or duration under which an individual can perform a particular major life activity as compared to the condition, manner, or duration under which the average person in the general population can perform that same major life activity.
>
> (2) The following factors should be considered in determining whether an individual is substantially limited in a major life activity:
>
> (i) The nature and severity of the impairment;
> (ii) The duration or expected duration of the impairment; and
> (iii) The permanent or long term impact, or the expected permanent or long term impact of or resulting from the impairment.

29 C.F.R. § 1630.2(j).

As the regulations make clear, a determination of whether an impairment substantially limits any of an individual's major life activities depends upon the extent, duration, and impact of the impairment. The factors to consider when making this determination will be discussed in more detail below.

(c) Extent to Which an Impairment Restricts a Major Life Activity—An impairment is substantially limiting when it prevents an individual from performing a major life activity or when it significantly restricts the condition, manner, or duration under which an individual can perform a major life activity. 29 C.F.R. § 1630.2(j). The individual's ability to perform the major life activity must be restricted as compared to the ability of the average person in the general population to perform the activity. Id. The reference to the "average person" does not "imply a precise mathematical 'average.'" 29 C.F.R. pt. 1630 app. § 1630.2(j).

Example 1—CP has a permanent knee impairment that causes him pain when he walks for extended periods. He can walk for ten miles at a time without discomfort, but he experiences pain on the eleventh mile. CP's knee impairment does not substantially limit his ability to walk. The average person in the general population would not be able to walk for eleven miles without experiencing some discomfort.

Example 2—CP, who has sickle cell anemia, frequently experiences severe back and joint pain. As a result of the sickle cell disease, CP often cannot walk for more than very short distances. CP's impairment (sickle cell anemia) substantially limits his ability to walk. The average person in the general population can walk for more than very short distances. (Note that allegations of employment discrimination based on sickle cell anemia also may be covered by Title VII of the Civil Rights Act of 1964, 42 U.S.C. § 2000e. See EEOC Dec. No. 81-8, 1983 EEOC Decisions (CCH) Par. 6764 (Nov. 18, 1980).)

Further, the limitation must be substantial, rather than minor. Not every impairment affects an individual's life to the extent that it is a substantially limiting impairment. A minor impairment, such as an infected finger, is not a disability. Senate Report at 23; House Education and Labor Report at 52.

Most of the discussion and analysis of the concept of substantial limitation has focused on its meaning as applied to the major life activity of working. This is largely because there has been little dispute about what is meant by such terms as "breathing," "walking," "hearing," or "seeing" but much dispute about what is meant by the term "working." Consequently, the determination of whether a person's impairment is substantially limiting should first address major life activities other than working. If it is clear that a person's impairment substantially limits a major life activity other than working, then one need not determine whether the impairment substantially limits the person's ability to work. See 29 C.F.R. pt. 1630 app. § 1630.2(j). On the other hand, if an impairment does not substantially limit any of the other major life activities, then one must determine whether the person is substantially limited in working. See id.

For example, if an individual's arthritis makes it unusually difficult (as compared to most people or to the average person in the general population) to walk, then the individual is substantially limited in the ability to walk. In that case, one would not need to ascertain whether the individual is also substantially limited in working. If, however, it was not clear whether the person's impairment substantially limited his/her ability to walk (or to perform other major life activities), then one would have to analyze whether the impairment substantially limited the person's ability to work.

(1) *Substantial Limitation of Major Life Activities Generally*—In most cases, a careful, case-by-case analysis is necessary to determine whether an impairment substantially limits any of a person's major life activities. This analysis focuses on the individual in question and analyzes whether the individual's impairment is substantially limiting for that individual.

The key here is the extent to which the impairment restricts a major life activity. If there is no showing that the impairment significantly restricts a major life activity, then the impairment is not a disability. Thus, an individual who alleged that he had asthma but did not even assert that the asthma substantially limited a major life activity did not establish that he was an individual with a disability. *Harris v. Adams*, 873 F.2d 929, 933, 50 EPD Par. 38,973 at 57,217, 1 AD Cas. (BNA) 1475, 1477 (6th Cir. 1989). Similarly, an employee failed to establish that he was an individual with a disability when he presented no credible evidence to establish that his sinusitis and hypertension substantially limited major life activities. *Thomas v. General Services Administration*, 49 Fair Empl. Prac. Cas. (BNA) 1602, 1607, 51 EPD Par. 39,221 at 58,685 (D.D.C. 1989).

The investigator, therefore, should conduct a careful analysis of whether a charging party's impairment substantially limits one or more major life activities. The investigator should conduct this analysis even if the charging party does not make a specific allegation that his/her impairment is substantially limiting. (For guidance on how to conduct this analysis, refer to the suggestions for investigators at the end of this subsection, infra.)

> *Example*—CP alleges that her employer discriminated against her on the basis of disability. She defines her disability as a "knee injury." When the investigator asks how the injury affects her, CP responds, "I don't know." She provides no information in response to the investigator's inquiries about the extent to which the injury restricts her ability to walk or to perform any other activities. There is no showing that the knee injury limits CP in any way. As a result, there is no evidence that CP's knee injury substantially limits one or more of her major life activities.

To rise to the level of a disability, an impairment must significantly restrict an individual's major life activities. Impairments that result in only mild limitations are not disabilities. Thus, a mild case of varicose veins that moderately affect an individual's ability to stand and to sit is not a disability. *Oesterling v. Walters*, 760 F.2d 859, 861, 36 EPD Par. 35,201 at 37,485, 1 AD Cas. (BNA) 722, 723-24 (8th Cir. 1985). Similarly, a "borderline" case of cerebral palsy that only slightly interferes with an individual's ability to read (because of poor control over ocular muscles) and to speak also is not a disability. *Pridemore v. Rural Legal Aid Society*, 625 F. Supp. 1180, 1183-84, 40 EPD Par. 36,184 at 42,659, 2 AD Cas. (BNA) 382, 384 (S.D. Ohio 1985). In both instances, impairments may affect major life activities, but they do not substantially restrict those activities.

One of the reasons an individualized approach is necessary is because the same types of impairments often vary in severity and often restrict different people to different degrees or in different ways.

> The determination of whether an individual has a disability is not necessarily based on the name or diagnosis of the impairment the person has, but rather on the effect of that impairment on the life of the individual. Some impairments may be disabling for particular individuals but not for others, depending on the stage of the disease or disorder, the presence of other impairments that combine to make the impairment disabling or any number of other factors.

29 C.F.R. pt. 1630 app. § 1630.2(j). For example, the plaintiff in *Perez v. Philadelphia Housing Authority*, 677 F. Supp. 357, 1 AD Cas. (BNA) 1170 (E.D. Pa. 1987), aff'd, 841 F.2d 1120, 2 AD Cas. (BNA) 1104 (3d Cir. 1988), sustained a back injury that resulted in considerable pain. The evidence indicated that the plaintiff's back pain restricted "her ability to walk, sit, stand, drive, care for her home and child, and engage in leisure pastimes." 677 F. Supp. at 360, 1 AD Cas. at 1173. As a result, the court found that the plaintiff was an individual with a disability. 677 F. Supp. at 360-61, 1 AD Cas. at 1173. In another case, however, a court determined that a general laborer who had sustained a back injury was not an individual with a disability. *Fuqua v. Unisys Corp.*, 716 F. Supp. 1201 (D. Minn. 1989) (applying state law similar to Rehabilitation Act). The plaintiff in that case had been able to continue an active life that included weight lift-

ing and other recreational activities. *Id.* at 1203. In addition, he had obtained alternative employment as a security guard and had not been significantly restricted in employment. *Id.* Accordingly, the court found that the plaintiff's back injury did not rise to the level of a disability. *Id.* at 1206.

> *Example 1*—CP has a mild form of Type II, non-insulin-dependent diabetes. She does not need to take insulin or other medication, and her physician has placed no significant restrictions on her activities. Instead, her physician simply has advised CP to maintain a well balanced diet and to reduce her consumption of foods that are high in sugar or starch. Although diabetes often substantially limits an individual's major life activities, CP's diabetes does not substantially limit any of her major life activities. It has only a moderate effect on what she eats, and it does not restrict her in any other way.

> *Example 2*—Same as Example 1, above, except CP's condition requires CP to follow a strict regimen. She must adhere to a stringent diet, eat meals on a regular schedule, and ensure a proper balance between her caloric intake and her level of physical activity. A change of routine, such as a high-calorie meal or unexpected strenuous exercise, could result in blood-sugar levels that are dangerously high or low. CP's condition significantly restricts how she functions in her day-to-day life. CP, therefore, has an impairment (diabetes) that substantially limits one or more of her major life activities.

In very rare instances, impairments are so severe that there is no doubt that they substantially limit major life activities. In those cases, it is undisputed that the complainant is an individual with a disability. Thus, courts accepted without discussion that a person was an individual with a disability when the impairment was insulin-dependent diabetes, *Bentivegna v. United States Department of Labor*, 694 F.2d 619, 621, 30 EPD Par. 33,211 at 27,791, 1 AD Cas. (BNA) 403, 405 (9th Cir. 1982); legal blindness, *Norcross v. Sneed*, 755 F.2d 113, 36 EPD Par. 35,006, 1 AD Cas. (BNA) 689 (8th Cir. 1985); deafness, *Davis v. Frank*, 711 F. Supp. 447, 453, 50 EPD Par. 39,157 at 58,339 (N.D. Ill. 1989), manic depressive syndrome, *Gardner v. Morris*, 752 F.2d 1271, 35 EPD Par. 34,906, 1 AD Cas. (BNA) 673 (8th Cir. 1985), and alcoholism, *Whitlock v. Donovan*, 598 F. Supp. 126, 129, 35 EPD Par. 34,815 at 35,533, 1 AD Cas. (BNA) 630, 632 (D.D.C. 1984), aff'd sub nom. *Whitlock v. Brock*, 790 F.2d 964, 1 AD Cas. (BNA) 1050 (D.C. Cir. 1986). Further, according to the legislative history, an individual who has HIV infection (including asymptomatic HIV infection) is an individual with a disability. Senate Report at 22; House Education and Labor Report at 52; House Judiciary Report at 28 n.18; see also *Doe v. Kohn Nast & Graf*, 862 F. Supp. 1310, 1321, 3 AD Cas. (BNA) 879, 885 (E.D. Pa. 1994); *Doe v. District of Columbia*, 796 F. Supp. 559, 59 EPD Par. 41,656, 2 AD Cas. (BNA) 197 (D.D.C. 1992); Memorandum from Douglas W. Kmiec, Acting Assistant Attorney General, to Arthur B. Culvahouse, Jr., Counsel to President Reagan, 8 Fair Empl. Prac. Manual (BNA) No. 641, at 405:1 (Sept. 27, 1988); Federal Contract Compliance Manual App. 6D, 8 Fair Empl. Prac. Manual (BNA) No. 694, at 405:352 (Dec. 23, 1988).

Just as medical documentation submitted by a charging party is relevant to determining whether the charging party has an impairment, see supra § 902.2(b), it also is a good starting point for determining the extent to which a physical or mental impairment limits any of the charging party's major life activities. Such documentation often describes the restrictions that the impairment places on the charging party. For example, the documentation may state that the charging party cannot lift objects weighing more than a few pounds, cannot walk unassisted, or cannot hear at all. On the other hand, the documentation may state that the charging party's impairment results in only minimal limitations. The investigator should ask the charging party for copies of medical statements that describe the charging party's restrictions. In addition, the investigator should ask the respondent for copies of relevant medical documentation in the respondent's possession. Such documentation may include medical information that accompanied a request for light or limited duty as well as information obtained through fitness-for-duty examinations conducted or ordered by the respondent. If the investigator requests the information directly from a third party, rather than from the charging party or the respondent, then the investigator should obtain a signed medical release from the charging party and should submit the release with the request.

Although medical documentation can provide important information about the restrictions that an impairment places on an individual, the investigator should not rely solely on this information. The investigator should obtain other available relevant information that describes the restrictions resulting from the impairment. In this regard, it is essential that the investigator obtain a statement in which the charging party describes the nature of his/her condition and explains how the condition limits his/her performance of major life activities. In addition, the investigator should obtain statements from other persons who have direct knowledge of the individual's restrictions. For example, persons such as friends and family members, supervisors, rehabilitation counselors, and occupational or physical therapists may be able to describe the restrictions that the individual's impairment places on the individual. Further, the investigator's own observations of the charging party may supply or confirm information about the charging party's restrictions.

The information that the investigator obtains should be specific. For example, it is insufficient for the charging party merely to state that his/her condition interferes with the ability to walk. The charging party should explain the extent of the interference; that is, the charging party should provide such information as whether the condition prevents him/her from walking at all, whether (s)he can walk under certain conditions, and whether (s)he can walk for short or long distances and periods.

(2) *Substantial Limitation of Major Life Activity of Working*—As noted previously, supra, one need not determine whether an impairment substantially limits an individual's ability to work if the impairment substantially limits another major life activity. If the individual is not substantially limited with respect to any other major life activity, then one should consider whether the individual is substantially limited in working.

The Commission has provided regulatory guidance for determining whether an impairment substantially limits an individual in the major life activity of working. The regulation states,

> (3) With respect to the major life activity of working—
>
> (i) The term *substantially limits* means significantly restricted in the ability to perform either a class of jobs or a broad range of jobs in various classes as compared to the average person having comparable training, skills and abilities. The inability to perform a single, particular job does not constitute a substantial limitation in the major life activity of working.
>
> (ii) In addition to the factors listed in paragraph (j)(2) of this section, the following factors may be considered in determining whether an individual is substantially limited in the major life activity of "working":
>
> (A) The geographical area to which the individual has reasonable access;
>
> (B) The job from which the individual has been disqualified because of an impairment, and the number and types of jobs utilizing similar training, knowledge, skills or abilities, within that geographical area, from which the individual is also disqualified because of the impairment (class of jobs); and/or
>
> (C) The job from which the individual has been disqualified because of an impairment, and the number and types of other jobs not utilizing similar training, knowledge, skills or abilities, within that geographical area, from which the individual is also disqualified because of the impairment (broad range of jobs in various classes).

29 C.F.R. § 1630.2(j)(3) (emphasis in the original).

As the regulation makes clear, an impairment that prevents an individual from working at one particular job, because of circumstances or materials unique to that job, does not substantially limit that individual's ability to work. See House Judiciary Report at 29. A person is not substantially limited in the ability to work simply because (s)he cannot perform one particular job for one particular employer. See *E.E. Black, Ltd. v. Marshall*, 497 F. Supp. 1088, 1099, 24 EPD Par. 31,260 at 17,650, 1 AD Cas. (BNA) 220, 229 (D. Hawaii 1980). Rather, an individual is substantially limited in working if (s)he is prevented or significantly restricted (when compared to the average person having similar qualifications) from performing a class of jobs or a wide range of various jobs. See *id.;* see also 29 C.F.R. § 1630.2(j)(3).

In *E.E. Black*, an apprentice carpenter was denied employment after a preemployment physical examination disclosed a congenital back anomaly. The court held that the term "substantial limitation" means more than an inability to perform one particular job but less than a general inability to work. It suggested that the evaluation of whether an individual is substantially limited in working focus on such factors as the number and type of jobs from which the individual is disqualified and the geographical area to which the individual has reasonable access. 497 F. Supp. at 1099-1101, 24 EPD at 17,650-52, 1 AD Cas. at 229-30.

These criteria, when read together, indicate that an impairment is a substantial limitation to working if it disqualifies an individual from a class of jobs or a broad range of jobs in various classes. For example, a charging party is substantially limited in working if (s)he has a back impairment that precludes him/her from heavy lifting and, therefore, from the class of heavy labor jobs. See 497 F. Supp. at 1102, 24 EPD at 17,652, 1 AD Cas. at 231. Conversely, a postal clerk with a mild case of crossed eyes that caused him to develop eye strain and headaches after operating a particular machine that required detailed eye work was not substantially limited in working. *Jasany v. United States Postal Service*, 755 F.2d 1244, 1250, 36 EPD Par. 35,070 at 36,835, 1 AD Cas. (BNA) 706, 710 (6th Cir. 1985). Unlike the charging party in the first example, this complainant did not have an impairment that precluded him from performing any other job or duty within a class of jobs. In fact, the parties agreed that his impairment had not affected his past work history or his ability to perform other duties at the post office. *Id.* The impairment had limited only his ability to perform this one particular job and perhaps a narrow range of like jobs. For the same reason, an individual whose vision impairment and high-tone hearing loss disqualified him from a position as a detention deputy but did not disqualify him from other positions (e.g., corrections officer) was not substantially limited in working. See *State v. Hennepin County*, 441 N.W.2d 106, 51 EPD Par. 39,383, 1 AD Cas. (BNA) 1490 (Minn. 1989) (applying state law with same definition of "disability").

Example 1—CP is a computer programmer. She develops a vision impairment that does not substantially limit her ability to see but does prevent her from distinguishing characters on computer screens (without reasonable accommodation). As a result, she cannot perform any work that requires her to read characters on computer screens. Her vision impairment prevents her from working as a computer programmer, a systems analyst, a computer instructor, and a computer operator. CP is substantially limited in working because her impairment prevents her from working in the class of jobs requiring use of a computer.

Example 2—Same as Example 1, above, except CP's vision impairment does not interfere with her ability to distinguish characters on most computer screens. It does prevent her, however, from distinguishing characters on the peculiar type of computer screens that R uses. Although CP cannot work with the unique screens that R uses, she can work with other computer screens. CP, therefore, is not substantially limited in working. Her impairment prevents her from being a computer programmer for one particular employer (R), but it does not prevent her from performing similar jobs for other employers.

Impairments that preclude an individual from performing a broad range of jobs in various classes also may substantially limit the major life activity of working. For example, an individual could be substantially limited in working if (s)he has a severe allergy to a substance found in many high-rise office buildings. If the allergy prevents the individual from working in many of the high-rise office buildings in the geographical area to which the individual has reasonable access, then the individual is substantially limited in working. This is so because a great number of positions within many classes of jobs would be performed in those buildings. 29 C.F.R. pt. 1630 app. § 1630.2(j).

By contrast, a severe allergy to the peculiar type or amount of dust found within one office is not an impairment that substantially limits the ability to work. *Wright v. Tisch*, 45 Fair Empl. Prac. Cas. (BNA) 151, 1 AD Cas. (BNA) 1157 (E.D. Va. 1987). In Wright, the court determined that a complainant's inability to tolerate the dusty environment in the unit where she worked did not constitute a disability. 45 Fair Empl. Prac. Cas. at 152-53, 1 AD Cas. at 1158. The court noted that none of the complainant's other work activities was affected by her allergy. 45 Fair Empl. Prac. Cas. at 152, 1 AD Cas. at 1158. It also noted that the complainant's allergy did not restrict her from working in other offices with dust and that she had, in fact, worked in the presence of dust in other offices within the agency. *Id.*

Example 1—CP has a hearing impairment that only mildly affects his ability to hear. The impairment, however, makes CP extremely sensitive to very loud noises. CP experiences severe pain when he is exposed to loud noises for more than a brief period. Because of this sensitivity, CP cannot work in environments where noise levels routinely exceed a certain decibel level. As a result, R refused to hire CP for a welder's position. Further, CP could not work in carpentry or auto repair shops and could not be a heavy equipment operator, a demolitions expert, or a member of an airport ground crew. CP's impairment, therefore, prevents CP from working in a broad range of jobs in various classes. Accordingly, CP has an impairment that substantially limits his ability to work.

Example 2—CP has a hearing impairment that does not significantly restrict his ability to hear but does make him very sensitive to sound at one particular pitch. CP works on an assembly line at an automobile plant in an area that has several such plants. His employer has installed a new conveyor belt that has a unique whistle that sounds approximately every ten minutes, every time the conveyor belt stops and starts. CP experiences severe pain in his ears whenever the whistle sounds. As a result, CP can no longer work at that plant. CP's impairment, however, does not substantially limit his ability to work. Although the impairment prevents him from performing this particular job for this particular employer, it does not prevent him from performing similar jobs for other employers in his geographical area.

Example 3—CP has an impairment that requires radiation therapy, which results in an abnormal rate or degree of exhaustion. CP becomes very tired very easily and cannot engage in continuous activity for long periods. Assume that CP's impairment does not substantially limit her ability to perform any major life activity other than working. As a result of the impairment, however, CP cannot work more than four hours per day. This prevents CP from working in all jobs requiring full-time work. Since those jobs constitute a wide range of jobs in various classes, CP is substantially limited in working. (A reasonable accommodation of a part-time or modified work schedule might enable CP to work in a number of jobs from which she otherwise would be excluded. When determining whether an impairment is substantially limiting, however, one does not consider the ameliorative effects of reasonable accommodation or other mitigating measures. See § 902.5, infra.)

As the Commission's regulation notes, a number of factors may help to determine whether an individual is substantially limited in working. 29 C.F.R. § 1630.2(j)(3)(ii). Although a showing with respect to each factor is not a required element of proof, information relating to the factors is relevant to whether an individual is significantly restricted in the ability to perform a class of jobs or a broad range of jobs in various classes. Thus, information about the geographical area to which an individual has access and the number and types of jobs from which an individual is disqualified because of his/her impairment may be considered when determining whether an impairment substantially limits the individual's ability to work. See *id.*

The reference to the "number and types" of jobs is not meant to require an onerous evidentiary showing. 29 C.F.R. pt. 1630 app. § 1630.2(j). The reference does not mean that an individual must identify the exact number of jobs using similar or dissimilar skills in a certain geographic area. Further, the reference does not mean that an individual must count positions or otherwise present a precise number of jobs from which (s)he is disqualified because of an impairment. Instead, the reference to the "number and types" of jobs "only require[s] the presentation of evidence of general employment demographics and/or of recognized occupational classifications that indicate the approximate number of jobs (e.g., 'few,' 'many,' 'most') from which an individual would be excluded because of an impairment." Id. Furthermore, in cases where it is clear that an individual is excluded from a class of jobs or a broad range of jobs in various classes, only minimal evidence will be required.

An assessment of whether an impairment substantially limits an individual's ability to work focuses on whether the individual is significantly restricted in the ability to perform a class of jobs or a broad range of jobs in various classes as compared to the average person having comparable training, skills, and abilities. 29 C.F.R. § 1630.2(j)(3)(i). For example, suppose that an individual has an impairment that interferes with his/her ability to work in the class of clerical jobs. The individual is substantially limited in working if (s)he is significantly restricted in performing clerical work as compared to the average person having comparable clerical skills. Thus, if the individual has clerical skills and training and the impairment prevents him/her from performing many of the clerical jobs that the average person with comparable clerical skills can perform, then the individual is substantially limited in working. On the other hand, if the individual wants to work as a clerk but has no clerical skills or training, then (s)he is substantially limited in working only if the impairment significantly restricts his/her ability to work in the clerical class as compared to the ability of the average person with a similar lack of clerical skills. (It is likely in that case that the average person with a lack of clerical skills can perform only a limited number of clerical jobs and that the individual is not significantly restricted when compared to the average person.)

The investigator often can begin to obtain information relevant to a determination of whether the charging party's impairment significantly restricts his/her ability to perform either a class of jobs or a broad range of jobs in various classes from: a position description of the job at issue, the respondent's explanation of the requirements of the job, and the charging party's description of his/her qualifications and his/her experience in similar positions. This information, which helps to identify the skills relevant to the job, may be useful in identifying other jobs using similar or dissimilar skills. In addition, the investigator should attempt to determine the number and types of jobs in the geographical area from which the charging party is disqualified because of the impairment. Information about other jobs where the charging party has worked, or for which the charging party has or has not applied, may be relevant to this inquiry. For example, other employers may have refused to employ the charging party because of his/her impairment, or the charging party may not have applied for certain jobs because the impairment disqualified him/her from those jobs. Similarly, an employment agency or an employment counselor may have told the charging party that the impairment prevents him/her from working in certain jobs. On the other hand, the fact that the charging party performed certain jobs successfully may indicate that the impairment—if it existed at the time that the charging party performed those jobs—does not disqualify him/her from that type of work.[21]

(d) Duration and Impact of Impairment—One of the factors that may be relevant to whether an impairment is substantially limiting is the duration of the impairment. The length of time that an impairment affects major life activities may help to determine whether the impairment substantially limits those activities. As with all other matters, the determination must be made on a case-by-case basis. There are no set time limits for determining whether an impairment is of sufficient duration to be considered substantially limiting. There are, however, a few basic guidelines.

Generally, conditions that last for only a few days or weeks and have no permanent or long-term effects on an individual's health are not substantially limiting impairments. Examples of such transitory conditions are common colds, influenza, and most broken bones and sprains. The mere fact that an individual may have required absolute bed rest or hospitalization for such a condition does not alter the transitory nature of the condition. Even the necessity of surgery, without more, is not sufficient to raise a short-term condition to the level of a disability. Thus, for example, an employee who had an undisclosed temporary illness that required exploratory surgery but who was expected to recover completely in six to eight weeks did not have an impairment that substantially limited major life activities. *Stevens v. Stubbs*, 576 F. Supp. 1409, 1 AD Cas. (BNA) 546 (N.D. Ga. 1983). In that case, a temporary illness with no permanent effects on the individual's health was not a substantially limiting impairment. 576 F. Supp. at 1414, 1 AD Cas. at 549-50. Similarly, an employee who incurred a knee injury that required surgery was not an individual with a disability. *Evans v. City of Dallas*, 861 F.2d 846, 49 EPD Par. 38,674, 1 AD Cas. (BNA) 1394 (5th Cir. 1988). Although the injury may have limited the employee's major life activities during his recuperation, it did not continue to do so after his recuperation. See 861 F.2d at 852-53, 49 EPD at 55,700, 1 AD Cas. at 1398-99 (quoting district court opinion). For the same reason, an attack of appendicitis accompanied by a "routine" appendectomy would not constitute a disability. The condition might restrict an individual's activities for a few days or weeks, but the restrictions would be only temporary.

> *Example 1*—CP has laryngitis. It is very painful for her to speak, and she cannot talk above a whisper when she does speak. Her physician has prescribed medication for her, has instructed her to drink plenty of fluids, and has advised her to stay home from work. She should be fully recovered within seven to ten days. CP does not have a disability. Although the laryngitis significantly restricts her ability to speak, it does so only on a very short-term basis and has no long-lasting or permanent effects on CP.

> *Example 2*—CP sustains a compound fracture of her arm and must undergo surgery to set the bone. She is hospitalized for one week and will have a cast on her arm for five additional weeks. During these six weeks, CP must wear a sling and must keep her arm immobilized. She will have full use of her arm after the cast is removed. CP's broken arm is not a disability. Instead, it is a short-term, temporary impairment with no long-lasting or permanent effects.

Although short-term, temporary restrictions generally are not substantially limiting, an impairment does not necessarily have to be permanent to rise to the level of a disability. Some conditions may be long-term, or potentially long-term, in that their duration is indefinite and unknowable or is expected to be at least several months. Such conditions, if severe, may constitute disabilities. Thus, a person who has been blinded or paralyzed but is expected to recover fully "eventually" is an individual with a disability,

---

[21] If the charging party does not have an impairment that substantially limits his or her ability to work (or to perform any other major life activity), then the investigator should determine whether the charging party has a record of such an impairment (see § 902.7, infra) or is regarded as having such an impairment (see § 902.8, infra). An individual who in fact does not have an impairment that substantially limits the major life activity of working nonetheless may be regarded as having such an impairment (see § 902.8(f), infra).

despite the prognosis for full recovery at some indeterminable time in the future.

Example 1—CP has nodes on his vocal chords. His doctor has told CP that he must rest his vocal chords and that he will lose his ability to speak unless he refrains from talking for more than one hour per day for the next one-and-one-half years. If CP follows his doctor's advice, his vocal chords will heal and he will have full use of his voice. CP, whose impairment will last for many months and will significantly restrict his ability to speak during that time, has a disability.

Example 2—CP recently was released from the hospital following a ten-month stay for treatment for a mood disorder. The disorder significantly restricted CP's ability to interact with people and to care for herself. She will require two months of daily treatment, on an out-patient basis, to ensure that she can deal with people on a day-to-day basis and then four to six months of less intensive out-patient treatment. Her doctor anticipates that CP will be fully recovered when she completes her treatment. CP has a disability. Although her impairment (a mood disorder) is not permanent, it is long lasting and has significantly restricted her major life activities for an extended period (at least ten months during her hospitalization and possibly for the two months of intensive out-patient treatment).

Example 3—CP recently was diagnosed as having Guillain-Barre syndrome, a neurological disorder of unknown origin. As a result of the condition, she cannot walk. Her doctor has told her that she must undergo extensive rehabilitation and that the rehabilitation period will last for several months. The doctor tells CP that there is a good chance that she will regain total use of her legs after she completes her rehabilitation. CP has a disability because she has an impairment (Guillain-Barre syndrome) that substantially limits her ability to walk. The impairment prevents CP from walking, and it will be at least several months before she will be able to walk again. Although CP is expected to recover at some point in the future, her restrictions are significant and long-lasting.

Example 4—CP fractured her left ankle as the result of a skiing accident. Immediately after the accident, she underwent surgery on her ankle. She was hospitalized for one week and has been using crutches for two weeks. Her physician has directed her to use crutches for another two weeks, after which time she should be able to walk unaided. Her prognosis for a full recovery is excellent. CP does not have an impairment that substantially limits her major life activities. Although her ankle injury has restricted her ability to walk, it has done so for only a relatively short time (five weeks). The injury is a transitory impairment that has no long-term effects on CP.

Example 5—Same as Example 4, above, except the surgery was not successful. Although CP can now walk unaided, she can do so only for three to five minutes without experiencing excruciating pain. Her physician predicts that CP's condition, which may improve at some point in the future, will remain like this indefinitely. CP has an ankle impairment that substantially limits her ability to walk. Most people can walk for three to five minutes without pain. Although the condition may not be permanent, it is long-term. CP is an individual with a disability.

Sometimes a temporary impairment that usually is not substantially limiting because it generally heals within a few weeks will take longer than the normal healing period to heal. In that case, the impairment may be substantially limiting if it goes on for a long period and significantly restricts the performance of a major life activity during that time. Thus, an impairment that takes significantly longer than the normal healing period to heal and prevents or significantly restricts the performance of a major life activity for an extended time during the healing process is a disability.

Example—CP sustains a broken leg. Although broken legs generally heal within a few months, CP's leg will require eleven months to heal. CP will be unable to walk without the use of crutches during the eleven-month healing period. CP, whose impairment will take significantly longer than the normal healing period to heal and will significantly restrict CP's ability to perform a major life activity (walking) during the healing period, has a disability.

In some cases, an impairment that appears to be temporary may have residual effects. That is, the impairment may have a long-term impact on an individual's ability to perform one or more major life activities. For example, a person may sustain an injury that heals but nonetheless leaves a permanent or long-term residual effect. Although a short-term impairment that does not have a long-lasting impact is not a disability, an impairment that results in a long-term, substantial limitation is a disability.

Example 1—CP sustained a head injury in an automobile accident. He felt dizzy and disoriented immediately after the accident and was hospitalized overnight for observation. His doctor told him that x-rays revealed a slight concussion but no permanent injury. He was released from the hospital the next day, and he has experienced no side effects from the injury. CP's head injury was not substantially limiting. The impairment lasted for only a brief time and had no permanent or long-term impact on CP's major life activities. CP, therefore, does not have a disability.

Example 2—Same as Example 1, above, except CP sustained a serious concussion that resulted in permanent brain damage. Because of this, CP has a short-term memory deficit, has trouble processing information, cannot concentrate, and has great difficulty learning. CP's concussion resulted in long-term, significant restrictions on his major life activities. CP, therefore, has a disability.

Further, some chronic conditions may constitute substantially limiting impairments. Such conditions may be substantially limiting when active or may have a high likelihood of recurrence in substantially limiting forms. In addition, such conditions may require a substantial limitation of a major life activity to prevent or to lessen the likelihood or severity of recurrence. Some severe back problems and most forms of heart disease and cancer fall into this category. This category also includes illnesses, such as tuberculosis, that may lay dormant for long periods but can reemerge at any time in a substantially limiting manner. Similarly, episodic disorders, such as bipolar disorder, which remit and then intensify also fall into this category.

Finally, the duration of an impairment does not, by itself, determine whether the impairment substantially limits an individual's major life activities. It is just one factor to be considered with all of the other relevant information. An impairment may be long lasting or permanent but still not constitute a substantial limitation to major life activities. For example, a permanently injured finger is not substantially limiting if it does not significantly restrict an individual's ability to perform a major life activity such as performing manual tasks or caring for oneself. Thus, when determining whether an impairment substantially limits a major life activity, one must consider the severity of the limitation caused by the impairment as well as the duration of the limitation. An impairment is substantially limiting if it lasts for more than several months and significantly restricts the performance of one or more major life activities during that time. It is not substantially limiting if it lasts for only a brief time or does not significantly restrict an individual's ability to perform a major life activity.

In sum, relatively brief and transitory illnesses or injuries that have no permanent or long-term effects on an individual's major life activities are not disabilities. Temporary impairments may be disabilities if they take significantly longer than normal to heal and significantly restrict the performance of major life activities during the healing period. Similarly, long-term impairments, or potentially long-term impairments of indefinite duration, may be disabilities if they are severe. Chronic conditions that are substantially limiting when active, and conditions with a high likelihood of recurrence in substantially limiting form, also are disabilities.

Because the duration of an impairment may be relevant to determining whether the impairment is a disability, the investigator should ask the charging party how long (s)he has had the impairment at issue. In addition, the investigator should obtain copies of any available medical documentation that indicates the length of time the charging party has had the impairment, describes the long-term effects of the impairment, or gives a prognosis for recovery.

(e) Multiple Impairments—An individual may have two or more impairments that are not substantially limiting by themselves but that together substantially limit one or more major life activities. In that situation, the individual has a disability. "Multiple impairments that combine to substantially limit one or more of an individual's major life activities also constitute a disability." 29 C.F.R. pt. 1630 app. § 1630.2(j).

Example—CP has a mild form of arthritis in her wrists and hands and a mild form of osteoporosis (a reduction in bone quantity). Neither impairment, by itself, would significantly restrict any of CP's major life activities. Together, however, the two impairments affect CP's manual dexterity to such an extent that they significantly restrict her ability to perform manual tasks. Thus, the combination of the two impairments substantially limits one or more of CP's major life activities. CP, therefore, has a disability.

902.5 Mitigating Measures—The determination of whether a condition constitutes an impairment must be made without regard to mitigating measures. 29 C.F.R. pt. 1630 app. § 1630.2(h). The availability of reasonable accommodation or auxiliary aids such as hearing aids to alleviate the effects of a condition has no bearing on whether the condition is an impairment. It is the scope or perceived scope of the condition itself, not its origin or capacity for being corrected, that determines whether a particular condition is an impairment.

Further, the extent to which the impairment limits the individual's major life activities should be assessed without regard to the availability of mitigating measures. 29 C.F.R. pt. 1630 app. § 1630.2(j); see also Senate Report at 23; House Education and Labor Report at 52; House Judiciary Report at 28. Thus, an individual who has experienced a significant loss of hearing is substantially limited in his/her ability to hear, even if the use of a hearing aid would improve the individual's level of hearing. House Education and Labor Report at 52; see also House Judiciary Report at 28-29. Similarly, individuals with impairments (such as epilepsy or diabetes) that substantially limit major life activities are individuals with disabilities, even if medication controls the effects of the impairments. House Education and Labor Report at 52; see also House Judiciary Report at 28-29. Accordingly, an individual who received dialysis treatments for polycystic kidney disease had a substantially limiting impairment, even though the disease was adequately treated through dialysis. *Gilbert v. Frank*, 949 F.2d 637, 641, 57 EPD Par. 41,106 at 68,909, 2 AD Cas. (BNA) 60, 63 (2d Cir. 1991) ("We are inclined to view persons whose kidneys would cease to function without mechanical assistance, or whose kidneys do not function sufficiently to rid their bodies of waste matter without regular dialysis, as substantially limited in their ability to care for themselves.")

Example 1—CP, who has schizophrenia, takes medication to control the disorder. With medication, CP can function well in his everyday life. Without medication, however, CP cannot care for himself. CP has an impairment, schizophrenia, that substantially limits his major life activities. Although CP can function well with medication, he cannot care for himself without medication.

Example 2—CP has systemic lupus, which often results in acute anemia and arthritis-like symptoms. CP's physician has prescribed medication to control the effects of the disease. Without medication, CP is very lethargic, develops a skin rash, and experiences severe swelling and stiffness in her joints. With medication, CP experiences none of these symptoms. CP has a disability. Her impairment, when evaluated without regard to the effects of medication, substantially limits her major life activities.

Example 3—CP's right leg was amputated below the knee. Using a prosthesis, he can walk for a long distance without discomfort. CP has an impairment that substantially limits his ability to walk, even though he can walk with the use of a prosthesis. CP is an individual with a disability.

Note, finally, that the mere use of a mitigating measure does not automatically indicate the presence of a disability. Some individuals may use medication, prosthetic devices, or auxiliary aids to alleviate impairments that are not substantially limiting. For example, an individual who uses a hearing aid to correct a slight hearing impairment may not have a disability under the first part of the definition of the term "disability." The individual's impairment may only mildly affect his/her hearing and may not substantially limit the individual's ability to hear.

902.6 Statutory Exceptions to the Definition of "Disability"—The statute specifies that certain conditions are not disabilities covered by the ADA. Since homosexuality and bisexuality are not impairments, those conditions are not disabilities. 42 U.S.C. § 12211(a); see also 29 C.F.R. § 1630.3(e). In addition, "the term 'individual with a disability' does not include an individual who is currently engaging in the illegal use of drugs, when the covered entity acts on the basis of such use." 42 U.S.C. § 12210(a); see also 29 C.F.R. § 1630.3(a). Further, the term "disability" does not include

(1) transvestism, transsexualism, pedophilia, exhibitionism, voyeurism, gender identity disorders not resulting from physical impairments, or other sexual behavior disorders;
(2) compulsive gambling, kleptomania, or pyromania; or
(3) psychoactive substance use disorders resulting from current illegal use of drugs.

42 U.S.C. § 12211(b); see also 29 C.F.R. § 1630.3(d).

The term "illegal use of drugs" refers to drugs whose possession or distribution is unlawful under the Controlled Substances Act, 21 U.S.C. § 812.[22] It "does not include the use of a drug taken under supervision by a licensed health care professional, or other uses authorized by the Controlled Substances Act or

---

[22] Medications required by law to be prescribed by licensed health care professionals are not necessarily "controlled substances." "Controlled substances" are those which are addictive or have potential for abuse and which are listed on Schedules I-V of the Controlled Substances Act. Many prescription medications, therefore, are not "controlled substances."

other provision of Federal law." 42 U.S.C. §§ 12111(6)(A), 12110(d)(1); see also 29 C.F.R. § 1630.3(a)(2). The term does include, however, the unlawful use of prescription controlled substances. 29 C.F.R. pt. 1630 app. § 1630.3(a)-(c).

The reference to a person "currently engaging" in the illegal use of drugs does not mean that this exclusion is limited to a person who illegally used drugs "on the day of, or within a matter of days or weeks before, the employment action in question." Id. Rather, the exclusion applies to any individual whose "illegal use of drugs . . . has occurred recently enough to indicate that the individual is actively engaged in such conduct." Id. If an individual tests positive on a test for the illegal use of drugs, the individual will be considered a current drug user under the ADA where the test correctly indicates that the individual is engaging in the current illegal use of a controlled substance.

Although the ADA excludes individuals currently engaging in the illegal use of drugs, it does not exclude individuals who have a record of such use or who are erroneously regarded as engaging in such use. 42 U.S.C. § 12110(b); see also 29 C.F.R. § 1630.3(b). It is important to remember, however, that an individual who has a record of the illegal use of drugs or who is erroneously regarded as engaging in such use is not automatically an individual with a disability. One still must evaluate whether the record or erroneous perception pertains to a substantially limiting impairment. Only addiction or perceived addiction to a controlled substance meets this standard. Occasional, casual illegal use of drugs does not constitute a disability. Similarly, a record or perception of such casual use does not constitute a disability. See *Hartman v. City of Petaluma*, 841 F. Supp. 946, 949, 2 AD Cas. (BNA) 1860, 1862-63 (N.D. Cal. 1994) (ADA provisions "require some indicia of dependence sufficient to substantially limit a major life activity").

Example 1—Several years ago, CP was hospitalized for treatment for a cocaine addiction. He has been rehabilitated successfully and has not engaged in the illegal use of drugs since receiving treatment. CP, who has a record of an impairment that substantially limited his major life activities, is covered by the ADA.

Example 2—Three years ago, CP was arrested and convicted of the possession of cocaine. He had used the substance occasionally, perhaps three or four times over a sixteen-month period. CP has not used cocaine or any other illegal drug since his arrest. CP is not covered by the ADA. Although CP has a record of cocaine use, the use was not an addiction and did not substantially limit any of CP's major life activities.

Example 3—CP applies for a job with R, which requires job applicants to undergo a test to determine the current illegal use of drugs. CP's drug test falsely indicates that CP is using cocaine. R's personnel manager informs CP that the test came back positive for cocaine use and that R will not hire CP because "we don't want drug addicts working here." CP is not currently using cocaine and does not use any other drug illegally. R, which erroneously regards CP as being addicted to cocaine, erroneously regards CP as having a substantially limiting impairment. CP, therefore, meets the definition of "disability."

Example 4– Same as Example 3, above, except the personnel manager tells CP that the test came back showing marijuana use and that R will not hire CP because "we don't hire anybody who uses drugs illegally." The personnel manager tells the EEOC investigator that she did not hire CP because of R's strict policy against hiring anyone who tests positive for the illegal use of drugs and that she had not considered or been concerned about the extent of CP's use. "All I know is that his test showed marijuana use. I didn't think about anything beyond that." Since there is no evidence that R regarded CP as being addicted to marijuana, there is no evidence that R erroneously regarded CP as having a substantially limiting impairment. CP, therefore, does not meet the definition of disability.

A person who alleges disability based on one of the excluded conditions is not an individual with a disability under the ADA. Note, however, that a person who has one of these conditions is an individual with a disability if (s)he has another condition that rises to the level of a disability. See House Education and Labor Report at 142. Thus, a compulsive gambler who has a heart impairment that substantially limits his/her major life activities is an individual with a disability. Although compulsive gambling is not a disability, the individual's heart impairment is a disability.

902.7 Record of an Impairment that Substantially Limits Major Life Activities

(a) General—The second part of the statutory definition of the term "disability" applies to persons who have a record of a substantially limiting impairment. This part covers persons who have a history of, or have been classified or misclassified as having, a physical or mental impairment that substantially limits one or more major life activities. It includes persons who have had a disabling impairment but have recovered in whole or in part and are not now substantially limited. It also includes persons who have been incorrectly classified as having a disability. See 29 C.F.R. § 1630.2(k).

> The legislative history of the ADA emphasizes that this part of the definition is intended to prevent discrimination against individuals who have been classified or labeled, correctly or incorrectly, as having a disability. It also makes clear that the coverage of the Act extends to persons who have recovered, in whole or in part, from a disability but are subjected to discrimination because of their history of a substantially limiting impairment. Senate Report at 23; House Education and Labor Report at 52-53; House Judiciary Report at 29.

When determining whether an individual is covered by this part of the definition of the term "disability," one must remember that the record at issue must be a record of an impairment that substantially limited a major life activity. A record of a condition that is not an impairment, or of an impairment that was not substantially limiting, does not satisfy this part of the definition. See *Byrne v. Board of Educ.*, 979 F.2d 560, 566-67, 60 EPD Par. 41,862 at 73,020-21, 2 AD Cas. (BNA) 284, 289-90 (7th Cir. 1992) (single hospital stay for administration of allergy tests is not a record of a such an impairment). Further, a record of a condition, such as transvestism or compulsive gambling, that is specifically excluded from ADA coverage also does not satisfy this part of the definition. (Note, however, that a record of addiction to the illegal use of drugs is a disability, even though current illegal use of drugs is specifically excluded from ADA coverage. See § 902.6, supra.)

> *Example 1*—For several years, CP was twenty-to-thirty pounds beyond the target weight for men of his height and bone structure. His condition did not rise to the level of morbid obesity and did not cause or result from a physiological disorder. Further, his condition did not restrict any of his activities. CP recently completed a weight-loss program and is now at his target weight. CP does not have a record of a disability. He has a history of obesity, but his obesity was not an impairment and did not substantially limit any of his major life activities.

> *Example 2*—CP was recently hospitalized for appendicitis. She underwent a routine appendectomy, was hospitalized for one week, and recovered fully within the normal healing period. Although CP has a hospital record of treatment for appendicitis, she does not have a record of a disability. The appendicitis restricted CP's activities for only a brief period and had no long-term or permanent effects on CP. The impairment, therefore, did not substantially limit any of CP's major life activities. As a result, CP does not have a history of a disability and the hospital record does not constitute a record of a disability.

> *Example 3*—CP was convicted several times of shoplifting. He received treatment for kleptomania and has recovered from the condition. CP has a record of kleptomania, but he does not have a record of a disability. Kleptomania is specifically excluded from the statutory definition of the term "disability."

An individual who has a record of a disability under other laws or regulations does not necessarily have a record of a disability for purposes of the ADA. Other laws may define the term "disability" differently from the way the ADA defines the term. See § 902.1(a), supra. The investigator, therefore, should not assume that an individual who has been certified as having a disability or a handicap for other purposes, such as veterans programs, state vocational rehabilitation programs, or disability retirement programs, also has a disability under the ADA. The investigator, however, should obtain a copy of the certification and other similar available documents. Such certification is not dispositive for the purposes of the ADA, but it may provide relevant information. For example, medical information supporting the certification may be relevant to whether the charging party has a "disability" under the ADA. Further, the respondent's knowledge of and attitude toward the certification may be relevant to whether the respondent regarded the charging party as having a substantially limiting impairment. See § 902.8, infra.

(b) History of Such an Impairment—The term "disability" covers persons who have recovered from substantially limiting physical or mental impairments. Examples of persons who would fall under this part of the definition of the term "disability" include individuals who have histories of substantially limiting forms of heart disease or mental or emotional illness. Senate Report at 23; House Education and Labor Report at 52-53.

In *School Bd. of Nassau County v. Arline*, 480 U.S. 273, 281, 42 EPD Par. 36,791 at 45,635, 1 AD Cas. (BNA) 1026, 1029 (1987), the United States Supreme

Court stated that the plaintiff's hospitalization for an acute form of tuberculosis, an illness that had substantially limited one or more of the plaintiff's major life activities, sufficed to establish a record of a substantially limiting impairment.[23] Similarly, a district court found that an individual who had incurred four or five shoulder dislocations prior to undergoing corrective surgery had a "history" of a substantially limiting impairment. *Mahoney v. Ortiz*, 645 F. Supp. 22, 24, 1 AD Cas. (BNA) 924, 925 (S.D.N.Y. 1986).

Example—CP, who is thirty, had a severe form of depression when he was in his early twenties. He lost his appetite, could not sleep, was always tired, and rarely left his home. The depression became so serious that he could not function in day-to-day life. CP was hospitalized for four months and then received therapy on an out-patient basis for six months. The treatment was successful, and CP has had no recurrence of the depression. Although CP does not currently have an impairment that substantially limits a major life activity, he has a history of such an impairment. CP, therefore, falls under the second part of the definition of the term "disability."

(c) Misclassified as Having Such an Impairment— The term "disability" covers persons who are not, and may have never actually been, impaired but nonetheless have been misclassified as having a disability. Thus, school or other institutional documents labeling or classifying an individual as having a substantially limiting impairment would establish a "record" of a disability. Individuals who have been misclassified by a school or a hospital as having mental retardation or a substantially limiting learning disability would be covered by this part of the definition of the term "disability." See Senate Report at 23; House Education and Labor Report at 52-53; House Judiciary Report at 29.

902.8 Regarded as Having a Substantially Limiting Impairment

(a) General—The third part of the statutory definition of the term "disability" applies to individuals who are regarded as having impairments that substantially limit one or more major life activities. This part covers persons who have impairments that do not substantially limit major life activities but are treated by covered entities as constituting substantially limiting impairments. It also covers persons whose impairments are substantially limiting only as the result of the attitudes of others toward the impairment and persons who have no impairments but nonetheless are treated as having substantially limiting impairments. 29 C.F.R. pt. 1630 app. § 1630.2(l); see also Senate Report at 23; House Education and Labor Report at 53.

The inclusion of persons regarded as having a substantially limiting impairment reflects Congressional intent to protect all persons who are subjected to discrimination based on disability, even if they do not in fact have a disability. It also reflects a recognition by Congress that the reactions of others to an impairment or a perceived impairment can be just as disabling as the limitations caused by an actual impairment. See House Judiciary Report at 30. As noted in the legislative history of the ADA (see Senate Report at 23-24; House Education and Labor Report at 53; House Judiciary Report at 30), the United States Supreme Court effectively explained the rationale for this aspect of the definition of the term "disability" in *School Bd. of Nassau County v. Arline*, 480 U.S. 273, 42 EPD Par. 36,791, 1 AD Cas. (BNA) 1026 (1987). The Court stated,

> By amending the definition of "handicapped individual" to include not only those who are actually physically impaired, but also those who are regarded as impaired and who, as a result, are substantially limited in a major life activity, Congress acknowledged that society's accumulated myths and fears about disability and disease are as handicapping as are the physical limitations that flow from actual impairment.

480 U.S. at 284, 42 EPD at 45,637, 1 AD Cas. at 1030 (footnote omitted).

This aspect of the definition of the term "disability," therefore, is designed to protect against myths, fears, stereotypes, and other attitudinal barriers about disability. Common attitudinal barriers include, but are not limited to, "concerns about productivity, safety, insurance, liability, attendance, cost of accommodation and accessibility, and acceptance by co-workers and customers." House Judiciary Report at 30. Quite often, employers will assume, without any objective evidence, that a person's physical or mental condition will cause problems in these areas. The ADA is

---

[23] The plaintiff had been hospitalized for tuberculosis from May 1957 until August 1958. *Arline v. School Board of Nassau County*, 692 F. Supp. 1286, 1289, 48 EPD Par. 38,397 at 54,248, 1 AD Cas. (BNA) 1345, 1348 (M.D. Fla. 1988). The plaintiff's tuberculosis, which required lengthy hospitalization, was a substantially limiting impairment. See § 902.4(d), supra.

designed to prevent employment discrimination based on mere speculation and unfounded fears about disability. Thus, the third part of the definition is designed to protect individuals who experience employment discrimination because of myths, fears, and stereotypes associated with disabilities, even if the individuals' physical or mental conditions do not meet the criteria of the first or second part of the definition. *Id.*

In contrast to the first two parts of the statutory definition of the term "disability," this part of the definition is directed at the employer rather than at the individual alleging discrimination. The issue is whether the employer treats the individual as having an impairment that substantially limits major life activities. Thus, as the legislative history to the ADA notes, "[t]he perception of the covered entity is a key element of this test." House Judiciary Report at 30. Because it is the employer's perception that is at issue, it is not necessary that the individual alleging discrimination actually have a disability or an impairment. It also is not necessary that the employer's perception of the individual be shared by other employers. The individual is covered by this part of the definition if (s)he can show that the employer "made an employment decision because of a perception of disability based on 'myth, fear or stereotype'. . . . If the employer cannot articulate a non-discriminatory reason for the employment action, an inference that the employer is acting on the basis of 'myth, fear or stereotype' can be drawn." 29 C.F.R. pt. 1630 app. § 1630.2(l); see also House Judiciary Report at 30-31.

The legislative history to the Act makes clear that the individual does not have to demonstrate that the employer's perception is wrong. As the legislative history notes, A person who is covered because of being regarded as having an impairment is not required to show that the employer's perception is inaccurate, e.g., that he will be accepted by others, or that insurance rates will not increase, in order to be qualified for the job.

> For example, many people are rejected from jobs because a back x-ray reveals some anomaly, even though the person has no symptoms of a back impairment. The reasons for the rejection are often the fear of injury, as well as increased insurance or worker's compensation costs. These reasons for rejection rely on common barriers to employment for persons with disabilities and therefore, the person is perceived to be disabled under the third test.

House Judiciary Report at 31.

This part of the definition of "disability" applies to individuals who are subjected to discrimination on the basis of genetic information relating to illness, disease, or other disorders. Covered entities that discriminate against individuals on the basis of such genetic information are regarding the individuals as having impairments that substantially limit a major life activity. Those individuals, therefore, are covered by the third part of the definition of "disability." See 136 Cong. Rec. H4623 (daily ed. July 12, 1990) (statement of Rep. Owens); id. at H4624-25 (statement of Rep. Edwards); id. at H4627 (statement of Rep. Waxman).

> *Example*—CP's genetic profile reveals an increased susceptibility to colon cancer. CP is currently asymptomatic and may never in fact develop colon cancer. After making CP a conditional offer of employment, R learns about CP's increased susceptibility to colon cancer. R then withdraws the job offer because of concerns about matters such as CP's productivity, insurance costs, and attendance. R is treating CP as having an impairment that substantially limits a major life activity. Accordingly, CP is covered by the third part of the definition of "disability."

To determine whether an employer regards an individual as having an impairment that substantially limits major life activities, one must examine the employer's perception and treatment of the charging party. Toward that end, the investigator may obtain a statement in which the respondent explains his/her perceptions of the charging party's physical or mental condition. The statement should describe the type of condition that the respondent perceives the charging party to have and the extent to which the respondent believes the condition to limit the charging party's major life activities. Further, if the charging party has been classified as having a disability or handicap under another law or benefit program, then the investigator may determine if the respondent was aware of the classification and, if so, how the respondent interpreted the classification. For example, if the charging party has a veterans' disability rating, then the investigator may determine whether the respondent was aware of that rating. The investigator also may determine whether the respondent viewed the rating as indicative of an impairment that substantially limited a major life activity. A respondent might, for example, believe that all individuals who have ten-percent veterans' disability ratings are substantially limited in a major life activity. In addition, the investigator may ascertain the information that the employer had about the charging party's condition at the time of the employment action at issue. Other information, such as statements from other individuals in the work place or evidence that the employer has a pattern of not hiring individuals with the same or similar impairment, also may help to determine how the employer perceived the charging party.

Further, the investigator should examine carefully the employer's treatment of the charging party. An employer may claim that it does not perceive an individual as having an impairment that substantially limits a major life activity but nonetheless may treat the individual as having such an impairment. In such a case, actions may speak louder than words. For example, an employer may assert that it does not regard an individual as substantially limited in working but nonetheless may treat an individual as having an impairment that disqualifies him or her from a class of jobs or a broad range of jobs in various classes. The employer in that case regards the individual as substantially limited in the major life activity of working. See § 902.8(f), infra.

The investigator should remember that a determination that an employer regarded a charging party as having an impairment that substantially limits a major life activity does not automatically require a finding of discrimination. The determination of whether the charging party is covered by the third part of the definition of "disability" and the determination of whether the respondent discriminated against the charging party are two separate determinations. In each charge involving the third part of the definition of "disability," the investigator should engage in a careful evidentiary analysis to determine whether the respondent (1) regarded the individual as having a substantially limiting impairment and (2) acted on that basis in violation of the ADA. Although the same facts may be relevant to both determinations, a finding of coverage does not necessarily lead to a finding of liability. An employer that erroneously regards an individual as having a substantially limiting impairment may nonetheless take an employment action for a legitimate reason. For example, evidence may show that an employer that gave an employee a low performance rating erroneously regarded the employee as having AIDS. The evidence also may show, however, that the employee's work objectively warranted the rating, that other employees with comparable performances received comparable ratings, and that the employer has had employees who actually had AIDS and has never discriminated against them on that basis. In that situation, there is coverage but no liability.

(b) Regulatory Definition—An individual is covered by this part of the definition if (s)he

> (1) [h]as a physical or mental impairment that does not substantially limit major life activities but is treated by a covered entity as constituting such limitation;
>
> (2) [h]as a physical or mental impairment that substantially limits major life activities only as a result of the attitudes of others toward such impairment; or
>
> (3) [h]as none of the impairments defined in [the definition of the term "impairment"] but is treated by the covered entity as having a substantially limiting impairment.

29 C.F.R. § 1630.2(l). Each of these three subparts of the third part of the definition of the term "disability" is discussed below in detail.

(c) Persons with Impairments Regarded as Substantially Limiting—This subpart of the regulatory definition covers individuals who have impairments that do not substantially limit major life activities but who are perceived as being substantially limited. For example, an individual who has a slight limp that does not substantially limit any major life activities but who is rejected for employment because the employer believes that the limp significantly restricts the individual's ability to walk is covered by this part of the definition. Although the individual's limp does not in fact substantially limit major life activities, the employer perceives the limp as substantially limiting the individual's ability to walk. The individual meets the definition of an individual with a disability because (s)he is regarded as having an impairment that substantially limits his/her major life activity of walking.

> *Example*—CP has a mild form of strabismus (crossed eyes). The impairment only slightly affects CP's ability to see. CP's employer, however, thinks that the impairment prevents CP from seeing all printed material. As a result, the employer refuses to promote CP to a supervisory position that would require CP to review the written work of others. Although CP does not actually have a disability, she is regarded as having an impairment that substantially limits her ability to see. CP, therefore, is covered by the third part of the definition of "disability."

(d) Persons Who Are Substantially Limited as a Result of Others' Attitudes—This subpart covers individuals who have stigmatic conditions that constitute physical or mental impairments but that do not by themselves substantially limit a major life activity. The impairments become substantially limiting only because of the negative reactions of others toward the impairments. For example, a person who has experienced severe burns may have an impairment that is substantially limiting solely because of the attitudes of others. Similarly, a person who has a cosmetic disfigurement may be continuously refused employment because of employers' fears about the negative reactions of co-workers or clients. These persons would be covered under the third part of the definition of the term "disability." See Senate Report at 24; House Education and Labor Report at 53; House Judiciary Report at 30-31.

Example—CP, who has a facial scar that runs from the base of his left ear to his chin, applies for a job as a sales representative in a home appliance store. The sales manager of the store refuses to consider CP for the position because she fears that CP's presence on the showroom floor will dissuade customers from shopping at the store. CP is covered by the third part of the definition of the term "disability." He has an impairment, a facial scar, that is substantially limiting only as a result of the negative attitudes of others.

(e) Unimpaired Persons Regarded as Having Substantially Limiting Impairments— This subpart covers persons who have no actual physical or mental impairments but nonetheless are treated as having substantially limiting impairments. For example, an individual who is rejected for employment because the employer erroneously believes that the individual is infected with the Human Immunodeficiency Virus is an individual with a disability. Even though the individual has no impairment, (s)he is regarded as having a substantially limiting impairment.

Similarly, in a nonemployment case under the Rehabilitation Act, a court ruled that a parent whose children had been erroneously placed in a class for mentally retarded students had standing to sue. Although the children had no actual impairments, they were regarded as having disabilities. *Carter v. Orleans Parish Pub. Sch.*, 725 F.2d 261, 262-63 (5th Cir. 1984).

Example 1—R refuses to consider CP for a position as a lifeguard because R believes that CP has a serious heart condition that significantly restricts her ability to engage in physical activity. CP, in fact, has no heart condition. Although CP does not have an impairment, CP is regarded as having an impairment that substantially limits her major life activities. CP, therefore, is covered by this part of the definition of the term "disability."

Example 2—CP and her spouse have recently completed couples counseling by a clinical psychologist in an effort to remedy problems in their marriage. Neither CP nor her spouse has any psychological disabilities. CP's employer, however, believes that anyone who sees or has seen a psychologist "must be crazy." He finds a pretext under which to fire her. CP, therefore, is covered by the third part of the definition of "disability," because she is being treated by her employer as though she has a substantially limiting impairment although, in fact, she does not.

Example 3—CP has high normal blood pressure. Her blood pressure is within "normal" range, and she does not have hypertension. Nonetheless, R fires CP because R thinks this means that CP cannot perform everyday activities without risking a massive stroke. Although CP does not have an impairment, she is regarded as having an impairment that substantially limits major life activities. CP, therefore, is covered by the third part of the definition of "disability."

Example 4—CP had abdominal surgery a few years ago to treat a hernia. The hernia was fully corrected, and CP has no residual effects. R, however, thinks that this means that CP cannot lift anything weighing more than a few pounds and refuses to hire CP. R regards CP as having an impairment that substantially limits the major life activity of lifting. CP, therefore, is covered by this part of the definition of the term "disability."

(f) Regarded as Substantially Limited in the Major Life Activity of Working—If an individual is not regarded as having an impairment that substantially limits any other major life activities (and does not fall under either of the first two parts of the definition of "disability"), then the investigator should consider whether (s)he is regarded as having an impairment that substantially limits the major life activity of working. An employer regards an individual as substantially limited in the ability to work if, as the result of myths, fears, stereotypes, or other attitudinal barriers commonly associated with disability, it treats the individual as having an impairment that disqualifies or significantly restricts him or her from working in a class of jobs or in a broad range of jobs in various classes. An employer does not regard an individual as substantially limited in the ability to work simply because it finds the individual unsuitable for one particular job. *Forrisi v. Bowen,* 794 F.2d 931, 934, 40 EPD Par. 36,307 at 43,277-78, 1 AD Cas. (BNA) 921, 923 (9th Cir. 1986); see also *E.E. Black, Ltd. v. Marshall*, 497 F. Supp. 1088, 24 EPD Par. 31,260, 1 AD Cas. (BNA) 220 (D.

Hawaii 1980). Rather, an employer regards an individual as substantially limited in working if it perceives the individual to have an impairment that "foreclose[s] generally the type of employment involved." *Forrisi*, 794 F.2d at 935, 40 EPD Par. at 43,278, 1 AD Cas. at 923.

In Forrisi, an employer discharged a newly hired utility systems repairer who had acrophobia (fear of heights). The condition had not previously interfered with the individual's employability. It did, however, prevent the individual from performing the job at issue, a utility systems repairer position at the employer's plant, which required work at high elevations. The employer viewed the individual as qualified for and generally capable of doing utility systems repair work but as unable to perform one particular job. Noting that the individual "was seen as unsuited for one position in one plant—and nothing more," the court found that he was not regarded as substantially limited in working. *Id.*

To determine whether an employer regards an individual as substantially limited in working, one must determine whether the employer (1) perceives the individual as having an impairment that precludes or significantly restricts work only in a particular job or a narrow range of jobs or (2) perceives the individual as having an impairment that disqualifies or significantly restricts the individual from a class of jobs or a broad range of jobs. This means that one must determine what the employer thinks about the impairment and how the employer believes the impairment affects the individual's ability to work. That is, one must identify the work limitations that the employer believes result from the impairment.

To do this, one first should identify the qualification standard or other criterion that the employer has used to disqualify or restrict the individual from employment. For example, the *Forrisi* employer disqualified the plaintiff because he could not perform utility systems repair work at certain heights, 794 F. 2d at 933, 40 EPD at 43,276, 1 AD Cas. at 922, and the *E.E. Black* employer disqualified the plaintiff because he had a congenital back anomaly that the employer thought made him "a poor risk for heavy labor," 497 F. Supp. at 1091, 24 EPD at 17,644, 1 AD Cas. at 222. Other disqualifying criteria include such requirements as a certain level of hearing or vision, an ability to carry objects for a certain distance, an ability to lift a certain amount of weight, an ability to work with a certain substance, and an ability to handle particularly stressful situations.

Next, one should determine whether the criterion pertains uniquely to the peculiar job or work site of one particular employer. If the criterion pertains only to the peculiar job or work site, then an employer who refuses to employ an individual who does not meet the criterion regards the individual as disqualified only from work in that particular job or at that particular work site. The employer, who perceives the individual to be unsuited for one particular job, does not regard the individual as substantially limited in working.

For example, the *Forrisi* criterion, an ability to perform utility systems repair work at certain heights, was unique to that employer's job. The criterion did not measure the employee's ability to perform a class of jobs; rather, the criterion measured the employee's ability to perform utility repair work at the employer's plant, which exposed the employee to certain heights. See 794 F.2d at 935, 40 EPD at 43,278, 1 AD Cas. at 923 (employer doubted plaintiff's ability to perform utility repair work above certain heights in employer's plant, not plaintiff's ability to perform such work in general). The *Forrisi* employer did not regard the plaintiff as substantially limited in the ability to work. Instead, the employer regarded the plaintiff as unable to meet a unique criterion that pertained to the location of one specific job for one specific employer.

If the criterion does not pertain to the peculiar job or work site of one particular employer, then the investigator should determine whether the criterion pertains to a class of jobs or a broad range of jobs in various classes. To do this, the investigator should look at the number and types of jobs, in the geographical area to which the individual has reasonable access, that use similar training, knowledge, skills, and abilities (a class of jobs) and that do not use similar training, knowledge, skills, and abilities (a broad range of jobs). 29 C.F.R. § 1630.2(j)(3)(ii). If the criterion pertains to a class of jobs or to a broad range of jobs, then the employer that applied the criterion has treated the individual as having an impairment that disqualifies or restricts him or her from a class of jobs or from a broad range of jobs in various classes. The employer's actions, therefore, demonstrate that the employer regards the individual as having an impairment that precludes or significantly restricts work in a class of jobs or a broad range of jobs in various classes. Accordingly, the employer regards the individual as substantially limited in working.

For example, the *E.E. Black* criterion that the plaintiff could not meet because of a back anomaly did not pertain uniquely to the peculiar job or work site of one particular employer. Instead, the requirement that employees not be "a poor risk for heavy labor" pertained to the plaintiff's ability to perform all jobs involving heavy labor and not just to a particular job of the employer. See 497 F. Supp. at 1091, 24 EPD at 17,644, 1 AD Cas. at 222 (noting that plaintiff was disqualified from employment because he "was a poor risk for heavy labor"). The criterion, therefore, pertained to a class of jobs, heavy labor jobs. By applying the criterion to exclude the plaintiff from employment, the employer treated the plaintiff as having an impairment that disqualified him from a class of jobs. As a result, the employer demonstrated that it regarded the plaintiff as having an impairment that disqualified him from a class of jobs and, therefore, as substantially limited in the ability to work.

On the other hand, an employer that disqualifies an individual from employment on the basis of a criterion that does not pertain to a class of jobs or a broad range of jobs (for example, a criterion that pertains only to a narrow range of jobs) does not regard the individual as substantially limited in working. See 29 C.F.R. pt. 1630 app. § 1630.2(j). An employer that applies such a criterion to disqualify an individual because of an impairment is treating the individual as having an impairment that disqualifies him or her only from a narrow range of jobs. The employer, therefore, regards the individual as having an impairment that precludes work only in a narrow range of jobs (rather than in a class of jobs or a broad range of jobs). Accordingly, the employer, which does not regard the individual as disqualified from a class of jobs or a broad range of jobs, does not regard the individual as substantially limited in working.

In summary, an employer that disqualifies an individual from a job on the basis of a criterion that pertains to a unique aspect of the job at issue does not regard the individual as substantially limited in the ability to work. Instead, the employer merely regards the individual as unsuitable for one particular job. The individual, therefore, does not meet the third, "regarded as" part of the definition of the term "disability" with respect to the major life activity of working. On the other hand, an employer that disqualifies an individual on the basis of a criterion that does not pertain to a unique aspect of one particular job does regard the individual as substantially limited in working if the criterion pertains to a class of jobs or to a broad range of jobs. In that case, the individual is covered by the third part of the definition of "disability."

Example 1—CP is an industrial painter who has extensive experience painting factories, warehouses, aircraft hangars, and other large structures. He applies for a position with R, a company with a contract to paint all of the buildings at a nuclear power facility. R plans to paint the buildings with a unique type of paint that contains a substance designed to help insulate buildings from radiation. R erroneously believes that CP is allergic to that substance and cannot use paint that contains it. As a result, R does not hire CP. In this case, the exclusionary criterion—the requirement that employees be able to work with paint that contains a certain substance—is unique to this job. The criterion pertains specifically to R's work site. By disqualifying CP from employment on the basis of a criterion that pertains to a unique aspect of R's job, R has shown that it finds CP to be unsuitable only for one particular job for one particular employer. R, therefore, does not regard CP as substantially limited in working.

Example 2—CP is a warehouse worker whose duties include loading and unloading vehicles, moving heavy boxes from one part of the warehouse to another, and keeping an inventory of the items stored in one section of the warehouse. R requires its warehouse workers to be able to lift packages weighing up to seventy pounds, to carry those packages for up to one hundred yards, to bend repeatedly, and to climb up and down ladders several times each day. CP recently learned that she has arthritis in her left knee. The arthritis does not significantly restrict her in any way, and her physician has placed no limitations on her activities. Nevertheless, R believes that the arthritis prevents CP from meeting the lifting, carrying, bending, and climbing requirements of the warehouse position. R has no objective evidence about any limitations that CP might have but instead bases its belief on its views about arthritis in general. R fires CP on the grounds that she can no longer meet the climbing, lifting, bending, and carrying requirements of her warehouse job. The exclusionary criteria—R's climbing, lifting, bending, and carrying requirements—do not apply to some unique aspect of R's warehouse. Instead, the criteria apply to the class of jobs that involve manual labor. By disqualifying CP from employment on the basis of criteria that apply to manual labor jobs, R has shown that it finds CP to be unsuitable for work in a class of jobs. R, therefore, regards CP as substantially limited in the ability to work.

Example 3—CP, a bank teller, has a mild form of clinically diagnosed depression. The depression does not substantially limit any of CP's major life activities. R, CP's employer, learns of CP's clinically diagnosed depression and assumes that the depression will prevent CP from working well with customers and other members of the public. There is no factual basis to R's assumption. Nevertheless, R reassigns CP to a clerical position in a back office. In this case, the exclusionary criterion—the requirement that employees be able to work well with members of the public—does not pertain to a unique aspect of the job or work site. Rather, since a wide variety of jobs involves working with the public, the exclusionary criterion applies to a broad range of jobs. By disqualifying CP from the teller position on the basis of a criterion that applies to a broad range of jobs in various classes, R has demonstrated that it finds CP to be unsuitable for work in a broad range of jobs. Accordingly, R regards CP as substantially limited in the ability to work.

Example 4—CP applies for a job as a laborer at R's construction site. A post-offer medical examination reveals that CP has a congenital back anomaly. CP is asymptomatic; the back anomaly does not limit any of her activities. Nonetheless, R withdraws the job offer because it believes that the back anomaly makes CP a poor risk for heavy labor jobs. That is, R thinks that CP will injure her back on the job and will increase R's workers' compensation costs. The criterion—a requirement that employees not pose a risk of injury in heavy labor jobs—does not apply to a unique aspect of R's job or work site. Instead, the criterion applies to a class of jobs—heavy labor jobs. By disqualifying CP from employment on the basis of a criterion that applies to all heavy labor jobs, R has shown that it finds CP to be unsuitable for work in a class of jobs. R, therefore, regards CP as substantially limited in working.

To determine whether a respondent regards a charging party as having an impairment that substantially limits the major life activity of working, the investigator should take the following steps:

(1) identify the impairment that CP has or is regarded as having;

(2) identify the criterion that disqualifies or significantly restricts CP because of the impairment;

(3) determine whether the criterion pertains uniquely to the peculiar job or work site of R;

(a) if the criterion pertains uniquely to the peculiar job or work site of R, then R does not regard CP as substantially limited in working; instead, R regards CP as unsuitable for one particular job for one particular employer;

(b) if the criterion does not pertain uniquely to the peculiar job or work site of R, then

(4) determine whether the criterion pertains to a class of jobs or a broad range of jobs in various classes;

(a) if the criterion pertains to a class of jobs or a broad range of jobs in various classes, then R regards CP as substantially limited in working;

(b) if the criterion does not pertain to a class of jobs or a broad range of jobs in various classes, then R does not regard CP as substantially limited in working.

902.9 Cross-References

(a) How to investigate, § 602
(b) Definition of the term "qualified individual with a disability," § ____.

Index [Omitted.]

APPLICATION OF THE AMERICANS WITH DISABILITIES ACT OF 1990 TO DISABILITY-BASED DISTINCTIONS IN EMPLOYER PROVIDED HEALTH INSURANCE.

EEOC NOTICE
Number 915.002
Date 6/8/93

1. Interim Enforcement Guidance on the application of the Americans with Disabilities Act of 1990 to disability-based distinctions in employer provided health insurance.
2. PURPOSE: This interim enforcement guidance sets forth the Commission's position on the application of the Americans with Disabilities Act to disability-based distinctions in employer provided health insurance.
3. EFFECTIVE DATE: Upon issuance.
4. EXPIRATION DATE: As an exception to EEOC Order 205.001, Appendix B, Attachment 4, § a(5), this Notice will remain in effect until rescinded or superseded.
5. ORIGINATOR: Americans with Disabilities Act Division, Office of Legal Counsel.
6. INSTRUCTIONS: This enforcement guidance is to be used on an interim basis until the Commission issues final guidance after publication for notice and comment. File after [ ] of Volume II of the Compliance Manual.
7. SUBJECT MATTER:

I. INTRODUCTION

The interplay between the nondiscrimination principles of the ADA and employer provided health insurance, which is predicated on the ability to make health-related distinctions, is both unique and complex. This interplay is, undoubtedly, most complex when a health insurance plan contains distinctions that are based on disability. The purpose of this interim guidance is to assist Commission investigators in analyzing ADA charges which allege that a disability-based distinction in the terms or provisions of an employer provided health insurance plan violates the ADA.[1] This interim guidance does not address the application of the ADA to other issues arising in the context of employer provided health insurance. Nor does it address the application of the ADA to other types of "fringe benefits," such as employer provided pension plans, life insurance, and disability insurance. These subjects will be addressed in future documents.

II. BACKGROUND AND LEGAL FRAMEWORK

The ADA provides that it is unlawful for an employer[2] to discriminate on the basis of disability against a qualified individual with a disability in regard to "job application procedures, the hiring, advancement, or discharge of employees, employee compensation, job training, and other terms, conditions, and privileges of employment." 42 U.S.C. § 12112(a). Section 1630.4 of the Commission's regulations implementing the employment provisions of the ADA further provides, in pertinent part, that it is unlawful for an employer to discriminate on the basis of disability against a qualified individual with a disability in regard to "[f]ringe benefits available by virtue of employment, whether or not administered by the [employer]." 29 C.F.R. § 1630.4(f). Employee benefit plans, including health insurance plans provided by an employer to its employees, are a fringe benefit available by virtue of employment. Generally speaking, therefore, the ADA prohibits employers from discriminating on the basis of disability in the provision of health insurance to their employees.

The ADA also prohibits employers from indirectly discriminating on the basis of disability in the provision of health insurance. Employers may not enter into, or participate in, a contractual or other arrangement or relationship that has the effect of discriminating against their own qualified applicants or employees with disabilities. 42 U.S.C. § 12112(b)(2); 29 C.F.R. § 1630.6(a). Contractual or other relationships with organizations that provide fringe benefits to employees are expressly included in this prohibition. 42 U.S.C. § 12112(b)(2); 29 C.F.R. § 1630.6(b). This means that an employer will be liable for any discrimination resulting from a contract or agreement with an insurance company, health maintenance organization (HMO), third party administrator (TPA), stop-loss car-

[1] In light of the recent amendments to the Rehabilitation Act of 1973, the analysis in this interim guidance also applies to federal sector complaints of discrimination arising under section 501 of that statute.

[2] The ADA also prohibits employment agencies, labor organizations, and joint labor management committees from discriminating in employment against qualified individuals with disabilities. However, for convenience, only the term "employer" is used throughout this document.

rier, or other organization to provide or administer a health insurance plan on behalf of its employees.

Another provision of the ADA makes it unlawful for an employer to limit, segregate, or classify an applicant or employee in a way that adversely affects his or her employment opportunities or status on the basis of disability. 42 U.S.C. § 12112(b)(1); 29 C.F.R. § 1630.5. Both the legislative history and the interpretive Appendix to the regulations indicate that this prohibition applies to employer provided health insurance. S. Rep. No. 116, 101st Cong., 1st Sess. (Senate Report) (1989) at 28-29; H.R. Rep. No. 485 part 2, 101st Cong., 2nd Sess. (House Labor Report) (1990) at 58-59; H.R. Rep. No. 485 part 3, 101st Cong., 2nd Sess. (House Judiciary Report) (1990) at 36; Appendix to 29 C.F.R. § 1630.5.

Several consequences result from the application of these statutory provisions. First, disability-based insurance plan distinctions are permitted only if they are within the protective ambit of section 501(c) of the ADA. (See the discussion in Section III, infra.) Second, decisions about the employment of an individual with a disability cannot be motivated by concerns about the impact of the individual's disability on the employer's health insurance plan. Appendix to 29 C.F.R. § 1630.15(a). Third, employees with disabilities must be accorded "equal access" to whatever health insurance the employer provides to employees without disabilities. See Appendix to 29 C.F.R. § 1630.16(f). Fourth, in view of the statute's "association provision," 42 U.S.C. § 12112(b)(4); 29 C.F.R. § 1630.8, it would violate the ADA for an employer to make an employment decision about any person, whether or not that person has a disability, because of concerns about the impact on the health insurance plan of the disability of someone else with whom that person has a relationship.

As previously noted, this interim guidance is devoted solely to the ADA implications of disability-based health insurance plan distinctions. The ADA implications of other issues arising in the context of employer provided health insurance will be addressed in future guidance.

III. DISABILITY-BASED DISTINCTIONS

A. Framework of Analysis

Whenever it is alleged that a health-related term or provision of an employer provided health insurance plan violates the ADA, the first issue is whether the challenged term or provision is, in fact, a disability-based distinction. If the Commission determines that a challenged health insurance plan term or provision is a disability-based distinction, the respondent will be required to prove that that disability-based distinction is within the protective ambit of section 501(c) of the ADA.

In pertinent part, section 501(c) permits employers, insurers, and plan administrators to establish and/or observe the terms of an insured[3] health insurance plan that is "bona fide,"[4] based on "underwriting risks, classifying risks, or administering such risks that are based on or not inconsistent with State law," and that is not being used as a "subterfuge" to evade the purposes of the ADA. Section 501(c) likewise permits employers, insurers, and plan administrators to establish and/or observe the terms of a "bona fide" self-insured health insurance plan that is not used as a "subterfuge." 42 U.S.C. § 12201(c). The text of section 501(c) is incorporated into § 1630.16(f) of the Commission's regulations.[5]

Consequently, if the Commission determines that the challenged term or provision is a disability-based distinction, the respondent will be required to prove that: 1) the health insurance plan is either a bona fide

---

3 An "insured" health insurance plan is a health insurance plan or policy that is purchased from an insurance company or other organization, such as a health maintenance organization (HMO). This is in contrast to a "self-insured" health plan, where the employer directly assumes the liability of an insurer. Insured health insurance plans are regulated by both ERISA and state law. Self-insured plans are typically subject to ERISA, but are not subject to state laws that regulate insurance.

4 The term "bona fide" is defined in Section III (C)(1), infra.

5 Section 1630.16(f) states:

(f) Health insurance, life insurance and other benefit plans—

(1) An insurer, hospital, or medical service company, health maintenance organization, or any agent or entity that administers benefit plans, or similar organizations may underwrite risks, classify risks, or administer such risks that are based on or not inconsistent with State law.

(2) A covered entity may establish, sponsor, observe, or administer the terms of a bona fide benefit plan that are based on underwriting risks, classifying risks, or administering such risks that are based on or not inconsistent with State law.

insured health insurance plan that is not inconsistent with state law, or a bona fide self-insured health insurance plan;[6] and 2) the challenged disability-based distinction is not being used as a subterfuge. If the respondent so demonstrates, the Commission will conclude that the challenged disability-based distinction is within the protective ambit of section 501(c) and does not violate the ADA. If, on the other hand, the respondent is unable to make this two-pronged demonstration, the Commission will conclude that the respondent has violated the ADA.

B. What Is a Disability-Based Distinction?

It is important to note that not all health-related plan distinctions discriminate on the basis of disability. Insurance distinctions that are not based on disability, and that are applied equally to all insured employees, do not discriminate on the basis of disability and so do not violate the ADA.[7]

For example, a feature of some employer provided health insurance plans is a distinction between the benefits provided for the treatment of physical conditions on the one hand, and the benefits provided for the treatment of "mental/nervous" conditions on the other. Typically, a lower level of benefits is provided for the treatment of mental/nervous conditions than is provided for the treatment of physical conditions. Similarly, some health insurance plans provide fewer benefits for "eye care" than for other physical conditions. Such broad distinctions, which apply to the treatment of a multitude of dissimilar conditions and which constrain individuals both with and without disabilities, are not distinctions based on disability. Consequently, although such distinctions may have a greater impact on certain individuals with disabilities, they do not intentionally discriminate on the basis of disability[8] and do not violate the ADA.[9]

Blanket pre-existing condition clauses that exclude from the coverage of a health insurance plan the treatment of conditions that pre-date an individual's eligibility for benefits under that plan also are not distinctions based on disability, and do not violate the ADA. Universal limits or exclusions from coverage of all experimental drugs and/or treatments, or of all "elective surgery," are likewise not insurance distinctions based on disability. Similarly, coverage limits on medical procedures that are not exclusively, or nearly exclusively, utilized for the treatment of a particular disability are not distinctions based on disability. Thus, for example, it would not violate the ADA for an employer to limit the number of blood transfusions or X-rays that it will pay for, even though this may have an adverse effect on individuals with certain disabilities.

---

(3) A covered entity may establish, sponsor, observe, or administer the terms of a bona fide benefit plan that is not subject to State laws that regulate insurance.

(4) The activities described in paragraphs (f)(1), (2) and (3). are permitted unless these activities are being used as a subterfuge to evade the purposes of [Title I of the ADA].

6 If an employer provided health insurance plan is a "multiple employer welfare arrangement" (MEWA) pursuant to section 3(40) of ERISA, it may be subject to certain state insurance laws even if it is self-insured. See footnote 13, infra.

7 The term "discriminates" refers only to disparate treatment. The adverse impact theory of discrimination is unavailable in this context. See *Alexander v. Choate*, 469 U.S. 287 (1985), a case brought under § 504 of the Rehabilitation Act of 1973. See also the discussion of Choate in the Senate Report at 85; House Labor Report at 137.

8 However, it would violate the ADA for an employer to selectively apply a universal or "neutral" non-disability based insurance distinction only to individuals with disabilities. Thus, for example, it would violate the ADA for an employer to apply a "neutral" health insurance plan limitation on "eye care" only to an employee seeking treatment for a vision disability, but not to other employees who do not have vision disabilities. Charges alleging that a universal or "neutral" non-disability based insurance distinction has been selectively applied to individuals with disabilities should be processed using traditional disparate treatment theory and analysis.

9 This position is consistent with the case law developed pursuant to § 504 of the Rehabilitation Act of 1973, as amended, 29 U.S.C. § 794, the statute on which the ADA is patterned. Courts faced with challenges to insurance plan distinctions between physical benefits and mental/nervous benefits under the Rehabilitation Act have held that such distinctions are rational and do not discriminate on the basis of disability. See, e.g., *Doe v. Colautti*, 592 F.2d 704 (3d Cir. 1979) (holding that Pennsylvania's medical assistance statute was not required by the Rehabilitation Act to provide the same level of benefits for inpatient hospital treatment of mental illness as for inpatient hospital treatment of physical illness; the court noted that care for physical illness and care for mental illness were two different benefits), and *Doe v. Devine,* 545 F. Supp. 576 (D.D.C. 1982), aff'd on other grounds, 703 F. 2d 1319 (D.C. Cir. 1983) (holding that Blue Cross "cutbacks" in mental health benefits for federal employees are reasonable and do not discriminate on the basis of disability).

Example 1. The R Company health insurance plan limits the benefits provided for the treatment of any physical conditions to a maximum of $25,000 per year. CP, an employee of R, files a charge of discrimination alleging that the $25,000 cap violates the ADA because it is insufficient to cover the cost of treatment for her cancer. The $25,000 cap does not single out a specific disability, discrete group of disabilities, or disability in general. It is therefore not a disability-based distinction. If it is applied equally to all insured employees, it does not violate the ADA.

In contrast, however, health-related insurance distinctions that are based on disability may violate the ADA. A term or provision is "disability-based" if it singles out a particular disability (e.g., deafness, AIDS, schizophrenia), a discrete group of disabilities (e.g., cancers, muscular dystrophies, kidney diseases), or disability in general (e.g., non-coverage of all conditions that substantially limit a major life activity).

As previously noted, employers may establish and/or observe the terms and provisions of a bona fide benefit plan, including terms or provisions based on disability, that are not a "subterfuge to evade the purposes" of the ADA. Such terms and provisions do not violate the ADA. However, disability-based insurance distinctions that are a "subterfuge" do intentionally discriminate on the basis of disability and so violate the ADA.

Example 2. R Company's new self-insured health insurance plan caps benefits for the treatment of all physical conditions, except AIDS, at $100,000 per year. The treatment of AIDS is capped at $5,000 per year. CP, an employee with AIDS enrolled in the health insurance plan, files a charge alleging that the lower AIDS cap violates the ADA. The lower AIDS cap is a disability-based distinction. Accordingly, if R is unable to demonstrate that its health insurance plan is bona fide and that the AIDS cap is not a subterfuge, a violation of the ADA will be found.

Example 3. R Company has a health insurance plan that excludes from coverage treatment for any pre-existing blood disorders for a period of 18 months, but does not exclude the treatment of any other pre-existing conditions. R's pre-existing condition clause only excludes treatment for a discrete group of related disabilities, e.g., hemophilia, leukemia, and is thus a disability-based distinction. CP, an individual with acute leukemia who recently joined R Company and enrolled in its health insurance plan, files a charge of discrimination alleging that the disability-based pre-existing condition clause violates the ADA. If R is unable to demonstrate that its health insurance plan is bona fide and that the disability-specific pre-existing condition clause is not a subterfuge, a violation of the ADA will be found.

It should be noted that the ADA does not provide a "safe harbor" for health insurance plans that were adopted prior to its July 26, 1990 enactment. As the Senate Report states, subterfuge is to be determined "regardless of the date an insurance or employer benefit plan was adopted." Senate Report at 85; see also House Labor report at 136-138; House Judiciary Report at 70-71; Appendix to 29 C.F.R. § 1630.16(f). Consequently, the challenged disability-based terms and provisions of a pre-ADA health insurance plan will be scrutinized under the same subterfuge standard as are the challenged disability-based terms, provisions, and conditions of post-ADA health insurance plans.[10]

C. The Respondent's Burden of Proof

Once the Commission has determined that a challenged health insurance term or provision constitutes a disability-based distinction, the respondent must prove that the health insurance plan is either a bona fide insured plan that is not inconsistent with state law, or a bona fide self-insured plan. The respondent must also prove that the challenged disability-based distinction is not being used as a subterfuge. Requiring the respondent to bear this burden of proving entitlement to the protection of section 501(c) is consistent with the well-established principle that the burden of proof

---

[10] It has been suggested that the Commission should interpret "subterfuge" under the ADA as having the same meaning as was accorded that term under the Age Discrimination in Employment Act (ADEA) of 1967, 29 U.S.C. § 621 et seq. In *Ohio Public Employees Retirement System v. Betts*, 492 U.S. 158 (1989), the Court held that a pre-ADEA benefit plan could not be a subterfuge, and that, since the ADEA did not expressly apply to fringe benefits, subterfuge required a showing of the employer's specific intent to discriminate in some non-fringe aspect of the employment relationship. However, both the language of the ADA, expressly covering "fringe benefits," and the Act's legislative history, rejecting the concept of a "safe harbor" for pre-ADA plans, make plain congressional intent that the Betts approach not be applied in the context of the ADA.

should rest with the party who has the greatest access to the relevant facts.[11] In the health insurance context, it is the respondent employer (and/or the employer's insurer, if any) who has control of the risk assessment, actuarial, and/or claims data relied upon in adopting the challenged disability-based distinction. Charging party employees have no access to such data, and, generally speaking, have no information about the employer provided health insurance plan beyond that contained in the employer provided health insurance plan description. Consequently, it is the employer who should bear the burden of proving that the challenged disability-based insurance distinction is within the protective ambit of section 501(c).

1. The Health Insurance Plan Is "Bona Fide" and Consistent with Applicable Law

In order to gain the protection of section 501(c) for a challenged disability-based insurance distinction, the respondent must first prove that the health insurance plan in which the challenged distinction is contained is either a bona fide insured health insurance plan that is not inconsistent with state law, or a bona fide self-insured health insurance plan.[12] If the health insurance plan is an insured plan, the respondent will be able to satisfy this requirement by proving that: 1) the health insurance plan is bona fide in that it exists and pays benefits, and its terms have been accurately communicated to eligible employees; and 2) the health insurance plan's terms are not inconsistent with applicable state law as interpreted by the appropriate state authorities.[13] If the health insurance plan is a self-insured plan, the respondent will only be required to prove that the health insurance plan is bona fide in that it exists and pays benefits, and that its terms have been accurately communicated to covered employees.

2. The Disability-Based Distinction Is Not a Subterfuge

The second demonstration that the respondent must make in order to gain the protection of section 501(c) is that the challenged disability-based distinction is not a subterfuge to evade the purposes of the ADA. "Subterfuge" refers to disability-based disparate treatment that is not justified by the risks or costs associated with the disability. Whether a particular challenged disability-based insurance distinction is being used as a subterfuge will be determined on a case by case basis, considering the totality of the circumstances.

The respondent can prove that a challenged disability-based insurance distinction is not a subterfuge in several ways. A non-exclusive list of potential business/insurance justifications follows.

a. The respondent may prove that it has not engaged in the disability-based disparate treatment alleged. For example, where a charging party has alleged that a benefit cap of a particular catastrophic disability is discriminatory, the respondent may prove that its health insurance plan actually treats all similarly catastrophic conditions in the same way.

b. The respondent may prove that the disparate treatment is justified by legitimate actuarial data,[14]

---

[11] See *Morgado v. Birmingham-Jefferson County Civil Defense Corps.*, 706 F.2d 1184, 1189 (11th Cir. 1983), *cert. denied*, 464 U.S. 1045 (1984) (employer relying on Equal Pay Act provision allowing pay differentials for reasons other than sex must prove entitlement to provision's protection because such facts "are peculiarly within the knowledge of the employer"); *EEOC v. Whitin Machine Works, Inc.*, 635 F.2d 1095, 1097 (4th Cir. 1980) (when facts are "within [the] unique knowledge" of the employer, it bears burden of proof concerning those facts); *EEOC v. Radiator Specialty* Co., 610 F.2d 178, 185 n. 8 (4th Cir. 1979) ("general principle of allocation of proof to the party with the most ready access to the relevant information" requires Title VII defendant to show inappropriateness of labor pool statistics).

[12] See footnote 3, supra, for a discussion of the difference between "insured" and "self-insured" insurance plans.

[13] The term "applicable state law" refers both to the determination of: 1) which state's laws are applicable to the particular charge (e.g., which state's laws are applicable in the event that the health insurance policy was drawn up in accordance with the laws of the state of Maryland, but the insured employee resides in the state of Virginia) and 2) which laws of that appropriate state are relevant to the particular charge. With respect to health insurance plans that are MEWAs, applicable state law is determined with reference to ERISA section 514 (b)(6)(A). Questions concerning the "applicable state law" should be directed to the Regional Attorney.

[14] Actuarial data that is seriously outdated and/or inaccurate is not legitimate actuarial data. The respondent, for example, will not be able to rely on actuarial data about a disability that is based on myths, fears, or stereotypes about the disability. Nor will a respondent be able to rely on actuarial data that is based on false assumptions about disability, or on assumptions that may have once been, but are no longer, true. For example, a respondent would not be able to justify an exclusion of epilepsy from its insurance plan that is based on an erroneous assumption that people with epilepsy are more likely to have serious accidents (and thus file more claims for insurance benefits) than are individuals who do not have epilepsy.

or by actual or reasonably anticipated experience, and that conditions with comparable actuarial data and/or experience are treated in the same fashion. In other words, the respondent may prove that the disability-based disparate treatment is attributable to the application of legitimate risk classification and underwriting[15] procedures to the increased risks (and thus increased cost to the health insurance plan) of the disability, and not to the disability per se.

c. The respondent may prove that the disparate treatment is necessary (i.e., that there is no nondisability-based health insurance plan change that could be made) to ensure that the challenged health insurance plan satisfies the commonly accepted or legally required standards for the fiscal soundness of such an insurance plan. The respondent, for example, may prove that it limited coverage for the treatment of a discrete group of disabilities because continued unlimited coverage would have been so expensive as to cause the health insurance plan to become financially insolvent, and there was no nondisability-based health insurance plan alteration that would have avoided insolvency.

d. The respondent may prove that the challenged insurance practice or activity is necessary (i.e., that there is no nondisability-based change that could be made) to prevent the occurrence of an unacceptable change either in the coverage of the health insurance plan, or in the premiums charged for the health insurance plan. An "unacceptable" change is a drastic increase in premium payments (or in co-payments or deductibles), or a drastic alteration to the scope of coverage or level of benefits provided, that would: 1) make the health insurance plan effectively unavailable to a significant number of other employees, 2) make the health insurance plan so unattractive as to result in significant adverse selection,[16] or 3) make the health insurance plan so unattractive that the employer cannot compete in recruiting and maintaining qualified workers due to the superiority of health insurance plans offered by other employers in the community.

e. Where the charging party is challenging the respondent's denial of coverage for a disability-specific treatment, the respondent may prove that this treatment does not provide any benefit (i.e., has no medical value). The respondent, in other words, may prove by reliable scientific evidence that the disability-specific treatment does not cure the condition, slow the degeneration/deterioration or harm attributable to the condition, alleviate the symptoms of the condition, or maintain the current health status of individuals with the disability who receive the treatment.[17]

IV. COVERAGE OF DEPENDENTS

The coverage of an employee's dependents under an employer provided health insurance plan is a benefit available to the employee by virtue of employment. Consequently, insurance terms, provisions, and conditions concerning dependent coverage are subject to the same ADA standards, including the application of section 501(c) to disability-based distinctions, as are other insurance terms, provisions, and conditions.

The ADA, however, does not require that the coverage accorded dependents be the same in scope as the coverage accorded the employee. For example, it would not violate the ADA for a health insurance plan to cover prescription drugs for employees, but not to include such coverage for employee dependents. Nor does the ADA require that dependents be accorded the same level of benefits as that accorded the employee. Thus, it would not violate the ADA for a health insurance plan to have a $100,000 benefit cap for employees, but only a $50,000 benefit cap for employee dependents.

---

15 Risk classification refers to the identification of risk factors and the grouping of those factors that pose similar risks. Risk factors may include characteristics such as age, occupation, personal habits (e.g., smoking), and medical history. Underwriting refers to the application of the various risk factors or risk classes to a particular individual or group (usually only if the group is small) for the purpose of determining whether to provide insurance.

16 Adverse selection is the tendency of people who represent poorer-than-average health risks to apply for and/or retain health insurance to a greater extent than people who represent average or above average health risks. Drastic increases in premiums and/or drastic decreases in insurance benefits foster an increase in adverse selection, as those who are considered to be "good" insurance risks drop out and seek enrollment in an insurance plan with lower premiums and/or better benefits. An insurance plan that is subjected to a significant rate of adverse selection may, as a result of the increase in the proportion of "poor risk/high use" enrollees to "good risk/low use" enrollees, become not viable or financially unsound.

17 However, the respondent may be found to have violated the ADA if the evidence reveals that the respondent's health insurance plan covers treatments for other conditions that are likewise of no medical value.

V. CHARGE PROCESSING

1. In General

Charges alleging that a term or provision of an employer provided health insurance plan discriminates on the basis of disability should be processed in accordance with the foregoing guidance. When confronted with a charge alleging that a health insurance plan distinction is a disability-based distinction that violates the ADA, the investigator should initially determine whether the challenged insurance term or provision is, in fact, a disability-based distinction . To do this, the investigator should determine whether:

1) the insurance term, provision, or condition singles out a particular disability, discrete group of disabilities, or disability in general; and/or

2) the insurance term, provision, or condition singles out a procedure or treatment used exclusively, or nearly exclusively, for the treatment of a particular disability or discrete group of disabilities (e.g., exclusion of a drug used only to treat AIDS). (Section III. B, supra.)

If it is determined that the challenged insurance term or provision is not a disability-based distinction and is applied equally to all insured employees, the investigator should conclude that the health insurance plan distinction does not violate the ADA.

On the other hand, if the challenged insurance term or provision is found to be a disability-based distinction, the investigator should determine whether the respondent can justify the disability-based distinction by satisfying the requirements of section 501(c) of the ADA. To make this determination, the investigator should take the steps described below.

1) The investigator should obtain evidence from the respondent that the health insurance plan is a bona fide plan. (Section III.C.1, supra.)

2) If the health insurance plan is an insured plan, the investigator should also obtain evidence from the respondent that the health insurance plan is not inconsistent with the applicable state law(s). (Section III.C.1, supra.)

3) The investigator should obtain evidence from the respondent relevant to any business/insurance justification proffered to justify the disability-based insurance distinction. The evidence obtained should be specific and detailed. For example, if the respondent is relying on actuarial data to justify the disability-based distinction, the investigator should require a detailed explanation of the rationale underlying the disability-based distinction, including the actuarial conclusions arrived at, the actuarial assumptions relied upon to reach those conclusions, and the factual data that supports the assumptions and/or conclusions.

Similarly, if the respondent asserts that the disability-based distinction is justified by actual or reasonably anticipated experience, the investigator should obtain evidence about the respondent's insurance claims experience, and the way in which the respondent has reacted to similar previous experience situations. If the respondent asserts that the disability-based distinction was necessary to prevent the occurrence of an unacceptable change in coverage or premiums, or to assure the fiscal soundness of the health insurance plan, the investigator should obtain evidence of the nondisability-based options for modifying the health insurance plan that were considered and the reason(s) for the rejection of these options. If the respondent asserts that its health insurance plan excludes a disability-specific treatment because it is of no medical value, the investigator should obtain evidence regarding the scientific evidence relied upon by the respondent in reaching that determination. (Section III.C.2, supra.)

Commission staff should direct questions concerning the guidance or its application in particular cases to the Office of Legal Counsel Attorney of the Day.

Date

Approved: Tony Gallegos
Chairman

The U.S. Equal Employment Opportunity Commission

EEOC	DIRECTIVES TRANSMITTAL	Number 915.003
		October 3, 2000

SUBJECT: EEOC COMPLIANCE MANUAL

PURPOSE: This transmittal covers the issuance of Section 3 of the new Compliance Manual on "Employee Benefits." The section provides guidance and instructions for investigating and analyzing issues that arise with regard to life and health insurance benefits, long-term and short-term disability benefits, severance benefits, pension or other retirement benefits, and early retirement incentives.

EFFECTIVE DATE: Upon receipt

DISTRIBUTION: EEOC Compliance Manual holders

OBSOLETE DATA: This section of the new Compliance Manual supersedes the following Commission policy documents: EEOC Compliance Manual, Volume II, Section 627, "Employee Benefit Plans"; *Application of Section 4(f)(2) of the ADEA to Life Insurance and Long-Term Disability Plans* (No. 87-15, September 1987); *Application of Section 4(f)(2) of the ADEA to Defined Contribution Pension Plans* (No. 87-21, September 1987); *Effect of 1986 Amendments to ADEA on Commission's Enforcement Activities* (No. N-915-024, April 1988); *Application of Section 4(g) of the ADEA (Coverage of Older Workers Under Group Health Plans)* (No. 88-8, May 1988); *Cases Involving the Extension of Additional Benefits to Older Workers* (No. 88-11, June 1988); *Maternity and Pregnancy Benefits as Wages* (Compliance Manual Section 633, Appendix B, January 1989); and *Questions and Answers About Disability and Service Retirement Plans Under the ADA* (May 1995).

FILING INSTRUCTIONS: This is the third section issued as part of the new Compliance Manual.

/s/
Ida L. Castro
Chairwoman

CHAPTER 3: EMPLOYEE BENEFITS

* * *

ADA ISSUES

I. Introduction

An employer may not discriminate against a qualified individual with a disability, on the basis of disability, with respect to fringe benefits.[71] Congress recognized, however, that some types of benefit plans rest on an assessment of the risks and costs associated with various health conditions in accordance with accepted principles of risk assessment.[72] As a result, the ADA permits employers to make disability-based distinctions in employee benefit plans where the distinctions are based on sound actuarial principles or are related to actual or reasonably anticipated experience.[73] This Section addresses some of the circumstances in which those distinctions are lawful and some in which they are not.

If a charge alleges that the terms of an employee benefit plan discriminate on the basis of disability, the first question is whether the employer has provided benefits to a qualified employee with a disability that are equal to the benefits provided to employees generally under the plan. Benefits will be equal only if all employees participating in the plan, regardless of disability, receive the same types of benefits, the same payment options, and the same amounts of coverage—for the same cost.

If the employer has provided equal benefits, there is no ADA violation. If, on the other hand, the employer has provided benefits to a qualified employee with a disability that are *unequal* to the benefits provided to other employees, the next question is whether the difference is based on the employee's disability. If the difference in the benefits is not a result of a disability-based distinction, and if the challenged provision is

71 42 U.S.C. § 12112(b)(2) (defining prohibited discrimination to include participation in a contractual relationship with, *inter alia*, an entity "providing fringe benefits to an employee" with the effect of subjecting a qualified applicant or employee to prohibited discrimination); 29 C.F.R. § 1630.6(b) (same); 29 C.F.R. § 1630.4(f) (unlawful to discriminate based on disability with regard to "fringe benefits available by virtue of employment").

72 *See* S. Rep. No. 116, 101st Cong., 1st Sess. 85-86 (1989); H.R. Rep. No. 485 part 2, 101st Cong., 2d Sess. 137-138 (1990), *reprinted in* 1990 U.S.C.C.A.N. 267, 420-21.

73 42 U.S.C. § 12201(c); 29 C.F.R. § 1630.16(f).

applied equally to all employees participating in the plan, then there is no violation of the law.

If the unequal benefits provided to a qualified employee with a disability are based on disability, the benefit plan will be unlawful unless the employer can show that the disability-based distinction is not a "subterfuge" to evade the purposes of the ADA. There are several ways an employer can make this showing. *See* Section IV, *infra*.

Thus, if the charge challenges discrimination in the terms or provisions of a benefit plan, the relevant questions are the following:

- Has the employer provided equal benefits to employees with disabilities and to other employees covered by the plan?

If not,

- **Is the difference in benefits the result of a disability-based distinction in the plan?**

If so,

- **Can the employer show that the benefit plan is *bona fide* and that the disability-based distinction is not a subterfuge to evade the purposes of the ADA?**

II. Equal Benefits

For benefits to be equal, the same coverage must be provided, on the same terms, to all similarly situated employees. For example, benefit plans must be the same with regard to:

- **premiums;**
- **deductibles;**
- **caps on coverage; and**
- **waiting periods.**

EXAMPLE—Employer X's health insurance plan has a separate lifetime cap of $50,000 for the treatment of HIV/AIDS, but a general lifetime cap of $2,000,000 for the treatment of all other medical conditions. These benefits are not equal.

EXAMPLE—Employer X's health insurance plan has an annual deductible of $250, but has a separate deductible of $300 for the treatment of mental disorders. People with mental disorders have not received equal benefits.[74]

III. Disability-Based Distinctions

Not all provisions of an employer's benefit plan that are related to health, and that result in unequal benefits for individuals with disabilities, are based on disability. A health-related distinction that is not disability-based, and that is applied equally to all employees, does not violate the ADA. Therefore, the next question is whether any difference in benefits arises from a disability-based distinction.

A health-related distinction in a benefit plan *is* disability-based if it singles out:

- **a particular disability;**
- **a discrete group of disabilities; or**
- **disability in general.**

The following are examples of disability-based distinctions.

EXAMPLE—Singles out a particular disability. Employer Z's disability retirement plan covers all physical and mental disorders except major depression.

EXAMPLE—Singles out a discrete group of disabilities. Employer Z's health insurance plan caps coverage for treatment of cancers at one million dollars but caps coverage for the treatment of all other physical conditions at 20 million dollars.

EXAMPLE—Singles out disability in general. Employer Z requires employees who are no longer able to work because of a physical or mental disorder to retire on disability retirement, even if they also are eligible to retire under the employer's service retirement plan.

Generally, a health-related distinction in a benefit plan *is not* disability-based if:

- **it is a broad distinction which applies to a multitude of dissimilar conditions,** ***and***
- **it constrains both individuals with and individuals without disabilities.**

EXAMPLE—Employer U's health insurance plan treats workers' compensation as primary, and provides only secondary coverage, for conditions which are attributable to occupational injury or ill-

74 The fact that individuals with particular disabilities have not received equal benefits does not necessarily mean that the plan violates the ADA. An investigator must still determine whether the distinction drawn by the plan is disability-based. In the context of health insurance, for example, differences in the coverage of expenses for mental and physical conditions are not disability-based distinctions. [*See* notes 75-77 and accompanying text.]

ness. Because many different types of impairments may result from occupational injury or illness, and because the limit on coverage affects employees with and without disabilities, this is not a disability-based distinction.

EXAMPLE—Employer U's long-term disability plan has a 6-month waiting period for all pre-existing conditions. This is not a disability-based distinction.

EXAMPLE—Employer U's health insurance plan covers only two Electronic Resonance Imaging (ERI) scans per year per patient. Because ERI scans are used for all kinds of conditions and because the limitation affects both individuals with and individuals without disabilities, this provision is not based on disability.

The Commission has also taken the position that it is not necessarily a disability-based distinction if an employer's health insurance plan provides unequal benefits for mental conditions compared to physical conditions.[75] This is because, in the context of health insurance, the term "mental conditions" covers, for example, not only impairments like schizophrenia and major depression—which likely would be disabilities under the ADA—but also counseling for grief, self-esteem, or marital problems, which are not impairments and so are not ADA disabilities.[76] As a result, a distinction in a health insurance plan's coverage of expenses for treatment of physical, as compared with mental, conditions (a) constitutes a broad distinction that covers a multitude of dissimilar conditions, and (b) limits both individuals with and those without disabilities. Such distinctions in health insurance plans thus will not generally violate the ADA.[77]

IV. Justifications for Disability-Based Distinctions

If an employer has made a disability-based distinction in a benefit plan, it will be liable for a violation of the ADA unless it can show that the distinction is justified. The ADA sets forth two elements to the defense. An employer must demonstrate that:

- **the benefit plan is *bona fide*; and**
- **the plan is not a subterfuge to evade the purposes of the ADA.**[78]

A. *Bona fide* plans

Under the first prong of the defense, an employer must demonstrate that its plan is either a *bona fide* insured plan that is not inconsistent with state law, or a *bona fide* self-insured plan.[79] To be *bona fide*, a plan must exist and pay benefits; in addition, the terms of the plan must have been accurately communicated to eligible employees. To determine whether a plan meets this standard, investigators typically need simply obtain a copy of the employer's plan documents and

---

75 *Interim Enforcement Guidance on the Application of the Americans with Disabilities Act of 1990 to Disability-Based Distinctions in Employer Provided Health Insurance*, No. N-915.002 (June 8, 1993), at p. 6.

76 Mental conditions are "impairments" only if they are based on a mental or psychological "disorder." 29 C.F.R. § 1630.2(h) (1998).

77 The Commission has taken the position in litigation, on the other hand, that distinctions between mental and physical conditions in long-term disability (LTD) plans are disability-based. Generally, an employee becomes eligible for LTD benefits when s/he is no longer able to work because of a serious permanent or long-term illness or injury. This means that in most instances employees who are eligible for or are receiving LTD benefits have disabilities as defined by the ADA, because their impairments substantially limit their ability to work or to engage in one or more other major life activities. Courts have disagreed with the Commission's position and have held that treating physical and mental conditions differently in an LTD plan does not violate the ADA. *See, e.g.*, *EEOC v. Staten Island Savings Bank*, 207 F.3d 144 (2d Cir. 2000) (equal coverage of all disabilities not required by ADA); *Lewis v. Kmart Corp.*, 180 F.3d 166, 170 (4th Cir. 1999) (ADA does not require a long-term disability plan sponsored by a private employer to provide the same level of benefits for mental and physical disabilities), *cert. denied*, 68 U.S.L.W. 3311 (U.S. Jan. 24, 2000); *Ford v. Schering-Plough Corp.*, 145 F.3d 601, 611 (3d Cir. 1998) (*en banc*) (employer and insurance company need not justify actuarial basis for difference in benefits in long-term disability plan for mental and physical conditions), *cert. denied*, 119 S. Ct. 850 (1999); *but see Olmstead v. L.C.*, 527 U.S. 581 (1999) (ADA prohibits discrimination between different types of disabilities).

78 42 U.S.C. § 12201.

79 An "insured" benefit plan is a plan that is purchased from an insurance company or other entity. In a "self-insured" plan, the employer directly assumes the liability of an insurer. Insured benefit plans are regulated by both ERISA and state law. Self-insured benefit plans are typically subject to ERISA, but are not subject to state laws that regulate insurance.

confirm that benefits have in fact been paid.[80]

B. Subterfuge

The term "subterfuge" refers to disability-based disparate treatment in an employee benefit plan that is not justified by the risks or costs associated with the disability—that is, to disability-based distinctions that are not "based on sound actuarial principles or related to actual or reasonably anticipated experience."[81] Whether a provision of a benefit plan is a subterfuge must be determined on a case-by-case basis.

There are several ways that an employer can prove that a disability-based distinction in a benefit plan is *not* a subterfuge. Among possible justifications are the following.

- **The employer may prove that it has not engaged in the disability-based disparate treatment alleged.**

> **EXAMPLE**—CP alleges that Employer N has refused to cover treatment for her diabetes, despite the fact that it has covered a coworker's costs for treatment of her rheumatoid arthritis. Employer N shows that it refused to cover CP's diabetes because the condition predated her enrollment in the insurance plan, and further that it treats all pre-existing conditions similarly.

- **The employer may prove that the disability-based disparate treatment is justified by legitimate actuarial data, or by actual or reasonably anticipated experience, and that conditions with comparable actuarial data and/or experience are treated the same way.**

Actuarial data will measure both the likelihood that the employer will incur insurance costs related to the disability and magnitude of those costs as they arise. Thus, employers must show that the reduction in coverage for the disability or disabilities is required to account for an increased possibility that the benefit will be claimed or that the amounts required for coverage will be higher. Employers may not, however, rely on actuarial data that is outdated or that is based on myths, fears, stereotypes, or assumptions about the disability at issue.

Even where employers can produce actuarial data that demonstrates that the risks and costs of treatment of a condition justify differential treatment of it, employers must also show that they have treated other conditions that pose the same risks and costs the same way. If there is evidence that an employer has treated other conditions differently from the disability at issue, the employer has discriminated by singling out a particular disability for disadvantageous treatment. Investigators should find cause.

- **The employer may prove that the disability-based disparate treatment is necessary to maintain the solvency of the plan.** To establish this defense, employers must show:
  - **that covering the disability or disabilities at issue would require such substantial payments of benefits that it would threaten the fiscal soundness of the plan under commonly accepted or legally required standards, *and***
  - **that there is no non-disability-based benefit plan change that could be made to limit those fiscal consequences.**

If an employer raises this defense, contact the Office of Legal Counsel.

- **The employer may prove that the challenged practice or activity is necessary to avoid unacceptable changes in the coverage of, or the premiums for, a benefit plan.** An "unacceptable" change is a drastic increase in premium payments (or in co-payments or deductibles), or a drastic alteration to the scope of coverage or level of benefits provided, that would:
  - **increase the cost to other employees so substantially that the benefit plan would be effectively unavailable to a significant number of them;**

---

[80] If questions arise concerning whether a *bona fide* insured plan is consistent with state law, contact the Regional Attorney.

[81] H.R. Rep. No. 485, part 3, 101st Cong., 2d Sess. 7 (1990), *reprinted in* 1990 U.S.C.C.A.N. 267, 494; *see also* S. Rep. No. 116, 101st Cong., 1st Sess. 85-86 (1989) (benefit plan protected under the ADA only if administered in a manner consistent with basic principles of insurance risk classification).

- **make the benefit plan so unattractive as to result in significant adverse selection;**[82] **or**
- **make the benefit plan so unattractive that the employer cannot compete in recruiting and maintaining qualified workers due to the superiority of benefit plans offered by other employers in the community.**

- **The employer may prove that a particular treatment that it has excluded from a health insurance plan provides *no* medical benefit.** The employer, in other words, may prove by reliable scientific evidence that the disability-specific treatment does not cure the condition, slow the degeneration/deterioration or harm attributable to the condition, alleviate the symptoms of the condition, or maintain the current health status of individuals with the disability who receive the treatment. The employer may not rely on this argument, however, if it covers treatments for other conditions that are likewise of no medical value when judged by these tests.

For a disability-based distinction to be a subterfuge, it is not necessary that it have been adopted (a) after enactment of the ADA; or (b) with the intent to discriminate in hiring, promotion, termination, or other non-benefit employment decisions.[83] First, the legislative history shows that Congress intended to reach insurance or benefit plans that were adopted prior to enactment of the ADA.[84] In addition, the ADA explicitly bans discrimination in fringe benefits, and is not limited to discrimination in hiring, firing, or other non-benefit aspects of employment. As a result, it is not necessary to prove that discrimination in fringe benefits was intended as a means to discriminate in other employment decisions.[85]

V. Disability Retirement and Service Retirement Plans

Employers are not *required* to provide disability and/or service retirement plans for their employees. In addition, it does not violate the ADA for an employer to offer only a service retirement—but not a disability retirement—plan. Where an employer establishes either or both types of plans, however, it may not discriminate against employees with disabilities.

An employer will violate the ADA if it does any of the following:

- **Excludes employees from participation in a service retirement or disability retirement plan because of their disabilities.**

> **EXAMPLE**—Employer F requires employees covered by the ADA who qualify for both service and disability retirement plans to take the disability retirement benefit. This violates the ADA.

- **Requires different lengths of employment for participation by individuals with disabilities and individuals without disabilities in the employer's service retirement or disability retirement plans.**

---

82 Adverse selection is the tendency of people who represent greater risks to apply for and/or retain a fringe benefit to a greater extent than people who represent average or below average risks. Drastic increases in premiums and/or drastic decreases in benefits foster an increase in adverse selection, as those who are considered to be "good" risks drop out and seek enrollment in a benefit plan with lower premiums and/or better benefits. A benefit plan that is subjected to a significant rate of adverse selection may, as a result of the increase in the proportion of "poor risk/high use" enrollees to "good risk/low use" enrollees, become not viable or financially unsound.

83 This showing was required under a prior version of the ADEA in order to prove that an age-based distinction in benefits was a subterfuge to evade the purposes of that law. *See Ohio Public Employees Retirement Syst. v. Betts*, 492 U.S. 158 (1989). Congress legislatively superseded *Betts* by enacting amendments to the ADEA in the Older Workers Benefit Protection Act of 1990, *codified at* 29 U.S.C. § 623(f)(2).

84 *See* H.R. Rep. No. 485, part 2, 101st Cong., 2d Sess. 137, *reprinted in* 1990 U.S.C.C.A.N. at 420; S. Rep. No. 116, 101st Cong., 1st Sess. 85 (1989).

85 Courts are split on the issue of whether the *Betts* analysis applies to disability-based distinctions in fringe benefits. *Compare, e.g., Cloutier v. Prudential Ins. Co. of Am.*, 964 F. Supp. 299, 304 (N.D. Cal. 1996) (*Betts* inapplicable; to meet defense, insurers must show that underwriting decisions accord with either sound actuarial principles or with actual or reasonably anticipated experience), *with, e.g., Ford v. Schering-Plough Corp.*, 145 F.3d 601, 611 (3d Cir. 1998) (*en banc*) (*Betts* applies and bars most challenges to LTD plans adopted after enactment of the ADA), *cert. denied*, 119 S. Ct. 850 (1999). The Commission disagrees with cases applying the *Betts* analysis because the ADA makes clear that discrimination in fringe benefits is covered, regardless of the date of adoption of the plan, and is unlawful absent an actuarial justification for disability-based distinctions in coverage.

EXAMPLE—Employer F requires that employees with disabilities complete 12 years of service before being allowed to enroll in its service retirement plan; the employer permits employees without disabilities to enroll in the service retirement plan after 10 years of service. This is discriminatory.

- **Sets different levels or types of coverage for individuals with and without disabilities in a service retirement plan.**

EXAMPLE—In its service retirement plan, Employer G gives cost-of-living increases to employees without disabilities every three years, but gives such increases to employees with disabilities only every five years. This violates the ADA.
EXAMPLE—Under Employer G's service retirement plan, employees with AIDS receive a benefit equal to 33% of their highest annual compensation. All other eligible employees receive 50% of their highest annual compensation. This discriminates against individuals with a particular disability and is unlawful.

However, the ADA does not require that service retirement and disability retirement plans provide the same level of benefits, because they are two separate benefits which serve two different purposes. As long as all employees may participate in the service retirement plan on the same terms, regardless of the existence of a disability, an employer will not violate the ADA if it provides lower levels of benefits in its disability than in its service retirement plans.

EXAMPLE—Employer Q's service retirement plan enables any employee with 20 or more years of service to retire with an annuity equal to 30% of the individual's highest annual compensation. Employer Q's disability retirement plan, payable when illness or injury prevent the individual from continuing work, provides an annuity equal only to 25% of the employee's highest annual compensation. This does not violate the ADA, as long as employees who are eligible for both have the right to choose between disability and service retirement programs.

EXAMPLE—Under Employer Q's service retirement plan, retirees receive periodic increases (*e.g.*, based on inflation or an increased return on invested pension funds). Under the employer's disability retirement plan, disability retirees get fixed benefits. This is not unlawful.

In addition, it does not violate the ADA for an employer to deny service retirement benefits to those who have previously chosen voluntarily to take disability retirement benefits. Investigators should find no cause if charges challenging such denials arise and the charging party voluntarily opted for disability retirement benefits.[86]

QUESTIONS AND ANSWERS: COMPLIANCE MANUAL SECTION ON EMPLOYEE BENEFITS

INTRODUCTION

What does this Compliance Manual section address?

- This Compliance Manual section explains how the employment discrimination laws apply to life and health insurance benefits, long-term and short-term disability benefits, severance benefits, pension or other retirement benefits, and early retirement incentives. The section covers discrimination in these benefits under the Age Discrimination in Employment Act (ADEA), the Americans with Disabilities Act (ADA), Title VII of the Civil Rights Act of 1964 (Title VII), and the Equal Pay Act (EPA).

Why did the EEOC issue this Compliance Manual section?

- The section first defines the types of benefits it discusses and then provides an overview of applicable rules. It then separately explains the requirements regarding benefits under the ADEA, the ADA, and Title VII and the EPA. The section contains a detailed Table of Contents to permit users to quickly find relevant information.

The following Questions and Answers summarize the most important points in this chapter of the

86 *See Castellano v. City of New York*, 142 F.3d 58, 70 (2d Cir.), *cert. denied*, 119 S. Ct. 60 (1998).

Compliance Manual.

AMERICANS WITH DISABILITIES ACT

Does the ADA bar discrimination on the basis of disability in benefits?

- Yes. Employers may not make disability-based distinctions in employee benefits unless they can show that the distinction is not a subterfuge to evade the purposes of the ADA.

What is a disability-based distinction?

- A disability-based distinction singles out for different treatment (a) a particular disability; (b) a discrete group of disabilities; or (c) disability in general. For example, a cap on the health insurance benefits that an employer will pay for AIDS is a disability-based distinction.

A benefit plan provision that applies to a number of dissimilar conditions, and that affects both individuals with and individuals without disabilities, is not a disability-based distinction. It is not a disability-based distinction, for example, if an employer's health insurance plan has a waiting period for pre-existing conditions.

Distinctions that are not disability-based do not violate the ADA.

What is a subterfuge to evade the purposes of the ADA?

- A subterfuge is a disability-based distinction that an employer cannot justify. The ADA provides for several types of justifications. For example, an employer will not violate the ADA if a disability-based distinction is justified by actuarial data or is necessary to avoid prohibitive increases in the premiums for other employees.

May an employer provide different benefits in its disability retirement and service retirement plans?

- Yes. Because disability retirement and service retirement plans serve two different purposes, the ADA does not require that they each provide the same benefits. The ADA is satisfied as long as all employees may participate in the service retirement plan on the same terms, regardless of the existence of a disability.

The U.S. Equal Employment Opportunity Commission

EEOC	NOTICE	Number 915.002
		Date 7/27/00

1. SUBJECT: EEOC Enforcement Guidance on Disability-Related Inquiries and Medical Examinations of Employees Under the Americans with Disabilities Act (ADA)
2. PURPOSE: This enforcement guidance explains when it is permissible for employers to make disability-related inquiries or require medical examinations of employees.
3. EFFECTIVE DATE: Upon receipt.
4. EXPIRATION DATE: As an exception to EEOC Order 205.001, Appendix B, Attachment 4, § a(5), this Notice will remain in effect until rescinded or superseded.
5. ORIGINATOR: ADA Division, Office of Legal Counsel.
6. INSTRUCTIONS: File after Section 902 of Volume II of the Compliance Manual.

7/27/00 /s/
Date Ida L. Castro
Chairwoman

DISTRIBUTION: CM Holders

ENFORCEMENT GUIDANCE: DISABILITY-RELATED INQUIRIES AND MEDICAL EXAMINATIONS OF EMPLOYEES UN-DER THE AMERICANS WITH DISABILITIES ACT (ADA)

TABLE OF CONTENTS

INTRODUCTION

Title I of the Americans with Disabilities Act of 1990 (the "ADA")[1] limits an employer's ability to make disability-related inquiries or require medical examinations at three stages: pre-offer, post-offer, and during employment. In its guidance on preemployment disability-related inquiries and medical examinations, the Commission addressed the ADA's restrictions on disability-related inquiries and medical examinations at the pre- and post-offer stages.[2] This enforcement guidance focuses on the ADA's limitations on disability-related inquiries and medical examinations during employment.[3]

Disability-related inquiries and medical examinations of employees must be "job-related and consistent with business necessity." This guidance gives examples of the kinds of questions that are and are not "disability-related" and examples of tests and procedures

1 42 U.S.C. §§ 12101-12117, 12201-12213 (1994) (codified as amended).

2 Enforcement Guidance: Preemployment Disability-Related Questions and Medical Examinations Under the Americans with Disabilities Act of 1990, 8 FEP Manual (BNA) 405:7191 (1995) [hereinafter Preemployment Questions and Medical Examinations]. This and other ADA guidances are available through the Internet at http://www.eeoc.gov.

3 Pursuant to the Rehabilitation Act Amendment of 1992, the ADA's employment standards apply to all nonaffirmative action employment discrimination claims of individuals with disabilities who are federal employees or applicants for federal employment. Pub. L. No. 102-569 § 503(b), 106 Stat. 4344, 4424 (1992) (codified as amended at 29 U.S.C. § 791(g) (1994)). Accordingly, the analysis in the guidance applies to federal sector complaints of nonaffirmative action employment discrimination arising under section 501 of the Rehabilitation Act of 1973. It also applies to complaints of nonaffirmative action employment discrimination arising under section 503 and to employment discrimination under section 504 of the Rehabilitation Act. *Id.* at §§ 793(d), 794(d) (1994).

that generally are and are not "medical." The guidance also defines what the term "job-related and consistent with business necessity" means and addresses situations in which an employer would meet the general standard for asking an employee a disability-related question or requiring a medical examination. Other acceptable inquiries and examinations of employees, such as inquiries and examinations required by federal law and those that are part of voluntary wellness and health screening programs, as well as invitations to voluntarily self-identify as persons with disabilities for affirmative action purposes, also are addressed.[4]

GENERAL PRINCIPLES

A. Background

Historically, many employers asked applicants and employees to provide information concerning their physical and/or mental condition. This information often was used to exclude and otherwise discriminate against individuals with disabilities—particularly non-visible disabilities, such as diabetes, epilepsy, heart disease, cancer, and mental illness—despite their ability to perform the job. The ADA's provisions concerning disability-related inquiries and medical examinations reflect Congress's intent to protect the rights of applicants and employees to be assessed on merit alone, while protecting the rights of employers to ensure that individuals in the workplace can efficiently perform the essential functions of their jobs.[5]

Under the ADA, an employer's ability to make disability-related inquiries or require medical examinations is analyzed in three stages: pre-offer, post-offer, and employment. At the first stage (**prior to an offer of employment**), the ADA prohibits all disability-related inquiries and medical examinations, *even if* they are related to the job.[6] At the second stage (**after an applicant is given a conditional job offer, but before s/he starts work**), an employer may make disability-related inquiries and conduct medical examinations, regardless of whether they are related to the job, as long as it does so for all entering employees in the same job category.[7] At the third stage (**after employment begins**), an employer may make disability-related inquiries and require medical examinations *only* if they are job-related and consistent with business necessity.[8]

The ADA requires employers to treat any medical information obtained from a disability-related inquiry or medical examination (including medical information from voluntary health or wellness programs[9]) as well as any medical information voluntarily disclosed by an employee, as a confidential medical record. Employers may share such information only in limited circumstances with supervisors, managers, first aid

---

4 The purpose of this guidance is to explain when it is permissible for an employer to make a disability-related inquiry or require a medical examination of an employee. It does not focus on what actions an employer may take based on what it learns in response to such an inquiry or after it receives the result of a medical examination.

5 In the ADA legislative history, Congress stated that an employee's "actual performance on the job is, of course, the best measure of ability to do the job." S. Rep. No. 101-116, at 39 (1989); H.R. Rep. No. 101-485, pt. 2, at 75 (1990).

6 However, where an applicant has an obvious disability, and the employer has a reasonable belief that s/he will need a reasonable accommodation to perform specific job functions, the employer may ask whether the applicant needs a reasonable accommodation and, if so, what type of accommodation. These same two questions may be asked when an individual voluntarily discloses a nonvisible disability or voluntarily tells the employer that s/he will need a reasonable accommodation to perform a job. 42 U.S.C. § 12112(c)(B) (1994); 29 C.F.R. § 1630.13(a) (1998); *see also* Preemployment Questions and Medical Examinations, *supra* note 2, at 6-8, 8 FEP at 405:7193-94; EEOC Enforcement Guidance on the Americans with Disabilities Act and Psychiatric Disabilities at 13-15, 8 FEP Manual (BNA) 405:7461, 7467-68 (1997) [hereinafter The ADA and Psychiatric Disabilities]; Enforcement Guidance: Reasonable Accommodation and Undue Hardship Under the Americans with Disabilities Act at 20-21, 8 FEP Manual (BNA) 405:7601, 7611 (1999) [hereinafter Reasonable Accommodation Under the ADA]. Under certain circumstances, an employer also may ask applicants to self-identify as individuals with disabilities for purposes of its affirmative action program. *See* Preemployment Questions and Medical Examinations, *supra* note 2, at 12-13, 8 FEP at 405:7196-97.

7 42 U.S.C. § 12112(d)(3) (1994); 29 C.F.R. § 1630.14(b) (1998). However, if an individual is screened out because of a disability, the employer must show that the exclusionary criterion is job-related and consistent with business necessity. 42 U.S.C. § 12112(b)(6) (1994); 29 C.F.R. §§ 1630.10, 1630.14(b)(3) (1998).

8 42 U.S.C. § 12112(d)(4)(A) (1994); 29 C.F.R. § 1630.14(c) (1998).

9 *See infra* note 77.

and safety personnel, and government officials investigating compliance with the ADA.[10]

B. Disability-Related Inquiries and Medical Examinations of Employees

The ADA states, in relevant part:

> A covered entity[11] shall not require a medical examination and shall not make inquiries of an employee as to whether such employee is an individual with a disability or as to the nature and severity of the disability, unless such examination or inquiry is shown to be job-related and consistent with business necessity.[12]

This statutory language makes clear that the ADA's restrictions on inquiries and examinations apply to all employees, not just those with disabilities. Unlike other provisions of the ADA which are limited to qualified individuals with disabilities,[13] the use of the term "employee" in this provision reflects Congress's intent to cover a broader class of individuals and to prevent employers from asking questions and conducting medical examinations that serve no legitimate purpose.[14] Requiring an individual to show that s/he is a person with a disability in order to challenge a disability-related inquiry or medical examination would defeat this purpose.[15] Any employee, therefore, has a right to challenge a disability-related inquiry or medical exam-

---

[10] 42 U.S.C. §§ 12112(d)(3)(B), (4)(C) (1994); 29 C.F.R. § 1630.14(b)(1) (1998). The Commission also has interpreted the ADA to allow employers to disclose medical information to state workers' compensation offices, state second injury funds, workers' compensation insurance carriers, and to health care professionals when seeking advice in making reasonable accommodation determinations. 29 C.F.R. pt. 1630, app. § 1630.14(b) (1998). Employers also may use medical information for insurance purposes. *Id. See also* Preemployment Questions and Medical Examinations, *supra* note 2, at 21-23, 8 FEP at 405:7201; EEOC Enforcement Guidance: Workers' Compensation and the ADA at 7, 8 FEP Manual (BNA) 405:7391, 7394 (1996) [hereinafter Workers' Compensation and the ADA].

[11] "Covered entity" means an employer, employment agency, labor organization, or joint labor management committee. 29 C.F.R. § 1630.2(b) (1998). For simplicity, this guidance refers to all covered entities as "employers." The definition of "employer" includes persons who are "agents" of the employer, such as managers, supervisors, or others who act for the employer (*e.g.*, agencies used to conduct background checks on applicants and employees). 42 U.S.C. § 12111(5) (1994).

[12] 42 U.S.C. § 12112(d)(4)(A) (1994); 29 C.F.R. § 1630.14(c) (1998). *See infra* Question 5 and accompanying text for a discussion of what the "job-related and consistent with business necessity" standard means.

[13] *See, e.g.,* 42 U.S.C. § 12112(a) (1994) (no entity shall discriminate against a qualified individual with a disability because of the disability of such individual).

[14] Congress was particularly concerned about questions that allowed employers to learn which employees have disabilities that are not apparent from observation. It concluded that the only way to protect employees with nonvisible disabilities is to prohibit employers from making disability-related inquiries and requiring medical examinations that are not job-related and consistent with business necessity. *See* S. Rep. No. 101-116 at 39-40 (1989); H.R. Rep. No. 101-485, pt. 2, at 75 (1990) ("An inquiry or medical examination that is not job-related serves no legitimate employer purpose, but simply serves to stigmatize the person with a disability." A person with cancer "may object merely to being identified, independent of the consequences [since] being identified as [a person with a disability] often carries both blatant and subtle stigma").

[15] *See Roe v. Cheyenne Mountain Resort,* 124 F.3d 1221, 1229, 7 AD Cas. (BNA) 779, 783 (10th Cir. 1997) ("it makes little sense to require an employee to demonstrate that he has a disability to prevent his employer from inquiring as to whether or not he has a disability"). Although *Roe* involved only the issue of disability-related inquiries of employees, the same rationale applies to medical examinations of employees and to disability-related inquiries and medical examinations of applicants. The ADA's restrictions on disability-related inquiries and medical examinations apply to individuals both with and without disabilities at all three stages: pre-offer, post-offer, and during employment. *See also Griffin v. Steeltek, Inc.*, 160 F.3d 591, 595, 8 AD Cas. 1249, 1252 (10th Cir. 1998), *cert. denied,* 119 S. Ct. 1455, 9 AD Cas. 416 (1999) (a job applicant without a disability can sue under the ADA regarding medical history questions); *Gonzales v. Sandoval County*, 2 F. Supp. 2d 1442, 1445, 8 AD Cas. 1337, 1340 (D. N.M. 1998) (plaintiff need not establish disability to state a claim for a prohibited inquiry under the ADA); *Fredenburg v. Contra Costa County Department of Health Services*, 172 F.3d 1176, 9 AD Cas. 385 (9th Cir. 1999) (requiring plaintiffs to prove that they are persons with disabilities to challenge a medical examination would render § 12112(d)(4)(A) of the ADA "nugatory"; thus, plaintiffs need not prove that they are qualified individuals with a disability to bring claims challenging the scope of medical examinations under the ADA). Some courts, however, have held that to bring a claim alleging a violation of the ADA's prohibition against disability-related inquiries and medical examinations, an individual must demonstrate that s/he is a qualified individual with a disability. *See, e.g., Armstrong v. Turner Industries, Inc.*, 141 F.3d 554, 558, 8 AD Cas. (BNA) 118, 124 (5th Cir. 1998), *aff'g* 950 F. Supp. 162, 7 AD Cas. 875 (M.D. La. 1996) (plaintiff must be a qualified individual with a disability to challenge an illegal preemployment inquiry); *Hunter v. Habegger Corp.*, 139 F.3d 901 (7th Cir.

ination that is not job-related and consistent with business necessity.

Only disability-related inquiries and medical examinations are subject to the ADA's restrictions. Thus, the first issue that must be addressed is whether the employer's question is a "disability-related inquiry" or whether the test or procedure it is requiring is a "medical examination." The next issue is whether the person being questioned or asked to submit to a medical examination is an "employee." If the person is an employee (rather than an applicant or a person who has received a conditional job offer), the final issue is whether the inquiry or examination is "job-related and consistent with business necessity" or is otherwise permitted by the ADA.[16]

1. What is a **"disability-related inquiry"**?

In its guidance on Preemployment Questions and Medical Examinations, the Commission explained in detail what is and is not a disability-related inquiry.[17] A "disability-related inquiry" is a **question (or series of questions) that is likely to elicit information about a disability.**[18] The same standards for determining whether a question is disability-related in the pre- and post-offer stages apply to the employment stage.[19]

Disability-related inquiries may include the following:

- asking an employee whether s/he has (or ever had) a disability or how s/he became disabled or inquiring about the nature or severity of an employee's disability;[20]
- asking an employee to provide medical documentation regarding his/her disability;
- asking an employee's co-worker, family member, doctor, or another person about an employee's disability;
- asking about an employee's genetic information;[21]
- asking about an employee's prior workers' compensation history;[22]
- asking an employee whether s/he currently is taking any prescription drugs or medications, whether s/he has taken any such drugs or medications in the past, or monitoring an employee's taking of such drugs or medications;[23] and,

---

1998) ("it seems clear that in order to assert that one has been discriminated against because of an improper inquiry, that person must also have been otherwise qualified"). For the reasons stated above, it is the Commission's position that the plain language of the statute explicitly protects individuals with and *without* disabilities from improper disability-related inquiries and medical examinations.

[16] For example, employers may make disability-related inquiries and require medical examinations that are required or necessitated by another federal law or regulation. *See infra* Question 21 and accompanying text. Employers also may make disability-related inquiries and conduct medical examinations that are part of their voluntary wellness programs. *See infra* Question 22 and accompanying text.

[17] Preemployment Questions and Medical Examinations, *supra* note 2, at 4-13, 8 FEP at 405:7191, 7192-97.

[18] *Id.* at 4, 8 FEP at 405:7192.

[19] *Id.* at 4-13, 8 FEP at 405:7192-97.

[20] The prohibition against making disability-related inquiries applies to inquiries made directly to an employee, as well as to indirect or surreptitious inquiries such as a search through an employee's belongings to confirm an employer's suspicions about an employee's medical condition. *See Doe v. Kohn Nast & Graf, P.C.*, 866 F. Supp. 190, 3 AD Cas. (BNA) 1322 (E.D. Pa. 1994) (employer conducted an unlawful medical inquiry when it searched the office of an employee it knew was sick and discovered a letter indicating the employee had AIDS).

[21] As used in this guidance, the term "genetic information" has the same definition as "protected genetic information" in Executive Order 13145. In general, genetic information is information about an individual's genetic tests, information about the genetic tests of an individual's family members, or information about the occurrence of a disease, medical condition, or disorder in family members of the individual. *See* Exec. Order No. 13,145, To Prohibit Discrimination in Federal Employment Based on Genetic Information, 65 Fed. Reg. 6877 (Feb. 8, 2000).

[22] *See Griffin v. Steeltek, Inc.*, 160 F.3d 591, 594, 8 AD Cas. (BNA) 1249, 1252 (10th Cir. 1998), *cert. denied,* 119 S.Ct. 1455, 9 AD. Cas. 416 (1999) (on its application for employment, employer unlawfully asked: "Have you received workers' compensation or disability payments? If yes, describe.").

[23] *See Roe v. Cheyenne Mountain Conference Resort, Inc.*, 124 F.3d 1221, 7 AD Cas. (BNA) 779 (10th Cir. 1997) (employer had a policy of requiring all employees to report every drug, including legal prescription drugs); *Krocka v. Bransfield*, 969 F. Supp. 1073 (N.D. Ill. 1997) (police department implemented a policy of monitoring employees taking psychotropic medication).

- asking an employee a **broad** question about his/her impairments that is likely to elicit information about a disability (*e.g.*, What impairments do you have?).[24]

Questions that are not likely to elicit information about a disability are *not* disability-related inquiries and, therefore, are not prohibited under the ADA.

Questions that are permitted include the following:

- asking generally about an employee's **well being** (*e.g.*, How are you?), asking an employee who looks tired or ill if s/he is feeling okay, asking an employee who is sneezing or coughing whether s/he has a cold or allergies, or asking how an employee is doing following the death of a loved one or the end of a marriage/relationship;
- asking an employee about nondisability-related impairments (*e.g.*, How did you break your leg?)[25]
- asking an employee whether s/he can perform job functions;
- asking an employee whether s/he has been drinking;[26]
- asking an employee about his/her **current illegal use of drugs**;[27]
- asking a pregnant employee how she is feeling or when her baby is due;[28]and,
- asking an employee to provide the name and telephone number of a person to contact in case of a medical emergency.

2. What is a **"medical examination"**?

A "medical examination" is a **procedure or test that seeks information about an individual's physical or mental impairments or health**.[29] The guidance on Preemployment Questions and Medical Examinations lists the following factors that should be considered to determine whether a test (or procedure) is a medical examination: (1) whether the test is administered by a health care professional; (2) whether the test is interpreted by a health care professional; (3) whether the test is designed to reveal an impairment or physical or mental health; (4) whether the test is invasive; (5) whether the test measures an employee's performance of a task or measures his/her physiological responses to performing the task; (6) whether the test normally is given in a medical setting; and, (7) whether medical equipment is used.[30]

In many cases, a combination of factors will be relevant in determining whether a test or procedure is a medical examination. In other cases, one factor may be enough to determine that a test or procedure is medical.

Medical examinations include, but are not limited to, the following:

- vision tests conducted and analyzed by an ophthalmologist or optometrist;
- blood, urine, and breath analyses to check for alcohol use;[31]
- blood, urine, saliva, and hair analyses to detect disease or genetic markers (*e.g.*, for conditions such as sickle cell trait, breast cancer, Huntington's disease);
- blood pressure screening and cholesterol

---

[24] Preemployment Questions and Medical Examinations, *supra* note 2, at 9, 8 FEP at 405:7195.

[25] Preemployment Questions and Medical Examinations, *supra* note 2, at 9, 8 FEP at 405:7195.

[26] Employers also may maintain and enforce rules prohibiting employees from being under the influence of alcohol in the workplace and may conduct alcohol testing for this purpose if they have a reasonable belief that an employee may be under the influence of alcohol at work.

[27] An individual who currently uses drugs illegally is not protected under the ADA; therefore, questions about current illegal drug use are not disability-related inquiries. 42 U.S.C. § 12114(a) (1994); 29 C.F.R. § 1630.3(a) (1998). However, questions about *past* addiction to illegal drugs or questions about whether an employee ever has participated in a rehabilitation program *are* disability-related because past drug addiction generally is a disability. Individuals who were addicted to drugs, but are not currently using drugs illegally, are protected under the ADA. 29 C.F.R. § 1630.3(b)(1), (2) (1998).

[28] Pregnancy is not a disability for purposes of the ADA. 29 C.F.R. pt. 1630, app. § 1630.2(h) (1998). However, discrimination on that basis may violate the Pregnancy Discrimination Act amendments to Title VII. 42 U.S.C. § 2000e(k) (1994).

[29] Preemployment Questions and Medical Examinations *supra* note 2, at 14, 8 FEP at 405:7197.

[30] *Id.*

[31] *See supra* note 26.

testing;

- nerve conduction tests (*i.e.*, tests that screen for possible nerve damage and susceptibility to injury, such as carpal tunnel syndrome);
- range-of-motion tests that measure muscle strength and motor function;
- pulmonary function tests (*i.e.*, tests that measure the capacity of the lungs to hold air and to move air in and out);
- psychological tests that are designed to identify a mental disorder or impairment; and,
- diagnostic procedures such as x-rays, computerized axial tomography (CAT) scans, and magnetic resonance imaging (MRI).

There are a **number of procedures and tests employers may require that generally are not considered medical examinations**, including:

- tests to determine the **current illegal use of drugs**;[32]
- **physical agility tests**, which measure an employee's ability to perform actual or simulated job tasks, and **physical fitness tests**, which measure an employee's performance of physical tasks, such as running or lifting, as long as these tests do not include examinations that could be considered medical (*e.g.*, measuring heart rate or blood pressure);
- tests that evaluate an employee's ability to read labels or distinguish objects as part of a demonstration of the ability to perform actual job functions;
- **psychological tests** that measure personality traits such as honesty, preferences, and habits; and,
- polygraph examinations.[33]

3. Who is an **"employee"**?

The ADA defines the term "employee" as "an individual employed by an employer."[34] As a general rule, an individual is an employee if an entity controls the means and manner of his/her work performance.[35]

Where more than one entity controls the means and manner of how an individual's work is done, the individual is an employee of each entity.

<u>Example</u>: XYZ, a temporary employment agency, hires a computer programmer and assigns him to Business Systems, Inc. (BSI), one of its clients. XYZ determines when the programmer's assignment begins and pays him a salary based on the number of hours worked as reported by BSI. XYZ also withholds social security and taxes and provides workers' compensation coverage. BSI sets the hours of work, the duration of the job, and oversees the programmer's work. XYZ can terminate the programmer if his performance is unacceptable to BSI.

The programmer is an employee of both XYZ and BSI. Thus, XYZ and BSI may ask the programmer disability-related questions and require a medical examination only if they are job-related and consistent with business necessity.

4. How should an employer treat an employee who **applies for a new (*i.e.*, different) job with the same employer**?

An employer should treat an employee who *applies* for a new job as an **applicant** for the new job.[36] The employer, therefore, is prohibited from asking disability-related questions or requiring a medical examination before making the individual a conditional offer of the new position.[37] Further, where a current supervisor has medical information regarding an employee

---

[32] *See supra* note 27.

[33] Under the ADA, polygraph examinations, which purportedly measure whether a person believes s/he is telling the truth in response to a particular inquiry, are not medical examinations. However, an employer cannot ask disability-related questions as part of the examination. *See* Preemployment Questions and Medical Examinations, *supra* note 2, at 17, 8 FEP at 405:7199.

[34] 42 U.S.C. § 12111(4) (1994); 29 C.F.R. § 1630.2(f) (1998). This term has the same meaning as it does under Title VII of the Civil Rights Act of 1964. 42 U.S.C. § 2000e(f) (1994).

[35] In its guidance on contingent workers, the Commission lists additional factors that indicate when a worker is an employee and explains that other aspects of the relationship between the parties may affect the determination of whether an employee-employer relationship exists. *See* EEOC Enforcement Guidance: Application of EEO Laws to Contingent Workers Placed by Temporary Employment Agencies and Other Staffing Firms at 4-7, 8 FEP Manual (BNA) 405:7551, 7554-55 (1997).

[36] An employee in this situation is an applicant with respect to rules concerning disability-related inquiries and medical examinations but *not* for employee benefits (*e.g.*, retirement, health and life insurance, leave accrual) or other purposes.

[37] Where the employer already has medical information concerning an individual at the pre-offer stage for the new position (*e.g.*, information obtained in connection with the individual's request for reasonable accommodation in his/her current

who is applying for a new job, s/he may not disclose that information to the person interviewing the employee for the new job or to the supervisor of that job.

After the employer extends an offer for the new position, it may ask the individual disability-related questions or require a medical examination as long as it does so for all entering employees in the same job category. If an employer withdraws the offer based on medical information (*i.e.*, screens him/her out because of a disability), it must show that the reason for doing so was job-related and consistent with business necessity.

An individual is *not* an applicant where s/he is **noncompetitively** entitled to another position with the same employer (*e.g.*, because of seniority or satisfactory performance in his/her current position). An individual who is temporarily assigned to another position and then returns to his/her regular job also is not an applicant. These individuals are employees and, therefore, the employer only may make a disability-related inquiry or require a medical examination that is job-related and consistent with business necessity.

Example A: Ruth, an inventory clerk for a retail store, applies for a position as a sales associate at the same store. Ruth is an applicant for the new job. Accordingly, her employer may not ask any disability-related questions or require a medical examination before extending her a conditional offer of the sales associate position. Following a conditional offer of employment, the employer may ask disability-related questions and conduct medical examinations, regardless of whether they are related to the job, as long as it does so for all entering employees in the same job category.[38]

Example B: A grade 4 clerk typist has worked in the same position for one year and received a rating of outstanding on her annual performance appraisal. When she was hired, she was told that she automatically would be considered for promotion to the next grade after 12 months of satisfactory performance. Because the clerk typist is noncompetitively entitled to a promotion, she is an employee and not an applicant. The employer, therefore, only may make a disability-related inquiry or require a medical examination that is job-related and consistent with business necessity.

Example C: A newspaper reporter, who regularly works out of his employer's New York headquarters, is temporarily assigned to its bureau in South Africa to cover the political elections. Because the reporter is on a temporary assignment doing the same job, he is an employee; the employer, therefore, may make disability-related inquiries or require medical examinations only if they are job-related and consistent with business necessity.

JOB-RELATED AND CONSISTENT WITH BUSINESS NECESSITY

Once an employee is on the job, his/her actual performance is the best measure of ability to do the job. When a need arises to question the ability of an employee to do the essential functions of his/her job or to question whether the employee can do the job without posing a direct threat due to a medical condition, it may be job-related and consistent with business necessity for an employer to make disability-related inquiries or require a medical examination.

A. In General

5. When may a disability-related inquiry or medical examination of an employee be **"job-related and consistent with business necessity"**?

Generally, a disability-related inquiry or medical examination of an employee may be "job-related and consistent with business necessity" when an employer "has a reasonable belief, based on objective evidence, that: (1) an employee's ability to perform essential job

position) and this information causes the employer to have a reasonable belief that the individual will need a reasonable accommodation to perform the functions of the *new* job, the employer may ask what type of reasonable accommodation would be needed to perform the functions of the new job, before extending an offer for that job. An employer, however, may not use its knowledge of an applicant's disability to discriminate against him/her. The employer also may not use the fact that the individual will need a reasonable accommodation in the new position to deny him/her the new job unless it can show that providing the accommodation would cause an undue hardship.

[38] 42 U.S.C. § 12112(d)(3) (1994); 29 C.F.R. § 1630.14(b) (1998).

functions will be impaired by a medical condition; or (2) an employee will pose a direct threat[39] due to a medical condition."[40] Disability-related inquiries and medical examinations that follow up on a request for reasonable accommodation when the disability or need for accommodation is not known or obvious also may be job-related and consistent with business necessity. In addition, periodic medical examinations and other monitoring under specific circumstances may be job-related and consistent with business necessity.[41]

Sometimes this standard may be met when an employer knows about a particular employee's medical condition, has observed performance problems, and reasonably can attribute the problems to the medical condition. An employer also may be given **reliable information** by a credible third party that an employee has a medical condition,[42]or the employer may observe symptoms indicating that an employee may have a medical condition that will impair his/her ability to perform essential job functions or will pose a direct threat. In these situations, it may be job-related and consistent with business necessity for an employer to make disability-related inquiries or require a medical examination.

Example A: For the past two months, Sally, a tax auditor for a federal government agency, has done a third fewer audits than the average employee in her unit. She also has made numerous mistakes in assessing whether taxpayers provided appropriate documentation for claimed deductions. When questioned about her poor performance, Sally tells her supervisor that the medication she takes for her lupus makes her lethargic and unable to concentrate.

Based on Sally's explanation for her performance problems, the agency has a reasonable belief that her ability to perform the essential functions of her job will be impaired because of a medical condition.[43] Sally's supervisor, therefore, may make disability-related inquiries (*e.g.*, ask her whether she is taking a new medication and how long the medication's side effects are expected to last), or the supervisor may ask Sally to provide documentation from her health care provider explaining the effects of the medication on Sally's ability to perform her job.

Example B: A crane operator works at construction sites hoisting concrete panels weighing several tons. A rigger on the ground helps him load the panels, and several other workers help him position them. During a break, the crane operator appears to become lightheaded, has to sit down abruptly, and seems to have some difficulty catching his breath. In response to a question from his supervisor about whether he is feeling all right, the crane operator says that this has happened to him a few times during the past several months, but he does not know why.

The employer has a reasonable belief, based on objective evidence, that the employee will pose a direct threat and, therefore, may require the crane operator to have a medical examination to ascertain whether the symptoms he is experiencing make him unfit to perform his job. To ensure that it receives sufficient information to make this determination, the employer may want to provide the doctor who does the examination with a description of the employee's duties, including any physical qualification standards, and require that the employee provide documentation of his ability to work following the examination.[44]

Example C: Six months ago, a supervisor heard a secretary tell her co-worker that she discovered a lump in her breast and is afraid that she may have breast cancer. Since that conversation, the secretary still comes to work every day and performs her duties in her nor-

---

39 "Direct threat" means a significant risk of substantial harm that cannot be eliminated or reduced by reasonable accommodation. 29 C.F.R. § 1630.2(r) (1998). Direct threat determinations must be based on an individualized assessment of the individual's present ability to safely perform the essential functions of the job, considering a reasonable medical judgment relying on the most current medical knowledge and/or best available objective evidence. *Id.* To determine whether an employee poses a direct threat, the following factors should be considered: (1) the duration of the risk; (2) the nature and severity of the potential harm; (3) the likelihood that potential harm will occur; and, (4) the imminence of the potential harm. *Id.*

40 The Commission explained this standard in its enforcement guidance on The ADA and Psychiatric Disabilities, *supra* note 6, at 15, 8 FEP at 405:7468-69.

41 *See infra* Questions 18 and 19 and accompanying text.

42 *See infra* Question 6 and accompanying text.

43 *See Yin v. State of California*, 95 F.3d 864, 868, 5 AD Cas. (BNA) 1487, 1489 (9th Cir. 1996) (where employee missed an inordinate number of days and her performance declined, employer's request that she submit to a medical examination was job-related and consistent with business necessity).

44 *See also infra* Question 12.

mal efficient manner.

In this case, the employer does not have a reasonable belief, based on objective evidence, either that the secretary's ability to perform her essential job functions will be impaired by a medical condition or that she will pose a direct threat due to a medical condition. The employer, therefore, may not make any disability-related inquiries or require the employee to submit to a medical examination.

An employer's reasonable belief that an employee's ability to perform essential job functions will be impaired by a medical condition or that s/he will pose a direct threat due to a medical condition must be based on *objective evidence* obtained, or reasonably available to the employer, prior to making a disability-related inquiry or requiring a medical examination. Such a belief requires an assessment of the employee and his/her position and cannot be based on general assumptions.

Example D: An employee who works in the produce department of a large grocery store tells her supervisor that she is HIV-positive. The employer is concerned that the employee poses a direct threat to the health and safety of others because she frequently works with sharp knives and might cut herself while preparing produce for display. The store requires any employee working with sharp knives to wear gloves and frequently observes employees to determine whether they are complying with this policy. Available scientific evidence shows that the possibility of transmitting HIV from a produce clerk to other employees or the public, assuming the store's policy is observed, is virtually nonexistent. Moreover, the Department of Health and Human Services (HHS), which has the responsibility under the ADA for preparing a list of infectious and communicable diseases that may be transmitted through food handling,[45] does not include HIV on the list.[46]

In this case, the employer does *not* have a reasonable belief, based on objective evidence, that this employee's ability to perform the essential functions of her position will be impaired or that she will pose a direct threat due to her medical condition. The employer, therefore, may not make any disability-related inquiries or require the employee to submit to a medical examination.[47]

6. May an employer make disability-related inquiries or require a medical examination of an employee **based, in whole or in part, on information learned from another person**?

Yes, if the information learned is **reliable** and would give rise to a reasonable belief that the employee's ability to perform essential job functions will be impaired by a medical condition or that s/he will pose a direct threat due to a medical condition, an employer may make disability-related inquiries or require a medical examination.

Factors that an employer might consider in assessing whether information learned from another person is sufficient to justify asking disability-related questions or requiring a medical examination of an employee include: (1) the relationship of the person providing the information to the employee about whom it is being provided; (2) the seriousness of the medical condition at issue; (3) the possible motivation of the person providing the information; (4) how the person learned the information (*e.g.*, directly from the employee whose medical condition is in question or from someone else); and (5) other evidence that the employer has that bears on the reliability of the information provided.

Example A: Bob and Joe are close friends who work as copy editors for an advertising firm. Bob tells Joe that he is worried because he has just learned that he had a positive reaction to a tuberculin skin test and believes that he has tuberculosis. Joe encourages Bob to tell

---

45 42 U.S.C. § 12113(d) (1994).

46 The most current list was published by HHS, Centers for Disease Control and Prevention (CDC), in 1998. 63 Fed.Reg. 49359 (Sept. 15, 1998).

47 *But see EEOC v. Prevo's Family Market, Inc.*, 135 F.3d 1089, 1097, 8 AD Cas. (BNA) 401, 408 (6th Cir. 1998) (employer did not violate the ADA when it required a produce clerk, who claimed to be HIV-positive, to submit to a medical examination to determine whether he posed a direct threat). The Commission believes that *Prevo's* was wrongly decided because the employer did not base its belief that the employee posed a direct threat on reasonably available objective evidence and, therefore, its request that the employee submit to a medical examination was not job-related and consistent with business necessity. A number of sources, such as the Centers for Disease Control (www.cdc.gov), a physician or health care provider knowledgeable about HIV and other infectious diseases, a state or local health department, a public or university library, or a state or county medical association can provide information about the likelihood of an employee transmitting HIV or other infectious diseases to co-workers or the public.

their supervisor, but Bob refuses. Joe is reluctant to breach Bob's trust but is concerned that he and the other editors may be at risk since they all work closely together in the same room. After a couple of sleepless nights, Joe tells his supervisor about Bob. The supervisor questions Joe about how he learned of Bob's alleged condition and finds Joe's explanation credible.

Because tuberculosis is a potentially life-threatening medical condition and can be passed from person to person by coughing or sneezing, the supervisor has a reasonable belief, based on objective evidence, that Bob will pose a direct threat if he in fact has active tuberculosis. Under these circumstances, the employer may make disability-related inquiries or require a medical examination to the extent necessary to determine whether Bob has tuberculosis and is contagious.[48]

Example B: Kim works for a small computer consulting firm. When her mother died suddenly, she asked her employer for three weeks off, in addition to the five days that the company customarily provides in the event of the death of a parent or spouse, to deal with family matters. During her extended absence, a rumor circulated among some employees that Kim had been given additional time off to be treated for depression. Shortly after Kim's return to work, Dave, who works on the same team with Kim, approached his manager to say that he had heard that some workers were concerned about their safety. According to Dave, people in the office claimed that Kim was talking to herself and threatening to harm them. Dave said that he had not observed the strange behavior himself but was not surprised to hear about it given Kim's alleged recent treatment for depression. Dave's manager sees Kim every day and never has observed this kind of behavior. In addition, none of the co-workers to whom the manager spoke confirmed Dave's statements.

In this case, the employer does not have a reasonable belief, based on objective evidence, that Kim's ability to perform essential functions will be impaired or that s/he will pose a direct threat because of a medical condition. The employer, therefore, would not be justified in asking Kim disability-related questions or requiring her to submit to a medical examination because the information provided by Dave is not reliable.

Example C: Several customers have complained that Richard, a customer service representative for a mail order company, has made numerous errors on their orders. They consistently have complained that Richard seems to have a problem hearing because he always asks them to repeat the item number(s), color(s), size(s), credit card number(s), etc., and frequently asks them to speak louder. They also have complained that he incorrectly reads back their addresses even when they have enunciated clearly and spelled street names.

In this case, the employer has a reasonable belief, based on objective evidence, that Richard's ability to correctly process mail orders will be impaired by a medical condition (*i.e.*, a problem with his hearing). The employer, therefore, may make disability-related inquiries of Richard or require him to submit to a medical examination to determine whether he can perform the essential functions of his job.

7. May an employer ask an employee for **documentation** when s/he requests a **reasonable accommodation?**

Yes. The employer is entitled to know that an employee has a covered disability that requires a reasonable accommodation.[49] Thus, when the **disability or the need for the accommodation is not known or obvious,** it is job-related and consistent with business necessity for an employer to ask an employee for reasonable documentation about his/her disability and its functional limitations that require reasonable accommodation.[50]

---

[48] This guidance does not affect the obligation of a physician, under any state law, to report cases of active tuberculosis to appropriate public health authorities.

[49] *See* Reasonable Accommodation Under the ADA, *supra* note 6, at 14-15, 8 FEP at 405:7608 for examples of other situations where employers may ask for documentation; *see also id.* at 16-17, 8 FEP at 405: 7609 for examples of situations in which an employer **cannot** ask for documentation in response to a request for reasonable accommodation.

[50] 29 C.F.R. pt. 1630 app. § 1630.9 (1998); *see also* Preemployment Questions and Medical Examinations, *supra* note 2, at 6, 8 FEP at 405: 7193; ADA and Psychiatric Disabilities, *supra* note 6, at 22-23, 8 FEP at 405:7472-73; Reasonable Accommodation Under the ADA, *supra* note 6, at 12-13, 8 FEP at 405: 7607. *See also Templeton v. Neodata Services, Inc.*, 162 F.3d 617, 618, 8 AD Cas. (BNA) 1615, 1616 (10th Cir. 1998) (employer's request for updated medical information was reasonable in light of treating physician's letter indicating doubt as to employee's ability to return to work as scheduled, and employer needed the requested information to determine appropriate reasonable accommodation for employee in event she was able to return to work).

8. May an employer ask **all employees what prescription medications** they are taking?

Generally, no. Asking all employees about their use of prescription medications is not job-related and consistent with business necessity.[51] In limited circumstances, however, certain employers may be able to demonstrate that it *is* job-related and consistent with business necessity to require employees in positions affecting public safety to report when they are taking medication that may affect their ability to perform essential functions. **Under these limited circumstances, an employer must be able to demonstrate that an employee's inability or impaired ability to perform essential functions will result in a direct threat.** For example, a police department could require armed officers to report when they are taking medications that may affect their ability to use a firearm or to perform other essential functions of their job. Similarly, an airline could require its pilots to report when they are taking any medications that may impair their ability to fly. A fire department, however, could not require fire department employees who perform only administrative duties to report their use of medications because it is unlikely that it could show that these employees would pose a direct threat as a result of their inability or impaired ability to perform their essential job functions.

9. **What action may an employer take if an employee fails to respond to a disability-related inquiry or fails to submit to a medical examination** that is job-related and consistent with business necessity?

The action the employer may take depends on its reason for making the disability-related inquiry or requiring a medical examination.

Example A: A supervisor notices that the quality of work from an ordinarily outstanding employee has deteriorated over the past several months. Specifically, the employee requires more time to complete routine reports, which frequently are submitted late and contain numerous errors. The supervisor also has observed during this period of time that the employee appears to be squinting to see her computer monitor, is holding printed material close to her face to read it, and takes frequent breaks during which she sometimes is seen rubbing her eyes. Concerned about the employee's declining performance, which appears to be due to a medical condition, the supervisor tells her to go see the company doctor, but she does not.

Any discipline that the employer decides to impose should focus on the employee's **performance problems**. Thus, the employer may discipline the employee for past and future performance problems in accordance with a uniformly applied policy.

Example B: An accountant with no known disability asks for an ergonomic chair because she says she is having back pain. The employer asks the employee to provide documentation from her treating physician that: (1) describes the nature, severity, and duration of her impairment, the activity or activities that the impairment limits, and the extent to which the impairment limits her ability to perform the activity or activities; and (2) substantiates why an ergonomic chair is needed.

Here, the employee's possible disability and **need for reasonable accommodation** are not obvious. Therefore, if the employee fails to provide the requested documentation or if the documentation does not demonstrate the existence of a disability, the employer can refuse to provide the chair.[52]

B. Scope and Manner of Disability-Related Inquiries and Medical Examinations

10. **What documentation** may an employer require from an employee who requests a **reasonable accommodation**?

An employer may require an employee to provide documentation that is **sufficient** to substantiate that s/he has an ADA disability and needs the reasonable accommodation requested, but cannot ask for unrelated documentation. This means that, in most circumstances, an employer cannot ask for an employee's complete medical records because they are likely to

---

51 *See Roe v. Cheyenne Mountain Conference Resort*, 124 F.3d 1221, 1229, 7 AD Cas. (BNA) 779, 784 (10th Cir. 1997) (employer, who implemented a drug and alcohol policy that included many permissible inquiries but also asked employees to inform the employer of every drug they were taking, including legal prescription drugs, violated the ADA by failing to demonstrate that this inquiry was job-related and consistent with business necessity).

52 *See* Reasonable Accommodation Under the ADA, *supra* note 6, at 15, 8 FEP at 405:7608.

contain information unrelated to the disability at issue and the need for accommodation.[53]

Documentation is sufficient if it: (1) describes the nature, severity, and duration of the employee's impairment, the activity or activities that the impairment limits, and the extent to which the impairment limits the employee's ability to perform the activity or activities; and, (2) substantiates why the requested reasonable accommodation is needed.

Example: An employee, who has exhausted all of his available leave, telephones his supervisor on Monday morning to inform him that he had a severe pain episode on Saturday due to his sickle cell anemia, is in the hospital, and needs time off. Prior to this call, the supervisor was unaware of the employee's medical condition.

The employer can ask the employee to send in documentation from his treating physician that substantiates that the employee has a disability, confirms that his hospitalization is related to his disability, and provides information on how long he may be absent from work.[54]

11. May an employer **require an employee to go to a health care professional of the employer's (rather than the employee's) choice** when the employee requests a **reasonable accommodation?**

The ADA does not prevent an employer from requiring an employee to go to an appropriate health care professional of the employer's choice if the employee provides **insufficient documentation** from his/her treating physician (or other health care professional) to substantiate that s/he has an ADA disability and needs a reasonable accommodation.[55] However, if an employee provides insufficient documentation in response to the employer's initial request, the employer should explain why the documentation is insufficient and allow the employee an opportunity to provide the missing information in a timely manner.[56] The employer also should consider consulting with the employee's doctor (with the employee's consent) before requiring the employee to go to a health care professional of its choice.[57]

Documentation is insufficient if it does not specify the existence of an ADA disability and explain the need for reasonable accommodation.[58] Documentation also might be insufficient where, for example: (1) the health care professional does not have the expertise to give an opinion about the employee's medical condition and the limitations imposed by it; (2) the information does not specify the functional limitations due to the disability; or, (3) other factors indicate that the information provided is not credible or is fraudulent. If an employee provides insufficient documentation, an employer does not have to provide reasonable accommodation until sufficient documentation is provided.

Any medical examination conducted by the employer's health care professional must be job-related and consistent with business necessity. This means that the examination must be limited to determining the existence of an ADA disability and the functional limitations that require reasonable accommodation. If an employer requires an employee to go to a health care professional of the employer's choice, the employer must pay all costs associated with the visit(s).[59]

---

53 *See id.* at 13, 8 FEP at 405:7607. (An "employer may require only the documentation that is needed to establish that a person has an ADA disability, and that the disability necessitates a reasonable accommodation." If an employee has more than one disability, an employer can request information pertaining only to the disability for which the employee is requesting an accommodation.)

54 *See* Reasonable Accommodation Under the ADA, *supra* note 6, at 14-15, 16-17, 8 FEP at 405:7607-09. If the employee subsequently should request another reasonable accommodation related to his sickle cell anemia, the employer may ask for reasonable documentation relating to the new request (if the need is not obvious). The employer, however, cannot ask again for documentation that the employee has an ADA disability where the medical information the employee provided in support of his first reasonable accommodation request established the existence of a long-term impairment that substantially limits a major life activity. *Id.* at 16-17, 8 FEP at 405:7609.

55 *See* Reasonable Accommodation Under the ADA, *supra* note 6, at 15-16, 8 FEP at 405:7698; The ADA and Psychiatric Disabilities, *supra* note 6, at 23, 8 FEP at 405:7473.

56 *See* Reasonable Accommodation Under the ADA, *supra* note 6, at 15, 8 FEP at 405:7608.

57 Since a doctor cannot disclose information about a patient without his/her permission, an employer must obtain a release from the employee that will permit the doctor to answer questions. The release should be clear as to what information will be requested. *See* Reasonable Accommodation Under the ADA, *supra* note 6, at 13-14, 8 FEP at 405:7607.

58 *Id.* at 15, 8 FEP at 405:7608-09.

59 *Id.* at 16, 8 FEP at 405:7609; The ADA and Psychiatric Disabilities, *supra* note 6, at 23, 8 FEP at 405:7473.

The Commission has previously stated that when an employee provides sufficient evidence of the existence of a disability and the need for reasonable accommodation, continued efforts by the employer to require that the individual provide more documentation and/or submit to a medical examination could be considered retaliation.[60] However, an employer that requests additional information or requires a medical examination based on a good faith belief that the documentation the employee submitted is insufficient would *not* be liable for retaliation.

12. May an employer require that an **employee, who it reasonably believes will pose a direct threat, be examined by an appropriate health care professional of the employer's choice?**

Yes. The determination that an employee poses a direct threat must be based on an individualized assessment of the employee's present ability to safely perform the essential functions of the job. This assessment must be based on a reasonable medical judgment that relies on the most current medical knowledge and/or best objective evidence.[61] To meet this burden, an employer may want to have the employee examined by a health care professional of its choice who has expertise in the employee's specific condition and can provide medical information that allows the employer to determine the effects of the condition on the employee's ability to perform his/her job. Any medical examination, however, must be limited to determining whether the employee can perform his/her job without posing a direct threat, with or without reasonable accommodation. An employer also must pay all costs associated with the employee's visit(s) to its health care professional.[62]

An employer should be cautious about relying solely on the opinion of its own health care professional that an employee poses a direct threat where that opinion is contradicted by documentation from the employee's own treating physician, who is knowledgeable about the employee's medical condition and job functions, and/or other objective evidence. In evaluating conflicting medical information, the employer may find it helpful to consider: (1) the area of expertise of each medical professional who has provided information; (2) the kind of information each person providing documentation has about the job's essential functions and the work environment in which they are performed; (3) whether a particular opinion is based on speculation or on current, objectively verifiable information about the risks associated with a particular condition; and, (4) whether the medical opinion is contradicted by information known to or observed by the employer (*e.g.*, information about the employee's actual experience in the job in question or in previous similar jobs).

13. **How much** medical information can an employer obtain about an employee when it reasonably believes that an employee's **ability to perform the essential functions** of his/her job will be impaired by a medical condition or that s/he **will pose a direct threat** due to a medical condition?

An employer is entitled only to the information necessary to determine whether the employee can do the essential functions of the job or work without posing a direct threat. This means that, in most situations, an employer cannot request an employee's complete medical records because they are likely to contain information unrelated to whether the employee can perform his/her essential functions or work without posing a direct threat.

14. May an employer require an employee to provide **medical certification that s/he can safely perform a physical agility or physical fitness test**?

Yes. Employers that require physical agility or physical fitness tests may ask an employee to have a physician certify whether s/he can safely perform the test.[63] In this situation, however, the employer is entitled to obtain only **a note simply stating that the employee can safely perform the test or, alternatively, an explanation of the reason(s) why the employee cannot perform the test.** An employer may not obtain the employee's complete medical records or information about any conditions that do not affect the employee's ability to perform the physical agility or physical fitness test safely.

---

60 *See* Reasonable Accommodation Under the ADA, *supra* note 6, at 15 (n.30), 8 FEP at 405:7609.

61 29 C.F.R. § 1630.2(r) (1998).

62 *See* Reasonable Accommodation Under the ADA, *supra* note 6, at 16, 8 FEP at 405:7609; The ADA and Psychiatric Disabilities, *supra* note 6, at 23, 8 FEP at 405:7473.

63 *See* Preemployment Questions and Medical Examinations, *supra* note 2, at 16, 8 FEP at 405:7198.

C. Disability-Related Inquiries and Medical Examinations Relating to Leave[64]

15. May an employer request an employee to provide a **doctor's note or other explanation** to substantiate his/her use of sick leave?

Yes. An employer is entitled to know why an employee is requesting sick leave. An employer, therefore, may ask an employee to justify his/her use of sick leave by providing a doctor's note or other explanation, as long as it has a policy or practice of requiring all employees, with and without disabilities, to do so.

16. May an employer require **periodic updates** when an employee is on extended leave because of a medical condition?

Yes. If the employee's request for leave did not specify an exact or fairly specific return date (*e.g.*, October 4 or around the second week of November) or if the employee needs continued leave beyond what was originally granted, the employer may require the employee to provide periodic updates on his/her condition and possible date of return.[65] However, where the employer has granted a fixed period of extended leave and the employee has not requested additional leave, the employer *cannot* require the employee to provide periodic updates. Employers, of course, may call employees on extended leave to check on their progress or to express concern for their health.

17. May an employer make disability-related inquiries or require a medical examination **when an employee who has been on leave for a medical condition seeks to return to work**?

Yes. If an employer has a reasonable belief that an employee's **present** ability to perform essential job functions will be impaired by a medical condition or that s/he will pose a direct threat due to a medical condition, the employer may make disability-related inquiries or require the employee to submit to a medical examination. Any inquiries or examination, however, must be limited in scope to what is needed to make an assessment of the employee's ability to work. Usually, inquiries or examinations related to the specific medical condition for which the employee took leave will be all that is warranted. The employer may not use the employee's leave as a justification for making far-ranging disability-related inquiries or requiring an unrelated medical examination.

Example A: A data entry clerk broke her leg while skiing and was out of work for four weeks, after which time she returned to work on crutches. In this case, the employer does not have a reasonable belief, based on objective evidence, either that the clerk's ability to perform her essential job functions will be impaired by a medical condition or that she will pose a direct threat due to a medical condition. The employer, therefore, may not make any disability-related inquiries or require a medical examination but generally may ask the clerk how she is doing and express concern about her injury.

Example B: As the result of problems he was having with his medication, an employee with a known psychiatric disability threatened several of his co-workers and was disciplined. Shortly thereafter, he was hospitalized for six weeks for treatment related to the condition. Two days after his release, the employee returns to work with a note from his doctor indicating only that he is "cleared to return to work." Because the employer has a reasonable belief, based on objective evidence, that the employee will pose a direct threat due to a medical condition, it may ask the employee for additional documentation regarding his medication(s) or treatment or request that he submit to a medical examination.

D. Periodic Testing and Monitoring

In most instances, an employer's need to make disability-related inquiries or require medical examinations will be triggered by evidence of **current** performance problems or observable evidence suggesting that a particular employee will pose a direct threat. The

64 The questions and answers in this section address situations in which an employee has used sick, annual, or some other kind of leave because of a medical condition, but has **not** taken leave under the **Family and Medical Leave Act (FMLA)**. 29 U.S.C. § 2601 (1994). Where an employee has been on leave under the FMLA, the employer must comply with the requirements of that statute. For example, the FMLA generally does not authorize an employer to make its own determination of whether an employee is fit to return to work but, rather, states that the employer must rely on the evaluation done by the employee's own health care provider. *Id.* at § 2613(b).

65 *See* Reasonable Accommodation Under the ADA, *supra* note 6, at 57, 8 FEP at 405:7632.

following questions, however, address situations in which disability-related inquiries and medical examinations of employees may be permissible absent such evidence.

18. May **employers** require **periodic medical examinations** of employees in **positions affecting public safety** (***e.g.*, police officers and firefighters**)?

Yes. In limited circumstances, periodic medical examinations of employees in positions affecting public safety that are narrowly tailored to address specific job-related concerns are permissible.[66]

Example A: A fire department requires employees for whom firefighting is an essential job function to have a comprehensive visual examination every two years and to have an annual electrocardiogram because it is concerned that certain visual disorders and heart problems will affect their ability to do their job without posing a direct threat. These periodic medical examinations are permitted by the ADA.

Example B: A police department may not periodically test all of its officers to determine whether they are HIV-positive because a diagnosis of that condition alone is not likely to result in an inability or impaired ability to perform essential functions that would result in a direct threat.

Example C: A private security company may require its armed security officers who are expected to pursue and detain fleeing criminal suspects to have periodic blood pressure screenings and stress tests because it is concerned about the risk of harm to the public that could result if an officer has a sudden stroke.

If an employer decides to terminate or take other adverse action against an employee with a disability based on the results of a medical examination, it must demonstrate that the employee is unable to perform his/her essential job functions or, in fact, poses a direct threat that cannot be eliminated or reduced by reasonable accommodation.[67] Therefore, when an employer discovers that an employee has a condition for which it lawfully may test as part of a periodic medical examination, it may make additional inquiries or require additional medical examinations that are **necessary to determine whether the employee currently is unable to perform his/her essential job functions or poses a direct threat due to the condition.**

19. May an employer subject an employee, who has been off from work in an alcohol rehabilitation program, to **periodic alcohol testing** when s/he returns to work?

Yes, but only if the employer has a reasonable belief, based on objective evidence, that the employee will pose a direct threat in the absence of periodic testing. Such a reasonable belief requires an individualized assessment of the employee and his/her position and cannot be based on general assumptions. Employers also may conduct periodic alcohol testing pursuant to "last chance" agreements.[68]

In determining whether to subject an employee to periodic alcohol testing (in the absence of a "last chance" agreement), the employer should consider the safety risks associated with the position the employee holds, the consequences of the employee's inability or impaired ability to perform his/her job functions, and how recently the event(s) occurred that cause the employer to believe that the employee will pose a direct threat (*e.g.*, how long the individual has been an employee, when s/he completed rehabilitation, whether s/he previously has relapsed). Further, the duration and frequency of the testing must be designed to address particular safety concerns and should not be used to harass, intimidate, or retaliate against the employee because of his/her disability. Where the employee repeatedly has tested negative for alcohol, continued testing may not be job-related and consistent with business necessity because the employer no longer may have a *reasonable* belief that the employee will pose a direct threat.

Example A: Three months after being hired, a city bus driver informed his supervisor of his alcoholism and requested leave to enroll in a rehabilitation program. The driver explained that he had not had a drink in

---

66 *See* The ADA and Psychiatric Disabilities, *supra* note 6, at 16 (n.41), 8 FEP at 405:7469.

67 *See supra* note 39.

68 Some employers, including some federal government agencies, commonly use "last chance agreements" in disciplinary actions involving employee use of alcohol. Such agreements typically provide that, as a condition of continued employment, employees must enter into a rehabilitation program and submit to periodic alcohol testing.

more than 10 years until he recently started having a couple of beers before bed to deal with the recent separation from his wife. After four months of rehabilitation and counseling, the driver was cleared to return to work. Given the safety risks associated with the bus driver's position, his short period of employment, and recent completion of rehabilitation, the city can show that it would be job-related and consistent with business necessity to subject the driver to frequent periodic alcohol tests following his return to work.

Example B: An attorney has been off from work in a residential alcohol treatment program for six weeks and has been cleared to return to work. Her supervisor wants to perform periodic alcohol tests to determine whether the attorney has resumed drinking. Assuming that there is no evidence that the attorney will pose a direct threat, the employer cannot show that periodic alcohol testing would be job-related and consistent with business necessity.[69]

OTHER ACCEPTABLE DISABILITY-RELATED INQUIRIES AND MEDICAL EXAMINATIONS OF EMPLOYEES

20. May an **Employee Assistance Program (EAP)**[70] **counselor ask** an employee seeking help for personal problems about any physical or mental condition(s) s/he may have?

Yes. An EAP counselor may ask employees about their medical condition(s) if s/he: (1) does not act for or on behalf of the employer; (2) is obligated to shield any information the employee reveals from decision makers; and, (3) has no power to affect employment decisions. Many employers contract with EAP counselors so that employees can voluntarily and confidentially seek professional counseling for personal or work-related problems without having to be concerned that their employment status will be affected because they sought help.[71]

21. May an employer make disability-related inquiries and require medical examinations that are required or necessitated by another **federal law or regulation**?

Yes. An employer may make disability-related inquiries and require employees to submit to medical examinations that are mandated or necessitated by another federal law or regulation.[72] For example, under federal safety regulations, interstate bus and truck drivers must undergo medical examinations at least once every two years. Similarly, airline pilots and flight attendants must continually meet certain medical requirements.[73] Other federal laws that require medical examinations or medical inquiries of employees without violating the ADA include:

- the Occupational Safety and Health Act;[74]
- the Federal Mine Health and Safety Act;[75] and
- other federal statutes that require employees

---

69 The employer, however, may require the attorney to submit to an alcohol test if it has objective evidence that she is violating a workplace policy prohibiting all employees from being under the influence of alcohol on the job. *See supra* note 26.

70 Generally, EAPs are confidential programs designed to assist employees in coping with personal issues (*e.g.*, substance abuse, grief) that may interfere with their job performance.

71 *See Vardiman v. Ford Motor Co.*, 981 F. Supp. 1279, 1283, 7 AD Cas. (BNA) 1068, 1072 (E.D. Mo. 1997) (EAP representative had no power to affect employment decisions and, in fact, was obligated to shield the decision makers from an employee's personal or substance abuse problems).

72 29 C.F.R. § 1630.15(e) (1998) ("it may be a defense to a charge of discrimination . . . that a challenged action is required or necessitated by another Federal law or regulation . . . .").

73 *See e.g.*, 14 C.F.R. pt. 67 (1999) (Federal Aviation Administration (FAA) and Department of Transportation (DOT) medical certifications); 14 C.F.R. pt. 121, app. I (1999) (FAA and DOT drug testing program); 49 C.F.R. pt. 40 and app. (1999) (procedures for transportation workplace drug testing programs); 49 C.F.R. 240.207 (1996) (Federal Railroad Administration and DOT procedures for making determination on hearing and visual acuity); 49 C.F.R. pt. 391 (1999) (Federal Highway Administration and DOT medical certification requirements); 49 C.F.R. pt. 653 (1999) (Federal Transit Administration (FTA) procedures for prevention of prohibited drug use in transit operations); 49 C.F.R. pt. 654 (1999) (FTA procedures for prevention of alcohol abuse in transit operations).

74 29 U.S.C. §§ 651-678 (1994).

75 30 U.S.C. §§ 801-962 (1994).

exposed to toxic or hazardous substances to be medically monitored at specific intervals.[76]

22. May an employer make disability-related inquiries or conduct medical examinations that are part of its **voluntary wellness program**?

Yes. The ADA allows employers to conduct voluntary medical examinations and activities, including voluntary medical histories, which are part of an employee health program without having to show that they are job-related and consistent with business necessity, as long as any medical records acquired as part of the wellness program are kept confidential and separate from personnel records.[77] These programs often include blood pressure screening, cholesterol testing, glaucoma testing, and cancer detection screening. Employees may be asked disability-related questions and may be given medical examinations pursuant to such voluntary wellness programs.[78]

A **wellness program is "voluntary"** as long as an employer neither requires participation nor penalizes employees who do not participate.

23. May an employer ask employees to **voluntarily self-identify as persons with disabilities for affirmative action purposes?**

Yes. An employer may ask employees to voluntarily self-identify as individuals with disabilities when the employer is:

- undertaking affirmative action because of a federal, state, or local law (including a veterans' preference law) that requires affirmative action for individuals with disabilities (*i.e.*, the law requires some action to be taken on behalf of such individuals); or,
- *voluntarily* using the information to benefit individuals with disabilities.[79]

If an employer invites employees to voluntarily self-identify in connection with the above-mentioned situations, the employer must indicate clearly and conspicuously on any written questionnaire used for this purpose, or state clearly (if no written questionnaire is used), that: (1) the specific information requested is intended for use solely in connection with its affirmative action obligations or its voluntary affirmative action efforts; and, (2) the specific information is being requested on a voluntary basis, that it will be kept confidential in accordance with the ADA, that refusal to provide it will not subject the employee to any adverse treatment, and that it will be used only in accordance with the ADA.[80]

In order to invite self-identification for purposes of an affirmative action program that is voluntarily undertaken or undertaken pursuant to a law that encourages (rather than requires) affirmative action, an employer must be taking some action that actually benefits individuals with disabilities. The invitation to self-identify also must be *necessary* in order to provide the benefit.

---

76 *See e.g,* The Comprehensive Environmental Response, Compensation and Liability Act, 42 U.S.C. § 9601 (1994).

77 *See* H.R. Rep. No. 101-485, pt. 2, at 75 (1990) ("As long as the programs are voluntary and the medical records are maintained in a confidential manner and not used for the purpose of limiting health insurance eligibility or preventing occupational advancement, these activities would fall within the purview of accepted activities.").

78 If a program simply promotes a healthier life style but does not ask any disability-related questions or require medical examinations (*e.g.*, a smoking cessation program that is available to anyone who smokes and only asks participants to disclose how much they smoke), it is not subject to the ADA's requirements concerning disability-related inquiries and medical examinations.

79 *See* Preemployment Questions and Medical Examinations, *supra* note 2, at 12, 8 FEP at 405:7196-97.

80 *Id.*

AMERICANS WITH DISABILITIES ACT AND PSYCHIATRIC DISABILITIES

EEOC NOTICE
Number 915.002
Date 3-25-97

1. SUBJECT: Enforcement Guidance on the Americans with Disabilities Act and Psychiatric Disabilities.
2. PURPOSE: This enforcement guidance sets forth the Commission's position on the application of Title I of the Americans with Disabilities Act of 1990 to individuals with psychiatric disabilities.
3. EFFECTIVE DATE: Upon receipt.
4. EXPIRATION DATE: As an exception to EEOC Order 205.001, Appendix B, Attachment 4, § a(5), this Notice will remain in effect until rescinded or superseded.
5. ORIGINATOR: ADA Division, Office of Legal Counsel.
6. INSTRUCTIONS: File after Section 902 of Volume II of the Compliance Manual.

3-25-97 /S/

Date Gilbert F. Casellas
Chairman

TABLE OF CONTENTS

THE AMERICANS WITH DISABILITIES ACT AND PSYCHIATRIC DISABILITIES

INTRODUCTION

The workforce includes many individuals with psychiatric disabilities who face employment discrimination because their disabilities are stigmatized or misunderstood. Congress intended Title I of the Americans with Disabilities Act (ADA)[1] to combat such employment discrimination as well as the myths, fears, and stereotypes upon which it is based.[2]

The Equal Employment Opportunity Commission ("EEOC" or "Commission") receives a large number of charges under the ADA alleging employment discrimination based on psychiatric disability.[3] These charges raise a wide array of legal issues including, for example, whether an individual has a psychiatric disability as defined by the ADA and whether an employer may ask about an individual's psychiatric disability. People with psychiatric disabilities and employers also have posed numerous questions to the EEOC about this topic.

This guidance is designed to:

* facilitate the full enforcement of the ADA with respect to individuals alleging employment discrimination based on psychiatric disability;

---

1 42 U.S.C. §§ 12101-12117, 12201-12213 (1994) (codified as amended).

2 H.R. Rep. No. 101-485, pt. 3, at 31-32 (1990) [hereinafter House Judiciary Report].

3 Between July 26, 1992, and September 30, 1996, approximately 12.7% of ADA charges filed with EEOC were based on emotional or psychiatric impairment. These included charges based on anxiety disorders, depression, bipolar disorder (manic depression), schizophrenia, and other psychiatric impairments.

* respond to questions and concerns expressed by individuals with psychiatric disabilities regarding the ADA; and
* answer questions posed by employers about how principles of ADA analysis apply in the context of psychiatric disabilities.[4]

WHAT IS A PSYCHIATRIC DISABILITY UNDER THE ADA?

Under the ADA, the term "disability" means: "(a) A physical or mental impairment that substantially limits one or more of the major life activities of [an] individual; (b) a record of such an impairment; or (c) being regarded as having such an impairment."[5]

This guidance focuses on the first prong of the ADA's definition of "disability" because of the great number of questions about how it is applied in the context of psychiatric conditions.

Impairment

1. What is a **"mental impairment"** under the ADA?

The ADA rule defines "mental impairment" to include "[a]ny mental or psychological disorder, such as . . . emotional or mental illness."[6] Examples of "emotional or mental illness[es]" include major depression, bipolar disorder, anxiety disorders (which include panic disorder, obsessive compulsive disorder, and post-traumatic stress disorder), schizophrenia, and personality disorders. The current edition of the American Psychiatric Association's *Diagnostic and Statistical Manual of Mental Disorders* (now the fourth edition, DSM-IV) is relevant for identifying these disorders. The DSM-IV has been recognized as an important reference by courts[7] and is widely used by American mental health professionals for diagnostic and insurance reimbursement purposes.

Not all conditions listed in the DSM-IV, however, are disabilities, or even impairments, for purposes of the ADA. For example, the DSM-IV lists several conditions that Congress expressly excluded from the ADA's definition of "disability."[8] While DSM-IV covers conditions involving drug abuse, the ADA provides that the term "individual with a disability" does not include an individual who is currently engaging in the illegal use of drugs, when the covered entity acts on the basis of that use.[9] The DSM-IV also includes conditions that are not mental disorders but for which people may seek treatment (for example, problems with a spouse or child).[10] Because these conditions are not disor-

---

4 The analysis in this guidance applies to federal sector complaints of non-affirmative action employment discrimination arising under section 501 of the Rehabilitation Act of 1973. 29 U.S.C. § 791(g) (1994). It also applies to complaints of non-affirmative action employment discrimination arising under section 503 and employment discrimination under section 504 of the Rehabilitation Act. 29 U.S.C. §§ 793(d), 794(d) (1994).

5 42 U.S.C. § 12102(2) (1994); 29 C.F.R. § 1630.2(g) (1996). *See generally* EEOC Compliance Manual § 902, Definition of the Term "Disability," 8 FEP Manual (BNA) 405:7251 (1995).

6 29 C.F.R. § 1630.2(h)(2) (1996). This ADA regulatory definition also refers to mental retardation, organic brain syndrome, and specific learning disabilities. These additional mental conditions, as well as other neurological disorders such as Alzheimer's disease, are not the primary focus of this guidance.

7 *See, e.g., Boldini v. Postmaster Gen.*, 928 F. Supp. 125, 130, 5 AD Cas. (BNA) 11, 14 (D.N.H. 1995) (stating, under section 501 of the Rehabilitation Act, that "in circumstances of mental impairment, a court may give weight to a diagnosis of mental impairment which is described in the Diagnostic and Statistical Manual of Mental Disorders of the American Psychiatric Association . . . .").

8 These include various sexual behavior disorders, compulsive gambling, kleptomania, pyromania, and psychoactive substance use disorders resulting from current illegal use of drugs. 42 U.S.C. § 12211(b) (1994); 29 C.F.R. § 1630.3(d) (1996).

9 42 U.S.C. § 12210(a) (1994). However, individuals who are not currently engaging in the illegal use of drugs and who are participating in, or have successfully completed, a supervised drug rehabilitation program (or who have otherwise been successfully rehabilitated) may be covered by the ADA. Individuals who are erroneously regarded as engaging in the current illegal use of drugs, but who are not engaging in such use, also may be covered. *Id.* at § 12210(b).

Individuals with psychiatric disabilities may, either as part of their condition or separate from their condition, engage in the illegal use of drugs. In such cases, EEOC investigators may need to make a factual determination about whether an employer treated an individual adversely because of his/her psychiatric disability or because of his/her illegal use of drugs.

10 See DSM-IV chapter "Other Conditions That May Be a Focus of Clinical Attention."

ders, they are not impairments under the ADA.[11]

Even if a condition is an impairment, it is not automatically a "disability." To rise to the level of a "disability," an impairment must "substantially limit" one or more major life activities of the individual.[12]

2. Are **traits or behaviors** in themselves mental impairments?

No. Traits or behaviors are not, in themselves, mental impairments. For example, stress, in itself, is not automatically a mental impairment. Stress, however, may be shown to be related to a mental or physical impairment. Similarly, traits like **irritability, chronic lateness, and poor judgment** are not, in themselves, mental impairments, although they may be linked to mental impairments.[13]

Major Life Activities

An impairment must substantially limit one or more major life activities to rise to the level of a "disability" under the ADA.[14]

3. What **major life activities** are limited by mental impairments?

The major life activities limited by mental impairments **differ from person to person**. There is no exhaustive list of major life activities. For some people, mental impairments restrict *major life activities* such as learning, thinking, concentrating, interacting with others,[15] caring for oneself, speaking, performing manual tasks, or working. Sleeping is also a major life activity that may be limited by mental impairments.[16]

4. To establish a psychiatric disability, must an individual always show that s/he is substantially limited in **working**?

No. The first question is whether an individual is substantially limited in a major life activity **other than working** (*e.g.*, sleeping, concentrating, caring for oneself). Working should be analyzed only **if no other major life activity** is substantially limited by an impairment.[17]

Substantial Limitation

Under the ADA, an impairment rises to the level of a disability if it substantially limits a major life activity.[18] "Substantial limitation" is evaluated in terms of the severity of the limitation and the **length of time** it restricts a major life activity.[19]

The determination that a particular individual has a substantially limiting impairment should be based on information about how the impairment affects that

---

11 Individuals who do not have a mental impairment but are treated by their employers as having a substantially limiting impairment have a disability as defined by the ADA because they are regarded as having a substantially limiting impairment. See EEOC Compliance Manual § 902.8, Definition of the Term "Disability," 8 FEP Manual (BNA) 405:7282 (1995).

12 This discussion refers to the terms "impairment" and "substantially limit" in the present tense. These references are not meant to imply that the determinations of whether a condition is an impairment, or of whether there is substantial limitation, are relevant only to whether an individual meets the first part of the definition of "disability," i.e., actually has a physical or mental impairment that substantially limits a major life activity. These determinations also are relevant to whether an individual has a record of a substantially limiting impairment or is regarded as having a substantially limiting impairment. See id. §§ 902.7, 902.8, Definition of the Term "Disability," 8 FEP Manual (BNA) 405:7276-78, 7281 (1995).

13 *Id.* § 902.2(c)(4), Definition of the Term "Disability," 8 FEP Manual (BNA) 405:7258 (1995).

14 42 U.S.C. § 12102(2)(A) (1994); 29 C.F.R. § 1630.2(g)(1) (1996). See also EEOC Compliance Manual § 902.3, Definition of the Term "Disability," 8 FEP Manual (BNA) 405:7261 (1995).

15 Interacting with others, as a major life activity, is not substantially limited just because an individual is irritable or has some trouble getting along with a supervisor or coworker.

16 Sleeping is not substantially limited just because an individual has some trouble getting to sleep or occasionally sleeps fitfully.

17 *See* 29 C.F.R. pt. 1630 app. § 1630.2(j) (1996) ("[i]f an individual is not substantially limited with respect to any other major life activity, the individual's ability to perform the major life activity of working should be considered . . . ."); *see also* EEOC Compliance Manual § 902.4(c)(2), Definition of the Term "Disability," 8 FEP Manual (BNA) 405:7266 (1995).

18 42 U.S.C. § 12102(2) (1994).

19 *See generally* EEOC Compliance Manual § 902.4, Definition of the Term "Disability," 8 FEP Manual (BNA) 405:7262 (1995).

individual and not on generalizations about the condition. Relevant evidence for EEOC investigators includes descriptions of an individual's typical level of functioning at home, at work, and in other settings, as well as evidence showing that the individual's functional limitations are linked to his/her impairment. Expert testimony about substantial limitation is not necessarily required. Credible testimony from the individual with a disability and his/her family members, friends, or coworkers may suffice.

5. When is an impairment sufficiently severe to substantially limit a major life activity?

An impairment is sufficiently severe to substantially limit a major life activity if it **prevents** an individual from performing a major life activity or **significantly restricts the condition, manner, or duration** under which an individual can perform a major life activity, as compared to **the average person in the general population.**[20] **An impairment does not significantly restrict** major life activities if it results in only **mild limitations**.

6. Should the corrective effects of **medications** be considered when deciding if an impairment is so severe that it substantially limits a major life activity?

No. The ADA legislative history unequivocally states that the extent to which an impairment limits performance of a major life activity is assessed without regard to mitigating measures, including medications.[21] Thus, an individual who is taking medication for a mental impairment has an ADA disability if there is evidence that the mental impairment, when left untreated, substantially limits a major life activity.[22] Relevant evidence for EEOC investigators includes, for example, a description of how an individual's condition changed when s/he went off medication[23] or needed to have dosages adjusted, or a description of his/her condition before starting medication.[24]

7. How long does a mental impairment have to last to be substantially limiting?

An impairment is substantially limiting if it lasts for more than several months and significantly restricts the performance of one or more major life activities during that time. It is not substantially limiting if it lasts for only a brief time or does not significantly restrict an individual's ability to perform a major life activity.[25] Whether the impairment is substantially limiting is assessed without regard to mitigating measures such as medication.

Example A: An employee has had major depression for almost a year. He has been intensely sad and socially withdrawn (except

---

20 See 29 C.F.R. § 1630.2(j) (1996).

21 S. Rep. No. 101-116, at 23 (1989); H.R. Rep. No. 101-485, pt. 2, at 52 (1990); House Judiciary Report, *supra* n.2, at 28-29. *See also* 29 C.F.R. pt. 1630 app. § 1630.2(j) (1996).

22 ADA cases in which courts have disregarded the positive effects of medications or other treatment in the determination of disability include *Canon v. Clark*, 883 F. Supp. 718, 4 AD Cas. (BNA) 734 (S.D. Fla. 1995) (finding that individual with insulin-dependent diabetes stated an ADA claim), and *Sarsycki v. United Parcel Ser.*, 862 F. Supp. 336, 340, 3 AD Cas. (BNA) 1039 (W.D. Okla. 1994) (stating that substantial limitation should be evaluated without regard to medication and finding that an individual with insulin-dependent diabetes had a disability under the ADA). Pertinent Rehabilitation Act cases in which courts have made similar determinations include *Liff v. Secretary of Transp.*, 1994 WL 579912, at *3-*4 (D.D.C. 1994) (deciding under the Rehabilitation Act, after acknowledging pertinent ADA guidance, that depression controlled by medication is a disability), and *Gilbert v. Frank*, 949 F.2d 637, 641, 2 AD Cas. (BNA) 60 (2d Cir. 1991) (determining under the Rehabilitation Act that an individual who could not function without kidney dialysis had a substantially limiting impairment).

Cases in which courts have found that individuals are *not* substantially limited after considering the positive effects of medication are, in the Commission's view, incorrectly decided. *See, e.g., Mackie v. Runyon*, 804 F. Supp. 1508,1510-11, 2 AD Cas. (BNA) 260 (M.D. Fla. 1992) (holding under section 501 of the Rehabilitation Act that bipolar disorder stabilized by medication is not substantially limiting); *Chandler v. City of Dallas*, 2 F.3d 1385, 1390-91, 2 AD Cas. (BNA) 1326 (5th Cir. 1993) (holding under section 504 of the Rehabilitation Act that an individual with insulin-dependent diabetes did not have a disability), *cert. denied*,114 S. Ct. 1386, 3 AD Cas. (BNA) 512 (1994).

23 Some individuals do not experience renewed symptoms when they stop taking medication. These individuals are still covered by the ADA, however, if they have a record of a substantially limiting impairment (*i.e.*, if their psychiatric impairment was sufficiently severe and long-lasting to be substantially limiting).

24 If medications cause negative side effects, these side effects should be considered in assessing whether the individual is substantially limited. *See, e.g., Guice-Mills v. Derwinski*, 967 F.2d 794, 2 AD Cas. (BNA) 187 (2d Cir. 1992).

25 EEOC Compliance Manual § 902.4(d), Definition of the Term "Disability," 8 FEP Manual (BNA) 405:7273 (1995).

for going to work), has developed serious insomnia, and has had severe problems concentrating. This employee has an impairment (major depression) that significantly restricts his ability to interact with others, sleep, and concentrate. The effects of this impairment are severe and have lasted long enough to be substantially limiting.

In addition, some conditions may be long-term, or potentially long-term, in that their duration is indefinite and unknowable or is expected to be at least several months. Such conditions, if severe, may constitute disabilities.[26]

Example B: An employee has taken medication for bipolar disorder for a few months. For some time before starting medication, he experienced increasingly severe and frequent cycles of depression and mania; at times, he became extremely withdrawn socially or had difficulty caring for himself. His symptoms have abated with medication, but his doctor says that the duration and course of his bipolar disorder is indefinite, although it is potentially long-term. This employee's impairment (bipolar disorder) significantly restricts his major life activities of interacting with others and caring for himself, when considered without medication. The effects of his impairment are severe, and their duration is indefinite and potentially long-term.

However, conditions that are temporary and have no permanent or long-term effects on an individual's major life activities are not substantially limiting.

Example C: An employee was distressed by the end of a romantic relationship. Although he continued his daily routine, he sometimes became agitated at work. He was most distressed for about a month during and immediately after the breakup. He sought counseling and his mood improved within weeks. His counselor gave him a diagnosis of "adjustment disorder" and stated that he was not expected to experience any long-term problems associated with this event. While he has an impairment (adjustment disorder), his impairment was short-term, did not significantly restrict major life activities during that time, and was not expected to have permanent or long-term effects. This employee does not have a disability for purposes of the ADA.

8. Can **chronic, episodic disorders** be substantially limiting?

Yes. Chronic, episodic conditions may constitute substantially limiting impairments if they are substantially limiting when active or have a high likelihood of recurrence in substantially limiting forms. For some individuals, psychiatric impairments such as bipolar disorder, major depression, and schizophrenia may remit and intensify, sometimes repeatedly, over the course of several months or several years.[27]

9. When does an impairment substantially limit an individual's ability to **interact with others**?

An impairment substantially limits an individual's ability to interact with others if, due to the impairment, s/he is **significantly restricted as compared to the average person in the general population**. Some unfriendliness with coworkers or a supervisor would not, standing alone, be sufficient to establish a **substantial limitation** in interacting with others. An individual would be substantially limited, however, if his/her relations with others were characterized **on a regular basis by severe** problems, for example, consistently high levels of hostility, social withdrawal, or failure to communicate when necessary.

These limitations must be long-term or potentially long-term, as opposed to temporary, to justify a finding of ADA disability.

Example: An individual diagnosed with schizophrenia now works successfully as a computer programmer for a large company. Before finding an effective medication, however, he stayed in his room at home for several months, usually refusing to talk to family and close friends. After finding an effective medication, he was able to return to school, graduate, and start his career. This individual has a mental impairment, schizophrenia, which substantially limits his

---

[26] *Id.*, 8 FEP Manual (BNA) 405:7271.

[27] *See, e.g.*, *Clark v. Virginia Bd. of Bar Exam'rs*, 861 F. Supp. 512, 3 AD Cas. (BNA) 1066 (E.D. Va. 1994) (vacating its earlier ruling (at 3 AD Cas. (BNA) 780) that plaintiff's recurrent major depression did not constitute a "disability" under the ADA).

ability to interact with others when evaluated without medication. Accordingly, he is an individual with a disability as defined by the ADA.

10. When does an impairment substantially limit an individual's ability to concentrate?

An impairment substantially limits an individual's ability to concentrate if, due to the impairment, s/he is **significantly restricted as compared to the average person in the general population**.[28] For example, an individual would be substantially limited if s/he was easily and frequently distracted, meaning that his/her attention was frequently drawn to irrelevant sights or sounds or to intrusive thoughts; or if s/he experienced his/her "mind going blank" on a frequent basis.

Such limitations must be long-term or potentially long-term, as opposed to temporary, to justify a finding of ADA disability.[29]

Example A: An employee who has an anxiety disorder says that his mind wanders frequently and that he is often distracted by irrelevant thoughts. As a result, he makes repeated errors at work on detailed or complex tasks, even after being reprimanded. His doctor says that the errors are caused by his anxiety disorder and may last indefinitely. This individual has a disability because, as a result of an anxiety disorder, his ability to concentrate is significantly restricted as compared to the average person in the general population.

Example B: An employee states that he has trouble concentrating when he is tired or during long meetings. He attributes this to his chronic depression. Although his ability to concentrate may be slightly limited due to depression (a mental impairment), it is not significantly restricted as compared to the average person in the general population. Many people in the general population have difficulty concentrating when they are tired or during long meetings.

11. When does an impairment substantially limit an individual's ability to sleep?

An impairment substantially limits an individual's ability to sleep if, due to the impairment, his/her sleep is **significantly restricted as compared to the average person in the general population**. These limitations must be long-term or potentially long-term as opposed to temporary to justify a finding of ADA disability.

For example, an individual who sleeps only a negligible amount without medication for many months, due to post-traumatic stress disorder, would be significantly restricted as compared to the average person in the general population and therefore would be substantially limited in sleeping.[30] Similarly, an individual who for several months typically slept about two to three hours per night without medication, due to depression, also would be substantially limited in sleeping.

By contrast, an individual would not be substantially limited in sleeping if s/he had some trouble getting to sleep or sometimes slept fitfully because of a mental impairment. Although this individual may be slightly restricted in sleeping, s/he is not significantly restricted as compared to the average person in the general population.

12. When does an impairment substantially limit an individual's ability to care for him/herself?

An impairment substantially limits an individual's ability to care for him/herself if, due to the impairment, an individual is **significantly restricted as compared to the average person in the general population** in performing basic activities such as getting up in the morning, bathing, dressing, and preparing or obtaining food. These limitations must be long-term or potentially long-term as opposed to temporary to justify a finding of ADA disability.

Some psychiatric impairments, for example major depression, may result in an individual sleeping too much. In such cases, an individual may be substan-

[28] 29 C.F.R. § 1630.2(j)(ii) (1996); EEOC Compliance Manual§ 902.3(b), Definition of the Term "Disability," 8 FEP Manual (BNA) 405:7261 (1995).

[29] Substantial limitation in concentrating also may be associated with learning disabilities, neurological disorders, and physical trauma to the brain (*e.g.*, stroke, brain tumor, or head injury in a car accident). Although this guidance does not focus on these particular impairments, the analysis of basic ADA issues is consistent regardless of the nature of the condition.

[30] A 1994 survey of 1,000 American adults reports that 71% averaged 5-8 hours of sleep a night on weeknights and that 55% averaged 5-8 hours a night on weekends (with 37% getting more than 8 hours a night on weekends). *See The Cutting Edge: Vital Statistics—America's Sleep Habits*, Washington Post, May 24, 1994, Health Section at 5.

tially limited if, as a result of the impairment, s/he sleeps so much that s/he does not effectively care for him/herself. Alternatively, the individual may be substantially limited in working.

DISCLOSURE OF DISABILITY

Individuals with psychiatric disabilities may have questions about whether and when they must disclose their disability to their employer under the ADA. They may have concerns about the potential negative consequences of disclosing a psychiatric disability in the workplace, and about the confidentiality of information that they do disclose.

13. May an employer ask **questions on a job application** about history of treatment of mental illness, hospitalization, or the existence of mental or emotional illness or psychiatric disability?

No. An employer may not ask questions that are likely to elicit information about a disability before making an offer of employment.[31] Questions on a job application about psychiatric disability or mental or emotional illness or about treatment are likely to elicit information about a psychiatric disability and therefore are prohibited before an offer of employment is made.

14. When may an employer lawfully ask an individual about a **psychiatric disability** under the ADA?

An employer may ask for disability-related information, including information about psychiatric disability, only in the following limited circumstances:

* **Application Stage.** Employers are prohibited from asking disability-related questions before making an offer of employment. An exception, however, is if an applicant asks for **reasonable accommodation for the hiring process**. If the need for this accommodation is not obvious, an employer may ask an applicant for **reasonable** documentation about his/her disability. The employer may require the applicant to provide documentation from an appropriate professional concerning his/her disability and functional limitations.[32] A variety of health professionals may provide such documentation regarding psychiatric disabilities including primary health care professionals,[33] psychiatrists, psychologists, psychiatric nurses, and licensed mental health professionals such as licensed clinical social workers and licensed professional counselors.[34]

An employer should make clear to the applicant why it is requesting such information, *i.e.*, to verify the existence of a disability and the need for an accommodation. Furthermore, the employer may request only information necessary to accomplish these limited purposes.

Example A: An applicant for a secretarial job asks to take a typing test in a quiet location rather than in a busy reception area "because of a medical condition." The employer may make disability-related inquiries at this point because the applicant's need for reasonable accommodation under the ADA is not obvious based on the statement that an accommodation is needed "because of a medical condition." Specifically, the employer may ask the applicant to provide documentation showing that she has an impairment that substantially limits a major life activity and that she needs to take the typing test in a quiet location because of disability-related functional limitations.[35]

Although an employer may not ask an applicant if s/he will need reasonable accommodation **for the job**, there is an exception if the employer could **reasonably believe**, before making a job offer, that the applicant will need accommodation to perform the functions of the job. For an individual with a

---

[31] See 42 U.S.C. § 12112(d)(2) (1994); 29 C.F.R. § 1630.13(a) (1996). See also EEOC Enforcement Guidance: Preemployment Disability-Related Questions and Medical Examinations at 4, 8 FEP Manual (BNA) 405:7192 (1995).

[32] Enforcement Guidance: Preemployment Disability-Related Questions and Medical Examinations at 6, 8 FEP Manual (BNA) 405:7193 (1995).

[33] When a primary health care professional supplies documentation about a psychiatric disability, his/her credibility depends on how well s/he knows the individual and on his/her knowledge about the psychiatric disability.

[34] Important information about an applicant's functional limitations also may be obtained from non-professionals, such as the applicant, his/her family members, and friends.

[35] In response to the employer's request for documentation, the applicant may elect to revoke the request for accommodation and to take the test in the reception area. In these circumstances, where the request for reasonable accommodation has been withdrawn, the employer cannot continue to insist on obtaining the documentation.

non-visible disability, this may occur if the individual voluntarily discloses his/her disability or if s/he voluntarily tells the employer that s/he needs reasonable accommodation to perform the job. The employer may then ask certain limited questions, specifically:

* whether the applicant needs reasonable accommodation; and what type of reasonable accommodation would be needed to perform the functions of the job.[36]

* **After making an offer of employment, if the employer requires a post-offer, preemployment medical examination or inquiry.** After an employer extends an offer of employment, the employer **may** require a medical examination (including a psychiatric examination) or ask questions related to disability (including questions about psychiatric disability) *if* the employer subjects all entering employees in the same job category to the same inquiries or examinations regardless of disability. The inquiries and examinations do not need to be related to the job.[37]

* **During employment, when a disability-related inquiry or medical examination of an employee is "job-related and consistent with business necessity."**[38] This requirement may be met when an employer has a reasonable belief, based on objective evidence, that: (1) an employee's ability to perform essential job functions[39] will be impaired by a medical condition; or (2) an employee will pose a direct threat due to a medical condition. Thus, for example, inquiries or medical examinations are permitted if they follow-up on a request for reasonable accommodation when the need for accommodation is not obvious, or if they address reasonable concerns about whether an individual is fit to perform essential functions of his/her position. In addition, inquiries or examinations are permitted if they are required by another Federal law or regulation.[40] In these situations, the inquiries or examinations **must not exceed the scope of the specific medical condition and its effect on the employee's ability, with or without reasonable accommodation, to perform essential job functions or to work without posing a direct threat**.[41]

Example B: A delivery person does not learn the route he is required to take when he makes deliveries in a particular neighborhood. He often does not deliver items at all or delivers them to the wrong address. He is not adequately performing his essential function of making deliveries. There is no indication, however, that his failure to learn his route is related in any way to a medical condition. Because the employer does not have a reasonable belief, **based on objective evidence**, that this individual's ability to perform his essential job function is impaired by a medical condition, a medical examination (including a psychiatric examination) or disability-related inquiries would not be job-related and consistent with business necessity.[42]

Example C: A limousine service knows that one

---

36 EEOC Enforcement Guidance: Preemployment Disability-RelatedQuestions and Medical Examinations at 6-7, 8 FEP Manual (BNA) 405:7193-94 (1995).

37 If an employer uses the results of these inquiries or examinations to screen out an individual because of disability, the employer must prove that the exclusionary criteria are job-related and consistent with business necessity, and cannot be met with reasonable accommodation, in order to defend against a charge of employment discrimination. 42 U.S.C. § 12112(b)(6) (1994); 29 C.F.R.§§ 1630.10, 1630.14(b)(3), 1630.15(b) (1996).

38 42 U.S.C. § 12112(d)(4) (1994); 29 C.F.R. § 1630.14(c) (1996).

39 A "qualified" individual with a disability is one who can perform the essential functions of a position with or without reasonable accommodation. 42 U.S.C. § 12111(8) (1994). An employer does not have to lower production standards, whether qualitative or quantitative, to enable an individual with a disability to perform an essential function. *See* 29 C.F.R. pt. 1630 app. § 1630.2(n) (1996).

40 29 C.F.R. § 1630.15(e) (1996) ("It may be a defense to a charge of discrimination . . . that a challenged action is required or necessitated by another Federal law or regulation . . . .").

41 There may be additional situations which could meet the "job-related and consistent with business necessity" standard. For example, periodic medical examinations for public safety positions that are narrowly tailored to address specific job-related concerns and are shown to be consistent with business necessity would be permissible.

42 Of course, an employer would be justified in taking disciplinary action in these circumstances.

of its best drivers has bipolar disorder and had a manic episode last year, which started when he was driving a group of diplomats to around-the-clock meetings. During the manic episode, the chauffeur engaged in behavior that posed a direct threat to himself and others (he repeatedly drove a company limousine in a reckless manner). After a short leave of absence, he returned to work and to his usual high level of performance. The limousine service now wants to assign him to drive several business executives who may begin around-the-clock labor negotiations during the next several weeks. The employer is concerned, however, that this will trigger another manic episode and that, as a result, the employee will drive recklessly and pose a significant risk of substantial harm to himself and others. There is no indication that the employee's condition has changed in the last year, or that his manic episode last year was not precipitated by the assignment to drive to around-the-clock meetings. The employer may make disability-related inquiries, or require a medical examination, because it has a reasonable belief, based on objective evidence, that the employee will pose a direct threat to himself or others due to a medical condition.

Example D: An employee with depression seeks to return to work after a leave of absence during which she was hospitalized and her medication was adjusted. Her employer may request a fitness-for-duty examination because it has a reasonable belief, based on the employee's hospitalization and medication adjustment, that her ability to perform essential job functions may continue to be impaired by a medical condition. This examination, however, must be limited to the effect of her depression on her ability, with or without reasonable accommodation, to perform essential job functions. Inquiries about her entire psychiatric history or about the details of her therapy sessions would, for example, exceed this limited scope.

15. Do ADA **confidentiality requirements** apply to information about a psychiatric disability disclosed to an employer?

Yes. Employers must keep all information concerning the medical condition or history of its applicants or employees, including information about psychiatric disability, confidential under the ADA. This includes medical information that an individual voluntarily tells his/her employer. Employers must collect and maintain such information on separate forms and in separate medical files, apart from the usual personnel files.[43] There are limited exceptions to the ADA confidentiality requirements:

* supervisors and managers may be told about necessary restrictions on the work or duties of the employee and about necessary accommodations;
* first aid and safety personnel may be told if the disability might require emergency treatment; and
* government officials investigating compliance with the ADA must be given relevant information on request.[44]

16. How can an employer respond **when employees ask questions about a coworker who has a disability?**

If employees ask questions about a coworker who has a disability, the employer must not disclose any medical information in response. Apart from the limited exceptions listed in Question 15, the ADA confidentiality provisions prohibit such disclosure.

An employer also may not tell employees whether it is providing a reasonable accommodation for a particular individual. A statement that an individual receives a reasonable accommodation discloses that the individual probably has a disability because only individuals with disabilities are entitled to reasonable accommodation under the ADA. In response to coworker questions, however, the employer may explain that it is acting for legiti-

43 For a discussion of other confidentiality issues, see EEOC Enforcement Guidance: Preemployment Disability-Related Questions and Medical Examinations at 21-23, 8 FEP Manual (BNA) 405:7201-02 (1995).

44 42 U.S.C. § 12112(d)(3)(B), (4)(C) (1994); 29 C.F.R. § 1630.14(b)(1) (1996). The Commission has interpreted the ADA to allow employers to disclose medical information to state workers' compensation offices, state second injury funds, or workers' compensation insurance carriers in accordance with state workers' compensation laws. 29 C.F.R. pt. 1630 app. § 1630.14(b) (1996). The Commission also has interpreted the ADA to permit employers to use medical information for insurance purposes. *Id. See also* EEOC Enforcement Guidance: Preemployment Disability-Related Questions and Medical Examinations at 21 nn.24, 25, 8 FEP Manual (BNA) 405:7201 nn.24, 25 (1995).

mate business reasons or in compliance with federal law.

As background information for all employees, an employer may find it helpful to explain the requirements of the ADA, including the obligation to provide reasonable accommodation, in its employee handbook or in its employee orientation or training.

REQUESTING REASONABLE ACCOMMODATION

An employer must provide a reasonable accommodation to the known physical or mental limitations of a qualified individual with a disability unless it can show that the accommodation would impose an undue hardship.[45] An employee's decision about requesting reasonable accommodation may be influenced by his/her concerns about the potential negative consequences of disclosing a psychiatric disability at work. Employees and employers alike have posed numerous questions about what constitutes a request for reasonable accommodation.

17. When an individual decides to **request reasonable accommodation**, what must s/he say to make the request and start the reasonable accommodation process?

When an individual decides to request accommodation, the individual or his/her representative must let the employer know that s/he needs an adjustment or change at work for a reason related to a medical condition. To request accommodation, an individual may use "plain English" and need not mention the ADA or use the phrase "reasonable accommodation."[46]

Example A: An employee asks for time off because he is "depressed and stressed." The employee has communicated a request for a change at work (time off) for a reason related to a medical condition (being "depressed and stressed" may be "plain English" for a medical condition). This statement is sufficient to put the employer on notice that the employee is requesting reasonable accommodation. However, if the employee's need for accommodation is not obvious, the employer may ask for reasonable documentation concerning the employee's disability and functional limitations.[47]

Example B: An employee submits a note from a health professional stating that he is having a stress reaction and needs one week off. Subsequently, his wife telephones the Human Resources department to say that the employee is disoriented and mentally falling apart and that the family is having him hospitalized. The wife asks about procedures for extending the employee's leave and states that she will provide the necessary information as soon as possible but that she may need a little extra time. The wife's statement is sufficient to constitute a request for reasonable accommodation. The wife has asked for changes at work (an exception to the procedures for requesting leave and more time off) for a reason related to a medical condition (her husband had a stress reaction and is so mentally disoriented that he is being hospitalized). As in the previous example, if the need for accommodation is not obvious, the employer may request documentation of disability and clarification of the need for accommodation.[48]

Example C: An employee asks to take a few days off to rest after the completion of a major project. The employee does not link her need for a few days off to a medical condition. Thus, even though she has requested a change at work

---

[45] *See* 42 U.S.C. §§ 12111(9), 12112(b)(5)(A) (1994); 29 C.F.R.§ 1630.2(o), .9 (1996); 29 C.F.R. pt. 1630 app. § 1630.9 (1996).

[46] *Schmidt v. Safeway, Inc.*, 864 F. Supp. 991, 3 AD Cas. (BNA) 1141 (D. Or. 1994) (an employee's request for reasonable accommodation need not use "magic words" and can be in plain English). *See Bultemeyer v. Ft. Wayne Community Schs.*, 6 AD Cas. (BNA) 67 (7th Cir. 1996) (an employee with a known psychiatric disability requested reasonable accommodation by stating that he could not do a particular job and by submitting a note from his psychiatrist).

[47] *See* Question 21 *infra* about employers requesting documentation after receiving a request for reasonable accommodation.

[48] In the Commission's view, *Miller v. Nat'l Cas. Co.*, 61 F.3d 627, 4 AD Cas. (BNA) 1089 (8th Cir. 1995) was incorrectly decided. The court in *Miller* held that the employer was not alerted to Miller's disability and need for accommodation despite the fact that Miller's sister phoned the employer repeatedly and informed it that Miller was falling apart mentally and that the family was trying to get her into a hospital. See also *Taylor v. Principal Financial Group*, 5 AD Cas. (BNA) 1653(5th Cir. 1996).

(time off), her statement is not sufficient to put the employer on notice that she is requesting reasonable accommodation.

18. May someone **other than the employee request a reasonable accommodation** on behalf of an individual with a disability?

Yes, a family member, friend, health professional, or other representative may request a reasonable accommodation on behalf of an individual with a disability.[49] Of course, an employee may refuse to accept an accommodation that is not needed.

19. Do requests for reasonable accommodation need to be **in writing**?

No. Requests for reasonable accommodation do not need to be in writing. Employees may request accommodations in conversation or may use any other mode of communication.[50]

20. When should an individual with a disability **request a reasonable accommodation** to do the job?

An individual with a disability is not required to request a reasonable accommodation at the beginning of employment. S/he may request a reasonable accommodation at any time during employment.[51]

21. May an employer ask an employee for documentation when the employee requests reasonable accommodation for the job?

Yes. When the need **for accommodation is not obvious**, an employer may ask an employee for **reasonable** documentation about his/her disability and functional limitations. The employer is entitled to know that the employee has a covered disability for which s/he needs a reasonable accommodation.[52] A variety of health professionals may provide such documentation with regard to psychiatric disabilities.[53]

Example A: An employee asks for time off because he is "depressed and stressed." Although this statement is sufficient to put the employer on notice that he is requesting accommodation,[54] the employee's need for accommodation is not obvious based on this statement alone. Accordingly, the employer may require **reasonable** documentation that the employee has a disability within the meaning of the ADA and, if he has such a disability, that the functional limitations of the disability necessitate time off.

Example B: Same as Example A, except that the employer requires the employee to submit **all** of the records from his health professional regarding his mental health history, including materials that are not relevant to disability and reasonable accommodation under the ADA. This is not a request for reasonable documentation. All of these records are not required to determine if the employee has a disability as defined by the ADA and needs the requested reasonable accommodation because of his disability-related functional limitations. As one

[49] Cf. *Beck v. Univ. of Wis.*, 75 F.3d 1130, 5 AD Cas. (BNA) 304(7th Cir. 1996) (assuming, without discussion, that a doctor's note requesting reasonable accommodation on behalf of his patient triggered the reasonable accommodation process); *Schmidt v. Safeway, Inc.*, 864 F. Supp. 991, 3 AD Cas. (BNA) 1141 (D. Or. 1994) (stating that a doctor need not be expressly authorized to request accommodation on behalf of an employee in order to make a valid request).

In addition, because the reasonable accommodation process presumes open communication between the employer and the employee with the disability, the employer should be receptive to any relevant information or requests it receives from a third party acting on the employee's behalf. 29 C.F.R. pt. 1630 app. § 1630.9 (1996).

[50] Although individuals with disabilities are not required to keep records, they may find it useful to document requests for reasonable accommodation in the event there is a dispute about whether or when they requested accommodation. Of course, employers must keep all employment records, including records of requests for reasonable accommodation, for one year from the making of the record or the personnel action involved, whichever occurs later. 29 C.F.R. § 1602.14 (1996).

[51] As a practical matter, it may be in the employee's interest to request a reasonable accommodation before performance suffers or conduct problems occur.

[52] EEOC Enforcement Guidance: Preemployment Disability-Related Questions and Medical Examinations at 6, 8 FEP Manual (BNA) 405:7193 (1995).

[53] *See supra* nn.32-34 and accompanying text. *See also Bultemeyer v. Ft. Wayne Community Schs.*, 6 AD Cas. (BNA) 67 (7th Cir. 1996) (stating that, if employer found the precise meaning of employee's request for reasonable accommodation unclear, employer should have spoken to the employee or his psychiatrist, thus properly engaging in the interactive process).

[54] *See* Question 17, Example A, *supra*.

alternative, in order to determine the scope of its ADA obligations, the employer may ask the employee to sign a limited release allowing the employer to submit a list of specific questions to the employee's health care professional about his condition and need for reasonable accommodation.

22. May an employer require an employee to go to a health care professional of the **employer's (rather than the employee's) choice** for purposes of documenting need for accommodation and disability?

The ADA does not prevent an employer from requiring an employee to go to an appropriate health professional of the employer's choice if the employee initially provides insufficient information to substantiate that s/he has an ADA disability and needs a reasonable accommodation. Of course, any examination must be job-related and consistent with business necessity.[55] If an employer requires an employee to go to a health professional of the employer's choice, the employer must pay all costs associated with the visit(s).

SELECTED TYPES OF REASONABLE ACCOMMODATION

Reasonable accommodations for individuals with disabilities must be determined on a case-by-case basis because workplaces and jobs vary, as do people with disabilities. Accommodations for individuals with psychiatric disabilities may involve changes to workplace policies, procedures, or practices. Physical changes to the workplace or extra equipment also may be effective reasonable accommodations for some people. In some instances, the precise nature of an effective accommodation for an individual may not be immediately apparent. Mental health professionals, including psychiatric rehabilitation counselors, may be able to make suggestions about particular accommodations and, of equal importance, help employers and employees communicate effectively about reasonable accommodation.[56] The questions below discuss selected types of reasonable accommodation that may be effective for certain individuals with psychiatric disabilities.[57]

23. Does reasonable accommodation include giving an individual with a disability **time off** from work or **a modified work schedule**?

Yes. Permitting the use of accrued paid leave or providing additional unpaid leave for treatment or recovery related to a disability is a reasonable accommodation, unless (or until) the employee's absence imposes an undue hardship on the operation of the employer's business.[58] This includes leaves of absence, occasional leave (*e.g.*, a few hours at a time), and part-time scheduling.

A related reasonable accommodation is to allow an individual with a disability to change his/her regularly scheduled working hours, for example, to work 10 AM to 6 PM rather than 9 AM to 5 PM, barring undue hardship. Some medications taken for psychiatric disabilities cause extreme grogginess and lack of concentration in the morning. Depending on the job, a later schedule can enable the employee to perform essential job functions.

24. What types of **physical changes to the workplace**

---

55 Employers also may consider alternatives like having their health professional consult with the employee's health professional, with the employee's consent.

56 The Job Accommodation Network (JAN) also provides advice free-of-charge to employers and employees contemplating reasonable accommodation. JAN is a service of the President's Committee on Employment of People with Disabilities which, in turn, is funded by the U.S. Department of Labor. JAN can be reached at 1-800-ADA-WORK.

57 Some of the accommodations discussed in this section also may prove effective for individuals with traumatic brain injuries, stroke, and other mental disabilities. As a general matter, a covered employer must provide reasonable accommodation to the known physical or mental limitations of an otherwise qualified individual with a disability, barring undue hardship. 42 U.S.C. § 12112(b)(5)(A) (1994).

58 29 C.F.R. pt. 1630 app. § 1630.2(o) (1996). Courts have recognized leave as a reasonable accommodation. *See, e.g., Vande Zande v. Wis. Dep't of Admin.*, 44 F.3d 538, 3 AD Cas. (BNA) 1636 (7th Cir. 1995) (defendant had duty to accommodate plaintiff's pressure ulcers resulting from her paralysis which required her to stay home for several weeks); *Vializ v. New York City Bd. of Educ.*, 1995 WL 110112, 4 AD Cas. (BNA) 345 (S.D.N.Y. 1995) (plaintiff stated claim under ADA where she alleged that she would be able to return to work after back injury if defendant granted her a temporary leave of absence); *Schmidt v. Safeway, Inc.*, 864 F. Supp. 991, 3 AD Cas. (BNA) 1141 (D. Or. 1994) ("[A] leave of absence to obtain medical treatment is a reasonable accommodation if it is likely that, following treatment, [the employee] would have been able to safely perform his duties . . . .").

or equipment can serve as accommodations for people with psychiatric disabilities?

Simple physical changes to the workplace may be effective accommodations for some individuals with psychiatric disabilities. For example, room dividers, partitions, or other soundproofing or visual barriers between workspaces may accommodate individuals who have disability-related limitations in concentration. Moving an individual away from noisy machinery or reducing other workplace noise that can be adjusted (*e.g.*, lowering the volume or pitch of telephones) are similar reasonable accommodations. Permitting an individual to wear headphones to block out noisy distractions also may be effective.

Some individuals who have disability-related limitations in concentration may benefit from access to equipment like a tape recorder for reviewing events such as training sessions or meetings.

25. Is it a reasonable accommodation to **modify a workplace policy**?

Yes. It is a reasonable accommodation to modify a workplace policy when necessitated by an individual's disability-related limitations, barring undue hardship.[59] For example, it would be a reasonable accommodation to allow an individual with a disability, who has difficulty concentrating due to the disability, to take detailed notes during client presentations even though company policy discourages employees from taking extensive notes during such sessions.

Example: A retail employer does not allow individuals working as cashiers to drink beverages at checkout stations. The retailer also limits cashiers to two 15-minute breaks during an eight-hour shift, in addition to a meal break. An individual with a psychiatric disability needs to drink beverages approximately once an hour in order to combat dry mouth, a side-effect of his psychiatric medication. This individual requests reasonable accommodation. In this example, the employer should consider either modifying its policy against drinking beverages at checkout stations or modifying its policy limiting cashiers to two 15-minute breaks each day plus a meal break, barring undue hardship.

Granting an employee time off from work or an adjusted work schedule as a reasonable accommodation may involve modifying leave or attendance procedures or policies. As an example, it would be a reasonable accommodation to modify a policy requiring employees to schedule vacation time in advance if an otherwise qualified individual with a disability needed to use accrued vacation time on an unscheduled basis because of disability-related medical problems, barring undue hardship.[60] In addition, an employer, in spite of a "no-leave" policy, may, in appropriate circumstances, be required to provide leave to an employee with a disability as a reasonable accommodation, unless the provision of leave would impose an undue hardship.[61]

26. Is adjusting **supervisory methods** a form of reasonable accommodation?

Yes. Supervisors play a central role in achieving effective reasonable accommodations for their employees. In some circumstances, supervisors may be able to adjust their methods as a reasonable accommodation by, for example, communicating assignments, instructions, or training by the medium that is most effective for a particular individual (*e.g.*, in writing, in conversation, or by electronic mail). Supervisors also may provide or arrange additional training or modified training materials.

Adjusting the level of supervision or structure sometimes may enable an otherwise qualified individual with a disability to perform essential job functions. For example, an otherwise qualified individual with a disability who experiences limitations in concentration may request more detailed day-to-day guidance, feedback, or structure in order to perform his job.[62]

Example: An employee requests more daily

---

[59] 42 U.S.C. § 12111(9)(B) (1994); 29 C.F.R. § 1630.2(o)(2)(ii) (1996).

[60] *See Dutton v. Johnson County Bd.*, 1995 WL 337588, 3 AD Cas. (BNA) 1614 (D. Kan. 1995) (it was a reasonable accommodation to permit an individual with a disability to use unscheduled vacation time to cover absence for migraine headaches, where that did not pose an undue hardship and employer knew about the migraine headaches and the need for accommodation).

[61] *See* 29 C.F.R. pt. 1630 app. § 1630.15(b), (c) (1996).

guidance and feedback as a reasonable accommodation for limitations associated with a psychiatric disability. In response to his request, the employer consults with the employee, his health care professional, and his supervisor about how his limitations are manifested in the office (the employee is unable to stay focused on the steps necessary to complete large projects) and how to make effective and practical changes to provide the structure he needs. As a result of these consultations, the supervisor and employee work out a long-term plan to initiate weekly meetings to review the status of large projects and identify which steps need to be taken next.

27. Is it a reasonable accommodation to provide a **job coach**?

Yes. An employer may be required to provide a temporary job coach to assist in the training of a qualified individual with a disability as a reasonable accommodation, barring undue hardship.[63] An employer also may be required to allow a job coach paid by a public or private social service agency to accompany the employee at the job site as a reasonable accommodation.

28. Is it a reasonable accommodation to make sure that an individual takes **medication** as prescribed?

No. Medication monitoring is not a reasonable accommodation. Employers have no obligation to monitor medication because doing so does not remove a barrier that is unique to the workplace. When people do not take medication as prescribed, it affects them on and off the job.

29. When is **reassignment** to a different position required as a reasonable accommodation?

In general, reassignment **must** be considered as a reasonable accommodation when accommodation in the present job would cause undue hardship[64] or would not be possible.[65] Reassignment may be considered if there are circumstances under which both the employer and employee voluntarily agree that it is preferable to accommodation in the present position.[66]

Reassignment should be made to an equivalent position that is vacant or will become vacant within a reasonable amount of time. If an equivalent position is not available, the employer must look for a vacant position at a lower level for which the employee is qualified. Reassignment is not required if a vacant position at a lower level is also unavailable.

CONDUCT

Maintaining satisfactory conduct and performance typically is not a problem for individuals with psychi-

---

62 Reasonable accommodation, however, does not require lowering standards or removing essential functions of the job. *Bolstein v. Reich*, 1995 WL 46387, 3 AD Cas. (BNA) 1761 (D.D.C. 1995) (attorney with chronic depression and severe personality disturbance was not a qualified individual with a disability because his requested accommodations of more supervision, less complex assignments, and the exclusion of appellate work would free him of the very duties that justified his GS-14 grade), motion for summary affirmance granted, 1995 WL 686236 (D.C. Cir. 1995). The court in Bolstein noted that the plaintiff objected to a reassignment to a lower grade in which he could have performed the essential functions of the position. 1995 WL 46387, * 4, 3 AD Cas. (BNA) 1761, 1764 (D.D.C. 1995).

63 *See* 29 C.F.R. pt. 1630 app. § 1630.9 (1996) (discussing supported employment); U.S. Equal Employment Opportunity Commission, "A Technical Assistance Manual on the Employment Provisions (Title I) of the Americans with Disabilities Act," at 3.4, 8 FEP Manual (BNA) 405:7001 (1992) [hereinafter Technical Assistance Manual]. A job coach is a professional who assists individuals with severe disabilities with job placement and job training.

64 For example, it may be an undue hardship to provide extra supervision as a reasonable accommodation in the present job if the employee's current supervisor is already very busy supervising several other individuals and providing direct service to the public.

65 42 U.S.C. § 12111(9)(B) (1994). For example, it may not be possible to accommodate an employee in his present position if he works as a salesperson on the busy first floor of a major department store and needs a reduction in visual distractions and ambient noise as a reasonable accommodation.

See EEOC Enforcement Guidance: Workers' Compensation and the ADA at 17, 8 FEP Manual (BNA) 405:7399-7400 (1996) (where an employee can no longer perform the essential functions of his/her original position, with or without a reasonable accommodation, because of a disability, an employer must reassign him/her to an equivalent vacant position for which s/he is qualified, absent undue hardship).

66 Technical Assistance Manual, *supra* note 63, at 3.10(5), 8 FEP Manual (BNA) 405:7011-12 (reassignment to a vacant position as a reasonable accommodation); *see also* 42 U.S.C. § 12111(9)(B) (1994); 29 C.F.R. § 1630.2(o)(2)(ii) (1996).

atric disabilities. Nonetheless, circumstances arise when employers need to discipline individuals with such disabilities for misconduct.

30. May an employer **discipline** an individual with a disability for **violating a workplace conduct standard** if the misconduct **resulted from a disability**?

Yes, provided that the workplace conduct standard is job-related for the position in question and is consistent with business necessity.[67] For example, nothing in the ADA prevents an employer from maintaining a workplace free of violence or threats of violence, or from disciplining an employee who steals or destroys property. Thus, an employer may discipline an employee with a disability for engaging in such misconduct if it would impose the same discipline on an employee without a disability.[68] Other conduct standards, however, may not be job-related for the position in question and consistent with business necessity. If they are not, imposing discipline under them could violate the ADA.

Example A: An employee steals money from his employer. Even if he asserts that his misconduct was caused by a disability, the employer may discipline him consistent with its uniform disciplinary policies because the individual violated a conduct standard—a prohibition against employee theft—that is job-related for the position in question and consistent with business necessity.

Example B: An employee at a clinic tampers with and incapacitates medical equipment. Even if the employee explains that she did this because of her disability, the employer may discipline her consistent with its uniform disciplinary policies because she violated a conduct standard—a rule prohibiting intentional damage to equipment—that is job-related for the position in question and consistent with business necessity. However, if the employer disciplines her even though it has not disciplined people without disabilities for the same misconduct, the employer would be treating her differently because of disability in violation of the ADA.

Example C: An employee with a psychiatric disability works in a warehouse loading boxes onto pallets for shipment. He has no customer contact and does not come into regular contact with other employees. Over the course of several weeks, he has come to work appearing increasingly disheveled. His clothes are ill-fitting and often have tears in them. He also has become increasingly anti-social. Coworkers have complained that when they try to engage him in casual conversation, he walks away or gives a curt reply. When he has to talk to a coworker, he is abrupt and rude. His work, however, has not suffered. The employer's company handbook states that employees should have a neat appearance at all times. The handbook also states that employees should be courteous to each other. When told that he is being disciplined for his appearance and treatment of coworkers, the employee explains that his appearance and demeanor have deteriorated because of his disability which was exacerbated during this time period.

The dress code and coworker courtesy rules are not job-related for the position in question and consistent with business necessity because this employee has no customer contact and does not come into regular contact with other employees. Therefore, rigid application of these rules to this employee would violate the ADA.

31. Must an employer make reasonable accommodation for an individual with a disability who violated a conduct rule that is job-related for the position in question and consistent with business necessity?

An employer must make reasonable accommodation to enable **an otherwise qualified individual with a disability** to meet such a conduct standard **in the future**, barring undue hardship.[69] Because reasonable accommodation is always prospective, however, an employer is not required to excuse

[67] 42 U.S.C. § 12112(b)(6) (1994); 29 C.F.R. § 1630.10, .15(c) (1996).

[68] See EEOC Compliance Manual § 902.2, n.11, Definition of the Term "Disability," 8 FEP Manual (BNA) 405:7259, n.11 (1995) (an employer "does not have to excuse . . . misconduct, even if the misconduct results from an impairment that rises to the level of a disability, if it does not excuse similar misconduct from its other employees"); see 56 Fed. Reg. 35,733 (1991) (referring to revisions to proposed ADA rule that "clarify that employers may hold all employees, disabled (including those disabled by alcoholism or drug addiction) and nondisabled, to the same performance and conduct standards").

[69] See 29 C.F.R. § 1630.15(d) (1996).

past misconduct.[70]

Example A: A reference librarian frequently loses her temper at work, disrupting the library atmosphere by shouting at patrons and coworkers. After receiving a suspension as the second step in uniform, progressive discipline, she discloses her disability, states that it causes her behavior, and requests a leave of absence for treatment. The employer may discipline her because she violated a conduct standard—a rule prohibiting disruptive behavior towards patrons and coworkers—that is job-related for the position in question and consistent with business necessity. The employer, however, must grant her request for a leave of absence as a reasonable accommodation, barring undue hardship, to enable her to meet this conduct standard in the future.

Example B: An employee with major depression is often late for work because of medication side-effects that make him extremely groggy in the morning. His scheduled hours are 9:00 AM to 5:30 PM, but he arrives at 9:00, 9:30, 10:00 or even 10:30 on any given day. His job responsibilities involve telephone contact with the company's traveling sales representatives, who depend on him to answer urgent marketing questions and expedite special orders. The employer disciplines him for tardiness, stating that continued failure to arrive promptly during the next month will result in termination of his employment. The individual then explains that he was late because of a disability and needs to work on a later schedule. In this situation, the employer may discipline the employee because he violated a conduct standard addressing tardiness that is job-related for the position in question and consistent with business necessity. The employer, however, must consider reasonable accommodation, barring undue hardship, to enable this individual to meet this standard in the future. For example, if this individual can serve the company's sales representatives by regularly working a schedule of 10:00 AM to 6:30 PM, a reasonable accommodation would be to modify his schedule so that he is not required to report for work until 10:00 AM.

Example C: An employee has a hostile altercation with his supervisor and threatens the supervisor with physical harm. The employer immediately terminates the individual's employment, consistent with its policy of immediately terminating the employment of anyone who threatens a supervisor. When he learns that his employment has been terminated, the employee asks the employer to put the termination on hold and to give him a month off for treatment instead. This is the employee's first request for accommodation and also the first time the employer learns about the employee's disability. The employer is not required to rescind the discharge under these circumstances, because the employee violated a conduct standard—a rule prohibiting threats of physical harm against supervisors—that is job-related for the position in question and consistent with business necessity. The employer also is not required to offer reasonable accommodation for the future because this individual is no longer a qualified individual with a disability. His employment was terminated under a uniformly applied conduct standard that is job-related for the position in question and consistent with business necessity.[71]

32. How should an employer deal with an employee with a disability who is engaging in misconduct because s/he is **not taking his/her medication**?

The employer should focus on the employee's conduct and explain to the employee the consequences of continued misconduct in terms of uniform disciplinary procedures. It is the **employee's** responsibility to decide about medication and to consider the consequences of not taking medication.[72]

DIRECT THREAT

Under the ADA, an employer may lawfully exclude an individual from employment for safety reasons only if the employer can show that employment of the indi-

[70] Therefore, it may be in the employee's interest to request a reasonable accommodation before performance suffers or conduct problems occur. See Question 20 supra.

[71] Regardless of misconduct, an individual with a disability must be allowed to file a grievance or appeal challenging his/her termination when that is a right normally available to other employees.

[72] If the employee requests reasonable accommodation in order to address the misconduct, the employer must grant the request, subject to undue hardship.

vidual would pose a "direct threat."[73] Employers must apply the "direct threat" standard uniformly and may not use safety concerns to justify exclusion of persons with disabilities when persons without disabilities would not be excluded in similar circumstances.[74]

The EEOC's ADA regulations explain that "direct threat" means "a significant risk of substantial harm to the health or safety of the individual or others that cannot be eliminated or reduced by reasonable accommodation."[75] A "significant" risk is a high, and not just a slightly increased, risk.[76] The determination that an individual poses a "direct threat" must be based on an individualized assessment of the individual's present ability to safely perform the functions of the job, considering a reasonable medical judgment relying on the most current medical knowledge and/or the best available objective evidence.[77] With respect to the employment of individuals with psychiatric disabilities, the employer must identify the specific behavior that would pose a direct threat.[78] An individual does not pose a "direct threat" simply by virtue of having a history of psychiatric disability or being treated for a psychiatric disability.[79]

33. Does an individual pose a direct threat in operating machinery solely because s/he takes **medication** that may as a side effect diminish concentration and/or coordination for some people?

> No. An individual does not pose a direct threat solely because s/he takes a medication that may diminish coordination or concentration for some people as a side effect. Whether such an individual poses a direct threat must be determined on a case-by-case basis, based on a reasonable medical judgment relying on the most current medical knowledge and/or on the best available objective evidence. Therefore, an employer must determine the nature and severity of this individual's side effects, how those side effects influence his/her ability to safely operate the machinery, and whether s/he has had safety problems in the past when operating the same or similar machinery while taking the medication. If a significant risk of substantial harm exists, then an employer must determine if there is a reasonable accommodation that will reduce or eliminate the risk.
>
> *Example*: An individual receives an offer for a job in which she will operate an electric saw, conditioned on a post-offer medical examination. In response to questions at this medical examination, the individual discloses her psychiatric disability and states that she takes a medication to control it. This medication is known to sometimes affect coordination and concentration. The company doctor determines that the individual experiences negligible side effects from the medication because she takes a relatively low dosage. She also had an excellent safety record at a previous job, where she operated similar machinery while taking the same medication. This individual does not pose a direct threat.

34. When can an employer refuse to hire someone based on his/her **history of violence or threats of violence**?

> An employer may refuse to hire someone based on his/her history of violence or threats of violence if it can show that the individual poses a direct threat. A determination of "direct threat" must be based on an individualized assessment of the individual's present ability to safely perform the functions of the job, considering the most current medical knowledge and/or the best available objective evidence. To find that an individual with a psychiatric disability poses a direct threat, the employer must identify the specific behavior on the part of the individual that would pose the direct threat. This includes an assessment of the likelihood and imminence of future violence.
>
> *Example*: An individual applies for a position with Employer X. When Employer X checks his employment background, she learns that he was terminated two weeks ago by Employer Y, after

---

73 See 42 U.S.C. § 12113(b) (1994).

74 29 C.F.R. pt. 1630 app. § 1630.2(r) (1996).

75 29 C.F.R. § 1630.2(r) (1996). To determine whether an individual would pose a direct threat, the factors to be considered include: (1) duration of the risk; (2) nature and severity of the potential harm; (3) likelihood that the potential harm will occur; and (4) imminence of the potential harm. *Id.*

76 29 C.F.R. pt. 1630 app. § 1630.2(r) (1996).

77 29 C.F.R. § 1630.2(r) (1996).

78 29 C.F.R. pt. 1630 app. § 1630.2(r) (1996).

79 House Judiciary Report, *supra* n.2, at 45.

he told a coworker that he would get a gun and "get his supervisor if he tries anything again." Employer X also learns that these statements followed three months of escalating incidents in which this individual had had several altercations in the workplace, including one in which he had to be restrained from fighting with a coworker. He then revealed his disability to Employer Y. After being given time off for medical treatment, he continued to have trouble controlling his temper and was seen punching the wall outside his supervisor's office. Finally, he made the threat against the supervisor and was terminated. Employer X learns that, since then, he has not received any further medical treatment. Employer X does not hire him, stating that this history indicates that he poses a direct threat.

This individual poses a direct threat as a result of his disability because his recent overt acts and statements (including an attempted fight with a coworker, punching the wall, and making a threatening statement about the supervisor) support the conclusion that he poses a "significant risk of substantial harm." Furthermore, his prior treatment had no effect on his behavior, he had received no subsequent treatment, and only two weeks had elapsed since his termination, all supporting a finding of direct threat.

35. Does an individual who has attempted suicide pose a direct threat when s/he seeks to return to work?

No, in most circumstances. As with other questions of direct threat, an employer must base its determination on an individualized assessment of the person's ability to safely perform job functions when s/he returns to work. Attempting suicide does not mean that an individual poses an imminent risk of harm to him/herself when s/he returns to work. In analyzing direct threat (including the likelihood and imminence of any potential harm), the employer must seek reasonable medical judgments relying on the most current medical knowledge and/or the best available factual evidence concerning the employee.

Example: An employee with a known psychiatric disability was hospitalized for two suicide attempts, which occurred within several weeks of each other. When the employee asked to return to work, the employer allowed him to return pending an evaluation of medical reports to determine his ability to safely perform his job. The individual's therapist and psychiatrist both submitted documentation stating that he could safely perform all of his job functions. Moreover, the employee performed his job safely after his return, without reasonable accommodation. The employer, however, terminated the individual's employment after evaluating the doctor's and therapist's reports, without citing any contradictory medical or factual evidence concerning the employee's recovery. Without more evidence, this employer cannot support its determination that this individual poses a direct threat.[80]

PROFESSIONAL LICENSING

Individuals may have difficulty obtaining state-issued professional licenses if they have, or have a record of, a psychiatric disability. When a psychiatric disability results in denial or delay of a professional license, people may lose employment opportunities.

36. Would an individual have grounds for filing an ADA charge if an employer refused to hire him/her (or revoked a job offer) because s/he did not have a professional license due to a psychiatric disability?

If an individual filed a charge on these grounds, EEOC would investigate to determine whether the professional license was required by law for the position at issue, and whether the employer in fact did not hire the individual because s/he lacked the license. If the employer did not hire the individual because s/he lacked a legally-required professional license, and the individual claims that the licensing process discriminates against individuals with psychiatric disabilities, EEOC would coordinate with the Department of Justice, Civil Rights Division, Disability Rights Section, which enforces Title II of the ADA covering state licensing requirements.

INDEX [Omitted.]

---

80 Cf. Ofat v. Ohio Civ. Rights Comm'n, 1995 WL 310051, 4 AD Cas. (BNA) 753 (Ohio Ct. App. 1995) (finding against employer, under state law, on issue of whether employee who had panic disorder with agoraphobia could safely return to her job after disability-related leave, where employer presented no expert evidence about employee's disability or its effect on her ability to safely perform her job but only provided copies of pages from a medical text generally discussing the employee's illness).

APPLICATIONS FOR BENEFITS ON THE DETERMINATION OF WHETHER A PERSON IS A "QUALIFIED INDIVIDUAL WITH A DISABILITY" UNDER THE AMERICANS WITH DISABILITIES ACT OF 1990 (ADA).

EEOC NOTICE
Number 915.002
Date 2-12-97

1. SUBJECT: Enforcement Guidance on the Effect of Representations Made in Applications for Benefits on the Determination of Whether a Person Is a "Qualified Individual with a Disability" Under the Americans with Disabilities Act of 1990 (ADA).
2. PURPOSE: This enforcement guidance sets forth the Commission's position that representations made in connection with an application for disability benefits should not be an automatic bar to an ADA claim.
3. EFFECTIVE DATE: Upon receipt.
4. EXPIRATION DATE: As an exception to EEOC Order 205.001, Appendix B, Attachment 4, § a(5), this Notice will remain in effect until rescinded or superseded.
5. ORIGINATOR: ADA Division, Office of Legal Counsel
6. INSTRUCTIONS: File after Section 902 of Volume II of the Compliance Manual.

____

Date — Gilbert F. Casellas
Chairman

Table of Contents

Representations.

1. Context
2. Timing

III. Public Policy Supports the Conclusion that Representations Made in Connection with an Application for Disability Benefits Are Never an Absolute Bar to an ADA Claim.

A. Permitting Individuals to Go Forward with Their ADA Claims Is Critical to the ADA's Goal of Eradicating Discrimination Against Individuals with Disabilities.

B. Individuals Should Not Have to Choose Between Applying for Disability Benefits and Vindicating Their Rights Under the ADA.

IV. Instructions to Investigators

Executive Summary: Enforcement Guidance on the Effect of Representations Made in Applications for Benefits on the Determination of Whether a Person Is a "Qualified Individual with a Disability" Under the Americans with Disabilities Act of 1990 (ADA or Act)

Introduction

This Enforcement Guidance explains why representations about the ability to work made in the course of applying for social security, workers' compensation, disability insurance, and other disability benefits do not bar the filing of an ADA charge. It provides instructions to EEOC investigators for assessing what weight, if any, to give to such representations in determining whether a charging party (CP) is a "qualified individual with a disability" for purposes of the ADA.

A "qualified individual with a disability" is "an individual with a disability who satisfies the requisite skill, experience, education and other job-related requirements of the employment position such individual holds or desires and who, with or without reasonable accommodation, can perform the essential functions of such position." Because of the fundamental differences in the definitions used in the ADA and the terms used in disability benefits programs, an individual can meet the eligibility requirements for receipt of disability benefits and still be a "qualified individual with a disability" for ADA purposes. Thus, a person's representations that s/he is "totally disabled" or "unable to work" for purposes of disability benefits are never an absolute bar to an ADA claim.

Americans with Disabilities Act

The definition of the term "qualified individual with a disability" reflects the ADA's broad remedial purpose to prohibit discrimination against individuals with disabilities who want to work and are qualified to work. Accordingly, the definition:

- requires an individualized assessment of a particular individual's capabilities;
- focuses on the essential functions of a particular position;
- looks at particular positions, not work in general; and
- considers whether a person can work with reasonable accommodation.

The ADA definition of "qualified individual with a disability" differs from the definitions used in the Social Security Act, state workers' compensation laws, disability insurance plans, and other disability benefits programs designed for different purposes.

Social Security Act

Disability programs established under the Social Security Act are designed to provide income to individuals with disabilities who generally are unable to work. Unlike the ADA definition of "qualified individual with a disability," the Social Security Administration (SSA) definition of "disability":

- permits general presumptions about an individual's ability to work;
- considers all tasks as jobs are customarily performed without focusing on the essential functions of a particular position;
- looks generally at whether an individual can do work which exists in the national economy rather than whether s/he can perform the essential functions of a particular position; and
- does not consider whether a person can work with reasonable accommodation.

Workers' Compensation Laws

The purpose of workers' compensation laws is to provide benefits to individuals whose earning capacity has been reduced because of a work-related injury or illness. Unlike the ADA definition of "qualified individual with a disability," the workers' compensation definitions of "disability" generally:

- permit generalized presumptions about an individual's ability to work;
- do not distinguish between marginal and essen-

tial functions;

- focus on whether an individual is unable to do any kind of work for which there is a reasonably stable employment market rather than whether s/he can perform the essential functions of a particular position; and
- do not consider whether an individual can work with reasonable accommodation.

Disability Insurance Plans

Disability insurance plans provide partial wage replacement when an employee becomes unable to work as a result of illness, injury, or disease. Frequently, the definitions of "disability" under such plans:

- do not distinguish between essential and marginal functions of a position; and
- make no allowance for an individual's ability to work with reasonable accommodation.

Relevant Factors for Determining Whether CP Is a "Qualified Individual with a Disability"

When assessing the effect of representations made in connection with an application for benefits on the determination of whether CP is a "qualified individual with disability," investigators should consider the following factors:

- the definitions of terms such as "disability," "permanent disability," "total disability," "inability to work," etc., under the relevant statute or contract pursuant to which CP applied for disability benefits (e.g., do they look at specific positions or general kinds of work? do these terms take into account reasonable accommodation?);
- the specific content of the representations, who made them, and the purpose for which they were made;
- whether the representations are in CP's own words;
- whether the representations about CP's inability to work are qualified in any way (e.g., "I am able to work with certain restrictions");
- when the representations were made, the period of time to which they refer, and whether CP's physical or mental condition has changed since the representations were made;
- whether CP was working during the period of time referred to as a period of total disability;
- whether the employer suggested that CP apply for benefits;
- whether CP asked for and was denied reasonable accommodation;
- when the employer learned of the representations; and
- other relevant factors, such as advances in technology or changes in the employer's operations that may have occurred since representations were made that may make it possible for CP to perform the essential functions of the position, with or without reasonable accommodation.

Enforcement Guidance: Effect of Representations Made in Applications for Disability Benefits on the Determination of Whether a Person Is a "Qualified Individual with a Disability" Under the Americans with Disabilities Act of 1990 (ADA)

Introduction The Americans with Disabilities Act of 1990 (herein after ADA or Act)[1] prohibits employers from discriminating against qualified individuals with disabilities in all aspects of employment. To be protected by the ADA, a person must meet the definition of the term "qualified individual with a disability."[2] A "qualified individual with a disability" is "an individual with a disability who satisfies the requisite skill, experience, education and other job-related

---

1 Codified as amended at 42 U.S.C. §§ 12101-17, 12201-13 (1994).

2 By including the phrase "qualified individual with a disability," Congress intended to reaffirm that the ADA "does not undermine an employer's ability to choose and maintain qualified workers." S. Rep. No. 101-116, at 26 (1989) [hereinafter Senate Report]; H.R. Rep. No. 101-485, pt. 2, at 55 (1990) [hereinafter House Education and Labor Report]. Rather, the ADA simply provides that employment decisions must not subject a "qualified individual with a disability" to discrimination on the basis of his/her disability. *Id.*

The ADA also protects individuals from discrimination on the basis of their relationship or association with a person with a disability and prohibits certain disability-related inquiries and medical examinations. 42 U.S.C. § 12112(b)(4), (d). Further, the Act prohibits retaliation or coercion against individuals because they have opposed any act that the ADA makes unlawful, have participated in the enforcement process, or have encouraged others to exercise their rights secured by the ADA. *Id.* § 12203. A person need not be a "qualified individual with a disability" to be protected by these sections of the Act.

requirements of the employment position such individual holds or desires, and who, with or without reasonable accommodation, can perform the essential functions of such position."[3]

The issue of whether a person is a "qualified individual with a disability" arises when an individual brings an ADA claim alleging that s/he was subjected to an adverse employment action because of his/her disability. For example, in many charges received by the EEOC, individuals claim that they were not hired or were fired because of disability even though they were able to perform the essential functions of the position at issue. Often, the individual has requested but been denied a reasonable accommodation. Frequently, the individual also has filed for disability benefits, sometimes at the suggestion of the employer, and has represented that s/he meets the relevant eligibility requirements (e.g., that s/he is "totally disabled" or "unable to work"). In such cases, questions may arise as to whether the individual is barred from claiming that s/he is a "qualified individual with a disability" under the ADA.[4]

This enforcement guidance explains why representations made in other contexts about the ability to work are not necessarily a bar to an ADA claim.[5] In this regard, the guidance:

- analyzes the differences between the ADA's purposes and standards and those of other statutory schemes, disability benefits programs, and contracts;
- discusses recent and significant court decisions that have addressed this issue;
- explains why the doctrine of judicial estoppel and summary judgment procedures should not be used to bar the ADA claims of individuals who have applied for disability benefits;
- delineates why public policy supports the Commission's position; and
- explains how to assess what weight, if any, to give to such representations in determining whether an individual is a "qualified individual with a disability" for purposes of the ADA.

I. The ADA's Purposes and Standards Are Fundamentally Different from the Purposes and Standards of Other Statutory Schemes and Contractual Rights.

The primary purposes underlying the ADA are the elimination of barriers that prevent individuals with disabilities from participating in "the economic and social mainstream of American life"[6] and the provision of equal employment and other opportunities for persons with disabilities. In addition, Congress enacted the ADA to provide legal remedies to individuals who have experienced discrimination on the basis of disability.[7] Consistent with these goals, the ADA establishes specific standards for assessing whether an individual has a disability and whether s/he is a "qualified individual with a disability."

Because the ADA definitions of the terms "disability" and "qualified individual with a disability" are tailored to the broad remedial purposes of the Act, they differ from the definitions of the same or similar terms used in other laws and benefits programs designed for other purposes. The definitions of the terms used in the Social Security Act, state workers' compensation laws, disability insurance plans, and other disability benefits programs are tailored to the purposes of those laws and programs. Therefore, representations made under those laws and programs are not determinative of coverage under the ADA. Although representations made in connection with an application for disability benefits may be relevant to such a determination, they are never an absolute bar to a finding that a person is a "qualified individual with a disability" for purposes of the ADA.

---

3 29 C.F.R. § 1630.2(m)(1996); see also 42 U.S.C. § 12111(8).

4 Similar questions also arise where individuals have filed claims for state disability, disability retirement, Railroad Retirement Board, and Federal Employee Compensation Act benefits. The analysis in this guidance also applies to representations concerning the ability to work made in other situations, such as applications for scholarships or admission to education programs and exemptions from, or deferments of, student loan repayments.

5 The analysis in this guidance also applies to federal sector complaints of non-affirmative action employment discrimination arising under section 501 of the Rehabilitation Act of 1973, 29 U.S.C. § 791(g) (1994), and to complaints of non-affirmative action employment discrimination arising under sections 503 and 504 of the Rehabilitation Act of 1973, 29 U.S.C. §§ 793(d), 794(d) (1994).

6 Senate Report at 20; House Education and Labor Report at 50.

7 See 42 U.S.C. § 12101(a)(3).

A. Americans with Disabilities Act

1. Purposes

The ADA is a sweeping civil rights law designed "to provide a clear and comprehensive national mandate for the elimination of discrimination against individuals with disabilities."[8] It also is designed "to provide clear, strong, consistent, enforceable standards addressing discrimination against individuals with disabilities."[9]

In enacting the ADA, Congress made clear that "the Nation's proper goals regarding individuals with disabilities are to assure equality of opportunity, full participation, independent living, and economic self-sufficiency for such individuals."[10] Congress found that many of the more than 43 million Americans with disabilities "continually encounter various forms of discrimination" and that this invidious discrimination "persists in such critical areas as employment. . . ."[11] Unlike other discrete and insular minorities, however, individuals with disabilities "have often had no legal recourse to redress such discrimination."[12] As a result, this discrimination and denial of equal employment opportunity have "cost[] the United States billions of dollars in unnecessary expenses resulting from dependency and nonproductivity."[13] Accordingly, Congress passed the ADA to enable individuals with disabilities to participate fully in all aspects of society, particularly employment. Underlying the ADA is the recognition that equal employment opportunity is the only way that this country can accomplish its "proper goal" of ensuring economic self- sufficiency for individuals with disabilities. It is this fundamental principle—that individuals with disabilities who want to work and are qualified to work must have an equal opportunity to work—that guides the Title I employment provisions of the ADA.[14]

The definition of the term "qualified individual with a disability" reflects this principle and the broad remedial purposes of the ADA. It focuses on what an individual with a disability can do, rather than on what s/he cannot do.[15] In addition, reflecting the Act's focus on individual rather than group characteristics,[16] the definition requires an individualized assessment of a person's abilities. Moreover, the definition looks at whether an individual with a disability is qualified for the specific position at issue, not at whether s/he is qualified for work in general.

2. Standards

Under the ADA, a "qualified individual with a disability," is

> an individual with a disability[17] who satisfies the requisite skill, experience, education and other job-related requirements of the employment position such individual holds or desires, and, who, with or without reasonable accommodation, can perform the essential functions of such position.[18]

The determination of whether an individual with a disability is "qualified" should be made in two steps.[19] The first step is to determine if the individual has the

---

[8] 42 U.S.C. § 12101(b)(1).

[9] *Id.* § 12101(b)(2).

[10] *Id.* § 12101(a)(8).

[11] *Id.* § 12101(a)(5),(3).

[12] *Id.* § 12101(a)(4).

[13] *Id.* § 12101(a)(9).

[14] *See id.* § 12101(a)(9) (noting that discrimination "denies people with disabilities the opportunity to compete on an equal basis and to pursue those opportunities for which our free society is justifiably famous").

[15] *See* 135 Cong. Rec. S10,711 (daily ed. Sept. 7, 1989) (statement of Sen. Harkin).

[16] *See* 42 U.S.C. § 12101(a)(7) (denouncing "stereotypic assumptions not truly indicative of the *individual ability* of [people with disabilities] to participate in, and contribute to, society") (emphasis added).

[17] The ADA defines "disability" as:

> (1) a physical or mental impairment that substantially limits one or more of the major life activities of [an] individual; (2) a record of such an impairment; or (3) being regarded as having such an impairment.

Id. § 12102(2); 29 C.F.R. § 1630.2(g).

[18] 29 C.F.R. § 1630.3(m); *see also* 42 U.S.C. § 12111(8).

[19] 29 C.F.R. pt. 1630 app. § 1630.2(m) (Interpretive Guidance on Title I of the Americans with Disabilities Act).

education, training, skills, experience, and other job-related credentials for the position. The second step is to determine whether the individual can perform the essential functions of the position held or desired, with or without accommodation.[20] The purpose of this second step is to ensure that individuals with disabilities who can perform a position's essential or fundamental functions are not denied employment opportunities simply because they are not able to perform the position's marginal or peripheral functions.[21]

The determination of whether a person is a "qualified individual with a disability" requires an individualized, case-by- case assessment of the specific abilities of the person, the specific requirements of the position that the person holds or desires, and the manner in which the person may be able or enabled to meet those requirements.[22] The issue is whether a particular individual with a disability is qualified for a particular position, not whether the individual or a group of individuals with a disability is qualified for a class of positions.[23]

Further, the definition of the term "qualified individual with a disability" expressly requires consideration of whether the individual can perform essential functions with reasonable accommodation. The ADA requires employers to provide reasonable accommodation to the known physical or mental limitations of otherwise qualified individuals with disabilities unless doing so would result in undue hardship.[24] This reasonable accommodation requirement is critical to achieving the goals of the ADA.[25]

In general, a reasonable accommodation is any change in the work environment or in the way things are customarily done that enables an individual with a disability to enjoy equal employment opportunities.[26] Some of the most common accommodations an employer may be required to provide are job restructuring, part-time or modified work schedules, modifications of equipment or devices, and other similar accommodations.[27]

The assessment of whether an individual with a disability is qualified should be based on the capabilities of the individual with a disability at the time of the employment decision. It should not be based on speculation that the individual may become incapacitated in the future.[28]

B. Other Statutory Schemes and Contractual Rights

1. Social Security Act

The Social Security Act establishes a social insurance program designed to provide guaranteed income to individuals with disabilities when they are found to be generally incapable of gainful employment. Its purpose is to provide a basic level of financial support for people who, because of disability, cannot support themselves. In adding disability as a basis for benefits administered by the Social Security Administration (SSA) in 1956, Congress recognized society's obligation to provide assistance to people whose disabilities prevent them from achieving economic self-sufficiency.[29]

The SSA definition of the term "disability," therefore, reflects the obligation to provide benefits to peo-

---

[20] *Id.*

[21] *See generally id.* app. § 1630.2(n); Senate Report at 26; House Education and Labor Report at 55; H.R. Rep. No. 101-485, pt. 3, at 33 (1990) [hereinafter House Judiciary Report].

[22] *See School Bd. of Nassau County v. Arline*, 480 U.S. 273, 287 (1987) (noting that an individualized inquiry into whether a person is "otherwise qualified" for purposes of section 504 of the Rehabilitation Act is essential to the goal of protecting individuals with disabilities "from deprivations based on prejudice, stereotypes, or unfounded fear").

[23] *See* 29 C.F.R. pt. 1630 app. (noting in "Background" section that "the determination of whether an individual is qualified for a particular position must necessarily be made on a case-by-case basis" and that a "case-by-case approach is essential if qualified individuals of varying disabilities are to receive equal opportunities to compete for an infinitely diverse range of jobs").

[24] 42 U.S.C. § 12112(b)(5)(A); 29 C.F.R. § 1630.9.

[25] *See* Senate Report at 10 ("the provision of all types of reasonable accommodations is essential to accomplishing the critical goal of this legislation—to allow individuals with disabilities to be part of the economic mainstream of our society"); House Education and Labor Report at 34 (same); House Judiciary Report at 39 (the "reasonable accommodation requirement is central to the non-discrimination mandate of the ADA").

[26] 29 C.F.R. pt. 1630 app. § 1630.2(o).

[27] 29 C.F.R. § 1630.2(o).

[28] 29 C.F.R. pt. 1630 app. § 1630.2(m); *see also* Senate Report at 26; House Education and Labor Report at 55.

[29] *See generally* 42 U.S.C. §§ 1381, 1382c(a)(3)(B).

ple who generally are unable to work. As a result, the definition focuses on what a person cannot do and on whether s/he cannot find work in the national economy in general.

To receive SSA disability benefits, an individual must prove that s/he is disabled under the Social Security Disability Insurance (SSDI) or the Supplemental Security Income (SSI) program.[30] The essential requirement for both programs is that the claimant be unable to engage in "any substantial gainful activity by reason of any medically determinable physical or mental impairment which can be expected to result in death or which has lasted or can be expected to last for a continuous period of not less than 12 months."[31] Under the statute, a person is entitled to disability benefits if his/her impairment is "of such severity that [s/he] is not only unable to do [his/her] previous work but cannot, considering [his/her] age, education, and work experience, engage in any other kind of substantial gainful work which exists in the national economy."[32]

The SSA itself, however, recognizes that an individual may be found to be unable to engage in substantial gainful activity and yet still may be able to work in a particular position. Although the SSA program is designed to provide a guaranteed income to individuals who are found to meet SSA disability eligibility criteria, Congress has recognized the importance of encouraging individuals with disabilities to work whenever possible.[33] Accordingly, the Social Security Act contains numerous work incentive provisions. For example, the SSA has a trial work period that allows beneficiaries to work for nine months while their benefit entitlement and payment levels remain unchanged.[34] Similarly, the SSA has an extended period of eligibility that provides individuals who return to work with benefits in any month in which earnings fall below a statutory level.[35] Thus, even the SSA does not view a person who meets its definition of "disability" as someone who is totally unable to work.

To determine if an individual meets the SSA definition of "disability," the SSA uses a sequential evaluation process.[36] This five-step process requires the SSA to ask the following questions:

(1) Is the claimant currently engaging in "substantial gainful activity"?[37] (If the answer is yes, the claim is denied; if the answer is no, the claim continues to the next step.)

(2) Does the claimant have a "severe" impairment? (If the answer is no, the claim is denied; if the claimant has an impairment that significantly limits his/her ability to work—that is, it is "severe"—the claim continues to step 3.)

---

30 The Social Security Act provides for several disability benefit programs administered by the SSA, including the SSDI and SSI programs. The SSDI program provides benefits to disabled workers, dependents, and widows/widowers if the worker is insured under the provisions of the program. The SSI program provides benefits to disabled individuals whose incomes and assets fall below a specified level. See 42 U.S.C. §§ 413-15, 1381-83. Although the eligibility criteria under the two programs are different (i.e., SSDI is insurance based and SSI is based on need), the determinations of disability are virtually identical. For purposes of this guidance, the phrase "social security disability benefits" or "SSA benefits" refers to both the SSDI and SSI programs.

31 42 U.S.C. § 423(d)(1)(A); 20 C.F.R. § 404.1505 (1996).

32 *Id.* § 423(d)(1)(A), (d)(2)(A); 20 C.F.R. § 404.1505. "Work which exists in the national economy" means work which exists in significant numbers, either in the region where such individual lives or in several regions of the country. *Id.* § 423(d)(2)(A). Isolated jobs which exist only in limited numbers in relatively few locations outside the region where the claimant lives are not considered "work which exists in the national economy." *Id.*

33 *Id.* § 422(c); *see also Mohamed v. Marriott*, 1996 WL 631687, at *7 (S.D.N.Y. Oct. 30, 1996) (noting that "the Social Security Act shares the goal of encouraging individuals to engage in remunerative employment, because it permits an individual to receive benefits while working").

34 Under SSA regulations, a beneficiary may evaluate whether his/her condition has improved by doing some work without fear of losing disability benefits. 20 C.F.R. § 404.1592(a).

35 *Id.*

36 *Id.* §§ 404.1520, 404.920.

37 Substantial gainful activity refers to work activity that is both substantial and gainful. *Id.* §§ 404.1572, 416.972. Work activity is substantial if it requires the performance of significant physical and mental activities. *Id.* §§ 404.1572(a), 416.972(a). Work activity is gainful if it is engaged in for profit. *Id.* §§ 404.1572(b), 416.972(b). In determining whether work actually performed is substantial gainful activity, the SSA considers factors such as the nature of the work performed, how well the claimant performs that work, whether the work is performed under special conditions, and the amount of time spent working. *Id.* §§ 404.1573, 416.973.

(3) Does the claimant have an impairment that is equivalent to any impairment the SSA has listed as so severe that it automatically precludes substantial gainful activity? (If the claimant has an impairment that is medically the equivalent of a listed impairment, the claimant is presumed disabled by the SSA and benefits are granted; if the claimant does not have a listed impairment, the claim proceeds to step 4.)

(4) Does the impairment prevent the claimant from performing his/her "past relevant work"?[38] (If the claimant can perform his/her past relevant work, the claim is denied; if the claimant cannot perform such work, the claim continues to step 5.)

(5) Does the impairment prevent the claimant from performing any other type of work? (If the SSA determines that the claimant is able to perform other work which exists in the national economy,[39] the claim is denied; if the SSA determines that the claimant is unable to perform any work, considering his/her age, education, and past work experience, benefits are granted.)

The SSA acknowledges the differences between its standards and those of other statutory schemes. In that regard, SSA regulations note that a decision by any other entity about whether an individual is disabled is based on the other entity's rules and may not be the same as the SSA's determination, which is based on social security law.[40]

The SSA definition of "disability" is inherently different from the ADA definition of "qualified individual with a disability." First, whereas the ADA always requires an individualized inquiry into the ability of a particular person to meet the requirements of a particular position, the SSA permits general presumptions about an individual's ability to work. In that regard, the SSA considers some conditions to be presumptively disabling. If a claimant has an impairment that is medically the equivalent of a listed impairment, then the SSA presumes that the disorder is so severe as to prevent the claimant from doing any substantial gainful activity, without considering his/her age, education, and past work experience.[41] Thus, an individual can have a "disability" under the SSA definition and yet in fact still be able to work.

Second, in determining whether a person meets the SSA definition of disability, the SSA looks at the customary requirements of jobs as usually performed in the national economy without focusing on the essential functions of a particular position.[42] All tasks required

---

38 "Past relevant work" is substantial gainful activity which was performed within the 15 years prior to the claim for benefits. *See generally id.* §§ 404.1560-61.

39 To determine whether a claimant can perform any work which exists in the national economy, the SSA considers what the individual still can do, given his/her functional limitations and vocational capabilities (age, education, and past work experience). *Id.* § 404.1520(f)(1). Individuals who have marginal education, long work experience (*i.e.*, 35 years or more) in only arduous unskilled physical labor, and can no longer do this kind of work may have adisability for SSA purposes and be eligible for benefits even though they are capable of performing sedentary work. *Id.* §§ 404.1520(f)(2), .1562.

40 *Id.* § 404.1504.

41 *See id.* § 404.1520(d); 20 C.F.R. pt. 404, subpt. p, app. 1 (listings of impairments). The listings consist of medical criteria for specified disorders for each of the major body systems (*e.g.*, musculoskeletal system, respiratory system, immune system). 20 C.F.R. § 404.1525(d). Most of the listed impairments are permanent or expected to result in death. For all others, the evidence must show that the impairment has lasted or is expected to last for a continuous period of at least 12 months. *Id.* The listings contain more than 150 categories of medical conditions that, according to the SSA, are severe enough ordinarily to prevent an individual from engaging in substantial gainful activity. For example, listed impairments under the musculoskeletal system include the loss of both hands or feet. 20 C.F.R. pt. 404, subpt. p, app. 1 § 1.09(A), (B). Under the ADA, however, a person with no hands or feet may well be a "qualified individual with a disability" who is able to work with or without reasonable accommodation.

In addition, the Social Security Act provides a special disability eligibility for individuals who are blind. Any claimant age 55 or older who has a visual impairment that meets the statutory definition of blindness (*i.e.*, central visual acuity of 20/200 or less in the better eye with use of correcting lens) is presumed to be incapable of engaging in substantial gainful activity and is deemed eligible for disability benefits. *See* 20 C.F.R. §§ 404.1581, .1583. Again, under the ADA, many persons who are blind are qualified to perform the essential functions of numerous positions with or without reasonable accommodation.

42 *See Eback v. Chater,* 94 F.3d 410, 412 (8th Cir. 1996) (the inquiry into whether an individual with a disability can engage in substantial gainful activity "is based on the functional demands and duties of jobs as ordinarily required by employers throughout the national economy" and not on the requirements of a particular position); *Overton v. Reilly,* 977 F.2d 1190, 1196 (7th Cir. 1992) (a determination of disability for SSA purposes cannot be construed as a judgment that an individual cannot do a particular job).

to perform the job are considered with no distinction made between fundamental and peripheral functions.[43] Thus, a person who is able to perform the essential functions of a particular position, but not the marginal functions, may be found to be unable to work and eligible for disability benefits. Accordingly, the SSA's determination that a person is unable to engage in any substantial gainful activity in the national economy does not mean that there is no job the person can perform. The person still may be able to perform the essential functions of a particular position.

Third, unlike the ADA definition, the SSA definition does not consider whether the individual can work with reasonable accommodation. An SSA interpretative guidance addressing the effect of the ADA on SSA's disability determination process states,

> The fact that an individual may be able to return to a past relevant job, provided that the employer makes accommodations, is not relevant to the issue(s) to be resolved. . . . [H]ypothetical inquiries about whether an employer would or could make accommodations that would allow return to a prior job would not be appropriate.[44]

Thus, the SSA may find that a person is unable to do any work which exists in the national economy even though s/he can work with a reasonable accommodation.[45] In those instances, the person is both a person with a "disability" under SSA and a "qualified individual with a disability" under the ADA. Accordingly, a person claiming to be disabled or found to be disabled under SSA programs still may be entitled to protection under the ADA.

2. Workers' Compensation

The workers' compensation definitions of "disability" reflect the purposes of workers' compensation laws. Those laws provide a system for securing prompt and fair settlement of employees' claims against employers for occupational injury and illness.[46] In that regard, the laws generally require employers to compensate employees who are injured in the course of employment for the resulting loss of earning capacity and for medical care.[47] Thus, workers' compensation provides benefits to individuals whose earning capacity has been reduced because of a work-related injury. Because of the emphasis on lost earning capacity, the workers' compensation definitions of disability generally focus on what a person can no longer do rather than on what s/he still is capable of doing with or without reasonable accommodation.

To receive workers' compensation benefits, an employee generally must prove that s/he has a compensable "disability" as defined by the applicable workers' compensation statute.[48] The term "disability" in this context most commonly means loss or reduction of earning power that results from a work-related injury.[49]

Some statutes, however, do not define "disability" in terms of lost earning capacity. Instead, under these statutes, an injured worker has a "disability" if his/her physical efficiency has been substantially reduced, or if s/he is unable to perform the same work with the same ease as before the injury or is unable to do heavy work that s/he could do before the injury.[50] Under these statutes, the worker has a "disability" even if s/he is employed at the same work and at the same wages as before the injury.

Although workers' compensation laws vary from state to state, the typical statute ordinarily provides the following four classifications of disability, determined by duration (i.e., permanent or temporary) and severi-

---

43 *See generally* 70A Am. Jur. 2d Social Security § 984 (all tasks required in the job must be considered).

44 *See* "Americans with Disabilities Act of 1990—INFORMATION," Memorandum from the Associate Commissioner, Social Security Administration 1 (June 2, 1993).

45 *See Eback v. Chater*, 94 F.3d at 412 (since the ADA and Social Security Act have different purposes, the SSA's determination whether there are available jobs that the claimant can do is based on broad vocational patterns and not on an assumption that an employer would be willing to make accommodations under the ADA); *Mohamed v. Marriott*, 1996 WL 631687 at *6 (S.D.N.Y. Oct. 30, 1996)(an individual may be "disabled" for purposes of receiving SSA benefits because few jobs which s/he might be able to perform are currently structured to accommodate his/her disability, but still be within the ADA's protected class because a particular position in which s/he has an interest could be modified to accommodate his/her disability).

46 *See generally* 1 Arthur Larson, The Law of Workmen's Compensation, § 1-1.10 (1994).

47 *Id.*

48 *See id*

49 82 Am. Jur. 2d *Workers' Compensation* § 380.

50 *Id.; see, e.g.,* W. Va. Code § 23-4-6(n).

ty or extent (i.e., partial or total): temporary partial, temporary total, permanent partial, and permanent total.[51] Generally, a disability is partial rather than total where the claimant is still capable of gainful employment, even though the disability is found to prevent the claimant from returning to his/her former employment. Conversely, a worker generally is considered "totally disabled" when the injury is found to render the worker temporarily or permanently unable to do any kind of work for which there is a reasonably stable employment market.[52]

Unlike the ADA, which always requires an individualized inquiry into the ability of a particular person to meet the requirements of a particular position, some workers' compensation statutes presume that some conditions are so severe as to prevent the claimant from doing any kind of work. In such instances, a claimant does not have to make any representations about ability to work and need not show a loss of earning capacity to prove permanent total disability. For example, under some workers' compensation statutes, a person who has lost vision in both eyes or has lost both arms or legs may have a "permanent total disability" and be deemed to be unable to work.[53] Such a person, however, clearly can perform the essential functions of many positions with or without reasonable accommodation.

Moreover, unlike the ADA definition of "qualified individual with a disability," the workers' compensation definitions of "disability" do not distinguish between marginal and essential functions and do not consider whether an individual can work with reasonable accommodation. In many workers' compensation cases, a person has a "total disability" when s/he is unable to do certain tasks, even if those tasks are marginal functions or if s/he could perform them with reasonable accommodation. Thus, a person may be "totally disabled" for workers' compensation purposes and yet still be able to perform a position's essential functions with or without reasonable accommodation.

Similarly, a person can receive workers' compensation benefits for a temporary total disability from which she is expected to recover if, during the time of incapacitation, s/he is unable to perform his/her duties in the occupation in which s/he was employed at the time of injury.[54] The person is found to have a "temporary total disability" even if the duties s/he cannot perform are marginal functions or s/he could perform duties with reasonable accommodation.

Further, some statutes permit a finding of "total disability" where a person can work but the work that s/he can do is of such limited availability that a reasonably stable and continuous market for such labor does not exist.[55] Thus, a determination under a workers' compensation statute that a person cannot do any kind of work for which a reasonably stable employment market exists, and therefore is totally disabled, does not necessarily mean that there is no job that the person can perform. Accordingly, an individual receiving workers' compensation benefits still may be entitled to protection under the ADA.

3. Disability Insurance Plans

Many employers offer disability insurance plans to their employees as benefits of employment.[56] Receipt of benefits pursuant to such plans is a contractual, rather than a statutory, right. The purpose of disability insurance plans is to provide partial wage replacement when an employee becomes unable to work as a result of illness, injury, or disease.[57] As a result, the plans' definitions of "disability" focus on individuals' inabilities rather than abilities.

To receive disability benefits, an individual must meet the eligibility requirements outlined by the terms of the contract (i.e., insurance policy). Disability insurance plans usually require that an individual have been

---

51 For the purposes of workers' compensation statutes, a disability is permanent if it appears to be of lasting or indefinite duration, as distinguished from a temporary condition from which a person usually recovers after normal healing. 82 Am. Jur. 2d Workers' Compensation § 381.

52 *Id.*

53 *See generally* 82 Am. Jur. 2d *Workers' Compensation* §§ 379-80.

54 Temporary total disability benefits are designed to provide compensation to an injured or ill employee for the economic losses incurred during recuperation. 99 C.J.S. *Workers' Compensation* § 304.

55 *Id.*

56 Short-term disability (STD) plans pay benefits for disability up to a specified period, generally not exceeding two years; long-term disability (LTD) plans pay extended benefits, generally until retirement age, but may require a higher showing of disability. *Employment Benefits Law* 947 (ABA Section of Labor & Employment Law) (Steven J. Sacher *et al.* eds. 1991).

57 *See id.*

employed for a set period and that s/he be "disabled." Disability benefits often are paid on a "residual" basis, meaning that they are payable in proportion to the earnings lost as a result of the disability. Benefits may be limited to "total disability," meaning generally that the insured is unable to perform any of the duties of his/her own occupation or any other type of remunerative work, or may be payable for "partial disability," where the insured is unable to perform one or more functions of his/her regular job.

The definition of "disability" depends on what the contract states and varies from contract to contract. Generally, "disability" is defined as the incapacity to perform one or more duties of the insured's regular occupation.

When assessing an individual's ability to perform job duties, disability insurance plans frequently do not distinguish between essential and marginal functions. For example, under one typical contract, an employee may be considered "totally disabled" if s/he is "unable to perform the duties of the job [s/he] held when [s/he] became disabled or any comparable job within [the company]."[58] Under this definition, an individual who could perform the essential, but not all the marginal, functions of a position would be considered "totally disabled." Some plans, however, may acknowledge the relative importance of different duties. Thus, one plan defined "total disability" as the inability of an individual "to perform the material and substantial duties of his or her own job during the Benefit Waiting Period plus the next 24 months . . . due to Injury or Sickness which requires regular care of a Physician."[59] Whether a contract's definition of "disability" distinguishes between essential and marginal functions is a key consideration when comparing a plan's definition of "disability" to the ADA definition of "qualified individual with a disability."

Another important consideration is whether the contract's definition of "disability" takes into account whether an individual can work with reasonable accommodation. Frequently, the definition makes no allowance for an individual's ability to work with reasonable accommodation.[60] In some cases, the definition expressly eliminates consideration of reasonable accommodations, such as modified or part-time work schedules.[61] For example, one disability plan defined a "totally disabled" individual as an employee "who is unable to perform the material duties of his/her job for the *entire regularly scheduled work week* as the result of illness or injury and requires the ongoing care of a physician. . . ."[62] Under such a plan, an individual with a disability who is able to work only part time may be both "totally disabled" under the plan and a "qualified individual with a disability" under the ADA. Accordingly, an individual receiving disability insurance benefits still may be entitled to protection under the ADA.

C. Analysis

Several important elements distinguish the definition of the term "qualified individual with a disability" under the ADA from the definitions of "disability" under other statutory schemes and contracts. Because of these inherent differences, an individual may be able to meet the eligibility requirements for receipt of disability benefits and still be a "qualified individual with a disability" for ADA purposes. That is, an individual may be "unable to work" for the purposes of a disability benefits program and yet still be able to perform the essential functions of a particular position with or without reasonable accommodation.[63]

---

58 See Miller v. U.S. Bancorp, 926 F. Supp. 994, 998, 5 AD Cas. (BNA) 968, 971 (D. Or. 1996).

59 *See Reiff v. Interim Personnel, Inc.*, 906 F. Supp. 1280, 1289, 5 AD Cas. (BNA) 740, 745 (D. Minn. 1995).

60 *See, e.g., Miller v. U.S. Bancorp*, 926 F. Supp. at 998, 5 AD Cas. at 971.

61 A part-time or modified work schedule is a form of reasonable accommodation under the ADA. 42 U.S.C. § 12111(9)(B); 29 C.F.R. § 1630.2(o).

62 *See D'Aprile v. Fleet Services Corp.*, 92 F.3d 1, 4-5 (1st Cir. 1996) (emphasis added).

63 *See, e.g., Robinson v. Neodata Services, Inc.*, 94 F.3d 499, 502 n. 2, 5 AD Cas. (BNA) 1441, 1442 n.2 (8th Cir. 1996) (SSA determinations of disability "are not synonymous with a determination of whether a plaintiff is a 'qualified person' for purposes of the ADA"); *Overton v. Reilly*, 977 F.2d 1190, 1196, 2 AD Cas. 254, 260 (7th Cir. 1992) (SSA's finding that a person is disabled "is consistent with a claim that the disabled person is 'qualified' to do his job under the Rehabilitation Act"); *Pegues v. Emerson Electric Co.*, 913 F. Supp. 976, 980, 5 AD Cas. 376, 379 (N.D. Miss. 1996) (a finding of disability by a state workers' compensation commission or the SSA does not necessarily foreclose an ADA claim); *Palmer v. Circuit Court of Cook County, Soc. Serv. Dep't*, 905 F. Supp. 499, 508 n.10 (N.D. Ill. 1995) (citing Overton v. Reilly and Smith v. Dovenmuehle) (determinations made by the SSA concerning disability "are not dispositive findings for claims arising under the ADA"); *Smith v. Dovenmuehle Mortgage, Inc.*, 859 F. Supp. 1138, 1141-42, 4 AD Cas. 132, 135 (N.D. Ill. 1994) (citing *Overton v. Reilly*) (a finding of disability by the SSA "cannot be construed as a judgment that the plaintiff is unable to do his job").

An individual's representations in connection with an application for disability benefits, therefore, do not preclude a determination that the individual is a "qualified individual with a disability." Although the representations that an individual has made in support of his/her application for benefits may be relevant to such a determination, they are never an absolute bar to a finding that the individual is a "qualified individual with a disability."

1. The ADA Definition of "Qualified Individual with a Disability" Always Requires an Individualized Assessment of the Particular Individual and the Particular Position; Other Definitions Permit Generalized Inquiries and Presumptions.

Unlike the definitions under other statutory and contractual schemes, which permit generalized inquiries, the definition of "qualified individual with a disability" under the ADA always requires an individualized inquiry into the ability of a particular person to meet the requirements of a particular position.[64] The ADA inquiry into whether a person is a "qualified individual with a disability" looks at whether an individual can perform the essential functions of a particular position, not whether s/he is able to work in general. Further, unlike the SSA and other statutory and contractual schemes, the ADA never presumes that some impairments are so severe as to prevent an individual from working. To the contrary, the ADA presumes that individuals with disabilities can work.[65]

The Seventh Circuit recognized this obvious and significant distinction in *Overton v. Reilly*, 977 F.2d 1190, 2 AD Cas. (BNA) 254 (7th Cir. 1992), when it ruled that a person could have a disability for SSA purposes and still be a "qualified individual with a disability" for Rehabilitation Act purposes. The SSA had granted benefits to the *Overton* plaintiff, who had an emotional disability, on a trial basis shortly after he began working for the defendant. The court made clear that the plaintiff's Rehabilitation Act claim of discriminatory discharge was not precluded by the SSA's decision to award him disability benefits.

In refusing to find that the plaintiff's receipt of benefits precluded his claim, the Seventh Circuit relied heavily on the fact that the SSA definition of disability permits generalized presumptions. First, the court noted that "the SSA may award disability benefits on a finding that the claimant meets the criteria for a listed disability, without inquiring into his ability to find work within the economy." 977 F.2d at 1196, 2 AD Cas. at 260. This, the court found, was the basis for the plaintiff's receipt of benefits. In addition, the Seventh Circuit emphasized that, "even if the SSA had looked into [the plaintiff's] ability to find work in the national economy, its inquiry would necessarily have been generalized." *Id.* Such a general inquiry, the court noted, may determine that a claimant is unlikely to find a job, but that does not mean that there is no work the claimant can do. Thus, a determination of disability for SSA purposes "can hardly be construed as a judgment that [the plaintiff] could not do [the particular job at issue]." *Id.*

Rather than be swayed by generalized presumptions, the Seventh Circuit looked specifically at the plaintiff's particular situation. In so doing, the circuit court found that the plaintiff's actual, adequate performance of work for the defendant refuted the district court's assertion that the plaintiff had not offered evidence that he could perform substantial gainful activity. The Seventh Circuit therefore concluded that the plaintiff had presented a genuine issue of material fact whether he was a "qualified individual with a disability." Id. By refusing to bar the plaintiff's claim of disability discrimination, the Seventh Circuit recognized that the individualized inquiry mandated by the definition of "qualified individual with a disability" differs significantly from the generalized inquiry permitted under the SSA definition of "disability." *Id.*; *see also Smith v. Dovenmuehle Mortgage, Inc.*, 859 F. Supp. 1138, 1141, 4 AD Cas. (BNA) 132, 135 (N.D. Ill. 1994) (holding that the SSA's decision to award disability benefits, based on its determination that the plaintiff could not find work in the economy, did not mean that he was not a "qualified individual with a disability" under the ADA, particularly since he found another position after being terminated by the defendant).

Similarly, a district court in the Second Circuit recognized the fundamental differences between the ADA's individualized approach and the SSA assessment. In refusing to grant the defendant's motion for summary judgment, the court in *Mohamed v. Marriott*, 1996 WL 631687 (S.D.N.Y. Oct. 30, 1996), emphasized that the SSA awarded the plaintiff benefits based on a "listed disability" (profound deafness) and did not

---

64 *See School Bd. of Nassau County v. Arline*, 480 U.S. 273, 287 n.17 (1987).

65 *See* 42 U.S.C. § 12101(a)(9) (noting that discrimination "denies people with disabilities the opportunity to compete on an equal basis and to pursue those opportunities for which our free society is justifiably famous").

inquire into his capability to work. *Id.* at *6. In that regard, the court noted that the plaintiff did not make any specific representations about his ability to perform the essential functions of the job from which he was terminated and, in fact, represented to the SSA that he continued to seek work. *Id.* Like the Seventh Circuit, the *Mohamed* court refused to be swayed by generalized presumptions and looked at the plaintiff's particular situation. Noting that the plaintiff consistently had received positive evaluations and had no record of disciplinary actions prior to his termination, the court found that there was "ample evidence" that the plaintiff was capable of performing the essential functions of the job from which he was discharged. *Id.* at *5. The court further concluded that barring the plaintiff's ADA claim based on the SSA's determination that he was eligible for benefits "would undermine the legislative policy of providing [persons with disabilities] with both protection against destitution and a genuine opportunity to participate fully in the job market." *Id.* at *7.

The Third Circuit, in *McNemar v. The Disney Store, Inc.*, 91 F.3d 610, 5 AD Cas.(BNA) 1227 (3d Cir. 1996), however, ignored this fundamental difference between the ADA and SSA and failed to conduct the individualized inquiry mandated by the ADA definition of "qualified individual with a disability." The *McNemar* plaintiff, who had AIDS, applied for and received SSA and state disability benefits after he was fired from his position of assistant manager. He certified on his benefits application that he had become unable to work approximately five weeks before his discharge. In affirming the district court's grant of summary judgment for the defendant, the Third Circuit found that it was irrelevant that AIDS is a presumptive disability that automatically renders a person "unable to work" for purposes of SSA benefits, since the plaintiff claimed that he was physically unable to work. The court also rejected the argument that the ADA's standards and purposes are fundamentally different from the SSA's. In reaching these conclusions, the court overlooked the fact that "unable to work" for SSA purposes does not mean unable to perform the essential functions of a particular position with or without reasonable accommodation.

The court's failure to acknowledge these inherent differences between the ADA definition of "qualified individual with a disability" and the SSA definition of "disability" is especially troubling here, where it is undisputed that the plaintiff was performing the essential functions of his assistant manager's position at the time of his discharge. It therefore also should have been undisputed that the plaintiff met the ADA definition of "qualified individual with a disability" at the time of the alleged discrimination. *See Daffron v. McDonnell Douglas Corp.*, 874 S.W.2d 482, 486, 3 AD Cas. (BNA) 183, 187 (Mo. Ct. App. 1994)(based on the plaintiff's assertions that he was capable of performing his job duties and was, in fact, performing those duties until the day he was laid off, the court found that there was evidence that could establish that the plaintiff was capable of performing his duties, even though he filed an application for disability benefits).

Moreover, the *McNemar* defendant's asserted reason for the discharge was unrelated to the issues raised by the benefits application. At the time of the discharge, the defendant maintained that the plaintiff was fired for theft; the defendant did not claim that the plaintiff's disability prevented the plaintiff from performing the essential functions of his position with or without reasonable accommodation. *McNemar*, 91 F.3d at 614, 5 AD Cas. at 1229. In fact, the defendant consistently disavowed any reliance on the plaintiff's disability. Since the plaintiff applied for disability benefits after his termination, the defendant obviously was unaware of the application when it decided to terminate him. Accordingly, under these circumstances, the defendant should not have been permitted to use benefits information acquired after the adverse action to challenge whether the plaintiff was a "qualified individual with a disability." *Cf. McKennon v. Nashville Banner Pub. Co.*, 115 S. Ct. 879, 885 (1995)(employer liability is determined solely by information available to employer "'at the time of the decision'"). For all these reasons, the Commission believes that *McNemar* was wrongly decided.[66]

Other courts have recognized that the ADA's focus on a particular individual's ability to perform the essential functions of a particular position is different from disability benefits programs' definitions of "disability." For example, in *Pressman v. Brigham Medical Group Foundation, Inc.*, 919 F. Supp. 516, 5 AD Cas. (BNA) 609 (D. Mass. 1996), the court concluded that a physician who consistently claimed that he was "totally disabled" under his private disability insurance plan still could be a "qualified individual

[66] Further, although the Third Circuit used the doctrine of judicial estoppel to reject the plaintiff's claim, it stressed that judicial estoppel is a discretionary doctrine. The court also emphasized that "each case must be decided upon its own particular facts and circumstances." *McNemar,* 91 F.3d at 617, 5 AD Cas. at 1232.

with a disability" with respect to the particular internist position for which he had applied. In that case, the plaintiff, who had a heart disability, maintained that he was capable of performing the essential functions of the internist position even though he had a "total disability" for purposes of the insurance plan. 919 F. Supp. at 523, 5 AD Cas. at 613. According to the plaintiff, the plan permitted him to receive total disability benefits as long as there were restrictions on his ability to practice his sub-specialty of cardiology. 919 F. Supp. at 522, 5 AD Cas. at 613. Since there were genuine issues of material fact whether the definition of "total disability" under the plaintiff's disability plan meant that he generally was unable to practice medicine, or whether it meant that he specifically was unable "to conduct a solo practice with emergency room duties," the court denied the defendant's motion for summary judgment. *Id.*

As *Pressman, Mohamed, Smith,* and *Overton* illustrate, the definitions under the SSA and other statutory and contractual schemes do not focus on whether a particular person can meet the requirements of a particular position. As a result, an individual can both meet the requirements for disability benefits and be a "qualified individual with a disability" for purposes of the ADA.

2. The ADA Definition of "Qualified Individual with a Disability" Requires Consideration of Reasonable Accommodation; Other Definitions Do Not Consider Whether an Individual Can Work with Reasonable Accommodation.

Assessing whether a person can work with reasonable accommodation is a key part of determining if the person meets the ADA definition of the term "qualified individual with a disability." Unlike the ADA definition, however, the definitions of disability under the SSA, workers' compensation laws, and disability insurance plans do not consider whether a person can work with reasonable accommodation.[67] Thus, a person may be deemed unable to work and be awarded disability benefits even though s/he can perform the essential functions of a particular position with reasonable accommodation.

Courts have recognized this important difference between the ADA definition of "qualified individual with a disability" and other definitions of "disability" or "totally disabled." For example, in *D'Aprile v. Fleet Services Corp.*, 92 F.3d 1 (1st Cir. 1996), the First Circuit reversed a district court's grant of summary judgment where the plaintiff had sought disability benefits after the defendant refused her request to work on a part-time basis.[68] In *D'Aprile*, the plaintiff had unofficially worked part time (through the use of accrued vacation leave) for two months after the defendant denied her request to be converted to a part-time status. After the plaintiff exhausted her vacation time, she submitted a doctor's note "stating that she was 'unable to work at this time and should be placed on disability.'" *Id.* at 3. The plaintiff then received disability benefits under an insurance plan that defined a "totally disabled" individual as an employee "who is unable to perform the material duties of his/her job for the entire regularly scheduled work week as the result of injury or illness . . . ." *Id.* at 4-5.

The First Circuit found that the plaintiff's contention that she was unable to work because her employer had refused her request for a modified schedule was "entirely consistent with her claim to have been 'totally disabled' within the meaning of the policy." *Id.* at 5. Noting that the plaintiff asserted that she could work on a part-time basis and that she in fact had worked part time, the court found that there existed a genuine issue of material fact whether the plaintiff could have worked with reasonable accommodation. In so doing, the court expressly ruled that the plaintiff's application for benefits "sheds no light on how [the plaintiff] would have fared had the accommodation been made." *Id.* In addition, the *D'Aprile* court explicitly stated that *August v. Offices Unlimited, Inc.*, 981 F.2d 576, 2 AD Cas. (BNA) 401 (1st Cir. 1992), does not stand for the broad proposition that a plaintiff who claims that s/he is "totally disabled" within the context of applying for disability benefits is barred from bringing an ADA claim but, rather, "stands for the narrow proposition that the plaintiff's ability to work with reasonable accommodation" is key in determining whether a person meets the ADA definition of "qualified individual with a disability."

---

67 See, e.g., Eback v. Chater, 94 F.3d 410, 412 (8th Cir. 1996) (since the ADA and Social Security Act have different purposes, the SSA's determination whether there are available jobs that the claimant can do is based on broad vocational patterns and not on an assumption that an employer would be willing to make accommodations under the ADA).

68 The *D'Aprile* decision interpreted the Rhode Island Fair Employment Practices Act, R.I. Gen. Laws § 28-5-1, et seq., which includes a reasonable accommodation requirement. *D'Aprile*, 92 F.3d at 2. (The defendant removed the case to federal district court based on diversity of jurisdiction.)

Id. at 3.[69] The Commission believes that *D'Aprile* is correct in recognizing that an individual can meet a disability benefits program definition of "totally disabled" and still be able to perform the essential functions of a particular position with reasonable accommodation.

Similarly, in *Anzalone v. Allstate Ins. Co.*, 5 AD Cas. (BNA) 223 (E.D. La. 1995), the court correctly recognized the differences between the ADA definition of "qualified individual with a disability" and a disability insurance plan's definition of "total disability" in refusing to grant defendant's motion for summary judgment. The plaintiff in *Anzalone* applied for and received LTD benefits after the defendant had refused his request to work at home. Noting that the plaintiff had consistently stated that he could perform the essential functions of his claims adjuster position with certain modifications, the court found that his receipt of disability benefits did not bar his ADA claim. According to the court, the plaintiff's receipt of benefits was relevant—but not dispositive—evidence of whether the plaintiff could perform essential functions with or without reasonable accommodation. *Anzalone*, 5 AD Cas. at 225.[70] *See also Ward v. Westvaco Corp.*, 859 F. Supp. 608, 615, 3 AD Cas. (BNA) 739, 745 (D. Mass. 1994) (in denying the employer's motion for summary judgment, the court found that there was a genuine issue of material fact whether the plaintiff would have been able to perform his job duties with reasonable accommodation); *Patel v. Everett Industries*, No. 88-BEM-0451 (Mass. Comm'n Against Discrimination Sept. 18, 1996)(injured employee who received workers' compensation benefits was not precluded from proving that she was a "qualified individual with a disability" under state law where she did not claim that she was disabled from all work but only that she could not perform the heavy tasks to which she was assigned).[71]

As *Patel, Ward, Anzalone*, and *D'Aprile* demonstrate, an individual can meet the eligibility requirements for disability benefits and still be able to perform the essential functions of particular positions with reasonable accommodation.

---

69 In *August,* a furniture salesperson applied for disability insurance benefits after his employer refused his request to return to work on a part-time basis following an extended leave of absence for severe depression. The First Circuit affirmed the district court's grant of summary judgment on the grounds that the plaintiff could not show that he was a "qualified individual with a disability" because he had conceded that he was totally disabled. 981 F.2d at 581, 2 AD Cas. at 406. The dissent, however, pointed out the weakness in the majority's reasoning, noting that it was not clear how "total disability" was defined in the plaintiff's insurance policy. Thus, the dissent correctly concluded that the plaintiff's inability to return to work after the employer denied his request for a part-time schedule "only demonstrates that, absent accommodations by [the employer, the plaintiff] could not work. It does not prove that he would have been incapable of working had his request[] been granted." *August,* 981 F.2d at 586, 2 AD Cas. at 408.

70 Compare *Anzalone* with *Kennedy v. Applause Inc.*, 90 F.3d 1477, 5 AD Cas. (BNA) 1249 (9th Cir. 1996), where the court looked not only at the plaintiff's statements in support of her application for disability benefits but at all of the relevant evidence in assessing whether the plaintiff was a "qualified individual with a disability." In *Kennedy*, a sales representative who had returned to work after a three-month leave of absence was discharged after she submitted a doctor's note stating that she could not work and needed another leave of absence. She then applied for state disability benefits, stating that her symptoms forced her to stop working. She also stated in a subsequent SSA "Daily Activities Questionnaire" that she barely could get out of bed. In her deposition on her ADA claim, however, the plaintiff testified that she could have continued to perform her job duties on a part-time or adjusted work schedule.

In affirming the district court's grant of summary judgment, the Ninth Circuit based its holding on the fact that there was no evidence, other than the plaintiff's "self-serving" deposition testimony that she was capable of continuing to work, to show that she could have performed the essential functions of her job. 90 F.3d at 1481, 5 AD Cas. at 1251. Although the court cited to the plaintiff's application for disability benefits, it did so only to point out that the plaintiff's statements "corroborate[d]" her treating physician's assessment that she was totally unable to perform her job. *Id. But see Garcia-Paz v. Swift Textiles*, 873 F. Supp. 547, 3 AD Cas. (BNA) 1844 (D. Kan. 1995)(in granting the defendant's motion for summary judgment, the court failed to consider whether the plaintiff could have done her job with reasonable accommodation).

Thus, *Kennedy* supports the Commission's view that the plaintiff's statements might be relevant to—but not dispositive of—whether s/he was qualified for the job at issue. Such statements alone cannot defeat the plaintiff's case, especially where countervailing evidence otherwise supports a finding that the plaintiff is a "qualified individual with a disability."

71 The *Patel* decision interpreted the Massachusetts discrimination statute, Mass. Gen. Laws ch. 151B, § 1(16), which defines a "qualified individual with a disability" in language nearly identical to the ADA.

II. Because of the Fundamental Differences Between the ADA and Other Statutory and Contractual Disability Benefits Programs, Representations Made in Connection with an Application for Benefits May Be Relevant to—but Are Never Determinative of—Whether a Person Is a "Qualified Individual with a Disability."

A. Representations Made in Connection with an Application for Disability Benefits Are Not Determinative of Whether a Person Is a "Qualified Individual with a Disability."

Because of the inherent differences in the definitions of the term "qualified individual with a disability" under the ADA and the terms used in the SSA, state workers' compensation laws, disability insurance plans, and other disability benefits programs, and because the ADA considers whether a person can work with reasonable accommodation, an individual can meet both the eligibility requirements for receipt of disability benefits and the definition of a "qualified individual with a disability" for ADA purposes. Thus, a person's representations that s/he is "disabled" or "totally disabled" for purposes of disability benefits are not necessarily inconsistent with his/her representations that s/he is a "qualified individual with a disability."[72] Accordingly, they should never be an automatic bar to an ADA claim. Thus, for example, the doctrine of judicial estoppel should not be used to bar the ADA claim of an individual who has applied for disability benefits. Similarly, granting summary judgment to bar such claims also is inappropriate.[73]

1. Judicial Estoppel

The common law doctrine of judicial estoppel prevents a party who has successfully maintained a position in one judicial proceeding from asserting a contrary position in another proceeding. It is a "principle of fairness" designed to preserve the integrity of the judicial process. 18 C. WRIGHT, A. MILLER & E. COOPER, FEDERAL PRACTICE AND PROCEDURE § 4477 at, 779-88 (1981). "Judicial estoppel applies where a party tries to contradict in a second lawsuit his sworn statement in previous litigation." *Grant v. Lone Star Co.*, 21 F.3d 649, 651 n.2 (5th Cir. 1994). The doctrine protects the integrity of the judicial process by "minimiz[ing] the danger of a party contradicting a court's determination based on the party's prior position," thereby resulting in "inconsistent court determinations." *United States ex. rel. Am. Bank v. C.I.T. Constr. Inc.*, 944 F.2d 253, 258 (5th Cir. 1991).[74]

As explained above, an individual who asserts that s/he is both "totally disabled" and a "qualified individual with a disability" has not necessarily made inconsistent representations. Accordingly, the doctrine of judicial estoppel should not be used to prevent the individual from raising an ADA claim. Thus, courts that have recognized the inherent differences between the definitions of "qualified individual with a disability" and "totally disabled" or "disabled" have refused to apply this doctrine to bar claims of disability discrimination. *See, e.g., Smith v. Dovenmuehle Mortgage Co.*, 859 F. Supp. 1138, 4 AD Cas. (BNA) 132 (N.D. Ill. 1994) (judicial estoppel inappropriate where genuine issue of material fact whether position that plaintiff with AIDS took before SSA is inconsistent with assertion that plaintiff is a "qualified individual with a disability"); *Mohamed v. Marriott*, 1996 WL 631687, at *6 (S.D.N.Y. Oct. 30, 1996) ("it would be inappropriate to invoke the fact-sensitive and limited doctrine of judicial estoppel to erect a per se bar to ADA protection for individuals who have also applied for and/or received [SSA] benefits").

Generally, the doctrine of judicial estoppel applies only when an individual took his/her earlier position in a prior judicial proceeding. *See, e.g., Shell Oil Co. v. Trailer & Truck Repair Co.*, 828 F.2d 205, 209-210 (3d Cir. 1987); *Smith v. Travelers Ins. Co.*, 438 F.2d 373, 377 (6th Cir.), *cert. denied*, 404 U.S. 832 (1971).

---

72 Further, representations made in the context of applying for disability benefits should not be construed as an evidentiary admission that a person is not a "qualified individual with a disability" for purposes of coverage under the ADA (i.e., an individual who represents that s/he meets the eligibility requirements for disability benefits is not necessarily admitting that s/he cannot perform the essential functions of a particular position with or without accommodation).

73 EEOC investigators should note that, while the doctrine of judicial estoppel and summary judgment procedures are relevant to litigating civil lawsuits, they are not relevant to Commission charge processing.

74 The doctrine of judicial estoppel has not been universally embraced. At least two circuit courts have refused to recognize the doctrine. *See United Mine Workers of America 1974 Pension v. Pittston Co.*, 984 F.2d 469, 477 (D.C. Cir.), *cert. denied*, 113 S. Ct. 3039 (1993); *Chrysler Credit Corp. v. Country Chrysler, Inc.*, 928 F.2d 1509, 1520 n.10 (10th Cir. 1991). Other courts have warned that the doctrine should be "applied with caution to avoid impugning on the truth-seeking function of the court." *Teledyne Indus., Inc. v. NLRB*, 911 F.2d 1214, 1218 (6th Cir. 1990).

However, in many cases, the individual has not made his/her representations before a judicial forum. Accordingly, courts that have recognized the significant differences in judicial proceedings and administrative determinations have declined to apply judicial estoppel to bar claims of disability discrimination. *See, e.g., Mohamed v. Marriott*, 1996 WL 631687, at *7 (S.D.N.Y. Oct. 30, 1996)("[t]he streamlined procedures giving rise to the SSA's determination of disability should, at a minimum, give pause to a court considering barring the courtroom door to a plaintiff alleging employment discrimination"); *see also EEOC v. MTS Corp. d/b/a Supercuts*, No. 94-1473 LH/WWD (D.N.M. July 26, 1996) (the court noted that, even if the Tenth Circuit recognized judicial estoppel, it would not apply the doctrine to the facts of this case where the plaintiff completed his SSA application over the telephone).[75]

Public policy considerations also preclude the application of judicial estoppel in the types of cases to which this guidance applies. *See Marvello v. Chemical Bank*, 923 F. Supp. 487, 491-92, 5 AD Cas. (BNA) 1400, 1403 (S.D.N.Y. 1996) (applying judicial estoppel to bar the ADA claim of individuals who have applied for disability benefits could undermine the policy goals of the ADA without advancing the separate goals of the Social Security Act); *Mohamed v. Marriott*, 1996 WL 531687, at *7 (S.D.N.Y. Oct. 30, 1996) (the ADA's overriding purpose of encouraging individuals with disabilities to seek employment would be thwarted by the application of judicial estoppel to the facts of this case). Because "[j]udicial estoppel is a technical rule designed to meet the needs of broad public policy," *Johnson Serv. Co. v. Transamerica Ins. Co.*, 485 F.2d 164, 175 (5th Cir. 1973), courts have been reluctant to apply the doctrine where doing so would undermine the public policy goals of a federal statute. *See City of Alma v. United States*, 744 F. Supp. 1546, 1556 (S.D. Ga. 1990). In fact, some courts have declined to apply the doctrine where barring the plaintiff's suit "implicates not only the relevant interests of the litigating parties, but also the public's interest in promoting the underlying statute." *Matter of Morristown & Erie R.R. Co.*, 677 F.2d 360, 368 n.10 (3d Cir. 1982); *cf. McKennon v. Nashville Banner Co.*, 115 S. Ct. 879, 885 (1995) (the Supreme Court noted that "the broader objectives of [the anti-discrimination statutes] are furthered when even a single employee establishes that an employer has discriminated against him or her").

2. Summary Judgment

The inherent differences between the definitions of the term "qualified individual with a disability" under the ADA and the terms used in other statutory and contractual schemes also make summary judgment inappropriate. Granting summary judgment is only proper when there is no genuine issue of material fact and the moving party is entitled to judgment as a matter of law. Fed. R. Civ. P. 56(c). In deciding whether a factual dispute is "genuine," the court must determine whether the evidence is such that a reasonable jury could return a verdict for the nonmoving party." *Anderson v. Liberty Lobby, Inc.*, 477 U.S. 242, 248 (1986). A court must review the facts in the light most favorable to the nonmoving party and accord the nonmoving party the benefit of all reasonable inferences to be drawn from the evidence. *See, e.g., United States v. O'Block*, 788 F.2d 1433 (10th Cir. 1986) (stating that "[t]he court must consider factual inferences tending to show triable issues in the light most favorable to the existence of those issues"). The court's function is not to weigh the evidence but, rather, merely to determine whether there is sufficient evidence favoring the nonmoving party for a finder of fact to return a verdict in that party's favor. *Anderson*, 477 U.S. at 249. Essentially, the court performs the threshold inquiry of determining whether a trial is necessary. *Id.* at 250.

As discussed in detail in this guidance, because the ADA's purposes and standards are fundamentally different from those of disability benefits programs, an individual's representations made in connection with an application for disability benefits do not mean that the individual cannot perform the essential functions of the position held or desired with or without reasonable accommodation. Accordingly, the application for disability benefits does not mean that there does not exist a genuine issue of material fact concerning whether a person is a "qualified individual with a disability." Thus, for example, in *Overton*, the court held that summary judgment was inappropriate. Overton, 977 F.2d at 1194. *See also Smith v. Dovenmuehle Mortgage Co.*, 859 F. Supp. 1138, 4 AD Cas. (BNA) 132 (N.D. Ill. 1994) (genuine issue of material fact whether position that plaintiff with AIDS took before

---

[75] Other courts, however, have ignored this difference and have inappropriately applied the doctrine to dismiss ADA claims. See, e.g., *McNemar v. The Disney Stores*, 91 F.3d 610, 5 AD Cas. (BNA) 1227 (3d Cir. 1996) (discussed supra § I.C.1); *August v. Offices, Unlimited, Inc.*, 981 F.2d 576 (1st Cir. 1992) (discussed supra § I.C.2).

SSA is inconsistent with assertion that plaintiff is a "qualified individual with a disability"); *Oswald v. Larouche Chemicals, Inc.*, 894 F. Supp. 988 (E.D. La. 1995) (genuine issue of material fact whether the doctor, whose conclusion that the plaintiff could not perform any jobs formed the basis of the grant of disability retirement benefits to the plaintiff, properly assessed the plaintiff's ability to perform the essential functions of the modified position); *Kupperschmidt v. Runyon*, 827 F. Supp. 570, 3 AD Cas. (BNA) 52 (E.D. Wis. 1993) (genuine issue of material fact whether plaintiff, who received SSA and federal employee retirement system disability benefits, was a "qualified individual with a disability" for purposes of the Rehabilitation Act); *EEOC v. MTS Corp. d/b/a Supercuts*, No. 94-1473 LH/WWD (D.N.M. July 26, 1996) (genuine issue of material fact regarding when plaintiff with AIDS, who applied for SSA disability benefits, became incapable of performing the essential functions of his position).

B. A Determination of What, if Any, Weight to Give to Representations Made in Support of Applications for Disability Benefits Depends on the Context and Timing of the Representations.

In assessing the extent to which representations made in connection with an application for disability benefits are relevant to a determination of whether a person is a "qualified individual with a disability" under the ADA, it is necessary to look at the context and timing of the representations. Often, applications for disability benefits do not use precise terminology and do not clearly define terms such as "total disability."[76] In addition, these forms or applications may require an individual merely to check off boxes and not allow him/her to fully describe his/her disabling condition or may be taken over the telephone. Even during depositions or hearings, questions concerning an individual's disability and/or ability to work are not always posed with precision. Accordingly, courts declining to dismiss the ADA claims of individuals who have applied for disability benefits have looked behind the "labels" or terms used in various forums and have considered other factors (*e.g.*, the content of the representations, who made them, the purpose for which they were made, when the representations were made, the period of time to which they refer, and any changes in the individual's physical or mental condition between the time of his/her application for benefits and the time of the adverse employment action at issue) in determining that a genuine issue of material fact exists as to whether an individual is a "qualified individual with a disability" for purposes of the ADA.

1. Context

Representations on a benefits application should not be viewed in a vacuum but, rather, considered in the context of all other relevant documents (*e.g.*, disability reports, doctors' reports, depositions). In addition, the circumstances under which the individual applied for benefits should be considered (*e.g.*, did the individual apply for benefits because s/he could not work because the employer denied reasonable accommodation?; did the individual maintain, at the time of application for benefits, that s/he could perform the essential functions of the position in question with accommodation?; did the individual apply for benefits based on a doctor's assessment that s/he was totally disabled?; did the individual apply for benefits at the suggestion of the employer?;[77] did the individual apply for benefits because s/he believed s/he was unable to work because of discrimination?).

For example, in *Anzalone v. Allstate Ins. Co.*, 5 AD Cas. (BNA) 223 (E.D. La. 1995), the plaintiff applied for disability benefits only after the defendant refused to allow him to return to work with certain restrictions. The court reviewed the context in which the plaintiff's statements were made and found that he did not unambiguously characterize himself as totally and completely disabled; rather, the plaintiff consistently took the position that he was capable of working under certain restrictions (i.e., with reasonable accommodation). *Anzalone*, 5 AD Cas. at 225. Similarly, in *Ward v. Westvaco Corp.*, 859 F. Supp. 608, 614-15, 3 AD Cas. (BNA) 738, 744-45 (D. Mass. 1994), although the plaintiff applied for disability retirement benefits under the SSA and his company's disability insurance plan, stating on the applications that he was "totally and permanently disabled," he explained that he would have been able to perform his job had his employer

---

76 See, e.g., *August v. Offices Unlimited, Inc.*, 981 F.2d 576, 586, 2 AD Cas. (BNA) 401, 408 (1st Cir. 1992) (Pettine, J., dissenting) (noting that the "disability insurance forms [at issue] are not legally or medically precise").

77 *See, e.g., Muellner v. Mars, Inc.*, 714 F. Supp. 351 (N.D. Ill. 1989)(in conjunction with the plaintiff's application for benefits under the employer's disability insurance plan, the employer and the insurer instructed the plaintiff to apply for SSA benefits because any such benefits would be set off against the disability insurance payments).

made reasonable accommodations.[78] The court held that the plaintiff's testimony, in the context of his ADA claim, was not inherently inconsistent with his former statements made in the course of obtaining disability benefits.

In addition, in some cases, the plaintiff applies for disability benefits based on a doctor's assessment that s/he is disabled, although the plaintiff believes that s/he can still work with reasonable accommodation. Doctors, however, can be wrong in assessing a person's condition and/or ability to work. For example, in *Oswald v. Larouche Chemicals, Inc.*, 894 F. Supp. 988 (E.D. La. 1995), the plaintiff, as well as his physical therapist, believed that he could perform the essential functions of a modified position, but the defendant's medical review officer determined that he could not. The court held that, because the employer's medical review officer's conclusion that the plaintiff could not perform any available jobs was the basis for the grant of disability benefits, there was a genuine issue of material fact whether the medical review officer properly assessed the plaintiff's abilities. *Oswald*, 894 F. Supp. at 996. Accordingly, it was possible that the plaintiff was a "qualified individual with a disability" capable of performing the essential functions of one or more positions with accommodation despite the medical review officer's determination that he was totally disabled.

In other cases, the plaintiff applies for disability benefits because the employer's alleged discriminatory conduct causes him/her to be unable to work or to believe that s/he cannot work because of discrimination. For example, in *EEOC v. MTS Corp. d/b/a Supercuts*, No. 94-1473 LH/WWD (D.N.M. July 26, 1996), after other employees became concerned about working with the plaintiff who had AIDS, the defendant excluded the plaintiff from a meeting at which his condition was discussed, denied his request to return to his "home base" salon, refused to pay his travel expenses to an annual company convention, and, after terminating him, informed him that he was no longer permitted on the premises. The defendant moved for summary judgment on the plaintiff's ADA claim, arguing that he was not a "qualified individual with a disability" because he applied for and received SSA benefits. In declining to grant the defendant's motion, the court noted that the plaintiff had completed "the application over the phone, outside of judicial machinery, without the benefit of counsel, and arguably under a great deal of emotional distress." *MTS Corp. d/b/a Supercuts*, No. 94-1473 LH/WWD at 2. Moreover, crediting the EEOC's version of the facts, the court noted that the defendants had forced the plaintiff "into the unenviable position of being unemployed . . . and emotionally devastated by their discriminatory conduct." *Id.*

Similarly, in *EEOC v. AIC Security*, 820 F. Supp. 1060, 2 AD Cas. (BNA) 561 (N.D. Ill. 1993), the plaintiff, who had cancer, maintained that he was qualified to perform the essential functions of the position from which he was terminated. The plaintiff's doctor also agreed that the plaintiff still could perform his job and explained that the information he supplied to the SSA, in support of the plaintiff's application for disability benefits, "was premised on the fact that [the plaintiff] had been fired from his job and that he should be able to get some compensation because no one [was] going to hire him." *AIC Security*, 820 F. Supp. at 1066-67, 2 AD Cas. at 567; *see also Mohamed v. Marriott*, 1996 WL 631687, at *2 (S.D.N.Y. Oct. 30, 1996) (in response to a question on the SSA application requesting an explanation of how his condition prevented him from working, the plaintiff, who was deaf, stated that he had tried to get another job but had been "frustrated" any place he looked because there were not "enough jobs open").

2. Timing

It is possible that an individual can be "totally disabled" at one point and can later be able to return to work or become totally disabled after a period of being able to work. It is therefore necessary to review what the person said about his/her condition at the time of his/her application for disability benefits and what s/he maintained his/her condition was at the time of the alleged discrimination (*i.e.*, was the condition at time to which the application refers different from condition at time of alleged discrimination?).[79]

---

[78] The plaintiff also attached a letter to his application for disability retirement, stating that his submission of his application and statements made on it were not intended as a waiver of his position that he would have been able to continue to perform his duties with reasonable accommodation. *Ward*, 859 F. Supp. at 614, 3 AD Cas. at 745.

[79] Moreover, some individuals with disabilities who have applied for disability benefits later seek employment when they learn of jobs that they can do with reasonable accommodation. Where such individuals believe that they were not hired for such positions because of discrimination, they should not be precluded from bringing an ADA claim merely because they previously applied for disability benefits stating that they were "totally disabled" or "unable to work."

For example, in *Lundstedt v. City of Miami*, 5 AD Cas. (BNA) 568 (S.D. Fla. 1995), the plaintiff applied for and was granted disability retirement benefits in 1980, based on his work-related accident in 1978 and subsequent related physical problems. The plaintiff also began receiving workers' compensation benefits in 1982 and received a lump sum payment in 1988 based on his total permanent disability. In 1992, the plaintiff requested to be reinstated to his former fire-fighter position, but the defendant denied his request.[80] In refusing to grant the defendant's motion for summary judgment with respect to the plaintiff's ADA claim, the court held that it was "perfectly consistent for [p]laintiff to assert that he was disabled in the past, but after time he became rehabilitated and is now able to return to work." *Lundstedt*, 5 AD Cas. at 577-78.

Similarly, in *Smith v. Dovenmuehle Mortgage Co.*, 859 F. Supp. 1138, 4 AD Cas. (BNA) 132 (N.D. Ill. 1994), the plaintiff, who had AIDS, claimed that, about one month after his discharge, he improved enough to perform the functions of his position (although he was receiving SSA benefits). The court found that, because the plaintiff's condition had improved, his position with respect to his ADA claim was not inconsistent with his position before the SSA. *Smith*, 859 F. Supp. at 1142, 4 AD Cas. at 136.

In addition, in *Lawrence v. United States I.C.C.*, 629 F. Supp. 819 (E.D. Pa. 1985), the plaintiff completed a disability retirement application, stating that he was "totally disabled" and "unable to carry out the vigorous activity required by [his] position"; later, he filed an ADA claim alleging that he was currently able to work. Since 22 months had lapsed between the plaintiff's application for SSA benefits and the filing of his ADA claim, the court reasoned that the plaintiff's claim that he was now able to work did not contradict his position at the time he applied for disability benefits. *Lawrence*, 629 F. Supp. at 822.[81]

III. Public Policy Supports the Conclusion that Representations Made in Connection with an Application for Disability Benefits Are Never an Absolute Bar to an ADA Claim.

A. Permitting Individuals to Go Forward with Their ADA Claims Is Critical to the ADA's Goal of Eradicating Discrimination Against Individuals with Disabilities.

The ADA's essential goal is "to provide a clear and comprehensive national mandate for the elimination of discrimination against individuals with disabilities."[82] Recognizing that individuals who have experienced discrimination on the basis of a disability "have often had no legal recourse to redress such discrimination,"[83] Congress enacted the ADA to provide legal remedies for the pervasive discrimination that "persists in such critical areas as employment . . . ."[84] Private lawsuits, therefore, play a critical role in the enforcement of the ADA.[85]

An individual who brings an employment discrimination case "acts not only to vindicate his or her personal interests in being made whole, but also acts as a 'private attorney general' to enforce the paramount public interest in eradicating invidious discrimination." *Mardell v. Harleysville Life Ins. Co.*, 31 F.3d 1221, 1235 (3d Cir. 1994), vacated, 115 S. Ct. 1397 (1995), *modified on other grounds*, 65 F.3d 1072 (3d Cir. 1995). Accordingly, when the EEOC acts on allegations of discrimination, at the behest of and for the benefit of specific individuals, it also acts to vindicate the public interest in preventing employment discrim-

---

80 The defendant's Fire Fighters' and Police Officers' Retirement Trust Board of Trustees had the authority to recommend to the defendant that any retiree who is no longer incapacitated for service be returned to his former classification. Lundstedt, 5 AD Cas. at 571.

81 *Compare Lawrence with McNeill v. Atchison, Topeka, and Santa Fe Railway Co.*, 4 AD Cas. (BNA) 300 (S.D. Tex. 1995). In *McNeill*, eight days after receiving a $305,000 award under the Federal Employer's Liability Act for a back injury that allegedly prevented him from working, the plaintiff filed an ADA suit against the defendant for failure to reinstate him. "[A]stonished by the audacity of the plaintiff in asserting that he was 'rehabilitated' from a 'permanent disability' within eight days," the court granted the defendant's motion for summary judgment. Id. at 303. The court stated, however, that if the plaintiff had filed his ADA claim "after a protracted period of convalescence, or vigorous and successful rehabilitation," or if his condition had changed because of new medical treatments or scientific technology, it would have considered the merits of his claim. *Id.*

82 42 U.S.C. § 12101(b)(1).

83 *Id.* § 12101(a)(4).

84 *Id.* § 12101(a)(3).

85 *Id.* § 12117(a).

ination. Barring individuals who apply for disability benefits from pursuing ADA claims would impede EEOC's enforcement of the ADA and deny individuals the right to have the court hear the merits of their claims. Moreover, it also would permit the continuation of the invidious discrimination that the ADA is designed to eradicate.

The Supreme Court has made clear that general equitable doctrines, such as judicial estoppel, cannot be applied as absolute bars to suits brought under the federal anti-discrimination statutes, given the important "'public purposes' furthered when even a single [person] establishes that an employer has discriminated against him or her." *McKennon v. Nashville Banner Publishing Co.*, __U.S.__, 115 S. Ct. 879, 885 (1995). This is so because "[t]he private litigator who seeks redress for his injuries vindicates both the deterrence and compensation objectives of [the Act in question]." *Id.*

In addition, as the *McKennon* court explained:

> The disclosure through litigation of incidents or practices which violate national policies respecting nondiscrimination in the work force is itself important, for the occurrence of violations may disclose patterns of noncompliance resulting from a misappreciation of the Act's operation or entrenched resistance to its commands, either of which can be of industry-wide significance.

Id. at 885.

Thus, if an individual is prevented from bringing an ADA claim because s/he has applied for disability benefits, discrimination is not deterred and the plaintiff's interests are not vindicated. Instead, "patterns of noncompliance" and pervasive discrimination against people with disabilities continue. *See also Smith v. Dovenmuehle Mortgage Co.*, 859 F. Supp. 1138, 1142, 4 AD Cas. (BNA) 132, 135 (N.D. Ill. 1994) (barring ADA claim of individual who received disability benefits would conflict with ADA's stated purpose "to combat the 'continuing existence of unfair and unnecessary discrimination and prejudice [which denies] people with disabilities the opportunity to compete on an equal basis'") (quoting 42 U.S.C. § 12101(a)(9)).

B. Individuals Should Not Have to Choose Between Applying for Disability Benefits and Vindicating Their Rights Under the ADA.

All persons have a right to be free from discrimination. In addition, each individual who meets the eligibility requirements for disability benefits has a right to receive such benefits. Barring an individual who applies for disability benefits from bringing a claim under the ADA would "place [him/her] in the untenable position of choosing between his right to seek disability benefits and his right to seek redress for an alleged violation of the ADA." *Smith v. Dovenmuehle Mortgage Co.*, 859 F. Supp. 1138, 1142, 4 AD Cas. (BNA) 132, 135 (N.D. Ill. 1994).

Moreover, an individual who applies for SSA, workers' compensation, and/or disability insurance benefits is not knowingly relinquishing his/her right to bring an ADA claim but, rather, is exercising independent rights. *Cf. Alexander v. Gardner-Denver*, 415 U.S. 36, 94 S. Ct. 1011 (1974) (the court held that an employee who had pursued a discrimination claim through union arbitration could not be prevented by the arbitrator's decision from bringing an independent cause of action under Title VII). The ADA was passed with the assumption that individuals with disabilities who want to work and are qualified to work must have an equal opportunity to work. The SSA operates from the same presumption by providing work incentive programs for disability beneficiaries that permit individuals to retain benefits while transitioning into employment. Accordingly, both the ADA and the SSA seek to promote the employment of individuals with disabilities whenever possible. *See Mohamed v. Marriott*, 1996 WL 631687, at *6 (S.D.N.Y. Oct. 30, 1996)(noting that since the Social Security Act itself permits individuals to receive benefits and work at the same time, "the classes of individuals entitled to protection under the [Social Security Act and the ADA] are not mutually exclusive"). Thus, because neither the ADA nor the SSA assumes that individuals are either totally able or unable to work, a person should not have to choose between applying for disability benefits or challenging an alleged adverse employment action under the ADA.

IV. Instructions to Investigators

As explained above, representations made in connection with an application for disability benefits are not dispositive of whether a person is a "qualified individual with a disability" for purposes of the ADA. Therefore, those representations, and the application for disability benefits, do not bar the filing of an ADA charge, nor should they prevent an investigator from recommending a cause determination if the evidence supports such a determination.

When determining whether a charging party (CP) is a "qualified individual with a disability," the investigator must conduct an individualized, case-by-case inquiry into whether CP can perform the essential functions of the position held or desired with or without reasonable accommodation. This inquiry must focus on the particular individual and the particular position at issue.

Although applying for disability benefits does not preclude CP from bringing an ADA claim, the representations made while pursuing such benefits may be relevant—but not dispositive—evidence of whether CP is a "qualified individual with a disability." As explained in this guidance, it is essential to look not only at CP's application for disability benefits but at all of the relevant evidence (*e.g.*, the facts surrounding the alleged discrimination, disability reports, doctors' reports, depositions) when determining whether CP meets this definition.

When assessing the effect that representations made in the context of applying for disability benefits may have on this determination, it is crucial to focus on the exact definition used by the benefits program, the precise content of the individual's representations, and the specific circumstances surrounding the application for disability benefits. It also is important to look at whether CP was "a qualified individual with a disability" at the time of the alleged discrimination and whether s/he maintained that s/he was still able to perform the essential functions of his/her position, with or without reasonable accommodation, at the time of the application for benefits. When deciding what, if any, weight to give to CP's representations made while pursuing disability benefits, investigators should consider the following factors:[86]

- the definitions of terms such as "disability," "permanent disability," "total disability," "inability to work," etc. under the relevant statute or contract pursuant to which CP applied for disability benefits (*e.g.*, do they look at specific positions or general kinds of work? do these terms take into account reasonable accommodation?);
- the specific content of the representations, who made them, and the purpose for which they were made;
- whether the representations are in CP's own words;
- whether the representations about CP's inability to work are qualified in any way (*e.g.*, "I am able to work with certain restrictions");
- when the representations were made, the period of time to which they refer, and whether CP's physical or mental condition has changed since the representations were made;
- whether CP was working during the period of time referred to as a period of total disability;
- whether the employer suggested that CP apply for benefits;
- whether CP asked for and was denied a reasonable accommodation;
- when the employer learned of the representations; and
- other relevant factors, such as advances in technology or changes in the employer's operations that may have occurred since representations were made that may make it possible for CP to perform the essential functions of the position, with or without reasonable accommodation.

[86] No one factor is necessarily determinative of whether CP is a "qualified individual with a disability." Rather, the investigator should consider all relevant evidence.

QUESTIONS AND ANSWERS ABOUT DISABILITY AND SERVICE RETIREMENT PLANS UNDER THE ADA

EEOC NOTICE
Number 915.002
Date 5/11/95

1. SUBJECT: Questions and Answers About Disability and Service Retirement Plans Under the ADA.
2. PURPOSE: EEOC has received a large number of discrimination charges and many informal inquiries concerning the application of the Americans with Disabilities Act (ADA) to disability and service retirement plans. The following questions and answers provide guidance to EEOC field offices on some issues that have been raised in this area.
3. EFFECTIVE DATE: Upon issuance.
4. EXPIRATION DATE: As an exception to EEOC Order 205.001, Appendix B, Attachment 4, § a(5), this Notice will remain in effect until rescinded or superseded.
5. ORIGINATOR: ADEA Division, Office of Legal Counsel.
6. INSTRUCTIONS: File after "Definition of Disability," in the 900 Series of Volume II of the Compliance Manual.
7. QUESTIONS AND ANSWERS

A. Q. What is the difference between a disability retirement plan and a service retirement plan?
A disability retirement plan provides a lifetime income for an employee who becomes unable to work because of illness or injury, without regard to the employee's age. A service retirement plan provides a lifetime income to employees who have reached a minimum age stated in the plan (most commonly age 60 or age 65) and/or who have completed specified years of service with the employer.

B. Q. Is it a violation of the ADA if an employer offers only a service retirement plan and does not offer a disability retirement plan?
A. Nothing in the ADA requires an employer to provide a disability retirement plan, whether or not the employer offers a service retirement plan. Where an employer offers only a service retirement plan, there is no ADA violation as long as the service retirement plan treats persons who are covered by the ADA the same as other employees.

C. Q. If an employer provides a disability retirement plan, is it permissible under the ADA for that plan to provide lower levels of benefits than the same employer's service retirement plan? Lower benefit levels may take different forms.

For example:

- a service retirement plan might enable any employee with 20 or more years of service to retire with an annuity equal to 50% of the individual's highest annual compensation. But, the disability retirement plan, payable when illness or injury prevents the individual from continuing work, might provide an annuity equal only to 45% of the individual's highest annual compensation;
- service retirees might receive periodic increases (for example, based on inflation or an increased return on invested pension funds) while disability retirees remain at a fixed benefit level;
- a service retirement plan might disregard outside earnings while a disability retirement plan contains an outside earnings offset provision.
- None of these examples would violate the ADA under any theory of discrimination. The ADA does not require that service retirement plans and disability retirement plans provide the same level of benefits, because they are two separate benefits which serve different purposes.

D. Q. Why don't differences in the plans cited above constitute discrimination against a qualified individual with a disability?
A. There is no disability discrimination because none of the plans make distinctions based on whether or not an individual is covered under the ADA. Thus, in the first example, the service retirement plan is available to all employees who have attained 20 or more years of service, without regard to the presence or absence of a disability. A qualified individual with a disability who works 20 or more years receives the same service retirement benefit as a person not covered by the ADA who works 20 or more years. Similarly, the disability retirement plan is available to everyone who becomes unable to work because of illness or injury. Therefore, the employer does not violate the ADA simply by providing different benefits under service and disability retirement plans.

E. Q. What types of plans offering disability retirement or service retirement benefits would violate the ADA?

A. Violations will occur under either type of plan when the employer treats a qualified individual with a disability less favorably because of that individual's disability or when an employer denies persons covered by the ADA access to a plan which would be available to persons not covered by the ADA. Some examples are:

- persons covered by the ADA who qualify for both a service retirement and disability retirement plan are required to take a disability benefit which is less advantageous;
- an employer requires persons covered by the ADA to serve 25 years to obtain a service retirement benefit, while persons not covered by the ADA are eligible for service retirement after 20 years;
- persons covered by the ADA when hired are eligible for disability retirement protection after 5 years on the job, while persons not covered by the ADA when hired are eligible for disability retirement protection after 1 year on the job;
- persons covered by the ADA who take disability retirement are provided a benefit equal to 33% of their highest annual compensation, while all others are eligible for a disability retirement benefit equal to 50% of their highest annual compensation;
- persons covered by the ADA who earn a service retirement benefit are given a cost of living increase every third year of retirement, while all other service retirees receive an annual cost of living increase;
- an employer excludes from the disability retirement plan an employee who otherwise meets the plan's criteria but who has a particular disability (such as insulin-dependent diabetes or paraplegia.)

When the Commission is confronted with such disability discrimination, it will seek relief for the aggrieved persons unless the employer shows that it did not act on the basis of disability or proves that the plan is sheltered by the ADA's defense for certain bona fide employee benefit plans. See § 501(c) of the ADA. The reach of that defense is beyond the scope of these questions and answers.

For additional guidance on these issues, contact the Office of Legal Counsel's Attorney-of-the-Day at 202-663-4691.

Date Gilbert F. Casellas

WORKERS' COMPENSATION AND THE ADA

EEOC NOTICE
Number 915.002
Date

1. SUBJECT: EEOC Enforcement Guidance: Workers' Compensation and the ADA.
2. PURPOSE: This enforcement guidance sets forth the Commission's position on the interaction between Title I of the Americans with Disabilities Act of 1990 and state workers' compensation laws.
3. EFFECTIVE DATE: Upon receipt.
4. EXPIRATION DATE: As an exception to EEOC Order 205.001, Appendix B, Attachment 4, § a(5), this Notice will remain in effect until rescinded or superseded.
5. ORIGINATOR: ADA Division, Office of Legal Counsel.
6. INSTRUCTIONS: File after Section 902 of Volume II of the Compliance Manual.

____

Date Gilbert F. Casellas
Chairman

WORKERS' COMPENSATION AND THE ADA

TABLE OF CONTENTS

WORKERS' COMPENSATION AND THE ADA

INTRODUCTION

This enforcement guidance concerns the interaction between Title I of the Americans with Disabilities Act of 1990 (ADA)[1] and state workers' compensation laws.[2] The purpose of Title I of the ADA is to prohibit employers from discriminating against qualified individuals because of disability in all aspects of employment.[3] On the other hand, the purpose of a workers' compensation law is to provide a system for securing prompt and fair settlement of employees' claims against employers for occupational injury and illness.[4] While the purposes of the two laws are not in conflict, the simultaneous application of the laws has raised questions for EEOC investigators, for employers, and for individuals with disabilities in a number of

---

1 Codified as amended at 42 U.S.C. §§ 12101-12117, 12201-12213 (1994).

2 The analysis in this guidance also applies to federal sector complaints of non-affirmative action employment discrimination arising from the interaction between the Federal Employee's Compensation Act, 5 U.S.C. §§ 8101-8193 (1994), and section 501 of the Rehabilitation Act of 1973, 29 U.S.C. § 791(g) (1994), and to complaints of non-affirmative action employment discrimination arising from the interaction between sections 503 and 504 of the Rehabilitation Act of 1973, 29 U.S.C. §§ 793(d), 794(d) (1994), and state workers' compensation laws.

3 42 U.S.C. § 12112(a); 29 C.F.R. § 1630.4.

4 Workers' compensation laws generally require employers to compensate employees who are injured or become ill in the course of employment for the resulting loss of earning capacity and for medical care. *See* 1 ARTHUR LARSON, THE LAW OF WORKMEN'S COMPENSATION, § 1-1.10 (1994).

areas.[5] In this document, the Commission provides guidance concerning the following issues:

* whether a person with an occupational injury has a disability as defined by the ADA;
* disability-related questions and medical examinations relating to occupational injury and workers' compensation claims;
* hiring of persons with a history of occupational injury, return to work of persons with occupational injury, and application of the direct threat standard;
* reasonable accommodation for persons with disability-related occupational injuries;
* light duty issues; and
* exclusive remedy provisions in workers' compensation laws.

DISABILITY

The Commission has provided general guidance on the definition of the term "disability" under the ADA in EEOC: Definition of the Term "Disability," 8 FEP Manual (BNA) 405:7251 (1995). This section applies that guidance in the context of occupational injury and workers' compensation. The definition of "disability" under the ADA is no different in the workers' compensation context than in any other context.

1. Does everyone with an occupational injury have a disability within the meaning of the ADA?

No. Even if an employee with an occupational injury has a "disability" as defined by a workers' compensation statute, s/he may not have a "disability" for ADA purposes.

The ADA defines "disability" as: (1) a physical or mental impairment that substantially limits a major life activity, (2) a record of such an impairment, or (3) being regarded as having such an impairment. Impairments resulting from occupational injury may not be severe enough to substantially limit a major life activity, or they may be only temporary, non-chronic, and have little or no long term impact.

2. Does every person who has filed a workers' compensation claim have a disability under the "record of" portion of the ADA definition?

No. A person has a disability under the "record of" portion of the ADA definition only if s/he has a history of, or has been misclassified as having, a mental or physical impairment that substantially limits one or more major life activities.

3. When does a person with an occupational injury have a disability under the "regarded as" portion of the ADA definition?

A person with an occupational injury has a disability under the "regarded as" portion of the ADA definition if s/he: (1) has an impairment that does not substantially limit a major life activity but is treated by an employer as if it were substantially limiting, (2) has an impairment that substantially limits a major life activity because of the attitude of others towards the impairment, or (3) has no impairment but is treated as having a substantially limiting impairment.[6]

Example A: An employee has an occupational injury that has resulted in a temporary back impairment that does not substantially limit a major life activity. However, the employer views her as not being able to lift more than a few pounds and refuses to return her to her position. The employer regards her as having an impairment that substantially limits the major life activity of lifting. The employee has a disability as defined by the ADA.

Example B: An employer refuses to allow an employee whose occupational injury results in a facial disfigurement to return to his position because the employer fears negative reactions by co-workers or customers. The employer regards him as having an impairment that substantially limits the major life activities of interacting with others and working. The employee has a disability as defined by the ADA.

Example C: An employee is fully recovered from an occupational injury that resulted in a

---

5 Basic information on this topic may be found in EEOC: Technical Assistance Manual on the Employment Provisions (Title I) of the Americans with Disabilities Act at 9.0, 8 FEP Manual (BNA) 405:7055 (1992) [hereinafter Technical Assistance Manual].

6 For a detailed discussion of whether an individual is covered under the "regarded as" portion of the ADA definition of disability, see EEOC: Definition of the Term "Disability" at 902.8(a), 8 FEP Manual (BNA) 405:7278-405:7286 (1995).

temporary back impairment. The employer fires the employee because it believes that, if he returns to his heavy labor job, he will severely injure his back and be totally incapacitated. The employer regards the employee as having an impairment that disqualifies him from a class of jobs (heavy labor) and therefore as substantially limited in the major life activity of working. The employee has a disability as defined by the ADA.

QUESTIONS AND EXAMINATIONS

The Commission has provided general guidance on disability-related questions and medical examinations in ADA Enforcement Guidance: Preemployment Disability-Related Questions and Medical Examinations, 8 FEP Manual (BNA) 405:7191 (1995). The guidance provided here pertains particularly to disability-related questions and medical examinations related to workers' compensation and occupational injuries.

4. When may an employer ask questions about an applicant's prior workers' compensation claims or occupational injuries?

An employer may ask questions about an applicant's prior workers' compensation claims or occupational injuries after it has made a conditional offer of employment, but before employment has begun, as long as it asks the same questions of all entering employees in the same job category.

5. When may an employer require a medical examination of an applicant to obtain information about the existence or nature of prior occupational injuries?

An employer may require a medical examination to obtain information about the existence or nature of an applicant's prior occupational injuries, after it has made a conditional offer of employment, but before employment has begun, as long as it requires all entering employees in the same job category to have a medical examination. Where an employer has already obtained basic medical information from all entering employees in a job category, it may require specific individuals to have follow-up medical examinations only if they are medically related to the previously obtained medical information.

6. Before making a conditional offer of employment, may an employer obtain information about an applicant's prior workers' compensation claims or occupational injuries from third parties, such as former employers, state workers' compensation offices, or a service that provides workers' compensation information?

No. At the pre-offer stage, as at any other time, an employer may not obtain from third parties any information that it could not lawfully obtain directly from the applicant.

7. May an employer ask disability-related questions or require a medical examination of an employee either at the time s/he experiences an occupational injury or when s/he seeks to return to the job following such an injury?

Yes, in both instances, provided that the disability-related questions or medical examinations are job-related and consistent with business necessity. This requirement is met where an employer reasonably believes that the occupational injury will impair the employee's ability to perform essential job functions or raises legitimate concerns about direct threat. However, the questions and examinations must not exceed the scope of the specific occupational injury and its effect on the employee's ability, with or without reasonable accommodation, to perform essential job functions or to work without posing a direct threat.[7]

8. May an employer ask disability-related questions or require a medical examination of an employee with an occupational injury in order to ascertain the extent of its workers' compensation liability?

Yes. The ADA does not prohibit an employer or its agent from asking disability-related questions or requiring medical examinations that are

---

[7] If, as a result of an examination or inquiry, an employer refuses to return an employee to work because of a disability, the reason for doing so must be job-related and consistent with business necessity. See 29 C.F.R. § 1630.10 and Appendix (1995). Where safety considerations are implicated, the employer can only refuse to return the employee to work where his/her employment in the position would pose a "direct threat." Direct threat is discussed in questions 11, 12, 14, and 15, below.

necessary to ascertain the extent of its workers' compensation liability.[8]

However, the questions and examinations must be consistent with the state law's intended purpose of determining an employee's eligibility for workers' compensation benefits. An employer may not use an employee's occupational injury as an opportunity to ask far-ranging disability-related questions or to require unrelated medical examinations. Examinations and questions must be limited in scope to the specific occupational injury and its impact on the individual and may not be required more often than is necessary to determine an individual's initial or continued eligibility for workers' compensation benefits. Excessive questioning or imposition of medical examinations may constitute disability-based harassment which is prohibited by the ADA.

9. If an employee with a disability-related occupational injury requests a reasonable accommodation, may the employer ask for documentation of his/her disability?

Yes. If an employee with a disability-related occupational injury[9] requests reasonable accommodation and the need for accommodation is not obvious, the employer may require reasonable documentation of the employee's entitlement to reasonable accommodation. While the employer may require documentation showing that the employee has a covered disability and stating his/her functional limitations, it is not entitled to medical records that are unnecessary to the request for reasonable accommodation.

CONFIDENTIALITY OF MEDICAL INFORMATION

10. Do the ADA's confidentiality requirements apply to medical information regarding an applicant's or employee's occupational injury or workers' compensation claim?

Yes. Medical information regarding an applicant's or employee's occupational injury or workers' compensation claim must be collected and maintained on separate forms and kept in a separate medical file along with other information required to be kept confidential under the ADA. An employer must keep medical information confidential even if someone is no longer an applicant or an employee.

The ADA allows disclosure of this information only in the following circumstances:

* supervisors and managers may be told about necessary restrictions on the work or duties of the employee and about necessary accommodations;[10]
* first aid and safety personnel may be told, when appropriate, if the disability might require emergency treatment;[11]
* government officials investigating compliance with the ADA must be given relevant information on request;[12]
* employers may give information to state workers' compensation offices, state second injury funds, and workers' compensation insurance carriers in accordance with state workers' compensation laws;[13] and
* employers may use the information for insurance purposes.[14]

---

8 This is because the ADA does not invalidate the procedures of any federal, state, or local law "that provides greater or equal protection for the rights of individuals with disabilities" than is provided by the ADA. 42 U.S.C. § 12201(b) (1994). Those portions of state workers' compensation laws that protect the rights of individuals to be compensated for work-related injury provide such greater or equal protection. The same is true for the analogous portions of the Federal Employee's Compensation Act, 5 U.S.C. §§ 8101-8193 (1994).

9 An individual with a disability may have an occupational injury that has nothing to do with the disability. The term "disability-related occupational injury" is used herein when the ADA and workers' compensation statutes apply simultaneously, *i.e.*, where there is a connection between an occupational injury and a disability as defined by the ADA.

10 42 U.S.C. § 12112(d)(3)(B)(i) (1994); 29 C.F.R. § 1630.14(b)(1)(i), (c)(1)(i) (1995).

11 42 U.S.C. § 12112(d)(3)(B)(ii); 29 C.F.R. § 1630.14(b)(1)(ii), (c)(1)(ii).

12 42 U.S.C. § 12112(d)(3)(B)(iii); 29 C.F.R. § 1630.14(b)(1)(iii), (c)(1)(iii).

13 *See* 42 U.S.C. § 12201(b); 29 C.F.R. pt. 1630 app. § 1630.14(b).

14 See 42 U.S.C. § 12201(c); 29 C.F.R. pt. 1630 app. §§ 1630.14(b) and 1630.16(f). For example, an employer may submit medical information to the company's health insurance carrier if the information is needed to administer a health insurance plan in accordance with § 501(c) of the ADA.

HIRING DECISIONS

11. May an employer refuse to hire a person with a disability simply because it assumes, correctly or incorrectly, that s/he poses some increased risk of occupational injury and increased workers' compensation costs?

No, unless the employer can show that employment of the person in the position poses a "direct threat." In enacting the ADA, Congress sought to address stereotypes regarding disability, including assumptions about workers' compensation costs.[15] Where an employer refuses to hire a person because it assumes, correctly or incorrectly, that, because of a disability, s/he poses merely some increased risk of occupational injury (and, therefore, increased workers' compensation costs), the employer discriminates against that person on the basis of disability. The employer can refuse to hire the person only if it can show that his/her employment in the position poses a "direct threat." This means that an employer may not "err on the side of safety" simply because of a potential health or safety risk. Rather, the employer must demonstrate that the risk rises to the level of a direct threat.

"Direct threat" means a significant risk of substantial harm to the health or safety of the individual or others that cannot be eliminated or reduced by reasonable accommodation.[16] The determination that a direct threat exists must be the result of a fact-based, individualized inquiry that takes into account the specific circumstances of the individual with a disability.

In determining whether employment of a person in a particular position poses a direct threat, the factors to be considered are:

* the duration of the risk;
* the nature and severity of the potential harm;
* the likelihood that the potential harm will occur; and
* the imminence of the potential harm.[17]

Some state health or safety laws may permit or require an employer to exclude a person with a disability from employment in cases where the ADA would not permit exclusion because employment of the person in the position does not pose a direct threat. Because the ADA supersedes such state laws, an employer may not defend its exclusion of a person with a disability on the basis of such a law.

12. May an employer refuse to hire a person with a disability simply because s/he sustained a prior occupational injury?

No. The mere fact that a person with a disability experienced an occupational injury in the past does not, by itself, establish that his/her current employment in the position in question poses a direct threat, i.e., a significant risk of substantial harm that cannot be lowered or eliminated by a reasonable accommodation. However, evidence about a person's prior occupational injury, in some circumstances, may be relevant to the direct threat analysis discussed in question 11, above.

An investigator should consider the following factors regarding a prior occupational injury in applying the direct threat analysis set forth in question 11, above:

* whether the prior injury is related to the person's disability (e.g., if employees without disabilities in the person's prior job had similar injuries, this may indicate that the injury is not related to the disability and, thus, is irrelevant to the direct threat inquiry);
* the circumstances surrounding the prior injury (e.g., the actions of others in the workplace or the lack of appropriate safety devices or procedures may have caused or contributed to the injury);
* the similarities and differences between the position in question and the position in which the prior injury occurred (e.g., the prior position may have involved hazards

---

15 H.R. Rep. No. 485 pt. 3, 101st Cong., 2d Sess. 31 (1990).

16 29 C.F.R. § 1630.2(r) (1995).

17 "Direct threat" is discussed more fully in the Commission's ADA regulations and interpretive guidance, 29 C.F.R. § 1630.2(r) and Appendix (1995), and in the Technical Assistance Manual at 4.5, 8 FEP Manual (BNA) 405:7022-405:7026 (1992).

not present in the position under consideration);
* whether the current condition of the person with a disability is similar to his/her condition at the time of the prior injury (e.g., if the person's condition has improved, the prior injury may have little significance);
* the number and frequency of prior occupational injuries;
* the nature and severity of the prior injury (e.g., if the injury was minor, it may have little or no significance);
* the amount of time the person has worked in the same or a similar position since the prior injury without subsequent injury; and
* whether the risk of harm can be lowered or eliminated by a reasonable accommodation.

Example A: CP applies for a position operating a large saw with R, a lumber mill. After making a conditional job offer, R discovers that CP, who has insulin-dependent diabetes, was seriously injured while operating a similar saw for another lumber mill. The injury was caused by the failure of a safety device and was unrelated to CP's diabetes. R assumes, however, that the injury was related to the diabetes and refuses to hire CP for safety reasons. CP's prior occupational injury, which was unrelated to her disability, does not constitute evidence that she poses a direct threat in the saw operator position because of her disability.

Example B: CP, who has a shoulder disability, applies to R restaurant for the position of bus person which requires frequent carrying of basins full of dirty dishes weighing 40-45 pounds. After a conditional job offer, R discovers that CP has had five serious injuries to his left shoulder while carrying basins full of dirty dishes in other bussing jobs over the past four years. A medical examination and physical fitness test show that the condition of CP's shoulder has significantly deteriorated with each injury. They also show that, if CP carries heavy basins, there is a high probability that his left shoulder will be immediately and permanently injured to the point where his left arm will be useless. Assume that there is no reasonable accommodation that will enable CP to perform the essential functions of the bussing position. The objective medical and other evidence (the number, frequency, nature, and severity of the prior injuries; the similarity of the position at issue to the positions in which the injuries occurred; the progressive deterioration of CP's shoulder with each injury; and the evidence that a further injury will render CP's arm useless) supports a finding that CP's employment in the position of bus person poses a significant risk of substantial harm. The evidence further shows that the risk cannot be lowered or eliminated through a reasonable accommodation. Therefore, CP's employment in the position of bus person poses a direct threat.

Example C: CP applies for a position as a laborer with R, a construction company. The position requires lifting equipment and other items weighing up to 100 pounds. After making a conditional offer of employment to CP, R requires him to undergo its standard medical examination. As a result, R discovers that CP previously injured his back while working for an automotive repair shop. CP's prior on-the-job injury, which occurred when CP was helping a co-worker push a stalled vehicle, was not serious. CP has completely recovered from the back injury. Nevertheless, R rescinds its offer of employment because it is worried about increased workers' compensation costs and considers CP to be a poor risk for heavy labor.[18] CP's prior occupational injury, which was not serious and which occurred in a position involving hazards not present in R's position, does not constitute evidence that employment of CP in the laborer position would pose a direct threat.

RETURN TO WORK DECISIONS

13. May an employer require that an employee with a disability-related occupational injury be able to return to "full duty" before allowing him/her to return to work?

No. The term "full duty" may include marginal

[18] CP has a disability as defined by the ADA because R regards CP as having a substantially limiting impairment. R, which disqualified CP from the heavy laborer position because it believed that CP was a poor risk for heavy labor, treated CP as unsuitable for the class of heavy labor jobs. Accordingly, R regards CP as substantially limited in the major life activity of working. See EEOC: Definition of the Term "Disability" at 902.8(f), 8 FEP Manual (BNA) 405:7282 (1995).

as well as essential job functions or may mean performing job functions without any accommodation. An employer may not require that an employee with a disability-related occupational injury who can perform essential functions be able to return to "full duty" if, because of the disability, s/he is unable to perform marginal functions of the position[19] or requires a reasonable accommodation that would not impose an undue hardship.

14. May an employer refuse to return to work an employee with a disability-related occupational injury simply because it assumes, correctly or incorrectly, that s/he poses some increased risk of reinjury and increased workers' compensation costs?

No, unless an employer can show that employment of the person in the position poses a "direct threat." Where an employer refuses to return an employee to work because it assumes, correctly or incorrectly, that his/her disability-related occupational injury creates merely some increased risk of further occupational injury and increased workers' compensation costs, it discriminates on the basis of disability. The employer may not refuse to return to work an employee who is able to perform the essential functions of the job, with or without a reasonable accommodation, unless it can show that returning the person to the position poses a "direct threat." (See the discussion of direct threat in questions 11 and 12, above.)

The fact that an employee has had a disability-related occupational injury does not, by itself, indicate that s/he is unable to perform the essential functions of the job or that returning him/her to work poses a direct threat. In some circumstances, evidence about an employee's disability-related occupational injury may be relevant to whether s/he can perform the essential functions of the job, with or without a reasonable accommodation, or it may be relevant to the direct threat analysis. An employer should consider the pertinent factors listed in questions 11 and 12, above, in applying the direct threat analysis in this context.

Example A: CP, a clerk/typist, breaks her wrist while trying to move heavy office equipment with a co-worker. CP is unable to work for six weeks and receives workers' compensation. After CP's wrist completely heals, she asks to return to work. A physician indicates that there is little risk that repetitive motion will damage CP's wrist. However, R refuses her request to return to the clerk/typist position because it believes that any repetitive motion will cause serious and permanent reinjury of her wrist.[20] The following objective evidence supports a finding that returning CP to the clerk/typist position does not pose a significant risk of substantial harm (i.e., direct threat): (1) her injury was not caused by repetitive motion, (2) her wrist has completely healed, and (3) there is little risk that she will reinjure her wrist through repetitive motion. R has violated the ADA by not returning CP to her clerk/typist position.

Example B: CP, a maintenance worker, badly fractures both ankles in a workplace accident. She is unable to work for six months and receives workers' compensation. Although CP's ankles partially heal, she is unable to walk and stand for more than short periods of time. CP's maintenance job requires extensive walking and standing on cement floors. The report from CP's most recent medical examination shows that there is a high probability of immediate, severe, and permanent damage to CP's ankles if she walks or stands for more than short periods of time, especially on hard surfaces. Assume that there is no accommodation that will lower the risk of harm. R may refuse to return CP to her maintenance position because there is sufficient evidence to support a finding that her employment in the position poses a direct threat, i.e., a significant risk of substantial harm that cannot be eliminated or reduced through a reasonable accommodation. (However, R must reassign CP, as set forth in question 22, below, absent undue hardship.)

---

[19] The employer can reallocate or redistribute to other employees the marginal functions that the employee is unable to perform because of the disability.

[20] CP has a disability because R regards her as having an impairment that disqualifies her from a class of jobs (clerk/typist) and therefore as substantially limited in the major life activity of working. *See* EEOC: Definition of the Term "Disability" at 902.8(f), 8 FEP Manual (BNA) 405:7282 (1995).

15. May an employer refuse to return to work an employee with a disability-related occupational injury simply because of a workers' compensation determination that s/he has a "permanent disability" or is "totally disabled"?

No. Workers' compensation laws are different in purpose from the ADA and may utilize different standards for evaluating whether an individual has a "disability" or whether s/he is capable of working. For example, under a workers' compensation statute, a person who loses vision in both eyes or has loss of use of both arms or both legs may have a "permanent total disability," although s/he may be able to work. A workers' compensation determination also may relate to a different time period. Such a determination is never dispositive regarding an individual's ability to return to work, although it may provide relevant evidence regarding an employee's ability to perform the essential functions of the position in question or to return to work without posing a direct threat.

16. Under the ADA, is a rehabilitation counselor, physician, or other specialist responsible for deciding whether an employee with a disability-related occupational injury is ready to return to work?

No. The employer bears the ultimate responsibility for deciding whether an employee with a disability-related occupational injury is ready to return to work. Therefore, the employer, rather than a rehabilitation counselor, physician, or other specialist, must determine whether the employee can perform the essential functions of the job, with or without reasonable accommodation, or can work without posing a direct threat.

On the other hand, the employer may find it helpful to seek information from the rehabilitation counselor, physician, or other specialist regarding the employee's specific functional limitations, abilities, and possible reasonable accommodations.

In order to obtain useful and accurate information from a rehabilitation counselor, physician, or other specialist in making a return to work decision, an employer may wish to provide him/her with specific information about the following:

* the essential functions of the employee's position and the nature of the work to be performed;
* the work environment and the employer's operations, including any unavoidable health or safety hazards which may exist; and
* possible reasonable accommodations.

An employer also may obtain useful information from others who are not experts but who are knowledgeable about the employee's current abilities, limitations, and possible reasonable accommodations. Such information will enable the employer to make an independent and accurate determination about the employee's ability to return to work.

REASONABLE ACCOMMODATION

The ADA requires that an employer make reasonable accommodation to the known physical or mental limitations of an otherwise qualified individual with a disability, unless the employer can demonstrate that the accommodation would impose an undue hardship. The general principles regarding reasonable accommodation and undue hardship are discussed in the Commission's ADA regulations and interpretive guidance (29 C.F.R. §§ 1630.2, 1630.9 and Appendix (1995)), and in the Technical Assistance Manual at 3.0, 8 FEP Manual (BNA) 405:6998 (1992). This section provides specific guidance regarding reasonable accommodation in the context of workers' compensation.

17. Does the ADA require an employer to provide reasonable accommodation for an employee with an occupational injury who does not have a disability as defined by the ADA?

No. The ADA does not require an employer to provide a reasonable accommodation for an employee with an occupational injury who does not have a disability as defined by the ADA.

18. May an employer discharge an employee who is temporarily unable to work because of a disability-related occupational injury?

No. An employer may not discharge an employee who is temporarily unable to work because of a disability-related occupational injury where it would not impose an undue hardship to provide leave as a reasonable accommodation.[21]

[21] Under the ADA, permitting the use of accrued paid leave or providing additional unpaid leave for treatment and/or recovery are forms of reasonable accommodation that an employer must provide, absent undue hardship. See 29 C.F.R. pt. 1630

19. What are the reinstatement rights of an employee with a disability-related occupational injury?

An employee with a disability-related occupational injury is entitled to return to his/her same position unless the employer demonstrates that holding open the position would impose an undue hardship.

In some instances, an employee may request more leave even after the employer has communicated that it would impose an undue hardship to hold open the employee's position any longer. In this situation, the employer must consider whether it has a vacant, equivalent position for which the employee is qualified and to which the employee can be reassigned without undue hardship to continue his/her leave for a specific period of time. For example, suppose that an employee needs six months to recover from a disability-related occupational injury, but holding his/her original position open for more than four months will impose an undue hardship. The employer must consider whether it has a vacant equivalent position to which the employee can be reassigned for the remaining two months of leave. If an equivalent position is not available, the employer must look for a vacant position at a lower level. Continued leave is not required as a reasonable accommodation if a vacant position at a lower level is also unavailable.[22]

20. Must an employer, as a reasonable accommodation, reallocate job duties of an employee with a disability-related occupational injury?

Yes, if the duties to be reallocated are marginal functions[23] of the position that the employee cannot perform because of the disability. Reasonable accommodation includes restructuring a position by reallocating or redistributing the marginal functions that the employee cannot perform because of the disability. However, an employer need not eliminate essential functions of the position.

21. May an employer unilaterally reassign an employee with a disability-related occupational injury to a different position instead of first trying to accommodate the employee in the position s/he held at the time the injury occurred?

No. An employer must first assess whether the employee can perform the essential functions of his/her original position, with or without a reasonable accommodation. Examples of reasonable accommodation include job restructuring, modification of equipment, or a part-time work schedule. Reassignment should be considered only when accommodation within the employee's original position is not possible or would impose an undue hardship.[24]

22. Must an employer reassign an employee who is no longer able to perform the essential functions of his/her original position, with or without a reasonable accommodation, because of a disability-related occupational injury?

Yes. Where an employee can no longer perform the essential functions of his/her original position, with or without a reasonable accommodation, because of a disability-related occupational injury, an employer must reassign him/her to an equivalent vacant position for which s/he is qualified, absent undue hardship.[25] If no equivalent vacant position (in terms of pay, status,

---

app. § 1630.2(o) (1995); Technical Assistance Manual at 3.10(4), 8 FEP Manual (BNA) 405:7011 (1992). In addition, an injured employee may be entitled to leave under the Family and Medical Leave Act of 1993, 29 U.S.C. §§ 2601-2654 (1994), which is enforced by the United States Department of Labor.

22 For further information on an employer's obligations regarding reassignment, see questions 21 and 22, below.

23 For a discussion of essential and marginal job functions see 29 C.F.R. § 1630.2(n) and Appendix (1995) and the Technical Assistance Manual at 2.3(a)-(c), 8 FEP Man. (BNA) 405:6993-405:6998 (1992).

24 29 C.F.R. pt. 1630 app. § 1630.2(o); Technical Assistance Manual at 3.10(5), 8 FEP Manual (BNA) 405:7011-405:7012 (1992). Note, however, that the ADA does not prohibit an employer and an employee from choosing reassignment rather than accommodation in the original position, if *both parties* voluntarily agree that reassignment is preferable.

25 *Id.* Note, however, that the ADA does not prohibit an employer from removing an essential function that an employee is no longer able to perform, in lieu of reassignment, if removing the essential function does not result in a diminution of an employment opportunity or status. Where removing an essential function results in a diminution of an employment opportunity or status, an employer may remove the essential function in lieu of reassignment only if both parties voluntarily agree that it is preferable to reassignment. Of course, the ADA does not require an employer to remove an essential job function as a reasonable accommodation.

etc.) exists, then the employee must be reassigned to a lower graded position for which s/he is qualified, absent undue hardship.

23. If there is no vacancy for an employee who can no longer perform his/her original position because of a disability-related occupational injury, must an employer create a new position or "bump" another employee from his/her position?

No. The ADA does not require an employer to create a new position or to bump another employee from his/her position in order to reassign an employee who can no longer perform the essential functions of his/her original position, with or without a reasonable accommodation.

24. When an employee requests leave as a reasonable accommodation under the ADA because of a disability-related occupational injury, may an employer provide an accommodation that requires him/her to remain on the job instead?

Yes. An employer need not provide an employee's preferred accommodation as long as the employer provides an effective accommodation—one that is sufficient to meet the employee's job-related needs.

Accordingly, an employer may provide a reasonable accommodation that requires an employee to remain on the job, in lieu of providing leave (*e.g.*, reallocating marginal functions, or providing temporary reassignment).

The employer is obligated, however, to restore the employee's full duties or to return the employee to his/her original position once s/he has recovered sufficiently to perform its essential functions, with or without a reasonable accommodation.

However, if an employee with a disability-related occupational injury does not request a reasonable accommodation, but simply requests leave that is routinely granted to other employees (*e.g.*, accrued paid leave or leave without pay), an employer may not require him/her to remain on the job with some type of adjustment unless it also requires employees without disabilities who request such leave to remain on the job with some type of adjustment.

(Note that, if an employee qualifies for leave under the Family and Medical Leave Act, an employer may *not* require him/her to remain on the job with an adjustment in lieu of taking a leave of absence. 29 C.F.R. § 825.702(d)(1) (1995).)

25. May an employer satisfy its ADA obligation to provide reasonable accommodation for an employee with a disability-related occupational injury by placing him/her in a workers' compensation vocational rehabilitation program?

No. An employer cannot substitute vocational rehabilitation services in place of a reasonable accommodation required by the ADA for an employee with a disability-related occupational injury. An employee's rights under the ADA are separate from his/her entitlements under a workers' compensation law. The ADA requires employers to accommodate an employee in his/her current position through job restructuring or some other modification, absent undue hardship.[26] If it would impose an undue hardship to accommodate an employee in his/her current position, then the ADA requires that an employer reassign the employee to a vacant position s/he can perform, absent undue hardship.[27] (See question 22, above.)

26. May an employer make a workplace modification that is not a required form of reasonable accommodation under the ADA in order to offset workers' compensation costs?

Yes. Nothing in the ADA prohibits an employer from making a workplace modification that is not a required form of reasonable accommodation under the ADA for an employee with an occupational injury in order to offset workers' compensation costs. For example, the ADA does not require employers to lower production standards to accommodate individuals with dis-

---

26 29 C.F.R. pt. 1630 app. § 1630.2(o) (1995); Technical Assistance Manual at 3.10(5), 8 FEP Manual (BNA) 405:7011-405:7012 (1992).

27 However, the ADA does not prohibit an employer and an employee from choosing vocational rehabilitation as an alternative to accommodating the employee in his/her current position, if both parties voluntarily agree that vocational rehabilitation is preferable.

abilities. However, an employer is clearly permitted to lower production standards for an occupationally injured employee as a way of returning him/her to work more quickly.

LIGHT DUTY

The term "light duty" has a number of different meanings in the employment setting. Generally, "light duty" refers to temporary or permanent work that is physically or mentally less demanding than normal job duties. Some employers use the term "light duty" to mean simply excusing an employee from performing those job functions that s/he is unable to perform because of an impairment. "Light duty" also may consist of particular positions with duties that are less physically or mentally demanding created specifically for the purpose of providing alternative work for employees who are unable to perform some or all of their normal duties. Further, an employer may refer to any position that is sedentary or is less physically or mentally demanding as "light duty."

In the following questions and answers, the term "light duty" refers only to particular positions created specifically for the purpose of providing work for employees who are unable to perform some or all of their normal duties.

27. Does the ADA prohibit an employer from creating a light duty position for an employee when s/he is injured on the job?

No, in most instances. An employer may recognize a special obligation arising out of the employment relationship to create a light duty position for an employee when s/he has been injured while performing work for the employer and, as a consequence, is unable to perform his/her regular job duties. Such a policy, on its face, does not treat an individual with a disability less favorably than an individual without a disability; nor does it screen out an individual on the basis of disability.[28]

Of course, an employer must apply its policy of creating a light duty position for an employee when s/he is occupationally injured on a non-discriminatory basis. In other words, an employer may not use disability as a reason to refuse to create a light duty position when an employee is occupationally injured.

An employer need not create a light duty position for a non-occupationally injured employee with a disability as a reasonable accommodation. The principle that the ADA does not require employers to create positions as a form of reasonable accommodation applies equally to the creation of light duty positions. However, an employer must provide other forms of reasonable accommodation required under the ADA. For example, subject to undue hardship, an employer must: (1) restructure a position by redistributing marginal functions which an individual cannot perform because of a disability, (2) provide modified scheduling (including part time work), or (3) reassign a non-occupationally injured employee with a disability to an equivalent existing vacancy for which s/he is qualified. Accordingly, an employer may not avoid its obligation to accommodate an individual with a disability simply by asserting that the disability did not derive from an occupational injury.

In some cases, the only effective reasonable accommodation available for an individual with a disability may be similar or equivalent to a light duty position. The employer would have to provide that reasonable accommodation unless the employer can demonstrate that doing so would impose an undue hardship.

Example: R creates light duty positions for employees when they are occupationally injured if they are unable to perform one or more of their regular job duties. CP can no longer perform functions of her position because of a disability caused by an off-the-job accident. She requests that R create a light duty position for her as a reasonable accommodation. R denies CP's request because she has not been injured on the job. R has not violated the ADA. However, R must provide another reasonable accommodation, absent undue hard-

---

28 A policy of creating light duty jobs for employees when they are occupationally injured in some instances may disproportionately exclude a class of individuals with disabilities. Where this is established by appropriate evidence of adverse impact, an employer must show that the policy is job-related and consistent with business necessity. Similarly, where such a policy has a disparate impact on a protected class under Title VII of the Civil Rights Act of 1964, as amended, 42 U.S.C. §§ 2000e-2000e-17 (1994), or the Age Discrimination in Employment Act of 1967, 29 U.S.C. §§ 621-634 (1994), the employer must show that the policy is job-related and consistent with business necessity.

ship. If it is determined that the only effective accommodation is to restructure CP's position by redistributing the marginal functions, and the restructured position resembles a light duty position, R must provide the reasonable accommodation unless it can prove that it imposes an undue hardship.

28. If an employer reserves light duty positions for employees with occupational injuries, does the ADA require it to consider reassigning an employee with a disability who is not occupationally injured to such positions as a reasonable accommodation?

Yes.[29] If an employee with a disability who is not occupationally injured becomes unable to perform the essential functions of his/her job, and there is no other effective accommodation available, the employer must reassign him/her to a vacant reserved light duty position as a reasonable accommodation if (1) s/he can perform its essential functions, with or without a reasonable accommodation; and (2) the reassignment would not impose an undue hardship. This is because reassignment to a vacant position and appropriate modification of an employer's policy are forms of reasonable accommodation required by the ADA, absent undue hardship.[30] An employer cannot establish that the reassignment to a vacant reserved light duty position imposes an undue hardship simply by showing that it would have no other vacant light duty positions available if an employee became injured on the job and needed light duty.

Example: R has light duty positions which it reserves for employees in its manufacturing department when they are unable to perform their regular job duties because of on-the-job injuries. CP, an assembly line worker, has multiple sclerosis (MS) which substantially limits a number of major life activities. Eventually CP is unable to perform the essential functions of her position, with or without a reasonable accommodation, because of the MS. As a reasonable accommodation, CP requests that she be reassigned to a vacant light duty position for which she is qualified. R says that the vacant light duty position is reserved for employees who are injured on the job and refuses to reassign CP, although it would not impose an undue hardship to do so. R has violated the ADA by refusing to reassign her to the vacant light duty position.

29. If an employer has only temporary light duty positions, must it still provide a permanent light duty position for an employee with a disability-related occupational injury?

No. The ADA typically does not limit an employer's ability to establish or change the content, nature, or functions of its positions. So, for example, an employer is free to determine that a light duty position will be temporary rather than permanent.[31] Thus, if an employer provides light duty positions only on a temporary basis, it need only provide a temporary light duty position for an employee with a disability-related occupational injury.

EXCLUSIVE REMEDY PROVISIONS

30. Do exclusive remedy provisions in workers' compensation laws bar employees from pursuing ADA claims?

No. The purpose of workers' compensation exclusivity clauses is to protect employers from being sued under common law theories of personal injury for occupational injury. Courts have generally held that the exclusive remedy provisions of state workers' compensation laws cannot bar claims arising under federal civil

[29] If it is established by appropriate evidence that a policy of reserving light duty jobs for employees who have been occupationally injured has an adverse impact on a protected class under any of the laws enforced by the EEOC, an employer must show that the policy is job-related and consistent with business necessity. See footnote 28, above. Of course, an employer may not apply the policy in a discriminatory manner.

[30] 29 C.F.R. § 1630.2(o)(2)(ii) (1995).

[31] Technical Assistance Manual at 9.4, 8 FEP Manual (BNA) 405:7057-405:7058 (1992).

rights laws,[32] even where a state workers' compensation law provides some relief for disability discrimination. Applying a state workers' compensation law's exclusivity provision to bar an individual's ADA claim would violate the Supremacy Clause of the U.S. Constitution and seriously diminish the civil rights protection Congress granted to persons with disabilities.

---

[32] The only federal court to have addressed the issue under the ADA has held that an individual's ADA rights are not precluded by a state workers' compensation exclusive remedy provision. *Wood v. County of Alameda*, 875 F. Supp. 659, 664, 4 AD Cas. (BNA) 43 (N.D. Cal. 1995). Prior to enactment of the ADA, it was well established that the exclusive remedy provisions of state workers' compensation laws could not bar claims arising under federal civil rights laws, including the Rehabilitation Act. See, e.g., *Lopez v. S.B. Thomas, Inc.*, 831 F.2d 1184, 1190 (2d Cir. 1987) (while workers' compensation law might bar plaintiff's state common law claim, it cannot bar relief under 42 U.S.C. § 1981 for discriminatory discharge); *Rosa v. Cantrell*, 705 F.2d 1208, 1221 (10th Cir. 1982), *cert. denied*, 464 U.S. 821 (1983) (state statute's exclusivity provision does not bar a federal civil rights claim under 42 U.S.C. § 1983); *Smith v. Lake City Nursing Home*, 771 F. Supp. 985, 987, 1 AD Cas. (BNA) 1874 (D. Minn. 1991) (federal remedy under section 504 of Rehabilitation Act for disability discrimination cannot be limited by a state workers' compensation act).

The U.S. Equal Employment Opportunity Commission

EEOC	NOTICE	Number 915.002
		October 17, 2002

1. SUBJECT: EEOC Enforcement Guidance on Reasonable Accommodation and Undue Hardship Under the Americans with Disabilities Act
2. PURPOSE: This enforcement guidance supersedes the enforcement guidance issued by the Commission on 03/01/99. Most of the original guidance remains the same, but limited changes have been made as a result of: (1) the Supreme Court's decision in US Airways, Inc. v. Barnett, 535 U.S. ___, 122 S. Ct. 1516 (2002), and (2) the Commission's issuance of new regulations under section 501 of the Rehabilitation Act. The major changes in response to the *Barnett* decision are found on pages 4-5, 44-45, and 61-62. In addition, minor changes were made to certain footnotes and the Instructions for Investigators as a result of the *Barnett* decision and the new section 501 regulations.
3. EFFECTIVE DATE: Upon receipt.
4. EXPIRATION DATE: As an exception to EEOC Order 205.001, Appendix B, Attachment 4, a(5), this Notice will remain in effect until rescinded or superseded.
5. ORIGINATOR: ADA Division, Office of Legal Counsel.
6 INSTRUCTIONS: File after Section 902 of Volume II of the Compliance Manual.

ENFORCEMENT GUIDANCE: REASONABLE ACCOMMODATION AND UNDUE HARDSHIP UNDER THE AMERICANS WITH DISABILITIES ACT

Table of Contents

ENFORCEMENT GUIDANCE: REASONABLE ACCOMMODATION AND UNDUE HARDSHIP UNDER THE AMERICANS WITH DISABILITIES ACT

INTRODUCTION

This Enforcement Guidance clarifies the rights and responsibilities of employers and individuals with disabilities regarding reasonable accommodation and undue hardship. Title I of the ADA requires an employer to provide reasonable accommodation to qualified individuals with disabilities who are employees or applicants for employment, except when such accommodation would cause an undue hardship. This Guidance sets forth an employer's legal obligations regarding reasonable accommodation; however, employers may provide more than the law requires.

This Guidance examines what "reasonable accommodation" means and who is entitled to receive it. The Guidance addresses what constitutes a request for reasonable accommodation, the form and substance of the request, and an employer's ability to ask questions and seek documentation after a request has been made.

The Guidance discusses reasonable accommodations applicable to the hiring process and to the benefits and privileges of employment. The Guidance also covers different types of reasonable accommodations related to job performance, including job restructuring, leave, modified or part-time schedules, modified workplace policies, and reassignment. Questions concerning the relationship between the ADA and the Family and Medical Leave Act (FMLA) are examined as they affect leave and modified schedules. Reassignment issues addressed include who is entitled to reassignment and the extent to which an employer must search for a vacant position. The Guidance also examines issues concerning the interplay between reasonable accommodations and conduct rules.

The final section of this Guidance discusses undue hardship, including when requests for schedule modifications and leave may be denied.

GENERAL PRINCIPLES

Reasonable Accommodation

Title I of the Americans with Disabilities Act of 1990 (the "ADA")[1] requires an employer[2] to provide reasonable accommodation to qualified individuals with disabilities who are employees or applicants for employment, unless to do so would cause undue hardship. "In general, an accommodation is any change in the work environment or in the way things are customarily done that enables an individual with a disability to enjoy equal employment opportunities."[3] There are three categories of "reasonable accommodations":

"(i) modifications or adjustments to a job application process that enable a qualified applicant with a disability to be considered for the position such qualified applicant desires; or

(ii) modifications or adjustments to the work environment, or to the manner or circumstances under which the position held or desired is customarily performed, that enable a qualified individual with a disability to perform the essential functions of that position; or

(iii) modifications or adjustments that enable a covered entity's employee with a disability to enjoy equal benefits and privileges of employment as are enjoyed by its other similarly situated employees without disabilities."[4]

The duty to provide reasonable accommodation is a fundamental statutory requirement because of the nature of discrimination faced by individuals with disabilities. Although many individuals with disabilities can apply for and perform jobs without any reasonable accommodations, there are workplace barriers that keep others from performing jobs which they could do with some form of accommodation. These barriers may be physical obstacles (such as inaccessible facilities or equipment), or they may be procedures or rules (such as rules concerning when work is performed, when breaks are taken, or how essential or marginal functions are performed). Reasonable accommodation removes workplace barriers for individuals with disabilities.

Reasonable accommodation is available to qualified applicants and employees with disabilities.[5] Reasonable accommodations must be provided to

---

1 42 U.S.C. §§ 12101-12117, 12201-12213 (1994) (codified as amended). The analysis in this guidance applies to federal sector complaints of non-affirmative action employment discrimination arising under section 501 of the Rehabilitation Act of 1973. 29 U.S.C. § 791(g) (1994). It also applies to complaints of non-affirmative action employment discrimination arising under section 503 and employment discrimination under section 504 of the Rehabilitation Act. 29 U.S.C. §§ 793(d), 794(d) (1994). The ADA's requirements regarding reasonable accommodation and undue hardship supercede any state or local disability antidiscrimination laws to the extent that they offer less protection than the ADA. See 29 C.F.R. § 1630.1(c)(2) (1997).

2 In addition to employers, the ADA requires employment agencies, labor organizations, and joint labor-management committees to provide reasonable accommodations. See 42 U.S.C. § 12112(a), (b)(5)(A) (1994).

3 29 C.F.R. pt. 1630 app. § 1630.2(o) (1997).

4 29 C.F.R. § 1630.2(o)(1)(i-iii) (1997). The notices that employers and labor unions must post informing applicants, employees, and members of labor organizations of their ADA rights must include a description of the reasonable accommodation requirement. These notices, which must be in an accessible format, are available from the EEOC. See the Appendix [not produced here.—Eds.].

5 All examples used in this document assume that the applicant or employee has an ADA "disability." Individuals with a relationship or association with a person with a disability are not entitled to receive reasonable accommodations. See Den Hartog v. Wasatch Academy, 129 F.3d 1076, 1084, 7 AD Cas. (BNA) 764, 772 (10th Cir. 1997).

qualified employees regardless of whether they work part-time or full-time, or are considered "probationary." Generally, the individual with a disability must inform the employer that an accommodation is needed.[6]

There are a number of possible reasonable accommodations that an employer may have to provide in connection with modifications to the work environment or adjustments in how and when a job is performed. These include:

- making existing facilities accessible;
- job restructuring;
- part-time or modified work schedules;
- acquiring or modifying equipment;
- changing tests, training materials, or policies;
- providing qualified readers or interpreters; and
- reassignment to a vacant position.[7]

A modification or adjustment is "reasonable" if it "seems reasonable on its face, i.e., ordinarily or in the run of cases;"[8] this means it is "reasonable" if it appears to be "feasible" or "plausible."[9] An accommodation also must be effective in meeting the needs of the individual.[10] In the context of job performance, this means that a reasonable accommodation enables the individual to perform the essential functions of the position. Similarly, a reasonable accommodation enables an applicant with a disability to have an equal opportunity to participate in the application process and to be considered for a job. Finally, a reasonable accommodation allows an employee with a disability an equal opportunity to enjoy the benefits and privileges of employment that employees without disabilities enjoy.

Example A: An employee with a hearing disability must be able to contact the public by telephone. The employee proposes that he use a TTY[11] to call a relay service operator who can then place the telephone call and relay the conversation between the parties. This is "reasonable" because a TTY is a common device used to facilitate communication between hearing and hearing-impaired individuals. Moreover, it would be effective in enabling the employee to perform his job.

Example B: A cashier easily becomes fatigued because of lupus and, as a result, has difficulty making it through her shift. The employee requests a stool because sitting greatly reduces the fatigue. This accommodation is reasonable because it is a common-sense solution to remove a workplace barrier—being required to stand—when the job can be effectively performed sitting down. This "reasonable" accommodation is effective because it addresses the employee's fatigue and enables her to perform her job.

Example C: A cleaning company rotates its staff to different floors on a monthly basis. One crew member has a psychiatric disability. While his mental illness does not affect his ability to perform the various cleaning functions, it does make it difficult to adjust to alterations in his

6 See 29 C.F.R. pt. 1630 app. § 1630.9 (1997); see also H.R. Rep. No. 101-485, pt. 3, at 39 (1990) [hereinafter House Judiciary Report]; H.R. Rep. No. 101-485, pt. 2, at 65 (1990) [hereinafter House Education and Labor Report]; S. Rep. No. 101-116, at 34 (1989) [hereinafter Senate Report]. For more information concerning requests for a reasonable accommodation, see Questions 1-4, infra. For a discussion of the limited circumstance under which an employer would be required to ask an individual with a disability whether s/he needed a reasonable accommodation, see Question 40, infra.

7 42 U.S.C. § 12111(9) (1994); 29 C.F.R. § 1630.2(o)(2)(i-ii) (1997).

8 US Airways, Inc. v. Barnett, 535 U.S ___, 122 S. Ct. 1516, 1523 (2002).

9 Id. Some courts have said that in determining whether an accommodation is "reasonable," one must look at the costs of the accommodation in relation to its benefits. See, e.g., Monette v. Electronic Data Sys. Corp., 90 F.3d 1173, 1184 n.10, 5 AD Cas. (BNA) 1326, 1335 n.10 (6th Cir. 1996); Vande Zande v. Wisconsin Dept. of Admin., 44 F.3d 538, 543, 3 AD Cas. (BNA) 1636, 1638-39 (7th Cir. 1995). This "cost/benefit" analysis has no foundation in the statute, regulations, or legislative history of the ADA. See 42 U.S.C. § 12111(9), (10) (1994); 29 C.F.R. § 1630.2(o), (p) (1997); see also Senate Report, supra note 6, at 31-35; House Education and Labor Report, supra note 6, at 57-58.

10 See US Airways, Inc. v. Barnett, 535 U.S. ___, 122 S. Ct. 1516, 1522 (2002). The Court explained that "in ordinary English the word 'reasonable' does not mean 'effective.' It is the word 'accommodation,' not the word 'reasonable,' that conveys the need for effectiveness." Id.

11 A TTY is a device that permits individuals with hearing and speech impairments to communicate by telephone.

daily routine. The employee has had significant difficulty adjusting to the monthly changes in floor assignments. He asks for a reasonable accommodation and proposes three options: staying on one floor permanently, staying on one floor for two months and then rotating, or allowing a transition period to adjust to a change in floor assignments. These accommodations are reasonable because they appear to be feasible solutions to this employee's problems dealing with changes to his routine. They also appear to be effective because they would enable him to perform his cleaning duties.

There are several modifications or adjustments that are not considered forms of reasonable accommodation.[12] An employer does not have to eliminate an essential function, i.e., a fundamental duty of the position. This is because a person with a disability who is unable to perform the essential functions, with or without reasonable accommodation,[13] is not a "qualified" individual with a disability within the meaning of the ADA. Nor is an employer required to lower production standards—whether qualitative or quantitative[14]—that are applied uniformly to employees with and without disabilities. However, an employer may have to provide reasonable accommodation to enable an employee with a disability to meet the production standard. While an employer is not required to eliminate an essential function or lower a production standard, it may do so if it wishes.

An employer does not have to provide as reasonable accommodations personal use items needed in accomplishing daily activities both on and off the job. Thus, an employer is not required to provide an employee with a prosthetic limb, a wheelchair, eyeglasses, hearing aids, or similar devices if they are also needed off the job. Furthermore, an employer is not required to provide personal use amenities, such as a hot pot or refrigerator, if those items are not provided to employees without disabilities. However, items that might otherwise be considered personal may be required as reasonable accommodations where they are specifically designed or required to meet job-related rather than personal needs.[15]

Undue Hardship

The only statutory limitation on an employer's obligation to provide "reasonable accommodation" is that no such change or modification is required if it would cause "undue hardship" to the employer.[16] "Undue hardship" means significant difficulty or expense and focuses on the resources and circumstances of the particular employer in relationship to the cost or difficulty of providing a specific accommodation. Undue hardship refers not only to financial difficulty, but to reasonable accommodations that are unduly extensive, substantial, or disruptive, or those that would fundamentally alter the nature or operation of the business.[17] An employer must assess on a case-by-case basis whether a particular reasonable accommodation would cause undue hardship. The ADA's "undue hardship" standard is different from that applied by courts under Title VII of the Civil Rights Act of 1964 for religious accommodation.[18]

---

12 In US Airways, Inc. v. Barnett, the Supreme Court held that it was unreasonable, absent "special circumstances," for an employer to provide a reassignment that conflicts with the terms of a seniority system. 535 U.S. ___, 122 S. Ct. 1516, 1524-25 (2002). For a further discussion of this issue, see Question 31, infra.

13 "[W]ith or without reasonable accommodation" includes, if necessary, reassignment to a vacant position. Thus, if an employee is no longer qualified because of a disability to continue in his/her present position, an employer must reassign him/her as a reasonable accommodation. See the section on "Reassignment," infra n.77 [and accompanying text].

14 29 C.F.R. pt. 1630 app. § 1630.2(n) (1997).

15 29 C.F.R. pt. 1630 app. § 1630.9 (1997).

16 See 42 U.S.C. § 12112 (b)(5)(A) (1994) (it is a form of discrimination to fail to provide a reasonable accommodation "unless such covered entity can demonstrate that the accommodation would impose an undue hardship . . ."); see also 42 U.S.C. § 12111(10) (1994) (defining "undue hardship" based on factors assessing cost and difficulty). The legislative history discusses financial, administrative, and operational limitations on providing reasonable accommodations only in the context of defining "undue hardship." Compare Senate Report, supra note 6, at 31-34 with 35-36; House Education and Labor Report, supra note 6, at 57-58 with 67-70.

17 See 42 U.S.C. § 12111(10) (1994); 29 C.F.R. § 1630.2(p) (1997); 29 C.F.R. pt. 1630 app. § 1630.2(p) (1997).

18 See 29 C.F.R. pt. 1630 app. § 1630.15(d) (1997). See also Eckles v. Consolidated Rail Corp., 94 F.3d 1041, 1048-49, 5 AD Cas. (BNA) 1367, 1372-73 (7th Cir. 1996); Bryant v. Better Business Bureau of Maryland, 923 F. Supp. 720, 740, 5 AD Cas. (BNA) 625, 638 (D. Md. 1996).

REQUESTING REASONABLE ACCOMMODATION

1. How must an individual request a reasonable accommodation?

When an individual decides to request accommodation, the individual or his/her representative must let the employer know that s/he needs an adjustment or change at work for a reason related to a medical condition. To request accommodation, an individual may use "plain English" and need not mention the ADA or use the phrase "reasonable accommodation."[19]

Example A: An employee tells her supervisor, "I'm having trouble getting to work at my scheduled starting time because of medical treatments I'm undergoing." This is a request for a reasonable accommodation.

Example B: An employee tells his supervisor, "I need six weeks off to get treatment for a back problem." This is a request for a reasonable accommodation.

Example C: A new employee, who uses a wheelchair, informs the employer that her wheelchair cannot fit under the desk in her office. This is a request for reasonable accommodation.

Example D: An employee tells his supervisor that he would like a new chair because his present one is uncomfortable. Although this is a request for a change at work, his statement is insufficient to put the employer on notice that he is requesting reasonable accommodation. He does not link his need for the new chair with a medical condition.

While an individual with a disability may request a change due to a medical condition, this request does not necessarily mean that the employer is required to provide the change. A request for reasonable accommodation is the first step in an informal, interactive process between the individual and the employer. In some instances, before addressing the merits of the accommodation request, the employer needs to determine if the individual's medical condition meets the ADA definition of "disability,"[20] a prerequisite for the individual to be entitled to a reasonable accommodation.

2. May someone other than the individual with a disability request a reasonable accommodation on behalf of the individual?

Yes, a family member, friend, health professional, or other representative may request a reasonable accommodation on behalf of an individual with a disability.[21] Of course, the individual with a disability may refuse to accept an accommodation that is not needed.

---

19 See, e.g., Schmidt v. Safeway Inc., 864 F. Supp. 991, 997, 3 AD Cas. (BNA) 1141, 1146-47 (D. Or. 1994) ("statute does not require the plaintiff to speak any magic words. . . . The employee need not mention the ADA or even the term 'accommodation.'"). See also Hendricks-Robinson v. Excel Corp., 154 F.3d 685, 694, 8 AD Cas. (BNA) 875, 882 (7th Cir. 1998) ("[a] request as straightforward as asking for continued employment is a sufficient request for accommodation"); Bultemeyer v. Ft. Wayne Community Schs., 100 F.3d 1281, 1285, 6 AD Cas. (BNA) 67, 71 (7th Cir. 1996) (an employee with a known psychiatric disability requested reasonable accommodation by stating that he could not do a particular job and by submitting a note from his psychiatrist); McGinnis v. Wonder Chemical Co., 5 AD Cas. (BNA) 219 (E.D. Pa. 1995) (employer on notice that accommodation had been requested because: (1) employee told supervisor that his pain prevented him from working and (2) employee had requested leave under the Family and Medical Leave Act). Nothing in the ADA requires an individual to use legal terms or to anticipate all of the possible information an employer may need in order to provide a reasonable accommodation. The ADA avoids a formulistic approach in favor of an interactive discussion between the employer and the individual with a disability, after the individual has requested a change due to a medical condition. Nevertheless, some courts have required that individuals initially provide detailed information in order to trigger the employer's duty to investigate whether reasonable accommodation is required. See, e.g., Taylor v. Principal Fin. Group, Inc., 93 F.3d 155, 165, 5 AD Cas. (BNA) 1653, 1660 (5th Cir. 1996); Miller v. Nat'l Cas. Co., 61 F.3d 627, 629-30, 4 AD Cas. (BNA) 1089, 1090-91 (8th Cir. 1995).

20 See Questions 5 - 7, infra, for a further discussion on when an employer may request reasonable documentation about a person's "disability" and the need for reasonable accommodation.

21 Cf. Beck v. Univ. of Wis. Bd. of Regents, 75 F.3d 1130, 5 AD Cas. (BNA) 304 (7th Cir. 1996); Schmidt v. Safeway Inc., 864 F. Supp. 991, 997, 3 AD Cas. (BNA) 1141, 1146 (D. Or. 1994). But see Miller v. Nat'l Casualty Co., 61 F.3d 627, 630,

Example A: An employee's spouse phones the employee's supervisor on Monday morning to inform her that the employee had a medical emergency due to multiple sclerosis, needed to be hospitalized, and thus requires time off. This discussion constitutes a request for reasonable accommodation.

Example B: An employee has been out of work for six months with a workers' compensation injury. The employee's doctor sends the employer a letter, stating that the employee is released to return to work, but with certain work restrictions. (Alternatively, the letter may state that the employee is released to return to a light duty position.) The letter constitutes a request for reasonable accommodation.

3. Do requests for reasonable accommodation need to be in writing?

No. Requests for reasonable accommodation do not need to be in writing. Individuals may request accommodations in conversation or may use any other mode of communication.[22] An employer may choose to write a memorandum or letter confirming the individual's request. Alternatively, an employer may ask the individual to fill out a form or submit the request in written form, but the employer cannot ignore the initial request. An employer also may request reasonable documentation that the individual has an ADA disability and needs a reasonable accommodation. (See Question 6).

4. When should an individual with a disability request a reasonable accommodation?

An individual with a disability may request a reasonable accommodation at any time during the application process or during the period of employment. The ADA does not preclude an employee with a disability from requesting a reasonable accommodation because s/he did not ask for one when applying for a job or after receiving a job offer. Rather, an individual with a disability should request a reasonable accommodation when s/he knows that there is a workplace barrier that is preventing him/her, due to a disability, from effectively competing for a position, performing a job, or gaining equal access to a benefit of employment.[23] As a practical matter, it may be in an employee's interest to request a reasonable accommodation before performance suffers or conduct problems occur.

5. What must an employer do after receiving a request for reasonable accommodation?

The employer and the individual with a disability should engage in an informal process to clarify what the individual needs and identify the appropriate reasonable accommodation.[24] The employer may ask the

---

4 AD Cas. (BNA) 1089, 1091 (8th Cir. 1995) (employer had no duty to investigate reasonable accommodation despite the fact that the employee's sister notified the employer that the employee "was mentally falling apart and the family was trying to get her into the hospital"). The employer should be receptive to any relevant information or requests it receives from a third party acting on the individual's behalf because the reasonable accommodation process presumes open communication in order to help the employer make an informed decision. See 29 C.F.R. §§ 1630.2(o), 1630.9 (1997); 29 C.F.R. pt. 1630 app. §§ 1630.2(o), 1630.9 (1997).

22 Although individuals with disabilities are not required to keep records, they may find it useful to document requests for reasonable accommodation in the event there is a dispute about whether or when they requested accommodation. Employers, however, must keep all employment records, including records of requests for reasonable accommodation, for one year from the making of the record or the personnel action involved, whichever occurs later. If a charge is filed, records must be preserved until the charge is resolved. 29 C.F.R. § 1602.14 (1997).

23 Cf. Masterson v. Yellow Freight Sys., Inc., Nos. 98-6126, 98-6025, 1998 WL 856143 (10th Cir. Dec. 11, 1998) (fact that an employee with a disability does not need a reasonable accommodation all the time does not relieve employer from providing an accommodation for the period when he does need one).

24 See 29 C.F.R. § 1630.2(o)(3) (1997); 29 C.F.R. pt. 1630 app. §§ 1630.2(o), 1630.9 (1997); see also Haschmann v. Time Warner Entertainment Co., 151 F.3d 591, 601, 8 AD Cas. (BNA) 692, 700 (7th Cir. 1998); Dalton v. Subaru-Isuzu, 141 F.3d 667, 677, 7 AD Cas. (BNA) 1872, 1880-81 (7th Cir. 1998). The appendix to the regulations at § 1630.9 provides a detailed discussion of the reasonable accommodation process. Engaging in an interactive process helps employers to discover and provide reasonable accommodation. Moreover, in situations where an employer fails to provide a reasonable accommodation (and undue hardship would not be a valid defense), evidence that the employer engaged in an interactive process can demonstrate a "good faith" effort which can protect an employer from having to pay punitive and certain compensatory damages. See 42 U.S.C. § 1981a(a)(3) (1994).

individual relevant questions that will enable it to make an informed decision about the request. This includes asking what type of reasonable accommodation is needed.[25]

The exact nature of the dialogue will vary. In many instances, both the disability and the type of accommodation required will be obvious, and thus there may be little or no need to engage in any discussion. In other situations, the employer may need to ask questions concerning the nature of the disability and the individual's functional limitations in order to identify an effective accommodation. While the individual with a disability does not have to be able to specify the precise accommodation, s/he does need to describe the problems posed by the workplace barrier. Additionally, suggestions from the individual with a disability may assist the employer in determining the type of reasonable accommodation to provide. Where the individual or the employer are not familiar with possible accommodations, there are extensive public and private resources to help the employer identify reasonable accommodations once the specific limitations and workplace barriers have been ascertained.[26]

6. May an employer ask an individual for documentation when the individual requests reasonable accommodation?

Yes. When the disability and/or the need for accommodation is not obvious, the employer may ask the individual for reasonable documentation about his/her disability and functional limitations.[27] The employer is entitled to know that the individual has a covered disability for which s/he needs a reasonable accommodation.

Reasonable documentation means that the employer may require only the documentation that is needed to establish that a person has an ADA disability, and that the disability necessitates a reasonable accommodation. Thus, an employer, in response to a request for reasonable accommodation, cannot ask for documentation that is unrelated to determining the existence of a disability and the necessity for an accommodation. This means that in most situations an employer cannot request a person's complete medical records because they are likely to contain information unrelated to the disability at issue and the need for accommodation. If an individual has more than one disability, an employer can request information pertaining only to the disability that requires a reasonable accommodation.

An employer may require that the documentation about the disability and the functional limitations come from an appropriate health care or rehabilitation professional. The appropriate professional in any particular situation will depend on the disability and the type of functional limitation it imposes. Appropriate professionals include, but are not limited to, doctors (including psychiatrists), psychologists, nurses, physical therapists, occupational therapists, speech therapists, vocational rehabilitation specialists, and licensed mental health professionals.

In requesting documentation, employers should specify what types of information they are seeking regarding the disability, its functional limitations, and the need for reasonable accommodation. The individual can be asked to sign a limited release allowing the employer to submit a list of specific questions to the health care or vocational professional.[28]

As an alternative to requesting documentation, an employer may simply discuss with the person the

---

25 The burden-shifting framework outlined by the Supreme Court in US Airways, Inc. v. Barnett, 535 U.S. ___, 122 S. Ct. 1516, 1523 (2002), does not affect the interactive process between an employer and an individual seeking reasonable accommodation. See [footnotes 125-127 and accompanying text], infra, for a further discussion.

26 See 29 C.F.R. pt. 1630 app. § 1630.9 (1997). The Appendix to this Guidance provides a list of resources to identify possible accommodations.

27 29 C.F.R. pt. 1630 app. § 1630.9 (1997); see also EEOC Enforcement Guidance: Preemployment Disability-Related Questions and Medical Examinations at 6, 8 FEP Manual (BNA) 405:7191, 7193 (1995) [hereinafter Preemployment Questions and Medical Examinations]; EEOC Enforcement Guidance: The Americans with Disabilities Act and Psychiatric Disabilities at 22-23, 8 FEP Manual (BNA) 405:7461, 7472-73 (1997) [hereinafter ADA and Psychiatric Disabilities]. Although the latter Enforcement Guidance focuses on psychiatric disabilities, the legal standard under which an employer may request documentation applies to disabilities generally. When an employee seeks leave as a reasonable accommodation, an employer's request for documentation about disability and the need for leave may overlap with the certification requirements of the Family and Medical Leave Act (FMLA), 29 C.F.R. §§ 825.305-.308, 825.310-.311 (1997).

28 Since a doctor cannot disclose information about a patient without his/her permission, an employer must obtain a release from the individual that will permit his/her doctor to answer questions. The release should be clear as to what information will be requested. Employers must maintain the confidentiality of all medical information collected during this process, regardless of where the information comes from. See Question 42 and note 111, infra

nature of his/her disability and functional limitations. It would be useful for the employer to make clear to the individual why it is requesting information, i.e., to verify the existence of an ADA disability and the need for a reasonable accommodation.

Example A: An employee says to an employer, "I'm having trouble reaching tools because of my shoulder injury." The employer may ask the employee for documentation describing the impairment; the nature, severity, and duration of the impairment; the activity or activities that the impairment limits; and the extent to which the impairment limits the employee's ability to perform the activity or activities (i.e., the employer is seeking information as to whether the employee has an ADA disability).

Example B: A marketing employee has a severe learning disability. He attends numerous meetings to plan marketing strategies. In order to remember what is discussed at these meetings he must take detailed notes but, due to his disability, he has great difficulty writing. The employee tells his supervisor about his disability and requests a laptop computer to use in the meetings. Since neither the disability nor the need for accommodation are obvious, the supervisor may ask the employee for reasonable documentation about his impairment; the nature, severity, and duration of the impairment; the activity or activities that the impairment limits; and the extent to which the impairment limits the employee's ability to perform the activity or activities. The employer also may ask why the disability necessitates use of a laptop computer (or any other type of reasonable accommodation, such as a tape recorder) to help the employee retain the information from the meetings.[29]

Example C: An employee's spouse phones the employee's supervisor on Monday morning to inform her that the employee had a medical emergency due to multiple sclerosis, needed to be hospitalized, and thus requires time off. The supervisor can ask the spouse to send in documentation from the employee's treating physician that confirms that the hospitalization was related to the multiple sclerosis and provides information on how long an absence may be required from work.[30]

If an individual's disability or need for reasonable accommodation is not obvious, and s/he refuses to provide the reasonable documentation requested by the employer, then s/he is not entitled to reasonable accommodation.[31] On the other hand, failure by the employer to initiate or participate in an informal dialogue with the individual after receiving a request for reasonable accommodation could result in liability for failure to provide a reasonable accommodation.[32]

7. May an employer require an individual to go to a health care professional of the employer's (rather than the employee's) choice for purposes of documenting need for accommodation and disability?

The ADA does not prevent an employer from requiring an individual to go to an appropriate health professional of the employer's choice if the individual provides insufficient information from his/her treating physician (or other health care professional) to substantiate that s/he has an ADA disability and needs a reasonable accommodation. However, if an individual provides insufficient documentation in response to the employer's initial request, the employer should explain why the documentation is insufficient and allow the individual an opportunity to provide the missing information in a timely manner. Documentation is insufficient if it does not specify the existence of an ADA disability and explain the need for reasonable accommodation.[33]

---

29 See Question 9, infra, for information on choosing between two or more effective accommodations.

30 This employee also might be covered under the Family and Medical Leave Act, and if so, the employer would need to comply with the requirements of that statute.

31 See Templeton v. Neodata Servs., Inc., No. 98-1106, 1998 WL 852516 (10th Cir. Dec. 10, 1998); Beck v. Univ. of Wis. Bd. of Regents, 75 F.3d 1130, 1134, 5 AD Cas. (BNA) 304, 307 (7th Cir. 1996); McAlpin v. National Semiconductor Corp., 921 F. Supp. 1518, 1525, 5 AD Cas. (BNA) 1047, 1052 (N.D. Tex. 1996).

32 See Hendricks-Robinson v. Excel Corp., 154 F.3d 685, 700, 8 AD Cas. (BNA) 875, 887 (7th Cir. 1998).

33 If an individual provides sufficient documentation to show the existence of an ADA disability and the need for reasonable accommodation, continued efforts by the employer to require that the individual see the employer's health professional could be considered retaliation.

Any medical examination conducted by the employer's health professional must be job-related and consistent with business necessity. This means that the examination must be limited to determining the existence of an ADA disability and the functional limitations that require reasonable accommodation.[34] If an employer requires an employee to go to a health professional of the employer's choice, the employer must pay all costs associated with the visit(s).

8. Are there situations in which an employer cannot ask for documentation in response to a request for reasonable accommodation?

Yes. An employer cannot ask for documentation when: (1) both the disability and the need for reasonable accommodation are obvious, or (2) the individual has already provided the employer with sufficient information to substantiate that s/he has an ADA disability and needs the reasonable accommodation requested.

Example A: An employee brings a note from her treating physician explaining that she has diabetes and that, as a result, she must test her blood sugar several times a day to ensure that her insulin level is safe in order to avoid a hyperglycemic reaction. The note explains that a hyperglycemic reaction can include extreme thirst, heavy breathing, drowsiness, and flushed skin, and eventually would result in unconsciousness. Depending on the results of the blood test, the employee might have to take insulin. The note requests that the employee be allowed three or four 10-minute breaks each day to test her blood, and if necessary, to take insulin. The doctor's note constitutes sufficient documentation that the person has an ADA disability because it describes a substantially limiting impairment and the reasonable accommodation needed as a result. The employer cannot ask for additional documentation.

Example B: One year ago, an employer learned that an employee had bipolar disorder after he requested a reasonable accommodation. The documentation provided at that time from the employee's psychiatrist indicated that this was a permanent condition which would always involve periods in which the disability would remit and then intensify. The psychiatrist's letter explained that during periods when the condition flared up, the person's manic moods or depressive episodes could be severe enough to create serious problems for the individual in caring for himself or working, and that medication controlled the frequency and severity of these episodes.

Now, one year later, the employee again requests a reasonable accommodation related to his bipolar disorder. Under these facts, the employer may ask for reasonable documentation on the need for the accommodation (if the need is not obvious), but it cannot ask for documentation that the person has an ADA disability. The medical information provided one year ago established the existence of a long-term impairment that substantially limits a major life activity.

Example C: An employee gives her employer a letter from her doctor, stating that the employee has asthma and needs the employer to provide her with an air filter. This letter contains insufficient information as to whether the asthma is an ADA disability because it does not provide any information as to its severity (i.e., whether it substantially limits a major life activity). Furthermore, the letter does not identify precisely what problem exists in the workplace that requires an air filter or any other reasonable accommodation. Therefore, the employer can request additional documentation.

9. Is an employer required to provide the reasonable accommodation that the individual wants?

The employer may choose among reasonable accommodations as long as the chosen accommodation is effective.[35] Thus, as part of the interactive process, the employer may offer alternative suggestions for reasonable accommodations and discuss their

---

34 Employers also may consider alternatives like having their health professional consult with the individual's health professional, with the employee's consent.

35 See 29 C.F.R. pt. 1630 app. § 1630.9 (1997); see also Stewart v. Happy Herman's Cheshire Bridge, Inc., 117 F.3d 1278, 1285-86, 6 AD Cas. (BNA) 1834, 1839 (11th Cir. 1997); Hankins v. The Gap, Inc., 84 F.3d 797, 800, 5 AD Cas. (BNA) 924, 926-27 (6th Cir. 1996); Gile v. United Airlines, Inc., 95 F.3d 492, 499, 5 AD Cas. (BNA) 1466, 1471 (7th Cir. 1996).

effectiveness in removing the workplace barrier that is impeding the individual with a disability.

If there are two possible reasonable accommodations, and one costs more or is more burdensome than the other, the employer may choose the less expensive or burdensome accommodation as long as it is effective (i.e., it would remove a workplace barrier, thereby providing the individual with an equal opportunity to apply for a position, to perform the essential functions of a position, or to gain equal access to a benefit or privilege of employment). Similarly, when there are two or more effective accommodations, the employer may choose the one that is easier to provide. In either situation, the employer does not have to show that it is an undue hardship to provide the more expensive or more difficult accommodation. If more than one accommodation is effective, "the preference of the individual with a disability should be given primary consideration. However, the employer providing the accommodation has the ultimate discretion to choose between effective accommodations."[36]

Example A: An employee with a severe learning disability has great difficulty reading. His supervisor sends him many detailed memoranda which he often has trouble understanding. However, he has no difficulty understanding oral communication. The employee requests that the employer install a computer with speech output and that his supervisor send all memoranda through electronic mail which the computer can then read to him. The supervisor asks whether a tape recorded message would accomplish the same objective and the employee agrees that it would. Since both accommodations are effective, the employer may choose to provide the supervisor and employee with a tape recorder so that the supervisor can record her memoranda and the employee can listen to them.

Example B: An attorney with a severe vision disability requests that her employer provide someone to read printed materials that she needs to review daily. The attorney explains that a reader enables her to review substantial amounts of written materials in an efficient manner. Believing that this reasonable accommodation would be too costly, the employer instead provides the attorney with a device that allows her to magnify print so that she can read it herself. The attorney can read print using this device, but with such great difficulty it significantly slows down her ability to review written materials. The magnifying device is ineffective as a reasonable accommodation because it does not provide the attorney with an equal opportunity to attain the same level of performance as her colleagues. Without an equal opportunity to attain the same level of performance, this attorney is denied an equal opportunity to compete for promotions. In this instance, failure to provide the reader, absent undue hardship, would violate the ADA.

10. How quickly must an employer respond to a request for reasonable accommodation?

An employer should respond expeditiously to a request for reasonable accommodation. If the employer and the individual with a disability need to engage in an interactive process, this too should proceed as quickly as possible.[37] Similarly, the employer should act promptly to provide the reasonable accommodation. Unnecessary delays can result in a violation of the ADA.[38]

Example A: An employer provides parking for all employees. An employee who uses a wheelchair requests from his supervisor an accessible parking space, explaining that the spaces are so narrow that there is insufficient room for his van to extend the ramp that allows him to get in and out. The supervisor does not act on the request and does not forward it to someone with authority to respond. The employee makes a second request to the supervisor. Yet, two months after the initial request, nothing has been done. Although the supervisor never definitively denies the request, the lack of action under these circumstances amounts to a denial, and thus violates the ADA.

---

36 29 C.F.R. pt. 1630 app. § 1630.9 (1997).

37 See Dalton v. Subaru-Isuzu Automotive, Inc., 141 F.3d 667, 677, 7 AD Cas. (BNA) 1872, 1880 (7th Cir. 1998).

38 In determining whether there has been an unnecessary delay in responding to a request for reasonable accommodation, relevant factors would include: (1) the reason(s) for the delay, (2) the length of the delay, (3) how much the individual with a disability and the employer each contributed to the delay, (4) what the employer was doing during the delay, and (5) whether the required accommodation was simple or complex to provide.

Example B: An employee who is blind requests adaptive equipment for her computer as a reasonable accommodation. The employer must order this equipment and is informed that it will take three months to receive delivery. No other company sells the adaptive equipment the employee needs. The employer notifies the employee of the results of its investigation and that it has ordered the equipment. Although it will take three months to receive the equipment, the employer has moved as quickly as it can to obtain it and thus there is no ADA violation resulting from the delay. The employer and employee should determine what can be done so that the employee can perform his/her job as effectively as possible while waiting for the equipment.

11. May an employer require an individual with a disability to accept a reasonable accommodation that s/he does not want?

No. An employer may not require a qualified individual with a disability to accept an accommodation. If, however, an employee needs a reasonable accommodation to perform an essential function or to eliminate a direct threat, and refuses to accept an effective accommodation, s/he may not be qualified to remain in the job.[39]

REASONABLE ACCOMMODATION AND JOB APPLICANTS

12. May an employer ask whether a reasonable accommodation is needed when an applicant has not asked for one?

An employer may tell applicants what the hiring process involves (e.g., an interview, timed written test, or job demonstration), and may ask applicants whether they will need a reasonable accommodation for this process.

During the hiring process and before a conditional offer is made, an employer generally may not ask an applicant whether s/he needs a reasonable accommodation for the job, except when the employer knows that an applicant has a disability—either because it is obvious or the applicant has voluntarily disclosed the information—and could reasonably believe that the applicant will need a reasonable accommodation to perform specific job functions. If the applicant replies that s/he needs a reasonable accommodation, the employer may inquire as to what type.[40]

After a conditional offer of employment is extended, an employer may inquire whether applicants will need reasonable accommodations related to anything connected with the job (i.e., job performance or access to benefits/privileges of the job) as long as all entering employees in the same job category are asked this question. Alternatively, an employer may ask a specific applicant if s/he needs a reasonable accommodation if the employer knows that this applicant has a disability—either because it is obvious or the applicant has voluntarily disclosed the information—and could reasonably believe that the applicant will need a reasonable accommodation. If the applicant replies that s/he needs a reasonable accommodation, the employer may inquire as to what type.[41]

13. Does an employer have to provide a reasonable accommodation to an applicant with a disability even if it believes that it will be unable to provide this individual with a reasonable accommodation on the job?

Yes. An employer must provide a reasonable accommodation to a qualified applicant with a disability that will enable the individual to have an equal opportunity to participate in the application process and to be considered for a job (unless it can show undue hardship). Thus, individuals with disabilities who meet initial requirements to be considered for a job should not be excluded from the application process because the employer speculates, based on a request for reasonable accommodation for the application process, that it will be unable to provide the individual with reasonable accommodation to perform the

---

39 See 29 C.F.R. pt. 1630 app. § 1630.9 (1997); see also Hankins v. The Gap, Inc., 84 F.3d 797, 801, 5 AD Cas. (BNA) 924, 927 (6th Cir. 1996).

40 42 U.S.C. § 12112(d)(2)(A) (1994); 29 C.F.R. § 1630.13(a) (1997). For a thorough discussion of these requirements, see Preemployment Questions and Medical Examinations, supra note 27, at 6-8, 8 FEP Manual (BNA) 405:7193-94.

41 42 U.S.C. § 12112(d)(3) (1994); 29 C.F.R. § 1630.14(b) (1997); see also Preemployment Questions and Medical Examinations, supra note 27, at 20, 8 FEP Manual (BNA) 405:7201.

job. In many instances, employers will be unable to determine whether an individual needs reasonable accommodation to perform a job based solely on a request for accommodation during the application process. And even if an individual will need reasonable accommodation to perform the job, it may not be the same type or degree of accommodation that is needed for the application process. Thus, an employer should assess the need for accommodations for the application process separately from those that may be needed to perform the job.[42]

Example A: An employer is impressed with an applicant's resume and contacts the individual to come in for an interview. The applicant, who is deaf, requests a sign language interpreter for the interview. The employer cancels the interview and refuses to consider further this applicant because it believes it would have to hire a full-time interpreter. The employer has violated the ADA. The employer should have proceeded with the interview, using a sign language interpreter (absent undue hardship), and at the interview inquired to what extent the individual would need a sign language interpreter to perform any essential functions requiring communication with other people.

Example B: An individual who has paraplegia applies for a secretarial position. Because the office has two steps at the entrance, the employer arranges for the applicant to take a typing test, a requirement of the application process, at a different location. The applicant fails the test. The employer does not have to provide any further reasonable accommodations for this individual because she is no longer qualified to continue with the application process.

REASONABLE ACCOMMODATION RELATED TO THE BENEFITS AND PRIVILEGES OF EMPLOYMENT[43]

The ADA requires employers to provide reasonable accommodations so that employees with disabilities can enjoy the "benefits and privileges of employment" equal to those enjoyed by similarly-situated employees without disabilities. Benefits and privileges of employment include, but are not limited to, employer-sponsored: (1) training, (2) services (e.g., employee assistance programs (EAP's), credit unions, cafeterias, lounges, gymnasiums, auditoriums, transportation), and (3) parties or other social functions (e.g., parties to celebrate retirements and birthdays, and company outings).[44] If an employee with a disability needs a reasonable accommodation in order to gain access to, and have an equal opportunity to participate in, these benefits and privileges, then the employer must provide the accommodation unless it can show undue hardship.

14. Does an employer have to provide reasonable accommodation to enable an employee with a disability to have equal access to information communicated in the workplace to non-disabled employees?

Yes. Employers provide information to employees through different means, including computers, bulletin boards, mailboxes, posters, and public address systems. Employers must ensure that employees with disabilities have access to information that is provided to other similarly-situated employees without disabilities, regardless of whether they need it to perform their jobs.

Example A: An employee who is blind has adaptive equipment for his computer that integrates him into the network with other employees, thus allowing communication via electronic mail and access to the computer bulletin board. When the employer installs upgraded computer equipment, it must provide new adaptive equipment in order for the employee to be integrated into the new networks, absent undue hardship. Alternative methods of communication (e.g., sending written or telephone messages to the employee instead of electronic mail) are likely to be ineffective substitutes since electronic mail is used by every employee and there is no effective way to ensure that each

---

42 See Question 12, supra, for the circumstances under which an employer may ask an applicant whether s/he will need reasonable accommodation to perform specific job functions.

43 The discussions and examples in this section assume that there is only one effective accommodation and that the reasonable accommodation will not cause undue hardship.

44 See 29 C.F.R. pt. 1630 app. § 1630.9 (1997).

one will always use alternative measures to ensure that the blind employee receives the same information that is being transmitted via computer.

Example B: An employer authorizes the Human Resources Director to use a public address system to remind employees about special meetings and to make certain announcements. In order to make this information accessible to a deaf employee, the Human Resources Director arranges to send in advance an electronic mail message to the deaf employee conveying the information that will be broadcast. The Human Resources Director is the only person who uses the public address system; therefore, the employer can ensure that all public address messages are sent, via electronic mail, to the deaf employee. Thus, the employer is providing this employee with equal access to office communications.

15. Must an employer provide reasonable accommodation so that an employee may attend training programs?

Yes. Employers must provide reasonable accommodation (e.g., sign language interpreters; written materials produced in alternative formats, such as braille, large print, or on audio-cassette) that will provide employees with disabilities with an equal opportunity to participate in employer-sponsored training, absent undue hardship. This obligation extends to in-house training, as well as to training provided by an outside entity. Similarly, the employer has an obligation to provide reasonable accommodation whether the training occurs on the employer's premises or elsewhere.

Example A: XYZ Corp. has signed a contract with Super Trainers, Inc., to provide mediation training at its facility to all of XYZ's Human Resources staff. One staff member is blind and requests that materials be provided in braille. Super Trainers refuses to provide the materials in braille. XYZ maintains that it is the responsibility of Super Trainers and sees no reason why it should have to arrange and pay for the braille copy.

Both XYZ (as an employer covered under Title I of the ADA) and Super Trainers (as a public accommodation covered under Title III of the ADA)[45] have obligations to provide materials in alternative formats. This fact, however, does not excuse either one from their respective obligations. If Super Trainers refuses to provide the braille version, despite its Title III obligations, XYZ still retains its obligation to provide it as a reasonable accommodation, absent undue hardship.

Employers arranging with an outside entity to provide training may wish to avoid such problems by specifying in the contract who has the responsibility to provide appropriate reasonable accommodations. Similarly, employers should ensure that any offsite training will be held in an accessible facility if they have an employee who, because of a disability, requires such an accommodation.

Example B: XYZ Corp. arranges for one of its employees to provide CPR training. This three-hour program is optional. A deaf employee wishes to take the training and requests a sign language interpreter. XYZ must provide the interpreter because the CPR training is a benefit that XYZ offers all employees, even though it is optional.

TYPES OF REASONABLE ACCOMMODATIONS RELATED TO JOB PERFORMANCE[46]

Below are discussed certain types of reasonable accommodations related to job performance.

Job Restructuring

Job restructuring includes modifications such as:

---

45 42 U.S.C. §§ 12181(7), 12182(1)(A), (2)(A)(iii) (1994).

46 The discussions and examples in this section assume that there is only one effective accommodation and that the reasonable accommodation will not cause undue hardship. The types of reasonable accommodations discussed in this section are not exhaustive. For example, employees with disabilities may request reasonable accommodations to modify the work environment, such as changes to the ventilation system or relocation of a work space. See the Appendix [not reproduced here—Eds.] for additional resources to identify other possible reasonable accommodations.

- reallocating or redistributing marginal job functions that an employee is unable to perform because of a disability; and
- altering when and/or how a function, essential or marginal, is performed.[47]

An employer never has to reallocate essential functions as a reasonable accommodation, but can do so if it wishes.

16. If, as a reasonable accommodation, an employer restructures an employee's job to eliminate some marginal functions, may the employer require the employee to take on other marginal functions that s/he can perform?

Yes. An employer may switch the marginal functions of two (or more) employees in order to restructure a job as a reasonable accommodation.

Example: A cleaning crew works in an office building. One member of the crew wears a prosthetic leg which enables him to walk very well, but climbing steps is painful and difficult. Although he can perform his essential functions without problems, he cannot perform the marginal function of sweeping the steps located throughout the building. The marginal functions of a second crew member include cleaning the small kitchen in the employee's lounge, which is something the first crew member can perform. The employer can switch the marginal functions performed by these two employees.

Leave

Permitting the use of accrued paid leave, or unpaid leave, is a form of reasonable accommodation when necessitated by an employee's disability.[48] An employer does not have to provide paid leave beyond that which is provided to similarly-situated employees. Employers should allow an employee with a disability to exhaust accrued paid leave first and then provide unpaid leave.[49] For example, if employees get 10 days of paid leave, and an employee with a disability needs 15 days of leave, the employer should allow the individual to use 10 days of paid leave and 5 days of unpaid leave.

An employee with a disability may need leave for a number of reasons related to the disability, including, but not limited to:

- obtaining medical treatment (e.g., surgery, psychotherapy, substance abuse treatment, or dialysis); rehabilitation services; or physical or occupational therapy;
- recuperating from an illness or an episodic manifestation of the disability;
- obtaining repairs on a wheelchair, accessible van, or prosthetic device;
- avoiding temporary adverse conditions in the work environment (for example, an air-conditioning breakdown causing unusually warm temperatures that could seriously harm an employee with multiple sclerosis);
- training a service animal (e.g., a guide dog); or
- receiving training in the use of braille or to learn sign language.

17. May an employer apply a "no-fault" leave policy, under which employees are automatically terminated after they have been on leave for a certain period of time, to an employee with a disability who needs leave beyond the set period?

No. If an employee with a disability needs additional unpaid leave as a reasonable accommodation, the employer must modify its "no-fault" leave policy to provide the employee with the additional leave, unless it can show that: (1) there is another effective accommodation that would enable the person to perform the essential functions of his/her position, or (2) granting additional leave would cause an undue hardship. Modifying workplace policies, including leave

47 42 U.S.C. § 12111(9)(B) (1994); 29 C.F.R. pt. 1630 app. §§ 1630.2(o), 1630.9 (1997); see Benson v. Northwest Airlines, Inc., 62 F.3d 1108, 1112-13, 4 AD Cas. (BNA) 1234, 1236-37 (8th Cir. 1995).

48 29 C.F.R. pt. 1630 app. § 1630.2(o) (1997). See Cehrs v. Northeast Ohio Alzheimer's, 155 F.3d 775, 782, 8 AD Cas. (BNA) 825, 830-31 (6th Cir. 1998). An employee who needs leave, or a part-time or modified schedule, as a reasonable accommodation also may be entitled to leave under the Family and Medical Leave Act. See Questions 21 and 23, infra.

49 See A Technical Assistance Manual on the Employment Provisions (Title I) of the Americans with Disabilities Act, at 3.10(4), 8 FEP Manual (BNA) 405:6981, 7011 (1992) [hereinafter TAM].

policies, is a form of reasonable accommodation.[50]

18. Does an employer have to hold open an employee's job as a reasonable accommodation?

Yes. An employee with a disability who is granted leave as a reasonable accommodation is entitled to return to his/her same position unless the employer demonstrates that holding open the position would impose an undue hardship.[51]

If an employer cannot hold a position open during the entire leave period without incurring undue hardship, the employer must consider whether it has a vacant, equivalent position for which the employee is qualified and to which the employee can be reassigned to continue his/her leave for a specific period of time and then, at the conclusion of the leave, can be returned to this new position.[52]

Example: An employee needs eight months of leave for treatment and recuperation related to a disability. The employer grants the request, but after four months the employer determines that it can no longer hold open the position for the remaining four months without incurring undue hardship. The employer must consider whether it has a vacant, equivalent position to which the employee can be reassigned for the remaining four months of leave, at the end of which time the employee would return to work in that new position. If an equivalent position is not available, the employer must look for a vacant position at a lower level. Continued leave is not required as a reasonable accommodation if a vacant position at a lower level is also unavailable.

19. Can an employer penalize an employee for work missed during leave taken as a reasonable accommodation?

No. To do so would be retaliation for the employee's use of a reasonable accommodation to which s/he is entitled under the law.[53] Moreover, such punishment would make the leave an ineffective accommodation, thus making an employer liable for failing to provide a reasonable accommodation.[54]

Example A: A salesperson took five months of leave as a reasonable accommodation. The company compares the sales records of all salespeople over a one-year period, and any employee whose sales fall more than 25% below the median sales performance of all employees is automatically terminated. The employer terminates the salesperson because she had fallen below the required performance standard. The company did not consider that the reason for her lower sales performance was her five-month leave of absence; nor did it assess her productivity during the period she did work (i.e., prorate her productivity).

Penalizing the salesperson in this manner constitutes retaliation and a denial of reasonable accommodation.

Example B: Company X is having a reduction-in-force. The company decides that any employee who has missed more than four weeks in the past year will be terminated. An employee took five weeks of leave for treatment of his disability. The company cannot count those five weeks in determining whether to ter-

---

50 42 U.S.C. § 12111(9)(B) (1994); 29 C.F.R. § 1630.2(o)(2)(ii) (1997). See US Airways, Inc. v. Barnett, 535 U.S. ___, 122 S. Ct. 1516, 1521 (2002). See also Question 24, infra. While undue hardship cannot be based solely on the existence of a no-fault leave policy, the employer may be able to show undue hardship based on an individualized assessment showing the disruption to the employer's operations if additional leave is granted beyond the period allowed by the policy. In determining whether undue hardship exists, the employer should consider how much additional leave is needed (e.g., two weeks, six months, one year?).

51 See Schmidt v. Safeway Inc., 864 F. Supp. 991, 996-97, 3 AD Cas. (BNA) 1141, 1145-46 (D. Or. 1994); Corbett v. National Products Co., 4 AD Cas. (BNA) 987, 990 (E.D. Pa. 1995).

52 See EEOC Enforcement Guidance: Workers' Compensation and the ADA at 16, 8 FEP Manual (BNA) 405:7391, 7399 (1996) [hereinafter Workers' Compensation and the ADA]. See also [footnotes 79-96 and accompanying text], infra, for information on reassignment as a reasonable accommodation.

53 Cf. Kiel v. Select Artificials, 142 F.3d 1077, 1080, 8 AD Cas. (BNA) 43, 44 (8th Cir. 1998).

54 See Criado v. IBM, 145 F.3d 437, 444-45, 8 AD Cas. (BNA) 336, 341 (1st Cir. 1998).

minate this employee.[55]

20. When an employee requests leave as a reasonable accommodation, may an employer provide an accommodation that requires him/her to remain on the job instead?

Yes, if the employer's reasonable accommodation would be effective and eliminate the need for leave.[56] An employer need not provide an employee's preferred accommodation as long as the employer provides an effective accommodation.[57] Accordingly, in lieu of providing leave, an employer may provide a reasonable accommodation that requires an employee to remain on the job (e.g., reallocation of marginal functions or temporary transfer) as long as it does not interfere with the employee's ability to address his/her medical needs. The employer is obligated, however, to restore the employee's full duties or to return the employee to his/her original position once s/he no longer needs the reasonable accommodation.

Example A: An employee with emphysema requests ten weeks of leave for surgery and recuperation related to his disability. In discussing this request with the employer, the employee states that he could return to work after seven weeks if, during his first three weeks back, he could work part-time and eliminate two marginal functions that require lots of walking. If the employer provides these accommodations, then it can require the employee to return to work after seven weeks.

Example B: An employee's disability is getting more severe and her doctor recommends surgery to counteract some of the effects. After receiving the employee's request for leave for the surgery, the employer proposes that it provide certain equipment which it believes will mitigate the effects of the disability and delay the need for leave to get surgery. The employer's proposed accommodation is not effective because it interferes with the employee's ability to get medical treatment.

21. How should an employer handle leave for an employee covered by both the ADA and the Family and Medical Leave Act (FMLA)?[58]

An employer should determine an employee's rights under each statute separately, and then consider whether the two statutes overlap regarding the appropriate actions to take.[59]

Under the ADA, an employee who needs leave related to his/her disability is entitled to such leave if there is no other effective accommodation and the leave will not cause undue hardship. An employer must allow the individual to use any accrued paid leave first, but, if that is insufficient to cover the entire period, then the employer should grant unpaid leave. An employer must continue an employee's health insurance benefits during his/her leave period only if it does so for other employees in a similar leave status. As for the employee's position, the ADA requires that the employer hold it open while the employee is on leave unless it can show that doing so causes undue hardship. When the employee is ready to return to work, the employer must allow the individual to return to the same position (assuming that there was no undue hardship in holding it open) if the employee is still qualified (i.e., the employee can perform the essential functions of the position with or without reasonable accommodation).

---

55 But see Matthews v. Commonwealth Edison Co., 128 F.3d 1194, 1197-98, 7 AD Cas. (BNA) 1651, 1653-54 (7th Cir. 1997) (an employee who, because of a heart attack, missed several months of work and returned on a part-time basis until health permitted him to work full-time, could be terminated during a RIF based on his lower productivity). In reaching this decision, the Seventh Circuit failed to consider that the employee needed leave and a modified schedule as reasonable accommodations for his disability, and that the accommodations became meaningless when he was penalized for using them.

56 If an employee, however, qualifies for leave under the Family and Medical Leave Act, an employer may not require him/her to remain on the job with an adjustment in lieu of taking leave. See 29 C.F.R. § 825.702(d)(1) (1997).

57 See Question 9, supra.

58 For more detailed information on issues raised by the interplay between these statutes, refer to the FMLA/ADA Fact Sheet listed in the Appendix [not reproduced here—Eds.].

59 Employers should remember that many employees eligible for FMLA leave will not be entitled to leave as a reasonable accommodation under the ADA, either because they do not meet the ADA's definition of disability or, if they do have an ADA disability, the need for leave is unrelated to that disability.

If it is an undue hardship under the ADA to hold open an employee's position during a period of leave, or an employee is no longer qualified to return to his/her original position, then the employer must reassign the employee (absent undue hardship) to a vacant position for which s/he is qualified.

Under the FMLA, an eligible employee is entitled to a maximum of 12 weeks of leave per 12 month period. The FMLA guarantees the right of the employee to return to the same position or to an equivalent one.[60] An employer must allow the individual to use any accrued paid leave first, but if that is insufficient to cover the entire period, then the employer should grant unpaid leave. The FMLA requires an employer to continue the employee's health insurance coverage during the leave period, provided the employee pays his/her share of the premiums.

Example A: An employee with an ADA disability needs 13 weeks of leave for treatment related to the disability. The employee is eligible under the FMLA for 12 weeks of leave (the maximum available), so this period of leave constitutes both FMLA leave and a reasonable accommodation. Under the FMLA, the employer could deny the employee the thirteenth week of leave. But, because the employee is also covered under the ADA, the employer cannot deny the request for the thirteenth week of leave unless it can show undue hardship. The employer may consider the impact on its operations caused by the initial 12-week absence, along with other undue hardship factors.[61]

Example B: An employee with an ADA disability has taken 10 weeks of FMLA leave and is preparing to return to work. The employer wants to put her in an equivalent position rather than her original one. Although this is permissible under the FMLA, the ADA requires that the employer return the employee to her original position. Unless the employer can show that this would cause an undue hardship, or that the employee is no longer qualified for her original position (with or without reasonable accommodation), the employer must reinstate the employee to her original position.

Example C: An employee with an ADA disability has taken 12 weeks of FMLA leave. He notifies his employer that he is ready to return to work, but he no longer is able to perform the essential functions of his position or an equivalent position. Under the FMLA, the employer could terminate his employment,[62] but under the ADA the employer must consider whether the employee could perform the essential functions with reasonable accommodation (e.g., additional leave, part-time schedule, job restructuring, or use of specialized equipment). If not, the ADA requires the employer to reassign the employee if there is a vacant position available for which he is qualified, with or without reasonable accommodation, and there is no undue hardship.

Modified or Part-Time Schedule

22. Must an employer allow an employee with a disability to work a modified or part-time schedule as a reasonable accommodation, absent undue hardship?

Yes.[63] A modified schedule may involve adjusting arrival or departure times, providing periodic breaks, altering when certain functions are performed, allowing an employee to use accrued paid leave, or providing additional unpaid leave. An employer must provide a modified or part-time schedule when required as a reasonable accommodation, absent undue hardship, even if it does not provide such schedules for other employees.[64]

Example A: An employee with HIV infection must take medication on a strict schedule. The

60 29 C.F.R. §§ 825.214(a), 825.215 (1997).

61 For further information on the undue hardship factors, see infra [text accompanying notes 112-124].

62 29 C.F.R. § 825.702(c)(4) (1997).

63 42 U.S.C. § 12111(9)(B) (1994); see Ralph v. Lucent Technologies, Inc., 135 F.3d 166, 172, 7 AD Cas. (BNA) 1345, 1349 (1st Cir. 1998) (a modified schedule is a form of reasonable accommodation).

64 See US Airways, Inc. v. Barnett, 535 U.S. ___, 122 S. Ct. 1516, 1521 (2002).

medication causes extreme nausea about one hour after ingestion, and generally lasts about 45 minutes. The employee asks that he be allowed to take a daily 45-minute break when the nausea occurs. The employer must grant this request absent undue hardship.

For certain positions, the time during which an essential function is performed may be critical. This could affect whether an employer can grant a request to modify an employee's schedule.[65] Employers should carefully assess whether modifying the hours could significantly disrupt their operations—that is, cause undue hardship—or whether the essential functions may be performed at different times with little or no impact on the operations or the ability of other employees to perform their jobs.

If modifying an employee's schedule poses an undue hardship, an employer must consider reassignment to a vacant position that would enable the employee to work during the hours requested.[66]

Example B: A day care worker requests that she be allowed to change her hours from 7:00 a.m. - 3:00 p.m. to 10:00 a.m. - 6:00 p.m. because of her disability. The day care center is open from 7:00 a.m. - 7:00 p.m. and it will still have sufficient coverage at the beginning of the morning if it grants the change in hours. In this situation, the employer must provide the reasonable accommodation.

Example C: An employee works for a morning newspaper, operating the printing presses which run between 10 p.m. and 3 a.m. Due to her disability, she needs to work in the daytime. The essential function of her position, operating the printing presses, requires that she work at night because the newspaper cannot be printed during the daytime hours. Since the employer cannot modify her hours, it must consider whether it can reassign her to a different position.

23. How should an employer handle requests for modified or part-time schedules for an employee covered by both the ADA and the Family and Medical Leave Act (FMLA)?[67]

An employer should determine an employee's rights under each statute separately, and then consider whether the two statutes overlap regarding the appropriate actions to take.

Under the ADA, an employee who needs a modified or part-time schedule because of his/her disability is entitled to such a schedule if there is no other effective accommodation and it will not cause undue hardship. If there is undue hardship, the employer must reassign the employee if there is a vacant position for which s/he is qualified and which would allow the employer to grant the modified or part-time schedule (absent undue hardship).[68] An employee receiving a part-time schedule as a reasonable accommodation is entitled only to the benefits, including health insurance, that other part-time employees receive. Thus, if non-disabled part-time workers are not provided with health insurance, then the employer does not have to provide such coverage to an employee with a disability who is given a part-time schedule as a reasonable accommodation.

Under the FMLA, an eligible employee is entitled

---

65 Certain courts have characterized attendance as an "essential function." See, e.g., Carr v. Reno, 23 F.3d 525, 530, 3 AD Cas. (BNA) 434, 438 (D.C. Cir. 1994); Jackson v. Department of Veterans Admin., 22 F.3d 277, 278-79, 3 AD Cas. (BNA) 483, 484 (11th Cir. 1994). Attendance, however, is not an essential function as defined by the ADA because it is not one of "the fundamental job *duties* of the employment position." 29 C.F.R. § 1630.2(n)(1) (1997) (emphasis added). As the regulations make clear, essential functions are duties to be performed. 29 C.F.R. § 1630.2(n)(2) (1997). See Haschmann v. Time Warner Entertainment Co., 151 F.3d 591, 602, 8 AD Cas. (BNA) 692, 701 (7th Cir. 1998); Cehrs v. Northeast Ohio Alzheimer's, 155 F.3d 775, 782-83, 8 AD Cas. (BNA) 825, 830-31 (6th Cir. 1998). On the other hand, attendance is relevant to job performance and employers need not grant all requests for a modified schedule. To the contrary, if the time during which an essential function is performed is integral to its successful completion, then an employer may deny a request to modify an employee's schedule as an undue hardship.

66 Employers covered under the Family and Medical Leave Act (FMLA) should determine whether any denial of leave or a modified schedule is also permissible under that law. See 29 C.F.R. § 825.203 (1997).

67 For more detailed information on issues raised by the interplay between these statutes, refer to the FMLA/ADA Fact Sheet listed in the Appendix [not reproduced here—Eds.].

68 See infra [text accompanying notes 75-96] for more information on reassignment, including under what circumstances an employer and employee may voluntarily agree that a transfer is preferable to having the employee remain in his/her current position.

to take leave intermittently or on a part-time basis, when medically necessary, until s/he has used up the equivalent of 12 workweeks in a 12-month period. When such leave is foreseeable based on planned medical treatment, an employer may require the employee to temporarily transfer (for the duration of the leave) to an available alternative position, with equivalent pay and benefits, for which the employee is qualified and which better suits his/her reduced hours.[69] An employer always must maintain the employee's existing level of coverage under a group health plan during the period of FMLA leave, provided the employee pays his/her share of the premium.[70]

Example: An employee with an ADA disability requests that she be excused from work one day a week for the next six months because of her disability. If this employee is eligible for a modified schedule under the FMLA, the employer must provide the requested leave under that statute if it is medically necessary, even if the leave would be an undue hardship under the ADA.

Modified Workplace Policies

24. Is it a reasonable accommodation to modify a workplace policy?

Yes. It is a reasonable accommodation to modify a workplace policy when necessitated by an individual's disability-related limitations,[71] absent undue hardship. But, reasonable accommodation only requires that the employer modify the policy for an employee who requires such action because of a disability; therefore, the employer may continue to apply the policy to all other employees.

Example: An employer has a policy prohibiting employees from eating or drinking at their workstations. An employee with insulin-dependent diabetes explains to her employer that she may occasionally take too much insulin and, in order to avoid going into insulin shock, she must immediately eat a candy bar or drink fruit juice. The employee requests permission to keep such food at her workstation and to eat or drink when her insulin level necessitates. The employer must modify its policy to grant this request, absent undue hardship. Similarly, an employer might have to modify a policy to allow an employee with a disability to bring in a small refrigerator, or to use the employer's refrigerator, to store medication that must be taken during working hours.

Granting an employee time off from work or an adjusted work schedule as a reasonable accommodation may involve modifying leave or attendance procedures or policies. For example, it would be a reasonable accommodation to modify a policy requiring employees to schedule vacation time in advance if an otherwise qualified individual with a disability needed to use accrued vacation time on an unscheduled basis because of disability-related medical problems, barring undue hardship.[72] Furthermore, an employer may be required to provide additional leave to an employee with a disability as a reasonable accommodation in spite of a "no-fault" leave policy, unless the provision of such leave would impose an undue hardship.[73]

In some instances, an employer's refusal to modify a workplace policy, such as a leave or attendance policy, could constitute disparate treatment as well as a failure to provide a reasonable accommodation. For example, an employer may have a policy requiring employees to notify supervisors before 9:00 a.m. if they are unable to report to work. If an employer would excuse an employee from complying with this policy because of emergency hospitalization due to a

---

69 29 C.F.R. § 825.204 (1997); see also special rules governing intermittent leave for instructional employees at §§ 825.601, 825.602.

70 29 C.F.R. §§ 825.209, 825.210 (1997).

71 42 U.S.C. § 12111(9)(B) (1994); 29 C.F.R. § 1630.2(o)(2)(ii) (1997). See US Airways, Inc. v. Barnett, 535 U.S. ___, 122 S. Ct. 1516, 1521 (2002).

72 See Dutton v. Johnson County Bd. of Comm'rs, 868 F. Supp. 1260, 1264-65, 3 AD Cas. (BNA) 1614, 1618 (D. Kan. 1994).

73 See 29 C.F.R. pt. 1630 app. § 1630.15(b), (c) (1997). See also Question 17, supra.

car accident, then the employer must do the same thing when the emergency hospitalization is due to a disability.[74]

Reassignment[75]

The ADA specifically lists "reassignment to a vacant position" as a form of reasonable accommodation.[76] This type of reasonable accommodation must be provided to an employee who, because of a disability, can no longer perform the essential functions of his/her current position, with or without reasonable accommodation, unless the employer can show that it would be an undue hardship.[77]

An employee must be "qualified" for the new position. An employee is "qualified" for a position if s/he: (1) satisfies the requisite skill, experience, education, and other job-related requirements of the position, and (2) can perform the essential functions of the new position, with or without reasonable accommodation.[78] The employee does not need to be the best qualified individual for the position in order to obtain it as a reassignment.

There is no obligation for the employer to assist the individual to become qualified. Thus, the employer does not have to provide training so that the employee acquires necessary skills to take a job.[79] The employer, however, would have to provide an employee with a disability who is being reassigned with any training that is normally provided to anyone hired for or transferred to the position.

Example A: An employer is considering reassigning an employee with a disability to a position which requires the ability to speak Spanish in order to perform an essential function. The employee never learned Spanish and wants the employer to send him to a course to learn Spanish. The employer is not required to provide this training as part of the obligation to make a reassignment. Therefore, the employee is not qualified for this position.

Example B: An employer is considering reassigning an employee with a disability to a position in which she will contract for goods and services. The employee is qualified for the position. The employer has its own specialized rules regarding contracting that necessitate training all individuals hired for these positions. In this situation, the employer must provide the employee with this specialized training.

Before considering reassignment as a reasonable accommodation, employers should first consider those accommodations that would enable an employee to

---

74 But cf. Miller v. Nat'l Casualty Co., 61 F.3d 627, 629-30, 4 AD Cas. (BNA) 1089, 1090 (8th Cir. 1995) (court refuses to find that employee's sister had requested reasonable accommodation despite the fact that the sister informed the employer that the employee was having a medical crisis necessitating emergency hospitalization).

75 For information on how reassignment may apply to employers who provide light duty positions, see Workers' Compensation and the ADA, supra note 52, at 20-23, 8 FEP Manual (BNA) 405:7401-03.

76 42 U.S.C. § 12111(9)(B) (1994); 29 C.F.R. § 1630.2(o)(2)(ii) (1997). See Benson v. Northwest Airlines, Inc., 62 F.3d 1108, 1114, 4 AD Cas. (BNA) 1234, 1238 (8th Cir. 1995); Monette v. Electronic Data Sys. Corp., 90 F.3d 1173, 1187, 5 AD Cas. (BNA) 1326, 1338 (6th Cir. 1996); Gile v. United Airlines, Inc., 95 F.3d 492, 498, 5 AD Cas. (BNA) 1466, 1471 (7th Cir. 1996). Reassignment is available only to employees, not to applicants. 29 C.F.R. pt. 1630 app. § 1630.2(o) (1997).

77 29 C.F.R. pt. 1630 app. § 1630.2(o) (1997); see Haysman v. Food Lion, Inc., 893 F. Supp. 1092, 1104, 4 AD Cas. (BNA) 1297, 1305 (S.D. Ga. 1995). Some courts have found that an employee who is unable to perform the essential functions of his/her current position is unqualified to receive a reassignment. See, e.g., Schmidt v. Methodist Hosp. of Indiana, Inc., 89 F.3d 342, 345, 5 AD Cas. (BNA) 1340, 1342 (7th Cir. 1996); Pangalos v. Prudential Ins. Co. of Am., 5 AD Cas. (BNA) 1825, 1826 (E.D. Pa. 1996). These decisions, however, nullify Congress' inclusion of reassignment in the ADA. An employee requires a reassignment only if s/he is unable to continue performing the essential functions of his/her current position, with or without reasonable accommodation. Thus, an employer must provide reassignment either when reasonable accommodation in an employee's current job would cause undue hardship or when it would not be possible. See Aka v. Washington Hosp. Ctr., 156 F.3d 1284, 1300-01, 8 AD Cas. (BNA) 1093, 1107-08 (D.C. Cir. 1998); Dalton v. Subaru-Isuzu Automotive, Inc., 141 F.3d 667, 678, 7 AD Cas. (BNA) 1872, 1880 (7th Cir. 1998); see also ADA and Psychiatric Disabilities, supra note 27, at 28, 8 FEP Manual (BNA) 405:7476; Workers' Compensation and the ADA, supra note 52, at 17-18, 8 FEP Manual (BNA) 405:7399-7400.

78 29 C.F.R. § 1630.2(m) (1997); 29 C.F.R. pt. 1630 app. §§ 1630.2(m), 1630.2(o) (1997). See Stone v. Mount Vernon, 118 F.3d 92, 100-01, 6 AD Cas. (BNA) 1685, 1693 (2d Cir. 1997).

79 See Quintana v. Sound Distribution Corp., 6 AD Cas. (BNA) 842, 846 (S.D.N.Y. 1997).

remain in his/her current position. Reassignment is the reasonable accommodation of last resort and is required only after it has been determined that: (1) there are no effective accommodations that will enable the employee to perform the essential functions of his/her current position, or (2) all other reasonable accommodations would impose an undue hardship.[80] However, if both the employer and the employee voluntarily agree that transfer is preferable to remaining in the current position with some form of reasonable accommodation, then the employer may transfer the employee.

"Vacant" means that the position is available when the employee asks for reasonable accommodation, or that the employer knows that it will become available within a reasonable amount of time. A "reasonable amount of time" should be determined on a case-by-case basis considering relevant facts, such as whether the employer, based on experience, can anticipate that an appropriate position will become vacant within a short period of time.[81] A position is considered vacant even if an employer has posted a notice or announcement seeking applications for that position. The employer does not have to bump an employee from a job in order to create a vacancy; nor does it have to create a new position.[82]

> Example C: An employer is seeking a reassignment for an employee with a disability. There are no vacant positions today, but the employer has just learned that another employee resigned and that that position will become vacant in four weeks. The impending vacancy is equivalent to the position currently held by the employee with a disability. If the employee is qualified for that position, the employer must offer it to him.

> Example D: An employer is seeking a reassignment for an employee with a disability. There are no vacant positions today, but the employer has just learned that an employee in an equivalent position plans to retire in six months. Although the employer knows that the employee with a disability is qualified for this position, the employer does not have to offer this position to her because six months is beyond a "reasonable amount of time." (If, six months from now, the employer decides to advertise the position, it must allow the individual to apply for that position and give the application the consideration it deserves.)

The employer must reassign the individual to a vacant position that is equivalent in terms of pay, status, or other relevant factors (e.g., benefits, geographical location) if the employee is qualified for the position. If there is no vacant equivalent position, the employer must reassign the employee to a vacant lower level position for which the individual is qualified. Assuming there is more than one vacancy for which the employee is qualified, the employer must place the individual in the position that comes closest to the employee's current position in terms of pay, status, etc.[83] If it is unclear which position comes closest, the employer should consult with the employee about his/her preference before determining the position to which the employee will be reassigned. Reassignment does not include giving an employee a promotion. Thus, an employee must compete for any vacant position that would constitute a promotion.

25. Is a probationary employee entitled to reassignment?

Employers cannot deny a reassignment to an employee solely because s/he is designated as "probationary." An employee with a disability is eligible for reassignment to a new position, regardless of whether s/he is considered "probationary," as long as the employee adequately performed the essential functions of the position, with or without reasonable accommodation, before the need for a reassignment arose.

The longer the period of time in which an employee has adequately performed the essential functions, with or without reasonable accommodation, the more

---

80 See 29 C.F.R. pt. 1630 app. § 1630.2(o) (1997); Senate Report, supra note 6, at 31; House Education and Labor Report, supra note 6, at 63.

81 For suggestions on what the employee can do while waiting for a position to become vacant within a reasonable amount of time, see note 89, infra.

82 See 29 C.F.R. pt. 1630 app. § 1630.2(o) (1997); see also White v. York Int'l Corp., 45 F.3d 357, 362, 3 AD Cas. (BNA) 1746, 1750 (10th Cir. 1995).

83 See 29 C.F.R. pt. 1630 app. § 1630.2(o) (1997).

likely it is that reassignment is appropriate if the employee becomes unable to continue performing the essential functions of the current position due to a disability. If, however, the probationary employee has never adequately performed the essential functions, with or without reasonable accommodation, then s/he is not entitled to reassignment because s/he was never "qualified" for the original position. In this situation, the employee is similar to an applicant who applies for a job for which s/he is not qualified, and then requests reassignment. Applicants are not entitled to reassignment.

Example A: An employer designates all new employees as "probationary" for one year. An employee has been working successfully for nine months when she becomes disabled in a car accident. The employee, due to her disability, is unable to continue performing the essential functions of her current position, with or without reasonable accommodation, and seeks a reassignment. She is entitled to a reassignment if there is a vacant position for which she is qualified and it would not pose an undue hardship.

Example B: A probationary employee has been working two weeks, but has been unable to perform the essential functions of the job because of his disability. There are no reasonable accommodations that would permit the individual to perform the essential functions of the position, so the individual requests a reassignment. The employer does not have to provide a reassignment (even if there is a vacant position) because, as it turns out, the individual was never qualified—i.e., the individual was never able to perform the essential functions of the position, with or without reasonable accommodation, for which he was hired.

26. Must an employer offer reassignment as a reasonable accommodation if it does not allow any of its employees to transfer from one position to another?

Yes. The ADA requires employers to provide reasonable accommodations to individuals with disabilities, including reassignment, even though they are not available to others. Therefore, an employer who does not normally transfer employees would still have to reassign an employee with a disability, unless it could show that the reassignment caused an undue hardship. And, if an employer has a policy prohibiting transfers, it would have to modify that policy in order to reassign an employee with a disability, unless it could show undue hardship.[84]

27. Is an employer's obligation to offer reassignment to a vacant position limited to those vacancies within an employee's office, branch, agency, department, facility, personnel system (if the employer has more than a single personnel system), or geographical area?

No. This is true even if the employer has a policy prohibiting transfers from one office, branch, agency, department, facility, personnel system, or geographical area to another. The ADA contains no language limiting the obligation to reassign only to positions within an office, branch, agency, etc.[85] Rather, the extent to which an employer must search for a vacant position will be an issue of undue hardship.[86] If an employee is being reassigned to a different geographical area, the

---

84 See US Airways, Inc. v. Barnett, 535 U.S. ___, 122 S. Ct. 1516, 1521, 1524 (2002); see also Aka v. Washington Hosp. Ctr., 156 F.3d 1284, 1304-05, 8 AD Cas. (BNA) 1093, 1110-11 (D.C. Cir. 1998); United States v. Denver, 943 F. Supp. 1304, 1312, 6 AD Cas. (BNA) 245, 252 (D. Colo. 1996). See also Question 24, supra.

85 42 U.S.C. § 12111(9)(B) (1994); 29 C.F.R. § 1630.2(o)(2)(ii) (1997); see Hendricks-Robinson v. Excel Corp., 154 F.3d 685, 695, 8 AD Cas. (BNA) 875, 883 (7th Cir. 1998); see generally Dalton v. Subaru-Isuzu Automotive, Inc., 141 F.3d 667, 677-78, 7 AD Cas. (BNA) 1872, 1880-81 (7th Cir. 1998).

86 See Gile v. United Airlines, Inc., 95 F.3d 492, 499, 5 AD Cas. (BNA) 1466, 1472 (7th Cir. 1996); see generally United States v. Denver, 943 F. Supp. 1304, 1311-13, 6 AD Cas. (BNA) 245, 251-52 (D. Colo. 1996). Some courts have limited the obligation to provide a reassignment to positions within the same department or facility in which the employee currently works, except when the employer's standard practice is to provide inter-department or inter-facility transfers for all employees. See, e.g., Emrick v. Libbey-Owens-Ford Co., 875 F. Supp. 393, 398, 4 AD Cas. (BNA) 1, 4-5 (E.D. Tex. 1995). However, the ADA requires modification of workplace policies, such as transfer policies, as a form of reasonable accommodation. See Question 24, supra. Therefore, policies limiting transfers cannot be a per se bar to reassigning someone outside his/her department or facility. Furthermore, the ADA requires employers to provide reasonable accommodations, including reassignment, regardless of whether such accommodations are routinely granted to non-disabled employees. See Question 26, supra.

employee must pay for any relocation expenses unless the employer routinely pays such expenses when granting voluntary transfers to other employees.

28. Does an employer have to notify an employee with a disability about vacant positions, or is it the employee's responsibility to learn what jobs are vacant?

The employer is in the best position to know which jobs are vacant or will become vacant within a reasonable period of time.[87] In order to narrow the search for potential vacancies, the employer, as part of the interactive process, should ask the employee about his/her qualifications and interests. Based on this information, the employer is obligated to inform an employee about vacant positions for which s/he may be eligible as a reassignment. However, an employee should assist the employer in identifying appropriate vacancies to the extent that the employee has access to information about them. If the employer does not know whether the employee is qualified for a specific position, the employer can discuss with the employee his/her qualifications.[88]

An employer should proceed as expeditiously as possible in determining whether there are appropriate vacancies. The length of this process will vary depending on how quickly an employer can search for and identify whether an appropriate vacant position exists. For a very small employer, this process may take one day; for other employers this process may take several weeks.[89] When an employer has completed its search, identified whether there are any vacancies (including any positions that will become vacant in a reasonable amount of time), notified the employee of the results, and either offered an appropriate vacancy to the employee or informed him/her that no appropriate vacancies are available, the employer will have fulfilled its obligation.

29. Does reassignment mean that the employee is permitted to compete for a vacant position?

No. Reassignment means that the employee gets the vacant position if s/he is qualified for it. Otherwise, reassignment would be of little value and would not be implemented as Congress intended.[90]

---

87 See Hendricks-Robinson v. Excel Corp., 154 F.3d 685, 695-96, 697-98, 8 AD Cas. (BNA) 875, 883, 884 (7th Cir. 1998) (employer cannot mislead disabled employees who need reassignment about full range of vacant positions; nor can it post vacant positions for such a short period of time that disabled employees on medical leave have no realistic chance to learn about them); Mengine v. Runyon, 114 F.3d 415, 420, 6 AD Cas. (BNA) 1530, 1534 (3d Cir. 1997) (an employer has a duty to make reasonable efforts to assist an employee in identifying a vacancy because an employee will not have the ability or resources to identify a vacant position absent participation by the employer); Woodman v. Runyon, 132 F.3d 1330, 1344, 7 AD Cas. (BNA) 1189, 1199 (10th Cir. 1997) (federal employers are far better placed than employees to investigate in good faith the availability of vacant positions).

88 See Dalton v. Subaru-Isuzu Automotive, Inc., 141 F.3d 667, 678, 7 AD Cas. (BNA) 1872, 1881 (7th Cir. 1998) (employer must first identify full range of alternative positions and then determine which ones employee qualified to perform, with or without reasonable accommodation); Hendricks-Robinson v. Excel Corp., 154 F.3d 685, 700, 8 AD Cas. (BNA) 875, 886-87 (7th Cir. 1998) (employer's methodology to determine if reassignment is appropriate does not constitute the "interactive process" contemplated by the ADA if it is directive rather than interactive); Mengine v. Runyon, 114 F.3d 415, 419-20, 6 AD Cas. (BNA) 1530, 1534 (3d Cir. 1997) (once an employer has identified possible vacancies, an employee has a duty to identify which one he is capable of performing).

89 If it will take several weeks to determine whether an appropriate vacant position exists, the employer and employee should discuss the employee's status during that period. There are different possibilities depending on the circumstances, but they may include: use of accumulated paid leave, use of unpaid leave, or a temporary assignment to a light duty position. Employers also may choose to take actions that go beyond the ADA's requirements, such as eliminating an essential function of the employee's current position, to enable an employee to continue working while a reassignment is sought.

90 42 U.S.C. § 12111(9)(b) (1994); 29 C.F.R. pt. 1630 app. § 1630.2(o) (1997). See Senate Report, supra note 6, at 31 ("If an employee, because of disability, can no longer perform the essential functions of the job that she or he has held, a transfer to another vacant job for which the person is qualified may prevent the employee from being out of work and the employer from losing a valuable worker."). See Wood v. County of Alameda, 5 AD Cas. (BNA) 173, 184 (N.D. Cal. 1995) (when employee could no longer perform job because of disability, she was entitled to reassignment to a vacant position, not simply an opportunity to "compete"); cf. Aka v. Washington Hosp. Ctr., 156 F.3d 1284, 1304-05, 8 AD Cas. (BNA) 1093, 1110-11 (D.C. Cir. 1998) (the court, in interpreting a collective bargaining agreement provision authorizing reassignment of disabled employees, states that "[a]n employee who is allowed to compete for jobs precisely like any other applicant has not been 'reas-

30. If an employee is reassigned to a lower level position, must an employer maintain his/her salary from the higher level position?

No, unless the employer transfers employees without disabilities to lower level positions and maintains their original salaries.[91]

31. Must an employer provide a reassignment if it would violate a seniority system?

Generally, it will be "unreasonable" to reassign an employee with a disability if doing so would violate the rules of a seniority system.[92] This is true both for collectively bargained seniority systems and those unilaterally imposed by management. Seniority systems governing job placement give employees expectations of consistent, uniform treatment, expectations that would be undermined if employers had to make the type of individualized, case-by-case assessment required by the reasonable accommodation process.[93]

However, if there are "special circumstances" that "undermine the employees' expectations of consistent, uniform treatment," it may be a "reasonable accommodation," absent undue hardship, to reassign an employee despite the existence of a seniority system. For example, "special circumstances" may exist where an employer retains the right to alter the seniority system unilaterally, and has exercised that right fairly frequently, thereby lowering employee expectations in the seniority system.[94] In this circumstance, one more exception (i.e., providing the reassignment to an employee with a disability) may not make a difference.[95] Alternatively, a seniority system may contain exceptions, such that one more exception is unlikely to matter.[96] Another possibility is that a seniority system might contain procedures for making exceptions, thus suggesting to employees that seniority does not automatically guarantee access to a specific job.

OTHER REASONABLE ACCOMMODATION ISSUES[97]

32. If an employer has provided one reasonable accommodation, does it have to provide additional reasonable accommodations requested by an individual with a disability?

The duty to provide reasonable accommodation is an ongoing one.[98] Certain individuals require only one reasonable accommodation, while others may need more than one. Still others may need one reasonable accommodation for a period of time, and then at a later date, require another type of reasonable accommodation. If an individual requests multiple reasonable

---

signed'); United States v. Denver, 943 F. Supp. 1304, 1310-11, 6 AD Cas. (BNA) 245, 250 (D. Colo. 1996) (the ADA requires employers to move beyond traditional analysis and consider reassignment as a method of enabling a disabled worker to do a job). Some courts have suggested that reassignment means simply an opportunity to compete for a vacant position. See, e.g., Daugherty v. City of El Paso, 56 F.3d 695, 700, 4 AD Cas. (BNA) 993, 997 (5th Cir. 1995). Such an interpretation nullifies the clear statutory language stating that reassignment is a form of reasonable accommodation. Even without the ADA, an employee with a disability may have the right to compete for a vacant position.

91 29 C.F.R. pt. 1630 app. § 1630.2(o) (1997).

92 See US Airways, Inc. v. Barnett, 535 U.S. ___, 122 S. Ct. 1516, 1524-25 (2002).

93 Id.

94 Id. at 1525. In a lawsuit, the plaintiff/employee bears the burden of proof to show the existence of "special circumstances" that warrant a jury's finding that a reassignment is "reasonable" despite the presence of a seniority system. If an employee can show "special circumstances," then the burden shifts to the employer to show why the reassignment would pose an undue hardship. See id.

95 Id.

96 Id. The Supreme Court made clear that these two were examples of "special circumstances" and that they did not constitute an exhaustive list of examples. Furthermore, Justice Stevens, in a concurring opinion, raised additional issues that could be relevant to show special circumstances that would make it reasonable for an employer to make an exception to its seniority system. See id. at 1526.

97 The discussions and examples in this section assume that there is only one effective accommodation and that the reasonable accommodation will not cause an undue hardship.

98 See Ralph v. Lucent Technologies, Inc., 135 F.3d 166, 171, 7 AD Cas. (BNA) 1345, 1349 (1st Cir. 1998).

accommodations, s/he is entitled only to those accommodations that are necessitated by a disability and that will provide an equal employment opportunity.

An employer must consider each request for reasonable accommodation and determine: (1) whether the accommodation is needed, (2) if needed, whether the accommodation would be effective, and (3) if effective, whether providing the reasonable accommodation would impose an undue hardship. If a reasonable accommodation turns out to be ineffective and the employee with a disability remains unable to perform an essential function, the employer must consider whether there would be an alternative reasonable accommodation that would not pose an undue hardship. If there is no alternative accommodation, then the employer must attempt to reassign the employee to a vacant position for which s/he is qualified, unless to do so would cause an undue hardship.

33. Does an employer have to change a person's supervisor as a form of reasonable accommodation?

No. An employer does not have to provide an employee with a new supervisor as a reasonable accommodation. Nothing in the ADA, however, prohibits an employer from doing so. Furthermore, although an employer is not required to change supervisors, the ADA may require that supervisory methods be altered as a form of reasonable accommodation.[99] Also, an employee with a disability is protected from disability-based discrimination by a supervisor, including disability-based harassment.

Example: A supervisor frequently schedules team meetings on a day's notice often notifying staff in the afternoon that a meeting will be held on the following morning. An employee with a disability has missed several meetings because they have conflicted with previously-scheduled physical therapy sessions. The employee asks that the supervisor give her two to three days' notice of team meetings so that, if necessary, she can reschedule the physical therapy sessions. Assuming no undue hardship would result, the supervisor must make this reasonable accommodation.

34. Does an employer have to allow an employee with a disability to work at home as a reasonable accommodation?

An employer must modify its policy concerning where work is performed if such a change is needed as a reasonable accommodation, but only if this accommodation would be effective and would not cause an undue hardship.[100] Whether this accommodation is effective will depend on whether the essential functions of the position can be performed at home. There are certain jobs in which the essential functions can only be performed at the work site—e.g., food server, cashier in a store. For such jobs, allowing an employee to work at home is not effective because it does not enable an employee to perform his/her essential functions. Certain considerations may be critical in determining whether a job can be effectively performed at home, including (but not limited to) the employer's ability to adequately supervise the employee and the employee's need to work with certain equipment or tools that cannot be replicated at home. In contrast, employees may be able to perform the essential functions of certain types of jobs at home (e.g., telemarketer, proofreader).[101] For these types of jobs, an employer may deny a request to work at home if it can

---

99 For a discussion on ways to modify supervisory methods, see ADA and Psychiatric Disabilities, supra note 27, at 26-27, 8 FEP Manual (BNA) 405:7475.

100 See 29 C.F.R. § 1630.2(o)(1)(ii), (2)(ii) (1997) (modifications or adjustments to the manner or circumstances under which the position held or desired is customarily performed that enable a qualified individual with a disability to perform the essential functions).

101 Courts have differed regarding whether "work-at-home" can be a reasonable accommodation. Compare Langon v. Department of Health and Human Servs., 959 F.2d 1053, 1060, 2 AD Cas. (BNA) 152, 159 (D.C. Cir. 1992); Anzalone v. Allstate Insurance Co., 5 AD Cas. (BNA) 455, 458 (E.D. La. 1995); Carr v. Reno, 23 F.3d 525, 530, 3 AD Cas. (BNA) 434, 437-38 (D.D.C. 1994), with Vande Zande v. Wisconsin Dep't of Admin., 44 F.3d 538, 545, 3 AD Cas. (BNA) 1636, 1640 (7th Cir. 1995). Courts that have rejected working at home as a reasonable accommodation focus on evidence that personal contact, interaction, and coordination are needed for a specific position. See, e.g., Whillock v. Delta Air Lines, 926 F. Supp. 1555, 1564, 5 AD Cas. (BNA) 1027 (N.D. Ga. 1995), aff'd, 86 F.3d 1171, 7 AD Cas. (BNA) 1267 (11th Cir. 1996); Misek-Falkoff v. IBM Corp., 854 F. Supp. 215, 227-28, 3 AD Cas. (BNA) 449, 457-58 (S.D.N.Y. 1994), aff'd, 60 F.3d 811, 6 AD Cas. (BNA) 576 (2d Cir. 1995).

show that another accommodation would be effective or if working at home will cause undue hardship.

35. Must an employer withhold discipline or termination of an employee who, because of a disability, violated a conduct rule that is job-related for the position in question and consistent with business necessity?

No. An employer never has to excuse a violation of a uniformly applied conduct rule that is job-related and consistent with business necessity. This means, for example, that an employer never has to tolerate or excuse violence, threats of violence, stealing, or destruction of property. An employer may discipline an employee with a disability for engaging in such misconduct if it would impose the same discipline on an employee without a disability.

36. Must an employer provide a reasonable accommodation for an employee with a disability who violated a conduct rule that is job-related for the position in question and consistent with business necessity?

An employer must make reasonable accommodation to enable an otherwise qualified employee with a disability to meet such a conduct standard in the future, barring undue hardship, except where the punishment for the violation is termination.[102] Since reasonable accommodation is always prospective, an employer is not required to excuse past misconduct even if it is the result of the individual's disability.[103] Possible reasonable accommodations could include adjustments to starting times, specified breaks, and leave if these accommodations will enable an employee to comply with conduct rules.[104]

Example: An employee with major depression is often late for work because of medication side-effects that make him extremely groggy in the morning. His scheduled hours are 9:00 a.m. to 5:30 p.m., but he arrives at 9:00, 9:30, 10:00, or even 10:30 on any given day. His job responsibilities involve telephone contact with the company's traveling sales representatives, who depend on him to answer urgent marketing questions and expedite special orders. The employer disciplines him for tardiness, stating that continued failure to arrive promptly during the next month will result in termination of his employment. The individual then explains that he was late because of a disability and needs to work on a later schedule. In this situation, the employer may discipline the employee because he violated a conduct standard addressing tardiness that is job-related for the position in question and consistent with business necessity. The employer, however, must consider reasonable accommodation, barring undue hardship, to enable this individual to meet this standard in the future. For example, if this individual can serve the company's sales representatives by regularly working a schedule of 10:00 a.m. to 6:30 p.m., a reasonable accommodation would be to modify his schedule so that he is not required to report for work until 10:00 a.m.

37. Is it a reasonable accommodation to make sure that an employee takes medication as prescribed?

No. Medication monitoring is not a reasonable accommodation. Employers have no obligation to monitor medication because doing so does not remove a workplace barrier. Similarly, an employer has no

102 See 29 C.F.R. § 1630.15(d) (1997).

103 See Siefken v. Arlington Heights, 65 F.3d 664, 666, 4 AD Cas. (BNA) 1441, 1442 (7th Cir. 1995). Therefore, it may be in the employee's interest to request a reasonable accommodation before performance suffers or conduct problems occur. For more information on conduct standards, including when they are job-related and consistent with business necessity, see ADA and Psychiatric Disabilities, supra note 27, at 29-32, 8 FEP Manual (BNA) 405:7476-78. An employer does not have to offer a "firm choice" or a "last chance agreement" to an employee who performs poorly or who has engaged in misconduct because of alcoholism. "Firm choice" or "last chance agreements" involve excusing past performance or conduct problems resulting from alcoholism in exchange for an employee's receiving substance abuse treatment and refraining from further use of alcohol. Violation of such an agreement generally warrants termination. Since the ADA does not require employers to excuse poor performance or violation of conduct standards that are job-related and consistent with business necessity, an employer has no obligation to provide "firm choice" or a "last chance agreement" as a reasonable accommodation. See Johnson v. Babbitt, EEOC Docket No. 03940100 (March 28, 1996). However, an employer may choose to offer an employee a "firm choice" or a "last chance agreement."

104 See ADA and Psychiatric Disabilities, supra note 27, at 31-32, 8 FEP Manual (BNA) 405:7477-78.

responsibility to monitor an employee's medical treatment or ensure that s/he is receiving appropriate treatment because such treatment does not involve modifying workplace barriers.[105]

It may be a form of reasonable accommodation, however, to give an employee a break in order that s/he may take medication, or to grant leave so that an employee may obtain treatment.

38. Is an employer relieved of its obligation to provide reasonable accommodation for an employee with a disability who fails to take medication, to obtain medical treatment, or to use an assistive device (such as a hearing aid)?

No. The ADA requires an employer to provide reasonable accommodation to remove workplace barriers, regardless of what effect medication, other medical treatment, or assistive devices may have on an employee's ability to perform the job.[106]

However, if an employee with a disability, with or without reasonable accommodation, cannot perform the essential functions of the position or poses a direct threat in the absence of medication, treatment, or an assistive device, then s/he is unqualified.

39. Must an employer provide a reasonable accommodation that is needed because of the side effects of medication or treatment related to the disability, or because of symptoms or other medical conditions resulting from the underlying disability?

Yes. The side effects caused by the medication that an employee must take because of the disability are limitations resulting from the disability. Reasonable accommodation extends to all limitations resulting from a disability.

Example A: An employee with cancer undergoes chemotherapy twice a week, which causes her to be quite ill afterwards. The employee requests a modified schedule—leave for the two days a week of chemotherapy. The treatment will last six weeks. Unless it can show undue hardship, the employer must grant this request.

Similarly, any symptoms or related medical conditions resulting from the disability that cause limitations may also require reasonable accommodation.[107]

Example B: An employee, as a result of insulin-dependent diabetes, has developed background retinopathy (a vision impairment). The employee, who already has provided documentation showing his diabetes is a disability, requests a device to enlarge the text on his computer screen. The employer can request documentation that the retinopathy is related to the diabetes but the employee does not have to show that the retinopathy is an independent disability under the ADA. Since the retinopathy is a consequence of the diabetes (an ADA disability), the request must be granted unless undue hardship can be shown.

40. Must an employer ask whether a reasonable accommodation is needed when an employee has not asked for one?

Generally, no. As a general rule, the individual with a disability—who has the most knowledge about the need for reasonable accommodation—must inform the employer that an accommodation is needed.[108]

---

105 See Robertson v. The Neuromedical Ctr., 161 F.3d 292, 296 (5th Cir. 1998); see also ADA and Psychiatric Disabilities, supra note 27, at 27-28, 8 FEP Manual (BNA) 405:7475.

106 While from an employer's perspective it may appear that an employee is "failing" to use medication or follow a certain treatment, such questions can be complex. There are many reasons why a person would choose to forgo treatment, including expense and serious side effects.

107 See Vande Zande v. Wisconsin Dep't of Admin., 44 F.3d 538, 544, 3 AD Cas. (BNA) 1636, 1639 (7th Cir. 1995).

108 See 29 C.F.R. pt. 1630 app. § 1630.9 (1997); see also House Judiciary Report, supra note 6, at 39; House Education and Labor Report, supra note 6, at 65; Senate Report, supra note 6, at 34. See, e.g., Taylor v. Principal Fin. Group, Inc., 93 F.3d 155, 165, 5 AD Cas. (BNA) 1653, 1659 (5th Cir. 1996); Tips v. Regents of Texas Tech Univ., 921 F. Supp. 1515, 1518 (N.D. Tex. 1996); Cheatwood v. Roanoke Indus., 891 F. Supp. 1528, 1538, 5 AD Cas. (BNA) 141, 147 (N.D. Ala. 1995); Mears v. Gulfstream Aerospace Corp., 905 F. Supp. 1075, 1080, 5 AD Cas. (BNA) 1295, 1300 (S.D. Ga. 1995), aff'd, 87 F.3d 1331, 6 AD Cas. (BNA) 1152 (11th Cir. 1996). But see Schmidt v. Safeway Inc., 864 F. Supp. 991, 997, 3 AD Cas. (BNA) 1141, 1146-47 (D. Or. 1994) (employer had obligation to provide reasonable accommodation because it knew of the employee's alcohol problem and had reason to believe that an accommodation would permit the employee to perform the job). An employer may

However, an employer should initiate the reasonable accommodation interactive process[109] without being asked if the employer: (1) knows that the employee has a disability, (2) knows, or has reason to know, that the employee is experiencing workplace problems because of the disability, and (3) knows, or has reason to know, that the disability prevents the employee from requesting a reasonable accommodation. If the individual with a disability states that s/he does not need a reasonable accommodation, the employer will have fulfilled its obligation.

Example: An employee with mental retardation delivers messages at a law firm. He frequently mixes up messages for "R. Miller" and "T. Miller." The employer knows about the disability, suspects that the performance problem is a result of the disability, and knows that this employee is unable to ask for a reasonable accommodation because of his mental retardation. The employer asks the employee about mixing up the two names and asks if it would be helpful to spell the first name of each person. When the employee says that would be better, the employer, as a reasonable accommodation, instructs the receptionist to write the full first name when messages are left for one of the Messrs. Miller.

41. May an employer ask whether a reasonable accommodation is needed when an employee with a disability has not asked for one?

An employer may ask an employee with a known disability whether s/he needs a reasonable accommodation when it reasonably believes that the employee may need an accommodation. For example, an employer could ask a deaf employee who is being sent on a business trip if s/he needs reasonable accommodation. Or, if an employer is scheduling a luncheon at a restaurant and is uncertain about what questions it should ask to ensure that the restaurant is accessible for an employee who uses a wheelchair, the employer may first ask the employee. An employer also may ask an employee with a disability who is having performance or conduct problems if s/he needs reasonable accommodation.[110]

42. May an employer tell other employees that an individual is receiving a reasonable accommodation when employees ask questions about a coworker with a disability?

No. An employer may not disclose that an employee is receiving a reasonable accommodation because this usually amounts to a disclosure that the individual has a disability. The ADA specifically prohibits the disclosure of medical information except in certain limited situations, which do not include disclosure to coworkers.[111]

An employer may certainly respond to a question from an employee about why a coworker is receiving what is perceived as "different" or "special" treatment by emphasizing its policy of assisting any employee who encounters difficulties in the workplace. The employer also may find it helpful to point out that many of the workplace issues encountered by employees are personal, and that, in these circumstances, it is the employer's policy to respect employee privacy. An employer may be able to make this point effectively by reassuring the employee asking the question that his/her privacy would similarly be respected if s/he

---

not assert that it never received a request for reasonable accommodation, as a defense to a claim of failure to provide reasonable accommodation, if it actively discouraged an individual from making such a request. For more information about an individual requesting reasonable accommodation, see Questions 1-4, supra.

109 See Question 5, supra, for information on the interactive process.

110 29 C.F.R. pt. 1630 app. § 1630.9 (1997).

111 42 U.S.C. § 12112(d)(3)(B), (d)(4)(C) (1994); 29 C.F.R. § 1630.14(b)(1) (1997). The limited exceptions to the ADA confidentiality requirements are: (1) supervisors and managers may be told about necessary restrictions on the work or duties of the employee and about necessary accommodations; (2) first aid and safety personnel may be told if the disability might require emergency treatment; and (3) government officials investigating compliance with the ADA must be given relevant information on request. In addition, the Commission has interpreted the ADA to allow employers to disclose medical information in the following circumstances: (1) in accordance with state workers' compensation laws, employers may disclose information to state workers' compensation offices, state second injury funds, or workers' compensation insurance carriers; and (2) employers are permitted to use medical information for insurance purposes. See 29 C.F.R. pt. 1630 app. § 1630.14(b) (1997); Preemployment Questions and Medical Examinations, supra note 27, at 23, 8 FEP Manual (BNA) 405:7201; Workers' Compensation and the ADA, supra note 52, at 7, 8 FEP Manual (BNA) 405:7394.

found it necessary to ask the employer for some kind of workplace change for personal reasons.

Since responding to specific coworker questions may be difficult, employers might find it helpful before such questions are raised to provide all employees with information about various laws that require employers to meet certain employee needs (e.g., the ADA and the Family and Medical Leave Act), while also requiring them to protect the privacy of employees. In providing general ADA information to employees, an employer may wish to highlight the obligation to provide reasonable accommodation, including the interactive process and different types of reasonable accommodations, and the statute's confidentiality protections. Such information could be delivered in orientation materials, employee handbooks, notices accompanying paystubs, and posted flyers. Employers may wish to explore these and other alternatives with unions because they too are bound by the ADA's confidentiality provisions. Union meetings and bulletin boards may be further avenues for such educational efforts.

As long as there is no coercion by an employer, an employee with a disability may voluntarily choose to disclose to coworkers his/her disability and/or the fact that s/he is receiving a reasonable accommodation.

UNDUE HARDSHIP ISSUES[112]

An employer does not have to provide a reasonable accommodation that would cause an "undue hardship" to the employer. Generalized conclusions will not suffice to support a claim of undue hardship. Instead, undue hardship must be based on an individualized assessment of current circumstances that show that a specific reasonable accommodation would cause significant difficulty or expense.[113] A determination of undue hardship should be based on several factors, including:

- the nature and cost of the accommodation needed;
- the overall financial resources of the facility making the reasonable accommodation; the number of persons employed at this facility; the effect on expenses and resources of the facility;
- the overall financial resources, size, number of employees, and type and location of facilities of the employer (if the facility involved in the reasonable accommodation is part of a larger entity);
- the type of operation of the employer, including the structure and functions of the workforce, the geographic separateness, and the administrative or fiscal relationship of the facility involved in making the accommodation to the employer;
- the impact of the accommodation on the operation of the facility.[114]

The ADA's legislative history indicates that Congress wanted employers to consider all possible sources of outside funding when assessing whether a particular accommodation would be too costly.[115] Undue hardship is determined based on the net cost to the employer. Thus, an employer should determine whether funding is available from an outside source, such as a state rehabilitation agency, to pay for all or part of the accommodation.[116] In addition, the employer should determine whether it is eligible for certain tax credits or deductions to offset the cost of the accommodation. Also, to the extent that a portion of the cost of an accommodation causes undue hardship, the employer should ask the individual with a disability if s/he will pay the difference.

If an employer determines that one particular reasonable accommodation will cause undue hardship, but a second type of reasonable accommodation will be effective and will not cause an undue hardship, then the employer must provide the second accommodation.

An employer cannot claim undue hardship based

---

[112] The discussions and examples in this section assume that there is only one effective accommodation.

[113] See 29 C.F.R. pt. 1630 app. § 1630.15(d) (1996); see also Stone v. Mount Vernon, 118 F.3d 92, 101, 6 AD Cas. (BNA) 1685, 1693 (2d Cir. 1997) (an employer who has not hired any persons with disabilities cannot claim undue hardship based on speculation that if it were to hire several people with disabilities it may not have sufficient staff to perform certain tasks); Bryant v. Better Business Bureau of Greater Maryland, 923 F. Supp. 720, 735, 5 AD Cas. (BNA) 625, 634 (D. Md. 1996).

[114] See 42 U.S.C. § 12111(10)(B) (1994); 29 C.F.R. § 1630.2(p)(2) (1997); 29 C.F.R. pt. 1630 app. § 1630.2(p) (1997); TAM, supra note 49, at 3.9, 8 FEP Manual (BNA) 405:7005-07.

[115] See Senate Report, supra note 6, at 36; House Education and Labor Report, supra note 6, at 69. See also 29 C.F.R. pt. 1630 app. § 1630.2(p) (1997).

[116] See the Appendix [not reproduced here] on how to obtain information about the tax credit and deductions.

on employees' (or customers') fears or prejudices toward the individual's disability.[117] Nor can undue hardship be based on the fact that provision of a reasonable accommodation might have a negative impact on the morale of other employees. Employers, however, may be able to show undue hardship where provision of a reasonable accommodation would be unduly disruptive to other employees's ability to work.

Example A: An employee with breast cancer is undergoing chemotherapy. As a consequence of the treatment, the employee is subject to fatigue and finds it difficult to keep up with her regular workload. So that she may focus her reduced energy on performing her essential functions, the employer transfers three of her marginal functions to another employee for the duration of the chemotherapy treatments. The second employee is unhappy at being given extra assignments, but the employer determines that the employee can absorb the new assignments with little effect on his ability to perform his own assignments in a timely manner. Since the employer cannot show significant disruption to its operation, there is no undue hardship.[118]

Example B: A convenience store clerk with multiple sclerosis requests that he be allowed to go from working full-time to part-time as a reasonable accommodation because of his disability. The store assigns two clerks per shift, and if the first clerk's hours are reduced, the second clerk's workload will increase significantly beyond his ability to handle his responsibilities. The store determines that such an arrangement will result in inadequate coverage to serve customers in a timely manner, keep the shelves stocked, and maintain store security. Thus, the employer can show undue hardship based on the significant disruption to its operations and, therefore, can refuse to reduce the employee's hours. The employer, however, should explore whether any other reasonable accommodation will assist the store clerk without causing undue hardship.

43. Must an employer modify the work hours of an employee with a disability if doing so would prevent other employees from performing their jobs?

No. If the result of modifying one employee's work hours (or granting leave) is to prevent other employees from doing their jobs, then the significant disruption to the operations of the employer constitutes an undue hardship.

Example A: A crane operator, due to his disability, requests an adjustment in his work schedule so that he starts work at 8:00 a.m. rather than 7:00 a.m., and finishes one hour later in the evening. The crane operator works with three other employees who cannot perform their jobs without the crane operator. As a result, if the employer grants this requested accommodation, it would have to require the other three workers to adjust their hours, find other work for them to do from 7:00 to 8:00, or have the workers do nothing. The ADA does not require the employer to take any of these actions because they all significantly disrupt the operations of the business. Thus, the employer can deny the requested accommodation, but should discuss with the employee if there are other possible accommodations that would not result in undue hardship.

Example B: A computer programmer works with a group of people to develop new software. There are certain tasks that the entire group must perform together, but each person also has individual assignments. It is through habit, not necessity, that they have often worked together first thing in the morning.

The programmer, due to her disability, requests an adjustment in her work schedule so that she works from 10:00 a.m. - 7:00 p.m. rather than 9:00 a.m. - 6:00 p.m. In this situation, the employer could grant the adjustment in hours because it would not significantly disrupt the operations of the business. The effect of the reasonable accommodation would be to alter when the group worked together and when they performed their individual assignments.

117 See 29 C.F.R. pt. 1630 app. § 1630.15(d) (1997).

118 Failure to transfer marginal functions because of its negative impact on the morale of other employees also could constitute disparate treatment when similar morale problems do not stop an employer from reassigning tasks in other situations.

44. Can an employer deny a request for leave when an employee cannot provide a fixed date of return?

Providing leave to an employee who is unable to provide a fixed date of return is a form of reasonable accommodation. However, if an employer is able to show that the lack of a fixed return date causes an undue hardship, then it can deny the leave. In certain circumstances, undue hardship will derive from the disruption to the operations of the entity that occurs because the employer can neither plan for the employee's return nor permanently fill the position. If an employee cannot provide a fixed date of return, and an employer determines that it can grant such leave at that time without causing undue hardship, the employer has the right to require, as part of the interactive process, that the employee provide periodic updates on his/her condition and possible date of return. After receiving these updates, employers may reevaluate whether continued leave constitutes an undue hardship.

In certain situations, an employee may be able to provide only an approximate date of return.[119] Treatment and recuperation do not always permit exact timetables. Thus, an employer cannot claim undue hardship solely because an employee can provide only an approximate date of return. In such situations, or in situations in which a return date must be postponed because of unforeseen medical developments, employees should stay in regular communication with their employers to inform them of their progress and discuss, if necessary, the need for continued leave beyond what might have been granted originally.[120]

Example A: An experienced chef at a top restaurant requests leave for treatment of her disability but cannot provide a fixed date of return. The restaurant can show that this request constitutes undue hardship because of the difficulty of replacing, even temporarily, a chef of this caliber. Moreover, it leaves the employer unable to determine how long it must hold open the position or to plan for the chef's absence. Therefore, the restaurant can deny the request for leave as a reasonable accommodation.

Example B: An employee requests eight weeks of leave for surgery for his disability. The employer grants the request. During surgery, serious complications arise that require a lengthier period of recuperation than originally anticipated, as well as additional surgery. The employee contacts the employer after three weeks of leave to ask for an additional ten to fourteen weeks of leave (i.e., a total of 18 to 22 weeks of leave). The employer must assess whether granting additional leave causes an undue hardship.

45. Does a cost-benefit analysis determine whether a reasonable accommodation will cause undue hardship?

No. A cost-benefit analysis assesses the cost of a reasonable accommodation in relation to the perceived benefit to the employer and the employee. Neither the statute nor the legislative history supports a cost-benefit analysis to determine whether a specific accommodation causes an undue hardship.[121] Whether the cost of a reasonable accommodation imposes an undue hardship depends on the employer's resources, not on the individual's salary, position, or status (e.g., full-time versus part-time, salary versus hourly wage, permanent versus temporary).

---

119 See Haschmann v. Time Warner Entertainment Co., 151 F.3d 591, 600-02, 8 AD Cas. (BNA) 692, 699-701 (7th Cir. 1998).

120 See Criado v. IBM, 145 F.3d 437, 444-45, 8 AD Cas. (BNA) 336, 341 (1st Cir. 1998).

121 The ADA's definition of undue hardship does not include any consideration of a cost-benefit analysis. See 42 U.S.C. § 12111(10) (1994); see also House Education and Labor Report, supra note 6, at 69 ("[T]he committee wishes to make clear that the fact that an accommodation is used by only one employee should not be used as a negative factor counting in favor of a finding of undue hardship."). Furthermore, the House of Representatives rejected a cost-benefit approach by defeating an amendment which would have presumed undue hardship if a reasonable accommodation cost more than 10% of the employee's annual salary. See 136 Cong. Rec. H2475 (1990), see also House Judiciary Report, supra note 6, at 41; 29 C.F.R. pt. 1630 app. § 1630.15(d) (1997). Despite the statutory language and legislative history, some courts have applied a cost-benefit analysis. See, e.g., Monette v. Electronic Data Sys. Corp., 90 F.3d 1173, 1184 n.10, 5 AD Cas. (BNA) 1326, 1335 n.10 (6th Cir. 1996); Vande Zande v. Wisconsin Dep't of Admin., 44 F.3d 538, 543, 3 AD Cas. (BNA) 1636, 1638-39 (7th Cir. 1995).

46. Can an employer claim undue hardship solely because a reasonable accommodation would require it to make changes to property owned by someone else?

No, an employer cannot claim undue hardship solely because a reasonable accommodation would require it to make changes to property owned by someone else. In some situations, an employer will have the right under a lease or other contractual relationship with the property owner to make the type of changes that are needed. If this is the case, the employer should make the changes, assuming no other factors exist that would make the changes too difficult or costly. If the contractual relationship between the employer and property owner requires the owner's consent to the kinds of changes that are required, or prohibits them from being made, then the employer must make good faith efforts either to obtain the owner's permission or to negotiate an exception to the terms of the contract. If the owner refuses to allow the employer to make the modifications, the employer may claim undue hardship. Even in this situation, however, the employer must still provide another reasonable accommodation, if one exists, that would not cause undue hardship.

Example A: X Corp., a travel agency, leases space in a building owned by Z Co. One of X Corp.'s employees becomes disabled and needs to use a wheelchair. The employee requests as a reasonable accommodation that several room dividers be moved to make his work space easily accessible. X Corp.'s lease specifically allows it to make these kinds of physical changes, and they are otherwise easy and inexpensive to make. The fact that X Corp. does not own the property does not create an undue hardship and therefore it must make the requested accommodation.

Example B: Same as Example A, except that X Corp.'s lease requires it to seek Z Co.'s permission before making any physical changes that would involve reconfiguring office space. X Corp. requests that Z Co. allow it to make the changes, but Z Co. denies the request. X Corp. can claim that making the physical changes would constitute an undue hardship. However, it must provide any other type of reasonable accommodation that would not involve making physical changes to the facility, such as finding a different location within the office that would be accessible to the employee.

An employer should remember its obligation to make reasonable accommodation when it is negotiating contracts with property owners.[122] Similarly, a property owner should carefully assess a request from an employer to make physical changes that are needed as a reasonable accommodation because failure to permit the modification might constitute "interference" with the rights of an employee with a disability.[123] In addition, other ADA provisions may require the property owner to make the modifications.[124]

BURDENS OF PROOF

In US Airways, Inc. v. Barnett, 535 U.S. ___, 122 S. Ct. 1516 (2002), the Supreme Court laid out the burdens of proof for an individual with a disability (plaintiff) and an employer (defendant) in an ADA lawsuit alleging failure to provide reasonable accommodation. The "plaintiff/employee (to defeat a defendant/employer's motion for summary judgment) need only show that an 'accommodation' seems reasonable on its face, i.e., ordinarily or in the run of cases."[125] Once the plaintiff has shown that the accommodation s/he needs is "reasonable," the burden shifts to the defendant/ employer to provide case-specific evidence proving that reasonable accommodation would cause an undue hardship in the particular circumstances.[126]

122 See 42 U.S.C. § 12112(b)(2) (1994); 29 C.F.R. § 1630.6 (1997) (prohibiting an employer from participating in a contractual relationship that has the effect of subjecting qualified applicants or employees with disabilities to discrimination).

123 See 42 U.S.C. § 12203(b) (1994); 29 C.F.R. § 1630.12(b) (1997).

124 For example, under Title III of the ADA a private entity that owns a building in which goods and services are offered to the public has an obligation, subject to certain limitations, to remove architectural barriers so that people with disabilities have equal access to these goods and services. 42 U.S.C. § 12182(b)(2)(A)(iv) (1994). Thus, the requested modification may be something that the property owner should have done to comply with Title III.

125 US Airways, Inc. v. Barnett, 535 U.S. ___, 122 S. Ct. 1516, 1523 (2002).

126 Id.

The Supreme Court's burden-shifting framework does not affect the interactive process triggered by an individual's request for accommodation.[127] An employer should still engage in this informal dialogue to obtain relevant information needed to make an informed decision.

INSTRUCTIONS FOR INVESTIGATORS

When assessing whether a Respondent has violated the ADA by denying a reasonable accommodation to a Charging Party, investigators should consider the following:

- Is the Charging Party "otherwise qualified" (i.e., is the Charging Party qualified for the job except that, because of disability, s/he needs a reasonable accommodation to perform the position's essential functions)?
- Did the Charging Party, or a representative, request a reasonable accommodation (i.e., did the Charging Party let the employer know that s/he needed an adjustment or change at work for a reason related to a medical condition)? [see Questions 1-4]
  - Did the Respondent request documentation of the Charging Party's disability and/or functional limitations? If yes, was the documentation provided? Did the Respondent have a legitimate reason for requesting documentation? [see Questions 6-8]
  - What specific type of reasonable accommodation, if any, did the Charging Party request?
  - Was there a nexus between the reasonable accommodation requested and the functional limitations resulting from the Charging Party's disability? [see Question 6]
  - Was the need for reasonable accommodation related to the use of medication, side effects from treatment, or symptoms related to a disability? [see Questions 36-38]
- For what purpose did the Charging Party request a reasonable accommodation:
  - for the application process? [see Questions 12-13]
  - in connection with aspects of job performance? [see Questions 16-24, 32-33]
  - in order to enjoy the benefits and privileges of employment? [see Questions 14-15]
- Should the Respondent have initiated the interactive process, or provided a reasonable accommodation, even if the Charging Party did not ask for an accommodation? [see Questions 11, 39]
- What did the Respondent do in response to the Charging Party's request for reasonable accommodation (i.e., did the Respondent engage in an interactive process with the Charging Party and if so, describe both the Respondent's and the Charging Party's actions/statements during this process)? [see Questions 5-11]
- If the Charging Party asked the Respondent for a particular reasonable accommodation, and the Respondent provided a different accommodation, why did the Respondent provide a different reasonable accommodation than the one requested by the Charging Party? Why does the Respondent believe that the reasonable accommodation it provided was effective in eliminating the workplace barrier at issue, thus providing the Charging Party with an equal employment opportunity? Why does the Charging Party believe that the reasonable accommodation provided by the Respondent was ineffective? [see Question 9]
- What type of accommodation could the Respondent have provided that would have been "reasonable" and effective in eliminating the workplace barrier at issue, thus providing the Charging Party with an equal employment opportunity?
- Does the charge involve allegations concerning reasonable accommodation and violations of any conduct rules? [see Questions 34-35]
- If the Charging Party alleges that the Respondent failed to provide a reassignment as a reasonable accommodation [see generally Questions 25-30 and accompanying text]:
  - did the Respondent and the Charging Party first discuss other forms of reasonable accommodation that would enable the Charging Party to remain in his/her current position before discussing reassignment?
  - did the Respondent have any vacant positions? [see Question 27]
  - did the Respondent notify the Charging Party about possible vacant positions? [see Question 28]
  - was the Charging Party qualified for a vacant position?

---

127 See Questions 5-10 for a discussion of the interactive process.

- if there was more than one vacant position, did the Respondent place the Charging Party in the one that was most closely equivalent to the Charging Party's original position?
- if the reassignment would conflict with a seniority system, are there "special circumstances" that would make it "reasonable" to reassign the Charging Party? [see Question 31]

• If the Respondent is claiming undue hardship [see generally Questions 42-46 and accompanying text]:
  - what evidence has the Respondent produced showing that providing a specific reasonable accommodation would entail significant difficulty or expense?
  - if a modified schedule or leave is the reasonable accommodation, is undue hardship based on the impact on the ability of other employees to do their jobs? [see Question 42]
  - if leave is the reasonable accommodation, is undue hardship based on the amount of leave requested? [see Question 43]
  - if there are "special circumstances" that would make it "reasonable" to reassign the Charging Party, despite the apparent conflict with a seniority system, would it nonetheless be an undue hardship to make the reassignment? [see Question 31]
  - is undue hardship based on the fact that providing the reasonable accommodation requires changes to property owned by an entity other than the Respondent? [see Question 46]
  - if the Respondent claims that a particular reasonable accommodation would result in undue hardship, is there another reasonable accommodation that Respondent could have provided that would not have resulted in undue hardship?

• Based on the evidence obtained in answers to the questions above, is the Charging Party a qualified individual with a disability (i.e., can the Charging Party perform the essential functions of the position with or without reasonable accommodation)?

ADA TITLE II

PUBLIC SERVICES

PROHIBITION AGAINST DISCRIMINATION AND OTHER GENERALLY APPLICABLE PROVISIONS

ACTIONS APPLICABLE TO PUBLIC TRANSPORTATION PROVIDED BY PUBLIC ENTITIES CONSIDERED DISCRIMINATORY

Public Transportation Other Than by Aircraft or Certain Rail Operations

ADA TITLE II

PUBLIC SERVICES

PROHIBITION AGAINST DISCRIMINATION AND OTHER GENERALLY APPLICABLE PROVISIONS

§ 12131. Definition

As used in this subchapter:

(1) Public entity

The term "public entity" means—

(A) any State or local government;

(B) any department, agency, special purpose district, or other instrumentality of a State or States or local government; and

(C) the National Railroad Passenger Corporation, and any commuter authority (as defined in section 502(8) of Title 45).

(2) Qualified individual with a disability

The term "qualified individual with a disability" means an individual with a disability who, with or without reasonable modifications to rules, policies, or practices, the removal of architectural, communication, or transportation barriers, or the provision of auxiliary aids and services, meets the essential eligibility requirements for the receipt of services or the participation in programs or activities provided by a public entity.

§ 12132. Discrimination

Subject to the provisions of this subchapter, no qualified individual with a disability shall, by reason of such disability, be excluded from participation in or be denied the benefits of the services, programs, or activities of a public entity, or be subjected to discrimination by any such entity.

§ 12133. Enforcement

The remedies, procedures, and rights set forth in section 794a of Title 29 shall be the remedies, procedures, and rights this subchapter provides to any person alleging discrimination on the basis of disability in violation of section 12132 of this title.

§ 12134. Regulations

(a) In general. Not later than 1 year after the date of enactment of this Act [enacted July 26, 1990], the Attorney General shall promulgate regulations in an accessible format that implement this subtitle. Such regulations shall not include any matter within the scope of the authority of the Secretary of Transportation under section 223, 229, or 244 [42 USCS § 12143, 12149, or 12164].

(b) Relationship to other regulations. Except for "program accessibility, existing facilities", and "communications", regulations under subsection (a) shall be consistent with this Act and with the coordination regulations under part 41 of title 28, Code of Federal Regulations (as promulgated by the Department of Health, Education, and Welfare on January 13, 1978), applicable to recipients of Federal financial assistance under section 504 of the Rehabilitation Act of 1973 (29 U.S.C. 794). With respect to "program accessibility, existing facilities", and "communications", such regulations shall be consistent with regulations and analysis as in part 39 of title 28 of the Code of Federal

Regulations, applicable to federally conducted activities under such section 504.

(c) Standards. Regulations under subsection (a) shall include standards applicable to facilities and vehicles covered by this subtitle, other than facilities, stations, rail passenger cars, and vehicles covered by subtitle B. Such standards shall be consistent with the minimum guidelines and requirements issued by the Architectural and Transportation Barriers Compliance Board in accordance with section 504(a) of this Act [42 USCS § 12204(a)].

ACTIONS APPLICABLE TO PUBLIC TRANSPORTATION PROVIDED BY PUBLIC ENTITIES CONSIDERED DISCRIMINATORY

Public Transportation Other Than by Aircraft or Certain Rail Operations

§ 12141. Definitions

As used in this sub-part:

(1) Demand responsive system

The term "demand responsive system" means any system of providing designated public transportation which is not a fixed route system.

(2) Designated public transportation

The term "designated public transportation" means transportation (other than public school transportation) by bus, rail, or any other conveyance (other than transportation by aircraft or intercity or commuter rail transportation (as defined in section 12161 of this title) that provides the general public with general or special service (including charter service) on a regular and continuing basis.

(3) Fixed route system

The term "fixed route system" means a system of providing designated public transportation on which a vehicle is operated along a prescribed route according to a fixed schedule.

(4) Operates

The term "operates", as used with respect to a fixed route system or demand responsive system, includes operation of such system by a person under a contractual or other arrangement or relationship with a public entity.

(5) Public school transportation

The term "public school transportation" means transportation by school bus vehicles of schoolchildren, personnel, and equipment to and from a public elementary or secondary school and school-related activities.

(6) Secretary

The term "Secretary" means the Secretary of Transportation.

§ 12142. Public entities operating fixed route systems

(a) Purchase and lease of new vehicles

It shall be considered discrimination for purposes of section 12132 of this title and section 794 of Title 29 for a public entity which operates a fixed route system to purchase or lease a new bus, a new rapid rail vehicle, a new light rail vehicle, or any other new vehicle to be used on such system, if the solicitation for such purchase or lease is made after the 30th day following July 26, 1990, and if such bus, rail vehicle, or other vehicle is not readily accessible to and usable by individuals with disabilities, including individuals who use wheelchairs.

(b) Purchase and lease of used vehicles

Subject to subsection (c)(1) of this section, it shall be considered discrimination for purposes of section 12132 of this title and section 794 of Title 29 for a public entity which operates a fixed route system to purchase or lease, after the 30th day following July 26, 1990, a used vehicle for use on such system unless such entity makes demonstrated good faith efforts to purchase or lease a used vehicle for use on such system that is readily accessible to and usable by individuals with disabilities, including individuals who use wheelchairs.

(c) Remanufactured vehicles

(1) General rule

Except as provided in paragraph (2), it shall be considered discrimination for purposes of section 12132 of this title and section 794 of Title 29 for a public entity which operates a fixed route system—

(A) to remanufacture a vehicle for use on such system so as to extend its usable life for 5 years or more, which remanufacture begins (or for which the solicitation is made) after the 30th day following July 26, 1990; or

(B) to purchase or lease for use on such system a remanufactured vehicle which has been remanufactured so as to extend its usable life for 5 years or more, which purchase or lease occurs after such 30th day and during the period in which the usable life is extended; unless, after remanufacture, the vehicle is, to the maximum extent feasible, readily accessible to and usable by individuals with disabilities, including individuals who use wheelchairs.

(2) Exception for historic vehicles

(A) General rule

If a public entity operates a fixed route system any segment of which is included on the National Register of Historic Places and if making a vehicle of historic character to be used solely on such segment readily accessible to and usable by individuals with disabilities would significantly alter the historic character of such vehicle, the public entity only has to make (or to purchase or lease a remanufactured vehicle with) those modifications which are necessary to meet the requirements of paragraph (1) and which do not significantly alter the historic character of such vehicle.

(B) Vehicles of historic character defined by regulations

For purposes of this paragraph and section 12148(b) of this title, a vehicle of historic character shall be defined by the regulations issued by the Secretary to carry out this subsection.

§ 12143. Paratransit as a complement to fixed route service

(a) General rule

It shall be considered discrimination for purposes of section 12132 of this title and section 794 of Title 29 for a public entity which operates a fixed route system (other than a system which provides solely commuter bus service) to fail to provide with respect to the operations of its fixed route system, in accordance with this section, paratransit and other special transportation services to individuals with disabilities, including individuals who use wheelchairs, that are sufficient to provide to such individuals a level of service (1) which is comparable to the level of designated public transportation services provided to individuals without disabilities using such system; or (2) in the case of response time, which is comparable, to the extent practicable, to the level of designated public transportation services provided to individuals without disabilities using such system.

(b) Issuance of regulations

Not later than 1 year after July 26, 1990, the Secretary shall issue final regulations to carry out this section.

(c) Required contents of regulations

(1) Eligible recipients of service

The regulations issued under this section shall require each public entity which operates a fixed route system to provide the paratransit and other special transportation services required under this section—

(A)(i) to any individual with a disability who is unable, as a result of a physical or mental impairment (including a vision impairment) and without the assistance of another individual (except an operator of a wheelchair lift or other boarding assistance device), to board, ride, or disembark from any vehicle on the system which is readily accessible to and usable by individuals with disabilities;

(ii) to any individual with a disability who needs the assistance of a wheelchair lift or other boarding assistance device (and is able with such assistance) to board, ride, and disembark from any vehicle which is readily accessible to and usable by individuals with disabilities if the individual wants to travel on a route on the system during the hours of operation of the system at a time (or within a reasonable period of such time) when such a vehicle is not being used to provide designated public transportation on the route; and

(iii) to any individual with a disability who has a specific impairment-related condition which prevents such individual from traveling to a boarding location or from a disembarking location on such system;

(B) to one other individual accompanying the individual with the disability; and

(C) to other individuals, in addition to the one individual described in subparagraph (B), accompanying the individual with a disability provided that space for these additional individuals is available on the paratransit vehicle carrying the individual with a disability and that the transportation of such additional individuals will not result in a denial of service to individuals with disabilities.

For purposes of clauses (i) and (ii) of subparagraph (A), boarding or disembarking from a vehicle does not include travel to the boarding location or from the disembarking location.

(2) Service area

The regulations issued under this section shall require the provision of paratransit and special transportation services required under this section in the service area of each public entity which operates a fixed route system, other than any portion of the service area in which the public entity solely provides commuter bus service.

(3) Service criteria

Subject to paragraphs (1) and (2), the regulations issued under this section shall establish minimum service criteria for determining the level of services to be required under this section.

(4) Undue financial burden limitation

The regulations issued under this section shall provide that, if the public entity is able to demonstrate to the satisfaction of the Secretary that the provision of paratransit and other special transportation services otherwise required under this section would impose an undue financial burden on the public entity, the public entity, notwithstanding any other provision of this section (other than paragraph (5)), shall only be required to provide such services to the extent that providing such services would not impose such a burden.

(5) Additional services

The regulations issued under this section shall establish circumstances under which the Secretary may require a public entity to provide, notwithstanding paragraph (4), paratransit and other special transportation services under this section beyond the level of paratransit and other special transportation services which would otherwise be required under paragraph (4).

(6) Public participation

The regulations issued under this section shall require that each public entity which operates a fixed route system hold a public hearing, provide an opportunity for public comment, and consult with individuals with disabilities in preparing its plan under paragraph (7).

(7) Plans

The regulations issued under this section shall require that each public entity which operates a fixed route system—

(A) within 18 months after July 26, 1990, submit to the Secretary, and commence implementation of, a plan for providing paratransit and other special transportation services which meets the requirements of this section; and

(B) on an annual basis thereafter, submit to the Secretary, and commence implementation of, a plan for providing such services.

(8) Provision of services by others

The regulations issued under this section shall—

(A) require that a public entity submitting a plan to the Secretary under this section identify in the plan any person or other public entity which is providing a paratransit or other special transportation service for individuals with disabilities in the service area to which the plan applies; and

(B) provide that the public entity submitting the plan does not have to provide under the plan such service for individuals with disabilities.

(9) Other provisions

The regulations issued under this section shall include such other provisions and requirements as the Secretary determines are necessary to carry out the objectives of this section.

(d) Review of plan

(1) General rule

The Secretary shall review a plan submitted under this section for the purpose of determining whether or not such plan meets the requirements of this section, including the regulations issued under this section.

(2) Disapproval

If the Secretary determines that a plan reviewed under this subsection fails to meet the requirements of this section, the Secretary shall disapprove the plan and notify the public entity which submitted the plan of such disapproval and the reasons therefor.

(3) Modification of disapproved plan

Not later than 90 days after the date of disapproval of a plan under this subsection, the public entity which submitted the plan shall modify the plan to meet the requirements of this section and shall submit to the Secretary, and commence implementation of, such modified plan.

(e) Discrimination defined

As used in subsection (a) of this section, the term "discrimination" includes—

(1) a failure of a public entity to which the regulations issued under this section apply to submit, or commence implementation of, a plan in accordance with subsections (c)(6) and (c)(7) of this section;

(2) a failure of such entity to submit, or commence implementation of, a modified plan in accordance with subsection (d)(3) of this section;

(3) submission to the Secretary of a modified plan under subsection (d)(3) of this section which does not meet the requirements of this section; or

(4) a failure of such entity to provide paratransit or other special transportation services in accordance with the plan or modified plan the public entity submitted to the Secretary under this section.

(f) Statutory construction

Nothing in this section shall be construed as preventing a public entity—

(1) from providing paratransit or other special transportation services at a level which is greater than the level of such services which are required by this section,

(2) from providing paratransit or other special transportation services in addition to those paratransit and special transportation services required by this section, or

(3) from providing such services to individuals in addition to those individuals to whom such services are required to be provided by this section.

§ 12144. Public entity operating a demand responsive system

If a public entity operates a demand responsive system, it shall be considered discrimination, for purposes of section 12132 of this title and section 794 of Title 29, for such entity to purchase or lease a new vehicle for use on such system, for which a solicitation is made after the 30th day following July 26, 1990, that is not readily accessible to and usable by individuals with disabilities, including individuals who use wheelchairs, unless such system, when viewed in its entirety, provides a level of service to such individuals equivalent to the level of service such system provides to individuals without disabilities.

§ 12145. Temporary relief where lifts are unavailable

(a) Granting

With respect to the purchase of new buses, a public entity may apply for, and the Secretary may temporarily relieve such public entity from the obligation under section 12142(a) or 12144 of this title to purchase new buses that are readily accessible to and usable by individuals with disabilities if such public entity demonstrates to the satisfaction of the Secretary—

(1) that the initial solicitation for new buses made by the public entity specified that all new buses were to be lift-equipped and were to be otherwise accessible to and usable by individuals with disabilities;

(2) the unavailability from any qualified manufacturer of hydraulic, electromechanical, or other lifts for such new buses;

(3) that the public entity seeking temporary relief has made good faith efforts to locate a qualified manufacturer to supply the lifts to the manufacturer of such buses in sufficient time to comply with such solicitation; and

(4) that any further delay in purchasing new buses necessary to obtain such lifts would significantly impair transportation services in the community served by the public entity.

(b) Duration and notice to Congress

Any relief granted under subsection (a) of this section shall be limited in duration by a specified date, and the appropriate committees of Congress shall be notified of any such relief granted.

(c) Fraudulent application

If, at any time, the Secretary has reasonable cause to believe that any relief granted under subsection (a) of this section was fraudulently applied for, the Secretary shall—

(1) cancel such relief if such relief is still in effect; and

(2) take such other action as the Secretary considers appropriate.

§ 12146. New facilities

For purposes of section 12132 of this title and section 794 of Title 29, it shall be considered discrimination for a public entity to construct a new facility to be used in the provision of designated public transportation services unless such facility is readily accessible to and usable by individuals with disabilities, including individuals who use wheelchairs.

§ 12147. Alterations of existing facilities

(a) General rule

With respect to alterations of an existing facility or part thereof used in the provision of designated public transportation services that affect or could affect the usability of the facility or part thereof, it shall be considered discrimination, for purposes of section 12132 of this title and section 794 of Title 29, for a public entity to fail to make such alterations (or to ensure that the alterations are made) in such a manner that, to the maximum extent feasible, the altered portions of the facility are readily accessible to and usable by individuals with disabilities, including individuals who use wheelchairs, upon the completion of such alterations. Where the public entity is undertaking an alteration that affects or could affect usability of or access to an area of the facility containing a primary function, the entity shall also make the alterations in such a manner that, to the maximum extent feasible, the path of travel to the altered area and the bathrooms, telephones, and drinking fountains serving the altered area, are readily accessible to and usable by individuals with disabilities, including individuals who use wheelchairs, upon completion of such alterations, where such alterations to the path of travel or the bathrooms, telephones, and drinking fountains serving the altered area are not disproportionate to the overall alterations in terms of cost and scope (as determined under criteria established by the Attorney General).

(b) Special rule for stations

(1) General rule

For purposes of section 12132 of this title and section 794 of Title 29, it shall be considered discrimination for a public entity that provides designated public transportation to fail, in accordance with the provisions of this subsection, to make key stations (as determined under criteria established by the Secretary by regulation) in rapid rail and light rail systems readily accessible to and usable by individuals with disabilities, including individuals who use wheelchairs.

(2) Rapid rail and light rail key stations

(A) Accessibility

Except as otherwise provided in this paragraph, all key stations (as determined under criteria established by the Secretary by regulation) in rapid rail and light rail systems shall be made readily accessible to and usable by individuals with disabilities, including individuals who use wheelchairs, as soon as practicable but in no event later than the last day of the 3-year period beginning on July 26, 1990.

(B) Extension for extraordinarily expensive structural changes

The Secretary may extend the 3-year period under subparagraph (A) up to a 30-year period for key stations in a rapid rail or light rail system which stations need extraordinarily expensive structural changes to, or replacement of, existing facilities; except that by the last day of the 20th year following July 26, 1990, at least 2/3 of such key stations must be readily accessible to and usable by individuals with disabilities.

(3) Plans and milestones

The Secretary shall require the appropriate public entity to develop and submit to the Secretary a plan for compliance with this subsection—

(A) that reflects consultation with individuals with disabilities affected by such plan and the results of a public hearing and public comments on such plan, and

(B) that establishes milestones for achievement of the requirements of this subsection.

§ 12148. Public transportation programs and activities in existing facilities and one car per train rule

(a) Public transportation programs and activities in existing facilities

(1) In general

With respect to existing facilities used in the provision of designated public transportation services, it shall be considered discrimination, for purposes of section 12132 of this title and section 794 of Title 29, for a public entity to fail to operate a designated public transportation program or activity conducted in such facilities so that, when viewed in the entirety, the program or activity is readily accessible to and usable by individuals with disabilities.

(2) Exception

Paragraph (1) shall not require a public entity to make structural changes to existing facilities in order to make such facilities accessible to individuals who use wheelchairs, unless and to the extent required by section 12147(a) of this title (relating to alterations) or section 12147(b) of this title (relating to key stations).

(3) Utilization

Paragraph (1) shall not require a public entity to which paragraph (2) applies, to provide to individuals who use wheelchairs services made available to the general public at such facilities when such individuals could not utilize or benefit from such services provided at such facilities.

(b) One car per train rule

(1) General rule

Subject to paragraph (2), with respect to 2 or more vehicles operated as a train by a light or rapid rail system, for purposes of section 12132 of this title and section 794 of Title 29, it shall be considered discrimination for a public entity to fail to have at least 1 vehicle per train that is accessible to individuals with disabilities, including individuals who use wheelchairs, as soon as practicable but in no event later than the last day of the 5-year period beginning on the effective date of this section.

(2) Historic trains

In order to comply with paragraph (1) with respect to the remanufacture of a vehicle of historic character which is to be used on a segment of a light or rapid rail system which is included on the National Register of Historic Places, if making such vehicle readily accessible to and usable by individuals with disabilities would significantly alter the historic character of such vehicle, the public entity which operates such system only has to make (or to purchase or lease a remanufactured vehicle with) those modifications which are necessary to meet the requirements of section 12142(c)(1) of this title and which do not significantly alter the historic character of such vehicle.

§ 12149. Regulations

(a) In general. Not later than 1 year after the date of enactment of this Act [enacted July 26, 1990], the Secretary of Transportation shall issue regulations, in an accessible format, necessary for carrying out this part [42 USCS §§ 12141 et seq.] (other than section 223).

(b) Standards. The regulations issued under this section and section 223 [42 USCS § 12143] shall include standards applicable to facilities and vehicles covered by this subtitle [42 USCS §§ 12141 et seq.]. The standards shall be consistent with the minimum guidelines and requirements issued by the Architectural and Transportation Barriers Compliance Board in accordance with section 504 of this Act [42 USCS § 12204].

§ 12150. Interim accessibility requirements

If final regulations have not been issued pursuant to section 229 [42 USCS § 12149] for new construction or alterations for which a valid and appropriate State or local building permit is obtained prior to the issuance of final regulations under such section, and for which the construction or alteration authorized by such permit begins within one year of the receipt of such permit and is completed under the terms of such permit, compliance with the Uniform Federal Accessibility Standards in effect at the time the building permit is issued shall suffice to satisfy the requirement that facilities be readily accessible to and usable by persons with disabilities as required under sections 226 and 227 [42 USCS §§ 12146, 12147], except that, if such final regulations have not been issued one year after the Architectural and Transportation Barriers Compliance Board has issued the supplemental minimum guidelines required under section 504(a) of this Act [42 USCS § 12204(a)], compliance with such supplemental minimum guidelines shall be necessary to satisfy the requirement that facilities be readily accessible to and usable by persons with disabilities prior to issuance of the final regulations.

ADA TITLE II DOJ REGULATIONS

28 C.F.R. §

ADA TITLE II DOJ REGULATIONS

Subpart A—General

§ 35.102 Application.

(a) Except as provided in paragraph (b) of this section, this part applies to all services, programs, and activities provided or made available by public entities.

(b) To the extent that public transportation services, programs, and activities of public entities are covered by subtitle B of title II of the ADA (42 U.S.C. 12141), they are not subject to the requirements of this part.

§ 35.103 Relationship to other laws.

(a) Rule of interpretation. Except as otherwise provided in this part, this part shall not be construed to apply a lesser standard than the standards applied under title V of the Rehabilitation Act of 1973 (29 U.S.C. 791) or the regulations issued by Federal agencies pursuant to that title.

(b) Other laws. This part does not invalidate or limit the remedies, rights, and procedures of any other Federal laws, or State or local laws (including State common law) that provide greater or equal protection for the rights of individuals with disabilities or individuals associated with them.

§ 35.104 Definitions.

For purposes of this part, the term—

Act means the Americans with Disabilities Act (Pub. L. 101-336, 104 Stat. 327, 42 U.S.C. 12101-12213 and 47 U.S.C. 225 and 611).

Assistant Attorney General means the Assistant Attorney General, Civil Rights Division, United States Department of Justice.

Auxiliary aids and services includes—

(1) Qualified interpreters, note takers, transcription services, written materials, telephone handset amplifiers, assistive listening devices, assistive listening systems, telephones compatible with hearing aids, closed caption decoders, open and closed captioning, telecommunications devices for deaf persons (TDD's), videotext displays, or other effective methods of making aurally delivered materials available to individuals with hearing impairments;

(2) Qualified readers, taped texts, audio recordings, Brailled materials, large print materials, or other effective methods of making visually delivered materials available to individuals with visual impairments;

(3) Acquisition or modification of equipment or devices; and

(4) Other similar services and actions.

Complete complaint means a written statement that contains the complainant's name and address and describes the public entity's alleged discriminatory action in sufficient detail to inform the agency of the nature and date of the alleged violation of this part. It shall be signed by the complainant or by someone authorized to do so on his or her behalf. Complaints filed on behalf of classes or third parties shall describe or identify (by name, if possible) the alleged victims of discrimination.

Current illegal use of drugs means illegal use of drugs that occurred recently enough to justify a reasonable belief that a person's drug use is current or that continuing use is a real and ongoing problem.

Designated agency means the Federal agency designated under sub-part G of this part to oversee compliance activities under this part for particular components of State and local governments.

Disability means, with respect to an individual, a physical or mental impairment that substantially limits one or more of the major life activities of such individual; a record of such an impairment; or being regarded as having such an impairment.

(1)(i) The phrase physical or mental impairment means—

(A) Any physiological disorder or condition, cosmetic disfigurement, or anatomical loss affecting one or more of the following body systems: Neurological, musculoskeletal, special sense organs, respiratory (including speech organs), cardiovascular, reproductive, digestive, genitourinary, hemic and lymphatic, skin, and endocrine;

(B) Any mental or psychological disorder such as mental retardation, organic brain syndrome, emotional or mental illness, and specific learning disabilities.

(ii) The phrase physical or mental impairment includes, but is not limited to, such contagious and noncontagious diseases and conditions as orthopedic, visual, speech and hearing impairments, cerebral palsy, epilepsy, muscular dystrophy, multiple sclerosis, cancer, heart disease, diabetes, mental retardation, emotional illness, specific learning disabilities, HIV disease (whether symptomatic or asymptomatic), tuberculosis, drug addiction, and alcoholism.

(iii) The phrase physical or mental impairment does not include homosexuality or bisexuality.

(2) The phrase major life activities means functions such as caring for one's self, performing manual tasks, walking, seeing, hearing, speaking, breathing, learning, and working.

(3) The phrase has a record of such an impairment means has a history of, or has been misclassified as having, a mental or physical impairment that substantially limits one or more major life activities.

(4) The phrase is regarded as having an impairment means—

(i) Has a physical or mental impairment that does not substantially limit major life activities but that is treated by a public entity as constituting such a limitation;

(ii) Has a physical or mental impairment that substantially limits major life activities only as a result of the attitudes of others toward such impairment; or

(iii) Has none of the impairments defined in paragraph (1) of this definition but is treated by a public entity as having such an impairment.

(5) The term disability does not include—

(i) Transvestism, transsexualism, pedophilia, exhibitionism, voyeurism, gender identity disorders not resulting from physical impairments, or other sexual behavior disorders;

(ii) Compulsive gambling, kleptomania, or pyromania; or

(iii) Psychoactive substance use disorders resulting from current illegal use of drugs.

Drug means a controlled substance, as defined in schedules I through V of section 202 of the Controlled Substances Act (21 U.S.C. 812).

Facility means all or any portion of buildings, structures, sites, complexes, equipment, rolling stock or other conveyances, roads, walks, passageways, parking lots, or other real or personal property, including the site where the building, property, structure, or equipment is located.

Historic preservation programs means programs conducted by a public entity that have preservation of historic properties as a primary purpose.

Historic Properties means those properties that are listed or eligible for listing in the National Register of Historic Places or properties designated as historic under State or local law.

Illegal use of drugs means the use of one or more drugs, the possession or distribution of which is unlawful under the Controlled Substances Act (21 U.S.C. 812). The term illegal use of drugs does not include the use of a drug taken under supervision by a licensed health care professional, or other uses authorized by the Controlled Substances Act or other provisions of Federal law.

Individual with a disability means a person who has a disability. The term individual with a disability does not include an individual who is currently engaging in the illegal use of drugs, when the public entity acts on the basis of such use.

Public entity means—

(1) Any State or local government;

(2) Any department, agency, special purpose district, or other instrumentality of a State or States or local government; and

(3) The National Railroad Passenger Corporation, and any commuter authority (as defined in section 103(8) of the Rail Passenger Service Act).

Qualified individual with a disability means an individual with a disability who, with or without reasonable modifications to rules, policies, or practices, the removal of architectural, communication, or transportation barriers, or the provision of auxiliary aids and services, meets the essential eligibility requirements for the receipt of services or the participation in programs or activities provided by a public entity.

Qualified interpreter means an interpreter who is able to interpret effectively, accurately, and impartially both receptively and expressively, using any necessary specialized vocabulary.

Section 504 means section 504 of the Rehabilitation Act of 1973 (Pub. L. 93-112, 87 Stat. 394 (29 U.S.C. 794)), as amended.

State means each of the several States, the District of Columbia, the Commonwealth of Puerto Rico, Guam, American Samoa, the Virgin Islands, the Trust Territory of the Pacific Islands, and the Commonwealth of the Northern Mariana Islands.

Subpart B—General Requirements

§ 35.130 General prohibitions against discrimination.

(a) No qualified individual with a disability shall, on the basis of disability, be excluded from participation in or be denied the benefits of the services, programs, or activities of a public entity, or be subjected to discrimination by any public entity.

(b)(1) A public entity, in providing any aid, benefit, or service, may not, directly or through contractual, licensing, or other arrangements, on the basis of disability—

(i) Deny a qualified individual with a disability the opportunity to participate in or benefit from the aid, benefit, or service;

(ii) Afford a qualified individual with a disability an opportunity to participate in or benefit from the aid, benefit, or service that is not equal to that afforded others;

(iii) Provide a qualified individual with a disability with an aid, benefit, or service that is not as effective in affording equal opportunity to obtain the same result, to gain the same benefit, or to reach the same level of achievement as that provided to others;

(iv) Provide different or separate aids, benefits, or services to individuals with disabilities or to any class of individuals with disabilities than is provided to others unless such action is necessary to provide qualified individuals with disabilities with aids, benefits, or services that are as effective as those provided to others;

(v) Aid or perpetuate discrimination against a qualified individual with a disability by providing significant assistance to an agency, organization, or person that discriminates on the basis of disability in providing any aid, benefit, or service to beneficiaries of the public entity's program;

(vi) Deny a qualified individual with a disability the opportunity to participate as a member of planning or advisory boards;

(vii) Otherwise limit a qualified individual with a disability in the enjoyment of any right, privilege, advantage, or opportunity enjoyed by others receiving the aid, benefit, or service.

(2) A public entity may not deny a qualified individual with a disability the opportunity to participate in services, programs, or activities that are not separate or different, despite the existence of permissibly separate or different programs or activities.

(3) A public entity may not, directly or through contractual or other arrangements, utilize criteria or methods of administration:

(i) That have the effect of subjecting qualified individuals with disabilities to discrimination on the basis of disability;

(ii) That have the purpose or effect of defeating or substantially impairing accomplishment of the objectives of the public entity's program with respect to individuals with disabilities; or

(iii) That perpetuate the discrimination of another public entity if both public entities are subject to common administrative control or are agencies of the same State.

(4) A public entity may not, in determining the site or location of a facility, make selections—

(i) That have the effect of excluding individuals with disabilities from, denying them the benefits of, or otherwise subjecting them to discrimination; or

(ii) That have the purpose or effect of defeating or substantially impairing the accomplishment of the objectives of the service, program, or activity with respect to individuals with disabilities.

(5) A public entity, in the selection of procurement contractors, may not use criteria that subject qualified individuals with disabilities to discrimination on the basis of disability.

(6) A public entity may not administer a licensing or certification program in a manner that subjects qualified individuals with disabilities to discrimination on the basis of disability, nor may a public entity establish requirements for the programs or activities of licensees or certified entities that subject qualified individuals with disabilities to discrimination on the

basis of disability. The programs or activities of entities that are licensed or certified by a public entity are not, themselves, covered by this part.

(7) A public entity shall make reasonable modifications in policies, practices, or procedures when the modifications are necessary to avoid discrimination on the basis of disability, unless the public entity can demonstrate that making the modifications would fundamentally alter the nature of the service, program, or activity.

(8) A public entity shall not impose or apply eligibility criteria that screen out or tend to screen out an individual with a disability or any class of individuals with disabilities from fully and equally enjoying any service, program, or activity, unless such criteria can be shown to be necessary for the provision of the service, program, or activity being offered.

(c) Nothing in this part prohibits a public entity from providing benefits, services, or advantages to individuals with disabilities, or to a particular class of individuals with disabilities beyond those required by this part.

(d) A public entity shall administer services, programs, and activities in the most integrated setting appropriate to the needs of qualified individuals with disabilities.

(e)(1) Nothing in this part shall be construed to require an individual with a disability to accept an accommodation, aid, service, opportunity, or benefit provided under the ADA or this part which such individual chooses not to accept.

(2) Nothing in the Act or this part authorizes the representative or guardian of an individual with a disability to decline food, water, medical treatment, or medical services for that individual.

(f) A public entity may not place a surcharge on a particular individual with a disability or any group of individuals with disabilities to cover the costs of measures, such as the provision of auxiliary aids or program accessibility, that are required to provide that individual or group with the nondiscriminatory treatment required by the Act or this part.

(g) A public entity shall not exclude or otherwise deny equal services, programs, or activities to an individual or entity because of the known disability of an individual with whom the individual or entity is known to have a relationship or association.

§ 35.131 Illegal use of drugs.

(a) General.

(1) Except as provided in paragraph (b) of this section, this part does not prohibit discrimination against an individual based on that individual's current illegal use of drugs.

(2) A public entity shall not discriminate on the basis of illegal use of drugs against an individual who is not engaging in current illegal use of drugs and who—

(i) Has successfully completed a supervised drug rehabilitation program or has otherwise been rehabilitated successfully;

(ii) Is participating in a supervised rehabilitation program; or

(iii) Is erroneously regarded as engaging in such use.

(b) Health and drug rehabilitation services.

(1) A public entity shall not deny health services, or services provided in connection with drug rehabilitation, to an individual on the basis of that individual's current illegal use of drugs, if the individual is otherwise entitled to such services.

(2) A drug rehabilitation or treatment program may deny participation to individuals who engage in illegal use of drugs while they are in the program.

(c) Drug testing.

(1) This part does not prohibit a public entity from adopting or administering reasonable policies or procedures, including but not limited to drug testing, designed to ensure that an individual who formerly engaged in the illegal use of drugs is not now engaging in current illegal use of drugs.

(2) Nothing in paragraph (c) of this section shall be construed to encourage, prohibit, restrict, or authorize the conduct of testing for the illegal use of drugs.

§ 35.132 Smoking.

This part does not preclude the prohibition of, or the imposition of restrictions on, smoking in transportation covered by this part.

§ 35.133 Maintenance of accessible features.

(a) A public entity shall maintain in operable working condition those features of facilities and equipment that are required to be readily accessible to and usable by persons with disabilities by the Act or this part.

(b) This section does not prohibit isolated or temporary interruptions in service or access due to maintenance or repairs.

§ 35.134 Retaliation or coercion.

(a) No private or public entity shall discriminate against any individual because that individual has opposed any act or practice made unlawful by this part, or because that individual made a charge, testified, assisted, or participated in any manner in an investigation, proceeding, or hearing under the Act or this part.

(b) No private or public entity shall coerce, intimidate, threaten, or interfere with any individual in the exercise or enjoyment of, or on account of his or her having exercised or enjoyed, or on account of his or her having aided or encouraged any other individual in the exercise or enjoyment of, any right granted or protected by the Act or this part.

§ 35.135 Personal devices and services.

This part does not require a public entity to provide to individuals with disabilities personal devices, such as wheelchairs; individually prescribed devices, such as prescription eyeglasses or hearing aids; readers for personal use or study; or services of a personal nature including assistance in eating, toileting, or dressing.

Subpart C—Employment

§ 35.140 Employment discrimination prohibited.

(a) No qualified individual with a disability shall, on the basis of disability, be subjected to discrimination in employment under any service, program, or activity conducted by a public entity.

(b)(1) For purposes of this part, the requirements of title I of the Act, as established by the regulations of the Equal Employment Opportunity Commission in 29 CFR part 1630, apply to employment in any service, program, or activity conducted by a public entity if that public entity is also subject to the jurisdiction of title I.

(2) For the purposes of this part, the requirements of section 504 of the Rehabilitation Act of 1973, as established by the regulations of the Department of Justice in 28 CFR part 41, as those requirements pertain to employment, apply to employment in any service, program, or activity conducted by a public entity if that public entity is not also subject to the jurisdiction of title I

Subpart D—Program Accessibility

§ 35.149 Discrimination prohibited.

Except as otherwise provided in § 35.150, no qualified individual with a disability shall, because a public entity's facilities are inaccessible to or unusable by individuals with disabilities, be excluded from participation in, or be denied the benefits of the services, programs, or activities of a public entity, or be subjected to discrimination by any public entity.

§ 35.150 Existing facilities.

(a) General. A public entity shall operate each service, program, or activity so that the service, program, or activity, when viewed in its entirety, is readily accessible to and usable by individuals with disabilities. This paragraph does not—

(1) Necessarily require a public entity to make each of its existing facilities accessible to and usable by individuals with disabilities;

(2) Require a public entity to take any action that would threaten or destroy the historic significance of an historic property; or

(3) Require a public entity to take any action that it can demonstrate would result in a fundamental alteration in the nature of a service, program, or activity or in undue financial and administrative burdens. In those circumstances where personnel of the public entity believe that the proposed action would fundamentally alter the service, program, or activity or would result in undue financial and administrative burdens, a public entity has the burden of proving that compliance with § 35.150(a) of this part would result in such alteration or burdens. The decision that compliance would result in such alteration or burdens must be made by the head of a public entity or his or her designee after considering all resources available for use in the funding and operation of the service, program, or activity, and must be accompanied by a written statement of the reasons for reaching that conclusion. If an action would result in such an alteration or such burdens, a public entity shall take any other action that would not result in such an alteration or such burdens but would nevertheless ensure that individuals with disabilities receive the benefits or services provided by the public entity.

(b) Methods—

(1) General. A public entity may comply with the requirements of this section through such means as redesign of equipment, reassignment of services to accessible buildings, assignment of aides to beneficiaries, home visits, delivery of services at alternate accessible sites, alteration of existing facilities and construction of new facilities, use of accessible rolling stock or other conveyances, or any other methods that result in making its services, programs, or activities readily accessible to and usable by individuals with disabilities. A public entity is not required to make

structural changes in existing facilities where other methods are effective in achieving compliance with this section. A public entity, in making alterations to existing buildings, shall meet the accessibility requirements of § 35.151. In choosing among available methods for meeting the requirements of this section, a public entity shall give priority to those methods that offer services, programs, and activities to qualified individuals with disabilities in the most integrated setting appropriate.

(2) Historic preservation programs. In meeting the requirements of § 35.150(a) in historic preservation programs, a public entity shall give priority to methods that provide physical access to individuals with disabilities. In cases where a physical alteration to an historic property is not required because of paragraph (a)(2) or (a)(3) of this section, alternative methods of achieving program accessibility include—

(i) Using audio-visual materials and devices to depict those portions of an historic property that cannot otherwise be made accessible;

(ii) Assigning persons to guide individuals with handicaps into or through portions of historic properties that cannot otherwise be made accessible; or

(iii) Adopting other innovative methods.

(c) Time period for compliance. Where structural changes in facilities are undertaken to comply with the obligations established under this section, such changes shall be made within three years of January 26, 1992, but in any event as expeditiously as possible.

(d) Transition plan.

(1) In the event that structural changes to facilities will be undertaken to achieve program accessibility, a public entity that employs 50 or more persons shall develop, within six months of January 26, 1992, a transition plan setting forth the steps necessary to complete such changes. A public entity shall provide an opportunity to interested persons, including individuals with disabilities or organizations representing individuals with disabilities, to participate in the development of the transition plan by submitting comments. A copy of the transition plan shall be made available for public inspection.

(2) If a public entity has responsibility or authority over streets, roads, or walkways, its transition plan shall include a schedule for providing curb ramps or other sloped areas where pedestrian walks cross curbs, giving priority to walkways serving entities covered by the Act, including State and local government offices and facilities, transportation, places of public accommodation, and employers, followed by walkways serving other areas.

(3) The plan shall, at a minimum—

(i) Identify physical obstacles in the public entity's facilities that limit the accessibility of its programs or activities to individuals with disabilities;

(ii) Describe in detail the methods that will be used to make the facilities accessible;

(iii) Specify the schedule for taking the steps necessary to achieve compliance with this section and, if the time period of the transition plan is longer than one year, identify steps that will be taken during each year of the transition period; and

(iv) Indicate the official responsible for implementation of the plan.

(4) If a public entity has already complied with the transition plan requirement of a Federal agency regulation implementing section 504 of the Rehabilitation Act of 1973, then the requirements of this paragraph (d) shall apply only to those policies and practices that were not included in the previous transition plan.

(Approved by the Office of Management and Budget under control number 1190-0004)

§ 35.151 New construction and alterations.

(a) Design and construction. Each facility or part of a facility constructed by, on behalf of, or for the use of a public entity shall be designed and constructed in such manner that the facility or part of the facility is readily accessible to and usable by individuals with disabilities, if the construction was commenced after January 26, 1992.

(b) Alteration. Each facility or part of a facility altered by, on behalf of, or for the use of a public entity in a manner that affects or could affect the usability of the facility or part of the facility shall, to the maximum extent feasible, be altered in such manner that the altered portion of the facility is readily accessible to and usable by individuals with disabilities, if the alteration was commenced after January 26, 1992.

(c) Accessibility standards. Design, construction, or alteration of facilities in conformance with the Uniform Federal Accessibility Standards (UFAS) (Appendix A to 41 CFR part 101-19.6) or with the Americans with Disabilities Act Accessibility Guidelines for Buildings and Facilities (ADAAG) (Appendix A to 28 CFR part 36) shall be deemed to comply with the requirements of this section with respect to those facilities, except that the elevator exemption contained at section 4.1.3(5) and section 4.1.6(1)(k) of ADAAG shall not apply. Departures from particular requirements of either standard by the use of other methods shall be permitted when it is clearly evident that equivalent access to the facility or part of the facility is thereby provided.

(d) Alterations: Historic properties.

(1) Alterations to historic properties shall comply, to the maximum extent feasible, with section 4.1.7 of UFAS or section 4.1.7 of ADAAG.

(2) If it is not feasible to provide physical access to an historic property in a manner that will not threaten or destroy the historic significance of the building or facility, alternative methods of access shall be provided pursuant to the requirements of § 35.150.

(e) Curb ramps.

(1) Newly constructed or altered streets, roads, and highways must contain curb ramps or other sloped areas at any intersection having curbs or other barriers to entry from a street level pedestrian walkway.

(2) Newly constructed or altered street level pedestrian walkways must contain curb ramps or other sloped areas at intersections to streets, roads, or highways.

Subpart E—Communications

§ 35.160 General.

(a) A public entity shall take appropriate steps to ensure that communications with applicants, participants, and members of the public with disabilities are as effective as communications with others.

(b)(1) A public entity shall furnish appropriate auxiliary aids and services where necessary to afford an individual with a disability an equal opportunity to participate in, and enjoy the benefits of, a service, program, or activity conducted by a public entity.

(2) In determining what type of auxiliary aid and service is necessary, a public entity shall give primary consideration to the requests of the individual with disabilities.

§ 35.161 Telecommunication devices for the deaf (TDD's).

Where a public entity communicates by telephone with applicants and beneficiaries, TDD's or equally effective telecommunication systems shall be used to communicate with individuals with impaired hearing or speech.

§ 35.162 Telephone emergency services.

Telephone emergency services, including 911 services, shall provide direct access to individuals who use TDD's and computer modems.

§ 35.163 Information and signage.

(a) A public entity shall ensure that interested persons, including persons with impaired vision or hearing, can obtain information as to the existence and location of accessible services, activities, and facilities.

(b) A public entity shall provide signage at all inaccessible entrances to each of its facilities, directing users to an accessible entrance or to a location at which they can obtain information about accessible facilities. The international symbol for accessibility shall be used at each accessible entrance of a facility.

§ 35.164 Duties.

This subpart does not require a public entity to take any action that it can demonstrate would result in a fundamental alteration in the nature of a service, program, or activity or in undue financial and administrative burdens. In those circumstances where personnel of the public entity believe that the proposed action would fundamentally alter the service, program, or activity or would result in undue financial and administrative burdens, a public entity has the burden of proving that compliance with this subpart would result in such alteration or burdens. The decision that compliance would result in such alteration or burdens must be made by the head of the public entity or his or her designee after considering all resources available for use in the funding and operation of the service, program, or activity and must be accompanied by a written statement of the reasons for reaching that conclusion. If an action required to comply with this subpart would result in such an alteration or such burdens, a public entity shall take any other action that would not result in such an alteration or such burdens but would nevertheless ensure that, to the maximum extent possible, individuals with disabilities receive the benefits or services provided by the public entity.

Subpart F—Compliance Procedures

§ 35.178 State immunity.

A State shall not be immune under the eleventh amendment to the Constitution of the United States from an action in Federal or State court of competent jurisdiction for a violation of this Act. In any action against a State for a violation of the requirements of this Act, remedies (including remedies both at law and in equity) are available for such a violation to the same extent as such remedies are available for such a violation in an action against any public or private entity other than a State.

ADA TITLE II DOJ INTERPRETIVE GUIDANCE

28 C.F.R §

ADA TITLE II DOJ INTERPRETIVE GUIDANCE

Subpart A—General

Section 35.104 Definitions

"Act." The word "Act" is used in this part to refer to the Americans with Disabilities Act of 1990, Public Law 101-336, which is also referred to as the "ADA." "Assistant Attorney General." The term "Assistant Attorney General" refers to the Assistant Attorney General of the Civil Rights Division of the Department of Justice.

"Auxiliary aids and services." Auxiliary aids and services include a wide range of services and devices for ensuring effective communication. The proposed definition in § 35.104 provided a list of examples of auxiliary aids and services that were taken from the definition of auxiliary aids and services in section 3(1) of the ADA and were supplemented by examples from regulations implementing section 504 in federally conducted programs (see 28 CFR 39.103).

A substantial number of commenters suggested that additional examples be added to this list. The Department has added several items to this list but wishes to clarify that the list is not an all-inclusive or exhaustive catalogue of possible or available auxiliary aids or services. It is not possible to provide an exhaustive list, and an attempt to do so would omit the new devices that will become available with emerging technology.

Subparagraph (1) lists several examples, which would be considered auxiliary aids and services to make aurally delivered materials available to individuals with hearing impairments. The Department has changed the phrase used in the proposed rules, "orally delivered materials," to the statutory phrase, "aurally delivered materials," to track section 3 of the ADA and to include non-verbal sounds and alarms, and computer generated speech.

The Department has added videotext displays, transcription services, and closed and open captioning to the list of examples. Videotext displays have become an important means of accessing auditory communications through a public address system. Transcription services are used to relay aurally delivered material almost simultaneously in written form to persons who are deaf or hearing-impaired. This technology is often used at conferences, conventions, and hearings. While the proposed rule expressly included television decoder equipment as an auxiliary aid or service, it did not mention captioning itself. The final rule rectifies this omission by mentioning both closed and open captioning.

Several persons and organizations requested that the Department replace the term "telecommunications devices for deaf persons" or "TDD's" with the term "text telephone." The Department has declined to do so. The Department is aware that the Architectural and Transportation Barriers Compliance Board (ATBCB) has used the phrase "text telephone" in lieu of the statutory term "TDD" in its final accessibility guidelines. Title IV of the ADA, however, uses the term "Telecommunications Device for the Deaf" and the Department believes it would be inappropriate to abandon this statutory term at this time.

Several commenters urged the Department to include in the definition of "auxiliary aids and services" devices that are now available or that may become available with emerging technology. The Department declines to do so in the rule. The Department, however, emphasizes that, although the definition would include "state of the art" devices, public entities are not required to use the newest or most advanced technologies as long as the auxiliary aid or service that is selected affords effective communication.

Subparagraph (2) lists examples of aids and services for making visually delivered materials accessible to persons with visual impairments. Many commenters proposed additional examples, such as signage or mapping, audio description services, secondary auditory programs, telebraillers, and reading machines. While the Department declines to add these items to the list, they are auxiliary aids and services and may be appropriate depending on the circumstances.

Subparagraph (3) refers to acquisition or modification of equipment or devices. Several commenters suggested the addition of current technological innovations in microelectronics and computerized control systems (e.g., voice recognition systems, automatic dialing telephones, and infrared elevator and light control systems) to the list of auxiliary aids. The Department interprets auxiliary aids and services as those aids and services designed to provide effective communications, i.e., making aurally and visually delivered information available to persons with hearing, speech, and vision impairments. Methods of making services, programs, or activities accessible to, or usable by, individuals with mobility or manual dexterity impairments are addressed by other sections of this part, including the provision for modifications in policies, practices, or procedures (s 35.130 (b)(7)).

Paragraph (b)(4) deals with other similar services and actions. Several commenters asked for clarification that "similar services and actions" include retrieving items from shelves, assistance in reaching a marginally accessible seat, pushing a barrier aside in order to provide an accessible route, or assistance in removing a sweater or coat. While retrieving an item from a shelf might be an "auxiliary aid or service" for a blind person who could not locate the item without assistance, it might be a method of providing program access for a person using a wheelchair who could not reach the shelf, or a reasonable modification to a self-service policy for an individual who lacked the ability to grasp the item. As explained above, auxiliary aids and services are those aids and services required to provide effective communications. Other forms of assistance are more appropriately addressed by other provisions of the final rule.

"Complete complaint." "Complete complaint" is defined to include all the information necessary to enable the Federal agency designated under subpart G as responsible for investigation of a complaint to initiate its investigation.

"Current illegal use of drugs." The phrase "current illegal use of drugs" is used in § 35.131. Its meaning is discussed in the preamble for that section.

"Designated agency." The term "designated agency" is used to refer to the Federal agency designated under subpart G of this rule as responsible for carrying out the administrative enforcement responsibilities established by subpart F of the rule.

"Disability." The definition of the term "disability" is the same as the definition in the title III regulation codified at 28 CFR part 36. It is comparable to the definition of the term "individual with handicaps" in section 7(8) of the Rehabilitation Act and section 802(h) of the Fair Housing Act. The Education and Labor Committee report makes clear that the analysis of the term "individual with handicaps" by the Department of Health, Education, and Welfare (HEW) in its regulations implementing section 504 (42 FR 22685 (May 4, 1977)) and the analysis by the Department of Housing and Urban Development in its regulation implementing the Fair Housing Amendments Act of 1988 (54 FR 3232 (Jan. 23, 1989)) should also apply fully to the term "disability" (Education and Labor report at 50).

The use of the term "disability" instead of "handicap" and the term "individual with a disability" instead of "individual with handicaps" represents an effort by Congress to make use of up-to-date, currently accepted terminology. As with racial and ethnic epithets, the choice of terms to apply to a person with a disability is overlaid with stereotypes, patronizing attitudes, and other emotional connotations. Many individuals with disabilities, and organizations representing such individuals, object to the use of such terms as "handicapped person" or "the handicapped." In other recent legislation, Congress also recognized this shift in terminology, e.g., by changing the name of the National Council on the Handicapped to the National Council on Disability (Pub. L. 100-630).

In enacting the Americans with Disabilities Act, Congress concluded that it was important for the current legislation to use terminology most in line with the sensibilities of most Americans with disabilities. No change in definition or substance is intended nor should one be attributed to this change in phraseology. The term "disability" means, with respect to an individual—

(A) A physical or mental impairment that substantially limits one or more of the major life activities of such individual;

(B) A record of such an impairment; or

(C) Being regarded as having such an impairment.

If an individual meets any one of these three tests, he or she is considered to be an individual with a disability for purposes of coverage under the Americans with Disabilities Act.

Congress adopted this same basic definition of "disability," first used in the Rehabilitation Act of 1973 and in the Fair Housing Amendments Act of 1988, for a number of reasons. First, it has worked well since it was adopted in 1974. Second, it would not be possible to guarantee comprehensiveness by providing a list of specific disabilities, especially because new disorders may be recognized in the future, as they have since the definition was first established in 1974.

Test A—A physical or mental impairment that substantially limits one or more of the major life activities of such individual

Physical or mental impairment. Under the first test, an individual must have a physical or mental impairment. As explained in paragraph (1)(i) of the definition, "impairment" means any physiological disorder or condition, cosmetic disfigurement, or anatomical loss affecting one or more of the following body systems: neurological; musculoskeletal; special sense organs (which would include speech organs that are not respiratory such as vocal cords, soft palate, tongue, etc.); respiratory, including speech organs; cardiovascular; reproductive; digestive; genitourinary; hemic and lymphatic; skin; and endocrine. It also means any mental or psychological disorder, such as mental retardation, organic brain syndrome, emotional or mental illness, and specific learning disabilities. This list closely tracks the one used in the regulations for section 504 of the Rehabilitation Act of 1973 (see, e.g., 45 CFR 84.3(j)(2)(i)).

Many commenters asked that "traumatic brain injury" be added to the list in paragraph (1)(i). Traumatic brain injury is already included because it is a physiological condition affecting one of the listed body systems, i.e., "neurological." Therefore, it was unnecessary to add the term to the regulation, which only provides representative examples of physiological disorders.

It is not possible to include a list of all the specific conditions, contagious and noncontagious diseases, or infections that would constitute physical or mental impairments because of the difficulty of ensuring the comprehensiveness of such a list, particularly in light of the fact that other conditions or disorders may be identified in the future. However, the list of examples in paragraph (1)(ii) of the definition includes: orthopedic, visual, speech and hearing impairments, cerebral palsy, epilepsy, muscular dystrophy, multiple sclerosis, cancer, heart disease, diabetes, mental retardation, emotional illness, specific learning disabilities, HIV disease (symptomatic or asymptomatic), tuberculosis, drug addiction, and alcoholism. The phrase "symptomatic or asymptomatic" was inserted in the final rule after "HIV disease" in response to commenters who suggested the clarification was necessary.

The examples of "physical or mental impairments" in paragraph (1)(ii) are the same as those contained in many section 504 regulations, except for the addition of the phrase "contagious and noncontagious" to describe the types of diseases and conditions included, and the addition of "HIV disease (symptomatic or asymptomatic)" and "tuberculosis" to the list of examples. These additions are based on the committee reports, caselaw, and official legal opinions interpreting section 504. In *School Board of Nassau County v. Arline*, 480 U.S. 273 (1987), a case involving an individual with tuberculosis, the Supreme Court held that people with contagious diseases are entitled to the protections afforded by section 504. Following the Arline decision, this Department's Office of Legal Counsel issued a legal opinion that concluded that symptomatic HIV disease is an impairment that substantially limits a major life activity; therefore it has been included in the definition of disability under this part. The opinion also concluded that asymptomatic HIV disease is an impairment that substantially limits a major life activity, either because of its actual effect on the individual with HIV disease or because the reactions of other people to individuals with HIV disease cause such individuals to be treated as though they are disabled. See Memorandum from Douglas W. Kmiec, Acting Assistant Attorney General, Office of Legal Counsel, Department of Justice, to Arthur B. Culvahouse, Jr., Counsel to the President (Sept. 27, 1988), reprinted in Hearings on S. 933, the Americans with Disabilities Act, Before the Subcomm. on the Handicapped of the Senate Comm. on Labor and Human Resources, 101st. Cong., 1st Sess. 346 (1989).

Paragraph (1)(iii) states that the phrase "physical or mental impairment" does not include homosexuality or bisexuality. These conditions were never considered impairments under other Federal disability laws. Section 511(a) of the statute makes clear that they are likewise not to be considered impairments under the Americans with Disabilities Act.

Physical or mental impairment does not include simple physical characteristics, such as blue eyes or black hair. Nor does it include environmental, cultural, economic, or other disadvantages, such as having a prison record, or being poor. Nor is age a disability. Similarly, the definition does not include common personality traits such as poor judgment or a quick temper where these are not symptoms of a mental or psychological disorder. However, a person who has these characteristics and also has a physical or mental impairment may be considered as having a disability for purposes of the Americans with Disabilities Act based on the impairment. Substantial Limitation of a Major Life Activity. Under Test A, the impairment must be one that "substantially limits a major life activity." Major life activities include such things as caring for one's self, performing manual tasks, walking, seeing, hearing, speaking, breathing, learning, and working.

For example, a person who is paraplegic is substantially limited in the major life activity of walking, a person who is blind is substantially limited in the major life activity of seeing, and a person who is mentally retarded is substantially limited in the major life activity of learning. A person with traumatic brain injury is substantially limited in the major life activities of caring for one's self, learning, and working because of memory deficit, confusion, contextual difficulties, and inability to reason appropriately.

A person is considered an individual with a disability for purposes of Test A, the first prong of the definition, when the individual's important life activities are restricted as to the conditions, manner, or duration under which they can be performed in comparison to most people. A person with a minor, trivial impairment, such as a simple infected finger, is not impaired in a major life activity. A person who can walk for 10 miles continuously is not substantially limited in walking merely because, on the eleventh mile, he or she begins to experience pain, because most people would not be able to walk eleven miles without experiencing some discomfort.

The Department received many comments on the proposed rule's inclusion of the word "temporary" in the definition of "disability." The preamble indicated that impairments are not necessarily excluded from the definition of "disability" simply because they are temporary, but that the duration, or expected duration, of an impairment is one factor that may properly be considered in determining whether the impairment substantially limits a major life activity. The preamble recognized, however, that temporary impairments, such as a broken leg, are not commonly regarded as disabilities, and only in rare circumstances would the degree of the limitation and its expected duration be substantial. Nevertheless, many commenters objected to inclusion of the word "temporary" both because it is not in the statute and because it is not contained in the definition of "disability" set forth in the title I regulations of the Equal Employment Opportunity Commission (EEOC). The word "temporary" has been deleted from the final rule to conform with the statutory language.

The question of whether a temporary impairment is a disability must be resolved on a case-by-case basis, taking into consideration both the duration (or expected duration) of the impairment and the extent to which it actually limits a major life activity of the affected individual.

The question of whether a person has a disability should be assessed without regard to the availability of mitigating measures, such as reasonable modification or auxiliary aids and services. For example, a person with hearing loss is substantially limited in the major life activity of hearing, even though the loss may be improved through the use of a hearing aid. Likewise, persons with impairments, such as epilepsy or diabetes, that substantially limit a major life activity, are covered under the first prong of the definition of disability, even if the effects of the impairment are controlled by medication.

Many commenters asked that environmental illness (also known as multiple chemical sensitivity) as well as allergy to cigarette smoke be recognized as disabilities. The Department, however, declines to state categorically that these types of allergies or sensitivities are disabilities, because the determination as to whether an impairment is a disability depends on whether, given the particular circumstances at issue, the impairment substantially limits one or more major life activities (or has a history of, or is regarded as having such an effect).

Sometimes respiratory or neurological functioning is so severely affected that an individual will satisfy the requirements to be considered disabled under the regulation. Such an individual would be entitled to all of the protections afforded by the Act and this part. In other cases, individuals may be sensitive to environmental elements or to smoke but their sensitivity will not rise to the level needed to constitute a disability. For example, their major life activity of breathing may be somewhat, but not substantially, impaired. In such circumstances, the individuals are not disabled and are not entitled to the protections of the statute despite their sensitivity to environmental agents.

In sum, the determination as to whether allergies to cigarette smoke, or allergies or sensitivities characterized by the commenters as environmental illness are disabilities covered by the regulation must be made using the same case-by-case analysis that is applied to all other physical or mental impairments. Moreover, the addition of specific regulatory provisions relating to environmental illness in the final rule would be inappropriate at this time pending future consideration of the issue by the Architectural and Transportation Barriers Compliance Board, the Environmental Protection Agency, and the Occupational Safety and Health Administration of the Department of Labor.

Test B—A record of such an impairment

This test is intended to cover those who have a record of an impairment. As explained in paragraph (3) of the rule's definition of disability, this includes a person who has a history of an impairment that substantially limited a major life activity, such as someone who has recovered from an impairment. It also includes persons who have been misclassified as having an impairment.

This provision is included in the definition in part to protect individuals who have recovered from a physical or mental impairment that previously substantially limited them in a major life activity. Discrimination on the basis of such a past impairment is prohibited. Frequently occurring examples of the first group (those who have a history of an impairment) are persons with histories of mental or emotional illness, heart disease, or cancer; examples of the second group (those who have been misclassified as having an impairment) are persons who have been misclassified as having mental retardation or mental illness.

Test C—Being regarded as having such an impairment

This test, as contained in paragraph (4) of the definition, is intended to cover persons who are treated by a public entity as having a physical or mental impairment that substantially limits a major life activity. It applies when a person is treated as if he or she has an impairment that substantially limits a major life activity, regardless of whether that person has an impairment.

The Americans with Disabilities Act uses the same "regarded as" test set forth in the regulations implementing section 504 of the Rehabilitation Act. See, e.g., 28 CFR 42.540(k)(2)(iv), which provides:

(iv) "Is regarded as having an impairment" means (A) Has a physical or mental impairment that does not substantially limit major life activities but that is treated by a recipient as constituting such a limitation; (B) Has a physical or mental impairment that substantially limits major life activities only as a result of the attitudes of others toward such impairment; or (C) Has none of the impairments defined in paragraph (k)(2)(i) of this section but is treated by a recipient as having such an impairment.

The perception of the covered entity is a key element of this test. A person who perceives himself or herself to have an impairment, but does not have an impairment, and is not treated as if he or she has an impairment, is not protected under this test.

A person would be covered under this test if a public entity refused to serve the person because it perceived that the person had an impairment that limited his or her enjoyment of the goods or services being offered.

For example, persons with severe burns often encounter discrimination in community activities, resulting in substantial limitation of major life activities. These persons would be covered under this test based on the attitudes of others towards the impairment, even if they did not view themselves as "impaired."

The rationale for this third test, as used in the Rehabilitation Act of 1973, was articulated by the Supreme Court in *Arline,* 480 U.S. 273 (1987). The Court noted that although an individual may have an impairment that does not in fact substantially limit a major life activity, the reaction of others may prove just as disabling. "Such an impairment might not diminish a person's physical or mental capabilities, but could nevertheless substantially limit that person's ability to work as a result of the negative reactions of others to the impairment." *Id.* at 283. The Court concluded that, by including this test in the Rehabilitation Act's definition, "Congress acknowledged that society's accumulated myths and fears about disability and diseases are as handicapping as are the physical limitations that flow from actual impairment." *Id.* at 284.

Thus, a person who is denied services or benefits by a public entity because of myths, fears, and stereotypes associated with disabilities would be covered under this third test whether or not the person's physical or mental condition would be considered a disability under the first or second test in the definition.

If a person is refused admittance on the basis of an actual or perceived physical or mental condition, and the public entity can articulate no legitimate reason for the refusal (such as failure to meet eligibility criteria), a perceived concern about admitting persons with disabilities could be inferred and the individual would qualify for coverage under the "regarded as" test. A person who is covered because of being regarded as having an impairment is not required to show that the public entity's perception is inaccurate (e.g., that he will be accepted by others) in order to receive benefits from the public entity.

Paragraph (5) of the definition lists certain conditions that are not included within the definition of "disability." The excluded conditions are: Transvestism, transsexualism, pedophilia, exhibitionism, voyeurism, gender identity disorders not resulting from physical impairments, other sexual behavior disorders, compulsive gambling, kleptomania, pyromania, and psychoactive substance use disorders resulting from current illegal use of drugs. Unlike homosexuality and bisexuality, which are not considered impairments under either section 504 or the Americans with Disabilities Act (see the definition of "disability," paragraph (1)(iv)), the conditions listed in paragraph (5), except for transvestism, are not necessarily excluded as impairments under section 504. (Transvestism was excluded from the definition of disability for section 504 by the Fair Housing Amendments Act of 1988, Pub. L. 100-430, section 6(b)).

"Drug." The definition of the term "drug" is taken from section 510(d)(2) of the ADA.

"Facility." "Facility" means all or any portion of buildings, structures, sites, complexes, equipment, rolling stock or other conveyances, roads, walks, passageways, parking lots, or other real or personal property, including the site where the building, property, structure, or equipment is located. It includes both indoor and outdoor areas where human-constructed improvements, structures, equipment, or property have been added to the natural environment.

Commenters raised questions about the applicability of this part to activities operated in mobile facilities, such as bookmobiles or mobile health screening units. Such activities would be covered by the requirement for program accessibility in § 35.150, and would be included in the definition of "facility" as "other real or personal property," although standards for new construction and alterations of such facilities are not yet included in the accessibility standards adopted by § 35.151. Sections 35.150 and 35.151 specifically address the obligations of public entities to ensure accessibility by providing curb ramps at pedestrian walkways.

"Historic preservation programs" and "Historic properties" are defined in order to aid in the interpretation of §§ 35.150 (a)(2) and (b)(2), which relate to accessibility of historic preservation programs, and § 35.151(d), which relates to the alteration of historic properties.

"Illegal use of drugs." The definition of "illegal use of drugs" is taken from section 510(d)(1) of the Act and clarifies that the term includes the illegal use of one or more drugs.

"Individual with a disability" means a person who has a disability but does not include an individual who is currently illegally using drugs, when the public entity acts on the basis of such use. The phrase "current illegal use of drugs" is explained in § 35.131.

"Public entity." The term "public entity" is defined in accordance with section 201(1) of the ADA as any State or local government; any department, agency, special purpose district, or other instrumentality of a State or States or local government; or the National Railroad Passenger Corporation, and any commuter authority (as defined in section 103(8) of the Rail Passenger Service Act).

"Qualified individual with a disability." The definition of "qualified individual with a disability" is taken from section 201(2) of the Act, which is derived from the definition of "qualified handicapped person" in the Department of Health and Human Services' regulation implementing section 504 (45 CFR § 84.3(k)). It combines the definition at 45 CFR 84.3(k)(1) for employment ("a handicapped person who, with reasonable accommodation, can perform the essential functions of the job in question") with the definition for other services at 45 CFR 84.3(k)(4) ("a handicapped person who meets the essential eligibility requirements for the receipt of such services").

Some commenters requested clarification of the term "essential eligibility requirements." Because of the variety of situations in which an individual's qualifications will be at issue, it is not possible to include more specific criteria in the definition. The "essential eligibility requirements" for participation in some activities covered under this part may be minimal. For example, most public entities provide information about their operations as a public service to anyone who requests it. In such situations, the only "eligibility requirement" for receipt of such information would be the request for it. Where such information is provided by telephone, even the ability to use a voice telephone is not an "essential eligibility requirement," because § 35.161 requires a public entity to provide equally effective telecommunication systems for individuals with impaired hearing or speech.

For other activities, identification of the "essential eligibility requirements" may be more complex. Where questions of safety are involved, the principles established in § 36.208 of the Department's regulation implementing title III of the ADA, to be codified at 28 CFR, part 36, will be applicable. That section implements section 302(b)(3) of the Act, which provides that a public accommodation is not required to permit an individual to participate in or benefit from the goods, services, facilities, privileges, advantages and accommodations of the public accommodation, if that individual poses a direct threat to the health or safety of others.

A "direct threat" is a significant risk to the health or safety of others that cannot be eliminated by a modification of policies, practices, or procedures, or by the provision of auxiliary aids or services. In *School Board of Nassau County v. Arline*, 480 U.S. 273 (1987), the Supreme Court recognized that there is a need to balance the interests of people with disabilities against legitimate concerns for public safety. Although persons with disabilities are generally entitled to the protection of this part, a person who poses a significant risk to others will not be "qualified," if reasonable modifications to the public entity's policies, practices, or procedures will not eliminate that risk.

The determination that a person poses a direct threat to the health or safety of others may not be based on generalizations or stereotypes about the effects of a particular disability. It must be based on an individualized assessment, based on reasonable judgment that relies on current medical evidence or on the best available objective evidence, to determine: the nature, duration, and severity of the risk; the probability that the potential injury will actually occur; and whether reasonable modifications of policies, practices, or procedures will mitigate the risk. This is the test established by the Supreme Court in Arline. Such an inquiry is essential if the law is to achieve its goal of protecting disabled individuals from discrimination based on prejudice, stereotypes, or unfounded fear, while giving appropriate weight to legitimate concerns, such as the need to avoid exposing others to significant health and safety risks. Making this assessment will not usually require the services of a physician. Sources for medical knowledge include guidance from public health authorities, such as the U.S. Public Health Service, the Centers for Disease Control, and the National Institutes of Health, including the National Institute of Mental Health.

"Qualified interpreter." The Department received substantial comment regarding the lack of a definition of "qualified interpreter." The proposed rule defined auxiliary aids and services to include the statutory term, "qualified interpreters" (§ 35.104), but did not define it. Section 35.160 requires the use of auxiliary aids including qualified interpreters and commenters stated that a lack of guidance on what the term means would create confusion among those trying to secure interpreting services and often result in less than effective communication.

Many commenters were concerned that, without clear guidance on the issue of "qualified" interpreter, the rule would be interpreted to mean "available, rather than qualified" interpreters. Some claimed that few public entities would understand the difference between a qualified interpreter and a person who simply knows a few signs or how to fingerspell.

In order to clarify what is meant by "qualified interpreter" the Department has added a definition of the term to the final rule. A qualified interpreter means an interpreter who is able to interpret effectively, accurately, and impartially both receptively and expressively, using any necessary specialized vocabulary. This definition focuses on the actual ability of the interpreter in a particular interpreting context to facilitate effective communication between the public entity and the individual with disabilities.

Public comment also revealed that public entities have at times asked persons who are deaf to provide family members or friends to interpret. In certain circumstances, notwithstanding that the family member of friend is able to interpret or is a certified interpreter, the family member or friend may not be qualified to render the necessary interpretation because of factors such as emotional or personal involvement or considerations of confidentiality that may adversely affect the ability to interpret "effectively, accurately, and impartially."

The definition of "qualified interpreter" in this rule does not invalidate or limit standards for interpreting services of any State or local law that are equal to or more stringent than those imposed by this definition. For instance, the definition would not supersede any requirement of State law for use of a certified interpreter in court proceedings.

"Section 504." The Department added a definition of "section 504" because the term is used extensively in subpart F of this part.

"State." The definition of "State" is identical to the statutory definition in section 3(3) of the ADA.

Subpart B—General Requirements

Section 35.130 General Prohibitions Against Discrimination

The general prohibitions against discrimination in the rule are generally based on the prohibitions in existing regulations implementing section 504 and, therefore, are already familiar to State and local entities covered by section 504. In addition, § 35.130

includes a number of provisions derived from title III of the Act that are implicit to a certain degree in the requirements of regulations implementing section 504.

Several commenters suggested that this part should include the section of the proposed title III regulation that implemented section 309 of the Act, which requires that courses and examinations related to applications, licensing, certification, or credentialing be provided in an accessible place and manner or that alternative accessible arrangements be made. The Department has not adopted this suggestion. The requirements of this part, including the general prohibitions of discrimination in this section, the program access requirements of subpart D, and the communications requirements of subpart E, apply to courses and examinations provided by public entities. The Department considers these requirements to be sufficient to ensure that courses and examinations administered by public entities meet the requirements of section 309. For example, a public entity offering an examination must ensure that modifications of policies, practices, or procedures or the provision of auxiliary aids and services furnish the individual with a disability an equal opportunity to demonstrate his or her knowledge or ability. Also, any examination specially designed for individuals with disabilities must be offered as often and in as timely a manner as are other examinations. Further, under this part, courses and examinations must be offered in the most integrated setting appropriate. The analysis of § 35.130(d) is relevant to this determination.

A number of commenters asked that the regulation be amended to require training of law enforcement personnel to recognize the difference between criminal activity and the effects of seizures or other disabilities such as mental retardation, cerebral palsy, traumatic brain injury, mental illness, or deafness. Several disabled commenters gave personal statements about the abuse they had received at the hands of law enforcement personnel. Two organizations that commented cited the Judiciary report at 50 as authority to require law enforcement training.

The Department has not added such a training requirement to the regulation. Discriminatory arrests and brutal treatment are already unlawful police activities. The general regulatory obligation to modify policies, practices, or procedures requires law enforcement to make changes in policies that result in discriminatory arrests or abuse of individuals with disabilities. Under this section law enforcement personnel would be required to make appropriate efforts to determine whether perceived strange or disruptive behavior or unconsciousness is the result of a disability. The Department notes that a number of States have attempted to address the problem of arresting disabled persons for noncriminal conduct resulting from their disability through adoption of the Uniform Duties to Disabled Persons Act, and encourages other jurisdictions to consider that approach.

Paragraph (a) restates the nondiscrimination mandate of section 202 of the ADA. The remaining paragraphs in § 35.130 establish the general principles for analyzing whether any particular action of the public entity violates this mandate.

Paragraph (b) prohibits overt denials of equal treatment of individuals with disabilities. A public entity may not refuse to provide an individual with a disability with an equal opportunity to participate in or benefit from its program simply because the person has a disability.

Paragraph (b)(1)(i) provides that it is discriminatory to deny a person with a disability the right to participate in or benefit from the aid, benefit, or service provided by a public entity. Paragraph (b)(1)(ii) provides that the aids, benefits, and services provided to persons with disabilities must be equal to those provided to others, and paragraph (b)(1)(iii) requires that the aids, benefits, or services provided to individuals with disabilities must be as effective in affording equal opportunity to obtain the same result, to gain the same benefit, or to reach the same level of achievement as those provided to others. These paragraphs are taken from the regulations implementing section 504 and simply restate principles long established under section 504.

Paragraph (b)(1)(iv) permits the public entity to develop separate or different aids, benefits, or services when necessary to provide individuals with disabilities with an equal opportunity to participate in or benefit from the public entity's programs or activities, but only when necessary to ensure that the aids, benefits, or services are as effective as those provided to others. Paragraph (b)(1)(iv) must be read in conjunction with paragraphs (b)(2), (d), and (e). Even when separate or different aids, benefits, or services would be more effective, paragraph (b)(2) provides that a qualified individual with a disability still has the right to choose to participate in the program that is not designed to accommodate individuals with disabilities. Paragraph (d) requires that a public entity administer services, programs, and activities in the most integrated setting appropriate to the needs of qualified individuals with disabilities.

Paragraph (b)(2) specifies that, notwithstanding the existence of separate or different programs or activities provided in accordance with this section, an individual with a disability shall not be denied the opportunity to participate in such programs or activities that are not separate or different. Paragraph (e), which is derived from section 501(d) of the Americans with Disabilities Act, states that nothing in this part shall be construed to require an individual with a disability to accept an accommodation, aid, service, opportunity, or benefit that he or she chooses not to accept.

Taken together, these provisions are intended to prohibit exclusion and segregation of individuals with disabilities and the denial of equal opportunities enjoyed by others, based on, among other things, presumptions, patronizing attitudes, fears, and stereotypes about individuals with disabilities. Consistent with these standards, public entities are required to ensure that their actions are based on facts applicable to individuals and not on presumptions as to what a class of individuals with disabilities can or cannot do.

Integration is fundamental to the purposes of the Americans with Disabilities Act. Provision of segregated accommodations and services relegates persons with disabilities to second-class status. For example, it would be a violation of this provision to require persons with disabilities to eat in the back room of a government cafeteria or to refuse to allow a person with a disability the full use of recreation or exercise facilities because of stereotypes about the person's ability to participate.

Many commenters objected to proposed paragraphs (b)(1)(iv) and (d) as allowing continued segregation of individuals with disabilities. The Department recognizes that promoting integration of individuals with disabilities into the mainstream of society is an important objective of the ADA and agrees that, in most instances, separate programs for individuals with disabilities will not be permitted. Nevertheless, section 504 does permit separate programs in limited circumstances, and Congress clearly intended the regulations issued under title II to adopt the standards of section 504. Furthermore, Congress included authority for separate programs in the specific requirements of title III of the Act. Section 302(b)(1)(A)(iii) of the Act provides for separate benefits in language similar to that in § 35.130(b)(1)(iv), and section 302(b)(1)(B) includes the same requirement for "the most integrated setting appropriate" as in § 35.130(d).

Even when separate programs are permitted, individuals with disabilities cannot be denied the opportunity to participate in programs that are not separate or different. This is an important and overarching principle of the Americans with Disabilities Act. Separate, special, or different programs that are designed to provide a benefit to persons with disabilities cannot be used to restrict the participation of persons with disabilities in general, integrated activities.

For example, a person who is blind may wish to decline participating in a special museum tour that allows persons to touch sculptures in an exhibit and instead tour the exhibit at his or her own pace with the museum's recorded tour. It is not the intent of this section to require the person who is blind to avail himself or herself of the special tour. Modified participation for persons with disabilities must be a choice, not a requirement.

In addition, it would not be a violation of this section for a public entity to offer recreational programs specially designed for children with mobility impairments. However, it would be a violation of this section if the entity then excluded these children from other recreational services for which they are qualified to participate when these services are made available to nondisabled children, or if the entity required children with disabilities to attend only designated programs.

Many commenters asked that the Department clarify a public entity's obligations within the integrated program when it offers a separate program but an individual with a disability chooses not to participate in the separate program. It is impossible to make a blanket statement as to what level of auxiliary aids or modifications would be required in the integrated program. Rather, each situation must be assessed individually. The starting point is to question whether the separate program is in fact necessary or appropriate for the individual. Assuming the separate program would be appropriate for a particular individual, the extent to which that individual must be provided with modifications in the integrated program will depend not only on what the individual needs but also on the limitations and defenses of this part. For example, it may constitute an undue burden for a public accommodation, which provides a full-time interpreter in its special guided tour for individuals with hearing impairments, to hire an additional interpreter for those individuals who choose to attend the integrated program. The Department cannot identify categorically the level of assistance or aid required in the integrated program.

Paragraph (b)(1)(v) provides that a public entity may not aid or perpetuate discrimination against a qualified individual with a disability by providing significant assistance to an agency, organization, or person that discriminates on the basis of disability in providing any aid, benefit, or service to beneficiaries of the public entity's program. This paragraph is taken from the regulations implementing section 504 for federally assisted programs.

Paragraph (b)(1)(vi) prohibits the public entity

from denying a qualified individual with a disability the opportunity to participate as a member of a planning or advisory board.

Paragraph (b)(1)(vii) prohibits the public entity from limiting a qualified individual with a disability in the enjoyment of any right, privilege, advantage, or opportunity enjoyed by others receiving any aid, benefit, or service.

Paragraph (b)(3) prohibits the public entity from utilizing criteria or methods of administration that deny individuals with disabilities access to the public entity's services, programs, and activities or that perpetuate the discrimination of another public entity, if both public entities are subject to common administrative control or are agencies of the same State. The phrase "criteria or methods of administration" refers to official written policies of the public entity and to the actual practices of the public entity. This paragraph prohibits both blatantly exclusionary policies or practices and nonessential policies and practices that are neutral on their face, but deny individuals with disabilities an effective opportunity to participate. This standard is consistent with the interpretation of section 504 by the U.S. Supreme Court in *Alexander v. Choate*, 469 U.S. 287 (1985). The Court in *Choate* explained that members of Congress made numerous statements during passage of section 504 regarding eliminating architectural barriers, providing access to transportation, and eliminating discriminatory effects of job qualification procedures. The Court then noted: "These statements would ring hollow if the resulting legislation could not rectify the harms resulting from action that discriminated by effect as well as by design." *Id.* at 297 (footnote omitted).

Paragraph (b)(4) specifically applies the prohibition enunciated in § 35.130(b)(3) to the process of selecting sites for construction of new facilities or selecting existing facilities to be used by the public entity. Paragraph (b)(4) does not apply to construction of additional buildings at an existing site.

Paragraph (b)(5) prohibits the public entity, in the selection of procurement contractors, from using criteria that subject qualified individuals with disabilities to discrimination on the basis of disability.

Paragraph (b)(6) prohibits the public entity from discriminating against qualified individuals with disabilities on the basis of disability in the granting of licenses or certification. A person is a "qualified individual with a disability" with respect to licensing or certification if he or she can meet the essential eligibility requirements for receiving the license or certification (see § 35.104).

A number of commenters were troubled by the phrase "essential eligibility requirements" as applied to State licensing requirements, especially those for health care professions. Because of the variety of types of programs to which the definition of "qualified individual with a disability" applies, it is not possible to use more specific language in the definition. The phrase "essential eligibility requirements," however, is taken from the definitions in the regulations implementing section 504, so caselaw under section 504 will be applicable to its interpretation. In *Southeastern Community College v. Davis*, 442 U.S. 397, for example, the Supreme Court held that section 504 does not require an institution to "lower or effect substantial modifications of standards to accommodate a handicapped person," 442 U.S. at 413, and that the school had established that the plaintiff was not "qualified" because she was not able to "serve the nursing profession in all customary ways," id. Whether a particular requirement is "essential" will, of course, depend on the facts of the particular case.

In addition, the public entity may not establish requirements for the programs or activities of licensees or certified entities that subject qualified individuals with disabilities to discrimination on the basis of disability. For example, the public entity must comply with this requirement when establishing safety standards for the operations of licensees. In that case the public entity must ensure that standards that it promulgates do not discriminate against the employment of qualified individuals with disabilities in an impermissible manner.

Paragraph (b)(6) does not extend the requirements of the Act or this part directly to the programs or activities of licensees or certified entities themselves. The programs or activities of licensees or certified entities are not themselves programs or activities of the public entity merely by virtue of the license or certificate.

Paragraph (b)(7) is a specific application of the requirement under the general prohibitions of discrimination that public entities make reasonable modifications in policies, practices, or procedures where necessary to avoid discrimination on the basis of disability. Section 302(b)(2)(A)(ii) of the ADA sets out this requirement specifically for public accommodations covered by title III of the Act, and the House Judiciary Committee Report directs the Attorney General to include those specific requirements in the title II regulation to the extent that they do not conflict with the regulations implementing section 504. Judiciary report at 52.

Paragraph (b)(8), a new paragraph not contained in the proposed rule, prohibits the imposition or application of eligibility criteria that screen out or tend to screen out an individual with a disability or any class of individuals with disabilities from fully and equally enjoying any service, program, or activity, unless such criteria can be shown to be necessary for the provision of the service, program, or activity being offered. This prohibition is also a specific application of the general prohibitions of discrimination and is based on section 302(b)(2)(A)(i) of the ADA. It prohibits overt denials of equal treatment of individuals with disabilities, or establishment of exclusive or segregative criteria that would bar individuals with disabilities from participation in services, benefits, or activities.

Paragraph (b)(8) also prohibits policies that unnecessarily impose requirements or burdens on individuals with disabilities that are not placed on others. For example, public entities may not require that a qualified individual with a disability be accompanied by an attendant. A public entity is not, however, required to provide attendant care, or assistance in toileting, eating, or dressing to individuals with disabilities, except in special circumstances, such as where the individual is an inmate of a custodial or correctional institution.

In addition, paragraph (b)(8) prohibits the imposition of criteria that "tend to" screen out an individual with a disability. This concept, which is derived from current regulations under section 504 (see, e.g., 45 CFR 84.13), makes it discriminatory to impose policies or criteria that, while not creating a direct bar to individuals with disabilities, indirectly prevent or limit their ability to participate. For example, requiring presentation of a driver's license as the sole means of identification for purposes of paying by check would violate this section in situations where, for example, individuals with severe vision impairments or developmental disabilities or epilepsy are ineligible to receive a driver's license and the use of an alternative means of identification, such as another photo I.D. or credit card, is feasible.

A public entity may, however, impose neutral rules and criteria that screen out, or tend to screen out, individuals with disabilities if the criteria are necessary for the safe operation of the program in question. Examples of safety qualifications that would be justifiable in appropriate circumstances would include eligibility requirements for drivers' licenses, or a requirement that all participants in a recreational rafting expedition be able to meet a necessary level of swimming proficiency. Safety requirements must be based on actual risks and not on speculation, stereotypes, or generalizations about individuals with disabilities.

Paragraph (c) provides that nothing in this part prohibits a public entity from providing benefits, services, or advantages to individuals with disabilities, or to a particular class of individuals with disabilities, beyond those required by this part. It is derived from a provision in the section 504 regulations that permits programs conducted pursuant to Federal statute or Executive order that are designed to benefit only individuals with disabilities or a given class of individuals with disabilities to be limited to those individuals with disabilities. Section 504 ensures that federally assisted programs are made available to all individuals, without regard to disabilities, unless the Federal program under which the assistance is provided is specifically limited to individuals with disabilities or a particular class of individuals with disabilities. Because coverage under this part is not limited to federally assisted programs, paragraph (c) has been revised to clarify that State and local governments may provide special benefits, beyond those required by the nondiscrimination requirements of this part, that are limited to individuals with disabilities or a particular class of individuals with disabilities, without thereby incurring additional obligations to persons without disabilities or to other classes of individuals with disabilities.

Paragraphs (d) and (e), previously referred to in the discussion of paragraph (b)(1)(iv), provide that the public entity must administer services, programs, and activities in the most integrated setting appropriate to the needs of qualified individuals with disabilities, i.e., in a setting that enables individuals with disabilities to interact with nondisabled persons to the fullest extent possible, and that persons with disabilities must be provided the option of declining to accept a particular accommodation.

Some commenters expressed concern that § 35.130(e), which states that nothing in the rule requires an individual with a disability to accept special accommodations and services provided under the ADA, could be interpreted to allow guardians of infants or older people with disabilities to refuse medical treatment for their wards. Section 35.130(e) has been revised to make it clear that paragraph (e) is inapplicable to the concern of the commenters. A new paragraph (e)(2) has been added stating that nothing in the regulation authorizes the representative or guardian of an individual with a disability to decline food, water, medical treatment, or medical services for that individual. New paragraph (e) clarifies that neither the ADA nor the regulation alters current Federal law ensuring the rights of incompetent individuals with disabilities to receive food, water, and medical treatment. See, e.g., Child Abuse Amendments of 1984 (42 U.S.C. 5106a(b)(10), 5106g(10)); Rehabilitation Act of 1973, as amended (29 U.S.C. 794); the Developmentally Disabled Assistance and Bill of

Rights Act (42 U.S.C. 6042).

Sections 35.130(e) (1) and (2) are based on section 501(d) of the ADA. Section 501(d) was designed to clarify that nothing in the ADA requires individuals with disabilities to accept special accommodations and services for individuals with disabilities that may segregate them:

The Committee added this section [501(d)] to clarify that nothing in the ADA is intended to permit discriminatory treatment on the basis of disability, even when such treatment is rendered under the guise of providing an accommodation, service, aid or benefit to the individual with disability. For example, a blind individual may choose not to avail himself or herself of the right to go to the front of a line, even if a particular public accommodation has chosen to offer such a modification of a policy for blind individuals. Or, a blind individual may choose to decline to participate in a special museum tour that allows persons to touch sculptures in an exhibit and instead tour the exhibits at his or her own pace with the museum's recorded tour.

Judiciary report at 71-72. The Act is not to be construed to mean that an individual with disabilities must accept special accommodations and services for individuals with disabilities when that individual can participate in the regular services already offered. Because medical treatment, including treatment for particular conditions, is not a special accommodation or service for individuals with disabilities under section 501(d), neither the Act nor this part provides affirmative authority to suspend such treatment. Section 501(d) is intended to clarify that the Act is not designed to foster discrimination through mandatory acceptance of special services when other alternatives are provided; this concern does not reach to the provision of medical treatment for the disabling condition itself.

Paragraph (f) provides that a public entity may not place a surcharge on a particular individual with a disability, or any group of individuals with disabilities, to cover any costs of measures required to provide that individual or group with the nondiscriminatory treatment required by the Act or this part. Such measures may include the provision of auxiliary aids or of modifications required to provide program accessibility.

Several commenters asked for clarification that the costs of interpreter services may not be assessed as an element of "court costs." The Department has already recognized that imposition of the cost of courtroom interpreter services is impermissible under section 504. The preamble to the Department's section 504 regulation for its federally assisted programs states that where a court system has an obligation to provide qualified interpreters, "it has the corresponding responsibility to pay for the services of the interpreters." (45 FR 37630 (June 3, 1980)). Accordingly, recouping the costs of interpreter services by assessing them as part of court costs would also be prohibited.

Paragraph (g), which prohibits discrimination on the basis of an individual's or entity's known relationship or association with an individual with a disability, is based on sections 102(b)(4) and 302(b)(1)(E) of the ADA. This paragraph was not contained in the proposed rule. The individuals covered under this paragraph are any individuals who are discriminated against because of their known association with an individual with a disability. For example, it would be a violation of this paragraph for a local government to refuse to allow a theater company to use a school auditorium on the grounds that the company had recently performed for an audience of individuals with HIV disease.

This protection is not limited to those who have a familial relationship with the individual who has a disability. Congress considered, and rejected, amendments that would have limited the scope of this provision to specific associations and relationships. Therefore, if a public entity refuses admission to a person with cerebral palsy and his or her companions, the companions have an independent right of action under the ADA and this section.

During the legislative process, the term "entity" was added to section 302(b)(1)(E) to clarify that the scope of the provision is intended to encompass not only persons who have a known association with a person with a disability, but also entities that provide services to or are otherwise associated with such individuals. This provision was intended to ensure that entities such as health care providers, employees of social service agencies, and others who provide professional services to persons with disabilities are not subjected to discrimination because of their professional association with persons with disabilities.

Section 35.131 Illegal Use of Drugs

Section 35.131 effectuates section 510 of the ADA, which clarifies the Act's application to people who use drugs illegally. Paragraph (a) provides that this part does not prohibit discrimination based on an individual's current illegal use of drugs.

The Act and the regulation distinguish between illegal use of drugs and the legal use of substances, whether or not those substances are "controlled substances," as defined in the Controlled Substances Act

(21 U.S.C. 812). Some controlled substances are prescription drugs that have legitimate medical uses. Section 35.131 does not affect use of controlled substances pursuant to a valid prescription under supervision by a licensed health care professional, or other use that is authorized by the Controlled Substances Act or any other provision of Federal law. It does apply to illegal use of those substances, as well as to illegal use of controlled substances that are not prescription drugs. The key question is whether the individual's use of the substance is illegal, not whether the substance has recognized legal uses. Alcohol is not a controlled substance, so use of alcohol is not addressed by § 35.131 (although alcoholics are individuals with disabilities, subject to the protections of the statute).

A distinction is also made between the use of a substance and the status of being addicted to that substance. Addiction is a disability, and addicts are individuals with disabilities protected by the Act. The protection, however, does not extend to actions based on the illegal use of the substance. In other words, an addict cannot use the fact of his or her addiction as a defense to an action based on illegal use of drugs. This distinction is not artificial. Congress intended to deny protection to people who engage in the illegal use of drugs, whether or not they are addicted, but to provide protection to addicts so long as they are not currently using drugs.

A third distinction is the difficult one between current use and former use. The definition of "current illegal use of drugs" in § 35.104, which is based on the report of the Conference Committee, H.R. Conf. Rep. No. 596, 101st Cong., 2d Sess. 64 (1990) (hereinafter "Conference report"), is "illegal use of drugs that occurred recently enough to justify a reasonable belief that a person's drug use is current or that continuing use is a real and ongoing problem."

Paragraph (a)(2)(i) specifies that an individual who has successfully completed a supervised drug rehabilitation program or has otherwise been rehabilitated successfully and who is not engaging in current illegal use of drugs is protected. Paragraph (a)(2)(ii) clarifies that an individual who is currently participating in a supervised rehabilitation program and is not engaging in current illegal use of drugs is protected. Paragraph (a)(2)(iii) provides that a person who is erroneously regarded as engaging in current illegal use of drugs, but who is not engaging in such use, is protected.

Paragraph (b) provides a limited exception to the exclusion of current illegal users of drugs from the protections of the Act. It prohibits denial of health services, or services provided in connection with drug rehabilitation to an individual on the basis of current illegal use of drugs, if the individual is otherwise entitled to such services. A health care facility, such as a hospital or clinic, may not refuse treatment to an individual in need of the services it provides on the grounds that the individual is illegally using drugs, but it is not required by this section to provide services that it does not ordinarily provide. For example, a health care facility that specializes in a particular type of treatment, such as care of burn victims, is not required to provide drug rehabilitation services, but it cannot refuse to treat a individual's burns on the grounds that the individual is illegally using drugs.

Some commenters pointed out that abstention from the use of drugs is an essential condition of participation in some drug rehabilitation programs, and may be a necessary requirement in inpatient or residential settings. The Department believes that this comment is well-founded. Congress clearly intended to prohibit exclusion from drug treatment programs of the very individuals who need such programs because of their use of drugs, but, once an individual has been admitted to a program, abstention may be a necessary and appropriate condition to continued participation. The final rule therefore provides that a drug rehabilitation or treatment program may prohibit illegal use of drugs by individuals while they are participating in the program.

Paragraph (c) expresses Congress' intention that the Act be neutral with respect to testing for illegal use of drugs. This paragraph implements the provision in section 510(b) of the Act that allows entities "to adopt or administer reasonable policies or procedures, including but not limited to drug testing," that ensure that an individual who is participating in a supervised rehabilitation program, or who has completed such a program or otherwise been rehabilitated successfully is no longer engaging in the illegal use of drugs. The section is not to be "construed to encourage, prohibit, restrict, or authorize the conducting of testing for the illegal use of drugs."

Paragraph 35.131(c) clarifies that it is not a violation of this part to adopt or administer reasonable policies or procedures to ensure that an individual who formerly engaged in the illegal use of drugs is not currently engaging in illegal use of drugs. Any such policies or procedures must, of course, be reasonable, and must be designed to identify accurately the illegal use of drugs. This paragraph does not authorize inquiries, tests, or other procedures that would disclose use of substances that are not controlled substances or are taken under supervision by a licensed health care professional, or other uses authorized by the Controlled Substances Act or other provisions of Federal law, because such uses are not included in the definition of "illegal use of drugs." A commenter argued that the rule should permit testing for lawful use of prescription drugs, but most commenters preferred that tests must be limited to unlawful use in order to avoid revealing the lawful use of prescription medicine used to treat disabilities.

Section 35.132 Smoking

Section 35.132 restates the clarification in section 501(b) of the Act that the Act does not preclude the prohibition of, or imposition of restrictions on, smoking in transportation covered by title II. Some commenters argued that this section is too limited in scope, and that the regulation should prohibit smoking in all facilities used by public entities. The reference to smoking in section 501, however, merely clarifies that the Act does not require public entities to accommodate smokers by permitting them to smoke in transportation facilities.

35.133 Maintenance of Accessible Features

Section 35.133 provides that a public entity shall maintain in operable working condition those features of facilities and equipment that are required to be readily accessible to and usable by persons with disabilities by the Act or this part. The Act requires that, to the maximum extent feasible, facilities must be accessible to, and usable by, individuals with disabilities. This section recognizes that it is not sufficient to provide features such as accessible routes, elevators, or ramps, if those features are not maintained in a manner that enables individuals with disabilities to use them. Inoperable elevators, locked accessible doors, or "accessible" routes that are obstructed by furniture, filing cabinets, or potted plants are neither "accessible to" nor "usable by" individuals with disabilities.

Some commenters objected that this section appeared to establish an absolute requirement and suggested that language from the preamble be included in the text of the regulation. It is, of course, impossible to guarantee that mechanical devices will never fail to operate. Paragraph (b) of the final regulation provides that this section does not prohibit isolated or temporary interruptions in service or access due to maintenance or repairs. This paragraph is intended to clarify that temporary obstructions or isolated instances of mechanical failure would not be considered violations of the Act or this part. However, allowing obstructions or "out of service" equipment to persist beyond a reasonable period of time would violate this part, as would repeated mechanical failures due to improper or inadequate maintenance. Failure of the public entity to ensure that accessible routes are properly maintained and free of obstructions, or failure to arrange prompt repair of inoperable elevators or other equipment intended to provide access would also violate this part.

Other commenters requested that this section be expanded to include specific requirements for inspection and maintenance of equipment, for training staff in the proper operation of equipment, and for maintenance of specific items. The Department believes that this section properly establishes the general requirement for maintaining access and that further details are not necessary.

Section 35.134 Retaliation or Coercion

Section 35.134 implements section 503 of the ADA, which prohibits retaliation against any individual who exercises his or her rights under the Act. This section is unchanged from the proposed rule. Paragraph (a) of § 35.134 provides that no private or public entity shall discriminate against any individual because that individual has exercised his or her right to oppose any act or practice made unlawful by this part, or because that individual made a charge, testified, assisted, or participated in any manner in an investigation, proceeding, or hearing under the Act or this part.

Paragraph (b) provides that no private or public entity shall coerce, intimidate, threaten, or interfere with any individual in the exercise of his or her rights under this part or because that individual aided or encouraged any other individual in the exercise or enjoyment of any right granted or protected by the Act or this part. This section protects not only individuals who allege a violation of the Act or this part, but also any individuals who support or assist them. This section applies to all investigations or proceedings initiated under the Act or this part without regard to the ultimate resolution of the underlying allegations. Because this section prohibits any act of retaliation or coercion in response to an individual's effort to exercise rights established by the Act and this part (or to support the efforts of another individual), the section applies not only to public entities subject to this part, but also to persons acting in an individual capacity or to private entities. For example, it would be a violation of the Act and this part for a private individual to harass or intimidate an individual with a disability in an effort to prevent that individual from attending a concert in a State-owned park. It would, likewise, be a violation of the Act and this part for a private entity to take adverse action against an employee who appeared as a witness on behalf of an individual who sought to enforce the Act.

Section 35.135 Personal Devices and Services

The final rule includes a new § 35.135, entitles "Personal devices and services," which states that the provision of personal devices and services is not required by title II. This new section, which serves as a limitation on all of the requirements of the regulation, replaces § 35.160(b)(2) of the proposed rule, which addressed the issue of personal devices and services explicitly only in the context of communications. The personal devices and services limitation was intended to have general application in the proposed rule in all contexts where it was relevant. The final rule, therefore, clarifies this point by including a general provision that will explicitly apply not only to auxiliary aids and services but across-the-board to include other relevant areas such as, for example, modifications in policies, practices, and procedures (§ 35.130(b)(7)). The language of § 35.135 parallels an analogous provision in the Department's title III regulations (28 CFR 36.306) but preserves the explicit reference to "readers for personal use or study" in § 35.160(b)(2) of the proposed rule. This section does not preclude the short-term loan of personal receivers that are part of an assistive listening system.

Subpart C—Employment

Section 35.140

Employment Discrimination Prohibited

Title II of the ADA applies to all activities of public entities, including their employment practices. The proposed rule cross-referenced the definitions, requirements, and procedures of title I of the ADA, as established by the Equal Employment Opportunity Commission in 29 CFR part 1630. This proposal would have resulted in use, under § 35.140, of the title I definition of "employer," so that a public entity with 25 or more employees would have become subject to the requirements of § 35.140 on July 26, 1992, one with 15 to 24 employees on July 26, 1994, and one with fewer than 15 employees would have been excluded completely.

The Department received comments objecting to this approach. The commenters asserted that Congress intended to establish nondiscrimination requirements for employment by all public entities, including those that employ fewer than 15 employees; and that Congress intended the employment requirements of title II to become effective at the same time that the other requirements of this regulation become effective, January 26, 1992. The Department has reexamined the statutory language and legislative history of the ADA on this issue and has concluded that Congress intended to cover the employment practices of all public entities and that the applicable effective date is that of title II.

The statutory language of section 204(b) of the ADA requires the Department to issue a regulation that is consistent with the ADA and the Department's coordination regulation under section 504, 28 CFR part 41. The coordination regulation specifically requires nondiscrimination in employment, 28 CFR 41.52-41.55, and does not limit coverage based on size of employer. Moreover, under all section 504 implementing regulations issued in accordance with the Department's coordination regulation, employment coverage under section 504 extends to all employers with federally assisted programs or activities, regardless of size, and the effective date for those employment requirements has always been the same as the effective date for nonemployment requirements established in the same regulations. The Department therefore concludes that § 35.140 must apply to all public entities upon the effective date of this regulation.

In the proposed regulation the Department cross-referenced the regulations implementing title I of the ADA, issued by the Equal Employment Opportunity Commission at 29 CFR part 1630, as a compliance standard for § 35.140 because, as proposed, the scope of coverage and effective date of coverage under title II would have been coextensive with title I. In the final regulation this language is modified slightly. Subparagraph (1) of new paragraph (b) makes it clear that the standards established by the Equal Employment Opportunity Commission in 29 CFR part 1630 will be the applicable compliance standards if the public entity is subject to title I. If the public entity is not covered by title I, or until it is covered by title I, subparagraph (b)(2) cross-references section 504 standards for what constitutes employment discrimination, as established by the Department of Justice in 28 CFR part 41. Standards for title I of the ADA and section 504 of the Rehabilitation Act are for the most part identical because title I of the ADA was based on requirements set forth in regulations implementing section 504.

The Department, together with the other Federal agencies responsible for the enforcement of Federal laws prohibiting employment discrimination on the basis of disability, recognizes the potential for jurisdictional overlap that exists with respect to coverage of public entities and the need to avoid problems related to overlapping coverage. The other Federal agencies include the Equal Employment Opportunity Commission, which is the agency primarily responsible for enforcement of title I of the ADA, the Department of Labor, which is the agency responsible for enforcement of section 503 of the Rehabilitation Act of 1973, and 26 Federal agencies with programs of Federal financial assistance, which are responsible for enforcing section 504 in those programs. Section 107 of the ADA requires that coordination mechanisms be developed in connection with the administrative enforcement of complaints alleging discrimination under title I and complaints alleging discrimination in employment in violation of the Rehabilitation Act. Although the ADA does not specifically require inclusion of employment complaints under title II in the coordinating mechanisms required by title I, Federal investigations of title II employment complaints will be coordinated on a government-wide basis also. The Department is currently working with the EEOC and other affected Federal agencies to develop effective coordinating mechanisms, and final regulations on this issue will be issued on or before January 26, 1992.

Subpart D—Program Accessibility

Section 35.149 Discrimination Prohibited

Section 35.149 states the general nondiscrimination principle underlying the program accessibility requirements of ss 35.150 and 35.151.

Section 35.150 Existing Facilities

Consistent with section 204(b) of the Act, this regulation adopts the program accessibility concept found in the section 504 regulations for federally conducted programs or activities (e.g., 28 CFR part 39). The concept of "program accessibility" was first used in the section 504 regulation adopted by the Department of Health, Education, and Welfare for its federally assisted programs and activities in 1977. It allowed recipients to make their federally assisted programs and activities available to individuals with disabilities without extensive retrofitting of their existing buildings and facilities, by offering those programs through alternative methods. Program accessibility has proven to be a useful approach and was adopted in the regulations issued for programs and activities conducted by Federal Executive agencies. The Act provides that the concept of program access will continue to apply with respect to facilities now in existence, because the cost of retrofitting existing facilities is often prohibitive.

Section 35.150 requires that each service, program, or activity conducted by a public entity, when viewed in its entirety, be readily accessible to and usable by individuals with disabilities. The regulation makes clear, however, that a public entity is not required to make each of its existing facilities accessible (s 35.150(a)(1)). Unlike title III of the Act, which requires public accommodations to remove architectural barriers where such removal is "readily achievable," or to provide goods and services through alternative methods, where those methods are "readily achievable," title II requires a public entity to make its programs accessible in all cases, except where to do so would result in a fundamental alteration in the nature of the program or in undue financial and administrative burdens. Congress intended the "undue burden" standard in title II to be significantly higher than the "readily achievable" standard in title III. Thus, although title II may not require removal of barriers in some cases where removal would be required under title III, the program access requirement of title II should enable individuals with disabilities to participate in and benefit from the services, programs, or activities of public entities in all but the most unusual cases.

Paragraph (a)(2), which establishes a special limitation on the obligation to ensure program accessibility in historic preservation programs, is discussed below in connection with paragraph (b).

Paragraph (a)(3), which is taken from the section 504 regulations for federally conducted programs, generally codifies case law that defines the scope of the public entity's obligation to ensure program accessibility. This paragraph provides that, in meeting the program accessibility requirement, a public entity is not required to take any action that would result in a fundamental alteration in the nature of its service, program, or activity or in undue financial and administrative burdens. A similar limitation is provided in § 35.164.

This paragraph does not establish an absolute defense; it does not relieve a public entity of all obligations to individuals with disabilities. Although a public entity is not required to take actions that would result in a fundamental alteration in the nature of a service, program, or activity or in undue financial and administrative burdens, it nevertheless must take any other steps necessary to ensure that individuals with disabilities receive the benefits or services provided by the public entity.

It is the Department's view that compliance with § 35.150(a), like compliance with the corresponding provisions of the section 504 regulations for federally conducted programs, would in most cases not result in undue financial and administrative burdens on a public entity. In determining whether financial and administrative burdens are undue, all public entity resources available for use in the funding and operation of the service, program, or activity should be considered. The burden of proving that compliance with paragraph (a) of § 35.150 would fundamentally alter the nature of a service, program, or activity or would result in undue financial and administrative burdens rests with the public entity.

The decision that compliance would result in such alteration or burdens must be made by the head of the public entity or his or her designee and must be accompanied by a written statement of the reasons for reaching that conclusion. The Department recognizes the difficulty of identifying the official responsible for this determination, given the variety of organizational forms that may be taken by public entities and their components. The intention of this paragraph is that the determination must be made by a high level official, no lower than a Department head, having budgetary authority and responsibility for making spending decisions.

Any person who believes that he or she or any specific class of persons has been injured by the public entity head's decision or failure to make a decision may file a complaint under the compliance procedures established in subpart F.

Paragraph (b)(1) sets forth a number of means by which program accessibility may be achieved, including redesign of equipment, reassignment of services to accessible buildings, and provision of aides.

The Department wishes to clarify that, consistent with longstanding interpretation of section 504, carrying an individual with a disability is considered an ineffective and therefore an unacceptable method for achieving program accessibility. Department of Health, Education, and Welfare, Office of Civil Rights, Policy Interpretation No. 4, 43 FR 36035 (August 14, 1978). Carrying will be permitted only in manifestly exceptional cases, and only if all personnel who are permitted to participate in carrying an individual with a disability are formally instructed on the safest and least humiliating means of carrying. "Manifestly exceptional" cases in which carrying would be permitted might include, for example, programs conducted in unique facilities, such as an oceanographic vessel, for which structural changes and devices necessary to adapt the facility for use by individuals with mobility impairments are unavailable or prohibitively expensive. Carrying is not permitted as an alternative to structural modifications such as installation of a ramp or a chairlift.

In choosing among methods, the public entity shall give priority consideration to those that will be consistent with provision of services in the most integrated setting appropriate to the needs of individuals with disabilities. Structural changes in existing facilities are required only when there is no other feasible way to make the public entity's program accessible. (It should be noted that "structural changes" include all physical changes to a facility; the term does not refer only to changes to structural features, such as removal of or alteration to a load-bearing structural member.) The requirements of § 35.151 for alterations apply to structural changes undertaken to comply with this section. The public entity may comply with the program accessibility requirement by delivering services at alternate accessible sites or making home visits as appropriate.

Section 35.151 New Construction and Alterations

Section 35.151 provides that those buildings that are constructed or altered by, on behalf of, or for the use of a public entity shall be designed, constructed, or altered to be readily accessible to and usable by individuals with disabilities if the construction was commenced after the effective date of this part. Facilities under design on that date will be governed by this section if the date that bids were invited falls after the effective date. This interpretation is consistent with Federal practice under section 504.

Section 35.151(c) establishes two standards for accessible new construction and alteration. Under paragraph (c), design, construction, or alteration of facilities in conformance with the Uniform Federal Accessibility Standards (UFAS) or with the Americans with Disabilities Act Accessibility Guidelines for Buildings and Facilities (hereinafter ADAAG) shall be deemed to comply with the requirements of this section with respect to those facilities except that, if ADAAG is chosen, the elevator exemption contained at ss 36.40l(d) and 36.404 does not apply. ADAAG is the standard for private buildings and was issued as guidelines by the Architectural and Transportation Barriers Compliance Board (ATBCB) under title III of the ADA. It has been adopted by the Department of Justice and is published as appendix A to the Department's title III rule in today's Federal Register. Departures from particular requirements of these standards by the use of other methods shall be permitted when it is clearly evident that equivalent access to the facility or part of the facility is thereby provided. Use of two standards is a departure from the proposed rule.

The proposed rule adopted UFAS as the only interim accessibility standard because that standard was referenced by the regulations implementing section 504 of the Rehabilitation Act promulgated by most Federal funding agencies. It is, therefore, familiar to many State and local government entities subject to this rule. The Department, however, received many comments objecting to the adoption of UFAS. Commenters pointed out that, except for the elevator exemption, UFAS is not as stringent as ADAAG. Others suggested that the standard should be the same to lessen confusion.

Section 204(b) of the Act states that title II regulations must be consistent not only with section 504 regulations but also with "this Act." Based on this provision, the Department has determined that a public entity should be entitled to choose to comply either with ADAAG or UFAS.

Public entities who choose to follow ADAAG, however, are not entitled to the elevator exemption contained in title III of the Act and implemented in the title III regulation at § 36.401(d) for new construction and § 36.404 for alterations. Section 303(b) of title III states that, with some exceptions, elevators are not required in facilities that are less than three stories or have less than 3000 square feet per story. The section 504 standard, UFAS, contains no such exemption. Section 501 of the ADA makes clear that nothing in the Act may be construed to apply a lesser standard to public entities than the standards applied under section 504. Because permitting the elevator exemption would clearly result in application of a lesser standard than that applied under section 504, paragraph (c) states that the elevator exemption does not apply when public entities choose to follow ADAAG. Thus, a two-story courthouse, whether built according to UFAS or ADAAG, must be constructed with an elevator. It should be noted that Congress did not include an elevator exemption for public transit facilities covered by subtitle B of title II, which covers public transportation provided by public entities, providing further evidence that Congress intended that public buildings have elevators.

Section 504 of the ADA requires the ATBCB to issue supplemental Minimum Guidelines and Requirements for Accessible Design of buildings and facilities subject to the Act, including title II. Section 204(c) of the ADA provides that the Attorney General shall promulgate regulations implementing title II that are consistent with the ATBCB's ADA guidelines. The ATBCB has announced its intention to issue title II guidelines in the future. The Department anticipates that, after the ATBCB's title II guidelines have been published, this rule will be amended to adopt new accessibility standards consistent with the ATBCB's rulemaking. Until that time, however, public entities will have a choice of following UFAS or ADAAG, without the elevator exemption.

Existing buildings leased by the public entity after the effective date of this part are not required by the regulation to meet accessibility standards simply by virtue of being leased. They are subject, however, to the program accessibility standard for existing facilities in § 35.150. To the extent the buildings are newly constructed or altered, they must also meet the new construction and alteration requirements of § 35.151.

The Department received many comments urging that the Department require that public entities lease only accessible buildings. Federal practice under section 504 has always treated newly leased buildings as subject to the existing facility program accessibility standard. Section 204(b) of the Act states that, in the area of "program accessibility, existing facilities," the title II regulations must be consistent with section 504 regulations. Thus, the Department has adopted the section 504 principles for these types of leased buildings. Unlike the construction of new buildings where architectural barriers can be avoided at little or no cost, the application of new construction standards to an existing building being leased raises the same prospect of retrofitting buildings as the use of an existing Federal facility, and the same program accessibility standard should apply to both owned and leased existing buildings. Similarly, requiring that public entities only lease accessible space would significantly restrict the options of State and local governments in seeking leased space, which would be particularly burdensome in rural or sparsely populated areas.

On the other hand, the more accessible the leased space is, the fewer structural modifications will be required in the future for particular employees whose disabilities may necessitate barrier removal as a reasonable accommodation. Pursuant to the requirements for leased buildings contained in the Minimum Guidelines and Requirements for Accessible Design published under the Architectural Barriers Act by the ATBCB, 36 CFR 1190.34, the Federal Government may not lease a building unless it contains (1) One accessible route from an accessible entrance to those areas in which the principal activities for which the building is leased are conducted, (2) accessible toilet facilities, and (3) accessible parking facilities, if a parking area is included within the lease (36 CFR 1190.34). Although these requirements are not applicable to buildings leased by public entities covered by this regulation, such entities are encouraged to look for the most accessible space available to lease and to attempt to find space complying at least with these minimum Federal requirements.

Section 35.151(d) gives effect to the intent of Congress, expressed in section 504(c) of the Act, that this part recognize the national interest in preserving significant historic structures. Commenters criticized the Department's use of descriptive terms in the proposed rule that are different from those used in the ADA to describe eligible historic properties. In addition, some commenters criticized the Department's decision to use the concept of "substantially impairing" the historic features of a property, which is a concept employed in regulations implementing section 504 of the Rehabilitation Act of 1973. Those commenters recommended that the Department adopt the criteria of "adverse effect" published by the Advisory Council on Historic Preservation under the National Historic Preservation Act, 36 CFR 800.9, as the standard for determining whether an historic property may be altered.

The Department agrees with these comments to the extent that they suggest that the language of the rule should conform to the language employed by Congress in the ADA. A definition of "historic property," drawn from section 504 of the ADA, has been added to § 35.104 to clarify that the term applies to those properties listed or eligible for listing in the National Register of Historic Places, or properties designated as historic under State or local law.

The Department intends that the exception created by this section be applied only in those very rare situations in which it is not possible to provide access to an historic property using the special access provisions established by UFAS and ADAAG. Therefore, paragraph (d)(1) of § 35.151 has been revised to clearly state that alterations to historic properties shall comply, to the maximum extent feasible, with section 4.1.7 of UFAS or section 4.1.7 of ADAAG. Paragraph (d)(2) has been revised to provide that, if it has been determined under the procedures established in UFAS and ADAAG that it is not feasible to provide physical access to an historic property in a manner that will not threaten or destroy the historic significance of the property, alternative methods of access shall be provided pursuant to the requirements of § 35.150.

In response to comments, the Department has added to the final rule a new paragraph (e) setting out the requirements of § 36.151 as applied to curb ramps. Paragraph (e) is taken from the statement contained in the preamble to the proposed rule that all newly constructed or altered streets, roads, and highways must contain curb ramps at any intersection having curbs or other barriers to entry from a street level pedestrian walkway, and that all newly constructed or altered street level pedestrian walkways must have curb ramps at intersections to streets, roads, or highways.

Section 35.178 State Immunity

Section 35.178 restates the provision of section 502 of the Act that a State is not immune under the eleventh amendment to the Constitution of the United States from an action in Federal or State court for violations of the Act, and that the same remedies are available for any such violations as are available in an action against an entity other than a State.

ADA TITLE II DOJ TECHNICAL ASSISTANCE MANUAL

TABLE OF CONTENTS

II-1.0000 COVERAGE

II-1.1000 General.

Title II of the ADA covers programs, activities, and services of public entities. It is divided into two subtitles. This manual focuses on subtitle A of title II, which is implemented by the Department of Justice's title II regulation. Subtitle B, covering public transportation, and the Department of Transportation's regulation implementing that subtitle, are not addressed in this manual.

Subtitle A is intended to protect qualified individuals with disabilities from discrimination on the basis of disability in the services, programs, or activities of all State and local governments. It additionally extends the prohibition of discrimination on the basis of disability established by section 504 of the Rehabilitation Act of 1973, as amended, to all activities of State and local governments, including those that do not receive Federal financial assistance. By law, the Department of Justice's title II regulation adopts the general prohibitions of discrimination established under section 504, and incorporates specific prohibitions of discrimination from the ADA.

Subtitle B is intended to clarify the requirements of section 504 for public transportation entities that receive Federal financial assistance. Also it extends coverage to all public entities that provide public transportation, whether or not they receive Federal financial assistance. It establishes detailed and complex standards for the operation of public transit systems, including commuter and intercity rail (AMTRAK). The Department of Transportation is responsible for the implementation of the second subtitle of Title II and issued a regulation implementing that subtitle.

II-1.2000 Public entity.

A public entity covered by title II is defined as—

1) Any State or local government;

2) Any department, agency, special purpose district, or other instrumentality of a State or local government; or

3) Certain commuter authorities as well as AMTRAK.

As defined, the term "public entity" does not include the Federal Government. Title II, therefore, does not apply to the Federal Government, which is covered by sections 501 and 504 of the Rehabilitation Act of 1973.

Title II is intended to apply to all programs, activities, and services provided or operated by State and local governments. Currently, section 504 of the Rehabilitation Act only applies to programs or activities receiving Federal financial assistance. Because many State and local government operations, such as courts, licensing, and legislative facilities and proceedings do not receive Federal funds, they are beyond the reach of section 504.

In some cases it is difficult to determine whether a particular entity that is providing a public service, such as a library, museum, or volunteer fire department, is in fact a public entity. Where an entity appears to have both public and private features, it is necessary to examine the relationship between the entity and the governmental unit to determine whether the entity is public or private. Factors to be considered in this determination include—

1) Whether the entity is operated with public funds;

2) Whether the entity's employees are considered government employees;

3) Whether the entity receives significant assistance from the government by provision of property or equipment; and

4) Whether the entity is governed by an independent board selected by members of a private organization or a board elected by the voters or appointed by elected officials.

II-1.3000 Relationship to title III.

Public entities are not subject to title III of the ADA, which covers only private entities. Conversely, private entities are not subject to title II. In many situations, however, public entities have a close relationship to private entities that are covered by title III, with the result that certain activities may be at least indirectly affected by both titles.

ILLUSTRATION 1: A privately owned restaurant in a State park operates for the convenience of park users under a concession agreement with a State department of parks. As a public accommodation, the restaurant is subject to title III and must meet those obligations. The State department of parks, a public entity, is subject to title II. The parks department is obligated to ensure by contract that the restaurant is operated in a manner that enables the parks department to meet its title II obligations, even though the restaurant is not directly subject to title II.

ILLUSTRATION 2: A city owns a downtown office building occupied by its department of human resources. The building's first floor, however, is leased to a restaurant, a newsstand, and a travel agency. The city, as a public entity and landlord of the office building, is subject to title II. As a public entity, it is not subject to title III, even though its tenants are public accommodations that are covered by title III.

Similarly, if an existing building is owned by a private entity covered by title III and rented to a public entity covered by title II, the private landlord does not become subject to the public entity's title II program access requirement by virtue of the leasing relationship. The private landlord only has title III obligations. These extend to the commercial facility as a whole and to any places of public accommodation contained in the facility. The governmental entity is responsible for ensuring that the programs offered in its renteed space meet the requirements of title II.

ILLUSTRATION 3: A city engages in a joint venture with a private corporation to build a new professional sports stadium. Where public and private entities act jointly, the public entity must ensure that the relevant requirements of title II are met; and the private entity must ensure compliance with title III. Consequently, the new stadium would have to be built in compliance with the accessibility guidelines of both titles II and III. In cases where the standards differ, the stadium would have to meet the standard that provides the highest degree of access to individuals with disabilities.

ILLUSTRATION 4: A private, nonprofit corporation operates a number of group homes under contract with a State agency for the benefit of individuals with mental disabilities. These particular homes provide a significant enough level of social services to be considered places of public accommodation under title III. The State agency must ensure that its contracts are carried out in accordance with title II, and the private entity must ensure that the homes comply with title III.

II-1.4000 Relationship to other laws

II-1.4100 Rehabilitation Act.

Title II provides protections to individuals with disabilities that are at least equal to those provided by the nondiscrimination provisions of title V of the Rehabilitation Act. Title V includes such provisions as section 501, which prohibits discrimination on the basis of disability in Federal employment; section 503, which addresses the employment practices of Federal contractors; and section 504, which covers all programs receiving Federal financial assistance and all the operations of Federal Executive agencies. Title II may not be interpreted to provide a lesser degree of protection to individuals with disabilities than is provided under these laws.

II-1.4200 Other Federal and State laws.

Title II does not disturb other Federal laws or any State laws that provide protection for individuals with disabilities at a level greater or equal to that provided by the ADA. It does, however, prevail over any conflicting State laws.

II-2.0000 QUALIFIED INDIVIDUALS WITH DISABILITIES

II-2.1000 General.

Title II of the ADA prohibits discrimination against any "qualified individual with a disability." Whether a particular individual is protected by title II requires a careful analysis first, of whether an individual is an "individual with a disability," and then whether that individual is "qualified."

People commonly refer to disabilities or disabling conditions in a broad sense. For example, poverty or lack of education may impose real limitations on an individual's opportunities. Likewise, being only five feet in height may prove to be an insurmountable barrier to an individual whose ambition is to play professional basketball. Although one might loosely characterize these conditions as "disabilities" in relation to the aspirations of the particular individual, the disabilities reached by title II are limited to those that meet the ADA's legal definition—those that place substantial limitations on an individual's major life activities. Title II protects three categories of individuals with disabilities:

1) Individuals who have a physical or mental impairment that substantially limits one or more major life activities;

2) Individuals who have a record of a physical or mental impairment that substantially limited one or more of the individual's major life activities; and

3) Individuals who are regarded as having such an impairment, whether they have the impairment or not.

II-2.2000 Physical or mental impairments.

The first category of persons covered by the definition of an individual with a disability is restricted to those with "physical or mental impairments." Physical impairments include—

1) Physiological disorders or conditions;

2) Cosmetic disfigurement; or

3) Anatomical loss

affecting one or more of the following body systems: neurological; musculoskeletal; special sense organs (which would include speech organs that are not respiratory such as vocal cords, soft palate, tongue, etc.); respiratory, including speech organs; cardiovascular; reproductive; digestive;, genito-urinary; hemic and lymphatic; skin; and endocrine.

Specific examples of physical impairments include orthopedic, visual, speech, and hearing impairments, cerebral palsy, epilepsy, muscular dystrophy, multiple sclerosis, cancer, heart disease, diabetes, HIV disease (symptomatic or asymptomatic), tuberculosis, drug addiction, and alcoholism.

Mental impairments include mental or psychological disorders, such as mental retardation, organic brain syndrome, emotional or mental illness, and specific learning disabilities.

Simple physical characteristics such as the color of one's eyes, hair, or skin; baldness; left-handedness; or age do not constitute physical impairments. Similarly, disadvantages attributable to environmental, cultural, or economic factors are not the type of impairments covered by title II. Moreover, the definition does not include common personality traits such as poor judgment or a quick temper, where these are not symptoms of a mental or psychological disorder.

Does title II prohibit discrimination against individuals based on their sexual orientation? No. The phrase "physical or mental impairment" does not include homosexuality or bisexuality.

II-2.3000 Drug addiction as an impairment.

Drug addiction is an impairment under the ADA. A public entity, however, may base a decision to with hold services or benefits in most cases on the fact that an addict is engaged in the current and illegal use of drugs.

What is "illegal use of drugs"? Illegal use of drugs means the use of one or more drugs, the possession or distribution of which is unlawful under the Controlled Substances Act. It does not include use of controlled substances pursuant to a valid prescription, or other uses that are authorized by the Controlled Substances Act or other Federal law. Alcohol is not a "controlled substance," but alcoholism is a disability.

What is "current use"? "Current use" is the illegal use of controlled substances that occurred recently enough to justify a reasonable belief that a person's drug use is current or that continuing use is a real and ongoing problem. A public entity should review carefully all the facts surrounding its belief that an individual is currently taking illegal drugs to ensure that its belief is a reasonable one.

Does title II protect drug addicts who no longer take controlled substances? Yes. Title II prohibits discrimination against drug addicts based solely on the fact that they previously illegally used controlled substances. Protected individuals include persons who have successfully completed a supervised drug rehabilitation program or have otherwise been rehabilitated successfully and who are not engaging in current illegal use of drugs. Additionally, discrimination is prohibited against an individual who is currently participating in a supervised rehabilitation program and is not engaging in current illegal use of drugs. Finally, a person who is erroneously regarded as engaging in current illegal use of drugs is protected.

Is drug testing permitted under the ADA? Yes. Public entities may utilize reasonable policies or procedures, including but not limited to drug testing, designed to ensure that an individual who formerly engaged in the illegal use of drugs is not now engaging in current illegal use of drugs.

II-2.4000 Substantial limitation of a major life activity.

To constitute a "disability," a condition must substantially limit a major life activity. Major life activities include such activities as caring for one's self, performing manual tasks, walking, seeing, hearing, speaking, breathing, learning, and working.

When does an impairment "substantially limit" a major life activity? There is no absolute standard for determining when an impairment is a substantial limitation. Some impairments obviously or by their nature substantially limit the ability of an individual to engage in a major life activity.

ILLUSTRATION 1: A person who is deaf is substantially limited in the major life activity of hearing. A person with a minor hearing impairment, on the other hand, may not be substantially limited.

ILLUSTRATION 2: A person with traumatic brain injury may be substantially limited in the major life activities of caring for one's self, learning, and working because of memory deficit, confusion, contextual difficulties, and inability to reason appropriately.

An impairment substantially interferes with the accomplishment of a major life activity when the individual's important life activities are restricted as to the conditions, manner, or duration under which they can be performed in comparison to most people.

ILLUSTRATION 1: A person with a minor vision impairment, such as 20/40 vision, does not have a substantial impairment of the major life activity of seeing.

ILLUSTRATION 2: A person who can walk for 10 miles continuously is not substantially limited in walking merely because, on the eleventh mile, he or she begins to experience pain, because most people would not be able to walk eleven miles without experiencing some discomfort.

Are "temporary" mental or physical impairments covered by title II? Yes, if the impairment substantially limits a major life activity. The issue of whether a temporary impairment is significant enough to be a disability must be resolved on a case-by-case basis, taking into consideration both the duration (or expected duration) of the impairment and the extent to which it actually limits a major life activity of the affected individual.

ILLUSTRATION: During a house fire, M received burns affecting his hands and arms. While it is expected that, with treatment, M will eventually recover full use of his hands, in the meantime he requires assistance in performing basic tasks required to care for himself such as eating and dressing. Because M's burns are expected to substantially limit a major life activity (caring for one's self) for a significant period of time, M would be considered to have a disability covered by title II.

If a person's impairment is greatly lessened or eliminated through the use of aids or devices, would the person still be considered an individual with a disability? Whether a person has a disability is assessed without regard to the availability of mitigating measures, such as reasonable modifications, auxiliary aids and services, services and devices of a personal nature, or medication. For example, a person with severe hearing loss is substantially limited in the major life activity of hearing, even though the loss may be improved through the use of a hearing aid. Likewise, persons with impairments, such as epilepsy or diabetes, that, if untreated, would substantially limit a major life activity, are still individuals with disabilities under the ADA, even if the debilitating consequences of the impairment are controlled by medication.

II-2.5000 Record of a physical or mental impairment that substantially limited a major life activity.

The ADA protects not only those individuals with disabilities who actually have a physical or mental impairment that substantially limits a major life activity, but also those with a record of such an impairment.

This protected group includes—

1) A person who has a history of an impairment that substantially limited a major life activity but who has recovered from the impairment. Examples of individuals who have a history of an impairment are persons who have histories of mental or emotional illness, drug addiction, alcoholism, heart disease, or cancer.

2) Persons who have been misclassified as having an impairment. Examples include persons who have been erroneously diagnosed as mentally retarded or mentally ill.

II-2.6000 "Regarded as."

The ADA also protects certain persons who are regarded by a public entity as having a physical or mental impairment that substantially limits a major life activity, whether or not that person actually has an impairment. Three typical situations are covered by this category:

1) An individual who has a physical or mental impairment that does not substantially limit major life activities, but who is treated as if the impairment does substantially limit a major life activity;

ILLUSTRATION: A, an individual with mild diabetes controlled by medication, is barred by the staff of a county-sponsored summer camp from participation in certain sports because of her diabetes. Even though A does not actually have an impairment that substantially limits a major life activity, she is protected under the ADA because she is treated as though she does.

2) An individual who has a physical or mental impairment that substantially limits major life activities only as a result of the attitudes of others towards the impairment;

ILLUSTRATION: B, a three-year old child born with a prominent facial disfigurement, has been refused admittance to a county-run day care program on the grounds that her presence in the program might upset the other children. B is an individual with a physical impairment that substantially limits her major life activities only as the result of the attitudes of others toward her impairment.

3) An individual who has no impairments but who is treated by a public entity as having an impairment that substantially limits a major life activity.

ILLUSTRATION: C is excluded from a county-sponsored soccer team because the coach believes rumors that C is infected with the HIV virus. Even though these rumors are untrue, C is protected under the ADA, because he is being subjected to discrimination by the county based on the belief that he has an impairment that substantially limits major life activities (i.e., the belief that he is infected with HIV).

II-2.7000 Exclusions.

The following conditions are specifically excluded from the definition of "disability": transvestism, transsexualism, pedophilia, exhibitionism, voyeurism, gender identity disorders not resulting from physical impairments, other sexual behavior disorders, compulsive gambling, kleptomania, pyromania, and psychoactive substance use disorders resulting from current illegal use of drugs.

II-2.8000 Qualified individual with a disability.

In order to be an individual protected by title II, the individual must be a "qualified" individual with a disability. To be qualified, the individual with a disability must meet the essential eligibility requirements for receipt of services or participation in a public entity's programs, activities, or services with or without—

1) Reasonable modifications to a public entity's rules, policies, or practices;

2) Removal of architectural, communication, or transportation barriers; or

3) Provision of auxiliary aids and services.

The "essential eligibility requirements" for participation in many activities of public entities may be minimal. For example, most public entities provide information about their programs, activities, and services upon request. In such situations, the only "eligibility requirement" for receipt of such information would be the request for it. However, under other circumstances, the "essential eligibility requirements" imposed by a public entity may be quite stringent.

ILLUSTRATION: The medical school at a public university may require those admitted to its program to have successfully completed specified undergraduate science courses.

Can a visitor, spectator, family member, or associate of a program participant be a qualified individual with a disability under title II? Yes. Title II protects any qualified individual with a disability involved in any capacity in a public entity's programs, activities, or services.

ILLUSTRATION: Public schools generally operate programs and activities that are open to students' parents, such as parent-teacher conferences, school plays, athletic events, and graduation ceremonies. A parent who is a qualified individual with a disability with regard to these activities would be entitled to title II protection.

Can health and safety factors be taken into account in determining who is qualified? Yes. An individual who poses a direct threat to the health or safety of others will not be "qualified."

What is a "direct threat"? A "direct threat" is a significant risk to the health or safety of others that cannot be eliminated or reduced to an acceptable level by the public entity's modification of its policies, practices, or procedures, or by the provision of auxiliary aids or services. The public entity's determination that a person poses a direct threat to the health or safety of others may not be based on generalizations or stereotypes about the effects of a particular disability.

How does one determine whether a direct threat exists? The determination must be based on an individualized assessment that relies on current medical evidence, or on the best available objective evidence, to assess—

1) The nature, duration, and severity of the risk;

2) The probability that the potential injury will actually occur; and,

3) Whether reasonable modifications of policies, practices, or procedures will mitigate or eliminate the risk.

Making this assessment will not usually require the services of a physician. Medical guidance may be obtained from public health authorities, such as the U.S. Public Health Service, the Centers for Disease Control, and the National Institutes of Health, including the National Institute of Mental Health.

ILLUSTRATION: An adult individual with tuberculosis wishes to tutor elementary school children in a volunteer mentor program operated by a local public school board. Title II permits the board to refuse to allow the individual to participate on the grounds that the mentor's condition would be a direct threat to the health or safety of the children participating in the program, if the condition is contagious and the threat cannot be mitigated or eliminated by reasonable modifications in policies, practices, or procedures.

II–3.0000 GENERAL REQUIREMENTS

II-3.1000 General.

Most requirements of title II are based on section 504 of the Rehabilitation Act of 1973, which prohibits discrimination on the basis of handicap in federally assisted programs and activities. Section 504 also applies to programs and activities "conducted" by Federal Executive agencies. The ADA similarly extends section 504's nondiscrimination requirement to all activities of State and local governments, not only those that receive Federal financial assistance.

Section 504 was implemented in 1977 for federally assisted programs in regulations issued by the Department of Health, Education, and Welfare. Later, other Federal agencies issued their own regulations for the programs and activities that they funded. Public entities should be familiar with those regulations from their experience in applying for Federal grant programs. As mandated by the ADA, the requirements for public entities under title II are consistent with and, in many areas, identical to the requirements of the section 504 regulations.

The ADA, however, also mandates that the title II regulations be consistent with the concepts of the ADA. Therefore, the title II regulations include language that is adapted from other parts of the ADA but not specifically found in section 504 regulations.

II-3.2000 Denial of participation.

The ADA, like other civil rights statutes, prohibits the denial of services or benefits on specified discriminatory grounds. Just as a government office cannot refuse to issue food stamps or other benefits to an individual on the basis of his or her race, it cannot refuse to provide benefits solely because an individual has a disability.

ILLUSTRATION: A city cannot refuse to admit an individual to a city council meeting that is open to the public merely because the individual is deaf.

II-3.3000 Equality in participation/benefits.

The ADA provides for equality of opportunity, but does not guarantee equality of results. The foundation of many of the specific requirements in the Department's regulations is the principle that individuals with disabilities must be provided an equally effective opportunity to participate in or benefit from a public entity's aids, benefits, and services.

ILLUSTRATION 1: A deaf individual does not receive an equal opportunity to benefit from attending a city council meeting if he or she does not have access to what is said.

ILLUSTRATION 2: An individual who uses a

wheelchair will not have an equal opportunity to participate in a program if applications must be filed in a second-floor office of a building without an elevator, because he or she would not be able to reach the office.

ILLUSTRATION 3: Use of printed information alone is not "equally effective" for individuals with vision impairments who cannot read written material.

On the other hand, as long as persons with disabilities are afforded an equally effective opportunity to participate in or benefit from a public entity's aids, benefits, and services, the ADA's guarantee of equal opportunity is not violated.

ILLUSTRATION 4: A person who uses a wheelchair seeks to run for a State elective office. State law requires the candidate to collect petition signatures in order to qualify for placement on the primary election ballot. Going door-to-door to collect signatures is difficult or, in many cases, impossible for the candidate because of the general inaccessibility of private homes. The law, however, provides over five months to collect the signatures and allows them to be collected by persons other than the candidate both through the mail and at any site where registered voters congregate. With these features, the law affords an equally effective opportunity for the individual who uses a wheelchair to seek placement on the ballot and to participate in the primary election process.

Also, the ADA generally does not require a State or local government entity to provide additional services for individuals with disabilities that are not provided for individuals without disabilities.

ILLUSTRATION 5: The ADA does not require a city government to provide snow removal service for the private driveways of residents with disabilities, if the city does not provide such service for residents without disabilities.

Finally, the ADA permits a public entity to offer benefits to individuals with disabilities, or a particular class of individuals without disabilities. This allows State and local governments to provide special benefits, beyond those required by the ADA, that are limited to individuals with disabilities or a particular class of individuals with disabilities, without thereby incurring additional obligations to persons without disabilities or to other classes of individuals with disabilities.

ILLUSTRATION 6: The ADA does not require a State government to continue providing medical support payments to dependent children with schizophrenia, if other dependent children without disabilities are also ineligible for continued coverage. This is true even if the State chooses to provide continued coverage to a particular class of children with disabilities (e.g., those with physical impairments, or those who have mental retardation).

Specific requirements for physical access to programs and communications are discussed in detail below, but the general principle underlying these obligations is the mandate for an equal opportunity to participate in and benefit from a public entity's services, programs, and activities.

II-3.4000 Separate benefit/integrated setting.

A primary goal of the ADA is the equal participation of individuals with disabilities in the "mainstream" of American society. The major principles of mainstreaming are—

1) Individuals with disabilities must be integrated to the maximum extent appropriate.

2) Separate programs are permitted where necessary to ensure equal opportunity. A separate program must be appropriate to the particular individual.

3) Individuals with disabilities cannot be excluded from the regular program, or required to accept special services or benefits.

II-3.4100 Separate programs.

A public entity may offer separate or special programs when necessary to provide individuals with disabilities an equal opportunity to benefit from the programs. Such programs must, however, be specifically designed to meet the needs of the individuals with disabilities for whom they are provided.

ILLUSTRATION 1: Museums generally do not allow visitors to touch exhibits because handling can cause damage to the objects. A municipal museum may offer a special tour for individuals with vision impairments on which they are permitted to touch and handle specific objects on a limited basis. (It cannot, however, exclude a blind person from the standard museum tour.)

ILLUSTRATION 2: A city recreation department may sponsor a separate basketball league for individuals who use wheelchairs.

II-3.4200 Relationship to "program accessibility" requirement.

The integrated setting requirement may conflict with the obligation to provide program accessibility, which may not necessarily mandate physical access to all parts of all facilities (see II-5.0000). Provision of services to individuals with disabilities in a different location, for example, is one method of achieving program accessibility. Public entities should make every effort to ensure that alternative methods of providing program access do not result in unnecessary segregation.

ILLUSTRATION: A school system should provide for wheelchair access at schools dispersed throughout its service area so that children who use wheelchairs can attend school at locations comparable in convenience to those available to other children. Also, where "magnet" schools, or schools offering different curricula or instruction techniques are available, the range of choice provided to students with disabilities must be comparable to that offered to other students.

II-3.4300 Right to participate in the regular program.

Even if a separate or special program for individuals with disabilities is offered, a public entity cannot deny a qualified individual with a disability participation in its regular program.

Qualified individuals with disabilities are entitled to participate in regular programs, even if the public entity could reasonably believe that they cannot benefit from the regular program.

ILLUSTRATION: A museum cannot exclude a person who is blind from a tour because of assumptions about his or her inability to appreciate and benefit from the tour experience. Similarly, a deaf person may not be excluded from a museum concert because of a belief that deaf persons cannot enjoy the music.

The fact that a public entity offers special programs does not affect the right of an individual with a disability to participate in regular programs. The requirements for providing access to the regular program, including the requirement that the individual be "qualified" for the program, still apply.

ILLUSTRATION: Where a State offers special drivers' licenses with limitations or restrictions for individuals with disabilities, an individual with a disability is not eligible for an unrestricted license, unless he or she meets the essential eligibility requirements for the unrestricted license.

BUT: If an individual is qualified for the regular program, he or she cannot be excluded from that program simply because a special program is available.

Individuals with disabilities may not be required to accept special "benefits" if they choose not to do so.

ILLUSTRATION: A State that provides optional special automobile license plates for individuals with disabilities and requires appropriate documentation for eligibility for the special plates cannot require an individual who qualifies for a special plate to present documentation or accept a special plate, if he or she applies for a plate without the special designation.

II-3.4400 Modifications in the regular program.

When a public entity offers a special program for individuals with a particular disability, but an individual with that disability elects to participate in the regular program rather than in the separate program, the public entity may still have obligations to provide an opportunity for that individual to benefit from the regular program. The fact that a separate program is offered may be a factor in determining the extent of the obligations under the regular program, but only if the separate program is appropriate to the needs of the particular individual with a disability.

ILLUSTRATION: If a museum provides a sign language interpreter for one of its regularly scheduled tours, the availability of the signed tour may be a factor in determining whether it would be an undue burden to provide an interpreter for a deaf person who wants to take the tour at a different time.

BUT: The availability of the signed tour would not affect the museum's obligation to provide an interpreter for a different tour, or the museum's obligation to provide a different auxiliary aid, such as an assistive listening device, for an individual with impaired hearing who does not use sign language.

II-3.5000 Eligibility criteria

II-3.5100 General.

A public entity may not impose eligibility criteria for participation in its programs, services, or activities that either screen out or tend to screen out persons with disabilities, unless it can show that such requirements are necessary for the provision of the service, program, or activity.

ILLUSTRATION 1: The director of a county recreation program prohibits persons who use wheelchairs from participating in county-sponsored scuba diving classes because he believes that persons who use wheelchairs probably cannot swim well enough to participate. An unnecessary blanket exclusion of this nature would violate the ADA.

ILLUSTRATION 2: A community college requires students with certain disabilities to be accompanied to class by attendants, even when such individuals prefer to attend classes unaccompanied. The college also requires individuals with disabilities to provide extensive medical histories, although such histories are not required from other students. Unless the college can demonstrate that it is necessary for some compelling reason to adopt these policies, the policies would not be permitted by the ADA.

II-3.5200 Safety.

A public entity may impose legitimate safety requirements necessary for the safe operation of its services, programs, or activities. However, the public entity must ensure that its safety requirements are based on real risks, not on speculation, stereotypes, or generalizations about individuals with disabilities.

ILLUSTRATION: A county recreation program may require that all participants in its scuba program pass a swimming test, if it can demonstrate that being able to swim is necessary for safe participation in the class. This is permitted even if requiring such a test would tend to screen out people with certain kinds of disabilities.

II-3.5300 Unnecessary inquiries.

A public entity may not make unnecessary inquiries into the existence of a disability.

ILLUSTRATION: A municipal recreation department summer camp requires parents to fill out a questionnaire and to submit medical documentation regarding their children's ability to participate in various camp activities. The questionnaire is acceptable, if the recreation department can demonstrate that each piece of information requested is needed to ensure safe participation in camp activities. The Department, however, may not use this information to screen out children with disabilities from admittance to the camp.

ILLUSTRATION 2: An essential eligibility requirement for obtaining a license to practice medicine is the ability to practice medicine safely and competently. State Agency X requires applicants for licenses to practice medicine to disclose whether they have ever had any physical and mental disabilities. A much more rigorous investigation is undertaken of applicants answering in the affirmative than of others. This process violates title II because of the additional burdens placed on individuals with disabilities, and because the disclosure requirement is not limited to conditions that currently impair one's ability to practice medicine.

II-3.5400 Surcharges.

Although compliance may result in some additional cost, a public entity may not place a surcharge only on particular individuals with disabilities or groups of individuals with disabilities to cover these expenses.

ILLUSTRATION: A community college provides interpreter services to deaf students, removes a limited number of architectural barriers, and relocates inaccessible courses and activities to more accessible locations. The college cannot place a surcharge on either an individual student with a disability (such as a deaf student who benefited from interpreter services) or on groups of students with disabilities (such as students with mobility impairments who benefited from barrier removal). It may, however, adjust its tuition or fees for all students.

II-3.6000 Reasonable modifications

II-3.6100 General.

A public entity must reasonably modify its policies, practices, or procedures to avoid discrimination. If the public entity can demonstrate, however, that the modifications would fundamentally alter the nature of its service, program, or activity, it is not required to make the modification.

ILLUSTRATION 1: A municipal zoning ordinance requires a set-back of 12 feet from the curb in the central business district. In order to install a ramp to the front entrance of a pharmacy, the owner must encroach on the set- back by three feet. Granting a variance in the zoning requirement may be a reasonable modification of town policy.

ILLUSTRATION 2: A county general relief program provides emergency food, shelter, and cash grants to individuals who can demonstrate their eligibility. The application process, however, is extremely lengthy and complex. When many individuals with mental disabilities apply for benefits, they are unable to complete the application process successfully. As a result, they are effectively denied benefits to which they are otherwise entitled. In this case, the county has an obligation to make reasonable modifications to its application process to ensure that otherwise eligible individuals are not denied needed benefits. Modifications to the relief program might include simplifying the application process or providing applicants who have mental disabilities with individualized assistance to complete the process.

ILLUSTRATION 3: A county ordinance prohibits the use of golf carts on public highways. An individual with a mobility impairment uses a golf cart as a mobility device. Allowing use of the golf cart as a mobility device on the shoulders of public highways where pedestrians are permitted, in limited circumstances that do not involve a significant risk to the health or safety of others, is a reasonable modification of the county policy.

ILLUSTRATION 4: C, a person with a disability, stops at a rest area on the highway. C requires assistance in order to use the toilet facilities and his only companion is a person of the opposite sex. Permitting a person of the opposite sex to assist C in a toilet room designated for one sex may be a required reasonable modification of policy.

ILLUSTRATION 5: S, an individual with an environmental illness, requests a public entity to adopt a policy prohibiting the use of perfume or other scented products by its employees who come into contact with the public. Such a requirement is not a 'reasonable' modification of the public entity's personnel policy.

II-3.6200 Personal services and devices.

A public entity is not required to provide individuals with disabilities with personal or individually prescribed devices, such as wheelchairs, prescription eyeglasses, or hearing aids, or to provide services of a personal nature, such as assistance in eating, toileting, or dressing. Of course, if personal services or devices are customarily provided to the individuals served by a public entity, such as a hospital or nursing home, then these personal services should also be provided to individuals with disabilities.

II-3.7000 Contracting and licensing

II-3.7100 Contracting.

A public entity may not discriminate on the basis of disability in contracting for the purchase of goods and services.

ILLUSTRATION 1: A municipal government may not refuse to contract with a cleaning service company to clean its government buildings because the company is owned by an individual with disabilities or employs individuals with disabilities.

II-3.7200 Licensing.

A public entity may not discriminate on the basis of disability in its licensing, certification, and regulatory activities. A person is a "qualified individual with a disability" with respect to licensing or certification, if he or she can meet the essential eligibility requirements for receiving the license or certification.

The phrase "essential eligibility requirements" is particularly important in the context of State licensing requirements. While many programs and activities of public entities do not have significant qualification requirements, licensing programs often do require applicants to demonstrate specific skills, knowledge, and abilities. Public entities may not discriminate against qualified individuals with disabilities who apply for licenses, but may consider factors related to the disability in determining whether the individual is "qualified."

ILLUSTRATION: An individual is not "qualified" for a driver's license unless he or she can operate a motor vehicle safely. A public entity may establish requirements, such as vision requirements, that would exclude some individuals with disabilities, if those requirements are essential for the safe operation of a motor vehicle.

BUT: The public entity may only adopt "essential" requirements for safe operation of a motor vehicle. Denying a license to all individuals who have missing limbs, for example, would be discriminatory if an individual who could operate a vehicle safely without use of the missing limb were denied a license. A public entity, however, could impose appropriate restrictions as a condition to obtaining a license, such as requiring an individual who is unable to use foot controls to use hand controls when operating a vehicle.

A public entity does not have to lower or eliminate licensing standards that are essential to the licensed activity to accommodate an individual with a disability. Whether a specific requirement is "essential" will depend on the facts of the particular case. Where a public entity administers licensing examinations, it must provide auxiliary aids for applicants with disabilities and administer the examinations in accessible locations.

In addition, a public entity may not establish requirements for the programs or activities of licensees that would result in discrimination against qualified individuals with disabilities. For example, a public entity's safety standards may not require the licensee to discriminate against qualified individuals with disabilities in its employment practices.

ILLUSTRATION: A State prohibits the licensing of transportation companies that employ individuals with missing limbs as drivers. XYZ company refuses to hire an individual with a missing limb who is "qualified" to perform the essential functions of the job, because he is able to drive safely with hand controls. The State's licensing requirements violate title II.

BUT: The State is not accountable for discrimination in the employment or other practices of XYZ company, if those practices are not the result of requirements or policies established by the State.

Although licensing standards are covered by title II, the licensee's activities themselves are not covered. An activity does not become a "program or activity" of a public entity merely because it is licensed by the public entity.

II-3.8000 Illegal use of drugs.

Discrimination based on an individual's current illegal use of drugs is not prohibited (see II-2.3000). Although individuals currently using illegal drugs are not protected from discrimination, the ADA does prohibit denial of health services, or services provided in connection with drug rehabilitation, to an individual on the basis of current illegal use of drugs, if the individual is otherwise entitled to such services.

ILLUSTRATION 1: A hospital emergency room may not refuse to provide emergency services to an individual because the individual is using drugs.

ILLUSTRATION 2: A municipal medical facility that specializes in care of burn patients may not refuse to treat an individual's burns on the grounds that the individual is illegally using drugs.

Because abstention from the use of drugs is an essential condition for participation in some drug rehabilitation programs, and may be a necessary requirement in inpatient or residential settings, a drug rehabilitation or treatment program may deny participation to individuals who use drugs while they are in the program.

ILLUSTRATION: A residential drug and alcohol treatment program may expel an individual for using drugs in a treatment center.

II-3.9000 Discrimination on the basis of association.

A State or local government may not discriminate against individuals or entities because of their known relationship or association with persons who have disabilities. This prohibition applies to cases where the public entity has knowledge of both the individual's disability and his or her relationship to another individual or entity. In addition to familial relationships, the prohibition covers any type of association between the individual or entity that is discriminated against and the individual or individuals with disabilities, if the discrimination is actually based on the disability.

ILLUSTRATION 1: A county recreation center may not refuse admission to a summer camp program to a child whose brother has HIV disease.

ILLUSTRATION 2: A local government could not refuse to allow a theater company to use a school auditorium on the grounds that the company has recently performed at an HIV hospice.

ILLUSTRATION 3: If a county-owned sports arena refuses to admit G, an individual with cerebral palsy, as well as H (his sister) because G has cerebral palsy, the arena would be illegally discriminating against H on the basis of her association with G.

II-3.10000 Maintenance of accessible features

Public entities must maintain in working order equipment and features of facilities that are required to provide ready access to individuals with disabilities. Isolated or temporary interruptions in access due to maintenance and repair of accessible features are not prohibited.

Where a public entity must provide an accessible route, the route must remain accessible and not blocked by obstacles such as furniture, filing cabinets, or potted plants. An isolated instance of placement of an object on an accessible route, however, would not be a violation, if the object is promptly removed. Similarly, accessible doors must be unlocked when the public entity is open for business.

Mechanical failures in equipment such as elevators or automatic doors will occur from time to time. The obligation to ensure that facilities are readily accessible to and usable by individuals with disabilities would be violated, if repairs are not made promptly or if improper or inadequate maintenance causes repeated and persistent failures.

ILLUSTRATION 1: It would be a violation for a building manager of a three- story building to turn off the only passenger elevator in order to save energy during the hours when the building is open.

ILLUSTRATION 2: A public high school has a lift to provide access for persons with mobility impairments to an auditorium stage. The lift is not working. If the lift normally is functional and reasonable steps have been taken to repair the lift, then the school has not violated its obligations to maintain accessible features. On the other hand, if the lift frequently does not work and reasonable steps have not been taken to maintain the lift, then the school has violated the maintenance of accessible features requirement.

ILLUSTRATION 3: Because of lack of space, a city office manager places tables and file cabinets in the hallways, which interferes with the usability of the hallway by individuals who use wheelchairs. By rendering a previously accessible hallway inaccessible, the city has violated the maintenance requirement, if that hallway is part of a required accessible route.

II-3.11000 Retaliation or coercion.

Individuals who exercise their rights under the ADA, or assist others in exercising their rights, are protected from retaliation. The prohibition against retaliation or coercion applies broadly to any individual or entity that seeks to prevent an individual from exercising his or her rights or to retaliate against him or her for having exercised those rights. Any form of retaliation or coercion, including threats, intimidation, or interference, is prohibited if it interferes with the exercise of rights under the Act.

ILLUSTRATION 1: A, a private individual, harasses X, an individual with cerebral palsy, in an effort to prevent X from attending a concert in a State park. A has violated the ADA.

ILLUSTRATION 2: A State tax official delays a tax refund for M, because M testified in a title II grievance proceeding involving the inaccessibility of the tax information office. The State has illegally retaliated against M in violation of title II.

II-3.12000 Smoking.

A public entity may prohibit smoking, or may impose restrictions on smoking, in its facilities.

II-4.0000 EMPLOYMENT

II-4.1000 General.

Beginning January 26, 1992, title II prohibits all public entities, regardless of size of workforce, from discriminating in their employment practices against qualified individuals with disabilities.

II-4.2000 Relationship among title II and other Federal laws that prohibit employment discrimination by public entities on the basis of disability.

In addition to title II's employment coverage, title I of the ADA and section 504 of the Rehabilitation Act of 1973 prohibit employment discrimination against qualified individuals with disabilities by certain public entities.

Title I of the ADA, which is primarily enforced by the Equal Employment Opportunity Commission (EEOC), prohibits job discrimination-

1) Effective July 26, 1992, by State and local employers with 25 or more employees; and

2) Effective July 26, 1994, by State and local employers with 15 or more employees.

Section 504 of the Rehabilitation Act prohibits discrimination in employment in programs or activities that receive Federal financial assistance, including federally funded State or local programs or activities. Each Federal agency that extends financial assistance is responsible for enforcement of section 504 in the programs it funds.

What standards are used to determine compliance under title II? For those public entities that are subject to title I of the ADA, title II adopts the standards of title I. In all other cases, the section 504 standards for employment apply. On October 29, 1992, legislation reauthorizing the Rehabilitation Act of 1973 was signed by the President. The law amended section 504 to conform its provisions barring employment discrimination to those applied under title I of the ADA. Thus, employment standards under section 504 are now identical to those under title I.

II-4.3000 Basic employment requirements.

The following sections set forth examples of the basic title II employment requirements. Additional information on employment issues is available in "A Technical Assistance Manual on the Employment Provisions (Title I) of the Americans with Disabilities Act," issued by the EEOC. (For information about obtaining this document or other information about title I, contact the EEOC at 800-669-EEOC (voice) or 800-800-3302 (TDD)).

II-4.3100 Nondiscriminatory practices and policies.

As of January 26, 1992, all public entities must ensure that their employment practices and policies do not discriminate on the basis of disability against qualified individuals with disabilities in every aspect of employment, including recruitment, hiring, promotion, demotion, layoff and return from layoff, compensation, job assignments, job classifications, paid or unpaid leave, fringe benefits, training, and employer-sponsored activities, including recreational or social programs.

II-4.3200 Reasonable accommodation.

All public entities must make "reasonable accommodation" to the known physical or mental limitations of otherwise qualified applicants or employees with disabilities, unless the public entity can show that the accommodation would impose an "undue hardship" on the operation of its program.

"Reasonable accommodation" means any change or adjustment to a job or work environment that permits a qualified applicant or employee with a disability to participate in the job application process, to perform the essential functions of a job, or to enjoy benefits and privileges of employment equal to those enjoyed by employees without disabilities. Examples include—

1) Acquiring or modifying equipment or devices;
2) Job restructuring;
3) Part-time or modified work schedules;
4) Providing readers or interpreters;
5) Making the workplace accessible to and usable by individuals with disabilities.

However, any particular change or adjustment would not be required if, under the circumstances involved, it would result in an undue hardship.

"Undue hardship" means significant difficulty or expense relative to the operation of a public entity's program. Where a particular accommodation would result in an undue hardship, the public entity must determine if another accommodation is available that would not result in an undue hardship.

II-4.3300 Nondiscrimination in selection criteria and the administration of tests.

Public entities may not use employment selection criteria that have the effect of subjecting individuals with disabilities to discrimination. In addition, public entities are required to ensure that, where necessary to avoid discrimination, employment tests are modified so that the test results reflect job skills or aptitude or whatever the test purports to measure, rather than the applicant's or employee's hearing, visual, speaking, or manual skills (unless the test is designed to measure hearing, visual, speaking, or manual skills).

II-4.3400 Preemployment medical examinations and medical inquiries.

During the hiring process, public entities may ask about an applicant's ability to perform job-related functions but may not ask whether an applicant is disabled or about the nature or severity of an applicant's disability.

Public entities may not conduct preemployment medical examinations, but they may condition a job offer on the results of a medical examination conducted prior to an individual's entrance on duty if—

1) All entering employees in the same job category, regardless of disability, are required to take the same medical examination, and
2) The results of the medical examination are not used to impermissibly discriminate on the basis of disability.

The results of a medical entrance examination must be kept confidential and maintained in separate medical files.

II-5.0000 PROGRAM ACCESSIBILITY

II-5.1000 General.

A public entity may not deny the benefits of its programs, activities, and services to individuals with disabilities because its facilities are inaccessible. A public entity's services, programs, or activities, when viewed in their entirety, must be readily accessible to and usable by individuals with disabilities. This standard, known as "program accessibility," applies to all existing facilities of a public entity. Public entities, however, are not necessarily required to make each of their existing facilities accessible.

ILLUSTRATION 1: When a city holds a public meeting in an existing building, it must provide ready access to, and use of, the meeting facilities to individuals with disabilities. The city is not required to make all areas in the building accessible, as long as the meeting room is accessible. Accessible telephones and bathrooms should also be provided where these services are available for use of meeting attendees.

ILLUSTRATION 2: D, a defendant in a civil suit, has a respiratory condition that prevents her from climbing steps. Civil suits are routinely heard in a courtroom on the second floor of the courthouse. The courthouse has no elevator or other means of access to the second floor. The public entity must relocate the proceedings to an accessible ground floor courtroom or take alternative steps, including moving the proceedings to another building, in order to allow D to participate in the civil suit.

ILLUSTRATION 3: A State provides ten rest areas approximately 50 miles apart along an interstate highway. Program accessibility requires that an accessible toilet room for each sex with at least one accessible stall, or a unisex bathroom, be provided at each rest area.

Is a public entity relieved of its obligation to make its programs accessible if no individual with a disability is known to live in a particular area? No. The absence of individuals with disabilities living in an area cannot be used as the test of whether programs and activities must be accessible.

ILLUSTRATION: A rural school district has only one elementary school and it is located in a one-room schoolhouse accessible only by steps. The school board asserts that there are no students in the district who use wheelchairs. Students, however, who currently do not have a disability may become individuals with disabilities through, for example, accidents or disease. In addition, persons other than students, such as parents and other school visitors, may be qualified individuals with disabilities who are entitled to participate in school programs. Consequently, the apparent lack of students with disabilities in a school district's service area does not excuse the school district from taking whatever appropriate steps are necessary to ensure that its programs, services, and activities are accessible to qualified individuals with disabilities.

Does the program accessibility requirement prevent a public entity from renting existing inaccessible space to a private entity? Not necessarily. For example, if a State leases space to a public accommodation in a downtown office building in a purely commercial transaction, i.e., the private entity does not provide any services as part of a State program, the State may rent out inaccessible space without violating its program access requirement. The private entity, though, would be responsible for compliance with title III. On the other hand, if a State highway authority leases a facility in one of its highway rest areas to a privately owned restaurant, the public entity would be responsible for making the space accessible, because the restaurant is part of the State's program of providing services to the monitoring public. The private entity operating the restaurant would have an independent obligation to meet the requirements of title III.

Can back doors and freight elevators be used to satisfy the program accessibility requirement? Yes, but only as a last resort and only if such an arrangement provides accessibility comparable to that provided to persons without disabilities, who generally use front doors and passenger elevators. For example, a back door is acceptable if it is kept unlocked during the same hours the front door remains unlocked; the passageway to and from the floor is accessible, well-lit, and neat and clean; and the individual with a mobility impairment does not have to travel excessive distances or through nonpublic areas such as kitchens and storerooms to gain access. A freight elevator would be acceptable if it were upgraded so as to be usable by passengers generally and if the passageways leading to and from the elevator are well-lit and neat and clean.

Are there any limitations on the program accessibility requirement? Yes. A public entity does not have to take any action that it can demonstrate would result in a fundamental alteration in the nature of its program or activity or in undue financial and administrative burdens. This determination can only be made by the head of the public entity or his or her designee and must be accompanied by a written statement of the reasons for reaching that conclusion. The determination that undue burdens would result must be based on all resources available for use in the program. If an action would result in such an alteration or such burdens, the public entity must take any other action that would not result in such an alteration or such burdens but would nevertheless ensure that individuals with disabilities receive the benefits and services of the program or activity.

II-5.2000 Methods for providing program accessibility.

Public entities may achieve program accessibility by a number of methods. In many situations, providing access to facilities through structural methods, such as alteration of existing facilities and acquisition or construction of additional facilities, may be the most efficient method of providing program accessibility. The public entity may, however, pursue alternatives to structural changes in order to achieve program accessibility. Nonstructural methods include acquisition or redesign of equipment, assignment of aides to beneficiaries, and provision of services at alternate accessible sites.

ILLUSTRATION 1: The office building housing a public welfare agency may only be entered by climbing a flight of stairs. If an individual with a mobility impairment seeks information about welfare benefits, the agency can provide the information in an accessible ground floor location or in another accessible building.

ILLUSTRATION 2: A public library's open stacks are located on upper floors having no elevator. As an alternative to installing a lift or elevator, library staff may retrieve books for patrons who use wheelchairs. The aides must be available during the operating hours of the library.

ILLUSTRATION 3: A public university that conducts a French course in an inaccessible building may relocate the course to a building that is readily accessible.

ILLUSTRATION 4: A municipal performing arts center provides seating at two prices—inexpensive balcony seats and more expensive orchestra seats. All of the accessible seating is located on the higher priced orchestra level. In lieu of providing accessible seating on the balcony level, the city must make a reasonable number of accessible orchestra-level seats available at the lower price of balcony seats.

When choosing a method of providing program access, a public entity must give priority to the one that results in the most integrated setting appropriate to encourage interaction among all users, including individuals with disabilities.

ILLUSTRATION: A rural, one-room library has an entrance with several steps. The library can make its services accessible in several ways. It may construct a simple wooden ramp quickly and at relatively low cost. Alternatively, individuals with mobility impairments may be provided access to the library's services through a bookmobile, by special messenger service, through use of clerical aides, or by any other method that makes the resources of the library "readily accessible." Priority should be given, however, to constructing a ramp because that is the method that offers library services to individuals with disabilities and others in the same setting.

Is carrying an individual with a disability considered an acceptable method of achieving program access? Generally, it is not. Carrying persons with mobility impairments to provide program accessibility is permitted in only two cases. First, when program accessibility in existing facilities can be achieved only through structural alterations (that is, physical changes to the facilities), carrying may serve as a temporary expedient until construction is completed. Second, carrying is permitted in manifestly exceptional cases if (a) carriers are formally instructed on the safest and least humiliating means of carrying and (b) the service is provided in a reliable manner. Carrying is contrary to the goal of providing accessible programs, which is to foster independence.

How is "program accessibility" under title II different than "readily achievable barrier removal" under title III? Unlike private entities under title III, public entities are not required to remove barriers from each facility, even if removal is readily achievable. A public entity must make its "programs" accessible. Physical changes to a building are required only when there is no other feasible way to make the program accessible. In contrast, barriers must be removed from places of public accommodation under title III where such removal is "readily achievable," without regard to whether the public accommodation's services can be made accessible through other methods.

II-5.3000 Curb ramps.

Public entities that have responsibility or authority over streets, roads, or walkways must prepare a schedule for providing curb ramps where pedestrian walkways cross curbs. Public entities must give priority to walkways serving State and local government offices and facilities, transportation, places of public accommodation, and employees, followed by walkways serving other areas. This schedule must be included as part of a transition plan (see II-8.3000).

To promote both efficiency and accessibility, public entities may choose to construct curb ramps at every point where a pedestrian walkway intersects a curb. However, public entities are not necessarily required to construct a curb ramp at every such intersection.

Alternative routes to buildings that make use of existing curb cuts may be acceptable under the concept of program accessibility in the limited circumstances where individuals with disabilities need only travel a marginally longer route. In addition, the fundamental alteration and undue burdens limitations may limit the number of curb ramps required.

To achieve or maintain program accessibility, it may be appropriate to establish an ongoing procedure for installing curb ramps upon request in areas frequented by individuals with disabilities as residents, employees, or visitors.

What are walkways? Pedestrian walkways include locations where access is required for use of public transportation, such as bus stops that are not located at intersections or crosswalks.

II-5.4000 Existing parking lots or garages.

A public entity should provide an adequate number

of accessible parking spaces in existing parking lots or garages over which it has jurisdiction.

II-5.5000 Historic preservation programs.

Special program accessibility requirements and limitations apply to historic preservation programs. Historic preservation programs are programs conducted by a public entity that have preservation of historic properties as a primary purpose. An historic property is a property that is listed or eligible for listing in the National Register of Historic Places or a property designated as historic under State or local law.

In achieving program accessibility in historic preservation programs, a public entity must give priority to methods that provide physical access to individuals with disabilities. Physical access is particularly important in an historic preservation program, because a primary benefit of the program is uniquely the experience of the historic property itself.

Are there any special limitations on measures required to achieve program accessibility in historic preservation programs in addition to the general fundamental alteration/undue financial and administrative burdens limitations? Yes, a public entity is not required to take any action that would threaten or destroy the historic significance of an historic property. In cases where physical access cannot be provided because of either this special limitation, or because an undue financial burden or fundamental alteration would result, alternative measures to achieve program accessibility must be undertaken.

ILLUSTRATION: Installing an elevator in an historic house museum to provide access to the second floor bedrooms would destroy architectural features of historic significance on the first floor. Providing an audio-visual display of the contents of the upstairs rooms in an accessible location on the first floor would be an alternative way of achieving program accessibility.

Does the special limitation apply to programs that are not historic preservation programs, but just happen to be located in historic properties? No. In these cases, nonstructural methods of providing program accessibility, such as relocating all or part of a program or making home visits, are available to ensure accessibility, and no special limitation protecting the historic structure is provided.

II-5.6000 Time periods for achieving program accessibility.

Public entities must achieve program accessibility by January 26, 1992. If structural changes are needed to achieve program accessibility, they must be made as expeditiously as possible, but in no event later than January 26, 1995. This three-year time period is not a grace period; all changes must be accomplished as expeditiously as possible. A public entity that employs 50 or more persons must develop a transition plan by July 26, 1992, setting forth the steps necessary to complete such changes. For guidance on transition plan requirements, see II-8.3000.

II-6.0000 NEW CONSTRUCTION AND ALTERATIONS

II-6.1000 General.

All facilities designed, constructed, or altered by, on behalf of, or for the use of a public entity must be readily accessible and usable by individuals with disabilities, if the construction or alteration is begun after January 26, 1992.

What is "readily accessible and usable?" This means that the facility must be designed, constructed, or altered in strict compliance with a design standard. The regulation gives a choice of two standards that may be used (see II-6.2000).

II-6.2000 Choice of design standard: UFAS or ADAAG

II-6.2100 General.

Public entities may choose from two design standards for new construction and alterations. They can choose either the Uniform Federal Accessibility Standards (UFAS) or the Americans with Disabilities Act Accessibility Guidelines for Buildings and Facilities (ADAAG), which is the standard that must be used for public accommodations and commercial facilities under title III of the ADA. If ADAAG is chosen, however, public entities are not entitled to the elevator exemption (which permits certain buildings under three stories or under 3,000 square feet per floor to be constructed without an elevator).

Many public entities that are recipients of Federal funds are already subject to UFAS, which is the accessibility standard referenced in most section 504 regulations.

On December 21, 1992, the Access Board published proposed title II accessibility guidelines that will generally adopt ADAAG for State and local government facilities. The proposed guidelines also set specific requirements for judicial, legislative, and regulatory facilities; detention and correctional facilities; accessible residential housing; and public rights-of-way. The proposed guidelines are subject to a 90-day comment period. It is anticipated that the Department of Justice will amend its title II rule to eliminate the choice between ADAAG and UFAS and, instead, mandate that public entities follow the amended ADAAG.

Which standard is stricter, UFAS or ADAAG? The many differences between the standards are highlighted below. In some areas, UFAS may appear to be more stringent. In other areas ADAAG may appear to be more stringent. Because of the many differences, one standard is not stricter than the other.

Can a public entity follow ADAAG on one floor of a new building and then follow UFAS on the next floor? No. Each facility or project must follow one standard completely.

Can a public entity follow UFAS for one alteration project and then follow ADAAG for another alteration project in the same building? No. All alterations in the same building must be done in accordance with the same standard.

What if neither ADAAG nor UFAS contain specific standards for a particular type of facility? In such cases the technical requirements of the chosen standard should be applied to the extent possible. If no standard exists for particular features, those features need not comply with a particular design standard. However, the facility must still be designed and operated to meet other title II requirements, including program accessibility (see II5.0000).

ILLUSTRATION 1: A public entity is designing and constructing a playground. Because there are no UFAS or ADAAG standards for playground equipment, the equipment need not comply with any specific design standard. The title II requirements for equal opportunity and program accessibility, however, may obligate the public entity to provide an accessible route to the playground, some accessible equipment, and an accessible surface for the playground.

ILLUSTRATION 2: A public entity is designing and constructing a new baseball stadium that will feature a photographers' moat running around the perimeter of the playing field. While there are no specific standards in either ADAAG or UFAS for either dugouts or photographer's moats, the chosen standard should be applied to the extent that it contains appropriate technical standards. For example, an accessible route must be provided and any ramps or changes in level must meet the chosen standard. The public entity may have additional obligations under other title II requirements.

II-6.3000 Major differences between ADAAG and UFAS.

Set forth below is a summary of some of the major differences between ADAAG and UFAS.

II-6.3100 General principles

1) Work areas

ADAAG: Requires that areas used only by employees as work areas be designed and constructed so that individuals with disabilities can approach, enter, and exit the areas. There is, then, only a limited application of the standards to work areas (§ 4.1.1(3)).

UFAS: Contains no special limited requirement for work areas. The UFAS standards apply (as provided in the Architectural Barriers Act) in all areas frequented by the public or which "may result in employment . . . of physically handicapped persons" (§ 1).

2) Equivalent facilitation

ADAAG: Departures from particular standards are permitted where alternatives will provide substantially equivalent or greater access (§ 2.2).

UFAS: UFAS itself does not contain a statement concerning equivalent facilitation. However, section 504 regulations, as well as the Department's title II regulation (28 CFR 35.151(c)), state that departures are permitted where it is "clearly evident that equivalent access" is provided.

3) Exemption from application of standards in new construction

ADAAG: Contains a structural impracticability exception for new construction: full compliance with the new construction standards is not required in the rare case where the terrain prevents compliance (§ 4.1.1(5)(a)).

UFAS: Does not contain a structural impracticability exception (or any other exception) for new construction.

4) Exemption from application of standards in alterations

ADAAG: For alterations, application of standards is not required where it would be "technically infeasible" (i.e., where application of the standards would involve removal of a load-bearing structural member or where existing physical or site restraints prevent compliance). Cost is not a factor (§ 4.1.6(1)(j)).

UFAS: Application of standards is not required for

alterations where "structurally impracticable," i.e., where removal of a load-bearing structural member is involved or where the result would be an increased cost of 50 percent or more of the value of the element involved (§§ 4.1.6(3); 3.5 ("structural impractibility")). Cost is a factor. (Note that the similar term, "structural impracticability," is used in ADAAG (see item #3 above), but in ADAAG it is used in relation to new construction. In UFAS, it is used in relation to alterations, and it has a different meaning.)

5) Alterations triggering additional requirements

ADAAG: Alterations to primary function areas (where major activities take place) trigger a "path of travel" requirement, that is, a requirement to make the path of travel from the entrance to the altered area—and telephones, restrooms, and drinking fountains serving the altered area—accessible (§ 4.1.6(2)). But, under the Department of Justice title III rule, a public entity is not required to spend more than 20% of the cost of the original alteration on making the path of travel accessible, even if this cost limitation results in less than full accessibility (28 CFR 36.403(f)).

UFAS: If a building undergoes a "substantial alteration" (where the total cost of all alterations in a 12-month period amounts to 50% or more of the value of the building), the public entity must provide an accessible route from public transportation, parking, streets, and sidewalks to all accessible parts of the building; an accessible entrance; and accessible restrooms (§ 4.1.6(3)).

6) Additions

ADAAG: Each addition to an existing building is regarded as an alteration subject to the ADAAG alterations requirements (including triggering of path of travel obligations, if applicable). If the addition does not have an accessible entrance, the path of travel obligation may require an accessible route from the addition through the existing building, including its entrance and exterior approaches, subject to the 20% disproportionality limitation. Moreover, to the extent that a space or element is newly constructed as part of an addition, it is also regarded as new construction and must comply with the applicable new construction provisions of ADAAG (§ 4.1.5).

UFAS: Has specific requirements for additions, including requirements for entrances, routes, restrooms, and common areas. An accessible route from the addition through the existing building, including its entrance, is required if the addition does not have an accessible entrance (§ 4.1.5).

II-6.3200 Elements.

The following requirements apply in new construction, unless otherwise indicated.

1) Van parking

ADAAG: One in every eight accessible spaces must be wide enough and high enough for a van lift to be deployed. The space must be marked as "van accessible" with a supplementary sign. Alternatively, "universal parking" is permitted, in which all spaces can accommodate van widths (§ 4.1.2(5)(b)).

UFAS: Van parking is not required. Universal parking is not addressed.

2) Valet parking

ADAAG: Facilities with valet parking must have an accessible passenger loading zone on an accessible route to the exterior of the facility (§ 4.1.2(5)(e)).

UFAS: No requirements for valet parking.

3) Signs

ADAAG:

- Signs designating permanent rooms and spaces (men's and women's rooms; room numbers; exit signs) must have raised and Brailled letters; must comply with finish and contrast standards; and must be mounted at a certain height and location (§ 4.1.3(16)(a)).
- Signs that provide direction to or information about functional spaces of a building (e.g., "cafeteria this way;" "copy room") need not comply with requirements for raised and Brailled letters, but they must comply with requirements for character proportion, finish, and contrast. If suspended or projected overhead, they must also comply with character height requirements (§ 4.1.3(16)(b)).
- Building directories and other signs providing temporary information (such as current occupant's name) do not have to comply with any ADAAG requirements (§ 4.1.3(16)).
- Has requirements not only for the standard international symbol of accessibility, but also for symbols of accessibility identifying volume control telephones, text telephones, and assistive listening systems (§§ 4.1.2(7); 4.30.7).

UFAS:

- Signs designating permanent rooms and spaces must be raised (Braille is not required) and must be mounted at a certain height and location (§ 4.1.2(15)).

- All other signs (including temporary signs) must comply with requirements for letter proportion and color contrast, but not with requirements for raised letters or mounting height (§ 4.1.2(15)).
- Requires only the standard international symbol of accessibility (§ 4.30.5).

4) Entrances

ADAAG: At least 50 percent of all public entrances must be accessible with certain qualifications. In addition, there must be accessible entrances to enclosed parking, pedestrian tunnels, and elevated walkways (§ 4.1.3(8)).

UFAS: At least one principal entrance at each grade floor level must be accessible. In addition, there must be an accessible entrance to transportation facilities, passenger loading zones, accessible parking, taxis, streets, sidewalks, and interior accessible areas, if the building has entrances that normally serve those functions (§ 4.1.2(8)). (This latter requirement could result in all entrances having to be accessible in many cases.)

5) Areas of rescue assistance or places of refuge

ADAAG: Areas of rescue assistance (safe areas in which to await help in an emergency) are generally required on each floor, other than the ground floor, of a multistory building. An accessible egress route or an area of rescue assistance is required for each exit required by the local fire code. Specific requirements are provided for such features as location, size, stairway width, and two-way communications. Areas of rescue assistance are not required in buildings with supervised automatic sprinkler systems, nor are they required in alternations (§ 4.1.3(9)).

UFAS: Accessible routes must serve as a means of egress or connect to an accessible "place of refuge." No specific requirements for places of refuge are included. Rather, UFAS refers to local administrative authority for specific provisions on location, size, etc. UFAS requires more than one means of accessible egress when more than one exit is required (§ 4.3.10).

6) Water fountains

ADAAG: Where there is more than one fountain on a floor, 50% must be accessible to persons using wheelchairs. If there is only one drinking fountain on a floor, it must be accessible both to individuals who use wheelchairs and to individuals who have trouble bending or stooping (for example, a "hi-lo fountain" or fountain and water cooler may be used) (§ 4.1.3(10)).

UFAS: Approximately 50% on each floor must be accessible. If there is only one fountain on a floor, it must be accessible to individuals who use wheelchairs (§ 4.1.3(9)).

7) Storage and shelves

ADAAG: One of each type of fixed storage facility must be accessible. Self-service shelves and displays must be on an accessible route but need not comply with reach-range requirements (§ 4.1.3(12)).

UFAS: Has the same requirements as ADAAG for fixed storage, but does not contain the reach requirement exemption for self-service shelves and displays (§ 4.1.2(11)).

8) Volume controls

ADAAG: All accessible public phones must be equipped with volume controls. In addition, 25%, but never less than one, of all other public phones must have volume controls (§ 4.1.3(17)(b)).

UFAS: At least one accessible telephone must have a volume control (§ 4.1.2(16)(b)).

9) Telecommunication Devices for the Deaf (TDD's)

ADAAG: One TDD (also known as a "text telephone") must be provided inside any building that has at least one interior pay phone and four or more public pay telephones, counting both interior and exterior phones. In addition, one TDD or text telephone (per facility) must be provided whenever there is an interior public pay phone in a stadium or arena; convention center; hotel with a convention center; covered shopping mall; or hospital emergency, recovery, or waiting room (§ 4.1.3(17)(c)).

UFAS: No requirement for TDD's.

10) Assembly areas

ADAAG:

- Wheelchair seating: Requirements triggered in any assembly area with fixed seating that seats four or more people. The number of wheelchair locations required depends upon the size of the assembly area. When the area has over 300 seats, there are requirements for dispersal of wheelchair seating. ADAAG also contains requirements for aisle seats without armrests (or with removable armrests) and fixed seating for companions located adjacent to each wheelchair seating area

(§ 4.1.3(19)(a)).

- Assistive listening systems: Certain fixed seating assembly areas that accommodate 50 or more people or have audio-amplification systems must have permanently installed assistive listening systems. Other assembly areas must have permanent systems or an adequate number of electrical outlets or other wiring to support a portable system. A special sign indicating the availability of the system is required. The minimum number of receivers must be equal to four percent of the total number of seats, but never less than two (§ 4.1.3(19)(b)).

UFAS:

- Wheelchair seating: No requirements for wheelchair seating are triggered, unless the assembly area has 50 or more seats. Seating must be dispersed and provide comparable lines of sight (§ 4.1.2(18)(a)).
- Assistive listening systems: Assembly areas with audio-amplification systems must have a listening system that serves a reasonable number of people, but at least two. If it has no amplification system or is used primarily as meeting or conference room, it must have a permanent or portable system. No special signs are required (§ 4.1.2(18)(b)).

11) Automated teller machines (ATM's)

ADAAG: Where ATM's are provided, each must be accessible, except that only one need comply when two or more ATM's are at the same location. Accessible machines must have, among other features, accessible controls and instructions and other information accessible to persons with sight impairments (§ 4.1.3(20)).

UFAS: No requirements for ATM's.

12) Bathrooms

ADAAG: Every public and common use bathroom must be accessible. Generally only one stall must be accessible (standard five-by-five feet). When there are six or more stalls, there must be one accessible stall and one stall that is three feet wide (§§ 4.1.3(11); 4.22.4).

UFAS: Same general requirements but no requirement for an additional three-foot-wide stall (§§ 4.1.2(10); 4.22.4).

13) Detectable warnings

ADAAG: Required on curb ramps, hazardous vehicular areas, and reflecting pools, but not on doors to hazardous areas. The warnings must be truncated domes (§ 4.29).

UFAS: "Tactile warnings" (uses different terminology) required only on doors to hazardous areas. Must be a textured surface on the door handle or hardware (§ 4.29).

14) Carpet and carpet tile

ADAAG: Same standards for carpet and carpet tile: maximum pile height of 1/2" (§ 4.5.3).

UFAS: Carpet must have maximum pile height of 1/2". Carpet tile must have maximum combined thickness of pile, cushion, and backing height of 1/2" (§ 4.5.3).

15) Curb ramps

ADAAG: Curb ramps must have detectable warnings (which must be raised truncated domes) (§ 4.7.7).

UFAS: No requirement for detectable warnings on curb ramps.

16) Elevator hoistway floor designations and car controls

ADAAG: Must have raised and Brailled characters (§§ 4.10.5; 4.10.12).

UFAS: Must have raised characters; no requirement for Braille (§§ 4.10.5; 4.10.12).

17) Visual alarms

ADAAG: Contains details about features required on visual alarms for individuals with hearing impairments, including type of lamp, color, intensity, and location. Flash rate must be at a minimum of 1Hz and maximum of 3Hz (§ 4.28.3).

UFAS: Contains much less detail. Allows faster flash rate of up to 5Hz (§ 4.28.3).

18) Elevators and platform lifts in new construction and alterations

ADAAG: The elevator exemption for two-story places of public accommodation or commercial facilities does not apply to buildings and facilities subject to title II. Therefore, elevators are required in all new multilevel buildings or facilities, but vertical access to elevator pits, elevator penthouses, mechanical rooms, and piping or equipment catwalks is not required. Platform lifts may be used instead of elevators under certain conditions in new construction and may always be used in alterations (§ 4.1.3(5)). Individuals must be able to enter unassisted, operate, and exit the lift without assistance (§ 4.11.3).

UFAS: Has same general requirement for elevators and exceptions similar to those in ADAAG. Platform lifts may be substituted for elevators in new construction or alterations "if no other alternative is feasible" (§ 4.1.2(5)). Lifts must facilitate unassisted entry and exit (but not "operation" of the lift as in ADAAG) (§ 4.11.3).

II-6.3300 Types of facilities

1) Historic buildings

ADAAG: Contains procedures for buildings eligible for listing in the National Register of Historic Places under the National Historic Preservation Act and for historic buildings designated under State or local law (§ 4.1.7).

UFAS: Contains requirements for buildings eligible for listing in the National Register of Historic Places under the National Historic Preservation Act that are also subject to the Architectural Barriers Act. UFAS does not contain provisions applicable to buildings and facilities that are designated as "historic" under State or local law. (Under title II, the UFAS provisions may be applied to any building that is eligible for listing on the National Register of Historic Places, regardless of whether it is also subject to the Architectural Barriers Act.) (§ 4.1.7).

2) Residential facilities/transient lodging

ADAAG:

- Hotels, motels, dormitories, and other similar establishments: Four percent of the first 100 rooms and approximately two percent of rooms in excess of 100 must be accessible to both persons with hearing impairments (i.e., contain visual alarms, visual notification devices, volume-control telephones, and an accessible electrical outlet for a text telephone) and to persons with mobility impairments. Moreover, a similar percentage of additional rooms must be accessible to persons with hearing impairments. In addition, where there are more than 50 rooms, approximately one percent of rooms must be accessible rooms with a special roll-in/transfer shower. There are special provisions for alterations (§§ 9.1-9.4).
- Homeless shelters, halfway houses, and similar social service establishments: Homeless shelters and other social service entities must provide the same percentage of accessible sleeping accommodations as above. At least one type of amenity in each common area must be accessible. Alterations are subject to less stringent standards (§ 9.5).

UFAS: Contains requirements for residential occupancies with technical requirements for "dwelling units." No requirements for sleeping rooms for individuals with hearing impairments. No requirements for roll-in showers as in ADAAG. No standards for alterations (§§ 4.1.4(11); 4.34).

3) Restaurants

ADAAG: In restaurants, generally all dining areas and five percent of fixed tables (but not less than one) must be accessible. While raised or sunken dining areas must be accessible, inaccessible mezzanines are permitted under certain conditions. Contains requirements for counters and bars, access aisles, food service lines, tableware and condiment areas, raised speaker's platforms, and vending machine areas (but not controls). Contains some less stringent requirements for alterations (§ 5).

UFAS: Less detailed requirements. Does not address counters and bars. Raised platforms are allowed if same service and decor are provided. Vending machines and controls are covered. No special, less stringent requirements for alterations (§ 5).

4) Medical or health care facilities

ADAAG: In medical care facilities, all public and common use areas must be accessible. In general purpose hospitals and in psychiatric and detoxification facilities, 10 percent of patient bedrooms and toilets must be accessible. The required percentage is 100 percent for special facilities treating conditions that affect mobility, and 50 percent for long-term care facilities and nursing homes. Uses terms clarified by the Department of Health and Human Services to describe types of facilities. Some descriptive information was added. Contains special, less stringent requirements for alterations (§ 6).

UFAS: Uses different terms to describe types of facilities. Required clearances in rooms exceed ADAAG requirements. No special, less stringent requirements for alterations (§ 6).

5) Mercantile

ADAAG:

Counters:

- At least one of each type of sales or service counter where a cash register is located must be accessible. Accessible counters must be dispersed throughout the facility. Auxiliary counters are permissible in alterations (§ 7.2(1)).

- At counters without cash registers, such as bank teller windows and ticketing counters, three alternatives are possible: (1) a portion of the counter may be lowered, (2) an auxiliary counter may be provided, or (3) equivalent facilitation may be provided by installing a folding shelf on the front of a counter to provide a work surface for a person using a wheelchair (§ 7.2(2)).

Check-out aisles:

- At least one of each design of check-out aisle must be accessible, and, in many cases, additional check-out aisles are required to be accessible (i.e., from 20 to 40 percent) depending on the number of check-out aisles and the size of the facility. There are less stringent standards for alterations (§ 7.3).

UFAS:

Much less detail. At service counters, must provide an accessible portion of the counter or a nearby accessible counter. At least one check-out aisle must be accessible (§ 7).

6) Jails and prisons

ADAAG: No scoping requirements indicating how many cells need to be accessible.

UFAS: Five percent of residential units in jails, prisons, reformatories, and other detention or correctional facilities must be accessible (§ 4.1.4(9)(c)).

II-6.4000 Leased buildings.

Public entities are encouraged, but not required, to lease accessible space. The availability of accessible private commercial space will steadily increase over time as the title III requirements for new construction and alterations take effect. Although a public entity is not required to lease accessible space, once it occupies a facility, it must provide access to all of the programs conducted in that space (see II-5.0000). Thus, the more accessible the space is to begin with, the easier and less costly it will be later on to make programs available to individuals with disabilities and to provide reasonable accommodations for employees who may need them.

II-6.5000 Alterations to historic properties.

Alterations to historic properties must comply with the specific provisions governing historic properties in ADAAG or UFAS, to the maximum extent feasible. Under those provisions, alterations should be done in full compliance with the alterations standards for other types of buildings. However, if following the usual standards would threaten or destroy the historic significance of a feature of the building, alternative standards may be used. The decision to use alternative standards for that feature must be made in consultation with the appropriate historic advisory board designated in ADAAG or UFAS, and interested persons should be invited to participate in the decisionmaking process.

What are "historic properties?" These are properties listed or eligible for listing in the National Register of Historic Places, or properties designated as historic under State or local law.

What are the alternative requirements? The alternative requirements for historic buildings or facilities provide a minimal level of access. For example—

1) An accessible route is only required from one site access point (such as the parking lot).

2) A ramp may be steeper than is ordinarily permitted.

3) The accessible entrance does not need to be the one used by the general public.

4) Only one accessible toilet is required and it may be unisex.

5) Accessible routes are only required on the level of the accessible entrance.

But what if complying with even these minimal alternative requirements will threaten or destroy the historic significance? In such a case, which is rare, the public entity need not make the structural changes required by UFAS or ADAAG. But, if structural modifications that comply with UFAS or ADAAG cannot be undertaken, the Department's regulation requires that "program accessibility" be provided.

ILLUSTRATION: A town owns a one-story historic house and decides to make certain alterations in it so that the house can be used as a museum. The town architect concludes that most of the normal standards for alterations can be applied during the renovation process without threatening or destroying historic features. There appears, however, to be a problem if one of the interior doors is widened, because historic decorative features on the door might be destroyed. The town architect consults the standards and determines that the appropriate historic body with jurisdiction over the particular historic home is the State Historic Preservation Officer. The architect then sets up a meeting with that officer, to which the local disability group and the designated title II coordinator are invited.

At the meeting the participants agree with the town architect's conclusion that the normal alterations standards cannot be applied to the interior door. They then review the special alternative requirements, which require an accessible route throughout the level of the accessible entrance. The meeting participants determine that application of the alternative minimal requirements is likewise not possible.

In this situation, the town is not required to widen the interior door. Instead, the town provides access to the program offered in that room by making available a video presentation of the items within the inaccessible room. The video can be viewed in a nearby accessible room in the museum.

II-6.6000 Curb ramps.

When streets, roads, or highways are newly built or altered, they must have ramps or sloped areas wherever there are curbs or other barriers to entry from a sidewalk or path. Likewise, when new sidewalks or paths are built or are altered, they must contain curb ramps or sloped areas wherever they intersect with streets, roads, or highways.

Resurfacing beyond normal maintenance is an alteration Merely filling potholes is considered to be normal maintenance.

II-7.0000 COMMUNICATIONS

II-7.1000 Equally effective communication.

A public entity must ensure that its communications with individuals with disabilities are as effective as communications with others. This obligation, however, does not require a public entity to take any action that it can demonstrate would result in a fundamental alteration in the nature of its services, programs, or activities, or in undue financial and administrative burdens.

In order to provide equal access, a public accommodation is required to make available appropriate auxiliary aids and services where necessary to ensure effective communication.

What are auxiliary aids and services? Auxiliary aids and services include a wide range of services and devices that promote effective communication.

Examples of auxiliary aids and services for individuals who are deaf or hard of hearing include qualified interpreters, notetakers, computer-aided transcription services, written materials, telephone handset amplifiers, assistive listening systems, telephones compatible with hearing aids, closed caption decoders, open and closed captioning, telecommunications devices for deaf persons (TDD's), videotext displays, and exchange of written notes.

Examples for individuals with vision impairments include qualified readers, taped texts, audio recordings, Brailled materials, large print materials, and assistance in locating items.

Examples for individuals with speech impairments include TDD's, computer terminals, speech synthesizers, and communication boards.

The type of auxiliary aid or service necessary to ensure effective communication will vary in accordance with the length and complexity of the communication involved.

ILLUSTRATION 1: Some individuals who have difficulty communicating because of a speech impairment can be understood if individuals dealing with them merely listen carefully and take the extra time that is necessary.

ILLUSTRATION 2: For individuals with vision impairments, employees can provide oral directions or read written instructions. In many simple transactions, such as paying bills or filing applications, communications provided through such simple methods will be as effective as the communications provided to other individuals in similar transactions.

ILLUSTRATION: S, who is blind, wants to use the laundry facilities in his State university dormitory. Displayed on the laundry machine controls are written instructions for operating the machines. The university could make the machines accessible to S by Brailling the instructions onto adhesive labels and placing the labels (or a Brailled template) on the machines. An alternative method of ensuring effective communication with S would be to arrange for a laundry room attendant to read the instructions printed on the machines to S. Any one particular method is not required, so long as effective communication is provided.

Many transactions with public entities, however, involve more complex or extensive communications than can be provided through such simple methods. Sign language or oral interpreters, for example, may be required when the information being communicated in a transaction with a deaf individual is complex, or is exchanged for a lengthy period of time. Factors to be considered in determining whether an interpreter is required include the context in which the communication is taking place, the number of people involved, and the importance of the communication.

ILLUSTRATION 1: A municipal hospital emergency room must be able to communicate with patients about symptoms and patients must be able to understand information provided about their conditions and treatment. In this situation, an interpreter is likely to be necessary for communications with individuals who are deaf.

ILLUSTRATION 2: Because of the importance of effective communication in State and local court proceedings, special attention must be given to the communications needs of individuals with disabilities involved in such proceedings. Qualified interpreters will usually be necessary to ensure effective communication with parties, jurors, and witnesses who have hearing impairments and use sign language. For individuals with hearing impairments who do not use sign language, other types of auxiliary aids or services, such as assistive listening devices or computer-assisted transcription services, which allow virtually instantaneous transcripts of courtroom argument and testimony to appear on displays, may be required.

ILLUSTRATION 3: A municipal police department encounters many situations where effective communication with members of the public who are deaf or hard of hearing is critical. Such situations include interviewing suspects prior to arrest (when an officer is attempting to establish probable cause); interrogating arrestees; and interviewing victims or critical witnesses. In these situations, appropriate qualified interpreters must be provided when necessary to ensure effective communication.

The obligation of public entities to provide necessary auxiliary aids and services is not limited to individuals with a direct interest in the proceedings or outcome. Courtroom spectators with disabilities are also participants in the court program and are entitled to such aids or services as will afford them an equal opportunity to follow the court proceedings.

ILLUSTRATION: B, an individual who is hard of hearing, wishes to observe proceedings in the county courthouse. Even though the county believes that B has no personal or direct involvement in the courtroom proceedings at issue, the county must provide effective communication, which in this case may involve the provision of an assistive listening device, unless it can demonstrate that undue financial and administrative burdens would result.

Must public service announcements or other television programming produced by public entities be captioned? Audio portions of television and videotape programming produced by public entities are subject to the requirement to provide equally effective communication for individuals with hearing impairments. Closed captioning of such programs is sufficient to meet this requirement.

Brailled documents are not required if effective communication is provided by other means.

Must tax bills from public entities be available in Braille and/or large print? What about other documents? Tax bills and other written communications provided by public entities are subject to the requirement for effective communication. Thus, where a public entity provides information in written form, it must, when requested, make that information available to individuals with vision impairments in a form that is usable by them. "Large print" versions of written documents may be produced on a copier with enlargement capacities. Brailled versions of documents produced by computers may be produced with a Braille printer, or audio tapes may be provided for individuals who are unable to read large print or do not use Braille.

II-7.1100 Primary consideration.

When an auxiliary aid or service is required, the public entity must provide an opportunity for individuals with disabilities to request the auxiliary aids and services of their choice and must give primary consideration to the choice expressed by the individual. "Primary consideration" means that the public entity must honor the choice, unless it can demonstrate that another equally effective means of communication is available, or that use of the means chosen would result in a fundamental alteration in the service, program, or activity or in undue financial and administrative burdens.

ILLUSTRATION: A county's Supervisor of Elections provides magnifying lenses and readers for individuals with vision impairments seeking to vote. The election assistance will be aided by two poll workers, or by one person selected by the voter. C, a voter who is blind, protests that this method does not allow a blind voter to cast a secret ballot, and requests that the County provide him with a Brailled ballot. A Brailled ballot, however, would have to be counted separately and would be readily identifiable, and thus would not resolve the problem of ballot secrecy. Because County X can demonstrate that its current system or providing assistance is an effective means of affording an individual with a disability an equal opportunity to vote, the County need not provide ballots in Braille.

It is important to consult with the individual to determine the most appropriate auxiliary aid or service, because the individual with a disability is most familiar with his or her disability and is in the best position to determine what type of aid or service will be effective. Some individuals who were deaf at birth or who lost their hearing before acquiring language, for example, use sign language as their primary form of communication and may be uncomfortable or not proficient with written English, making use of a notepad an ineffective means of communication.

Individuals who lose their hearing later in life, on the other hand, may not be familiar with sign language and can communicate effectively through writing. For these individuals, use of a word processor with a videotext display may provide effective communication in transactions that are long or complex, and computer-assisted simultaneous transcription may be necessary in courtroom proceedings. Individuals with less severe hearing impairments are often able to communicate most effectively with voice amplification provided by an assistive listening device.

For individuals with vision impairments, appropriate auxiliary aids include readers, audio recordings, Brailled materials, and large print materials. Brailled materials, however, are ineffective for many individuals with vision impairments who do not read Braille, just as large print materials would be ineffective for individuals with severely impaired vision who rely on Braille or on audio communications. Thus, the requirement for consultation and primary consideration to the individual's expressed choice applies to information provided in visual formats as well as to aurally communicated information.

II-7.1200 Qualified interpreter.

There are a number of sign language systems in use by individuals who use sign language. (The most common systems of sign language are American Sign Language and signed English.) Individuals who use a particular system may not communicate effectively through an interpreter who uses a different system. When an interpreter is required, therefore, the public entity should provide a qualified interpreter, that is, an interpreter who is able to sign to the individual who is deaf what is being said by the hearing person and who can voice to the hearing person what is being signed by the individual who is deaf. This communication must be conveyed effectively, accurately, and impartially, through the use of any necessary specialized vocabulary.

May friends or relatives be asked to interpret? Often, friends or relatives of the individual can provide interpreting services, but the public entity may not require the individual to provide his or her own interpreter, because it is the responsibility of the public entity to provide a qualified interpreter. Also, in many situations, requiring a friend or family member to interpret may not be appropriate, because his or her presence at the transaction may violate the individual's right to confidentiality, or because the friend or family member may have an interest in the transaction that is different from that of the individual involved. The obligation to provide "impartial" interpreting services requires that, upon request, the public entity provide an interpreter who does not have a personal relationship to the individual with a disability.

Are certified interpreters considered to be more qualified than interpreters without certification? Certification is not required in order for an interpreter to be considered to have the skills necessary to facilitate communication. Regardless of the professionalism or skills that a certified interpreter may possess, that particular individual may not feel comfortable or possess the proper vocabulary necessary for interpreting for a computer class, for example. Another equally skilled, but noncertified interpreter might have the necessary vocabulary, thus making the noncertified person the qualified interpreter for that particular situation.

Can a public entity use a staff member who signs "pretty well" as an interpreter for meetings with individuals who use sign language to communicate? Signing and interpreting are not the same thing. Being able to sign does not mean that a person can process spoken communication into the proper signs, nor does it mean that he or she possesses the proper skills to observe someone signing and change their signed or fingerspelled communication into spoken words. The interpreter must be able to interpret both receptively and expressively.

II-7.2000 Telephone communications.

Public entities that communicate by telephone must provide equally effective communication to individuals with disabilities, including hearing and speech impairments. If telephone relay services, such as those required by title IV of the ADA, are available, these services generally may be used to meet this requirement.

Relay services involve a relay operator who uses both a standard telephone and a TDD to type the voice messages to the TDD user and read the TDD messages to the standard telephone user. Where such services are available, public employees must be instructed to accept and handle relayed calls in the normal course of business.

II-7.3000 Emergency telephone services

II-7.3100 General.

Many public entities provide telephone emergency services by which individuals can seek immediate assistance from police, fire, ambulance, and other emergency services. These telephone emergency services-including "911" services-are clearly an important public service whose reliability can be a matter of life or death. Public entities must ensure that these services, including 911 services, are accessible to persons with impaired hearing and speech.

State and local agencies that provide emergency telephone services must provide "direct access" to individuals who rely on a TDD or computer modem for telephone communication. Telephone access through a third party or through a relay service does not satisfy the requirement for direct access. (However, if an individual places a call to the emergency service through a relay service, the emergency service should accept the call rather than require the caller to hang up and call the emergency service directly without using the relay.) A public entity may, however, operate its own relay service within its emergency system, provided that the services for nonvoice calls are as effective as those provided for voice calls.

What emergency telephone services are covered by title II? The term "telephone emergency services" applies to basic emergency services—police, fire, and ambulance—that are provided by public entities, including 911 (or, in some cases, seven-digit) systems. Direct access must be provided to all services included in the system, including services such as emergency poison control information. Emergency services that are not provided by public entities are not subject to the requirement for "direct access."

What is "direct access? "Direct access" means that emergency telephone services can directly receive calls from TDD's and computer modem users without relying on outside relay services or third party services.

Does title II require that telephone emergency service systems be compatible with all formats used for nonvoice communications? No. At present, telephone emergency services must only be compatible with the Baudot format. Until it can be technically proven that communications in another format can operate in a reliable and compatible manner in a given telephone emergency environment, a public entity would not be required to provide direct access to computer modems using formats other than Baudot.

Are any additional dialing or space bar requirements permissible for 911 systems? No. Additional dialing or space bar requirements are not permitted. Operators should be trained to recognize incoming TDD signals and respond appropriately. In addition, they also must be trained to recognize that "silent" calls may be TDD or computer modem calls and to respond appropriately to such calls as well.

A caller, however, is not prohibited from announcing to the answerer that the call is being made on a TDD by pressing the space bar or keys. A caller may transmit tones if he or she chooses to do so. However, a public entity may not require such a transmission.

II-7.3200 911 lines.

Where a 911 telephone line is available, a separate seven-digit telephone line must not be substituted as the sole means for nonvoice users to access 911 services. A public entity may, however, provide a separate seven-digit line for use exclusively by nonvoice calls in addition to providing direct access for such calls to the 911 line. Where such a separate line is provided, callers using TDD's or computer modems would have the option of calling either 911 or the seven-digit number.

II-7.3300 Seven-digit lines.

Where a 911 line is not available and the public entity provides emergency services through a seven-digit number, it may provide two separate lines—one for voice calls, and another for nonvoice calls—rather than providing direct access for nonvoice calls to the line used for voice calls, provided that the services for nonvoice calls are as effective as those offered for voice calls in terms of time response and availability in hours. Also, the public entity must ensure that the nonvoice number is publicized as effectively as the voice number, and is displayed as prominently as the voice number wherever the emergency numbers are listed.

ILLUSTRATION: Some States may operate a statewide 911 system for both voice and nonvoice calls and, in addition, permit voice callers only to dial seven- digit numbers to obtain assistance from particular emergency service providers. Such an arrangement does not violate title II so long as nonvoice callers whose calls are directed through 911 receive emergency attention as quickly as voice callers who dial local emergency seven-digit numbers for assistance.

II-7.3400 Voice amplification.

Public entities are encouraged, but not required, to provide voice amplification for the operator's voice. In an emergency, a person who has a hearing loss may be using a telephone that does not have an amplification device. Installation of speech amplification devices on the handsets of operators would be one way to respond to this situation.

II-8.0000 ADMINISTRATIVE REQUIREMENTS

II-8.1000 General.

Title II requires that public entities take several steps designed to achieve compliance. These include the preparation of a self-evaluation. In addition, public entities with 50 or more employees are required to—

1) Develop a grievance procedure;
2) Designate an individual to oversee title II compliance;
3) Develop a transition plan if structural changes are necessary for achieving program accessibility; and
4) Retain the self-evaluation for three years.

How does a public entity determine whether it has "50 or more employees"? Determining the number of employees will be based on a governmentwide total of employees, rather than by counting the number of employees of a subunit, department, or division of the local government. Part-time employees are included in the determination.

ILLUSTRATION: Town X has 55 employees (including 20 part-time employees). Its police department has 10 employees, and its fire department has eight employees. The police and fire department are subject to title II's administrative requirements applicable to public entities with 50 or more employees because Town X, as a whole, has 50 or more employees.

Because all States have at least 50 employees, all State departments, agencies, and other divisional units are subject to title II's administrative requirements applicable to public entities with 50 or more employees.

II-8.2000 Self-evaluation.

All public entities subject to title II of the ADA must complete a self- evaluation by January 26, 1993 (one year from the effective date of the Department's regulation).

Does the fact that a public entity has not completed its self-evaluation until January 26, 1993, excuse interim compliance? No. A public entity is required to comply with the requirements of title II on January 26, 1992, whether or not it has completed its self-evaluation.

Which public entities must retain a copy of the self-evaluation? A public entity that employs 50 or more employees must retain its self-evaluation for three years. Other public entities are not required to retain their self- evaluations but are encouraged to do so because these documents evidence a public entity's good faith efforts to comply with title II's requirements.

What if a public entity already did a self-evaluation as part of its obligations under section 504 of the Rehabilitation Act of 1973? The title II self-evaluation requirement applies only to those policies and practices that previously had not been included in a self-evaluation required by section 504. Because most section 504 self-evaluations were done many years ago, however, the Department expects that many public entities will re-examine all their policies and practices. Programs and functions may have changed significantly since the section 504 self-evaluation was completed. Actions that were taken to comply with section 504 may not have been implemented fully or may no longer be effective. In addition, section 504's coverage has been changed by statutory amendment, particularly the Civil Rights Restoration Act of 1987, which expanded the definition of a covered "program or activity." Therefore, public entities should ensure that all programs, activities, and services are examined fully, except where there is evidence that all policies were previously scrutinized under section 504.

What should a self-evaluation contain? A self-evaluation is a public entity's assessment of its current policies and practices. The self-evaluation identifies and corrects those policies and practices that are inconsistent with title II's requirements. As part of the self-evaluation, a public entity should:

1) Identify all of the public entity's programs, activities, and services; and
2) Review all the policies and practices that govern the administration of the public entity's programs, activities, and services.

Normally, a public entity's policies and practices are reflected in its laws, ordinances, regulations, administrative manuals or guides, policy directives, and memoranda. Other practices, however, may not be recorded and may be based on local custom.

Once a public entity has identified its policies and practices, it should analyze whether these policies and practices adversely affect the full participation of individuals with disabilities in its programs, activities, and services. In this regard, a public entity should be mindful that although its policies and practices may appear harmless, they may result in denying individuals with disabilities the full participation of its programs, activities, or services. Areas that need careful examination include the following:

1) A public entity must examine each program to determine whether any physical barriers to access exist. It should identify steps that need to be taken to enable these programs to be made accessible when viewed in their entirety. If structural changes are necessary, they should be included in the transition plan (see II-8.3000).

2) A public entity must review its policies and practices to determine whether any exclude or limit the participation of individuals with disabilities in its programs, activities, or services. Such policies or practices must be modified, unless they are necessary for the operation or provision of the program, service, or activity. The self-evaluation should identify policy modifications to be implemented and include complete justifications for any exclusionary or limiting policies or practices that will not be modified.

3) A public entity should review its policies to ensure that it communicates with applicants, participants, and members of the public with disabilities in a manner that is as effective as its communications with others. If a public entity communicates with applicants and beneficiaries by telephone, it should ensure that TDD's or equally effective telecommunication systems are used to communicate with individuals with impaired hearing or speech. Finally, if a public entity provides telephone emergency services, it should review its policies to ensure direct access to individuals who use TDD's and computer modems.

4) A public entity should review its policies to ensure that they include provisions for readers for individuals with visual impairments; interpreters or other alternative communication measures, as appropriate, for individuals with hearing impairments; and amanuenses for individuals with manual impairments. A method for securing these services should be developed, including guidance on when and where these services will be provided. Where equipment is used as part of a public entity's program, activity, or service, an assessment should be made to ensure that the equipment is usable by individuals with disabilities, particularly individuals with hearing, visual, and manual impairments. In addition, a public entity should have policies that ensure that its equipment is maintained in operable working order.

5) A review should be made of the procedures to evacuate individuals with disabilities during an emergency. This may require the installation of visual and audible warning signals and special procedures for assisting individuals with disabilities from a facility during an emergency.

6) A review should be conducted of a public entity's written and audio- visual materials to ensure that individuals with disabilities are not portrayed in an offensive or demeaning manner.

7) If a public entity operates historic preservation programs, it should review its policies to ensure that it gives priority to methods that provide physical access to individuals with disabilities.

8) A public entity should review its policies to ensure that its decisions concerning a fundamental alteration in the nature of a program, activity, or service, or a decision that an undue financial and administrative burden will be imposed by title II, are made properly and expeditiously.

9) A public entity should review its policies and procedures to ensure that individuals with mobility impairments are provided access to public meetings.

10) A public entity should review its employment practices to ensure that they comply with other applicable nondiscrimination requirements, including section 504 of the Rehabilitation Act and the ADA regulation issued by the Equal Employment Opportunity Commission.

11) A public entity should review its building and construction policies to ensure that the construction of each new facility or part of a facility, or the alteration of existing facilities after January 26, 1992, conforms to the standards designated under the title II regulation.

12) A review should be made to ascertain whether measures have been taken to ensure that employees of a public entity are familiar with the policies and practices for the full participation of individuals with disabilities. If appropriate, training should be provided to employees.

13) If a public entity limits or denies participation in its programs, activities, or services based on drug usage, it should make sure that such policies do not discriminate against former drug users, as opposed to individuals who are currently engaged in illegal use of drugs.

If a public entity identifies policies and practices that deny or limit the participation of individuals with disabilities in its programs, activities, and services, when should it make changes? Once a public entity has identified policies and practices that deny or limit the participation of individuals with disabilities in its programs, activities, and services, it should take immediate remedial action to eliminate the impediments to full and equivalent participation. Structural modifications that are required for program accessibility should be made as expeditiously as possible but no later than January 26, 1995.

Is there a requirement for public hearings on a public entity's self- evaluation? No, but public entities are required to accept comments from the public on the self-evaluation and are strongly encouraged to consult with individuals with disabilities and organizations that represent them to assist in the self-evaluation process. Many individuals with disabilities have unique perspectives on a public entity's programs, activities, and services. For example, individuals with mobility impairments can readily identify barriers preventing their full enjoyment of the public entity's programs, activities, and services. Similarly, individuals with hearing impairments can identify the communication barriers that hamper participation in a public entity's programs, activities, and services.

II-8.3000 Transition plan.

Where structural modifications are required to achieve program accessibility, a public entity with 50 or more employees must do a transition plan by July 26, 1992, that provides for the removal of these barriers. Any structural modifications must be completed as expeditiously as possible, but, in any event, by July 26, 1995.

What if a public entity has already done a transition plan under section 504 of the Rehabilitation Act of 1973? If a public entity previously completed a section 504 transition plan, then, at a minimum, a title II transition plan must cover those barriers to accessibility that were not addressed by its prior transition plan. Although not required, it may be simpler to include all of a public entity's operations in its transition plan rather than identifying and excluding those barriers that were addressed in its previous plan.

Must the transition plan be made available to the public? If a public entity has 50 or more employees, a copy of the transition plan must be made available for public inspection.

What are the elements of an acceptable transition plan? A transition plan should contain at a minimum-

1) A list of the physical barriers in a public entity's facilities that limit the accessibility of its programs, activities, or services to individuals with disabilities;

2) A detailed outline of the methods to be utilized to remove these barriers and make the facilities accessible;

3) The schedule for taking the necessary steps to achieve compliance with title II. If the time period for achieving compliance is longer than one year, the plan should identify the interim steps that will be taken during each year of the transition period; and,

4) The name of the official responsible for the plan's implementation.

II-8.4000 Notice to the public.

A public entity must provide information on title II's requirements to applicants, participants, beneficiaries, and other interested persons. The notice shall explain title II's applicability to the public entity's services, programs, or activities. A public entity shall provide such information as the head of the public entity determines to be necessary to apprise individuals of title II's prohibitions against discrimination.

What methods can be used to provide this information? Methods include the publication of information in handbooks, manuals, and pamphlets that are distributed to the public to describe a public entity's programs and activities; the display of informative posters in service centers and other public places; or the broadcast of information by television or radio. In providing the notice, a public entity must comply with the title II requirements for effective communication, including alternate formats, as appropriate.

II-8.5000 Designation of responsible employee and development of grievance procedures.

A public entity that employs 50 or more persons shall designate at least one employee to coordinate its efforts to comply with and fulfill its responsibilities under title II, including the investigation of complaints. A public entity shall make available the name, office address, and telephone number of any designated employee.

In addition, the public entity must adopt and publish grievance procedures providing for prompt and equitable resolution of complaints alleging any action that would be prohibited by title II.

II-9.0000 INVESTIGATION OF COMPLAINTS AND ENFORCEMENT

II-9.1000 General.

Individuals wishing to file title II complaints may either file—

1) An administrative complaint with an appropriate Federal agency; or

2) A lawsuit in Federal district court.

If an individual files an administrative complaint, an appropriate Federal agency will investigate the allegations of discrimination. Should the agency conclude that the public entity violated title II, it will attempt to negotiate a settlement with the public entity to remedy the violations. If settlement efforts fail, the matter will be referred to the Department of Justice for a decision whether to institute litigation.

How does title II relate to section 504? Many public entities are subject to section 504 of the Rehabilitation Act as well as title II. Section 504 covers those public entities operating programs or activities that receive Federal financial assistance. Title II does not displace any existing section 504 jurisdiction.

The substantive standards adopted for title II are generally the same as those required under section 504 for federally assisted programs. In those situations where title II provides greater protection of the rights of individuals with disabilities, however, the funding agencies will also apply the substantive requirements established under title II in processing complaints covered by both title II and section 504.

Individuals may continue to file discrimination complaints against recipients of Federal financial assistance with the agencies that provide that assistance, and the funding agencies will continue to process those complaints under their existing procedures for enforcing section 504. The funding agencies will be enforcing both title II and section 504, however, for recipients that are also public entities.

II-9.2000 Complaints.

A person or a specific class of individuals or their representative may file a complaint alleging discrimination on the basis of disability.

What must be included in a complaint? First, a complaint must be in writing. Second, it should contain the name and address of the individual or the representative filing the complaint. Third, the complaint should describe the public entity's alleged discriminatory action in sufficient detail to inform the Federal agency of the nature and date of the alleged violation. Fourth, the complaint must be signed by the complainant or by someone authorized to do so on his or her behalf. Finally, complaints filed on behalf of classes or third parties shall describe or identify (by name, if possible) the alleged victims of discrimination.

Is there a time period in which a complaint must be filed? Yes. A complaint must be filed within 180 days of the date of the alleged act(s) of discrimination, unless the time for filing is extended by the Federal agency for good cause. As long as the complaint is filed with any Federal agency, the 180-day requirement will be considered satisfied.

Where should a complaint be filed? A complaint may be filed with either—

1) Any Federal agency that provides funding to the public entity that is the subject of the complaint;

2) A Federal agency designated in the title II regulation to investigate title II complaints; or

3) The Department of Justice.

Complainants may file with a Federal funding agency that has section 504 jurisdiction, if known. If no Federal funding agency is known, then complainants should file with the appropriate designated agency. In any event, complaints may always be filed with the Department of Justice, which will refer the complaint to the appropriate agency. The Department's regulation designates eight Federal agencies to investigate title II complaints primarily in those cases where there is no Federal agency with section 504 jurisdiction.

How will employment complaints be handled? Individuals who believe that they have been discriminated against in employment by a State or local government in violation of title II may file a complaint—

1) With a Federal agency that provides financial assistance, if any, to the State or local program in which the alleged discrimination took place; or

2) With the EEOC, if the State or local government is also subject to title I of the ADA (see II—4.0000); or

3) With the Federal agency designated in the title II regulation to investigate complaints in the type of program in which the alleged discrimination took place.

As is the case with complaints related to nonemployment issues, employment complaints may be filed with the Department of Justice, which will refer the complaint to the appropriate agency.

Which are the designated Federal agencies and what are their areas of responsibility? The eight designated Federal agencies, the functional areas covered by these agencies, and the addresses for filing a complaint are the—

1) Department of Agriculture: All programs, services, and regulatory activities relating to farming and the raising of livestock, including extension services. Complaints should be sent to: Complaints Adjudication Division, Office of Advocacy and Enterprise, Room 1353—South Building, Department

of Agriculture, 14th & Independence Avenue, S.W., Washington, D.C. 20250.

2) Department of Education: All programs, services, and regulatory activities relating to the operation of elementary and secondary education systems and institutions, institutions of higher education and vocational education (other than schools of medicine, dentistry, nursing, and other health-related schools), and libraries. Complaints should be sent to: Office for Civil Rights, Department of Education, 330 C Street, S.W., Suite 5000, Washington, D.C. 20202.

3) Department of Health and Human Services: All programs, services, and regulatory activities relating to the provision of health care and social services, including schools of medicine, dentistry, nursing, and other health-related schools, the operation of health care and social service providers and institutions, including "grass-roots" and community services organizations and programs, and preschool and day care programs. Complaints should be sent to: Office for Civil Rights, Department of Health & Human Services, 330 Independence Avenue, S.W., Washington, D.C. 20201.

4) Department of Housing and Urban Development: All programs, services, and regulatory activities relating to State and local public housing, and housing assistance and referral. Complaints should be sent to: Assistant Secretary for Fair Housing and Equal Opportunity, Department of Housing and Urban Development, 451 7th Street, S.W., Room 5100, Washington, D.C. 20410.

5) Department of the Interior: All programs, services, and regulatory activities relating to lands and natural resources, including parks and recreation, water and waste management, environmental protection, energy, historic and cultural preservation, and museums. Complaints should be sent to: Office for Equal Opportunity, Office of the Secretary, Department of the Interior, 18th & C Streets, N.W., Washington, D.C. 20547.

6) Department of Justice: All programs, services, and regulatory activities relating to law enforcement, public safety, and the administration of justice, including courts and correctional institutions; commerce and industry, including general economic development, banking and finance, consumer protection, insurance, and small business; planning, development, and regulation (unless assigned to other designated agencies); State and local government support services (e.g., audit, personnel, comptroller, administrative services); all other government functions not assigned to other designated agencies. Complaints should be sent to: Coordination and Review Section, P.O. Box 66118, Civil Rights Division, U.S. Department of Justice, Washington, D.C. 20035-6118.

7) Department of Labor: All programs, services, and regulatory activities relating to labor and the work force. Complaints should be sent to: Directorate of Civil Rights, Department of Labor, 200 Constitution Avenue, N.W., Room N-4123, Washington, D.C. 20210.

8) Department of Transportation: All programs, services, and regulatory activities relating to transportation, including highways, public transportation, traffic management (non-law enforcement), automobile licensing and inspection, and driver licensing. Complaints should be sent to: Office for Civil Rights, Office of the Secretary, Department of Transportation, 400 Seventh Street, S.W., Room 10215, Washington, D.C. 20590.

Where should a complaint be filed if more than one designated agency has responsibility for a complaint because it concerns more than one department or agency of a public entity? Complaints involving more than one area should be filed with the Department of Justice. If two or more agencies have apparent responsibility for a complaint, the Assistant Attorney General for Civil Rights of the Department of Justice shall determine which one of the agencies shall be the designated agency for purposes of that complaint. Complaints involving more than one area of a public entity should be sent to: Coordination and Review Section, Civil Rights Division, U.S. Department of Justice, P.O. Box 66118, Washington, D.C. 20035-6118.

How will complaints be resolved? The Federal agency processing the complaint will resolve the complaint through informal means or issue a detailed letter containing findings of fact and conclusions of law and, where appropriate, a description of the actions necessary to remedy each violation. Where voluntary compliance cannot be achieved, the complaint may be referred to the Department of Justice for enforcement. In cases where there is Federal funding, fund termination is also an enforcement option.

If a public entity has a grievance procedure, must an individual use that procedure before filing a complaint with a Federal agency or a court? No. Exhaustion of a public entity's grievance procedure is not a prerequisite to filing a complaint with either a Federal agency or a court.

Must the complainant file a complaint with a Federal agency prior to filing an action in court? No. The ADA does not require complainants to exhaust administrative remedies prior to instituting litigation.

Are attorney's fees available? Yes. The prevailing

party (other than the United States) in any action or administrative proceeding under the Act may recover attorney's fees in addition to any other relief granted. The "prevailing party" is the party that is successful and may be either the complainant (plaintiff) or the covered entity against which the action is brought (defendant). The defendant, however, may not recover attorney's fees unless the court finds that the plaintiff's action was frivolous, unreasonable, or without foundation, although it does not have to find that the action was brought in subjective bad faith . Attorney's fees include litigation expenses, such as expert witness fees, travel expenses, and costs. The United States is liable for attorney's fees in the same manner as any other party, but is not entitled to them when it is the prevailing party.

Is a State immune from suit under the ADA? No. A State is not immune from an action in Federal court for violations of the ADA.

Is a private plaintiff entitled to compensatory damages? A private plaintiff under title II is entitled to all of the remedies available under section 504 of the Rehabilitation Act of 1973, including compensatory damage.

ILLUSTRATION: A county court system is found by a Federal court to have violated title II of the ADA by excluding a blind individual from a jury because of his blindness. The individual is entitled to compensatory damages for any injuries suffered, including compensation, when appropriate, for any emotional distress caused by the discrimination.

ADA TITLE III

PUBLIC ACCOMMODATIONS AND SERVICES OPERATED BY PRIVATE ENTITIES

42 U.S.C. §

ADA TITLE III

PUBLIC ACCOMMODATIONS AND SERVICES OPERATED BY PRIVATE ENTITIES

§ 12181. Definitions

As used in this subchapter:

(1) Commerce

The term "commerce" means travel, trade, traffic, commerce, transportation, or communication—

(A) among the several States;

(B) between any foreign country or any territory or possession and any State; or

(C) between points in the same State but through another State or foreign country.

(2) Commercial facilities

The term "commercial facilities" means facilities—

(A) that are intended for nonresidential use; and

(B) whose operations will affect commerce.

Such term shall not include railroad locomotives, railroad freight cars, railroad cabooses, railroad cars described in section 242 or covered under this subchapter, railroad rights-of-way, or facilities that are covered or expressly exempted from coverage under the Fair Housing Act of 1968 (42 U.S.C. 3601 et seq.).

(3) Demand responsive system

The term "demand responsive system" means any system of providing transportation of individuals by a vehicle, other than a system which is a fixed route system.

(4) Fixed route system

The term "fixed route system" means a system of providing transportation of individuals (other than by aircraft) on which a vehicle is operated along a prescribed route according to a fixed schedule.

(5) Over-the-road bus

The term "over-the-road bus" means a bus characterized by an elevated passenger deck located over a baggage compartment.

(6) Private entity

The term "private entity" means any entity other than a public entity (as defined in section 12131(1) of this title).

(7) Public accommodation

The following private entities are considered public accommodations for purposes of this subchapter, if the operations of such entities affect commerce

(A) an inn, hotel, motel, or other place of lodging, except for an establishment located within a building that contains not more than five rooms for rent or hire and that is actually occupied by the proprietor of such establishment as the residence of such proprietor;

(B) a restaurant, bar, or other establishment serving food or drink;

(C) a motion picture house, theater, concert hall, stadium, or other place of exhibition or entertainment;

(D) an auditorium, convention center, lecture hall, or other place of public gathering;

(E) a bakery, grocery store, clothing store, hardware store, shopping center, or other sales or rental establishment;

(F) a laundromat, dry-cleaner, bank, barber shop, beauty shop, travel service, shoe repair service, funeral parlor, gas station, office of an accountant or lawyer, pharmacy, insurance office, professional office of a health care provider, hospital, or other service establishment;

(G) a terminal, depot, or other station used for specified public transportation;

(H) a museum, library, gallery, or other place of public display or collection;

(I) a park, zoo, amusement park, or other place of recreation;

(J) a nursery, elementary, secondary, undergraduate, or postgraduate private school, or other place of education;

(K) a day care center, senior citizen center, homeless shelter, food bank, adoption agency, or other social service center establishment; and

(L) a gymnasium, health spa, bowling alley, golf course, or other place of exercise or recreation.

(8) Rail and railroad

The terms "rail" and "railroad" have the meaning given the term "railroad" in section 431(e) of Title 45.

(9) Readily achievable

The term "readily achievable" means easily accomplishable and able to be carried out without much difficulty or expense. In determining whether an action is readily achievable, factors to be considered include—

(A) the nature and cost of the action needed under this chapter;

(B) the overall financial resources of the facility or facilities involved in the action; the number of persons employed at such facility; the effect on expenses and resources, or the impact otherwise of such action upon the operation of the facility;

(C) the overall financial resources of the covered entity; the overall size of the business of a covered entity with respect to the number of its employees; the number, type, and location of its facilities; and

(D) the type of operation or operations of the covered entity, including the composition, structure, and functions of the work force of such entity; the geographic separateness, administrative or fiscal relationship of the facility or facilities in question to the covered entity.

(10) Specified public transportation

The term "specified public transportation" means transportation by bus, rail, or any other conveyance (other than by aircraft) that provides the general public with general or special service (including charter service) on a regular and continuing basis.

(11) Vehicle

The term "vehicle" does not include a rail passenger car, railroad locomotive, railroad freight car, railroad caboose, or a railroad car described in section 12162 of this title or covered under this subchapter.

§ 12182. Prohibition of discrimination by public accommodations

(a) General rule

No individual shall be discriminated against on the basis of disability in the full and equal enjoyment of the goods, services, facilities, privileges, advantages, or accommodations of any place of public accommodation by any person who owns, leases (or leases to), or operates a place of public accommodation.

(b) Construction

(1) General prohibition

(A) Activities

(i) Denial of participation

It shall be discriminatory to subject an individual or class of individuals on the basis of a disability or disabilities of such individual or class, directly, or through contractual, licensing, or other arrangements, to a denial of the opportunity of the individual or class to participate in or benefit from the goods, services, facilities, privileges, advantages, or accommodations of an entity.

(ii) Participation in unequal benefit

It shall be discriminatory to afford an individual or class of individuals, on the basis of a disability or disabilities of such individual or class, directly, or through contractual, licensing, or other arrangements with the opportunity to participate in or benefit from a good, service, facility, privilege, advantage, or accommodation that is not equal to that afforded to other individuals.

(iii) Separate benefit

It shall be discriminatory to provide an individual or class of individuals, on the basis of a disability or disabilities of such individual or class, directly, or through contractual, licensing, or other arrangements with a good, service, facility, privilege, advantage, or accommodation that is different or separate from that provided to other individuals, unless such action is necessary to provide the individual or class of individuals with a good, service, facility, privilege, advantage, or accommodation, or other opportunity that is as effective as that provided to others.

(iv) Individual or class of individuals

For purposes of clauses (i) through (iii) of this subparagraph, the term "individual or class of individuals" refers to the clients or customers of the covered public accommodation that enters into the contractual, licensing or other arrangement.

(B) Integrated settings

Goods, services, facilities, privileges, advantages, and accommodations shall be afforded to an individual with a disability in the most integrated setting appropriate to the needs of the individual.

(C) Opportunity to participate

Notwithstanding the existence of separate or different programs or activities provided in accordance with this section, an individual with a disability shall not be denied the opportunity to participate in such programs or activities that are not separate or different.

(D) Administrative methods

An individual or entity shall not, directly or through contractual or other arrangements, utilize standards or criteria or methods of administration—

(i) that have the effect of discriminating on the basis of disability; or

(ii) that perpetuate the discrimination of others who are subject to common administrative control.

(E) Association

It shall be discriminatory to exclude or otherwise deny equal goods, services, facilities, privileges, advantages, accommodations, or other opportunities to an individual or entity because of the known disability of an individual with whom the individual or entity is known to have a relationship or association.

(2) Specific prohibitions

(A) Discrimination

For purposes of subsection (a) of this section, discrimination includes—

(i) the imposition or application of eligibility criteria that screen out or tend to screen out an individual with a disability or any class of individuals with disabilities from fully and equally enjoying any goods, services, facilities, privileges, advantages, or accommodations, unless such criteria can be shown to be necessary for the provision of the goods, services, facilities, privileges, advantages, or accommodations being offered;

(ii) a failure to make reasonable modifications in policies, practices, or procedures, when such modifications are necessary to afford such goods, services, facilities, privileges, advantages, or accommodations to individuals with disabilities, unless the entity can demonstrate that making such modifications would fundamentally alter the nature of such goods, services, facilities, privileges, advantages, or accommodations;

(iii) a failure to take such steps as may be necessary to ensure that no individual with a disability is excluded, denied services, segregated or otherwise treated differently than other individuals because of the absence of auxiliary aids and services, unless the entity can demonstrate that taking such steps would fundamentally alter the nature of the good, service, facility, privilege, advantage, or accommodation being offered or would result in an undue burden;

(iv) a failure to remove architectural barriers, and communication barriers that are structural in nature, in existing facilities, and transportation barriers in existing vehicles and rail passenger cars used by an establishment for transporting individuals (not including barriers that can only be removed through the retrofitting of vehicles or rail passenger cars by the installation of a hydraulic or other lift), where such removal is readily achievable; and

(v) where an entity can demonstrate that the removal of a barrier under clause (iv) is not readily achievable, a failure to make such goods, services, facilities, privileges, advantages, or accommodations available through alternative methods if such methods are readily achievable.

(B) Fixed route system

(i) Accessibility

It shall be considered discrimination for a private entity which operates a fixed route system and which is not subject to section 12184 of this title to purchase or lease a vehicle with a seating capacity in excess of 16 passengers (including the driver) for use on such system, for which a solicitation is made after the 30th day following the effective date of this subparagraph, that is not readily accessible to and usable by individuals with disabilities, including individuals who use wheelchairs.

(ii) Equivalent service

If a private entity which operates a fixed route system and which is not subject to section 12184 of this title purchases or leases a vehicle with a seating capacity of 16 passengers or less (including the driver) for use on such system after the effective date of this subparagraph that is not readily accessible to or usable by individuals with disabilities, it shall be considered discrimination for such entity to fail to operate such system so that, when viewed in its entirety, such system ensures a level of service to individuals with disabilities, including individuals who use wheelchairs, equivalent to the level of service provided to individuals without disabilities.

(C) Demand responsive system

For purposes of subsection (a) of this section, discrimination includes—

(i) a failure of a private entity which operates a demand responsive system and which is not subject to section 12184 of this title to operate such system so that, when viewed in its entirety, such system ensures a level of service to individuals with disabilities, including individuals who use wheelchairs, equivalent to the level of service provided to individuals without disabilities; and

(ii) the purchase or lease by such entity for use on such system of a vehicle with a seating capacity in excess of 16 passengers (including the driver), for which solicitations are made after the 30th day following the effective date of this subparagraph, that is not readily accessible to and usable by individuals with disabilities (including individuals who use wheelchairs) unless such entity can demonstrate that such system, when viewed in its entirety, provides a level of service to individuals with disabilities equivalent to that provided to individuals without disabilities.

(D) Over-the-road buses

(i) Limitation on applicability

Subparagraphs (B) and (C) do not apply to over-the-road buses.

(ii) Accessibility requirements

For purposes of subsection (a) of this section, discrimination includes (I) the purchase or lease of an over-the-road bus which does not comply with the regulations issued under section 12186(a)(2) of this title by a private entity which provides transportation of individuals and which is not primarily engaged in the business of transporting people, and (II) any other failure of such entity to comply with such regulations.

(3) Specific construction

Nothing in this subchapter shall require an entity to permit an individual to participate in or benefit from the goods, services, facilities, privileges, advantages and accommodations of such entity where such individual poses a direct threat to the health or safety of others. The term "direct threat" means a significant risk to the health or safety of others that cannot be eliminated by a modification of policies, practices, or procedures or by the provision of auxiliary aids or services.

§ 12183. New construction and alterations in public accommodations and commercial facilities

(a) Application of term

Except as provided in subsection (b) of this section, as applied to public accommodations and commercial facilities, discrimination for purposes of section 12182(a) of this title includes—

(1) a failure to design and construct facilities for first occupancy later than 30 months after July 26, 1990, that are readily accessible to and usable by individuals with disabilities, except where an entity can demonstrate that it is structurally impracticable to meet the requirements of such subsection in accordance with standards set forth or incorporated by reference in regulations issued under this subchapter; and

(2) with respect to a facility or part thereof that is altered by, on behalf of, or for the use of an establishment in a manner that affects or could affect the usability of the facility or part thereof, a failure to make alterations in such a manner that, to the maximum extent feasible, the altered portions of the facility are readily accessible to and usable by individuals with disabilities, including individuals who use wheelchairs. Where the entity is undertaking an alteration that affects or could affect usability of or access to an area of the facility containing a primary function, the entity shall also make the alterations in such a manner that, to the maximum extent feasible, the path of travel to the altered area and the bathrooms, telephones, and drinking fountains serving the altered area, are readily accessible to and usable by individuals with disabilities where such alterations to the path of travel or the bathrooms, telephones, and drinking fountains serving the altered area are not disproportionate to the overall alterations in terms of cost and scope (as determined under criteria established by the Attorney General).

(b) Elevator

Subsection (a) of this section shall not be construed to require the installation of an elevator for facilities that are less than three stories or have less than 3,000 square feet per story unless the building is a shopping center, a shopping mall, or the professional office of a health care provider or unless the Attorney General determines that a particular category of such facilities requires the installation of elevators based on the usage of such facilities.

§ 12184. Prohibition of discrimination in specified public transportation services provided by private entities

(a) General rule. No individual shall be discriminated against on the basis of disability in the full and equal enjoyment of specified public transportation services provided by a private entity that is primarily engaged in the business of transporting people and whose operations affect commerce.

(b) Construction. For purposes of subsection (a), discrimination includes—

(1) the imposition or application by a entity described in subsection (a) of eligibility criteria that screen out or tend to screen out an individual with a disability or any class of individuals with disabilities from fully enjoying the specified public transportation services provided by the entity, unless such criteria can be shown to be necessary for the provision of the services being offered;

(2) the failure of such entity to—

(A) make reasonable modifications consistent with those required under section 302(b)(2)(A)(ii) [42 USCS § 12182(b)(2)(A)(ii)];

(B) provide auxiliary aids and services consistent with the requirements of section 302(b)(2)(A)(iii) [42 USCS § 12182(b)(2)(A)(iii)]; and

(C) remove barriers consistent with the requirements of section 302(b)(2)(A) [42 USCS § 12182(b)(2)(A)]and with the requirements of section 303(a)(2) [42 USCS § 12183(a)(2)];

(3) the purchase or lease by such entity of a new vehicle (other than an automobile, a van with a seating capacity of less than 8 passengers, including the driver, or an over-the-road bus) which is to be used to provide specified public transportation and for which a solici-

tation is made after the 30th day following the effective date of this section, that is not readily accessible to and usable by individuals with disabilities, including individuals who use wheelchairs; except that the new vehicle need not be readily accessible to and usable by such individuals if the new vehicle is to be used solely in a demand responsive system and if the entity can demonstrate that such system, when viewed in its entirety, provides a level of service to such individuals equivalent to the level of service provided to the general public;

(4)(A) the purchase or lease by such entity of an over-the-road bus which does not comply with the regulations issued under section 306(a)(2) [42 USCS § 12186(a)(2)]; and

(B) any other failure of such entity to comply with such regulations; and

(5) the purchase or lease by such entity of a new van with a seating capacity of less than 8 passengers, including the driver, which is to be used to provide specified public transportation and for which a solicitation is made after the 30th day following the effective date of this section that is not readily accessible to or usable by individuals with disabilities, including individuals who use wheelchairs; except that the new van need not be readily accessible to and usable by such individuals if the entity can demonstrate that the system for which the van is being purchased or leased, when viewed in its entirety, provides a level of service to such individuals equivalent to the level of service provided to the general public;

(6) the purchase or lease by such entity of a new rail passenger car that is to be used to provide specified public transportation, and for which a solicitation is made later than 30 days after the effective date of this paragraph, that is not readily accessible to and usable by individuals with disabilities, including individuals who use wheelchairs; and

(7) the remanufacture by such entity of a rail passenger car that is to be used to provide specified public transportation so as to extend its usable life for 10 years or more, or the purchase or lease by such entity of such a rail car, unless the rail car, to the maximum extent feasible, is made readily accessible to and usable by individuals with disabilities, including individuals who use wheelchairs.

(c) Historical or antiquated cars.

(1) Exception. To the extent that compliance with subsection (b)(2)(C) or (b)(7) would significantly alter the historic or antiquated character of a historical or antiquated rail passenger car, or a rail station served exclusively by such cars, or would result in violation of any rule, regulation, standard, or order issued by the Secretary of Transportation under the Federal Railroad Safety Act of 1970 [45 USCS §§ 431 et seq.], such compliance shall not be required.

(2) Definition. As used in this subsection, the term "historical or antiquated rail passenger car" means a rail passenger car—

(A) which is not less than 30 years old at the time of its use for transporting individuals;

(B) the manufacturer of which is no longer in the business of manufacturing rail passenger cars; and

(C) which—

(i) has a consequential association with events or persons significant to the past; or

(ii) embodies, or is being restored to embody, the distinctive characteristics of a type of rail passenger car used in the past, or to represent a time period which has passed.

§ 12185. Study

(a) Purposes. The Office of Technology Assessment shall undertake a study to determine—

(1) the access needs of individuals with disabilities to over-the-road buses and over-the-road bus service; and

(2) the most cost-effective methods for providing access to over-the-road buses and over-the-road bus service to individuals with disabilities, particularly individuals who use wheelchairs, through all forms of boarding options.

(b) Contents. The study shall include, at a minimum, an analysis of the following:

(1) The anticipated demand by individuals with disabilities for accessible over-the-road buses and over-the-road bus service.

(2) The degree to which such buses and service, including any service required under sections 304(b)(4) and 306(a)(2) [42 USCS §§ 12184(b)(4), 12186(a)(2)], are readily accessible to and usable by individuals with disabilities.

(3) The effectiveness of various methods of providing accessibility to such buses and service to individuals with disabilities.

(4) The cost of providing accessible over-the-road buses and bus service to individuals with disabilities, including consideration of recent technological and cost saving developments in equipment and devices.

(5) Possible design changes in over-the-road buses that could enhance accessibility, including the installation of accessible restrooms which do not result in a loss of seating capacity.

(6) The impact of accessibility requirements on the continuation of over-the-road bus service, with particular consideration of the impact of such requirements on such service to rural communities.

(c) Advisory committee. In conducting the study required by subsection (a), the Office of Technology Assessment shall establish an advisory committee, which shall consist of—

(1) members selected from among private operators and manufacturers of over-the-road buses;

(2) members selected from among individuals with disabilities, particularly individuals who use wheelchairs, who are potential riders of such buses; and

(3) members selected for their technical expertise on issues included in the study, including manufacturers of boarding assistance equipment and devices. The number of members selected under each of paragraphs (1) and (2) shall be equal, and the total number of members selected under paragraphs (1) and (2) shall exceed the number of members selected under paragraph (3).

(d) Deadline. The study required by subsection (a), along with recommendations by the Office of Technology Assessment, including any policy options for legislative action, shall be submitted to the President and Congress within 36 months after the date of the enactment of this Act [enacted July 26, 1990]. If the President determines that compliance with the regulations issued pursuant to section 306(a)(2)(B) [42 USCS § 12186(a)(2)(B)]on or before the applicable deadlines specified in section 306(a)(2)(B) [42 USCS § 12186(a)(2)(B)] will result in a significant reduction in intercity over-the-road bus service, the President shall extend each such deadline by 1 year.

(e) Review. In developing the study required by subsection (a), the Office of Technology Assessment shall provide a preliminary draft of such study to the Architectural and Transportation Barriers Compliance Board established under section 502 of the Rehabilitation Act of 1973 (29 U.S.C. 792). The Board shall have an opportunity to comment on such draft study, and any such comments by the Board made in writing within 120 days after the Board's receipt of the draft study shall be incorporated as part of the final study required to be submitted under subsection (d).

§ 12186. Regulations

(a) Transportation provisions.

(1) General rule. Not later than 1 year after the date of the enactment of this Act [enacted July 26, 1990], the Secretary of Transportation shall issue regulations in an accessible format to carry out sections 302(b)(2)(B) and (C) [42 USCS § 12182(b)(2)(B), (C)] and to carry out section 304 [42 USCS § 12184] (other than subsection (b)(4)).

(2) Special rules for providing access to over-the-road buses.

(A) Interim requirements.

(i) Issuance. Not later than 1 year after the date of the enactment of this Act [enacted July 26, 1990], the Secretary of Transportation shall issue regulations in an accessible format to carry out sections 304(b)(4) and 302(b)(2)(D)(ii) [42 USCS §§ 12184(b)(4), 12182(b)(2)(D)(ii)] that require each private entity which uses an over-the-road bus to provide transportation of individuals to provide accessibility to such bus; except that such regulations shall not require any structural changes in over-the-road buses in order to provide access to individuals who use wheelchairs during the effective period of such regulations and shall not require the purchase of boarding assistance devices to provide access to such individuals.

(ii) Effective period. The regulations issued pursuant to this subparagraph shall be effective until the effective date of the regulations issued under subparagraph (B).

(B) Final requirement.

(i) Review of study and interim requirements. The Secretary shall review the study submitted under section 305 [42 USCS § 12185] and the regulations issued pursuant to subparagraph (A).

(ii) Issuance. Not later than 1 year after the date of the submission of the study under section 305 [42 USCS § 12185], the Secretary shall issue in an accessible format new regulations to carry out sections 304(b)(4) and 302(b)(2)(D)(ii) [42 USCS §§ 12184(b)(4), 12182(b)(2)(D)(ii)] that require, taking into account the purposes of the study under section 305 [42 USCS § 12185] and any recommendations resulting from such study, each private entity which uses an over-the-road bus to provide transportation to individuals to provide accessibility to such bus to individuals with disabilities, including individuals who use wheelchairs.

(iii) Effective period. Subject to section 305(d) [42 USCS § 12185(d)], the regulations issued pursuant to this subparagraph shall take effect—

(I) with respect to small providers of transportation (as defined by the Secretary), 3 years after the date of issuance of final regulations under clause (ii) [October 29, 2001]; and

(II) with respect to other providers of transportation, 2 years after the date of issuance of such final regulations [October 30, 2000].

(C) Limitation on requiring installation of accessible restrooms. The regulations issued pursuant to this paragraph shall not require the installation of accessible restrooms in over-the-road buses if such installation would result in a loss of seating capacity.

(3) Standards. The regulations issued pursuant to this subsection shall include standards applicable to facilities and vehicles covered by sections 302(b)(2) and 304 [42 USCS §§ 12182(b)(2), 12184].

(b) Other provisions. Not later than 1 year after the date of the enactment of this Act [enacted July 26, 1990], the Attorney General shall issue regulations in an accessible format to carry out the provisions of this title not referred to in subsection (a) that include standards applicable to facilities and vehicles covered under section 302 [42 USCS § 12182].

(c) Consistency with ATBCB guidelines. Standards included in regulations issued under subsections (a) and (b) shall be consistent with the minimum guidelines and requirements issued by the Architectural and Transportation Barriers Compliance Board in accordance with section 504 of this Act [42 USCS § 12204].

(d) Interim accessibility standards.

(1) Facilities. If final regulations have not been issued pursuant to this section, for new construction or alterations for which a valid and appropriate State or local building permit is obtained prior to the issuance of final regulations under this section, and for which the construction or alteration authorized by such permit begins within one year of the receipt of such permit and is completed under the terms of such permit, compliance with the Uniform Federal Accessibility Standards in effect at the time the building permit is issued shall suffice to satisfy the requirement that facilities be readily accessible to and usable by persons with disabilities as required under section 303 [42 USCS § 12183], except that, if such final regulations have not been issued one year after the Architectural and Transportation Barriers Compliance Board has issued the supplemental minimum guidelines required under section 504(a) of this Act [42 USCS § 12204(a)], compliance with such supplemental minimum guidelines shall be necessary to satisfy the requirement that facilities be readily accessible to and usable by persons with disabilities prior to issuance of the final regulations.

(2) Vehicles and rail passenger cars. If final regulations have not been issued pursuant to this section, a private entity shall be considered to have complied with the requirements of this title, if any, that a vehicle or rail passenger car be readily accessible to and usable by individuals with disabilities, if the design for such vehicle or car complies with the laws and regulations (including the Minimum Guidelines and Requirements for Accessible Design and such supplemental minimum guidelines as are issued under section 504(a) of this Act [42 USCS § 12204(a)] governing accessibility of such vehicles or cars, to the extent that such laws and regulations are not inconsistent with this title and are in effect at the time such design is substantially completed.

§ 12187. Exemptions for private clubs and religious organizations

The provisions of this subchapter shall not apply to private clubs or establishments exempted from coverage under title II of the Civil Rights Act of 1964 (42 U.S.C. 2000-a(e)) [FN1PP] or to religious organizations or entities controlled by religious organizations, including places of worship.

§ 12188. Enforcement

(a) In general

(1) Availability of remedies and procedures

The remedies and procedures set forth in section 2000a-3(a) of this title are the remedies and procedures this subchapter provides to any person who is being subjected to discrimination on the basis of disability in violation of this subchapter or who has reasonable grounds for believing that such person is about to be subjected to discrimination in violation of section 12183 of this title. Nothing in this section shall require a person with a disability to engage in a futile gesture if such person has actual notice that a person or organization covered by this subchapter does not intend to comply with its provisions.

(2) Injunctive relief

In the case of violations of sections 12182(b)(2)(A)(iv) of this title and section 12183(a) of this title, injunctive relief shall include an order to alter facilities to make such facilities readily accessible to and usable by individuals with disabilities to the extent required by this subchapter. Where appropriate, injunctive relief shall also include requiring the provision of an auxiliary aid or service, modification of a policy, or provision of alternative methods, to the extent required by this subchapter.

(b) Enforcement by the Attorney General

(1) Denial of rights

(A) Duty to investigate

(i) In general

The Attorney General shall investigate alleged violations of this subchapter, and shall undertake periodic reviews of compliance of covered entities under this subchapter.

(ii) Attorney General certification

On the application of a State or local government, the Attorney General may, in consultation with the Architectural and Transportation Barriers Compliance Board, and after prior notice and a public hearing at which persons, including individuals with disabilities, are provided an opportunity to testify against such certification, certify that a State law or local building code or similar ordinance that establishes accessibility requirements meets or exceeds the minimum requirements of this chapter for the accessibility and usability of covered facilities under this subchapter. At any enforcement proceeding under this section, such certification by the Attorney General shall be rebuttable evidence that such State law or local ordinance does meet or exceed the minimum requirements of this chapter.

(B) Potential violation

If the Attorney General has reasonable cause to believe that—

(i) any person or group of persons is engaged in a pattern or practice of discrimination under this subchapter; or

(ii) any person or group of persons has been discriminated against under this subchapter and such discrimination raises an issue of general public importance, the Attorney General may commence a civil action in any appropriate United States district court.

(2) Authority of court

In a civil action under paragraph (1)(B), the court—

(A) may grant any equitable relief that such court considers to be appropriate, including, to the extent required by this subchapter—

(i) granting temporary, preliminary, or permanent relief;

(ii) providing an auxiliary aid or service, modification of policy, practice, or procedure, or alternative method; and

(iii) making facilities readily accessible to and usable by individuals with disabilities;

(B) may award such other relief as the court considers to be appropriate, including monetary damages to persons aggrieved when requested by the Attorney General; and

(C) may, to vindicate the public interest, assess a civil penalty against the entity in an amount—

(i) not exceeding $50,000 for a first violation; and

(ii) not exceeding $100,000 for any subsequent violation.

(3) Single violation

For purposes of paragraph (2)(C), in determining whether a first or subsequent violation has occurred, a determination in a single action, by judgment or settlement, that the covered entity has engaged in more than one discriminatory act shall be counted as a single violation.

(4) Punitive damages

For purposes of subsection (b)(2)(B) of this section, the term "monetary damages" and "such other relief" does not include punitive damages.

(5) Judicial consideration

In a civil action under paragraph (1)(B), the court, when considering what amount of civil penalty, if any, is appropriate, shall give consideration to any good faith effort or attempt to comply with this chapter by the entity. In evaluating good faith, the court shall consider, among other factors it deems relevant, whether the entity could have reasonably anticipated the need for an appropriate type of auxiliary aid needed to accommodate the unique needs of a particular individual with a disability.

§ 12189. Examinations and courses

Any person that offers examinations or courses related to applications, licensing, certification, or credentialing for secondary or post-secondary education, professional, or trade purposes shall offer such examinations or courses in a place and manner accessible to persons with disabilities or offer alternative accessible arrangements for such individuals.

ADA TITLE III DOJ REGULATIONS

28 C.F.R. §

ADA TITLE III DOJ REGULATIONS

Subpart A—General

§ 36.104 Definitions.

For purposes of this part, the term—

Act means the Americans with Disabilities Act of 1990 (Pub. L. 101-336, 104 Stat. 327, 42 U.S.C. 12101-12213 and 47 U.S.C. 225 and 611).

Commerce means travel, trade, traffic, commerce, transportation, or communication—

(1) Among the several States;

(2) Between any foreign country or any territory or possession and any State; or

(3) Between points in the same State but through another State or foreign country.

Commercial facilities means facilities—

(1) Whose operations will affect commerce;

(2) That are intended for nonresidential use by a private entity; and

(3) That are not—

(i) Facilities that are covered or expressly exempted from coverage under the Fair Housing Act of 1968, as amended (42 U.S.C. 3601-3631);

(ii) Aircraft; or

(iii) Railroad locomotives, railroad freight cars, railroad cabooses, commuter or intercity passenger rail cars (including coaches, dining cars, sleeping cars, lounge cars, and food service cars), any other railroad cars described in section 242 of the Act or covered under title II of the Act, or railroad rights-of-way. For purposes of this definition, "rail" and "railroad" have the meaning given the term "railroad" in section 202(e) of the Federal Railroad Safety Act of 1970 (45 U.S.C. 431(e)).

Current illegal use of drugs means illegal use of drugs that occurred recently enough to justify a reasonable belief that a person's drug use is current or that continuing use is a real and ongoing problem.

Disability means, with respect to an individual, a physical or mental impairment that substantially limits one or more of the major life activities of such individual; a record of such an impairment; or being regarded as having such an impairment.

(1) The phrase physical or mental impairment means—

(i) Any physiological disorder or condition, cosmetic disfigurement, or anatomical loss affecting one or more of the following body systems: neurological; musculoskeletal; special sense organs; respiratory, including speech organs; cardiovascular; reproductive; digestive; genitourinary; hemic and lymphatic; skin;

and endocrine;

(ii) Any mental or psychological disorder such as mental retardation, organic brain syndrome, emotional or mental illness, and specific learning disabilities;

(iii) The phrase physical or mental impairment includes, but is not limited to, such contagious and noncontagious diseases and conditions as orthopedic, visual, speech, and hearing impairments, cerebral palsy, epilepsy, muscular dystrophy, multiple sclerosis, cancer, heart disease, diabetes, mental retardation, emotional illness, specific learning disabilities, HIV disease (whether symptomatic or asymptomatic), tuberculosis, drug addiction, and alcoholism;

(iv) The phrase physical or mental impairment does not include homosexuality or bisexuality.

(2) The phrase major life activities means functions such as caring for one's self, performing manual tasks, walking, seeing, hearing, speaking, breathing, learning, and working.

(3) The phrase has a record of such an impairment means has a history of, or has been misclassified as having, a mental or physical impairment that substantially limits one or more major life activities.

(4) The phrase is regarded as having an impairment means—

(i) Has a physical or mental impairment that does not substantially limit major life activities but that is treated by a private entity as constituting such a limitation;

(ii) Has a physical or mental impairment that substantially limits major life activities only as a result of the attitudes of others toward such impairment; or

(iii) Has none of the impairments defined in paragraph (1) of this definition but is treated by a private entity as having such an impairment.

(5) The term disability does not include—

(i) Transvestism, transsexualism, pedophilia, exhibitionism, voyeurism, gender identity disorders not resulting from physical impairments, or other sexual behavior disorders;

(ii) Compulsive gambling, kleptomania, or pyromania; or

(iii) Psychoactive substance use disorders resulting from current illegal use of drugs.

Drug means a controlled substance, as defined in schedules I through V of section 202 of the Controlled Substances Act (21 U.S.C. 812).

Facility means all or any portion of buildings, structures, sites, complexes, equipment, rolling stock or other conveyances, roads, walks, passageways, parking lots, or other real or personal property, including the site where the building, property, structure, or equipment is located.

Illegal use of drugs means the use of one or more drugs, the possession or distribution of which is unlawful under the Controlled Substances Act (21 U.S.C. 812). The term "illegal use of drugs" does not include the use of a drug taken under supervision by a licensed health care professional, or other uses authorized by the Controlled Substances Act or other provisions of Federal law.

Individual with a disability means a person who has a disability. The term "individual with a disability" does not include an individual who is currently engaging in the illegal use of drugs, when the private entity acts on the basis of such use.

Place of public accommodation means a facility, operated by a private entity, whose operations affect commerce and fall within at least one of the following categories—

(1) An inn, hotel, motel, or other place of lodging, except for an establishment located within a building that contains not more than five rooms for rent or hire and that is actually occupied by the proprietor of the establishment as the residence of the proprietor;

(2) A restaurant, bar, or other establishment serving food or drink;

(3) A motion picture house, theater, concert hall, stadium, or other place of exhibition or entertainment;

(4) An auditorium, convention center, lecture hall, or other place of public gathering;

(5) A bakery, grocery store, clothing store, hardware store, shopping center, or other sales or rental establishment;

(6) A laundromat, dry-cleaner, bank, barber shop, beauty shop, travel service, shoe repair service, funeral parlor, gas station, office of an accountant or lawyer, pharmacy, insurance office, professional office of a health care provider, hospital, or other service establishment;

(7) A terminal, depot, or other station used for specified public transportation;

(8) A museum, library, gallery, or other place of public display or collection;

(9) A park, zoo, amusement park, or other place of recreation;

(10) A nursery, elementary, secondary, undergraduate, or postgraduate private school, or other place of education;

(11) A day care center, senior citizen center, homeless shelter, food bank, adoption agency, or other social service center establishment; and

(12) A gymnasium, health spa, bowling alley, golf course, or other place of exercise or recreation.

Private club means a private club or establishment

exempted from coverage under title II of the Civil Rights Act of 1964 (42 U.S.C. 2000a(e)).

Private entity means a person or entity other than a public entity.

Public accommodation means a private entity that owns, leases (or leases to), or operates a place of public accommodation.

Public entity means—

(1) Any State or local government;

(2) Any department, agency, special purpose district, or other instrumentality of a State or States or local government; and

(3) The National Railroad Passenger Corporation, and any commuter authority (as defined in section 103(8) of the Rail Passenger Service Act). (45 U.S.C. 541)

Qualified interpreter means an interpreter who is able to interpret effectively, accurately and impartially both receptively and expressively, using any necessary specialized vocabulary.

Readily achievable means easily accomplishable and able to be carried out without much difficulty or expense. In determining whether an action is readily achievable factors to be considered include—

(1) The nature and cost of the action needed under this part;

(2) The overall financial resources of the site or sites involved in the action; the number of persons employed at the site; the effect on expenses and resources; legitimate safety requirements that are necessary for safe operation, including crime prevention measures; or the impact otherwise of the action upon the operation of the site;

(3) The geographic separateness, and the administrative or fiscal relationship of the site or sites in question to any parent corporation or entity;

(4) If applicable, the overall financial resources of any parent corporation or entity; the overall size of the parent corporation or entity with respect to the number of its employees; the number, type, and location of its facilities; and

(5) If applicable, the type of operation or operations of any parent corporation or entity, including the composition, structure, and functions of the work force of the parent corporation or entity.

Religious entity means a religious organization, including a place of worship.

Service animal means any guide dog, signal dog, or other animal individually trained to do work or perform tasks for the benefit of an individual with a disability, including, but not limited to, guiding individuals with impaired vision, alerting individuals with impaired hearing to intruders or sounds, providing minimal protection or rescue work, pulling a wheelchair, or fetching dropped items.

Specified public transportation means transportation by bus, rail, or any other conveyance (other than by aircraft) that provides the general public with general or special service (including charter service) on a regular and continuing basis.

State means each of the several States, the District of Columbia, the Commonwealth of Puerto Rico, Guam, American Samoa, the Virgin Islands, the Trust Territory of the Pacific Islands, and the Commonwealth of the Northern Mariana Islands.

Undue burden means significant difficulty or expense. In determining whether an action would result in an undue burden, factors to be considered include—

(1) The nature and cost of the action needed under this part;

(2) The overall financial resources of the site or sites involved in the action; the number of persons employed at the site; the effect on expenses and resources; legitimate safety requirements that are necessary for safe operation, including crime prevention measures; or the impact otherwise of the action upon the operation of the site;

(3) The geographic separateness, and the administrative or fiscal relationship of the site or sites in question to any parent corporation or entity;

(4) If applicable, the overall financial resources of any parent corporation or entity; the overall size of the parent corporation or entity with respect to the number of its employees; the number, type, and location of its facilities; and

(5) If applicable, the type of operation or operations of any parent corporation or entity, including the composition, structure, and functions of the work force of the parent corporation or entity.

Subpart B—General Requirements

§ 36.201 General.

(a) Prohibition of discrimination. No individual shall be discriminated against on the basis of disability in the full and equal enjoyment of the goods, services, facilities, privileges, advantages, or accommodations of any place of public accommodation by any private entity who owns, leases (or leases to), or operates a place of public accommodation.

(b) Landlord and tenant responsibilities. Both the landlord who owns the building that houses a place of public accommodation and the tenant who owns or operates the place of public accommodation are public accommodations subject to the requirements of this part. As between the parties, allocation of responsibility for complying with the obligations of this part may be determined by lease or other contract.

§ 36.202 Activities.

(a) Denial of participation. A public accommodation shall not subject an individual or class of individuals on the basis of a disability or disabilities of such individual or class, directly, or through contractual, licensing, or other arrangements, to a denial of the opportunity of the individual or class to participate in or benefit from the goods, services, facilities, privileges, advantages, or accommodations of a place of public accommodation.

(b) Participation in unequal benefit. A public accommodation shall not afford an individual or class of individuals, on the basis of a disability or disabilities of such individual or class, directly, or through contractual, licensing, or other arrangements, with the opportunity to participate in or benefit from a good, service, facility, privilege, advantage, or accommodation that is not equal to that afforded to other individuals.

(c) Separate benefit. A public accommodation shall not provide an individual or class of individuals, on the basis of a disability or disabilities of such individual or class, directly, or through contractual, licensing, or other arrangements with a good, service, facility, privilege, advantage, or accommodation that is different or separate from that provided to other individuals, unless such action is necessary to provide the individual or class of individuals with a good, service, facility, privilege, advantage, or accommodation, or other opportunity that is as effective as that provided to others.

(d) Individual or class of individuals. For purposes of paragraphs (a) through (c) of this section, the term "individual or class of individuals" refers to the clients or customers of the public accommodation that enters into the contractual, licensing, or other arrangement.

§ 36.203 Integrated settings.

(a) General. A public accommodation shall afford goods, services, facilities, privileges, advantages, and accommodations to an individual with a disability in the most integrated setting appropriate to the needs of the individual.

(b) Opportunity to participate. Notwithstanding the existence of separate or different programs or activities provided in accordance with this subpart, a public accommodation shall not deny an individual with a disability an opportunity to participate in such programs or activities that are not separate or different.

(c) Accommodations and services.

(1) Nothing in this part shall be construed to require an individual with a disability to accept an accommodation, aid, service, opportunity, or benefit available under this part that such individual chooses not to accept.

(2) Nothing in the Act or this part authorizes the representative or guardian of an individual with a disability to decline food, water, medical treatment, or medical services for that individual.

§ 36.204 Administrative methods.

A public accommodation shall not, directly or through contractual or other arrangements, utilize standards or criteria or methods of administration that have the effect of discriminating on the basis of disability, or that perpetuate the discrimination of others who are subject to common administrative control.

§ 36.205 Association.

A public accommodation shall not exclude or otherwise deny equal goods, services, facilities, privileges, advantages, accommodations, or other opportunities to an individual or entity because of the known disability of an individual with whom the individual or entity is known to have a relationship or association.

§ 36.206 Retaliation or coercion.

(a) No private or public entity shall discriminate against any individual because that individual has opposed any act or practice made unlawful by this part, or because that individual made a charge, testified, assisted, or participated in any manner in an investigation, proceeding, or hearing under the Act or this part.

(b) No private or public entity shall coerce, intimidate, threaten, or interfere with any individual in the exercise or enjoyment of, or on account of his or her having exercised or enjoyed, or on account of his or her having aided or encouraged any other individual in the exercise or enjoyment of, any right granted or protected by the Act or this part.

(c) Illustrations of conduct prohibited by this section include, but are not limited to:

(1) Coercing an individual to deny or limit the benefits, services, or advantages to which he or she is entitled under the Act or this part;

(2) Threatening, intimidating, or interfering with an individual with a disability who is seeking to

obtain or use the goods, services, facilities, privileges, advantages, or accommodations of a public accommodation;

(3) Intimidating or threatening any person because that person is assisting or encouraging an individual or group entitled to claim the rights granted or protected by the Act or this part to exercise those rights; or

(4) Retaliating against any person because that person has participated in any investigation or action to enforce the Act or this part.

§ 36.207 Places of public accommodation located in private residences.

(a) When a place of public accommodation is located in a private residence, the portion of the residence used exclusively as a residence is not covered by this part, but that portion used exclusively in the operation of the place of public accommodation or that portion used both for the place of public accommodation and for residential purposes is covered by this part.

(b) The portion of the residence covered under paragraph (a) of this section extends to those elements used to enter the place of public accommodation, including the homeowner's front sidewalk, if any, the door or entryway, and hallways; and those portions of the residence, interior or exterior, available to or used by customers or clients, including restrooms.

§ 36.208 Direct threat.

(a) This part does not require a public accommodation to permit an individual to participate in or benefit from the goods, services, facilities, privileges, advantages and accommodations of that public accommodation when that individual poses a direct threat to the health or safety of others.

(b) Direct threat means a significant risk to the health or safety of others that cannot be eliminated by a modification of policies, practices, or procedures, or by the provision of auxiliary aids or services.

(c) In determining whether an individual poses a direct threat to the health or safety of others, a public accommodation must make an individualized assessment, based on reasonable judgment that relies on current medical knowledge or on the best available objective evidence, to ascertain: the nature, duration, and severity of the risk; the probability that the potential injury will actually occur; and whether reasonable modifications of policies, practices, or procedures will mitigate the risk.

§ 36.209 Illegal use of drugs.

(a) General.

(1) Except as provided in paragraph (b) of this section, this part does not prohibit discrimination against an individual based on that individual's current illegal use of drugs.

(2) A public accommodation shall not discriminate on the basis of illegal use of drugs against an individual who is not engaging in current illegal use of drugs and who—

(i) Has successfully completed a supervised drug rehabilitation program or has otherwise been rehabilitated successfully;

(ii) Is participating in a supervised rehabilitation program; or

(iii) Is erroneously regarded as engaging in such use.

(b) Health and drug rehabilitation services.

(1) A public accommodation shall not deny health services, or services provided in connection with drug rehabilitation, to an individual on the basis of that individual's current illegal use of drugs, if the individual is otherwise entitled to such services.

(2) A drug rehabilitation or treatment program may deny participation to individuals who engage in illegal use of drugs while they are in the program.

(c) Drug testing.

(1) This part does not prohibit a public accommodation from adopting or administering reasonable policies or procedures, including but not limited to drug testing, designed to ensure that an individual who formerly engaged in the illegal use of drugs is not now engaging in current illegal use of drugs.

(2) Nothing in this paragraph (c) shall be construed to encourage, prohibit, restrict, or authorize the conducting of testing for the illegal use of drugs.

§ 36.210 Smoking.

This part does not preclude the prohibition of, or the imposition of restrictions on, smoking in places of public accommodation.

§ 36.211 Maintenance of accessible features.

(a) A public accommodation shall maintain in operable working condition those features of facilities and equipment that are required to be readily accessible to and usable by persons with disabilities by the Act or this part.

(b) This section does not prohibit isolated or temporary interruptions in service or access due to maintenance or repairs.

§ 36.212 Insurance.

(a) This part shall not be construed to prohibit or restrict—

(1) An insurer, hospital or medical service company, health maintenance organization, or any agent, or entity that administers benefit plans, or similar organizations from underwriting risks, classifying risks, or administering such risks that are based on or not inconsistent with State law; or

(2) A person or organization covered by this part from establishing, sponsoring, observing or administering the terms of a bona fide benefit plan that are based on underwriting risks, classifying risks, or administering such risks that are based on or not inconsistent with State law; or

(3) A person or organization covered by this part from establishing, sponsoring, observing or administering the terms of a bona fide benefit plan that is not subject to State laws that regulate insurance.

(b) Paragraphs (a) (1), (2), and (3) of this section shall not be used as a subterfuge to evade the purposes of the Act or this part.

(c) A public accommodation shall not refuse to serve an individual with a disability because its insurance company conditions coverage or rates on the absence of individuals with disabilities.

Subpart C—Specific Requirements

§ 36.301 Eligibility criteria.

(a) General. A public accommodation shall not impose or apply eligibility criteria that screen out or tend to screen out an individual with a disability or any class of individuals with disabilities from fully and equally enjoying any goods, services, facilities, privileges, advantages, or accommodations, unless such criteria can be shown to be necessary for the provision of the goods, services, facilities, privileges, advantages, or accommodations being offered.

(b) Safety. A public accommodation may impose legitimate safety requirements that are necessary for safe operation. Safety requirements must be based on actual risks and not on mere speculation, stereotypes, or generalizations about individuals with disabilities.

(c) Charges. A public accommodation may not impose a surcharge on a particular individual with a disability or any group of individuals with disabilities to cover the costs of measures, such as the provision of auxiliary aids, barrier removal, alternatives to barrier removal, and reasonable modifications in policies, practices, or procedures, that are required to provide that individual or group with the nondiscriminatory treatment required by the Act or this part.

§ 36.302 Modifications in policies, practices, or procedures.

(a) General. A public accommodation shall make reasonable modifications in policies, practices, or procedures, when the modifications are necessary to afford goods, services, facilities, privileges, advantages, or accommodations to individuals with disabilities, unless the public accommodation can demonstrate that making the modifications would fundamentally alter the nature of the goods, services, facilities, privileges, advantages, or accommodations.

(b) Specialties—

(1) General. A public accommodation may refer an individual with a disability to another public accommodation, if that individual is seeking, or requires, treatment or services outside of the referring public accommodation's area of specialization, and if, in the normal course of its operations, the referring public accommodation would make a similar referral for an individual without a disability who seeks or requires the same treatment or services.

(2) Illustration—medical specialties. A health care provider may refer an individual with a disability to another provider, if that individual is seeking, or requires, treatment or services outside of the referring provider's area of specialization, and if the referring provider would make a similar referral for an individual without a disability who seeks or requires the same treatment or services. A physician who specializes in treating only a particular condition cannot refuse to treat an individual with a disability for that condition, but is not required to treat the individual for a different condition.

(c) Service animals—

(1) General. Generally, a public accommodation shall modify policies, practices, or procedures to permit the use of a service animal by an individual with a disability.

(2) Care or supervision of service animals. Nothing in this part requires a public accommodation to supervise or care for a service animal.

(d) Check-out aisles. A store with check-out aisles shall ensure that an adequate number of accessible check-out aisles are kept open during store hours, or shall otherwise modify its policies and practices, in order to ensure that an equivalent level of convenient service is provided to individuals with disabilities as is provided to others. If only one check-out aisle is accessible, and it is generally used for express service, one way of providing equivalent service is to allow persons with mobility impairments to make all their purchases at that aisle.

§ 36.303 Auxiliary aids and services.

(a) General. A public accommodation shall take those steps that may be necessary to ensure that no individual with a disability is excluded, denied services, segregated or otherwise treated differently than other individuals because of the absence of auxiliary aids and services, unless the public accommodation can demonstrate that taking those steps would fundamentally alter the nature of the goods, services, facilities, privileges, advantages, or accommodations being offered or would result in an undue burden, i.e., significant difficulty or expense.

(b) Examples. The term "auxiliary aids and services" includes—

(1) Qualified interpreters, notetakers, computer-aided transcription services, written materials, telephone handset amplifiers, assistive listening devices, assistive listening systems, telephones compatible with hearing aids, closed caption decoders, open and closed captioning, telecommunications devices for deaf persons (TDD's), videotext displays, or other effective methods of making aurally delivered materials available to individuals with hearing impairments;

(2) Qualified readers, taped texts, audio recordings, Brailled materials, large print materials, or other effective methods of making visually delivered materials available to individuals with visual impairments;

(3) Acquisition or modification of equipment or devices; and

(4) Other similar services and actions.

(c) Effective communication. A public accommodation shall furnish appropriate auxiliary aids and services where necessary to ensure effective communication with individuals with disabilities.

(d) Telecommunication devices for the deaf (TDD's).

(1) A public accommodation that offers a customer, client, patient, or participant the opportunity to make outgoing telephone calls on more than an incidental convenience basis shall make available, upon request, a TDD for the use of an individual who has impaired hearing or a communication disorder.

(2) This part does not require a public accommodation to use a TDD for receiving or making telephone calls incident to its operations.

(e) Closed caption decoders. Places of lodging that provide televisions in five or more guest rooms and hospitals that provide televisions for patient use shall provide, upon request, a means for decoding captions for use by an individual with impaired hearing.

(f) Alternatives. If provision of a particular auxiliary aid or service by a public accommodation would result in a fundamental alteration in the nature of the goods, services, facilities, privileges, advantages, or accommodations being offered or in an undue burden, i.e., significant difficulty or expense, the public accommodation shall provide an alternative auxiliary aid or service, if one exists, that would not result in an alteration or such burden but would nevertheless ensure that, to the maximum extent possible, individuals with disabilities receive the goods, services, facilities, privileges, advantages, or accommodations offered by the public accommodation.

§ 36.304 Removal of barriers.

(a) General. A public accommodation shall remove architectural barriers in existing facilities, including communication barriers that are structural in nature, where such removal is readily achievable, i.e., easily accomplishable and able to be carried out without much difficulty or expense.

(b) Examples. Examples of steps to remove barriers include, but are not limited to, the following actions—

(1) Installing ramps;

(2) Making curb cuts in sidewalks and entrances;

(3) Repositioning shelves;

(4) Rearranging tables, chairs, vending machines, display racks, and other furniture;

(5) Repositioning telephones;

(6) Adding raised markings on elevator control buttons;

(7) Installing flashing alarm lights;

(8) Widening doors;

(9) Installing offset hinges to widen doorways;

(10) Eliminating a turnstile or providing an alternative accessible path;

(11) Installing accessible door hardware;

(12) Installing grab bars in toilet stalls;

(13) Rearranging toilet partitions to increase maneuvering space;

(14) Insulating lavatory pipes under sinks to prevent burns;

(15) Installing a raised toilet seat;

(16) Installing a full-length bathroom mirror;

(17) Repositioning the paper towel dispenser in a bathroom;

(18) Creating designated accessible parking spaces;

(19) Installing an accessible paper cup dispenser at an existing inaccessible water fountain;

(20) Removing high pile, low density carpeting; or

(21) Installing vehicle hand controls.

(c) Priorities. A public accommodation is urged to take measures to comply with the barrier removal requirements of this section in accordance with the following order of priorities.

(1) First, a public accommodation should take measures to provide access to a place of public accommodation from public sidewalks, parking, or public transportation. These measures include, for example, installing an entrance ramp, widening entrances, and providing accessible parking spaces.

(2) Second, a public accommodation should take measures to provide access to those areas of a place of public accommodation where goods and services are made available to the public. These measures include, for example, adjusting the layout of display racks, rearranging tables, providing Brailled and raised character signage, widening doors, providing visual alarms, and installing ramps.

(3) Third, a public accommodation should take measures to provide access to restroom facilities. These measures include, for example, removal of obstructing furniture or vending machines, widening of doors, installation of ramps, providing accessible signage, widening of toilet stalls, and installation of grab bars.

(4) Fourth, a public accommodation should take any other measures necessary to provide access to the goods, services, facilities, privileges, advantages, or accommodations of a place of public accommodation.

(d) Relationship to alterations requirements of subpart D of this part.

(1) Except as provided in paragraph (d)(2) of this section, measures taken to comply with the barrier removal requirements of this section shall comply with the applicable requirements for alterations in § 36.402 and ss 36.404-36.406 of this part for the element being altered. The path of travel requirements of § 36.403 shall not apply to measures taken solely to comply with the barrier removal requirements of this section.

(2) If, as a result of compliance with the alterations requirements specified in paragraph (d)(1) of this section, the measures required to remove a barrier would not be readily achievable, a public accommodation may take other readily achievable measures to remove the barrier that do not fully comply with the specified requirements. Such measures include, for example, providing a ramp with a steeper slope or widening a doorway to a narrower width than that mandated by the alterations requirements. No measure shall be taken, however, that poses a significant risk to the health or safety of individuals with disabilities or others.

(e) Portable ramps. Portable ramps should be used to comply with this section only when installation of a permanent ramp is not readily achievable. In order to avoid any significant risk to the health or safety of individuals with disabilities or others in using portable ramps, due consideration shall be given to safety features such as nonslip surfaces, railings, anchoring, and strength of materials.

(f) Selling or serving space. The rearrangement of temporary or movable structures, such as furniture, equipment, and display racks is not readily achievable to the extent that it results in a significant loss of selling or serving space.

(g) Limitation on barrier removal obligations.

(1) The requirements for barrier removal under § 36.304 shall not be interpreted to exceed the standards for alterations in subpart D of this part.

(2) To the extent that relevant standards for alterations are not provided in subpart D of this part, then the requirements of § 36.304 shall not be interpreted to exceed the standards for new construction in subpart D of this part.

(3) This section does not apply to rolling stock and other conveyances to the extent that § 36.310 applies to rolling stock and other conveyances.

§ 36.305 Alternatives to barrier removal.

(a) General. Where a public accommodation can demonstrate that barrier removal is not readily achievable, the public accommodation shall not fail to make its goods, services, facilities, privileges, advantages, or accommodations available through alternative methods, if those methods are readily achievable.

(b) Examples. Examples of alternatives to barrier removal include, but are not limited to, the following actions—

(1) Providing curb service or home delivery;

(2) Retrieving merchandise from inaccessible shelves or racks;

(3) Relocating activities to accessible locations;

(c) Multiscreen cinemas. If it is not readily achievable to remove barriers to provide access by persons with mobility impairments to all of the theaters of a multiscreen cinema, the cinema shall establish a film rotation schedule that provides reasonable access for individuals who use wheelchairs to all films. Reasonable notice shall be provided to the public as to the location and time of accessible showings.

§ 36.306 Personal devices and services.

This part does not require a public accommodation to provide its customers, clients, or participants with personal devices, such as wheelchairs; individually prescribed devices, such as prescription eyeglasses or hearing aids; or services of a personal nature including assistance in eating, toileting, or dressing.

§ 36.307 Accessible or special goods.

(a) This part does not require a public accommodation to alter its inventory to include accessible or special goods that are designed for, or facilitate use by, individuals with disabilities.

(b) A public accommodation shall order accessible or special goods at the request of an individual with disabilities, if, in the normal course of its operation, it makes special orders on request for unstocked goods, and if the accessible or special goods can be obtained from a supplier with whom the public accommodation customarily does business.

(c) Examples of accessible or special goods include items such as Brailled versions of books, books on audio cassettes, closed-captioned video tapes, special sizes or lines of clothing, and special foods to meet particular dietary needs.

§ 36.308 Seating in assembly areas.

(a) Existing facilities.

(1) To the extent that it is readily achievable, a public accommodation in assembly areas shall—

(i) Provide a reasonable number of wheelchair seating spaces and seats with removable aisle-side arm rests; and

(ii) Locate the wheelchair seating spaces so that they—

(A) Are dispersed throughout the seating area;

(B) Provide lines of sight and choice of admission prices comparable to those for members of the general public;

(C) Adjoin an accessible route that also serves as a means of egress in case of emergency; and

(D) Permit individuals who use wheelchairs to sit with family members or other companions.

(2) If removal of seats is not readily achievable, a public accommodation shall provide, to the extent that it is readily achievable to do so, a portable chair or other means to permit a family member or other companion to sit with an individual who uses a wheelchair.

(3) The requirements of paragraph (a) of this section shall not be interpreted to exceed the standards for alterations in subpart D of this part.

(b) New construction and alterations. The provision and location of wheelchair seating spaces in newly constructed or altered assembly areas shall be governed by the standards for new construction and alterations in subpart D of this part.

§ 36.309 Examinations and courses.

(a) General. Any private entity that offers examinations or courses related to applications, licensing, certification, or credentialing for secondary or postsecondary education, professional, or trade purposes shall offer such examinations or courses in a place and manner accessible to persons with disabilities or offer alternative accessible arrangements for such individuals.

(b) Examinations.

(1) Any private entity offering an examination covered by this section must assure that—

(i) The examination is selected and administered so as to best ensure that, when the examination is administered to an individual with a disability that impairs sensory, manual, or speaking skills, the examination results accurately reflect the individual's aptitude or achievement level or whatever other factor the examination purports to measure, rather than reflecting the individual's impaired sensory, manual, or speaking skills (except where those skills are the factors that the examination purports to measure);

(ii) An examination that is designed for individuals with impaired sensory, manual, or speaking skills is offered at equally convenient locations, as often, and in as timely a manner as are other examinations; and

(iii) The examination is administered in facilities that are accessible to individuals with disabilities or alternative accessible arrangements are made.

(2) Required modifications to an examination may include changes in the length of time permitted for completion of the examination and adaptation of the manner in which the examination is given.

(3) A private entity offering an examination covered by this section shall provide appropriate auxiliary aids for persons with impaired sensory, manual, or speaking skills, unless that private entity can demonstrate that offering a particular auxiliary aid would fundamentally alter the measurement of the skills or knowledge the examination is intended to test

or would result in an undue burden. Auxiliary aids and services required by this section may include taped examinations, interpreters or other effective methods of making orally delivered materials available to individuals with hearing impairments, Brailled or large print examinations and answer sheets or qualified readers for individuals with visual impairments or learning disabilities, transcribers for individuals with manual impairments, and other similar services and actions.

(4) Alternative accessible arrangements may include, for example, provision of an examination at an individual's home with a proctor if accessible facilities or equipment are unavailable. Alternative arrangements must provide comparable conditions to those provided for nondisabled individuals.

(c) Courses.

(1) Any private entity that offers a course covered by this section must make such modifications to that course as are necessary to ensure that the place and manner in which the course is given are accessible to individuals with disabilities.

(2) Required modifications may include changes in the length of time permitted for the completion of the course, substitution of specific requirements, or adaptation of the manner in which the course is conducted or course materials are distributed.

(3) A private entity that offers a course covered by this section shall provide appropriate auxiliary aids and services for persons with impaired sensory, manual, or speaking skills, unless the private entity can demonstrate that offering a particular auxiliary aid or service would fundamentally alter the course or would result in an undue burden. Auxiliary aids and services required by this section may include taped texts, interpreters or other effective methods of making orally delivered materials available to individuals with hearing impairments, Brailled or large print texts or qualified readers for individuals with visual impairments and learning disabilities, classroom equipment adapted for use by individuals with manual impairments, and other similar services and actions.

(4) Courses must be administered in facilities that are accessible to individuals with disabilities or alternative accessible arrangements must be made.

(5) Alternative accessible arrangements may include, for example, provision of the course through videotape, cassettes, or prepared notes. Alternative arrangements must provide comparable conditions to those provided for nondisabled individuals.

Subpart D—New Construction and Alterations

§ 36.401 New construction.

(a) General.

(1) Except as provided in paragraphs (b) and (c) of this section, discrimination for purposes of this part includes a failure to design and construct facilities for first occupancy after January 26, 1993, that are readily accessible to and usable by individuals with disabilities.

(2) For purposes of this section, a facility is designed and constructed for first occupancy after January 26, 1993, only—

(i) If the last application for a building permit or permit extension for the facility is certified to be complete, by a State, County, or local government after January 26, 1992 (or, in those jurisdictions where the government does not certify completion of applications, if the last application for a building permit or permit extension for the facility is received by the State, County, or local government after January 26, 1992); and

(ii) If the first certificate of occupancy for the facility is issued after January 26, 1993.

(b) Commercial facilities located in private residences.

(1) When a commercial facility is located in a private residence, the portion of the residence used exclusively as a residence is not covered by this subpart, but that portion used exclusively in the operation of the commercial facility or that portion used both for the commercial facility and for residential purposes is covered by the new construction and alterations requirements of this subpart.

(2) The portion of the residence covered under paragraph (b)(1) of this section extends to those elements used to enter the commercial facility, including the homeowner's front sidewalk, if any, the door or entryway, and hallways; and those portions of the residence, interior or exterior, available to or used by employees or visitors of the commercial facility, including restrooms.

(c) Exception for structural impracticability.

(1) Full compliance with the requirements of this section is not required where an entity can demonstrate that it is structurally impracticable to meet the requirements. Full compliance will be considered structurally impracticable only in those rare circumstances when the unique characteristics of terrain prevent the incorporation of accessibility features.

(2) If full compliance with this section would be structurally impracticable, compliance with this sec-

tion is required to the extent that it is not structurally impracticable. In that case, any portion of the facility that can be made accessible shall be made accessible to the extent that it is not structurally impracticable.

(3) If providing accessibility in conformance with this section to individuals with certain disabilities (e.g., those who use wheelchairs) would be structurally impracticable, accessibility shall nonetheless be ensured to persons with other types of disabilities (e.g., those who use crutches or who have sight, hearing, or mental impairments) in accordance with this section.

(d) Elevator exemption.

(1) For purposes of this paragraph (d)—

(i) Professional office of a health care provider means a location where a person or entity regulated by a State to provide professional services related to the physical or mental health of an individual makes such services available to the public. The facility housing the "professional office of a health care provider" only includes floor levels housing at least one health care provider, or any floor level designed or intended for use by at least one health care provider.

(ii) Shopping center or shopping mall means—

(A) A building housing five or more sales or rental establishments; or

(B) A series of buildings on a common site, either under common ownership or common control or developed either as one project or as a series of related projects, housing five or more sales or rental establishments. For purposes of this section, places of public accommodation of the types listed in paragraph (5) of the definition of "place of public accommodation" in section § 36.104 are considered sales or rental establishments. The facility housing a "shopping center or shopping mall" only includes floor levels housing at least one sales or rental establishment, or any floor level designed or intended for use by at least one sales or rental establishment.

(2) This section does not require the installation of an elevator in a facility that is less than three stories or has less than 3000 square feet per story, except with respect to any facility that houses one or more of the following:

(i) A shopping center or shopping mall, or a professional office of a health care provider.

(ii) A terminal, depot, or other station used for specified public transportation, or an airport passenger terminal. In such a facility, any area housing passenger services, including boarding and debarking, loading and unloading, baggage claim, dining facilities, and other common areas open to the public, must be on an accessible route from an accessible entrance.

(3) The elevator exemption set forth in this paragraph (d) does not obviate or limit, in any way the obligation to comply with the other accessibility requirements established in paragraph (a) of this section. For example, in a facility that houses a shopping center or shopping mall, or a professional office of a health care provider, the floors that are above or below an accessible ground floor and that do not house sales or rental establishments or a professional office of a health care provider, must meet the requirements of this section but for the elevator.

§ 36.402 Alterations.

(a) General.

(1) Any alteration to a place of public accommodation or a commercial facility, after January 26, 1992, shall be made so as to ensure that, to the maximum extent feasible, the altered portions of the facility are readily accessible to and usable by individuals with disabilities, including individuals who use wheelchairs.

(2) An alteration is deemed to be undertaken after January 26, 1992, if the physical alteration of the property begins after that date.

(b) Alteration. For the purposes of this part, an alteration is a change to a place of public accommodation or a commercial facility that affects or could affect the usability of the building or facility or any part thereof.

(1) Alterations include, but are not limited to, remodeling, renovation, rehabilitation, reconstruction, historic restoration, changes or rearrangement in structural parts or elements, and changes or rearrangement in the plan configuration of walls and full-height partitions. Normal maintenance, reroofing, painting or wallpapering, asbestos removal, or changes to mechanical and electrical systems are not alterations unless they affect the usability of the building or facility.

(2) If existing elements, spaces, or common areas are altered, then each such altered element, space, or area shall comply with the applicable provisions of appendix A to this part.

(c) To the maximum extent feasible. The phrase "to the maximum extent feasible," as used in this section, applies to the occasional case where the nature of an existing facility makes it virtually impossible to comply fully with applicable accessibility standards through a planned alteration. In these circumstances, the alteration shall provide the maximum physical accessibility feasible. Any altered features of the facility that can be made accessible shall be made accessible. If providing accessibility in conformance with this section to individuals with certain disabilities (e.g., those who use wheelchairs) would not be feasible, the facility shall be made accessible to persons with other types of disabilities (e.g., those who use crutches, those who have impaired vision or hearing, or those who have other impairments).

§ 36.403 Alterations: Path of travel.

(a) General. An alteration that affects or could affect the usability of or access to an area of a facility that contains a primary function shall be made so as to ensure that, to the maximum extent feasible, the path of travel to the altered area and the restrooms, telephones, and drinking fountains serving the altered area, are readily accessible to and usable by individuals with disabilities, including individuals who use wheelchairs, unless the cost and scope of such alterations is disproportionate to the cost of the overall alteration.

(b) Primary function. A "primary function" is a major activity for which the facility is intended. Areas that contain a primary function include, but are not limited to, the customer services lobby of a bank, the dining area of a cafeteria, the meeting rooms in a conference center, as well as offices and other work areas in which the activities of the public accommodation or other private entity using the facility are carried out. Mechanical rooms, boiler rooms, supply storage rooms, employee lounges or locker rooms, janitorial closets, entrances, corridors, and restrooms are not areas containing a primary function.

(c) Alterations to an area containing a primary function.

(1) Alterations that affect the usability of or access to an area containing a primary function include, but are not limited to—

(i) Remodeling merchandise display areas or employee work areas in a department store;

(ii) Replacing an inaccessible floor surface in the customer service or employee work areas of a bank;

(iii) Redesigning the assembly line area of a factory; or

(iv) Installing a computer center in an accounting firm.

(2) For the purposes of this section, alterations to windows, hardware, controls, electrical outlets, and signage shall not be deemed to be alterations that affect the usability of or access to an area containing a primary function.

(d) Landlord/tenant: If a tenant is making alterations as defined in § 36.402 that would trigger the requirements of this section, those alterations by the tenant in areas that only the tenant occupies do not trigger a path of travel obligation upon the landlord with respect to areas of the facility under the landlord's authority, if those areas are not otherwise being altered.

(e) Path of travel.

(1) A "path of travel" includes a continuous, unobstructed way of pedestrian passage by means of which the altered area may be approached, entered, and exited, and which connects the altered area with an exterior approach (including sidewalks, streets, and parking areas), an entrance to the facility, and other parts of the facility.

(2) An accessible path of travel may consist of walks and sidewalks, curb ramps and other interior or exterior pedestrian ramps; clear floor paths through lobbies, corridors, rooms, and other improved areas; parking access aisles; elevators and lifts; or a combination of these elements.

(3) For the purposes of this part, the term "path of travel" also includes the restrooms, telephones, and drinking fountains serving the altered area.

(f) Disproportionality.

(1) Alterations made to provide an accessible path of travel to the altered area will be deemed disproportionate to the overall alteration when the cost exceeds 20% of the cost of the alteration to the primary function area.

(2) Costs that may be counted as expenditures required to provide an accessible path of travel may include:

(i) Costs associated with providing an accessible entrance and an accessible route to the altered area, for example, the cost of widening doorways or installing ramps;

(ii) Costs associated with making restrooms accessible, such as installing grab bars, enlarging toilet stalls, insulating pipes, or installing accessible faucet controls;

(iii) Costs associated with providing accessible telephones, such as relocating the telephone to an accessible height, installing amplification devices, or installing a telecommunications device for deaf persons (TDD);

(iv) Costs associated with relocating an inaccessible drinking fountain.

(g) Duty to provide accessible features in the event of disproportionality.

(1) When the cost of alterations necessary to make the path of travel to the altered area fully acces-

sible is disproportionate to the cost of the overall alteration, the path of travel shall be made accessible to the extent that it can be made accessible without incurring disproportionate costs.

(2) In choosing which accessible elements to provide, priority should be given to those elements that will provide the greatest access, in the following order:

(i) An accessible entrance;

(ii) An accessible route to the altered area;

(iii) At least one accessible restroom for each sex or a single unisex restroom;

(iv) Accessible telephones;

(v) Accessible drinking fountains; and

(vi) When possible, additional accessible elements such as parking, storage, and alarms.

(h) Series of smaller alterations.

(1) The obligation to provide an accessible path of travel may not be evaded by performing a series of small alterations to the area served by a single path of travel if those alterations could have been performed as a single undertaking.

(2)(i) If an area containing a primary function has been altered without providing an accessible path of travel to that area, and subsequent alterations of that area, or a different area on the same path of travel, are undertaken within three years of the original alteration, the total cost of alterations to the primary function areas on that path of travel during the preceding three year period shall be considered in determining whether the cost of making that path of travel accessible is disproportionate.

(ii) Only alterations undertaken after January 26, 1992, shall be considered in determining if the cost of providing an accessible path of travel is disproportionate to the overall cost of the alterations.

§ 36.404 Alterations: Elevator exemption.

(a) This section does not require the installation of an elevator in an altered facility that is less than three stories or has less than 3,000 square feet per story, except with respect to any facility that houses a shopping center, a shopping mall, the professional office of a health care provider, a terminal, depot, or other station used for specified public transportation, or an airport passenger terminal.

(1) For the purposes of this section, "professional office of a health care provider" means a location where a person or entity regulated by a State to provide professional services related to the physical or mental health of an individual makes such services available to the public. The facility that houses a "professional office of a health care provider" only includes floor levels housing by at least one health care provider, or any floor level designed or intended for use by at least one health care provider.

(2) For the purposes of this section, shopping center or shopping mall means—

(i) A building housing five or more sales or rental establishments; or

(ii) A series of buildings on a common site, connected by a common pedestrian access route above or below the ground floor, that is either under common ownership or common control or developed either as one project or as a series of related projects, housing five or more sales or rental establishments. For purposes of this section, places of public accommodation of the types listed in paragraph (5) of the definition of "place of public accommodation" in § 36.104 are considered sales or rental establishments. The facility housing a "shopping center or shopping mall" only includes floor levels housing at least one sales or rental establishment, or any floor level designed or intended for use by at least one sales or rental establishment.

(b) The exemption provided in paragraph (a) of this section does not obviate or limit in any way the obligation to comply with the other accessibility requirements established in this subpart. For example, alterations to floors above or below the accessible ground floor must be accessible regardless of whether the altered facility has an elevator.

§ 36.405 Alterations: Historic preservation.

(a) Alterations to buildings or facilities that are eligible for listing in the National Register of Historic Places under the National Historic Preservation Act (16 U.S.C. 470 et seq.), or are designated as historic under State or local law, shall comply to the maximum extent feasible with section 4.1.7 of appendix A to this part.

(b) If it is determined under the procedures set out in section 4.1.7 of appendix A that it is not feasible to provide physical access to an historic property that is a place of public accommodation in a manner that will not threaten or destroy the historic significance of the building or facility, alternative methods of access shall be provided pursuant to the requirements of subpart C of this part.

§ 36.406 Standards for new construction and alterations.

(a) New construction and alterations subject to this part shall comply with the standards for accessible design published as appendix A to this part (ADAAG).

(b) The chart in the appendix to this section provides guidance to the user in reading appendix A to this part (ADAAG) together with subparts A through D of this part, when determining requirements for a particular facility.

Subpart E—Enforcement

§ 36.501 Private suits.

(a) General. Any person who is being subjected to discrimination on the basis of disability in violation of the Act or this part or who has reasonable grounds for believing that such person is about to be subjected to discrimination in violation of section 303 of the Act or subpart D of this part may institute a civil action for preventive relief, including an application for a permanent or temporary injunction, restraining order, or other order. Upon timely application, the court may, in its discretion, permit the Attorney General to intervene in the civil action if the Attorney General or his or her designee certifies that the case is of general public importance. Upon application by the complainant and in such circumstances as the court may deem just, the court may appoint an attorney for such complainant and may authorize the commencement of the civil action without the payment of fees, costs, or security. Nothing in this section shall require a person with a disability to engage in a futile gesture if the person has actual notice that a person or organization covered by title III of the Act or this part does not intend to comply with its provisions.

(b) Injunctive relief. In the case of violations of § 36.304, § 36.308, § 36.310(b), § 36.401, § 36.402, § 36.403, and § 36.405 of this part, injunctive relief shall include an order to alter facilities to make such facilities readily accessible to and usable by individuals with disabilities to the extent required by the Act or this part. Where appropriate, injunctive relief shall also include requiring the provision of an auxiliary aid or service, modification of a policy, or provision of alternative methods, to the extent required by the Act or this part.

§ 36.502 Investigations and compliance reviews.

(a) The Attorney General shall investigate alleged violations of the Act or this part.

(b) Any individual who believes that he or she or a specific class of persons has been subjected to discrimination prohibited by the Act or this part may request the Department to institute an investigation.

(c) Where the Attorney General has reason to believe that there may be a violation of this part, he or she may initiate a compliance review.

§ 36.503 Suit by the Attorney General.

Following a compliance review or investigation under § 36.502, or at any other time in his or her discretion, the Attorney General may commence a civil action in any appropriate United States district court if the Attorney General has reasonable cause to believe that—

(a) Any person or group of persons is engaged in a pattern or practice of discrimination in violation of the Act or this part; or

(b) Any person or group of persons has been discriminated against in violation of the Act or this part and the discrimination raises an issue of general public importance.

§ 36.504 Relief.

(a) Authority of court. In a civil action under § 36.503, the court—

(1) May grant any equitable relief that such court considers to be appropriate, including, to the extent required by the Act or this part—

(i) Granting temporary, preliminary, or permanent relief;

(ii) Providing an auxiliary aid or service, modification of policy, practice, or procedure, or alternative method; and

(iii) Making facilities readily accessible to and usable by individuals with disabilities;

(2) May award other relief as the court considers to be appropriate, including monetary damages to persons aggrieved when requested by the Attorney General; and

(3) May, to vindicate the public interest, assess a civil penalty against the entity in an amount

(i) Not exceeding $50,000 for a first violation occurring before September 29, 1999, and not exceeding $55,000 for a first violation occurring on or after September 29, 1999; and

(ii) Not exceeding $100,000 for any subsequent violation occurring before September 29, 1999, and not exceeding $110,000 for any subsequent violation occurring on or after September 29, 1999.

(b) Single violation. For purposes of paragraph (a)(3) of this section, in determining whether a first or subsequent violation has occurred, a determination in a single action, by judgment or settlement, that the covered entity has engaged in more than one discriminatory act shall be counted as a single violation.

(c) Punitive damages. For purposes of paragraph (a)(2) of this section, the terms "monetary damages" and "such other relief" do not include punitive damages.

(d) Judicial consideration. In a civil action under § 36.503, the court, when considering what amount of civil penalty, if any, is appropriate, shall give consideration to any good faith effort or attempt to comply with this part by the entity. In evaluating good faith, the court shall consider, among other factors it deems relevant, whether the entity could have reasonably anticipated the need for an appropriate type of auxiliary aid needed to accommodate the unique needs of a particular individual with a disability.

§ 36.505 Attorneys fees.

In any action or administrative proceeding commenced pursuant to the Act or this part, the court or agency, in its discretion, may allow the prevailing party, other than the United States, a reasonable attorney's fee, including litigation expenses, and costs, and the United States shall be liable for the foregoing the same as a private individual.

ADA TITLE III
DOJ INTERPRETIVE GUIDANCE

CODE OF FEDERAL REGULATIONS TITLE 28—JUDICIAL ADMINISTRATION CHAPTER I—DEPARTMENT OF JUSTICE PART 36—NONDISCRIMINATION ON THE BASIS OF DISABILITY BY PUBLIC ACCOMMODATIONS AND IN COMMERCIAL FACILITIES

Current through June 2, 1998; 63 FR 29958

Appendix B to Part 36—Preamble to Regulation on Nondiscrimination on the Basis of Disability by Public Accommodations and in Commercial Facilities (Published July 26, 1991)

Note: For the convenience of the reader, this appendix contains the text of the preamble to the final regulation on nondiscrimination on the basis of disability by public accommodations and in commercial facilities beginning at the heading "Section-by-Section Analysis and Response to Comments" and ending before "List of Subjects in 28 CFR part 36" (56 FR July 26, 1991).

Section-By-Section Analysis and Response to Comments

Subpart A—General

Section 36.101 Purpose

Section 36.101 states the purpose of the rule, which is to effectuate title III of the Americans with Disabilities Act of 1990. This title prohibits discrimination on the basis of disability by public accommodations, requires places of public accommodation and commercial facilities to be designed, constructed, and altered in compliance with the accessibility standards established by this part, and requires that examinations or courses related to licensing or certification for professional or trade purposes be accessible to persons with disabilities.

Section 36.102 Application

Section 36.102 specifies the range of entities and facilities that have obligations under the final rule. The rule applies to any public accommodation or commercial facility as those terms are defined in § 36.104. It also applies, in accordance with section 309 of the ADA, to private entities that offer examinations or courses related to applications, licensing, certification, or credentialing for secondary or postsecondary education, professional, or trade purposes. Except as provided in § 36.206, "Retaliation or coercion," this part does not apply to individuals other than public accommodations or to public entities. Coverage of private individuals and public entities is discussed in the preamble to § 36.206.

As defined in § 36.104, a public accommodation is a private entity that owns, leases or leases to, or operates a place of public accommodation. Section 36.102(b)(2) emphasizes that the general and specific public accommodations requirements of subparts B and C obligate a public accommodation only with respect to the operations of a place of public accommodation. This distinction is drawn in recognition of the fact that a private entity that meets the regulatory definition of public accommodation could also own, lease or lease to, or operate facilities that are not places of public accommodation. The rule would exceed the reach of the ADA if it were to apply the public accommodations requirements of subparts B and C to the operations of a private entity that do not involve a place of public accommodation. Similarly, § 36.102(b)(3) provides that the new construction and alterations requirements of subpart D obligate a public accommodation only with respect to facilities used as, or designed or constructed for use as, places of public accommodation or commercial facilities.

On the other hand, as mandated by the ADA and reflected in § 36.102(c), the new construction and alterations requirements of subpart D apply to a commercial facility whether or not the facility is a place of public accommodation, or is owned, leased, leased to, or operated by a public accommodation.

Section 36.102(e) states that the rule does not apply to any private club, religious entity, or public entity. Each of these terms is defined in § 36.104. The exclusion of private clubs and religious entities is derived from section 307 of the ADA; and the exclusion of public entities is based on the statutory definition of public accommodation in section 301(7) of the ADA, which excludes entities other than private entities from coverage under title III of the ADA.

Section 36.103 Relationship to Other Laws

Section 36.103 is derived from sections 501 (a) and (b) of the ADA. Paragraph (a) provides that, except as otherwise specifically provided by this part, the ADA is not intended to apply lesser standards than are required under title V of the Rehabilitation Act of 1973, as amended (29 U.S.C. 790-794), or the regulations implementing that title. The standards of title V of the Rehabilitation Act apply for purposes of the ADA to the extent that the ADA has not explicitly adopted a different standard from title V. Where the ADA explicitly provides a different standard from section 504, the ADA standard applies to the ADA, but not to section 504. For example, section 504 requires that all federally assisted programs and activities be readily accessible to and usable by individuals with handicaps, even if major structural alterations are necessary to make a program accessible. Title III of the ADA, in contrast, only requires alterations to existing facilities if the modifications are "readily achievable," that is, able to be accomplished easily and without much difficulty or expense. A public accommodation that is covered under both section 504 and the ADA is still required to meet the "program accessibility" standard in order to comply with section 504, but would not be in violation of the ADA unless it failed to make "readily achievable" modifications. On the other hand, an entity covered by the ADA is required to make "readily achievable" modifications, even if the program can be made accessible without any architectural modifications. Thus, an entity covered by both section 504 and title III of the ADA must meet both the "program accessibility" requirement and the "readily achievable" requirement.

Paragraph (b) makes explicit that the rule does not affect the obligation of recipients of Federal financial assistance to comply with the requirements imposed under section 504 of the Rehabilitation Act of 1973.

Paragraph (c) makes clear that Congress did not intend to displace any of the rights or remedies provided by other Federal laws or other State or local laws (including State common law) that provide greater or equal protection to individuals with disabilities. A plaintiff may choose to pursue claims under a State law that does not confer greater substantive rights, or even confers fewer substantive rights, if the alleged violation is protected under the alternative law and the remedies are greater. For example, assume that a person with a physical disability seeks damages under a State law that allows compensatory and punitive damages for discrimination on the basis of physical disability, but does not allow them on the basis of mental disability. In that situation, the State law would provide narrower coverage, by excluding mental disabilities, but broader remedies, and an individual covered by both laws could choose to bring an action under both laws. Moreover, State tort claims confer greater remedies and are not preempted by the ADA. A plaintiff may join a State tort claim to a case brought under the ADA. In such a case, the plaintiff must, of course, prove all the elements of the State tort claim in order to prevail under that cause of action.

A commenter had concerns about privacy requirements for banking transactions using telephone relay services. Title IV of the Act provides adequate protections for ensuring the confidentiality of communications using the relay services. This issue is more appropriately addressed by the Federal Communications Commission in its regulation implementing title IV of the Act.

Section 36.104 Definitions

"Act." The word "Act" is used in the regulation to refer to the Americans with Disabilities Act of 1990, Pub.L. 101-336, which is also referred to as the "ADA."

"Commerce." The definition of "commerce" is identical to the statutory definition provided in section 301(l) of the ADA. It means travel, trade, traffic, commerce, transportation, or communication among the several States, between any foreign country or any territory or possession and any State, or between points in the same State but through another State or foreign country. Commerce is defined in the same manner as in title II of the Civil Rights Act of 1964, which prohibits racial discrimination in public accommodations.

The term "commerce" is used in the definition of "place of public accommodation." According to that definition, one of the criteria that an entity must meet before it can be considered a place of public accommodation is that its operations affect commerce. The term "commerce" is similarly used in the definition of "commercial facility."

The use of the phrase "operations affect commerce" applies the full scope of coverage of the Commerce Clause of the Constitution in enforcing the ADA. The Constitution gives Congress broad authority to regulate interstate commerce, including the activities of local business enterprises (e.g., a physician's office, a neighborhood restaurant, a laundromat, or a bakery) that affect interstate commerce through the purchase or sale of products manufactured in other States, or by providing services to individuals from other States. Because of the integrated nature of the national economy, the ADA and this final rule will have extremely broad application.

"Commercial facilities" are those facilities that are intended for nonresidential use by a private entity and whose operations affect commerce. As explained under § 36.401, "New construction," the new construction and alteration requirements of subpart D of the rule apply to all commercial facilities, whether or not they are places of public accommodation. Those commercial facilities that are not places of public accommodation are not subject to the requirements of subparts B and C (e.g., those requirements concerning auxiliary aids and general nondiscrimination provisions).

Congress recognized that the employees within commercial facilities would generally be protected under title I (employment) of the Act. However, as the House Committee on Education and Labor pointed out, "[t]o the extent that new facilities are built in a manner that make[s] them accessible to all individuals, including potential employees, there will be less of a need for individual employers to engage in reasonable accommodations for particular employees." H.R. Rep. No. 485, 101st Cong., 2d Sess., pt. 2, at 117 (1990) [hereinafter "Education and Labor report"]. While employers of fewer than 15 employees are not covered by title I's employment discrimination provisions, there is no such limitation with respect to new construction covered under title III. Congress chose not to so limit the new construction provisions because of its desire for a uniform requirement of accessibility in new construction, because accessibility can be accomplished easily in the design and construction stage, and because future expansion of a business or sale or lease of the property to a larger employer or to a business that is a place of public accommodation is always a possibility.

The term "commercial facilities" is not intended to be defined by dictionary or common industry definitions. Included in this category are factories, warehouses, office buildings, and other buildings in which employment may occur. The phrase, "whose operations affect commerce," is to be read broadly, to include all types of activities reached under the commerce clause of the Constitution.

Privately operated airports are also included in the category of commercial facilities. They are not, however, places of public accommodation because they are not terminals used for "specified public transportation." (Transportation by aircraft is specifically excluded from the statutory definition of "specified public transportation.") Thus, privately operated airports are subject to the new construction and alteration requirements of this rule (subpart D) but not to subparts B and C. (Airports operated by public entities are covered by title II of the Act.) Places of public accommodation located within airports, such as restaurants, shops, lounges, or conference centers, however, are covered by subparts B and C of this part.

The statute's definition of "commercial facilities" specifically includes only facilities "that are intended for nonresidential use" and specifically exempts those facilities that are covered or expressly exempted from coverage under the Fair Housing Act of 1968, as amended (42 U.S.C. 3601-3631). The interplay between the Fair Housing Act and the ADA with respect to those facilities that are "places of public accommodation" was the subject of many comments and is addressed in the preamble discussion of the definition of "place of public accommodation."

"Current illegal use of drugs." The phrase "current illegal use of drugs" is used in § 36.209. Its meaning is discussed in the preamble for that section.

"Disability." The definition of the term "disability" is comparable to the definition of the term "individual with handicaps" in section 7(8)(B) of the Rehabilitation Act and section 802(h) of the Fair Housing Act. The Education and Labor Committee report makes clear that the analysis of the term "individual with handicaps" by the Department of Health, Education, and Welfare in its regulations implementing section 504 (42 FR 22685 (May 4, 1977)) and the analysis by the Department of Housing and Urban Development in its regulation implementing the Fair Housing Amendments Act of 1988 (54 FR 3232 (Jan. 23, 1989)) should also apply fully to the term "disability" (Education and Labor report at 50).

The use of the term "disability" instead of "handicap" and the term "individual with a disability" instead of "individual with handicaps" represents an effort by the Congress to make use of up-to-date, currently accepted terminology. The terminology applied to individuals with disabilities is a very significant and sensitive issue. As with racial and ethnic terms, the choice of words to describe a person with a disability is overlaid with stereotypes, patronizing attitudes, and other emotional connotations. Many individuals with disabilities, and organizations representing such individuals, object to the use of such terms as "handicapped person" or "the handicapped." In other recent legislation, Congress also recognized this shift in terminology, e.g., by changing the name of the National Council on the Handicapped to the National Council on Disability (Pub.L. 100-630).

In enacting the Americans with Disabilities Act, Congress concluded that it was important for the current legislation to use terminology most in line with the sensibilities of most Americans with disabilities. No change in definition or substance is intended nor should be attributed to this change in phraseology.

The term "disability" means, with respect to an individual—

(A) A physical or mental impairment that substantially limits one or more of the major life activities of such individual;

(B) A record of such an impairment; or

(C) Being regarded as having such an impairment.

If an individual meets any one of these three tests, he or she is considered to be an individual with a disability for purposes of coverage under the Americans with Disabilities Act.

Congress adopted this same basic definition of "disability," first used in the Rehabilitation Act of 1973 and in the Fair Housing Amendments Act of 1988, for a number of reasons. It has worked well since it was adopted in 1974. There is a substantial body of administrative interpretation and judicial precedent on this definition. Finally, it would not be possible to guarantee comprehensiveness by providing a list of specific disabilities, especially because new disorders may be recognized in the future, as they have since the definition was first established in 1974.

Test A—A Physical or Mental Impairment That Substantially Limits One or More of the Major Life Activities of Such Individual

Physical or mental impairment. Under the first test, an individual must have a physical or mental impairment. As explained in paragraph (1) (i) of the definition, "impairment" means any physiological disorder or condition, cosmetic disfigurement, or anatomical loss affecting one or more of the following body systems: Neurological; musculoskeletal; special sense organs (including speech organs that are not respiratory, such as vocal cords, soft palate, and tongue); respiratory, including speech organs; cardiovascular; reproductive; digestive; genitourinary; hemic and lymphatic; skin; and endocrine. It also means any mental or psychological disorder, such as mental retardation, organic brain syndrome, emotional or mental illness, and specific learning disabilities. This list closely tracks the one used in the regulations for section 504 of the Rehabilitation Act of 1973 (see, e.g., 45 CFR 84.3(j)(2)(i)).

Many commenters asked that "traumatic brain injury" be added to the list in paragraph (1)(i). Traumatic brain injury is already included because it is a physiological condition affecting one of the listed body systems, i.e., "neurological." Therefore, it was unnecessary for the Department to add the term to the regulation.

It is not possible to include a list of all the specific conditions, contagious and noncontagious diseases, or infections that would constitute physical or mental impairments because of the difficulty of ensuring the comprehensiveness of such a list, particularly in light of the fact that other conditions or disorders may be identified in the future. However, the list of examples in paragraph (1)(iii) of the definition includes: Orthopedic, visual, speech and hearing impairments; cerebral palsy; epilepsy, muscular dystrophy, multiple sclerosis, cancer, heart disease, diabetes, mental retardation, emotional illness, specific learning disabilities, HIV disease (symptomatic or asymptomatic), tuberculosis, drug addiction, and alcoholism.

The examples of "physical or mental impairments" in paragraph (1)(iii) are the same as those contained in many section 504 regulations, except for the addition of the phrase "contagious and noncontagious" to describe the types of diseases and conditions included, and the addition of "HIV disease (symptomatic or asymptomatic)" and "tuberculosis" to the list of examples. These additions are based on the ADA committee reports, caselaw, and official legal opinions interpreting section 504. In *School Board of Nassau County v. Arline*, 480 U.S. 273 (1987), a case involving an individual with tuberculosis, the Supreme Court held that people with contagious diseases are entitled to the protections afforded by section 504. Following the *Arline* decision, this Department's Office of Legal Counsel issued a legal opinion that concluded that symptomatic HIV disease is an impairment that substantially limits a major life activity; therefore it has been included in the definition of disability under this part. The opinion also concluded that asymptomatic HIV disease is an impairment that substantially limits a major life activity, either because of its actual effect on the individual with HIV disease or because the reactions of other people to individuals with HIV disease cause such individuals to be treated as though they are disabled. See Memorandum from Douglas W. Kmiec, Acting Assistant Attorney General, Office of Legal Counsel, Department of Justice, to Arthur B. Culvahouse, Jr., Counsel to the President (Sept. 27, 1988), reprinted in Hearings on S. 933, the Americans with Disabilities Act, Before the Subcomm. on the Handicapped of the Senate Comm. on Labor and Human Resources, 101st Cong., 1st Sess. 346 (1989). The phrase "symptomatic or asymptomatic" was inserted in the final rule after "HIV disease" in response to commenters who suggested that the clarification was necessary to give full meaning to the Department's opinion.

Paragraph (1)(iv) of the definition states that the phrase "physical or mental impairment" does not include homosexuality or bisexuality. These conditions were never considered impairments under other Federal disability laws. Section 511(a) of the statute makes clear that they are likewise not to be considered impairments under the Americans with Disabilities

Act.

Physical or mental impairment does not include simple physical characteristics, such as blue eyes or black hair. Nor does it include environmental, cultural, economic, or other disadvantages, such as having a prison record, or being poor. Nor is age a disability. Similarly, the definition does not include common personality traits such as poor judgment or a quick temper where these are not symptoms of a mental or psychological disorder. However, a person who has these characteristics and also has a physical or mental impairment may be considered as having a disability for purposes of the Americans with Disabilities Act based on the impairment.

Substantial limitation of a major life activity. Under Test A, the impairment must be one that "substantially limits a major life activity." Major life activities include such things as caring for one's self, performing manual tasks, walking, seeing, hearing, speaking, breathing, learning, and working. For example, a person who is paraplegic is substantially limited in the major life activity of walking, a person who is blind is substantially limited in the major life activity of seeing, and a person who is mentally retarded is substantially limited in the major life activity of learning. A person with traumatic brain injury is substantially limited in the major life activities of caring for one's self, learning, and working because of memory deficit, confusion, contextual difficulties, and inability to reason appropriately.

A person is considered an individual with a disability for purposes of Test A, the first prong of the definition, when the individual's important life activities are restricted as to the conditions, manner, or duration under which they can be performed in comparison to most people. A person with a minor, trivial impairment, such as a simple infected finger, is not impaired in a major life activity. A person who can walk for 10 miles continuously is not substantially limited in walking merely because, on the eleventh mile, he or she begins to experience pain, because most people would not be able to walk eleven miles without experiencing some discomfort.

The Department received many comments on the proposed rule's inclusion of the word "temporary" in the definition of "disability." The preamble indicated that impairments are not necessarily excluded from the definition of "disability" simply because they are temporary, but that the duration, or expected duration, of an impairment is one factor that may properly be considered in determining whether the impairment substantially limits a major life activity. The preamble recognized, however, that temporary impairments, such as a broken leg, are not commonly regarded as disabilities, and only in rare circumstances would the degree of the limitation and its expected duration be substantial: Nevertheless, many commenters objected to inclusion of the word "temporary" both because it is not in the statute and because it is not contained in the definition of "disability" set forth in the title I regulations of the Equal Employment Opportunity Commission (EEOC). The word "temporary" has been deleted from the final rule to conform with the statutory language. The question of whether a temporary impairment is a disability must be resolved on a case-by-case basis, taking into consideration both the duration (or expected duration) of the impairment and the extent to which it actually limits a major life activity of the affected individual.

The question of whether a person has a disability should be assessed without regard to the availability of mitigating measures, such as reasonable modifications or auxiliary aids and services. For example, a person with hearing loss is substantially limited in the major life activity of hearing, even though the loss may be improved through the use of a hearing aid. Likewise, persons with impairments, such as epilepsy or diabetes, that substantially limit a major life activity, are covered under the first prong of the definition of disability, even if the effects of the impairment are controlled by medication.

Many commenters asked that environmental illness (also known as multiple chemical sensitivity) as well as allergy to cigarette smoke be recognized as disabilities. The Department, however, declines to state categorically that these types of allergies or sensitivities are disabilities, because the determination as to whether an impairment is a disability depends on whether, given the particular circumstances at issue, the impairment substantially limits one or more major life activities (or has a history of, or is regarded as having such an effect).

Sometimes respiratory or neurological functioning is so severely affected that an individual will satisfy the requirements to be considered disabled under the regulation. Such an individual would be entitled to all of the protections afforded by the Act and this part. In other cases, individuals may be sensitive to environmental elements or to smoke but their sensitivity will not rise to the level needed to constitute a disability. For example, their major life activity of breathing may be somewhat, but not substantially, impaired. In such circumstances, the individuals are not disabled and are not entitled to the protections of the statute despite their sensitivity to environmental agents.

In sum, the determination as to whether allergies to

cigarette smoke, or allergies or sensitivities characterized by the commenters as environmental illness are disabilities covered by the regulation must be made using the same case-by-case analysis that is applied to all other physical or mental impairments. Moreover, the addition of specific regulatory provisions relating to environmental illness in the final rule would be inappropriate at this time pending future consideration of the issue by the Architectural and Transportation Barriers Compliance Board, the Environmental Protection Agency, and the Occupational Safety and Health Administration of the Department of Labor.

Test B—A Record of Such an Impairment

This test is intended to cover those who have a record of an impairment. As explained in paragraph (3) of the rule's definition of disability, this includes a person who has a history of an impairment that substantially limited a major life activity, such as someone who has recovered from an impairment. It also includes persons who have been misclassified as having an impairment.

This provision is included in the definition in part to protect individuals who have recovered from a physical or mental impairment that previously substantially limited them in a major life activity. Discrimination on the basis of such a past impairment is prohibited. Frequently occurring examples of the first group (those who have a history of an impairment) are persons with histories of mental or emotional illness, heart disease, or cancer; examples of the second group (those who have been misclassified as having an impairment) are persons who have been misclassified as having mental retardation or mental illness.

Test C—Being Regarded as Having Such an Impairment

This test, as contained in paragraph (4) of the definition, is intended to cover persons who are treated by a private entity or public accommodation as having a physical or mental impairment that substantially limits a major life activity. It applies when a person is treated as if he or she has an impairment that substantially limits a major life activity, regardless of whether that person has an impairment.

The Americans with Disabilities Act uses the same "regarded as" test set forth in the regulations implementing section 504 of the Rehabilitation Act. See, e.g., 28 CFR 42.540(k)(2)(iv), which provides:

(iv) "Is regarded as having an impairment" means (A) Has a physical or mental impairment that does not substantially limit major life activities but that is treated by a recipient as constituting such a limitation; (B) Has a physical or mental impairment that substantially limits major life activities only as a result of the attitudes of others toward such impairment; or (C) Has none of the impairments defined in paragraph (k)(2)(i) of this section but is treated by a recipient as having such an impairment.

The perception of the private entity or public accommodation is a key element of this test. A person who perceives himself or herself to have an impairment, but does not have an impairment, and is not treated as if he or she has an impairment, is not protected under this test. A person would be covered under this test if a restaurant refused to serve that person because of a fear of "negative reactions" of others to that person. A person would also be covered if a public accommodation refused to serve a patron because it perceived that the patron had an impairment that limited his or her enjoyment of the goods or services being offered.

For example, persons with severe burns often encounter discrimination in community activities, resulting in substantial limitation of major life activities. These persons would be covered under this test based on the attitudes of others towards the impairment, even if they did not view themselves as "impaired."

The rationale for this third test, as used in the Rehabilitation Act of 1973, was articulated by the Supreme Court in *Arline,* 480 U.S. 273 (1987). The Court noted that, although an individual may have an impairment that does not in fact substantially limit a major life activity, the reaction of others may prove just as disabling. "Such an impairment might not diminish a person's physical or mental capabilities, but could nevertheless substantially limit that person's ability to work as a result of the negative reactions of others to the impairment." *Id.* at 283. The Court concluded that, by including this test in the Rehabilitation Act's definition, "Congress acknowledged that society's accumulated myths and fears about disability and disease are as handicapping as are the physical limitations that flow from actual impairment." *Id.* at 284.

Thus, a person who is not allowed into a public accommodation because of the myths, fears, and stereotypes associated with disabilities would be covered under this third test whether or not the person's physical or mental condition would be considered a disability under the first or second test in the definition.

If a person is refused admittance on the basis of an

actual or perceived physical or mental condition, and the public accommodation can articulate no legitimate reason for the refusal (such as failure to meet eligibility criteria), a perceived concern about admitting persons with disabilities could be inferred and the individual would qualify for coverage under the "regarded as" test. A person who is covered because of being regarded as having an impairment is not required to show that the public accommodation's perception is inaccurate (e.g., that he will be accepted by others, or that insurance rates will not increase) in order to be admitted to the public accommodation.

Paragraph (5) of the definition lists certain conditions that are not included within the definition of "disability." The excluded conditions are: transvestism, transsexualism, pedophilia, exhibitionism, voyeurism, gender identity disorders not resulting from physical impairments, other sexual behavior disorders, compulsive gambling, kleptomania, pyromania, and psychoactive substance use disorders resulting from current illegal use of drugs. Unlike homosexuality and bisexuality, which are not considered impairments under either the Americans with Disabilities Act (see the definition of "disability," paragraph (1)(iv)) or section 504, the conditions listed in paragraph (5), except for transvestism, are not necessarily excluded as impairments under section 504. (Transvestism was excluded from the definition of disability for section 504 by the Fair Housing Amendments Act of 1988, Pub.L. 100-430, § 6(b).) The phrase "current illegal use of drugs" used in this definition is explained in the preamble to § 36.209.

"Drug." The definition of the term "drug" is taken from section 510(d)(2) of the ADA.

"Facility." "Facility" means all or any portion of buildings, structures, sites, complexes, equipment, rolling stock or other conveyances, roads, walks, passageways, parking lots, or other real or personal property, including the site where the building, property, structure, or equipment is located. Committee reports made clear that the definition of facility was drawn from the definition of facility in current Federal regulations (see, e.g., Education and Labor report at 114). It includes both indoor and outdoor areas where human-constructed improvements, structures, equipment, or property have been added to the natural environment.

The term "rolling stock or other conveyances" was not included in the definition of facility in the proposed rule. However, commenters raised questions about the applicability of this part to places of public accommodation operated in mobile facilities (such as cruise ships, floating restaurants, or mobile health units). Those places of public accommodation are covered under this part, and would be included in the definition of "facility." Thus the requirements of subparts B and C would apply to those places of public accommodation. For example, a covered entity could not discriminate on the basis of disability in the full and equal enjoyment of the facilities (§ 36.201). Similarly, a cruise line could not apply eligibility criteria to potential passengers in a manner that would screen out individuals with disabilities, unless the criteria are "necessary," as provided in § 36.301.

However, standards for new construction and alterations of such facilities are not yet included in the Americans with Disabilities Act Accessibility Guidelines for Buildings and Facilities (ADAAG) adopted by § 36.406 and incorporated in Appendix A. The Department therefore will not interpret the new construction and alterations provisions of subpart D to apply to the types of facilities discussed here, pending further development of specific requirements.

Requirements pertaining to accessible transportation services provided by public accommodations are included in § 36.310 of this part; standards pertaining to accessible vehicles will be issued by the Secretary of Transportation pursuant to section 306 of the Act, and will be codified at 49 CFR part 37.

A public accommodation has obligations under this rule with respect to a cruise ship to the extent that its operations are subject to the laws of the United States.

The definition of "facility" only includes the site over which the private entity may exercise control or on which a place of public accommodation or a commercial facility is located. It does not include, for example, adjacent roads or walks controlled by a public entity that is not subject to this part. Public entities are subject to the requirements of title II of the Act. The Department's regulation implementing title II, which will be codified at 28 CFR part 35, addresses the obligations of public entities to ensure accessibility by providing curb ramps at pedestrian walkways.

"Illegal use of drugs." The definition of "illegal use of drugs" is taken from section 510(d)(1) of the Act and clarifies that the term includes the illegal use of one or more drugs.

"Individual with a disability" means a person who has a disability but does not include an individual who is currently illegally using drugs, when the public accommodation acts on the basis of such use. The phrase "current illegal use of drugs" is explained in the preamble to § 36.209.

"Place of public accommodation." The term "place of public accommodation" is an adaptation of the statutory definition of "public accommodation" in section 301(7) of the ADA and appears as an element of the regulatory definition of public accommodation. The final rule defines "place of public accommodation" as a facility, operated by a private entity, whose operations affect commerce and fall within at least one of 12 specified categories. The term "public accommodation," on the other hand, is reserved by the final rule for the private entity that owns, leases (or leases to), or operates a place of public accommodation. It is the public accommodation, and not the place of public accommodation, that is subject to the regulation's nondiscrimination requirements. Placing the obligation not to discriminate on the public accommodation, as defined in the rule, is consistent with section 302(a) of the ADA, which places the obligation not to discriminate on any person who owns, leases (or leases to), or operates a place of public accommodation.

Facilities operated by government agencies or other public entities as defined in this section do not qualify as places of public accommodation. The actions of public entities are governed by title II of the ADA and will be subject to regulations issued by the Department of Justice under that title. The receipt of government assistance by a private entity does not by itself preclude a facility from being considered as a place of public accommodation.

The definition of place of public accommodation incorporates the 12 categories of facilities represented in the statutory definition of public accommodation in section 301(7) of the ADA:

1. Places of lodging.
2. Establishments serving food or drink.
3. Places of exhibition or entertainment.
4. Places of public gathering.
5. Sales or rental establishments.
6. Service establishments.
7. Stations used for specified public transportation.
8. Places of public display or collection.
9. Places of recreation.
10. Places of education.
11. Social service center establishments.
12. Places of exercise or recreation.

In order to be a place of public accommodation, a facility must be operated by a private entity, its operations must affect commerce, and it must fall within one of these 12 categories. While the list of categories is exhaustive, the representative examples of facilities within each category are not. Within each category only a few examples are given. The category of social service center establishments would include not only the types of establishments listed, day care centers, senior citizen centers, homeless shelters, food banks, adoption agencies, but also establishments such as substance abuse treatment centers, rape crisis centers, and halfway houses. As another example, the category of sales or rental establishments would include an innumerable array of facilities that would sweep far beyond the few examples given in the regulation. For example, other retail or wholesale establishments selling or renting items, such as bookstores, videotape rental stores, car rental establishment, pet stores, and jewelry stores would also be covered under this category, even though they are not specifically listed.

Several commenters requested clarification as to the coverage of wholesale establishments under the category of "sales or rental establishments." The Department intends for wholesale establishments to be covered under this category as places of public accommodation except in cases where they sell exclusively to other businesses and not to individuals. For example, a company that grows food produce and supplies its crops exclusively to food processing corporations on a wholesale basis does not become a public accommodation because of these transactions. If this company operates a road side stand where its crops are sold to the public, the road side stand would be a sales establishment covered by the ADA. Conversely, a sales establishment that markets its goods as "wholesale to the public" and sells to individuals would not be exempt from ADA coverage despite its use of the word "wholesale" as a marketing technique.

Of course, a company that operates a place of public accommodation is subject to this part only in the operation of that place of public accommodation. In the example given above, the wholesale produce company that operates a road side stand would be a public accommodation only for the purposes of the operation of that stand. The company would be prohibited from discriminating on the basis of disability in the operation of the road side stand, and it would be required to remove barriers to physical access to the extent that it is readily achievable to do so (see § 36.304); however, in the event that it is not readily achievable to remove barriers, for example, by replacing a gravel surface or regrading the area around the stand to permit access by persons with mobility impairments, the company could meet its obligations through alternative methods of making its goods available, such as delivering produce to a customer in his or her car (see § 36.305). The concepts of readily achievable barrier removal and alternatives to barrier removal are discussed further in the preamble discussion of §§ 36.304 and 36.305.

Even if a facility does not fall within one of the 12 categories, and therefore does not qualify as a place of public accommodation, it still may be a commercial facility as defined in § 36.104 and be subject to the new construction and alterations requirements of subpart D.

A number of commenters questioned the treatment of residential hotels and other residential facilities in the Department's proposed rule. These commenters were essentially seeking resolution of the relationship between the Fair Housing Act and the ADA concerning facilities that are both residential in nature and engage in activities that would cause them to be classified as "places of public accommodation" under the ADA. The ADA's express exemption relating to the Fair Housing Act applies only to "commercial facilities" and not to "places of public accommodation."

A facility whose operations affect interstate commerce is a place of public accommodation for purposes of the ADA to the extent that its operations include those types of activities engaged in or services provided by the facilities contained on the list of 12 categories in section 301(7) of the ADA. Thus, a facility that provides social services would be considered a "social service center establishment." Similarly, the category "places of lodging" would exclude solely residential facilities because the nature of a place of lodging contemplates the use of the facility for short-term stays.

Many facilities, however, are mixed use facilities. For example, in a large hotel that has a separate residential apartment wing, the residential wing would not be covered by the ADA because of the nature of the occupancy of that part of the facility. This residential wing would, however, be covered by the Fair Housing Act. The separate nonresidential accommodations in the rest of the hotel would be a place of lodging, and thus a public accommodation subject to the requirements of this final rule. If a hotel allows both residential and short-term stays, but does not allocate space for these different uses in separate, discrete units, both the ADA and the Fair Housing Act may apply to the facility. Such determinations will need to be made on a case-by-case basis. Any place of lodging of the type described in paragraph (1) of the definition of place of public accommodation and that is an establishment located within a building that contains not more than five rooms for rent or hire and is actually occupied by the proprietor of the establishment as his or her residence is not covered by the ADA. (This exclusion from coverage does not apply to other categories of public accommodations, for example, professional offices or homeless shelters, that are located in a building that is also occupied as a private residence.)

A number of commenters noted that the term "residential hotel" may also apply to a type of hotel commonly known as a "single room occupancy hotel." Although such hotels or portions of such hotels may fall under the Fair Housing Act when operated or used as long-term residences, they are also considered "places of lodging" under the ADA when guests of such hotels are free to use them on a short-term basis. In addition, "single room occupancy hotels" may provide social services to their guests, often through the operation of Federal or State grant programs. In such a situation, the facility would be considered a "social service center establishment" and thus covered by the ADA as a place of public accommodation, regardless of the length of stay of the occupants.

A similar analysis would also be applied to other residential facilities that provide social services, including homeless shelters, shelters for people seeking refuge from domestic violence, nursing homes, residential care facilities, and other facilities where persons may reside for varying lengths of time. Such facilities should be analyzed under the Fair Housing Act to determine the application of that statute. The ADA, however, requires a separate and independent analysis. For example, if the facility, or a portion of the facility, is intended for or permits short-term stays, or if it can appropriately be categorized as a service establishment or as a social service establishment, then the facility or that portion of the facility used for the covered purpose is a place of public accommodation under the ADA. For example, a homeless shelter that is intended and used only for long-term residential stays and that does not provide social services to its residents would not be covered as a place of public accommodation. However, if this facility permitted short-term stays or provided social services to its residents, it would be covered under the ADA either as a "place of lodging" or as a "social service center establishment," or as both.

A private home, by itself, does not fall within any of the 12 categories. However, it can be covered as a place of public accommodation to the extent that it is used as a facility that would fall within one of the 12 categories. For example, if a professional office of a dentist, doctor, or psychologist is located in a private home, the portion of the home dedicated to office use (including areas used both for the residence and the office, e.g., the entrance to the home that is also used as the entrance to the professional office) would be considered a place of public accommodation. Places of public accommodation located in residential facilities are specifically addressed in § 36.207.

If a tour of a commercial facility that is not otherwise a place of public accommodation, such as, for example, a factory or a movie studio production set, is open to the general public, the route followed by the tour is a place of public accommodation and the tour must be operated in accordance with the rule's requirements for public accommodations. The place of public accommodation defined by the tour does not include those portions of the commercial facility that are merely viewed from the tour route. Hence, the barrier removal requirements of § 36.304 only apply to the physical route followed by the tour participants and not to work stations or other areas that are merely adjacent to, or within view of, the tour route. If the tour is not open to the general public, but rather is conducted, for example, for selected business colleagues, partners, customers, or consultants, the tour route is not a place of public accommodation and the tour is not subject to the requirements for public accommodations.

Public accommodations that receive Federal financial assistance are subject to the requirements of section 504 of the Rehabilitation Act as well as the requirements of the ADA.

Private schools, including elementary and secondary schools, are covered by the rule as places of public accommodation. The rule itself, however, does not require a private school to provide a free appropriate education or develop an individualized education program in accordance with regulations of the Department of Education implementing section 504 of the Rehabilitation Act of 1973, as amended (34 CFR part 104), and regulations implementing the Individuals with Disabilities Education Act (34 CFR part 300). The receipt of Federal assistance by a private school, however, would trigger application of the Department of Education's regulations to the extent mandated by the particular type of assistance received.

"Private club." The term "private club" is defined in accordance with section 307 of the ADA as a private club or establishment exempted from coverage under title II of the Civil Rights Act of 1964. Title II of the 1964 Act exempts any "private club or other establishment not in fact open to the public, except to the extent that the facilities of such establishment are made available to the customers or patrons of [a place of public accommodation as defined in title II]." The rule, therefore, as reflected in § 36.102(e) of the application section, limits the coverage of private clubs accordingly. The obligations of a private club that rents space to any other private entity for the operation of a place of public accommodation are discussed further in connection with § 36.201.

In determining whether a private entity qualifies as a private club under title II, courts have considered such factors as the degree of member control of club operations, the selectivity of the membership selection process, whether substantial membership fees are charged, whether the entity is operated on a nonprofit basis, the extent to which the facilities are open to the public, the degree of public funding, and whether the club was created specifically to avoid compliance with the Civil Rights Act. See e.g., *Tillman v. Wheaton-Haven Recreation Ass'n*, 410 U.S. 431 (1973); *Daniel v. Paul*, 395 U.S. 298 (1969); *Olzman v. Lake Hills Swim Club, Inc.*, 495 F.2d 1333 (2d Cir. 1974); *Anderson v. Pass Christian Isles Golf Club, Inc.*, 488 F.2d 855 (5th Cir. 1974); *Smith v. YMCA*, 462 F.2d 634 (5th Cir. 1972); *Stout v. YMCA*, 404 F.2d 687 (5th Cir. 1968); *United States v. Richberg*, 398 F.2d 523 (5th Cir. 1968); *Nesmith v. YMCA*, 397 F.2d 96 (4th Cir. 1968); *United States v. Lansdowne Swim Club*, 713 F. Supp. 785 (E.D. Pa. 1989); *Durham v. Red Lake Fishing and Hunting Club, Inc.*, 666 F. Supp. 954 (W.D. Tex. 1987); *New York v. Ocean Club, Inc.*, 602 F. Supp. 489 (E.D.N.Y. 1984); *Brown v. Loudoun Golf and Country Club, Inc.*, 573 F. Supp. 399 (E.D. Va. 1983); *United States v. Trustees of Fraternal Order of Eagles*, 472 F. Supp. 1174 (E.D. Wis. 1979); *Cornelius v. Benevolent Protective Order of Elks*, 382 F. Supp. 1182 (D. Conn. 1974).

"Private entity." The term "private entity" is defined as any individual or entity other than a public entity. It is used as part of the definition of "public accommodation" in this section.

The definition adds "individual" to the statutory definition of private entity (see section 301(6) of the ADA). This addition clarifies that an individual may be a private entity and, therefore, may be considered a public accommodation if he or she owns, leases (or leases to), or operates a place of public accommodation. The explicit inclusion of individuals under the definition of private entity is consistent with section 302(a) of the ADA, which broadly prohibits discrimination on the basis of disability by any person who owns, leases (or leases to), or operates a place of public accommodation.

"Public accommodation." The term "public accommodation" means a private entity that owns, leases (or leases to), or operates a place of public accommodation. The regulatory term, "public accommodation," corresponds to the statutory term, "person," in section 302(a) of the ADA. The ADA prohibits discrimination "by any person who owns, leases (or leases to), or operates a place of public accommodation." The text of the regulation consequently places the ADA's nondiscrimination obligations on "public accommodations" rather than on "persons" or on "places of public accommodation."

As stated in § 36.102(b)(2), the requirements of subparts B and C obligate a public accommodation only with respect to the operations of a place of public accommodation. A public accommodation must also meet the requirements of subpart D with respect to facilities used as, or designed or constructed for use as, places of public accommodation or commercial facilities.

"Public entity." The term "public entity" is defined in accordance with section 201(1) of the ADA as any State or local government; any department, agency, special purpose district, or other instrumentality of a State or States or local government; and the National Railroad Passenger Corporation, and any commuter authority (as defined in section 103(8) of the Rail Passenger Service Act). It is used in the definition of "private entity" in § 36.104. Public entities are excluded from the definition of private entity and therefore cannot qualify as public accommodations under this regulation. However, the actions of public entities are covered by title II of the ADA and by the Department's title II regulations codified at 28 CFR part 35.

"Qualified interpreter." The Department received substantial comment regarding the lack of a definition of "qualified interpreter." The proposed rule defined auxiliary aids and services to include the statutory term, "qualified interpreters" (§ 36.303(b)), but did not define that term. Section 36.303 requires the use of a qualified interpreter where necessary to achieve effective communication, unless an undue burden or fundamental alteration would result. Commenters stated that a lack of guidance on what the term means would create confusion among those trying to secure interpreting services and often result in less than effective communication.

Many commenters were concerned that, without clear guidance on the issue of "qualified" interpreter, the rule would be interpreted to mean "available, rather than qualified" interpreters. Some claimed that few public accommodations would understand the difference between a qualified interpreter and a person who simply knows a few signs or how to fingerspell.

In order to clarify what is meant by "qualified interpreter" the Department has added a definition of the term to the final rule. A qualified interpreter means an interpreter who is able to interpret effectively, accurately, and impartially both receptively and expressively, using any necessary specialized vocabulary. This definition focuses on the actual ability of the interpreter in a particular interpreting context to facilitate effective communication between the public accommodation and the individual with disabilities.

Public comment also revealed that public accommodations have at times asked persons who are deaf to provide family members or friends to interpret. In certain circumstances, notwithstanding that the family member or friend is able to interpret or is a certified interpreter, the family member or friend may not be qualified to render the necessary interpretation because of factors such as emotional or personal involvement or considerations of confidentiality that may adversely affect the ability to interpret "effectively, accurately, and impartially."

"Readily achievable." The definition of "readily achievable" follows the statutory definition of that term in section 301(9) of the ADA. Readily achievable means easily accomplishable and able to be carried out without much difficulty or expense. The term is used as a limitation on the obligation to remove barriers under §§ 36.304(a), 36.305(a), 36.308(a), and 36.310(b). Further discussion of the meaning and application of the term "readily achievable" may be found in the preamble section for § 36.304.

The definition lists factors to be considered in determining whether barrier removal is readily achievable in any particular circumstance. A significant number of commenters objected to § 36.306 of the proposed rule, which listed identical factors to be considered for determining "readily achievable" and "undue burden" together in one section. They asserted that providing a consolidated section blurred the distinction between the level of effort required by a public accommodation under the two standards. The readily achievable standard is a "lower" standard than the "undue burden" standard in terms of the level of effort required, but the factors used in determining whether an action is readily achievable or would result in an undue burden are identical (See Education and Labor report at 109). Although the preamble to the proposed rule clearly delineated the relationship between the two standards, to eliminate any confusion the Department has deleted § 36.306 of the proposed rule. That section, in any event, as other commenters noted, had merely repeated the lists of factors contained in the definitions of readily achievable and undue burden.

The list of factors included in the definition is derived from section 301(9) of the ADA. It reflects the congressional intention that a wide range of factors be considered in determining whether an action is readily achievable. It also takes into account that many local facilities are owned or operated by parent corporations or entities that conduct operations at many different sites. This section makes clear that, in some instances, resources beyond those of the local facility where the barrier must be removed may be relevant in determining whether an action is readily achievable. One must also evaluate the degree to which any parent entity has resources that may be allocated to the local facility.

The statutory list of factors in section 301(9) of the Act uses the term "covered entity" to refer to the larger entity of which a particular facility may be a part. "Covered entity" is not a defined term in the ADA and is not used consistently throughout the Act. The definition, therefore, substitutes the term "parent entity" in place of "covered entity" in paragraphs (3), (4), and (5) when referring to the larger private entity whose overall resources may be taken into account. This usage is consistent with the House Judiciary Committee's use of the term "parent company" to describe the larger entity of which the local facility is a part (H.R. Rep. No. 485, 101st Cong., 2d Sess., pt. 3, at 40-41, 54-55 (1990) (hereinafter "Judiciary report")).

A number of commenters asked for more specific guidance as to when and how the resources of a parent corporation or entity are to be taken into account in determining what is readily achievable. The Department believes that this complex issue is most appropriately resolved on a case-by-case basis. As the comments reflect, there is a wide variety of possible relationships between the site in question and any parent corporation or other entity. It would be unwise to posit legal ramifications under the ADA of even generic relationships (e.g., banks involved in foreclosures or insurance companies operating as trustees or in other similar fiduciary relationships), because any analysis will depend so completely on the detailed fact situations and the exact nature of the legal relationships involved. The final rule does, however, reorder the factors to be considered. This shift and the addition of the phrase "if applicable" make clear that the line of inquiry concerning factors will start at the site involved in the action itself. This change emphasizes that the overall resources, size, and operations of the parent corporation or entity should be considered to the extent appropriate in light of "the geographic separateness, and the administrative or fiscal relationship of the site or sites in question to any parent corporation or entity."

Although some commenters sought more specific numerical guidance on the definition of readily achievable, the Department has declined to establish in the final rule any kind of numerical formula for determining whether an action is readily achievable. It would be difficult to devise a specific ceiling on compliance costs that would take into account the vast diversity of enterprises covered by the ADA's public accommodations requirements and the economic situation that any particular entity would find itself in at any moment. The final rule, therefore, implements the flexible case-by-case approach chosen by Congress.

A number of commenters requested that security considerations be explicitly recognized as a factor in determining whether a barrier removal action is readily achievable. The Department believes that legitimate safety requirements, including crime prevention measures, may be taken into account so long as they are based on actual risks and are necessary for safe operation of the public accommodation. This point has been included in the definition.

Some commenters urged the Department not to consider acts of barrier removal in complete isolation from each other in determining whether they are readily achievable. The Department believes that it is appropriate to consider the cost of other barrier removal actions as one factor in determining whether a measure is readily achievable.

"Religious entity." The term "religious entity" is defined in accordance with section 307 of the ADA as a religious organization or entity controlled by a religious organization, including a place of worship. Section 36.102(e) of the rule states that the rule does not apply to any religious entity.

The ADA's exemption of religious organizations and religious entities controlled by religious organizations is very broad, encompassing a wide variety of situations. Religious organizations and entities controlled by religious organizations have no obligations under the ADA. Even when a religious organization carries out activities that would otherwise make it a public accommodation, the religious organization is exempt from ADA coverage. Thus, if a church itself operates a day care center, a nursing home, a private school, or a diocesan school system, the operations of the center, home, school, or schools would not be subject to the requirements of the ADA or this part. The religious entity would not lose its exemption merely because the services provided were open to the general public. The test is whether the church or other religious organization operates the public accommodation, not which individuals receive the public accommodation's services.

Religious entities that are controlled by religious organizations are also exempt from the ADA's requirements. Many religious organizations in the United States use lay boards and other secular or corporate mechanisms to operate schools and an array of social services. The use of a lay board or other mechanism does not itself remove the ADA's religious exemption. Thus, a parochial school, having religious doctrine in its curriculum and sponsored by a religious order, could be exempt either as a religious organization or as an entity controlled by a religious organization, even if it has a lay board. The test remains a factual one—whether the church or other religious organization controls the operations of the school or of the service or whether the school or service is itself a religious organization.

Although a religious organization or a religious entity that is controlled by a religious organization has no obligations under the rule, a public accommodation that is not itself a religious organization, but that operates a place of public accommodation in leased space on the property of a religious entity, which is not a place of worship, is subject to the rule's requirements if it is not under control of a religious organization. When a church rents meeting space, which is not a place of worship, to a local community group or to a private, independent day care center, the ADA applies to the activities of the local community group and day care center if a lease exists and consideration is paid.

"Service animal." The term "service animal" encompasses any guide dog, signal dog, or other animal individually trained to provide assistance to an individual with a disability. The term is used in § 36.302(c), which requires public accommodations generally to modify policies, practices, and procedures to accommodate the use of service animals in places of public accommodation.

"Specified public transportation." The definition of "specified public transportation" is identical to the statutory definition in section 301(10) of the ADA. The term means transportation by bus, rail, or any other conveyance (other than by aircraft) that provides the general public with general or special service (including charter service) on a regular and continuing basis. It is used in category (7) of the definition of "place of public accommodation," which includes stations used for specified public transportation.

The effect of this definition, which excludes transportation by aircraft, is that it excludes privately operated airports from coverage as places of public accommodation. However, places of public accommodation located within airports would be covered by this part. Airports that are operated by public entities are covered by title II of the ADA and, if they are operated as part of a program receiving Federal financial assistance, by section 504 of the Rehabilitation Act. Privately operated airports are similarly covered by section 504 if they are operated as part of a program receiving Federal financial assistance. The operations of any portion of any airport that are under the control of an air carrier are covered by the Air Carrier Access Act. In addition, airports are covered as commercial facilities under this rule.

"State." The definition of "State" is identical to the statutory definition in section 3(3) of the ADA. The term is used in the definitions of "commerce" and "public entity" in § 36.104.

"Undue burden." The definition of "undue burden" is analogous to the statutory definition of "undue hardship" in employment under section 101(10) of the ADA. The term undue burden means "significant difficulty or expense" and serves as a limitation on the obligation to provide auxiliary aids and services under § 36.303 and §§ 36.309 (b)(3) and (c)(3). Further discussion of the meaning and application of the term undue burden may be found in the preamble discussion of § 36.303.

The definition lists factors considered in determining whether provision of an auxiliary aid or service in any particular circumstance would result in an undue burden. The factors to be considered in determining whether an action would result in an undue burden are identical to those to be considered in determining whether an action is readily achievable. However, "readily achievable" is a lower standard than "undue burden" in that it requires a lower level of effort on the part of the public accommodation (see Education and Labor report at 109).

Further analysis of the factors to be considered in determining undue burden may be found in the preamble discussion of the definition of the term "readily achievable."

Subpart B—General Requirements

Subpart B includes general prohibitions restricting a public accommodation from discriminating against people with disabilities by denying them the opportunity to benefit from goods or services, by giving them unequal goods or services, or by giving them different or separate goods or services. These general prohibitions are patterned after the basic, general prohibitions that exist in other civil rights laws that prohibit discrimination on the basis of race, sex, color, religion, or national origin.

Section 36.201 General

Section 36.201(a) contains the general rule that prohibits discrimination on the basis of disability in the full and equal enjoyment of goods, services, facilities, privileges, advantages, and accommodations of any place of public accommodation.

Full and equal enjoyment means the right to participate and to have an equal opportunity to obtain the same results as others to the extent possible with such accommodations as may be required by the Act and these regulations. It does not mean that an individual with a disability must achieve an identical result or level of achievement as persons without a disability. For example, an exercise class cannot exclude a person who uses a wheelchair because he or she cannot do all of the exercises and derive the same result from the class as persons without a disability.

Section 302(a) of the ADA states that the prohibition against discrimination applies to "any person who owns, leases (or leases to), or operates a place of public accommodation," and this language is reflected in § 36.201(a). The coverage is quite extensive and would include sublessees, management companies, and any other entity that owns, leases, leases to, or operates a place of public accommodation, even if the operation is only for a short time.

The first sentence of paragraph (b) of § 36.201 reiterates the general principle that both the landlord that owns the building that houses the place of public accommodation, as well as the tenant that owns or operates the place of public accommodation, are public accommodations subject to the requirements of this part. Although the statutory language could be interpreted as placing equal responsibility on all private entities, whether lessor, lessee, or operator of a public accommodation, the committee reports suggest that liability may be allocated. Section 36.201(b) of that section of the proposed rule attempted to allocate liability in the regulation itself. Paragraph (b)(2) of that section made a specific allocation of liability for the obligation to take readily achievable measures to remove barriers, and paragraph (b)(3) made a specific allocation for the obligation to provide auxiliary aids.

Numerous commenters pointed out that these allocations would not apply in all situations. Some asserted that paragraph (b)(2) of the proposed rule only addressed the situation when a lease gave the tenant the right to make alterations with permission of the landlord, but failed to address other types of leases, e.g., those that are silent on the right to make alterations, or those in which the landlord is not permitted to enter a tenant's premises to make alterations. Several commenters noted that many leases contain other clauses more relevant to the ADA than the alterations clause. For example, many leases contain a "compliance clause," a clause which allocates responsibility to a particular party for compliance with all relevant Federal, State, and local laws. Many commenters pointed out various types of relationships that were left unaddressed by the regulation, e.g., sale and leaseback arrangements where the landlord is a financial institution with no control or responsibility for the building; franchises; subleases; and management companies which, at least in the hotel industry, often have control over operations but are unable to make modifications to the premises.

Some commenters raised specific questions as to how the barrier removal allocation would work as a practical matter. Paragraph (b)(2) of the proposed rule provided that the burden of making readily achievable modifications within the tenant's place of public accommodation would shift to the landlord when the modifications were not readily achievable for the tenant or when the landlord denied a tenant's request for permission to make such modifications. Commenters noted that the rule did not specify exactly when the burden would actually shift from tenant to landlord and whether the landlord would have to accept a tenant's word that a particular action is not readily achievable. Others questioned if the tenant should be obligated to use alternative methods of barrier removal before the burden shifts. In light of the fact that readily achievable removal of barriers can include such actions as moving of racks and displays, some commenters doubted the appropriateness of requiring a landlord to become involved in day-to-day operations of its tenants' businesses.

The Department received widely differing comments in response to the preamble question asking whether landlord and tenant obligations should vary depending on the length of time remaining on an existing lease. Many suggested that tenants should have no responsibilities in "shorter leases," which commenters defined as ranging anywhere from 90 days to three years. Other commenters pointed out that the time remaining on the lease should not be a factor in the rule's allocation of responsibilities, but is relevant in determining what is readily achievable for the tenant. The Department agrees with this latter approach and will interpret the rule in that manner.

In recognition of the somewhat limited applicability of the allocation scheme contained in the proposed rule, paragraphs (b)(2) and (b)(3) have been deleted from the final rule. The Department has substituted instead a statement that allocation of responsibility as between the parties for taking readily achievable measures to remove barriers and to provide auxiliary aids and services both in common areas and within places of public accommodation may be determined by the lease or other contractual relationships between the parties. The ADA was not intended to change existing landlord/tenant responsibilities as set forth in the lease. By deleting specific provisions from the rule, the Department gives full recognition to this principle. As between the landlord and tenant, the extent of responsibility for particular obligations may be, and in many cases probably will be, determined by contract.

The suggested allocation of responsibilities contained in the proposed rule may be used if appropriate in a particular situation. Thus, the landlord would generally be held responsible for making readily achievable changes and providing auxiliary aids and services in common areas and for modifying policies, practices, or procedures applicable to all tenants, and the tenant would generally be responsible for readily achievable changes, provision of auxiliary aids, and modification of policies within its own place of public accommodation.

Many commenters objected to the proposed rule's allocation of responsibility for providing auxiliary aids and services solely to the tenant, pointing out that this exclusive allocation may not be appropriate in the case of larger public accommodations that operate their businesses by renting space out to smaller public accommodations. For example, large theaters often rent to smaller traveling companies and hospitals often rely on independent contractors to provide childbirth classes. Groups representing persons with disabilities objected to the proposed rule because, in their view, it permitted the large theater or hospital to evade ADA responsibilities by leasing to independent smaller entities. They suggested that these types of public accommodations are not really landlords because they are in the business of providing a service, rather than renting space, as in the case of a shopping center or office building landlord. These commenters believed that responsibility for providing auxiliary aids should shift to the landlord, if the landlord relies on a smaller public accommodation or independent contractor to provide services closely related to those of the larger public accommodation, and if the needed auxiliary aids prove to be an undue burden for the smaller public accommodation. The final rule no longer lists specific allocations to specific parties but, rather, leaves allocation of responsibilities to the lease negotiations. Parties are, therefore, free to allocate the responsibility for auxiliary aids.

Section 36.201(b)(4) of the proposed rule, which provided that alterations by a tenant on its own premises do not trigger a path of travel obligation on the landlord, has been moved to § 36.403(d) of the final rule.

An entity that is not in and of itself a public accommodation, such as a trade association or performing artist, may become a public accommodation when it leases space for a conference or performance at a hotel, convention center, or stadium. For an entity to become a public accommodation when it is the lessee of space, however, the Department believes that consideration in some form must be given. Thus, a Boy Scout troop that accepts donated space does not become a public accommodation because the troop has not "leased" space, as required by the ADA.

As a public accommodation, the trade association or performing artist will be responsible for compliance with this part. Specific responsibilities should be allocated by contract, but, generally, the lessee should be responsible for providing auxiliary aids and services (which could include interpreters, Braille programs, etc.) for the participants in its conference or performance as well as for assuring that displays are accessible to individuals with disabilities.

Some commenters suggested that the rule should allocate responsibilities for areas other than removal of barriers and auxiliary aids. The final rule leaves allocation of all areas to the lease negotiations. However, in general landlords should not be given responsibility for policies a tenant applies in operating its business, if such policies are solely those of the tenant. Thus, if a restaurant tenant discriminates by refusing to seat a patron, it would be the tenant, and not the landlord, who would be responsible, because the discriminatory policy is imposed solely by the tenant and not by the landlord. If, however, a tenant refuses to modify a "no pets" rule to allow service animals in its restaurant because the landlord mandates such a rule, then both the landlord and the tenant would be liable for violation of the ADA when a person with a service dog is refused entrance. The Department wishes to emphasize, however, that the parties are free to allocate responsibilities in any way they choose.

Private clubs are also exempt from the ADA. However, consistent with title II of the Civil Rights Act (42 U.S.C. 2000a(e), a private club is considered a public accommodation to the extent that "the facilities of such establishment are made available to the customers or patrons" of a place of public accommodation. Thus, if a private club runs a day care center that is open exclusively to its own members, the club, like the church in the example above, would have no responsibility for compliance with the ADA. Nor would the day care center have any responsibilities because it is part of the private club exempt from the ADA.

On the other hand, if the private club rents to a day care center that is open to the public, then the private club would have the same obligations as any other public accommodation that functions as a landlord with respect to compliance with title III within the day care center. In such a situation, both the private club that "leases to" a public accommodation and the public accommodation lessee (the day care center) would be subject to the ADA. This same principle would apply if the private club were to rent to, for example, a bar association, which is not generally a public accommodation but which, as explained above, becomes a public accommodation when it leases space for a conference.

Section 36.202 Activities

Section 36.202 sets out the general forms of discrimination prohibited by title III of the ADA. These general prohibitions are further refined by the specific prohibitions in subpart C. Section 36.213 makes clear that the limitations on the ADA's requirements contained in subpart C, such as "necessity" (§ 36.301(a)) and "safety" (§ 36.301(b)), are applicable to the prohibitions in § 36.202. Thus, it is unnecessary to add these limitations to § 36.202 as has been requested by some commenters. In addition, the language of § 36.202 very closely tracks the language of section 302(b)(1)(A) of the Act, and that statutory provision does not expressly contain these limitations.

Deny participation—Section 36.202(a) provides that it is discriminatory to deny a person with a disability the right to participate in or benefit from the goods, services, facilities, privileges, advantages, or accommodations of a place of public accommodation.

A public accommodation may not exclude persons with disabilities on the basis of disability for reasons other than those specifically set forth in this part. For example, a public accommodation cannot refuse to serve a person with a disability because its insurance company conditions coverage or rates on the absence of persons with disabilities. This is a frequent basis of exclusion from a variety of community activities and is prohibited by this part.

Unequal benefit—Section 36.202(b) prohibits services or accommodations that are not equal to those provided others. For example, persons with disabilities must not be limited to certain performances at a theater.

Separate benefit—Section 36.202(c) permits different or separate benefits or services only when necessary to provide persons with disabilities opportunities as effective as those provided others. This paragraph permitting separate benefits "when necessary" should be read together with § 36.203(a), which requires integration in "the most integrated setting appropriate to the needs of the individual." The preamble to that section provides further guidance on separate programs. Thus, this section would not prohibit the designation of parking spaces for persons with disabilities.

Each of the three paragraphs (a)-(c) prohibits discrimination against an individual or class of individuals "either directly or through contractual, licensing, or other arrangements." The intent of the contractual prohibitions of these paragraphs is to prohibit a public accommodation from doing indirectly, through a contractual relationship, what it may not do directly. Thus, the "individual or class of individuals" referenced in the three paragraphs is intended to refer to the clients and customers of the public accommodation that entered into a contractual arrangement. It is not intended to encompass the clients or customers of other entities. A public accommodation, therefore, is not liable under this provision for discrimination that may be practiced by those with whom it has a contractual relationship, when that discrimination is not directed against its own clients or customers. For example, if an amusement park contracts with a food service company to operate its restaurants at the park, the amusement park is not responsible for other operations of the food service company that do not involve clients or customers of the amusement park. Section 36.202(d) makes this clear by providing that the term "individual or class of individuals" refers to the clients or customers of the public accommodation that enters into the contractual, licensing, or other arrangement.

Section 36.203 Integrated Settings

Section 36.203 addresses the integration of persons with disabilities. The ADA recognizes that the provision of goods and services in an integrated manner is a fundamental tenet of nondiscrimination on the basis of disability. Providing segregated accommodations and services relegates persons with disabilities to the status of second-class citizens. For example, it would be a violation of this provision to require persons with mental disabilities to eat in the back room of a restaurant or to refuse to allow a person with a disability the full use of a health spa because of stereotypes about the person's ability to participate. Section 36.203(a) states that a public accommodation shall afford goods, services, facilities, privileges, advantages, and accommodations to an individual with a disability in the most integrated setting appropriate to the needs of the individual. Section 36.203(b) specifies that, notwithstanding the existence of separate or different programs or activities provided in accordance with this section, an individual with a disability shall not be denied the opportunity to participate in such programs or activities that are not separate or different. Section

306.203(c), which is derived from section 501(d) of the Americans with Disabilities Act, states that nothing in this part shall be construed to require an individual with a disability to accept an accommodation, aid, service, opportunity, or benefit that he or she chooses not to accept.

Taken together, these provisions are intended to prohibit exclusion and segregation of individuals with disabilities and the denial of equal opportunities enjoyed by others, based on, among other things, presumptions, patronizing attitudes, fears, and stereotypes about individuals with disabilities. Consistent with these standards, public accommodations are required to make decisions based on facts applicable to individuals and not on the basis of presumptions as to what a class of individuals with disabilities can or cannot do.

Sections 36.203 (b) and (c) make clear that individuals with disabilities cannot be denied the opportunity to participate in programs that are not separate or different. This is an important and overarching principle of the Americans with Disabilities Act. Separate, special, or different programs that are designed to provide a benefit to persons with disabilities cannot be used to restrict the participation of persons with disabilities in general, integrated activities.

For example, a person who is blind may wish to decline participating in a special museum tour that allows persons to touch sculptures in an exhibit and instead tour the exhibit at his or her own pace with the museum's recorded tour. It is not the intent of this section to require the person who is blind to avail himself or herself of the special tour. Modified participation for persons with disabilities must be a choice, not a requirement.

Further, it would not be a violation of this section for an establishment to offer recreational programs specially designed for children with mobility impairments in those limited circumstances. However, it would be a violation of this section if the entity then excluded these children from other recreational services made available to nondisabled children, or required children with disabilities to attend only designated programs.

Many commenters asked that the Department clarify a public accommodation's obligations within the integrated program when it offers a separate program, but an individual with a disability chooses not to participate in the separate program. It is impossible to make a blanket statement as to what level of auxiliary aids or modifications are required in the integrated program. Rather, each situation must be assessed individually. Assuming the integrated program would be appropriate for a particular individual, the extent to which that individual must be provided with modifications will depend not only on what the individual needs but also on the limitations set forth in subpart C. For example, it may constitute an undue burden for a particular public accommodation, which provides a full-time interpreter in its special guided tour for individuals with hearing impairments, to hire an additional interpreter for those individuals who choose to attend the integrated program. The Department cannot identify categorically the level of assistance or aid required in the integrated program.

The preamble to the proposed rule contained a statement that some interpreted as encouraging the continuation of separate schools, sheltered workshops, special recreational programs, and other similar programs. It is important to emphasize that § 36.202(c) only calls for separate programs when such programs are "necessary" to provide as effective an opportunity to individuals with disabilities as to other individuals. Likewise, § 36.203(a) only permits separate programs when a more integrated setting would not be "appropriate." Separate programs are permitted, then, in only limited circumstances. The sentence at issue has been deleted from the preamble because it was too broadly stated and had been erroneously interpreted as Departmental encouragement of separate programs without qualification.

The proposed rule's reference in § 36.203(b) to separate programs or activities provided in accordance with "this section" has been changed to "this subpart" in recognition of the fact that separate programs or activities may, in some limited circumstances, be permitted not only by § 36.203(a) but also by § 36.202(c).

In addition, some commenters suggested that the individual with the disability is the only one who can decide whether a setting is "appropriate" and what the "needs" are. Others suggested that only the public accommodation can make these determinations. The regulation does not give exclusive responsibility to either party. Rather, the determinations are to be made based on an objective view, presumably one which would take into account views of both parties.

Some commenters expressed concern that § 36.203(c), which states that nothing in the rule requires an individual with a disability to accept special accommodations and services provided under the ADA, could be interpreted to allow guardians of infants or older people with disabilities to refuse medical treatment for their wards. Section 36.203(c) has been revised to make it clear that paragraph (c) is inapplicable to the concern of the commenters. A new paragraph (c)(2) has been added stating that nothing in the regulation authorizes the representative or guardian of an individual with a disability to decline food, water, medical treatment, or medical services for that individual. New paragraph (c) clarifies that neither the ADA nor the regulation alters current Federal law ensuring the rights of incompetent individuals with disabilities to receive food, water, and medical treatment. See, e.g., Child Abuse Amendments of 1984 (42 U.S.C. 5106a(b)(10), 5106g(10)); Rehabilitation Act of 1973, as amended (29 U.S.C 794); Developmentally Disabled Assistance and Bill of Rights Act (42 U.S.C. 6042).

Sections 36.203(c) (1) and (2) are based on section 501(d) of the ADA. Section § 501(d) was designed to clarify that nothing in the ADA requires individuals with disabilities to accept special accommodations and services for individuals with disabilities that may segregate them:

> The Committee added this section (501(d)) to clarify that nothing in the ADA is intended to permit discriminatory treatment on the basis of disability, even when such treatment is rendered under the guise of providing an accommodation, service, aid or benefit to the individual with disability. For example, a blind individual may choose not to avail himself or herself of the right to go to the front of a line, even if a particular public accommodation has chosen to offer such a modification of a policy for blind individuals. Or, a blind individual may choose to decline to participate in a special museum tour that allows persons to touch sculptures in an exhibit and instead tour the exhibits at his or her own pace with the museum's recorded tour.

(Judiciary report at 71-72.) The Act is not to be construed to mean that an individual with disabilities must accept special accommodations and services for individuals with disabilities when that individual chooses to participate in the regular services already offered. Because medical treatment, including treatment for particular conditions, is not a special accommodation or service for individuals with disabilities under section 501(d), neither the Act nor this part provides affirmative authority to suspend such treatment. Section 501(d) is intended to clarify that the Act is not designed to foster discrimination through mandatory acceptance of special services when other alternatives are provided; this concern does not reach to the provision of medical treatment for the disabling condition itself.

Section 36.213 makes clear that the limitations contained in subpart C are to be read into subpart B. Thus, the integration requirement is subject to the various defenses contained in subpart C, such as safety, if eligibility criteria are at issue (§ 36.301(b)), or fundamental alteration and undue burden, if the concern is provision of auxiliary aids (§ 36.303(a)).

Section 36.204 Administrative Methods

Section 36.204 specifies that an individual or entity shall not, directly, or through contractual or other arrangements, utilize standards or criteria or methods of administration that have the effect of discriminating on the basis of disability or that perpetuate the discrimination of others who are subject to common administrative control. The preamble discussion of § 36.301 addresses eligibility criteria in detail.

Section 36.204 is derived from section 302(b)(1)(D) of the Americans with Disabilities Act, and it uses the same language used in the employment section of the ADA (section 102(b)(3)). Both sections incorporate a disparate impact standard to ensure the effectiveness of the legislative mandate to end discrimination. This standard is consistent with the interpretation of section 504 by the U.S. Supreme Court in *Alexander v. Choate*, 469 U.S. 287 (1985). The Court in *Choate* explained that members of Congress made numerous statements during passage of section 504 regarding eliminating architectural barriers, providing access to transportation, and eliminating discriminatory effects of job qualification procedures. The Court then noted: "These statements would ring hollow if the resulting legislation could not rectify the harms resulting from action that discriminated by effect as well as by design." *Id* at 297 (footnote omitted).

Of course, § 36.204 is subject to the various limitations contained in subpart C including, for example, necessity (§ 36.301(a)), safety (§ 36.301(b)), fundamental alteration (§ 36.302(a)), readily achievable (§ 36.304(a)), and undue burden (§ 36.303(a)).

Section 36.205 Association

Section 36.205 implements section 302(b)(1)(E) of the Act, which provides that a public accommodation shall not exclude or otherwise deny equal goods, services, facilities, privileges, advantages, accommodations, or other opportunities to an individual or entity because of the known disability of an individual with whom the individual or entity is known to have a relationship or association. This section is unchanged from the proposed rule.

The individuals covered under this section include any individuals who are discriminated against because of their known association with an individual with a disability. For example, it would be a violation of this part for a day care center to refuse admission to a child because his or her brother has HIV disease.

This protection is not limited to those who have a familial relationship with the individual who has a disability. If a place of public accommodation refuses admission to a person with cerebral palsy and his or her companions, the companions have an independent right of action under the ADA and this section.

During the legislative process, the term "entity" was added to section 302(b)(1)(E) to clarify that the scope of the provision is intended to encompass not only persons who have a known association with a person with a disability, but also entities that provide services to or are otherwise associated with such individuals. This provision was intended to ensure that entities such as health care providers, employees of social service agencies, and others who provide professional services to persons with disabilities are not subjected to discrimination because of their professional association with persons with disabilities. For example, it would be a violation of this section to terminate the lease of a entity operating an independent living center for persons with disabilities, or to seek to evict a health care provider because that individual or entity provides services to persons with mental impairments.

Section 36.206 Retaliation or Coercion

Section 36.206 implements section 503 of the ADA, which prohibits retaliation against any individual who exercises his or her rights under the Act. This section is unchanged from the proposed rule. Paragraph (a) of § 36.206 provides that no private entity or public entity shall discriminate against any individual because that individual has exercised his or her right to oppose any act or practice made unlawful by this part, or because that individual made a charge, testified, assisted, or participated in any manner in an investigation, proceeding, or hearing under the Act or this part.

Paragraph (b) provides that no private entity or public entity shall coerce, intimidate, threaten, or interfere with any individual in the exercise of his or her rights under this part or because that individual aided or encouraged any other individual in the exercise or enjoyment of any right granted or protected by the Act or this part.

Illustrations of practices prohibited by this section are contained in paragraph (c), which is modeled on a similar provision in the regulations issued by the Department of Housing and Urban Development to implement the Fair Housing Act (see 24 CFR 100.400(c)(l)). Prohibited actions may include:

(1) Coercing an individual to deny or limit the benefits, services, or advantages to which he or she is entitled under the Act or this part;

(2) Threatening, intimidating, or interfering with an individual who is seeking to obtain or use the goods, services, facilities, privileges, advantages, or accommodations of a public accommodation;

(3) Intimidating or threatening any person because that person is assisting or encouraging an individual or group entitled to claim the rights granted or protected by the Act or this part to exercise those rights; or

(4) Retaliating against any person because that person has participated in any investigation or action to enforce the Act or this part.

This section protects not only individuals who allege a violation of the Act or this part, but also any individuals who support or assist them. This section applies to all investigations or proceedings initiated under the Act or this part without regard to the ultimate resolution of the underlying allegations. Because this section prohibits any act of retaliation or coercion in response to an individual's effort to exercise rights established by the Act and this part (or to support the efforts of another individual), the section applies not only to public accommodations that are otherwise subject to this part, but also to individuals other than public accommodations or to public entities. For example, it would be a violation of the Act and this part for a private individual, e.g., a restaurant customer, to harass or intimidate an individual with a disability in an effort to prevent that individual from patronizing the restaurant. It would, likewise, be a violation of the Act and this part for a public entity to take adverse action against an employee who appeared as a witness on behalf of an individual who sought to enforce the Act.

Section 36.207 Places of Public Accommodation Located in Private Residences

A private home used exclusively as a residence is not covered by title III because it is neither a "commercial facility" nor a "place of public accommodation." In some situations, however, a private home is not used exclusively as a residence, but houses a place of public accommodation in all or part of a home (e.g., an accountant who meets with his or her clients at his or her residence). Section 36.207(a) provides that those portions of the private residence used in the operation of the place of public accommodation are covered by this part.

For instance, a home or a portion of a home may be

used as a day care center during the day and a residence at night. If all parts of the house are used for the day care center, then the entire residence is a place of public accommodation because no part of the house is used exclusively as a residence. If an accountant uses one room in the house solely as his or her professional office, then a portion of the house is used exclusively as a place of public accommodation and a portion is used exclusively as a residence. Section 36.207 provides that when a portion of a residence is used exclusively as a residence, that portion is not covered by this part. Thus, the portions of the accountant's house, other than the professional office and areas and spaces leading to it, are not covered by this part. All of the requirements of this rule apply to the covered portions, including requirements to make reasonable modifications in policies, eliminate discriminatory eligibility criteria, take readily achievable measures to remove barriers or provide readily achievable alternatives (e.g., making house calls), provide auxiliary aids and services and undertake only accessible new construction and alterations.

Paragraph (b) was added in response to comments that sought clarification on the extent of coverage of the private residence used as the place of public accommodation. The final rule makes clear that the place of accommodation extends to all areas of the home used by clients and customers of the place of public accommodation. Thus, the ADA would apply to any door or entry way, hallways, a restroom, if used by customers and clients; and any other portion of the residence, interior or exterior, used by customers or clients of the public accommodation. This interpretation is simply an application of the general rule for all public accommodations, which extends statutory requirements to all portions of the facility used by customers and clients, including, if applicable, restrooms, hallways, and approaches to the public accommodation. As with other public accommodations, barriers at the entrance and on the sidewalk leading up to the public accommodation, if the sidewalk is under the control of the public accommodation, must be removed if doing so is readily achievable.

The Department recognizes that many businesses that operate out of personal residences are quite small, often employing only the homeowner and having limited total revenues. In these circumstances the effect of ADA coverage would likely be quite minimal. For example, because the obligation to remove existing architectural barriers is limited to those that are easily accomplishable without much difficulty or expense (see § 36.304), the range of required actions would be quite modest. It might not be readily achievable for such a place of public accommodation to remove any existing barriers. If it is not readily achievable to remove existing architectural barriers, a public accommodation located in a private residence may meet its obligations under the Act and this part by providing its goods or services to clients or customers with disabilities through the use of alternative measures, including delivery of goods or services in the home of the customer or client, to the extent that such alternative measures are readily achievable (See § 36.305).

Some commenters asked for clarification as to how the new construction and alteration standards of subpart D will apply to residences. The new construction standards only apply to the extent that the residence or portion of the residence was designed or intended for use as a public accommodation. Thus, for example, if a portion of a home is designed or constructed for use exclusively as a lawyer's office or for use both as a lawyer's office and for residential purposes, then it must be designed in accordance with the new construction standards in the appendix. Likewise, if a homeowner is undertaking alterations to convert all or part of his residence to a place of public accommodation, that work must be done in compliance with the alterations standards in the appendix.

The preamble to the proposed rule addressed the applicable requirements when a commercial facility is located in a private residence. That situation is now addressed in § 36.401(b) of subpart D.

Section 36.208 Direct Threat

Section 36.208(a) implements section 302(b)(3) of the Act by providing that this part does not require a public accommodation to permit an individual to participate in or benefit from the goods, services, facilities, privileges, advantages and accommodations of the public accommodation, if that individual poses a direct threat to the health or safety of others. This section is unchanged from the proposed rule.

The Department received a significant number of comments on this section. Commenters representing individuals with disabilities generally supported this provision, but suggested revisions to further limit its application. Commenters representing public accommodations generally endorsed modifications that would permit a public accommodation to exercise its own judgment in determining whether an individual poses a direct threat.

The inclusion of this provision is not intended to imply that persons with disabilities pose risks to others. It is intended to address concerns that may arise in this area. It establishes a strict standard that must be met before denying service to an individual with a disability or excluding that individual from participation.

Paragraph (b) of this section explains that a "direct threat" is a significant risk to the health or safety of others that cannot be eliminated by a modification of policies, practices, or procedures, or by the provision of auxiliary aids and services. This paragraph codifies the standard first applied by the Supreme Court in *School Board of Nassau County v. Arline*, 480 U.S. 273 (1987), in which the Court held that an individual with a contagious disease may be an "individual with handicaps" under section 504 of the Rehabilitation Act. In *Arline,* the Supreme Court recognized that there is a need to balance the interests of people with disabilities against legitimate concerns for public safety. Although persons with disabilities are generally entitled to the protection of this part, a person who poses a significant risk to others may be excluded if reasonable modifications to the public accommodation's policies, practices, or procedures will not eliminate that risk. The determination that a person poses a direct threat to the health or safety of others may not be based on generalizations or stereotypes about the effects of a particular disability; it must be based on an individual assessment that conforms to the requirements of paragraph (c) of this section.

Paragraph (c) establishes the test to use in determining whether an individual poses a direct threat to the health or safety of others. A public accommodation is required to make an individualized assessment, based on reasonable judgment that relies on current medical evidence or on the best available objective evidence, to determine: The nature, duration, and severity of the risk; the probability that the potential injury will actually occur; and whether reasonable modifications of policies, practices, or procedures will mitigate the risk. This is the test established by the Supreme Court in *Arline.* Such an inquiry is essential if the law is to achieve its goal of protecting disabled individuals from discrimination based on prejudice, stereotypes, or unfounded fear, while giving appropriate weight to legitimate concerns, such as the need to avoid exposing others to significant health and safety risks. Making this assessment will not usually require the services of a physician. Sources for medical knowledge include guidance from public health authorities, such as the U.S. Public Health Service, the Centers for Disease Control, and the National Institutes of Health, including the National Institute of Mental Health.

Many of the commenters sought clarification of the inquiry requirement. Some suggested that public accommodations should be prohibited from making any inquiries to determine if an individual with a disability would pose a direct threat to other persons. The Department believes that to preclude all such inquiries would be inappropriate. Under § 36.301 of this part, a public accommodation is permitted to establish eligibility criteria necessary for the safe operation of the place of public accommodation. Implicit in that right is the right to ask if an individual meets the criteria. However, any eligibility or safety standard established by a public accommodation must be based on actual risk, not on speculation or stereotypes; it must be applied to all clients or customers of the place of public accommodation; and inquiries must be limited to matters necessary to the application of the standard.

Some commenters suggested that the test established in the *Arline* decision, which was developed in the context of an employment case, is too stringent to apply in a public accommodations context where interaction between the public accommodation and its client or customer is often very brief. One suggested alternative was to permit public accommodations to exercise "good faith" judgment in determining whether an individual poses a direct threat, particularly when a public accommodation is dealing with a client or customer engaged in disorderly or disruptive behavior.

The Department believes that the ADA clearly requires that any determination to exclude an individual from participation must be based on an objective standard. A public accommodation may establish neutral eligibility criteria as a condition of receiving its goods or services. As long as these criteria are necessary for the safe provision of the public accommodation's goods and services and applied neutrally to all clients or customers, regardless of whether they are individuals with disabilities, a person who is unable to meet the criteria may be excluded from participation without inquiry into the underlying reason for the inability to comply. In places of public accommodation such as restaurants, theaters, or hotels, where the contact between the public accommodation and its clients is transitory, the uniform application of an eligibility standard precluding violent or disruptive behavior by any client or customer should be sufficient to enable a public accommodation to conduct its business in an orderly manner.

Some other commenters asked for clarification of the application of this provision to persons, particularly children, who have short-term, contagious illnesses, such as fevers, influenza, or the common cold. It is common practice in schools and day care settings to exclude persons with such illnesses until the symptoms subside. The Department believes that these commenters misunderstand the scope of this rule. The ADA only prohibits discrimination against an individual with a disability. Under the ADA and this part, a "disability" is defined as a physical or mental impairment that substantially limits one or more major life activities. Common, short-term illnesses that predictably resolve themselves within a matter of days do not "substantially limit" a major life activity; therefore, it is not a violation of this part to exclude an individual from receiving the services of a public accommodation because of such transitory illness. However, this part does apply to persons who have long-term illnesses. Any determination with respect to a person who has a chronic or long-term illness must be made in compliance with the requirements of this section.

Section 36.209 Illegal Use of Drugs

Section 36.209 effectuates section 510 of the ADA, which clarifies the Act's application to people who use drugs illegally. Paragraph (a) provides that this part does not prohibit discrimination based on an individual's current illegal use of drugs.

The Act and the regulation distinguish between illegal use of drugs and the legal use of substances, whether or not those substances are "controlled substances," as defined in the Controlled Substances Act (21 U.S.C. 812). Some controlled substances are prescription drugs that have legitimate medical uses. Section 36.209 does not affect use of controlled substances pursuant to a valid prescription, under supervision by a licensed health care professional, or other use that is authorized by the Controlled Substances Act or any other provision of Federal law. It does apply to illegal use of those substances, as well as to illegal use of controlled substances that are not prescription drugs. The key question is whether the individual's use of the substance is illegal, not whether the substance has recognized legal uses. Alcohol is not a controlled substance, so use of alcohol is not addressed by § 36.209. Alcoholics are individuals with disabilities, subject to the protections of the statute.

A distinction is also made between the use of a substance and the status of being addicted to that substance. Addiction is a disability, and addicts are individuals with disabilities protected by the Act. The protection, however, does not extend to actions based on the illegal use of the substance. In other words, an addict cannot use the fact of his or her addiction as a defense to an action based on illegal use of drugs. This distinction is not artificial. Congress intended to deny protection to people who engage in the illegal use of drugs, whether or not they are addicted, but to provide protection to addicts so long as they are not currently using drugs.

A third distinction is the difficult one between current use and former use. The definition of "current illegal use of drugs" in § 36.104, which is based on the report of the Conference Committee, H.R. Conf. Rep. No. 596, 101st Cong., 2d Sess. 64 (1990), is "illegal use of drugs that occurred recently enough to justify a reasonable belief that a person's drug use is current or that continuing use is a real and ongoing problem."

Paragraph (a)(2)(i) specifies that an individual who has successfully completed a supervised drug rehabilitation program or has otherwise been rehabilitated successfully and who is not engaging in current illegal use of drugs is protected. Paragraph (a)(2)(ii) clarifies that an individual who is currently participating in a supervised rehabilitation program and is not engaging in current illegal use of drugs is protected. Paragraph (a)(2)(iii) provides that a person who is erroneously regarded as engaging in current illegal use of drugs, but who is not engaging in such use, is protected.

Paragraph (b) provides a limited exception to the exclusion of current illegal users of drugs from the protections of the Act. It prohibits denial of health services, or services provided in connection with drug rehabilitation, to an individual on the basis of current illegal use of drugs, if the individual is otherwise entitled to such services. As explained further in the discussion of § 36.302, a health care facility that specializes in a particular type of treatment, such as care of burn victims, is not required to provide drug rehabilitation services, but it cannot refuse to treat an individual's burns on the grounds that the individual is illegally using drugs.

A commenter argued that health care providers should be permitted to use their medical judgment to postpone discretionary medical treatment of individuals under the influence of alcohol or drugs. The regulation permits a medical practitioner to take into account an individual's use of drugs in determining appropriate medical treatment. Section 36.209 provides that the prohibitions on discrimination in this part do not apply when the public accommodation acts on the basis of current illegal use of drugs. Although those prohibitions do apply under paragraph (b), the limitations established under this part also apply. Thus, under § 36.208, a health care provider or other public accommodation covered under § 36.209(b) may exclude an individual whose current illegal use of drugs poses a direct threat to the health or safety of others, and, under § 36.301, a public accommodation may impose or apply eligibility criteria that are necessary for the provision of the services being offered, and may impose legitimate safety requirements that are necessary for safe operation. These same limitations also apply to individuals with disabilities who use alcohol or prescription drugs. The Department believes that these provisions address this commenter's concerns.

Other commenters pointed out that abstention from the use of drugs is an essential condition for participation in some drug rehabilitation programs, and may be a necessary requirement in inpatient or residential settings. The Department believes that this comment is well-founded. Congress clearly did not intend to exclude from drug treatment programs the very individuals who need such programs because of their use of drugs. In such a situation, however, once an individual has been admitted to a program, abstention may be a necessary and appropriate condition to continued participation. The final rule therefore provides that a drug rehabilitation or treatment program may deny participation to individuals who use drugs while they are in the program.

Paragraph (c) expresses Congress' intention that the Act be neutral with respect to testing for illegal use of drugs. This paragraph implements the provision in section 510(b) of the Act that allows entities "to adopt or administer reasonable policies or procedures, including but not limited to drug testing," that ensure an individual who is participating in a supervised rehabilitation program, or who has completed such a program or otherwise been rehabilitated successfully, is no longer engaging in the illegal use of drugs. Paragraph (c) is not to be construed to encourage, prohibit, restrict, or authorize the conducting of testing for the illegal use of drugs.

Paragraph (c) of § 36.209 clarifies that it is not a violation of this part to adopt or administer reasonable policies or procedures to ensure that an individual who formerly engaged in the illegal use of drugs is not currently engaging in illegal use of drugs. Any such policies or procedures must, of course, be reasonable, and must be designed to identify accurately the illegal use of drugs. This paragraph does not authorize inquiries, tests, or other procedures that would disclose use of substances that are not controlled substances or are taken under supervision by a licensed health care professional, or other uses authorized by the Controlled Substances Act or other provisions of Federal law, because such uses are not included in the definition of "illegal use of drugs."

One commenter argued that the rule should permit testing for lawful use of prescription drugs, but most favored the explanation that tests must be limited to unlawful use in order to avoid revealing the use of prescription medicine used to treat disabilities. Tests revealing legal use of prescription drugs might violate the prohibition in § 36.301 of attempts to unnecessarily identify the existence of a disability.

Section 36.210 Smoking

Section 36.210 restates the clarification in section 501(b) of the Act that the Act does not preclude the prohibition of, or imposition of restrictions on, smoking. Some commenters argued that § 36.210 does not go far enough, and that the regulation should prohibit smoking in all places of public accommodation. The reference to smoking in section 501 merely clarifies that the Act does not require public accommodations to accommodate smokers by permitting them to smoke in places of public accommodations.

Section 36.211 Maintenance of Accessible Features

Section 36.211 provides that a public accommodation shall maintain in operable working condition those features of facilities and equipment that are required to be readily accessible to and usable by persons with disabilities by the Act or this part. The Act requires that, to the maximum extent feasible, facilities must be accessible to, and usable by, individuals with disabilities. This section recognizes that it is not sufficient to provide features such as accessible routes, elevators, or ramps, if those features are not maintained in a manner that enables individuals with disabilities to use them. Inoperable elevators, locked accessible doors, or "accessible" routes that are obstructed by furniture, filing cabinets, or potted plants are neither "accessible to" nor "usable by" individuals with disabilities.

Some commenters objected that this section appeared to establish an absolute requirement and suggested that language from the preamble be included in the text of the regulation. It is, of course, impossible to guarantee that mechanical devices will never fail to operate. Paragraph (b) of the final regulation provides that this section does not prohibit isolated or temporary interruptions in service or access due to maintenance or repairs. This paragraph is intended to clarify that temporary obstructions or isolated instances of mechanical failure would not be considered violations of the Act or this part. However, allowing obstructions or "out of service" equipment to persist beyond a reasonable period of time would violate this part, as would repeated mechanical failures due to improper or inadequate maintenance. Failure of the public accommodation to ensure that accessible routes are properly maintained and free of obstructions, or failure to arrange prompt repair of inoperable elevators or other equipment intended to provide access, would also violate this part.

Other commenters requested that this section be expanded to include specific requirements for inspection and maintenance of equipment, for training staff in the proper operation of equipment, and for maintenance of specific items. The Department believes that this section properly establishes the general requirement for maintaining access and that further, more detailed requirements are not necessary.

Section 36.212 Insurance

The Department received numerous comments on proposed § 36.212. Most supported the proposed regulation but felt that it did not go far enough in protecting individuals with disabilities and persons associated with them from discrimination. Many commenters argued that language from the preamble to the proposed regulation should be included in the text of the final regulation. Other commenters argued that even that language was not strong enough, and that more stringent standards should be established. Only a few commenters argued that the Act does not apply to insurance underwriting practices or the terms of insurance contracts. These commenters cited language from the Senate committee report (S. Rep. No. 116, 101st Cong., 1st Sess., at 84-86 (1989) (hereinafter "Senate report")), indicating that Congress did not intend to affect existing insurance practices.

The Department has decided to adopt the language of the proposed rule without change. Sections 36.212 (a) and (b) restate section 501(c) of the Act, which provides that the Act shall not be construed to restrict certain insurance practices on the part of insurance companies and employers, as long as such practices are not used to evade the purposes of the Act. Section 36.212(c) is a specific application of § 36.202(a), which prohibits denial of participation on the basis of disability. It provides that a public accommodation may not refuse to serve an individual with a disability because of limitations on coverage or rates in its insurance policies (see Judiciary report at 56).

Many commenters supported the requirements of § 36.212(c) in the proposed rule because it addressed an important reason for denial of services by public accommodations. One commenter argued that services could be denied if the insurance coverage required exclusion of people whose disabilities were reasonably related to the risks involved in that particular place of public accommodation. Sections 36.208 and 36.301 establish criteria for denial of participation on the basis of legitimate safety concerns. This paragraph does not prohibit consideration of such concerns in insurance policies, but provides that any exclusion on the basis of disability must be based on the permissible criteria, rather than on the terms of the insurance contract.

Language in the committee reports indicates that Congress intended to reach insurance practices by prohibiting differential treatment of individuals with disabilities in insurance offered by public accommodations unless the differences are justified. "Under the ADA, a person with a disability cannot be denied insurance or be subject to different terms or conditions of insurance based on disability alone, if the disability does not pose increased risks" (Senate report at 84; Education and Labor report at 136). Section 501(c) (1) of the Act was intended to emphasize that "insurers may continue to sell to and underwrite individuals applying for life, health, or other insurance on an individually underwritten basis, or to service such insurance products, so long as the standards used are based on sound actuarial data and not on speculation" (Judiciary report at 70 (emphasis added); see also Senate report at 85; Education and Labor report at 137).

The committee reports indicate that underwriting and classification of risks must be "based on sound actuarial principles or be related to actual or reasonably anticipated experience" (see, e.g., Judiciary report at 71). Moreover, "while a plan which limits certain kinds of coverage based on classification of risk would be allowed * * *, the plan may not refuse to insure, or refuse to continue to insure, or limit the amount, extent, or kind of coverage available to an individual, or charge a different rate for the same coverage solely because of a physical or mental impairment, except where the refusal, limitation, or rate differential is based on sound actuarial principles or is related to actual or reasonably anticipated experience" (Senate report at 85; Education and Labor report at 136-37; Judiciary report at 71). The ADA, therefore, does not prohibit use of legitimate actuarial considerations to justify differential treatment of individuals with disabilities in insurance.

The committee reports provide some guidance on how nondiscrimination principles in the disability rights area relate to insurance practices. For example, a person who is blind may not be denied coverage based on blindness independent of actuarial risk classification. With respect to group health insurance coverage, an individual with a pre-existing condition may be denied coverage for that condition for the period specified in the policy, but cannot be denied coverage for illness or injuries unrelated to the pre-existing condition. Also, a public accommodation may offer insurance policies that limit coverage for certain procedures or treatments, but may not entirely deny coverage to a person with a disability.

The Department requested comment on the extent to which data that would establish statistically sound correlations are available. Numerous commenters cited pervasive problems in the availability and cost of insurance for individuals with disabilities and parents of children with disabilities. No commenters cited specific data, or sources of data, to support specific exclusionary practices. Several commenters reported that, even when statistics are available, they are often outdated and do not reflect current medical technology and treatment methods. Concern was expressed that adequate efforts are not made to distinguish those individuals who are high users of health care from individuals in the same diagnostic groups who may be low users of health care. One insurer reported that "hard data and actuarial statistics are not available to provide precise numerical justifications for every underwriting determination," but argued that decisions may be based on "logical principles generally accepted by actuarial science and fully consistent with state insurance laws." The commenter urged that the Department recognize the validity of information other than statistical data as a basis for insurance determinations.

The most frequent comment was a recommendation that the final regulation should require the insurance company to provide a copy of the actuarial data on which its actions are based when requested by the applicant. Such a requirement would be beyond anything contemplated by the Act or by Congress and has therefore not been included in the Department's final rule. Because the legislative history of the ADA clarifies that different treatment of individuals with disabilities in insurance may be justified by sound actuarial data, such actuarial data will be critical to any potential litigation on this issue. This information would presumably be obtainable in a court proceeding where the insurer's actuarial data was the basis for different treatment of persons with disabilities. In addition, under some State regulatory schemes, insurers may have to file such actuarial information with the State regulatory agency and this information may be obtainable at the State level.

A few commenters representing the insurance industry conceded that underwriting practices in life and health insurance are clearly covered, but argued that property and casualty insurance are not covered. The Department sees no reason for this distinction. Although life and health insurance are the areas where the regulation will have its greatest application, the Act applies equally to unjustified discrimination in all types of insurance provided by public accommodations. A number of commenters, for example, reported difficulties in obtaining automobile insurance because of their disabilities, despite their having good driving records.

Section 36.213 Relationship of Subpart 8 to Subparts C and D

This section explains that subpart B sets forth the general principles of nondiscrimination applicable to all entities subject to this regulation, while subparts C and D provide guidance on the application of this part to specific situations. The specific provisions in subparts C and D, including the limitations on those provisions, control over the general provisions in circumstances where both specific and general provisions apply. Resort to the general provisions of subpart B is only appropriate where there are no applicable specific rules of guidance in subparts C or D. This interaction between the specific requirements and the general requirements operates with regard to contractual obligations as well.

One illustration of this principle is its application to the obligation of a public accommodation to provide access to services by removal of architectural barriers or by alternatives to barrier removal. The general requirement, established in subpart B by § 36.203, is that a public accommodation must provide its services to individuals with disabilities in the most integrated setting appropriate. This general requirement would appear to categorically prohibit "segregated" seating for persons in wheelchairs. Section 36.304, however, only requires removal of architectural barriers to the extent that removal is "readily achievable." If providing access to all areas of a restaurant, for example, would not be "readily achievable," a public accommodation may provide access to selected areas only. Also, § 36.305 provides that, where barrier removal is not readily achievable, a public accommodation may use alternative, readily achievable methods of making services available, such as curbside service or home delivery. Thus, in this manner, the specific requirements of §§ 36.304 and 36.305 control over the general requirement of § 36.203.

Subpart C—Specific Requirements

In general, subpart C implements the "specific prohibitions" that comprise section 302(b)(2) of the ADA. It also addresses the requirements of section 309 of the ADA regarding examinations and courses.

Section 36.301 Eligibility Criteria

Section 36.301 of the rule prohibits the imposition or application of eligibility criteria that screen out or tend to screen out an individual with a disability or any class of individuals with disabilities from fully and equally enjoying any goods, services, facilities, privileges, advantages, and accommodations, unless such criteria can be shown to be necessary for the provision of the goods, services, facilities, privileges, advantages, or accommodations being offered. This prohibition is based on section 302(b)(2)(A)(i) of the ADA.

It would violate this section to establish exclusive or segregative eligibility criteria that would bar, for example, all persons who are deaf from playing on a golf course or all individuals with cerebral palsy from attending a movie theater, or limit the seating of individuals with Down's syndrome to only particular areas of a restaurant. The wishes, tastes, or preferences of other customers may not be asserted to justify criteria that would exclude or segregate individuals with disabilities.

Section 36.301 also prohibits attempts by a public accommodation to unnecessarily identify the existence of a disability; for example, it would be a violation of this section for a retail store to require an individual to state on a credit application whether the applicant has epilepsy, mental illness, or any other disability, or to inquire unnecessarily whether an individual has HIV disease.

Section 36.301 also prohibits policies that unnecessarily impose requirements or burdens on individuals with disabilities that are not placed on others. For example, public accommodations may not require that an individual with a disability be accompanied by an attendant. As provided by § 36.306, however, a public accommodation is not required to provide services of a personal nature including assistance in toileting, eating, or dressing.

Paragraph (c) of § 36.301 provides that public accommodations may not place a surcharge on a particular individual with a disability or any group of individuals with disabilities to cover the costs of measures, such as the provision of auxiliary aids and services, barrier removal, alternatives to barrier removal, and reasonable modifications in policies, practices, and procedures, that are required to provide that individual or group with the nondiscriminatory treatment required by the Act or this part.

A number of commenters inquired as to whether deposits required for the use of auxiliary aids, such as assistive listening devices, are prohibited surcharges. It is the Department's view that reasonable, completely refundable, deposits are not to be considered surcharges prohibited by this section. Requiring deposits is an important means of ensuring the availability of equipment necessary to ensure compliance with the ADA.

Other commenters sought clarification as to whether § 36.301(c) prohibits professionals from charging for the additional time that it may take in certain cases to provide services to an individual with disabilities. The Department does not intend § 36.301(c) to prohibit professionals who bill on the basis of time from charging individuals with disabilities on that basis. However, fees may not be charged for the provision of auxiliary aids and services, barrier removal, alternatives to barrier removal, reasonable modifications in policies, practices, and procedures, or any other measures necessary to ensure compliance with the ADA.

Other commenters inquired as to whether day care centers may charge for extra services provided to individuals with disabilities. As stated above, § 36.302(c) is intended only to prohibit charges for measures necessary to achieve compliance with the ADA.

Another commenter asserted that charges may be assessed for home delivery provided as an alternative to barrier removal under § 36.305, when home delivery is provided to all customers for a fee. Charges for home delivery are permissible if home delivery is not considered an alternative to barrier removal. If the public accommodation offers an alternative, such as curb, carry-out, or sidewalk service for which no surcharge is assessed, then it may charge for home delivery in accordance with its standard pricing for home delivery.

In addition, § 36.301 prohibits the imposition of criteria that "tend to" screen out an individual with a disability. This concept, which is derived from current regulations under section 504 (see, e.g., 45 CFR 84.13), makes it discriminatory to impose policies or criteria that, while not creating a direct bar to individuals with disabilities, indirectly prevent or limit their ability to participate. For example, requiring presentation of a driver's license as the sole means of identification for purposes of paying by check would violate this section in situations where, for example, individuals with severe vision impairments or developmental disabilities or epilepsy are ineligible to receive a driver's license and the use of an alternative means of identification, such as another photo I.D. or credit card, is feasible.

A public accommodation may, however, impose neutral rules and criteria that screen out, or tend to screen out, individuals with disabilities, if the criteria are necessary for the safe operation of the public accommodation. Examples of safety qualifications that would be justifiable in appropriate circumstances would include height requirements for certain amusement park rides or a requirement that all participants in a recreational rafting expedition be able to meet a necessary level of swimming proficiency. Safety requirements must be based on actual risks and not on speculation, stereotypes, or generalizations about individuals with disabilities.

Section 36.302 Modifications in Policies, Practices, or Procedures

Section 36.302 of the rule prohibits the failure to make reasonable modifications in policies, practices, and procedures when such modifications may be necessary to afford any goods, services, facilities, privileges, advantages, or accommodations, unless the entity can demonstrate that making such modifications would fundamentally alter the nature of such goods, services, facilities, privileges, advantages, or accommodations. This prohibition is based on section 302(b)(2)(A)(ii) of the ADA.

For example, a parking facility would be required to modify a rule barring all vans or all vans with raised roofs, if an individual who uses a wheelchair- accessible van wishes to park in that facility, and if overhead structures are high enough to accommodate the height of the van. A department store may need to modify a policy of only permitting one person at a time in a dressing room, if an individual with mental retardation needs and requests assistance in dressing from a companion. Public accommodations may need to revise operational policies to ensure that services are available to individuals with disabilities. For instance, a hotel may need to adopt a policy of keeping an accessible room unoccupied until an individual with a disability arrives at the hotel, assuming the individual has properly reserved the room.

One example of application of this principle is specifically included in a new § 36.302(d) on check-out aisles. That paragraph provides that a store with check-out aisles must ensure that an adequate number of accessible check-out aisles is kept open during store hours, or must otherwise modify its policies and practices, in order to ensure that an equivalent level of convenient service is provided to individuals with disabilities as is provided to others. For example, if only one check-out aisle is accessible, and it is generally used for express service, one way of providing equivalent service is to allow persons with mobility impairments to make all of their purchases at that aisle. This principle also applies with respect to other accessible elements and services. For example, a particular bank may be in compliance with the accessibility guidelines for new construction incorporated in appendix A with respect to automated teller machines (ATM) at a new branch office by providing one accessible walk-up machine at that location, even though an adjacent walk-up ATM is not accessible and the drive-up ATM is not accessible. However, the bank would be in violation of this section if the accessible ATM was located in a lobby that was locked during evening hours while the drive-up ATM was available to customers without disabilities during those same hours. The bank would need to ensure that the accessible ATM was available to customers during the hours that any of the other ATM's was available.

A number of commenters inquired as to the relationship between this section and § 36.307, "Accessible or special goods." Under § 36.307, a public accommodation is not required to alter its inventory to include accessible or special goods that are designed for, or facilitate use by, individuals with disabilities. The rule enunciated in § 36.307 is consistent with the "fundamental alteration" defense to the reasonable modifications requirement of § 36.302. Therefore, § 36.302 would not require the inventory of goods provided by a public accommodation to be altered to include goods with accessibility features. For example, § 36.302 would not require a bookstore to stock Brailled books or order Brailled books, if it does not do so in the normal course of its business.

The rule does not require modifications to the legitimate areas of specialization of service providers. Section 36.302(b) provides that a public accommodation may refer an individual with a disability to another public accommodation, if that individual is seeking, or requires, treatment or services outside of the referring public accommodation's area of specialization, and if, in the normal course of its operations, the referring public accommodation would make a similar referral for an individual without a disability who seeks or requires the same treatment or services.

For example, it would not be discriminatory for a physician who specializes only in burn treatment to refer an individual who is deaf to another physician for treatment of an injury other than a burn injury. To require a physician to accept patients outside of his or her specialty would fundamentally alter the nature of the medical practice and, therefore, not be required by this section.

A clinic specializing exclusively in drug rehabilitation could similarly refuse to treat a person who is not a drug addict, but could not refuse to treat a person who is a drug addict simply because the patient tests positive for HIV. Conversely, a clinic that specializes in the treatment of individuals with HIV could refuse to treat an individual that does not have HIV, but could not refuse to treat a person for HIV infection simply because that person is also a drug addict.

Some commenters requested clarification as to how this provision would apply to situations where manifestations of the disability in question, itself, would raise complications requiring the expertise of a different practitioner. It is not the Department's intention in § 36.302(b) to prohibit a physician from referring an individual with a disability to another physician, if the disability itself creates specialized complications for the patient's health that the physician lacks the experience or knowledge to address (see Education and Labor report at 106).

Section 36.302(c)(1) requires that a public accommodation modify its policies, practices, or procedures to permit the use of a service animal by an individual with a disability in any area open to the general public. The term "service animal" is defined in § 36.104 to include guide dogs, signal dogs, or any other animal individually trained to provide assistance to an individual with a disability.

A number of commenters pointed to the difficulty of making the distinction required by the proposed rule between areas open to the general public and those that are not. The ambiguity and uncertainty surrounding these provisions has led the Department to adopt a single standard for all public accommodations.

Section 36.302(c)(1) of the final rule now provides that "[g]enerally, a public accommodation shall modify policies, practices, and procedures to permit the use of a service animal by an individual with a disability." This formulation reflects the general intent of Congress that public accommodations take the necessary steps to accommodate service animals and to ensure that individuals with disabilities are not separated from their service animals. It is intended that the broadest feasible access be provided to service animals in all places of public accommodation, including movie theaters, restaurants, hotels, retail stores, hospitals, and nursing homes (see Education and Labor report at 106; Judiciary report at 59). The section also acknowledges, however, that, in rare circumstances, accommodation of service animals may not be required because a fundamental alteration would result in the nature of the goods, services, facilities, privileges, or accommodations offered or provided, or the safe operation of the public accommodation would be jeopardized.

As specified in § 36.302(c)(2), the rule does not require a public accommodation to supervise or care for any service animal. If a service animal must be separated from an individual with a disability in order to avoid a fundamental alteration or a threat to safety, it is the responsibility of the individual with the disability to arrange for the care and supervision of the animal during the period of separation.

A museum would not be required by § 36.302 to modify a policy barring the touching of delicate works of art in order to enhance the participation of individuals who are blind, if the touching threatened the integrity of the work. Damage to a museum piece would clearly be a fundamental alteration that is not required by this section.

Section 36.303 Auxiliary Aids and Services.

Section 36.303 of the final rule requires a public accommodation to take such steps as may be necessary to ensure that no individual with a disability is excluded, denied services, segregated or otherwise treated differently than other individuals because of the absence of auxiliary aids and services, unless the public accommodation can demonstrate that taking such steps would fundamentally alter the nature of the goods, services, facilities, advantages, or accommodations being offered or would result in an undue burden. This requirement is based on section 302(b)(2)(A)(iii) of the ADA.

Implicit in this duty to provide auxiliary aids and services is the underlying obligation of a public accommodation to communicate effectively with its customers, clients, patients, or participants who have disabilities affecting hearing, vision, or speech. To give emphasis to this underlying obligation, § 36.303(c) of the rule incorporates language derived from section 504 regulations for federally conducted programs (see e.g., 28 CFR 39.160(a)) that requires that appropriate auxiliary aids and services be furnished to ensure that communication with persons with disabilities is as effective as communication with others.

Auxiliary aids and services include a wide range of services and devices for ensuring effective communication. Use of the most advanced technology is not required so long as effective communication is ensured. The Department's proposed § 36.303(b) provided a list of examples of auxiliary aids and services that was taken from the definition of auxiliary aids and services in section 3(1) of the ADA and was supplemented by examples from regulations implementing section 504 in federally conducted programs (see e.g., 28 CFR 39.103). A substantial number of commenters suggested that additional examples be added to this list. The Department has added several items to this list but wishes to clarify that the list is not an all-inclusive or exhaustive catalogue of possible or available auxiliary aids or services. It is not possible to provide an exhaustive list, and such an attempt would omit new devices that will become available with emerging technology.

The Department has added videotext displays, computer-aided transcription services, and open and closed captioning to the list of examples. Videotext displays have become an important means of accessing auditory communications through a public address system. Transcription services are used to relay aurally delivered material almost simultaneously in written form to persons who are deaf or hard of hearing. This technology is often used at conferences, conventions, and hearings. While the proposed rule expressly included television decoder equipment as an auxiliary aid or service, it did not mention captioning itself. The final rule rectifies this omission by mentioning both closed and open captioning.

In this section, the Department has changed the proposed rule's phrase, "orally delivered materials," to the phrase, "aurally delivered materials." This new phrase tracks the language in the definition of "auxiliary aids and services" in section 3 of the ADA and is meant to include nonverbal sounds and alarms and computer-generated speech.

Several persons and organizations requested that the Department replace the term "telecommunications devices for deaf persons" or "TDD's" with the term "text telephone." The Department has declined to do so. The Department is aware that the Architectural and Transportation Barriers Compliance Board has used the phrase "text telephone" in lieu of the statutory term "TDD" in its final accessibility guidelines. Title IV of the ADA, however, uses the term "Telecommunications Device for the Deaf," and the Department believes it would be inappropriate to abandon this statutory term at this time.

Paragraph (b)(2) lists examples of aids and services for making visually delivered materials accessible to persons with visual impairments. Many commenters proposed additional examples such as signage or mapping, audio description services, secondary auditory programs (SAP), telebraillers, and reading machines. While the Department declines to add these items to the list in the regulation, they may be considered appropriate auxiliary aids and services.

Paragraph (b)(3) refers to the acquisition or modification of equipment or devices. For example, tape players used for an audio-guided tour of a museum exhibit may require the addition of Brailled adhesive labels to the buttons on a reasonable number of the tape players to facilitate their use by individuals who are blind. Similarly, permanent or portable assistive listening systems for persons with hearing impairments may be required at a hotel conference center.

Several commenters suggested the addition of current technological innovations in microelectronics and computerized control systems (e.g., voice recognition systems, automatic dialing telephones, and infrared elevator and light control systems) to the list of auxiliary aids and services. The Department interprets auxiliary aids and services as those aids and services designed to provide effective communications, i.e., making aurally and visually delivered information available to persons with hearing, speech, and vision impairments. Methods of making services, programs, or activities accessible to, or usable by, individuals with mobility or manual dexterity impairments are addressed by other sections of this part, including the requirements for modifications in policies, practices, or procedures (§ 36.302), the elimination of existing architectural barriers (§ 36.304), and the provision of alternatives to barriers removal (§ 36.305).

Paragraph (b)(4) refers to other similar services and actions. Several commenters asked for clarification that "similar services and actions" include retrieving items from shelves, assistance in reaching a marginally accessible seat, pushing a barrier aside in order to provide an accessible route, or assistance in removing a sweater or coat. While retrieving an item from a shelf might be an "auxiliary aid or service" for a blind person who could not locate the item without assistance, it might be a readily achievable alternative to barrier removal for a person using a wheelchair who could not reach the shelf, or a reasonable modification to a self-service policy for an individual who lacked the ability to grasp the item. (Of course, a store would not be required to provide a personal shopper.) As explained above, auxiliary aids and services are those aids and services required to provide effective communications. Other forms of assistance are more appropriately addressed by other provisions of the final rule.

The auxiliary aid requirement is a flexible one. A public accommodation can choose among various alternatives as long as the result is effective communication. For example, a restaurant would not be required to provide menus in Braille for patrons who are blind, if the waiters in the restaurant are made available to read the menu. Similarly, a clothing boutique would not be required to have Brailled price tags if sales personnel provide price information orally upon request; and a bookstore would not be required to make available a sign language interpreter, because effective communication can be conducted by notepad.

A critical determination is what constitutes an effective auxiliary aid or service. The Department's proposed rule recommended that, in determining what auxiliary aid to use, the public accommodation consult with an individual before providing him or her with a particular auxiliary aid or service. This suggestion sparked a significant volume of public comment. Many persons with disabilities, particularly persons who are deaf or hard of hearing, recommended that the rule should require that public accommodations give "primary consideration" to the "expressed choice" of an individual with a disability. These commenters asserted that the proposed rule was inconsistent with congressional intent of the ADA, with the Department's proposed rule implementing title II of the ADA, and with longstanding interpretations of section 504 of the Rehabilitation Act.

Based upon a careful review of the ADA legislative history, the Department believes that Congress did not intend under title III to impose upon a public accommodation the requirement that it give primary consideration to the request of the individual with a disability. To the contrary, the legislative history demonstrates congressional intent to strongly encourage consulting with persons with disabilities. In its analysis of the ADA's auxiliary aids requirement for public accommodations, the House Education and Labor Committee stated that it "expects" that "public accommodation(s) will consult with the individual with a disability before providing a particular auxiliary aid or service" (Education and Labor report at 107). Some commenters also cited a different committee statement that used mandatory language as evidence of legislative intent to require primary consideration. However, this statement was made in the context of reasonable accommodations required by title I with respect to employment (Education and Labor report at 67). Thus, the Department finds that strongly encouraging consultation with persons with disabilities, in lieu of mandating primary consideration of their expressed choice, is consistent with congressional intent.

The Department wishes to emphasize that public accommodations must take steps necessary to ensure that an individual with a disability will not be excluded, denied services, segregated or otherwise treated differently from other individuals because of the use of inappropriate or ineffective auxiliary aids. In those situations requiring an interpreter, the public accommodations must secure the services of a qualified interpreter, unless an undue burden would result.

In the analysis of § 36.303(c) in the proposed rule, the Department gave as an example the situation where a note pad and written materials were insufficient to permit effective communication in a doctor's office when the matter to be decided was whether major surgery was necessary. Many commenters objected to this statement, asserting that it gave the impression that only decisions about major surgery would merit the provision of a sign language interpreter. The statement would, as the commenters also claimed, convey the impression to other public accommodations that written communications would meet the regulatory requirements in all but the most extreme situations. The Department, when using the example of major surgery, did not intend to limit the provision of interpreter services to the most extreme situations.

Other situations may also require the use of interpreters to ensure effective communication depending on the facts of the particular case. It is not difficult to imagine a wide range of communications involving areas such as health, legal matters, and finances that would be sufficiently lengthy or complex to require an interpreter for effective communication. In some situations, an effective alternative to use of a notepad or an interpreter may be the use of a computer terminal upon which the representative of the public accommodation and the customer or client can exchange typewritten messages.

Section 36.303(d) specifically addresses requirements for TDD's. Partly because of the availability of telecommunications relay services to be established under title IV of the ADA, § 36.303(d)(2) provides that a public accommodation is not required to use a telecommunication device for the deaf (TDD) in receiving or making telephone calls incident to its operations. Several commenters were concerned that relay services would not be sufficient to provide effective access in a number of situations. Commenters argued that relay systems (1) do not provide effective access to the automated systems that require the caller to respond by pushing a button on a touch tone phone, (2) cannot operate fast enough to convey messages on answering machines, or to permit a TDD user to leave a recorded message, and (3) are not appropriate for calling crisis lines relating to such matters as rape, domestic violence, child abuse, and drugs where confidentiality is a concern. The Department believes that it is more appropriate for the Federal Communications Commission to address these issues in its rulemaking under title IV.

A public accommodation is, however, required to make a TDD available to an individual with impaired hearing or speech, if it customarily offers telephone service to its customers, clients, patients, or participants on more than an incidental convenience basis. Where entry to a place of public accommodation requires use of a security entrance telephone, a TDD or other effective means of communication must be provided for use by an individual with impaired hearing or speech.

In other words, individual retail stores, doctors' offices, restaurants, or similar establishments are not required by this section to have TDD's, because TDD users will be able to make inquiries, appointments, or reservations with such establishments through the relay system established under title IV of the ADA. The public accommodation will likewise be able to contact TDD users through the relay system. On the other hand, hotels, hospitals, and other similar establishments that offer nondisabled individuals the opportunity to make outgoing telephone calls on more than an incidental convenience basis must provide a TDD on request.

Section 36.303(e) requires places of lodging that provide televisions in five or more guest rooms and hospitals to provide, upon request, a means for decoding closed captions for use by an individual with impaired hearing. Hotels should also provide a TDD or similar device at the front desk in order to take calls from guests who use TDD's in their rooms. In this way guests with hearing impairments can avail themselves of such hotel services as making inquiries of the front desk and ordering room service. The term "hospital" is used in its general sense and should be interpreted broadly.

Movie theaters are not required by § 36.303 to present open-captioned films. However, other public accommodations that impart verbal information through soundtracks on films, video tapes, or slide shows are required to make such information accessible to persons with hearing impairments. Captioning is one means to make the information accessible to individuals with disabilities.

The rule specifies that auxiliary aids and services include the acquisition or modification of equipment or devices. For example, tape players used for an audio-guided tour of a museum exhibit may require the addition of Brailled adhesive labels to the buttons on a reasonable number of the tape players to facilitate their use by individuals who are blind. Similarly, a hotel conference center may need to provide permanent or portable assistive listening systems for persons with hearing impairments.

As provided in § 36.303(f), a public accommodation is not required to provide any particular aid or service that would result either in a fundamental alteration in the nature of the goods, services, facilities, privileges, advantages, or accommodations offered or in an undue burden. Both of these statutory limitations are derived from existing regulations and caselaw under section 504 and are to be applied on a case-by-case basis (see, e.g., 28 CFR 39.160(d) and *Southeastern Community College v. Davis*, 442 U.S. 397 (1979)). Congress intended that "undue burden" under § 36.303 and "undue hardship," which is used in the employment provisions of title I of the ADA, should be determined on a case-by-case basis under the same standards and in light of the same factors (Judiciary report at 59). The rule, therefore, in accordance with the definition of undue hardship in section 101(10) of the ADA, defines undue burden as "significant difficulty or expense" (see §§ 36.104 and 36.303(a)) and requires that undue burden be determined in light of the factors listed in the definition in 36.104.

Consistent with regulations implementing section 504 in federally conducted programs (see, e.g., 28 CFR 39.160(d)), § 36.303(f) provides that the fact that the provision of a particular auxiliary aid or service would result in an undue burden does not relieve a public accommodation from the duty to furnish an alternative auxiliary aid or service, if available, that would not result in such a burden.

Section 36.303(g) of the proposed rule has been deleted from this section and included in a new § 36.306. That new section continues to make clear that the auxiliary aids requirement does not mandate the provision of individually prescribed devices, such as prescription eyeglasses or hearing aids.

The costs of compliance with the requirements of this section may not be financed by surcharges limited to particular individuals with disabilities or any group of individuals with disabilities (§ 36.301(c)).

Section 36.304 Removal of Barriers

Section 36.304 requires the removal of architectural barriers and communication barriers that are structural in nature in existing facilities, where such removal is readily achievable, i.e., easily accomplishable and able to be carried out without much difficulty or expense. This requirement is based on section

302(b)(2)(A)(iv) of the ADA.

A number of commenters interpreted the phrase "communication barriers that are structural in nature" broadly to encompass the provision of communications devices such as TDD's, telephone handset amplifiers, assistive listening devices, and digital check-out displays. The statute, however, as read by the Department, limits the application of the phrase "communications barriers that are structural in nature" to those barriers that are an integral part of the physical structure of a facility. In addition to the communications barriers posed by permanent signage and alarm systems noted by Congress (see Education and Labor report at 110), the Department would also include among the communications barriers covered by § 36.304 the failure to provide adequate sound buffers, and the presence of physical partitions that hamper the passage of sound waves between employees and customers. Given that § 36.304's proper focus is on the removal of physical barriers, the Department believes that the obligation to provide communications equipment and devices such as TDD's, telephone handset amplifiers, assistive listening devices, and digital check- out displays is more appropriately determined by the requirements for auxiliary aids and services under § 36.303 (see Education and Labor report at 107-108). The obligation to remove communications barriers that are structural in nature under § 36.304, of course, is independent of any obligation to provide auxiliary aids and services under § 36.303.

The statutory provision also requires the readily achievable removal of certain barriers in existing vehicles and rail passenger cars. This transportation requirement is not included in § 36.304, but rather in § 36.310(b) of the rule.

In striking a balance between guaranteeing access to individuals with disabilities and recognizing the legitimate cost concerns of businesses and other private entities, the ADA establishes different standards for existing facilities and new construction. In existing facilities, which are the subject of § 36.304, where retrofitting may prove costly, a less rigorous degree of accessibility is required than in the case of new construction and alterations (see §§ 36.401-36.406) where accessibility can be more conveniently and economically incorporated in the initial stages of design and construction.

For example, a bank with existing automatic teller machines (ATM's) would have to remove barriers to the use of the ATM's, if it is readily achievable to do so. Whether or not it is necessary to take actions such as ramping a few steps or raising or lowering an ATM would be determined by whether the actions can be accomplished easily and without much difficulty or expense.

On the other hand, a newly constructed bank with ATM's would be required by § 36.401 to have an ATM that is "readily accessible to and usable by" persons with disabilities in accordance with accessibility guidelines incorporated under § 36.406.

The requirement to remove architectural barriers includes the removal of physical barriers of any kind. For example, § 36.304 requires the removal, when readily achievable, of barriers caused by the location of temporary or movable structures, such as furniture, equipment, and display racks. In order to provide access to individuals who use wheelchairs, for example, restaurants may need to rearrange tables and chairs, and department stores may need to reconfigure display racks and shelves. As stated in § 36.304(f), such actions are not readily achievable to the extent that they would result in a significant loss of selling or serving space. If the widening of all aisles in selling or serving areas is not readily achievable, then selected widening should be undertaken to maximize the amount of merchandise or the number of tables accessible to individuals who use wheelchairs. Access to goods and services provided in any remaining inaccessible areas must be made available through alternative methods to barrier removal, as required by § 36.305.

Because the purpose of title III of the ADA is to ensure that public accommodations are accessible to their customers, clients, or patrons (as opposed to their employees, who are the focus of title I), the obligation to remove barriers under § 36.304 does not extend to areas of a facility that are used exclusively as employee work areas.

Section 36.304(b) provides a wide-ranging list of the types of modest measures that may be taken to remove barriers and that are likely to be readily achievable. The list includes examples of measures, such as adding raised letter markings on elevator control buttons and installing flashing alarm lights, that would be used to remove communications barriers that are structural in nature. It is not an exhaustive list, but merely an illustrative one. Moreover, the inclusion of a measure on this list does not mean that it is readily achievable in all cases. Whether or not any of these measures is readily achievable is to be determined on a case-by-case basis in light of the particular circumstances presented and the factors listed in the definition of readily achievable (§ 36.104).

A public accommodation generally would not be required to remove a barrier to physical access posed by a flight of steps, if removal would require extensive ramping or an elevator. Ramping a single step, however, will likely be readily achievable, and ramping several steps will in many circumstances also be readily achievable. The readily achievable standard does not require barrier removal that requires extensive restructuring or burdensome expense. Thus, where it is not readily achievable to do, the ADA would not require a restaurant to provide access to a restroom reachable only by a flight of stairs.

Like § 36.405, this section permits deference to the national interest in preserving significant historic structures. Barrier removal would not be considered "readily achievable" if it would threaten or destroy the historic significance of a building or facility that is eligible for listing in the National Register of Historic Places under the National Historic Preservation Act (16 U.S.C. 470, et seq.), or is designated as historic under State or local law.

The readily achievable defense requires a less demanding level of exertion by a public accommodation than does the undue burden defense to the auxiliary aids requirements of § 36.303. In that sense, it can be characterized as a "lower" standard than the undue burden standard. The readily achievable defense is also less demanding than the undue hardship defense in section 102(b)(5) of the ADA, which limits the obligation to make reasonable accommodation in employment. Barrier removal measures that are not easily accomplishable and are not able to be carried out without much difficulty or expense are not required under the readily achievable standard, even if they do not impose an undue burden or an undue hardship.

Section 36.304(f)(1) of the proposed rule, which stated that "barrier removal is not readily achievable if it would result in significant loss of profit or significant loss of efficiency of operation," has been deleted from the final rule. Many commenters objected to this provision because it impermissibly introduced the notion of profit into a statutory standard that did not include it. Concern was expressed that, in order for an action not to be considered readily achievable, a public accommodation would inappropriately have to show, for example, not only that the action could not be done without "much difficulty or expense", but that a significant loss of profit would result as well. In addition, some commenters asserted use of the word "significant," which is used in the definition of undue hardship under title I (the standard for interpreting the meaning of undue burden as a defense to title III's auxiliary aids requirements) (see §§ 36.104, 36.303(f)), blurs the fact that the readily achievable standard requires a lower level of effort on the part of a public accommodation than does the undue burden standard.

The obligation to engage in readily achievable barrier removal is a continuing one. Over time, barrier removal that initially was not readily achievable may later be required because of changed circumstances. Many commenters expressed support for the Department's position that the obligation to comply with § 36.304 is continuing in nature. Some urged that the rule require public accommodations to assess their compliance on at least an annual basis in light of changes in resources and other factors that would be relevant to determining what barrier removal measures would be readily achievable.

Although the obligation to engage in readily achievable barrier removal is clearly a continuing duty, the Department has declined to establish any independent requirement for an annual assessment or self-evaluation. It is best left to the public accommodations subject to § 36.304 to establish policies to assess compliance that are appropriate to the particular circumstances faced by the wide range of public accommodations covered by the ADA. However, even in the absence of an explicit regulatory requirement for periodic self-evaluations, the Department still urges public accommodations to establish procedures for an ongoing assessment of their compliance with the ADA's barrier removal requirements. The Department recommends that this process include appropriate consultation with individuals with disabilities or organizations representing them. A serious effort at self-assessment and consultation can diminish the threat of litigation and save resources by identifying the most efficient means of providing required access.

The Department has been asked for guidance on the best means for public accommodations to comply voluntarily with this section. Such information is more appropriately part of the Department's technical assistance effort and will be forthcoming over the next several months. The Department recommends, however, the development of an implementation plan designed to achieve compliance with the ADA's barrier removal requirements before they become effective on January 26, 1992. Such a plan, if appropriately designed and diligently executed, could serve as evidence of a good faith effort to comply with the requirements of § 36.104. In developing an implementation plan for readily achievable barrier removal, a public accommodation should consult with local organizations representing persons with disabilities and solicit their suggestions for cost-effective means of making individual places of public accommodation accessible. Such organizations may also be helpful in allocating scarce resources and establishing priorities. Local associations of businesses may want to encourage this process and serve as the forum for discussions on the local level between disability rights organizations and local businesses.

Section 36.304(c) recommends priorities for public accommodations in removing barriers in existing facilities. Because the resources available for barrier removal may not be adequate to remove all existing barriers at any given time, § 36.304(c) suggests priorities for determining which types of barriers should be mitigated or eliminated first. The purpose of these priorities is to facilitate long-term business planning and to maximize, in light of limited resources, the degree of effective access that will result from any given level of expenditure.

Although many commenters expressed support for the concept of establishing priorities, a significant number objected to their mandatory nature in the proposed rule. The Department shares the concern of these commenters that mandatory priorities would increase the likelihood of litigation and inappropriately reduce the discretion of public accommodations to determine the most effective mix of barrier removal measures to undertake in particular circumstances. Therefore, in the final rule the priorities are no longer mandatory.

In response to comments that the priorities failed to address communications issues, the Department wishes to emphasize that the priorities encompass the removal of communications barriers that are structural in nature. It would be counter to the ADA's carefully wrought statutory scheme to include in this provision the wide range of communication devices that are required by the ADA's provisions on auxiliary aids and services. The final rule explicitly includes Brailled and raised letter signage and visual alarms among the examples of steps to remove barriers provided in § 36.304(c)(2).

Section 36.304(c)(1) places the highest priority on measures that will enable individuals with disabilities to physically enter a place of public accommodation. This priority on "getting through the door" recognizes that providing actual physical access to a facility from public sidewalks, public transportation, or parking is generally preferable to any alternative arrangements in terms of both business efficiency and the dignity of individuals with disabilities.

The next priority, which is established in § 36.304(c)(2), is for measures that provide access to those areas of a place of public accommodation where goods and services are made available to the public. For example, in a hardware store, to the extent that it is readily achievable to do so, individuals with disabilities should be given access not only to assistance at the front desk, but also access, like that available to other customers, to the retail display areas of the store.

The Department agrees with those commenters who argued that access to the areas where goods and services are provided is generally more important than the provision of restrooms. Therefore, the final rule reverses priorities two and three of the proposed rule in order to give lower priority to accessible restrooms. Consequently, the third priority in the final rule (§ 36.304(c)(3)) is for measures to provide access to restroom facilities and the last priority is placed on any remaining measures required to remove barriers.

Section 36.304(d) requires that measures taken to remove barriers under § 36.304 be subject to subpart D's requirements for alterations (except for the path of travel requirements in § 36.403). It only permits deviations from the subpart D requirements when compliance with those requirements is not readily achievable. In such cases, § 36.304(d) permits measures to be taken that do not fully comply with the subpart D requirements, so long as the measures do not pose a significant risk to the health or safety of individuals with disabilities or others.

This approach represents a change from the proposed rule which stated that "readily achievable" measures taken solely to remove barriers under § 36.304 are exempt from the alterations requirements of subpart D. The intent of the proposed rule was to maximize the flexibility of public accommodations in undertaking barrier removal by allowing deviations from the technical standards of subpart D. It was thought that allowing slight deviations would provide access and release additional resources for expanding the amount of barrier removal that could be obtained under the readily achievable standard.

Many commenters, however, representing both businesses and individuals with disabilities, questioned this approach because of the likelihood that unsafe or ineffective measures would be taken in the absence of the subpart D standards for alterations as a reference point. Some advocated a rule requiring strict compliance with the subpart D standard.

The Department in the final rule has adopted the view of many commenters that (1) public accommodations should in the first instance be required to comply with the subpart D standards for alterations where it is readily achievable to do so and (2) safe, readily achievable measures must be taken when compliance with the subpart D standards is not readily achievable. Reference to the subpart D standards in this manner will promote certainty and good design at the same time that permitting slight deviations will expand the amount of barrier removal that may be achieved under

§ 36.304.

Because of the inconvenience to individuals with disabilities and the safety problems involved in the use of portable ramps, § 36.304(e) permits the use of a portable ramp to comply with § 36.304(a) only when installation of a permanent ramp is not readily achievable. In order to promote safety, § 36.304(e) requires that due consideration be given to the incorporation of features such as nonslip surfaces, railings, anchoring, and strength of materials in any portable ramp that is used.

Temporary facilities brought in for use at the site of a natural disaster are subject to the barrier removal requirements of § 36.304.

A number of commenters requested clarification regarding how to determine when a public accommodation has discharged its obligation to remove barriers in existing facilities. For example, is a hotel required by § 36.304 to remove barriers in all of its guest rooms? Or is some lesser percentage adequate? A new paragraph (g) has been added to § 36.304 to address this issue. The Department believes that the degree of barrier removal required under § 36.304 may be less, but certainly would not be required to exceed, the standards for alterations under the ADA Accessibility Guidelines incorporated by subpart D of this part (ADAAG). The ADA's requirements for readily achievable barrier removal in existing facilities are intended to be substantially less rigorous than those for new construction and alterations. It, therefore, would be obviously inappropriate to require actions under § 36.304 that would exceed the ADAAG requirements. Hotels, then, in order to satisfy the requirements of § 36.304, would not be required to remove barriers in a higher percentage of rooms than required by ADAAG. If relevant standards for alterations are not provided in ADAAG, then reference should be made to the standards for new construction.

Section 36.305 Alternatives to Barrier Removal

Section 36.305 specifies that where a public accommodation can demonstrate that removal of a barrier is not readily achievable, the public accommodation must make its goods, services, facilities, privileges, advantages, or accommodations available through alternative methods, if such methods are readily achievable. This requirement is based on section 302(b)(2)(A)(v) of the ADA.

For example, if it is not readily achievable for a retail store to raise, lower, or remove shelves or to rearrange display racks to provide accessible aisles, the store must, if readily achievable, provide a clerk or take other alternative measures to retrieve inaccessible merchandise. Similarly, if it is not readily achievable to ramp a long flight of stairs leading to the front door of a restaurant or a pharmacy, the restaurant or the pharmacy must take alternative measures, if readily achievable, such as providing curb service or home delivery. If, within a restaurant, it is not readily achievable to remove physical barriers to a certain section of a restaurant, the restaurant must, where it is readily achievable to do so, offer the same menu in an accessible area of the restaurant.

Where alternative methods are used to provide access, a public accommodation may not charge an individual with a disability for the costs associated with the alternative method (see § 36.301(c)). Further analysis of the issue of charging for alternative measures may be found in the preamble discussion of § 36.301(c).

In some circumstances, because of security considerations, some alternative methods may not be readily achievable. The rule does not require a cashier to leave his or her post to retrieve items for individuals with disabilities, if there are no other employees on duty.

Section 36.305(c) of the proposed rule has been deleted and the requirements have been included in a new § 36.306. That section makes clear that the alternative methods requirement does not mandate the provision of personal devices, such as wheelchairs, or services of a personal nature.

In the final rule, § 36.305(c) provides specific requirements regarding alternatives to barrier removal in multiscreen cinemas. In some situations, it may not be readily achievable to remove enough barriers to provide access to all of the theaters of a multiscreen cinema. If that is the case, § 36.305(c) requires the cinema to establish a film rotation schedule that provides reasonable access for individuals who use wheelchairs to films being presented by the cinema. It further requires that reasonable notice be provided to the public as to the location and time of accessible showings. Methods for providing notice include appropriate use of the international accessibility symbol in a cinema's print advertising and the addition of accessibility information to a cinema's recorded telephone information line.

Section 36.306 Personal Devices and Services

The final rule includes a new § 36.306, entitled "Personal devices and services." Section 36.306 of the proposed rule, "Readily achievable and undue burden: Factors to be considered," was deleted for the reasons described in the preamble discussion of the definition of the term "readily achievable" in § 36.104. In place of §§ 36.303(g) and 36.305(c) of the proposed rule, which addressed the issue of personal devices and services in the contexts of auxiliary aids and alternatives to barrier removal, § 36.306 provides a general statement that the regulation does not require the provision of personal devices and services. This section states that a public accommodation is not required to provide its customers, clients, or participants with personal devices, such as wheelchairs; individually prescribed devices, such as prescription eyeglasses or hearing aids; or services of a personal nature including assistance in eating, toileting, or dressing.

This statement serves as a limitation on all the requirements of the regulation. The personal devices and services limitation was intended to have general application in the proposed rule in all contexts where it was relevant. The final rule, therefore, clarifies, this point by including a general provision that will explicitly apply not just to auxiliary aids and services and alternatives to barrier removal, but across-the-board to include such relevant areas as modifications in policies, practices, and procedures (§ 36.302) and examinations and courses (§ 36.309), as well.

The Department wishes to clarify that measures taken as alternatives to barrier removal, such as retrieving items from shelves or providing curb service or home delivery, are not to be considered personal services. Similarly, minimal actions that may be required as modifications in policies, practices, or procedures under § 36.302, such as a waiter's removing the cover from a customer's straw, a kitchen's cutting up food into smaller pieces, or a bank's filling out a deposit slip, are not services of a personal nature within the meaning of § 36.306. (Of course, such modifications may be required under § 36.302 only if they are "reasonable.") Similarly, this section does not preclude the short-term loan of personal receivers that are part of an assistive listening system.

Of course, if personal services are customarily provided to the customers or clients of a public accommodation, e.g., in a hospital or senior citizen center, then these personal services should also be provided to persons with disabilities using the public accommodation.

Section 36.307 Accessible or Special Goods.

Section 36.307 establishes that the rule does not require a public accommodation to alter its inventory to include accessible or special goods with accessibility features that are designed for, or facilitate use by, individuals with disabilities. As specified in § 36.307(c), accessible or special goods include such items as Brailled versions of books, books on audio-cassettes, closed captioned video tapes, special sizes or lines of clothing, and special foods to meet particular dietary needs.

The purpose of the ADA's public accommodations requirements is to ensure accessibility to the goods offered by a public accommodation, not to alter the nature or mix of goods that the public accommodation has typically provided. In other words, a bookstore, for example, must make its facilities and sales operations accessible to individuals with disabilities, but is not required to stock Brailled or large print books. Similarly, a video store must make its facilities and rental operations accessible, but is not required to stock closed-captioned video tapes. The Department has been made aware, however, that the most recent titles in video-tape rental establishments are, in fact, closed captioned.

Although a public accommodation is not required by § 36.307(a) to modify its inventory, it is required by § 36.307(b), at the request of an individual with disabilities, to order accessible or special goods that it does not customarily maintain in stock if, in the normal course of its operation, it makes special orders for unstocked goods, and if the accessible or special goods can be obtained from a supplier with whom the public accommodation customarily does business. For example, a clothing store would be required to order specially- sized clothing at the request of an individual with a disability, if it customarily makes special orders for clothing that it does not keep in stock, and if the clothing can be obtained from one of the store's customary suppliers.

One commenter asserted that the proposed rule could be interpreted to require a store to special order accessible or special goods of all types, even if only one type is specially ordered in the normal course of its business. The Department, however, intends for § 36.307(b) to require special orders only of those particular types of goods for which a public accommodation normally makes special orders. For example, a book and recording store would not have to specially order Brailled books if, in the normal course of its business, it only specially orders recordings and not books.

Section 36.308 Seating in Assembly Areas.

Section 36.308 establishes specific requirements for removing barriers to physical access in assembly areas, which include such facilities as theaters, concert halls, auditoriums, lecture halls, and conference rooms. This section does not address the provision of auxiliary aids or the removal of communications barriers that are structural in nature. These communications requirements are the focus of other provisions of the regulation (see §§ 36.303-36.304).

Individuals who use wheelchairs historically have been relegated to inferior seating in the back of assembly areas separate from accompanying family members and friends. The provisions of § 36.308 are intended to promote integration and equality in seating.

In some instances it may not be readily achievable for auditoriums or theaters to remove seats to allow individuals with wheelchairs to sit next to accompanying family members or friends. In these situations, the final rule retains the requirement that the public accommodation provide portable chairs or other means to allow the accompanying individuals to sit with the persons in wheelchairs. Persons in wheelchairs should have the same opportunity to enjoy movies, plays, and similar events with their families and friends, just as other patrons do. The final rule specifies that portable chairs or other means to permit family members or companions to sit with individuals who use wheelchairs must be provided only when it is readily achievable to do so.

In order to facilitate seating of wheelchair users who wish to transfer to existing seating, paragraph (a)(1) of the final rule adds a requirement that, to the extent readily achievable, a reasonable number of seats with removable aisle-side armrests must be provided. Many persons in wheelchairs are able to transfer to existing seating with this relatively minor modification. This solution avoids the potential safety hazard created by the use of portable chairs and fosters integration. The final ADA Accessibility Guidelines incorporated by subpart D (ADAAG) also add a requirement regarding aisle seating that was not in the proposed guidelines. In situations when a person in a wheelchair transfers to existing seating, the public accommodation shall provide assistance in handling the wheelchair of the patron with the disability.

Likewise, consistent vith ADAAG, the final rule adds in § 36.308(a)(1)(ii)(B) a requirement that, to the extent readily achievable, wheelchair seating provide lines of sight and choice of admission prices comparable to those for members of the general public.

Finally, because Congress intended that the requirements for barrier removal in existing facilities be substantially less rigorous than those required for new construction and alterations, the final rule clarifies in § 36.308(a)(3) that in no event can the requirements for existing facilities be interpreted to exceed the standards for alterations under ADAAG. For example, § 4.33 of ADAAG only requires wheelchair spaces to be provided in more than one location when the seating capacity of the assembly area exceeds 300. Therefore, paragraph (a) of § 36.308 may not be interpreted to require readily achievable dispersal of wheelchair seating in assembly areas with 300 or fewer seats. Similarly, § 4.1.3(19) of ADAAG requires six accessible wheelchair locations in an assembly area with 301 to 500 seats. The reasonable number of wheelchair locations required by paragraph (a), therefore, may be less than six, but may not be interpreted to exceed six.

Proposed Section 36.309
Purchase of Furniture and Equipment

Section 36.309 of the proposed rule would have required that newly purchased furniture or equipment made available for use at a place of public accommodation be accessible, to the extent such furniture or equipment is available, unless this requirement would fundamentally alter the goods, services, facilities, privileges, advantages, or accommodations offered, or would not be readily achievable. Proposed § 36.309 has been omitted from the final rule because the Department has determined that its requirements are more properly addressed under other sections, and because there are currently no appropriate accessibility standards addressing many types of furniture and equipment.

Some types of equipment will be required to meet the accessibility requirements of subpart D. For example, ADAAG establishes technical and scoping requirements in new construction and alterations for automated teller machines and telephones. Purchase or modification of equipment is required in certain instances by the provisions in §§ 36.201 and 36.202. For example, an arcade may need to provide accessible video machines in order to ensure full and equal enjoyment of the facilities and to provide an opportunity to participate in the services and facilities it provides. The barrier removal requirements of § 36.304 will apply as well to furniture and equipment (lowering shelves, rearranging furniture, adding Braille labels to a vending machine).

Section 36.309 Examinations and Courses

Section 36.309(a) sets forth the general rule that any private entity that offers examinations or courses related to applications, licensing, certification, or credentialing for secondary or postsecondary education, professional, or trade purposes shall offer such examinations or courses in a place and manner accessible to persons with disabilities or offer alternative accessible arrangements for such individuals.

Paragraph (a) restates section 309 of the Americans with Disabilities Act. Section 309 is intended to fill the gap that is created when licensing, certification, and other testing authorities are not covered by section 504 of the Rehabilitation Act or title II of the ADA. Any such authority that is covered by section 504, because of the receipt of Federal money, or by title II, because it is a function of a State or local government, must make all of its programs accessible to persons with disabilities, which includes physical access as well as modifications in the way the test is administered, e.g., extended time, written instructions, or assistance of a reader.

Many licensing, certification, and testing authorities are not covered by section 504, because no Federal money is received; nor are they covered by title II of the ADA because they are not State or local agencies. However, States often require the licenses provided by such authorities in order for an individual to practice a particular profession or trade. Thus, the provision was included in the ADA in order to assure that persons with disabilities are not foreclosed from educational, professional, or trade opportunities because an examination or course is conducted in an inaccessible site or without needed modifications.

As indicated in the "Application" section of this part (§ 36.102), § 36.309 applies to any private entity that offers the specified types of examinations or courses. This is consistent with section 309 of the Americans with Disabilities Act, which states that the requirements apply to "any person" offering examinations or courses.

The Department received a large number of comments on this section, reflecting the importance of ensuring that the key gateways to education and employment are open to individuals with disabilities. The most frequent comments were objections to the fundamental alteration and undue burden provisions in §§ 36.309 (b)(3) and (c)(3) and to allowing courses and examinations to be provided through alternative accessible arrangements, rather than in an integrated setting.

Although section 309 of the Act does not refer to a fundamental alteration or undue burden limitation, those limitations do appear in section 302(b)(2)(A)(iii) of the Act, which establishes the obligation of public accommodations to provide auxiliary aids and services. The Department, therefore, included it in the paragraphs of § 36.309 requiring the provision of auxiliary aids. One commenter argued that similar limitations should apply to all of the requirements of § 36.309, but the Department did not consider this extension appropriate.

Commenters who objected to permitting "alternative accessible arrangements" argued that such arrangements allow segregation and should not be permitted, unless they are the least restrictive available alternative, for example, for someone who cannot leave home. Some commenters made a distinction between courses, where interaction is an important part of the educational experience, and examinations, where it may be less important. Because the statute specifically authorizes alternative accessible arrangements as a method of meeting the requirements of section 309, the Department has not adopted this suggestion. The Department notes, however, that, while examinations of the type covered by § 36.309 may not be covered elsewhere in the regulation, courses will generally be offered in a "place of education," which is included in the definition of "place of public accommodation" in § 36.104, and, therefore, will be subject to the integrated setting requirement of § 36.203.

Section 36.309(b) sets forth specific requirements for examinations. Examinations covered by this section would include a bar exam or the Scholastic Aptitude Test prepared by the Educational Testing Service. Paragraph (b)(1) is adopted from the Department of Education's section 504 regulation on admission tests to postsecondary educational programs (34 CFR 104.42(b)(3)). Paragraph (b)(1)(i) requires that a private entity offering an examination covered by the section must assure that the examination is selected and administered so as to best ensure that the examination accurately reflects an individual's aptitude or achievement level or other factor the examination purports to measure, rather than reflecting the individual's impaired sensory, manual, or speaking skills (except where those skills are the factors that the examination purports to measure).

Paragraph (b)(1)(ii) requires that any examination specially designed for individuals with disabilities be offered as often and in as timely a manner as other examinations. Some commenters noted that persons with disabilities may be required to travel long distances when the locations for examinations for individuals with disabilities are limited, for example, to only one city in a State instead of a variety of cities. The Department has therefore revised this paragraph to add a requirement that such examinations be offered at locations that are as convenient as the location of other examinations.

Commenters representing organizations that

administer tests wanted to be able to require individuals with disabilities to provide advance notice and appropriate documentation, at the applicants' expense, of their disabilities and of any modifications or aids that would be required. The Department agrees that such requirements are permissible, provided that they are not unreasonable and that the deadline for such notice is no earlier than the deadline for others applying to take the examination. Requiring individuals with disabilities to file earlier applications would violate the requirement that examinations designed for individuals with disabilities be offered in as timely a manner as other examinations.

Examiners may require evidence that an applicant is entitled to modifications or aids as required by this section, but requests for documentation must be reasonable and must be limited to the need for the modification or aid requested. Appropriate documentation might include a letter from a physician or other professional, or evidence of a prior diagnosis or accommodation, such as eligibility for a special education program. The applicant may be required to bear the cost of providing such documentation, but the entity administering the examination cannot charge the applicant for the cost of any modifications or auxiliary aids, such as interpreters, provided for the examination.

Paragraph (b)(1)(iii) requires that examinations be administered in facilities that are accessible to individuals with disabilities or alternative accessible arrangements are made.

Paragraph (b)(2) gives examples of modifications to examinations that may be necessary in order to comply with this section. These may include providing more time for completion of the examination or a change in the manner of giving the examination, e.g., reading the examination to the individual.

Paragraph (b)(3) requires the provision of auxiliary aids and services, unless the private entity offering the examination can demonstrate that offering a particular auxiliary aid would fundamentally alter the examination or result in an undue burden. Examples of auxiliary aids include taped examinations, interpreters or other effective methods of making aurally delivered materials available to individuals with hearing impairments, readers for individuals with visual impairments or learning disabilities, and other similar services and actions. The suggestion that individuals with learning disabilities may need readers is included, although it does not appear in the Department of Education regulation, because, in fact, some individuals with learning disabilities have visual perception problems and would benefit from a reader.

Many commenters pointed out the importance of ensuring that modifications provide the individual with a disability an equal opportunity to demonstrate his or her knowledge or ability. For example, a reader who is unskilled or lacks knowledge of specific terminology used in the examination may be unable to convey the information in the questions or to follow the applicant's instructions effectively. Commenters pointed out that, for persons with visual impairments who read Braille, Braille provides the closest functional equivalent to a printed test. The Department has, therefore, added Brailled examinations to the examples of auxiliary aids and services that may be required. For similar reasons, the Department also added to the list of examples of auxiliary aids and services large print examinations and answer sheets; "qualified" readers; and transcribers to write answers.

A commenter suggested that the phrase "fundamentally alter the examination" in this paragraph of the proposed rule be revised to more accurately reflect the function affected. In the final rule the Department has substituted the phrase "fundamentally alter the measurement of the skills or knowledge the examination is intended to test."

Paragraph (b)(4) gives examples of alternative accessible arrangements. For instance, the private entity might be required to provide the examination at an individual's home with a proctor. Alternative arrangements must provide conditions for individuals with disabilities that are comparable to the conditions under which other individuals take the examinations. In other words, an examination cannot be offered to an individual with a disability in a cold, poorly lit basement, if other individuals are given the examination in a warm, well lit classroom.

Some commenters who provide examinations for licensing or certification for particular occupations or professions urged that they be permitted to refuse to provide modifications or aids for persons seeking to take the examinations if those individuals, because of their disabilities, would be unable to perform the essential functions of the profession or occupation for which the examination is given, or unless the disability is reasonably determined in advance as not being an obstacle to certification. The Department has not changed its rule based on this comment. An examination is one stage of a licensing or certification process. An individual should not be barred from attempting to pass that stage of the process merely because he or she might be unable to meet other requirements of the process. If the examination is not the first stage of the qualification process, an applicant may be required to complete the earlier stages prior to being admitted to the examination. On the other hand, the applicant may not be denied admission to the examination on the basis of doubts about his or her abilities to meet requirements that the examination is not designed to test.

Paragraph (c) sets forth specific requirements for courses. Paragraph (c)(1) contains the general rule that any course covered by this section must be modified to ensure that the place and manner in which the course is given is accessible. Paragraph (c)(2) gives examples of possible modifications that might be required, including extending the time permitted for completion of the course, permitting oral rather than written delivery of an assignment by a person with a visual impairment, or adapting the manner in which the course is conducted (i.e., providing cassettes of class handouts to an individual with a visual impairment). In response to comments, the Department has added to the examples in paragraph (c)(2) specific reference to distribution of course materials. If course materials are published and available from other sources, the entity offering the course may give advance notice of what materials will be used so as to allow an individual to obtain them in Braille or on tape but materials provided by the course offerer must be made available in alternative formats for individuals with disabilities.

In language similar to that of paragraph (b), paragraph (c)(3) requires auxiliary aids and services, unless a fundamental alteration or undue burden would result, and paragraph (c)(4) requires that courses be administered in accessible facilities. Paragraph (c)(5) gives examples of alternative accessible arrangements. These may include provision of the course through videotape, cassettes, or prepared notes. Alternative arrangements must provide comparable conditions to those provided to others, including similar lighting, room temperature, and the like. An entity offering a variety of courses, to fulfill continuing education requirements for a profession, for example, may not limit the selection or choice of courses available to individuals with disabilities.

Section 36.310 Transportation Provided by Public Accommodations

Section 36.310 contains specific provisions relating to public accommodations that provide transportation to their clients or customers. This section has been substantially revised in order to coordinate the requirements of this section with the requirements applicable to these transportation systems that will be contained in the regulations issued by the Secretary of Transportation pursuant to section 306 of the ADA, to be codified at 49 CFR part 37. The Department notes that, although the responsibility for issuing regulations applicable to transportation systems operated by public accommodations is divided between this Department and the Department of Transportation, enforcement authority is assigned only to the Department of Justice.

The Department received relatively few comments on this section of the proposed rule. Most of the comments addressed issues that are not specifically addressed in this part, such as the standards for accessible vehicles and the procedure for determining whether equivalent service is provided. Those standards will be contained in the regulation issued by the Department of Transportation. Other commenters raised questions about the types of transportation that will be subject to this section. In response to these inquiries, the Department has revised the list of examples contained in the regulation.

Paragraph (a)(1) states the general rule that covered public accommodations are subject to all of the specific provisions of subparts B, C, and D, except as provided in § 36.310. Examples of operations covered by the requirements are listed in paragraph (a)(2). The stated examples include hotel and motel airport shuttle services, customer shuttle bus services operated by private companies and shopping centers, student transportation, and shuttle operations of recreational facilities such as stadiums, zoos, amusement parks, and ski resorts. This brief list is not exhaustive. The section applies to any fixed route or demand responsive transportation system operated by a public accommodation for the benefit of its clients or customers. The section does not apply to transportation services provided only to employees. Employee transportation will be subject to the regulations issued by the Equal Employment Opportunity Commission to implement title I of the Act. However, if employees and customers or clients are served by the same transportation system, the provisions of this section will apply.

Paragraph (b) specifically provides that a public accommodation shall remove transportation barriers in existing vehicles to the extent that it is readily achievable to do so, but that the installation of hydraulic or other lifts is not required.

Paragraph (c) provides that public accommodations subject to this section shall comply with the requirements for transportation vehicles and systems contained in the regulations issued by the Secretary of Transportation.

Subpart D—New Construction and Alterations

Subpart D implements section 303 of the Act, which requires that newly constructed or altered places of public accommodation or commercial facilities be readily accessible to and usable by individuals with disabilities. This requirement contemplates a high degree of convenient access. It is intended to ensure that patrons and employees of places of public accommodation and employees of commercial facilities are able to get to, enter, and use the facility.

Potential patrons of places of public accommodation, such as retail establishments, should be able to get to a store, get into the store, and get to the areas where goods are being provided. Employees should have the same types of access, although those individuals require access to and around the employment area as well as to the area in which goods and services are provided.

The ADA is geared to the future—its goal being that, over time, access will be the rule, rather than the exception. Thus, the Act only requires modest expenditures, of the type addressed in § 36.304 of this part, to provide access to existing facilities not otherwise being altered, but requires all new construction and alterations to be accessible.

The Act does not require new construction or alterations; it simply requires that, when a public accommodation or other private entity undertakes the construction or alteration of a facility subject to the Act, the newly constructed or altered facility must be made accessible. This subpart establishes the requirements for new construction and alterations.

As explained under the discussion of the definition of "facility," § 36.104, pending development of specific requirements, the Department will not apply this subpart to places of public accommodation located in mobile units, boats, or other conveyances.

Section 36.401 New Construction

General

Section 36.401 implements the new construction requirements of the ADA. Section 303 (a)(1) of the Act provides that discrimination for purposes of section 302(a) of the Act includes a failure to design and construct facilities for first occupancy later than 30 months after the date of enactment (i.e., after January 26, 1993) that are readily accessible to and usable by individuals with disabilities.

Paragraph 36.401(a)(1) restates the general requirement for accessible new construction. The proposed rule stated that "any public accommodation or other private entity responsible for design and construction" must ensure that facilities conform to this requirement. Various commenters suggested that the proposed language was not consistent with the statute because it substituted "private entity responsible for design and construction" for the statutory language; because it did not address liability on the part of architects, contractors, developers, tenants, owners, and other entities; and because it limited the liability of entities responsible for commercial facilities. In response, the Department has revised this paragraph to repeat the language of section 303(a) of the ADA. The Department will interpret this section in a manner consistent with the intent of the statute and with the nature of the responsibilities of the various entities for design, for construction, or for both.

Designed and Constructed for First Occupancy

According to paragraph (a)(2), a facility is subject to the new construction requirements only if a completed application for a building permit or permit extension is filed after January 26, 1992, and the facility is occupied after January 26, 1993.

The proposed rule set forth for comment two alternative ways by which to determine what facilities are subject to the Act and what standards apply. Paragraph (a)(2) of the final rule is a slight variation on Option One in the proposed rule. The reasons for the Department's choice of Option One are discussed later in this section.

Paragraph (a)(2) acknowledges that Congress did not contemplate having actual occupancy be the sole trigger for the accessibility requirements, because the statute prohibits a failure to "design and construct for first occupancy," rather than requiring accessibility in facilities actually occupied after a particular date.

The commenters overwhelmingly agreed with the Department's proposal to use a date certain; many cited the reasons given in the preamble to the proposed rule. First, it is helpful for designers and builders to have a fixed date for accessible design, so that they can determine accessibility requirements early in the planning and design stage. It is difficult to determine accessibility requirements in anticipation of the actual date of first occupancy because of unpredictable and uncontrollable events (e.g., strikes affecting suppliers or labor, or natural disasters) that may delay occupancy. To redesign or reconstruct portions of a facility if it begins to appear that occupancy will be later than anticipated would be quite costly. A fixed date also assists those responsible for enforcing, or monitoring compliance with, the statute, and those protected by it.

The Department considered using as a trigger date for application of the accessibility standards the date on which a permit is granted. The Department chose instead the date on which a complete permit application is certified as received by the appropriate government entity. Almost all commenters agreed with this choice of a trigger date. This decision is based partly on information that several months or even years can pass between application for a permit and receipt of a permit. Design is virtually complete at the time an application is complete (i.e., certified to contain all the information required by the State, county, or local government). After an application is filed, delays may occur before the permit is granted due to numerous factors (not necessarily relating to accessibility): for example, hazardous waste discovered on the property, flood plain requirements, zoning disputes, or opposition to the project from various groups. These factors should not require redesign for accessibility if the application was completed before January 26, 1992. However, if the facility must be redesigned for other reasons, such as a change in density or environmental preservation, and the final permit is based on a new application, the rule would require accessibility if that application was certified complete after January 26, 1992.

The certification of receipt of a complete application for a building permit is an appropriate point in the process because certifications are issued in writing by governmental authorities. In addition, this approach presents a clear and objective standard.

However, a few commenters pointed out that in some jurisdictions it is not possible to receive a "certification" that an application is complete, and suggested that in those cases the fixed date should be the date on which an application for a permit is received by the government agency. The Department has included such a provision in § 36.401(a)(2)(i).

The date of January 26, 1992, is relevant only with respect to the last application for a permit or permit extension for a facility. Thus, if an entity has applied for only a "foundation" permit, the date of that permit application has no effect, because the entity must also apply for and receive a permit at a later date for the actual superstructure. In this case, it is the date of the later application that would control, unless construction is not completed within the time allowed by the permit, in which case a third permit would be issued and the date of the application for that permit would be determinative for purposes of the rule.

Choice of Option One for Defining "Designed and Constructed for First Occupancy"

Under the option the Department has chosen for determining applicability of the new construction standards, a building would be considered to be "for first occupancy" after January 26, 1993, only (1) if the last application for a building permit or permit extension for the facility is certified to be complete (or, in some jurisdictions, received) by a State, county, or local government after January 26, 1992, and (2) if the first certificate of occupancy is issued after January 26, 1993. The Department also asked for comment on an Option Two, which would have imposed new construction requirements if a completed application for a building permit or permit extension was filed after the enactment of the ADA (July 26, 1990), and the facility was occupied after January 26, 1993.

The request for comment on this issue drew a large number of comments expressing a wide range of views. Most business groups and some disability rights groups favored Option One, and some business groups and most disability rights groups favored Option Two. Individuals and government entities were equally divided; several commenters proposed other options.

Those favoring Option One pointed out that it is more reasonable in that it allows time for those subject to the new construction requirements to anticipate those requirements and to receive technical assistance pursuant to the Act. Numerous commenters said that time frames for designing and constructing some types of facilities (for example, health care facilities) can range from two to four years or more. They expressed concerns that Option Two, which would apply to some facilities already under design or construction as of the date the Act was signed, and to some on which construction began shortly after enactment, could result in costly redesign or reconstruction of those facilities. In the same vein, some Option One supporters found Option Two objectionable on due process grounds. In their view, Option Two would mean that in July 1991 (upon issuance of the final DOJ rule) the responsible entities would learn that ADA standards had been in effect since July 26, 1990, and this would amount to retroactive application of standards. Numerous commenters characterized Option Two as having no support in the statute and Option One as being more consistent with congressional intent.

Those who favored Option Two pointed out that it would include more facilities within the coverage of the new construction standards. They argued that because similar accessibility requirements are in effect under State laws, no hardship would be imposed by this option. Numerous commenters said that hardship would also be eliminated in light of their view that the ADA requires compliance with the Uniform Federal Accessibility Standards (UFAS) until issuance of DOJ standards. Those supporting Option Two claimed that it was more consistent with the statute and its legislative history.

The Department has chosen Option One rather than Option Two, primarily on the basis of the language of three relevant sections of the statute. First, section 303(a) requires compliance with accessibility standards set forth, or incorporated by reference in, regulations to be issued by the Department of Justice. Standing alone, this section cannot be read to require compliance with the Department's standards before those standards are issued (through this rulemaking). Second, according to section 310 of the statute, section 303 becomes effective on January 26, 1992. Thus, section 303 cannot impose requirements on the design of buildings before that date. Third, while section 306(d) of the Act requires compliance with UFAS if final regulations have not been issued, that provision cannot reasonably be read to take effect until July 26, 1991, the date by which the Department of Justice must issue final regulations under title III.

Option Two was based on the premise that the interim standards in section 306(d) take effect as of the ADA's enactment (July 26, 1990), rather than on the date by which the Department of Justice regulations are due to be issued (July 26, 1991). The initial clause of section 306(d)(1) itself is silent on this question:

> If final regulations have not been issued pursuant to this section, for new construction for which a * * * building permit is obtained prior to the issuance of final regulations * * * (interim standards apply).

The approach in Option Two relies partly on the language of section 310 of the Act, which provides that section 306, the interim standards provision, takes effect on the date of enactment. Under this interpretation the interim standards provision would prevail over the operative provision, section 303, which requires that new construction be accessible and which becomes effective January 26, 1992. This approach would also require construing the language of section 306(d)(1) to take effect before the Department's standards are due to be issued. The preferred reading of section 306 is that it would require that, if the Department's final standards had not been issued by July 26, 1991, UFAS would apply to certain buildings until such time as the Department's standards were issued.

General Substantive Requirements of the New Construction Provisions

The rule requires, as does the statute, that covered newly constructed facilities be readily accessible to and usable by individuals with disabilities. The phrase "readily accessible to and usable by individuals with disabilities" is a term that, in slightly varied formulations, has been used in the Architectural Barriers Act of 1968, the Fair Housing Act, the regulations implementing section 504 of the Rehabilitation Act of 1973, and current accessibility standards. It means, with respect to a facility or a portion of a facility, that it can be approached, entered, and used by individuals with disabilities (including mobility, sensory, and cognitive impairments) easily and conveniently. A facility that is constructed to meet the requirements of the rule's accessibility standards will be considered readily accessible and usable with respect to construction. To the extent that a particular type or element of a facility is not specifically addressed by the standards, the language of this section is the safest guide.

A private entity that renders an "accessible" building inaccessible in its operation, through policies or practices, may be in violation of section 302 of the Act. For example, a private entity can render an entrance to a facility inaccessible by keeping an accessible entrance open only during certain hours (whereas the facility is available to others for a greater length of time). A facility could similarly be rendered inaccessible if a person with disabilities is significantly limited in her or his choice of a range of accommodations.

Ensuring access to a newly constructed facility will include providing access to the facility from the street or parking lot, to the extent the responsible entity has control over the route from those locations. In some cases, the private entity will have no control over access at the point where streets, curbs, or sidewalks already exist, and in those instances the entity is encouraged to request modifications to a sidewalk, including installation of curb cuts, from a public entity responsible for them. However, as some commenters pointed out, there is no obligation for a private entity subject to title III of the ADA to seek or ensure compliance by a public entity with title II. Thus, although a locality may have an obligation under title II of the Act to install curb cuts at a particular location, that responsibility is separate from the private entity's title III obligation, and any involvement by a private entity in seeking cooperation from a public entity is purely voluntary in this context.

Work Areas

Proposed paragraph 36.401(b) addressed access to employment areas, rather than to the areas where goods or services are being provided. The preamble noted that the proposed paragraph provided guidance for new construction and alterations until more specific guidance was issued by the ATBCB and reflected in this Department's regulation. The entire paragraph has been deleted from this section in the final rule. The concepts of paragraphs (b) (1), (2), and (5) of the proposed rule are included, with modifications and expansion, in ADAAG. Paragraphs (3) and (4) of the proposed rule, concerning fixtures and equipment, are not included in the rule or in ADAAG.

Some commenters asserted that questions relating to new construction and alterations of work areas should be addressed by the EEOC under title I, as employment concerns. However, the legislative history of the statute clearly indicates that the new construction and alterations requirements of title III were intended to ensure accessibility of new facilities to all individuals, including employees. The language of section 303 sweeps broadly in its application to all public accommodations and commercial facilities. EEOC's title I regulations will address accessibility requirements that come into play when "reasonable accommodation" to individual employees or applicants with disabilities is mandated under title I.

The issues dealt with in proposed § 36.401(b) (1) and (2) are now addressed in ADAAG section 4.1.1(3). The Department's proposed paragraphs would have required that areas that will be used only by employees as work stations be constructed so that individuals with disabilities could approach, enter, and exit the areas. They would not have required that all individual work stations be constructed or equipped (for example, with shelves that are accessible or adaptable) to be accessible. This approach was based on the theory that, as long as an employee with disabilities could enter the building and get to and around the employment area, modifications in a particular work station could be instituted as a "reasonable accommodation" to that employee if the modifications were necessary and they did not constitute an undue hardship.

Almost all of the commenters agreed with the proposal to require access to a work area but not to require accessibility of each individual work station. This principle is included in ADAAG 4.1.1(3). Several of the comments related to the requirements of the proposed ADAAG and have been addressed in the accessibility standards.

Proposed paragraphs (b) (3) and (4) would have required that consideration be given to placing fixtures and equipment at accessible heights in the first instance, and to purchasing new equipment and fixtures that are adjustable. These paragraphs have not been included in the final rule because the rule in most instances does not establish accessibility standards for purchased equipment. (See discussion elsewhere in the preamble of proposed § 36.309.) While the Department encourages entities to consider providing accessible or adjustable fixtures and equipment for employees, this rule does not require them to do so.

Paragraph (b)(5) of proposed § 36.401 clarified that proposed paragraph (b) did not limit the requirement that employee areas other than individual work stations must be accessible. For example, areas that are employee "common use" areas and are not solely used as work stations (e.g., employee lounges, cafeterias, health units, exercise facilities) are treated no differently under this regulation than other parts of a building; they must be constructed or altered in compliance with the accessibility standards. This principle is not stated in § 36.401 but is implicit in the requirements of this section and ADAAG.

Commercial Facilities in Private Residences

Section 36.401(b) of the final rule is a new provision relating to commercial facilities located in private residences. The proposed rule addressed these requirements in the preamble to § 36.207, "Places of public accommodation located in private residences." The preamble stated that the approach for commercial facilities would be the same as that for places of public accommodation, i.e., those portions used exclusively as a commercial facility or used as both a commercial facility and for residential purposes would be covered. Because commercial facilities are only subject to new construction and alterations requirements, however, the covered portions would only be subject to subpart D. This approach is reflected in § 36.401(b)(1).

The Department is aware that the statutory definition of "commercial facility" excludes private residences because they are "expressly exempted from coverage under the Fair Housing Act of 1968, as amended." However, the Department interprets that exemption as applying only to facilities that are exclusively residential. When a facility is used as both a residence and a commercial facility, the exemption does not apply.

Paragraph (b)(2) is similar to the new paragraph (b) under § 36.207, "Places of public accommodation located in private residences." The paragraph clarifies that the covered portion includes not only the space used as a commercial facility, but also the elements used to enter the commercial facility, e.g., the homeowner's front sidewalk, if any; the doorway; the hallways; the restroom, if used by employees or visitors of the commercial facility; and any other portion of the residence, interior or exterior, used by employees or visitors of the commercial facility.

As in the case of public accommodations located in private residences, the new construction standards only apply to the extent that a portion of the residence is designed or intended for use as a commercial facility. Likewise, if a homeowner alters a portion of his home to convert it to a commercial facility, that work must be done in compliance with the alterations standards in appendix A.

Structural Impracticability

Proposed § 36.401(c) is included in the final rule with minor changes. It details a statutory exception to the new construction requirement: the requirement that new construction be accessible does not apply where an entity can demonstrate that it is structurally impracticable to meet the requirements of the regulation. This provision is also included in ADAAG, at section 4.1.1(5)(a).

Consistent with the legislative history of the ADA, this narrow exception will apply only in rare and unusual circumstances where unique characteristics of terrain make accessibility unusually difficult. Such limitations for topographical problems are analogous to an acknowledged limitation in the application of the accessibility requirements of the Fair Housing Amendments Act (FHAA) of 1988.

Almost all commenters supported this interpretation. Two commenters argued that the DOJ requirement is too limiting and would not exempt some buildings that should be exempted because of soil conditions, terrain, and other unusual site conditions. These commenters suggested consistency with HUD's Fair Housing Accessibility Guidelines (56 FR 9472 (1991)), which generally would allow exceptions from accessibility requirements, or allow compliance with less stringent requirements, on sites with slopes exceeding 10%.

The Department is aware of the provisions in HUD's guidelines, which were issued on March 6, 1991, after passage of the ADA and publication of the Department's proposed rule. The approach taken in these guidelines, which apply to different types of construction and implement different statutory requirements for new construction, does not bind this Department in regulating under the ADA. The Department has included in the final rule the substance of the proposed provision, which is faithful to the intent of the statute, as expressed in the legislative history. (See Senate report at 70-71; Education and Labor report at 120.)

The limited structural impracticability exception means that it is acceptable to deviate from accessibility requirements only where unique characteristics of terrain prevent the incorporation of accessibility features and where providing accessibility would destroy the physical integrity of a facility. A situation in which a building must be built on stilts because of its location in marshlands or over water is an example of one of the few situations in which the exception for structural impracticability would apply.

This exception to accessibility requirements should not be applied to situations in which a facility is located in "hilly" terrain or on a plot of land upon which there are steep grades. In such circumstances, accessibility can be achieved without destroying the physical integrity of a structure, and is required in the construction of new facilities.

Some commenters asked for clarification concerning when and how to apply the ADA rules or the Fair Housing Accessibility Guidelines, especially when a facility may be subject to both because of mixed use. Guidance on this question is provided in the discussion of the definitions of place of public accommodation and commercial facility. With respect to the structural impracticability exception, a mixed-use facility could not take advantage of the Fair Housing exemption, to the extent that it is less stringent than the ADA exemption, except for those portions of the facility that are subject only to the Fair Housing Act.

As explained in the preamble to the proposed rule, in those rare circumstances in which it is structurally impracticable to achieve full compliance with accessibility retirements under the ADA, places of public accommodation and commercial facilities should still be designed and constructed to incorporate accessibility features to the extent that the features are structurally practicable. The accessibility requirements should not be viewed as an all-or- nothing proposition in such circumstances.

If it is structurally impracticable for a facility in its entirety to be readily accessible to and usable by people with disabilities, then those portions that can be made accessible should be made accessible. If a building cannot be constructed in compliance with the full range of accessibility requirements because of structural impracticability, then it should still incorporate those features that are structurally practicable. If it is structurally impracticable to make a particular facility accessible to persons who have particular types of disabilities, it is still appropriate to require it to be made accessible to persons with other types of disabilities. For example, a facility that is of necessity built on stilts and cannot be made accessible to persons who use wheelchairs because it is structurally impracticable to do so, must be made accessible for individuals with vision or hearing impairments or other kinds of disabilities.

Elevator Exemption

Section 36.401(d) implements the "elevator exemption" for new construction in section 303(b) of the ADA. The elevator exemption is an exception to the general requirement that new facilities be readily accessible to and usable by individuals with disabilities. Generally, an elevator is the most common way to provide individuals who use wheelchairs "ready access" to floor levels above or below the ground floor of a multi-story building. Congress, however, chose not to require elevators in new small buildings, that is, those with less than three stories or less than 3,000 square feet per story. In buildings eligible for the exemption, therefore, "ready access" from the building entrance to a floor above or below the ground floor is not required, because the statute does not require that an elevator be installed in such buildings. The elevator exemption does not apply, however, to a facility housing a shopping center, a shopping mall, or the professional office of a health care provider, or other categories of facilities as determined by the Attorney General. For example, a new office building that will have only two stories, with no elevator planned, will not be required to have an elevator, even if each story has 20,000 square feet. In other words, having either less than 3000 square feet per story or less than three stories qualifies a facility for the exemption; it need not qualify for the exemption on both counts. Similarly, a facility that has five stories of 2800 square feet each qualifies for the exemption. If a facility has three or more stories at any point, it is not eligible for the elevator exemption unless all the stories are less than 3000 square feet.

The terms "shopping center or shopping mall" and "professional office of a health care provider" are defined in this section. They are substantively identical to the definitions included in the proposed rule in § 36.104, "Definitions." They have been moved to this section because, as commenters pointed out, they are relevant only for the purposes of the elevator exemption, and inclusion in the general definitions section could give the incorrect impression that an office of a health care provider is not covered as a place of public accommodation under other sections of the rule, unless the office falls within the definition.

For purposes of § 36.401, a "shopping center or shopping mall" is (1) a building housing five or more sales or rental establishments, or (2) a series of buildings on a common site, either under common ownership or common control or developed either as one project or as a series of related projects, housing five or more sales or rental establishments. The term "shopping center or shopping mall" only includes floor levels containing at least one sales or rental establishment, or any floor level that was designed or intended for use by at least one sales or rental establishment.

Any sales or rental establishment of the type that is included in paragraph (5) of the definition of "place of public accommodation" (for example, a bakery, grocery store, clothing store, or hardware store) is considered a sales or rental establishment for purposes of this definition; the other types of public accommodations (e.g., restaurants, laundromats, banks, travel services, health spas) are not.

In the preamble to the proposed rule, the Department sought comment on whether the definition of "shopping center or mall" should be expanded to include any of these other types of public accommodations. The Department also sought comment on whether a series of buildings should fall within the definition only if they are physically connected.

Most of those responding to the first question (overwhelmingly groups representing people with disabilities, or individual commenters) urged that the definition encompass more places of public accommodation, such as restaurants, motion picture houses, laundromats, dry cleaners, and banks. They pointed out that often it is not known what types of establishments will be tenants in a new facility. In addition, they noted that malls are advertised as entities, that their appeal is in the "package" of services offered to the public, and that this package often includes the additional types of establishments mentioned.

Commenters representing business groups sought to exempt banks, travel services, grocery stores, drug stores, and freestanding retail stores from the elevator requirement. They based this request on the desire to continue the practice in some locations of incorporating mezzanines housing administrative offices, raised pharmacist areas, and raised areas in the front of supermarkets that house safes and are used by managers to oversee operations of check-out aisles and other functions. Many of these concerns are adequately addressed by ADAAG. Apart from those addressed by

ADAAG, the Department sees no reason to treat a particular type of sales or rental establishment differently from any other. Although banks and travel services are not included as "sales or rental establishments," because they do not fall under paragraph (5) of the definition of place of public accommodation, grocery stores and drug stores are included.

The Department has declined to include places of public accommodation other than sales or rental establishments in the definition. The statutory definition of "public accommodation" (section 301(7)) lists 12 types of establishments that are considered public accommodations. Category (E) includes "a bakery, grocery store, clothing store, hardware store, shopping center, or other sales or rental establishment." This arrangement suggests that it is only these types of establishments that would make up a shopping center for purposes of the statute. To include all types of places of public accommodation, or those from 6 or 7 of the categories, as commenters suggest, would overly limit the elevator exemption; the universe of facilities covered by the definition of "shopping center" could well exceed the number of multitenant facilities not covered, which would render the exemption almost meaningless.

For similar reasons, the Department is rctaining the requirement that a building or series of buildings must house five or more sales or rental establishments before it falls within the definition of "shopping center." Numerous commenters objected to the number and requested that the number be lowered from five to three or four. Lowering the number in this manner would include an inordinately large number of two-story multitenant buildings within the category of those required to have elevators.

The responses to the question concerning whether a series of buildings should be connected in order to be covered were varied. Generally, disability rights groups and some government agencies said a series of buildings should not have to be connected, and pointed to a trend in some areas to build shopping centers in a garden or village setting. The Department agrees that this design choice should not negate the elevator requirement for new construction. Some business groups answered the question in the affirmative, and some suggested a different definition of shopping center. For example, one commenter recommended the addition of a requirement that the five or more establishments be physically connected on the non-ground floors by a common pedestrian walkway or pathway, because otherwise a series of stand-alone facilities would have to comply with the elevator requirement, which would be unduly burdensome and perhaps infeasible. Another suggested use of what it characterized as the standard industry definition: "A group of retail stores and related business facilities, the whole planned, developed, operated and managed as a unit." While the rule's definition would reach a series of related projects that are under common control but were not developed as a single project, the Department considers such a facility to be a shopping center within the meaning of the statute. However, in light of the hardship that could confront a series of existing small stand-alone buildings if elevators were required in alterations, the Department has included a common access route in the definition of shopping center or shopping mall for purposes of § 36.404.

Some commenters suggested that access to restrooms and other shared facilities open to the public should be required even if those facilities were not on a shopping floor. Such a provision with respect to toilet or bathing facilities is included in the elevator exception in final ADAAG 4.1.3(5).

For purposes of this subpart, the rule does not distinguish between a "shopping mall" (usually a building with a roofed-over common pedestrian area serving more than one tenant in which a majority of the tenants have a main entrance from the common pedestrian area) and a "shopping center" (e.g., a "shopping strip"). Any facility housing five or more of the types of sales or rental establishments described, regardless of the number of other types of places of public accommodation housed there (e.g., offices, movie theatres, restaurants), is a shopping center or shopping mall.

For example, a two-story facility built for mixed-use occupancy on both floors (e.g., by sales and rental establishments, a movie theater, restaurants, and general office space) is a shopping center or shopping mall if it houses five or more sales or rental establishments. If none of these establishments is located on the second floor, then only the ground floor, which contains the sales or rental establishments, would be a "shopping center or shopping mall," unless the second floor was designed or intended for use by at least one sales or rental establishment. In determining whether a floor was intended for such use, factors to be considered include the types of establishments that first occupied the floor, the nature of the developer's marketing strategy, i.e., what types of establishments were sought, and inclusion of any design features particular to rental and sales establishments.

A "professional office of a health care provider" is defined as a location where a person or entity regulated by a State to provide professional services related to the physical or mental health of an individual makes such services available to the public. In a two-story development that houses health care providers only on the ground floor, the "professional office of a health care provider" is limited to the ground floor unless the second floor was designed or intended for use by a health care provider. In determining if a floor was intended for such use, factors to be considered include whether the facility was constructed with special plumbing, electrical, or other features needed by health care providers, whether the developer marketed the facility as a medical office center, and whether any of the establishments that first occupied the floor was, in fact, a health care provider.

In addition to requiring that a building that is a shopping center, shopping mall, or the professional office of a health care provider have an elevator regardless of square footage or number of floors, the ADA (section 303(b)) provides that the Attorney General may determine that a particular category of facilities requires the installation of elevators based on the usage of the facilities. The Department, as it proposed to do, has added to the nonexempt categories terminals, depots, or other stations used for specified public transportation, and airport passenger terminals. Numerous commenters in all categories endorsed this proposal; none opposed it. It is not uncommon for an airport passenger terminal or train station, for example, to have only two floors, with gates on both floors. Because of the significance of transportation, because a person with disabilities could be arriving or departing at any gate, and because inaccessible facilities could result in a total denial of transportation services, it is reasonable to require that newly constructed transit facilities be accessible, regardless of square footage or number of floors. One comment suggested an amendment that would treat terminals and stations similarly to shopping centers, by requiring an accessible route only to those areas used for passenger loading and unloading and for other passenger services. Paragraph (d)(2)(ii) has been modified accordingly.

Some commenters suggested that other types of facilities (e.g., educational facilities, libraries, museums, commercial facilities, and social service facilities) should be included in the category of nonexempt facilities. The Department has not found adequate justification for including any other types of facilities in the nonexempt category at this time.

Section 36.401(d)(2) establishes the operative requirements concerning the elevator exemption and its application to shopping centers and malls, professional offices of health care providers, transit stations, and airport passenger terminals. Under the rule's framework, it is necessary first to determine if a new facility (including one or more buildings) houses places of public accommodation or commercial facilities that are in the categories for which elevators are required. If so, and the facility is a shopping center or shopping mall, or a professional office of a health care provider, then any area housing such an office or a sales or rental establishment or the professional office of a health care provider is not entitled to the elevator exemption.

The following examples illustrate the application of these principles:

1. A shopping mall has an upper and a lower level. There are two "anchor stores" (in this case, major department stores at either end of the mall, both with exterior entrances and an entrance on each level from the common area). In addition, there are 30 stores (sales or rental establishments) on the upper level, all of which have entrances from a common central area. There are 30 stores on the lower level, all of which have entrances from a common central area. According to the rule, elevator access must be provided to each store and to each level of the anchor stores. This requirement could be satisfied with respect to the 60 stores through elevators connecting the two pedestrian levels, provided that an individual could travel from the elevator to any other point on that level (i.e., into any store through a common pedestrian area) on an accessible path.

2. A commercial (nonresidential) "townhouse" development is composed of 20 two-story attached buildings. The facility is developed as one project, with common ownership, and the space will be leased to retailers. Each building has one accessible entrance from a pedestrian walk to the first floor. From that point, one can enter a store on the first floor, or walk up a flight of stairs to a store on the second floor. All 40 stores must be accessible at ground floor level or by accessible vertical access from that level. This does not mean, however, that 20 elevators must be installed. Access could be provided to the second floor by an elevator from the pedestrian area on the lower level to an upper walkway connecting all the areas on the second floor.

3. In the same type of development, it is planned that retail stores will be housed exclusively on the ground floor, with only office space (not professional offices of health care providers) on the second. Elevator access need not be provided to the second floor because all the sales or rental establishments (the entities that make the facility a shopping center) are located on an accessible ground floor.

4. In the same type of development, the space is

designed and marketed as medical or office suites, or as a medical office facility. Accessible vertical access must be provided to all areas, as described in example 2.

Some commenters suggested that building owners who knowingly lease or rent space to nonexempt places of public accommodation would violate § 36.401. However, the Department does not consider leasing or renting inaccessible space in itself to constitute a violation of this part. Nor does a change in use of a facility, with no accompanying alterations (e.g., if a psychiatrist replaces an attorney as a tenant in a second-floor office, but no alterations are made to the office) trigger accessibility requirements.

Entities cannot evade the requirements of this section by constructing facilities in such a way that no story is intended to constitute a "ground floor." For example, if a private entity constructs a building whose main entrance leads only to stairways or escalators that connect with upper or lower floors, the Department would consider at least one level of the facility a ground story.

The rule requires in § 36.401(d)(3), consistent with the proposed rule, that, even if a building falls within the elevator exemption, the floor or floors other than the ground floor must nonetheless be accessible, except for elevator access, to individuals with disabilities, including people who use wheelchairs. This requirement applies to buildings that do not house sales or rental establishments or the professional offices of a health care provider as well as to those in which such establishments or offices are all located on the ground floor. In such a situation, little added cost is entailed in making the second floor accessible, because it is similar in structure and floor plan to the ground floor.

There are several reasons for this provision. First, some individuals who are mobility impaired may work on a building's second floor, which they can reach by stairs and the use of crutches; however, the same individuals, once they reach the second floor, may then use a wheelchair that is kept in the office. Secondly, because the first floor will be accessible, there will be little additional cost entailed in making the second floor, with the same structure and generally the same floor plan, accessible. In addition, the second floor must be accessible to those persons with disabilities who do not need elevators for level changes (for example, persons with sight or hearing impairments and those with certain mobility impairments). Finally, if an elevator is installed in the future for any reason, full access to the floor will be facilitated.

One commenter asserted that this provision goes beyond the Department's authority under the Act, and disagreed with the Department's claim that little additional cost would be entailed in compliance. However, the provision is taken directly from the legislative history (see Education and Labor report at 114).

One commenter said that where an elevator is not required, platform lifts should be required. Two commenters pointed out that the elevator exemption is really an exemption from the requirement for providing an accessible route to a second floor not served by an elevator. The Department agrees with the latter comment. Lifts to provide access between floors are not required in buildings that are not required to have elevators. This point is specifically addressed in the appendix to ADAAG (§ 4.1.3(5)). ADAAG also addresses in detail the situations in which lifts are permitted or required.

Section 36.402 Alterations

Sections 36.402-36.405 implement section 303(a)(2) of the Act, which requires that alterations to existing facilities be made in a way that ensures that the altered portion is readily accessible to and usable by individuals with disabilities. This part does not require alterations; it simply provides that when alterations are undertaken, they must be made in a manner that provides access.

Section 36.402(a)(1) provides that any alteration to a place of public accommodation or a commercial facility, after January 26, 1992, shall be made so as to ensure that, to the maximum extent feasible, the altered portions of the facility are readily accessible to and usable by individuals with disabilities, including individuals who use wheelchairs.

The proposed rule provided that an alteration would be deemed to be undertaken after January 26, 1992, if the physical alteration of the property is in progress after that date. Commenters pointed out that this provision would, in some cases, produce an unjust result by requiring the redesign or retrofitting of projects initiated before this part established the ADA accessibility standards. The Department agrees that the proposed rule would, in some instances, unfairly penalize projects that were substantially completed before the effective date. Therefore, paragraph (a)(2) has been revised to specify that an alteration will be deemed to be undertaken after January 26, 1992, if the physical alteration of the property begins after that date. As a matter of interpretation, the Department will construe this provision to apply to alterations that require a permit from a State, County or local government, if physical alterations pursuant to the terms of the permit begin after January 26, 1992. The Department recognizes that this application of the effective date may require redesign of some facilities that were planned prior to the publication of this part, but no retrofitting will be required of facilities on which the physical alterations were initiated prior to the effective date of the Act. Of course, nothing in this section in any way alters the obligation of any facility to remove architectural barriers in existing facilities to the extent that such barrier removal is readily achievable.

Paragraph (b) provides that, for the purposes of this part, an "alteration" is a change to a place of public accommodation or a commercial facility that affects or could affect the usability of the building or facility or any part thereof. One commenter suggested that the concept of usability should apply only to those changes that affect access by persons with disabilities. The Department remains convinced that the Act requires the concept of "usability" to be read broadly to include any change that affects the usability of the facility, not simply changes that relate directly to access by individuals with disabilities.

The Department received a significant number of comments on the examples provided in paragraphs (b)(1) and (b)(2) of the proposed rule. Some commenters urged the Department to limit the application of this provision to major structural modifications, while others asserted that it should be expanded to include cosmetic changes such as painting and wallpapering. The Department believes that neither approach is consistent with the legislative history, which requires this Department's regulation to be consistent with the accessibility guidelines (ADAAG) developed by the Architectural and Transportation Barriers Compliance Board (ATBCB). Although the legislative history contemplates that, in some instances, the ADA accessibility standards will exceed the current MGRAD requirements, it also clearly indicates the view of the drafters that "minor changes such as painting or papering walls * * * do not affect usability" (Education and Labor report at 111, Judiciary report at 64), and, therefore, are not alterations. The proposed rule was based on the existing MGRAD definition of "alteration." The language of the final rule has been revised to be consistent with ADAAG, incorporated as appendix A to this part.

Some commenters sought clarification of the intended scope of this section. The proposed rule contained illustrations of changes that affect usability and those that do not. The intent of the illustrations was to explain the scope of the alterations requirement; the effect was to obscure it. As a result of the illustrations, some commenters concluded that any alteration to a facility, even a minor alteration such as relocating an electrical outlet, would trigger an extensive obligation to provide access throughout an entire facility. That result was never contemplated.

Therefore, in this final rule paragraph (b)(1) has been revised to include the major provisions of paragraphs (b)(1) and (b)(2) of the proposed rule. The examples in the proposed rule have been deleted. Paragraph (b)(1) now provides that alterations include, but are not limited to, remodeling, renovation, rehabilitation, reconstruction, historic restoration, changes or rearrangement in structural parts or elements, and changes or rearrangement in the plan configuration of walls and full-height partitions. Normal maintenance, reroofing, painting or wallpapering, asbestos removal, or changes to mechanical and electrical systems are not alterations unless they affect the usability of building or facility.

Paragraph (b)(2) of this final rule was added to clarify the scope of the alterations requirement. Paragraph (b)(2) provides that if existing elements, spaces, or common areas are altered, then each such altered element, space, or area shall comply with the applicable provisions of appendix A (ADAAG). As provided in § 36.403, if an altered space or area is an area of the facility that contains a primary function, then the requirements of that section apply.

Therefore, when an entity undertakes a minor alteration to a place of public accommodation or commercial facility, such as moving an electrical outlet, the new outlet must be installed in compliance with ADAAG. (Alteration of the elements listed in § 36.403(c)(2) cannot trigger a path of travel obligation.) If the alteration is to an area, such as an employee lounge or locker room, that is not an area of the facility that contains a primary function, that area must comply with ADAAG. It is only when an alteration affects access to or usability of an area containing a primary function, as opposed to other areas or the elements listed in § 36.403(c)(2), that the path of travel to the altered area must be made accessible.

The Department received relatively few comments on paragraph (c), which explains the statutory phrase "to the maximum extent feasible." Some commenters suggested that the regulation should specify that cost is a factor in determining whether it is feasible to make an altered area accessible. The legislative history of the ADA indicates that the concept of feasibility only reaches the question of whether it is possible to make the alteration accessible in compliance with this part. Costs are to be considered only when an alteration to an area containing a primary function triggers an additional requirement to make the path of travel to the altered area accessible.

Section 36.402(c) is, therefore, essentially unchanged from the proposed rule. At the recommendation of a commenter, the Department has inserted the word "virtually" to modify "impossible" to conform to the language of the legislative history. It explains that the phrase "to the maximum extent feasible" as used in this section applies to the occasional case where the nature of an existing facility makes it virtually impossible to comply fully with applicable accessibility standards through a planned alteration. In the occasional cases in which full compliance is impossible, alterations shall provide the maximum physical accessibility feasible. Any features of the facility that are being altered shall be made accessible unless it is technically infeasible to do so. If providing accessibility in conformance with this section to individuals with certain disabilities (e.g., those who use wheelchairs) would not be feasible, the facility shall be made accessible to persons with other types of disabilities (e.g., those who use crutches or who have impaired vision or hearing, or those who have other types of impairments).

Section 36.403 Alterations: Path of Travel

Section 36.403 implements the statutory requirement that any alteration that affects or could affect the usability of or access to an area of a facility that contains a primary function shall be made so as to ensure that, to the maximum extent feasible, the path of travel to the altered area, and the restrooms, telephones, and drinking fountains serving the altered area, are readily accessible to and usable by individuals with disabilities, including individuals who use wheelchairs, unless the cost and scope of such alterations is disproportionate to the cost of the overall alteration. Paragraph (a) restates this statutory requirement.

Paragraph (b) defines a "primary function" as a major activity for which the facility is intended. This paragraph is unchanged from the proposed rule. Areas that contain a primary function include, but are not limited to, the customer services lobby of a bank, the dining area of a cafeteria, the meeting rooms in a conference center, as well as offices and all other work areas in which the activities of the public accommodation or other private entities using the facility are carried out. The concept of "areas containing a primary function" is analogous to the concept of "functional spaces" in § 3.5 of the existing Uniform Federal Accessibility Standards, which defines "functional spaces" as "[t]he rooms and spaces in a building or facility that house the major activities for which the building or facility is intended."

Paragraph (b) provides that areas such as mechanical rooms, boiler rooms, supply storage rooms, employee lounges and locker rooms, janitorial closets, entrances, corridors, and restrooms are not areas containing a primary function. There may be exceptions to this general rule. For example, the availability of public restrooms at a place of public accommodation at a roadside rest stop may be a major factor affecting customers' decisions to patronize the public accommodation. In that case, a restroom would be considered to be an "area containing a primary function" of the facility.

Most of the commenters who addressed this issue supported the approach taken by the Department; but a few commenters suggested that areas not open to the general public or those used exclusively by employees should be excluded from the definition of primary function. The preamble to the proposed rule noted that the Department considered an alternative approach to the definition of "primary function," under which a primary function of a commercial facility would be defined as a major activity for which the facility was intended, while a primary function of a place of public accommodation would be defined as an activity which involves providing significant goods, services, facilities, privileges, advantages, or accommodations. However, the Department concluded that, although portions of the legislative history of the ADA support this alternative, the better view is that the language now contained in § 36.403(b) most accurately reflects congressional intent. No commenter made a persuasive argument that the Department's interpretation of the legislative history is incorrect.

When the ADA was introduced, the requirement to make alterations accessible was included in section 302 of the Act, which identifies the practices that constitute discrimination by a public accommodation. Because section 302 applies only to the operation of a place of public accommodation, the alterations requirement was intended only to provide access to clients and customers of a public accommodation. It was anticipated that access would be provided to employees with disabilities under the "reasonable accommodation" requirements of title I. However, during its consideration of the ADA, the House Judiciary Committee amended the bill to move the alterations provision from section 302 to section 303, which applies to commercial facilities as well as public accommodations. The Committee report accompanying the bill explains that:

> New construction and alterations of both public accommodations and commercial facilities must be made readily accessible to and usable by individuals with disabilities * * *. Essentially, [this requirement] is designed to ensure that patrons and employees of public accommodations and commercial facilities are able to get to, enter and use the facility * * *. The rationale for making new construction accessible applies with equal force to alterations.

Judiciary report at 62-63 (emphasis added).

The ADA, as enacted, contains the language of section 303 as it was reported out of the Judiciary Committee. Therefore, the Department has concluded that the concept of "primary function" should be applied in the same manner to places of public accommodation and to commercial facilities, thereby including employee work areas in places of public accommodation within the scope of this section.

Paragraph (c) provides examples of alterations that affect the usability of or access to an area containing a primary function. The examples include: Remodeling a merchandise display area or employee work areas in a department store; installing a new floor surface to replace an inaccessible surface in the customer service area or employee work areas of a bank; redesigning the assembly line area of a factory; and installing a computer center in an accounting firm. This list is illustrative, not exhaustive. Any change that affects the usability of or access to an area containing a primary function triggers the statutory obligation to make the path of travel to the altered area accessible.

When the proposed rule was drafted, the Department believed that the rule made it clear that the ADA would require alterations to the path of travel only when such alterations are not disproportionate to the alteration to the primary function area. However, the comments that the Department received indicated that many commenters believe that even minor alterations to individual elements would require additional alterations to the path of travel. To address the concern of these commenters, a new paragraph (c)(2) has been added to the final rule to provide that alterations to such elements as windows, hardware, controls (e.g. light switches or thermostats), electrical outlets, or signage will not be deemed to be alterations that affect the usability of or access to an area containing a primary function. Of course, each element that is altered must comply with ADAAG (appendix A) . The cost of alterations to individual elements would be included in the overall cost of an alteration for purposes of determining disproportionality and would be counted when determining the aggregate cost of a series of small alterations in accordance with § 36.401(h) if the area is altered in a manner that affects access to or usability of an area containing a primary function.

Paragraph (d) concerns the respective obligations of landlords and tenants in the cases of alterations that trigger the path of travel requirement under § 36.403. This paragraph was contained in the landlord/tenant section of the proposed rule, § 36.201(b). If a tenant is making alterations upon its premises pursuant to terms of a lease that grant it the authority to do so (even if they constitute alterations that trigger the path of travel requirement), and the landlord is not making alterations to other parts of the facility, then the alterations by the tenant on its own premises do not trigger a path of travel obligation upon the landlord in areas of the facility under the landlord's authority that are not otherwise being altered. The legislative history makes clear that the path of travel requirement applies only to the entity that is already making the alteration, and thus the Department has not changed the final rule despite numerous comments suggesting that the tenant be required to provide a path of travel.

Paragraph (e) defines a "path of travel" as a continuous, unobstructed way of pedestrian passage by means of which an altered area may be approached, entered, and exited; and which connects the altered area with an exterior approach (including sidewalks, streets, and parking areas), an entrance to the facility, and other parts of the facility. This concept of an accessible path of travel is analogous to the concepts of "accessible route" and "circulation path" contained in section 3.5 of the current UFAS. Some commenters suggested that this paragraph should address emergency egress. The Department disagrees. "Path of travel" as it is used in this section is a term of art under the ADA that relates only to the obligation of the public accommodation or commercial facility to provide additional accessible elements when an area containing a primary function is altered. The Department recognizes that emergency egress is an important issue, but believes that it is appropriately addressed in ADAAG (appendix A), not in this paragraph. Furthermore, ADAAG does not require changes to emergency egress areas in alterations.

Paragraph (e)(2) is drawn from section 3.5 of UFAS. It provides that an accessible path of travel may consist of walks and sidewalks, curb ramps and other interior or exterior pedestrian ramps; clear floor paths through lobbies, corridors, rooms, and other improved areas; parking access aisles; elevators and lifts; or a combination of such elements. Paragraph (e)(3) provides that, for the purposes of this part, the term "path of travel" also includes the restrooms, telephones, and drinking fountains serving an altered area.

Although the Act establishes an expectation that an accessible path of travel should generally be included when alterations are made to an area containing a primary function, Congress recognized that, in some circumstances, providing an accessible path of travel to an altered area may be sufficiently burdensome in comparison to the alteration being undertaken to the area containing a primary function as to render this requirement unreasonable. Therefore, Congress provided, in section 303(a)(2) of the Act, that alterations to the path of travel that are disproportionate in cost and scope to the overall alteration are not required.

The Act requires the Attorney General to determine at what point the cost of providing an accessible path of travel becomes disproportionate. The proposed rule provided three options for making this determination.

Two committees of Congress specifically addressed this issue: the House Committee on Education and Labor and the House Committee on the Judiciary. The reports issued by each committee suggested that accessibility alterations to a path of travel might be "disproportionate" if they exceed 30% of the alteration costs (Education and Labor report at 113; Judiciary report at 64). Because the Department believed that smaller percentage rates might be appropriate, the proposed rule sought comments on three options: 10%, 20%, or 30%.

The Department received a significant number of comments on this section. Commenters representing individuals with disabilities generally supported the use of 30% (or more); commenters representing covered entities supported a figure of 10% (or less). The Department believes that alterations made to provide an accessible path of travel to the altered area should be deemed disproportionate to the overall alteration when the cost exceeds 20% of the cost of the alteration to the primary function area. This approach appropriately reflects the intent of Congress to provide access for individuals with disabilities without causing economic hardship for the covered public accommodations and commercial facilities.

The Department has determined that the basis for this cost calculation shall be the cost of the alterations to the area containing the primary function. This approach will enable the public accommodation or other private entity that is making the alteration to calculate its obligation as a percentage of a clearly ascertainable base cost, rather than as a percentage of the "total" cost, an amount that will change as accessibility alterations to the path of travel are made.

Paragraph (f)(2) (paragraph (e)(2) in the proposed rule) is unchanged. It provides examples of costs that may be counted as expenditures required to provide an accessible path of travel. They include:

• Costs associated with providing an accessible entrance and an accessible route to the altered area, for example, the cost of widening doorways or installing ramps;

• Costs associated with making restrooms accessible, such as installing grab bars, enlarging toilet stalls, insulating pipes, or installing accessible faucet controls;

• Costs associated with providing accessible telephones, such as relocating telephones to an accessible height, installing amplification devices, or installing telecommunications devices for deaf persons (TDD's);

• Costs associated with relocating an inaccessible drinking fountain.

Paragraph (f)(1) of the proposed rule provided that when the cost of alterations necessary to make the path of travel serving an altered area fully accessible is disproportionate to the cost of the overall alteration, the path of travel shall be made accessible to the maximum extent feasible. In response to the suggestion of a commenter, the Department has made an editorial change in the final rule (paragraph (g)(1)) to clarify that if the cost of providing a fully accessible path of travel is disproportionate, the path of travel shall be made accessible "to the extent that it can be made accessible without incurring disproportionate costs."

Paragraph (g)(2) (paragraph (f)(2) in the NPRM) establishes that priority should be given to those elements that will provide the greatest access, in the following order: An accessible entrance; an accessible route to the altered area; at least one accessible restroom for each sex or a single unisex restroom; accessible telephones; accessible drinking fountains; and, whenever possible, additional accessible elements such as parking, storage, and alarms. This paragraph is unchanged from the proposed rule.

Paragraph (h) (paragraph (g) in the proposed rule) provides that the obligation to provide an accessible path of travel may not be evaded by performing a series of small alterations to the area served by a single path of travel if those alterations could have been performed as a single undertaking. If an area containing a primary function has been altered without providing an accessible path of travel to serve that area, and subsequent alterations of that area, or a different area on the same path of travel, are undertaken within three years of the original alteration, the total cost of alterations to primary function areas on that path of travel during the preceding three year period shall be considered in determining whether the cost of making the path of travel serving that area accessible is disproportionate. Only alterations undertaken after January 26, 1992, shall be considered in determining if the cost of providing accessible features is disproportionate to the overall cost of the alterations.

Section 36.404 Alterations: Elevator Exemption

Section 36.404 implements the elevator exemption in section 303(b) of the Act as it applies to altered facilities. The provisions of section 303(b) are discussed in the preamble to § 36.401(d) above. The statute applies the same exemption to both new construction and alterations. The principal difference between the requirements of § 36.401(d) and § 36.404 is that, in altering an existing facility that is not eligible for the statutory exemption, the public accommodation or other private entity responsible for the alteration is not required to install an elevator if the installation of an elevator would be disproportionate in cost and scope to the cost of the overall alteration as provided in § 36.403(f)(1). In addition, the standards referenced in § 36.406 (ADAAG) provide that installation of an elevator in an altered facility is not required if it is "technically infeasible."

This section has been revised to define the terms "professional office of a health care provider" and "shopping center or shopping mall" for the purposes of this section. The definition of "professional office of a health care provider" is identical to the definition included in § 36.401(d).

It has been brought to the attention of the Department that there is some misunderstanding about the scope of the elevator exemption as it applies to the professional office of a health care provider. A public accommodation, such as the professional office of a health care provider, is required to remove architectural barriers to its facility to the extent that such barrier removal is readily achievable (see § 36.304), but it is not otherwise required by this part to undertake new construction or alterations. This part does not require that an existing two story building that houses the professional office of a health care provider be altered for the purpose of providing elevator access. If, however, alterations to the area housing the office of the health care provider are undertaken for other purposes, the installation of an elevator might be required, but only if the cost of the elevator is not disproportionate to the cost of the overall alteration. Neither the Act nor this part prohibits a health care provider from locating his or her professional office in an existing facility that does not have an elevator.

Because of the unique challenges presented in altering existing facilities, the Department has adopted a definition of "shopping center or shopping mall" for the purposes of this section that is slightly different from the definition adopted under § 36.401(d). For the purposes of this section, a "shopping center or shopping mall" is (1) a building housing five or more sales or rental establishments, or (2) a series of buildings on a common site, connected by a common pedestrian access route above or below the ground floor, either under common ownership or common control or developed either as one project or as a series of related projects, housing five or more sales or rental establishments. As is the case with new construction, the term "shopping center or shopping mall" only includes floor levels housing at least one sales or rental establishment, or any floor level that was designed or intended for use by at least one sales or rental establishment.

The Department believes that it is appropriate to use a different definition of "shopping center or shopping mall" for this section than for § 36.401, in order to make it clear that a series of existing buildings on a common site that is altered for the use of sales or rental establishments does not become a "shopping center or shopping mall" required to install an elevator, unless there is a common means of pedestrian access above or below the ground floor. Without this exemption, separate, but adjacent, buildings that were initially designed and constructed independently of each other could be required to be retrofitted with elevators, if they were later renovated for a purpose not contemplated at the time of construction.

Like § 36.401(d), § 36.404 provides that the exemptions in this paragraph do not obviate or limit in any way the obligation to comply with the other accessibility requirements established in this subpart. For example, alterations to floors above or below the ground floor must be accessible regardless of whether the altered facility has an elevator. If a facility that is not required to install an elevator nonetheless has an elevator, that elevator shall meet, to the maximum extent feasible, the accessibility requirements of this section.

Section 36.405 Alterations: Historic Preservation

Section 36.405 gives effect to the intent of Congress, expressed in section 504(c) of the Act, that this part recognize the national interest in preserving significant historic structures. Commenters criticized the Department's use of descriptive terms in the proposed rule that are different from those used in the ADA to describe eligible historic properties. In addition, some commenters criticized the Department's decision to use the concept of "substantially impairing" the historic features of a property, which is a concept employed in regulations implementing section 504 of the Rehabilitation Act of 1973. Those commenters recommended that the Department adopt the criteria of "adverse effect" published by the Advisory Council on Historic Preservation under the National Historic Preservation Act (36 CFR 800.9) as the standard for determining whether an historic property may be altered.

The Department agrees with these comments to the extent that they suggest that the language of the rule should conform to the language employed by Congress in the ADA. Therefore, the language of this section has been revised to make it clear that this provision applies to buildings or facilities that are eligible for listing in the National Register of Historic Places under the National Historic Preservation Act (16 U.S.C. 470 et seq.) and to buildings or facilities that are designated as historic under State or local law. The Department believes, however, that the criteria of adverse effect employed under the National Historic Preservation Act are inappropriate for this rule because section 504(c) of the ADA specifies that special alterations provisions shall apply only when an alteration would "threaten or destroy the historic significance of qualified historic buildings and facilities."

The Department intends that the exception created by this section be applied only in those very rare situations in which it is not possible to provide access to an historic property using the special access provisions in ADAAG. Therefore, paragraph (a) of § 36.405 has been revised to provide that alterations to historic properties shall comply, to the maximum extent feasible, with section 4.1.7 of ADAAG. Paragraph (b) of this section has been revised to provide that if it has been determined, under the procedures established in ADAAG, that it is not feasible to provide physical access to an historic property that is a place of public accommodation in a manner that will not threaten or destroy the historic significance of the property, alternative methods of access shall be provided pursuant to the requirements of Subpart C.

Section 36.406 Standards for New Construction and Alterations

Section 36.406 implements the requirements of sections 306(b) and 306(c) of the Act, which require the Attorney General to promulgate standards for accessible design for buildings and facilities subject to the Act and this part that are consistent with the supplemental minimum guidelines and requirements for accessible design published by the Architectural and Transportation Barriers Compliance Board (ATBCB or Board) pursuant to section 504 of the Act. This section of the rule provides that new construction and alterations subject to this part shall comply with the standards for accessible design published as appendix A to this part.

Appendix A contains the Americans with Disabilities Act Accessibility Guidelines for Buildings and Facilities (ADAAG) which is being published by the ATBCB as a final rule elsewhere in this issue of the Federal Register. As proposed in this Department's proposed rule, § 36.406(a) adopts ADAAG as the accessibility standard applicable under this rule.

Paragraph (b) was not included in the proposed rule. It provides, in chart form, guidance for using ADAAG together with subparts A through D of this part when determining requirements for a particular facility. This chart is intended solely as guidance for the user; it has no effect for purposes of compliance or enforcement. It does not necessarily provide complete or mandatory information.

Proposed § 36.406(b) is not included in the final rule. That provision, which would have taken effect only if the final rule had followed the proposed Option Two for § 36.401(a), is unnecessary because the Department has chosen Option One, as explained in the preamble for that section.

Section 504(a) of the ADA requires the ATBCB to issue minimum guidelines to supplement the existing Minimum Guidelines and Requirements for Accessible Design (MGRAD) (36 CFR part 1190) for purposes of title III. According to section 504(b) of the Act, the guidelines are to establish additional requirements, consistent with the Act, "to ensure that buildings and facilities are accessible, in terms of architecture and design, . . . and communication, to individuals with disabilities." Section 306(c) of the Act requires that the accessibility standards included in the Department's regulations be consistent with the minimum guidelines, in this case ADAAG.

As explained in the ATBCB's preamble to ADAAG, the substance and form of the guidelines are drawn from several sources. They use as their model the 1984 Uniform Federal Accessibility Standards (UFAS) (41 CFR part 101, subpart 101-19.6, appendix), which are the standards implementing the Architectural Barriers Act. UFAS is based on the Board's 1982 MGRAD. ADAAG follows the numbering system and format of the private sector American National Standard Institute's ANSI A117.1 standards. (American National Specifications for Making

Buildings and Facilities Accessible to and Usable by Physically Handicapped People (ANSI A117-1980) and American National Standard for Buildings and Facilities—Providing Accessibility and Usability for Physically Handicapped People (ANSI A117.1-1986).) ADAAG supplements MGRAD. In developing ADAAG, the Board made every effort to be consistent with MGRAD and the current and proposed ANSI Standards, to the extent consistent with the ADA.

ADAAG consists of nine main sections and a separate appendix. Sections 1 through 3 contain general provisions and definitions. Section 4 contains scoping provisions and technical specifications applicable to all covered buildings and facilities. The scoping provisions are listed separately for new construction of sites and exterior facilities; new construction of buildings; additions; alterations; and alterations to historic properties. The technical specifications generally reprint the text and illustrations of the ANSI A117.1 standard, except where differences are noted by italics. Sections 5 through 9 of the guidelines are special application sections and contain additional requirements for restaurants and cafeterias, medical care facilities, business and mercantile facilities, libraries, and transient lodging. The appendix to the guidelines contains additional information to aid in understanding the technical specifications. The section numbers in the appendix correspond to the sections of the guidelines to which they relate. An asterisk after a section number indicates that additional information appears in the appendix.

ADAAG's provisions are further explained under Summary of ADAAG below.

General Comments

One commenter urged the Department to move all or portions of subpart D, New Construction and Alterations, to the appendix (ADAAG) or to duplicate portions of subpart D in the appendix. The commenter correctly pointed out that subpart D is inherently linked to ADAAG, and that a self-contained set of rules would be helpful to users. The Department has attempted to simplify use of the two documents by deleting some paragraphs from subpart D (e.g., those relating to work areas), because they are included in ADAAG. However, the Department has retained in subpart D those sections that are taken directly from the statute or that give meaning to specific statutory concepts (e.g., structural impracticability, path of travel). While some of the subpart D provisions are duplicated in ADAAG, others are not. For example, issues relating to path of travel and disproportionality in alterations are not addressed in detail in ADAAG. (The structure and contents of the two documents are addressed below under Summary of ADAAG.) While the Department agrees that it would be useful to have one self-contained document, the different focuses of this rule and ADAAG do not permit this result at this time. However, the chart included in § 36.406(b) should assist users in applying the provisions of subparts A through D, and ADAAG together.

Numerous business groups have urged the Department not to adopt the proposed ADAAG as the accessibility standards, because the requirements established are too high, reflect the "state of the art," and are inflexible, rigid, and impractical. Many of these objections have been lodged on the basis that ADAAG exceeds the statutory mandate to establish "minimum" guidelines. In the view of the Department, these commenters have misconstrued the meaning of the term "minimum guidelines." The statute clearly contemplates that the guidelines establish a level of access—a minimum—that the standards must meet or exceed. The guidelines are not to be "minimal" in the sense that they would provide for a low level of access. To the contrary, Congress emphasized that the ADA requires a "high degree of convenient access." Education and Labor report at 117-18. The legislative history explains that the guidelines may not "reduce, weaken, narrow or set less accessibility standards than those included in existing MGRAD" and should provide greater guidance in communication accessibility for individuals with hearing and vision impairments. Id. at 139. Nor did Congress contemplate a set of guidelines less detailed than ADAAG; the statute requires that the ADA guidelines supplement the existing MGRAD. When it established the statutory scheme, Congress was aware of the content and purpose of the 1982 MGRAD; as ADAAG does with respect to ADA, MGRAD establishes a minimum level of access that the Architectural Barriers Act standards (i.e., UFAS) must meet or exceed, and includes a high level of detail.

Many of the same commenters urged the Department to incorporate as its accessibility standards the ANSI standard's technical provisions and to adopt the proposed scoping provisions under development by the Council of American Building Officials' Board for the Coordination of Model Codes (BCMC). They contended that the ANSI standard is familiar to and accepted by professionals, and that both documents are developed through consensus. They suggested that ADAAG will not stay current, because it does not follow an established cyclical review process, and that it is not likely to be adopted by nonfederal jurisdictions in State and local codes. They urged the Department and the Board to coordinate the ADAAG provisions and any substantive changes to them with the ANSI A117 committee in order to maintain a consistent and uniform set of accessibility standards that can be efficiently and effectively implemented at the State and local level through the existing building regulatory processes.

The Department shares the commenters' goal of coordination between the private sector and Federal standards, to the extent that coordination can lead to substantive requirements consistent with the ADA. A single accessibility standard, or consistent accessibility standards, that can be used for ADA purposes and that can be incorporated or referenced by State and local governments, would help to ensure that the ADA requirements are routinely implemented at the design stage. The Department plans to work toward this goal.

The Department, however, must comply with the requirements of the ADA, the Federal Advisory Committee Act (5 U.S.C app. 1 et seq.) and the Administrative Procedure Act (5 U.S.C 551 et seq.). Neither the Department nor the Board can adopt private requirements wholesale. Furthermore, neither the 1991 ANSI A117 Standard revision nor the BCMC process is complete. Although the ANSI and BCMC provisions are not final, the Board has carefully considered both the draft BCMC scoping provisions and draft ANSI technical standards and included their language in ADAAG wherever consistent with the ADA.

Some commenters requested that, if the Department did not adopt ANSI by reference, the Department declare compliance with ANSI/BCMC to constitute equivalency with the ADA standards. The Department has not adopted this recommendation but has instead worked as a member of the ATBCB to ensure that its accessibility standards are practical and usable. In addition, as explained under subpart F, Certification of State Laws or Local Building Codes, the proper forum for further evaluation of this suggested approach would be in conjunction with the certification process.

Some commenters urged the Department to allow an additional comment period after the Board published its guidelines in final form, for purposes of affording the public a further opportunity to evaluate the appropriateness of including them as the Departments accessibility standards. Such an additional comment period is unnecessary and would unduly delay the issuance of final regulations. The Department put the public on notice, through the proposed rule, of its intention to adopt the proposed ADAAG, with any changes made by the Board, as the accessibility standards. As a member of the Board and of its ADA Task Force, the Department participated actively in the public hearings held on the proposed guidelines and in preparation of both the proposed and final versions of ADAAG. Many individuals and groups commented directly to the Department's docket, or at its public hearings, about ADAAG. The comments received on ADAAG, whether by the Board or by this Department, were thoroughly analyzed and considered by the Department in the context of whether the proposed ADAAG was consistent with the ADA and suitable for adoption as both guidelines and standards. The Department is convinced that ADAAG as adopted in its final form is appropriate for these purposes. The final guidelines, adopted here as standards, will ensure the high level of access contemplated by Congress, consistent with the ADA's balance between the interests of people with disabilities and the business community.

A few commenters, citing the Senate report (at 70) and the Education and Labor report (at 119), asked the Department to include in the regulations a provision stating that departures from particular technical and scoping requirements of the accessibility standards will be permitted so long as the alternative methods used will provide substantially equivalent or greater access to and utilization of the facility. Such a provision is found in ADAAG 2.2 and by virtue of that fact is included in these regulations.

Comments on specific provisions of proposed ADAAG

During the course of accepting comments on its proposed rule, the Department received numerous comments on ADAAG. Those areas that elicited the heaviest response included assistive listening systems, automated teller machines, work areas, parking, areas of refuge, telephones (scoping for TDD's and volume controls) and visual alarms. Strenuous objections were raised by some business commenters to the proposed provisions of the guidelines concerning check-out aisles, counters, and scoping for hotels and nursing facilities. All these comments were considered in the same manner as other comments on the Department's proposed rule and, in the Department's view, have been addressed adequately in the final ADAAG.

Largely in response to comments, the Board made numerous changes from its proposal, including the following:

• Generally, at least 50% of public entrances to new buildings must be accessible, rather than all entrances, as would often have resulted from the proposed approach.

• Not all check-out aisles are required to be accessible.

• The final guidelines provide greater flexibility in providing access to sales counters, and no longer require a portion of every counter to be accessible.

• Scoping for TDD's or text telephones was increased. One TDD or text telephone, for speech and hearing impaired persons, must be provided at locations with 4, rather than 6, pay phones, and in hospitals and shopping malls. Use of portable (less expensive) TDD's is allowed.

• Dispersal of wheelchair seating areas in theaters will be required only where there are more than 300 seats, rather than in all cases. Seats with removable armrests (i.e., seats into which persons with mobility impairments can transfer) will also be required.

• Areas of refuge (areas with direct access to a stairway, and where people who cannot use stairs may await assistance during a emergency evacuation) will be required, as proposed, but the final provisions are based on the Uniform Building Code. Such areas are not required in alterations.

• Rather than requiring 5% of new hotel rooms to be accessible to people with mobility impairments, between 2 and 4% accessibility (depending on total number of rooms) is required. In addition, 1% of the rooms must have roll-in showers.

• The proposed rule reserved the provisions on alterations to homeless shelters. The final guidelines apply alterations requirements to homeless shelters, but the requirements are less stringent than those applied to other types of facilities.

• Parking spaces that can be used by people in vans (with lifts) will be required.

• As mandated by the ADA, the Board has established a procedure to be followed with respect to alterations to historic facilities.

Summary of ADAAG

This section of the preamble summarizes the structure of ADAAG, and highlights the more important portions.

Sections 1 Through 3

Sections 1 through 3 contain general requirements, including definitions.

Section 4.1.1, Application

Section 4 contains scoping requirements. Section 4.1.1, Application, provides that all areas of newly designed or newly constructed buildings and facilities and altered portions of existing buildings and facilities required to be accessible by § 4.1.6 must comply with the guidelines unless otherwise provided in § 4.1.1 or a special application section. It addresses areas used only by employees as work areas, temporary structures, and general exceptions.

Section 4.1.1(3) preserves the basic principle of the proposed rule: Areas that may be used by employees with disabilities shall be designed and constructed so that an individual with a disability can approach, enter, and exit the area. The language has been clarified to provide that it applies to any area used only as a work area (not just to areas "that may be used by employees with disabilities"), and that the guidelines do not require that any area used as an individual work station be designed with maneuvering space or equipped to be accessible. The appendix to ADAAG explains that work areas must meet the guidelines' requirements for doors and accessible routes, and recommends, but does not require, that 5% of individual work stations be designed to permit a person using a wheelchair to maneuver within the space.

Further discussion of work areas is found in the preamble concerning proposed § 36.401(b).

Section 4.1.1(5)(a) includes an exception for structural impracticability that corresponds to the one found in § 36.401(c) and discussed in that portion of the preamble.

Section 4.1.2, Accessible Sites and Exterior Facilities: New Construction

This section addresses exterior features, elements, or spaces such as parking, portable toilets, and exterior signage, in new construction. Interior elements and spaces are covered by § 4.1.3.

The final rule retains the UFAS scoping for parking but also requires that at least one of every eight accessible parking spaces be designed with adequate adjacent space to deploy a lift used with a van. These spaces must have a sign indicating that they are van-accessible, but they are not to be reserved exclusively for van users.

Section 4.1.3, Accessible Buildings: New Construction

This section establishes scoping requirements for new construction of buildings and facilities.

Sections 4.1.3 (1) through (4) cover accessible

routes, protruding objects, ground and floor surfaces, and stairs.

Section 4.1.3(5) generally requires elevators to serve each level in a newly constructed building, with four exceptions included in the subsection. Exception 1 is the "elevator exception" established in § 36.401(d), which must be read with this section. Exception 4 allows the use of platform lifts under certain conditions.

Section 4.1.3(6), Windows, is reserved. Section 4.1.3(7) applies to doors.

Under § 4.1.3(8), at least 50% of all public entrances must be accessible. In addition, if a building is designed to provide access to enclosed parking, pedestrian tunnels, or elevated walkways, at least one entrance that serves each such function must be accessible. Each tenancy in a building must be served by an accessible entrance. Where local regulations (e.g., fire codes) require that a minimum number of exits be provided, an equivalent number of accessible entrances must be provided. (The latter provision does not require a greater number of entrances than otherwise planned.)

ADAAG Section 4.1.3(9), with accompanying technical requirements in Section 4.3, requires an area of rescue assistance (i.e., an area with direct access to an exit stairway and where people who are unable to use stairs may await assistance during an emergency evacuation) to be established on each floor of a multistory building. This was one of the most controversial provisions in the guidelines. The final ADAAG is based on current Uniform Building Code requirements and retains the requirement that areas of refuge (renamed "areas of rescue assistance") be provided, but specifies that this requirement does not apply to buildings that have a supervised automatic sprinkler system. Areas of refuge are not required in alterations.

The next seven subsections deal with drinking fountains (§ 4.1.3(10)); toilet facilities (§ 4.1.3(11)); storage, shelving, and display units (§ 4.1.3(12)), controls and operating mechanisms (§ 4.1.3(13)), emergency warning systems (§ 4.1.3(14)), detectable warnings (§ 4.1.3(15)), and building signage (§ 4.1.3(16)). Paragraph 11 requires that toilet facilities comply with § 4.22, which requires one accessible toilet stall (60" x 60") in each newly constructed restroom. In response to public comments, the final rule requires that a second accessible stall (36" x 60") be provided in restrooms that have six or more stalls.

ADAAG Section 4.1.3(17) establishes requirements for accessibility of pay phones to persons with mobility impairments, hearing impairments (requiring some phones with volume controls), and those who cannot use voice telephones. It requires one interior "text telephone" to be provided at any facility that has a total of four or more public pay phones. (The term "text telephone" has been adopted to reflect current terminology and changes in technology.) In addition, text telephones will be required in specific locations, such as covered shopping malls, hospitals (in emergency rooms, waiting rooms, and recovery areas), and convention centers.

Paragraph 18 of Section 4.1.3 generally requires that at least five percent of fixed or built-in seating or tables be accessible.

Paragraph 19, covering assembly areas, specifies the number of wheelchair seating spaces and types and numbers of assistive listening systems required. It requires dispersal of wheelchair seating locations in facilities where there are more than 300 seats. The guidelines also require that at least one percent of all fixed seats be aisle seats without armrests (or with moveable armrests) on the aisle side to increase accessibility for persons with mobility impairments who prefer to transfer from their wheelchairs to fixed seating. In addition, the final ADAAG requires that fixed seating for a companion be located adjacent to each wheelchair location.

Paragraph 20 requires that where automated teller machines are provided, at least one must comply with section 4.34, which, among other things, requires accessible controls, and instructions and other information that are accessible to persons with sight impairments.

Under paragraph 21, where dressing rooms are provided, five percent or at least one must comply with section 4.35.

Section 4.1.5, Additions

Each addition to an existing building or facility is regarded as an alteration subject to §§ 36.402 through 36.406 of subpart D, including the date established in § 36.402(a). But additions also have attributes of new construction, and to the extent that a space or element in the addition is newly constructed, each new space or element must comply with the applicable scoping provisions of sections 4.1.1 to 4.1.3 for new construction, the applicable technical specifications of sections 4.2 through 4.34, and any applicable special provisions in sections 5 through 10. For instance, if a restroom is provided in the addition, it must comply with the requirements for new construction. Construction of an addition does not, however, create an obligation to retrofit the entire existing building or facility to meet requirements for new construction. Rather, the addition is to be regarded as an alteration and to the extent that it affects or could affect the usability of or access to an area containing a primary function, the requirements in section 4.1.6(2) are triggered with respect to providing an accessible path of travel to the altered area and making the restrooms, telephones, and drinking fountains serving the altered area accessible. For example, if a museum adds a new wing that does not have a separate entrance as part of the addition, an accessible path of travel would have to be provided through the existing building or facility unless it is disproportionate to the overall cost and scope of the addition as established in § 36.403(f).

Section 4.1.6, Alterations

An alteration is a change to a building or facility that affects or could affect the usability of or access to the building or facility or any part thereof. There are three general principles for alterations. First, if any existing element or space is altered, the altered element or space must meet new construction requirements (section 4.1.6(1)(b)). Second, if alterations to the elements in a space when considered together amount to an alteration of the space, the entire space must meet new construction requirements (section 4.1.6(1)(c)). Third, if the alteration affects or could affect the usability of or access to an area containing a primary function, the path of travel to the altered area and the restrooms, drinking fountains, and telephones serving the altered area must be made accessible unless it is disproportionate to the overall alterations in terms of cost and scope as determined under criteria established by the Attorney General (§ 4.1.6(2)).

Section 4.1.6 should be read with §§ 36.402 through 36.405. Requirements concerning alterations to an area serving a primary function are addressed with greater detail in the latter sections than in section 4.1.6(2). Section 4.1.6(1)(j) deals with technical infeasibility. Section 4.1.6(3) contains special technical provisions for alterations to existing buildings and facilities.

Section 4.1.7, Historic Preservation

This section contains scoping provisions and alternative requirements for alterations to qualified historic buildings and facilities. It clarifies the procedures under the National Historic Preservation Act and their application to alterations covered by the ADA. An individual seeking to alter a facility that is subject to the ADA guidelines and to State or local historic preservation statutes shall consult with the State Historic Preservation Officer to determine if the planned alteration would threaten or destroy the historic significance of the facility.

Sections 4.2 Through 4.35

Sections 4.2 through 4.35 contain the technical specifications for elements and spaces required to be accessible by the scoping provisions (sections 4.1 through 4.1.7) and special application sections (sections 5 through 10). The technical specifications are the same as the 1980 version of ANSI A117.1 standard, except as noted in the text by italics.

Sections 5 Through 9

These are special application sections and contain additional requirements for restaurants and cafeterias, medical care facilities, business and mercantile facilities, libraries, and transient lodging. For example, at least 5 percent, but not less than one, of the fixed tables in a restaurant must be accessible.

In section 7, Business and Mercantile, paragraph 7.2 (Sales and Service Counters, Teller Windows, Information Counters) has been revised to provide greater flexibility in new construction than did the proposed rule. At least one of each type of sales or service counter where a cash register is located shall be made accessible. Accessible counters shall be dispersed throughout the facility. At counters such as bank teller windows or ticketing counters, alternative methods of compliance are permitted. A public accommodation may lower a portion of the counter, provide an auxiliary counter, or provide equivalent facilitation through such means as installing a folding shelf on the front of the counter at an accessible height to provide a work surface for a person using a wheelchair.

Section 7.3., Check-out Aisles, provides that, in new construction, a certain number of each design of check-out aisle, as listed in a chart based on the total number of check-out aisles of each design, shall be accessible. The percentage of check-outs required to be accessible generally ranges from 20% to 40%. In a newly constructed or altered facility with less than 5,000 square feet of selling space, at least one of each type of check-out aisle must be accessible. In altered facilities with 5,000 or more square feet of selling space, at least one of each design of check-out aisle must be made accessible when altered, until the number of accessible aisles of each design equals the number that would be required for new construction.

Section 9, Accessible Transient Lodging

Section 9 addresses two types of transient lodging: hotels, motels, inns, boarding houses, dormitories, resorts, and other similar places (sections 9.1 through 9.4); and homeless shelters, halfway houses, transient group homes, and other social service establishments (section 9.5). The interplay of the ADA and Fair Housing Act with respect to such facilities is addressed in the preamble discussion of the definition of "place of public accommodation" in § 36.104.

The final rule establishes scoping requirements for accessibility of newly constructed hotels. Four percent of the first hundred rooms, and roughly two percent of rooms in excess of 100, must meet certain requirements for accessibility to persons with mobility or hearing impairments, and an additional identical percentage must be accessible to persons with hearing impairments. An additional 1% of the available rooms must be equipped with roll-in showers, raising the actual scoping for rooms accessible to persons with mobility impairments to 5% of the first hundred rooms and 3% thereafter. The final ADAAG also provides that when a hotel is being altered, one fully accessible room and one room equipped with visual alarms, notification devices, and amplified telephones shall be provided for each 25 rooms being altered until the number of accessible rooms equals that required under the new construction standard. Accessible rooms must be dispersed in a manner that will provide persons with disabilities with a choice of single or multiple-bed accommodations.

In new construction, homeless shelters and other social service entities must comply with ADAAG; at least one type of amenity in each common area must be accessible. In a facility that is not required to have an elevator, it is not necessary to provide accessible amenities on the inaccessible floors if at least one of each type of amenity is provided in accessible common areas. The percentage of accessible sleeping accommodations required is the same as that required for other places of transient lodging. Requirements for facilities altered for use as a homeless shelter parallel the current MGRAD accessibility requirements for leased buildings. A shelter located in an altered facility must have at least one accessible entrance, accessible sleeping accommodations in a number equivalent to that established for new construction, at least one accessible toilet and bath, at least one accessible common area, and an accessible route connecting all accessible areas. All accessible areas in a homeless shelter in an altered facility may be located on one level.

Section 10, Transportation Facilities

Section 10 of ADAAG is reserved. On March 20, 1991, the ATBCB published a supplemental notice of proposed rulemaking (56 FR 11874) to establish special access requirements for transportation facilities. The Department anticipates that when the ATBCB issues final guidelines for transportation facilities, this part will be amended to include those provisions.

Subpart E—Enforcement

Because the Department of Justice does not have authority to establish procedures for judicial review and enforcement, subpart E generally restates the statutory procedures for enforcement.

Section 36.501 describes the procedures for private suits by individuals and the judicial remedies available. In addition to the language in section 308(a)(1) of the Act, § 36.501(a) of this part includes the language from section 204(a) of the Civil Rights Act of 1964 (42 U.S.C. 2000a-3(a)) which is incorporated by reference in the ADA. A commenter noted that the proposed rule did not include the provision in section 204(a) allowing the court to appoint an attorney for the complainant and authorize the commencement of the civil action without the payment of fees, costs, or security. That provision has been included in the final rule.

Section 308(a)(1) of the ADA permits a private suit by an individual who has reasonable grounds for believing that he or she is "about to be" subjected to discrimination in violation of section 303 of the Act (subpart D of this part), which requires that new construction and alterations be readily accessible to and usable by individuals with disabilities. Authorizing suits to prevent construction of facilities with architectural barriers will avoid the necessity of costly retrofitting that might be required if suits were not permitted until after the facilities were completed. To avoid unnecessary suits, this section requires that the individual bringing the suit have 'reasonable grounds" for believing that a violation is about to occur, but does not require the individual to engage in a futile gesture if he or she has notice that a person or organization covered by title III of the Act does not intend to comply with its provisions.

Section 36.501(b) restates the provisions of section 308(a)(2) of the Act, which states that injunctive relief for the failure to remove architectural barriers in existing facilities or the failure to make new construction and alterations accessible "shall include" an order to alter these facilities to make them readily accessible to and usable by persons with disabilities to the extent required by title III. The Report of the Energy and Commerce Committee notes that "an order to make a facility readily accessible to and usable by individuals with disabilities is mandatory" under this standard. H.R. Rep. No. 485, 101st Cong., 2d Sess, pt 4, at 64 (1990). Also, injunctive relief shall include, where appropriate, requiring the provision of an auxiliary aid or service, modification of a policy, or provision of alternative methods, to the extent required by title III of the Act and this part.

Section 36.502 is based on section 308(b)(1)(A)(i) of the Act, which provides that the Attorney General shall investigate alleged violations of title III and undertake periodic reviews of compliance of covered entities. Although the Act does not establish a comprehensive administrative enforcement mechanism for investigation and resolution of all complaints received, the legislative history notes that investigation of alleged violations and periodic compliance reviews are essential to effective enforcement of title III, and that the Attorney General is expected to engage in active enforcement and to allocate sufficient resources to carry out this responsibility. Judiciary Report at 67.

Many commenters argued for inclusion of more specific provisions for administrative resolution of disputes arising under the Act and this part in order to promote voluntary compliance and avoid the need for litigation. Administrative resolution is far more efficient and economical than litigation, particularly in the early stages of implementation of complex legislation when the specific requirements of the statute are not widely understood. The Department has added a new paragraph (c) to this section authorizing the Attorney General to initiate a compliance review where he or she has reason to believe there may be a violation of this rule.

Section 36.503 describes the procedures for suits by the Attorney General set out in section 308(b)(1)(B) of the Act. If the Department has reasonable cause to believe that any person or group of persons is engaged in a pattern or practice of resistance to the full enjoyment of any of the rights granted by title III or that any person or group of persons has been denied any of the rights granted by title III and such denial raises an issue of general public importance, the Attorney General may commence a civil action in any appropriate United States district court. The proposed rule provided for suit by the Attorney General "or his or her designee." The reference to a "designee" has been omitted in the final rule because it is unnecessary. The Attorney General has delegated enforcement authority under the ADA to the Assistant Attorney General for Civil Rights. 55 FR 40653 (October 4, 1990) (to be codified at 28 CFR 0.50(l).)

Section 36.504 describes the relief that may be granted in a suit by the Attorney General under section 308(b)(2) of the Act. In such an action, the court may grant any equitable relief it considers to be appropriate, including granting temporary, preliminary, or permanent relief, providing an auxiliary aid or service, modification of policy or alternative method, or making facilities readily accessible to and usable by individuals with disabilities, to the extent required by title III. In addition, a court may award such other relief as the court considers to be appropriate, including monetary damages to persons aggrieved, when requested by the Attorney General.

Furthermore, the court may vindicate the public interest by assessing a civil penalty against the covered entity in an amount not exceeding $50,000 for a first violation and not exceeding $100,000 for any subsequent violation. Section 36.504(b) of the rule adopts the standard of section 308(b)(3) of the Act. This section makes it clear that, in counting the number of previous determinations of violations for determining whether a "first" or "subsequent" violation has occurred, determinations in the same action that the entity has engaged in more than one discriminatory act are to be counted as a single violation. A "second violation" would not accrue to that entity until the Attorney General brought another suit against the entity and the entity was again held in violation. Again, all of the violations found in the second suit would be cumulatively considered as a "subsequent violation."

Section 36.504(c) clarifies that the terms "monetary damages" and "other relief" do not include punitive damages. They do include, however, all forms of compensatory damages, including out-of-pocket expenses and damages for pain and suffering.

Section 36.504(a)(3) is based on section 308(b)(2)(C) of the Act, which provides that, "to vindicate the public interest," a court may assess a civil penalty against the entity that has been found to be in violation of the Act in suits brought by the Attorney General. In addition, § 36.504(d), which is taken from section 308(b)(5) of the Act, further provides that, in considering what amount of civil penalty, if any, is appropriate, the court shall give consideration to "any good faith effort or attempt to comply with this part." In evaluating such good faith, the court shall consider "among other factors it deems relevant, whether the entity could have reasonably anticipated the need for an appropriate type of auxiliary aid needed to accommodate the unique needs of a particular individual with a disability."

The "good faith" standard referred to in this section is not intended to imply a willful or intentional standard—that is, an entity cannot demonstrate good faith simply by showing that it did not willfully, intentionally, or recklessly disregard the law. At the same time, the absence of such a course of conduct would be a factor a court should weigh in determining the existence of good faith.

Section 36.505 states that courts are authorized to

award attorneys fees, including litigation expenses and costs, as provided in section 505 of the Act. Litigation expenses include items such as expert witness fees, travel expenses, etc. The Judiciary Committee Report specifies that such items are included under the rubric of "attorneys fees" and not "costs" so that such expenses will be assessed against a plaintiff only under the standard set forth in *Christiansburg Garment Co. v. Equal Employment Opportunity Commission*, 434 U.S. 412 (1978). (Judiciary report at 73.)

Section 36.506 restates section 513 of the Act, which encourages use of alternative means of dispute resolution. Section 36.507 explains that, as provided in section 506(e) of the Act, a public accommodation or other private entity is not excused from compliance with the requirements of this part because of any failure to receive technical assistance.

Section 36.305 Effective Date

In general, title III is effective 18 months after enactment of the Americans with Disabilities Act, i.e., January 26, 1992. However, there are several exceptions to this general rule contained throughout title III. Section 36.508 sets forth all of these exceptions in one place.

Paragraph (b) contains the rule on civil actions. It states that, except with respect to new construction and alterations, no civil action shall be brought for a violation of this part that occurs before July 26, 1992, against businesses with 25 or fewer employees and gross receipts of $1,000,000 or less; and before January 26, 1993, against businesses with 10 or fewer employees and gross receipts of $500,000 or less. In determining what constitutes gross receipts, it is appropriate to exclude amounts collected for sales taxes.

Paragraph (c) concerns transportation services provided by public accommodations not primarily engaged in the business of transporting people. The 18-month effective date applies to all of the transportation provisions except those requiring newly purchased or leased vehicles to be accessible. Vehicles subject to that requirement must be accessible to and usable by individuals with disabilities if the solicitation for the vehicle is made on or after August 26, 1990.

Subpart F—Certification of State Labs or Local Building Codes

Subpart F establishes procedures to implement section 308(b)(1)(A)(ii) of the Act, which provides that, on the application of a State or local government, the Attorney General may certify that a State law or local building code or similar ordinance meets or exceeds the minimum accessibility requirements of the Act. In enforcement proceedings, this certification will constitute rebuttable evidence that the law or code meets or exceeds the ADA's requirements.

Three significant changes, further explained below, were made from the proposed subpart, in response to comments. First, the State or local jurisdiction is required to hold a public hearing on its proposed request for certification and to submit to the Department, as part of the information and materials in support of a request for certification, a transcript of the hearing. Second, the time allowed for interested persons and organizations to comment on the request filed with the Department (§ 36.605(a)(1)) has been changed from 30 to 60 days. Finally, a new § 36.608, Guidance concerning model codes, has been added.

Section 36.601 establishes the definitions to be used for purposes of this subpart. Two of the definitions have been modified, and a definition of "model code" has been added. First, in response to a comment, a reference to a code "or part thereof" has been added to the definition of "code." The purpose of this addition is to clarify that an entire code need not be submitted if only part of it is relevant to accessibility, or if the jurisdiction seeks certification of only some of the portions that concern accessibility. The Department does not intend to encourage "piecemeal" requests for certification by a single jurisdiction. In fact, the Department expects that in some cases, rather than certifying portions of a particular code and refusing to certify others, it may notify a submitting jurisdiction of deficiencies and encourage a reapplication that cures those deficiencies, so that the entire code can be certified eventually. Second, the definition of "submitting official" has been modified. The proposed rule defined the submitting official to be the State or local official who has principal responsibility for administration of a code. Commenters pointed out that in some cases more than one code within the same jurisdiction is relevant for purposes of certification. It was also suggested that the Department allow a State to submit a single application on behalf of the State, as well as on behalf of any local jurisdictions required to follow the State accessibility requirements. Consistent with these comments, the Department has added to the definition language clarifying that the official can be one authorized to submit a code on behalf of a jurisdiction.

A definition of "model code" has been added in light of new § 36.608.

Most commenters generally approved of the proposed certification process. Some approved of what they saw as the Department's attempt to bring State and local codes into alignment with the ADA. A State agency said that this section will be the backbone of the intergovernmental cooperation essential if the accessibility provisions of the ADA are to be effective.

Some comments disapproved of the proposed process as time-consuming and laborious for the Department, although some of these comments pointed out that, if the Attorney General certified model codes on which State and local codes are based, many perceived problems would be alleviated. (This point is further addressed by new § 36.608.)

Many of the comments received from business organizations, as well as those from some individuals and disability rights groups, addressed the relationship of the ADA requirements and their enforcement, to existing State and local codes and code enforcement systems. These commenters urged the Department to use existing code-making bodies for interpretations of the ADA, and to actively participate in the integration of the ADA into the text of the national model codes that are adopted by State and local enforcement agencies. These issues are discussed in preamble section 36.406 under General comments.

Many commenters urged the Department to evaluate or certify the entire code enforcement system (including any process for hearing appeals from builders of denials by the building code official of requests for variances, waivers, or modifications). Some urged that certification not be allowed in jurisdictions where waivers can be granted, unless there is a clearly identified decision- making process, with written rulings and notice to affected parties of any waiver or modification request. One commenter urged establishment of a dispute resolution mechanism, providing for interpretation (usually through a building official) and an administrative appeals mechanism (generally called Boards of Appeal, Boards of Construction Appeals, or Boards of Review), before certification could be granted.

The Department thoroughly considered these proposals but has declined to provide for certification of processes of enforcement or administration of State and local codes. The statute clearly authorizes the Department to certify the codes themselves for equivalency with the statute; it would be ill-advised for the Department at this point to inquire beyond the face of the code and written interpretations of it. It would be inappropriate to require those jurisdictions that grant waivers or modifications to establish certain procedures before they can apply for certification, or to insist that no deviations can be permitted. In fact, the Department expects that many jurisdictions will allow slight variations from a particular code, consistent with ADAAG itself. ADAAG includes in § 2.2 a statement allowing departures from particular requirements where substantially equivalent or greater access and usability is provided. Several sections specifically allow for alternative methods providing equivalent facilitation and, in some cases, provide examples. (See, e.g., section 4.31.9, Text Telephones; section 7.2(2) (iii), Sales and Service Counters.) Section 4.1.6 includes less stringent requirements that are permitted in alterations, in certain circumstances.

However, in an attempt to ensure that it does not certify a code that in practice has been or will be applied in a manner that defeats its equivalency with the ADA, the Department will require that the submitting official include, with the application for certification, any relevant manuals, guides, or any other interpretive information issued that pertain to the code. (§ 36.603(c)(1).) The requirement that this information be provided is in addition to the NPRM's requirement that the official provide any pertinent formal opinions of the State Attorney General or the chief legal officer of the jurisdiction.

The first step in the certification process is a request for certification, filed by a "submitting official" (§ 36.603). The Department will not accept requests for certification until after January 26, 1992, the effective date of this part. The Department received numerous comments from individuals and organizations representing a variety of interests, urging that the hearing required to be held by the Assistant Attorney General in Washington, DC, after a preliminary determination of equivalency (§ 36.605(a)(2)), be held within the State or locality requesting certification, in order to facilitate greater participation by all interested parties. While the Department has not modified the requirement that it hold a hearing in Washington, it has added a new subparagraph 36.603(b)(3) requiring a hearing within the State or locality before a request for certification is filed. The hearing must be held after adequate notice to the public and must be on the record; a transcript must be provided with the request for certification. This procedure will insure input from the public at the State or local level and will also insure a Washington, DC, hearing as mentioned in the legislative history.

The request for certification, along with supporting documents (§ 36.603(c)), must be filed in duplicate with the office of the Assistant Attorney General for Civil Rights. The Assistant Attorney General may request further information. The request and supporting materials will be available for public examination at the office of the Assistant Attorney General and at the office of the State or local agency charged with administration and enforcement of the code. The submitting official must publish public notice of the request for certification.

Next, under § 36.604, the Assistant Attorney General's office will consult with the ATBCB and make a preliminary determination to either (1) find that the code is equivalent (make a "preliminary determination of equivalency") or (2) deny certification. The next step depends on which of these preliminary determinations is made.

If the preliminary determination is to find equivalency, the Assistant Attorney General, under § 36.605, will inform the submitting official in writing of the preliminary determination and publish a notice in the Federal Register informing the public of the preliminary determination and inviting comment for 60 days. (This time period has been increased from 30 days in light of public comment pointing out the need for more time within which to evaluate the code.) After considering the information received in response to the comments, the Department will hold an hearing in Washington. This hearing will not be subject to the formal requirements of the Administrative Procedure Act. In fact, this requirement could be satisfied by a meeting with interested parties. After the hearing, the Assistant Attorney General's office will consult again with the ATBCB and make a final determination of equivalency or a final determination to deny the request for certification, with a notice of the determination published in the Federal Register.

If the preliminary determination is to deny certification, there will be no hearing (§ 36.606). The Department will notify the submitting official of the preliminary determination, and may specify how the code could be modified in order to receive a preliminary determination of equivalency. The Department will allow at least 15 days for the submitting official to submit relevant material in opposition to the preliminary denial. If none is received, no further action will be taken. If more information is received, the Department will consider it and make either a final decision to deny certification or a preliminary determination of equivalency. If at that stage the Assistant Attorney General makes a preliminary determination of equivalency, the hearing procedures set out in § 36.605 will be followed.

Section 36.607 addresses the effect of certification. First, certification will only be effective concerning those features or elements that are both (1) covered by the certified code and (2) addressed by the regulations against which they are being certified. For example, if children's facilities are not addressed by the Department's standards, and the building in question is a private elementary school, certification will not be effective for those features of the building to be used by children. And if the Department's regulations addressed equipment but the local code did not, a building's equipment would not be covered by the certification.

In addition, certification will be effective only for the particular edition of the code that is certified. Amendments will not automatically be considered certified, and a submitting official will need to reapply for certification of the changed or additional provisions.

Certification will not be effective in those situations where a State or local building code official allows a facility to be constructed or altered in a manner that does not follow the technical or scoping provisions of the certified code. Thus, if an official either waives an accessible element or feature or allows a change that does not provide equivalent facilitation, the fact that the Department has certified the code itself will not stand as evidence that the facility has been constructed or altered in accordance with the minimum accessibility requirements of the ADA. The Department's certification of a code is effective only with respect to the standards in the code; it is not to be interpreted to apply to a State or local government's application of the code. The fact that the Department has certified a code with provisions concerning waivers, variances, or equivalent facilitation shall not be interpreted as an endorsement of actions taken pursuant to those provisions.

The final rule includes a new § 36.608 concerning model codes. It was drafted in response to concerns raised by numerous commenters, many of which have been discussed under General comments (§ 36.406). It is intended to assist in alleviating the difficulties posed by attempting to certify possibly tens of thousands of codes. It is included in recognition of the fact that many codes are based on, or incorporate, model or consensus standards developed by nationally recognized organizations (e.g., the American National Standards Institute (ANSI); Building Officials and Code Administrators (BOCA) International; Council of American Building Officials (CABO) and its Board for the Coordination of Model Codes (BCMC); Southern Building Code Congress International (SBCCI)). While the Department will not certify or "precertify" model codes, as urged by some commenters, it does wish to encourage the continued viability of the consensus and model code process consistent with the purposes of the ADA.

The new section therefore allows an authorized

representative of a private entity responsible for developing a model code to apply to the Assistant Attorney General for review of the code. The review process will be informal and will not be subject to the procedures of §§ 36.602 through 36.607. The result of the review will take the form of guidance from the Assistant Attorney General as to whether and in what respects the model code is consistent with the ADA's requirements. The guidance will not be binding on any entity or on the Department; it will assist in evaluations of individual State or local codes and may serve as a basis for establishing priorities for consideration of individual codes. The Department anticipates that this approach will foster further cooperation among various government levels, the private entities developing standards, and individuals with disabilities.

ADA TITLE III DOJ TECHNICAL ASSISTANCE MANUAL

TABLE OF CONTENTS

III-1.0000 COVERAGE

III-1.1000 General.

Title III of the ADA covers—

1) Places of public accommodation;

2) Commercial facilities; and

3) Examinations and courses related to applications, licensing, certification, or credentialing for secondary or postsecondary education, professional, or trade purposes.

The obligations of title III only extend to private entities. State and local government entities are public entities covered by title II of the ADA, not by title III.

Title III also covers private entities primarily engaged in transporting people. The Department of Transportation has issued regulations implementing that section of title III.

Is the Federal Government covered by title III because it is not a "public entity" under title II? The operations of the executive branch of the Federal Government are not covered by title III of the ADA. They are covered, however, by sections 501 and 504 of the Rehabilitation Act of 1973, as amended, which prohibit disability discrimination in programs and activities conducted by Federal Executive agencies or the United States Postal Service, and by the Architectural Barriers Act, which requires that the design, construction, and alteration of Federal buildings be done in an accessible manner. The activities of the legislative branch, including Congress, on the other hand, are covered under title V of the ADA.

Are places of public accommodation and commercial facilities subject to the same requirements? No. Both places of public accommodation and commercial facilities (which include many facilities that are not places of public accommodation) are subject to the title III requirements for new construction and alterations. In addition to these requirements, places of public accommodation must be operated in accordance with the full range of title III requirements, such as nondiscriminatory eligibility criteria; reasonable modifications in policies, practices, and procedures; provision of auxiliary aids; and removal of barriers in existing facilities.

Are continuing education courses sponsored by a State bar association subject to title III? Yes. Continuing education courses sponsored by a State bar association are related to licensing, certification, and credentialing of attorneys, and therefore are covered by title III's special requirements for certain examinations and courses, whether or not they are mandatory. Independent of these requirements, if a continuing education course is offered by a private entity that owns, operates, leases, or leases to a place of public accommodation, the entity offering that course would have to meet all of the requirements generally applicable to public accommodations.

III-1.2000 Public accommodations.

The broad range of title III obligations relating to "places of public accommodation"must be met by entities that the Department of Justice regulation labels as "public accommodations." In order to be considered a public accommodation with title III obligations, an entity must be private and it must—

Own;
Lease;
Lease to; or
Operate a place of public accommodation.

What is a place of public accommodation? A place of public accommodation whose operations—

Affect commerce; and

Fall within at least one of the following 12 categories:

1) Places of lodging (e.g., inns, hotels, motels) (except for owner- occupied establishments renting fewer than six rooms);

2) Establishments serving food or drink (e.g., restaurants and bars);

3) Places of exhibition or entertainment (e.g., motion picture houses, theaters, concert halls, stadiums);

4) Places of public gathering (e.g., auditoriums, convention centers, lecture halls);

5) Sales or rental establishments (e.g., bakeries, grocery stores, hardware stores, shopping centers);

6) Service establishments (e.g., laundromats, drycleaners, banks, barber shops, beauty shops, travel services, shoe repair services, funeral parlors, gas stations, offices of accountants or lawyers, pharmacies, insurance offices, professional offices of health care providers, hospitals);

7) Public transportation terminals, depots, or stations (not including facilities relating to air transportation);

8) Places of public display or collection (e.g., museums, libraries, galleries);

9) Places of recreation (e.g., parks, zoos, amusement parks);

10) Places of education (e.g., nursery schools, elementary, secondary, undergraduate, or post-graduate private schools);

11) Social service center establishments (e.g., day care centers, senior citizen centers, homeless shelters, food banks, adoption agencies); and

12) Places of exercise or recreation (e.g., gymnasiums, health spas, bowling alleys, golf courses).

Can a facility be considered a place of public accommodation if it does not fall under one of these 12 categories? No, the 12 categories are an exhaustive list. However, within each category the examples given are just illustrations. For example, the category "sales or rental establishments" would include many facilities other than those specifically listed, such as video stores, carpet showrooms, and athletic equipment stores.

What does it mean for a facility's operations to 'affect commerce'? The phrase 'affect commerce' is a constitutional law concept frequently used in Federal statutes enacted pursuant to Congress' power to regulate interstate commerce. Some factors to examine in determining whether a facility's operation affect commerce are:

(a) Whether the facility is open to out-of-State visitors;

(b) Whether the products it exhibits or sells originated out of State, or have travelled through other States;

(c) Whether facilities of this kind, in the aggregate, would affected interstate commerce.

ILLUSTRATION: A private restaurant, located near an interstate highway, serves customers who come from other States and offers food that contains ingredients grown or processed in a different State. This restaurant's operations affect commerce because of any one of the following factors, independently: (a) it serves out-of-State customers; (b) it serves products that originated out of State; or (c) the restaurant industry as a whole affects interstate commerce.

What if a private entity operates, or leases space to, many different types of facilities, of which only relatively few are places of public accommodation? Is the whole private entity still a public accommodation? The entire private entity is, legally speaking, a public accommodation, but it only has ADA title III obligations with respect to the operations of the places of public accommodation.

ILLUSTRATION: ZZ Oil Company owns a wide range of production and processing facilities that are not places of public accommodation. It also operates a large number of retail service stations that are places of public accommodation. In this case, ZZ Oil Company would be a public accommodation. However, only its operations relating to the retail service stations are subject to the broad title III requirements for public accommodations. The other facilities, however, are commercial facilities and would be subject only to the requirements for new construction and alterations.

Do both a landlord who leases space in a building to a tenant and the tenant who operates a place of public accommodation have responsibilities under the ADA? Both the landlord and the tenant are public accommodations and have full responsibility for complying with all ADA title III requirements applicable to that place of public accommodation. The title III regulation permits the landlord and the tenant to allocate responsibility, in the lease, for complying with particular provisions of the regulation. However, any allocation made in a lease or other contract is only effective as between the parties, and both landlord and tenant remain fully liable for compliance with all provisions of the ADA relating to that place of public accommodation.

ILLUSTRATION: ABC Company leases space in a shopping center it owns to XYZ Boutique. In their lease, the parties have allocated to XYZ Boutique the responsibility for complying with the barrier removal requirements of title III within that store. In this situation, if XYZ Boutique fails to remove barriers, both ABC Company (the landlord) and XYZ Boutique (the tenant) would be liable for violating the ADA and could be sued by an XYZ customer. Of course, in the lease, ABC could require XYZ to indemnify it against all losses caused by XYZ's failure to comply with its obligations under the lease, but again, such matters would be between the parties and would not affect their liability under the ADA.

If the owner of a building is not covered by the ADA, is it possible for a private tenant to still have title III responsibilities? Yes. The fact that a landlord in a particular case is not covered by the ADA does not necessarily negate title III's coverage of private entities that lease or operate places of public accommodation within the facility.

ILLUSTRATION: A Federal Executive agency owns a building in which several spaces are rented to retail stores. Although Federal executive agencies are not covered by the ADA, the private entities that rent and operate the retail stores, which are places of public accommodation, are covered by title III.

Is a bank that acquires ownership of a place of public accommodation through foreclosure subject to title III? Yes. Any owner of a place of public accommodation is covered as a public accommodation regardless of the intended or actual duration of its ownership.

Can a place of public accommodation be covered by both the ADA and the Fair Housing Act (FHA)? Yes. The analysis for determining whether a facility is covered by title III is entirely separate and independent from the analysis used to determine coverage under the FHA. A facility can be a residential dwelling under the FHA and still fall in whole or in part under at least one of the 12 categories of places of public accommodation.

ILLUSTRATION: LM, Inc., a private, nonsectarian, nonprofit organization operates a homeless shelter permitting stays ranging from overnight to those of sufficient length to result in coverage as a dwelling under the FHA. Because it permits short-term, overnight stays, the shelter may also be considered a place of public accommodation as a "place of lodging," and covered by title III of the ADA. In addition, if the shelter provides a significant enough level of social services, such as medical care, meals, counseling, transportation, or training, it may also be covered under title III as a "social service center establishment."

Are nursing homes, congregate care facilities, independent living centers, and retirement communities covered as places of public accommodation? Some may be. Nursing homes are expressly covered in the title III regulation as social service center establishments. Similar residential facilities, such as congregate care facilities, independent living centers, and retirement communities, are covered by title III, if they provide a significant enough level of social services that they can be considered social service center establishments. Social services in this context include medical care, assistance with daily living activities, provision of meals, transportation, counseling, and organized recreational activities. No one of these services will automatically trigger ADA coverage. Rather, the determination of whether a private entity provides a significant enough level of social services will depend on the nature and degree of the services.

If a facility provides a significant enough level of social services such that it can be considered a social service center establishment, all of those portions of the facility that are used in the provision of the social services are covered by the ADA. For example, if the social services are provided throughout the facility, including in the individual housing units, then the entire facility is a place of public accommodation, covered by Title III.

Are group homes covered by title III? Sometimes. Like congregate care facilities and the other dual residential/social service facilities discussed above, group homes are covered by title III if they provide a significant enough level of social services to be considered social service center establishments. The homes are not subject to title III if they simply provide family-like living arrangements without significant social services. Foster care provided by a family in its own home is covered.

Does title III apply to common areas within residential facilities? Although title III does not apply to strictly residential facilities, it covers places of public accommodation within residential facilities. Thus, areas within multifamily residential facilities that qualify as places of public accommodation are covered by the ADA if use of the areas is not limited exclusively to owners, residents, and their guests.

ILLUSTRATION 1: A private residential apartment complex includes a swimming pool for use by apartment tenants and their guests. The complex also sells pool "memberships" generally to the public. The pool qualifies as a place of public accommodation.

ILLUSTRATION 2: A residential condominium association maintains a longstanding policy of restricting use of its party room to owners, residents, and their guests. Consistent with that policy, it refuses to rent the room to local businesses and community organizations as a meeting place for educational seminars. The party room is not a place of public accommodation.

ILLUSTRATION 3: A private residential apartment complex contains a rental office. The rental office is a place of public accommodation.

Are model homes places of public accommodation? Generally, no. A model home does not fall under one of the 12 categories of places of public accommodation. If, however, the sales office for a residential housing development were located in a model home, the area used for the sales office would be considered a place of public accommodation. Although model homes are not covered, the Department encourages developers to voluntarily provide at least a minimal level of access to model homes for potential homebuyers with disabilities. For example, a developer could provide physical access (via ramp or lift) to the primary level of one of several model homes and make photographs of other levels within the home as well as of other models available to the customer.

Can a vacation timeshare property be a place of public accommodation? Yes. Whether a particular timeshare property is a place of public accommodation depends upon how much the timeshare operation resembles that of a hotel or other typical place of lodging. Among the factors to be considered in this determination are—

1) Whether the timeshare offers short-term ownership interests (for instance, stays of one week or less are considered short term);

2) The nature of the ownership interest conveyed (e.g., fee simple);

3) The degree of restrictions placed on the ownership (e.g., whether the timeshare owner has the right to occupy, alter, or exercise control over a particular unit over a period of time);

4) The extent to which the operations resemble those of a hotel, motel, or inn (e.g., reservations, central registration, meals, laundry service).

If a public accommodation operating two geographically separate facilities serves clients or customers at one location and has only administrative offices at another, are both sites places of public accommodation? No. Only the facility in which clients or customers are served is covered as a place of public accommodation. The geographically separate, employees-only facility is a commercial facility, but any activities undertaken in that facility that affect the operations of the place of public accommodation are subject to the title III requirements for public accommodations.

ILLUSTRATION: A medical care provider owns one building in which patients are seen, and another building in a different location that contains only administrative offices. At the building housing the administrative offices, no services are provided (no patients go there, only employees). The building where patients are treated is a place of public accommodation. The geographically separate administrative offices are a commercial facility, not a place of public accommodation. However, any policies or decisions made in the administrative offices that affect the treatment of patients would be subject to the requirements for public accommodations. For example, a protocol for the provision of auxiliary aids that is issued as a directive to medical staff by the administrative office must comply with the effective communication requirements for public accommodations.

BUT: If patients receive medical services in the same building where the administrative offices are located, the entire building is a place of public accommodation, even if one or more floors are reserved for the exclusive use of employees.

Are privately owned ships covered by title III? Yes. Ships operated by a private entity that is primarily engaged in the business of providing transportation are subject to ADA requirements established by the U.S. Department of Transportation (see III-4.4700). (Ships registered under foreign flags that operate in United States ports may be subject to domestic laws, such as the ADA, unless there are specific treaty prohibitions that preclude enforcement.) If a ship, or portion of a ship, functions as one of the twelve categories of places of public accommodation, the ship is also subject to the title III requirements for places of public accommodation.

ILLUSTRATION: A cruise ship is owned and operated by a private entity whose primary business is to operate cruise ships. On the ship are places of lodging, restaurants, bars, a health club, and a nightclub. The private entity is a public accommodation and must comply with the applicable requirements of title III.

Places of public accommodation aboard ships must comply with all of the title III requirements, including removal of barriers to access where readily achievable. Currently, however, a ship is not required to comply with specific accessibility standards for new construction or alterations, because specific accessibility standards for new construction or alteration or cruise ships have not yet been developed.

III-1.3000 Commercial Facilities.

The requirements of title III for new construction and alterations cover commercial facilities, which include nonresidential facilities, such as office buildings, factories, and warehouses, whose operations affect commerce. This category sweeps under ADA coverage a large number of potential places of employment that are not covered as places of public accommodation. A building may contain both commercial facilities and places of public accommodation.

ILLUSTRATION: A manufacturing company has an extensive customer services operation, which takes customer complaints and provides other services in connection with the retail sales of the company's products. The customer services operation is a 'service establishment,' and is thus separately covered as a place of public accommodation under the ADA. The manufacturing operation is covered as a commercial facility.

A commercial facility, such as a manufacturing facility, is not a place of business accommodation solely by virtue of its being open to vendors, salespersons, or job applicants. However, under title I of the ADA, the private entity operating a commercial facility may have accessibility obligations regarding its job applicants.

III-1.3100 Exceptions.

Commercial facilities do not include rail vehicles or any facility covered by the Fair Housing Act. Residential dwelling units, therefore, are not commercial facilities. In addition, facilities that are expressly exempted from coverage under the Fair Housing Act are also not considered to be commercial facilities. For example, owner-occupied rooming houses providing living quarters for four for fewer families, which are exempt from the Fair Housing Act, would not be commercial facilities.

Even though private air terminals are not considered to be places of public accommodation, are airports covered as commercial facilities? Yes, private air terminals are commercial facilities and, therefore, would be subject to the new construction and alterations requirements of title III. Moreover, while a private air terminal, itself, may not be a place of public accommodation (because the ADA statutory language exempts air transportation), the retail stores and service establishments located within a private airport would be places of public accommodation. (In addition, private airports that receive Federal financial assistance are subject to the requirements of section

504 of the Rehabilitation Act of 1973, which prohibits discrimination on the basis of disability in programs and activities of recipients of Federal funds. Airline operations at private airports may also be subject to the nondiscrimination requirements of the Air Carrier Access Act.) Air terminals operated by public entities would be covered by title II of the ADA, not title III; but any private retail stores operated within the terminal would be places of public accommodation covered by title III.

III-1.4000 Examinations and courses.

Private entities offering examinations or courses covered by title III are subject to the requirements discussed in III-4.6000 of this manual. If the private entity is also a public accommodation or has responsibility for a commercial facility, it would be subject to other applicable title III requirements as well.

III-1.5000 Religious entities.

Religious entities are exempt from the requirements of title III of the ADA. A religious entity, however, would be subject to the employment obligations of title I if it has enough employees to meet the requirements for coverage.

III-1.5100 Definition.

A religious entity is a religious organization or an entity controlled by a religious organization, including a place of worship.

If an organization has a lay board, is it automatically ineligible for the religious exemption? No. The exemption is intended to have broad application. For example, a parochial school that teaches religious doctrine and is sponsored by a religious order could be exempt, even if it has a lay board.

III-1.5200 Scope of exemption.

The exemption covers all of the activities of a religious entity, whether religious or secular.

ILLUSTRATION: A religious congregation operates a day care center and a private elementary school for members and nonmembers alike. Even though the congregation is operating facilities that would otherwise be places of public accommodation, its operations are exempt from title III requirements.

What if the congregation rents to a private day care center or elementary school? Is the tenant organization also exempt? The private entity that rents the congregation's facilities to operate a place of public accommodation is not exempt, unless it is also a religious entity. If it is not a religious entity, then its activities would be covered by title III. The congregation, however, would remain exempt, even if its tenant is covered. That is, the obligations of a landlord for a place of public accommodation do not apply if the landlord is a religious entity.

If a nonreligious entity operates a community theater or other place of public accommodation in donated space on the congregation's premises, is the nonreligious entity covered by title III? No. A nonreligious entity running a place of public accommodation in space donated by a religious entity is exempt from title III's requirements. The nonreligious tenant entity is subject to title III only if a lease exists under which rent or other consideration is paid.

III-1.6000 Private clubs.

The obligations of title III do not apply to any "private club." An entity is a private club for purposes of the ADA if it is a private club under title II of the Civil Rights Act of 1964, which prohibits discrimination on the basis of race, color, and national origin by public accommodations.

Courts have been most inclined to find private club status in cases where—

1) Members exercise a high degree of control over club operations.

2) The membership selection process is highly selective.

3) Substantial membership fees are charged.

4) The entity is operated on a nonprofit basis.

5) The club was not founded specifically to avoid compliance with Federal civil rights laws.

Facilities of a private club lose their exemption to the extent that they are made available for use by nonmembers as places of public accommodation.

ILLUSTRATION: A private country club that would be considered a "private club" for ADA purposes rents space to a private day care center that is also open to the children of nonmembers. Although the private club would maintain its exemption for its other operations, it would have title III obligations with respect to the operation of the day care center.

III-1.7000 Relationship to title II.

Public entities, by definition, can never be subject to title III of the ADA, which covers only private entities. Conversely, private entities cannot be covered by title II. There are many situations, however, in which public entities stand in very close relation to private entities that are covered by title III, with the result that certain activities may be affected, at least indirectly, by both titles.

ILLUSTRATION 1: A State department of parks provides a restaurant in one of its State parks. The restaurant is operated by X Corporation under a concession agreement. As a public accommodation, X Corporation is subject to title III of the ADA. The State department of parks, a public entity, is subject to title II. The parks department is obligated to ensure by contract that the restaurant will be operated in a manner that enables the parks department to meet its title II obligations, even though the restaurant is not directly subject to title II.

ILLUSTRATION 2: The City of W owns a downtown office building occupied by W's Department of Human Resources. The first floor is leased as commercial space to a restaurant, a newsstand, and a travel agency. The City of W, as a public entity, is subject to title II in its role as landlord of the office building. As a public entity, it cannot be subject to title III, even though its tenants are public accommodations that are covered by title III.

ILLUSTRATION 3: A private, nonprofit corporation operates a number of group homes under contract with a State agency for the benefit of individuals with mental disabilities. These particular homes provide a significant enough level of social services to be considered places of public accommodation under title III. The State agency must ensure that its contracts are carried out in accordance with title II, and the private entity must ensure that the homes comply with title III.

ILLUSTRATION 4: If an existing commercial facility is owned by a private entity covered by title III and rented to a public entity covered by title II, the private landlord does not become subject to the public entity's title II program access requirement by virtue of the leasing relationship. The private landlord only has title III obligations. These extend to the commercial facility as a whole and to any places of public accommodation contained in the facility. The governmental entity is responsible for ensuring that the governmental programs and services offered in its rented space meets the requirements of title II.

Where public and private entities act jointly, the public entity must ensure that the relevant requirements of title II are met; and the private entity must ensure compliance with title III.

ILLUSTRATION: The City of W engages in a joint venture with T Corporation to build a new professional football stadium. The new stadium would have to be built in compliance with the accessibility guidelines of both titles II and III. In cases where the standards differ, the stadium would have to meet the standard that provides the highest degree of access to individuals with disabilities.

III-1.8000 Relationship to other laws.

III-1.8100 Rehabilitation Act.

Title III is intended to provide protection to individuals with disabilities that is at least as great as that provided under title V of the Rehabilitation Act. Title V includes such provisions as section 504, which covers all the operations of Federal Executive agencies and programs receiving Federal financial assistance. Title III may not be interpreted to provide a lesser degree of protection to individuals with disabilities than is provided under section 504.

III-1.8200 Other Federal and State laws.

Title III does not disturb other Federal laws or any State law that provides protection for individuals with disabilities at a level greater or equal to that provided by the ADA. It does, however, prevail over any conflicting State laws.

ILLUSTRATION: A restaurant has constructed a new facility that is subject to both building code accessibility requirements and the requirements of the ADA. With respect to some building features, the local code contains more stringent technical requirements than the ADA; with respect to others, the ADA has the stronger standard. Each building element should comply with the requirement (local or ADA) that provides the greatest degree of accessibility.

Which law applies if the ADA provides broader remedies, but the other applicable law provides more stringent technical requirements? Both. An aggrieved individual may file a lawsuit under both the ADA and another law where both apply, but the ADA's remedies would be applicable only to the ADA claim, because the ADA enforcement process may be used only to enforce the requirements of the ADA. The ADA would not preempt the other law's requirements or remedies.

III-2.0000 INDIVIDUALS WITH DISABILITIES.

III-2.1000 General.

Title III of the ADA prohibits discrimination against any "individual with a disability." People commonly refer to disabilities or disabling conditions in a broad sense. For example, poverty or lack of education may impose real limitations on an individual's opportunities. Likewise, being only five feet in height may prove to be an insurmountable barrier to an individual whose ambition is to play professional basketball. Although one might loosely characterize these conditions as "disabilities" in relation to the aspirations of the particular individual, the disabilities reached by title III are limited to those that meet the ADA's legal definition-those that place substantial limitations on an individual's major life activities.

Title III protects three categories of individuals with disabilities:

1) Individuals who have a physical or mental impairment that substantially limits one or more major life activities;

2) Individuals who have a record of a physical or mental impairment that substantially limited one or more of the individual's major life activities; and

3) Individuals who are regarded as having such an impairment, whether they have the impairment or not.

III-2.2000 Physical or mental impairments.

The first category of persons covered by the definition of an individual with a disability is restricted to those with "physical or mental impairments." Physical impairments include—

1) Physiological disorders or conditions;
2) Cosmetic disfigurement; or
3) Anatomical loss

affecting one or more of the following body systems: neurological; musculoskeletal; special sense organs (which would include speech organs that are not respiratory such as vocal cords, soft palate, tongue, etc.); respiratory, including speech organs; cardiovascular; reproductive; digestive; genitourinary; hemic and lymphatic; skin; and endocrine.

Specific examples of physical impairments include orthopedic, visual, speech, and hearing impairments, cerebral palsy, epilepsy, muscular dystrophy, multiple sclerosis, cancer, heart disease, diabetes, HIV disease (symptomatic or asymptomatic), tuberculosis, drug addiction, and alcoholism.

Mental impairments include mental or psychological disorders, such as mental retardation, organic brain syndrome, emotional or mental illness, and specific learning disabilities.

Simple physical characteristics such as the color of one's eyes, hair, or skin; baldness; left-handedness; or age do not constitute physical impairments. Similarly, disadvantages attributable to environmental, cultural, or economic factors are not the type of impairments covered by title III. Moreover, the definition does not include common personality traits such as poor judgment or a quick temper, where these are not symptoms of a mental or psychological disorder.

Does title III prohibit discrimination against individuals based on their sexual orientation? No. The phrase "physical or mental impairment" does not include homosexuality or bisexuality.

III-2.3000 Drug addiction as an impairment.

Drug addiction is an impairment under the ADA. A public accommodation generally, however, may base a decision to withhold services or benefits in most cases on the fact that an addict is engaged in the current and illegal use of drugs.

What is "illegal use of drugs"? Illegal use of drugs means the use of one or more drugs, the possession or distribution of which is unlawful under the Controlled Substances Act. It does not include use of controlled substances pursuant to a valid prescription or other uses that are authorized by the Controlled Substances Act or other Federal law. Alcohol is not a "controlled substance," but alcoholism is a disability.

What is "current use"? "Current use" is the illegal use of controlled substances that occurred recently enough to justify a reasonable belief that a person's drug use is current or that continuing use is a real and ongoing problem. Therefore, a private entity should review carefully all the facts surrounding its belief that an individual is currently taking illegal drugs to ensure that its belief is a reasonable one.

Does title III protect drug addicts who no longer take controlled substances? Yes. Title III prohibits discrimination against drug addicts based solely on the fact that they previously illegally used controlled substances. Protected individuals include persons who have successfully completed a supervised drug rehabilitation program or have otherwise been rehabilitated successfully and who are not engaging in current illegal use of drugs. Additionally, discrimination is prohibited against an individual who is currently participating in a supervised rehabilitation program and is not engaging in current illegal use of drugs. Finally, a person who is erroneously regarded as engaging in current illegal use of drugs is protected.

Is drug testing permitted under the ADA? Yes. Public accommodations may utilize reasonable policies or procedures, including but not limited to drug testing, designed to ensure that an individual who formerly engaged in the illegal use of drugs is not now engaging in current illegal use of drugs.

III-2.4000 Substantial limitation of a major life activity.

To constitute a "disability," a condition must substantially limit a major life activity. Major life activities include such activities as caring for one's self, performing manual tasks, walking, seeing, hearing, speaking, breathing, learning, and working.

When does an impairment "substantially limit" a major life activity? There is no absolute standard for determining when an impairment is a substantial limitation. Some impairments obviously or by their nature substantially limit the ability of an individual to engage in a major life activity.

ILLUSTRATION 1: A person who is deaf is substantially limited in the major life activity of hearing. A person with a minor hearing impairment, on the other hand, may not be substantially limited.

ILLUSTRATION 2: A person with traumatic brain injury may be substantially limited in the major life activities of caring for one's self, learning, and working because of memory deficit, confusion, contextual difficulties, and inability to reason appropriately.

An impairment substantially interferes with the accomplishment of a major life activity when the individual's important life activities are restricted as to the conditions, manner, or duration under which they can be performed in comparison to most people.

ILLUSTRATION 1: A person with a minor vision impairment, such as 20/40 vision, does not have a substantial impairment of the major life activity of seeing.

ILLUSTRATION 2: A person who can walk for 10 miles continuously is not substantially limited in walking merely because, on the eleventh mile, he or she begins to experience pain, because most people would not be able to walk eleven miles without experiencing some discomfort.

Are "temporary" mental or physical impairments covered by title III? Yes, if the impairment substantially limits a major life activity. The issue of whether a temporary impairment is significant enough to be a disability must be resolved on a case-by-case basis, taking into consideration both the duration (or expected duration) of the impairment and the extent to which it actually limits a major life activity of the affected individual.

ILLUSTRATION: During a house fire, M received burns affecting his hands and arms. While it is expected that, with treatment, M will eventually recover full use of his hands, in the meantime he is substantially limited in performing basic tasks required to care for himself such as eating and dressing. Because M's burns are expected to substantially limit a major life activity (caring for one's self) for a significant period of time, M would be considered to have a disability covered by title III.

If a person's impairment is greatly lessened or eliminated through the use of aids or devices, would the person still be considered an individual with a disability? Whether a person has a disability is determined without regard to the availability of mitigating measures, such as reasonable modifications, auxiliary aids and services, services or devices of a personal nature, or medication. For example, a person with severe hearing loss is substantially limited in the major life activity of hearing, even though the loss may be improved through the use of a hearing aid. Likewise, persons with impairments, such as epilepsy or diabetes, that, if untreated, would substantially limit a major life activity, are still individuals with disabilities under the ADA, even if the debilitating consequences of the impairment are controlled by medication.

III-2.5000 Record of a physical or mental impairment that substantially limited a major life activity.

The ADA protects not only those individuals with disabilities who actually have a physical or mental impairment that substantially limits a major life activity, but also those with a record of such an impairment. This protected group includes—

1) A person who has a history of an impairment that substantially limited a major life activity but has recovered from the impairment. Examples of individuals who have a history of an impairment are persons who have histories of mental or emotional illness, drug addiction, alcoholism, heart disease, or cancer.

2) Persons who have been misclassified as having an impairment. Examples include persons who have been erroneously diagnosed as mentally retarded or mentally ill.

III-2.6000 "Regarded as."

The ADA also protects certain persons who are regarded by a public entity as having a physical or mental impairment that substantially limits a major life activity, whether or not that person actually has an impairment. Three typical situations are covered by this category:

1) An individual who has a physical or mental impairment that does not substantially limit major life activities, but who is treated as if the impairment does substantially limit a major life activity;

ILLUSTRATION: A, an individual with mild diabetes controlled by medication, is barred by the staff of a private summer camp from participation in certain sports because of her diabetes. Even though A does not actually have an impairment that substantially limits a major life activity, she is protected under the ADA because she is treated as though she does.

2) An individual who has a physical or mental impairment that substantially limits major life activities only as a result of the attitudes of others towards the impairment;

ILLUSTRATION: B, a three-year old child born with a prominent facial disfigurement, has been refused admittance to a private day care program on the grounds that her presence in the program might upset the other children. B is an individual with a physical impairment that substantially limits her major life activities only as the result of the attitudes of others toward her impairment.

3) An individual who has no impairments but who is treated by a public accommodation as having an impairment that substantially limits a major life activity.

ILLUSTRATION: C is excluded from a private elementary school because the principal believes rumors that C is infected with the HIV virus. Even though these rumors are untrue, C is protected under the ADA, because he is being subjected to discrimination by the school based on the belief that he has an impairment that substantially limits major life activities (i.e., the belief that he is infected with HIV).

III-2.7000 Exclusions.

The following conditions are specifically excluded from the definition of "disability": transvestism, transsexualism, pedophilia, exhibitionism, voyeurism, gender identity disorders not resulting from physical impairments, other sexual behavior disorders, compulsive gambling, kleptomania, pyromania, and psychoactive substance use disorders resulting from current illegal use of drugs.

III-3.0000 GENERAL REQUIREMENTS.

III-3.1000 General.

A public accommodation may not discriminate against an individual with a disability in the operation of a place of public accommodation. Individuals with disabilities may not be denied full and equal enjoyment of the "goods, services, facilities, privileges, advantages, or accommodations" offered by a place of public accommodation. The phrase "goods, services, facilities, privileges, advantages, or accommodations" applies to whatever type of good or service a public accommodation provides to its customers or clients. In other words, a public accommodation must ensure equal opportunity for individuals with disabilities.

Several broad principles underlie the nondiscrimination requirements of title III. These include—

1) Equal opportunity to participate;
2) Equal opportunity to benefit; and
3) Receipt of benefits in the most integrated setting appropriate.

The specific requirements discussed below in III-4.0000 are all designed to effectuate the general requirements. The specific provisions furnish guidance on how a public accommodation can meet its obligations in particular situations and establish standards for determining when the general requirement has been violated. Where a specific requirement applies, it controls over the general requirement.

ILLUSTRATION: Public accommodations are only required to remove architectural barriers in existing facilities if removal is "readily achievable" (see III-4.4200). If making the main entrance to a place of public accommodation accessible is not readily achievable, the public accommodation can provide access to the facility through another entrance, even though use of the alternative entrance for individuals with disabilities would not be the most integrated setting appropriate.

III-3.2000 Denial of participation.

The ADA prohibits discriminatory denial of services or benefits to individuals with disabilities. Just as under the Civil Rights Act of 1964 a restaurant cannot refuse to admit an individual because of his or her race under the ADA, it cannot refuse to admit an individual merely because he or she has a disability.

ILLUSTRATION: A theater cannot refuse to admit an individual with mental retardation to a performance merely because of the individual's mental disability.

III-3.3000 Equality in participation/benefits.

The ADA mandates an equal opportunity to participate in or benefit from the goods and services offered by a place of public accommodation, but does not guarantee that an individual with a disability must achieve an identical result or level of achievement as persons without disabilities.

ILLUSTRATION 1: Persons with disabilities must not be limited to certain performances at a theater.

ILLUSTRATION 2: An individual who uses a wheelchair may not be excluded from an exercise class at a health club because he or she cannot do all of the exercises and derive the same result from the class as persons without disabilities.

III-3.4000 Separate benefit/integrated setting.

A primary goal of the ADA is the equal participation of individuals with disabilities in the "mainstream" of American society. The major principles of mainstreaming include the following:

1) Individuals with disabilities must be integrated to the maximum extent appropriate.
2) Separate programs are permitted where necessary to ensure equal opportunity. A separate program must be appropriate to the particular individual.
3) Individuals with disabilities cannot be excluded from the regular program, or required to accept special services or benefits.

III-3.4100 Separate programs.

A public accommodation may offer separate or special programs necessary to provide individuals with disabilities an equal opportunity to benefit from the programs. Such programs must, however, be specifically designed to meet the needs of the individuals with disabilities for whom they are provided.

ILLUSTRATION 1: Museums generally do not allow visitors to touch exhibits because handling can cause damage to the objects. A municipal museum may offer a special tour for individuals with vision impairments during which they are permitted to touch and handle specific objects on a limited basis. (It cannot, however, exclude a blind person from the standard museum tour.)

ILLUSTRATION 2: A private athletic facility may sponsor a separate basketball league for individuals who use wheelchairs.

III-3.4200 Right to participate in the regular program.

Even if a separate or special program for individuals with disabilities is offered, a public accommodation cannot deny an individual with a disability participation in its regular program, unless some other limitation on the obligation to provide services applies. See, e.g., III-3.8000 (direct threat); III-4.1000 (eligibility criteria).

ILLUSTRATION: An individual who uses a wheelchair may be excluded from playing in a basketball league, if the recreation center can demonstrate that the exclusion is necessary for safe operation.

Individuals with disabilities are entitled to participate in regular programs, even if the public accommodation could reasonably believe that they cannot benefit from the regular program.

ILLUSTRATION: A museum cannot exclude a person who is blind from a tour because of assumptions about his or her inability to appreciate and benefit from the tour experience. Similarly, a deaf person may not be excluded from a museum concert because of a belief that deaf persons cannot enjoy the music.

The fact that a public accommodation offers special programs does not affect the right of an individual with a disability to participate in regular programs. The requirements for providing access to the regular program still apply.

ILLUSTRATION: A public accommodation cannot exclude a person who is blind from a standard museum tour, where touching objects is not permitted, if he or she prefers the standard tour.

Individuals with disabilities may not be required to accept special "benefits" if they choose not to do so.

ILLUSTRATION: ABC theater offers reduced rate tickets for individuals with disabilities and requires appropriate documentation for eligibility for the reduced rates. ABC cannot require an individual who qualifies for the reduced rate to present documentation or accept the reduced rate, if he or she chooses to pay the full price.

III-3.4300 Modifications in the regular program.

When a public accommodation offers a special program for individuals with a particular disability, but an individual with that disability elects to participate in the regular program rather than in the separate program, the public accommodation may still have obligations to provide an opportunity for that individual to benefit from the regular program. The fact that a separate program is offered may be a factor in determining the extent of the obligations under the regular program, but only if the separate program is appropriate to the needs of the particular individual with a disability.

ILLUSTRATION: If a museum provides a sign language interpreter for one of its regularly scheduled tours, the availability of the signed tour may be a factor in determining whether it would be an undue burden to provide an interpreter for a deaf person who wants to take the tour at a different time.

BUT: The availability of the signed tour would not affect the museum's obligation to provide an interpreter for a different tour, or the museum's obligation to provide a different auxiliary aid, such as an assistive listening device, for an individual with impaired hearing who does not use sign language.

III-3.5000 Discrimination on the basis of association.

A public accommodation may not discriminate against individuals or entities because of their known relationship or association with persons who have disabilities.

ILLUSTRATION: A day care center cannot refuse to admit a child because his or her brother is infected with HIV, even though the child seeking admission does not have a disability.

This prohibition applies to cases where the public accommodation has knowledge of both the individual's disability and his or her relationship to another individual or entity. In addition to familial relationships, the prohibition covers any type of association between the individual or entity that is discriminated against and the individual or individuals with disabilities, if the discrimination is actually based on the disability.

ILLUSTRATION 1: The owner of a building may not refuse to lease space to a medical facility because the facility specializes in treatment of individuals with HIV disease.

ILLUSTRATION 2: If a theater refuses to admit K, an individual with cerebral palsy, as well as L (his brother) because K has cerebral palsy, the theater would be illegally discriminating against L on the basis of his association with K.

III-3.6000 Retaliation or coercion.

Individuals who exercise their rights under the ADA, or assist others in exercising their rights, are protected from retaliation. The prohibition against retaliation or coercion applies broadly to any individual or entity that seeks to prevent an individual from exercising his or her rights or to retaliate against him or her for having exercised those rights.

ILLUSTRATION: A restaurant may not refuse to serve a customer because he or she filed an ADA complaint against the restaurant or against another public accommodation.

Protection is extended to those who assist others in exercising their rights.

ILLUSTRATION: A dry cleaner may not refuse to serve an individual because he encouraged another individual to file a complaint, or because he testified for that individual in a proceeding to enforce the ADA.

Any form of retaliation or coercion, including threats, intimidation, or interference, is prohibited if it is intended to interfere with the exercise of rights under the ADA.

ILLUSTRATION: It would be a violation for a restaurant customer to harass or intimidate an individual with a disability in an effort to prevent that individual from patronizing the restaurant.

III-3.7000 Maintenance of accessible features.

Public accommodations must maintain in working order equipment and features of facilities that are required to provide ready access to individuals with disabilities. Isolated or temporary interruptions in access due to maintenance and repair of accessible features are not prohibited.

Where a public accommodation must provide an accessible route, the route must remain accessible and not blocked by obstacles such as furniture, filing cabinets, or potted plants. Similarly, accessible doors must be unlocked when the place of public accommodation is open for business.

ILLUSTRATION 1: Placing a vending machine on the accessible route to an accessible restroom in a bowling alley would be a violation if it obstructed the accessible route.

ILLUSTRATION 2: Placing ornamental plants in an elevator lobby may be a violation if they block the approach to the elevator call buttons or obstruct access to the elevator cars.

ILLUSTRATION 3: Using an accessible route for storage of supplies would also be a violation, if it made the route inaccessible.

BUT: An isolated instance of placement of an object on an accessible route would not be a violation, if the object is promptly removed.

Although it is recognized that mechanical failures in equipment such as elevators or automatic doors will occur from time to time, the obligation to ensure that facilities are readily accessible to and usable by individuals with disabilities would be violated, if repairs are not made promptly or if improper or inadequate maintenance causes repeated and persistent failures. Inoperable or "out of service" equipment does not meet the requirements for providing access to a place of public accommodation.

ILLUSTRATION 1: It would be a violation for a building manager of a three-story building to turn off an elevator during business hours in order to save energy.

ILLUSTRATION 2: Deactivating accessible automatic doors because of inclement weather would not be permitted.

III-3.8000 Direct threat.

A public accommodation may exclude an individual with a disability from participation in an activity, if that individual's participation would result in a direct threat to the health or safety of others. The public accommodation must determine that there is a significant risk to others that cannot be eliminated or reduced to an acceptable level by reasonable modifications to the public accommodation's policies, practices, or procedures or by the provision of appropriate auxiliary aids or services. The determination that a person poses a direct threat to the health or safety of others may not be based on generalizations or stereotypes about the effects of a particular disability; it must be based on an individual assessment that considers the particular activity and the actual abilities and disabilities of the individual.

The individual assessment must be based on reasonable judgment that relies on current medical evidence, or on the best available objective evidence, to determine—

1) The nature, duration, and severity of the risk;

2) The probability that the potential injury will actually occur; and

3) Whether reasonable modifications of policies, practices, or procedures will mitigate or eliminate the risk.

Such an inquiry is essential to protect individuals with disabilities from discrimination based on prejudice, stereotypes, or unfounded fear, while giving appropriate weight to legitimate concerns, such as the need to avoid exposing others to significant health and safety risks. Making this assessment will not usually require the services of a physician. Sources for medical knowledge include public health authorities, such as the U.S. Public Health Service, the Centers for Disease Control, and the National Institutes of Health, including the National Institute of Mental Health.

ILLUSTRATION: Refusal to admit an individual to a restaurant because he or she is infected with HIV would be a violation, because the HIV virus cannot be transmitted through casual contact, such as that among restaurant patrons.

ILLUSTRATION 2: Denial of health club membership to an individual who is infected with HIV would be a violation, because current medical evidence indicates that the HIV virus cannot be contracted through casual contact, perspiration, or urine in an exercise room, sauna room, or pool.

ILLUSTRATION 3: Refusal to provide dental services to an individual who is infected with HIV because of the patient's HIV-positive status would be a violation. Current medical evidence indicates that the risk of HIV transmission from a patient to other patients and/or the dental staff is infinitesimal, and can be even further reduced by the use of universal precautions (infection control procedures that prevent the transmission of all infectious diseases, including HIV).

III-3.9000 Illegal use of drugs.

Discrimination based on an individual's current illegal use of drugs is not prohibited (see III-2.3000). Although individuals currently using illegal drugs are not protected from discrimination, the ADA does prohibit denial of health services, or services provided in connection with drug rehabilitation, to an individual on the basis of current illegal use of drugs, if the individual is otherwise entitled to such services.

ILLUSTRATION 1: A hospital emergency room may not refuse to provide emergency services to an individual because the individual is illegally using drugs.

ILLUSTRATION 2: A medical facility that specializes in care of burn patients may not refuse to treat an individual's burns on the grounds that the individual is illegally using drugs.

Because abstention from the use of drugs is an essential condition for participation in some drug rehabilitation programs, and may be a necessary requirement in inpatient or residential settings, a drug rehabilitation or treatment program may deny participation to individuals who use drugs while they are in the program.

ILLUSTRATION: A residential drug and alcohol treatment program may expel an individual for using drugs in a treatment center.

III-3.10000 Smoking.

A public accommodation may prohibit smoking, or may impose restrictions on smoking, in places of public accommodation.

III-3.11000 Insurance.

Insurance offices are places of public accommodation and, as such, may not discriminate on the basis of disability in the sale of insurance contracts or in the terms or conditions of the insurance contracts they offer. Because of the nature of the insurance business, however, consideration of disability in the sale of insurance contracts does not always constitute "discrimination." An insurer or other public accommodation may underwrite, classify, or administer risks that are based on or not inconsistent with State law, provided that such practices are not used to evade the purposes of the ADA.

Thus, a public accommodation may offer a plan that limits certain kinds of coverage based on classification of risk, but may not refuse to insure, or refuse to continue to insure, or limit the amount, extent, or kind of coverage available to an individual, or charge a different rate for the same coverage solely because of a physical or mental impairment, except where the refusal, limitation, or rate differential is based on sound actuarial principles or is related to actual or reasonably anticipated experience. The ADA, therefore, does not prohibit use of legitimate actuarial considerations to justify differential treatment of individuals with disabilities in insurance.

ILLUSTRATION: A person who has cerebral palsy may not be denied coverage based on disability independent of actuarial risk classification.

Can a group health insurance policy have a pre-existing condition exclusion? Yes. An individual with a pre-existing condition may be denied coverage for that condition for the period specified in the policy. However, the individual cannot be denied coverage for illness or injuries unrelated to the pre-existing condition.

Can an insurance policy limit coverage for certain procedures or treatments? Yes, but it may not entirely deny coverage to a person with a disability.

Does the ADA require insurance companies to provide a copy of the actuarial data on which its actions are based at the request of the applicant? The ADA does not require it. Under some State regulatory schemes, however, insurers may have to file such actuarial information with the State regulatory agency, and this information may be obtainable at the State level.

Does the ADA apply only to life and health insurance? No. Although life and health insurance are the areas where the ADA will have its greatest application, the ADA applies equally to unjustified discrimination in all types of insurance, including property and casualty insurance, provided by public accommodations.

ILLUSTRATION: Differential treatment of individuals with disabilities, including individuals who have been treated for , applying for automobile insurance would have to be justified by legitimate actuarial considerations.

BUT: An individual's driving record, including any alcohol-related violations, may be considered.

May a public accommodation refuse to serve an individual with a disability because of limitations on coverage or rates in its insurance policies? No. A public accommodation may not rely on such limitations to justify exclusion of individuals with disabilities. Any exclusion must be based on legitimate safety concerns (see III-4.1200), rather than on the terms of the insurance contract.

ILLUSTRATION: An amusement park requires individuals to meet a minimum height requirement that excludes some individuals with disabilities for certain rides because of a limitation in its liability insurance coverage. The limitation in insurance coverage is not a permissible basis for the exclusion.

BUT: The minimum height requirement would be a permissible safety criterion, if it is necessary for the safe operation of the ride.

III-3.12000 Places of public accommodation located in private residences.

When a place of public accommodation is located in a home, the portions of the home used as a place of public accommodation are covered by title III, even is those portions are also used for residential purposes. Coverage extends not only to those portions but also includes an accessible route from the sidewalk, through the doorway, through the hallway and other portions of the home, such as restrooms, used by clients and customers of the public accommodation.

ILLUSTRATION: J, a family day care provider, is having a new home built. J intends to use two of the rooms as a family day care center. In addition, the children will be using the master bathroom. Even though the two rooms and bathroom will be used for residential purposes when the children are not present, all three rooms are covered by the title III new construction requirements, because the rooms are not being used exclusively as a residence. Moreover, J must assure that there is an accessible route to the day care rooms and bathroom.

III-4.0000 SPECIFIC REQUIREMENTS.

III-4.1000 Eligibility criteria.

III-4.1100 General.

A public accommodation may not impose eligibility criteria that either screen out or tend to screen out persons with disabilities from fully and equally enjoying any goods, services, privileges, advantages, or accommodations offered to individuals without disabilities, unless it can show that such requirements are necessary for the provision of the goods, services, privileges, advantages, or accommodations.

ILLUSTRATION 1: A restaurant has an unofficial policy of seating individuals with visible disabilities in the least desirable parts of the restaurant. This policy violates the ADA because it establishes an eligibility criterion that discriminates against individuals with certain disabilities and that is not necessary for the operation of the restaurant. The restaurant may not justify its policy on the basis of the preferences of its other customers.

ILLUSTRATION 2: A parking garage refuses to allow vans to park inside even though the garage has adequate roof clearance and space for vans. Although the garage operator does not intend to discriminate against individuals with disabilities, the garage's policy unnecessarily tends to screen out people with certain mobility impairments who, in order to have enough space for mobility aids such as wheelchairs, use vans rather than cars.

ILLUSTRATION 3: A cruise ship subject to the ADA discovers that an individual who uses a wheelchair has made a reservation for a cruise and plans to travel independently. The cruise line notifies the individual that she must bring a "traveling companion" or her reservation will be cancelled. Requiring a traveling companion as an eligibility criterion violates the ADA, unless the cruise line demonstrates that its policy is necessary for some compelling reason.

ILLUSTRATION 4: A committee reviews applications from physicians seeking "admitting privileges" at a privately owned hospital. The hospital requires all applicants, no matter their specialty, to meet certain physical and mental health qualifications, because the hospital believes they will promote the safe and efficient delivery of medical care. The hospital must be able to show that the specific qualifications imposed are necessary.

ILLUSTRATION 5: A retail store has a policy of permitting only customers with driver's licenses to write checks for purchases. Customers without driver's licenses must complete credit applications before their checks will be accepted. This policy places an unnecessary burden on persons who have disabilities that prevent them from obtaining driver's licenses. The store must therefore allow customers who cannot obtain driver's licenses due to disability to present state identification cards for check-verification purposes.

III-4.1200 Safety.

A public accommodation may impose legitimate safety requirements necessary for safe operation. However, the public accommodation must ensure that its safety requirements are based on real risks, not on speculation, stereotypes, or generalizations about individuals with disabilities.

ILLUSTRATION: A wilderness tour company may require participants to meet a necessary level of swimming proficiency in order to participate in a rafting expedition.

III-4.1300 Unnecessary inquiries.

The ADA prohibits unnecessary inquiries into the existence of a disability.

ILLUSTRATION 1: A private summer camp requires parents to fill out a questionnaire and to submit medical documentation regarding their children's ability to participate in various camp activities. The questionnaire is acceptable if the summer camp can demonstrate that each piece of information requested is needed to ensure safe participation in camp activities. The camp, however, may not use this information to screen out children with disabilities from admittance to the camp.

ILLUSTRATION 2: A retail store requires applicants for a store credit card to supply information regarding their physical or mental health history. This policy violates the ADA because such information is not relevant to a determination of credit worthiness.

III-4.1400 Surcharges.

Although compliance may result in some additional cost, a public accommodation may not place a surcharge only on particular individuals with disabilities or groups of individuals with disabilities to cover these expenses.

ILLUSTRATION: The ABC pharmacy is located on the second floor of an older four-story building that does not have an elevator. Because the pharmacy's owner has determined that providing physical access to the pharmacy for those unable to climb stairs would not be readily achievable, she has chosen to provide home delivery as a readily achievable alternative to barrier removal. The pharmacy may not charge an individual who uses a wheelchair for the cost of providing home delivery.

ILLUSTRATION 2: In order to ensure effective communication with a deaf patient during an office visit, a doctor arranges for the services of a sign language interpreter. The cost of the interpreter's services must be absorbed by the doctor.

ILLUSTRATION 3: A community civic association arranges to provide interpreting services for a deaf individual wishing to attend a business seminar sponsored by the organization in rented space at a local motel. The interpreting service requires the organization to provide payment in full prior to the seminar. Due to a business emergency, the individual is unable to attend. The organization may not charge the deaf individual for the cost of the unused interpreting services.

III-4.2000 Reasonable modifications.

III-4.2100 General.

A public accommodation must reasonably modify its policies, practices, or procedures to avoid discrimination. If the public accommodation can demonstrate, however, that a modification would fundamentally alter the nature of the goods, services, facilities, privileges, advantages, or accommodations it provides, it is not required to make the modification.

ILLUSTRATION 1: A private health clinic, in collaboration with its local public safety officials, has developed an evacuation plan to be used in the event of fire or other emergency. The clinic occupies several floors of a multistory building. During an emergency, elevators, which are the normal means of exiting from the clinic, will be shut off. The health clinic is obligated to modify its evacuation procedures, if necessary, to provide alternative means for clients with mobility impairments to be safely evacuated from the clinic without using the elevator. The clinic should also modify its plan to take into account the needs of its clients with visual, hearing, and other disabilities.

ILLUSTRATION 2: Under its obligation to remove architectural barriers where it is readily achievable to do so, a local motel has greatly improved physical access in several of its rooms. However, under its present reservation system, the motel is unable to guarantee that, when a person requests an accessible room, one of the new rooms will actually be available when he or she arrives. The ADA requires the motel to make reasonable modifications in its reservation system to ensure the availability of the accessible room.

Also, if the motel's only available accessible rooms were offered at higher rates than the room initially requested, it may be a reasonable modification of policy for the hotel to make the more expensive rooms available at the lower rate.

ILLUSTRATION 3: A retail store has a policy of not taking special orders for out-of-stock merchandise unless the customer appears personally to sign the order. The store would be required to reasonably modify its procedures to allow the taking of special orders by phone from persons with disabilities who cannot visit the store. If the store's concern is obtaining a guarantee of payment that a signed order would provide, the store could, for example, take orders by mail or take credit card orders by telephone from persons with disabilities.

ILLUSTRATION 4: An individual requires assistance in order to use toilet facilities and his only companion is a person of the opposite sex. Permitting a person of the opposite sex to assist an individual with a disability in a toilet room designated for one sex may be a required reasonable modification of policy.

ILLUSTRATION 5: A car rental company has a policy that customers who wish to secure car rentals with cash must have been employed at their present jobs for a year or more. A responsible, cash-paying customer with other sources of income, who is unemployed due to a disability, applies to rent a car and is rejected. The ADA requires the car rental company to reasonably modify its procedures to permit rentals by individuals with other adequate sources of income, including disability-related sources of income such as SSI, SSDI, Veteran's Administration disability benefits, or employer's disability benefits.

ILLUSTRATION 6: An individual is unable to wait in a long line for an amusement park ride because of a disability that carries with it a heightened sensitivity to heat. Another individual cannot wait in line because the line moves along an inaccessible path. In both cases the park may be required to modify its policy requiring all patrons to wait in line for attractions. For example, the amusement park could make available a marker to hold an individual's place in line.

ILLUSTRATION 7: A movie theater has a policy prohibiting patrons from consuming food and beverages purchased outside the theater. The theater may be required to make an exception to permit a parent to bring in appropriate food for a child with diabetes.

III-4.2200 Specialties.

It is not considered discriminatory for a public accommodation with a specialty in a particular area to refer an individual with a disability to a different public accommodation if—

1) The individual is seeking a service or treatment outside the referring public accommodation's area of expertise; and

2) The public accommodation would make a similar referral for an individual who does not have a disability.

ILLUSTRATION: An individual who is blind initially visits a doctor who specializes in family medicine. The doctor discovers that the individual has a potentially cancerous growth. The family practice physician may refer the blind individual to a cancer specialist, if he or she has no expertise in that area, and if he or she would make a similar referral for an individual who is not blind. The cancer specialist who receives the referral may not refuse to treat the individual for cancer-related problems simply because the individual is blind.

III-4.2300 Service animals.

A public accommodation must modify its policies to permit the use of a service animal by an individual with a disability, unless doing so would result in a fundamental alteration or jeopardize the safe operation of the public accommodation.

Service animals include any animal individually trained to do work or perform tasks for the benefit of an individual with a disability. Tasks typically performed by service animals include guiding people with impaired vision, alerting individuals with impaired hearing to the presence of intruders or sounds, providing minimal protection or rescue work, pulling a wheelchair, or retrieving dropped items.

The care or supervision of a service animal is the responsibility of his or her owner, not the public accommodation. A public accommodation may not require an individual with a disability to post a deposit as a condition to permitting a service animal to accompany its owner in a place of public accommodation, even if such deposits are required for pets.

ILLUSTRATION: An individual who is blind wishes to be accompanied in a restaurant by her guide dog. The restaurant must permit the guide dog to accompany its owner in all areas of the restaurant open to other patrons and may not insist that the dog be separated from her.

A number of States have programs to certify service animals. A private entity, however, may not insist on proof of State certification before permitting the entry of a service animal to a place of public accommodation.

This regulation also acknowledges that in rare circumstances, if the nature of the goods and services provided or accommodations offered would be fundamentally altered or the safe operation of a public accommodation jeopardized, a service animal need not be allowed to enter.

ILLUSTRATION: A showing by appropriate medical personnel that the presence or use of a service animal would pose a significant health risk in certain designated areas of a hospital may serve as a basis for excluding service animals in those areas.

III-4.2400 Check-out aisles.

If a store has check-out aisles, customers with disabilities must be provided an equivalent level of convenience in access to check-out facilities as customers without disabilities. To accomplish this, the store must either keep an adequate number of accessible aisles open or otherwise modify its policies and practices.

ILLUSTRATION: PQR Foodmart has twenty narrow, inaccessible check-out aisles and one wider, accessible aisle. The accessible aisle is used as an express lane limited to customers purchasing fewer than ten items. K, who uses a wheelchair, wishes to make a larger purchase. PQR Foodmart must permit K to make his large purchase at the express lane.

III-4.2500 Accessible or special goods.

As a general rule, a public accommodation is not required to alter its inventory to carry accessible or special products that are designed for or easier to use by customers with disabilities. Examples of accessible goods include Brailled books, books on audio tape, closed-captioned video tapes, specially sized or designed clothing, and foods that meet special dietary needs.

ILLUSTRATION: A local book store has customarily carried only regular print versions of books. The ADA does not require the bookstore to expand its inventory to include large print books or books on audio tape.

On the other hand, a public accommodation may be required to special order accessible goods at the request of a customer with a disability if—

1) It makes special orders for unstocked goods in its regular course of business, and

2) The accessible or special goods requested can be obtained from one of its regular suppliers.

ILLUSTRATION: A customer of a local bookstore begins to experience some vision loss and has difficulty reading regular print. Upon request by the customer, the bookstore is required to try to obtain large print books, if it normally fills special orders (of any kind) for its other customers, and if large print books can be obtained from its regular suppliers.

The ADA does not require that manufacturers provide warranties or operating manuals that are packed with the product in accessible formats.

III-4.2600 Personal services and devices.

A public accommodation is not required to provide individuals with disabilities with personal or individually prescribed devices, such as wheelchairs, prescription eyeglasses, or hearing aids, or to provide services of a personal nature, such as assistance in eating, toileting, or dressing.

Although discussed here as a limit on the duty to make reasonable modifications, this provision applies to all aspects of the title III rule and limits the obligations of public accommodations in areas such as the provision of auxiliary aids and services, alternatives to barrier removal, and examinations and courses.

However, the phrase "services of a personal nature" is not to be interpreted as referring to minor assistance provided to individuals with disabilities. For example, measures taken as alternatives to barrier removal, such as retrieving items from shelves or providing curb service or home delivery, or actions required as modifications in policies, practices, and procedures, such as a waiter's removing the cover from a customer's straw, a kitchen's cutting up food into smaller pieces, or a bank's filling out a deposit slip, would not be considered "services of a personal nature." Also, if a public accommodation such as a hospital or nursing home customarily provides its clients with what might otherwise be considered services of a personal nature, it must provide the same services for individuals with disabilities.

ILLUSTRATION: An exclusive women's clothing shop provides individualized assistance to its customers in selecting and trying on garments. Although "dressing" might otherwise be considered a personal service, in this case the store must extend the same service to its customers with disabilities. However, a "no frills" merchandiser would not be required to provide assistance in trying on garments, because it does not provide such a service to any of its customers.

III-4.3000 Auxiliary aids.

III-4.3100 General.

A public accommodation is required to provide auxiliary aids and services that are necessary to ensure equal access to the goods, services, facilities, privileges, or accommodations that it offers, unless an undue burden or a fundamental alteration would result.

Who is entitled to auxiliary aids? This obligation extends only to individuals with disabilities who have physical or mental impairments, such as vision, hearing, or speech impairments, that substantially limit the ability to communicate. Measures taken to accommodate individuals with other types of disabilities are covered by other title III requirements such as "reasonable modifications" and "alternatives to barrier removal."

ILLUSTRATION: W, an individual who is blind, needs assistance in locating and removing an item from a grocery store shelf. A store employee who locates the desired item for W would be providing an "auxiliary aid or service."

BUT: If G, who uses a wheelchair, receives the same retrieval service, not because of a disability related to communication, but rather because of his inability to physically reach the desired item, the store would be making a required "reasonable modification" in its practices, as discussed in III- 4.2000 of this manual.

III-4.3200 Effective communication.

In order to provide equal access, a public accommodation is required to make available appropriate auxiliary aids and services where necessary to ensure effective communication. The type of auxiliary aid or service necessary to ensure effective communication will vary in accordance with the length and complexity of the communication involved.

ILLUSTRATION 1: H, an individual who is deaf, uses sign language as his primary means of communication and also communicates by writing. He is shopping for film at a camera store. Exchanging notes with the sales clerk would be adequate to ensure effective communication.

ILLUSTRATION 2: H then stops by a new car showroom to look at the latest models. The car dealer would be able to communicate effectively general information about the models available by providing brochures and exchanging notes by pen and notepad, or perhaps by means of taking turns at a computer terminal keyboard. If H becomes serious about making a purchase, the services of a qualified interpreter may be necessary because of the complicated nature of the communication involved in buying a car.

ILLUSTRATION 2a: H goes to his doctor for a biweekly check-up, during which the nurse records H's blood pressure and weight. Exchanging notes and using gestures are likely to provide an effective means of communication at this type of check-up.

BUT: Upon experiencing symptoms of a mild stroke, H returns to his doctor for a thorough examination and battery of tests and requests that an interpreter be provided. H's doctor should arrange for the services of a qualified interpreter, as an interpreter is likely to be necessary for effective communication with H, given the length and complexity of the communication involved.

ILLUSTRATION 3: S, an individual who is blind, visits an electronics store to purchase a clock radio and wishes to inspect the merchandise information cards next to the floor models in order to decide which one to buy. Reading the model information to S should be adequate to ensure effective communication. Of course, if S is unreasonably demanding or is shopping when the store is extremely busy, it may be an undue burden to spend extended periods of time reading price and product information.

ILLUSTRATION 4: S also has tickets to a play. When S arrives at the theater, the usher notices that S is an individual who is blind and guides S to her seat. An usher is also available to guide S to her seat following intermission. With the provision of these services, a Brailled ticket is not necessary for effective communication in seating S.

ILLUSTRATION 5: The same theater provides S with a tape-recorded version of its printed program for the evening's performance. A Brailled program is not necessary to effectively communicate the contents of the program to S, if an audio cassette and tape player are provided.

Who decides what type of auxiliary aid should be provided? Public accommodations should consult with individuals with disabilities wherever possible to determine what type of auxiliary aid is needed to ensure effective communication. In many cases, more than one type of auxiliary aid or service may make effective communication possible. While consultation is strongly encouraged, the ultimate decision as to what measures to take to ensure effective communication rests in the hands of the public accommodation, provided that the method chosen results in effective communication.

ILLUSTRATION: A patient who is deaf brings his own sign language interpreter for an office visit without prior consultation and bills the physician for the cost of the interpreter. The physician is not obligated to comply with the unilateral determination by the patient that an interpreter is necessary. The physician must be given an opportunity to consult with the patient and make an independent assessment of what type of auxiliary aid, if any, is necessary to ensure effective communication. If the patient believes that the physician's decision will not lead to effective communication, then the patient may challenge that decision under title III by initiating litigation or filing a complaint with the Department of Justice (see III-8.0000).

ILLUSTRATION 2: S, who is blind, goes to the corner laundromat. Displayed on the laundry machine controls are written instructions for operating the machines. The company that owns and operates the laundromat could make the machines accessible to S by Brailling the instructions onto adhesive labels and placing the labels (or a Brailled template) on the machines. Alternatively, the laundromat company could arrange for a laundry room attendant to read the instructions printed on the machines to S. Any one particular method is not required, so long as effective communication is provided.

Who is a qualified interpreter? There are a number of sign language systems in use by persons who use sign language. (The most common systems of sign language are American Sign Language and signed English.) Individuals who use a particular system may not communicate effectively through an interpreter who uses another system. When an interpreter is required, the public accommodation should provide a qualified interpreter, that is, an interpreter who is able to sign to the individual who is deaf what is being said by the hearing person and who can voice to the hearing person what is being signed by the individual who is deaf. This communication must be conveyed effectively, accurately, and impartially, through the use of any necessary specialized vocabulary.

Can a public accommodation use a staff member who signs "pretty well" as an interpreter for meetings with individuals who use sign language to communicate? Signing and interpreting are not the same thing. Being able to sign does not mean that a person can process spoken communication into the proper signs, nor does it mean that he or she possesses the proper skills to observe someone signing and change their signed or fingerspelled communication into spoken words. The interpreter must be able to interpret both receptively and expressively.

If a sign language interpreter is required for effective communication, must only a certified interpreter be provided? No. The key question in determining whether effective communication will result is whether the interpreter is "qualified," not whether he or she has been actually certified by an official licensing body. A qualified interpreter is one "who is able to interpret effectively, accurately and impartially, both receptively and expressively, using any necessary specialized vocabulary." An individual does not have to be certified in order to meet this standard. A certified interpreter may not meet this standard in all situations, e.g., where the interpreter is not familiar with the specialized vocabulary involved in the communication at issue.

III-4.3300 Examples of auxiliary aids and services.

Auxiliary aids and services include a wide range of services and devices that promote effective communication. Examples of auxiliary aids and services for individuals who are deaf or hard of hearing include qualified interpreters, notetakers, computer-aided transcription services, written materials, telephone handset amplifiers, assistive listening systems, telephones compatible with hearing aids, closed caption decoders, open and closed captioning, telecommunications devices for deaf persons (TDD's), videotext displays, and exchange of written notes.

Examples for individuals with vision impairments include qualified readers, taped texts, audio recordings, Brailled materials, large print materials, and assistance in locating items.

Examples for individuals with speech impairments include TDD's, computer terminals, speech synthesizers, and communication boards.

III-4.3400 Telecommunication devices for the deaf (TDD's).

In order to ensure effective communication by telephone, a public accommodation is required to provide TDD's in certain circumstances. Because TDD relay systems required by title IV of the ADA (which must be operational by July 26, 1993) will eliminate many telephone system barriers to TDD users, the auxiliary aids requirements relating to TDD's are limited in nature.

III-4.3410 Calls incident to business operations.

A public accommodation is not required to have a TDD available for receiving or making telephone calls that are part of its business operations. Even during the interim period between the effective date of title III and the date the TDD relay service becomes available, there is no requirement that public accommodations have TDD's. Of course, the ADA does not prevent a public accommodation from obtaining a TDD if, for business or other reasons, it chooses to do so.

III-4.3420 Outgoing calls by customers, clients, patients, or participants.

On the other hand, TDD's must be provided when customers, clients, patients, or participants are permitted to make outgoing calls on "more than an incidental convenience basis." For example, TDD's must be made available on request to hospital patients or hotel guests where in-room phone service is provided. A hospital or hotel front desk should also be equipped with a TDD so that patients or guests using TDD's in their rooms have the same access to in- house services as other patients or guests.

It is the hotel's or hospital's responsibility to monitor requests for TDD's to ensure that it has a sufficient supply of such devices. The facility should acquire what it reasonably predicts will be an adequate number of TDD's, and then acquire additional TDD's if experience shows that an increase is necessary to meet actual demand.

Newly constructed hotels must have a certain number of rooms that are accessible to persons who are deaf or hard of hearing (the exact number is dependent on the number of rooms in the hotel). This number of rooms is a useful reference point for a facility attempting to gauge the number of TDD's necessary for effective communication.

III-4.3500 Closed caption decoders.

Hospitals that provide televisions for use by patients, and hotels, motels, and other places of lodging that provide televisions in five or more guest rooms, must provide closed caption decoder service upon request.

III-4.3600 Limitations and alternatives.

A public accommodation is not required to provide any auxiliary aid or service that would fundamentally alter the nature of the goods or services offered or that would result in an undue burden.

However, the fact that providing a particular auxiliary aid or service would result in a fundamental alteration or undue burden does not necessarily relieve a public accommodation from its obligation to ensure effective communication. The public accommodation must still provide an alternative auxiliary aid or service that would not result in an undue burden or fundamental alteration but that would ensure effective communication to the maximum extent possible, if one is available.

ILLUSTRATION: It may be an undue burden for a small private historic house museum on a shoestring budget to provide a sign language interpreter for a deaf individual wishing to participate in a tour. Providing a written script of the tour, however, would be an alternative that would be unlikely to result in an undue burden.

What is a fundamental alteration? A fundamental alteration is a modification that is so significant that it alters the essential nature of the goods, services, facilities, privileges, advantages, or accommodations offered.

What is an undue burden? "Undue burden" is defined as "significant difficulty or expense." Among the factors to be considered in determining whether an action would result in an undue burden are the following—

1) The nature and cost of the action;

2) The overall financial resources of the site or sites involved; the number of persons employed at the site; the effect on expenses and resources; legitimate safety requirements necessary for safe operation, including crime prevention measures; or any other impact of the action on the operation of the site;

3) The geographic separateness, and the administrative or fiscal relationship of the site or sites in question to any parent corporation or entity;

4) If applicable, the overall financial resources of any parent corporation or entity; the overall size of the parent corporation or entity with respect to the number of its employees; the number, type, and location of its facilities; and

5) If applicable, the type of operation or operations of any parent corporation or entity, including the composition, structure, and functions of the workforce of the parent corporation or entity.

Does a public accommodation have to do more or less under the "undue burden" standard than under other ADA limitations such as "undue hardship" and "readily achievable"? The definition of undue burden is identical to the definition of undue hardship used in title I of the ADA as the limitation on an employer's obligation to reasonably accommodate an applicant or employee. Under both limitations, an action is not required if it results in "significant difficulty or expense." The undue burden standard, however, requires a greater level of effort by a public accommodation in providing auxiliary aids and services than does the "readily achievable" standard for removing barriers in existing facilities (see III-4.4200). Although "readily achievable" is therefore a "lesser" standard, the factors to be considered in determining what is readily achievable are identical to those listed above for determining undue burden.

III-4.4000 Removal of Barriers.

III-4.4100 General.

Public accommodations must remove architectural barriers and communication barriers that are structural in nature in existing facilities, when it is readily achievable to do so.

What is an architectural barrier? Architectural barriers are physical elements of a facility that impede access by people with disabilities. These barriers include more than obvious impediments such as steps and curbs that prevent access by people who use wheelchairs.

In many facilities, telephones, drinking fountains, mirrors, and paper towel dispensers are mounted at a height that makes them inaccessible to people using wheelchairs. Conventional doorknobs and operating controls may impede access by people who have limited manual dexterity. Deep pile carpeting on floors and unpaved exterior ground surfaces often are a barrier to access by people who use wheelchairs and people who use other mobility aids, such as crutches. Impediments caused by the location of temporary or movable structures, such as furniture, equipment, and display racks, are also considered architectural barriers.

What is a communication barrier that is structural in nature? Communication barriers that are "structural in nature" are barriers that are an integral part of the physical structure of a facility. Examples include conventional signage, which generally is inaccessible to people who have vision impairments, and audible alarm systems, which are inaccessible to people with hearing impairments. Structural communication barriers also include the use of physical partitions that hamper the passage of sound waves between employees and customers, and the absence of adequate sound buffers in noisy areas that would reduce the extraneous noise that interferes with communication with people who have limited hearing.

How does the communication barrier removal requirement relate to the obligation to provide auxiliary aids? Communications devices, such as TDD's, telephone handset amplifiers, assistive listening devices, and digital check- out displays, are not an integral part of the physical structure of the building and, therefore, are considered auxiliary aids under the Department's title III regulation. The failure to provide auxiliary aids is not a communication barrier that is structural in nature. The obligation to remove structural communications barriers is independent of any obligation to provide auxiliary aids and services.

What is a "facility"? The term "facility" includes all or any part of a building, structure, equipment, vehicle, site (including roads, walks, passageways, and parking lots), or other real or personal property. Both permanent and temporary facilities are subject to the barrier removal requirements.

III-4.4200 Readily achievable barrier removal.

Public accommodations are required to remove barriers only when it is "readily achievable" to do so. "Readily achievable" means easily accomplishable and able to be carried out without much difficulty or expense.

How does the "readily achievable" standard relate to other standards in the ADA? The ADA establishes different standards for existing facilities and new construction. In existing facilities, where retrofitting may be expensive, the requirement to provide access is less stringent than it is in new construction and alterations, where accessibility can be incorporated in the initial stages of design and construction without a significant increase in cost.

This standard also requires a lesser degree of effort on the part of a public accommodation than the "undue burden" limitation on the auxiliary aids requirements of the ADA. In that sense, it can be characterized as a lower standard. The readily achievable standard is also less demanding than the "undue hardship" standard in title I, which limits the obligation to make reasonable accommodation in employment.

How does a public accommodation determine when barrier removal is readily achievable? Determining if barrier removal is readily achievable is necessarily a case-by-case judgment. Factors to consider include:

1) The nature and cost of the action;

2) The overall financial resources of the site or sites involved; the number of persons employed at the site; the effect on expenses and resources; legitimate safety requirements necessary for safe operation, including crime prevention measures; or any other impact of the action on the operation of the site;

3) The geographic separateness, and the administrative or fiscal relationship of the site or sites in question to any parent corporation or entity;

4) If applicable, the overall financial resources of any parent corporation or entity; the overall size of the parent corporation or entity with respect to the number of its employees; the number, type, and location of its

facilities; and

5) If applicable, the type of operation or operations of any parent corporation or entity, including the composition, structure, and functions of the workforce of the parent corporation or entity.

If the public accommodation is a facility that is owned or operated by a parent entity that conducts operations at many different sites, the public accommodation must consider the resources of both the local facility and the parent entity to determine if removal of a particular barrier is "readily achievable." The administrative and fiscal relationship between the local facility and the parent entity must also be considered in evaluating what resources are available for any particular act of barrier removal.

What barriers will it be "readily achievable" to remove? There is no definitive answer to this question because determinations as to which barriers can be removed without much difficulty or expense must be made on a case-by- case basis.

The Department's regulation contains a list of 21 examples of modifications that may be readily achievable:

1) Installing ramps;
2) Making curb cuts in sidewalks and entrances;
3) Repositioning shelves;
4) Rearranging tables, chairs, vending machines, display racks, and other furniture;
5) Repositioning telephones;
6) Adding raised marking on elevator control buttons;
7) Installing flashing alarm lights;
8) Widening doors;
9) Installing offset hinges to widen doorways;
10) Eliminating a turnstile or providing an alternative accessible path;
11) Installing accessible door hardware;
12) Installing grab bars in toilet stalls;
13) Rearranging toilet partitions to increase maneuvering space;
14) Insulating lavatory pipes under sinks to prevent burns;
15) Installing a raised toilet seat;
16) Installing a full-length bathroom mirror;
17) Repositioning the paper towel dispenser in a bathroom;
18) Creating designated accessible parking spaces;
19) Installing an accessible paper cup dispenser at an existing inaccessible water fountain;
20) Removing high pile, low density carpeting; or
21) Installing vehicle hand controls.

Businesses such as restaurants may need to rearrange tables and department stores may need to adjust their layout of racks and shelves in order to permit wheelchair access, but they are not required to do so if it would result in a significant loss of selling or serving space.

The list is intended to be illustrative. Each of these modifications will be readily achievable in many instances, but not in all. Whether or not any of these measures is readily achievable is to be determined on a case-by-case basis in light of the particular circumstances presented and the factors discussed above.

Are public accommodations required to retrofit existing buildings by adding elevators? A public accommodation generally would not be required to remove a barrier to physical access posed by a flight of steps, if removal would require extensive ramping or an elevator. The readily achievable standard does not require barrier removal that requires extensive restructuring or burdensome expense. Thus, where it is not readily achievable to do, the ADA would not require a public accommodation to provide access to an area reachable only by a flight of stairs.

Does a public accommodation have an obligation to search for accessible space? A public accommodation is not required to lease space that is accessible. However, upon leasing, the barrier removal requirements for existing facilities apply. In addition, any alterations to the space must meet the accessibility requirements for alterations.

Does the ADA require barrier removal in historic buildings? Yes, if it is readily achievable. However, the ADA takes into account the national interest in preserving significant historic structures. Barrier removal would not be considered "readily achievable" if it would threaten or destroy the historic significance of a building or facility that is eligible for listing in the National Register of Historic Places under the National Historic Preservation Act (16 U.S.C. 470, et seq.), or is designated as historic under State or local law.

ILLUSTRATION 1: The installation of a platform lift in an historic facility that is preserved because of its unique place in American architecture, or because it is one of few surviving examples of the architecture of a particular period, would not be readily achievable, if the installation of the lift would threaten or destroy architecturally significant elements of the building.

ILLUSTRATION 2: The installation of a ramp or lift in a facility that has historic significance because of events that have occurred there, rather than because of unique architectural characteristics, may be readily achievable, if it does not threaten or destroy the historic significance of the building and is within appropriate cost constraints.

Does the ADA permit a public accommodation to consider the effect of a modification on the operation of its business? Yes. The ADA permits consideration of factors other than the initial cost of the physical removal of a barrier.

ILLUSTRATION 1: CDE convenience store determines that it would be inexpensive to remove shelves to provide access to wheelchair users throughout the store. However, this change would result in a significant loss of selling space that would have an adverse effect on its business. In this case, the removal of the shelves is not readily achievable and, thus, is not required by the ADA.

ILLUSTRATION 2: BCD Hardware Store provides three parking spaces for its customers. BCD determines that it would be inexpensive to restripe the parking lot to create an accessible space and reserve it for use by persons with disabilities. However, this change would reduce the available parking for individuals who do not have disabilities. The loss of parking (not just the cost of the paint for restriping) can be considered in determining whether the action is readily achievable.

ILLUSTRATION 3: A small car rental office for a national chain is located in a rural community. Title III requires the company to install vehicle hand controls if it is readily achievable to do so. However, this procedure may not be readily achievable in a rural, isolated area, unless the company is provided adequate notice by the customer. What constitutes adequate notice will vary depending on factors such as the remoteness of the location, the availability of trained mechanics, the availability of hand controls, and the size of the fleet. For example, notice of an hour or less may be adequate at a large city site where it is readily achievable to stock hand controls and to have a mechanic always available who is trained to install them properly. On the other hand, notice of two days may necessary for a small, rural site where it is not readily achievable to keep hand controls in stock and where there is only a part-time mechanic who has been trained in the proper installation of controls.

Does the requirement for readily achievable barrier removal apply to equipment? Yes. Manufacturers are not required by Title III to produce accessible equipment. Public accommodations, however, have the obligation, if readily achievable, to take measures, such as altering the height of equipment controls and operating devices, to provide access to goods and services.

ILLUSTRATION: Although manufacturers of washing machines are not obligated under the ADA to produce machines of a particular design, laundromats or resort guest laundry rooms must do what is readily achievable to remove barriers to the use of existing machines.

III-4.4300 Standards to apply.

Measures taken to remove barriers should comply with the ADA Accessibility Guidelines (ADAAG) contained in the appendix to the Department's rule. Barrier removal in existing facilities does not, however, trigger the accessible path of travel requirement (see III-6.2000). Deviations from ADAAG are acceptable only when full compliance with those requirements is not readily achievable. In such cases, barrier removal measures may be taken that do not fully comply with the standards, so long as the measures do not pose a significant risk to the health or safety of individuals with disabilities or others.

ILLUSTRATION: As a first step toward removing architectural barriers, the owner of a small shop decides to widen the shop's 26-inch wide front door. However, because of space constraints, he is unable to widen the door to the full 32-inch clearance required for alterations under ADAAG. Because full compliance with ADAAG is not readily achievable, the shop owner need not widen the door the full 32 inches but, rather, may widen the door to only 30 inches. The 30-inch door clearance does not pose a significant risk to health or safety.

Are portable ramps permitted? Yes, but only when the installation of a permanent ramp is not readily achievable. In order to promote safety, a portable ramp should have railings and a firm, stable, nonslip surface. It should also be properly secured.

III-4.4400 Continuing obligation.

The obligation to engage in readily achievable barrier removal is a continuing one. Over time, barrier removal that initially was not readily achievable may later be required because of changed circumstances.

If the obligation is continuing, are there any limits on what must be done? The obligation is continuing, but not unlimited. The obligation to remove barriers will never exceed the level of access required under the alterations standard (or the new construction standard if ADAAG does not provide specific standards for alterations).

ILLUSTRATION 1: A 100-room hotel is removing barriers in guest accommodations. If the hotel were newly constructed, it would be required to provide five fully accessible rooms (including one with a roll-in shower) and four rooms that are equipped with visual alarms and notification devices and telephones equipped with amplification devices. A hotel that is being altered is required to provide a number of accessible rooms in the area being altered that is proportionate to the number it would be required to provide in new construction.

A hotel that is engaged in barrier removal should meet this alterations standard, if it is readily achievable to do so. It is not required to exceed this level of access. Even if it is readily achievable to make more rooms accessible than would be required under the ADAAG alterations standards, once the hotel provides this level of access, it has no obligation to remove barriers in additional guest rooms.

ILLUSTRATION 2: A grocery store that has more than 5000 square feet of selling space and now has six inaccessible check-out aisles is assessing its obligations under the barrier removal requirement. ADAAG does not contain specific provisions applicable to the alteration of check-out aisles, but, in new construction, two of the six check-out aisles would be required to be accessible. The store is never required to provide more than two accessible check-out aisles, even if it would be readily achievable to do so.

ILLUSTRATION 3: An office building that houses places of public accommodation is removing barriers in common areas. If the building were newly constructed, the building would be required to contain areas of rescue assistance. However, the ADAAG alterations standard explicitly specifies that areas of rescue assistance are not required in buildings that are being altered. Because barrier removal is not required to exceed the alterations standard, the building owner need not establish areas of rescue assistance.

III-4.4500 Priorities for barrier removal.

The Department's regulation recommends priorities for removing barriers in existing facilities. Because the resources available for barrier removal may not be adequate to remove all existing barriers at any given time, the regulation suggests a way to determine which barriers should be mitigated or eliminated first. The purpose of these priorities is to facilitate long-term business planning and to maximize the degree of effective access that will result from any given level of expenditure. These priorities are not mandatory. Public accommodations are free to exercise discretion in determining the most effective "mix" of barrier removal measures to undertake in their facilities.

The regulation suggests that a public accommodation's first priority should be to enable individuals with disabilities to physically enter its facility. This priority on "getting through the door" recognizes that providing physical access to a facility from public sidewalks, public transportation, or parking is generally preferable to any alternative arrangements in terms of both business efficiency and the dignity of individuals with disabilities.

The next priority is for measures that provide access to those areas of a place of public accommodation where goods and services are made available to the public. For example, in a hardware store, to the extent that it is readily achievable to do so, individuals with disabilities should be given access not only to assistance at the front desk, but also access, like that available to other customers, to the retail display areas of the store.

The third priority should be providing access to restrooms, if restrooms are provided for use by customers or clients.

The fourth priority is to remove any remaining barriers to using the public accommodation's facility by, for example, installing visual alarms, adding Brailled floor indicators to elevator panels, or lowering telephones.

Must barriers be removed in areas used only by employees? No. The "readily achievable" obligation to remove barriers in existing facilities does not extend to areas of a facility that are used exclusively by employees as work areas.

How can a public accommodation decide what needs to be done? One effective approach is to conduct a "self-evaluation" of the facility to identify existing barriers. The Department's regulation does not require public accommodations to conduct a self-evaluation. However, public accommodations are urged to establish procedures for an ongoing assessment of their compliance with the ADA's barrier removal requirements. This process should include consultation with individuals with disabilities or organizations representing them. A serious effort at self-assessment and consultation can diminish the threat of litigation and save resources by identifying the most efficient means of providing required access.

If a public accommodation determines that its facilities have barriers that should be removed, but it is not readily achievable to undertake all of the modifications now, what should it do? The Department recommends that a public accommodation develop an implementation plan designed to achieve compliance with the ADA's barrier removal requirements. Such a plan, if appropriately designed and diligently executed, could serve as evidence of a good faith effort to comply with the ADA's barrier removal requirements.

In developing an implementation plan for readily achievable barrier removal, a public accommodation should consult with local organizations representing persons with disabilities to solicit their suggestions for cost- effective means of making individual places of public accommodation accessible. These organizations may provide useful guidance to public accommodations in identifying the most significant barriers to remove, and the most efficient means of removing them.

If readily achievable modifications are being made in a single facility that has more than one restroom for each sex, should the public accommodation focus its resources on making one restroom for each sex fully accessible or should the public accommodation make some changes (e.g., lowering towel dispensers or installing grab bars) in each restroom? This is a decision best made on a case-by-case basis after considering the specific barriers that need to be removed in that facility, and whether it is readily achievable to remove these barriers. It is likely that if it is readily achievable to make one restroom fully accessible, that option would be preferred by the clients or customers of the facility.

III-4.4600 Seating in assembly areas.

Public accommodations are required to remove barriers to physical access in assembly areas such as theaters, lecture halls, and conference rooms with fixed seating.

If it is readily achievable to do so, public accommodations that operate places of assembly must locate seating for individuals who use wheelchairs so that it—

1) Is dispersed throughout the seating area;

2) Provides lines of sight and choices of admission prices comparable to those offered to the general public;

3) Adjoins an accessible route for emergency egress; and

4) Permits people who use wheelchairs to sit with their friends or family.

If it is not readily achievable for auditoriums or theaters to remove seats to allow individuals who use wheelchairs to sit next to accompanying family members or friends, the public accommodation may meet its obligation by providing portable chairs or other means to allow the accompanying individuals to sit with the persons who use wheelchairs. Portable chairs or other means must be provided only when it is readily achievable to do so.

How many seating locations for persons who use wheelchairs must be provided? Under the general principles applicable to barrier removal in existing facilities, a public accommodation is never required to provide greater access than it would be required to provide under the alterations provisions of the ADAAG.

Must the seating locations be dispersed? The ADA accessibility standard for alterations requires wheelchair seating to be dispersed (i.e., provided in more than one location) only in assembly areas with fixed seating for more than 300 people. Because the requirements for making existing facilities accessible never exceed the ADAAG standard for alterations, public accommodations engaged in barrier removal are not required to disperse wheelchair seating in assembly areas with 300 or fewer seats, or in any case where it is technically infeasible.

Must a public accommodation permit a person who uses a wheelchair to leave his or her wheelchair and view the performance or program from a stationary seat? Yes. And in order to facilitate seating of wheelchair users who wish to transfer to existing seating when fixed seating is provided, a public accommodation must provide, to the extent readily achievable, a reasonable number of seats with removable aisle-side armrests. Many persons who use wheelchairs are able to transfer to fixed seating with this relatively minor modification. This solution avoids the potential safety hazard created by the use of portable chairs, and it also fosters integration. In situations when a person who uses a wheelchair transfers to existing seating, the public accommodation may provide assistance in handling the wheelchair of the patron with the disability.

May a public accommodation charge a wheelchair user a higher fee to compensate for the extra space required to accommodate a wheelchair or for storing or retrieving a wheelchair? No. People with disabilities may not be subjected to additional charges related to their use of a wheelchair. In fact, to the extent readily achievable, wheelchair seating should provide a choice of admission prices and lines of sight comparable to those for members of the general public.

III-4.4700 Transportation barriers.

Public accommodations that provide transportation to their clients or customers must remove barriers to the extent that it is readily achievable to do so. Public accommodations that provide transportation service must also comply with the applicable portions of the ADA regulation issued by the Department of Transportation (56 Fed. Reg. 45,884 (September 6, 1991) to the codified at 49 CFR Part 37)).

What kinds of transportation systems are covered by the Department of Justice's title III rule? The Department of Justice's rule covers any fixed route or demand responsive transportation system operated by a public accommodation that is not primarily engaged in the business of transporting people. Examples include airport shuttle services operated by hotels, customer bus or van services operated by shopping centers, transportation systems at colleges and universities, and transport systems in places of recreation, such as those at stadiums, zoos, and amusement parks. If a public accommodation is primarily engaged in the business of transporting people, its activities are not covered under the Department of Justice's title III regulation. Rather, its activities are subject to the Department of Transportation's ADA regulation.

What requirements apply to the acquisition of new vehicles? Requirements for the acquisition of new vehicles are found in the Department of Transportation regulation and vary depending on both the capacity of the vehicle and its intended use, as follows:

1) Fixed route system: Vehicle capacity over 16. Any vehicle with a capacity over 16 that is purchased or leased for a fixed route system must be "readily accessible to and usable by individuals with disabilities, including those who use wheelchairs."

2) Fixed route system: Vehicle capacity of 16 or less. Vehicles of this description must meet the same "readily accessible and usable" standard described in (1) above, unless they are part of a system that already meets the "equivalent service" standard.

3) Demand responsive system: Vehicle capacity over 16. These vehicles must meet the "readily accessible and usable" standard, unless they are part of a system that already meets the "equivalent service" standard.

4) Demand responsive system: Vehicle capacity of 16 or less. Vehicles of this description are not subject to any requirements for purchase of accessible vehicles. However, "equivalent service" must be provided.

What is "equivalent service"? A system is deemed to provide equivalent service if, when the system is viewed in its entirety, the service provided to individuals with disabilities, including those who use wheelchairs, is provided in the most integrated setting appropriate to the needs of the individual and is equivalent to the service provided other individuals. The Department of Transportation regulation lists eight service characteristics that must be equivalent. These include schedules/response time, fares, and places and times of service availability.

Is it necessary to install a lift in an existing vehicle? No. The ADA states that the installation of hydraulic lifts in existing vehicles is not required.

Are employee transportation systems covered? Transportation services provided only to employees of a place of public accommodation are not subject to the Department's title III regulation but are covered by the regulation issued by the Equal Employment Opportunity Commission to implement title I of the ADA. However, if employees and customers or clients are served by the same transportation system, the provisions of the title III regulation will also apply.

III-4.5000 Alternatives to Barrier Removal.

III-4.5100 General.

When a public accommodation can demonstrate that the removal of barriers is not readily achievable, the public accommodation must make its goods and services available through alternative methods, if such methods are readily achievable.

ILLUSTRATION 1: A retail store determines that it is not readily achievable to rearrange display racks to make every aisle accessible. However, the store is still required to make the goods and services that are located along inaccessible aisles available to individuals with disabilities through alternative methods. For example, the store could instruct a clerk to retrieve inaccessible merchandise, if it is readily achievable to do so.

ILLUSTRATION 2: A pharmacy that is located in a building that can be entered only by means of a long flight of stairs determines that it is not readily achievable to provide a ramp to that entrance; therefore, it is not required to provide access to its facility. However, the pharmacy is still required to provide access to its services, if any readily achievable alternative method of delivery is available. Therefore, the pharmacy must consider options, such as delivering goods to customers at curbside or at their homes.

ILLUSTRATION 3: A self-service gas station determines that it is not readily achievable to redesign gas pumps to enable people with disabilities to use them; therefore, the gas station is not required to make physical modifications to the gas pumps. However, the gas station is required to provide its services to individuals with disabilities through any readily achievable alternative method, such as providing refueling service upon request to an individual with a disability.

ILLUSTRATION 4: A restaurant determines that it is not readily achievable to remove physical barriers to access in a specific area of the restaurant. The restaurant must offer the same menu in an accessible area of the restaurant, unless it would not be readily achievable to do so.

ILLUSTRATION 5: A laundromat, if it is readily achievable to do so, must modify controls on existing washing machines to be within an accessible reach range. If modification is not readily achievable, then assistive devices or services must be provided, such as a wand, mechanical grabber, or assistance from an on-duty laundromat attendant, if it is readily achievable to do so.

ILLUSTRATION 6: A medical center that operates inaccessible mobile health care screening vans must consider readily achievable alternative methods of providing access to the van's services. Possible alternatives include providing equivalent services at accessible site in the medical center, using the van to deliver services to persons with disabilities in their own homes, or transporting people with disabilities from their homes or the van site to an accessible facility where they can receive equivalent services.

How can a public accommodation determine if an alternative to barrier removal is readily achievable? The factors to consider in determining if an alternative is readily achievable are the same as those that are considered in determining if barrier removal is readily achievable (see III-4.4200).

If a public accommodation provides its services through alternative measures, such as home delivery, may it charge its customers for this special service? No. When goods or services are provided to an individual with a disability through alternative methods because the public accommodation's facility is inaccessible, the public accommodation may not place a surcharge on the individual with a disability for the costs associated with the alternative method.

ILLUSTRATION 1: A gas station that chooses to provide refueling service to individuals with disabilities at a self-service island, rather than removing the barriers that preclude that individual from refueling his or her own vehicle, must provide the refueling service at the self-service price.

ILLUSTRATION 2: An inaccessible pharmacy that provides home delivery to individuals with disabilities, rather than removing the barriers that prevent those individuals from being served in the pharmacy, must provide the home delivery at no charge to the customer. However, a pharmacy that normally offers home delivery as an option to its customers and charges a fee for that service, may continue to charge a delivery fee to customers with disabilities, if the pharmacy provides at least one "no-cost" alternative, such as delivering its products to a customer at curbside.

May a public accommodation consider security issues when it is determining if an alternative is readily achievable? Yes. Security is a factor that may be considered when a public accommodation is determining if an alternative method of delivering its goods or services is readily achievable.

ILLUSTRATION 1: A service station is not required to provide refueling service to individuals with disabilities at any time when it is operating exclusively on a remote control basis with a single cashier.

ILLUSTRATION 2: A cashier working in a security booth in a convenience store when there are no other employees on duty is not required to leave his or her post to retrieve items for individuals with disabilities.

III-4.5200 Multiscreen cinemas.

The Department's regulation expressly recognizes that it may not be readily achievable to remove enough barriers to provide access to all of the theaters in a multiscreen cinema. In this situation, a cinema must make its services available by establishing a film rotation schedule that provides reasonable access for individuals who use wheelchairs to films being presented by the cinema. Public notice must be provided as to the location and time of accessible showings. Methods for providing notice include appropriate use of the international accessibility symbol in a cinema's print advertising and the addition of accessibility information to a cinema's recorded telephone information line.

III-4.6000 Examinations and courses.

Any private entity that offers examinations or courses related to applications, licensing, certification, or credentialing for secondary or postsecondary education, professional, or trade purposes must offer such examinations or courses in a place and manner accessible to persons with disabilities, or offer alternative accessible arrangements for such individuals.

III-4.6100 Examinations.

Examinations covered by this section include examinations for admission to secondary schools, college entrance examinations, examinations for admission to trade or professional schools, and licensing examinations such as bar exams, examinations for medical licenses, or examinations for certified public accountants.

A private entity offering an examination covered by this section is responsible for selecting and administering the examination in a place and manner that ensures that the examination accurately reflects an individual's aptitude or achievement level or other factor the examination purports to measure, rather than reflecting the individual's impaired sensory, manual, or speaking skills (except where those skills are the factors that the examination purports to measure).

Where necessary, an examiner may be required to provide auxiliary aids or services, unless it can demonstrate that offering a particular auxiliary aid or service would fundamentally alter the examination or result in an undue burden. For individuals with hearing impairments, for example, oral instructions or other aurally delivered materials could be provided through an interpreter, assistive listening device, or other effective method. For individuals with visual impairments, providing examinations and answer sheets on audio tape, in large print or Braille, or providing qualified readers or transcribers to record answers, may be appropriate. Also, some individuals with learning disabilities may need auxiliary aids or services, such as readers, because of problems in perceiving and processing written information. See III-4.3000 for a general discussion of auxiliary aids and services.

In order to ensure that the examination accurately measures the factors that it purports to measure, the entity administering the examination must ensure that the auxiliary aid or service provided is effective.

ILLUSTRATION 1: MNO Testing Service provides a reader for an applicant who is blind who is taking a bar examination, but the reader is unfamiliar with specific terminology used in the examination, mispronounces words, and, because he or she does not understand the questions, is unable to convey the information in the questions or to follow the applicant's instructions effectively. Because of the difficulty in communicating with the reader, the applicant is unable to complete the examination. MNO is not in compliance with the ADA, because the results of the examination will reflect the reader's lack of skill and familiarity with the material, rather than the applicant's knowledge.

ILLUSTRATION 2: ABC Testing Service administers written examinations designed to test specific skills or areas of knowledge. An individual with a vision impairment or learning disability that limits the ability to read written material may be unable to pass such an examination because of limited reading ability, regardless of his or her knowledge or ability in the area that the test is designed to measure. ABC must administer the test in a manner that enables the applicant to demonstrate his or her skill or knowledge, rather than the ability to read.

BUT: If the test is designed to measure the ability to read written material, it may be administered in written form because the result will accurately reflect the individual's reading ability.

Aside from auxiliary aids or services, what other types of modifications may be required? In order to ensure that an examination provides an accurate measurement of the applicant's aptitude or achievement level, or whatever other factor it purports to measure, the entity administering the examination may also be required to modify the manner in which it is administered.

ILLUSTRATION: X has a manual impairment that makes writing difficult. It may be necessary to provide X with more time to complete the exam and/or permit typing of answers.

What obligations does an examiner have if its facilities are inaccessible? Examinations must be administered in facilities that are accessible to individuals with disabilities or alternative accessible arrangements must be made. If the facility in which the examination is offered is not accessible, it may be administered to an individual with a disability in a different room or other location. For instance, the entity might provide the examination at an individual's home with a proctor. The alternative location must, however, provide comparable conditions to the conditions in which the test is administered to others.

ILLUSTRATION: A nurse licensing examination is administered in a warm, well-lit, second-floor classroom that is not accessible to an individual who uses a wheelchair. The Nursing Board may allow that individual to take it in a classroom or office on the first floor that is accessible, but must ensure that the accessible room is also well-lit and has adequate heat.

Must all testing locations be accessible and offer specially designed exams? No, but if an examination for individuals with disabilities is administered in an alternative accessible location, or in a manner specially designed for individuals with disabilities, it must be offered as often and in as timely a manner as other examinations. Examinations must be offered to individuals with disabilities at locations that are as convenient as the location of other examinations.

ILLUSTRATION: A college entrance examination is offered by LMN Testing Service in several cities in a State, but only one location has either an accessible facility or an alternative accessible facility. X, an individual who uses a wheelchair, lives near an inaccessible test location at which no alternative accessible facility is provided. The nearest test location with an accessible facility is 500 miles away. LMN has violated the ADA, because X is required to travel a longer distance to take the examination than other people who can take the examination in the city that is most convenient for them.

Can individuals with disabilities be required to file their applications to take an examination earlier than the deadline for other applicants? No. This would violate the requirement that examinations designed for individuals with disabilities be offered in as timely a manner as other examinations. Entities that administer tests may require individuals with disabilities to provide advance notice of their disabilities and of any modifications or aids that would be required, provided that the deadline for such notice is no earlier than the deadline for others applying to take the examination.

May an examiner require that an applicant provide documentation of the existence and nature of the disability as evidence that he or she is entitled to modifications or aids? Yes, but requests for documentation must be reasonable and must be limited to the need for the modification or aid requested. Appropriate documentation might include a letter from a physician or other professional, or evidence of a prior diagnosis or accommodation, such as eligibility for a special education program. The applicant may be required to bear the cost of providing such documentation, but the entity administering the examination cannot charge the applicant for the cost of any modifications or auxiliary aids, such as interpreters, provided for the examination.

ILLUSTRATION: A testing service may be required to provide individuals with dyslexia with more time to complete an examination. An individual who requests additional time may, however, be required to notify the testing service of the request at the time he or she applies to take the examination, and to furnish appropriate documentation to establish that the additional time is needed because of a disability.

Can an entity refuse to provide modifications or aids for applicants with disabilities on the grounds that those individuals, because of their disabilities, would be unable to meet other requirements of the profession or occupation for which the examination is given? No. When an examination is one step in qualifying for a license, an individual may not be barred from taking the examination merely because he or she might be unable to meet other requirements for the license. If the examination is not the first stage of the qualification process, an applicant may be required to complete the earlier stages prior to being admitted to the examination. On the other hand, the applicant may not be denied admission to the examination on the basis of doubts about his or her abilities to meet requirements that the examination is not designed to test.

ILLUSTRATION: An individual with a disability may not be required to demonstrate that he or she is capable of practicing medicine in order to be provided with an auxiliary aid in taking a test for admission to medical school.

BUT: An individual may be required to complete medical school before being admitted to a licensing examination for medical school graduates.

III-4.6200 Courses.

The requirements for courses under this section are generally the same as those for examinations. Any course covered by this section must be modified to ensure that the place and manner in which the course is given are accessible. Examples of possible modifications that might be required include extending the time permitted for completion of the course, providing auxiliary aids or services (except where to do so would fundamentally alter the course or result in an undue burden), or offering the course in an accessible location or making alternative accessible arrangements.

ILLUSTRATION: If the course is offered in an inaccessible location, alternative accessible arrangements may include provision of the course through videotape, cassettes, or prepared notes.

Alternative arrangements for courses, like those for examinations, must provide comparable conditions to those provided to others, including similar lighting, room temperature, and the like.

The entity offering the course must ensure that the course materials that it provides are available in alternate formats that individuals with disabilities can use.

ILLUSTRATION: Class handouts may be provided in Braille or on audio cassettes for individuals with visual impairments.

BUT: If the course uses published materials that are available from other sources, the entity offering the course is not responsible for providing them in alternate formats. It should, however, inform students in advance what materials will be used so that an individual with a disability can obtain them in a usable format, such as Braille or audio tape, before the class begins.

An entity offering a variety of courses covered by this section may not limit the selection or choice of courses available to individuals with disabilities. Courses offered to fulfill a continuing education requirement for a profession, for example, are covered by the requirement that they be offered in an accessible place and manner, and an entity that offers such courses may not designate particular courses for individuals with disabilities and refuse to make other courses accessible.

III-5.0000 NEW CONSTRUCTION.

III-5.1000 General.

All newly constructed places of public accommodation and commercial facilities must be readily accessible to and usable by individuals with disabilities to the extent that it is not structurally impracticable. This requirement, along with the requirement for accessible alterations, are the only requirements that apply to commercial facilities.

What is "readily accessible and usable"? This means that facilities must be built in strict compliance with the Americans with Disabilities Act Accessibility Guidelines (ADAAG). There is no cost defense to the new construction requirements.

What buildings are covered? The new construction requirements apply to any facility first occupied after January 26, 1993, for which the last application for a building permit or permit extension is certified as complete after January 26, 1992; or in those jurisdictions where the government does not certify completion of applications, the date that the last application for a building permit or permit extension is received by the government.

What if a building is occupied before January 26, 1993? It is not covered by the title III new construction requirements.

What does "structurally impracticable" mean? The phrase "structurally impracticable" means that unique characteristics of the land prevent the incorporation of accessibility features in a facility. In such a case, the new construction requirements apply, except where the private entity can demonstrate that it is structurally impracticable to meet those requirements. This exception is very narrow and should not be used in cases of merely hilly terrain. The Department expects that it will be used in only rare and unusual circumstances.

Even in those circumstances where the exception applies, portions of a facility that can be made accessible must still be made accessible. In addition, access should be provided for individuals with other types of disabilities, even if it may be structurally impracticable to provide access to individuals who use wheelchairs.

ILLUSTRATION: M owns a large piece of land on which he plans to build many facilities, including office buildings, warehouses, and stores. The eastern section of the land is fairly level, the central section of the land is extremely steep, and the western section of the land is marshland. M assumes that he only need comply with the new construction requirements in the eastern section. He notifies his architect and construction contractor to be sure that all buildings in the eastern section are built in full compliance with ADAAG. He further advises that no ADAAG requirements apply in the central and western sections.

M's advice as to two of the sections is incorrect. The central section may be extremely steep, but that is not sufficient to qualify for the "structural impracticability" exemption under the ADA. M should have advised his contractor to grade the land to provide an accessible slope at the entrance and apply all new construction requirements in the central section.

M's advice as to the western section is also incorrect. Because the land is marshy, provision of an accessible grade-level entrance may be structurally impracticable. This is one of the rare situations in which the exception applies, and full compliance with ADAAG is not required. However, M should have advised his contractor to nevertheless construct the facilities in compliance with other ADAAG requirements, including provision of features that serve individuals who use crutches or who have vision or hearing impairments. For instance, the facility needs to have stairs and railings that comply with ADAAG, and it should comply with the ADAAG signage and alarm requirements, as well.

Who is liable for violation of the ADA in the above example? Any of the entities involved in the design and construction of the central and western sections might be liable. Thus, in any lawsuit, M, the architect, and the construction contractor may all be held liable in an ADA lawsuit.

III-5.2000 Commercial facilities in a home.

When a commercial facility, such as a home sales office or production workshop, is located in a home, the portion used exclusively as a commercial facility, as well as the portion used both as a commercial facility and for residential purposes, are covered by the new construction and alterations requirements. The covered areas include not only the rooms used as a commercial facility but also an accessible route to the commercial facility from the sidewalk, through the doorway, through the hallway, and other portions of the home, such as restrooms, used by employees and visitors.

III-5.3000 Application of ADAAG.

The Department of Justice has adopted the ADA Accessibility Guidelines (ADAAG), issued by the Architectural and Transportation Barriers Compliance Board, as thc standard to be applied in new construction. The major provisions of ADAAG are summarized in III-7.0000.

What if ADAAG has no standards for a particular type of facility-such as bowling alleys, golf courses, exercise equipment, pool lifts, amusement park rides, and cruise ships? In such cases, the ADAAG standards should be applied to the extent possible. Where appropriate technical standards exist, they should be applied. If there are no applicable scoping requirements (i.e., how many features must be accessible), then a reasonable number, but at least one, must be accessible.

ILLUSTRATION 1: A swimming pool complex must comply fully with ADAAG in the parking facilities, route to the facility door, entrance to the facility, locker rooms, showers, common areas, and route to the pool. However, ADAAG does not contain technical standards for access to the pool itself. Thus, the owner cannot be found in violation of ADAAG for failure to install a lift or other means of access into the pool.

ILLUSTRATION 2: Most bowling alleys are inaccessible because they have a few steps down to the bowling area and a step up to the lanes. ADAAG requirements for ramping steps can be applied to the design of new bowling alleys, resulting in an accessible bowling alley. Unlike in the case of pool lifts above, appropriate technical standards for ramps are applicable. However, ADAAG contains no "scoping" for bowling alleys. In other words, it does not specify how many alleys need to be accessible. As a result, if a reasonable number, but at least one, of the alleys is designed to be accessible, no ADA violation will be found.

ILLUSTRATION 3: Because of the unique structure of ships, none of the ADAAG technical or scoping standards are appropriate. Until such time as the Architectural and Transportation Barriers Compliance Board issues specific standards applicable to ships, there is no requirement that ships be constructed accessibly. (Cruise ships would still be subject to other title III requirements.)

ILLUSTRATION 4: Although mobile health care screening vans are 'facilities' subject to the requirements of title III, there are no specific ADAAG standards for newly constructed or altered vans. The vehicles are, however, subject to the other title III requirements including the obligation to provide equal opportunity and the duty to remove architectural, communication, and transportation achievable to do so, and if it is not readily achievable to do so, to provide alternative methods of access to the services offered through the mobile vans.

Does ADAAG apply to equipment that is not built in to the facility? No. Only equipment that is fixed or built in to the facility, is covered by the accessibility standards (e.g., public pay telephones or built-in ATMs). Free- standing equipment is not covered by ADAAG, but public accommodations may be required to purchase accessible free-standing equipment in certain circumstances in order to provide equal opportunity. They may also be required to make existing free-standing equipment accessible to individuals with disabilities, if it is readily achievable to do so (see III14.4200).

III-5.4000 Elevator exemption.

Elevators are the most common way to provide access in multistory buildings. Title III of the ADA, however, contains an exception to the general rule requiring elevators. Elevators are not required in facilities under three stories or with fewer than 3000 square feet per floor, unless the building is a shopping center or mall; professional office of a health care provider; public transit station; or airport passenger terminal.

ILLUSTRATION 1: A two-story office building has 40,000 square feet on each floor. Because the building is less than three stories, an elevator is not required. (To qualify for the exemption, a building must either be under three stories or have fewer than 3000 square feet per floor; it need not meet both criteria.)

BUT: A two-story shopping center with 40,000 square feet on each floor is required to have an elevator, because shopping centers are not entitled to the exemption.

ILLUSTRATION 2: A four-story building has 2900 square feet per floor. An elevator is not required because each floor has less than 3000 square feet.

ILLUSTRATION 3: A four-story office building has 3500 square feet on the first floor and 2500 square feet on each of the other floors. An elevator is required. (All of the stories must be under 3000 square feet to qualify for the exemption.)

What is a "story"? A story is "occupiable" space, which means space designed for human occupancy and equipped with one or more means of egress, light, and ventilation. Basements designed or intended for occupancy are considered "stories." Mezzanines are not counted as stories, but are just levels within stories.

If a two-story building is not required to have an elevator to the second floor, must it provide a lift? No. The elevator exemption is a "vertical access" exemption. This means that no access by any means need be provided to the second floor. However, if an entity wishes to provide access by ramp or a lift, it is, of course, free to do so.

What if a building is not required to have an elevator, but the owner decides to install an elevator anyway? Must the elevator comply with ADAAG elevator requirements? Yes. And that elevator must serve every level of the building, unless it only provides service from a garage to one level of the building.

If a building is subject to the elevator exemption, do any other ADAAG requirements apply in the building? Yes. Even in buildings that are exempt from the elevator requirement, all other ADAAG requirements (apart from the requirement for an elevator) must still be met.

ILLUSTRATION: A two-story building will be used as real estate offices. There will be bathrooms on both the ground floor and the second floor. No elevator will be installed because it is not required in a building with less than three stories. However, the second floor bathrooms must still be accessible. In other words, both the ground floor and the second floor bathrooms must be accessible.

But why are accessible bathrooms and fountains required on the second floor when there is no way that an individual using a wheelchair can get to the second floor? There are many individuals who can walk up stairs by using crutches, but then use wheelchairs to get around once they reach the upper floor. Also, since the ground floor is being designed to be accessible, there is little additional cost involved in designing the second floor to be accessible as well. In addition, ADAAG contains accessibility features for individuals with disabilities other than those who use wheelchairs, and those features should be incorporated in building design. Finally, an elevator may be installed at a future date, or an addition with an elevator may be added later on. In addition, accessible design of bathroom facilities will foster ease of use by all persons.

III-5.4100 Shopping center or mall.

A "shopping center or mall" is either—

(1) A building with five or more "sales or retail establishments," or

(2) A series of buildings on a common site, either under common ownership or common control or developed together, with five or more "sales or retail establishments."

Included within the phrase "sales or retail establishments" are those types of stores listed in the fifth category of places of public accommodations, i.e., bakery, grocery store, clothing store, hardware store, etc. (see III-1.2000). The term includes floor levels containing at least one such establishment, or any floor that was designed or intended for use by at least one such establishment. The definition of "shopping center or mall" is slightly different for purposes of alterations (see III-6.3000).

ILLUSTRATION 1: A strip of stores includes a grocery store, a clothing store, a restaurant, a drycleaner, a bank, and a pharmacy. This is not a shopping center or mall because only two stores are in the fifth category of "sales or retail establishments" (the grocery store and the clothing store). The restaurant is an establishment serving food or drink (the second category of place of public accommodation). The remaining establishments are "service establishments" included under the sixth category in the definition of place of public accommodation.

ILLUSTRATION 2: A building has a card store, office supply store, video store, and a bakery on the first floor; and a hobby shop, accountant's office, and lawyer's office on the second floor. In this case, both the first and second floors qualify as a "shopping center or mall," because each of those floors has at least one sales establishment. Although no floor alone has five sales establishments, the first and second floor each have at least one such establishment and, together, the total is five. (The accountant's and lawyer's offices are "service establishments" and are not included in the number of "sales or retail establishments.")

When a building is being constructed, the owner or developer does not always know exactly what types of stores will be located in the facility. In such a situation, how will the Department of Justice determine whether a facility was intended as a shopping center? There are a number of factors that can be considered in determining whether a particular floor was designed or intended for use by at least one sales or rental establishment (which would mean that floor is a shopping center). Relevant questions include—

1) What type of businesses did the developer target in his advertising and marketing of the property? Was the developer trying to encourage sales establishments to join the property?

2) Was the facility designed with any special features for sales or rental establishments? For example, are there counters and large windows and check- out aisles?

3) What type of establishment actually first occupied the floor? Was it retail stores or was it offices, for example?

If a shopping mall has 25 stores on each level, how many elevators are needed? Generally, one is enough, as long as an individual could use the elevator and then be able to reach any of the stores on the second level during the hours that the mall is open.

III-5.4200 Professional office of a health care provider.

A "professional office of a health care provider" is a location where a State-regulated professional provides physical or mental health services to the public. The ADA's elevator exemption does not apply to buildings housing the offices of a health care provider.

ILLUSTRATION: A physician has offices on the first floor of a multistory building. The second floor has other types of offices. An elevator is not required.

BUT: If the second floor was designed or intended for use by a health care provider, an elevator would be required.

ILLUSTRATION 2: A newly constructed two-story building houses a business that provides home health care services. No health care services are actually provided at the company's offices. While the building must meet all other requirements for new construction, no elevator is required.

ILLUSTRATION 3: A newly constructed building intended for physical therapy offices will have two floors. The first floor will include patient treatment areas and the second floor will be reserved exclusively for private physician offices and storage space. Regardless of whether patients will receive treatment on each floor, both floors of the building together constitute the professional office of a health care provider, and an elevator must be installed to ensure that each floor is readily accessible to and usable by individuals with disabilities.

How will the Department of Justice determine whether a facility was designed or intended for occupancy by a health care provider? Factors that the Department of Justice will look at in making that determination include—

1) Whether the facility has special plumbing, electrical, or other features needed by health care providers;

2) Whether the facility was marketed as a medical office center; and

3) Whether any of the establishments that actually first occupied the floor were, in fact, health care providers.

III-5.4300 Transportation terminals.

The ADA's elevator exemption also does not apply to bus or train terminals or depots, or to airport passenger terminals. If, however, all passenger services in a two-story facility - including boarding, debarking, loading and unloading, baggage claim, dining facilities, and other common areas open to the public - are located on the same floor level and on an accessible route from an accessible entrance, an elevator is not required.

III-6.0000 ALTERATIONS.

III-6.1000 General.

If an alteration in a place of public accommodation or commercial facility is begun after January 26, 1992, that alteration must be readily accessible to and usable by individuals with disabilities in accordance with ADAAG to the maximum extent feasible.

What is an alteration? An alteration is any change that affects usability. It includes remodeling, renovation, rearrangements in structural parts, and changes or rearrangement of walls and full-height partitions. Normal maintenance, reroofing, painting, wallpapering, asbestos removal, and changes to electrical and mechanical systems are not "alterations," unless they affect usability.

ILLUSTRATION 1: Flooring in a store is being replaced. This is an alteration because it can affect whether or not an individual in a wheelchair can travel in the store. The new floor must comply with, for example, ADAAG requirements for a nonslip surface or with the ADAAG carpeting requirements, if applicable.

ILLUSTRATION 2: A doorway is being relocated and a new door will be installed. The new doorway must be wide enough to meet ADAAG. The new door must have appropriate hardware that can be used without grasping, twisting, or pinching of the wrist.

ILLUSTRATION 3: An electrical outlet is being relocated. The location of the new outlet can affect usability by an individual who uses a wheelchair because, if the outlet is placed too low, the individual will be unable to reach it. This, then, is an alteration that must be done in accordance with ADAAG reach requirements.

BUT: If the electrical wiring inside the wall is being changed, usability by an individual with disabilities is not affected. Thus, the wiring need not be done in compliance with ADAAG because it is not an "alteration."

ILLUSTRATION 4: A parking lot is restriped. Because the restriping may affect the ability of individuals with disabilities to gain access to the facility, the restriping project would be considered an alteration and therefore must include accessible spaces and access aisles in the number required by ADAAG.

What does "maximum extent feasible" mean? Occasionally, the nature of a facility makes it impossible to comply with all of the alterations standards. In such a case, features must only be made accessible to the extent that it is technically feasible to do so. The fact that adding accessibility features during an alteration may increase costs does not mean compliance is technically infeasible. Cost is not to be considered. Moreover, even when it may be technically infeasible to comply with standards for individuals with certain disabilities (for instance, those who use wheelchairs), the alteration must still comply with standards for individuals with other impairments.

ILLUSTRATION 1: A restaurant is undergoing a major renovation. Widening the entrance would affect the building structure because removal of an essential part of the structural frame would be required. In this case, it is "technically infeasible" to widen the entrance, and the action is not required. However, all other ADAAG alterations requirements apply to the renovation.

BUT: If the only problem with widening the entrance is that it would increase the cost of the renovation, the "technically infeasible" exception does not apply, and the entrance must be widened.

III-6.2000 Alterations: Path of travel.

When an alteration is made to a "primary function area," not only must that alteration be done in compliance with ADAAG, but there must also be an accessible path of travel from the altered area to the entrance. The "path of travel" requirement includes an accessible route to the altered area and the bathrooms, telephones, and drinking fountains serving the area. Alterations to provide an accessible path of travel are required to the extent that they are not "disproportionate" to the original alteration, that is, to the extent that the added accessibility costs do not exceed 20 percent of the cost of the original alteration to the primary function area.

What is a primary function area? It is any area where a major activity takes place. It includes both the customer services areas and work areas in places of public accommodation. It includes all offices and work areas in commercial facilities. It does not include mechanical rooms, boiler rooms, supply storage rooms, employee lounges or locker rooms, janitorial closets, entrances, corridors, or restrooms.

ILLUSTRATION 1: The customer service area of a dry cleaning store and the employee area behind the counter are both primary function areas.

ILLUSTRATION 2: Remodeling an office is an alteration to a primary function area. But remodeling the employee restrooms is not an alteration to a primary function area.

ILLUSTRATION 3: Installing a new floor surface in a factory work room is an alteration to a primary function area, but installing a new floor surface in the corridor leading to the work room is not.

What is a "path of travel"? It is a continuous route connecting the altered area to the entrance. It can include sidewalks, lobbies, corridors, rooms, and elevators. It also includes phones, restrooms, and drinking fountains serving the altered area.

Does this mean that every single time any minor alteration is made in a primary function area, the "path of travel" requirement is triggered? In other words, does a simple thing like changing door hardware trigger the path of travel requirement? No. There are some alterations that will never trigger the path of travel requirement. The Department's regulation states that alterations to windows, hardware, controls, electrical outlets, and signs do not trigger path of travel requirements. (If they affect usability, however, they are still considered to be "alterations" and must be done accessibly.) ADAAG gives some additional exceptions: the path of travel requirement is not triggered if alteration work is limited solely to the electrical, mechanical, or plumbing system, hazardous material abatement, or automatic sprinkler retrofitting, unless the project involves alteration to elements required to be accessible.

ILLUSTRATION 1: An office building manager is replacing all of the room number signs. This is an "alteration" because it can affect usability by an individual who is blind. Thus, the new signs must comply with ADAAG requirements for permanent signs. However, the path of travel requirement is not triggered. Even though an alteration is being made in a primary function area, alterations to "signs" are in the list of alterations that will never trigger the path of travel requirement.

ILLUSTRATION 2: The building manager now replaces the men's and women's room signs. Again this is an alteration because it can affect usability, and the new signs must comply with ADAAG. Here, the path of travel requirements are not triggered for two separate reasons. First, as in the above case, the alteration is to "signs" and thus will never trigger the path of travel requirement. In addition, in this case, the alteration is to the restroom. Restrooms are not primary function areas except in limited circumstances, such as highway rest stops.

What if a tenant remodels his store in a manner that would trigger the path of travel obligation, but the tenant has no authority to create an accessible path of travel because the common areas are under the control of the landlord? Does this mean the landlord must now make an accessible path of travel to the remodeled store? No. Alterations by a tenant do not trigger a path of travel obligation for the landlord. Nor is the tenant required to make changes in areas not under his control.

What costs can be included in determining whether the 20 percent disproportionality limitation has been met? Widening doorways, installing ramps, making bathrooms accessible, lowering telephones, relocating water fountains—as well as any other costs associated with making the path of travel accessible—can be included.

What if the cost of making an accessible path of travel would exceed the cost of the original alteration by much more than 20 percent? In such a case, is the entity exempt from the path of travel requirement? No. The entity must still make the path of travel accessible to the extent possible without going over 20 percent, giving priority to those elements that provide the greatest degree of access. Changes should be made in the following order: accessible entrance, accessible route to the altered area, at least one accessible restroom for each sex or single unisex restroom, phones, drinking fountains, and then other elements such as parking, storage, and alarms.

ILLUSTRATION: A library is remodeling its reading area for a total cost of $20,000. The library must spend, if necessary, up to an additional $4,000 (20 percent of $20,000) on "path of travel" costs. For $4,000 the library can install a ramp leading to the reading area, and it can lower telephones and drinking fountains. For $3,500 the library can create an accessible restroom. Because the most important path of travel element is the entrance and route to the area, the library should spend the money on the ramp, telephones, and drinking fountains.

Can an entity limit its path of travel obligation by engaging in a series of small alterations? No. An entity cannot evade the path of travel requirement by doing several small alterations (each of which, if considered by itself, would be so inexpensive that adding 20 percent would not result in addition of any path of travel features). Whenever an area containing a primary function is altered, other alterations to that area (or to other areas on the same path of travel) made within the preceding three years are considered together in determining disproportionality. Only alterations after January 26, 1992, are counted. In other words, all of the alterations to the same path of travel taken within the preceding three years are considered together in deciding whether the 20 percent has been reached.

ILLUSTRATION: On February 1, 1992, a nursery school with several steps at its entrance renovates one of its classrooms. The renovations total $500, triggering up to $100 worth of path of travel obligations (20 percent of $500). Because $100 will not buy a ramp and because no other accessible features needed in that particular nursery school can be added for $100, no path of travel features are added. On October 1, 1992, more renovations are done at a cost of $1,000, this time triggering path of travel obligations of up to $200. As before, no path of travel features are added. Then, on March 1, 1993, another minor renovation ($2,000) is made to the same area, this time triggering path of travel obligations of up to $400. Had the nursery school done all three small renovations at the same time, the cost would have been $3,500, triggering a path of travel obligation of up to $700. For $700, an accessible ramp could have been installed.

In determining amounts that must be spent on path of travel features at the time of the March 1, 1993, renovation, the nursery school must spend up to 20 percent not just of the $2,000 renovation taking place on March 1, but, rather, up to 20 percent of all of the renovations in the preceding three years put together. Thus, on March 1, 1993, the nursery school must spend up to 20 percent of $3,500 or $700 (the total cost of the three small renovations) rather than up to 20 percent of $2,000 or $400 (the cost of just the March 1, 1993, renovation).

III-6.3000 Alterations: Elevator exemption.

As under new construction, elevators are not required to be installed during alterations in facilities under three stories or with fewer than 3,000 square feet per floor, unless the building is a shopping center or mall; professional office of a health care provider; public transit station; or airport passenger terminal. As discussed below, "shopping center or mall" is defined differently for alterations than it is for new construction.

Does this mean that shopping centers, health care providers, and transit facilities have to install elevators every time they do alterations that would trigger a path of travel obligation involving vertical access? No. The 20 percent disproportionality limit discussed above applies and means that elevators are not required when installing them would exceed 20 percent of the cost of the original alteration (which will most often be the case).

BUT, if escalators or stairs are being planned where none existed before and major structural modifications are necessary, an elevator or platform lift may need to be installed, because ADAAG provides that, in such a situation, an accessible means of vertical access must be provided. However, elevators or lifts are never required to be installed during alterations if it is technically infeasible to do so.

Why is there a different definition of "shopping center or mall" for alterations as opposed to new construction? A "shopping center or mall" is defined in the alterations provisions as a series of existing buildings on a common site connected by a "common pedestrian route" above or below the ground floor. This definition was included to avoid a requirement for several separate elevators in buildings that were initially designed and built independently of one another. The common pedestrian route would allow access to all of the stores to be provided by a single elevator.

If an alteration is planned on the third floor of a building and an elevator is not required, do any other ADAAG requirements apply to the third floor? Yes. All other ADAAG requirements, aside from the requirement for an elevator, apply to the third floor.

III-6.4000 Alterations: Historic preservations.

Alterations to historic properties must comply with the historic property provisions of ADAAG, to the maximum extent feasible. Under those provisions, alterations should be done in full compliance with the alterations standards for other types of buildings. However, if following the usual standards would threaten or destroy the historic significance of a feature of the building, alternative standards may be used. The decision to use alternative standards for that feature must be made in consultation with the appropriate advisory board designated in ADAAG, and interested persons should be invited to participate in the decisionmaking process.

What are "historic properties"? These are properties that are listed or that are eligible for listing in the National Register or Historic Places, or properties designated as historic under State or local law.

What are the alternative requirements? The alternative requirements provide a minimal level of access. For example—

1) An accessible route is only required from one site access point (such as the parking lot).

2) A ramp may be steeper than is ordinarily permitted.

3) The accessible entrance does not need to be the one used by the general public.

4) Only one accessible toilet is required and it may be unisex.

5) Accessible routes are only required on the level of the accessible entrance.

But what if complying with even these minimal alternative requirements will threaten or destroy the historic significance? In such a case, which is rare, structural changes need not be made. Rather, alternative methods can be used to provide access, such as providing auxiliary aids or modifying policies.

ILLUSTRATION: A historic house is being altered to be used as a museum. The architect designing the project concludes that most of the normal standards for alterations can be applied during the renovation process without threatening or destroying historic features. There appears, however, to be a problem if one of the interior doors is widened, because historic decorative features on the door might be destroyed. After consulting ADAAG, the architect determines that the appropriate historic body with jurisdiction over the particular historic home is the Advisory Council on Historic Preservation. The architect sets up a meeting with the Council, to which a local disability group is invited.

At the meeting the participants agree with the architect's conclusion that the normal alterations standards cannot be applied to the interior door. They then review the special alternative requirements, which require an accessible entrance. The meeting participants determine that application of the alternative minimal requirements is likewise not possible.

In this situation, the museum owner is not required to widen the interior door. Instead, the owner modifies the usual operational policies and provides alternative access to the activities offered in the inaccessible room by making available a video presentation of the items within the inaccessible room. The video can be viewed in a nearby accessible room in the museum.

III-7.0000 THE AMERICANS WITH DISABILITIES ACT ACCESSIBILITY GUIDELINES (ADAAG).

III-7.1000 General.

The standards to be used in new construction and alterations covered by subpart D of the Department's title III regulation are those found in the Americans with Disabilities Act Accessibility Guidelines published by the Architectural and Transportation Barriers Compliance Board. These guidelines are incorporated as an appendix to the Department's regulations. The substance and form of ADAAG is drawn from several sources, particularly the Uniform Federal Accessibility Standards (UFAS) (the Federal standard for buildings constructed with Federal funds), and the private sector American National Standard Institute's ANSI A117.1 standards.

Does the ADA eliminate the accessibility provisions that State and local code officials now enforce? No. State and local code provisions remain in effect. However, if elements of a State or local code provide a lesser standard of access than the ADA requires, a public accommodation or commercial facility is still required to comply with the applicable ADA provision.

Who enforces ADAAG? The Department of Justice and private parties. ADAAG has been adopted as part of the Department's regulation implementing title III. Title III of the ADA is enforced through compliance reviews, complaint investigations, and litigation initiated by the Department of Justice, and through litigation initiated by private parties (see III-8.0000).

Can local building inspectors certify compliance with the ADA? No. The ADA is not enforced by State or local building inspectors. However, if a State or local accessibility code has been certified by the Department (see III-9.0000), compliance with that certified code will constitute rebuttable evidence of compliance with the ADA in any enforcement proceeding.

Will the Department review building plans for compliance with ADAAG? No. There is no Federal equivalent to the State code enforcement process. Neither the Department of Justice, nor any other Federal agency, functions as a "building department" to review plans, to issue building permits or occupancy certificates, or to provide interpretations of ADAAG during the building process.

How does ADAAG compare to ANSI? ADAAG's technical design standards (e.g., how many inches wide a doorway must be) resemble the 1986 ANSI A117.1 standards, in large part. Some design standards were adopted from the proposed new version of ANSI as it appeared in draft form when ADAAG was developed. The numbering and format of ADAAG also resemble ANSI. However, there are significant differences between ADAAG and the 1986 ANSI standards.

Perhaps the most important difference is in the new scoping requirements. ADAAG, unlike the 1986 ANSI standards, contains scoping requirements; that is, specifications as to how many, and under what circumstances, accessibility features must be incorporated. These requirements explain when to apply the technical standards.

Other differences reflect congressional intent that

the ADA guidelines focus on certain areas not specifically addressed in ANSI, such as dressing rooms, restaurants, automated teller machines, and mercantile establishments. ADAAG also reflects congressional intent that the guidelines place an increased emphasis on communications with individuals with vision or hearing impairments.

Does the new CABO/ANSI A117.1 standard replace ADAAG? No. The ADA requires the Department of Justice to adopt regulations consistent with the guidelines for the design and construction of accessible buildings and facilities published by the U.S. Architectural and Transportation Barriers Compliance Board (Access Board). The Department adopted ADAAG as the enforceable title III standard. The publication of the revised CABO/ANSI standard does not alter the legal obligation of a place of public accommodation or commercial facility to comply with ADAAG as published by the Department.

III-7.2000 General requirements/definitions.

III-7.2100 Equivalent facilitation (§2.2).

Departures are permitted from particular requirements where alternative designs and technologies will provide substantially equivalent or greater access to and usability of the facility.

Will the Department tell me if my design is "equivalent"? No. The ADA, like all other Federal civil rights laws, requires each covered entity to use its best professional judgment to comply with the statute and the implementing regulations. The Department of Justice does not have a mechanism to certify any specific variation from the standards as being "equivalent." Proposed alternative designs, when supported by available data, are not prohibited; but in any title III investigation or lawsuit, the covered entity would bear the burden of proving that any alternative design provides equal or greater access.

If a facility complies with a State or local building code, will it be considered in compliance with the ADA? Possibly. Compliance with a State or local code that has been certified by the Attorney General (see III-9.0000) to be equivalent will provide rebuttable evidence of compliance with the ADA. Compliance with a code that has not been certified will constitute ADA compliance only if it can be demonstrated that the specific code provision at issue provides accessibility that equals or exceeds the ADA requirement.

ADAAG itself provides various examples of equivalent facilitation, i.e., acceptable deviations from the standards. For instance—

1) In altered areas, elevator car dimensions can be smaller than the standards would mandate for new construction (§4.1.6(3)(c));

2) Rather than install a text telephone next to a pay phone, hotels may keep portable text telephones at the desk, if they are available 24 hours per day and certain other conditions are met (§4.31.9);

3) A folding shelf with space for handing materials back and forth can be used instead of providing an accessible ticketing or other similar counter (§7.2(2)(iii));

4) Accessible guest quarters in newly constructed hotels may all be "multiple-occupancy" rooms, provided that individuals with disabilities who request accessible single-occupancy rooms are allowed to use the multiple-occupancy rooms at the cost of a single-occupancy room (9.1.4(2));

5) If balconies or terraces cannot be made accessible because wind or water damage will result, a ramp or raised decking may be used (§9.2.2(6)).

Are these the only places where equivalent facilitation can be used? No. Departures from any provision in ADAAG are permitted as long as equivalent access is provided. However, portable ramps are not considered equivalent facilitation.

Is it permissible to deviate from the requirements for elements such as lavatories, operating controls and faucets, urinals, bathtubs, and shower stalls in order to follow State or local building code standards for these fixtures? Sometimes. Such deviations are permissible only if they provide access equal to or greater than that required by the ADA.

III-7.3000 Accessible elements and spaces: Scoping and technical requirements.

III-7.3100 Application (ADAAG §4.1.1(1)).

ADAAG applies to all areas in new construction and alterations, except where limited by scoping requirements.

III-7.3110 Work areas (ADAAG §4.1.1(3)).

Access to work areas, but not to individual work stations, is required. The requirement for work areas is that they be designed so that individuals with disabilities can approach, enter, and exit the areas.

Neither maneuvering within the work area nor accessible racks and shelves are required. It is recommended, however, that when there are identical work stations, five percent, but not less than one, should be constructed so that an individual with disabilities can maneuver within the work stations. This will facilitate reasonable accommodation that may later be required under title I for particular employees. There are no requirements concerning placement of fixtures and equipment.

What about areas such as hotel rooms that are work areas for cleaning people? Are they considered "work areas" subject to the limited requirements for approach, enter, and exit? No. The "work area" limited exception applies only to areas used exclusively by employees as work areas. Because the hotel room is also used by customers for sleeping, it is not a work area subject to the limited exemption.

What is included in the term "work area"? Does it include employee lounges, restrooms, cafeterias, health units, and exercise facilities? No. These common use areas are not considered work areas, and they must be constructed or altered in full compliance with ADAAG.

What if an owner of a building believes that an individual who uses a wheelchair could never do the kind of job that will be performed in the particular area? Does the area still have to be made accessible? Yes. The ADA does not permit such assumptions to be made about the capabilities of individuals with disabilities. Unless the area is exempt from accessibility requirements (see III-7.3130), it must be designed so that individuals with disabilities can approach, enter, and exit the area. Even if an individual with a certain type of disability would not be qualified for a particular job, access must be provided for other individuals with disabilities such as, for example, supervisors, maintenance workers, volunteers, or inspectors, who may need to approach, enter, and exit the work area.

Does the work area exemption apply only to areas that can be characterized as individual work stations, such as cubicles, counters, offices, or booths? Or does it also apply to larger work spaces, such as restaurant kitchens, factory production areas, and warehouse space? It applies to the larger spaces as well. Thus, the requirement for a restaurant kitchen, a factory production area, or warehouse space, is that it be constructed so that an individual with a disability can approach, enter, or exit the area. However, alterations within those work areas need not be done accessibly, because that interior area is not covered by ADAAG. On the other hand, if alterations are made in such work areas, the path of travel requirements will be triggered because those work areas are primary function areas (see III-6.2000).

Does this mean that there can no longer be raised platforms for grocery managers or pharmacists? If a raised platform for a grocery manager station or area for pharmacists is an "observation galler[y] used primarily for security purposes," it is one of the types of facilities that is totally exempt from any accessibility requirements (see III-7.3130) (although title I may later require a lift as a reasonable accommodation for a particular employee). Otherwise, the general ADAAG work area requirements apply, and an individual with disabilities must be able to approach, enter, and exit the area. This means that, if there is a change in level of over 1/2", a ramp or lift must be provided to the raised area. Note, however, that in many instances a raised platform is surrounded by another work area, such as a service counter. The work area accessibility requirement would be satisfied as long as that outer area could be approached, entered, and exited.

What if the raised area is a mezzanine (i.e., an actual floor level) used, for example, as an employee lounge area? In this case, whether there needs to be an elevator to the mezzanine depends upon whether the elevator exemption applies. If an elevator is not required (because, for example, the building is under three stories and is not a shopping center or other exempt facility), then access need not be provided to that mezzanine. Likewise, access to the mezzanine need not be provided in one-story buildings. However, if an elevator is required (because the facility is a shopping center, for example), then there will need to be access to the mezzanine.

ILLUSTRATION: A two-story grocery store is located next to a bakery and a card store. The grocery store has a mezzanine that is used as an employee lounge area. The lounge area can be built without a ramp or elevator, because the facility is subject to the elevator exemption. (It is not a shopping center because it does not have five stores in it.) Given that inaccessible floors are permitted, inaccessible mezzanines are also allowed.

BUT: If the grocery store were located in a complex with four other sales or rental establishments, it would be a "shopping center." As such, it would not be entitled to the elevator exemption and the employees' lounge on the mezzanine would have to be made fully accessible, either by ramp or elevator.

III-7.3120 Temporary structures (ADAAG §4.1.1(4)).

Temporary buildings that are extensively used or are essential for public use are covered. However, structures, sites, and equipment directly associated with major construction are not covered.

III-7.3130 General exceptions (ADAAG §4.1.1(5)).

Accessibility is not required to—

1) Observation galleries used primarily for security purposes; or

2) Nonoccupiable spaces accessed only by ladders, crawl spaces, very narrow passageways, or freight (nonpassenger) elevators, and frequented only by service personnel for repair purposes. This includes elevator pits, elevator penthouses, piping or equipment catwalks, cooling towers, and utility tunnels.

What about mechanical rooms or closets not accessed by ladders or narrow passageways? They are not exempt. However, they are work areas subject to the limited exemption discussed above. In addition, mechanical rooms are exempt from the elevator requirement (§4.1.3(5), Exception 2).

III-7.4000 Sites and exterior facilities.

III-7.4100 General.

This section addresses exterior features such as parking, portable toilets, and exterior signage in new construction.

III-7.4200 Accessible route (ADAAG §4.1.2(1)).

An accessible route must connect accessible public transportation stops, parking spaces, passenger loading zones, and public streets or sidewalks to an accessible building entrance.

The ADA, however, does not require the provision of an accessible route in cases where there is no pedestrian route for the general public.

ILLUSTRATION 1: A developer would not be required to provide an accessible route between an accessible entrance to a retail store and a major highway bordering the site, if customers only have access to the store by driving to the parking lot (i.e., where no pedestrian route exists from the highway to the store). An accessible route would have to be provided, however, for pedestrians to travel from the parking lot to the facility's entrance.

ILLUSTRATION 2: Where multiple accessible facilities are built on the same site, an accessible route between the facilities will be required only where a pedestrian route for the general public exists between the multiple facilities or where pedestrians typically walk between the facilities.

Whether a route for the general public exists within a site depends upon the unique characteristics of the site, including its geography and proximity to public transportation stops. Factors such as the presence of sidewalks, crosswalks, or significant pedestrian flow along a particular route should also be considered in determining whether a route for the general public exists. Creation of special accessible routes along paths not available to the general public is not required.

Note, however, that private entities often do not have control over streets and sidewalks. In such a case, the private entity is not responsible for compliance. However, it is encouraged to request public entities to modify sidewalks and install curb cuts.

III-7.4300 Parking (ADAAG §4.1.2(5)(b)).

If self-parking is provided for employees or guests of a public accommodation, accessible parking spaces must be provided in compliance with the ADA.

ADAAG provides a table with the number of accessible parking spaces required dependent on the size of the lot. For example, only four percent of the spaces in a 100-space lot must be accessible. Certain facilities, however, are subject to higher requirements.

Outpatient units are subject to a higher requirement if they are part of medical care facilities where persons may need assistance in responding to an emergency and where the period of stay may exceed twenty-four hours. For such facilities, ten percent of the total parking attributable to the outpatient unit or facility must be accessible.

In addition, any unit or facility providing medical care or other services, including occupational or physical therapy, or vocational rehabilitation, is subject to a higher accessible parking requirement, if it specializes in treatment or services for persons with mobility impairments. Twenty percent of the total number of parking spaces serving each such unit or facility must be accessible.

In addition to the general requirements for accessible automobile spaces, ADAAG requires that at least one of every eight accessible parking spaces have adequate adjacent space for a van lift to be deployed. Each such space must have a sign indicating that it is van-accessible, but it is not to be reserved exclusively for vans. Alternatively, "universal parking," in which all spaces can accommodate van widths, is permitted.

Accessible parking spaces must be located on the shortest accessible route of travel to the facility's entrance. Accessible parking spaces and the required accessible route should be located where individuals with disabilities do not have to cross vehicular lanes or pass behind parked vehicles to have access to the entrance. If it is necessary to cross a vehicular lane because, for example, local fire engine access requirements prohibit parking immediately adjacent to a building, then a marked crossing should be used as part of the accessible route to the entrance.

If valet parking is provided, there must be an accessible passenger loading zone.

If a lot is limited to the exclusive use of employees, and none of the employees are individuals with disabilities requiring accessible parking, accessible spaces may be assigned to employees without disabilities.

III- 7.4400 Signage (ADAAG §4.1.2(7)).

Requirements for exterior signs are essentially the same as those for interior signs (see §4.1.3(b) below). The international symbol of accessibility must be used to indicate accessible parking spaces; accessible passenger loading zones; and accessible entrances and toilet facilities, if all are not accessible.

III-7.5000 Buildings: New construction (ADAAG §4.1.3).

III-7.5100 General.

This section contains scoping requirements for new construction.

III-7.5105 Accessible route (ADAAG §4.1.3(1)).

An accessible route must connect all accessible elements within a building.

III-7.5110 Stairs (ADAAG §4.1.3(4)).

Interior and exterior stairs must comply if they go between levels not connected by an elevator, ramp, or lift.

III-7.5115 Elevators and platform lifts (ADAAG §4.1.3(5)).

Elevators are required to serve each level in a newly constructed building, with four exceptions:

1) Exception 1 is the "elevator exemption" discussed above (see III-5.4000).

2) Exception 2 exempts elevator pits, elevator penthouses, mechanical rooms, and piping or equipment catwalks.

3) Exception 3 permits the use of accessible ramps instead of elevators at any time.

4) Exception 4 permits the use of platform lifts under certain conditions. Lifts must permit unassisted entry, operation, and exit.

III-7.5120 Windows (ADAAG §4.1.3(6)).

There are currently no requirements for windows.

III-7.5125 Doors (ADAAG §4.1.3(7)).

The following doors must be accessible:

1) At least one at each accessible entrance and at each accessible space;

2) Each door that is part of an accessible route; and

3) Each door that is required for egress.

Automated doors are not required. Because of a wide variety of factors that affect door usability, no specific force limit for exterior doors is identified, although standards are provided for interior doors.

III-7.5130 Entrances (ADAAG §4.1.3(8)).

At least 50 percent of all public entrances must be accessible with certain qualifications. In addition, there must be accessible entrances to enclosed parking, pedestrian tunnels, and elevated walkways.

III-7.5135 Areas of rescue assistance (ADAAG §4.1.3(9)).

Areas of rescue assistance (safe areas in which to await help in an emergency) are generally required on each floor, other than the ground floor, of a multistory building. An accessible egress route or an area of rescue assistance is required for each exit required by the local fire code. Specific requirements are provided for such features as location, size, stairway width, and two-way communications. Areas of rescue assistance are not required in buildings with supervised automatic sprinkler systems, nor are they required in alterations.

III-7.5140 Drinking fountains (ADAAG §4.1.3(10)).

Where there is only one drinking fountain on a floor, it must be accessible both to individuals who use wheelchairs and to those who have difficulty bending or stooping (for example, by using a "hi-lo" fountain or a fountain and a water cooler). Where there is more than one fountain on a floor, 50 percent must be accessible to persons using wheelchairs.

III-7.5145 Bathrooms (ADAAG §§4.1.3(11); 4.22.4).

Every public and common use bathroom must be accessible. Generally only one stall must be accessible (standard five-by-five feet). When there are six or more stalls, there must be one accessible stall and one stall that is three feet wide.

III-7.5150 Storage, shelving, and display units (ADAAG §4.1.3(12)).

One of each type of storage facility must be accessible. Self-service shelves and displays must be on an accessible route but need not be lowered within reach ranges of individuals who use wheelchairs.

III-7.5155 Controls and operating mechanisms (ADAAG §4.1.3(13)).

All controls in accessible areas must comply with reach requirements and must be operable with one hand without tight grasping, pinching, or twisting of the wrist.

III-7.5160 Alarms (ADAAG §4.1.3(14)).

Both audible and visual alarms are required when emergency warning systems are provided. ADAAG has detailed requirements concerning features needed for visual alarms, including type of lamp, color, flash rate, and intensity.

III-7.5161 Detectable warnings (ADAAG 4.1.3(15)).

The requirement for detectable warnings at certain locations is under review by the Architectural and Transportation Barriers Compliance Board, and will be the subject of future rulemaking.

III-7.5165 Signage (ADAAG §§4.1.3(16); 4.30.7).

Different requirements apply to various types of signs:

1) Signs designating permanent rooms and spaces (e.g., men's and women's rooms, room numbers, exit signs) must have raised and Brailled letters; must comply with finish and contrast standards; and must be mounted at a certain height and location.

2) Signs that provide direction to or information about functional spaces of a building (e.g., "cafeteria this way;" "copy room") need not comply with requirements for raised and Brailled letters, but they must comply with requirements for character proportion, finish, and contrast. If suspended or projected overhead, they must also comply with character height requirements.

3) Building directories and other signs providing temporary information (such as current occupant's name) do not have to comply with any ADAAG requirements.

4) New symbols of accessibility identifying volume control telephones, text telephones, and assistive listening systems are required.

5) When pictograms (pictorial symbols) are used as a sign to designate a permanent room or space (e.g., a men's or women's room), they must be accompanied by an equivalent verbal description placed directly below the pictogram. The field used for the pictogram must be at least six inches in height (not counting the space used for the verbal description), and the verbal description must employ Braille and raised characters.

III-7.5170 Telephones (ADAAG §4.1.3(17)).

This section establishes requirements for accessibility of pay phones to persons with mobility impairments, hearing impairments (requiring some phones with volume controls), and those who cannot use voice telephones and need "text telephones" (referred to in the Department's rule as telecommunication devices for the deaf (TDD's)):

1) One accessible public phone must be provided for each floor, unless the floor has two or more banks of phones, in which case there must be one accessible phone for each bank.

2) All accessible public phones must be equipped with volume controls. In addition, 25 percent, but never less than one, of all other public phones must havc volumc controls.

3) One TDD or text telephone must be provided inside any building that has four or more public pay telephones, counting both interior and exterior phones. In addition, one TDD or text telephone (per facility) must be provided whenever there is an interior public pay phone in a stadium or arena; convention center; hotel with a convention center; covered shopping mall; or hospital emergency, recovery, or waiting room.

Moreover, if any of the public pay telephones provided in these locations are coin-operated, then a TDD or text telephone that can be used with a coin-operated telephone must be provided. If all of the public pay telephones provided in these locations are card-operated only, then it is permissible to provide a TDD or text telephone that can be used only with card-operated telephones.

III-7.5175 Fixed seating (ADAAG §4.1.3(18)).

At least five percent of fixed or built-in seating or tables must be accessible. Wheelchair seating spaces in assembly areas and restaurants are not subject to this requirement but, rather, are covered by specific requirements for "assembly areas" and "restaurants."

III-7.5180 Assembly areas (ADAAG §4.1.3(19)).

This section specifies the number of wheelchair seating spaces and types and numbers of assistive listening systems required in assembly areas.

In addition to requiring companion seating and dispersion of wheelchair locations, ADAAG requires that wheelchair locations provide people with disabilities lines of sight comparable to those for members of the general public. Thus, in assembly areas where spectators can be expected to stand during the event or show being viewed, the wheelchair locations must provide lines of sight over spectators who stand. This can be accomplished in many ways, including placing wheelchair locations at the front of a seating section, or by providing sufficient additional elevation for wheelchair locations placed at the rear of seating sections to allow those spectators to see over the spectators who stand in front of them.

1) Wheelchair seating: Requirements for wheelchair seating are triggered in any area that seats four or more people. The number of wheelchair locations required depends upon the size of the assembly area. Dispersal of wheelchair seating is required in assembly areas where there are more than 300 seats. In addition, at least one percent of all fixed seats must be aisle seats without armrests (or with removable armrests) to allow for transfer from a wheelchair. Fixed seating for companions must be located adjacent to each wheelchair location. Finally, wheelchair seating must adjoin an accessible route that serves a means of egress from the assembly area. Under circumstances where wheelchair seating will be located adjacent to a portion of an aisle that serves as an accessible means of egress, then other portions of that aisle and other aisles that do not serve the accessible wheelchair locations are not required to comply with the requirements for ramps. ADAAG does not specify the location of the accessible means of egress. Therefore, the accessible means of egress from wheelchair locations can be through the rear, the side, or the front of the theater. (The general requirements for accessible routes are discussed above in III-7.4200.)

2) Assistive listening systems: Certain fixed seating assembly areas that accommodate 50 or more people or have audio-amplification systems must have a permanently installed assistive listening system. Other assembly areas must have a permanent system or an adequate number of electrical outlets or other wiring to support a portable system. A special sign indicating the availability of the system is required. The minimum number of receivers must be equal to four percent of the total number of seats, but never less than two.

III-7.5185 Automated teller machines (ATM's) (ADAAG §4.1.3(20)).

Where ATM's are provided, each must be accessible, except that only one need comply when two or more ATM's are at the same location. Accessible machines must have, among other features, accessible controls as well as instructions and other information accessible to persons with sight impairments. This can include Braille and raised letters and/or audio handsets, along with tactile keys.

The ADAAG standard now in effect provides that ATM's must meet the requirements for both a forward and a side approach. That standard, however, is under review by the Architectural and Transportation Barriers Compliance Board, and is the subject of current rulemaking.

ADAAG permits departures from particular technical requirements by use of other designs and technologies where the alternative designs and technologies will provide substantially equivalent or greater access to and usability of the facility. It may be possible to show that meeting only one of the reach ranges with respect to a particular ATM, as installed, provides equivalent facilitation in compliance with ADAAG.

III-7.5190 Dressing and fitting rooms (ADAAG §4.1.3(21)).

Where dressing rooms are provided, five percent or at least one must be accessible. Technical standards are provided for doors, benches, and mirrors, with less stringent standards for alterations.

III-7.6000 Additions (ADAAG §4.1.5).

Each addition to an existing building is regarded as an alteration subject to the ADAAG alterations requirements (including triggering of path of travel obligations, if applicable). If the addition does not have an accessible entrance, the path of travel obligation may require an accessible route from the addition through the existing building, including its entrance and exterior approaches, subject to the 20 percent disproportionality limitation. Moreover, to the extent that a space or element is newly constructed as part of an addition, it is also regarded as new construction and must comply with the applicable new construction provisions of ADAAG.

ILLUSTRATION: A new multistory parking structure is planned as an addition to an existing shopping mall that is served by an elevator. Each floor of the parking garage will be connected by an accessible route to the shopping mall. As an addition, the parking structure is subject to both the new construction and alterations requirements of ADAAG. If the parking structure functions as a separate building and may be used independently of the shopping mall—for instance, when the shopping mall is not open for business—then it would not be sufficient to provide vertical access only through the shopping center. In that case, an elevator or accessible ramp would be required in the parking structure to serve each level of the garage. If, on the other hand, vertical access to each level of the garage may be achieved through the shopping mall at all times that the garage is open, an elevator or accessible ramp would not be required in the parking structure.

III-7.7000 Alterations (ADAAG §4.1.6).

Throughout ADAAG, there are numerous examples of areas where there are less stringent standards for alterations than for new construction. For instance—

1) Section 4.1.6(3) contains a detailed set of special technical provisions for alterations to be applied where it is technically infeasible to comply with other provisions of the guidelines. Entities are permitted to—

a) Install only one accessible unisex bathroom per floor;

b) Cluster wheelchair seating in altered assembly areas;

c) Use platform lifts as part of an accessible route, without having to meet any of the conditions for use of platform lifts applicable in the new construction context (§4.1.3(5)); and

d) Install only one accessible dressing room for each sex on each level.

2) Areas of rescue assistance are not required in alterations (§4.1.6(1)(g)).

3) There are special less stringent requirements for alterations in many other areas, including sales and service counters (§7.2(1)), check-out aisles (§7.3(1)), hotels (9.1.5), and homeless shelters (9.5.2(2)).

III-7.8000 Special facility types.

III-7.8100 Historic preservation (ADAAG §4.1.7).

This section contains requirements for alterations to qualified historic buildings and facilities (see III-6.4000).

III-7.8200 Restaurants and cafeterias (ADAAG §5).

In restaurants, generally all dining areas and five percent of fixed tables (but not less than one) must be accessible. While raised or sunken dining areas must be accessible, inaccessible mezzanines are permitted under certain conditions. ADAAG contains requirements for counters and bars, access aisles, food service lines, tableware and condiment areas, raised speaker's platforms, and vending machine areas (but not controls).

III-7.8300 Medical care facilities (ADAAG §6).

In medical care facilities, all public and common use areas must be accessible. In general purpose hospitals, and in psychiatric and detoxification facilities, 10 percent of patient bedrooms and toilets must be accessible. The required percentage is 100 percent for special facilities treating conditions that affect mobility, and 50 percent for long-term facilities and nursing homes. There are special, less stringent requirements for alterations.

III-7.8400 Business and mercantile (ADAAG §7).

1) Sales and service counters with cash registers: At least one of each type of sales or service counter where a cash register is located must be accessible. Accessible counters must be dispersed throughout the facility. Auxiliary counters are permissible in alterations.

Are frozen food and deli counters covered? No, but employees should be instructed to bring food items around to the front of high counters for individuals with disabilities.

What does "one of each type" mean in a store where computerized check-out permits universal service at any cash register? The size of the store and the number of floors will be relevant factors in determining how many counters need to be accessible.

ILLUSTRATION 1: A small one-story clothing store has four identical cash register counters, one in each department. Only one counter need be accessible, if all items can be purchased there.

ILLUSTRATION 2: A very narrow but six-story tall department store has identical cash register counters throughout the facility. ADAAG will be satisfied if there is one accessible counter per floor at which all purchases can be made.

BUT: If the same six-story department store is a full city block long, one per floor may not be enough. A reasonable number should be provided.

2) Other counters: At counters without cash registers, such as bank teller windows and ticketing counters, three alternatives are possible:

a) A portion of the counter may be lowered,

b) An auxiliary counter may be provided, or

c) Equivalent facilitation may be provided by installing a folding shelf on the front of a counter to provide a work surface for a person using a wheelchair.

3) Check-out aisles (§7.3): At least one of each design of check-out aisle must be accessible, and, in some cases, additional check-out aisles are required to be accessible (i.e., from 20 to 40 percent) depending on the number of check-out aisles and the size of the facility. There are less stringent standards for alterations.

III-7.8500 Libraries (ADAAG §8).

In libraries, all public areas must be accessible. In addition, five percent of fixed tables or study carrels (or at least one) must be accessible. At least one lane at the check-out area and aisles between card catalogs, magazine displays, and stacks must be accessible.

III-7.8600 Transient lodging (ADAAG §9).

1) Hotels, motels, dormitories, and similar places: Four percent of the first 100 rooms and approximately two percent of rooms in excess of 100 must be accessible to persons with mobility impairments and to persons with hearing impairments (i.e., contain visual alarms, visual notification devices, volume-control telephones, and an accessible electrical outlet for a text telephone). In hotels with more than 50 rooms, an additional one percent of the rooms must be accessible rooms equipped with roll-in showers. Moreover, additional rooms must be accessible to persons with hearing impairments in the same percentages as above (i.e., four percent of the first 100 rooms and approximately two percent of rooms in excess of 100). There are special provisions for alterations.

2) Homeless shelters, halfway houses, and other social service establishments: These entities must provide the same percentage of accessible sleeping accommodations as other places of transient lodging. At least one type of amenity in each common area must be accessible. Alterations are subject to less stringent standards.

III-7.8700 Transportation facilities (ADAAG §10).

ADAAG provides requirements for bus stops and terminals, rail stations, and airports. These requirements have been incorporated by the Department of Transportation in its regulations implementing the transportation provisions of titles II and III.

There are currently no standards for boats or ferry docks.

III-8.0000 ENFORCEMENT.

III-8.1000 General.

The ADA establishes two avenues for enforcement of the requirements of title III—

1) Private suits by individuals who are being subjected to discrimination or who have reasonable grounds for believing that they are about to be subjected to discrimination.

2) Suits by the Department of Justice, whenever it has reasonable cause to believe that there is a pattern or practice of discrimination, or discrimination that raises an issue of general public importance. The Department will investigate complaints and conduct compliance reviews of covered entities.

Do State or local civil rights agencies have any role in enforcing title III? There is no provision for State or local civil rights agencies to directly enforce title III of the ADA. They can, however, enforce State or local laws that incorporate the standards of the ADA, or they can set up alternative dispute resolution mechanisms (see III-8.6000).

III-8.2000 Private suits.

Any person who is being subjected to discrimination on the basis of disability in violation of title III of the Act may file a civil action for injunctive relief. Also, when a person has reasonable grounds for believing that he or she is "about to be subjected to discrimination" because of a violation of the new construction and alterations requirements of the ADA, he or she may file a civil action.

ILLUSTRATION: X has reasonable grounds for believing that the plans for a hotel complex are not in compliance with the ADA. X may file a lawsuit challenging the plans, even though construction has not begun.

An individual is not required to engage in a futile gesture, if he or she has notice that a person or organization does not intend to comply with its obligations under the Act.

At the request of the plaintiff or defendant, and if the court permits it, the Department of Justice can intervene in the civil action, if it determines that the case is of general public importance. The court may also appoint an attorney for the plaintiff and may permit him or her to commence the civil action without first paying fees, costs, or security.

Remedies available in a private suit may include a permanent or temporary injunction, restraining order, or other order, but not compensatory or punitive money damages or civil penalties. In the case of violations of the requirements for readily achievable barrier removal or for accessible new construction and alterations, remedies to correct a violation may, as appropriate, include an order to alter the facilities that do not meet the requirements of the Act to make them readily accessible to and usable by individuals with disabilities. Also, the remedies may include requiring the provision of an auxiliary aid or service, modification of a policy, or provision of alternative methods of barrier removal.

III-8.3000 Investigations and compliance reviews.

The Department of Justice will investigate alleged violations of title III and undertake periodic reviews of compliance of covered entities. An investigation may be requested by any individual who believes that he or she has been discriminated against or that a specific class of persons has been discriminated against in violation of title III. Where the Department has reason to believe that there may be a violation, it may initiate a compliance review.

Complaints may be sent to the following address:

Office on the Americans with Disabilities Act
Civil Rights Division
U.S. Department of Justice
P.O. Box 66738
Washington, D.C. 20035-9998

III-8.4000 Suit by the Attorney General.

The Department may bring a civil action in any appropriate United States district court if it has reasonable cause to believe that—

1) Any person or group of persons is engaged in a pattern or practice of discrimination in violation of title III; or

2) Any person or group of persons has been discriminated against in violation of title III and the discrimination raises an issue of general public importance.

What remedies are available in civil actions brought by the Department of Justice? The remedies available include those available in an action brought by an individual, such as an order granting temporary, preliminary, or permanent relief; requiring that facilities be made readily accessible to and usable by individuals with disabilities; requiring provision of an auxiliary aid or service; or modification of a policy, practice, or procedure.

In addition, in a suit brought by the Department, the court may award other appropriate relief, including, if requested by the Department, monetary damages to individual victims of discrimination. Monetary damages do not include punitive damages. They do include, however, all forms of compensatory damages, including out-of-pocket expenses and damages for pain and suffering.

Also, to vindicate the public interest, the court may assess a civil penalty against the covered entity in an amount—

1) Not exceeding $50,000 for a first violation; and

2) Not exceeding $100,000 for any subsequent violation.

How will violations be counted in determining whether a particular violation is "first" or "subsequent"? All violations found in the first suit against a covered entity are considered to be the first violation, so that the maximum penalty that may be assessed in that suit is $50,000. A "subsequent" violation would not be found until the Department brought a second suit against the same covered entity. The maximum penalty in each suit after the first suit is $100,000.

Will good faith efforts be considered in determining the amount of civil penalty? Yes. In considering what amount of civil penalty, if any, is appropriate, the court is required to give consideration to any good faith effort or attempt by the covered entity to comply with its obligations under the Act. One of the factors to be considered in evaluating good faith is whether the entity could have reasonably anticipated the need for an appropriate type of auxiliary aid needed to accommodate the unique needs of a particular individual with a disability.

III-8.5000 Attorney's fees.

The prevailing party (other than the United States) in any action or administrative proceeding under the Act may recover attorney's fees in addition to any other relief granted. The "prevailing party" is the party that is successful and may be either the complainant (plaintiff) or the covered entity against which the action is brought (defendant). The defendant, however, may not recover attorney's fees unless the court finds that the plaintiff's action was frivolous, unreasonable, or without foundation, although it does not have to find that the action was brought in subjective bad faith. Attorney's fees include litigation expenses, such as expert witness fees, travel expenses, and costs. The United States is liable for attorney's fees in the same manner as any other party, but is not entitled to them when it is the prevailing party.

III-8.6000 Alternative means of dispute resolution.

The ADA encourages the use of alternative means of dispute resolution, including settlement negotiations, conciliation, facilitation, mediation, factfinding, minitrials, and arbitration to resolve disputes, where appropriate and to the extent authorized by law. In appropriate cases, these types of procedures may be faster, more efficient, and less expensive than the judicial and administrative procedures available under the ADA. Alternative means of dispute resolution, however, are intended to supplement the procedures provided in the ADA, not to replace them. Use of alternative procedures is completely voluntary and must be agreed to by the parties involved.

III-8.7000 Technical assistance.

The ADA recognizes the necessity of educating the public about its rights and responsibilities under the Act and requires the Department of Justice, in consultation with other agencies, to provide technical assistance to assist covered entities and individuals with disabilities in understanding their rights and responsibilities under the ADA.

The Federal Government's experience in implementing section 504 of the Rehabilitation Act of 1973, as amended, has demonstrated that a publicized, readily available, comprehensive technical assistance program responsive to the problems and needs of its audience offers many advantages. Technical assistance that is designed to meet the needs of individuals with disabilities, covered entities, and the general public reduces misunderstandings regarding rights and responsibilities, facilitates voluntary compliance, and promotes the exchange of information and the development of more effective and less costly methods to address compliance issues. It also avoids an unnecessary reliance on enforcement and litigation to achieve compliance.

Technical assistance includes the provision of expert advice, and both general and specific information and assistance to individuals with disabilities, the general public, and entities covered by the ADA. The purposes of this technical assistance are two-fold: to inform the public (including individuals with rights protected under the Act) and covered entities about their rights and duties; and to provide information about cost-effective methods and procedures to achieve compliance.

The Department plans to provide technical assistance through publications, exhibits, videotapes and audiotapes, and public service announcements. It has developed a number of nontechnical publications, including this manual, explaining the requirements of the Act, and has established a Speakers Bureau to provide speakers for events such as conferences, workshops, and training programs. It is also operating a telephone information line to respond to inquiries and requests for publications and to provide advice to individuals about specific problems. The Department also engages in a variety of clearinghouse functions and operates an electronic bulletin board to distribute information.

The Department has awarded over $3,000,000 in technical assistance grants to 19 organizations to disseminate technical assistance to specific audiences. They include national associations of covered entities, such as restaurants, hotels and motels; and associations of individuals with disabilities representing individuals with speech, hearing, and vision impairments, mobility impairments, mental retardation, and epilepsy. Many of these organizations have also established telephone information lines to respond to inquiries and are producing publications and providing training directed to their specific audiences. The Architectural and Transportation Barriers Compliance Board (800-USA-ABLE [voice or TDD]), which was responsible for development of ADAAG, and the Equal Employment Opportunity Commission (800-669-EEOC [voice]; 800-800-3302 [TDD]) have also established telephone information services. In addition, the National Institute on Disability and

Rehabilitation Research has established ten Regional Disability and Business Accommodation Centers to serve as regional resources for ADA information.

The agencies involved in providing ADA technical assistance are making, and will continue to make, a sustained effort to ensure that effective technical assistance is available to all covered entities. Nevertheless, covered entities retain responsibility for ensuring that their activities comply with the requirements of the Act, and a public accommodation or other private entity is not excused from compliance because of any failure to receive technical assistance.

III-8.8000 Effective date.

The ADA requirements became effective on—

1) January 26, 1992, generally;

2) August 26, 1990, for purchase or lease of new vehicles that are required to be accessible.

New facilities designed and constructed for first occupancy later than January 26, 1993, must be accessible.

Is there any grace period for small business? No. All businesses must comply by January 26, 1992. Small businesses, however, do enjoy limited protection from lawsuits. Except with respect to new construction and alterations, no lawsuit may be filed until—

1) July 26, 1992, against businesses with 25 or fewer employees and gross receipts of $1 million or less.

2) January 26, 1993, against businesses with ten or fewer employees and gross receipts of $500,000 or less.

III-9.0000 CERTIFICATION.

III-9.1000 General.

The ADA authorizes the Attorney General to certify that State laws, local building codes, or similar ordinances meet or exceed the title III accessibility requirements. Certification is advantageous for the following reasons—

1) When an entity is designing, constructing, or altering a building in accordance with an applicable State or local code that has been certified by the Department, the designer or contractor will need to consult only that one code, in order to determine the applicable Federal, State, and local requirements.

2) The covered entity will have some degree of assurance in advance of construction or alteration that the ADA requirements will be met.

3) If a covered entity is subject to a lawsuit, compliance with a certified code will be rebuttable evidence of compliance with the ADA.

4) A State or local agency enforcing a certified code is for practical, but not legal, purposes facilitating compliance with the ADA and helping to eliminate confusion and possible inconsistencies in standards.

5) The amount of unnecessary litigation can be reduced, particularly if a State or local code agency has an administrative method of effectively handling complaints concerning violations of its code.

Does this mean that if an architectural firm follows a certified State or local code, it will be safe from any Federal lawsuits because the State or local government will be implementing the ADA? No, but the firm will be less likely to face a lawsuit; and if it is sued, it has the advantage of rebuttable evidence of compliance. Keep in mind that State and local agencies are not authorized to enforce the ADA—which is a Federal civil rights statute—on behalf of the Federal government. This is true even when those agencies are implementing a certified code.

Moreover, the existence of a certified code does not ensure that facilities will be constructed in accordance with the code. In addition, even if a building is built to a certified code, that does not prevent a lawsuit concerning the building's accessibility by the Department or by an individual.

III-9.2000 Relationship to State and local enforcement efforts.

There are tens of thousands of code jurisdictions in the United States that enforce some combination of State and local building codes. Some, but not all, of these include accessibility requirements. Although many are based on a model code, there are major variations among the State codes, and among local codes within some States. Design and construction to these codes will not constitute compliance with the ADA, unless the codes impose requirements equal to or greater than those of the ADA.

The enforcement of these codes is the responsibility of State or local officials. They usually review building plans and inspect projects at specific intervals during construction to ensure that the construction complies with State and local laws. State and local officials do not have the authority to enforce the ADA on behalf of the Federal government.

Architects, builders, and others involved with design and construction are accustomed to the State and local enforcement system, which lets them know before construction whether they need to make changes to their plans in order to achieve compliance. The ADA relies on the traditional method of case-by-case civil rights enforcement in response to complaints. It does not contemplate Federal ADA inspections similar to those done at the State or local level. The ADA certification provisions will help to moderate the effects of these differences in enforcement procedures and standards.

If a building has been designed, built, or altered in accordance with a certified code, and a lawsuit concerning violation of the ADA standards is brought, the defendant will be able to point to compliance with the certified code as "rebuttable evidence" of compliance with the ADA.

ILLUSTRATION: The JKL Hotel chain builds hotels to a standard plan throughout the United States. The State of C has had its code certified by the Department, and JKL has designed a hotel, according to its standard plan, to be built in that State. The State has approved the plans, with no waivers or modifications. If the Department brings a lawsuit challenging the hotel's compliance with ADAAG, JKL has the advantage of being able to introduce the approved plans as evidence that the design complies with the ADA. A hotel designed to the same plans in the State of S, which does not have a code with accessibility requirements, would also have that advantage because the hotel was designed in compliance with a certified code.

If a builder follows a State's certified code, and the building official grants a waiver of certain requirements, does that mean the waiver is good for ADA purposes too? No. State or local officials have no authority to waive ADA requirements. Many State or local codes allow the building official to grant waivers, variances, or other types of exceptions (e.g., in cases of "undue hardship," "impossibility," or "impracticability"). They may also allow compliance by means other than those required by the code if "equivalent facilitation" is provided.

The ADA standards also include some exceptions (e.g., for structural impracticability in new construction) and allow for equivalent facilitation. But no individual is authorized under the ADA to grant the exceptions in advance; and the defendant in a lawsuit would have to justify the use of any of those ADA exceptions.

The Department would not refuse to certify a code merely because it includes authority for or procedures for waivers and variances. A defendant, however, would not be entitled to rely on certification as rebuttable evidence of compliance, if a local or State official had granted a waiver or other type of exception on the point at issue.

May code officials issue binding interpretations of ADA accessibility provisions at the local level? No. Code officials may not take any action that purports to relieve a public accommodation or commercial facility of its obligation to comply fully with the ADA.

May code officials be sued to challenge their implementation of a certified code? The certification process is not intended to impose greater liabilities on State or local officials toward private parties than they now have in carrying out their responsibilities under State law. Title III of the ADA does not alter the personal liability of State or local officials enforcing State or local laws. The Department of Justice anticipates that State and local officials enforcing a certified code will continue to enforce that code under the same standard of care that would apply if the code was not certified.

Why should code officials seek certification of local accessibility codes? If the code in a local jurisdiction is certified, the designers, contractors, and building owners will have some assurance that compliance with those regulations will also satisfy ADA requirements. Through knowledgeable and professional plan review and inspection services, a covered entity may benefit from the technical assistance available from the local code official. Also, if there is an effective procedure for handling complaints at the local level, litigation will be minimized.

III-9.3000 Procedure: Application and preliminary review.

The certification process begins with an application to the Department by a "submitting official." The submitting official is one who has principal responsibility for administration of a code or who is authorized to submit a code on behalf of a jurisdiction.

In some States, the local jurisdictions are required to follow and enforce the State code. Can the State submit a single application on behalf of the State as well as on behalf of all the local jurisdictions? Yes, the State can submit one application on behalf of the State and on behalf of any local jurisdiction that has authorized the State to do so.

What does the State or local agency have to do before it applies for certification? Four things are required:

1) The code or law must have been formally approved by the issuing body. In those States where an administrative agency (rather than the legislature) is charged with developing a code, and it becomes law

on a certain date if it is not modified by the legislature before that time, the Department will accept an application based on the code as approved by the agency.

2) The agency has to give public notice of its intent to request certification and notice of a hearing.

3) The agency has to hold a hearing within the State or locality at which the public is invited to comment on the proposed request for certification. The hearing must be held after adequate notice to the public and must be on the record (that is, a transcript of the hearing must be produced). This procedure ensures input from the public at the State or local level.

4) The agency has to make the materials and the certification request available for public examination and copying.

What should the application include? The submitting official must include two copies of—

1) The code;

2) Standards or other documents referenced in the code;

3) The law creating the agency;

4) Any relevant manuals, guides, or other interpretive information;

5) Any formal legal opinions that pertain to the code;

6) Any model code or statute on which the code is based, along with an explanation of any differences between the model and the code being submitted for certification;

7) The transcript of the public hearing; and

8) Any other information that the submitting official wants to be considered.

III-9.4000 Preliminary determination.

After receiving the application, the Office of the Assistant Attorney General for Civil Rights will determine whether or not to begin considering the application for certification. If the Assistant Attorney General's office decides to proceed, the office will consult with the Architectural and Transportation Barriers Compliance Board. After that consultation, the office will make a preliminary determination to either—

1) Find that the code is equivalent (make a "preliminary determination of equivalency"); or

2) Deny certification.

The next step depends on which of these preliminary determinations is made.

III-9.5000 Procedure following preliminary determination of equivalency.

If the AAG makes a preliminary determination of equivalency, he or she will—

1) Inform the submitting official in writing;

2) Publish a notice in the Federal Register informing the public of the preliminary determination and inviting comment for 60 days;

3) Consider the comments, and then hold an informal hearing in Washington. In many cases, this "hearing" may consist of a meeting with those who are interested;

4) Consult again with the ATBCB and make a final determination of equivalency or a final determination to deny the request for certification.

5) Publish a notice of the final determination in the Federal Register.

III-9.6000 Procedure following preliminary denial of certification.

If the preliminary determination is to deny certification, then there will be no hearing.

The Department will notify the submitting official of the preliminary determination. In the notification, the Department may specify how the code could be modified so that it could receive a preliminary determination of equivalency.

The submitting official will have at least 15 days to submit relevant material in opposition to the preliminary denial. If no more information is received, no further action will be taken.

If more information is received, the Department will consider it. The Department will then make either a final decision to deny certification or a preliminary determination of equivalency. If at that stage the Assistant Attorney General makes a preliminary determination of equivalency, the hearing procedures described in III-9.5000 will be followed.

III-9.7000 Effect of certification.

Certification will only be effective concerning those features or elements that are both covered by the certified code and addressed by the Department's regulations.

ILLUSTRATION: The Department's standards currently do not include specific provisions concerning children's facilities. A private elementary school is built to the specifications of a code certified by the Department. Certification will not be effective for those features of the building especially designed to be used by children (e.g., children's restrooms, water fountains).

Will certification be effective only for the particular edition of the code that is certified? Yes. Amendments will not automatically be considered certified, and a submitting official will need to reapply for certification of the changed or additional provisions.

Will certification apply to the process by which a State or local code is administered or enforced? No. In other words, the Department will evaluate and certify only the code itself, not the process by which it is implemented. This is true even though the Department has certified a code with provisions concerning waivers, variances, or equivalent facilitation. Certification of a code with those provisions is not to be interpreted as an endorsement of actions taken pursuant to those provisions. The Department's certification of a code is effective only with respect to the standards in the code; it is not to be interpreted to apply to a State or local government's application of the code. For example, a local official's decision that a particular approach constitutes equivalent facilitation under a local code is not effective for ADA purposes.

Can a code that is consistent with ADAAG be certified if the local enforcement process allows deviations from ADAAG? Yes. The Department expects that many jurisdictions will allow slight variations from a particular code. ADAAG itself permits variations from its standards in certain limited circumstances. ADAAG includes in §2.2 a statement allowing departures from particular requirements where substantially equivalent or greater access and usability is provided. Several sections specifically allow for alternative methods of providing equivalent facilitation and, in some cases, provide examples.

What if a State or local official allows a facility to be constructed or altered in a manner that does not follow the technical or scoping provisions of the certified code? If an official either waives an accessible element or feature or allows a change that does not provide equivalent facilitation, the fact that the Department has certified the code itself will not constitute rebuttable evidence that the facility has been constructed or altered in accordance with the minimum accessibility requirements of the ADA.

III-9.8000 Certification and barrier removal in existing facilities.

The Department will measure equivalency against subpart D of the title III rule, New Construction and Alterations. The Department will not require that provisions concerning barrier removal in existing facilities be included in a code in order for it to be certified.

Will the Department certify a code that includes provisions similar to those in the Department's title III rule concerning removal of barriers in existing facilities (e.g., on priorities, portable ramps, seating in assembly areas)? The Department generally will not review these parts of a code.

III-9.9000 Review of model codes.

The Department will not certify model codes, but the Department will review models for equivalency with ADA requirements.

The Department's rule provides for review of model codes in recognition of the fact that many codes are based on, or incorporate, models or consensus standards developed by nationally recognized organizations. These organizations include, for example, the American National Standards Institute (ANSI), Building Officials and Code Administrators (BOCA) International, the Council of American Building Officials (CABO) and its Board for the Coordination of Model Codes (BCMC), Southern Building Code Congress International (SBCCI), and the International Conference of Building Officials (ICBO). The Department wishes to encourage the continued viability of the consensus and model code process consistent with the purposes of the ADA.

The model code review process will be informal. The Department will not necessarily hold a public hearing, but it has the discretion to do so and to ask for public comment. After the review, the Department may issue guidance as to whether and in what respects the model code is consistent with the ADA's requirements.

This guidance will not be binding on any entity or on the Department. It will assist in evaluations of individual State or local codes; and it may also serve as a basis for establishing priorities for consideration of individual codes.

Who can submit a model code for review? It must be submitted by an authorized representative of the private entity responsible for developing the code.

ILLUSTRATION: The ABC model code, which includes both scoping and technical provisions, is followed by 13 States. It contains its own unique scoping requirements, with technical provisions that were developed by XYZ, Inc., another private group. An authorized representative of ABC can submit the ABC code, including the XYZ technical provisions, for review, even if XYZ has not submitted its standard to the Department for review.

ADA TITLE IV

47 U.S.C. § 225. Telecommunications services for hearing-impaired and speech-impaired individuals

(a) Definitions

As used in this section—

(1) Common carrier or carrier

The term "common carrier" or "carrier" includes any common carrier engaged in interstate communication by wire or radio as defined in section 153 of this title and any common carrier engaged in intrastate communication by wire or radio, notwithstanding sections 152(b) and 221(b) of this title.

(2) TDD

The term "TDD" means a Telecommunications Device for the Deaf, which is a machine that employs graphic communication in the transmission of coded signals through a wire or radio communication system.

(3) Telecommunications relay services

The term "telecommunications relay services" means telephone transmission services that provide the ability for an individual who has a hearing impairment or speech impairment to engage in communication by wire or radio with a hearing individual in a manner that is functionally equivalent to the ability of an individual who does not have a hearing impairment or speech impairment to communicate using voice communication services by wire or radio. Such term includes services that enable two-way communication between an individual who uses a TDD or other nonvoice terminal device and an individual who does not use such a device.

(b) Availability of telecommunications relay services

(1) In general

In order to carry out the purposes established under section 151 of this title, to make available to all individuals in the United States a rapid, efficient nationwide communication service, and to increase the utility of the telephone system of the Nation, the Commission shall ensure that interstate and intrastate telecommunications relay services are available, to the extent possible and in the most efficient manner, to hearing-impaired and speech- impaired individuals in the United States.

(2) Use of general authority and remedies

For the purposes of administering and enforcing the provisions of this section and the regulations prescribed thereunder, the Commission shall have the same authority, power, and functions with respect to common carriers engaged in intrastate communication as the Commission has in administering and enforcing the provisions of this title with respect to any common carrier engaged in interstate communication. Any violation of this section by any common carrier engaged in intrastate communication shall be subject to the same remedies, penalties, and procedures as are applicable to a violation of this chapter by a common carrier engaged in interstate communication.

(c) Provision of services

Each common carrier providing telephone voice transmission services shall, not later than 3 years after July 26, 1990, provide in compliance with the regulations prescribed under this section, throughout the area in which it offers service, telecommunications relay services, individually, through designees, through a competitively selected vendor, or in concert with other carriers. A common carrier shall be considered to be in compliance with such regulations—

(1) with respect to intrastate telecommunications relay services in any State that does not have a certified program under subsection (f) of this section and with respect to interstate telecommunications relay services, if such common carrier (or other entity through which the carrier is providing such relay services) is in compliance with the Commission's regulations under subsection (d) of this section; or

(2) with respect to intrastate telecommunications relay services in any State that has a certified program under subsection (f) of this section for such State, if such common carrier (or other entity through which the carrier is providing such relay services) is in compliance with the program certified under subsection (f) of this section for such State.

(d) Regulations

(1) In general

The Commission shall, not later than 1 year after July 26, 1990, prescribe regulations to implement this section, including regulations that—

(A) establish functional requirements, guidelines, and operations procedures for telecommunications relay services;

(B) establish minimum standards that shall be met in carrying out subsection (c) of this section;

(C) require that telecommunications relay services operate every day for 24 hours per day;

(D) require that users of telecommunications relay services pay rates no greater than the rates paid for functionally equivalent voice communication services with respect to such factors as the duration of the call, the time of day, and the distance from point of origination to point of termination;

(E) prohibit relay operators from failing to fulfill the obligations of common carriers by refusing calls or limiting the length of calls that use telecommunications relay services;

(F) prohibit relay operators from disclosing the content of any relayed conversation and from keeping records of the content of any such conversation beyond the duration of the call; and

(G) prohibit relay operators from intentionally altering a relayed conversation.

(2) Technology

The Commission shall ensure that regulations prescribed to implement this section encourage, consistent with section 157(a) of this title, the use of existing technology and do not discourage or impair the development of improved technology.

(3) Jurisdictional separation of costs

(A) In general

Consistent with the provisions of section 410 of this title, the Commission shall prescribe regulations governing the jurisdictional separation of costs for the services provided pursuant to this section.

(B) Recovering costs

Such regulations shall generally provide that costs caused by interstate telecommunications relay services shall be recovered from all subscribers for every interstate service and costs caused by intrastate telecommunications relay services shall be recovered from the intrastate jurisdiction. In a State that has a certified program under subsection (f) of this section, a State commission shall permit a common carrier to recover the costs incurred in providing intrastate telecommunications relay services by a method consistent with the requirements of this section.

(e) Enforcement

(1) In general

Subject to subsections (f) and (g) of this section, the Commission shall enforce this section.

(2) Complaint

The Commission shall resolve, by final order, a complaint alleging a violation of this section within 180 days after the date such complaint is filed.

(f) Certification

(1) State documentation

Any State desiring to establish a State program under this section shall submit documentation to the Commission that describes the program of such State for implementing intrastate telecommunications relay services and the procedures and remedies available for enforcing any requirements imposed by the State program.

(2) Requirements for certification

After review of such documentation, the Commission shall certify the State program if the Commission determines that—

(A) the program makes available to hearing-impaired and speech-impaired individuals, either directly, through designees, through a competitively selected vendor, or through regulation of intrastate common carriers, intrastate telecommunications relay services in such State in a manner that meets or exceeds the requirements of regulations prescribed by the Commission under subsection (d) of this section; and

(B) the program makes available adequate procedures and remedies for enforcing the requirements of the State program.

(3) Method of funding

Except as provided in subsection (d) of this section, the Commission shall not refuse to certify a State program based solely on the method such State will implement for funding intrastate telecommunication relay services.

(4) Suspension or revocation of certification

The Commission may suspend or revoke such certification if, after notice and opportunity for hearing, the Commission determines that such certification is no longer warranted. In a State whose program has been suspended or revoked, the Commission shall take such steps as may be necessary, consistent with this section, to ensure continuity of telecommunications relay services.

(g) Complaint

(1) Referral of complaint

If a complaint to the Commission alleges a violation of this section with respect to intrastate telecommunications relay services within a State and certification of the program of such State under subsection (f) of this section is in effect, the Commission shall refer such complaint to such State.

(2) Jurisdiction of Commission

After referring a complaint to a State under paragraph (1), the Commission shall exercise jurisdiction over such complaint only if—

(A) final action under such State program has not been taken on such complaint by such State—

(i) within 180 days after the complaint is filed with such State; or

(ii) within a shorter period as prescribed by the regulations of such State; or

(B) the Commission determines that such State program is no longer qualified for certification under subsection (f) of this section.

ADA TITLE V

MISCELLANEOUS PROVISIONS

42 U.S.C. §

ADA TITLE V

MISCELLANEOUS PROVISIONS

§ 12201 Construction

(a) In general

Except as otherwise provided in this chapter, nothing in this chapter shall be construed to apply a lesser standard than the standards applied under title V of the Rehabilitation Act of 1973 (29 U.S.C. 790 et seq.) or the regulations issued by Federal agencies pursuant to such title.

(b) Relationship to other laws

Nothing in this chapter shall be construed to invalidate or limit the remedies, rights, and procedures of any Federal law or law of any State or political subdivision of any State or jurisdiction that provides greater or equal protection for the rights of individuals with disabilities than are afforded by this chapter. Nothing in this chapter shall be construed to preclude the prohibition of, or the imposition of restrictions on, smoking in places of employment covered by subchapter I of this chapter, in transportation covered by subchapter II or III of this chapter, or in places of public accommodation covered by subchapter III of this chapter.

(c) Insurance

Subchapters I through III of this chapter and title IV of this Act shall not be construed to prohibit or restrict—

(1) an insurer, hospital or medical service company, health maintenance organization, or any agent, or entity that administers benefit plans, or similar organizations from underwriting risks, classifying risks, or administering such risks that are based on or not inconsistent with State law; or

(2) a person or organization covered by this chapter from establishing, sponsoring, observing or administering the terms of a bona fide benefit plan that are based on underwriting risks, classifying risks, or administering such risks that are based on or not inconsistent with State law; or

(3) a person or organization covered by this chapter from establishing, sponsoring, observing or administering the terms of a bona fide benefit plan that is not subject to State laws that regulate insurance.

Paragraphs (1), (2), and (3) shall not be used as a subterfuge to evade the purposes of subchapters I and III of this chapter.

(d) Accommodations and services

Nothing in this chapter shall be construed to require an individual with a disability to accept an accommodation, aid, service, opportunity, or benefit which such individual chooses not to accept.

§ 12202 State immunity

A State shall not be immune under the eleventh amendment to the Constitution of the United States from an action in Federal or State court of competent jurisdiction for a violation of this chapter. In any action against a State for a violation of the requirements of this chapter, remedies (including remedies both at law and in equity) are available for such a violation to the same extent as such remedies are available for such a violation in an action against any public or private entity other than a State.

§ 12203 Prohibition against retaliation and coercion

(a) Retaliation

No person shall discriminate against any individual because such individual has opposed any act or practice made unlawful by this chapter or because such individual made a charge, testified, assisted, or participated in any manner in an investigation, proceeding, or hearing under this chapter.

(b) Interference, coercion, or intimidation

It shall be unlawful to coerce, intimidate, threaten, or interfere with any individual in the exercise or enjoyment of, or on account of his or her having exercised or enjoyed, or on account of his or her having aided or encouraged any other individual in the exercise or enjoyment of, any right granted or protected by this chapter.

(c) Remedies and procedures

The remedies and procedures available under sections 12117, 12133, and 12188 of this title shall be available to aggrieved persons for violations of subsections (a) and (b) of this section, with respect to subchapter I, subchapter II and subchapter III, respectively, of this chapter.

§ 12204 Regulations by the Architectural and Transportation Barriers Compliance Board

(a) Issuance of guidelines. Not later than 9 months after the date of enactment of this Act [enacted July 26, 1990], the Architectural and Transportation Barriers Compliance Board shall issue minimum guidelines that shall supplement the existing Minimum Guidelines and Requirements for Accessible Design for purposes of titles II and III of this Act [42 USCS §§ 12131 et seq., 12181 et seq.].

(b) Contents of guidelines. The supplemental guidelines issued under subsection (a) shall establish additional requirements, consistent with this Act, to ensure that buildings, facilities, rail passenger cars, and vehicles are accessible, in terms of architecture and design, transportation, and communication, to individuals with disabilities.

(c) Qualified historic properties.

(1) In general. The supplemental guidelines issued under subsection (a) shall include procedures and requirements for alterations that will threaten or destroy the historic significance of qualified historic buildings and facilities as defined in 4.1.7(1)(a) of the Uniform Federal Accessibility Standards.

(2) Sites eligible for listing in National Register. With respect to alterations of buildings or facilities that are eligible for listing in the National Register of Historic Places under the National Historic Preservation Act (16 U.S.C. 470 et seq.), the guidelines described in paragraph (1) shall, at a minimum, maintain the procedures and requirements established in 4.1.7 (1) and (2) of the Uniform Federal Accessibility Standards.

(3) Other sites. With respect to alterations of buildings or facilities designated as historic under State or local law, the guidelines described in paragraph (1) shall establish procedures equivalent to those established by 4.1.7(1)(b) and (c) of the Uniform Federal Accessibility Standards, and shall require, at a minimum, compliance with the requirements established in 4.1.7(2) of such standards.

§ 12205 Attorney's fees

In any action or administrative proceeding commenced pursuant to this Act, the court or agency, in its discretion, may allow the prevailing party, other than the United States, a reasonable attorney's fee, including litigation expenses, and costs, and the United States shall be liable for the foregoing the same as a private individual.

§ 12206 Technical assistance

(a) Plan for assistance.

(1) In general. Not later than 180 days after the date of enactment of this Act [enacted July 26, 1990], the Attorney General, in consultation with the Chair of the Equal Employment Opportunity Commission, the Secretary of Transportation, the Chair of the Architectural and Transportation Barriers Compliance Board, and the Chairman of the Federal Communications Commission, shall develop a plan to assist entities covered under this Act, and other Federal agencies, in understanding the responsibility of such entities and agencies under this Act.

(2) Publication of plan. The Attorney General shall publish the plan referred to in paragraph (1) for public comment in accordance with subchapter II of chapter 5 of title 5, United States Code [5 USCS §§ 551 et seq.] (commonly known as the Administrative Procedure Act).

(b) Agency and public assistance. The Attorney General may obtain the assistance of other Federal agencies in carrying out subsection (a), including the National Council on Disability, the President's Committee on Employment of People with Disabilities, the Small Business Administration, and the Department of Commerce.

(c) Implementation.

(1) Rendering assistance. Each Federal agency that has responsibility under paragraph (2) for implementing this Act may render technical assistance to individuals and institutions that have rights or duties under the respective title or titles for which such agency has responsibility.

(2) Implementation of Titles.

(A) Title I. The Equal Employment Opportunity Commission and the Attorney General shall implement the plan for assistance developed under subsection (a), for title I [42 USCS §§ 12111 et seq.].

(B) Title II.

(i) Subtitle A. The Attorney General shall implement such plan for assistance for subtitle A of title II [42 USCS §§ 12131 et seq.].

(ii) Subtitle B. The Secretary of Transportation shall implement such plan for assistance for subtitle B of title II [42 USCS §§ 12141 et seq.].

(C) Title III. The Attorney General, in coordination with the Secretary of Transportation and the Chair of the Architectural Transportation Barriers Compliance Board, shall implement such plan for assistance for title III [42 USCS §§ 12181 et seq.], except for section 304 [42 USCS § 12184], the plan for assistance for which shall be implemented by the Secretary of Transportation.

(D) Title IV. The Chairman of the Federal Communications Commission, in coordination with the Attorney General, shall implement such plan for assistance for title IV.

(3) Technical assistance manuals. Each Federal agency that has responsibility under paragraph (2) for implementing this Act shall, as part of its implementation responsibilities, ensure the availability and provision of appropriate technical assistance manuals to individuals or entities with rights or duties under this Act no later than six months after applicable final regulations are published under titles I, II, III, and IV.

(d) Grants and contracts.

(1) In general. Each Federal agency that has responsibility under subsection (c)(2) for implementing this Act may make grants or award contracts to effectuate the purposes of this section, subject to the availability of appropriations. Such grants and contracts may be awarded to individuals, institutions not organized for profit and no part of the net earnings of which inures to the benefit of any private shareholder or individual (including educational institutions), and associations representing individuals who have rights or duties under this Act. Contracts may be awarded to entities organized for profit, but such entities may not be the recipients or grants described in this paragraph.

(2) Dissemination of information. Such grants and contracts, among other uses, may be designed to ensure wide dissemination of information about the rights and duties established by this Act and to provide information and technical assistance about techniques for effective compliance with this Act.

(e) Failure to receive assistance. An employer, public accommodation, or other entity covered under this Act shall not be excused from compliance with the requirements of this Act because of any failure to receive technical assistance under this section, including any failure in the development or dissemination of any technical assistance manual authorized by this section.

§ 12207 Federal wilderness areas

(a) Study. The National Council on Disability shall conduct a study and report on the effect that wilderness designations and wilderness land management practices have on the ability of individuals with disabilities to use and enjoy the National Wilderness Preservation System as established under the Wilderness Act (16 U.S.C. 1131 et seq.).

(b) Submission of report. Not later than 1 year after the enactment of this Act [enacted July 26, 1990], the National Council on Disability shall submit the report required under subsection (a) to Congress.

(c) Specific wilderness access.

(1) In general. Congress reaffirms that nothing in the Wilderness Act is to be construed as prohibiting the use of a wheelchair in a wilderness area by an individual whose disability requires use of a wheelchair, and consistent with the Wilderness Act no agency is required to provide any form of special treatment or accommodation, or to construct any facilities or modify any conditions of lands within a wilderness area in order to facilitate such use.

(2) Definition. For purposes of paragraph (1), the term "wheelchair" means a device designed solely for use by a mobility-impaired person for locomotion, that is suitable for use in an indoor pedestrian area.

§ 12208 Transvestites

For the purposes of this Act, the term "disabled" or "disability" shall not apply to an individual solely because that individual is a transvestite.

§ 12209. Instrumentalities of the Congress

The General Accounting Office, the Government Printing Office, and the Library of Congress shall be covered as follows:

(1) In general

The rights and protections under this chapter shall, subject to paragraph (2), apply with respect to the conduct of each instrumentality of the Congress.

(2) Establishment of remedies and procedures by instrumentalities

The chief official of each instrumentality of the Congress shall establish remedies and procedures to be utilized with respect to the rights and protections provided pursuant to paragraph (1).

(3) Report to Congress

The chief official of each instrumentality of the Congress shall, after establishing remedies and procedures for purposes of paragraph (2), submit to the Congress a report describing the remedies and procedures.

(4) Definition of instrumentality

For purposes of this section, the term "instrumentality of the Congress" means the following: the General Accounting Office, the Government Printing Office, and the Library of Congress.

(5) Enforcement of employment rights

The remedies and procedures set forth in section 2000e-16 of this title shall be available to any employee of an instrumentality of the Congress who alleges a violation of the rights and protections under sections 12112 through 12114 of this title that are made applicable by this section, except that the authorities of the Equal Employment Opportunity Commission shall be exercised by the chief official of the instrumentality of the Congress.

(6) Enforcement of rights to public services and accommodations

The remedies and procedures set forth in section 2000e-16 of this title shall be available to any qualified person with a disability who is a visitor, guest, or patron of an instrumentality of Congress and who alleges a violation of the rights and protections under sections 12131 through 12150 or section 12182 or 12183 of this title that are made applicable by this section, except that the authorities of the Equal Employment Opportunity Commission shall be exercised by the chief official of the instrumentality of the Congress.

(7) Construction

Nothing in this section shall alter the enforcement procedures for individuals with disabilities provided in the General Accounting Office Personnel Act of 1980 and regulations promulgated pursuant to that Act.

§ 12210 Illegal use of drugs

(a) In general

For purposes of this chapter, the term "individual with a disability" does not include an individual who is currently engaging in the illegal use of drugs, when the covered entity acts on the basis of such use.

(b) Rules of construction

Nothing in subsection (a) of this section shall be construed to exclude as an individual with a disability an individual who—

(1) has successfully completed a supervised drug rehabilitation program and is no longer engaging in the illegal use of drugs, or has otherwise been rehabilitated successfully and is no longer engaging in such use;

(2) is participating in a supervised rehabilitation program and is no longer engaging in such use; or

(3) is erroneously regarded as engaging in such use, but is not engaging in such use;

except that it shall not be a violation of this chapter for a covered entity to adopt or administer reasonable policies or procedures, including but not limited to drug testing, designed to ensure that an individual described in paragraph (1) or (2) is no longer engaging in the illegal use of drugs; however, nothing in this section shall be construed to encourage, prohibit, restrict, or authorize the conducting of testing for the illegal use of drugs.

(c) Health and other services

Notwithstanding subsection (a) of this section and section 12211(b)(3) of this title, an individual shall not be denied health services, or services provided in connection with drug rehabilitation, on the basis of the current illegal use of drugs if the individual is otherwise entitled to such services.

(d) Definition of illegal use of drugs

(1) In general

The term "illegal use of drugs" means the use of drugs, the possession or distribution of which is unlawful under the Controlled Substances Act (21 U.S.C. 812). Such term does not include the use of a drug taken under supervision by a licensed health care professional, or other uses authorized by the Controlled Substances Act [21 U.S.C.A. § 801 et seq.] or other provisions of Federal law.

(2) Drugs

The term "drug" means a controlled substance, as defined in schedules I through V of section 202 of the Controlled Substances Act [21 U.S.C.A. § 812].

§ 12211 Definitions

(a) Homosexuality and bisexuality

For purposes of the definition of "disability" in section 12102(2) of this title, homosexuality and bisexuality are not impairments and as such are not disabilities under this chapter.

(b) Certain conditions

Under this chapter, the term "disability" shall not include—

(1) transvestism, transsexualism, pedophilia, exhibitionism, voyeurism, gender identity disorders not resulting from physical impairments, or other sexual behavior disorders;

(2) compulsive gambling, kleptomania, or pyromania; or

(3) psychoactive substance use disorders resulting from current illegal use of drugs.

§ 12212 Alternative means of dispute resolution

Where appropriate and to the extent authorized by law, the use of alternative means of dispute resolution, including settlement negotiations, conciliation, facilitation, mediation, factfinding, minitrials, and arbitration, is encouraged to resolve disputes arising under this chapter.

§ 12213 Severability

Should any provision in this chapter be found to be unconstitutional by a court of law, such provision shall be severed from the remainder of this chapter and such action shall not affect the enforceability of the remaining provisions of this chapter.

REHABILITATION ACT

SECTION 504 OF THE REHABILITATION ACT OF 1973

SECTION 504 OF THE REHABILITATION ACT OF 1973

§ 794 Nondiscrimination under federal grants and programs

(a) Promulgation of rules and regulations

No otherwise qualified individual with a disability in the United States, as defined in section 705(20) of this title, shall, solely by reason of her or his disability, be excluded from the participation in, be denied the benefits of, or be subjected to discrimination under any program or activity receiving Federal financial assistance or under any program or activity conducted by any Executive agency or by the United States Postal Service. The head of each such agency shall promulgate such regulations as may be necessary to carry out the amendments to this section made by the Rehabilitation, Comprehensive Services, and Developmental Disabilities Act of 1978. Copies of any proposed regulation shall be submitted to appropriate authorizing committees of the Congress, and such regulation may take effect no earlier than the thirtieth day after the date on which such regulation is so submitted to such committees.

(b) "Program or activity" defined

For the purposes of this section, the term "program or activity" means all of the operations of—

(1)(A) a department, agency, special purpose district, or other instrumentality of a State or of a local government; or

(B) the entity of such State or local government that distributes such assistance and each such department or agency (and each other State or local government entity) to which the assistance is extended, in the case of assistance to a State or local government;

(2)(A) a college, university, or other post-secondary institution, or a public system of higher education; or

(B) a local educational agency (as defined in section 7801 of Title 20) system of vocational education, or other school system;

(3)(A) an entire corporation, partnership, or other private organization, or an entire sole proprietorship—

(i) if assistance is extended to such corporation, partnership, private organization, or sole proprietorship as a whole; or

(ii) which is principally engaged in the business of providing education, health care, housing, social services, or parks and recreation; or

(B) the entire plant or other comparable, geographically separate facility to which Federal financial assistance is extended, in the case of any other corporation, partnership, private organization, or sole proprietorship; or

(4) any other entity which is established by two or more of the entities described in paragraph (1), (2), or (3); any part of which is extended Federal financial assistance.

(c) Significant structural alterations by small providers; exception

Small providers are not required by subsection (a) of this section to make significant structural alterations to their existing facilities for the purpose of assuring program accessibility, if alternative means of providing the services are available. The terms used in this subsection shall be construed with reference to the regulations existing on March 22, 1988.

(d) Standards used in determining violation of section

The standards used to determine whether this section has been violated in a complaint alleging employment discrimination under this section shall be the standards applied under title I of the Americans with Disabilities Act of 1990 (42 U.S.C. 12111 et seq.) and the provisions of sections 501 through 504, and 510, of the Americans with Disabilities Act of 1990 (42 U.S.C. 12201-12204 and 12210), as such sections relate to employment.

§ 794a Remedies and attorney fees

(a)(1) The remedies, procedures, and rights set forth in section 717 of the Civil Rights Act of 1964 (42 U.S.C. 2000e-16), including the application of sections 706(f) through 706(k) (42 U.S.C. 2000e-5(f) through (k)), shall be available, with respect to any complaint under section 791 of this title, to any employee or applicant for employment aggrieved by the final disposition of such complaint, or by the failure to take final action on such complaint. In fashioning an equitable or affirmative action remedy under such section, a court may take into account the reasonableness of the cost of any necessary work place accommodation, and the availability of alternatives therefor or other appropriate relief in order to achieve an equitable and appropriate remedy.

(2) The remedies, procedures, and rights set forth in title VI of the Civil Rights Act of 1964 [42 U.S.C.A. § 2000d et seq.] shall be available to any person aggrieved by any act or failure to act by any recipient of Federal assistance or Federal provider of such assistance under section 794 of this title.

(b) In any action or proceeding to enforce or charge a violation of a provision of this subchapter, the court, in its discretion, may allow the prevailing party, other than the United States, a reasonable attorney's fee as part of the costs.

GENERAL PROVISIONS

§ 705 Definitions

For the purposes of this chapter [29 USCS §§ 701 et seq.]:

(1) Administrative costs

The term "administrative costs" means expenditures incurred in the performance of administrative functions under the vocational rehabilitation program carried out under subchapter I of this chapter [29 USCS § 720 et seq.], including expenses related to program planning, development, monitoring, and evaluation, including expenses for—

(A) quality assurance;

(B) budgeting, accounting, financial management, information systems, and related data processing;

(C) providing information about the program to the public;

(D) technical assistance and support services to other State agencies, private nonprofit organizations, and businesses and industries, except for technical assistance and support services described in section 723(b)(5) of this title;

(E) the State Rehabilitation Council and other advisory committees;

(F) professional organization membership dues for designated State unit employees;

(G) the removal of architectural barriers in State vocational rehabilitation agency offices and State operated rehabilitation facilities;

(H) operating and maintaining designated State unit facilities, equipment, and grounds;

(I) supplies;

(J) administration of the comprehensive system of personnel development described in section 721(a)(7) of this title, including personnel administration, administration of affirmative action plans, and training and staff development;

(K) administrative salaries, including clerical and other support staff salaries, in support of these administrative functions;

(L) travel costs related to carrying out the program, other than travel costs related to the provision of services;

(M) costs incurred in conducting reviews of rehabilitation counselor or coordinator determinations under section 722(c) of this title; and

(N) legal expenses required in the administration of the program.

(2) Assessment for determining eligibility and vocational rehabilitation needs

The term "assessment for determining eligibility and vocational rehabilitation needs" means, as appropriate in each case—

(A)(i) a review of existing data—

(I) to determine whether an individual is eligible for vocational rehabilitation services; and

(II) to assign priority for an order of selection described in section 721(a)(5)(A) of this title in the States that use an order of selection pursuant to section 721(a)(5)(A) of this title; and

(ii) to the extent necessary, the provision of appropriate assessment activities to obtain necessary additional data to make such determination and assignment;

(B) to the extent additional data is necessary to make a determination of the employment outcomes, and the nature and scope of vocational rehabilitation services, to be included in the individualized plan for employment of an eligible individual, a comprehensive assessment to determine the unique strengths, resources, priorities, concerns, abilities, capabilities, interests, and informed choice, including the need for supported employment, of the eligible individual, which comprehensive assessment—

(i) is limited to information that is necessary to identify the rehabilitation needs of the individual and to develop the individualized plan for employment of the eligible individual;

(ii) uses, as a primary source of such information, to the maximum extent possible and appropriate and in accordance with confidentiality requirements—

(I) existing information obtained for the purposes of determining the eligibility of the individual and assigning priority for an order of selection described in section 721(a)(5)(A) of this title for the individual; and

(II) such information as can be provided by the individual and, where appropriate, by the family of the individual;

(iii) may include, to the degree needed to make such a determination, an assessment of the personality, interests, interpersonal skills, intelligence and related functional capacities, educational achievements, work experience, vocational aptitudes, personal and social adjustments, and employment opportunities of the individual, and the medical, psychiatric, psychological, and other pertinent vocational, educational, cultural, social, recreational, and environmental factors, that affect the employment and rehabilitation needs of the individual; and

(iv) may include, to the degree needed, an appraisal of the patterns of work behavior of the individual and services needed for the individual to acquire occupational skills, and to develop work attitudes, work habits, work tolerance, and social and behavior patterns necessary for successful job performance, including the utilization of work in real job situations to assess and develop the capacities of the individual to perform adequately in a work environment;

(C) referral, for the provision of rehabilitation technology services to the individual, to assess and develop the capacities of the individual to perform in a work environment; and

(D) an exploration of the individual's abilities, capabilities, and capacity to perform in work situations, which shall be assessed periodically during trial work experiences, including experiences in which the individual is provided appropriate supports and training.

(3) Assistive technology device

The term "assistive technology device" has the meaning given such term in section 3002 of this title, except that the reference in such section to the term "individuals with disabilities" shall be deemed to mean more than one individual with a disability as defined in paragraph (20)(A).

(4) Assistive technology service

The term "assistive technology service" has the meaning given such term in section 3002 of this title, except that the reference in such section—

(A) to the term "individual with a disability" shall be deemed to mean an individual with a disability, as defined in paragraph (20)(A); and

(B) to the term "individuals with disabilities" shall be deemed to mean more than one such individual.

(5) Community rehabilitation program

The term "community rehabilitation program" means a program that provides directly or facilitates the provision of vocational rehabilitation services to individuals with disabilities, and that provides, singly or in combination, for an individual with a disability to enable the individual to maximize opportunities for employment, including career advancement—

(A) medical, psychiatric, psychological, social, and vocational services that are provided under one management;

(B) testing, fitting, or training in the use of prosthetic and orthotic devices;

(C) recreational therapy;

(D) physical and occupational therapy;

(E) speech, language, and hearing therapy;

(F) psychiatric, psychological, and social services, including positive behavior management;

(G) assessment for determining eligibility and vocational rehabilitation needs;

(H) rehabilitation technology;

(I) job development, placement, and retention services;

(J) evaluation or control of specific disabilities;

(K) orientation and mobility services for individuals who are blind;

(L) extended employment;

(M) psychosocial rehabilitation services;

(N) supported employment services and extended services;

(O) services to family members when necessary to the vocational rehabilitation of the individual;

(P) personal assistance services; or

(Q) services similar to the services described in one of subparagraphs (A) through (P).

(6) Construction; cost of construction—

(A) Construction

The term "construction" means—

(i) the construction of new buildings;

(ii) the acquisition, expansion, remodeling, alteration, and renovation of existing buildings; and

(iii) initial equipment of buildings described in clauses (i) and (ii).

(B) Cost of construction

The term "cost of construction" includes architects' fees and the cost of acquisition of land in connection with construction but does not include the cost of off-site improvements.

(7) Repealed. 105-277, Div. A, § 101(f) [Title VIII, § 402(c)(1)(B)], Oct. 21, 1998, 112 Stat. 2681-415

(8) Designated State agency; designated State unit—

(A) Designated State agency

The term "designated State agency" means an agency designated under section 721(a)(2)(A) of this title.

(B) Designated State unit

The term "designated State unit" means—

(i) any State agency unit required under section

721(a)(2)(B)(ii) of this title; or

(ii) in cases in which no such unit is so required, the State agency described in section 721(a)(2)(B)(i) of this title.

(9) Disability

The term "disability" means—

(A) except as otherwise provided in subparagraph (B), a physical or mental impairment that constitutes or results in a substantial impediment to employment; or

(B) for purposes of sections 701, 711, and 712 of this title and subchapters II, IV, V, and VII of this chapter [29 USCS §§ 760 et seq., 780 et seq., 790 et seq., and 796 et seq.], a physical or mental impairment that substantially limits one or more major life activities.

(10) Drug and illegal use of drugs

(A) Drug

The term "drug" means a controlled substance, as defined in schedules I through V of section 202 of the Controlled Substances Act (21 U.S.C. 812).

(B) Illegal use of drugs

The term "illegal use of drugs" means the use of drugs, the possession or distribution of which is unlawful under the Controlled Substances Act. Such term does not include the use of a drug taken under supervision by a licensed health care professional, or other uses authorized by the Controlled Substances Act or other provisions of Federal law.

(11) Employment outcome

The term "employment outcome" means, with respect to an individual—

(A) entering or retaining full-time or, if appropriate, part-time competitive employment in the integrated labor market;

(B) satisfying the vocational outcome of supported employment; or

(C) satisfying any other vocational outcome the Secretary may determine to be appropriate (including satisfying the vocational outcome of self-employment, telecommuting, or business ownership), in a manner consistent with this chapter [29 USCS § 701 et seq.].

(12) Establishment of a community rehabilitation program

The term "establishment of a community rehabilitation program" includes the acquisition, expansion, remodeling, or alteration of existing buildings necessary to adapt them to community rehabilitation program purposes or to increase their effectiveness for such purposes (subject, however, to such limitations as the Secretary may determine, in accordance with regulations the Secretary shall prescribe, in order to prevent impairment of the objectives of, or duplication of, other Federal laws providing Federal assistance in the construction of facilities for community rehabilitation programs), and may include such additional equipment and staffing as the Commissioner considers appropriate.

(13) Extended services

The term "extended services" means ongoing support services and other appropriate services, needed to support and maintain an individual with a most significant disability in supported employment, that—

(A) are provided singly or in combination and are organized and made available in such a way as to assist an eligible individual in maintaining supported employment;

(B) are based on a determination of the needs of an eligible individual, as specified in an individualized plan for employment; and

(C) are provided by a State agency, a nonprofit private organization, employer, or any other appropriate resource, after an individual has made the transition from support provided by the designated State unit.

(14) Federal share

(A) In general

Subject to subparagraph (B), the term "Federal share" means 78.7 percent.

(B) Exception

The term "Federal share" means the share specifically set forth in section 731(a)(3) of this title, except that with respect to payments pursuant to part B of subchapter I of this chapter [29 USCS § 730 et seq.] to any State that are used to meet the costs of construction of those rehabilitation facilities identified in section 723(b)(2) of this title in such State, the Federal share shall be the percentages determined in accordance with the provisions of section 731(a)(3) of this title applicable with respect to the State.

(C) Relationship to expenditures by a political subdivision

For the purpose of determining the non-Federal share with respect to a State, expenditures by a political subdivision thereof or by a local agency shall be regarded as expenditures by such State, subject to such limitations and conditions as the Secretary shall by regulation prescribe.

(15) Governor

The term "Governor" means a chief executive officer of a State.

(16) Impartial hearing officer

(A) In general

The term "impartial hearing officer" means an individual—

(i) who is not an employee of a public agency (other than an administrative law judge, hearing examiner, or employee of an institution of higher education);

(ii) who is not a member of the State Rehabilitation Council described in section 725 of this title;

(iii) who has not been involved previously in the vocational rehabilitation of the applicant or eligible individual;

(iv) who has knowledge of the delivery of vocational rehabilitation services, the State plan under section 721 of this title, and the Federal and State rules governing the provision of such services and training with respect to the performance of official duties; and

(v) who has no personal or financial interest that would be in conflict with the objectivity of the individual.

(B) Construction

An individual shall not be considered to be an employee of a public agency for purposes of subparagraph (A)(i) solely because the individual is paid by the agency to serve as a hearing officer.

(17) Independent living core services

The term "independent living core services" means—

(A) information and referral services;

(B) independent living skills training;

(C) peer counseling (including cross-disability peer counseling); and

(D) individual and systems advocacy.

(18) Independent living services

The term "independent living services" includes—

(A) independent living core services; and

(B)(i) counseling services, including psychological, psychotherapeutic, and related services;

(ii) services related to securing housing or shelter, including services related to community group living, and supportive of the purposes of this chapter [29 USCS § 701 et seq.] and of the subchapters of this chapter, and adaptive housing services (including appropriate accommodations to and modifications of any space used to serve, or occupied by, individuals with disabilities);

(iii) rehabilitation technology;

(iv) mobility training;

(v) services and training for individuals with cognitive and sensory disabilities, including life skills training, and interpreter and reader services;

(vi) personal assistance services, including attendant care and the training of personnel providing such services;

(vii) surveys, directories, and other activities to identify appropriate housing, recreation opportunities, and accessible transportation, and other support services;

(viii) consumer information programs on rehabilitation and independent living services available under this chapter [29 USCS § 701 et seq.], especially for minorities and other individuals with disabilities who have traditionally been unserved or underserved by programs under this chapter;

(ix) education and training necessary for living in a community and participating in community activities;

(x) supported living;

(xi) transportation, including referral and assistance for such transportation and training in the use of public transportation vehicles and systems;

(xii) physical rehabilitation;

(xiii) therapeutic treatment;

(xiv) provision of needed prostheses and other appliances and devices;

(xv) individual and group social and recreational services;

(xvi) training to develop skills specifically designed for youths who are individuals with disabilities to promote self-awareness and esteem, develop advocacy and self-empowerment skills, and explore career options;

(xvii) services for children;

(xviii) services under other Federal, State, or local programs designed to provide resources, training, counseling, or other assistance, of substantial benefit in enhancing the independence, productivity, and quality of life of individuals with disabilities;

(xix) appropriate preventive services to decrease the need of individuals assisted under this chapter for similar services in the future;

(xx) community awareness programs to enhance the understanding and integration into society of individuals with disabilities; and

(xxi) such other services as may be necessary and not inconsistent with the provisions of this chapter.

(19) Indian; American Indian; Indian American; Indian tribe—

(A) In general

The terms "Indian", "American Indian", and "Indian American" mean an individual who is a member of an Indian tribe.

(B) Indian tribe

The term "Indian tribe" means any Federal or State Indian tribe, band, rancheria, pueblo, colony, or community, including any Alaskan native village or regional village corporation (as defined in or established pursuant to the Alaska Native Claims Settlement Act).

(20) Individual with a disability

(A) In general

Except as otherwise provided in subparagraph (B),

the term "individual with a disability" means any individual who—

(i) has a physical or mental impairment which for such individual constitutes or results in a substantial impediment to employment; and

(ii) can benefit in terms of an employment outcome from vocational rehabilitation services provided pursuant to subchapter I, III, or VI of this chapter [29 USCS § 720 et seq., 771 et seq., or 795 et seq.].

(B) Certain programs; limitations on major life activities

Subject to subparagraphs (C), (D), (E), and (F), the term "individual with a disability" means, for purposes of sections 701, 711, and 712 of this title and subchapters II, IV, V, and VII of this chapter [29 USCS §§ 760 et seq., 780 et seq., 790 et seq., and 796 et seq.], any person who—

(i) has a physical or mental impairment which substantially limits one or more of such person's major life activities;

(ii) has a record of such an impairment; or

(iii) is regarded as having such an impairment.

(C) Rights and advocacy provision.

(i) In general; exclusion of individuals engaging in drug use

For purposes of subchapter V of this chapter [29 USCS § 790 et seq.], the term "individual with a disability" does not include an individual who is currently engaging in the illegal use of drugs, when a covered entity acts on the basis of such use.

(ii) Exception for individuals no longer engaging in drug use

Nothing in clause (i) shall be construed to exclude as an individual with a disability an individual who—

(I) has successfully completed a supervised drug rehabilitation program and is no longer engaging in the illegal use of drugs, or has otherwise been rehabilitated successfully and is no longer engaging in such use;

(II) is participating in a supervised rehabilitation program and is no longer engaging in such use; or

(III) is erroneously regarded as engaging in such use, but is not engaging in such use; except that it shall not be a violation of this chapter [29 USCS § 701 et seq.] for a covered entity to adopt or administer reasonable policies or procedures, including but not limited to drug testing, designed to ensure that an individual described in subclause (I) or (II) is no longer engaging in the illegal use of drugs.

(iii) Exclusion for certain services

Notwithstanding clause (i), for purposes of programs and activities providing health services and services provided under subchapters I, II, and III of this chapter [29 USCS §§ 720 et seq., 760 et seq., and 771 et seq.], an individual shall not be excluded from the benefits of such programs or activities on the basis of his or her current illegal use of drugs if he or she is otherwise entitled to such services.

(iv) Disciplinary action

For purposes of programs and activities providing educational services, local educational agencies may take disciplinary action pertaining to the use or possession of illegal drugs or alcohol against any student who is an individual with a disability and who currently is engaging in the illegal use of drugs or in the use of alcohol to the same extent that such disciplinary action is taken against students who are not individuals with disabilities. Furthermore, the due process procedures at section 104.36 of title 34, Code of Federal Regulations (or any corresponding similar regulation or ruling) shall not apply to such disciplinary actions.

(v) Employment; exclusion of alcoholics

For purposes of sections 793 and 794 of this title as such sections relate to employment, the term "individual with a disability" does not include any individual who is an alcoholic whose current use of alcohol prevents such individual from performing the duties of the job in question or whose employment, by reason of such current alcohol abuse, would constitute a direct threat to property or the safety of others.

(D) Employment; exclusion of individuals with certain diseases or infections

For the purposes of sections 793 and 794 of this title, as such sections relate to employment, such term does not include an individual who has a currently contagious disease or infection and who, by reason of such disease or infection, would constitute a direct threat to the health or safety of other individuals or who, by reason of the currently contagious disease or infection, is unable to perform the duties of the job.

(E) Rights provisions; exclusion of individuals on basis of homosexuality or bisexuality

For the purposes of sections 791, 793, and 794 of this title—

(i) for purposes of the application of subparagraph (B) to such sections, the term "impairment" does not include homosexuality or bisexuality; and

(ii) therefore the term "individual with a disability" does not include an individual on the basis of homosexuality or bisexuality.

(F) Rights provisions; exclusion of individuals on basis of certain disorders

For the purposes of sections 791, 793, and 794 of this title, the term "individual with a disability" does not include an individual on the basis of—

(i) transvestism, transsexualism, pedophilia, exhibitionism, voyeurism, gender identity disorders not resulting from physical impairments, or other sexual behavior disorders;

(ii) compulsive gambling, kleptomania, or pyromania; or

(iii) psychoactive substance use disorders resulting from current illegal use of drugs.

(G) Individuals with disabilities

The term "individuals with disabilities" means more than one individual with a disability.

(21) Individual with a significant disability

(A) In general

Except as provided in subparagraph (B) or (C), the term "individual with a significant disability" means an individual with a disability—

(i) who has a severe physical or mental impairment which seriously limits one or more functional capacities (such as mobility, communication, self-care, self-direction, interpersonal skills, work tolerance, or work skills) in terms of an employment outcome;

(ii) whose vocational rehabilitation can be expected to require multiple vocational rehabilitation services over an extended period of time; and

(iii) who has one or more physical or mental disabilities resulting from amputation, arthritis, autism, blindness, burn injury, cancer, cerebral palsy, cystic fibrosis, deafness, head injury, heart disease, hemiplegia, hemophilia, respiratory or pulmonary dysfunction, mental retardation, mental illness, multiple sclerosis, muscular dystrophy, musculo-skeletal disorders, neurological disorders (including stroke and epilepsy), paraplegia, quadriplegia, and other spinal cord conditions, sickle cell anemia, specific learning disability, end-stage renal disease, or another disability or combination of disabilities determined on the basis of an assessment for determining eligibility and vocational rehabilitation needs described in subparagraphs (A) and (B) of paragraph (2) to cause comparable substantial functional limitation.

(B) Independent living services and centers for independent living

For purposes of subchapter VII of this chapter [29 USCS § 796 et seq.], the term "individual with a significant disability" means an individual with a severe physical or mental impairment whose ability to function independently in the family or community or whose ability to obtain, maintain, or advance in employment is substantially limited and for whom the delivery of independent living services will improve the ability to function, continue functioning, or move toward functioning independently in the family or community or to continue in employment, respectively.

(C) Research and training

For purposes of subchapter II of this chapter [29 USCS § 760 et seq.], the term "individual with a significant disability" includes an individual described in subparagraph (A) or (B).

(D) Individuals with significant disabilities

The term "individuals with significant disabilities" means more than one individual with a significant disability.

(E) Individual with a most significant disability

(i) In general

The term "individual with a most significant disability", used with respect to an individual in a State, means an individual with a significant disability who meets criteria established by the State under section 721(a)(5)(C) of this title.

(ii) Individuals with the most significant disabilities

The term "individuals with the most significant disabilities" means more than one individual with a most significant disability.

(22) Individual's representative; applicant's representative

The terms "individual's representative" and "applicant's representative" mean a parent, a family member, a guardian, an advocate, or an authorized representative of an individual or applicant, respectively.

(23) Institution of higher education

The term "institution of higher education" has the meaning given the term in section 1.01 of this title.

(24) Local agency

The term "local agency" means an agency of a unit of general local government or of an Indian tribe (or combination of such units or tribes) which has an agreement with the designated State agency to conduct a vocational rehabilitation program under the supervision of such State agency in accordance with the State plan approved under section 721 of this title. Nothing in the preceding sentence of this paragraph or in section 721 of this title shall be construed to prevent the local agency from arranging to utilize another local public or nonprofit agency to provide vocational rehabilitation services if such an arrangement is made part of the agreement specified in this paragraph.

(25) Local workforce investment board

The term "local workforce investment board" means a local workforce investment board established under section 117 of the Workforce Investment Act of 1998 [29 USCS § 2832].

(26) Nonprofit

The term "nonprofit', when used with respect to a community rehabilitation program, means a community rehabilitation program carried out by a corporation or association, no part of the net earnings of which inures, or may lawfully inure, to the benefit of any private shareholder or individual and the income of which is exempt from taxation under section 501(c)(3) of Title 26.

(27) Ongoing support services

The term "ongoing support services" means services—

(A) provided to individuals with the most significant disabilities;

(B) provided, at a minimum, twice monthly—

(i) to make an assessment, regarding the employment situation, at the worksite of each such individual in supported employment, or, under special circumstances, especially at the request of the client, off site; and

(ii) based on the assessment, to provide for the coordination or provision of specific intensive services, at or away from the worksite, that are needed to maintain employment stability; and

(C) consisting of—

(i) a particularized assessment supplementary to the comprehensive assessment described in paragraph (2)(B);

(ii) the provision of skilled job trainers who accompany the individual for intensive job skill training at the worksite;

(iii) job development, job retention, and placement services;

(iv) social skills training;

(v) regular observation or supervision of the individual;

(vi) followup services such as regular contact with the employers, the individuals, the individuals' representatives, and other appropriate individuals, in order to reinforce and stabilize the job placement;

(vii) facilitation of natural supports at the worksite;

(viii) any other service identified in section 723 of this title; or

(ix) a service similar to another service described in this subparagraph.

(28) Personal assistance services

The term "personal assistance services" means a range of services, provided by one or more persons, designed to assist an individual with a disability to perform daily living activities on or off the job that the individual would typically perform if the individual did not have a disability. Such services shall be designed to increase the individual's control in life and ability to perform everyday activities on or off the job.

(29) Public or nonprofit

The term "public or nonprofit", used with respect to an agency or organization, includes an Indian tribe.

(30) Rehabilitation technology

The term "rehabilitation technology" means the systematic application of technologies, engineering methodologies, or scientific principles to meet the needs of and address the barriers confronted by individuals with disabilities in areas which include education, rehabilitation, employment, transportation, independent living, and recreation. The term includes rehabilitation engineering, assistive technology devices, and assistive technology services.

(31) Secretary

The term "Secretary", except when the context otherwise requires, means the Secretary of Education.

(32) State

The term "State" includes, in addition to each of the several States of the United States, the District of Columbia, the Commonwealth of Puerto Rico, the United States Virgin Islands, Guam, American Samoa, and the Commonwealth of the Northern Mariana Islands.

(33) State workforce investment board

The term "State workforce investment board" means a State workforce investment board established under section 111 of the Workforce Investment Act of 1998 [29 USCS § 2821].

(34) Statewide workforce investment system

The term "statewide workforce investment system" means a system described in section 111(d)(2) of the Workforce Investment Act of 1998 [29 USCS § 2821(d)(2)].

(35) Supported employment

(A) In general

The term "supported employment" means competitive work in integrated work settings, or employment in integrated work settings in which individuals are working toward competitive work, consistent with the strengths, resources, priorities, concerns, abilities, capabilities, interests, and informed choice of the individuals, for individuals with the most significant disabilities—

(i)(I) for whom competitive employment has not traditionally occurred; or

(II) for whom competitive employment has been interrupted or intermittent as a result of a significant disability; and

(ii) who, because of the nature and severity of their disability, need intensive supported employment services for the period, and any extension, described in paragraph (36)(C) and extended services after the transition described in paragraph (13)(C) in order to perform such work.

(B) Certain transitional employment

Such term includes transitional employment for persons who are individuals with the most significant disabilities due to mental illness.

(36) Supported employment services

The term "supported employment services" means ongoing support services and other appropriate services needed to support and maintain an individual with a most significant disability in supported employment, that—

(A) are provided singly or in combination and are organized and made available in such a way as to assist an eligible individual to achieve competitive employment;

(B) are based on a determination of the needs of an eligible individual, as specified in an individualized plan for employment; and

(C) are provided by the designated State unit for a period of time not to extend beyond 18 months, unless under special circumstances the eligible individual and the rehabilitation counselor or coordinator involved jointly agree to extend the time in order to achieve the employment outcome identified in the individualized plan for employment.

(37) Transition services

The term "transition services" means a coordinated set of activities for a student, designed within an outcome-oriented process, that promotes movement from school to post school activities, including postsecondary education, vocational training, integrated employment (including supported employment), continuing and adult education, adult services, independent living, or community participation. The coordinated set of activities shall be based upon the individual student's needs, taking into account the student's preferences and interests, and shall include instruction, community experiences, the development of employment and other post school adult living objectives, and, when appropriate, acquisition of daily living skills and functional vocational evaluation.

(38) Vocational rehabilitation services

The term "vocational rehabilitation services" means those services identified in section 723 of this title which are provided to individuals with disabilities under this chapter [29 USCS § 701 et seq.].

(39) Workforce investment activities

The term "workforce investment activities" means workforce investment activities, as defined in section 101 of the Workforce Investment Act of 1998, that are carried out under that Act.

REHABILITATION ACT REGULATIONS

29 C.F.R. §

REHABILITATION ACT REGULATIONS
Subpart A—General Provisions

§ 32.1 Purpose.

Section 504 of the Rehabilitation Act of 1973 prohibits discrimination on the basis of handicap in any program or activity receiving Federal financial assistance. The purpose of this part is to implement section 504 with respect to programs or activities receiving or benefiting from Federal financial assistance from the Department of Labor.

§ 32.2 Application.

(a) This part applies to each recipient of Federal financial assistance from the Department of Labor, and to every program or activity that receives such assistance.

(b) A government contractor covered by the provisions of section 503 of the Act shall be deemed in compliance with the employment provisions of these regulations if it is in compliance with 41 CFR Part 60-741 (as amended after publication of these regulations) with respect to Federal financial assistance from the Department of Labor.

§ 32.3 Definitions.

As used in this part, the term:

The Act means the Rehabilitation Act of 1973, Pub.L. 93-112, as amended by the Rehabilitation Act Amendments of 1974, Pub.L. 93-516, and by the Rehabilitation, Comprehensive Services, and Developmental Disabilities Amendments of 1978, Pub.L. 95-602.

Assistant Secretary means the Assistant Secretary for Employment and Training Administration or his or her designee.

Applicant for assistance means one who submits an application, request, or plan required to be approved by a Department official or by a recipient as a condition to becoming a recipient.

Department means the Department of Labor.

Facility means all or any portion of the buildings, structures, equipment, roads, walks, parking lots or other real or personal property or interest in such property which are utilized in the execution of the program or activity for which Federal financial assistance is received.

Federal financial assistance means any grant, loan, contract (other than a procurement contract or a contract of insurance or guarantee), or any other arrangement by which the Department provides or otherwise makes available assistance in the form of:

(a) Funds;

(b) Services of Federal personnel; or

(c) Real and personal property or any interest in or use of such property, including:

(1) Transfers or leases of such property for less than fair market value or for reduced consideration; and

(2) Proceeds from a subsequent transfer or lease of such property if the Federal share of its fair market value is not returned to the Federal Government.

Government means the Government of the United States of America.

Handicap means any condition or characteristic that renders a person a handicapped individual as defined in this section.

Handicapped individual

(a) Handicapped individual means any person who—

(1) Has a physical or mental impairment which substantially limits one or more major life activities;

(2) Has a record of such an impairment; or

(3) Is regarded as having such an impairment.

(b) As used in the proceeding paragraph of this section, the phrase:

(1) Physical or mental impairment means—

(i) Any physiological disorder or condition, cosmetic disfigurement, or anatomical loss affecting one or more of the following body systems: neurological; musculoskeletal; special sense organs; respiratory, including speech organs; cardiovascular; reproductive; digestive; genito-urinary; hemic and lymphatic; skin; and endocrine;

(ii) Any mental or psychological disorder, such as mental retardation, organic brain syndrome, emotional or mental illness, and specific learning disabilities.

(iii) The term physical or mental impairment includes but is not limited to such diseases and conditions as orthopedic, visual, speech and hearing impairments, cerebral palsy, epilepsy, muscular dystrophy, multiple sclerosis, cancer, heart disease, diabetes, mental retardation, emotional illness, and drug addiction and alcoholism.

(2) Substantially limits means the degree that the impairment affects an individual becoming a beneficiary of a program or activity receiving Federal financial assistance or affects an individual's employability. A handicapped individual who is likely to experience difficulty in securing or retaining benefits or in securing, or retaining, or advancing in employment would be considered substantially limited.

(3) Major life activities means functions such as caring for one's self, performing manual tasks, walking, seeing, hearing, speaking, breathing, learning, working, and receiving education or vocational training.

(4) Has a record of such an impairment means that the individual has a history of, or has been misclassified as having, a mental or physical impairment that substantially limits one or more life activity.

(5) Is regarded as having such an impairment means that the individual—

(i) Has a physical or mental impairment that does not substantially limit major life activities but that is treated by a recipient as constituting such a limitation;

(ii) Has a physical or mental impairment that substantially limits major life activities only as a result of the attitudes of others toward such impairment; or

(iii) Has none of the impairments defined in paragraph (b)(1) of this section but is treated by a recipient as having such an impairment.

Program or activity means all of the operations of any entity described in paragraphs (1) through (4) of this definition, any part of which is extended Federal financial assistance:

(1)(i) A department, agency, special purpose district, or other instrumentality of a State or of a local government; or

(ii) The entity of such State or local government that distributes such assistance and each such department or agency (and each other State or local government entity) to which the assistance is extended, in the case of assistance to a State or local government;

(2)(i) A college, university, or other postsecondary institution, or a public system of higher education; or

(ii) A local educational agency (as defined in 20 U.S.C. 7801), system of vocational education, or other school system;

(3)(i) An entire corporation, partnership, or other private organization, or an entire sole proprietorship—

(A) If assistance is extended to such corporation, partnership, private organization, or sole proprietorship as a whole; or

(B) Which is principally engaged in the business of providing education, health care, housing, social services, or parks and recreation; or

(ii) The entire plant or other comparable, geographically separate facility to which Federal financial assistance is extended, in the case of any other corporation, partnership, private organization, or sole proprietorship; or

(4) Any other entity which is established by two or more of the entities described in paragraph (1), (2), or (3) of this definition.

Qualified handicapped individual means:

(a) With respect to employment, an individual with a handicap who is capable of performing the essential functions of the job or jobs for which he or she is being considered with reasonable accommodation to his or her handicap;

(b) With respect to services, a handicapped individual who meets eligibility requirements relevant to the receipt of services provided in the program or activity;

(c) With respect to employment and to employment related training, a handicapped individual who meets both the eligibility requirements for participation in the program or activity and valid job or training qualifications with reasonable accommodation.

Reasonable accommodation means the changes and modifications which can be made in the structure of a job or employment and training, or in the manner in which a job is performed or employment and training program is conducted, unless it would impose an undue hardship on the operation of the recipient's program or activity. Reasonable accommodation may include:

(a) Making the facilities used by the employees or participants in the area where the program or activity is conducted, including common areas used by all employees or participants such as hallways, restrooms, cafeterias and lounges, readily accessible to and usable by handicapped persons, and

(b) Job restructuring, part-time or modified work schedules, acquisition or modification of equipment or devices, the provision of readers or interpreters, and other similar actions.

Recipient means any state or its political subdivisions, any instrumentality of a State or its political subdivisions, any public or private agency, institution, organization, or other entity, or any person to which Federal financial assistance is extended directly or through another recipient, including any successor, assignee, or transferee of a recipient, but excluding the ultimate beneficiary of the assistance.

Secretary means the Secretary of Labor, U.S. Department of Labor, or his or her designee.Section 504 means section 504 of the Act.

Small recipient means a recipient who serves fewer than 15 beneficiaries, and employs fewer than 15 employees at all times during a grant year.

United States means the several States, the District of Columbia, the Virgin Islands, the Commonwealth of Puerto Rico, Guam, American Samoa and the Trust Territory of the Pacific Islands.

§ 32.4 Discrimination prohibited.

(a) General. No qualified handicapped individual shall, on the basis of handicap, be excluded from participation in, be denied the benefits of, or otherwise be subjected to discrimination under any program or activity which receives Federal financial assistance.

(b) Discriminatory actions prohibited.

(1) A recipient, in providing any aid, benefit, service or training, may not, directly or through contractual, licensing, or other arrangements, on the basis of handicap:

(i) Deny a qualified handicapped individual the opportunity to participate in or benefit from the aid, benefit, service or training;

(ii) Afford a qualified handicapped individual an opportunity to participate in or benefit from the aid, benefit, service or training that is not equal to that afforded others;

(iii) Provide a qualified handicapped individual with any aid, benefit, service or training that is not as effective as that provided to others;

(iv) Provide different or separate aid, benefits, or services to handicapped individuals or to any class of handicapped individuals unless such action is necessary to provide qualified handicapped individuals with aid, benefits, services or training that are as effective as those provided to others;

(v) Aid or perpetuate discrimination against a qualified handicapped individual by providing significant assistance to an agency, organization, or person that discriminates on the basis of handicap in providing any aid, benefit, service or training to beneficiaries of the recipient's program or activity;

(vi) Deny a qualified handicapped individual the opportunity to participate as a member of planning or advisory boards; or

(vii) Otherwise limit a qualified handicapped individual in enjoyment of any right, privilege, advantage, or opportunity enjoyed by others receiving any aid, benefit, service or training.

(2) For purposes of this part, aid, benefits, services or training, to be equally effective, are not required to produce the identical result or level of achievement for handicapped and nonhandicapped individuals, but must afford handicapped individuals equal opportunity to obtain the same result, to gain the same benefit, or to reach the same level of achievement, in the most integrated setting appropriate to the person's needs.

(3) A recipient may not deny a qualified handicapped individual the opportunity to participate in its regular aid, benefits, services, or training, despite the existence of separate or different aid, benefits, services, or training for the handicapped which are established in accordance with this Part.

(4) A recipient may not, directly or through contractual or other arrangements, utilize criteria or methods of administration:

(i) That have the effect of subjecting qualified handicapped individuals to discrimination on the basis of handicap;

(ii) That have the purpose or effect of defeating or substantially impairing accomplishment of the objectives of the recipient's program or activity with respect to handicapped individuals; or

(iii) That perpetuate the discrimination of another recipient if both recipients are subject to common administrative control or are agencies of the same State.

(5) In determining the site or location of a facility, an applicant for assistance or a recipient may not make selections:

(i) That have the effect of excluding handicapped individuals from, denying them the benefits of, or otherwise subjecting them to discrimination under any program or activity that receives Federal financial assistance; or

(ii) That have the purpose or effect of defeating or substantially impairing the accomplishment of the objectives of the program or activity with respect to handicapped individuals.

(6) As used in this section, the aid, benefit, service or training provided under a program or activity receiving Federal financial assistance includes any aid, benefit, service or training provided in or through a facility that has been constructed, expanded, altered, leased, rented, or otherwise acquired, in whole or in part, with Federal financial assistance.

(7)(i) In providing services receiving Federal financial assistance, except for employment-related training, a recipient to which this subpart applies, except small recipients, shall ensure that no handicapped participant is denied the benefits of, excluded from participation in, or otherwise subjected to discrimination under the program or activity operated by the recipient because of the absence of auxiliary aids for participants with impaired sensory, manual or speaking skills. In employment and employment-related training, this paragraph shall apply only to the intake, assessment and referral services. A recipient shall operate each program or activity to which this subpart applies so that, when viewed in its entirety, auxiliary aids are readily available.

(ii) Auxiliary aids may include brailled and taped written materials, interpreters or other effective methods of making orally delivered information available to persons with hearing impairments, readers for persons with visual impairments, equipment adapted for use by persons with manual impairments, and other similar services and actions. Recipients need not provide attendants, individually prescribed devices, readers for personal use or study, or other devices or services of a personal nature.

(c) Aid, benefits, services, or training limited by Federal law. The exclusion of nonhandicapped persons from aid, benefits, program services, or training limited by Federal statute or Executive Order to handicapped individuals or the exclusion of a specific class of handicapped individuals from aid, benefits, services, or training limited by Federal statute or Executive Order to a different class of handicapped individuals is not prohibited by this part.

(d) Integrated setting. Recipients shall administer programs or activities in the most integrated setting appropriate to the needs of qualified handicapped individuals.

(e) Communications with individuals with impaired vision and hearing. Recipients shall take appropriate steps to ensure that communications with their applicants, employees, and beneficiaries are available to persons with impaired vision and hearing.

§ 32.5 Assurances required.

(a) Assurances. An applicant for Federal financial assistance for a program or activity to which this part applies shall submit an assurance, on a form specified by the Assistant Secretary, that the program will be operated in compliance with this part. An applicant may incorporate these assurances by reference in subsequent applications to the Department.

(b) Duration of obligation.

(1) In the case of Federal financial assistance extended in the form of real property or structures on the property, the assurance will obligate the recipient or, in the case of a subsequent transfer, the transferee, for the period during which the real property or structures are used for the purpose involving the provision of similar services or benefits.

(2) In the case of Federal financial assistance extended to provide personal property, the assurance will obligate the recipient for the period during which it retains ownership or possession of the property.

(3) In all other cases the assurance will obligate the recipient for the period during which Federal financial assistance is extended or the federally-funded program is operated, whichever is longer.

(c) Covenants.

(1) Where Federal financial assistance is provided in the form of real property or interest in the property from the Department, the instrument effecting or recording this transfer shall contain a covenant running with the land to assure nondiscrimination for the period during which the real property is used for a purpose for which the Federal financial assistance is extended or for another purpose involving the provision of similar services or benefits.

(2) Where no Federal transfer of property is involved but property is purchased or improved with Federal financial assistance, the recipient shall agree to include the covenant described in paragraph (c)(1) of this section in the instrument effecting or recording any subsequent transfer of the property.

(3) Where Federal financial assistance is provided in the form of real property or interest in the property from the Department, the covenant shall also include a condition coupled with a right to be reserved by the Department to revert title to the property in the event of a breach of the covenant. If a transferee of real property proposes to mortgage or otherwise encumber the

real property as security to finance construction of new, or improvement of existing, facilities on the property for the purposes for which the property was transferred, the Assistant Secretary may agree to forbear the exercise of such right to revert title for so long as the lien of such mortgage or other encumbrance remains effective. Such an agreement by the Assistant Secretary may be entered into only upon the request of the transferee (recipient) if it is necessary to accomplish such financing and upon such terms and conditions as the Assistant Secretary deems appropriate.

(d) Interagency agreements. Where funds are granted by the Department to another Federal agency to carry out a program under a law administered by the Department, and where the grant obligates the recipient agency to comply with the rules and regulations of the Department applicable to that grant the provisions of this part shall apply to programs or activities operated with such funds.

§ 32.6 Remedial action, voluntary action, and self-evaluation.

(a) Remedial action.

(1) If the Assistant Secretary finds that a recipient has discriminated against persons on the basis of handicap in violation of section 504 [or] this part, the recipient shall take such remedial action as the Assistant Secretary deems necessary to overcome the effects of the discrimination.

(2) Where a recipient is found to have discriminated against persons on the basis of handicap in violation of section 504 or this part and where another recipient exercises control over the recipient that has discriminated, the Assistant Secretary, where appropriate, may require either or both recipients to take remedial action.

(3) The Assistant Secretary may, where necessary to overcome the effects of discrimination in violation of section 504 or this part, require a recipient to take remedial action:

(i) With respect to handicapped individuals who would have been participants in the program had the discrimination not occurred; and

(ii) With respect to handicapped persons who are no longer participants in the recipient's program but who were participants in the program when the discrimination occurred; and

(iii) With respect to employees and applicants for employment.

(b) Voluntary action. A recipient may take steps, in addition to any action that is required by this part, to overcome the effects of conditions that resulted in limited participation in the recipient's program or activity by qualified handicapped individuals.

(c) Self-evaluation.

(1) A recipient shall, within one year of the effective date of this part:

(i) Evaluate, with the assistance of interested persons who are selected by the recipient, including handicapped individuals or organizations representing handicapped individuals, its current policies and practices and the effects thereof that do not or may not meet the requirements of this part;

(ii) Modify, after consultation with interested persons who are selected by the recipient, including handicapped individuals or organizations representing handicapped individuals, any policies and practices that do not meet the requirements of this part; and

(iii) Take, after consultation with interested persons who are selected by the recipient, including handicapped individuals or organizations representing handicapped individuals, appropriate remedial steps to eliminate the effects of any discrimination that resulted from adherence to these policies and practices.

(2) A recipient, other than a small recipient, shall for at least three years following completion of the evaluation required under paragraph (c)(1) of this section, maintain on file, make available for public inspection, and provide to the Assistant Secretary upon request:

(i) A list of the interested persons consulted;

(ii) A description of areas examined and any problems identified; and

(iii) A description of any modifications made and of any remedial steps taken.

§ 32.7 Designation of responsible employee.

A recipient, other than a small recipient, shall designate at least one person to coordinate its efforts to comply with this part.

§ 32.8 Notice.

(a) A recipient, other than a small recipient, shall take appropriate initial and continuing steps to notify participants, beneficiaries, referral sources, applicants, and employees, including those with impaired vision or hearing, and unions or professional organizations which have collective bargaining or professional agreements with the recipient, that it does not discriminate on the basis of handicap in violation of section 504 and of this part. The notification shall state, where appropriate, that the recipient does not discriminate in the admission or access to, or treatment or employment in, its programs and activities. The notification shall also include an identification of the responsible employee designated pursuant to Sec. 32.7. A recipient shall make the initial notifications required by this paragraph within 90 days of the effective date of this part. Methods of initial and continuing notification may include the posting of notices, publication in newspapers and magazines, placement of notices in recipient's publications, and distribution of memoranda or other written communications.

(b) If a recipient publishes or uses recruitment materials or publications containing general information that it makes available to participants, beneficiaries, applicants, or employees, it shall include in those materials or publications a statement of the policy described in paragraph (a) of this section. A recipient may meet the requirement of this paragraph either by including appropriate inserts in existing materials and publications or by revising and reprinting the materials and publications.

§ 32.9 Administrative requirements for small recipients.

The Assistant Secretary may require any recipient that provides services to fewer than 15 beneficiaries or with fewer than 15 employees, or any class of such recipients, to comply with Secs. 32.7 and 32.8, in whole or in part, when the Assistant Secretary finds a violation of this part or finds that such compliance will not significantly impair the ability of the recipient or class of recipients to provide benefits or services.

§ 32.10 Effect of State or local law or other requirements and effect of employment opportunities.

(a) The obligation to comply with this part is not obviated or alleviated by the existence of any State or local law or other requirement that, on the basis of handicap, imposes prohibitions or limits upon the eligibility of qualified handicapped individuals to receive services, participate in programs or practice any occupation or profession.

(b) The obligation to comply with this part is not obviated or alleviated because employment opportunities in any occupation or profession are or may be more limited for handicapped individuals than for nonhandicapped persons.

Subpart B—Employment Practices and Employment Related Training Program Participation

§ 32.12 Discrimination prohibited.

(a) General.

(1) No qualified handicapped individual shall, on the basis of handicap, be subjected to discrimination in employment under any program or activity to which this part applies. This subpart is applicable to employees and applicants for employment with all recipients and to participants in employment and training programs financed in whole or in part by Federal financial assistance.

(2) A recipient shall make all decisions concerning employment or training under any program or activity to which this subpart applies in a manner which ensures that discrimination on the basis of handicap does not occur and may not limit, segregate, or classify applicants or employees or participants in any way that adversely affects their opportunities or status because of handicap.

(3) A recipient may not participate in a contractual or other relationship that has the effect of subjecting qualified handicapped applicants, employees or participants to discrimination prohibited by this subpart. The relationships referred to in this subparagraph include relationships with employment and referral agencies, with labor unions, with organizations providing or administering fringe benefits to employees of the recipient, and with organizations providing training and apprenticeship programs.

(b) Specific activities. The provisions of this subpart apply to:

(1) Recruitment advertising, and the processing of applicants for employment;

(2) Hiring, upgrading, promotion, award of tenure, demotion, transfer, layoff, termination, right of return from layoff and rehiring;

(3) Rates of pay or any other form of compensation and changes in compensation;

(4) Job assignments, job classifications, organizational structures, position descriptions, lines of progression, and seniority lists;

(5) Leaves of absence, sick leave, or any other leave;

(6) Fringe benefits available by virture of employment, whether or not administered by the recipient;

(7) Selection and financial support for training, including apprenticeship, professional meetings, conferences, and other related activities, and selection for leaves of absence to pursue training;

(8) Employer-sponsored activities, including social or recreational programs; and

(9) Any other term, condition, or privilege of employment.

(c) Collective bargaining agreements. Whenever a recipient's obligation to comply with this subpart and to correct discriminatory practices impacts on and/or necessitates changes in a term of a collective bargaining agreement(s) to which the recipient is a party, the recipient shall attempt to achieve compliance consistent with the provisions of Sec. 32.17(a). However a recipient's obligation to comply with this subpart is not relieved by a term of any such collective bargaining agreement(s).

(d) Compensation. In offering employment or promotions to handicapped individuals, the recipient shall not reduce the amount of compensation offered because of any disability income, pension or other benefit the applicant or employee receives from other source.

32.13 Reasonable accommodation.

(a) A recipient shall make reasonable accommodation to the known physical or mental limitations of an otherwise qualified handicapped applicant, employee or participant unless the recipient can demonstrate that the accommodation would impose an undue hardship on the operation of its program.

(b) In determining pursuant to paragraph (a) of this section whether an accommodation would impose an undue hardship on the operation of a recipient's program, factors to be considered include;

(1) The overall size of the recipient's program with respect to number of employees, number of participants, number and type of facilities, and size of budget;

(2) The type of the recipient's operation, including the composition and structure of the recipient's workforce, and duration and type of training program; and

(3) The nature and cost of the accommodation needed.

(c) A recipient may not deny any employment or training opportunity to a qualified handicapped employee, applicant or participant if the basis for the denial is the need to make reasonable accommodation to the physical or mental limitations of the employee, applicant or participant.

(d) Nothing in this paragraph shall relieve a recipient of its obligation to make its program accessible as required in subpart C of this part, or to provide auxiliary aids, as required by Sec. 32.4(b)(7).

§ 32.14 Job qualifications.

(a) The recipient shall provide for, and shall adhere to, a schedule for the review of the appropriateness of all job qualifications to ensure that to the extent job qualifications tend to exclude handicapped individuals because of their handicap, they are related to the performance of the job and are consistent with business necessity and safe performance.

(b) Whenever a recipient applies job qualifications in the selection of applicants, employees or participants for employment or training or other change in employment status such as promotion, demotion or training, which would tend to exclude handicapped individuals because of their handicap, the qualifications shall be related to the specific job or jobs for which the individual is being considered and shall be consistent with business necessity and safe performance. The recipient shall have the burden to demonstrate that it has complied with the requirements of this paragraph.

§ 32.15 Preemployment inquiries.

(a) Except as provided in paragraphs (b) and (c) of this section, a recipient may not conduct preemployment medical examinations or make preemployment inquiry of an applicant for employment or training as to whether the applicant is a handicapped person or as to the nature or the severity of a handicap. A recipient may, however, make preemployment inquiry into an applicant's ability to perform job-related functions.

(b) When a recipient is taking remedial action to correct the effects of past discrimination, when a recipient is taking voluntary action to overcome the effects of conditions that resulted in limited participation in its federally-assisted program or activity, or when a recipient is taking affirmative action pursuant to section 503 of the Act, the recipient may invite applicants for employment or training to indicate whether and to what extent they are handicapped if:

(1) The recipient states clearly on any written questionnaire used for this purpose or makes clear orally, if no written questionnaire is used, that the information requested is intended for use solely in connection with its remedial action obligations or its voluntary or affirmative action efforts.

(2) The recipient states clearly that the information is being requested on a voluntary basis, that it will be kept confidential as provided in paragraph (d) of this section, that refusal to provide it will not subject the applicant, employee or participant to any adverse treatment, and that it will be used only in accordance with this part.

(c) An employer who routinely requires medical examinations as part of the employment selection process must demonstrate that each of the requirements of this subsection are met:

(1) The medical examination shall be performed by a physician qualified to make functional assessments of individuals in a form which will express residual capacity for work or training. Such an assessment does not require clinical determinations of disease or disability, but shall provide selecting or referring officials sufficient information regarding any functional limitations relevant to proper job placement or referral to

appropriate training programs. Factors which may be assessed may include, for example, use of limbs and extremities, mobility and posture, endurance and energy expenditure, ability to withstand various working conditions and environments, use of senses and mental capacity;

(2) The results of the medical examination shall be specific and objective so as to be susceptible to review by independent medical evaluators and shall be transmitted to the applicant or employee at the same time as the employing official;

(3) The results of the medical examination shall not be used to screen out qualified applicants and employees but to determine proper placement and reasonable accommodation. The employing official using physical or mental information obtained pursuant to this section should be familiar with physical or mental activities involved in performing the job, and the working conditions and environment in which it is carried out. If the applicant is being considered for a variety of jobs having different requirements or skills, the employing official should make a functional assessment of the physical or mental demands of the jobs in order to match the applicant with the most suitable vacancy;

(4) All of potential employees for the jobs are subjected to the medical examination;

(5) The procedures for using medical examinations or the medical information shall be constructed in such a manner that:

(i) A conditional job offer was made or the individual was conditionally placed in a job pool or conditionally placed on an eligibility list prior to the medical examination being performed; or

(ii) The results of the medical examination were considered by the employing official only after a conditional decision to make a job offer or the individual had been placed conditionally in a job pool or conditionally placed on an eligibility list; that is the medical results were the last factor evaluated by the employing officials before a final decision to make an offer of employment was made.

(6) Unless a conditional job offer is made prior to the medical examination, all potential employees for the job shall be informed at the time of the medical examination that:

(i) The results of the medical examination are the last factor evaluated by the employing official before a final decision to make an offer of employment is made, and

(ii) The medical examination results shall be transmitted to the employing official and the applicant only after a conditional decision to make a job offer has been made.

(d) Information obtained in accordance with this section as to the medical condition or history of the applicant shall be collected and maintained on separate forms that shall be accorded confidentiality as medical records, except that:

(1) Employing officials may obtain the information after making a conditional decision to make a job offer to the applicant or the applicant was placed conditionally in a job pool or placed conditionally on an eligibility list;

(2) Supervisors and managers may be informed regarding restricions on the work or duties of qualified handicapped persons and regarding necessary accommodations;

(3) First aid and safety personnel may be informed, where appropriate, if the condition might require emergency treatment; and

(4) Government officials investigating compliance with the Act shall be provided information upon request.

§ 32.16 Listing of employment openings.

Recipients should request State employment security agencies to refer qualified handicapped individuals for consideration for employment.

§ 32.17 Labor unions and recruiting and training agencies.

The performance of a recipient's obligations under the nondiscrimination provisions of these regulations may necessitate a revision in a collective bargaining agreement(s). The policy of the Department of Labor is to use its best efforts, directly or through the recipients, subgrantees, local officials, vocational rehabilitation facilities, and other available instrumentalities, to cause any labor union, recruiting and training agency or other representative or workers who are or may be engaged in work under programs of Federal financial assistance to cooperate with, and to comply in the implementation of section 504.

(b) To effectuate the purposes of paragraph (a) of this section, the Assistant Secretary may hold hearings, public or private, with respect to the practices and policies of any such labor union or recruiting and training agency.

(c) Whenever compliance with section 504 necessitates a revision of a collective bargaining agreement or otherwise significantly affects a substantial number of employees represented by the union, the collective bargaining representatives shall be given an opportunity to present their views to the Assistant Secretary.

(d) The Assistant Secretary may notify any Federal,

State, or local agency of his/her conclusions and recommendations with respect to any such labor organization or recruiting and training agency which in his/her judgment has failed to cooperate with the Department of Labor, recipients, subgrantees or applicants in carrying out the purposes of section 504. The Assistant Secretary also may notify other appropriate Federal agencies when there is reason to believe that the practices of any such labor organization or agency violates other provisions of Federal law.

Subpart C—Program Accessibility

§ 32.26 Discrimination prohibited.

No qualified handicapped individual shall, because a recipient's facilities are inaccessible to or unusable by handicapped individuals, be denied the benefits of, be excluded from participation in, or otherwise be subjected to discrimination under any program or activity to which this part applies.

§ 32.27 Access to programs.

(a) Purpose. A recipient shall operate each program or activity to which this part applies so that the program or activity, when viewed in its entirety, is readily accessible to qualified handicapped individuals. This paragraph does not require a recipient to make each of its existing facilities or every part of a facility accessible to and usable by qualified handicapped individuals. However, if a particular program is available in only one location, that site must be made accessible or the program must be made available at an alternative accessible site or sites. Program accessibility requires nonpersonal aids to make the program accessible to mobility impaired persons. Reasonable accommodations, as defined in Sec. 32.3, are required for particular handicapped individuals in response to the specific limitations of their handicaps.

(b) Scope and application.

(1) For the purpose of this subpart, prime sponsors under the Comprehensive Employment and Training Act and any other individual or organization which receives a grant directly from the Department to establish or operate any program or activity shall assure that the program or activity, including Public Service Employment, Work Experience, Classroom Training and On-the-Job-Training, when viewed in its entirety, is readily accessible to qualified handicapped individuals.

(2) Job Corps. All agencies, grantees, or contractors which screen or recruit applicants for the Job Corps shall comply with the nondiscrimination provisions of this part. Each regional office of the Department of Labor's Employment and Training Administration which makes the decision on the assignment of a Job Corps applicant to a particular center may, where it finds, after consultation with the qualified handicapped person seeking Job Corps services, that there is no method of complying with Sec. 32.27(a) at a particular Job Corps Center, other than by making a significant alteration in its existing facilities or in its training programs, assign that individual to another Job Corps Center which is accessible in accordance with this section and which is offering comparable training. The Job Corps, and each regional office of the Employment and Training Administration, shall assure that the Job Corps Program, when viewed in its entirety, is readily accessible to qualified handicapped individuals and that all future construction, including improvements to existing Centers, be made accessible to the handicapped.

(3) If a small recipient finds, after consultation with a qualified handicapped person seeking its services, that there is no method of complying with Sec. 32.27(a) other than making a significant alteration in its existing facilities or facility the recipient may, as an alternative, refer the qualified handicapped person to other providers of those services that are accessible.

(c) Methods. A recipient may comply with the requirement of Sec. 32.27(a) through such means as redesign of equipment, reassignment of classes or other services to accessible buildings, assignment of aides to beneficiaries, home visits, delivery of services at alternate accessible sites, alteration of existing facilities and construction of new facilities in conformance with the requirements of Sec. 32.28, or any other method that results in making its program or activity accessible to handicapped individuals. A recipient is not required to make structural changes in existing facilities where other methods are effective in achieving compliance with Sec. 32.27(a). In choosing among available methods for meeting the requirement of Sec. 32.27(a), a recipient shall give priority to those methods that offer programs and activities to handicapped persons in the most integrated setting appropriate.

(d) Time period. A recipient shall comply with the requirements of Sec. 32.27(a) within 60 days of the effective date of this part except that where structural changes in facilities are necessary, such changes shall be made within three years of the effective date of this part, but in any even as expeditiously as possible.

(e) Transition plan. In the event that structural changes to facilities are necessary to meet the requirement of Sec. 32.27(a), a recipient shall develop, within six months of the effective date of this part, a transition plan setting forth the steps necessary to complete such changes. The plan shall be developed with the assistance of interested persons, including qualified handicapped individuals. A copy of the transition plan shall be made available for public inspection. The plan shall, at a minimum:

(1) Identify physical obstacles in the recipient's facilities that limit the accessibility of its program or activity to qualified handicapped individuals;

(2) Describe in detail the methods that will be used to make the facilities accessible;

(3) Specify the schedule for taking the steps necessary to achieve full program accessibility and, if the time period of the transition plan is longer than one year, identify steps that will be taken during each year of the transition period; and

(4) Indicate the person responsible for implementation of the plan.

(f) Notice. The recipient shall adopt and implement procedures to ensure that interested persons, including persons with impaired vision or hearing, can obtain information as to the existence and location of services, activities, and facilities that are accessible to and usable by qualified handicapped individuals.

§ 32.28 Architectural standards.

(a) Design and construction. Each facility or part of a facility constructed by, on behalf of, or for the use of a recipient shall be designed and constructed in such manner that the facility or part of the facility is readily accessible to and usable by qualified handicapped individuals, if the construction was commenced after the effective date of this part.

(b) Alteration. Each facility or part of a facility which is altered by, on behalf of, or for the use of a recipient after the effective date of this part in a manner that affects or could affect the usability of the facility or part of the facility shall, to the maximum extent feasible, be altered in such manner that the altered portion of the facility is readily accessible to and usable by qualified handicapped individuals.

(c) Standards for architectural accessibility. Design, construction, or alteration of facilities under this subpart shall meet the most current standards for physical accessibility prescribed by the General Services Administration under the Architectural Barriers Act at 41 CFR 101-19.6. Alternative standards may be adopted when it is clearly evident that equivalent or greater access to the facility or part of the facility is thereby provided.

FAIR HOUSING

FAIR HOUSING ACT AMENDMENTS OF 1988

FAIR HOUSING ACT AMENDMENTS OF 1988

§ 3601. Declaration of policy

It is the policy of the United States to provide, within constitutional limitations, for fair housing throughout the United States.

§ 3602. Definitions

As used in this subchapter—

(a) "Secretary" means the Secretary of Housing and Urban Development.

(b) "Dwelling" means any building, structure, or portion thereof which is occupied as, or designed or intended for occupancy as, a residence by one or more families, and any vacant land which is offered for sale or lease for the construction or location thereon of any such building, structure, or portion thereof.

(c) "Family" includes a single individual.

(d) "Person" includes one or more individuals, corporations, partnerships, associations, labor organizations, legal representatives, mutual companies, joint-stock companies, trusts, unincorporated organizations, trustees, trustees in cases under Title 11, receivers, and fiduciaries.

(e) "To rent" includes to lease, to sublease, to let and otherwise to grant for a consideration the right to occupy premises not owned by the occupant.

(f) "Discriminatory housing practice" means an act that is unlawful under section 3604, 3605, 3606, or 3617 of this title.

(g) "State" means any of the several States, the District of Columbia, the Commonwealth of Puerto Rico, or any of the territories and possessions of the United States.

(h) "Handicap" means, with respect to a person—

(1) a physical or mental impairment which substantially limits one or more of such person's major life activities,

(2) a record of having such an impairment, or

(3) being regarded as having such an impairment,

but such term does not include current, illegal use of or addiction to a controlled substance as defined in section 802 of Title 21.

(i) "Aggrieved person" includes any person who—

(1) claims to have been injured by a discriminatory housing practice; or

(2) believes that such person will be injured by a discriminatory housing practice that is about to occur.

(j) "Complainant" means the person (including the Secretary) who files a complaint under section 3610 of this title.

(k) "Familial status" means one or more individuals (who have not attained the age of 18 years) being domiciled with—

(1) a parent or another person having legal custody of such individual or individuals; or

(2) the designee of such parent or other person having such custody, with the written permission of such parent or other person.

The protections afforded against discrimination on the basis of familial status shall apply to any person who is pregnant or is in the process of securing legal custody of any individual who has not attained the age of 18 years.

(l) "Conciliation" means the attempted resolution of issues raised by a complaint, or by the investigation of such complaint, through informal negotiations involving the aggrieved person, the respondent, and the Secretary.

(m) "Conciliation agreement" means a written agreement setting forth the resolution of the issues in conciliation.

(n) "Respondent" means—

(1) the person or other entity accused in a complaint of an unfair housing practice; and

(2) any other person or entity identified in the course of investigation and notified as required with respect to respondents so identified under section 3610(a) of this title.

(o) "Prevailing party" has the same meaning as such term has in section 1988 of this title.

§ 3603. Effective dates of certain prohibitions

(a) Application to certain described dwellings

Subject to the provisions of subsection (b) of this section and section 3607 of this title, the prohibitions against discrimination in the sale or rental of housing set forth in section 3604 of this title shall apply:

(1) Upon enactment of this subchapter, to—

(A) dwellings owned or operated by the Federal Government;

(B) dwellings provided in whole or in part with the aid of loans, advances, grants, or contributions made by the Federal Government, under agreements entered into after November 20, 1962, unless payment due thereon has been made in full prior to April 11, 1968;

(C) dwellings provided in whole or in part by loans insured, guaranteed, or otherwise secured by the credit of the Federal Government, under agreements entered into after November 20, 1962, unless payment thereon has been made in full prior to April 11, 1968: Provided, That nothing contained in subparagraphs (B) and (C) of this subsection shall be applicable to dwellings solely by virtue of the fact that they are subject to mortgages held by an FDIC or FSLIC institution; and

(D) dwellings provided by the development or the redevelopment of real property purchased, rented, or otherwise obtained from a State or local public agency receiving Federal financial assistance for slum clearance or urban renewal with respect to such real property under loan or grant contracts entered into after November 20, 1962.

(2) After December 31, 1968, to all dwellings covered by paragraph (1) and to all other dwellings except as exempted by subsection (b) of this section.

(b) Exemptions

Nothing in section 3604 of this title (other than subsection (c)) shall apply to—

(1) any single-family house sold or rented by an owner: Provided, That such private individual owner does not own more than three such single-family houses at any one time: Provided further, That in the case of the sale of any such single-family house by a private individual owner not residing in such house at the time of such sale or who was not the most recent resident of such house prior to such sale, the exemption granted by this subsection shall apply only with respect to one such sale within any twenty-four month period: Provided further, That such bona fide private individual owner does not own any interest in, nor is there owned or reserved on his behalf, under any express or voluntary agreement, title to or any right to all or a portion of the proceeds from the sale or rental of, more than three such single-family houses at any one time: Provided further, That after December 31, 1969, the sale or rental of any such single-family house shall be excepted from the application of this subchapter only if such house is sold or rented (A) without the use in any manner of the sales or rental facilities or the sales or rental services of any real estate broker, agent, or salesman, or of such facilities or services of any person in the business of selling or renting dwellings, or of any employee or agent of any such broker, agent, salesman, or person and (B) without the publication, posting or mailing, after notice, of any advertisement or written notice in violation of section 3604(c) of this title; but nothing in this proviso shall prohibit the use of attorneys, escrow agents, abstractors, title companies, and other such professional assistance as necessary to perfect or transfer the title, or

(2) rooms or units in dwellings containing living quarters occupied or intended to be occupied by no more than four families living independently of each other, if the owner actually maintains and occupies one of such living quarters as his residence.

(c) Business of selling or renting dwellings defined

For the purposes of subsection (b) of this section, a person shall be deemed to be in the business of selling or renting dwellings if—

(1) he has, within the preceding twelve months, participated as principal in three or more transactions involving the sale or rental of any dwelling or any interest therein, or

(2) he has, within the preceding twelve months, participated as agent, other than in the sale of his own personal residence in providing sales or rental facilities or sales or rental services in two or more transactions involving the sale or rental of any dwelling or any interest therein, or

(3) he is the owner of any dwelling designed or intended for occupancy by, or occupied by, five or more families.

§ 3604. Discrimination in the sale or rental of housing and other prohibited practices

As made applicable by section 3603 of this title and except as exempted by sections 3603(b) and 3607 of this title, it shall be unlawful—

(a) To refuse to sell or rent after the making of a bona fide offer, or to refuse to negotiate for the sale or rental of, or otherwise make unavailable or deny, a dwelling to any person because of race, color, religion, sex, familial status, or national origin.

(b) To discriminate against any person in the terms, conditions, or privileges of sale or rental of a dwelling, or in the provision of services or facilities in connection therewith, because of race, color, religion, sex, familial status, or national origin.

(c) To make, print, or publish, or cause to be made, printed, or published any notice, statement, or advertisement, with respect to the sale or rental of a dwelling that indicates any preference, limitation, or discrimination based on race, color, religion, sex, handicap, familial status, or national origin, or an intention to make any such preference, limitation, or discrimination.

(d) To represent to any person because of race, color, religion, sex, handicap, familial status, or national origin that any dwelling is not available for inspection, sale, or rental when such dwelling is in fact so available.

(e) For profit, to induce or attempt to induce any person to sell or rent any dwelling by representations regarding the entry or prospective entry into the neighborhood of a person or persons of a particular race, color, religion, sex, handicap, familial status, or national origin.

(f)(1) To discriminate in the sale or rental, or to otherwise make unavailable or deny, a dwelling to any buyer or renter because of a handicap of—

(A) that buyer or renter;

(B) a person residing in or intending to reside in that dwelling after it is so sold, rented, or made available; or

(C) any person associated with that buyer or renter.

(2) To discriminate against any person in the terms, conditions, or privileges of sale or rental of a dwelling, or in the provision of services or facilities in connection with such dwelling, because of a handicap of—

(A) that person; or

(B) a person residing in or intending to reside in that dwelling after it is so sold, rented, or made available; or

(C) any person associated with that person.

(3) For purposes of this subsection, discrimination includes—

(A) a refusal to permit, at the expense of the handicapped person, reasonable modifications of existing premises occupied or to be occupied by such person if such modifications may be necessary to afford such person full enjoyment of the premises except that, in the case of a rental, the landlord may where it is reasonable to do so condition permission for a modification on the renter agreeing to restore the interior of the premises to the condition that existed before the modification, reasonable wear and tear excepted;

(B) a refusal to make reasonable accommodations in rules, policies, practices, or services, when such accommodations may be necessary to afford such person equal opportunity to use and enjoy a dwelling; or

(C) in connection with the design and construction of covered multifamily dwellings for first occupancy after the date that is 30 months after September 13, 1988, a failure to design and construct those dwellings in such a manner that—(i) the public use and common use portions of such dwellings are readily accessible to and usable by handicapped persons;

(ii) all the doors designed to allow passage into and within all premises within such dwellings are sufficiently wide to allow passage by handicapped persons in wheelchairs; and

(iii) all premises within such dwellings contain the following features of adaptive design:

(I) an accessible route into and through the dwelling;

(II) light switches, electrical outlets, thermostats, and other environmental controls in accessible locations;

(III) reinforcements in bathroom walls to allow later installation of grab bars; and

(IV) usable kitchens and bathrooms such that an individual in a wheelchair can maneuver about the space.

(4) Compliance with the appropriate requirements of the American National Standard for buildings and facilities providing accessibility and usability for physically handicapped people (commonly cited as "ANSI A117.1") suffices to satisfy the requirements of paragraph (3)(C)(iii).

(5)(A) If a State or unit of general local government has incorporated into its laws the requirements set forth in paragraph (3)(C), compliance with such laws shall be deemed to satisfy the requirements of that paragraph.

(B) A State or unit of general local government may review and approve newly constructed covered multifamily dwellings for the purpose of making determinations as to whether the design and construction requirements of paragraph (3)(C) are met.

(C) The Secretary shall encourage, but may not require, States and units of local government to include in their existing procedures for the review and approval of newly constructed covered multifamily dwellings, determinations as to whether the design and construction of such dwellings are consistent with paragraph (3)(C), and shall provide technical assistance to States and units of local government and other persons to implement the requirements of paragraph (3)(C).

(D) Nothing in this subchapter shall be construed to require the Secretary to review or approve the plans, designs or construction of all covered multifamily dwellings, to determine whether the design and construction of such dwellings are consistent with the requirements of paragraph 3(C).

(6)(A) Nothing in paragraph (5) shall be construed to affect the authority and responsibility of the

Secretary or a State or local public agency certified pursuant to section 3610(f)(3) of this title to receive and process complaints or otherwise engage in enforcement activities under this subchapter.

(B) Determinations by a State or a unit of general local government under paragraphs (5)(A) and (B) shall not be conclusive in enforcement proceedings under this subchapter.

(7) As used in this subsection, the term "covered multifamily dwellings" means—

(A) buildings consisting of 4 or more units if such buildings have one or more elevators; and

(B) ground floor units in other buildings consisting of 4 or more units.

(8) Nothing in this subchapter shall be construed to invalidate or limit any law of a State or political subdivision of a State, or other jurisdiction in which this subchapter shall be effective, that requires dwellings to be designed and constructed in a manner that affords handicapped persons greater access than is required by this subchapter.

(9) Nothing in this subsection requires that a dwelling be made available to an individual whose tenancy would constitute a direct threat to the health or safety of other individuals or whose tenancy would result in substantial physical damage to the property of others.

§ 3605. Discrimination in residential real estate-related transactions

(a) In general

It shall be unlawful for any person or other entity whose business includes engaging in residential real estate-related transactions to discriminate against any person in making available such a transaction, or in the terms or conditions of such a transaction, because of race, color, religion, sex, handicap, familial status, or national origin.

(b) Definition

As used in this section, the term "residential real estate-related transaction" means any of the following:

(1) The making or purchasing of loans or providing other financial assistance—

(A) for purchasing, constructing, improving, repairing, or maintaining a dwelling; or

(B) secured by residential real estate.

(2) The selling, brokering, or appraising of residential real property.

(c) Appraisal exemption

Nothing in this subchapter prohibits a person engaged in the business of furnishing appraisals of real property to take into consideration factors other than race, color, religion, national origin, sex, handicap, or familial status.

§ 3606. Discrimination in provision of brokerage services

After December 31, 1968, it shall be unlawful to deny any person access to or membership or participation in any multiple-listing service, real estate brokers' organization or other service, organization, or facility relating to the business of selling or renting dwellings, or to discriminate against him in the terms or conditions of such access, membership, or participation, on account of race, color, religion, sex, handicap, familial status, or national origin.

§ 3607. Exemption

(a) Religious organizations and private clubs

Nothing in this subchapter shall prohibit a religious organization, association, or society, or any nonprofit institution or organization operated, supervised or controlled by or in conjunction with a religious organization, association, or society, from limiting the sale, rental or occupancy of dwellings which it owns or operates for other than a commercial purpose to persons of the same religion, or from giving preference to such persons, unless membership in such religion is restricted on account of race, color, or national origin. Nor shall anything in this subchapter prohibit a private club not in fact open to the public, which as an incident to its primary purpose or purposes provides lodgings which it owns or operates for other than a commercial purpose, from limiting the rental or occupancy of such lodgings to its members or from giving preference to its members.

(b) Numbers of occupants; housing for older persons; persons convicted of making or distributing controlled substances

(1) Nothing in this subchapter limits the applicability of any reasonable local, State, or Federal restrictions regarding the maximum number of occupants permitted to occupy a dwelling. Nor does any provision in this subchapter regarding familial status apply with respect to housing for older persons.

(2) As used in this section, "housing for older persons" means housing—

(A) provided under any State or Federal program that the Secretary determines is specifically designed and operated to assist elderly persons (as defined in the State or Federal program); or

(B) intended for, and solely occupied by, persons 62 years of age or older; or

(C) intended and operated for occupancy by persons 55 years of age or older, and—

(i) at least 80 percent of the occupied units are occupied by at least one person who is 55 years of age or older;

(ii) the housing facility or community publishes and adheres to policies and procedures that demonstrate the intent required under this subparagraph; and

(iii) the housing facility or community complies with rules issued by the Secretary for verification of occupancy, which shall—

(I) provide for verification by reliable surveys and affidavits; and

(II) include examples of the types of policies and procedures relevant to a determination of compliance with the requirement of clause (ii). Such surveys and affidavits shall be admissible in administrative and judicial proceedings for the purposes of such verification.

(3) Housing shall not fail to meet the requirements for housing for older persons by reason of:

(A) persons residing in such housing as of September 13, 1988, who do not meet the age requirements of subsections (2)(B) or (C): Provided, That new occupants of such housing meet the age requirements of subsection (2)(B) or (C); or

(B) unoccupied units: Provided, That such units are reserved for occupancy by persons who meet the age requirements of subsection (2)(B) or (C).

(4) Nothing in this subchapter prohibits conduct against a person because such person has been convicted by any court of competent jurisdiction of the illegal manufacture or distribution of a controlled substance as defined in section 802 of Title 21.

(5)(A) A person shall not be held personally liable for monetary damages for a violation of this subchapter if such person reasonably relied, in good faith, on the application of the exemption under this subsection relating to housing for older persons.

(B) For the purposes of this paragraph, a person may only show good faith reliance on the application of the exemption by showing that—

(i) such person has no actual knowledge that the facility or community is not, or will not be, eligible for such exemption; and

(ii) the facility or community has stated formally, in writing, that the facility or community complies with the requirements for such exemption.

FAIR HOUSING ACT AMENDMENTS HUD REGULATIONS

24 C.F.R §

Subpart A—General

Subpart B—Discriminatory Housing Practices

Subpart C—Discrimination in Residential Real Estate-Related Transactions

Subpart D—Prohibition Against Discrimination Because of Handicap

FAIR HOUSING ACT AMENDMENTS HUD REGULATIONS

Subpart A—General

§ 100.1 Authority.

This regulation is issued under the authority of the Secretary of Housing and Urban Development to administer and enforce Title VIII of the Civil Rights Act of 1968, as amended by the Fair Housing Amendments Act of 1988 (the Fair Housing Act).

§ 100.5 Scope.

(a) It is the policy of the United States to provide, within constitutional limitations, for fair housing throughout the United States. No person shall be subjected to discrimination because of race, color, religion, sex, handicap, familial status, or national origin in the sale, rental, or advertising of dwellings, in the provision of brokerage services, or in the availability of residential real estate-related transactions.

(b) This part provides the Department's interpretation of the coverage of the Fair Housing Act regarding discrimination related to the sale or rental of dwellings, the provision of services in connection therewith, and the availability of residential real estate-related transactions.

(c) Nothing in this part relieves persons participating in a Federal or Federally-assisted program or activity from other requirements applicable to buildings and dwellings.

§ 100.10 Exemptions.

(a) This part does not:

(1) Prohibit a religious organization, association, or society, or any nonprofit institution or organization operated, supervised or controlled by or in conjunction with a religious organization, association, or society, from limiting the sale, rental or occupancy of dwellings which it owns or operates for other than a commercial purpose to persons of the same religion, or from giving preference to such persons, unless membership in such religion is restricted because of race, color, or national origin;

(2) Prohibit a private club, not in fact open to

the public, which, incident to its primary purpose or purposes, provides lodgings which it owns or operates for other than a commercial purpose, from limiting the rental or occupancy of such lodgings to its members or from giving preference to its members;

(3) Limit the applicability of any reasonable local, State or Federal restrictions regarding the maximum number of occupants permitted to occupy a dwelling; or

(4) Prohibit conduct against a person because such person has been convicted by any court of competent jurisdiction of the illegal manufacture or distribution of a controlled substance as defined in Section 102 of the Controlled Substances Act (21 U.S.C. 802).

(b) Nothing in this part regarding discrimination based on familial status applies with respect to housing for older persons as defined in Subpart E of this part.

(c) Nothing in this part, other than the prohibitions against discriminatory advertising, applies to:

(1) The sale or rental of any single family house by an owner, provided the following conditions are met:

(i) The owner does not own or have any interest in more than three single family houses at any one time.

(ii) The house is sold or rented without the use of a real estate broker, agent or salesperson or the facilities of any person in the business of selling or renting dwellings. If the owner selling the house does not reside in it at the time of the sale or was not the most recent resident of the house prior to such sale, the exemption in this paragraph (c)(1) of this section applies to only one such sale in any 24-month period.

(2) Rooms or units in dwellings containing living quarters occupied or intended to be occupied by no more than four families living independently of each other, if the owner actually maintains and occupies one of such living quarters as his or her residence.

§ 100.20 Definitions.

The terms "Department," "Fair Housing Act," and "Secretary" are defined in 24 CFR part 5. As used in this part:

"Aggrieved person" includes any person who—

(a) Claims to have been injured by a discriminatory housing practice; or

(b) Believes that such person will be injured by a discriminatory housing practice that is about to occur.

"Broker" or "Agent" includes any person authorized to perform an action on behalf of another person regarding any matter related to the sale or rental of dwellings, including offers, solicitations or contracts and the administration of matters regarding such offers, solicitations or contracts or any residential real estate-related transactions.

"Discriminatory housing practice" means an act that is unlawful under section 804, 805, 806, or 818 of the Fair Housing Act.

"Dwelling" means any building, structure or portion thereof which is occupied as, or designed or intended for occupancy as, a residence by one or more families, and any vacant land which is offered for sale or lease for the construction or location thereon of any such building, structure or portion thereof.

"Familial status" means one or more individuals (who have not attained the age of 18 years) being domiciled with—

(a) A parent or another person having legal custody of such individual or individuals; or

(b) The designee of such parent or other person having such custody, with the written permission of such parent or other person.

The protections afforded against discrimination on the basis of familial status shall apply to any person who is pregnant or is in the process of securing legal custody of any individual who has not attained the age of 18 years.

"Handicap" is defined in § 100.201.

"Person" includes one or more individuals, corporations, partnerships, associations, labor organizations, legal representatives, mutual companies, joint-stock companies, trusts, unincorporated organizations, trustees, trustees in cases under Title 11 of the United States Code, receivers, and fiduciaries.

"Person in the business of selling or renting dwellings" means any person who:

(a) Within the preceding twelve months, has participated as principal in three or more transactions involving the sale or rental of any dwelling or any interest therein;

(b) Within the preceding twelve months, has participated as agent, other than in the sale of his or her own personal residence, in providing sales or rental facilities or sales or rental services in two or more transactions involving the sale or rental of any dwelling or any interest therein; or

(c) Is the owner of any dwelling designed or intended for occupancy by, or occupied by, five or more families.

"State" means any of the several states, the District of Columbia, the Commonwealth of Puerto Rico, or any of the territories and possessions of the United States.

Subpart B—Discriminatory Housing Practices

§ 100.50 Real estate practices prohibited.

(a) This subpart provides the Department's interpretation of conduct that is unlawful housing discrimination under section 804 and section 806 of the Fair Housing Act. In general the prohibited actions are set forth under sections of this subpart which are most applicable to the discriminatory conduct described. However, an action illustrated in one section can constitute a violation under sections in the subpart. For example, the conduct described in § 100.60(b)(3) and (4) would constitute a violation of § 100.65(a) as well as § 100.60(a).

(b) It shall be unlawful to:

(1) Refuse to sell or rent a dwelling after a bona fide offer has been made, or to refuse to negotiate for the sale or rental of a dwelling because of race, color, religion, sex, familial status, or national origin, or to discriminate in the sale or rental of a dwelling because of handicap.

(2) Discriminate in the terms, conditions or privileges of sale or rental of a dwelling, or in the provision of services or facilities in connection with sales or rentals, because of race, color, religion, sex, handicap, familial status, or national origin.

(3) Engage in any conduct relating to the provision of housing which otherwise makes unavailable or denies dwellings to persons because of race, color, religion, sex, handicap, familial status, or national origin.

(4) Make, print or publish, or cause to be made, printed or published, any notice, statement or advertisement with respect to the sale or rental of a dwelling that indicates any preference, limitation or discrimination because of race, color, religion, sex, handicap, familial status, or national origin, or an intention to make any such preference, limitation or discrimination.

(5) Represent to any person because of race, color, religion, sex, handicap, familial status, or national origin that a dwelling is not available for sale or rental when such dwelling is in fact available.

(6) Engage in blockbusting practices in connection with the sale or rental of dwellings because of race, color, religion, sex, handicap, familial status, or national origin.

(7) Deny access to or membership or participation in, or to discriminate against any person in his or her access to or membership or participation in, any multiple-listing service, real estate brokers' association, or other service organization or facility relating to the business of selling or renting a dwelling or in the terms or conditions or membership or participation, because of race, color, religion, sex, handicap, familial status, or national origin.

(c) The application of the Fair Housing Act with respect to persons with handicaps is discussed in Subpart D of this part.

§ 100.60 Unlawful refusal to sell or rent or to negotiate for the sale or rental.

(a) It shall be unlawful for a person to refuse to sell or rent a dwelling to a person who has made a bona fide offer, because of race, color, religion, sex, familial status, or national origin or to refuse to negotiate with a person for the sale or rental of a dwelling because of race, color, religion, sex, familial status, or national origin, or to discriminate against any person in the sale or rental of a dwelling because of handicap.

(b) Prohibited actions under this section include, but are not limited to:

(1) Failing to accept or consider a bona fide offer because of race, color, religion, sex, handicap, familial status, or national origin.

(2) Refusing to sell or rent a dwelling to, or to negotiate for the sale or rental of a dwelling with, any person because of race, color, religion, sex, handicap, familial status, or national origin.

(3) Imposing different sales prices or rental charges for the sale or rental of a dwelling upon any person because of race, color, religion, sex, handicap, familial status, or national origin.

(4) Using different qualification criteria or applications, or sale or rental standards or procedures, such as income standards, application requirements, application fees, credit analysis or sale or rental approval procedures or other requirements, because of race, color, religion, sex, handicap, familial status, or national origin.

(5) Evicting tenants because of their race, color, religion, sex, handicap, familial status, or national origin or because of the race, color, religion, sex, handicap, familial status, or national origin of a tenant's guest.

§ 100.65 Discrimination in terms, conditions and privileges and in services and facilities.

(a) It shall be unlawful, because of race, color, religion, sex, handicap, familial status, or national origin, to impose different terms, conditions or privileges relating to the sale or rental of a dwelling or to deny or limit services or facilities in connection with the sale or rental of a dwelling.

(b) Prohibited actions under this section include, but are not limited to:

(1) Using different provisions in leases or contracts of sale, such as those relating to rental charges, security deposits and the terms of a lease and those relating to down payment and closing requirements, because of race, color, religion, sex, handicap, familial status, or national origin.

(2) Failing or delaying maintenance or repairs of sale or rental dwellings because of race, color, religion, sex, handicap, familial status, or national origin.

(3) Failing to process an offer for the sale or rental of a dwelling or to communicate an offer accurately because of race, color, religion, sex, handicap, familial status, or national origin.

(4) Limiting the use of privileges, services or facilities associated with a dwelling because of race, color, religion, sex, handicap, familial status, or national origin of an owner, tenant or a person associated with him or her.

(5) Denying or limiting services or facilities in connection with the sale or rental of a dwelling, because a person failed or refused to provide sexual favors.

§ 100.70 Other prohibited sale and rental conduct.

(a) It shall be unlawful, because of race, color, religion, sex, handicap, familial status, or national origin, to restrict or attempt to restrict the choices of a person by word or conduct in connection with seeking, negotiating for, buying or renting a dwelling so as to perpetuate, or tend to perpetuate, segregated housing patterns, or to discourage or obstruct choices in a community, neighborhood or development.

(b) It shall be unlawful, because of race, color, religion, sex, handicap, familial status, or national origin, to engage in any conduct relating to the provision of housing or of services and facilities in connection therewith that otherwise makes unavailable or denies dwellings to persons.

(c) Prohibited actions under paragraph (a) of this section, which are generally referred to as unlawful steering practices, include, but are not limited to:

(1) Discouraging any person from inspecting, purchasing or renting a dwelling because of race, color, religion, sex, handicap, familial status, or national origin, or because of the race, color, religion, sex, handicap, familial status, or national origin of persons in a community, neighborhood or development.

(2) Discouraging the purchase or rental of a dwelling because of race, color, religion, sex, handicap, familial status, or national origin, by exaggerating drawbacks or failing to inform any person of desirable fea-tures of a dwelling or of a community, neighborhood, or development.

(3) Communicating to any prospective purchaser that he or she would not be comfortable or compatible with existing residents of a community, neighborhood or development because of race, color, religion, sex, handicap, familial status, or national origin.

(4) Assigning any person to a particular section of a community, neighborhood or development, or to a particular floor of a building, because of race, color, religion, sex, handicap, familial status, or national origin.

(d) Prohibited activities relating to dwellings under paragraph (b) of this section include, but are not limited to:

(1) Discharging or taking other adverse action against an employee, broker or agent because he or she refused to participate in a discriminatory housing practice.

(2) Employing codes or other devices to segregate or reject applicants, purchasers or renters, refusing to take or to show listings of dwellings in certain areas because of race, color, religion, sex, handicap, familial status, or national origin, or refusing to deal with certain brokers or agents because they or one or more of their clients are of a particular race, color, religion, sex, handicap, familial status, or national origin.

(3) Denying or delaying the processing of an application made by a purchaser or renter or refusing to approve such a person for occupancy in a cooperative or condominium dwelling because of race, color, religion, sex, handicap, familial status, or national origin.

(4) Refusing to provide municipal services or property or hazard insurance for dwellings or providing such services or insurance differently because of race, color, religion, sex, handicap, familial status, or national origin.

§ 100.75 Discriminatory advertisements, statements and notices.

(a) It shall be unlawful to make, print or publish, or cause to be made, printed or published, any notice, statement or advertisement with respect to the sale or rental of a dwelling which indicates any preference, limitation or discrimination because of race, color, religion, sex, handicap, familial status, or national origin, or an intention to make any such preference, limitation or discrimination.

(b) The prohibitions in this section shall apply to all

written or oral notices or statements by a person engaged in the sale or rental of a dwelling. Written notices and statements include any applications, flyers, brochures, deeds, signs, banners, posters, billboards or any documents used with respect to the sale or rental of a dwelling.

(c) Discriminatory notices, statements and advertisements include, but are not limited to:

(1) Using words, phrases, photographs, illustrations, symbols or forms which convey that dwellings are available or not available to a particular group of persons because of race, color, religion, sex, handicap, familial status, or national origin.

(2) Expressing to agents, brokers, employees, prospective sellers or renters or any other persons a preference for or limitation on any purchaser or renter because of race, color, religion, sex, handicap, familial status, or national origin of such persons.

(3) Selecting media or locations for advertising the sale or rental of dwellings which deny particular segments of the housing market information about housing opportunities because of race, color, religion, sex, handicap, familial status, or national origin.

(4) Refusing to publish advertising for the sale or rental of dwellings or requiring different charges or terms for such advertising because of race, color, religion, sex, handicap, familial status, or national origin.

(d) 24 CFR Part 109 provides information to assist persons to advertise dwellings in a nondiscriminatory manner and describes the matters the Department will review in evaluating compliance with the Fair Housing Act and in investigating complaints alleging discriminatory housing practices involving advertising.

§ 100.80 Discriminatory representations on the availability of dwellings.

(a) It shall be unlawful, because of race, color, religion, sex, handicap, familial status, or national origin, to provide inaccurate or untrue information about the availability of dwellings for sale or rental.

(b) Prohibited actions under this section include, but are not limited to:

(1) Indicating through words or conduct that a dwelling which is available for inspection, sale, or rental has been sold or rented, because of race, color, religion, sex, handicap, familial status, or national origin.

(2) Representing that covenants or other deed, trust or lease provisions which purport to restrict the sale or rental of dwellings because of race, color, religion, sex, handicap, familial status, or national origin preclude the sale of rental of a dwelling to a person.

(3) Enforcing covenants or other deed, trust, or lease provisions which preclude the sale or rental of a dwelling to any person because of race, color, religion, sex, handicap, familial status, or national origin.

(4) Limiting information, by word or conduct, regarding suitably priced dwellings available for inspection, sale or rental, because of race, color, religion, sex, handicap, familial status, or national origin.

(5) Providing false or inaccurate information regarding the availability of a dwelling for sale or rental to any person, including testers, regardless of whether such person is actually seeking housing, because of race, color, religion, sex, handicap, familial status, or national origin.

§ 100.85 Blockbusting.

(a) It shall be unlawful, for profit, to induce or attempt to induce a person to sell or rent a dwelling by representations regarding the entry or prospective entry into the neighborhood of a person or persons of a particular race, color, religion, sex, familial status, or national origin or with a handicap.

(b) In establishing a discriminatory housing practice under this section it is not necessary that there was in fact profit as long as profit was a factor for engaging in the blockbusting activity.

(c) Prohibited actions under this section include, but are not limited to:

(1) Engaging, for profit, in conduct (including uninvited solicitations for listings) which conveys to a person that a neighborhood is undergoing or is about to undergo a change in the race, color, religion, sex, handicap, familial status, or national origin of persons residing in it, in order to encourage the person to offer a dwelling for sale or rental.

(2) Encouraging, for profit, any person to sell or rent a dwelling through assertions that the entry or prospective entry of persons of a particular race, color, religion, sex, familial status, or national origin, or with handicaps, can or will result in undesirable consequences for the project, neighborhood or community, such as a lowering of property values, an increase in criminal or antisocial behavior, or a decline in the quality of schools or other services or facilities.

§ 100.90 Discrimination in the provision of brokerage services.

(a) It shall be unlawful to deny any person access to or membership or participation in any multiple listing service, real estate brokers' organization or other service, organization, or facility relating to the business of selling or renting dwellings, or to discriminate against any person in the terms or conditions of such access, membership or participation, because of race, color, religion, sex, handicap, familial status, or national origin.

(b) Prohibited actions under this section include, but are not limited to:

(1) Setting different fees for access to or membership in a multiple listing service because of race, color, religion, sex, handicap, familial status, or national origin.

(2) Denying or limiting benefits accruing to members in a real estate brokers' organization because of race, color, religion, sex, handicap, familial status, or national origin.

(3) Imposing different standards or criteria for membership in a real estate sales or rental organization because of race, color, religion, sex, handicap, familial status, or national origin.

(4) Establishing geographic boundaries or office location or residence requirements for access to or membership or participation in any multiple listing service, real estate brokers' organization or other service, organization or facility relating to the business of selling or renting dwellings, because of race, color, religion, sex, handicap, familial status, or national origin.

Subpart C—Discrimination in Residential Real Estate-Related Transactions

§ 100.110 Discriminatory practices in residential real estate-related transactions.

(a) This subpart provides the Department's interpretation of the conduct that is unlawful housing discrimination under section 805 of the Fair Housing Act.

(b) It shall be unlawful for any person or other entity whose business includes engaging in residential real estate-related transactions to discriminate against any person in making available such a transaction, or in the terms or conditions of such a transaction, because of race, color, religion, sex, handicap, familial status, or national origin.

§ 100.115 Residential real estate-related transactions.

The term residential "real estate-related transactions" means:

(a) The making or purchasing of loans or providing other financial assistance—

(1) For purchasing, constructing, improving, repairing or maintaining a dwelling; or

(2) Secured by residential real estate; or

(b) The selling, brokering or appraising of residential real property.

§ 100.120 Discrimination in the making of loans and in the provision of other financial assistance.

(a) It shall be unlawful for any person or entity whose business includes engaging in residential real estate-related transactions to discriminate against any person in making available loans or other financial assistance for a dwelling, or which is or is to be secured by a dwelling, because of race, color, religion, sex, handicap, familial status, or national origin.

(b) Prohibited practices under this section include, but are not limited to, failing or refusing to provide to any person, in connection with a residential real estate-related transaction, information regarding the availability of loans or other financial assistance, application requirements, procedures or standards for the review and approval of loans or financial assistance, or providing information which is inaccurate or different from that provided others, because of race, color, religion, sex, handicap, familial status, or national origin.

§ 100.125 Discrimination in the purchasing of loans.

(a) It shall be unlawful for any person or entity engaged in the purchasing of loans or other debts or securities which support the purchase, construction, improvement, repair or maintenance of a dwelling, or which are secured by residential real estate, to refuse to purchase such loans, debts, or securities, or to impose different terms or conditions for such purchases, because of race, color, religion, sex, handicap, familial status, or national origin.

(b) Unlawful conduct under this section includes, but is not limited to:

(1) Purchasing loans or other debts or securities which relate to, or which are secured by dwellings in certain communities or neighborhoods but not in others because of the race, color, religion, sex, handicap, familial status, or national origin of persons in such neighborhoods or communities.

(2) Pooling or packaging loans or other debts or securities which relate to, or which are secured by, dwellings differently because of race, color, religion, sex, handicap, familial status, or national origin.

(3) Imposing or using different terms or conditions on the marketing or sale of securities issued on the basis of loans or other debts or securities which relate to, or which are secured by, dwellings because

of race, color, religion, sex, handicap, familial status, or national origin.

(c) This section does not prevent consideration, in the purchasing of loans, of factors justified by business necessity, including requirements of Federal law, relating to a transaction's financial security or to protection against default or reduction of the value of the security. Thus, this provision would not preclude considerations employed in normal and prudent transactions, provided that no such factor may in any way relate to race, color, religion, sex, handicap, familial status or national origin.

§ 100.130 Discrimination in the terms and conditions for making available loans or other financial assistance.

(a) It shall be unlawful for any person or entity engaged in the making of loans or in the provision of other financial assistance relating to the purchase, construction, improvement, repair or maintenance of dwellings or which are secured by residential real estate to impose different terms or conditions for the availability of such loans or other financial assistance because of race, color, religion, sex, handicap, familial status, or national origin.

(b) Unlawful conduct under this section includes, but is not limited to:

(1) Using different policies, practices or procedures in evaluating or in determining credit-worthiness of any person in connection with the provision of any loan or other financial assistance for a dwelling or for any loan or other financial assistance which is secured by residential real estate because of race, color, religion, sex, handicap, familial status, or national origin.

(2) Determining the type of loan or other financial assistance to be provided with respect to a dwelling, or fixing the amount, interest rate, duration or other terms for a loan or other financial assistance for a dwelling or which is secured by residential real estate, because of race, color, religion, sex, handicap, familial status, or national origin.

§ 100.135 Unlawful practices in the selling, brokering, or appraising of residential real property.

(a) It shall be unlawful for any person or other entity whose business includes engaging in the selling, brokering or appraising of residential real property to discriminate against any person in making available such services, or in the performance of such services, because of race, color, religion, sex, handicap, familial status, or national origin.

(b) For the purposes of this section, the term appraisal means an estimate or opinion of the value of a specified residential real property made in a business context in connection with the sale, rental, financing or refinancing of a dwelling or in connection with any activity that otherwise affects the availability of a residential real estate-related transaction, whether the appraisal is oral or written, or transmitted formally or informally. The appraisal includes all written comments and other documents submitted as support for the estimate or opinion of value.

(c) Nothing in this section prohibits a person engaged in the business of making or furnishing appraisals of residential real property from taking into consideration factors other than race, color, religion, sex, handicap, familial status, or national origin.

(d) Practices which are unlawful under this section include, but are not limited to, using an appraisal of residential real property in connection with the sale, rental, or financing of any dwelling where the person knows or reasonably should know that the appraisal improperly takes into consideration race, color, religion, sex, handicap, familial status or national origin.

Subpart D—Prohibition Against Discrimination Because of Handicap

§ 100.200 Purpose.

The purpose of this subpart is to effectuate sections 6 (a) and (b) and 15 of the Fair Housing Amendments Act of 1988.

§ 100.201 Definitions.

As used in this subpart:

"Accessible", when used with respect to the public and common use areas of a building containing covered multifamily dwellings, means that the public or common use areas of the building can be approached, entered, and used by individuals with physical handicaps. The phrase "readily accessible to and usable by" is synonymous with accessible. A public or common usc arca that complies with the appropriate requirements of ANSI A117.1-1986 or a comparable standard is "accessible" within the meaning of this paragraph.

"Accessible route" means a continuous unobstructed path connecting accessible elements and spaces in a building or within a site that can be negotiated by a person with a severe disability using a wheelchair and that is also safe for and usable by people with other disabilities. Interior accessible routes may include corridors, floors, ramps, elevators and lifts. Exterior accessible routes may include parking access aisles, curb ramps, walks, ramps and lifts. A route that complies with the appropriate requirements of ANSI A117.1-1986 or a comparable standard is an "accessible route".

"ANSI A117.1-1986" means the 1986 edition of the American National Standard for buildings and facilities providing accessibility and usability for physically handicapped people. This incorporation by reference was approved by the Director of the Federal Register in accordance with 5 U.S.C. 552(a) and 1 CFR Part 51. Copies may be obtained from American National Standards Institute, Inc., 1430 Broadway, New York, New York 10018. Copies may be inspected at the Department of Housing and Urban Development, 451 Seventh Street, S.W., Room 10276, Washington, D.C., or at the Office of the Federal Register, 1100 L Street, N.W., Room 8401, Washington, D.C.

"Building" means a structure, facility or portion thereof that contains or serves one or more dwelling units.

"Building entrance on an accessible route" means an accessible entrance to a building that is connected by an accessible route to public transportation stops, to accessible parking and passenger loading zones, or to public streets or sidewalks, if available. A building entrance that complies with ANSI A117.1-1986 or a comparable standard complies with the requirements of this paragraph.

"Common use areas" means rooms, spaces or elements inside or outside of a building that are made available for the use of residents of a building or the guests thereof. These areas include hallways, lounges, lobbies, laundry rooms, refuse rooms, mail rooms, recreational areas and passageways among and between buildings.

"Controlled substance" means any drug or other substance, or immediate precursor included in the definition in section 102 of the Controlled Substances Act (21 U.S.C. 802).

"Covered multifamily dwellings" means buildings consisting of 4 or more dwelling units if such buildings have one or more elevators; and ground floor dwelling units in other buildings consisting of 4 or more dwelling units.

"Dwelling unit" means a single unit of residence for a family or one or more persons. Examples of dwelling units include: a single family home; an apartment unit within an apartment building; and in other types of dwellings in which sleeping accommodations are provided but toileting or cooking facilities are shared by occupants of more than one room or portion of the dwelling, rooms in which people sleep. Examples of the latter include dormitory rooms and sleeping accommodations in shelters intended for occupancy as a residence for homeless persons.

"Entrance" means any access point to a building or portion of a building used by residents for the purpose of entering.

"Exterior" means all areas of the premises outside of an individual dwelling unit.

"First occupancy" means a building that has never before been used for any purpose.

"Ground floor" means a floor of a building with a building entrance on an accessible route. A building may have more than one ground floor.

"Handicap" means, with respect to a person, a physical or mental impairment which substantially limits one or more major life activities; a record of such an impairment; or being regarded as having such an impairment. This term does not include current, illegal use of or addiction to a controlled substance. For purposes of this part, an individual shall not be considered to have a handicap solely because that individual is a transvestite. As used in this definition:

(a) "Physical or mental impairment" includes:

(1) Any physiological disorder or condition, cosmetic disfigurement, or anatomical loss affecting one or more of the following body systems: Neurological; musculoskeletal; special sense organs; respiratory, including speech organs; cardiovascular; reproductive; digestive; genito-urinary; hemic and lymphatic; skin; and endocrine; or

(2) Any mental or psychological disorder, such as mental retardation, organic brain syndrome, emotional or mental illness, and specific learning disabilities. The term "physical or mental impairment" includes, but is not limited to, such diseases and conditions as orthopedic, visual, speech and hearing impairments, cerebral palsy, autism, epilepsy, muscular dystrophy, multiple sclerosis, cancer, heart disease, diabetes, Human Immunodeficiency Virus infection, mental retardation, emotional illness, drug addiction (other than addiction caused by current, illegal use of a controlled substance) and alcoholism.

(b) "Major life activities" means functions such as caring for one's self, performing manual tasks, walking, seeing, hearing, speaking, breathing, learning and working.

(c) "Has a record of such an impairment" means has a history of, or has been misclassified as having, a mental or physical impairment that substantially limits one or more major life activities.

(d) "Is regarded as having an impairment" means:

(1) Has a physical or mental impairment that does not substantially limit one or more major life

activities but that is treated by another person as constituting such a limitation;

(2) Has a physical or mental impairment that substantially limits one or more major life activities only as a result of the attitudes of other toward such impairment; or

(3) Has none of the impairments defined in paragraph (a) of this definition but is treated by another person as having such an impairment.

"Interior" means the spaces, parts, components or elements of an individual dwelling unit.

"Modification" means any change to the public or common use areas of a building or any change to a dwelling unit.

"Premises" means the interior or exterior spaces, parts, components or elements of a building, including individual dwelling units and the public and common use areas of a building.

"Public use areas" means interior or exterior rooms or spaces of a building that are made available to the general public. Public use may be provided at a building that is privately or publicly owned.

"Site" means a parcel of land bounded by a property line or a designated portion of a public right or way.

§ 100.202 General prohibitions against discrimination because of handicap.

(a) It shall be unlawful to discriminate in the sale or rental, or to otherwise make unavailable or deny, a dwelling to any buyer or renter because of a handicap of—

(1) That buyer or renter;

(2) A person residing in or intending to reside in that dwelling after it is so sold, rented, or made available; or

(3) Any person associated with that person.

(b) It shall be unlawful to discriminate against any person in the terms, conditions, or privileges of the sale or rental of a dwelling, or in the provision of services or facilities in connection with such dwelling, because of a handicap of—

(1) That buyer or renter;

(2) A person residing in or intending to reside in that dwelling after it is so sold, rented, or made available; or

(3) Any person associated with that person.

(c) It shall be unlawful to make an inquiry to determine whether an applicant for a dwelling, a person intending to reside in that dwelling after it is so sold, rented or made available, or any person associated with that person, has a handicap or to make inquiry as to the nature or severity of a handicap of such a person. However, this paragraph does not prohibit the following inquiries, provided these inquiries are made of all applicants, whether or not they have handicaps:

(1) Inquiry into an applicant's ability to meet the requirements of ownership or tenancy;

(2) Inquiry to determine whether an applicant is qualified for a dwelling available only to persons with handicaps or to persons with a particular type of handicap;

(3) Inquiry to determine whether an applicant for a dwelling is qualified for a priority available to persons with handicaps or to persons with a particular type of handicap;

(4) Inquiring whether an applicant for a dwelling is a current illegal abuser or addict of a controlled substance;

(5) Inquiring whether an applicant has been convicted of the illegal manufacture or distribution of a controlled substance.

(d) Nothing in this subpart requires that a dwelling be made available to an individual whose tenancy would constitute a direct threat to the health or safety of other individuals or whose tenancy would result in substantial physical damage to the property of others.

§ 100.203 Reasonable modifications of existing premises.

(a) It shall be unlawful for any person to refuse to permit, at the expense of a handicapped person, reasonable modifications of existing premises, occupied or to be occupied by a handicapped person, if the proposed modifications may be necessary to afford the handicapped person full enjoyment of the premises of a dwelling. In the case of a rental, the landlord may, where it is reasonable to do so, condition permission for a modification on the renter agreeing to restore the interior of the premises to the condition that existed before the modification, reasonable wear and tear excepted. The landlord may not increase for handicapped persons any customarily required security deposit. However, where it is necessary in order to ensure with reasonable certainty that funds will be available to pay for the restorations at the end of the tenancy, the landlord may negotiate as part of such a restoration agreement a provision requiring that the tenant pay into an interest bearing escrow account, over a reasonable period, a reasonable amount of money not to exceed the cost of the restorations. The interest in any such account shall accrue to the benefit of the tenant.

(b) A landlord may condition permission for a modification on the renter providing a reasonable description of the proposed modifications as well as reasonable assurances that the work will be done in a workmanlike manner and that any required building permits will be obtained.

(c) The application of paragraph (a) of this section may be illustrated by the following examples:

Example (1): A tenant with a handicap asks his or her landlord for permission to install grab bars in the bathroom at his or her own expense. It is necessary to reinforce the walls with blocking between studs in order to affix the grab bars. It is unlawful for the landlord to refuse to permit the tenant, at the tenant's own expense, from making the modifications necessary to add the grab bars. However, the landlord may condition permission for the modification on the tenant agreeing to restore the bathroom to the condition that existed before the modification, reasonable wear and tear excepted. It would be reasonable for the landlord to require the tenant to remove the grab bars at the end of the tenancy. The landlord may also reasonably require that the wall to which the grab bars are to be attached be repaired and restored to its original condition, reasonable wear and tear excepted. However, it would be unreasonable for the landlord to require the tenant to remove the blocking, since the reinforced walls will not interfere in any way with the landlord's or the next tenant's use and enjoyment of the premises and may be needed by some future tenant.

Example (2): An applicant for rental housing has a child who uses a wheelchair. The bathroom door in the dwelling unit is too narrow to permit the wheelchair to pass. The applicant asks the landlord for permission to widen the doorway at the applicant's own expense. It is unlawful for the landlord to refuse to permit the applicant to make the modification. Further, the landlord may not, in usual circumstances, condition permission for the modification on the applicant paying for the doorway to be narrowed at the end of the lease because a wider doorway will not interfere with the landlord's or the next tenant's use and enjoyment of the premises.

§ 100.204 Reasonable accommodations.

(a) It shall be unlawful for any person to refuse to make reasonable accommodations in rules, policies, practices, or services, when such accommodations may be necessary to afford a handicapped person equal opportunity to use and enjoy a dwelling unit, including public and common use areas.

(b) The application of this section may be illustrated by the following examples:

Example (1): A blind applicant for rental housing wants live in a dwelling unit with a seeing eye dog. The building has a "no pets" policy. It is a violation of § 100.204 for the owner or manager of the apartment complex to refuse to permit the applicant to live in the apartment with a seeing eye dog because, without the seeing eye dog, the blind person will not have an equal opportunity to use and enjoy a dwelling.

Example (2): Progress Gardens is a 300 unit apartment complex with 450 parking spaces which are available to tenants and guests of Progress Gardens on a "first come first served" basis. John applies for housing in Progress Gardens. John is mobility impaired and is unable to walk more than a short distance and therefore requests that a parking space near his unit be reserved for him so he will not have to walk very far to get to his apartment. It is a violation of § 100.204 for the owner or manager of Progress Gardens to refuse to make this accommodation. Without a reserved space, John might be unable to live in Progress Gardens at all or, when he has to park in a space far from his unit, might have great difficulty getting from his car to his apartment unit. The accommodation therefore is necessary to afford John an equal opportunity to use and enjoy a dwelling. The accommodation is reasonable because it is feasible and practical under the circumstances.

§ 100.205 Design and construction requirements.

(a) Covered multifamily dwellings for first occupancy after March 13, 1991 shall be designed and constructed to have at least one building entrance on an accessible route unless it is impractical to do so because of the terrain or unusual characteristics of the site. For purposes of this section, a covered multifamily dwelling shall be deemed to be designed and constructed for first occupancy on or before March 13, 1991, if the dwelling is occupied by that date, or if the last building permit or renewal thereof for the dwelling is issued by a State, County or local government on or before June 15, 1990. The burden of establishing impracticality because of terrain or unusual site characteristics is on the person or persons who designed or constructed the housing facility.

(b) The application of paragraph (a) of this section may be illustrated by the following examples:

Example (1): A real estate developer plans to construct six covered multifamily dwelling units on a site with a hilly terrain. Because of the terrain, it will be necessary to climb a long and steep stairway in order to enter the dwellings. Since there is no practical way to provide an accessible route to any of the dwellings, one need not be provided.

Example (2): A real estate developer plans to construct a building consisting of 10 units of multifamily housing on a waterfront site that floods frequently. Because of this unusual characteristic of the site, the builder plans to construct the building on stilts. It is customary for housing in the geographic area where the site is located to be built on stilts. The housing may lawfully be constructed on the proposed site on stilts even though this means that there will be no practical way to provide an accessible route to the building entrance.

Example (3): A real estate developer plans to construct a multifamily housing facility on a particular site. The developer would like the facility to be built on the site to contain as many units as possible. Because of the configuration and terrain of the site, it is possible to construct a building with 105 units on the site provided the site does not have an accessible route leading to the building entrance. It is also possible to construct a building on the site with an accessible route leading to the building entrance. However, such a building would have no more than 100 dwelling units. The building to be constructed on the site must have a building entrance on an accessible route because it is not impractical to provide such an entrance because of the terrain or unusual characteristics of the site.

(c) All covered multifamily dwellings for first occupancy after March 13, 1991 with a building entrance on an accessible route shall be designed and constructed in such a manner that—

(1) The public and common use areas are readily accessible to and usable by handicapped persons;

(2) All the doors designed to allow passage into and within all premises are sufficiently wide to allow passage by handicapped persons in wheelchairs; and

(3) All premises within covered multifamily dwelling units contain the following features of adaptable design:

(i) An accessible route into and through the covered dwelling unit;

(ii) Light switches, electrical outlets, thermostats, and other environmental controls in accessible locations;

(iii) Reinforcements in bathroom walls to allow later installation of grab bars around the toilet, tub, shower, stall and shower seat, where such facilities are provided; and

(iv) Usable kitchens and bathrooms such that an individual in a wheelchair can maneuver about the space.

(d) The application of paragraph (c) of this section may be illustrated by the following examples:

Example (1): A developer plans to construct a 100 unit condominium apartment building with one elevator. In accordance with paragraph (a), the building has at least one accessible route leading to an accessible entrance. All 100 units are covered multifamily dwelling units and they all must be designed and constructed so that they comply with the accessibility requirements of paragraph (c) of this section.

Example (2): A developer plans to construct 30 garden apartments in a three story building. The building will not have an elevator. The building will have one accessible entrance which will be on the first floor. Since the building does not have an elevator, only the "ground floor" units are covered multifamily units. The "ground floor" is the first floor because that is the floor that has an accessible entrance. All of the dwelling units on the first floor must meet the accessibility requirements of paragraph (c) of this section and must have access to at least one of each type of public or common use area available for residents in the building.

(e) Compliance with the appropriate requirements of ANSI A117.1-1986 suffices to satisfy the requirements of paragraph (c)(3) of this section.

(f) Compliance with a duly enacted law of a State or unit of general local government that includes the requirements of paragraphs (a) and (c) of this section satisfies the requirements of paragraphs (a) and (c) of this section.

(g)(1) It is the policy of HUD to encourage States and units of general local government to include, in their existing procedures for the review and approval of newly constructed covered multifamily dwellings, determinations as to whether the design and construction of such dwellings are consistent with paragraphs (a) and (c) of this section.

(2) A State or unit of general local government may review and approve newly constructed multifamily dwellings for the purpose of making determinations as to whether the requirements of paragraphs (a) and (c) of this section are met.

(h) Determinations of compliance or noncompliance by a State or a unit of general local government under paragraph (f) or (g) of this section are not conclusive in enforcement proceedings under the Fair Housing Amendments Act.

(i) This subpart does not invalidate or limit any law of a State or political subdivision of a State that requires dwellings to be designed and constructed in a manner that affords handicapped persons greater access than is required by this subpart.

DAMAGES

CIVIL RIGHTS ACT OF 1991

42 U.S.C. § 1981a. Damages in cases of intentional discrimination in employment

(a) Right of recovery

(1) Civil rights

In an action brought by a complaining party under section 706 or 717 of the Civil Rights Act of 1964 (42 U.S.C. 2000e-5) [42 U.S.C.A. § 2000e-5 or 42 U.S.C.A. § 2000e-16] against a respondent who engaged in unlawful intentional discrimination (not an employment practice that is unlawful because of its disparate impact) prohibited under section 703, 704, or 717 of the Act (42 U.S.C. 2000e-2 or 2000e-3) [42 U.S.C.A. § 2000e-2, 42 U.S.C.A. § 2000e-3, or 42 U.S.C.A. § 2000e-16], and provided that the complaining party cannot recover under section 1981 of this title, the complaining party may recover compensatory and punitive damages as allowed in subsection (b) of this section, in addition to any relief authorized by section 706(g) of the Civil Rights Act of 1964 [42 U.S.C.A. § 2000e-5(g)], from the respondent.

(2) Disability

In an action brought by a complaining party under the powers, remedies, and procedures set forth in section 706 or 717 of the Civil Rights Act of 1964 [42 U.S.C.A. § 2000e-5 or 42 U.S.C.A. § 2000e-16] (as provided in section 107(a) of the Americans with Disabilities Act of 1990 (42 U.S.C. 12117(a)), and section 794a(a)(1) of Title 29, respectively) against a respondent who engaged in unlawful intentional discrimination (not an employment practice that is unlawful because of its disparate impact) under section 791 of Title 29 and the regulations implementing section 791 of Title 29, or who violated the requirements of section 791 of Title 29 or the regulations implementing section 791 of Title 29 concerning the provision of a reasonable accommodation, or section 102 of the Americans with Disabilities Act of 1990 (42 U.S.C. 12112), or committed a violation of section 102(b)(5) of the Act [42 U.S.C.A. § 12112(b)(5)], against an individual, the complaining party may recover compensatory and punitive damages as allowed in subsection (b) of this section, in addition to any relief authorized by section 706(g) of the Civil Rights Act of 1964 [42 U.S.C.A. § 2000e-5(g)], from the respondent.

(3) Reasonable accommodation and good faith effort

In cases where a discriminatory practice involves the provision of a reasonable accommodation pursuant to section 102(b)(5) of the Americans with Disabilities Act of 1990 [42 U.S.C.A. § 12112(b)(5)] or regulations implementing section 791 of Title 29, damages may not be awarded under this section where the covered entity demonstrates good faith efforts, in consultation with the person with the disability who has informed the covered entity that accommodation is needed, to identify and make a reasonable accommodation that would provide such individual with an equally effective opportunity and would not cause an undue hardship on the operation of the business.

(b) Compensatory and punitive damages

(1) Determination of punitive damages

A complaining party may recover punitive damages under this section against a respondent (other than a government, government agency or political subdivision) if the complaining party demonstrates that the respondent engaged in a discriminatory practice or discriminatory practices with malice or with reckless indifference to the federally protected rights of an aggrieved individual.

(2) Exclusions from compensatory damages

Compensatory damages awarded under this section shall not include backpay, interest on backpay, or any other type of relief authorized under section 706(g) of the Civil Rights Act of 1964 [42 U.S.C.A. § 2000e-5(g)].

(3) Limitations

The sum of the amount of compensatory damages awarded under this section for future pecuniary losses, emotional pain, suffering, inconvenience, mental anguish, loss of enjoyment of life, and other nonpecuniary losses, and the amount of punitive damages awarded under this section, shall not exceed, for each complaining party—

(A) in the case of a respondent who has more than 14 and fewer than 101 employees in each of 20 or more calendar weeks in the current or preceding calendar year, $50,000;

(B) in the case of a respondent who has more than 100 and fewer than 201 employees in each of 20 or more calendar weeks in the current or preceding calendar year, $100,000; and

(C) in the case of a respondent who has more than 200 and fewer than 501 employees in each of 20 or more calendar weeks in the current or preceding calendar year, $200,000; and

(D) in the case of a respondent who has more than 500 employees in each of 20 or more calendar weeks in the current or preceding calendar year, $300,000.

(4) Construction

Nothing in this section shall be construed to limit the scope of, or the relief available under, section 1981 of this title.

(c) Jury trial

If a complaining party seeks compensatory or punitive damages under this section—

(1) any party may demand a trial by jury; and

(2) the court shall not inform the jury of the limitations described in subsection (b)(3) of this section.

(d) Definitions

As used in this section:

(1) Complaining party

The term "complaining party" means—

(A) in the case of a person seeking to bring an action under subsection (a)(1) of this section, the Equal Employment Opportunity Commission, the Attorney General, or a person who may bring an action or proceeding under title VII of the Civil Rights Act of 1964 (42 U.S.C. 2000e et seq.); or

(B) in the case of a person seeking to bring an action under subsection (a)(2) of this section, the Equal Employment Opportunity Commission, the Attorney General, a person who may bring an action or proceeding under section 794a(a)(1) of Title 29, or a person who may bring an action or proceeding under title I of the Americans with Disabilities Act of 1990 (42 U.S.C. 12101 et seq.).

(2) Discriminatory practice

The term "discriminatory practice" means the discrimination described in paragraph (1), or the discrimination or the violation described in paragraph (2), of subsection (a) of this section.

IDEA

Part A — General Provisions

IDEA
Part A — General Provisions

§ 1400. Short title; table of contents; findings; purposes

(a) Short title

This title may be cited as the "Individuals with Disabilities Education Act".

(b) Omitted

(c) Findings

Congress finds the following:

(1) Disability is a natural part of the human experience and in no way diminishes the right of individuals to participate in or contribute to society. Improving educational results for children with disabilities is an essential element of our national policy of ensuring equality of opportunity, full participation, independent living, and economic self-sufficiency for individuals with disabilities.

(2) Before the date of enactment of the Education for All Handicapped Children Act of 1975 (Public Law 94-142), the educational needs of millions of children with disabilities were not being fully met because —

(A) the children did not receive appropriate educational services;

(B) the children were excluded entirely from the public school system and from being educated with their peers;

(C) undiagnosed disabilities prevented the children from having a successful educational experience; or

(D) a lack of adequate resources within the public school system forced families to find services outside the public school system.

(d) Purposes

The purposes of this title are —

(1)(A) to ensure that all children with disabilities have available to them a free appropriate public education that emphasizes special education and related services designed to meet their unique needs and prepare them for further education, employment, and independent living;

(B) to ensure that the rights of children with disabilities and parents of such children are protected; and

(C) to assist States, localities, educational service agencies, and Federal agencies to provide for the education of all children with disabilities;

(2) to assist States in the implementation of a statewide, comprehensive, coordinated, multidisciplinary, interagency system of early intervention services for infants and toddlers with disabilities and their families;

(3) to ensure that educators and parents have the necessary tools to improve educational results for children with disabilities by supporting system improvement activities; coordinated research and personnel preparation; coordinated technical assistance, dissemination, and support; and technology development and media services; and

(4) to assess, and ensure the effectiveness of, efforts to educate children with disabilities.

§ 1401. Definitions

Except as otherwise provided, in this title:

(1) Assistive technology device

(A) In general

The term "assistive technology device" means any item, piece of equipment, or product system, whether acquired commercially off the shelf, modified, or customized, that is used to increase, maintain, or improve functional capabilities of a child with a disability.

(B) Exception

The term does not include a medical device that is surgically implanted, or the replacement of such device.

(2) Assistive technology service

The term "assistive technology service" means any service that directly assists a child with a disability in the selection, acquisition, or use of an assistive technology device. Such term includes —

(A) the evaluation of the needs of such child, including a functional evaluation of the child in the child's customary environment;

(B) purchasing, leasing, or otherwise providing for the acquisition of assistive technology devices by such child;

(C) selecting, designing, fitting, customizing, adapting, applying, maintaining, repairing, or replacing assistive technology devices;

(D) coordinating and using other therapies, interventions, or services with assistive technology devices, such as those associated with existing education and rehabilitation plans and programs;

(E) training or technical assistance for such child, or, where appropriate, the family of such child; and

(F) training or technical assistance for professionals (including individuals providing education and rehabilitation services), employers, or other individuals who provide services to, employ, or are otherwise substantially involved in the major life functions of such child.

(3) Child with a disability

(A) In general

The term "child with a disability" means a child —

(i) with mental retardation, hearing impairments (including deafness), speech or language impairments, visual impairments (including blindness), serious emotional disturbance (referred to in this title as "emotional disturbance"), orthopedic impairments, autism, traumatic brain injury, other health impairments, or specific learning disabilities; and

(ii) who, by reason thereof, needs special education and related services.

(B) Child aged 3 through 9

The term "child with a disability" for a child aged 3 through 9 (or any subset of that age range, including ages 3 through 5), may, at the discretion of the State and the local educational agency, include a child —

(i) experiencing developmental delays, as defined by the State and as measured by appropriate diagnostic instruments and procedures, in 1 or more of the following areas: physical development; cognitive development; communication development; social or emotional development; or adaptive development; and

(ii) who, by reason thereof, needs special education and related services.

(4) Core academic subjects

The term "core academic subjects" has the meaning given the term in section 9101 of the Elementary and Secondary Education Act of 1965.

(5) Educational service agency

The term "educational service agency" —

(A) means a regional public multiservice agency–

(i) authorized by State law to develop, manage, and provide services or programs to local educational agencies; and

(ii) recognized as an administrative agency for purposes of the provision of special education and related services provided within public elementary schools and secondary schools of the State; and

(B) includes any other public institution or agency having administrative control and direction over a public elementary school or secondary school.

(6) Elementary school

The term "elementary school" means a nonprofit institutional day or residential school, including a public elementary charter school, that provides elementary education, as determined under State law.

(7) Equipment

The term "equipment" includes —

(A) machinery, utilities, and built-in equipment, and any necessary enclosures or structures to house such machinery, utilities, or equipment; and

(B) all other items necessary for the functioning of a particular facility as a facility for the provision of educational services, including items such as instructional equipment and necessary furniture; printed, published, and audio-visual instructional materials; telecommunications, sensory, and other technological aids and devices; and books, periodicals, documents, and other related materials.

(8) Excess costs

The term "excess costs" means those costs that are in excess of the average annual per-student expenditure in a local educational agency during the preceding school year for an elementary school or secondary school student, as may be appropriate, and which shall be computed after deducting —

(A) amounts received —

(i) under part B [subchapter II of this chapter];

(ii) under part A of title I of the Elementary and Secondary Education Act of 1965; and

(iii) under parts A and B of title III of that Act; and

(B) any State or local funds expended for programs that would qualify for assistance under any of those parts.

(9) Free appropriate public education

The term "free appropriate public education" means special education and related services that —

(A) have been provided at public expense, under public supervision and direction, and without charge;

(B) meet the standards of the State educational agency;

(C) include an appropriate preschool, elementary school, or secondary school education in the State involved; and

(D) are provided in conformity with the individualized education program required under section 1414(d) of this title.

(10) Highly qualified

(A) In general

For any special education teacher, the term "highly qualified" has the meaning given the term in section 9101 of the Elementary and Secondary Education Act of 1965, except that such term also —

(i) includes the requirements described in subparagraph (B); and

(ii) includes the option for teachers to meet the requirements of section 9101 of such Act by meeting the requirements of subparagraph (C) or (D).

(B) Requirements for special education teachers

When used with respect to any public elementary school or secondary school special education teacher teaching in a State, such term means that —

(i) the teacher has obtained full State certification as a special education teacher (including certification obtained through alternative routes to certification), or passed the State special education teacher licensing examination, and holds a license to teach in the State as a special education teacher, except that when used with respect to any teacher teaching in a public charter school, the term means that the teacher meets the requirements set forth in the State's public charter school law;

(ii) the teacher has not had special education certification or licensure requirements waived on an emergency, temporary, or provisional basis; and

(iii) the teacher holds at least a bachelor's degree.

(C) Special education teachers teaching to alternate achievement standards

When used with respect to a special education teacher who teaches core academic subjects exclusively to children who are assessed against alternate achievement standards established under the regulations promulgated under section 1111(b)(1) of the Elementary and Secondary Education Act of 1965, such term means the teacher, whether new or not new to the profession, may either —

(i) meet the applicable requirements of section 9101 of such Act for any elementary, middle, or secondary school teacher who is new or not new to the profession; or

(ii) meet the requirements of subparagraph (B) or (C) of section 9101(23) of such Act as applied to an elementary school teacher, or, in the case of instruction above the elementary level, has subject matter knowledge appropriate to the level of instruction being provided, as determined by the State, needed to effectively teach to those standards.

(D) Special education teachers teaching multiple subjectsWhen used with respect to a special education teacher who teaches 2 or more core academic subjects exclusively to children with disabilities, such term means that the teacher may either —

(i) meet the applicable requirements of section 9101 of the Elementary and Secondary Education Act of 1965 for any elementary, middle, or secondary school teacher who is new or not new to the profession;

(ii) in the case of a teacher who is not new to the profession, demonstrate competence in all the core academic subjects in which the teacher teaches in the same manner as is required for an elementary, middle, or secondary school teacher who is not new to the profession under section 9101(23)(C)(ii) of such Act, which may include a single, high objective uniform State standard of evaluation covering multiple subjects; or

(iii) in the case of a new special education teacher who teaches multiple subjects and who is highly qualified in mathematics, language arts, or science, demonstrate competence in the other core academic subjects in which the teacher teaches in the same manner as is required for an elementary, middle, or secondary school teacher under section 9101(23)(C)(ii) of such Act, which may include a single, high objective uniform State standard of evaluation covering multiple subjects, not later than 2 years after the date of employment

(E) Rule of construction

Notwithstanding any other individual right of action that a parent or student may maintain under this subchapter, nothing in this section or subchapter shall be construed to create a right of action on behalf of an individual student or class of students for the failure of a particular State educational agency or local educational agency employee to be highly qualified.

(F) Definition for purposes of the ESEA

A teacher who is highly qualified under this paragraph shall be considered highly qualified for purposes of the Elementary and Secondary Education Act of 1965

(11) Homeless children

The term "homeless children" has the meaning given the term "homeless children and youths" in section 11434a of Title 42.

(12) Indian

The term "Indian" means an individual who is a member of an Indian tribe.

(13) Indian tribe

The term "Indian tribe" means any Federal or State Indian tribe, band, rancheria, pueblo, colony, or community, including any Alaska Native village or regional village corporation (as defined in or established under the Alaska Native Claims Settlement Act (43 U.S.C. 1601 et seq.)).

(14) Individualized education program; IEP

The term "individualized education program" or "IEP" means a written statement for each child with a disability that is developed, reviewed, and revised in accordance with section 1414(d) of this title.

(15) Individualized family service plan

The term "individualized family service plan" has the meaning given the term in section 1436 of this title.

(16) Infant or toddler with a disability

The term "infant or toddler with a disability" has the meaning given the term in section 1432 of this title.

(17) Institution of higher education

The term "institution of higher education" —

(A) has the meaning given the term in section 1001 of this title; and

(B) also includes any community college receiving funding from the Secretary of the Interior under the Tribally Controlled College or University Assistance Act of 1978.

(18) Limited English proficient

The term "limited English proficient" has the meaning given the term in section 9101 of the Elementary and Secondary Education Act of 1965.

(19) Local educational agency

(A) In general

The term "local educational agency" means a public board of education or other public authority legally constituted within a State for either administrative control or direction of, or to perform a service function for, public elementary schools or secondary schools in a city, county, township, school district, or other political subdivision of a State, or for such combination of school districts or counties as are recognized in a State as an administrative agency for its public elementary schools or secondary schools.

(B) Educational service agencies and other public institutions or agencies

The term includes —

(i) an educational service agency; and

(ii) any other public institution or agency having administrative control and direction of a public elementary school or secondary school.

(C) BIA funded schools

The term includes an elementary school or secondary school funded by the Bureau of Indian Affairs, but only to the extent that such inclusion makes the school eligible for programs for which specific eligibility is not provided to the school in another provision of law and the school does not have a student population that is smaller than the student population of the local educational agency receiving assistance under this chapter with the smallest student population, except that the school shall not be subject to the jurisdiction of any State educational agency other than the Bureau of Indian Affairs.

(20) Native language

The term "native language", when used with respect to an individual who is limited English proficient, means the language normally used by the individual or, in the case of a child, the language normally used by the parents of the child.

(21) Nonprofit

The term "nonprofit", as applied to a school, agency, organization, or institution, means a school, agency, organization, or institution owned and operated by 1 or more nonprofit corporations or associations no part of the net earnings of which inures, or may lawfully inure, to the benefit of any private shareholder or individual.

(22) Outlying area

The term "outlying area" means the United States Virgin Islands, Guam, American Samoa, and the Commonwealth of the Northern Mariana Islands.

(23) Parent

The term "parent" means —

(A) a natural, adoptive, or foster parent of a child (unless a foster parent is prohibited by State law from serving as a parent);

(B) a guardian (but not the State if the child is a ward of the State);

(C) an individual acting in the place of a natural or adoptive parent (including a grandparent, stepparent, or other relative) with whom the child lives, or an individual who is legally responsible for the child's welfare; or

(D) except as used in sections 1415(b)(2) of this title and 1439(a)(5) of this title, an individual assigned under either of those sections to be a surrogate parent.

(24) Parent organization

The term "parent organization" has the meaning given the term in section 1471(g) of this title.

(25) Parent training and information center

The term "parent training and information center" means a center assisted under section 1471 or 1472 of this title.

(26) Related service

(A) In general

The term "related services" means transportation, and such developmental, corrective, and other supportive services (including speech-language pathology and audiology services, interpreting services, psychological services, physical and occupational therapy, recreation, including therapeutic recreation, social work services, school nurse services designed to enable a child with a disability to receive a free appropriate public education as described in the individualized education program of the child, counseling services, including rehabilitation counseling, orientation and mobility services, and medical services, except that such medical services shall be for diagnostic and evaluation purposes only) as may be required to assist a child with a disability to benefit from special education, and includes the early identification and assessment of disabling conditions in children.

(B) Exception

The term does not include a medical device that is surgically implanted, or the replacement of such device.

(27) Secondary school

The term "secondary school" means a nonprofit institutional day or residential school, including a public secondary charter school, that provides secondary education, as determined under State law, except that it does not include any education beyond grade 12.

(28) Secretary

The term "Secretary" means the Secretary of Education.

(29) Special education

The term "special education" means specially designed instruction, at no cost to parents, to meet the unique needs of a child with a disability, including —

(A) instruction conducted in the classroom, in the home, in hospitals and institutions, and in other settings; and

(B) instruction in physical education.

(30) Specific learning disability

(A) In general

The term "specific learning disability" means a disorder in 1 or more of the basic psychological processes involved in understanding or in using language, spoken or written, which disorder may manifest itself in the imperfect ability to listen, think, speak, read, write, spell, or do mathematical calculations.

(B) Disorders included

Such term includes such conditions as perceptual disabilities, brain injury, minimal brain dysfunction, dyslexia, and developmental aphasia

(C) Disorders not included

Such term does not include a learning problem that is primarily the result of visual, hearing, or motor disabilities, of mental retardation, of emotional disturbance, or of environmental, cultural, or economic disadvantage.

(31) State

The term "State" means each of the 50 States, the District of Columbia, the Commonwealth of Puerto Rico, and each of the outlying areas.

(32) State educational agency

The term "State educational agency" means the State board of education or other agency or officer primarily responsible for the State supervision of public elementary schools and secondary schools, or, if there is no such officer or agency, an officer or agency designated by the Governor or by State law.

(33) Supplementary aids and services

The term "supplementary aids and services" means aids, services, and other supports that are provided in regular education classes or other education-related settings to enable children with disabilities to be educated with nondisabled children to the maximum extent appropriate in accordance with section 1412(a)(5) of this title.

(34) Transition services

The term "transition services" means a coordinated set of activities for a child with a disability that —

(A) is designed to be within a results-oriented process, that is focused on improving the academic and functional achievement of the child with a disability to facilitate the child's movement from school to post-school activities, including post-secondary education, vocational education, integrated employment (including supported employment), continuing and adult education, adult services, independent living, or community participation;

(B) is based on the individual child's needs, taking into account the child's strengths, preferences, and interests; and

(C) includes instruction, related services, community experiences, the development of employment and other post-school adult living objectives, and, when appropriate, acquisition of daily living skills and functional vocational evaluation.

(35) Universal design

The term "universal design" has the meaning given the term in section 3002 of Title 29.

(36) Ward of the State

(A) In general

The term "ward of the State" means a child who, as determined by the State where the child resides, is a foster child, is a ward of the State, or is in the custody of a public child welfare agency.

(B) Exception

The term does not include a foster child who has a foster parent who meets the definition of a parent in paragraph (23).

§ 1402. Office of Special Education Programs

(a) Establishment.

There shall be, within the Office of Special Education and Rehabilitative Services in the Department of Education, an Office of Special Education Programs, which shall be the principal agency in the Department for administering and carrying out this title and other programs and activities concerning the education of children with disabilities.

(b) Director.

The Office established under subsection (a) shall be headed by a Director who shall be selected by the Secretary and shall report directly to the Assistant Secretary for Special Education and Rehabilitative Services.

(c) Voluntary and uncompensated services.

Notwithstanding section 1342 of title 31, United States Code, the Secretary is authorized to accept voluntary and uncompensated services in furtherance of the purposes of this title.

§ 1403. Abrogation of State sovereign immunity

(a) In general.

A State shall not be immune under the 11th amendment to the Constitution of the United States from suit in Federal court for a violation of this title.

(b) Remedies.

In a suit against a State for a violation of this title, remedies (including remedies both at law and in equity) are available for such a violation to the same extent as those remedies are available for such a violation in the suit against any public entity other than a State.

(c) Effective date.

Subsections (a) and (b) apply with respect to violations that occur in whole or part after the date of enactment of the Education of the Handicapped Act Amendments of 1990.

§ 1404. Acquisition of equipment; construction or alteration of facilities

(a) In general.

If the Secretary determines that a program authorized under this title will be improved by permitting program funds to be used to acquire appropriate equipment, or to construct new facilities or alter existing facilities, the Secretary is authorized to allow the use of those funds for those purposes.

(b) Compliance with certain regulations.

Any construction of new facilities or alteration of existing facilities under subsection (a) shall comply with the requirements of —

(1) appendix A of part 36 of title 28, Code of Federal Regulations (commonly known as the "Americans with Disabilities Accessibility Guidelines for Buildings and Facilities"); or

(2) appendix A of subpart 101-19.6 of title 41, Code of Federal Regulations (commonly known as the "Uniform Federal Accessibility Standards").

§ 1405. Employment of individuals with disabilities

The Secretary shall ensure that each recipient of assistance under this title makes positive efforts to employ and advance in employment qualified individuals with disabilities in programs assisted under this title.

§ 1406. Requirements for prescribing regulations

(a) In general.

In carrying out the provisions of this title, the Secretary shall issue regulations under this title only to the extent that such regulations are necessary to ensure that there is compliance with the specific requirements of this title.

(b) Protections provided to children.

The Secretary may not implement, or publish in final form, any regulation prescribed pursuant to this title that —

(1) violates or contradicts any provision of this title; or

(2) procedurally or substantively lessens the protections provided to children with disabilities under this title, as embodied in regulations in effect on July 20, 1983 (particularly as such protections related to parental consent to initial evaluation or initial placement in special education, least restrictive environment, related services, timelines, attendance of evaluation personnel at individualized education program meetings, or qualifications of personnel), except to the extent that such regulation reflects the clear and unequivocal intent of Congress in legislation.

(c) Public comment period.

The Secretary shall provide a public comment period of not less than 75 days on any regulation proposed under part B or part C on which an opportunity for public comment is otherwise required by law.

(d) Policy letters and statements.

The Secretary may not issue policy letters or

other statements (including letters or statements regarding issues of national significance) that —

(1) violate or contradict any provision of this title; or

(2) establish a rule that is required for compliance with, and eligibility under, this title without following the requirements of section 553 of title 5, United States Code.

(e) Explanation and assurances.

Any written response by the Secretary under subsection (d) regarding a policy, question, or interpretation under part B shall include an explanation in the written response that —

(1) such response is provided as informal guidance and is not legally binding;

(2) when required, such response is issued in compliance with the requirements of section 553 of title 5, United States Code; and

(3) such response represents the interpretation by the Department of Education of the applicable statutory or regulatory requirements in the context of the specific facts presented.

(f) Correspondence from department of education describing interpretations of this title.

(1) In general.

The Secretary shall, on a quarterly basis, publish in the Federal Register, and widely disseminate to interested entities through various additional forms of communication, a list of correspondence from the Department of Education received by individuals during the previous quarter that describes the interpretations of the Department of Education of this title or the regulations implemented pursuant to this title.

(2) Additional information.

For each item of correspondence published in a list under paragraph (1), the Secretary shall —

(A) identify the topic addressed by the correspondence and shall include such other summary information as the Secretary determines to be appropriate; and

(B) ensure that all such correspondence is issued, where applicable, in compliance with the requirements of section 553 of title 5, United States Code.

§ 1407 State administration

(a) Rulemaking.

Each State that receives funds under this title shall —

(1) ensure that any State rules, regulations, and policies relating to this title conform to the purposes of this title;

(2) identify in writing to local educational agencies located in the State and the Secretary any such rule, regulation, or policy as a State-imposed requirement that is not required by this title and Federal regulations; and

(3) minimize the number of rules, regulations, and policies to which the local educational agencies and schools located in the State are subject under this title.

(b) Support and facilitation

State rules, regulations, and policies under this title shall support and facilitate local educational agency and school-level system improvement designed to enable children with disabilities to meet the challenging State student academic achievement standards.

§ 1408 Paperwork reduction

(a) Pilot program.

(1) Purpose.The purpose of this section is to provide an opportunity for States to identify ways to reduce paperwork burdens and other administrative duties that are directly associated with the requirements of this title, in order to increase the time and resources available for instruction and other activities aimed at improving educational and functional results for children with disabilities.

(2) Authorization.

(A) In general.

In order to carry out the purpose of this section, the Secretary is authorized to grant waivers of statutory requirements of, or regulatory requirements relating to, part B for a period of time not to exceed 4 years with respect to not more than 15 States based on proposals submitted by States to reduce excessive paperwork and noninstructional time burdens that do not assist in improving educational and functional results for children with disabilities.

(B) Exception.

The Secretary shall not waive under this section any statutory requirements of, or regulatory requirements relating to, applicable civil rights requirements.

(C) Rule of construction.

Nothing in this section shall be construed to —

(i) affect the right of a child with a disability to receive a free appropriate public education under part B; and

(ii) permit a State or local educational agency to waive procedural safeguards under section 615.

(3) Proposal.

(A) In general.

A State desiring to participate in the program under this section shall submit a proposal to the Secretary at such time and in such manner as the Secretary may reasonably require.

(B) Content.

The proposal shall include —

(i) a list of any statutory requirements of, or regulatory requirements relating to, part B that the State desires the Secretary to waive, in whole or in part; and

(ii) a list of any State requirements that the State proposes to waive or change, in whole or in part, to carry out a waiver granted to the State by the Secretary.

(4) Termination of waiver.

The Secretary shall terminate a State's waiver under this section if the Secretary determines that the State —

(A) needs assistance under section 616(d)(2)(A)(ii) and that the waiver has contributed to or caused such need for assistance;

(B) needs intervention under section 616(d)(2)(A)(iii) or needs substantial intervention under section 616(d)(2)(A)(iv); or

(C) failed to appropriately implement its waiver.

(b) Report.

Beginning 2 years after the date of enactment of the Individuals with Disabilities Education Improvement Act of 2004, the Secretary shall include in the annual report to Congress submitted pursuant to section 426 of the Department of Education Organization Act information related to the effectiveness of waivers granted under subsection (a), including any specific recommendations for broader implementation of such waivers, in —

(1) reducing —

(A) the paperwork burden on teachers, principals, administrators, and related service providers; and

(B) noninstructional time spent by teachers in complying with part B;

(2) enhancing longer-term educational planning;

(3) improving positive outcomes for children with disabilities;

(4) promoting collaboration between IEP Team members; and

(5) ensuring satisfaction of family members.

§ 1409 Freely associated states

The Republic of the Marshall Islands, the Federated States of Micronesia, and the Republic of Palau shall continue to be eligible for competitive grants administered by the Secretary under this title to the extent that such grants continue to be available to States and local educational agencies under this title.

PART B — ASSISTANCE FOR EDUCATION OF ALL CHILDREN WITH DISABILITIES

PART B — ASSISTANCE FOR EDUCATION OF ALL CHILDREN WITH DISABILITIES

§ 1411. Authorization; allotment; use of funds; authorization of appropriations

(a) Grants to States

(1) Purpose of grants.

The Secretary shall make grants to States, outlying areas, and freely associated States, and provide funds to the Secretary of the Interior, to assist them to provide special education and related services to children with disabilities in accordance with this part.

(2) Maximum amount.

The maximum amount of the grant a State may receive under this section —

(A) for fiscal years 2005 and 2006 is —

(i) the number of children with disabilities in the State who are receiving special education and related services —

(I) aged 3 through 5 if the State is eligible for a grant under section 619; and

(II) aged 6 through 21; multiplied by

(ii) 40 percent of the average per-pupil expenditure in public elementary schools and secondary schools in the United States; and

(B) for fiscal year 2007 and subsequent fiscal years is —

(i) the number of children with disabilities in the 2004-2005 school year in the State who received special education and related services —

(I) aged 3 through 5 if the State is eligible for a grant under section 619; and

(II) aged 6 through 21; multiplied by

(ii) 40 percent of the average per-pupil expenditure in public elementary schools and secondary schools in the United States; adjusted by

(iii) the rate of annual change in the sum of —

(I) 85 percent of such State's population described in subsection (d)(3)(A)(i)(II); and

(II) 15 percent of such State's population described in subsection (d)(3)(A)(i)(III).

(b) Outlying areas and freely associated states; Secretary of the Interior.

(1) Outlying areas and freely associated states.

(A) Funds reserved.

From the amount appropriated for any fiscal year under subsection (i), the Secretary shall reserve not more than 1 percent, which shall be used —

(i) to provide assistance to the outlying areas in accordance with their respective populations of individuals aged 3 through 21; and

(ii) to provide each freely associated State a grant in the amount that such freely associated State received for fiscal year 2003 under this part, but only if the freely associated State meets the applicable requirements of this part, as well as the requirements of section 611(b)(2)(C) as such section was in effect on the day before the date of enactment of the Individuals with Disabilities Education Improvement Act of 2004.

(B) Special rule.

The provisions of Public Law 95-134, permitting the consolidation of grants by the outlying areas, shall not apply to funds provided to the outlying areas or the freely associated States under this section.

(C) Definition.

In this paragraph, the term "freely associated States" means the Republic of the Marshall Islands, the Federated States of

Micronesia, and the Republic of Palau.

(2) Secretary of the Interior.

From the amount appropriated for any fiscal year under subsection (i), the Secretary shall reserve 1.226 percent to provide assistance to the Secretary of the Interior in accordance with subsection (h).

(c) Technical assistance.

(1) In general.

The Secretary may reserve not more than 1/2 of 1 percent of the amounts appropriated under this part for each fiscal year to provide technical assistance activities authorized under section 616(i).

(2) Maximum Amount.

The maximum amount the Secretary may reserve under paragraph (1) for any fiscal year is $25,000,000, cumulatively adjusted by the rate of inflation as measured by the percentage increase, if any, from the preceding fiscal year in the Consumer Price Index For All Urban Consumers, published by the Bureau of Labor Statistics of the Department of Labor.

(d) Allocations to states.

(1) In general.

After reserving funds for technical assistance, and for payments to the outlying areas, the freely associated States, and the Secretary of the Interior under subsections (b) and (c) for a fiscal year, the Secretary shall allocate the remaining amount among the States in accordance with this subsection.

(2) Special rule for use of fiscal year 1999 amount.

If a State received any funds under this section for fiscal year 1999 on the basis of children aged 3 through 5, but does not make a free appropriate public education available to all children with disabilities aged 3 through 5 in the State in any subsequent fiscal year, the Secretary shall compute the State's amount for fiscal year 1999, solely for the purpose of calculating the State's allocation in that subsequent year under paragraph (3) or (4), by subtracting the amount allocated to the State for fiscal year 1999 on the basis of those children.

(3) Increase in funds.

If the amount available for allocations to States under paragraph (1) for a fiscal year is equal to or greater than the amount allocated to the States under this paragraph for the preceding fiscal year, those allocations shall be calculated as follows:

(A) Allocation of increase.

(i) In general.

Except as provided in subparagraph (B), the Secretary shall allocate for the fiscal year —

(I) to each State the amount the State received under this section for fiscal year 1999;

(II) 85 percent of any remaining funds to States on the basis of the States' relative populations of children aged 3 through 21 who are of the same age as children with disabilities for whom the State ensures the availability of a free appropriate public education under this part; and

(III) 15 percent of those remaining funds to States on the basis of the States' relative populations of children described in subclause (II) who are living in poverty.

(ii) Data.

For the purpose of making grants under this paragraph, the Secretary shall use the most recent population data, including data on children living in poverty, that are available and satisfactory to the Secretary.

(B) Limitations.

Notwithstanding subparagraph (A), allocations under this paragraph shall be subject to the following:

(i) Preceding year allocation.

No State's allocation shall be less than its allocation under this section for the preceding fiscal year.

(ii) Minimum.

No State's allocation shall be less than the greatest of —

(I) the sum of —

(aa) the amount the State received under this section for fiscal year 1999; and

(bb) 1/3 of 1 percent of the amount by which the amount appropriated under subsection (i) for the fiscal year exceeds the amount appropriated for this section for fiscal year 1999;

(II) the sum of —

(aa) the amount the State received under this section for the preceding fiscal year; and

(bb) that amount multiplied by

the percentage by which the increase in the funds appropriated for this section from the preceding fiscal year exceeds 1.5 percent; or

(III) the sum of —

(aa) the amount the State received under this section for the preceding fiscal year; and

(bb) that amount multiplied by 90 percent of the percentage increase in the amount appropriated for this section from the preceding fiscal year.

(iii) Maximum.

Notwithstanding clause (ii), no State's allocation under this paragraph shall exceed the sum of —

(I) the amount the State received under this section for the preceding fiscal year; and

(II) that amount multiplied by the sum of 1.5 percent and the percentage increase in the amount appropriated under this section from the preceding fiscal year.

(C) Ratable reduction.

If the amount available for allocations under this paragraph is insufficient to pay those allocations in full, those allocations shall be ratably reduced, subject to subparagraph (B)(i).

(4) Decrease in funds.

If the amount available for allocations to States under paragraph (1) for a fiscal year is less than the amount allocated to the States under this section for the preceding fiscal year, those allocations shall be calculated as follows:

(A) Amounts greater than fiscal year 1999 allocations.

If the amount available for allocations is greater than the amount allocated to the States for fiscal year 1999, each State shall be allocated the sum of —

(i) the amount the State received under this section for fiscal year 1999; and

(ii) an amount that bears the same relation to any remaining funds as the increase the State received under this section for the preceding fiscal year over fiscal year 1999 bears to the total of all such increases for all States.

(B) Amounts equal to or less than fiscal year 1999 allocations.

(i) In general.

If the amount available for allocations under this paragraph is equal to or less than the amount allocated to the States for fiscal year 1999, each State shall be allocated the amount the State received for fiscal year 1999.

(ii) Ratable reduction.

If the amount available for allocations under this paragraph is insufficient to make the allocations described in clause (i), those allocations shall be ratably reduced.

(e) State-level activities.

(1) State Administration.

(A) In general.

For the purpose of administering this part, including paragraph (3), section 619, and the coordination of activities under this part with, and providing technical assistance to, other programs that provide services to children with disabilities —

(i) each State may reserve for each fiscal year not more than the maximum amount the State was eligible to reserve for State administration under this section for fiscal year 2004 or $800,000 (adjusted in accordance with subparagraph (B)), whichever is greater; and

(ii) each outlying area may reserve for each fiscal year not more than 5 percent of the amount the outlying area receives under subsection (b)(1) for the fiscal year or $35,000, whichever is greater.

(B) Cumulative annual adjustments.

For each fiscal year beginning with fiscal year 2005, the Secretary shall cumulatively adjust —

(i) the maximum amount the State was eligible to reserve for State administration under this part for fiscal year 2004; and

(ii) $800,000,

by the rate of inflation as measured by the percentage increase, if any, from the preceding fiscal year in the Consumer Price Index For All Urban Consumers, published by the Bureau of Labor Statistics of the Department of Labor.

(C) Certification.

Prior to expenditure of funds under this paragraph, the State shall certify to the Secretary that the arrangements to establish responsibility for services pursuant to section 612(a)(12)(A) are current.

(D) Part C.

Funds reserved under subparagraph (A) may be used for the administration of part C, if the State educational agency is the lead agency for the State under such part.

(2) Other state-level activities.

(A) State-level activities.

(i) In general.

Except as provided in clause (iii), for the purpose of carrying out State-level activities, each State may reserve for each of the fiscal years 2005 and 2006 not more than 10 percent from the amount of the State's allocation under subsection (d) for each of the fiscal years 2005 and 2006, respectively. For fiscal year 2007 and each subsequent fiscal year, the State may reserve the maximum amount the State was eligible to reserve under the preceding sentence for fiscal year 2006 (cumulatively adjusted by the rate of inflation as measured by the percentage increase, if any, from the preceding fiscal year in the Consumer Price Index For All Urban Consumers, published by the Bureau of Labor Statistics of the Department of Labor).

(ii) Small state adjustment.

Notwithstanding clause (i) and except as provided in clause (iii), in the case of a State for which the maximum amount reserved for State administration is not greater than $850,000, the State may reserve for the purpose of carrying out State-level activities for each of the fiscal years 2005 and 2006, not more than 10.5 percent from the amount of the State"s allocation under subsection (d) for each of the fiscal years 2005 and 2006, respectively. For fiscal year 2007 and each subsequent fiscal year, such State may reserve the maximum amount the State was eligible to reserve under the preceding sentence for fiscal year 2006 (cumulatively adjusted by the rate of inflation as measured by the percentage increase, if any, from the preceding fiscal year in the Consumer Price Index For All Urban Consumers, published by the Bureau of Labor Statistics of the Department of Labor).

(iii) Exception.

If a State does not reserve funds under paragraph (3) for a fiscal year, then —

(I) in the case of a State that is not described in clause (ii), for fiscal year 2005 or 2006, clause (i) shall be applied by substituting "9.0 percent" for "10 percent"; and

(II) in the case of a State that is described in clause (ii), for fiscal year 2005 or 2006, clause (ii) shall be applied by substituting "9.5 percent" for "10.5 percent".

(B) Required activities.

Funds reserved under subparagraph (A) shall be used to carry out the following activities:

(i) For monitoring, enforcement, and complaint investigation.

(ii) To establish and implement the mediation process required by section 615(e), including providing for the cost of mediators and support personnel.

(C) Authorized activities.

Funds reserved under subparagraph (A) may be used to carry out the following activities:

(i) For support and direct services, including technical assistance, personnel preparation, and professional development and training.

(ii) To support paperwork reduction activities, including expanding the use of technology in the IEP process.

(iii) To assist local educational agencies in providing positive behavioral interventions and supports and appropriate mental health services for children with disabilities

(iv) To improve the use of technology in the classroom by children with disabilities to enhance learning.

(v) To support the use of technology, including technology with universal design principles and assistive technology devices, to maximize accessibility to the general education curriculum for children with disabilities.

(vi) Development and implementation of transition programs, including coordination of services with agencies involved in supporting the transition of children with disabilities to postsecondary activities.

(vii) To assist local educational agencies in meeting personnel shortages.

(viii) To support capacity building activities and improve the delivery of services by local educational agencies to improve results for children with disabilities.

(ix) Alternative programming for children with disabilities who have been expelled from school, and services for children with disabilities in correctional facilities, children enrolled in State-operated or State-supported schools, and children with disabilities in charter schools.

(x) To support the development and provision of appropriate accommodations for children with disabilities, or the development and provision of alternate assessments that are valid and reliable for assessing the performance of children with disabilities, in accordance with sections 1111(b) and 6111 of the Elementary and Secondary Education Act of 1965.

(xi) To provide technical assistance to schools and local educational agencies, and direct services, including supplemental educational services as defined in 1116(e) of the Elementary and Secondary Education Act of 1965 to children with disabilities, in schools or local educational agencies identified for improvement under section 1116 of the Elementary and Secondary Education Act of 1965 on the sole basis of the assessment results of the disaggregated subgroup of children with disabilities, including providing professional development to special and regular education teachers, who teach children with disabilities, based on scientifically based research to improve educational instruction, in order to improve academic achievement to meet or exceed the objectives established by the State under section 1111(b)(2)(G) the Elementary and Secondary Education Act of 1965.

(3) Local educational agency risk pool.

(A) In general.

(i) Reservation of funds.

For the purpose of assisting local educational agencies (including a charter school that is a local educational agency or a consortium of local educational agencies) in addressing the needs of high need children with disabilities, each State shall have the option to reserve for each fiscal year 10 percent of the amount of funds the State reserves for State-level activities under paragraph (2)(A) —

(I) to establish and make disbursements from the high cost fund to local educational agencies in accordance with this paragraph during the first and succeeding fiscal years of the high cost fund; and

(II) to support innovative and effective ways of cost sharing by the State, by a local educational agency, or among a consortium of local educational agencies, as determined by the State in coordination with representatives from local educational agencies, subject to subparagraph (B)(ii).

(ii) Definition of local educational agency.

In this paragraph the term "local educational agency" includes a charter school that is a local educational agency, or a consortium of local educational agencies.

(B) Limitation on uses of funds.

(i) Establishment of high cost fund.

A State shall not use any of the funds the State reserves pursuant to subparagraph (A)(i), but may use the funds the State reserves under paragraph (1), to establish and support the high cost fund.

(ii) Innovative and effective cost sharing.

A State shall not use more than 5 percent of the funds the State reserves pursuant to subparagraph (A)(i) for each fiscal year to support innovative and effective ways of cost sharing among consortia of local educational agencies.

(C) State plan for high cost fund.

(i) Definition.

The State educational agency shall establish the State's definition of a high need child with a disability, which definition shall be developed in consultation with local educational agencies.

(ii) State plan.

The State educational agency shall develop, not later than 90 days after the State reserves funds under this paragraph, annually review, and amend as necessary, a State plan for the high cost fund. Such State plan shall —

(I) establish, in coordination with representatives from local educational agencies, a definition of a high need child with a disability that, at a minimum —

(aa) addresses the financial impact a high need child with a disability has on the budget of the child's local educational agency; and

(bb) ensures that the cost of the

high need child with a disability is greater than 3 times the average per pupil expenditure (as defined in section 9101 of the Elementary and Secondary Education Act of 1965) in that State;

(II) establish eligibility criteria for the participation of a local educational agency that, at a minimum, takes into account the number and percentage of high need children with disabilities served by a local educational agency;

(III) develop a funding mechanism that provides distributions each fiscal year to local educational agencies that meet the criteria developed by the State under subclause (II); and

(IV) establish an annual schedule by which the State educational agency shall make its distributions from the high cost fund each fiscal year.

(iii) Public availability.

The State shall make its final State plan publicly available not less than 30 days before the beginning of the school year, including dissemination of such information on the State website.

(D) Disbursements from the high cost fund.

(i) In general.

Each State educational agency shall make all annual disbursements from the high cost fund established under subparagraph (A)(i) in accordance with the State plan published pursuant to subparagraph (C).

(ii) Use of disbursements.

Each State educational agency shall make annual disbursements to eligible local educational agencies in accordance with its State plan under subparagraph (C)(ii).

(iii) Appropriate costs.

The costs associated with educating a high need child with a disability under subparagraph (C)(i) are only those costs associated with providing direct special education and related services to such child that are identified in such child's IEP.

(E) Legal fees.

The disbursements under subparagraph (D) shall not support legal fees, court costs, or other costs associated with a cause of action brought on behalf of a child with a disability to ensure a free appropriate public education for such child.

(F) Assurance of a Free Appropriate Public Education.

Nothing in this paragraph shall be construed

(i) to limit or condition the right of a child with a disability who is assisted under this part to receive a free appropriate public education pursuant to section 612(a)(1) in the least restrictive environment pursuant to section 612(a)(5); or

(ii) to authorize a State educational agency or local educational agency to establish a limit on what may be spent on the education of a child with a disability.

(G) Special rule for risk pool and high need assistance programs in effect as of January 1, 2004.

Notwithstanding the provisions of subparagraphs (A) through (F), a State may use funds reserved pursuant to this paragraph for implementing a placement neutral cost sharing and reimbursement program of high need, low incidence, catastrophic, or extraordinary aid to local educational agencies that provides services to high need students based on eligibility criteria for such programs that were created not later than January 1, 2004, and are currently in operation, if such program serves children that meet the requirement of the definition of a high need child with a disability as described in subparagraph (C)(ii)(I).

(H) Medicaid services not affected.

Disbursements provided under this paragraph shall not be used to pay costs that otherwise would be reimbursed as medical assistance for a child with a disability under the State medicaid program under title XIX of the Social Security Act.

(I) Remaining funds.

Funds reserved under subparagraph (A) in any fiscal year but not expended in that fiscal year pursuant to subparagraph (D) shall be allocated to local educational agencies for the succeeding fiscal year in the same manner as funds are allocated to local educational agencies under subsection (f) for the succeeding fiscal year.

(4) Inapplicability of certain prohibitions.

A State may use funds the State reserves under paragraphs (1) and (2) without regard to —

(A) the prohibition on commingling of funds in section 612(a)(17)(B); and

(B) the prohibition on supplanting other funds in section 612(a)(17)(C).

(5) Report on use of funds.

As part of the information required to be submitted to the Secretary under section 612, each State shall annually describe how amounts under this section —

(A) will be used to meet the requirements of this title; and

(B) will be allocated among the activities described in this section to meet State priorities based on input from local educational agencies.

(6) Special rule for increased funds.

A State may use funds the State reserves under paragraph (1)(A) as a result of inflationary increases under paragraph (1)(B) to carry out activities authorized under clause (i), (iii), (vii), or (viii) of paragraph (2)(C).

(7) Flexibility in using funds for Part C.

Any State eligible to receive a grant under section 619 may use funds made available under paragraph (1)(A), subsection (f)(3), or section 619(f)(5) to develop and implement a State policy jointly with the lead agency under part C and the State educational agency to provide early intervention services (which shall include an educational component that promotes school readiness and incorporates preliteracy, language, and numeracy skills) in accordance with part C to children with disabilities who are eligible for services under section 619 and who previously received services under part C until such children enter, or are eligible under State law to enter, kindergarten, or elementary school as appropriate.

(f) Subgrants to local educational agencies.

(1) Subgrants required.

Each State that receives a grant under this section for any fiscal year shall distribute any funds the State does not reserve under subsection (e) to local educational agencies (including public charter schools that operate as local educational agencies) in the State that have established their eligibility under section 613 for use in accordance with this part.

(2) Procedure for allocations to local educational agencies.

For each fiscal year for which funds are allocated to States under subsection (d), each State shall allocate funds under paragraph (1) as follows:

(A) Base payments.

The State shall first award each local educational agency described in paragraph (1) the amount the local educational agency would have received under this section for fiscal year 1999, if the State had distributed 75 percent of its grant for that year under section 611(d) as section 611(d) was then in effect.

(B) Allocation of remaining funds.

After making allocations under subparagraph (A), the State shall —

(i) allocate 85 percent of any remaining funds to those local educational agencies on the basis of the relative numbers of children enrolled in public and private elementary schools and secondary schools within the local educational agency's jurisdiction; and

(ii) allocate 15 percent of those remaining funds to those local educational agencies in accordance with their relative numbers of children living in poverty, as determined by the State educational agency.

(3) Reallocation of funds.

If a State educational agency determines that a local educational agency is adequately providing a free appropriate public education to all children with disabilities residing in the area served by that local educational agency with State and local funds, the State educational agency may reallocate any portion of the funds under this part that are not needed by that local educational agency to provide a free appropriate public education to other local educational agencies in the State that are not adequately providing special education and related services to all children with disabilities residing in the areas served by those other local educational agencies.

(g) Definitions.

In this section:

(1) Average per-pupil expenditure in public elementary schools and secondary schools in the United States.

The term "average per-pupil expenditure in public elementary schools and secondary schools in the United States" means —

(A) without regard to the source of funds —

(i) the aggregate current expenditures, during the second fiscal year preceding the fiscal year for which the determination is made (or, if satisfactory data for that year are not available, during the most recent preceding fiscal year for which satisfactory data are available) of all local educational agencies in the 50 States and the District of Columbia; plus

(ii) any direct expenditures by the State for the operation of those agencies; divided by

(B) the aggregate number of children in average daily attendance to whom those agencies provided free public education during that preceding year.

(2) State.

The term "State" means each of the 50 States, the District of Columbia, and the Commonwealth of Puerto Rico

(h) Use of amounts by Secretary of the Interior.

(1) Provision of amounts for assistance.

(A) In general.

The Secretary of Education shall provide amounts to the Secretary of the Interior to meet the need for assistance for the education of children with disabilities on reservations aged 5 to 21, inclusive, enrolled in elementary schools and secondary schools for Indian children operated or funded by the Secretary of the Interior. The amount of such payment for any fiscal year shall be equal to 80 percent of the amount allotted under subsection (b)(2) for that fiscal year. Of the amount described in the preceding sentence —

(i) 80 percent shall be allocated to such schools by July 1 of that fiscal year; and

(ii) 20 percent shall be allocated to such schools by September 30 of that fiscal year.

(B) Calculation of number of children.

In the case of Indian students aged 3 to 5, inclusive, who are enrolled in programs affiliated with the Bureau of Indian Affairs (referred to in this subsection as the "BIA") schools and that are required by the States in which such schools are located to attain or maintain State accreditation, and which schools have such accreditation prior to the date of enactment of the Individuals with Disabilities Education Act Amendments of 1991, the school shall be allowed to count those children for the purpose of distribution of the funds provided under this paragraph to the Secretary of the Interior. The Secretary of the Interior shall be responsible for meeting all of the requirements of this part for those children, in accordance with paragraph (2).

(C) Additional requirement.

With respect to all other children aged 3 to 21, inclusive, on reservations, the State educational agency shall be responsible for ensuring that all of the requirements of this part are implemented.

(2) Submission of information.

The Secretary of Education may provide the Secretary of the Interior amounts under paragraph (1) for a fiscal year only if the Secretary of the Interior submits to the Secretary of Education information that —

(A) demonstrates that the Department of the Interior meets the appropriate requirements, as determined by the Secretary of Education, of sections 612 (including monitoring and evaluation activities) and 613;

(B) includes a description of how the Secretary of the Interior will coordinate the provision of services under this part with local educational agencies, tribes and tribal organizations, and other private and Federal service providers;

(C) includes an assurance that there are public hearings, adequate notice of such hearings, and an opportunity for comment afforded to members of tribes, tribal governing bodies, and affected local school boards before the adoption of the policies, programs, and procedures related to the requirements described in subparagraph (A);

(D) includes an assurance that the Secretary of the Interior will provide such information as the Secretary of Education may require to comply with section 618;

(E) includes an assurance that the Secretary of the Interior and the Secretary of Health and Human Services have entered into a memorandum of agreement, to be provided to the Secretary of Education, for the coordination of services, resources, and personnel between their respective Federal, State, and local offices and with State and local educational agencies and other entities to facilitate the provision of services to Indian children with disabilities residing on or near reservations (such agreement shall provide for the apportionment of responsibilities and costs, including child find, evaluation, diagnosis, remediation or therapeutic measures, and (where appropriate) equipment and medical or personal supplies as needed for a child to remain in school or a program); and

(F) includes an assurance that the Department of the Interior will cooperate with the Department of Education in its exercise of monitoring and oversight of this application, and any agreements entered into between the Secretary of the Interior and other entities under this part, and will fulfill its duties under this part.

(3) Applicability.

The Secretary shall withhold payments under this subsection with respect to the information described in paragraph (2) in the same manner as the Secretary withholds payments under section 616(e)(6).

(4) Payments for education and services for Indian children with disabilities aged 3 through 5.

(A) In general.

With funds appropriated under subsection (i), the Secretary of Education shall make payments to the Secretary of the Interior to be distributed to tribes or tribal organizations (as defined under section 4 of the Indian Self-Determination and Education Assistance Act) or consortia of tribes or tribal organizations to provide for the coordination of assistance for special education and related services for children with disabilities aged 3 through 5 on reservations served by elementary schools and secondary schools for Indian children operated or funded by the Department of the Interior. The amount of such payments under subparagraph (B) for any fiscal year shall be equal to 20 percent of the amount allotted under subsection (b)(2).

(B) Distribution of funds.

The Secretary of the Interior shall distribute the total amount of the payment under subparagraph (A) by allocating to each tribe, tribal organization, or consortium an amount based on the number of children with disabilities aged 3 through 5 residing on reservations as reported annually, divided by the total of those children served by all tribes or tribal organizations.

(C) Submission of information.

To receive a payment under this paragraph, the tribe or tribal organization shall submit such figures to the Secretary of the Interior as required to determine the amounts to be allocated under subparagraph (B). This information shall be compiled and submitted to the Secretary of Education.

(D) Use of funds.

The funds received by a tribe or tribal organization shall be used to assist in child find, screening, and other procedures for the early identification of children aged 3 through 5, parent training, and the provision of direct services. These activities may be carried out directly or through contracts or cooperative agreements with the BIA, local educational agencies, and other public or private nonprofit organizations. The tribe or tribal organization is encouraged to involve Indian parents in the development and implementation of these activities. The tribe or tribal organization shall, as appropriate, make referrals to local, State, or Federal entities for the provision of services or further diagnosis.

(E) Biennial report.

To be eligible to receive a grant pursuant to subparagraph (A), the tribe or tribal organization shall provide to the Secretary of the Interior a biennial report of activities undertaken under this paragraph, including the number of contracts and cooperative agreements entered into, the number of children contacted and receiving services for each year, and the estimated number of children needing services during the 2 years following the year in which the report is made. The Secretary of the Interior shall include a summary of this information on a biennial basis in the report to the Secretary of Education required under this subsection. The Secretary of Education may require any additional information from the Secretary of the Interior.

(F) Prohibitions.

None of the funds allocated under this paragraph may be used by the Secretary of the Interior for administrative purposes, including child count and the provision of technical assistance.

(5) Plan for coordination of services.

The Secretary of the Interior shall develop and implement a plan for the coordination of services for all Indian children with disabilities residing on reservations covered under this title. Such plan shall provide for the coordination of services benefiting those children from whatever source, including tribes, the Indian Health Service, other BIA divisions, and other Federal agencies. In developing the plan, the Secretary of the Interior shall consult with all interested and involved parties. The plan shall be based on the needs of the children and the system best suited for meeting those needs, and may involve the establishment of cooperative agreements between the BIA, other Federal agencies, and other entities. The plan shall also be distributed upon request to States, State educational agencies and local educational agencies, and other agencies providing services to infants, toddlers, and children with disabilities, to tribes, and to other interested parties.

(6) Establishment of advisory board.

To meet the requirements of section 612(a)(21), the Secretary of the Interior shall establish, under the BIA, an advisory board composed of individuals involved in or concerned with the education and provision of services to Indian infants, toddlers, children, and youth with disabilities, including Indians with disabilities, Indian parents or guardians of such children, teachers, service providers, State and local educational officials, representatives of tribes or tribal organizations, representatives from State Interagency Coordinating Councils under section 641 in States having reservations, and other members representing the various divisions and entities of the BIA. The chairperson shall be selected by the Secretary of the Interior. The advisory board shall —

(A) assist in the coordination of services within the BIA and with other local, State, and Federal agencies in the provision of education for infants, toddlers, and children with disabilities;

(B) advise and assist the Secretary of the Interior in the performance of the Secretary of the Interior's responsibilities described in this subsection;

(C) develop and recommend policies concerning effective inter- and intra-agency collaboration, including modifications to regulations, and the elimination of barriers to inter- and intra-agency programs and activities;

(D) provide assistance and disseminate information on best practices, effective program coordination strategies, and recommendations for improved early intervention services or educational programming for Indian infants, toddlers, and children with disabilities; and

(E) provide assistance in the preparation of information required under paragraph (2)(D).

(7) Annual reports.

(A) In general.

The advisory board established under paragraph (6) shall prepare and submit to the Secretary of the Interior and to Congress an annual report containing a description of the activities of the advisory board for the preceding year.

(B) Availability.

The Secretary of the Interior shall make available to the Secretary of Education the report described in subparagraph (A).

(i) Authorization of appropriations.

For the purpose of carrying out this part, other than section 619, there are authorized to be appropriated —

(1) $12,358,376,571 for fiscal year 2005;

(2) $14,648,647,143 for fiscal year 2006;

(3) $16,938,917,714 for fiscal year 2007;

(4) $19,229,188,286 for fiscal year 2008;

(5) $21,519,458,857 for fiscal year 2009;

(6) $23,809,729,429 for fiscal year 2010;

(7) $26,100,000,000 for fiscal year 2011; and

(8) such sums as may be necessary for fiscal year 2012 and each succeeding fiscal year.

§ 1412. State eligibility

(a) In general.

A State is eligible for assistance under this part for a fiscal year if the State submits a plan that provides assurances to the Secretary that the State has in effect policies and procedures to ensure that the State meets each of the following conditions:

(1) Free appropriate public education.

(A) In general.

A free appropriate public education is available to all children with disabilities residing in the State between the ages of 3 and 21, inclusive, including children with disabilities who have been suspended or expelled from school.

(B) Limitation.

The obligation to make a free appropriate public education available to all children with disabilities does not apply with respect to children —

(i) aged 3 through 5 and 18 through 21 in a State to the extent that its application to those children would be inconsistent with State law or practice, or the order of any court, respecting the provision of public education to children in those age ranges; and

(ii) aged 18 through 21 to the extent that State law does not require that special education and related services under this part be provided to children with disabilities who, in the educational placement prior to their incarceration in an adult correctional facility —

(I) were not actually identified as being a child with a disability under section 602; or

(II) did not have an individualized education program under this part.

(C) State flexibility.

A State that provides early intervention services in accordance with part C to a child who is eligible for services under section 619, is not required to provide such child with a free appropriate public education.

(2) Full educational opportunity goal.

The State has established a goal of providing full educational opportunity to all children with disabilities and a detailed timetable for accomplishing that goal.

(3) Child find.

(A) In general.

All children with disabilities residing in the State, including children with disabilities who are homeless children or are wards of the State and children with disabilities attending private schools, regardless of the severity of their disabilities, and who are in need of special education and related services, are identified, located, and evaluated and a practical method is developed and implemented to determine which children with disabilities are currently receiving needed special education and related services.

(B) Construction.

Nothing in this title requires that children be classified by their disability so long as each child who has a disability listed in section 602 and who, by reason of that disability, needs special education and related services is regarded as a child with a disability under this part.

(4) Individualized education program.

An individualized education program, or an individualized family service plan that meets the requirements of section 636(d), is developed, reviewed, and revised for each child with a disability in accordance with section 614(d).

(5) Least restrictive environment.

(A) In general.

To the maximum extent appropriate, children with disabilities, including children in public or private institutions or other care facilities, are educated with children who are not disabled, and special classes, separate schooling, or other removal of children with disabilities from the regular educational environment occurs only when the nature or severity of the disability of a child is such that education in regular classes with the use of supplementary aids and services cannot be achieved satisfactorily.

(B) Additional requirement.

(i) In general.

A State funding mechanism shall not result in placements that violate the requirements of subparagraph (A), and a State shall not use a funding mechanism by which the State distributes funds on the basis of the type of setting in which a child is served that will result in the failure to provide a child with a disability a free appropriate public education according to the unique needs of the child as described in the child's IEP.

(ii) Assurance.

If the State does not have policies and procedures to ensure compliance with clause (i), the State shall provide the Secretary an assurance that the State will revise the funding mechanism as soon as feasible to ensure that such mechanism does not result in such placements.

(6) Procedural safeguards.

(A) In general.

Children with disabilities and their parents are afforded the procedural safeguards required by section 615.

(B) Additional procedural safeguards.

Procedures to ensure that testing and evaluation materials and procedures utilized for the purposes of evaluation and placement of children with disabilities for services under this title will be selected and administered so as not to be racially or culturally discriminatory. Such materials or procedures shall be provided and administered in the child's native language or mode of communication, unless it clearly is not feasible to do so, and no single procedure shall be the sole criterion for determining an appropriate educational program for a child.

(7) Evaluation.

Children with disabilities are evaluated in accordance with subsections (a) through (c) of section 614.

(8) Confidentiality.

Agencies in the State comply with section 617(c) (relating to the confidentiality of records and information).

(9) Transition from Part C to preschool programs.

Children participating in early intervention programs assisted under part C, and who will participate in preschool programs assisted under this part, experience a smooth and effective transition to those preschool programs in a manner consistent with section 637(a)(9). By the third birthday of such a child, an individualized education program or, if consistent with sections 614(d)(2)(B) and 636(d), an individualized family service plan, has been developed and is being implemented for the child. The local educational agency will participate in transition planning conferences arranged by the designated lead agency under section 635(a)(10).

(10) Children in private schools.

(A) Children enrolled in private schools by their parents.

(i) In general.

To the extent consistent with the number and location of children with disabilities in the State who are enrolled by their parents in private elementary schools and secondary schools in the school district served by a local educational agency, provision is made for the participation of those children in the program assisted or carried out under this part by providing for such children special education and related services in accordance with the following requirements, unless the Secretary has arranged for services to those children under subsection (f):

(I) Amounts to be expended for the provision of those services (including direct services to parentally placed private school children) by the local educational agency shall be equal to a proportionate amount of Federal funds made available under this part.

(II) In calculating the proportionate amount of Federal funds, the local educational agency, after timely and meaningful consultation with representatives of private schools as described in clause (iii), shall conduct a thorough and complete child find process to determine the number of parentally placed children with disabilities attending private schools located in the local educational agency.

(III) Such services to parentally placed private school children with disabilities may be provided to the children on the premises of private, including religious, schools, to the extent consistent with law.

(IV) State and local funds may supplement and in no case shall supplant the proportionate amount of Federal funds required to be expended under this subparagraph.

(V) Each local educational agency shall maintain in its records and provide to the State educational agency the number of children evaluated under this subparagraph, the number of children determined to be children with disabilities under this paragraph, and the number of children served under this paragraph.

(ii) Child find requirement.

(I) In general.

The requirements of paragraph (3) (relating to child find) shall apply with respect to children with disabilities in the State who are enrolled in private, including religious, elementary schools and secondary schools.

(II) Equitable participation.

The child find process shall be designed to ensure the equitable participation of parentally placed private school children with disabilities and an accurate count of such children.

(III) Activities.

In carrying out this clause, the local educational agency, or where applicable, the State educational agency, shall undertake activities similar to those activities undertaken for the agency's public school children.

(IV) Cost.

The cost of carrying out this clause, including individual evaluations, may not be considered in determining whether a local educational agency has met its obligations under clause (i).

(V) Completion period.

Such child find process shall be completed in a time period comparable to that for other students attending public schools in the local educational agency.

(iii) Consultation.

To ensure timely and meaningful consultation, a local educational agency, or where appropriate, a State educational agency, shall consult with private school representatives and representatives of parents of parentally placed private school children with disabilities during the design and development of special education and related services for the children, including regarding —

(I) the child find process and how parentally placed private school children suspected of having a disability can participate equitably, including how parents, teachers, and private school officials will be informed of the process;

(II) the determination of the proportionate amount of Federal funds available to serve parentally placed private school children with disabilities under this subparagraph, including the determination of how the amount was calculated;

(III) the consultation process among the local educational agency, private school officials, and representatives of parents of parentally placed private school children with disabilities, including how such process will operate throughout the school year to ensure that parentally placed private school children with disabilities identified through the child find process can meaningfully participate in special education and related services;

(IV) how, where, and by whom special education and related services will be provided for parentally placed private school children with disabilities, including a discussion of types of services, including direct services and alternate service delivery mechanisms, how such services will be apportioned if funds are insufficient to serve all children, and how and when these decisions will be made; and

(V) how, if the local educational agency disagrees with the views of the private school officials on the provision of services or the types of services, whether provided directly or through a contract, the local educational agency shall provide to the private school officials a written explanation of the reasons why the local educational agency chose not to provide services directly or through a contract.

(iv) Written affirmation.

When timely and meaningful consultation as required by clause (iii) has occurred, the local educational agency shall obtain a written affirmation signed by the representatives of participating private schools, and if such representatives do not provide such affirmation within a reasonable period of time, the local educational agency shall forward the documentation of the consultation process to the State educational agency.

(v) Compliance.

(I) In general.

A private school official shall have the right to submit a complaint to the State educational agency that the local educational agency did not engage in consultation that was meaningful and timely, or did not give due consideration to the views of the private school official.

(II) Procedure.

If the private school official wishes to submit a complaint, the official shall provide the basis of the noncompliance with this subparagraph by the local educational agency to the State educational agency, and the local educational agency shall forward the appropriate documentation to the State educational agency. If the private school official is dissatisfied with the decision of the State educational agency, such official may submit a complaint to the Secretary by providing the basis of the noncompliance with this subparagraph by the local educational agency to the Secretary, and the State educational agency shall forward the appropriate documentation to the Secretary.

(vi) Provision of equitable services.

(I) Directly or through contracts.

The provision of services pursuant to this subparagraph shall be provided —

(aa) by employees of a public agency; or

(bb) through contract by the public agency with an individual, association, agency, organization, or other entity.

(II) Secular, neutral, nonideological.

Special education and related services provided to parentally placed private school children with disabilities, including materials and equipment, shall be secular, neutral, and nonideological.

(vii) Public control of funds.

The control of funds used to provide special education and related services under this subparagraph, and title to materials, equipment, and property purchased with those funds, shall be in a public agency for the uses and purposes provided in this title, and a public agency shall administer the funds and property.

(B) Children placed in, or referred to, private schools by public agencies.

(i) In general.

Children with disabilities in private schools and facilities are provided special education and related services, in accordance with an individualized education program, at no cost to their parents, if such children are placed in, or referred to, such schools or facilities by the State or appropriate local educational agency as the means of carrying out the requirements of this part or any other applicable law requiring the provision of special education and related services to all children with disabilities within such State.

(ii) Standards.

In all cases described in clause (i), the State educational agency shall determine whether such schools and facilities meet standards that apply to State educational agencies and local educational agencies and that children so served have all the rights the children would have if served by such agencies.

(C) Payment for education of children enrolled in private schools without consent of or referral by the public agency.

(i) In general.

Subject to subparagraph (A), this part does not require a local educational agency to pay for the cost of education, including special education and related services, of a child with a disability at a private school or facility if that agency made a free appropriate public education available to the child and the parents elected to place the child in such private school or facility.

(ii) Reimbursement for private school placement.

If the parents of a child with a disability, who previously received special education and related services under the authority of a public agency, enroll the child in a private elementary school or secondary school without the consent of or referral by the public agency, a court or a hearing officer may require the agency to reimburse the parents for the cost of that enrollment if the court or hearing officer finds that the agency had not made a free appropriate public education available to the child in a timely manner prior to that enrollment.

(iii) Limitation on reimbursement.

The cost of reimbursement described in clause (ii) may be reduced or denied —

(I) if —

(aa) at the most recent IEP meeting that the parents attended prior to removal of the child from the public school, the parents did not inform the IEP Team that they were rejecting the placement proposed by the public agency to provide a free appropriate public education to their child, including stating their concerns and their intent to enroll their child in a private school at public expense; or

(bb) 10 business days (including any holidays that occur on a business day) prior to the removal of the child from the public school, the parents did not give written notice to the public agency of the information described in item (aa);

(II) if, prior to the parents' removal of the child from the public school, the public agency informed the parents, through the notice requirements described in section 615(b)(3), of its intent to evaluate the child (including a statement of the purpose of the evaluation that was appropriate and reasonable), but the parents did not make the child available for such evaluation; or

(III) upon a judicial finding of unreasonableness with respect to actions taken by the parents.

(iv) Exception.

Notwithstanding the notice requirement in clause (iii)(I), the cost of reimbursement —

(I) shall not be reduced or denied for failure to provide such notice if —

(aa) the school prevented the parent from providing such notice;

(bb) the parents had not received notice, pursuant to section 615, of the notice requirement in clause (iii)(I); or

(cc) compliance with clause (iii)(I) would likely result in physical harm to the child; and

(II) may, in the discretion of a court or a hearing officer, not be reduced or denied for failure to provide such notice if —

(aa) the parent is illiterate or cannot write in English; or

(bb) compliance with clause (iii)(I) would likely result in serious emotional harm to the child.

(11) State educational agency responsible for general supervision.

(A) In general.

The State educational agency is responsible for ensuring that —

(i) the requirements of this part are met;

(ii) all educational programs for children with disabilities in the State, including all such programs administered by any other State agency or local agency —

(I) are under the general supervision of individuals in the State who are responsible for educational programs for children with disabilities; and

(II) meet the educational standards of the State educational agency; and

(iii) in carrying out this part with respect to homeless children, the requirements of subtitle B of title VII of the McKinney-Vento Homeless Assistance Act (42 U.S.C. 11431 et seq.) are met.

(B) Limitation.

Subparagraph (A) shall not limit the responsibility of agencies in the State other than the State educational agency to provide, or pay for some or all of the costs of, a free appropriate public education for any child with a disability in the State.

(C) Exception.

Notwithstanding subparagraphs (A) and (B), the Governor (or another individual pursuant to State law), consistent with State law, may assign to any public agency in the State the responsibility of ensuring that the requirements of this part are met with respect to children with disabilities who are convicted as adults under State law and incarcerated in adult prisons.

(12) Obligations related to and methods of ensuring services.

(A) Establishing responsibility for services.

The Chief Executive Officer of a State or designee of the officer shall ensure that an interagency agreement or other mechanism for interagency coordination is in effect between each public agency described in subparagraph (B) and the State educational agency, in order to ensure that all services described in subparagraph (B)(i) that are needed to ensure a free appropriate public education are provided, including the provision of such services during the pendency of any dispute under clause (iii). Such agreement or mechanism shall include the following:

(i) Agency financial responsibility.

An identification of, or a method for defining, the financial responsibility of each agency for providing services described in subparagraph (B)(i) to ensure a free appropriate public education to children with disabilities, provided that the financial responsibility of each public agency described in subparagraph (B), including the State medicaid agency and other public insurers of children with disabilities, shall precede the financial responsibility of the local educational agency (or the State agency responsible for developing the child's IEP).

(ii) Conditions and terms of reimbursement.

The conditions, terms, and procedures under which a local educational agency shall be reimbursed by other agencies.

(iii) Interagency disputes.

Procedures for resolving interagency disputes (including procedures under which local educational agencies may initiate proceedings) under the agreement or other mechanism to secure reimbursement from other agencies or otherwise implement the provisions of the agreement or mechanism.

(iv) Coordination of services procedures.

Policies and procedures for agencies to determine and identify the interagency coordination responsibilities of each agency to promote the coordination and timely and appropriate delivery of services described in subparagraph (B)(i).

(B) Obligation of public agency.

(i) In general.

If any public agency other than an educational agency is otherwise obligated under Federal or State law, or assigned responsibility under State policy pursuant to subparagraph (A), to provide or pay for any services that are also considered special education or related services (such as, but not limited to, services described in section 602(1) relating to assistive technology devices, 602(2) relating to assistive technology services, 602(26) relating to related services, 602(33) relating to supplementary aids and services, and 602(34) relating to transition services) that are necessary for ensuring a free appropriate public education to children with disabilities within the State, such public agency shall fulfill that obligation or responsibility, either directly or through contract or other arrangement pursuant to subparagraph (A) or an agreement pursuant to subparagraph (C).

(ii) Reimbursement for services by public agency.

If a public agency other than an educational agency fails to provide or pay for the special education and related services described in clause (i), the local educational agency (or State agency responsible for developing the child's IEP) shall provide or pay for such services to the child. Such local educational agency or State agency is authorized to claim reimbursement for the services from the public agency that failed to provide or pay for such services and such public agency shall reimburse the local educational agency or State agency pursuant to the terms of the interagency agreement or other mechanism described in subparagraph (A)(i) according to the procedures established in such agreement pursuant to subparagraph (A)(ii).

(C) Special rule.

The requirements of subparagraph (A) may be met through —

(i) State statute or regulation;

(ii) signed agreements between respective agency officials that clearly identify the responsibilities of each agency relating to the provision of services; or

(iii) other appropriate written methods as determined by the Chief Executive Officer of the State or designee of the officer and approved by the Secretary.

(13) Procedural requirements relating to local educational agency eligibility.

The State educational agency will not make a final determination that a local educational agency is not eligible for assistance under this part without first affording that agency reasonable notice and an opportunity for a hearing.

(14) Personnel qualifications.

(A) In general.

The State educational agency has established and maintains qualifications to ensure that personnel necessary to carry out this part are appropriately and adequately prepared and trained, including that those personnel have the content knowledge and skills to serve children with disabilities.

(B) Related services personnel and paraprofessionals.

The qualifications under subparagraph (A) include qualifications for related services personnel and paraprofessionals that —

(i) are consistent with any State-approved or State-recognized certification, licensing, registration, or other comparable requirements that apply to the professional discipline in which those personnel are providing special education or related services;

(ii) ensure that related services personnel who deliver services in their discipline or profession meet the requirements of clause (i) and have not had certification or licensure requirements waived on an emergency, temporary, or provisional basis; and

(iii) allow paraprofessionals and assistants who are appropriately trained and supervised, in accordance with State law, regulation, or written policy, in meeting the requirements of this part to be used to assist in the provision of special education and related services under this part to children with disabilities.

(C) Qualifications for special education teachers.

The qualifications described in subparagraph (A) shall ensure that each person employed as a special education teacher in the State who teaches elementary school, middle school, or secondary school is highly qualified by the deadline established in section 1119(a)(2) of the Elementary and Secondary Education Act of 1965.

(D) Policy.

In implementing this section, a State shall adopt a policy that includes a requirement that local educational agencies in the State take measurable steps to recruit, hire, train, and retain highly qualified personnel to provide special education and related services under this part to children with disabilities.

(E) Rule of construction.

Notwithstanding any other individual right of action that a parent or student may maintain under this part, nothing in this paragraph shall be construed to create a right of action on behalf of an individual student for the failure of a particular State educational agency or local educational agency staff person to be highly qualified, or to prevent a parent from filing a complaint about staff qualifications with the State educational agency as provided for under this part.

(15) Performance goals and indicators.

The State —

(A) has established goals for the performance of children with disabilities in the State that —

(i) promote the purposes of this title, as stated in section 601(d);

(ii) are the same as the State's definition of adequate yearly progress, including the State's objectives for progress by children with disabilities, under section 1111(b)(2)(C) of the Elementary and Secondary Education Act of 1965;

(iii) address graduation rates and dropout rates, as well as such other factors as the State may determine; and

(iv) are consistent, to the extent appropriate, with any other goals and standards for children established by the State;

(B) has established performance indicators the State will use to assess progress toward achieving the goals described in subparagraph (A), including measurable annual objectives for progress by children with disabilities under section 1111(b)(2)(C)(v)(II)(cc) of the Elementary and Secondary Education Act of 1965; and

(C) will annually report to the Secretary and the public on the progress of the State, and of children with disabilities in the State, toward meeting the goals established under subparagraph (A), which may include elements of the reports required under section 1111(h) of the Elementary and Secondary Education Act of 1965.

(16) Participation in assessments.

(A) In general.

All children with disabilities are included in all general State and districtwide assessment programs, including assessments described under section 1111 of the Elementary and Secondary Education Act of 1965, with appropriate accommodations and alternate assessments where necessary and as indicated in their respective individualized education programs.

(B) Accommodation guidelines.

The State (or, in the case of a districtwide assessment, the local educational agency) has developed guidelines for the provision of appropriate accommodations.

(C) Alternate assessments.

(i) In general.

The State (or, in the case of a districtwide assessment, the local educational agency) has developed and implemented guidelines for the participation of children with disabilities in alternate assessments for those children who cannot participate in regular assessments under subparagraph (A) with accommodations as indicated in their respective individualized education programs.

(ii) Requirements for alternate assessments.

The guidelines under clause (i) shall provide for alternate assessments that —

(I) are aligned with the State's challenging academic content standards and challenging student academic achievement standards; and

(II) if the State has adopted alternate academic achievement standards permitted under the regulations promulgated to carry out section 1111(b)(1) of the Elementary and Secondary Education Act of 1965, measure the achievement of children with disabilities against those standards.

(iii) Conduct of alternate assessments.

The State conducts the alternate assessments described in this subparagraph.

(D) Reports.

The State educational agency (or, in the case of a districtwide assessment, the local educational agency) makes available to the public, and reports to the public with the same frequency and in the same detail as it reports on the assessment of nondisabled children, the following:

(i) The number of children with disabilities participating in regular assessments, and the number of those children who were provided accommodations in order to participate in those assessments.

(ii) The number of children with disabilities participating in alternate assessments described in subparagraph (C)(ii)(I).

(iii) The number of children with disabilities participating in alternate assessments described in subparagraph (C)(ii)(II).

(iv) The performance of children with disabilities on regular assessments and on alternate assessments (if the number of children with disabilities participating in those assessments is sufficient to yield statistically reliable information and reporting that information will not reveal personally identifiable information about an individual student), compared with the achievement of all children, including children with disabilities, on those assessments.

(E) Universal design.

The State educational agency (or, in the case of a districtwide assessment, the local educational agency) shall, to the extent feasible, use universal design principles in developing and administering any assessments under this paragraph.

(17) Supplementation of state, local, and other federal funds.

(A) Expenditures.

Funds paid to a State under this part will be expended in accordance with all the provisions of this part.

(B) Prohibition against commingling.

Funds paid to a State under this part will not be commingled with State funds.

(C) Prohibition against supplantation and conditions for waiver by secretary.

Except as provided in section 613, funds paid to a State under this part will be used to supplement the level of Federal, State, and local funds (including funds that are not under the direct control of State or local educational agencies) expended for special education and related services provided to children with disabilities under this part and in no case to supplant such Federal, State, and local funds, except that, where the State provides clear and convincing evidence that all children with disabilities have available to them a free appropriate public education, the Secretary may waive, in whole or in part, the requirements of this subparagraph if the Secretary concurs with the evidence provided by the State.

(18) Maintenance of state financial support.

(A) In general.

The State does not reduce the amount

of State financial support for special education and related services for children with disabilities, or otherwise made available because of the excess costs of educating those children, below the amount of that support for the preceding fiscal year.

(B) Reduction of funds for failure to maintain support.

The Secretary shall reduce the allocation of funds under section 611 for any fiscal year following the fiscal year in which the State fails to comply with the requirement of subparagraph (A) by the same amount by which the State fails to meet the requirement.

(C) Waivers for exceptional or uncontrollable circumstances.

The Secretary may waive the requirement of subparagraph (A) for a State, for 1 fiscal year at a time, if the Secretary determines that —

(i) granting a waiver would be equitable due to exceptional or uncontrollable circumstances such as a natural disaster or a precipitous and unforeseen decline in the financial resources of the State; or

(ii) the State meets the standard in paragraph (17)(C) for a waiver of the requirement to supplement, and not to supplant, funds received under this part.

(D) Subsequent years.

If, for any year, a State fails to meet the requirement of subparagraph (A), including any year for which the State is granted a waiver under subparagraph (C), the financial support required of the State in future years under subparagraph (A) shall be the amount that would have been required in the absence of that failure and not the reduced level of the State's support.

(19) Public participation.

Prior to the adoption of any policies and procedures needed to comply with this section (including any amendments to such policies and procedures), the State ensures that there are public hearings, adequate notice of the hearings, and an opportunity for comment available to the general public, including individuals with disabilities and parents of children with disabilities.

(20) Rule of construction.

In complying with paragraphs (17) and (18), a State may not use funds paid to it under this part to satisfy State-law mandated funding obligations to local educational agencies, including funding based on student attendance or enrollment, or inflation.

(21) State advisory panel.

(A) In general.

The State has established and maintains an advisory panel for the purpose of providing policy guidance with respect to special education and related services for children with disabilities in the State.

(B) Membership.

Such advisory panel shall consist of members appointed by the Governor, or any other official authorized under State law to make such appointments, be representative of the State population, and be composed of individuals involved in, or concerned with, the education of children with disabilities, including —

(i) parents of children with disabilities (ages birth through 26);

(ii) individuals with disabilities;

(iii) teachers;

(iv) representatives of institutions of higher education that prepare special education and related services personnel;

(v) State and local education officials, including officials who carry out activities under subtitle B of title VII of the McKinney-Vento Homeless Assistance Act (42 U.S.C. 11431 et seq.);

(vi) administrators of programs for children with disabilities;

(vii) representatives of other State agencies involved in the financing or delivery of related services to children with disabilities;

(viii) representatives of private schools and public charter schools;

(ix) not less than 1 representative of a vocational, community, or business organization concerned with the provision of transition services to children with disabilities;

(x) a representative from the State child welfare agency responsible for foster care; and

(xi) representatives from the State juvenile and adult corrections agencies.

(C) Special rule.

A majority of the members of the panel shall be individuals with disabilities or parents of children with disabilities (ages birth through 26).

(D) Duties.

The advisory panel shall —

(i) advise the State educational agency of unmet needs within the State in the education of children with disabilities;

(ii) comment publicly on any rules or regulations proposed by the State regarding the education of children with disabilities;

(iii) advise the State educational agency in developing evaluations and reporting on data to the Secretary under section 618;

(iv) advise the State educational agency in developing corrective action plans to address findings identified in Federal monitoring reports under this part; and

(v) advise the State educational agency in developing and implementing policies relating to the coordination of services for children with disabilities.

(22) Suspension and expulsion rates.

(A) In general.

The State educational agency examines data, including data disaggregated by race and ethnicity, to determine if significant discrepancies are occurring in the rate of long-term suspensions and expulsions of children with disabilities —

(i) among local educational agencies in the State; or

(ii) compared to such rates for nondisabled children within such agencies.

(B) Review and revision of policies.

If such discrepancies are occurring, the State educational agency reviews and, if appropriate, revises (or requires the affected State or local educational agency to revise) its policies, procedures, and practices relating to the development and implementation of IEPs, the use of positive behavioral interventions and supports, and procedural safeguards, to ensure that such policies, procedures, and practices comply with this title.

(23) Access to instructional materials.

(A) In general.

The State adopts the National Instructional Materials Accessibility Standard for the purposes of providing instructional materials to blind persons or other persons with print disabilities, in a timely manner after the publication of the National Instructional Materials Accessibility Standard in the Federal Register.

(B) Rights of state educational agency.

Nothing in this paragraph shall be construed to require any State educational agency to coordinate with the National Instructional Materials Access Center. If a State educational agency chooses not to coordinate with the National Instructional Materials Access Center, such agency shall provide an assurance to the Secretary that the agency will provide instructional materials to blind persons or other persons with print disabilities in a timely manner.

(C) Preparation and delivery of files.

If a State educational agency chooses to coordinate with the National Instructional Materials Access Center, not later than 2 years after the date of enactment of the Individuals with Disabilities Education Improvement Act of 2004, the agency, as part of any print instructional materials adoption process, procurement contract, or other practice or instrument used for purchase of print instructional materials, shall enter into a written contract with the publisher of the print instructional materials to —

(i) require the publisher to prepare and, on or before delivery of the print instructional materials, provide to the National Instructional Materials Access Center electronic files containing the contents of the print instructional materials using the National Instructional Materials Accessibility Standard; or

(ii) purchase instructional materials from the publisher that are produced in, or may be rendered in, specialized formats.

(D) Assistive technology.

In carrying out this paragraph, the State educational agency, to the maximum extent possible, shall work collaboratively with the State agency responsible for assistive technology programs.

(E) Definitions.

In this paragraph:

(i) National instructional materials access center.

The term "National Instructional Materials Access Center" means the center established pursuant to section 674(e).

(ii) National instructional materials accessibility standard.

The term "National Instructional Materials Accessibility Standard" has the meaning given the term in section 674(e)(3)(A).

(iii) Specialized formats.

The term "specialized formats" has the meaning given the term in section 674(e)(3)(D).

(24) Overidentification and disproportionality.

The State has in effect, consistent with the purposes of this title and with section 618(d), policies and procedures designed to prevent the inappropriate overidentification or disproportionate representation by race and ethnicity of children as children with disabilities, including children with disabilities with a particular impairment described in section 602.

(25) Prohibition on mandatory medication.

(A) In general.

The State educational agency shall prohibit State and local educational agency personnel from requiring a child to obtain a prescription for a substance covered by the Controlled Substances Act (21 U.S.C. 801 et seq.) as a condition of attending school, receiving an evaluation under subsection (a) or (c) of section 614, or receiving services under this title.

(B) Rule of construction.

Nothing in subparagraph (A) shall be construed to create a Federal prohibition against teachers and other school personnel consulting or sharing classroom-based observations with parents or guardians regarding a student's academic and functional performance, or behavior in the classroom or school, or regarding the need for evaluation for special education or related services under paragraph (3).

(b) State educational agency as provider of free appropriate public education or direct services.

If the State educational agency provides free appropriate public education to children with disabilities, or provides direct services to such children, such agency —

(1) shall comply with any additional requirements of section 613(a), as if such agency were a local educational agency; and

(2) may use amounts that are otherwise available to such agency under this part to serve those children without regard to section 613(a)(2)(A)(i) (relating to excess costs).

(c) Exception for prior state plans.

(1) In general.

If a State has on file with the Secretary policies and procedures that demonstrate that such State meets any requirement of subsection (a), including any policies and procedures filed under this part as in effect before the effective date of the Individuals with Disabilities Education Improvement Act of 2004, the Secretary shall consider such State to have met such requirement for purposes of receiving a grant under this part.

(2) Modifications made by state.

Subject to paragraph (3), an application submitted by a State in accordance with this section shall remain in effect until the State submits to the Secretary such modifications as the State determines necessary. This section shall apply to a modification to an application to the same extent and in the same manner as this section applies to the original plan.

(3) Modifications required by the secretary.

If, after the effective date of the Individuals with Disabilities Education Improvement Act of 2004, the provisions of this title are amended (or the regulations developed to carry out this title are amended), there is a new interpretation of this title by a Federal court or a State's highest court, or there is an official finding of noncompliance with Federal law or regulations, then the Secretary may require a State to modify its application only to the extent necessary to ensure the State's compliance with this part.

(d) Approval by the secretary.

(1) In general.

If the Secretary determines that a State is eligible to receive a grant under this part, the Secretary shall notify the State of that determination.

(2) Notice and hearing.

The Secretary shall not make a final determination that a State is not eligible to receive a grant under this part until after providing the State —

(A) with reasonable notice; and

(B) with an opportunity for a hearing.

(e) Assistance under other federal programs.

Nothing in this title permits a State to reduce medical and other assistance available, or to alter eligibility, under titles V and XIX of the Social Security Act with respect to the provision of a free appropriate public education for children with disabilities in the State.

(f) By-pass for children in private schools.

(1) In general.

If, on the date of enactment of the Education of the Handicapped Act Amendments of 1983, a State educational agency was prohibited by law from providing for the equitable participation in special programs of children with disabilities enrolled in private elementary schools and secondary schools as required by subsection (a)(10)(A), or if the Secretary determines that a State educational agency, local educational agency, or other entity has substantially failed or is unwilling to provide for such equitable participation, then the Secretary shall, notwithstanding such provision of law, arrange for the provision of services to such children through arrangements that shall be subject to the requirements of such subsection.

(2) Payments.

(A) Determination of amounts.

If the Secretary arranges for services pursuant to this subsection, the Secretary, after consultation with the appropriate public and private school officials, shall pay to the provider of such services for a fiscal year an amount per child that does not exceed the amount determined by dividing —

(i) the total amount received by the State under this part for such fiscal year; by

(ii) the number of children with disabilities served in the prior year, as reported to the Secretary by the State under section 618.

(B) Withholding of certain amounts.

Pending final resolution of any investigation or complaint that may result in a determination under this subsection, the Secretary may withhold from the allocation of the affected State educational agency the amount the Secretary estimates will be necessary to pay the cost of services described in subparagraph (A).

(C) Period of payments.

The period under which payments are made under subparagraph (A) shall continue until the Secretary determines that there will no longer be any failure or inability on the part of the State educational agency to meet the requirements of subsection (a)(10)(A).

(3) Notice and hearing.

(A) In general.

The Secretary shall not take any final action under this subsection until the State educational agency affected by such action has had an opportunity, for not less than 45 days after receiving written notice thereof, to submit written objections and to appear before the Secretary or the Secretary's designee to show cause why such action should not be taken.

(B) Review of action.

If a State educational agency is dissatisfied with the Secretary's final action after a proceeding under subparagraph (A), such agency may, not later than 60 days after notice of such action, file with the United States court of appeals for the circuit in which such State is located a petition for review of that action. A copy of the petition shall be forthwith transmitted by the clerk of the court to the Secretary. The Secretary thereupon shall file in the court the record of the proceedings on which the Secretary based the Secretary's action, as provided in section 2112 of title 28, United States Code.

(C) Review of findings of fact.

The findings of fact by the Secretary, if supported by substantial evidence, shall be conclusive, but the court, for good cause shown, may remand the case to the Secretary to take further evidence, and the Secretary may thereupon make new or modified findings of fact and may modify the Secretary's previous action, and shall file in the court the record of the further proceedings. Such new or modified findings of fact shall likewise be conclusive if supported by substantial evidence.

(D) Jurisdiction of court of appeals; review by united states supreme court.

Upon the filing of a petition under subparagraph (B), the United States court of appeals shall have jurisdiction to affirm the action of the Secretary or to set it aside, in whole or in part. The judgment of the court shall be subject to review by the Supreme Court of the United States upon certiorari or certification as provided in section 1254 of title 28, United States Code.

§ 1413. Local educational agency eligibility

(a) In general.

A local educational agency is eligible for assistance under this part for a fiscal year if such agency submits a plan that provides assurances to the State educational agency that the local educational agency meets each of the following conditions:

(1) Consistency with state policies.

The local educational agency, in providing for the education of children with disabilities within its jurisdiction, has in effect policies, procedures, and programs that are consistent with the State policies and procedures established under section 612.

(2) Use of amounts.

(A) In general.

Amounts provided to the local educational agency under this part shall be expended in accordance with the applicable provisions of this part and —

(i) shall be used only to pay the excess costs of providing special education and related services to children with disabilities;

(ii) shall be used to supplement State, local, and other Federal funds and not to supplant such funds; and

(iii) shall not be used, except as provided in subparagraphs (B) and (C), to reduce the level of expenditures for the education of children with disabilities made by the local educational agency from local funds below the level of those expenditures for the preceding fiscal year.

(B) Exception.

Notwithstanding the restriction in subparagraph (A)(iii), a local educational agency may reduce the level of expenditures where such reduction is attributable to —

(i) the voluntary departure, by retirement or otherwise, or departure for just cause, of special education personnel;

(ii) a decrease in the enrollment of children with disabilities;

(iii) the termination of the obligation of the agency, consistent with this part, to provide a program of special education to a particular child with a disability that is an exceptionally costly program, as determined by the State educational agency, because the child —

(I) has left the jurisdiction of the agency;

(II) has reached the age at which the obligation of the agency to provide a free appropriate public education to the child has terminated; or

(III) no longer needs such program of special education; or

(iv) the termination of costly expenditures for long-term purchases, such as the acquisition of equipment or the construction of school facilities.

(C) Adjustment to local fiscal effort in certain fiscal years.

(i) Amounts in excess.

Notwithstanding clauses (ii) and (iii) of subparagraph (A), for any fiscal year for which the allocation received by a local educational agency under section 611(f) exceeds the amount the local educational agency received for the previous fiscal year, the local educational agency may reduce the level of expenditures otherwise required by subparagraph (A)(iii) by not more than 50 percent of the amount of such excess.

(ii) Use of amounts to carry out activities under ESEA.

If a local educational agency exercises the authority under clause (i), the agency shall use an amount of local funds equal to the reduction in expenditures under clause (i) to carry out activities authorized under the Elementary and Secondary Education Act of 1965.

(iii) State prohibition.

Notwithstanding clause (i), if a State educational agency determines that a local educational agency is unable to establish and maintain programs of free appropriate public education that meet the requirements of subsection (a) or the State educational agency has taken action against the local educational agency under section 616, the State educational agency shall prohibit the local educational agency from reducing the level of expenditures under clause (i) for that fiscal year.

(iv) Special rule.

The amount of funds expended by a local educational agency under subsection (f) shall count toward the maximum amount of expenditures such local educational agency may reduce under clause (i).

(D) Schoolwide programs under Title I of the ESEA. —

Notwithstanding subparagraph (A) or any other provision of this part, a local educational agency may use funds received under this part for any fiscal year to carry out a schoolwide program under section 1114 of the Elementary and Secondary Education Act of 1965, except that the amount so used in any such program shall not exceed —

(i) the number of children with disabilities participating in the schoolwide program; multiplied by

(ii)(I) the amount received by the local educational agency under this part for that fiscal year; divided by

(II) the number of children with disabilities in the jurisdiction of that agency.

(3) Personnel development.

The local educational agency shall ensure that all personnel necessary to carry out this part are appropriately and adequately prepared, subject to the requirements of section 612(a)(14) and section 2122 of the Elementary and Secondary Education Act of 1965.

(4) Permissive use of funds.

(A) Uses.

Notwithstanding paragraph (2)(A) or section 612(a)(17)(B) (relating to commingled funds), funds provided to the local educational agency under this part may be used for the following activities:

(i) Services and aids that also benefit nondisabled children.

For the costs of special education and related services, and supplementary aids and services, provided in a regular class or other education-related setting to a child with a disability in accordance with the individualized education program of the child, even if 1 or more nondisabled children benefit from such services.

(ii) Early intervening services.

To develop and implement coordinated, early intervening educational services in accordance with subsection (f).

(iii) High cost education and related services.

To establish and implement cost or risk sharing funds, consortia, or cooperatives for the local educational agency itself, or for local educational agencies working in a consortium of which the local educational agency is a part, to pay for high cost special education and related services.

(B) Administrative case management.

A local educational agency may use funds received under this part to purchase appropriate technology for recordkeeping, data collection, and related case management activities of teachers and related services personnel providing services described in the individualized education program of children with disabilities, that is needed for the implementation of such case management activities.

(5) Treatment of charter schools and their students.

In carrying out this part with respect to charter schools that are public schools of the local educational agency, the local educational agency —

(A) serves children with disabilities attending those charter schools in the same manner as the local educational agency serves children with disabilities in its other schools, including providing supplementary and related services on site at the charter school to the same extent to which the local educational agency has a policy or practice of providing such services on the site to its other public schools; and

(B) provides funds under this part to those charter schools —

(i) on the same basis as the local educational agency provides funds to the local educational agency's other public schools, including proportional distribution based on relative enrollment of children with disabilities; and

(ii) at the same time as the agency distributes other Federal funds to the agency's other public schools, consistent with the State's charter school law.

(6) Purchase of instructional materials.

(A) In general.

Not later than 2 years after the date of enactment of the Individuals with Disabilities Education Improvement Act of 2004, a local educational agency that chooses to coordinate with the National Instructional Materials Access Center, when purchasing print instructional materials, shall acquire the print instructional materials in the same manner and subject to the same conditions as a State educational agency acquires print instructional materials under section 612(a)(23).

(B) Rights of local educational agency.

Nothing in this paragraph shall be construed to require a local educational agency to coordinate with the National Instructional Materials Access Center. If a local educational agency chooses not to coordinate with the National Instructional Materials Access Center, the local educational agency shall provide an assurance to the State educational agency that the local educational agency will provide instructional materials to blind persons or other persons with print disabilities in a timely manner.

(7) Information for state educational agency.

The local educational agency shall provide the State educational agency with information necessary to enable the State educational agency to carry out its duties under this part, including, with respect to paragraphs (15) and (16) of section 612(a), information relating to the performance of children with disabilities participating in programs carried out under this part.

(8) Public information.

The local educational agency shall make available to parents of children with disabilities and to the general public all documents relating to the eligibility of such agency under this part.

(9) Records regarding migratory children with disabilities.

The local educational agency shall cooperate in the Secretary's efforts under section 1308 of the Elementary and Secondary Education Act of 1965 to ensure the linkage of records pertaining to migratory children with a disability for the purpose of electronically exchanging, among the States, health and educational information regarding such children.

(b) Exception for prior local plans.

(1) In general.

If a local educational agency or State agency has on file with the State educational agency policies and procedures that demonstrate that such local educational agency, or such State agency, as the case may be, meets any requirement of subsection (a), including any policies and procedures filed under this part as in effect before the effective date of the Individuals with Disabilities Education Improvement Act of 2004, the State educational agency shall consider such local educational agency or State agency, as the case may be, to have met such requirement for purposes of receiving assistance under this part.

(2) Modification made by local educational agency.

Subject to paragraph (3), an application submitted by a local educational agency in accordance with this section shall remain in effect until the local educational agency submits to the State educational agency such modifications as the local educational agency determines necessary.

(3) Modifications required by state educational agency.

If, after the effective date of the Individuals with Disabilities Education Improvement Act of 2004, the provisions of this title are amended (or the regulations developed to carry out this title are amended), there is a new interpretation of this title by Federal or State courts, or there is an official finding of noncompliance with Federal or State law or regulations, then the State educational agency may require a local educational agency to modify its application only to the extent necessary to ensure the local educational agency's compliance with this part or State law.

(c) Notification of local educational agency or state agency in case of ineligibility.

If the State educational agency determines that a local educational agency or State agency is not eligible under this section, then the State educational agency shall notify the local educational agency or State agency, as the case may be, of that determination and shall provide such local educational agency or State agency with reasonable notice and an opportunity for a hearing.

(d) Local educational agency compliance.

(1) In general.

If the State educational agency, after reasonable notice and an opportunity for a hearing, finds that a local educational agency or State agency that has been determined to be eligible under this section is failing to comply with any requirement described in subsection (a), the State educational agency shall reduce or shall not provide any further payments to the local educational agency or State agency until the State educational agency is satisfied that the local educational agency or State agency, as the case may be, is complying with that requirement.

(2) Additional requirement.

Any State agency or local educational agency in receipt of a notice described in paragraph (1) shall, by means of public notice, take such measures as may be necessary to bring the pendency of an action pursuant to this subsection to the attention of the public within the jurisdiction of such agency.

(3) Consideration.

In carrying out its responsibilities under paragraph (1), the State educational agency shall consider any decision made in a hearing held under section 615 that is adverse to the local educational agency or State agency involved in that decision.

(e) Joint establishment of eligibility.

(1) Joint establishment.

(A) In general.

A State educational agency may require a local educational agency to establish its eligibility jointly with another local educational agency if the State educational agency determines that the local educational agency will be ineligible under this section because the local educational agency will not be able to establish and maintain programs of sufficient size and scope to effectively meet the needs of children with disabilities.

(B) Charter school exception.

A State educational agency may not require a charter school that is a local educational agency to jointly establish its eligibility under subparagraph (A) unless the charter school is explicitly permitted to do so under the State's charter school law.

(2) Amount of payments.

If a State educational agency requires the joint establishment of eligibility under paragraph (1), the total amount of funds made available to the affected local educational agencies shall be equal to the sum of the payments that each such local educational agency would have received under section 611(f) if such agencies were eligible for such payments.

(3) Requirements.

Local educational agencies that establish joint eligibility under this subsection shall —

(A) adopt policies and procedures that are consistent with the State's policies and procedures under section 612(a); and

(B) be jointly responsible for implementing programs that receive assistance under this part.

(4) Requirements for educational service agencies.

(A) In general.

If an educational service agency is required by State law to carry out programs under this part, the joint responsibilities given to local educational agencies under this subsection shall —

(i) not apply to the administration and disbursement of any payments received by that educational service agency; and

(ii) be carried out only by that educational service agency.

(B) Additional requirement.

Notwithstanding any other provision of this subsection, an educational service agency shall provide for the education of children with disabilities in the least restrictive environment, as required by section 612(a)(5).

(f) Early intervening services.

(1) In general.

A local educational agency may not use more than 15 percent of the amount such agency receives under this part for any fiscal year, less any amount reduced by the agency pursuant to subsection (a)(2)(C), if any, in combination with other amounts (which may include amounts other than education funds), to develop and implement coordinated, early intervening services, which may include interagency financing structures, for students in kindergarten through grade 12 (with a particular emphasis on students in kindergarten through grade 3) who have not been identified as needing special education or related services but who need additional academic and behavioral support to succeed in a general education environment.

(2) Activities.

In implementing coordinated, early intervening services under this subsection, a local educational agency may carry out activities that include —

(A) professional development (which may be provided by entities other than local educational agencies) for teachers and other school staff to enable such personnel to deliver scientifically based academic instruction and behavioral interventions, including scientifically based literacy instruction, and, where appropriate, instruction on the use of adaptive and instructional software; and

(B) providing educational and behavioral evaluations, services, and supports, including scientifically based literacy instruction.

(3) Construction.

Nothing in this subsection shall be construed to limit or create a right to a free appropriate public education under this part.

(4) Reporting.

Each local educational agency that develops and maintains coordinated, early intervening services under this subsection shall annually report to the State educational agency on —

(A) the number of students served under this subsection; and

(B) the number of students served under this subsection who subsequently receive special education and related services under this title during the preceding 2-year period.

(5) Coordination with Elementary and Secondary Education Act of 1965.

Funds made available to carry out this subsection may be used to carry out coordinated, early intervening services aligned with activities funded by, and carried out under, the Elementary and Secondary Education Act of 1965 if such funds are used to supplement, and not supplant, funds made available under the Elementary and Secondary Education Act of 1965 for the activities and services assisted under this subsection.

(g) Direct services by the state educational agency.

(1) In general.

A State educational agency shall use the payments that would otherwise have been available to a local educational agency or to a State agency to provide special education and related services directly to children with disabilities residing in the area served by that local educational agency, or for whom that State agency is responsible, if the State educational agency determines that the local educational agency or State agency, as the case may be —

(A) has not provided the information needed to establish the eligibility of such local educational agency or State agency under this section;

(B) is unable to establish and maintain programs of free appropriate public education that meet the requirements of subsection (a);

(C) is unable or unwilling to be consolidated with 1 or more local educational agencies in order to establish and maintain such programs; or

(D) has 1 or more children with disabilities who can best be served by a regional or State program or service delivery system designed to meet the needs of such children.

(2) Manner and location of education and services.

The State educational agency may provide special education and related services under paragraph (1) in such manner and at such locations (including regional or State centers) as the State educational agency considers appropriate. Such education and services shall be provided in accordance with this part.

(h) State agency eligibility.

Any State agency that desires to receive a subgrant for any fiscal year under section 611(f) shall demonstrate to the satisfaction of the State educational agency that —

(1) all children with disabilities who are

participating in programs and projects funded under this part receive a free appropriate public education, and that those children and their parents are provided all the rights and procedural safeguards described in this part; and

(2) the agency meets such other conditions of this section as the Secretary determines to be appropriate.

(i) Disciplinary information.

The State may require that a local educational agency include in the records of a child with a disability a statement of any current or previous disciplinary action that has been taken against the child and transmit such statement to the same extent that such disciplinary information is included in, and transmitted with, the student records of nondisabled children. The statement may include a description of any behavior engaged in by the child that required disciplinary action, a description of the disciplinary action taken, and any other information that is relevant to the safety of the child and other individuals involved with the child. If the State adopts such a policy, and the child transfers from 1 school to another, the transmission of any of the child's records shall include both the child's current individualized education program and any such statement of current or previous disciplinary action that has been taken against the child.

(j) State agency flexibility.

(1) Adjustment to state fiscal effort in certain fiscal years.

For any fiscal year for which the allotment received by a State under section 611 exceeds the amount the State received for the previous fiscal year and if the State in school year 2003-2004 or any subsequent school year pays or reimburses all local educational agencies within the State from State revenue 100 percent of the non-Federal share of the costs of special education and related services, the State educational agency, notwithstanding paragraphs (17) and (18) of section 612(a) and section 612(b), may reduce the level of expenditures from State sources for the education of children with disabilities by not more than 50 percent of the amount of such excess.

(2) Prohibition.

Notwithstanding paragraph (1), if the Secretary determines that a State educational agency is unable to establish, maintain, or oversee programs of free appropriate public education that meet the requirements of this part, or that the State needs assistance, intervention, or substantial intervention under section 616(d)(2)(A), the Secretary shall prohibit the State educational agency from exercising the authority in paragraph (1).

(3) Education activities.

If a State educational agency exercises the authority under paragraph (1), the agency shall use funds from State sources, in an amount equal to the amount of the reduction under paragraph (1), to support activities authorized under the Elementary and Secondary Education Act of 1965 or to support need based student or teacher higher education programs.

(4) Report.

For each fiscal year for which a State educational agency exercises the authority under paragraph (1), the State educational agency shall report to the Secretary the amount of expenditures reduced pursuant to such paragraph and the activities that were funded pursuant to paragraph (3).

(5) Limitation.

Notwithstanding paragraph (1), a State educational agency may not reduce the level of expenditures described in paragraph (1) if any local educational agency in the State would, as a result of such reduction, receive less than 100 percent of the amount necessary to ensure that all children with disabilities served by the local educational agency receive a free appropriate public education from the combination of Federal funds received under this title and State funds received from the State educational agency.

§ 1414. Evaluations, eligibility determinations, individualized education programs, and educational placements

(a) Evaluations and reevaluations

(1) Initial evaluations

(A) In general

A State educational agency, other State agency, or local educational agency shall conduct a full and individual initial evaluation in accordance with this paragraph and subsection (b), before the initial provision of special education and related services to a child with a disability under this part.

(B) Request for initial evaluation.

Consistent with subparagraph (D), either a parent of a child, or a State educational agency, other State agency, or local educational agency may initiate a request for an initial evaluation to determine if the child is a child with a disability.

(C) Procedures.

(i) In general.

Such initial evaluation shall consist of procedures —

(I) to determine whether a child is a child with a disability (as defined in section 602) within 60 days of receiving parental consent for the evaluation, or, if the State establishes a timeframe within which the evaluation must be conducted, within such timeframe; and

(II) to determine the educational needs of such child.

(ii) Exception.

The relevant timeframe in clause (i)(I) shall not apply to a local educational agency if —

(I) a child enrolls in a school served by the local educational agency after the relevant timeframe in clause (i)(I) has begun and prior to a determination by the child's previous local educational agency as to whether the child is a child with a disability (as defined in section 602), but only if the subsequent local educational agency is making sufficient progress to ensure a prompt completion of the evaluation, and the parent and subsequent local educational agency agree to a specific time when the evaluation will be completed; or

(II) the parent of a child repeatedly fails or refuses to produce the child for the evaluation.

(D) Parental consent.

(i) In general.

(I) Consent for initial evaluation.

The agency proposing to conduct an initial evaluation to determine if the child qualifies as a child with a disability as defined in section 602 shall obtain informed consent from the parent of such child before conducting the evaluation. Parental consent for evaluation shall not be construed as consent for placement for receipt of special education and related services.

(II) Consent for services.

An agency that is responsible for making a free appropriate public education available to a child with a disability under this part shall seek to obtain informed consent from the parent of such child before providing special education and related services to the child.

(ii) Absence of consent.

(I) For initial evaluation.

If the parent of such child does not provide consent for an initial evaluation under clause (i)(I), or the parent fails to respond to a request to provide the consent, the local educational agency may pursue the initial evaluation of the child by utilizing the procedures described in section 615, except to the extent inconsistent with State law relating to such parental consent.

(II) For services.

If the parent of such child refuses to consent to services under clause (i)(II), the local educational agency shall not provide special education and related services to the child by utilizing the procedures described in section 615.

(III) Effect on agency obligations.

If the parent of such child refuses to consent to the receipt of special education and related services, or the parent fails to respond to a request to provide such consent —

(aa) the local educational agency shall not be considered to be in violation of the requirement to make available a free appropriate public education to the child for the failure to provide such child with the special education and related services for which the local educational agency requests such consent; and

(bb) the local educational agency shall not be required to convene an IEP meeting or develop an IEP under this section for the child for the special education and related services for which the local educational agency requests such consent.

(iii) Consent for wards of the state.

(I) In general.

If the child is a ward of the State and is not residing with the child's parent, the agency shall make reasonable efforts to obtain the informed consent from the parent (as defined in section 602) of the child for an initial evaluation to determine whether the child is a child with a disability.

(II) Exception.

The agency shall not be required to obtain informed consent from the parent of a child for an initial evaluation to determine whether the child is a child with a disability if —

(aa) despite reasonable efforts to do so, the agency cannot discover the whereabouts of the parent of the child;

(bb) the rights of the parents of the child have been terminated in accordance with State law; or

(cc) the rights of the parent to make educational decisions have been subrogated by a judge in accordance with State law and consent for an initial evaluation has been given by an individual appointed by the judge to represent the child.

(E) Rule of construction.

The screening of a student by a teacher or specialist to determine appropriate instructional strategies for curriculum implementation shall not be considered to be an evaluation for eligibility for special education and related services.

(2) Reevaluations.

(A) In general.

A local educational agency shall ensure that a reevaluation of each child with a disability is conducted in accordance with subsections (b) and (c) —

(i) if the local educational agency determines that the educational or related services needs, including improved academic achievement and functional performance, of the child warrant a reevaluation; or

(ii) if the child's parents or teacher requests a reevaluation.

(B) Limitation.

A reevaluation conducted under subparagraph (A) shall occur —

(i) not more frequently than once a year, unless the parent and the local educational agency agree otherwise; and

(ii) at least once every 3 years, unless the parent and the local educational agency agree that a reevaluation is unnecessary.

(b) Evaluation procedures.

(1) Notice.

The local educational agency shall provide notice to the parents of a child with a disability, in accordance with subsections (b)(3), (b)(4), and (c) of section 615, that describes any evaluation procedures such agency proposes to conduct.

(2) Conduct of evaluation.

In conducting the evaluation, the local educational agency shall —

(A) use a variety of assessment tools and strategies to gather relevant functional, developmental, and academic information, including information provided by the parent, that may assist in determining —

(i) whether the child is a child with a disability; and

(ii) the content of the child's individualized education program, including information related to enabling the child to be involved in and progress in the general education curriculum, or, for preschool children, to participate in appropriate activities;

(B) not use any single measure or assessment as the sole criterion for determining whether a child is a child with a disability or determining an appropriate educational program for the child; and

(C) use technically sound instruments that may assess the relative contribution of cognitive and behavioral factors, in addition to physical or developmental factors.

(3) Additional requirements.

Each local educational agency shall ensure that —

(A) assessments and other evaluation materials used to assess a child under this section —

(i) are selected and administered so as not to be discriminatory on a racial or cultural basis;

(ii) are provided and administered in the language and form most likely to yield accurate information on what the child knows and can do academically, developmentally, and functionally, unless it is not feasible to so provide or administer;

(iii) are used for purposes for which the assessments or measures are valid and reliable;

(iv) are administered by trained and knowledgeable personnel; and

(v) are administered in accordance with any instructions provided by the producer of such assessments;

(B) the child is assessed in all areas of suspected disability;

(C) assessment tools and strategies that provide relevant information that directly assists persons in determining the educational needs of the child are provided; and

(D) assessments of children with disabilities who transfer from 1 school district to another school district in the same academic year are coordinated with such children's prior and subsequent schools, as necessary and as expeditiously as possible, to ensure prompt completion of full evaluations.

(4) Determination of eligibility and educational need.

Upon completion of the administration of assessments and other evaluation measures —

(A) the determination of whether the child is a child with a disability as defined in section 602(3) and the educational needs of the child shall be made by a team of qualified professionals and the parent of the child in accordance with paragraph (5); and

(B) a copy of the evaluation report and the documentation of determination of eligibility shall be given to the parent.

(5) Special rule for eligibility determination.

In making a determination of eligibility under paragraph (4)(A), a child shall not be determined to be a child with a disability if the determinant factor for such determination is —

(A) lack of appropriate instruction in reading, including in the essential components of reading instruction (as defined in section 1208(3) of the Elementary and Secondary Education Act of 1965);

(B) lack of instruction in math; or

(C) limited English proficiency.

(6) Specific learning disabilities.

(A) In general.

Notwithstanding section 607(b), when determining whether a child has a specific learning disability as defined in section 602, a local educational agency shall not be required to take into consideration whether a child has a severe discrepancy between achievement and intellectual ability in oral expression, listening comprehension, written expression, basic reading skill, reading comprehension, mathematical calculation, or mathematical reasoning.

(B) Additional authority.

In determining whether a child has a specific learning disability, a local educational agency may use a process that determines if the child responds to scientific, research-based intervention as a part of the evaluation procedures described in paragraphs (2) and (3).

(c) Additional requirements for evaluation and reevaluations.

(1) Review of existing evaluation data.

As part of an initial evaluation (if appropriate) and as part of any reevaluation under this section, the IEP Team and other qualified professionals, as appropriate, shall —

(A) review existing evaluation data on the child, including —

(i) evaluations and information provided by the parents of the child;

(ii) current classroom-based, local, or State assessments, and classroom-based observations; and

(iii) observations by teachers and related services providers; and

(B) on the basis of that review, and input from the child's parents, identify what additional data, if any, are needed to determine —

(i) whether the child is a child with a disability as defined in section 602(3), and the educational needs of the child, or, in case of a reevaluation of a child, whether the child continues to have such a disability and such educational needs;

(ii) the present levels of academic achievement and related developmental needs of the child;

(iii) whether the child needs special education and related services, or in the case of a reevaluation of a child, whether the child continues to need special education and related services; and

(iv) whether any additions or modifications to the special education and related services are needed to enable the child to meet the measurable annual goals set out in the individualized education program of the child and to participate, as appropriate, in the general education curriculum.

(2) Source of data.

The local educational agency shall administer such assessments and other evaluation measures as may be needed to produce the data identified by the IEP Team under paragraph (1)(B).

(3) Parental consent.

Each local educational agency shall obtain informed parental consent, in accordance with subsection (a)(1)(D), prior to conducting any reevaluation of a child with a disability, except that such informed parental consent need not be obtained if the local educational agency can demonstrate that it had taken reasonable measures to obtain such consent and the child's parent has failed to respond.

(4) Requirements if additional data are not needed.

If the IEP Team and other qualified professionals, as appropriate, determine that no additional data are needed to determine whether the child continues to be a child with a disability and to determine the child's educational needs, the local educational agency —

(A) shall notify the child's parents of —

(i) that determination and the reasons for the determination; and

(ii) the right of such parents to request an assessment to determine whether the child continues to be a child with a disability and to determine the child's educational needs; and

(B) shall not be required to conduct such an assessment unless requested to by the child's parents.

(5) Evaluations before change in eligibility.

(A) In general.

Except as provided in subparagraph (B), a local educational agency shall evaluate a child with a disability in accordance with this section before determining that the child is no longer a child with a disability.

(B) Exception.

(i) In general.

The evaluation described in subparagraph (A) shall not be required before the termination of a child's eligibility under this part due to graduation from secondary school with a regular diploma, or due to exceeding the age eligibility for a free appropriate public education under State law.

(ii) Summary of performance.

For a child whose eligibility under this part terminates under circumstances described in clause (i), a local educational agency shall provide the child with a summary of the child's academic achievement and functional performance, which shall include recommendations on how to assist the child in meeting the child's postsecondary goals.

(d) Individualized education programs.

(1) definitions.

In this title:

(A) Individualized education program.

(i) In general.

The term "individualized education program" or "IEP" means a written statement for each child with a disability that is developed, reviewed, and revised in accordance with this section and that includes —

(I) a statement of the child's present levels of academic achievement and functional performance, including —

(aa) how the child's disability affects the child's involvement and progress in the general education curriculum;

(bb) for preschool children, as appropriate, how the disability affects the child's participation in appropriate activities; and

(cc) for children with disabilities who take alternate assessments aligned to alternate achievement standards, a description of benchmarks or short-term objectives;

(II) a statement of measurable annual goals, including academic and functional goals, designed to —

(aa) meet the child's needs that result from the child's disability to enable the child to be involved in and make progress in the general education curriculum; and

(bb) meet each of the child's other educational needs that result from the child's disability;

(III) a description of how the child's progress toward meeting the annual goals described in subclause (II) will be measured and when periodic reports on the progress the child is making toward meeting the annual goals (such as through the use of quarterly or other periodic reports, concurrent with the issuance of report cards) will be provided;

(IV) a statement of the special education and related services and supplementary aids and services, based on peer-reviewed research to the extent practicable, to be provided to the child, or on behalf of the child, and a statement of the program modifications or supports for school personnel that will be provided for the child —

(aa) to advance appropriately toward attaining the annual goals;

(bb) to be involved in and make progress in the general education curriculum in accordance with subclause (I) and to participate in extracurricular and other nonacademic activities; and

(cc) to be educated and participate with other children with disabilities and nondisabled children in the activities described in this subparagraph;

(V) an explanation of the extent, if any, to which the child will not participate with nondisabled children in the regular class and in the activities described in subclause (IV)(cc);

(VI)(aa) a statement of any individual appropriate accommodations that are necessary to measure the academic achievement and functional performance of the child on State and districtwide assessments consistent with section 612(a)(16)(A); and

(bb) if the IEP Team determines that the child shall take an alternate assessment on a particular State or districtwide assessment of student achievement, a statement of why —

(AA) the child cannot participate in the regular assessment; and

(BB) the particular alternate assessment selected is appropriate for the child;

(VII) the projected date for the beginning of the services and modifications described in subclause (IV), and the anticipated frequency, location, and duration of those services and modifications; and

(VIII) beginning not later than the first IEP to be in effect when the child is 16, and updated annually thereafter —

(aa) appropriate measurable postsecondary goals based upon age appropriate transition assessments related to training, education, employment, and, where appropriate, independent living skills;

(bb) the transition services (including courses of study) needed to assist the child in reaching those goals; and

(cc) beginning not later than 1 year before the child reaches the age of majority under State law, a statement that the child has been informed of the child's rights under this title, if any, that will transfer to the child on reaching the age of majority under section 615(m).

(ii) Rule of construction.

Nothing in this section shall be construed to require —

(I) that additional information be included in a child's IEP beyond what is explicitly required in this section; and

(II) the IEP Team to include information under 1 component of a child's IEP that is already contained under another component of such IEP.

(B) Individualized education program team.

The term "individualized education program team" or "IEP Team" means a group of individuals composed of —

(i) the parents of a child with a disability;

(ii) not less than 1 regular education teacher of such child (if the child is, or may be, participating in the regular education environment);

(iii) not less than 1 special education teacher, or where appropriate, not less than 1 special education provider of such child;

(iv) a representative of the local educational agency who —

(I) is qualified to provide, or supervise the provision of, specially designed instruction to meet the unique needs of children with disabilities;

(II) is knowledgeable about the general education curriculum; and

(III) is knowledgeable about the availability of resources of the local educational agency;

(v) an individual who can interpret the instructional implications of evaluation results, who may be a member of the team described in clauses (ii) through (vi);

(vi) at the discretion of the parent or the agency, other individuals who have knowledge or special expertise regarding the child, including related services personnel as appropriate; and

(vii) whenever appropriate, the child with a disability.

(C) IEP team attendance.

(i) Attendance not necessary.

A member of the IEP Team shall not be required to attend an IEP meeting, in whole or in part, if the parent of a child with a disability and the local educational agency agree that the attendance of such member is not necessary because the member's area of the curriculum or related services is not being modified or discussed in the meeting.

(ii) Excusal.

A member of the IEP Team may be excused from attending an IEP meeting, in whole or in part, when the meeting involves a modification to or discussion of the member's area of the curriculum or related services, if —

(I) the parent and the local educational agency consent to the excusal; and

(II) the member submits, in writing to the parent and the IEP Team, input into the development of the IEP prior to the meeting.

(iii) Written agreement and consent required.

A parent's agreement under clause (i) and consent under clause (ii) shall be in writing.

(D) IEP team transition.

In the case of a child who was previously served under part C, an invitation to the initial IEP meeting shall, at the request of the parent, be sent to the part C service coordinator or other representatives of the part C system to assist with the smooth transition of services.

(2) Requirement that program be in effect—

(A) In general.

At the beginning of each school year, each local educational agency, State educational agency, or other State agency, as the case may be, shall have in effect, for each child with a disability in the agency's jurisdiction, an individualized education program, as defined in paragraph (1)(A).

(B) Program for child aged 3 through 5.

In the case of a child with a disability aged 3 through 5 (or, at the discretion of the State educational agency, a 2-year-old child with a disability who will turn age 3 during the school year), the IEP Team shall consider the individualized family service plan that contains the material described in section 636, and that is developed in accordance with this section, and the individualized family service plan may serve as the IEP of the child if using that plan as the IEP is —

(i) consistent with State policy; and

(ii) agreed to by the agency and the child's parents.

(C) Program for children who transfer school districts.

(i) In general.

(I) Transfer within the same state.

In the case of a child with a disability who transfers school districts within the same academic year, who enrolls in a new school, and who had an IEP that was in effect in the same State, the local educational agency shall provide such child with a free appropriate public education, including services comparable to those described in the previously held IEP, in consultation with the parents until such time as the local educational agency adopts the previously held IEP or develops, adopts, and implements a new IEP that is consistent with Federal and State law.

(II) Transfer outside state.

In the case of a child with a disability who transfers school districts within the same academic year, who enrolls in a new school, and who had an IEP that was in effect in another State, the local educational agency shall provide such child with a free appropriate public education, including services comparable to those described in the previously held IEP, in consultation with the parents until such time as the local educational agency conducts an evaluation pursuant to subsection (a)(1), if determined to be necessary by such agency, and develops a new IEP, if appropriate, that is consistent with Federal and State law.

(ii) Transmittal of records.

To facilitate the transition for a child described in clause (i) —

(I) the new school in which the child enrolls shall take reasonable steps to promptly obtain the child's records, including the IEP and supporting documents and any other records relating to the provision of special education or related services to the child, from the previous school in which the child was enrolled, pursuant to section 99.31(a)(2) of title 34, Code of Federal Regulations; and

(II) the previous school in which the child was enrolled shall take reasonable steps to promptly respond to such request from the new school.

(3) Development of IEP.

(A) In general. — In developing each child's IEP, the IEP Team, subject to subparagraph (C), shall consider —

(i) the strengths of the child;

(ii) the concerns of the parents for enhancing the education of their child;

(iii) the results of the initial evaluation or most recent evaluation of the child; and

(iv) the academic, developmental, and functional needs of the child.

(B) Consideration of special factors.

The IEP Team shall —

(i) in the case of a child whose behavior impedes the child's learning or that of others, consider the use of positive behavioral interventions and supports, and other strategies, to address that behavior;

(ii) in the case of a child with limited English proficiency, consider the language needs of the child as such needs relate to the child's IEP;

(iii) in the case of a child who is blind or visually impaired, provide for instruction in Braille and the use of Braille unless the IEP Team determines, after an evaluation of the child's reading and writing skills, needs, and appropriate reading and writing media (including an evaluation of the child's future needs for instruction in Braille or the use of Braille), that instruction in Braille or the use of Braille is not appropriate for the child;

(iv) consider the communication needs of the child, and in the case of a child who is deaf or hard of hearing, consider the child's language and communication needs, opportunities for direct communications with peers and professional personnel in the child's language and communication mode, academic level, and full range of needs, including opportunities for direct instruction in the child's language and communication mode; and

(v) consider whether the child needs assistive technology devices and services.

(C) Requirement with respect to regular education teacher.

A regular education teacher of the child, as a member of the IEP Team, shall, to the extent appropriate, participate in the development of the IEP of the child, including the determination of appropriate positive behavioral interventions and supports, and other strategies, and the determination of supplementary aids and services, program modifications, and support for school personnel consistent with paragraph (1)(A)(i)(IV).

(D) Agreement.

In making changes to a child's IEP after the annual IEP meeting for a school year, the parent of a child with a disability and the local educational agency may agree not to convene an IEP meeting for the purposes of making such changes, and instead may develop a written document to amend or modify the child's current IEP.

(E) Consolidation of iep team meetings.

To the extent possible, the local educational agency shall encourage the consolidation of reevaluation meetings for the child and other IEP Team meetings for the child.

(F) Amendments.

Changes to the IEP may be made either by the entire IEP Team or, as provided in subparagraph (D), by amending the IEP rather than by redrafting the entire IEP. Upon request, a parent shall be provided with a revised copy of the IEP with the amendments incorporated.

(4) Review and revision of IEP.

(A) In general.

The local educational agency shall

ensure that, subject to subparagraph (B), the IEP Team —

(i) reviews the child's IEP periodically, but not less frequently than annually, to determine whether the annual goals for the child are being achieved; and

(ii) revises the IEP as appropriate to address —

(I) any lack of expected progress toward the annual goals and in the general education curriculum, where appropriate;

(II) the results of any reevaluation conducted under this section;

(III) information about the child provided to, or by, the parents, as described in subsection (c)(1)(B);

(IV) the child's anticipated needs; or

(V) other matters.

(B) Requirement with respect to regular education teacher.

A regular education teacher of the child, as a member of the IEP Team, shall, consistent with paragraph (1)(C), participate in the review and revision of the IEP of the child.

(5) Multi-year IEP demonstration.

(A) Pilot program.

(i) Purpose.

The purpose of this paragraph is to provide an opportunity for States to allow parents and local educational agencies the opportunity for long-term planning by offering the option of developing a comprehensive multi-year IEP, not to exceed 3 years, that is designed to coincide with the natural transition points for the child.

(ii) Authorization.

In order to carry out the purpose of this paragraph, the Secretary is authorized to approve not more than 15 proposals from States to carry out the activity described in clause (I).

(iii) Proposal.

(I) In general.

A State desiring to participate in the program under this paragraph shall submit a proposal to the Secretary at such time and in such manner as the Secretary may reasonably require.

(II) Content.

The proposal shall include —

(aa) assurances that the development of a multi-year IEP under this paragraph is optional for parents;

(bb) assurances that the parent is required to provide informed consent before a comprehensive multi-year IEP is developed;

(cc) a list of required elements for each multi-year IEP, including —

(AA) measurable goals pursuant to paragraph (1)(A)(i)(II), coinciding with natural transition points for the child, that will enable the child to be involved in and make progress in the general education curriculum and that will meet the child's other needs that result from the child's disability; and

(BB) measurable annual goals for determining progress toward meeting the goals described in subitem (AA); and

(dd) a description of the process for the review and revision of each multi-year IEP, including —

(AA) a review by the IEP Team of the child's multi-year IEP at each of the child's natural transition points;

(BB) in years other than a child's natural transition points, an annual review of the child's IEP to determine the child's current levels of progress and whether the annual goals for the child are being achieved, and a requirement to amend the IEP, as appropriate, to enable the child to continue to meet the measurable goals set out in the IEP;

(CC) if the IEP Team determines on the basis of a review that the child is not making sufficient progress toward the goals described in the multi-year IEP, a requirement that the local educational agency shall ensure that the IEP Team carries out a more thorough review of the IEP in accordance with paragraph (4) within 30 calendar days; and

(DD) at the request of the parent, a requirement that the IEP Team shall conduct a review of the child's multi-year IEP rather than or subsequent to an annual review.

(B) Report.

Beginning 2 years after the date of enactment of the Individuals with Disabilities Education Improvement Act of 2004, the

Secretary shall submit an annual report to the Committee on Education and the Workforce of the House of Representatives and the Committee on Health, Education, Labor, and Pensions of the Senate regarding the effectiveness of the program under this paragraph and any specific recommendations for broader implementation of such program, including —

(i) reducing —

(I) the paperwork burden on teachers, principals, administrators, and related service providers; and

(II) noninstructional time spent by teachers in complying with this part;

(ii) enhancing longer-term educational plannin

(iii) improving positive outcomes for children with disabilities;

(iv) promoting collaboration between IEP Team members; and

(v) ensuring satisfaction of family members.

(C) Definition.

In this paragraph, the term "natural transition points" means those periods that are close in time to the transition of a child with a disability from preschool to elementary grades, from elementary grades to middle or junior high school grades, from middle or junior high school grades to secondary school grades, and from secondary school grades to post-secondary activities, but in no case a period longer than 3 years.

(6) Failure to meet transition objectives.

If a participating agency, other than the local educational agency, fails to provide the transition services described in the IEP in accordance with paragraph (1)(A)(i)(VIII), the local educational agency shall reconvene the IEP Team to identify alternative strategies to meet the transition objectives for the child set out in the IEP.

(7) Children with disabilities in adult prisons.

(A) In general.

The following requirements shall not apply to children with disabilities who are convicted as adults under State law and incarcerated in adult prisons:

(i) The requirements contained in section 612(a)(16) and paragraph (1)(A)(i)(VI) (relating to participation of children with disabilities in general assessments).

(ii) The requirements of items (aa) and (bb) of paragraph (1)(A)(i)(VIII) (relating to transition planning and transition services), do not apply with respect to such children whose eligibility under this part will end, because of such children's age, before such children will be released from prison.

(B) Additional requirement.

If a child with a disability is convicted as an adult under State law and incarcerated in an adult prison, the child's IEP Team may modify the child's IEP or placement notwithstanding the requirements of sections 612(a)(5)(A) and paragraph (1)(A) if the State has demonstrated a bona fide security or compelling penological interest that cannot otherwise be accommodated.

(e) Educational placements.

Each local educational agency or State educational agency shall ensure that the parents of each child with a disability are members of any group that makes decisions on the educational placement of their child.

(f) Alternative means of meeting participation.

When conducting IEP team meetings and placement meetings pursuant to this section, section 615(e), and section 615(f)(1)(B), and carrying out administrative matters under section 615 (such as scheduling, exchange of witness lists, and status conferences), the parent of a child with a disability and a local educational agency may agree to use alternative means of meeting participation, such as video conferences and conference calls.

§ 1415. Procedural safeguards

(a) Establishment of procedures

Any State educational agency, State agency, or local educational agency that receives assistance under this part shall establish and maintain procedures in accordance with this section to ensure that children with disabilities and their parents are guaranteed procedural safeguards with respect to the provision of a free appropriate public education by such agencies.

(b) Types of procedures.

The procedures required by this section shall include the following:

(1) An opportunity for the parents of a child with a disability to examine all records relating to such child and to participate in meetings with respect to the identification, evaluation, and educational placement of the child, and the provision of a free appropriate public education to such child, and to obtain an independent educational evaluation of the child.

(2)(A) Procedures to protect the rights of the child whenever the parents of the child are not known, the agency cannot, after reasonable efforts, locate the parents, or the child is a ward of the State, including the assignment of an individual to act as a surrogate for the parents, which surrogate shall not be an employee of the State educational agency, the local educational agency, or any other agency that is involved in the education or care of the child. In the case of —

(i) a child who is a ward of the State, such surrogate may alternatively be appointed by the judge overseeing the child's care provided that the surrogate meets the requirements of this paragraph; and

(ii) an unaccompanied homeless youth as defined in section 725(6) of the McKinney-Vento Homeless Assistance Act (42 U.S.C. 11434a(6)), the local educational agency shall appoint a surrogate in accordance with this paragraph.

(B) The State shall make reasonable efforts to ensure the assignment of a surrogate not more than 30 days after there is a determination by the agency that the child needs a surrogate.

(3) Written prior notice to the parents of the child, in accordance with subsection (c)(1), whenever the local educational agency —

(A) proposes to initiate or change; or

(B) refuses to initiate or change, the identification, evaluation, or educational placement of the child, or the provision of a free appropriate public education to the child.

(4) Procedures designed to ensure that the notice required by paragraph (3) is in the native language of the parents, unless it clearly is not feasible to do so.

(5) An opportunity for mediation, in accordance with subsection (e).

(6) An opportunity for any party to present a complaint —

(A) with respect to any matter relating to the identification, evaluation, or educational placement of the child, or the provision of a free appropriate public education to such child; and

(B) which sets forth an alleged violation that occurred not more than 2 years before the date the parent or public agency knew or should have known about the alleged action that forms the basis of the complaint, or, if the State has an explicit time limitation for presenting such a complaint under this part, in such time as the State law allows, except that the exceptions to the timeline described in subsection (f)(3)(D) shall apply to the timeline described in this subparagraph.

(7)(A) Procedures that require either party, or the attorney representing a party, to provide due process complaint notice in accordance with subsection (c)(2) (which shall remain confidential) —

(i) to the other party, in the complaint filed under paragraph (6), and forward a copy of such notice to the State educational agency; and

(ii) that shall include —

(I) the name of the child, the address of the residence of the child (or available contact information in the case of a homeless child), and the name of the school the child is attending;

(II) in the case of a homeless child or youth (within the meaning of section 725(2) of the McKinney-Vento Homeless Assistance Act (42 U.S.C. 11434a(2)), available contact information for the child and the name of the school the child is attending;

(III) a description of the nature of the problem of the child relating to such proposed initiation or change, including facts relating to such problem; and

(IV) a proposed resolution of the problem to the extent known and available to the party at the time.

(B) A requirement that a party may not have a due process hearing until the party, or the attorney representing the party, files a notice that meets the requirements of subparagraph (A)(ii).

(8) Procedures that require the State educational agency to develop a model form to assist parents in filing a complaint and due process complaint notice in accordance with paragraphs (6) and (7), respectively.

(c) Notification requirements.

(1) Content of prior written notice.

The notice required by subsection (b)(3) shall include —

(A) a description of the action proposed or refused by the agency;

(B) an explanation of why the agency proposes or refuses to take the action and a description of each evaluation procedure, assessment, record, or report the agency used as a basis for the proposed or refused action;

(C) a statement that the parents of a child with a disability have protection under the procedural safeguards of this part and, if this notice is not an initial referral for evaluation, the means by which a copy of a description of the procedural safeguards can be obtained;

(D) sources for parents to contact to obtain assistance in understanding the provisions of this part;

(E) a description of other options considered by the IEP Team and the reason why those options were rejected; and

(F) a description of the factors that are relevant to the agency's proposal or refusal.

(2) Due process complaint notice.

(A) Complaint.

The due process complaint notice required under subsection (b)(7)(A) shall be deemed to be sufficient unless the party receiving the notice notifies the hearing officer and the other party in writing that the receiving party believes the notice has not met the requirements of subsection (b)(7)(A).

(B) Response to complaint.

(i) Local educational agency response.

(I) In general.

If the local educational agency has not sent a prior written notice to the parent regarding the subject matter contained in the parent's due process complaint notice, such local educational agency shall, within 10 days of receiving the complaint, send to the parent a response that shall include —

(aa) an explanation of why the agency proposed or refused to take the action raised in the complaint;

(bb) a description of other options that the IEP Team considered and the reasons why those options were rejected;

(cc) a description of each evaluation procedure, assessment, record, or report the agency used as the basis for the proposed or refused action; and

(dd) a description of the factors that are relevant to the agency's proposal or refusal.

(II) Sufficiency.

A response filed by a local educational agency pursuant to subclause (I) shall not be construed to preclude such local educational agency from asserting that the parent's due process complaint notice was insufficient where appropriate.

(ii) Other party response.

Except as provided in clause (i), the non-complaining party shall, within 10 days of receiving the complaint, send to the complaint a response that specifically addresses the issues raised in the complaint.

(C) Timing.

The party providing a hearing officer notification under subparagraph (A) shall provide the notification within 15 days of receiving the complaint.

(D) Determination.

Within 5 days of receipt of the notification provided under subparagraph (C), the hearing officer shall make a determination on the face of the notice of whether the notification meets the requirements of subsection (b)(7)(A), and shall immediately notify the parties in writing of such determination.

(E) Amended complaint notice.

(i) In general.

A party may amend its due process complaint notice only if —

(I) the other party consents in writing to such amendment and is given the opportunity to resolve the complaint through a meeting held pursuant to subsection (f)(1)(B); or

(II) the hearing officer grants permission, except that the hearing officer may only grant such permission at any time not later than 5 days before a due process hearing occurs.

(ii) Applicable timeline.

The applicable timeline for a due process hearing under this part shall recommence at the time the party files an amended notice, including the timeline under subsection (f)(1)(B).

(d) Procedural safeguards notice.

(1) In general.

(A) Copy to parents.

A copy of the procedural safeguards available to the parents of a child with a disability shall be given to the parents only 1 time a year, except that a copy also shall be given to the parents —

(i) upon initial referral or parental request for evaluation;

(ii) upon the first occurrence of the filing of a complaint under subsection (b)(6); and

(iii) upon request by a parent.

(B) Internet website.

A local educational agency may place a current copy of the procedural safeguards notice on its Internet website if such website exists.

(2) Contents.

The procedural safeguards notice shall include a full explanation of the procedural safeguards, written in the native language of the parents (unless it clearly is not feasible to do so) and written in an easily understandable manner, available under this section and under regulations promulgated by the Secretary relating to —

(A) independent educational evaluation;

(B) prior written notice;

(C) parental consent;

(D) access to educational records;

(E) the opportunity to present and resolve complaints, including —

(i) the time period in which to make a complaint;

(ii) the opportunity for the agency to resolve the complaint; and

(iii) the availability of mediation;

(F) the child's placement during pendency of due process proceedings;

(G) procedures for students who are subject to placement in an interim alternative educational setting;

(H) requirements for unilateral placement by parents of children in private schools at public expense;

(I) due process hearings, including requirements for disclosure of evaluation results and recommendations;

(J) State-level appeals (if applicable in that State);

(K) civil actions, including the time period in which to file such actions; and

(L) attorneys' fees.

(e) Mediation.

(1) In general.

Any State educational agency or local educational agency that receives assistance under this part shall ensure that procedures are established and implemented to allow parties to disputes involving any matter, including matters arising prior to the filing of a complaint pursuant to subsection (b)(6), to resolve such disputes through a mediation process.

(2) Requirements.

Such procedures shall meet the following requirements:

(A) The procedures shall ensure that the mediation process —

(i) is voluntary on the part of the parties;

(ii) is not used to deny or delay a parent's right to a due process hearing under subsection (f), or to deny any other rights afforded under this part; and

(iii) is conducted by a qualified and impartial mediator who is trained in effective mediation techniques.

(B) Opportunity to meet with a disinterested party.

A local educational agency or a State agency may establish procedures to offer to parents and schools that choose not to use the mediation process, an opportunity to meet, at a time and location convenient to the parents, with a disinterested party who is under contract with —

(i) a parent training and information center or community parent resource center in the State established under section 671 or 672; or

(ii) an appropriate alternative dispute resolution entity, to encourage the use, and explain the benefits, of the mediation process to the parents.

(C) List of qualified mediators.

The State shall maintain a list of individuals who are qualified mediators and knowledgeable in laws and regulations relating to the provision of special education and related services.

(D) Costs.

The State shall bear the cost of the mediation process, including the costs of meetings described in subparagraph (B).

(E) Scheduling and location.

Each session in the mediation process shall be scheduled in a timely manner and shall be held in a location that is convenient to the parties to the dispute.

(F) Written agreement.

In the case that a resolution is reached to resolve the complaint through the mediation process, the parties shall execute a legally binding agreement that sets forth such resolution and that —

(i) states that all discussions that occurred during the mediation process shall be confidential and may not be used as evidence in any subsequent due process hearing or civil proceeding;

(ii) is signed by both the parent and a representative of the agency who has the authority to bind such agency; and

(iii) is enforceable in any State court of competent jurisdiction or in a district court of the United States.

(G) Mediation discussions.

Discussions that occur during the mediation process shall be confidential and may not be used as evidence in any subsequent due process hearing or civil proceeding.

(f) Impartial due process hearing.

(1) In general.

(A) Hearing.

Whenever a complaint has been received under subsection (b)(6) or (k), the parents or the local educational agency involved in such complaint shall have an opportunity for an impartial due process hearing, which shall be conducted by the State educational agency or by the local educational agency, as determined by State law or by the State educational agency.

(B) Resolution session.

(i) Preliminary meeting.

Prior to the opportunity for an impartial due process hearing under subparagraph (A), the local educational agency shall convene a meeting with the parents and the relevant member or members of the IEP Team who have specific knowledge of the facts identified in the complaint —

(I) within 15 days of receiving notice of the parents' complaint;

(II) which shall include a representative of the agency who has decisionmaking authority on behalf of such agency;

(III) which may not include an attorney of the local educational agency unless the parent is accompanied by an attorney; and

(IV) where the parents of the child discuss their complaint, and the facts that form the basis of the complaint, and the local educational agency is provided the opportunity to resolve the complaint unless the parents and the local educational agency agree in writing to waive such meeting, or agree to use the mediation process described in subsection (e).

(ii) Hearing.

If the local educational agency has not resolved the complaint to the satisfaction of the parents within 30 days of the receipt of the complaint, the due process hearing may occur, and all of the applicable timelines for a due process hearing under this part shall commence.

(iii) Written settlement agreement.

In the case that a resolution is reached to resolve the complaint at a meeting described in clause (i), the parties shall execute a legally binding agreement that is —

(I) signed by both the parent and a representative of the agency who has the authority to bind such agency; and

(II) enforceable in any State court of competent jurisdiction or in a district court of the United States.

(iv) Review period.

If the parties execute an agreement pursuant to clause (iii), a party may void such agreement within 3 business days of the agreement's execution.

(2) Disclosure of evaluations and recommendations.

(A) In general.

Not less than 5 business days prior to a hearing conducted pursuant to paragraph (1), each party shall disclose to all other parties all evaluations completed by that date, and recommendations based on the offering party's evaluations, that the party intends to use at the hearing.

(B) Failure to disclose.

A hearing officer may bar any party that fails to comply with subparagraph (A) from introducing the relevant evaluation or recommendation at the hearing without the consent of the other party.

(3) Limitations on hearing.

(A) Person conducting hearing.

A hearing officer conducting a hearing pursuant to paragraph (1)(A) shall, at a minimum —

(i) not be —

(I) an employee of the State educational agency or the local educational agency involved in the education or care of the child; or

(II) a person having a personal or professional interest that conflicts with the person's objectivity in the hearing;

(ii) possess knowledge of, and the ability to understand, the provisions of this title, Federal and State regulations pertaining to this title, and legal interpretations of this title by Federal and State courts;

(iii) possess the knowledge and ability to conduct hearings in accordance with appropriate, standard legal practice; and

(iv) possess the knowledge and ability to render and write decisions in accordance with appropriate, standard legal practice.

(B) Subject matter of hearing.

The party requesting the due process hearing shall not be allowed to raise issues at the due process hearing that were not raised in the notice filed under subsection (b)(7), unless the other party agrees otherwise.

(C) Timeline for requesting hearing.

A parent or agency shall request an impartial due process hearing within 2 years of the date the parent or agency knew or should have known about the alleged action that forms the basis of the complaint, or, if the State has an explicit time limitation for requesting such a hearing under this part, in such time as the State law allows.

(D) Exceptions to the timeline.

The timeline described in subparagraph (C) shall not apply to a parent if the parent was prevented from requesting the hearing due to —

(i) specific misrepresentations by the local educational agency that it had resolved the problem forming the basis of the complaint; or

(ii) the local educational agency's withholding of information from the parent that was required under this part to be provided to the parent.

(E) Decision of hearing officer.

(i) In general.

Subject to clause (ii), a decision made by a hearing officer shall be made on substantive grounds based on a determination of whether the child received a free appropriate public education.

(ii) Procedural issues.

In matters alleging a procedural violation, a hearing officer may find that a child did not receive a free appropriate public education only if the procedural inadequacies —

(I) impeded the child's right to a free appropriate public education;

(II) significantly impeded the parents' opportunity to participate in the decisionmaking process regarding the provision of a free appropriate public education to the parents' child; or

(III) caused a deprivation of educational benefits.

(iii) Rule of construction.

Nothing in this subparagraph shall be construed to preclude a hearing officer from ordering a local educational agency to comply with procedural requirements under this section.

(F) Rule of construction.

Nothing in this paragraph shall be construed to affect the right of a parent to file a complaint with the State educational agency.

(g) Appeal.

(1) In general.

If the hearing required by subsection (f) is conducted by a local educational agency, any party aggrieved by the findings and decision rendered in such a hearing may appeal such findings and decision to the State educational agency.

(2) Impartial review and independent decision.

The State educational agency shall conduct an impartial review of the findings and decision appealed under paragraph (1). The officer conducting such review shall make an independent decision upon completion of such review.

(h) Safeguards.

Any party to a hearing conducted pursuant to subsection (f) or (k), or an appeal conducted pursuant to subsection (g), shall be accorded —

(1) the right to be accompanied and advised by counsel and by individuals with special knowledge or training with respect to the problems of children with disabilities;

(2) the right to present evidence and confront, cross-examine, and compel the attendance of witnesses;

(3) the right to a written, or, at the option of the parents, electronic verbatim record of such hearing; and

(4) the right to written, or, at the option of the parents, electronic findings of fact and decisions, which findings and decisions —

(A) shall be made available to the public consistent with the requirements of section 617(b) (relating to the confidentiality of data, information, and records); and

(B) shall be transmitted to the advisory panel established pursuant to section 612(a)(21).

(i) Administrative procedures.

(1) In general.

(A) Decision made in hearing.

A decision made in a hearing conducted pursuant to subsection (f) or (k) shall be final, except that any party involved in such hearing may appeal such decision under the provisions of subsection (g) and paragraph (2).

(B) Decision made at appeal.

A decision made under subsection (g) shall be final, except that any party may bring an action under paragraph (2).

(2) Right to bring civil action.

(A) In general.

Any party aggrieved by the findings and decision made under subsection (f) or (k) who does not have the right to an appeal under subsection (g), and any party aggrieved by the findings and decision made under this subsection, shall have the right to bring a civil action with respect to the complaint presented pursuant to this section, which action may be brought in any State court of competent jurisdiction or in a district court of the United States, without regard to the amount in controversy.

(B) Limitation.

The party bringing the action shall have 90 days from the date of the decision of the hearing officer to bring such an action, or, if the State has an explicit time limitation for bringing such action under this part, in such time as the State law allows.

(C) Additional requirements.

In any action brought under this paragraph, the court —

(i) shall receive the records of the administrative proceedings;

(ii) shall hear additional evidence at the request of a party; and

(iii) basing its decision on the preponderance of the evidence, shall grant such relief as the court determines is appropriate.

(3) Jurisdiction of district courts; attorneys' fees.

(A) In general.

The district courts of the United States shall have jurisdiction of actions brought under this section without regard to the amount in controversy.

(B) Award of attorneys' fees.

(i) In general.

In any action or proceeding brought under this section, the court, in its discretion, may award reasonable attorneys' fees as part of the costs —

(I) to a prevailing party who is the parent of a child with a disability;

(II) to a prevailing party who is a State educational agency or local educational agency against the attorney of a parent who files a complaint or subsequent cause of action that is frivolous, unreasonable, or without foundation, or against the attorney of a parent who continued to litigate after the litigation clearly became frivolous, unreasonable, or without foundation; or

(III) to a prevailing State educational agency or local educational agency against the attorney of a parent, or against the parent, if the parent's complaint or subsequent cause of action was presented for any improper purpose, such as to harass, to cause unnecessary delay, or to needlessly increase the cost of litigation.

(ii) Rule of construction.

Nothing in this subparagraph shall be construed to affect section 327 of the District of Columbia Appropriations Act, 2005.

(C) Determination of amount of attorneys' fees.

Fees awarded under this paragraph shall be based on rates prevailing in the community in which the action or proceeding arose for the kind and quality of services furnished. No bonus or multiplier may be used in calculating the fees awarded under this subsection.

(D) Prohibition of attorneys' fees and related costs for certain services.

(i) In general.

Attorneys' fees may not be awarded and related costs may not be reimbursed in any action or proceeding under this section for services performed subsequent to the time of a written offer of settlement to a parent if —

(I) the offer is made within the time prescribed by Rule 68 of the Federal Rules of Civil Procedure or, in the case of an administrative proceeding, at any time more than 10 days before the proceeding begins;

(II) the offer is not accepted within 10 days; and

(III) the court or administrative hearing officer finds that the relief finally obtained by the parents is not more favorable to the parents than the offer of settlement.

(ii) IEP team meetings.

Attorneys' fees may not be awarded relating to any meeting of the IEP Team unless such meeting is convened as a result of an administrative proceeding or judicial action, or, at the discretion of the State, for a mediation described in subsection (e).

(iii) Opportunity to resolve complaints.

A meeting conducted pursuant to subsection (f)(1)(B)(i) shall not be considered —

(I) a meeting convened as a result of an administrative hearing or judicial action; or

(II) an administrative hearing or judicial action for purposes of this paragraph.

(E) Exception to prohibition on attorneys' fees and related costs.

Notwithstanding subparagraph (D), an award of attorneys' fees and related costs may be made to a parent who is the prevailing party and who was substantially justified in rejecting the settlement offer.

(F) Reduction in amount of attorneys' fees.

Except as provided in subparagraph (G), whenever the court finds that —

(i) the parent, or the parent's attorney, during the course of the action or proceeding, unreasonably protracted the final resolution of the controversy;

(ii) the amount of the attorneys' fees otherwise authorized to be awarded unreasonably exceeds the hourly rate prevailing in the community for similar services by attorneys of reasonably comparable skill, reputation, and experience;

(iii) the time spent and legal services furnished were excessive considering the nature of the action or proceeding; or

(iv) the attorney representing the parent did not provide to the local educational agency the appropriate information in the notice of the complaint described in subsection (b)(7)(A), the court shall reduce, accordingly, the amount of the attorneys' fees awarded under this section.

(G) Exception to reduction in amount of attorneys' fees.

The provisions of subparagraph (F) shall not apply in any action or proceeding if the court finds that the State or local educational agency unreasonably protracted the final resolution of the action or proceeding or there was a violation of this section.

(j) Maintenance of current educational placement.

Except as provided in subsection (k)(4), during the pendency of any proceedings conducted pursuant to this section, unless the State or local educational agency and the parents otherwise agree, the child shall remain in the then-current educational placement of the child, or, if applying for initial admission to a public school, shall, with the consent of the parents, be placed in the public school program until all such proceedings have been completed.

(k) Placement in alternative educational setting.

(1) Authority of school personnel.

(A) Case-by-case determination.

School personnel may consider any unique circumstances on a case-by-case basis when determining whether to order a change in placement for a child with a disability who violates a code of student conduct.

(B) Authority.

School personnel under this subsection may remove a child with a disability who violates a code of student conduct from their current placement to an appropriate interim alternative educational setting, another setting, or suspension, for not more than 10 school days (to the extent such alternatives are applied to children without disabilities).

(C) Additional authority.

If school personnel seek to order a change in placement that would exceed 10 school days and the behavior that gave rise to the violation of the school code is determined not to be a manifestation of the child's disability pursuant to subparagraph (E), the relevant disciplinary procedures applicable to children without disabilities may be applied to the child in the same manner and for the same duration in which the procedures would be applied to children without disabilities, except as provided in section 612(a)(1) although it may be provided in an interim alternative educational setting.

(D) Services.

A child with a disability who is removed from the child's current placement under subparagraph (G) (irrespective of whether the behavior is determined to be a manifestation of the child's disability) or subparagraph (C) shall —

(i) continue to receive educational services, as provided in section 612(a)(1), so as to enable the child to continue to participate in the general education curriculum, although in another setting, and to progress toward meeting the goals set out in the child's IEP; and

(ii) receive, as appropriate, a functional behavioral assessment, behavioral intervention services and modifications, that are designed to address the behavior violation so that it does not recur.

(E) Manifestation determination.

(i) In general.

Except as provided in subparagraph (B), within 10 school days of any decision to change the placement of a child with a disability because of a violation of a code of student conduct, the local educational agency, the parent, and relevant members of the IEP Team (as determined by the parent and the local educational agency) shall review all relevant information in the student's file, including the child's IEP, any teacher observations, and any relevant information provided by the parents to determine —

(I) if the conduct in question was caused by, or had a direct and substantial relationship to, the child's disability; or

(II) if the conduct in question was the direct result of the local educational agency's failure to implement the IEP.

(ii) Manifestation.

If the local educational agency, the parent, and relevant members of the IEP Team determine that either subclause (I) or (II) of clause (i) is applicable for the child, the conduct shall be determined to be a manifestation of the child's disability.

(F) Determination that behavior was a manifestation.

If the local educational agency, the parent, and relevant members of the IEP Team make the determination that the conduct was a manifestation of the child's disability, the IEP Team shall —

(i) conduct a functional behavioral assessment, and implement a behavioral intervention plan for such child, provided that the local educational agency had not conducted such assessment prior to such determination before the behavior that resulted in a change in placement described in subparagraph (C) or (G);

(ii) in the situation where a behavioral intervention plan has been developed, review the behavioral intervention plan if the child already has such a behavioral intervention plan, and modify it, as necessary, to address the behavior; and

(iii) except as provided in subparagraph (G), return the child to the placement from which the child was removed, unless the parent and the local educational agency agree to a change of placement as part of the modification of the behavioral intervention plan.

(G) special circumstances.

School personnel may remove a student to an interim alternative educational setting for not more than 45 school days without regard to whether the behavior is determined to be a manifestation of the child's disability, in cases where a child —

(i) carries or possesses a weapon to or at school, on school premises, or to or at a school function under the jurisdiction of a State or local educational agency;

(ii) knowingly possesses or uses illegal drugs, or sells or solicits the sale of a controlled substance, while at school, on school premises, or at a school function under the jurisdiction of a State or local educational agency; or

(iii) has inflicted serious bodily injury upon another person while at school, on school premises, or at a school function under the jurisdiction of a State or local educational agency.

(H) Notification.

Not later than the date on which the decision to take disciplinary action is made, the local educational agency shall notify the parents of that decision, and of all procedural safeguards accorded under this section.

(2) Determination of setting.

The interim alternative educational setting in subparagraphs (C) and (G) of paragraph (1) shall be determined by the IEP Team.

(3) Appeal.

(A) In general.

The parent of a child with a disability who disagrees with any decision regarding placement, or the manifestation determination under this subsection, or a local educational agency that believes that maintaining the current placement of the child is substantially likely to result in injury to the child or to others, may request a hearing.

(B) Authority of hearing officer.

(i) In general.

A hearing officer shall hear, and make a determination regarding, an appeal requested under subparagraph (A).

(ii) Change of placement order.

In making the determination under clause (i), the hearing officer may order a change in placement of a child with a disability. In such situations, the hearing officer may —

(I) return a child with a disability to the placement from which the child was removed; or

(II) order a change in placement of a child with a disability to an appropriate interim alternative educational setting for not more than 45 school days if the hearing officer determines that maintaining the current placement of such child is substantially likely to result in injury to the child or to others.

(4) Placement during appeals.

When an appeal under paragraph (3) has been requested by either the parent or the local educational agency —

(A) the child shall remain in the interim alternative educational setting pending the decision of the hearing officer or until the expiration of the time period provided for in paragraph (1)(C), whichever occurs first, unless the parent and the State or local educational agency agree otherwise; and

(B) the State or local educational agency shall arrange for an expedited hearing, which shall occur within 20 school days of the date the hearing is requested and shall result in a determination within 10 school days after the hearing.

(5) Protections for children not yet eligible for special education and related services.

(A) In general.

A child who has not been determined to be eligible for special education and related services under this part and who has engaged in behavior that violates a code of student conduct, may assert any of the protections provided for in this part if the local educational agency had knowledge (as determined in accordance with this paragraph) that the child was a child with a disability before the behavior that precipitated the disciplinary action occurred.

(B) Basis of knowledge.

A local educational agency shall be deemed to have knowledge that a child is a child with a disability if, before the behavior that precipitated the disciplinary action occurred —

(i) the parent of the child has expressed concern in writing to supervisory or administrative personnel of the appropriate educational agency, or a teacher of the child, that the child is in need of special education and related services;

(ii) the parent of the child has requested an evaluation of the child pursuant to section 614(a)(1)(B); or

(iii) the teacher of the child, or other personnel of the local educational agency, has expressed specific concerns about a pattern of behavior demonstrated by the child, directly to the director of special education of such agency or to other supervisory personnel of the agency.

(C) Exception.

A local educational agency shall not be deemed to have knowledge that the child is a child with a disability if the parent of the child has not allowed an evaluation of the child pursuant to section 614 or has refused services under this part or the child has been evaluated and it was determined that the child was not a child with a disability under this part.

(D) Conditions that apply if no basis of knowledge.

(i) In general.

If a local educational agency does not have knowledge that a child is a child with a disability (in accordance with subparagraph (B) or (C)) prior to taking disciplinary measures against the child, the child may be subjected to disciplinary measures applied to children without disabilities who engaged in comparable behaviors consistent with clause (ii).

(ii) Limitations.

If a request is made for an evaluation of a child during the time period in which the child is subjected to disciplinary measures under this subsection, the evaluation shall be conducted in an expedited manner. If the child is determined to be a child with a disability, taking into consideration information from the evaluation conducted by the agency and information provided by the parents, the agency shall provide special education and related services in accordance with this part, except that, pending the results of the evaluation, the child shall remain in the educational placement determined by school authorities.

(6) Referral to and action by law enforcement and judicial authorities.

(A) Rule of construction.

Nothing in this part shall be construed to prohibit an agency from reporting a crime committed by a child with a disability to appropriate authorities or to prevent State law enforcement and judicial authorities from exercising their responsibilities with regard to the application of Federal and State law to crimes committed by a child with a disability.

(B) Transmittal of records.

An agency reporting a crime committed by a child with a disability shall ensure that copies of the special education and disciplinary records of the child are transmitted for consideration by the appropriate authorities to whom the agency reports the crime.

(7) Definitions.

In this subsection:

(A) Controlled substance.

The term "controlled substance" means a drug or other substance identified under schedule I, II, III, IV, or V in section 202(c) of the Controlled Substances Act (21 U.S.C. 812(c)).

(B) Illegal drug.

The term "illegal drug" means a controlled substance but does not include a controlled substance that is legally possessed or used under the supervision of a licensed health-care professional or that is legally possessed or used under any other authority under that Act or under any other provision of Federal law.

(C) Weapon.

The term "weapon" has the meaning given the term "dangerous weapon" under section 930(g)(2) of title 18, United States Code.

(D) Serious bodily injury.

The term "serious bodily injury" has

the meaning given the term "serious bodily injury" under paragraph (3) of subsection (h) of section 1365 of title 18, United States Code.

(L) Rule of construction.

Nothing in this title shall be construed to restrict or limit the rights, procedures, and remedies available under the Constitution, the Americans with Disabilities Act of 1990, title V of the Rehabilitation Act of 1973, or other Federal laws protecting the rights of children with disabilities, except that before the filing of a civil action under such laws seeking relief that is also available under this part, the procedures under subsections (f) and (g) shall be exhausted to the same extent as would be required had the action been brought under this part.

(m) Transfer of parental rights at age of majority.

(1) In general.

A State that receives amounts from a grant under this part may provide that, when a child with a disability reaches the age of majority under State law (except for a child with a disability who has been determined to be incompetent under State law) —

(A) the agency shall provide any notice required by this section to both the individual and the parents;

(B) all other rights accorded to parents under this part transfer to the child;

(C) the agency shall notify the individual and the parents of the transfer of rights; and

(D) all rights accorded to parents under this part transfer to children who are incarcerated in an adult or juvenile Federal, State, or local correctional institution.

(2) Special rule.

If, under State law, a child with a disability who has reached the age of majority under State law, who has not been determined to be incompetent, but who is determined not to have the ability to provide informed consent with respect to the educational program of the child, the State shall establish procedures for appointing the parent of the child, or if the parent is not available, another appropriate individual, to represent the educational interests of the child throughout the period of eligibility of the child under this part.

(n) Electronic mail.

A parent of a child with a disability may elect to receive notices required under this section by an electronic mail (e-mail) communication, if the agency makes such option available.

(o) Separate complaint.

Nothing in this section shall be construed to preclude a parent from filing a separate due process complaint on an issue separate from a due process complaint already filed.

§ 1416. Withholding and judicial review

(a) Withholding of payments

(1) In general

The Secretary shall —

(A) monitor implementation of this part through —

(i) oversight of the exercise of general supervision by the States, as required in section 612(a)(11); and

(ii) the State performance plans, described in subsection (b);

(B) enforce this part in accordance with subsection (e); and

(C) require States to —

(i) monitor implementation of this part by local educational agencies; and

(ii) enforce this part in accordance with paragraph (3) and subsection (e).

(2) Focused monitoring.

The primary focus of Federal and State monitoring activities described in paragraph (1) shall be on —

(A) improving educational results and functional outcomes for all children with disabilities; and

(B) ensuring that States meet the program requirements under this part, with a particular emphasis on those requirements that are most closely related to improving educational results for children with disabilities.

(3) Monitoring priorities.

The Secretary shall monitor the States, and shall require each State to monitor the local educational agencies located in the State (except the State exercise of general supervisory responsibility), using quantifiable indicators in each of the following priority areas, and using such qualitative indicators as are needed to adequately measure performance in the following priority areas:

(A) Provision of a free appropriate public education in the least restrictive environment.

(B) State exercise of general supervisory authority, including child find, effective monitoring, the use of resolution sessions, mediation, voluntary binding arbitration, and a system of transition services as defined in sections 602(34) and 637(a)(9).

(C) Disproportionate representation of racial and ethnic groups in special education and related services, to the extent the representation is the result of inappropriate identification.

(4) Permissive areas of review.

The Secretary shall consider other relevant information and data, including data provided by States under section 618.

(b) State performance plans.

(1) Plan.

(A) In general.

Not later than 1 year after the date of enactment of the Individuals with Disabilities Education Improvement Act of 2004, each State shall have in place a performance plan that evaluates that State's efforts to implement the requirements and purposes of this part and describes how the State will improve such implementation.

(B) Submission for approval.

Each State shall submit the State's performance plan to the Secretary for approval in accordance with the approval process described in subsection (c).

(C) Review.

Each State shall review its State performance plan at least once every 6 years and submit any amendments to the Secretary.

(2) Targets.

(A) In general.

As a part of the State performance plan described under paragraph (1), each State shall establish measurable and rigorous targets for the indicators established under the priority areas described in subsection (a)(3).

(B) Data collection.

(i) In general.

Each State shall collect valid and reliable information as needed to report annually to the Secretary on the priority areas described in subsection (a)(3).

(ii) Rule of construction.

Nothing in this title shall be construed to authorize the development of a nationwide database of personally identifiable information on individuals involved in studies or other collections of data under this part.

(C) Public reporting and privacy.

(i) In general.

The State shall use the targets established in the plan and priority areas described in subsection (a)(3) to analyze the performance of each local educational agency in the State in implementing this part.

(ii) Report.

(I) Public report.

The State shall report annually to the public on the performance of each local educational agency located in the State on the targets in the State's performance plan. The State shall make the State's performance plan available through public means, including by posting on the website of the State educational agency, distribution to the media, and distribution through public agencies.

(II) State performance report.

The State shall report annually to the Secretary on the performance of the State under the State's performance plan.

(iii) Privacy.

The State shall not report to the public or the Secretary any information on performance that would result in the disclosure of personally identifiable information about individual children or where the available data is insufficient to yield statistically reliable information.

(c) Approval process.

(1) Deemed approval.

The Secretary shall review (including the specific provisions described in subsection (b)) each performance plan submitted by a State pursuant to subsection (b)(1)(B) and the plan shall be deemed to be approved by the Secretary unless the Secretary makes a written determination, prior to the expiration of the 120-day period beginning on the date on which the Secretary received the plan, that the plan does not meet the requirements of this section, including the specific provisions described in subsection (b).

(2) Disapproval.

The Secretary shall not finally disapprove a performance plan, except after giving the State notice and an opportunity for a hearing.

(3) Notification.

If the Secretary finds that the plan does not meet the requirements, in whole or in part, of this section, the Secretary shall —

(A) give the State notice and an opportunity for a hearing; and

(B) notify the State of the finding, and in such notification shall —

(i) cite the specific provisions in the plan that do not meet the requirements; and

(ii) request additional information, only as to the provisions not meeting the requirements, needed for the plan to meet the requirements of this section.

(4) Response.

If the State responds to the Secretary's notification described in paragraph (3)(B) during the 30-day period beginning on the date on which the State received the notification, and resubmits the plan with the requested information described in paragraph (3)(B)(ii), the Secretary shall approve or disapprove such plan prior to the later of —

(A) the expiration of the 30-day period beginning on the date on which the plan is resubmitted; or

(B) the expiration of the 120-day period described in paragraph (1).

(5) Failure to respond.

If the State does not respond to the Secretary's notification described in paragraph (3)(B) during the 30-day period beginning on the date on which the State received the notification, such plan shall be deemed to be disapproved.

(d) Secretary's review and determination.

(1) Review.

The Secretary shall annually review the State performance report submitted pursuant to subsection (b)(2)(C)(ii)(II) in accordance with this section.

(2) Determination.

(A) In general.

Based on the information provided by the State in the State performance report, information obtained through monitoring visits, and any other public information made available, the Secretary shall determine if the State —

(i) meets the requirements and purposes of this part;

(ii) needs assistance in implementing the requirements of this part;

(iii) needs intervention in implementing the requirements of this part; or

(iv) needs substantial intervention in implementing the requirements of this part.

(B) Notice and opportunity for a hearing.

For determinations made under clause (iii) or (iv) of subparagraph (A), the Secretary shall provide reasonable notice and an opportunity for a hearing on such determination.

(e) Enforcement.

(1) Needs assistance.

If the Secretary determines, for 2 consecutive years, that a State needs assistance under subsection (d)(2)(A)(ii) in implementing the requirements of this part, the Secretary shall take 1 or more of the following actions:

(A) Advise the State of available sources of technical assistance that may help the State address the areas in which the State needs assistance, which may include assistance from the Office of Special Education Programs, other offices of the Department of Education, other Federal agencies, technical assistance providers approved by the Secretary, and other federally funded nonprofit agencies, and require the State to work with appropriate entities. Such technical assistance may include —

(i) the provision of advice by experts to address the areas in which the State needs assistance, including explicit plans for addressing the area for concern within a specified period of time;

(ii) assistance in identifying and implementing professional development, instructional strategies, and methods of instruction that are based on scientifically based research;

(iii) designating and using distinguished superintendents, principals, special education administrators, special education teachers, and other teachers to provide advice, technical assistance, and support; and

(iv) devising additional approaches to providing technical assistance, such as collaborating with institutions of higher education, educational service agencies, national centers of technical assistance supported under part D, and private providers of scientifically based technical assistance.

(B) Direct the use of State-level funds under section 611(e) on the area or areas in which the State needs assistance.

(C) Identify the State as a high-risk grantee and impose special conditions on the State's grant under this part.

(2) Needs intervention.

If the Secretary determines, for 3 or more consecutive years, that a State needs intervention under subsection (d)(2)(A)(iii) in implementing the requirements of this part, the following shall apply:

(A) The Secretary may take any of the actions described in paragraph (1).

(B) The Secretary shall take 1 or more of the following actions:

(i) Require the State to prepare a corrective action plan or improvement plan if the Secretary determines that the State should be able to correct the problem within 1 year.

(ii) Require the State to enter into a compliance agreement under section 457 of the General Education Provisions Act, if the Secretary has reason to believe that the State cannot correct the problem within 1 year.

(iii) For each year of the determination, withhold not less than 20 percent and not more than 50 percent of the State's funds under section 611(e), until the Secretary determines the State has sufficiently addressed the areas in which the State needs intervention.

(iv) Seek to recover funds under section 452 of the General Education Provisions Act.

(v) Withhold, in whole or in part, any further payments to the State under this part pursuant to paragraph (5).

(vi) Refer the matter for appropriate enforcement action, which may include referral to the Department of Justice.

(3) Needs substantial intervention. —

Notwithstanding paragraph (1) or (2), at any time that the Secretary determines that a State needs substantial intervention in implementing the requirements of this part or that there is a substantial failure to comply with any condition of a State educational agency's or local educational agency's eligibility under this part, the Secretary shall take 1 or more of the following actions:

(A) Recover funds under section 452 of the General Education Provisions Act.

(B) Withhold, in whole or in part, any further payments to the State under this part.

(C) Refer the case to the Office of the Inspector General at the Department of Education.

(D) Refer the matter for appropriate enforcement action, which may include referral to the Department of Justice.

(4) Opportunity for hearing.

(A) Withholding funds.

Prior to withholding any funds under this section, the Secretary shall provide reasonable notice and an opportunity for a hearing to the State educational agency involved.

(B) Suspension.

Pending the outcome of any hearing to withhold payments under subsection (b), the Secretary may suspend payments to a recipient, suspend the authority of the recipient to obligate funds under this part, or both, after such recipient has been given reasonable notice and an opportunity to show cause why future payments or authority to obligate funds under this part should not be suspended.

(5) Report to congress.

The Secretary shall report to the Committee on Education and the Workforce of the House of Representatives and the Committee on Health, Education, Labor, and Pensions of the Senate within 30 days of taking enforcement action pursuant to paragraph (1), (2), or (3), on the specific action taken and the reasons why enforcement action was taken.

(6) Nature of withholding.

(A) Limitation.

If the Secretary withholds further payments pursuant to paragraph (2) or (3), the Secretary may determine —

(i) that such withholding will be limited to programs or projects, or portions of programs or projects, that affected the Secretary's determination under subsection (d)(2); or

(ii) that the State educational agency

shall not make further payments under this part to specified State agencies or local educational agencies that caused or were involved in the Secretary's determination under subsection (d)(2).

(B) Withholding until rectified.

Until the Secretary is satisfied that the condition that caused the initial withholding has been substantially rectified —

(i) payments to the State under this part shall be withheld in whole or in part; and

(ii) payments by the State educational agency under this part shall be limited to State agencies and local educational agencies whose actions did not cause or were not involved in the Secretary's determination under subsection (d)(2), as the case may be.

(7) Public attention.

Any State that has received notice under subsection (d)(2) shall, by means of a public notice, take such measures as may be necessary to bring the pendency of an action pursuant to this subsection to the attention of the public within the State.

(8) Judicial review.

(A) In general.

If any State is dissatisfied with the Secretary's action with respect to the eligibility of the State under section 612, such State may, not later than 60 days after notice of such action, file with the United States court of appeals for the circuit in which such State is located a petition for review of that action. A copy of the petition shall be transmitted by the clerk of the court to the Secretary. The Secretary thereupon shall file in the court the record of the proceedings upon which the Secretary's action was based, as provided in section 2112 of title 28, United States Code.

(B) Jurisdiction; review by united states supreme court.

Upon the filing of such petition, the court shall have jurisdiction to affirm the action of the Secretary or to set it aside, in whole or in part. The judgment of the court shall be subject to review by the Supreme Court of the United States upon certiorari or certification as provided in section 1254 of title 28, United States Code.

(C) Standard of review.

The findings of fact by the Secretary, if supported by substantial evidence, shall be conclusive, but the court, for good cause shown, may remand the case to the Secretary to take further evidence, and the Secretary may thereupon make new or modified findings of fact and may modify the Secretary's previous action, and shall file in the court the record of the further proceedings. Such new or modified findings of fact shall be conclusive if supported by substantial evidence.

(f) State enforcement.

If a State educational agency determines that a local educational agency is not meeting the requirements of this part, including the targets in the State's performance plan, the State educational agency shall prohibit the local educational agency from reducing the local educational agency's maintenance of effort under section 613(a)(2)(C) for any fiscal year.

(g) Rule of construction.

Nothing in this section shall be construed to restrict the Secretary from utilizing any authority under the General Education Provisions Act to monitor and enforce the requirements of this title.

(h) Divided state agency responsibility.

For purposes of this section, where responsibility for ensuring that the requirements of this part are met with respect to children with disabilities who are convicted as adults under State law and incarcerated in adult prisons is assigned to a public agency other than the State educational agency pursuant to section 612(a)(11)(C), the Secretary, in instances where the Secretary finds that the failure to comply substantially with the provisions of this part are related to a failure by the public agency, shall take appropriate corrective action to ensure compliance with this part, except that —

(1) any reduction or withholding of payments to the State shall be proportionate to the total funds allotted under section 611 to the State as the number of eligible children with disabilities in adult prisons under the supervision of the other public agency is proportionate to the number of eligible individuals with disabilities in the State under the supervision of the State educational agency; and

(2) any withholding of funds under paragraph (1) shall be limited to the specific

agency responsible for the failure to comply with this part.

(i) Data capacity and technical assistance review.

The Secretary shall —

(1) review the data collection and analysis capacity of States to ensure that data and information determined necessary for implementation of this section is collected, analyzed, and accurately reported to the Secretary; and

(2) provide technical assistance (from funds reserved under section 611(c)), where needed, to improve the capacity of States to meet the data collection requirements.

§ 1417. Administration

(a) Responsibilities of Secretary

In carrying out this subchapter, the Secretary shall —

(1) cooperate with, and (directly or by grant or contract) furnish technical assistance necessary to, a State in matters relating to —

(A) the education of children with disabilities; and

(B) carrying out this part; and

(2) provide short-term training programs and institutes.

(b) Prohibition against federal mandates, direction, or control.

Nothing in this title shall be construed to authorize an officer or employee of the Federal Government to mandate, direct, or control a State, local educational agency, or school's specific instructional content, academic achievement standards and assessments, curriculum, or program of instruction.

(c) Confidentiality.

The Secretary shall take appropriate action, in accordance with section 444 of the General Education Provisions Act, to ensure the protection of the confidentiality of any personally identifiable data, information, and records collected or maintained by the Secretary and by State educational agencies and local educational agencies pursuant to this part.

(d) Personnel.

The Secretary is authorized to hire qualified personnel necessary to carry out the Secretary's duties under subsection (a), under section 618, and under subpart 4 of part D, without regard to the provisions of title 5, United States Code, relating to appointments in the competitive service and without regard to chapter 51 and subchapter III of chapter 53 of such title relating to classification and general schedule pay rates, except that no more than 20 such personnel shall be employed at any time.

(e) Model forms.

Not later than the date that the Secretary publishes final regulations under this title, to implement amendments made by the Individuals with Disabilities Education Improvement Act of 2004, the Secretary shall publish and disseminate widely to States, local educational agencies, and parent and community training and information centers —

(1) a model IEP form;

(2) a model individualized family service plan (IFSP) form;

(3) a model form of the notice of procedural safeguards described in section 615(d); and

(4) a model form of the prior written notice described in subsections (b)(3) and (c)(1) of section 615 that is consistent with the requirements of this part and is sufficient to meet such requirements.

§ 1418. Program information

(a) In general

Each State that receives assistance under this part, and the Secretary of the Interior, shall provide data each year to the Secretary of Education and the public on the following:

(1)(A) The number and percentage of children with disabilities, by race, ethnicity, limited English proficiency status, gender, and disability category, who are in each of the following separate categories:

(i) Receiving a free appropriate public education.

(ii) Participating in regular education.

(iii) In separate classes, separate schools or facilities, or public or private residential facilities.

(iv) For each year of age from age 14 through 21, stopped receiving special education and related services because of program completion (including graduation with a regular secondary school diploma), or other reasons, and the reasons why those children stopped receiving special education and related services.

(v)(I) Removed to an interim alternative educational setting under section 615(k)(1).

(II) The acts or items precipitating those removals.

(III) The number of children with disabilities who are subject to long-term suspensions or expulsions.

(B) The number and percentage of children with disabilities, by race, gender, and ethnicity, who are receiving early intervention services.

(C) The number and percentage of children with disabilities, by race, gender, and ethnicity, who, from birth through age 2, stopped receiving early intervention services because of program completion or for other reasons.

(D) The incidence and duration of disciplinary actions by race, ethnicity, limited English proficiency status, gender, and disability category, of children with disabilities, including suspensions of 1 day or more.

(E) The number and percentage of children with disabilities who are removed to alternative educational settings or expelled as compared to children without disabilities who are removed to alternative educational settings or expelled.

(F) The number of due process complaints filed under section 615 and the number of hearings conducted.

(G) The number of hearings requested under section 615(k) and the number of changes in placements ordered as a result of those hearings.

(H) The number of mediations held and the number of settlement agreements reached through such mediations.

(2) The number and percentage of infants and toddlers, by race, and ethnicity, who are at risk of having substantial developmental delays (as defined in section 632), and who are receiving early intervention services under part C.

(3) Any other information that may be required by the Secretary.

(b) Data reporting.

(1) Protection of identifiable data.

The data described in subsection (a) shall be publicly reported by each State in a manner that does not result in the disclosure of data identifiable to individual children.

(2) Sampling.

The Secretary may permit States and the Secretary of the Interior to obtain the data described in subsection (a) through sampling.

(c) Technical assistance.

The Secretary may provide technical assistance to States to ensure compliance with the data collection and reporting requirements under this title.

(d) Disproportionality.

(1) In general.

Each State that receives assistance under this part, and the Secretary of the Interior, shall provide for the collection and examination of data to determine if significant disproportionality based on race and ethnicity is occurring in the State and the local educational agencies of the State with respect to —

(A) the identification of children as children with disabilities, including the identification of children as children with disabilities in accordance with a particular impairment described in section 602(3);

(B) the placement in particular educational settings of such children; and

(C) the incidence, duration, and type of disciplinary actions, including suspensions and expulsions.

(2) Review and revision of policies, practices, and procedures.

In the case of a determination of significant disproportionality with respect to the identification of children as children with disabilities, or the placement in particular educational settings of such children, in accordance with paragraph (1), the State or the Secretary of the Interior, as the case may be, shall —

(A) provide for the review and, if appropriate, revision of the policies, procedures, and practices used in such identification or placement to ensure that such policies, procedures, and practices comply with the requirements of this title;

(B) require any local educational agency identified under paragraph (1) to reserve the maximum amount of funds under section 613(f) to provide comprehensive coordinated early intervening services to serve children in the local educational agency, particularly children in those groups that were significantly overidentified under paragraph (1); and

(C) require the local educational agency to publicly report on the revision of policies, practices, and procedures described under subparagraph (A).

§ 1419. Preschool grants

(a) In general

The Secretary shall provide grants under this section to assist States to provide special education and related services, in accordance with this part —

(1) to children with disabilities aged 3 through 5, inclusive; and

(2) at the State's discretion, to 2-year-old children with disabilities who will turn 3 during the school year.

(b) Eligibility.

A State shall be eligible for a grant under this section if such State —

(1) is eligible under section 612 to receive a grant under this part; and

(2) makes a free appropriate public education available to all children with disabilities, aged 3 through 5, residing in the State.

(c) Allocations to states.

(1) In general.

The Secretary shall allocate the amount made available to carry out this section for a fiscal year among the States in accordance with paragraph (2) or (3), as the case may be.

(2) Increase in funds.

If the amount available for allocations to States under paragraph (1) for a fiscal year is equal to or greater than the amount allocated to the States under this section for the preceding fiscal year, those allocations shall be calculated as follows:

(A) Allocation.

(i) In general.

Except as provided in subparagraph (B), the Secretary shall —

(I) allocate to each State the amount the State received under this section for fiscal year 1997;

(II) allocate 85 percent of any remaining funds to States on the basis of the States' relative populations of children aged 3 through 5; and

(III) allocate 15 percent of those remaining funds to States on the basis of the States' relative populations of all children aged 3 through 5 who are living in poverty.

(ii) Data.

For the purpose of making grants under this paragraph, the Secretary shall use the most recent population data, including data on children living in poverty, that are available and satisfactory to the Secretary.

(B) Limitations.

Notwithstanding subparagraph (A), allocations under this paragraph shall be subject to the following:

(i) Preceding years.

No State's allocation shall be less than its allocation under this section for the preceding fiscal year.

(ii) Minimum.

No State's allocation shall be less than the greatest of —

(I) the sum of —

(aa) the amount the State received under this section for fiscal year 1997; and

(bb) 1/3 of 1 percent of the amount by which the amount appropriated under subsection (j) for the fiscal year exceeds the amount appropriated for this section for fiscal year 1997;

(II) the sum of —

(aa) the amount the State received under this section for the preceding fiscal year; and

(bb) that amount multiplied by the percentage by which the increase in the funds appropriated under this section from the preceding fiscal year exceeds 1.5 percent; or

(III) the sum of —

(aa) the amount the State received under this section for the preceding fiscal year; and

(bb) that amount multiplied by 90 percent of the percentage increase in the amount appropriated under this section from the preceding fiscal year.

(iii) Maximum.

Notwithstanding clause (ii), no State's allocation under this paragraph shall exceed the sum of —

(I) the amount the State received under this section for the preceding fiscal year; and

(II) that amount multiplied by the sum of 1.5 percent and the percentage increase in the amount appropriated under this section from the preceding fiscal year.

(C) Ratable reductions.

If the amount available for allocations under this paragraph is insufficient to pay those allocations in full, those allocations shall be ratably reduced, subject to subparagraph (B)(I).

(3) Decrease in funds.

If the amount available for allocations to States under paragraph (1) for a fiscal year is less than the amount allocated to the States under this section for the preceding fiscal year, those allocations shall be calculated as follows:

(A) Allocations.

If the amount available for allocations is greater than the amount allocated to the States for fiscal year 1997, each State shall be allocated the sum of —

(i) the amount the State received under this section for fiscal year 1997; and

(ii) an amount that bears the same relation to any remaining funds as the increase the State received under this section for the preceding fiscal year over fiscal year 1997 bears to the total of all such increases for all States.

(B) Ratable reductions.

If the amount available for allocations is equal to or less than the amount allocated to the States for fiscal year 1997, each State shall be allocated the amount the State received for fiscal year 1997, ratably reduced, if necessary.

(d) Reservation for state activities.

(1) In general.

Each State may reserve not more than the amount described in paragraph (2) for administration and other State-level activities in accordance with subsections (e) and (f).

(2) Amount described.

For each fiscal year, the Secretary shall determine and report to the State educational agency an amount that is 25 percent of the amount the State received under this section for fiscal year 1997, cumulatively adjusted by the Secretary for each succeeding fiscal year by the lesser of —

(A) the percentage increase, if any, from the preceding fiscal year in the State's allocation under this section; or

(B) the percentage increase, if any, from the preceding fiscal year in the Consumer Price Index For All Urban Consumers published by the Bureau of Labor Statistics of the Department of Labor.

(e) State administration.

(1) In general.

For the purpose of administering this section (including the coordination of activities under this part with, and providing technical assistance to, other programs that provide services to children with disabilities) a State may use not more than 20 percent of the maximum amount the State may reserve under subsection (d) for any fiscal year.

(2) Administration of part C.

Funds described in paragraph (1) may also be used for the administration of part C.

(f) Other state-level activities.

Each State shall use any funds the State reserves under subsection (d) and does not use for administration under subsection (e) —

(1) for support services (including establishing and implementing the mediation process required by section 615(e)), which may benefit children with disabilities younger than 3 or older than 5 as long as those services also benefit children with disabilities aged 3 through 5;

(2) for direct services for children eligible for services under this section;

(3) for activities at the State and local levels to meet the performance goals established by the State under section 612(a)(15);

(4) to supplement other funds used to develop and implement a statewide coordinated services system designed to improve results for children and families, including children with disabilities and their families, but not more than 1 percent of the amount received by the State under this section for a fiscal year;

(5) to provide early intervention services (which shall include an educational component that promotes school readiness and incor-

porates preliteracy, language, and numeracy skills) in accordance with part C to children with disabilities who are eligible for services under this section and who previously received services under part C until such children enter, or are eligible under State law to enter, kindergarten;

(6) at the State's discretion, to continue service coordination or case management for families who receive services under part C.

(g) Subgrants to local educational agencies.

(1) Subgrants required.

Each State that receives a grant under this section for any fiscal year shall distribute all of the grant funds that the State does not reserve under subsection (d) to local educational agencies in the State that have established their eligibility under section 613, as follows:

(A) Base payments.

The State shall first award each local educational agency described in paragraph (1) the amount that agency would have received under this section for fiscal year 1997 if the State had distributed 75 percent of its grant for that year under section 619(c)(3), as such section was then in effect.

(B) Allocation of remaining funds.

After making allocations under subparagraph (A), the State shall —

(i) allocate 85 percent of any remaining funds to those local educational agencies on the basis of the relative numbers of children enrolled in public and private elementary schools and secondary schools within the local educational agency's jurisdiction; and

(ii) allocate 15 percent of those remaining funds to those local educational agencies in accordance with their relative numbers of children living in poverty, as determined by the State educational agency.

(2) Reallocation of funds.

If a State educational agency determines that a local educational agency is adequately providing a free appropriate public education to all children with disabilities aged 3 through 5 residing in the area served by the local educational agency with State and local funds, the State educational agency may reallocate any portion of the funds under this section that are not needed by that local educational agency to provide a free appropriate public education to other local educational agencies in the State that are not adequately providing special education and related services to all children with disabilities aged 3 through 5 residing in the areas the other local educational agencies serve.

(h) Part C inapplicable.

Part C does not apply to any child with a disability receiving a free appropriate public education, in accordance with this part, with funds received under this section.

(i) State defined.

In this section, the term "State" means each of the 50 States, the District of Columbia, and the Commonwealth of Puerto Rico.

(j) Authorization of appropriations.

There are authorized to be appropriated to carry out this section such sums as may be necessary.

Part C — Infants and Toddlers with Disabilities

Part C — Infants and Toddlers with Disabilities

§1431. Findings and policy

(a) Findings

The Congress finds that there is an urgent and substantial need —

(1) to enhance the development of infants and toddlers with disabilities, to minimize their potential for developmental delay, and to recognize the significant brain development that occurs during a child's first 3 years of life;

(2) to reduce the educational costs to our society, including our Nation's schools, by minimizing the need for special education and related services after infants and toddlers with disabilities reach school age;

(3) to maximize the potential for individuals with disabilities to live independently in society;

(4) to enhance the capacity of families to meet the special needs of their infants and toddlers with disabilities; and

(5) to enhance the capacity of State and local agencies and service providers to identify, evaluate, and meet the needs of all children, particularly minority, low-income, inner city, and rural children, and infants and toddlers in foster care.

(b) Policy.

It is the policy of the United States to provide financial assistance to States —

(1) to develop and implement a statewide, comprehensive, coordinated, multidisciplinary, interagency system that provides early intervention services for infants and toddlers with disabilities and their families;

(2) to facilitate the coordination of payment for early intervention services from Federal, State, local, and private sources (including public and private insurance coverage);

(3) to enhance State capacity to provide quality early intervention services and expand and improve existing early intervention services being provided to infants and toddlers with disabilities and their families; and

(4) to encourage States to expand opportunities for children under 3 years of age who would be at risk of having substantial developmental delay if they did not receive early intervention services.

§ 1432. Definitions

As used in this subchapter:

(1) At-risk infant or toddler

The term "at-risk infant or toddler" means an individual under 3 years of age who would be at risk of experiencing a substantial developmental delay if early intervention services were not provided to the individual.

(2) Council.

The term "council" means a State interagency coordinating council established under section 641.

(3) Developmental delay.

The term "developmental delay", when used with respect to an individual residing in a State, has the meaning given such term by the State under section 635(a)(1).

(4) Early intervention services.

The term "early intervention services" means developmental services that —

(A) are provided under public supervision;

(B) are provided at no cost except where Federal or State law provides for a system of payments by families, including a schedule of sliding fees;

(C) are designed to meet the developmental needs of an infant or toddler with a disability, as identified by the individualized family service plan team, in any 1 or more of the following areas:

(i) physical development;

(ii) cognitive development;

(iii) communication development;

(iv) social or emotional development; or

(v) adaptive development;

(D) meet the standards of the State in which the services are provided, including the requirements of this part;

(E) include —

(i) family training, counseling, and home visits;

(ii) special instruction;

(iii) speech-language pathology and audiology services, and sign language and cued language services;

(iv) occupational therapy;

(v) physical therapy;

(vi) psychological services;

(vii) service coordination services;

(viii) medical services only for diagnostic or evaluation purposes;

(ix) early identification, screening, and assessment services;

(x) health services necessary to enable the infant or toddler to benefit from the other early intervention services;

(xi) social work services;

(xii) vision services;

(xiii) assistive technology devices and assistive technology services; and

(xiv) transportation and related costs that are necessary to enable an infant or toddler and the infant's or toddler's family to receive another service described in this paragraph;

(F) are provided by qualified personnel, including —

(i) special educators;

(ii) speech-language pathologists and audiologists;

(iii) occupational therapists;

(iv) physical therapists;

(v) psychologists;

(vi) social workers;

(vii) nurses;

(viii) registered dietitians;

(ix) family therapists;

(x) vision specialists, including ophthalmologists and optometrists;

(xi) orientation and mobility specialists; and

(xii) pediatricians and other physicians;

(G) to the maximum extent appropriate, are provided in natural environments, including the home, and community settings in which children without disabilities participate; and

(H) are provided in conformity with an individualized family service plan adopted in accordance with section 636.

(5) Infant or toddler with a disability.

The term "infant or toddler with a disability" —

(A) means an individual under 3 years of age who needs early intervention services because the individual —

(i) is experiencing developmental delays, as measured by appropriate diagnostic instruments and procedures in 1 or more of the areas of cognitive development, physical development, communication development, social or emotional development, and adaptive development; or

(ii) has a diagnosed physical or mental condition that has a high probability of resulting in developmental delay; and

(B) may also include, at a State's discretion —

(i) at-risk infants and toddlers; and

(ii) children with disabilities who are eligible for services under section 619 and who previously received services under this part until such children enter, or are eligible under State law to enter, kindergarten or elementary school, as appropriate, provided that any programs under this part serving such children shall include —

(I) an educational component that promotes school readiness and incorporates pre-literacy, language, and numeracy skills; and

(II) a written notification to parents of their rights and responsibilities in determining whether their child will continue to receive services under this part or participate in preschool programs under section 619.

§ 1433. General authority

The Secretary shall, in accordance with this part, make grants to States (from their allotments under section 643) to assist each State to maintain and implement a statewide, comprehensive, coordinated, multidisciplinary, interagency system to provide early intervention services for infants and toddlers with disabilities and their families.

§ 1434. Eligibility

In order to be eligible for a grant under section 633, a State shall provide assurances to the Secretary that the State —

(1) has adopted a policy that appropriate early intervention services are available to all infants and toddlers with disabilities in the State and their families, including Indian infants and toddlers with disabilities and their families residing on a reservation geographically located in the State, infants and toddlers with disabilities who are homeless children and their families, and infants and toddlers with disabilities who are wards of the State; and

(2) has in effect a statewide system that meets the requirements of section 635

§ 1435. Requirements for statewide system

(a) In general

A statewide system described in section 633 shall include, at a minimum, the following components:

(1) A rigorous definition of the term "developmental delay" that will be used by the State in carrying out programs under this part in order to appropriately identify infants and toddlers with disabilities that are in need of services under this part.

(2) A State policy that is in effect and that ensures that appropriate early intervention services based on scientifically based research, to the extent practicable, are available to all infants and toddlers with disabilities and their families, including Indian infants and toddlers with disabilities and their families residing on a reservation geographically located in the State and infants and toddlers with disabilities who are homeless children and their families.

(3) A timely, comprehensive, multidisciplinary evaluation of the functioning of each infant or toddler with a disability in the State, and a family-directed identification of the needs of each family of such an infant or toddler, to assist appropriately in the development of the infant or toddler.

(4) For each infant or toddler with a disability in the State, an individualized family service plan in accordance with section 636, including service coordination services in accordance with such service plan.

(5) A comprehensive child find system, consistent with part B, including a system for making referrals to service providers that includes timelines and provides for participation by primary referral sources and that ensures rigorous standards for appropriately identifying infants and toddlers with disabilities for services under this part that will reduce the need for future services.

(6) A public awareness program focusing on early identification of infants and toddlers with disabilities, including the preparation and dissemination by the lead agency designated or established under paragraph (10) to all primary referral sources, especially hospitals and physicians, of information to be given to parents, especially to inform parents with premature infants, or infants with other physical risk factors associated with learning or developmental complications, on the availability of early intervention services under this part and of services under section 619, and procedures for assisting such sources in disseminating such information to parents of infants and toddlers with disabilities.

(7) A central directory that includes information on early intervention services, resources, and experts available in the State and research and demonstration projects being conducted in the State.

(8) A comprehensive system of personnel development, including the training of paraprofessionals and the training of primary referral sources with respect to the basic components of early intervention services available in the State that —

(A) shall include —

(i) implementing innovative strategies and activities for the recruitment and retention of early education service providers;

(ii) promoting the preparation of early intervention providers who are fully and appropriately qualified provide early intervention services under this part; and

(iii) training personnel to coordinate transition services for infants and toddlers served under this part from a program providing early intervention services under this part and under part B (other than section 619), to a preschool program receiving funds under section 619, or another appropriate program; and

(B) may include —

(i) training personnel to work in rural and inner-city areas; and

(ii) training personnel in the emotional and social development of young children.

(9) Policies and procedures relating to the establishment and maintenance of qualifications to ensure that personnel necessary to carry out this part are appropriately and adequately prepared and trained, including the establishment and maintenance of qualifications that are consistent with any State-approved or recognized certification, licensing, registration, or other comparable requirements that apply to the area in which such personnel are providing early intervention services, except that nothing in this part (including this paragraph) shall be construed to prohibit the use of paraprofessionals and assistants who are appropriately trained and supervised in accordance with State law, regulation, or written policy, to assist in the provision of early intervention services under this part to infants and toddlers with disabilities.

(10) A single line of responsibility in a lead agency designated or established by the Governor for carrying out —

(A) the general administration and supervision of programs and activities receiving assistance under section 633, and the monitoring of programs and activities used by the State to carry out this part, whether or not such programs or activities are receiving assistance made available under section 633, to ensure that the State complies with this part;

(B) the identification and coordination of all available resources within the State from Federal, State, local, and private sources;

(C) the assignment of financial responsibility in accordance with section 637(a)(2) to the appropriate agencies;

(D) the development of procedures to ensure that services are provided to infants and toddlers with disabilities and their families under this part in a timely manner pending the resolution of any disputes among public agencies or service providers;

(E) the resolution of intra- and interagency disputes; and

(F) the entry into formal interagency agreements that define the financial responsibility of each agency for paying for early intervention services (consistent with State law) and procedures for resolving disputes and that include all additional components necessary to ensure meaningful cooperation and coordination.

(11) A policy pertaining to the contracting or making of other arrangements with service providers to provide early intervention services in the State, consistent with the provisions of this part, including the contents of the application used and the conditions of the contract or other arrangements.

(12) A procedure for securing timely reimbursements of funds used under this part in accordance with section 640(a).

(13) Procedural safeguards with respect to programs under this part, as required by section 639.

(14) A system for compiling data requested by the Secretary under section 618 that relates to this part.

(15) A State interagency coordinating council that meets the requirements of section 641.

(16) Policies and procedures to ensure that, consistent with section 636(d)(5) —

(A) to the maximum extent appropriate, early intervention services are provided in natural environments; and

(B) the provision of early intervention services for any infant or toddler with a disability occurs in a setting other than a natural environment that is most appropriate, as determined by the parent and the individualized family service plan team, only when early intervention cannot be achieved satisfactorily for the infant or toddler in a natural environment.

(b) Policy.

In implementing subsection (a)(9), a State may adopt a policy that includes making ongoing good-faith efforts to recruit and hire appropriately and adequately trained personnel to provide early intervention services to infants and toddlers with disabilities, including, in a geographic area of the State where there is a shortage of such personnel, the most qualified individuals available who are making satisfactory progress toward completing applicable course work necessary to meet the standards described in subsection (a)(9).

(c) Flexibility to serve children 3 years of age until entrance into elementary school.

(1) In general.

A statewide system described in section 633 may include a State policy, developed and implemented jointly by the lead agency and the State educational agency, under which parents of children with disabilities who are eligible for services under section 619 and previously received services under this part, may choose the continuation of early intervention services (which shall include an educational component that promotes school readiness and incorporates preliteracy, language, and numeracy skills) for such children under this part until such children enter, or are eligible under State law to enter, kindergarten.

(2) Requirements.

If a statewide system includes a State policy described in paragraph (1), the statewide system shall ensure that —

(A) parents of children with disabilities served pursuant to this subsection are provided annual notice that contains —

(i) a description of the rights of such parents to elect to receive services pursuant to this subsection or under part B; and

(ii) an explanation of the differences between services provided pursuant to this subsection and services provided under part B, including —

(I) types of services and the locations at which the services are provided;

(II) applicable procedural safeguards; and

(III) possible costs (including any fees to be charged to families as described in section 632(4)(B)), if any, to parents of infants or toddlers with disabilities;

(B) services provided pursuant to this subsection include an educational component that promotes school readiness and incorporates preliteracy, language, and numeracy skills;

(C) the State policy will not affect the right of any child served pursuant to this subsection to instead receive a free appropriate public education under part B;

(D) all early intervention services outlined in the child's individualized family service plan under section 636 are continued while any eligibility determination is being made for services under this subsection;

(E) the parents of infants or toddlers with disabilities (as defined in section 632(5)(A)) provide informed written consent to the State, before such infants or toddlers reach 3 years of age, as to whether such parents intend to choose the continuation of early intervention services pursuant to this subsection for such infants or toddlers;

(F) the requirements under section 637(a)(9) shall not apply with respect to a child who is receiving services in accordance with this subsection until not less than 90 days (and at the discretion of the parties to the conference, not more than 9 months) before the time the child will no longer receive those services; and

(G) there will be a referral for evaluation for early intervention services of a child who experiences a substantiated case of trauma due to exposure to family violence (as defined in section 320 of the Family Violence Prevention and Services Act).

(3) Reporting requirement.

If a statewide system includes a State policy described in paragraph (1), the State shall submit to the Secretary, in the State's report under section 637(b)(4)(A), a report on the number and percentage of children with disabilities who are eligible for services under section 619 but whose parents choose for such children to continue to receive early intervention services under this part.

(4) Available funds.

If a statewide system includes a State policy described in paragraph (1), the policy shall describe the funds (including an identification as Federal, State, or local funds) that will be used to ensure that the option described in paragraph (1) is available to eligible children and families who provide the consent described in paragraph (2)(E), including fees (if any) to be charged to families as described in section 632(4)(B).

(5) Rules of construction.

(A) Services under part B.

If a statewide system includes a State policy described in paragraph (1), a State that provides services in accordance with this subsection to a child with a disability who is eligible for services under section 619 shall not be required to provide the child with a free appropriate public education under part B for the period of time in which the child is receiving services under this part.

(B) Services under this part.

Nothing in this subsection shall be construed to require a provider of services under this part to provide a child served under this part with a free appropriate public education.

§ 1436. Individualized family service plan

(a) Assessment and program development

A statewide system described in section 633 shall provide, at a minimum, for each infant or toddler with a disability, and the infant's or toddler's family, to receive —

(1) a multidisciplinary assessment of the unique strengths and needs of the infant or toddler and the identification of services appropriate to meet such needs;

(2) a family-directed assessment of the resources, priorities, and concerns of the family and the identification of the supports and services necessary to enhance the family's capacity to meet the developmental needs of the infant or toddler; and

(3) a written individualized family service plan developed by a multidisciplinary team, including the parents, as required by subsection (e), including a description of the appropriate transition services for the infant or toddler.

(b) Periodic review.

The individualized family service plan shall be evaluated once a year and the family shall be provided a review of the plan at 6-month intervals (or more often where appropriate based on infant or toddler and family needs).

(c) Promptness after assessment.

The individualized family service plan shall be developed within a reasonable time after the assessment required by subsection (a)(1) is completed. With the parents' consent, early intervention services may commence prior to the completion of the assessment.

(d) Content of plan.

The individualized family service plan shall be in writing and contain —

(1) a statement of the infant's or toddler's present levels of physical development, cognitive development, communication development, social or emotional development, and adaptive development, based on objective criteria;

(2) a statement of the family's resources, priorities, and concerns relating to enancing the development of the family's infant or toddler with a disability;

(3) a statement of the measurable results or outcomes expected to be achieved for the infant or toddler and the family, including preliteracy and language skills, as developmentally appropriate for the child, and the criteria, procedures, and timelines used to determine the degree to which progress toward achieving the results or outcomes is being made and whether modifications or revisions of the results or outcomes or services are necessary;

(4) a statement of specific early intervention services based on peer-reviewed research, to the extent practicable, necessary to meet the unique needs of the infant or toddler and the family, including the frequency, intensity, and method of delivering services;

(5) a statement of the natural environments in which early intervention services will appropriately be provided, including a justification of the extent, if any, to which the services will not be provided in a natural environment;

(6) the projected dates for initiation of services and the anticipated length, duration, and frequency of the services;

(7) the identification of the service coordinator from the profession most immediately relevant to the infant's or toddler's or family's needs (or who is otherwise qualified to carry out all applicable responsibilities under this part) who will be responsible for the implementation of the plan and coordination with other agencies and persons, including transition services; and

(8) the steps to be taken to support the transition of the toddler with a disability to preschool or other appropriate services.

(e) Parental consent.

The contents of the individualized family service plan shall be fully explained to the parents and informed written consent from the parents shall be obtained prior to the provision of early intervention services described in such plan. If the parents do not provide consent with respect to a particular early intervention service, then only the early intervention services to which consent is obtained shall be provided.

§1437. State application and assurances

(a) Application

A State desiring to receive a grant under section 633 shall submit an application to the Secretary at such time and in such manner as the Secretary may reasonably require. The application shall contain —

(1) a designation of the lead agency in the State that will be responsible for the administration of funds provided under section 633;

(2) a certification to the Secretary that the arrangements to establish financial responsibility for services provided under this part pursuant to section 640(b) are current as of the date of submission of the certification;

(3) information demonstrating eligibility of the State under section 634, including —

(A) information demonstrating to the Secretary's satisfaction that the State has in effect the statewide system required by section 633; and

(B) a description of services to be provided to infants and toddlers with disabilities and their families through the system;

(4) if the State provides services to at-risk infants and toddlers through the statewide system, a description of such services;

(5) a description of the uses for which funds will be expended in accordance with this part;

(6) a description of the State policies and procedures that require the referral for early intervention services under this part of a child under the age of 3 who —

(A) is involved in a substantiated case of child abuse or neglect; or

(B) is identified as affected by illegal substance abuse, or withdrawal symptoms resulting from prenatal drug exposure;

(7) a description of the procedure used to ensure that resources are made available under this part for all geographic areas within the State;

(8) a description of State policies and procedures that ensure that, prior to the adoption by the State of any other policy or procedure necessary to meet the requirements of this part, there are public hearings, adequate notice of the hearings, and an opportunity for comment available to the general public, including individuals with disabilities and parents of infants and toddlers with disabilities;

(9) a description of the policies and procedures to be used —

(A) to ensure a smooth transition for toddlers receiving early intervention services under this part (and children receiving those services under section 635(c)) to preschool, school, other appropriate services, or exiting the program, including a description of how —

(i) the families of such toddlers and children will be included in the transition plans required by subparagraph (C); and

(ii) the lead agency designated or established under section 635(a)(10) will —

(I) notify the local educational agency for the area in which such a child resides that the child will shortly reach the age of eligibility for preschool services under part B, as determined in accordance with State law;

(II) in the case of a child who may be eligible for such preschool services, with the approval of the family of the child, convene a conference among the lead agency, the family, and the local educational agency not less than 90 days (and at the discretion of all such parties, not more than 9 months) before the child is eligible for the preschool services, to discuss any such services that the child may receive; and

(III) in the case of a child who may not be eligible for such preschool services, with the approval of the family, make reasonable efforts to convene a conference among the lead agency, the family, and providers of other appropriate services for children who are not eligible for preschool services under part B, to discuss the appropriate services that the child may receive;

(B) to review the child's program options for the period from the child's third birthday through the remainder of the school year; and

(C) to establish a transition plan, including, as appropriate, steps to exit from the program;

(10) a description of State efforts to promote collaboration among Early Head Start programs under section 645A of the Head Start Act, early education and child care programs, and services under part C; and

(11) such other information and assurances as the Secretary may reasonably require.

(b) Assurances.

The application described in subsection (a) —

(1) shall provide satisfactory assurance that Federal funds made available under section 643 to the State will be expended in accordance with this part;

(2) shall contain an assurance that the State will comply with the requirements of section 640;

(3) shall provide satisfactory assurance that the control of funds provided under section 643, and title to property derived from those funds, will be in a public agency for the uses and purposes provided in this part and that a public agency will administer such funds and property;

(4) shall provide for —

(A) making such reports in such form and containing such information as the Secretary may require to carry out the Secretary's functions under this part; and

(B) keeping such reports and affording such access to the reports as the Secretary may find necessary to ensure the correctness and verification of those reports and proper disbursement of Federal funds under this part;

(5) provide satisfactory assurance that Federal funds made available under section 643 to the State —

(A) will not be commingled with State funds; and

(B) will be used so as to supplement the level of State and local funds expended for infants and toddlers with disabilities and their families and in no case to supplant those State and local funds;

(6) shall provide satisfactory assurance that such fiscal control and fund accounting procedures will be adopted as may be necessary to ensure proper disbursement of, and accounting for, Federal funds paid under section 643 to the State;

(7) shall provide satisfactory assurance that policies and procedures have been adopted to ensure meaningful involvement of underserved groups, including minority, low-income, homeless, and rural families and children with disabilities who are wards of the State, in the planning and implementation of all the requirements of this part; and

(8) shall contain such other information and assurances as the Secretary may reasonably require by regulation.

(c) Standard for disapproval of application.

The Secretary may not disapprove such an application unless the Secretary determines, after notice and opportunity for a hearing, that the application fails to comply with the requirements of this section.

(d) Subsequent state application.

If a State has on file with the Secretary a policy, procedure, or assurance that demonstrates that the State meets a requirement of this section, including any policy or procedure filed under this part (as in effect before the date of enactment of the Individuals with Disabilities Education Improvement Act of 2004), the Secretary shall consider the State to have met the requirement for purposes of receiving a grant under this part.

(e) Modification of application.

An application submitted by a State in accordance with this section shall remain in effect until the State submits to the Secretary such modifications as the State determines necessary. This section shall apply to a modification of an application to the same extent and in the same manner as this section applies to the original application.

(f) Modifications required by the secretary.

The Secretary may require a State to modify its application under this section, but only to the extent necessary to ensure the State's compliance with this part, if —

(1) an amendment is made to this title, or a Federal regulation issued under this title;

(2) a new interpretation of this title is

made by a Federal court or the State's highest court; or

(3) an official finding of noncompliance with Federal law or regulations is made with respect to the State.

§ 1438. Uses of funds

In addition to using funds provided under section 633 to maintain and implement the statewide system required by such section, a State may use such funds —

(1) for direct early intervention services for infants and toddlers with disabilities, and their families, under this part that are not otherwise funded through other public or private sources;

(2) to expand and improve on services for infants and toddlers and their families under this part that are otherwise available;

(3) to provide a free appropriate public education, in accordance with part B, to children with disabilities from their third birthday to the beginning of the following school year;

(4) with the written consent of the parents, to continue to provide early intervention services under this part to children with disabilities from their 3rd birthday until such children enter, or are eligible under State law to enter, kindergarten, in lieu of a free appropriate public education provided in accordance with part B; and

(5) in any State that does not provide services for at-risk infants and toddlers under section 637(a)(4), to strengthen the statewide system by initiating, expanding, or improving collaborative efforts related to at-risk infants and toddlers, including establishing linkages with appropriate public or private community-based organizations, services, and personnel for the purposes of —

(A) identifying and evaluating at-risk infants and toddlers;

(B) making referrals of the infants and toddlers identified and evaluated under subparagraph (A); and

(C) conducting periodic follow-up on each such referral to determine if the status of the infant or toddler involved has changed with respect to the eligibility of the infant or toddler for services under this part.

§ 1439. Procedural safeguards

(a) Minimum procedures

The procedural safeguards required to be included in a statewide system under section 635(a)(13) shall provide, at a minimum, the following:

(1) The timely administrative resolution of complaints by parents. Any party aggrieved by the findings and decision regarding an administrative complaint shall have the right to bring a civil action with respect to the complaint in any State court of competent jurisdiction or in a district court of the United States without regard to the amount in controversy. In any action brought under this paragraph, the courtshall receive the records of the administrative proceedings, shall hear additional evidence at the request of a party, and, basing its decision on the preponderance of the evidence, shall grant such relief as the court determines is appropriate.

(2) The right to confidentiality of personally identifiable information, including the right of parents to written notice of and written consent to the exchange of such information among agencies consistent with Federal and State law.

(3) The right of the parents to determine whether they, their infant or toddler, or other family members will accept or decline any early intervention service under this part in accordance with State law without jeopardizing other early intervention services under this part.

(4) The opportunity for parents to examine records relating to assessment, screening, eligibility determinations, and the development and implementation of the individualized family service plan.

(5) Procedures to protect the rights of the infant or toddler whenever the parents of the infant or toddler are not known or cannot be found or the infant or toddler is a ward of the State, including the assignment of an individual (who shall not be an employee of the State lead agency, or other State agency, and who shall not be any person, or any employee of a person, providing early intervention services to the infant or toddler or any family member of the infant or toddler) to act as a surrogate for the parents.

(6) Written prior notice to the parents of

the infant or toddler with a disability whenever the State agency or service provider proposes to initiate or change, or refuses to initiate or change, the identification, evaluation, or placement of the infant or toddler with a disability, or the provision of appropriate early intervention services to the infant or toddler.

(7) Procedures designed to ensure that the notice required by paragraph (6) fully informs the parents, in the parents' native language, unless it clearly is not feasible to do so, of all procedures available pursuant to this section.

(8) The right of parents to use mediation in accordance with section 615, except that —

(A) any reference in the section to a State educational agency shall be considered to be a reference to a State's lead agency established or designated under section 635(a)(10);

(B) any reference in the section to a local educational agency shall be considered to be a reference to a local service provider or the State's lead agency under this part, as the case may be; and

(C) any reference in the section to the provision of a free appropriate public education to children with disabilities shall be considered to be a reference to the provision of appropriate early intervention services to infants and toddlers with disabilities.

(b) Services during pendency of proceedings.

During the pendency of any proceeding or action involving a complaint by the parents of an infant or toddler with a disability, unless the State agency and the parents otherwise agree, the infant or toddler shall continue to receive the appropriate early intervention services currently being provided or, if applying for initial services, shall receive the services not in dispute.

§ 1440. Payor of last resort

(a) Nonsubstitution

Funds provided under section 643 may not be used to satisfy a financial commitment for services that would have been paid for from another public or private source, including any medical program administered by the Secretary of Defense, but for the enactment of this part, except that whenever considered necessary to prevent a delay in the receipt of appropriate early intervention services by an infant, toddler, or family in a timely fashion, funds provided under section 643 may be used to pay the provider of services pending reimbursement from the agency that has ultimate responsibility for the payment.

(b) Obligations related to and methods of ensuring services.

(1) Establishing financial responsibility for services.

(A) In general.

The Chief Executive Officer of a State or designee of the officer shall ensure that an interagency agreement or other mechanism for interagency coordination is in effect between each public agency and the designated lead agency, in order to ensure —

(i) the provision of, and financial responsibility for, services provided under this part; and

(ii) such services are consistent with the requirements of section 635 and the State's application pursuant to section 637, including the provision of such services during the pendency of any such dispute.

(B) Consistency between agreements or mechanisms under part B.

The Chief Executive Officer of a State or designee of the officer shall ensure that the terms and conditions of such agreement or mechanism are consistent with the terms and conditions of the State's agreement or mechanism under section 612(a)(12), where appropriate.

(2) Reimbursement for services by public agency.

(A) In general.

If a public agency other than an educational agency fails to provide or pay for the services pursuant to an agreement required under paragraph (1), the local educational agency or State agency (as determined by the Chief Executive Officer or designee) shall provide or pay for the provision of such services to the child.

(B) Reimbursement.

Such local educational agency or State agency is authorized to claim reimbursement for the services from the public agency that failed to provide or pay for such services and such public agency shall reimburse the local educational agency or State agency pursuant to the terms of the interagency agreement or other mechanism required under paragraph (1).

(3) Special rule.

The requirements of paragraph (1) may be met through —

(A) State statute or regulation;

(B) signed agreements between respective agency officials that clearly identify the responsibilities of each agency relating to the provision of services; or

(C) other appropriate written methods as determined by the Chief Executive Officer of the State or designee of the officer and approved by the Secretary through the review and approval of the State's application pursuant to section 637.

(c) Reduction of other benefits.

Nothing in this part shall be construed to permit the State to reduce medical or other assistance available or to alter eligibility under title V of the Social Security Act (relating to maternal and child health) or title XIX of the Social Security Act (relating to medicaid for infants or toddlers with disabilities) within the State.

§ 1441. State interagency coordinating council

(a) Establishment

(1) In general

A State that desires to receive financial assistance under this part shall establish a State interagency coordinating council.

(2) Appointment.

The council shall be appointed by the Governor. In making appointments to the council, the Governor shall ensure that the membership of the council reasonably represents the population of the State.

(3) Chairperson.

The Governor shall designate a member of the council to serve as the chairperson of the council, or shall require the council to so designate such a member. Any member of the council who is a representative of the lead agency designated under section 635(a)(10) may not serve as the chairperson of the council.

(b) Composition.

(1) In general.

The council shall be composed as follows:

(A) Parents.

Not less than 20 percent of the members shall be parents of infants or toddlers with disabilities or children with disabilities aged 12 or younger, with knowledge of, or experience with, programs for infants and toddlers with disabilities. Not less than 1 such member shall be a parent of an infant or toddler with a disability or a child with a disability aged 6 or younger.

(B) Service providers.

Not less than 20 percent of the members shall be public or private providers of early intervention services.

(C) State legislature.

Not less than 1 member shall be from the State legislature.

(D) Personnel preparation.

Not less than 1 member shall be involved in personnel preparation.

(E) Agency for early intervention services.

Not less than 1 member shall be from each of the State agencies involved in the provision of, or payment for, early intervention services to infants and toddlers with disabilities and their families and shall have sufficient authority to engage in policy planning and implementation on behalf of such agencies.

(F) Agency for preschool services.

Not less than 1 member shall be from the State educational agency responsible for preschool services to children with disabilities and shall have sufficient authority to engage in policy planning and implementation on behalf of such agency.

(G) State medicaid agency.

Not less than 1 member shall be from the agency responsible for the State medicaid program.

(H) Head start agency.

Not less than 1 member shall be a representative from a Head Start agency or program in the State.

(I) Child care agency.

Not less than 1 member shall be a representative from a State agency responsible for child care.

(J) Agency for health insurance.

Not less than 1 member shall be from the agency responsible for the State regulation of health insurance.

(K) Office of the coordinator of education of homeless children and youth.

Not less than 1 member shall be a representative designated by the Office of Coordinator for Education of Homeless Children and Youths.

(L) State foster care representative.

Not less than 1 member shall be a representative from the State child welfare agency responsible for foster care.

(M) Mental health agency.

Not less than 1 member shall be a representative from the State agency responsible for children's mental health.

(2) Other members.

The council may include other members selected by the Governor, including a representative from the Bureau of Indian Affairs (BIA), or where there is no BIA-operated or BIA-funded school, from the Indian Health Service or the tribe or tribal council.

(c) Meetings.

The council shall meet, at a minimum, on a quarterly basis, and in such places as the council determines necessary. The meetings shall be publicly announced, and, to the extent appropriate, open and accessible to the general public.

(d) Management authority.

Subject to the approval of the Governor, the council may prepare and approve a budget using funds under this part to conduct hearings and forums, to reimburse members of the council for reasonable and necessary expenses for attending council meetings and performing council duties (including child care for parent representatives), to pay compensation to a member of the council if the member is not employed or must forfeit wages from other employment when performing official council business, to hire staff, and to obtain the services of such professional, technical, and clerical personnel as may be necessary to carry out its functions under this part.

(e) Functions of council.

(1) Duties.

The council shall —

(A) advise and assist the lead agency designated or established under section 635(a)(10) in the performance of the responsibilities set forth in such section, particularly the identification of the sources of fiscal and other support for services for early intervention programs, assignment of financial responsibility to the appropriate agency, and the promotion of the interagency agreements;

(B) advise and assist the lead agency in the preparation of applications and amendments thereto;

(C) advise and assist the State educational agency regarding the transition of toddlers with disabilities to preschool and other appropriate services; and

(D) prepare and submit an annual report to the Governor and to the Secretary on the status of early intervention programs for infants and toddlers with disabilities and their families operated within the State.

(2) Authorized activity.

The council may advise and assist the lead agency and the State educational agency regarding the provision of appropriate services for children from birth through age 5. The council may advise appropriate agencies in the State with respect to the integration of services for infants and toddlers with disabilities and at-risk infants and toddlers and their families, regardless of whether at-risk infants and toddlers are eligible for early intervention services in the State.

(f) Conflict of interest.

No member of the council shall cast a vote on any matter that is likely to provide a direct financial benefit to that member or otherwise give the appearance of a conflict of interest under State law.

§ 1442. Federal administration

Sections 616, 617, and 618 shall, to the extent not inconsistent with this part, apply to the program authorized by this part, except that —

(1) any reference in such sections to a State educational agency shall be considered to be a reference to a State's lead agency established or designated under section 635(a)(10);

(2) any reference in such sections to a local educational agency, educational service agency, or a State agency shall be considered to be a reference to an early intervention service provider under this part; and

(3) any reference to the education of children with disabilities or the education of all children with disabilities shall be considered to be a reference to the provision of appropriate early intervention services to infants and toddlers with disabilities.

§ 1443. Allocation of funds

(a) Reservation of funds for outlying areas

(1) In general

From the sums appropriated to carry out this part for any fiscal year, the Secretary may reserve not more than 1 percent for payments to Guam, American Samoa, the United States Virgin Islands, and the Commonwealth of the Northern Mariana Islands in accordance with their respective needs for assistance under this part.

(2) Consolidation of funds.

The provisions of Public Law 95-134, permitting the consolidation of grants to the outlying areas, shall not apply to funds those areas receive under this part.

(b) Payments to Indians.

(1) In general.

The Secretary shall, subject to this subsection, make payments to the Secretary of the Interior to be distributed to tribes, tribal organizations (as defined under section 4 of the Indian Self-Determination and Education Assistance Act), or consortia of the above entities for the coordination of assistance in the provision of early intervention services by the States to infants and toddlers with disabilities and their families on reservations served by elementary schools and secondary schools for Indian children operated or funded by the Department of the Interior. The amount of such payment for any fiscal year shall be 1.25 percent of the aggregate of the amount available to all States under this part for such fiscal year.

(2) Allocation.

For each fiscal year, the Secretary of the Interior shall distribute the entire payment received under paragraph (1) by providing to each tribe, tribal organization, or consortium an amount based on the number of infants and toddlers residing on the reservation, as determined annually, divided by the total of such children served by all tribes, tribal organizations, or consortia.

(3) Information.

To receive a payment under this subsection, the tribe, tribal organization, or consortium shall submit such information to the Secretary of the Interior as is needed to determine the amounts to be distributed under paragraph (2).

(4) Use of funds.

The funds received by a tribe, tribal organization, or consortium shall be used to assist States in child find, screening, and other procedures for the early identification of Indian children under 3 years of age and for parent training. Such funds may also be used to provide early intervention services in accordance with this part. Such activities may be carried out directly or through contracts or cooperative agreements with the Bureau of Indian Affairs, local educational agencies, and other public or private nonprofit organizations. The tribe, tribal organization, or consortium is encouraged to involve Indian parents in the development and implementation of these activities. The above entities shall, as appropriate, make referrals to local, State, or Federal entities for the provision of services or further diagnosis.

(5) Reports.

To be eligible to receive a payment under paragraph (2), a tribe, tribal organization, or consortium shall make a biennial report to the Secretary of the Interior of activities undertaken under this subsection, including the number of contracts and cooperative agreements entered into, the number of infants and toddlers contacted and receiving services for each year, and the estimated number of infants and toddlers needing services during the 2 years following the year in which the report is made. The Secretary of the Interior shall include a summary of this information on a biennial basis to the Secretary of Education along with such other information as required under section 611(h)(3)(E). The Secretary of Education may require any additional information from the Secretary of the Interior.

(6) Prohibited uses of funds.

None of the funds under this subsection may be used by the Secretary of the Interior for administrative purposes, including child count, and the provision of technical assistance.

(c) State allotments.

(1) In general.

Except as provided in paragraphs (2) and (3), from the funds remaining for each fiscal year after the reservation and payments under subsections (a), (b), and (e), the Secretary shall first allot to each State an amount that bears the same ratio to the amount of such remainder as the number of infants and toddlers in the State bears to the number of infants and toddlers in all States.

(2) Minimum allotments.

Except as provided in paragraph (3), no State shall receive an amount under this section for any fiscal year that is less than the greater of —

(A) 1/2 of 1 percent of the remaining amount described in paragraph (1); or

(B) $500,000.

(3) Ratable reduction.

(A) In general.

If the sums made available under this part for any fiscal year are insufficient to pay the full amounts that all States are eligible to receive under this subsection for such year, the Secretary shall ratably reduce the allotments to such States for such year.

(B) Additional funds.

If additional funds become available for making payments under this subsection for a fiscal year, allotments that were reduced under subparagraph (A) shall be increased on the same basis the allotments were reduced.

(4) Definitions.

In this subsection —

(A) the terms "infants" and "toddlers" mean children under 3 years of age; and

(B) the term "State" means each of the 50 States, the District of Columbia, and the Commonwealth of Puerto Rico.

(d) Reallotment of funds.

If a State elects not to receive its allotment under subsection (c), the Secretary shall reallot, among the remaining States, amounts from such State in accordance with such subsection.

(e) Reservation for state incentive grants.

(1) In general.

For any fiscal year for which the amount appropriated pursuant to the authorization of appropriations under section 644 exceeds $460,000,000, the Secretary shall reserve 15 percent of such appropriated amount to provide grants to States that are carrying out the policy described in section 635(c) in order to facilitate the implementation of such policy.

(2) Amount of grant.

(A) In general.

Notwithstanding paragraphs (2) and (3) of subsection (c), the Secretary shall provide a grant to each State under paragraph (1) in an amount that bears the same ratio to the amount reserved under such paragraph as the number of infants and toddlers in the State bears to the number of infants and toddlers in all States receiving grants under such paragraph.

(B) Maximum amount.

No State shall receive a grant under paragraph (1) for any fiscal year in an amount that is greater than 20 percent of the amount reserved under such paragraph for the fiscal year.

(3) Carryover of amounts.

(A) First succeeding fiscal year.

Pursuant to section 421(b) of the General Education Provisions Act, amounts under a grant provided under paragraph (1) that are not obligated and expended prior to the beginning of the first fiscal year succeeding the fiscal year for which such amounts were appropriated shall remain available for obligation and expenditure during such first succeeding fiscal year.

(B) Second succeeding fiscal year.

Amounts under a grant provided under paragraph (1) that are not obligated and expended prior to the beginning of the second fiscal year succeeding the fiscal year for which such amounts were appropriated shall be returned to the Secretary and used to make grants to States under section 633 (from their allotments under this section) during such second succeeding fiscal year.

§ 1444. Authorization of appropriations

For the purpose of carrying out this part, there are authorized to be appropriated such sums as may be necessary for each of the fiscal years 2005 through 2010.

Part D — National Activities to Improve Education of Children with Disabilities

20 U.S.C. §
1450 Findings

Part D — National Activities to Improve Education of Children with Disabilities

§ 1450. Findings and purpose

(a) Findings

The Congress finds the following:

(1) The Federal Government has an ongoing obligation to support activities that contribute to positive results for children with disabilities, enabling those children to lead productive and independent adult lives.

(2) Systemic change benefiting all students, including children with disabilities, requires the involvement of States, local educational agencies, parents, individuals with disabilities and their families, teachers and other service providers, and other interested individuals and organizations to develop and implement comprehensive strategies that improve educational results for children with disabilities.

(3) State educational agencies, in partnership with local educational agencies, parents of children with disabilities, and other individuals and organizations, are in the best position to improve education for children with disabilities and to address their special needs.

(4) An effective educational system serving students with disabilities should —

(A) maintain high academic achievement standards and clear performance goals for children with disabilities, consistent with the standards and expectations for all students in the educational system, and provide for appropriate and effective strategies and methods to ensure that all children with disabilities have the opportunity to achieve those standards and goals;

(B) clearly define, in objective, measurable terms, the school and post-school results that children with disabilities are expected to achieve; and

(C) promote transition services and coordinate State and local education, social, health, mental health, and other services, in addressing the full range of student needs, particularly the needs of children with disabilities who need significant levels of support to participate and learn in school and the community.

(5) The availability of an adequate number of qualified personnel is critical —

(A) to serve effectively children with disabilities;

(B) to assume leadership positions in administration and direct services;

(C) to provide teacher training; and

(D) to conduct high quality research to improve special education.

(6) High quality, comprehensive professional development programs are essential to ensure that the persons responsible for the education or transition of children with disabilities possess the skills and knowledge necessary to address the educational and related needs of those children.

(7) Models of professional development should be scientifically based and reflect successful practices, including strategies for recruiting, preparing, and retaining personnel.

(8) Continued support is essential for the development and maintenance of a coordinated and high quality program of research to inform successful teaching practices and model curricula for educating children with disabilities.

(9) Training, technical assistance, support, and dissemination activities are necessary to ensure that parts B and C are fully implemented and achieve high quality early intervention, educational, and transitional results for children with disabilities and their families.

(10) Parents, teachers, administrators, and related services personnel need technical assistance and information in a timely, coordinated, and accessible manner in order to improve early intervention, educational, and transitional services and results at the State and local levels for children with disabilities and their families.

(11) Parent training and information activities assist parents of a child with a disability in dealing with the multiple pressures of parenting such a child and are of particular importance in —

(A) playing a vital role in creating and preserving constructive relationships between parents of children with disabilities and schools by facilitating open communication between the parents and schools; encouraging dispute resolution at the earliest possible point in time; and discouraging the escalation of an adversarial process between the parents and schools;

(B) ensuring the involvement of parents in planning and decisionmaking with respect to early intervention, educational, and transitional services;

(C) achieving high quality early intervention, educational, and transitional results for children with disabilities;

(D) providing such parents information on their rights, protections, and responsibilities under this title to ensure improved early intervention, educational, and transitional results for children with disabilities;

(E) assisting such parents in the development of skills to participate effectively in the education and development of their children and in the transitions described in section 673(b)(6);

(F) supporting the roles of such parents as participants within partnerships seeking to improve early intervention, educational, and transitional services and results for children with disabilities and their families; and

(G) supporting such parents who may have limited access to services and supports, due to economic, cultural, or linguistic barriers.

(12) Support is needed to improve technological resources and integrate technology, including universally designed technologies, into the lives of children with disabilities, parents of children with disabilities, school personnel, and others through curricula, services, and assistive technologies.

Subpart 1 — State Personnel Development Grants

20 U.S.C. §

Subpart 1 — State Personnel Development Grants

§ 1451. Purpose; definition of personnel; program authority

(a) Purpose.

The purpose of this subpart is to assist State educational agencies in reforming and improving their systems for personnel preparation and professional development in early intervention, educational, and transition services in order to improve results for children with disabilities.

(b) Definition of personnel.

In this subpart the term "personnel" means special education teachers, regular education teachers, principals, administrators, related services personnel, paraprofessionals, and early intervention personnel serving infants, toddlers, preschoolers, or children with disabilities, except where a particular category of personnel, such as related services personnel, is identified.

(c) Competitive grants.

(1) In general.

Except as provided in subsection (d), for any fiscal year for which the amount appropriated under section 655, that remains after the Secretary reserves funds under subsection (e) for the fiscal year, is less than $100,000,000, the Secretary shall award grants, on a competitive basis, to State educational agencies to carry out the activities described in the State plan submitted under section 653.

(2) Priority.

In awarding grants under paragraph (1), the Secretary may give priority to State educational agencies that —

(A) are in States with the greatest personnel shortages; or

(B) demonstrate the greatest difficulty meeting the requirements of section 612(a)(14).

(3) Minimum amount.

The Secretary shall make a grant to each State educational agency selected under paragraph (1) in an amount for each fiscal year that is —

(A) not less than $500,000, nor more than $4,000,000, in the case of the 50 States, the District of Columbia, and the Commonwealth of Puerto Rico; and

(B) not less than $80,000 in the case of an outlying area.

(4) Increase in amount.

The Secretary may increase the amounts of grants under paragraph (4) to account for inflation.

(5) Factors.

The Secretary shall determine the amount of a grant under paragraph (1) after considering —

(A) the amount of funds available for making the grants;

(B) the relative population of the State or outlying area;

(C) the types of activities proposed by the State or outlying area;

(D) the alignment of proposed activities with section 612(a)(14);

(E) the alignment of proposed activities with the State plans and applications submitted under sections 1111 and 2112, respectively, of the Elementary and Secondary Education Act of 1965; and

(F) the use, as appropriate, of scientifically based research activities.

(d) Formula grants.

(1) In general.

Except as provided in paragraphs (2) and (3), for the first fiscal year for which the amount appropriated under section 655, that remains after the Secretary reserves funds under subsection (e) for the fiscal year, is equal to or greater than $100,000,000, and for each fiscal year thereafter, the Secretary shall allot to each State educational agency, whose application meets the requirements of this subpart, an amount that bears the same relation to the amount remaining as the amount the State received under section 611(d) for that fiscal year bears to the amount of funds received by all States (whose applications meet the requirements of this subpart) under section 611(d) for that fiscal year.

(2) Minimum allotments for states that received competitive grants.

(A) In general.

The amount allotted under this subsection to any State educational agency that received a competitive multi-year grant under subsection (c) for which the grant period has not expired shall be not less than the amount specified for that fiscal year in the State educational agency's grant award document under that subsection.

(B) Special rule.

Each such State educational agency shall use the minimum amount described in subparagraph (A) for the activities described in the State educational agency's competitive grant award document for that year, unless the Secretary approves a request from the State educational agency to spend the funds on other activities.

(3) Minimum allotment.

The amount of any State educational agency's allotment under this subsection for any fiscal year shall not be less than —

(A) the greater of $500,000 or 1/2 of 1 percent of the total amount available under this subsection for that year, in the case of each of the 50 States, the District of Columbia, and the Commonwealth of Puerto Rico; and

(B) $80,000, in the case of an outlying area.

(4) Direct benefit.

In using grant funds allotted under paragraph (1), a State educational agency shall, through grants, contracts, or cooperative agreements, undertake activities that significantly and directly benefit the local educational agencies in the State.

(e) Continuation awards.

(1) In general.

Notwithstanding any other provision of this subpart, from funds appropriated under section 655 for each fiscal year, the Secretary shall reserve the amount that is necessary to make a continuation award to any State educational agency (at the request of the State educational agency) that received a multi-year award under this part (as this part was in effect on the day before the date of enactment of the Individuals with Disabilities Education Improvement Act of 2004), to enable the State educational agency to carry out activities in accordance with the terms of the multi-year award.

(2) Prohibition.

A State educational agency that receives a continuation award under paragraph (1) for any fiscal year may not receive any other award under this subpart for that fiscal year.

§ 1452. Eligibility and collaborative process

(a) Eligible applicants

A State educational agency may apply for a grant under this subpart for a grant period of not less than 1 year and not more than 5 years.

(b) Partners.

(1) In general.

In order to be considered for a grant under this subpart, a State educational agency shall establish a partnership with local educational agencies and other State agencies involved in, or concerned with, the education of children with disabilities, including —

(A) not less than 1 institution of higher education; and

(B) the State agencies responsible for administering part C, early education, child care, and vocational rehabilitation programs.

(2) Other partners.

In order to be considered for a grant under this subpart, a State educational agency shall work in partnership with other persons and organizations involved in, and concerned with, the education of children with disabilities, which may include —

(A) the Governor;

(B) parents of children with disabilities ages birth through 26;

(C) parents of nondisabled children ages birth through 26;

(D) individuals with disabilities;

(E) parent training and information centers or community parent resource centers funded under sections 671 and 672, respectively;

(F) community based and other nonprofit organizations involved in the education and employment of individuals with disabilities;

(G) personnel as defined in section 651(b);

(H) the State advisory panel established under part B;

(I) the State interagency coordinating council established under part C;

(J) individuals knowledgeable about vocational education;

(K) the State agency for higher education;

(L) public agencies with jurisdiction in the areas of health, mental health, social services, and juvenile justice;

(M) other providers of professional development that work with infants, toddlers, preschoolers, and children with disabilities; and

(N) other individuals.

(3) Required partner.

If State law assigns responsibility for teacher preparation and certification to an individual, entity, or agency other than the State educational agency, the State educational agency shall —

(A) include that individual, entity, or agency as a partner in the partnership under this subsection; and

(B) ensure that any activities the State educational agency will carry out under this subpart that are within that partner's jurisdiction (which may include activities described in section 654(b)) are carried out by that partner.

§ 1453. Applications

(a) In general

(1) Submission

A State educational agency that desires to receive a grant under this subpart shall submit to the Secretary an application at such time, in such manner, and including such information as the Secretary may require.

(2) State plan.

The application shall include a plan that identifies and addresses the State and local needs for the personnel preparation and professional development of personnel, as well as individuals who provide direct supplementary aids and services to children with disabilities, and that —

(A) is designed to enable the State to meet the requirements of section 612(a)(14) and section 635(a) (8) and (9);

(B) is based on an assessment of State and local needs that identifies critical aspects and areas in need of improvement related to the preparation, ongoing training, and professional development of personnel who serve infants, toddlers, preschoolers, and children with disabilities within the State, including —

(i) current and anticipated personnel vacancies and shortages; and

(ii) the number of preservice and inservice programs; and

(C) is integrated and aligned, to the maximum extent possible, with State plans and activities under the Elementary and Secondary Education Act of 1965, the Rehabilitation Act of 1973, and the Higher Education Act of 1965.

(3) Requirement.

The State application shall contain an assurance that the State educational agency will carry out each of the strategies described in subsection (b)(4).

(b) Elements of state personnel development plan.

Each State personnel development plan under subsection (a)(2) shall —

(1) describe a partnership agreement that is in effect for the period of the grant, which agreement shall specify —

(A) the nature and extent of the partnership described in section 652(b) and the respective roles of each member of the partnership, including the partner described in section 652(b)(3) if applicable; and

(B) how the State educational agency will work with other persons and organizations involved in, and concerned with, the education of children with disabilities, including the respective roles of each of the persons and organizations;

(2) describe how the strategies and activities described in paragraph (4) will be coordinated with activities supported with other public resources (including part B and part C funds retained for use at the State level for personnel and professional development purposes) and private resources;

(3) describe how the State educational agency will align its personnel development plan under this subpart with the plan and application submitted under sections 1111 and 2112, respectively, of the Elementary and Secondary Education Act of 1965;

(4) describe those strategies the State educational agency will use to address the professional development and personnel needs identified under subsection (a)(2) and how such strategies will be implemented, including —

(A) a description of the programs and activities to be supported under this subpart that will provide personnel with the knowledge and skills to meet the needs of, and improve the performance and achievement of, infants, toddlers, preschoolers, and children with disabilities; and

(B) how such strategies will be integrated, to the maximum extent possible, with other activities supported by grants funded under section 662;

(5) provide an assurance that the State educational agency will provide technical assistance to local educational agencies to improve the quality of professional development available to meet the needs of personnel who serve children with disabilities;

(6) provide an assurance that the State educational agency will provide technical assistance to entities that provide services to infants and toddlers with disabilities to improve the quality of professional development available to meet the needs of personnel serving such children;

(7) describe how the State educational agency will recruit and retain highly qualified teachers and other qualified personnel in geographic areas of greatest need;

(8) describe the steps the State educational agency will take to ensure that poor and minority children are not taught at higher rates by teachers who are not highly qualified; and

(9) describe how the State educational agency will assess, on a regular basis, the extent to which the strategies implemented under this subpart have been effective in meeting the performance goals described in section 612(a)(15).

(c) Peer review.

(1) In general.

The Secretary shall use a panel of experts who are competent, by virtue of their training, expertise, or experience, to evaluate applications for grants under section 651(c)(1).

(2) Composition of panel.

A majority of a panel described in paragraph (1) shall be composed of individuals who are not employees of the Federal Government.

(3) payment of fees and expenses of certain members.

The Secretary may use available funds appropriated to carry out this subpart to pay the expenses and fees of panel members who are not employees of the Federal Government.

(d) Reporting procedures.

Each State educational agency that receives a grant under this subpart shall submit annual performance reports to the Secretary. The reports shall —

(1) describe the progress of the State educational agency in implementing its plan;

(2) analyze the effectiveness of the State educational agency's activities under this subpart and of the State educational agency's strategies for meeting its goals under section 612(a)(15); and

(3) identify changes in the strategies used by the State educational agency and described in subsection (b)(4), if any, to improve the State educational agency's performance.

§ 1454. Use of funds

(a) Professional development activities.

A State educational agency that receives a grant under this subpart shall use the grant funds to support activities in accordance with the State's plan described in section 653, including 1 or more of the following:

(1) Carrying out programs that provide support to both special education and regular education teachers of children with disabilities and principals, such as programs that —

(A) provide teacher mentoring, team teaching, reduced class schedules and case loads, and intensive professional development;

(B) use standards or assessments for guiding beginning teachers that are consistent with challenging State student academic achievement and functional standards and with the requirements for professional development, as defined in section 9101 of the Elementary and Secondary Education Act of 1965; and

(C) encourage collaborative and consultative models of providing early intervention, special education, and related services.

(2) Encouraging and supporting the training of special education and regular education teachers and administrators to effectively use and integrate technology —

(A) into curricula and instruction, including training to improve the ability to collect, manage, and analyze data to improve teaching, decisionmaking, school improvement efforts, and accountability;

(B) to enhance learning by children with disabilities; and

(C) to effectively communicate with parents.

(3) Providing professional development activities that —

(A) improve the knowledge of special education and regular education teachers concerning —

(i) the academic and developmental or functional needs of students with disabilities; or

(ii) effective instructional strategies, methods, and skills, and the use of State academic content standards and student academic achievement and functional standards, and State assessments, to improve teaching practices and student academic achievement;

(B) improve the knowledge of special education and regular education teachers and principals and, in appropriate cases, paraprofessionals, concerning effective instructional practices, and that —

(i) provide training in how to teach and address the needs of children with different learning styles and children who are limited English proficient;

(ii) involve collaborative groups of teachers, administrators, and, in appropriate cases, related services personnel;

(iii) provide training in methods of —

(I) positive behavioral interventions and supports to improve student behavior in the classroom;

(II) scientifically based reading instruction, including early literacy instruction;

(III) early and appropriate interventions to identify and help children with disabilities;

(IV) effective instruction for children with low incidence disabilities;

(V) successful transitioning to postsecondary opportunities; and

(VI) using classroom-based techniques to assist children prior to referral for special education;

(iv) provide training to enable personnel to work with and involve parents in their child's education, including parents of low income and limited English proficient children with disabilities;

(v) provide training for special education personnel and regular education personnel in planning, developing, and implementing effective and appropriate IEPs; and

(vi) provide training to meet the needs of students with significant health, mobility, or behavioral needs prior to serving such students;

(C) train administrators, principals, and other relevant school personnel in conducting effective IEP meetings; and

(D) train early intervention, preschool, and related services providers, and other relevant school personnel, in conducting effective individualized family service plan (IFSP) meetings.

(4) Developing and implementing initiatives to promote the recruitment and retention of highly qualified special education teachers, particularly initiatives that have been proven effective in recruiting and retaining highly qualified teachers, including programs that provide —

(A) teacher mentoring from exemplary special education teachers, principals, or superintendents;

(B) induction and support for special education teachers during their first 3 years of employment as teachers; or

(C) incentives, including financial incentives, to retain special education teachers who have a record of success in helping students with disabilities.

(5) Carrying out programs and activities that are designed to improve the quality of personnel who serve children with disabilities, such as —

(A) innovative professional development programs (which may be provided through partnerships that include institutions of higher education), including programs that train teachers and principals to integrate technology into curricula and instruction to improve teaching, learning, and technology literacy, which professional development shall be consistent with the definition of professional development in section 9101 of the Elementary and Secondary Education Act of 1965; and

(B) the development and use of proven, cost effective strategies for the implementation of professional development activities, such as through the use of technology and distance learning.

(6) Carrying out programs and activities that are designed to improve the quality of early intervention personnel, including paraprofessionals and primary referral sources, such as —

(A) professional development programs to improve the delivery of early intervention services;

(B) initiatives to promote the recruitment and retention of early intervention personnel; and

(C) interagency activities to ensure that early intervention personnel are adequately prepared and trained.

(b) Other activities.

A State educational agency that receives a grant under this subpart shall use the grant funds to support activities in accordance with the State's plan described in section 653, including 1 or more of the following:

(1) Reforming special education and regular education teacher certification (including recertification) or licensing requirements to ensure that —

(A) special education and regular education teachers have —

(i) the training and information necessary to address the full range of needs of children with disabilities across disability categories; and

(ii) the necessary subject matter knowledge and teaching skills in the academic subjects that the teachers teach;

(B) special education and regular education teacher certification (including recertification) or licensing requirements are aligned with challenging State academic content standards; and

(C) special education and regular education teachers have the subject matter knowledge and teaching skills, including technology literacy, necessary to help students with disabilities meet challenging State student academic achievement and functional standards.

(2) Programs that establish, expand, or improve alternative routes for State certification of special education teachers for highly qualified individuals with a baccalaureate or master's degree, including mid-career professionals from other occupations, paraprofessionals, and recent college or university graduates with records of academic distinction who demonstrate the potential to become highly effective special education teachers.

(3) Teacher advancement initiatives for special education teachers that promote professional growth and emphasize multiple career paths (such as paths to becoming a career teacher, mentor teacher, or exemplary teacher) and pay differentiation.

(4) Developing and implementing mechanisms to assist local educational agencies and schools in effectively recruiting and retaining highly qualified special education teachers.

(5) Reforming tenure systems, implementing teacher testing for subject matter knowledge, and implementing teacher testing for State certification or licensing, consistent with title II of the Higher Education Act of 1965.

(6) Funding projects to promote reciprocity of teacher certification or licensing between or among States for special education teachers, except that no reciprocity agreement developed under this paragraph or developed using funds provided under this subpart may lead to the weakening of any State teaching certification or licensing requirement.

(7) Assisting local educational agencies to serve children with disabilities through the development and use of proven, innovative strategies to deliver intensive professional development programs that are both cost effective and easily accessible, such as strategies that involve delivery through the use of technology, peer networks, and distance learning.

(8) Developing, or assisting local educational agencies in developing, merit based performance systems, and strategies that provide differential and bonus pay for special education teachers.

(9) Supporting activities that ensure that teachers are able to use challenging State academic content standards and student academic achievement and functional standards, and State assessments for all children with disabilities, to improve instructional practices and improve the academic achievement of children with disabilities.

(10) When applicable, coordinating with, and expanding centers established under, section 2113(c)(18) of the Elementary and Secondary Education Act of 1965 to benefit special education teachers.

(c) Contracts and subgrants.

A State educational agency that receives a grant under this subpart —

(1) shall award contracts or subgrants to local educational agencies, institutions of higher education, parent training and information centers, or community parent resource centers, as appropriate, to carry out its State plan under this subpart; and

(2) may award contracts and subgrants to other public and private entities, including the lead agency under part C, to carry out the State plan.

(d) Use of funds for professional development.

A State educational agency that receives a grant under this subpart shall use —

(1) not less than 90 percent of the funds the State educational agency receives under the grant for any fiscal year for activities under subsection (a); and

(2) not more than 10 percent of the funds the State educational agency receives under the grant for any fiscal year for activities under subsection (b).

(e) Grants to outlying areas.

Public Law 95-134, permitting the consolidation of grants to the outlying areas, shall not apply to funds received under this subpart.

§ 1455. Authorization of appropriations

There are authorized to be appropriated to carry out this subpart such sums as may be necessary for each of the fiscal years 2005 through 2010.

Subpart 2 — Personnel Preparation, Technical Assistance, Model Demonstration Projects, and Dissemination of Information

§ 1461. Purpose; definition of eligible entity.

(a) Purpose.

The purpose of this subpart is —

(1) to provide Federal funding for personnel preparation, technical assistance, model demonstration projects, information dissemination, and studies and evaluations, in order to improve early intervention, educational, and transitional results for children with disabilities; and

(2) to assist State educational agencies and local educational agencies in improving their education systems for children with disabilities.

(b) Definition of eligible entity.

(1) In general.

In this subpart, the term "eligible entity" means —

(A) a State educational agency;

(B) a local educational agency;

(C) a public charter school that is a local educational agency under State law;

(D) an institution of higher education;

(E) a public agency not described in subparagraphs (A) through (D);

(F) a private nonprofit organization;

(G) an outlying area;

(H) an Indian tribe or a tribal organization (as defined under section 4 of the Indian Self-Determination and Education Assistance Act); or

(I) a for-profit organization, if the Secretary finds it appropriate in light of the purposes of a particular competition for a grant, contract, or cooperative agreement under this subpart.

(2) Special rule.

The Secretary may limit which eligible entities described in paragraph (1) are eligible for a grant, contract, or cooperative agreement under this subpart to 1 or more of the categories of eligible entities described in paragraph (1).

§ 1462. Personnel development to improve services and results for children with disabilities.

(a) In general.

The Secretary, on a competitive basis, shall award grants to, or enter into contracts or cooperative agreements with, eligible entities to carry out 1 or more of the following objectives:

(1) To help address the needs identified in the State plan described in section 653(a)(2) for highly qualified personnel, as defined in section 651(b), to work with infants or toddlers with disabilities, or children with disabilities, consistent with the qualifications described in section 612(a)(14).

(2) To ensure that those personnel have the necessary skills and knowledge, derived from practices that have been determined, through scientifically based research, to be successful in serving those children.

(3) To encourage increased focus on academics and core content areas in special education personnel preparation programs.

(4) To ensure that regular education teachers have the necessary skills and knowledge to provide instruction to students with disabilities in the regular education classroom.

(5) To ensure that all special education teachers are highly qualified.

(6) To ensure that preservice and in-service personnel preparation programs include training in —

(A) the use of new technologies;

(B) the area of early intervention, educational, and transition services;

(C) effectively involving parents; and

(D) positive behavioral supports.

(7) To provide high-quality professional development for principals, superintendents, and other administrators, including training in —

(A) instructional leadership;

(B) behavioral supports in the school and classroom;

(C) paperwork reduction;

(D) promoting improved collaboration between special education and general education teachers;

(E) assessment and accountability;

(F) ensuring effective learning environments; and

(G) fostering positive relationships with parents.

(b) Personnel development; enhanced support for beginning special educators.

(1) In general.

In carrying out this section, the Secretary shall support activities —

(A) for personnel development, including activities for the preparation of personnel who will serve children with high incidence and low incidence disabilities, to prepare special education and general education teachers, principals, administrators, and related services personnel (and school board members, when appropriate) to meet the diverse and individualized instructional needs of children with disabilities and improve early intervention, educational, and transitional services and results for children with disabilities, consistent with the objectives described in subsection (a); and

(B) for enhanced support for beginning special educators, consistent with the objectives described in subsection (a).

(2) Personnel development.

In carrying out paragraph (1)(A), the Secretary shall support not less than 1 of the following activities:

(A) Assisting effective existing, improving existing, or developing new, collaborative personnel preparation activities undertaken by institutions of higher education, local educational agencies, and other local entities that incorporate best practices and scientifically based research, where applicable, in providing special education and general education teachers, principals, administrators, and related services personnel with the knowledge and skills to effectively support students with disabilities, including —

(i) working collaboratively in regular classroom settings;

(ii) using appropriate supports, accommodations, and curriculum modifications;

(iii) implementing effective teaching strategies, classroom-based techniques, and interventions to ensure appropriate identification of students who may be eligible for special education services, and to prevent the misidentification, inappropriate overidentification, or underidentification of children as having a disability, especially minority and limited English proficient children;

(iv) effectively working with and involving parents in the education of their children;

(v) utilizing strategies, including positive behavioral interventions, for addressing the conduct of children with disabilities that impedes their learning and that of others in the classroom;

(vi) effectively constructing IEPs, participating in IEP meetings, and implementing IEPs;

(vii) preparing children with disabilities to participate in statewide assessments (with or without accommodations) and alternate assessments, as appropriate, and to ensure that all children with disabilities are a part of all accountability systems under the Elementary and Secondary Education Act of 1965; and

(viii) working in high need elementary schools and secondary schools, including urban schools, rural schools, and schools operated by an entity described in section 7113(d)(1)(A)(ii) of the Elementary and Secondary Education Act of 1965, and schools that serve high numbers or percentages of limited English proficient children.

(B) Developing, evaluating, and disseminating innovative models for the recruitment, induction, retention, and assessment of new, highly qualified teachers to reduce teacher shortages, especially from groups that are underrepresented in the teaching profession, including individuals with disabilities.

(C) Providing continuous personnel preparation, training, and professional development designed to provide support and ensure retention of special education and general education teachers and personnel who teach and provide related services to children with disabilities.

(D) Developing and improving programs for paraprofessionals to become special education teachers, related services personnel, and early intervention personnel, including interdisciplinary training to enable the paraprofessionals to improve early intervention, educational, and transitional results for children with disabilities.

(E) In the case of principals and superintendents, providing activities to promote instructional leadership and improved collaboration between general educators, special education teachers, and related services personnel.

(F) Supporting institutions of higher education with minority enrollments of not less than 25 percent for the purpose of preparing personnel to work with children with disabilities.

(G) Developing and improving programs to train special education teachers to develop an expertise in autism spectrum disorders.

(H) Providing continuous personnel preparation, training, and professional development designed to provide support and improve the qualifications of personnel who provide related services to children with disabilities, including to enable such personnel to obtain advanced degrees.

(3) Enhanced support for beginning special educators.

In carrying out paragraph (1)(B), the Secretary shall support not less than 1 of the following activities:

(A) Enhancing and restructuring existing programs or developing preservice teacher education programs to prepare special education teachers, at colleges or departments of education within institutions of higher education, by incorporating an extended (such as an additional 5th year) clinical learning opportunity, field experience, or supervised practicum into such programs.

(B) Creating or supporting teacher-faculty partnerships (such as professional development schools) that —

(i) consist of not less than —

(I) 1 or more institutions of higher education with special education personnel preparation programs;

(II) 1 or more local educational agencies that serve high numbers or percentages of low-income students; or

(III) 1 or more elementary schools or secondary schools, particularly schools that have failed to make adequate yearly progress on the basis, in whole and in part, of the assessment results of the disaggregated subgroup of students with disabilities;

(ii) may include other entities eligible for assistance under this part; and

(iii) provide —

(I) high-quality mentoring and induction opportunities with ongoing support for beginning special education teachers; or

(II) inservice professional development to beginning and veteran special education teachers through the ongoing exchange of information and instructional strategies with faculty.

(c) Low incidence disabilities; authorized activities.

(1) In general.

In carrying out this section, the Secretary shall support activities, consistent with the objectives described in subsection (a), that benefit children with low incidence disabilities.

(2) Authorized activities.

Activities that may be carried out under this subsection include activities such as the following:

(A) Preparing persons who —

(i) have prior training in educational and other related service fields; and

(ii) are studying to obtain degrees, certificates, or licensure that will enable the persons to assist children with low incidence disabilities to achieve the objectives set out in their individualized education programs described in section 614(d), or to assist infants and toddlers with low incidence disabilities to achieve the outcomes described in their individualized family service plans described in section 636.

(B) Providing personnel from various disciplines with interdisciplinary training that will contribute to improvement in early intervention, educational, and transitional results for children with low incidence disabilities.

(C) Preparing personnel in the innovative uses and application of technology, including universally designed technologies, assistive technology devices, and assistive technology services —

(i) to enhance learning by children with low incidence disabilities through early intervention, educational, and transitional services; and

(ii) to improve communication with parents.

(D) Preparing personnel who provide services to visually impaired or blind children to teach and use Braille in the provision of services to such children.

(E) Preparing personnel to be qualified educational interpreters, to assist children with low incidence disabilities, particularly deaf and hard of hearing children in school and school related activities, and deaf and hard of hearing infants and toddlers and preschool children in early intervention and preschool programs.

(F) Preparing personnel who provide services to children with significant cognitive disabilities and children with multiple disabilities.

(G) Preparing personnel who provide services to children with low incidence disabilities and limited English proficient children.

(3) Definition.

In this section, the term "low incidence disability" means —

(A) a visual or hearing impairment, or simultaneous visual and hearing impairments;

(B) a significant cognitive impairment; or

(C) any impairment for which a small number of personnel with highly specialized skills and knowledge are needed in order for children with that impairment to receive early intervention services or a free appropriate public education.

(4) Selection of recipients.

In selecting eligible entities for assistance under this subsection, the Secretary may give preference to eligible entities submitting applications that include 1 or more of the following:

(A) A proposal to prepare personnel in more than 1 low incidence disability, such as deafness and blindness.

(B) A demonstration of an effective collaboration between an eligible entity and a local educational agency that promotes recruitment and subsequent retention of highly qualified personnel to serve children with low incidence disabilities.

(5) Preparation in use of braille.

The Secretary shall ensure that all recipients of awards under this subsection who will use that assistance to prepare personnel to provide services to visually impaired or blind children that can appropriately be provided in Braille, will prepare those individuals to provide those services in Braille.

(d) Leadership preparation; authorized activities.

(1) In general.

In carrying out this section, the Secretary shall support leadership preparation activities that are consistent with the objectives described in subsection (a).

(2) Authorized activities.

Activities that may be carried out under this subsection include activities such as the following:

(A) Preparing personnel at the graduate, doctoral, and postdoctoral levels of training to administer, enhance, or provide services to improve results for children with disabilities.

(B) Providing interdisciplinary training for various types of leadership personnel, including teacher preparation faculty, related services faculty, administrators, researchers, supervisors, principals, and other persons whose work affects early intervention, educational, and transitional services for children with disabilities, including children with disabilities who are limited English proficient children

(e) Applications.

(1) In general.

An eligible entity that wishes to receive a grant, or enter into a contract or cooperative agreement, under this section shall submit an application to the Secretary at such time, in such manner, and containing such information as the Secretary may require.

(2) Identified state needs.

(A) Requirement to address identified needs.

An application for assistance under subsection (b), (c), or (d) shall include information demonstrating to the satisfaction of the Secretary that the activities described in the application will address needs identified by the State or States the eligible entity proposes to serve.

(B) Cooperation with state educational agencies.

An eligible entity that is not a local educational agency or a State educational agency shall include in the eligible entity's application information demonstrating to the satisfaction of the Secretary that the eligible entity and 1 or more State educational agencies or local educational agencies will cooperate in carrying out and monitoring the proposed project.

(3) Acceptance by states of personnel preparation requirements.

The Secretary may require eligible entities to provide in the eligible entities' applications assurances from 1 or more States that such States intend to accept successful completion of the proposed personnel preparation program as meeting State personnel standards or other requirements in State law or regulation for serving children with disabilities or serving infants and toddlers with disabilities.

(f) Selection of recipients.

(1) Impact of project.

In selecting eligible entities for assistance under this section, the Secretary shall consider the impact of the proposed project described in the application in meeting the need for personnel identified by the States.

(2) Requirement for eligible entities to meet state and professional qualifications.

The Secretary shall make grants and enter into contracts and cooperative agreements under this section only to eligible entities that meet State and professionally recognized qualifications for the preparation of special education and related services personnel, if the purpose of the project is to assist personnel in obtaining degrees.

(3) Preferences.

In selecting eligible entities for assistance under this section, the Secretary may give preference to eligible entities that are institutions of higher education that are —

(A) educating regular education personnel to meet the needs of children with disabilities in integrated settings;

(B) educating special education personnel to work in collaboration with regular educators in integrated settings; and

(C) successfully recruiting and preparing individuals with disabilities and individuals from groups that are underrepresented in the profession for which the institution of higher education is preparing individuals.

(g) Scholarships.

The Secretary may include funds for scholarships, with necessary stipends and allowances, in awards under subsections (b), (c), and (d).

(h) Service obligation.

(1) In general.

Each application for assistance under subsections (b), (c), and (d) shall include an assurance that the eligible entity will ensure that individuals who receive a scholarship under the proposed project agree to subsequently provide special education and related services to children with disabilities, or in the case of leadership personnel to subsequently work in the appropriate field, for a period of 2 years for every year for which the scholarship was received or repay all or part of the amount of the scholarship, in accordance with regulations issued by the Secretary.

(2) Special rule.

Notwithstanding paragraph (1), the Secretary may reduce or waive the service obligation requirement under paragraph (1) if the Secretary determines that the service obligation is acting as a deterrent to the recruitment of students into special education or a related field.

(3) Secretary's responsibility.

The Secretary —

(A) shall ensure that individuals described in paragraph (1) comply with the requirements of that paragraph; and

(B) may use not more than 0.5 percent of the funds appropriated under subsection (i) for each fiscal year, to carry out subparagraph (A), in addition to any other funds that are available for that purpose.

(i) Authorization of appropriations.

There are authorized to be appropriated to carry out this section such sums as may be necessary for each of the fiscal years 2005 through 2010.

§ 1463 Technical assistance, demonstration projects, dissemination of information, and implementation of scientifically based research.

(a) In general.

The Secretary shall make competitive grants to, or enter into contracts or cooperative agreements with, eligible entities to provide technical assistance, support model demonstration projects, disseminate useful information, and implement activities that are supported by scientifically based research.

(b) Required activities.

Funds received under this section shall be used to support activities to improve services provided under this title, including the practices of professionals and others involved in providing such services to children with disabilities, that promote academic achievement and improve results for children with disabilities through —

(1) implementing effective strategies for addressing inappropriate behavior of students with disabilities in schools, including strategies to prevent children with emotional and behavioral problems from developing emotional disturbances that require the provision of special education and related services;

(2) improving the alignment, compatibility, and development of valid and reliable assessments and alternate assessments for assessing adequate yearly progress, as described under section 1111(b)(2)(B) of the Elementary and Secondary Education Act of 1965;

(3) providing training for both regular education teachers and special education teachers to address the needs of students with different learning styles;

(4) disseminating information about innovative, effective, and efficient curricula designs, instructional approaches, and strate-

gies, and identifying positive academic and social learning opportunities, that —

(A) provide effective transitions between educational settings or from school to post school settings; and

(B) improve educational and transitional results at all levels of the educational system in which the activities are carried out and, in particular, that improve the progress of children with disabilities, as measured by assessments within the general education curriculum involved; and

(5) applying scientifically based findings to facilitate systemic changes, related to the provision of services to children with disabilities, in policy, procedure, practice, and the training and use of personnel.

(c) Authorized activities.

Activities that may be carried out under this section include activities to improve services provided under this title, including the practices of professionals and others involved in providing such services to children with disabilities, that promote academic achievement and improve results for children with disabilities through —

(1) applying and testing research findings in typical settings where children with disabilities receive services to determine the usefulness, effectiveness, and general applicability of such research findings in such areas as improving instructional methods, curricula, and tools, such as textbooks and media;

(2) supporting and promoting the coordination of early intervention and educational services for children with disabilities with services provided by health, rehabilitation, and social service agencies;

(3) promoting improved alignment and compatibility of general and special education reforms concerned with curricular and instructional reform, and evaluation of such reforms;

(4) enabling professionals, parents of children with disabilities, and other persons to learn about, and implement, the findings of scientifically based research, and successful practices developed in model demonstration projects, relating to the provision of services to children with disabilities;

(5) conducting outreach, and disseminating information, relating to successful approaches to overcoming systemic barriers to the effective and efficient delivery of early intervention, educational, and transitional services to personnel who provide services to children with disabilities;

(6) assisting States and local educational agencies with the process of planning systemic changes that will promote improved early intervention, educational, and transitional results for children with disabilities;

(7) promoting change through a multistate or regional framework that benefits States, local educational agencies, and other participants in partnerships that are in the process of achieving systemic-change outcomes;

(8) focusing on the needs and issues that are specific to a population of children with disabilities, such as providing single-State and multi-State technical assistance and in-service training —

(A) to schools and agencies serving deaf-blind children and their families;

(B) to programs and agencies serving other groups of children with low incidence disabilities and their families;

(C) addressing the postsecondary education needs of individuals who are deaf or hard-of-hearing; and

(D) to schools and personnel providing special education and related services for children with autism spectrum disorders;

(9) demonstrating models of personnel preparation to ensure appropriate placements and services for all students and to reduce disproportionality in eligibility, placement, and disciplinary actions for minority and limited English proficient children; and

(10) disseminating information on how to reduce inappropriate racial and ethnic disproportionalities identified under section 618.

(d) Balance among activities and age ranges.

In carrying out this section, the Secretary shall ensure that there is an appropriate balance across all age ranges of children with disabilities.

(e) Linking states to information sources.

In carrying out this section, the Secretary shall support projects that link States to technical assistance resources, including special education and general education resources, and shall make research and related products available through libraries, electronic networks, parent training projects, and other information sources, including through the activities of the National Center for Education Evaluation and Regional Assistance established under part D of the Education Sciences Reform Act of 2002.

(f) Applications.

(1) In general.

An eligible entity that wishes to receive a grant, or enter into a contract or cooperative agreement, under this section shall submit an application to the Secretary at such time, in such manner, and containing such information as the Secretary may require.

(2) Standards.

To the maximum extent feasible, each eligible entity shall demonstrate that the project described in the eligible entity's application is supported by scientifically valid research that has been carried out in accordance with the standards for the conduct and evaluation of all relevant research and development established by the National Center for Education Research.

(3) Priority.

As appropriate, the Secretary shall give priority to applications that propose to serve teachers and school personnel directly in the school environment.

§ 1464. Studies and evaluations.

(a) Studies and evaluations.

(1) Delegation.

The Secretary shall delegate to the Director of the Institute of Education Sciences responsibility to carry out this section, other than subsections (d) and (f).

(2) Assessment.

The Secretary shall, directly or through grants, contracts, or cooperative agreements awarded to eligible entities on a competitive basis, assess the progress in the implementation of this title, including the effectiveness of State and local efforts to provide —

(A) a free appropriate public education to children with disabilities; and

(B) early intervention services to infants and toddlers with disabilities, and infants and toddlers who would be at risk of having substantial developmental delays if early intervention services were not provided to the infants and toddlers.

(b) Assessment of national activities.

(1) In general.

The Secretary shall carry out a national assessment of activities carried out with Federal funds under this title in order —

(A) to determine the effectiveness of this title in achieving the purposes of this title;

(B) to provide timely information to the President, Congress, the States, local educational agencies, and the public on how to implement this title more effectively; and

(C) to provide the President and Congress with information that will be useful in developing legislation to achieve the purposes of this title more effectively.

(2) Scope of assessment.

The national assessment shall assess activities supported under this title, including —

(A) the implementation of programs assisted under this title and the impact of such programs on addressing the developmental needs of, and improving the academic achievement of, children with disabilities to enable the children to reach challenging developmental goals and challenging State academic content standards based on State academic assessments;

(B) the types of programs and services that have demonstrated the greatest likelihood of helping students reach the challenging State academic content standards and developmental goals;

(C) the implementation of the professional development activities assisted under this title and the impact on instruction, student academic achievement, and teacher qualifications to enhance the ability of special education teachers and regular education teachers to improve results for children with disabilities; and

(D) the effectiveness of schools, local educational agencies, States, other recipients of assistance under this title, and the Secretary in achieving the purposes of this title by —

(i) improving the academic achievement of children with disabilities and their performance on regular statewide assessments as compared to nondisabled children, and the performance of children with disabilities on alternate assessments;

(ii) improving the participation of children with disabilities in the general education curriculum;

(iii) improving the transitions of children with disabilities at natural transition points;

(iv) placing and serving children with disabilities, including minority children, in the least restrictive environment appropriate;

(v) preventing children with disabilities, especially children with emotional disturbances and specific learning disabilities, from dropping out of school;

(vi) addressing the reading and literacy needs of children with disabilities;

(vii) reducing the inappropriate overidentification of children, especially minority and limited English proficient children, as having a disability;

(viii) improving the participation of parents of children with disabilities in the education of their children; and

(ix) resolving disagreements between education personnel and parents through alternate dispute resolution activities, including mediation.

(3) Interim and final reports.

The Secretary shall submit to the President and Congress —

(A) an interim report that summarizes the preliminary findings of the assessment not later than 3 years after the date of enactment of the Individuals with Disabilities Education Improvement Act of 2004; and

(B) a final report of the findings of the assessment not later than 5 years after the date of enactment of such Act.

(c) Study on ensuring accountability for students who are held to alternative achievement standards.

The Secretary shall carry out a national study or studies to examine —

(1) the criteria that States use to determine —

(A) eligibility for alternate assessments; and

(B) the number and type of children who take those assessments and are held accountable to alternative achievement standards;

(2) the validity and reliability of alternate assessment instruments and procedures;

(3) the alignment of alternate assessments and alternative achievement standards to State academic content standards in reading, mathematics, and science; and

(4) the use and effectiveness of alternate assessments in appropriately measuring student progress and outcomes specific to individualized instructional need.

(d) Annual report.

The Secretary shall provide an annual report to Congress that —

(1) summarizes the research conducted under part E of the Education Sciences Reform Act of 2002;

(2) analyzes and summarizes the data reported by the States and the Secretary of the Interior under section 618;

(3) summarizes the studies and evaluations conducted under this section and the timeline for their completion;

(4) describes the extent and progress of the assessment of national activities; and

(5) describes the findings and determinations resulting from reviews of State implementation of this title.

(e) Authorized activities.

In carrying out this section, the Secretary may support objective studies, evaluations, and assessments, including studies that —

(1) analyze measurable impact, outcomes, and results achieved by State educational agencies and local educational agencies through their activities to reform policies, procedures, and practices designed to improve educational and transitional services and results for children with disabilities;

(2) analyze State and local needs for professional development, parent training, and other appropriate activities that can reduce the need for disciplinary actions involving children with disabilities;

(3) assess educational and transitional services and results for children with disabilities from minority backgrounds, including —

(A) data on —

(i) the number of minority children who are referred for special education evaluation;

(ii) the number of minority children

who are receiving special education and related services and their educational or other service placement;

(iii) the number of minority children who graduated from secondary programs with a regular diploma in the standard number of years; and

(iv) the number of minority children who drop out of the educational system; and

(B) the performance of children with disabilities from minority backgrounds on State assessments and other performance indicators established for all students;

(4) measure educational and transitional services and results for children with disabilities served under this title, including longitudinal studies that —

(A) examine educational and transitional services and results for children with disabilities who are 3 through 17 years of age and are receiving special education and related services under this title, using a national, representative sample of distinct age cohorts and disability categories; and

(B) examine educational results, transition services, postsecondary placement, and employment status for individuals with disabilities, 18 through 21 years of age, who are receiving or have received special education and related services under this title; and

(5) identify and report on the placement of children with disabilities by disability category.

(f) Study.

The Secretary shall study, and report to Congress regarding, the extent to which States adopt policies described in section 635(c)(1) and on the effects of those policies.

§ 1465. Interim alternative educational settings, behavioral supports, and systemic school interventions.

(a) Program authorized.

The Secretary may award grants, and enter into contracts and cooperative agreements, to support safe learning environments that support academic achievement for all students by —

(1) improving the quality of interim alternative educational settings; and

(2) providing increased behavioral supports and research-based, systemic interventions in schools.

(b) Authorized activities.

In carrying out this section, the Secretary may support activities to —

(1) establish, expand, or increase the scope of behavioral supports and systemic interventions by providing for effective, research-based practices, including —

(A) training for school staff on early identification, prereferral, and referral procedures;

(B) training for administrators, teachers, related services personnel, behavioral specialists, and other school staff in positive behavioral interventions and supports, behavioral intervention planning, and classroom and student management techniques;

(C) joint training for administrators, parents, teachers, related services personnel, behavioral specialists, and other school staff on effective strategies for positive behavioral interventions and behavior management strategies that focus on the prevention of behavior problems;

(D) developing or implementing specific curricula, programs, or interventions aimed at addressing behavioral problems;

(E) stronger linkages between school-based services and community-based resources, such as community mental health and primary care providers; or

(F) using behavioral specialists, related services personnel, and other staff necessary to implement behavioral supports; or

(2) improve interim alternative educational settings by —

(A) improving the training of administrators, teachers, related services personnel, behavioral specialists, and other school staff (including ongoing mentoring of new teachers) in behavioral supports and interventions;

(B) attracting and retaining a high quality, diverse staff;

(C) providing for referral to counseling services;

(D) utilizing research-based interventions, curriculum, and practices;

(E) allowing students to use instructional technology that provides individualized instruction;

(F) ensuring that the services are fully

consistent with the goals of the individual student's IEP;

(G) promoting effective case management and collaboration among parents, teachers, physicians, related services personnel, behavioral specialists, principals, administrators, and other school staff;

(H) promoting interagency coordination and coordinated service delivery among schools, juvenile courts, child welfare agencies, community mental health providers, primary care providers, public recreation agencies, and community-based organizations; or

(I) providing for behavioral specialists to help students transitioning from interim alternative educational settings reintegrate into their regular classrooms.

(c) Definition of eligible entity.

In this section, the term "eligible entity" means —

(1) a local educational agency; or

(2) a consortium consisting of a local educational agency and 1 or more of the following entities:

(A) Another local educational agency.

(B) A community-based organization with a demonstrated record of effectiveness in helping children with disabilities who have behavioral challenges succeed.

(C) An institution of higher education.

(D) A community mental health provider.

(E) An educational service agency.

(d) Applications.

Any eligible entity that wishes to receive a grant, or enter into a contract or cooperative agreement, under this section shall —

(1) submit an application to the Secretary at such time, in such manner, and containing such information as the Secretary may require; and

(2) involve parents of participating students in the design and implementation of the activities funded under this section.

(e) Report and evaluation.

Each eligible entity receiving a grant under this section shall prepare and submit annually to the Secretary a report on the outcomes of the activities assisted under the grant.

§ 1466 Authorization of appropriations.

(a) In general.

There are authorized to be appropriated to carry out this subpart (other than section 662) such sums as may be necessary for each of the fiscal years 2005 through 2010.

(b) Reservation.

From amounts appropriated under subsection (a) for fiscal year 2005, the Secretary shall reserve $1,000,000 to carry out the study authorized in section 664(c). From amounts appropriated under subsection (a) for a succeeding fiscal year, the Secretary may reserve an additional amount to carry out such study if the Secretary determines the additional amount is necessary.

Subpart 3 — Supports To Improve Results for Children With Disabilities

Subpart 3 — Supports To Improve Results for Children With Disabilities

§ 1470. Purposes.

The purposes of this subpart are to ensure that —

(1) children with disabilities and their parents receive training and information designed to assist the children in meeting developmental and functional goals and challenging academic achievement goals, and in preparing to lead productive independent adult lives;

(2) children with disabilities and their parents receive training and information on their rights, responsibilities, and protections under this title, in order to develop the skills necessary to cooperatively and effectively participate in planning and decision making relating

to early intervention, educational, and transitional services;

(3) parents, teachers, administrators, early intervention personnel, related services personnel, and transition personnel receive coordinated and accessible technical assistance and information to assist such personnel in improving early intervention, educational, and transitional services and results for children with disabilities and their families; and

(4) appropriate technology and media are researched, developed, and demonstrated, to improve and implement early intervention, educational, and transitional services and results for children with disabilities and their families.

§ 1471. Parent training and information centers.

(a) Program authorized.

(1) In general.

The Secretary may award grants to, and enter into contracts and cooperative agreements with, parent organizations to support parent training and information centers to carry out activities under this section.

(2) Definition of parent organization.

In this section, the term "parent organization" means a private nonprofit organization (other than an institution of higher education) that —

(A) has a board of directors —

(i) the majority of whom are parents of children with disabilities ages birth through 26;

(ii) that includes —

(I) individuals working in the fields of special education, related services, and early intervention; and

(II) individuals with disabilities; and

(iii) the parent and professional members of which are broadly representative of the population to be served, including low-income parents and parents of limited English proficient children; and

(B) has as its mission serving families of children with disabilities who —

(i) are ages birth through 26; and

(ii) have the full range of disabilities described in section 602(3).

(b) Required activities.

Each parent training and information center that receives assistance under this section shall —

(1) provide training and information that meets the needs of parents of children with disabilities living in the area served by the center, particularly underserved parents and parents of children who may be inappropriately identified, to enable their children with disabilities to —

(A) meet developmental and functional goals, and challenging academic achievement goals that have been established for all children; and

(B) be prepared to lead productive independent adult lives, to the maximum extent possible;

(2) serve the parents of infants, toddlers, and children with the full range of disabilities described in section 602(3);

(3) ensure that the training and information provided meets the needs of low-income parents and parents of limited English proficient children;

(4) assist parents to —

(A) better understand the nature of their children's disabilities and their educational, developmental, and transitional needs;

(B) communicate effectively and work collaboratively with personnel responsible for providing special education, early intervention services, transition services, and related services;

(C) participate in decisionmaking processes and the development of individualized education programs under part B and individualized family service plans under part C;

(D) obtain appropriate information about the range, type, and quality of —

(i) options, programs, services, technologies, practices and interventions based on scientifically based research, to the extent practicable; and

(ii) resources available to assist children with disabilities and their families in school and at home;

(E) understand the provisions of this title for the education of, and the provision of early intervention services to, children with disabilities;

(F) participate in activities at the school level that benefit their children; and

(G) participate in school reform activities;

(5) in States where the State elects to contract with the parent training and information center, contract with State educational agencies to provide, consistent with subparagraphs (B) and (D) of section 615(e)(2), individuals who meet with parents to explain the mediation process to the parents;

(6) assist parents in resolving disputes in the most expeditious and effective way possible, including encouraging the use, and explaining the benefits, of alternative methods of dispute resolution, such as the mediation process described in section 615(e);

(7) assist parents and students with disabilities to understand their rights and responsibilities under this title, including those under section 615(m) upon the student's reaching the age of majority (as appropriate under State law);

(8) assist parents to understand the availability of, and how to effectively use, procedural safeguards under this title, including the resolution session described in section 615(e);

(9) assist parents in understanding, preparing for, and participating in, the process described in section 615(f)(1)(B);

(10) establish cooperative partnerships with community parent resource centers funded under section 672;

(11) network with appropriate clearinghouses, including organizations conducting national dissemination activities under section 663 and the Institute of Education Sciences, and with other national, State, and local organizations and agencies, such as protection and advocacy agencies, that serve parents and families of children with the full range of disabilities described in section 602(3); and

(12) annually report to the Secretary on —

(A) the number and demographics of parents to whom the center provided information and training in the most recently concluded fiscal year;

(B) the effectiveness of strategies used to reach and serve parents, including underserved parents of children with disabilities; and

(C) the number of parents served who have resolved disputes through alternative methods of dispute resolution.

(c) Optional activities.

A parent training and information center that receives assistance under this section may provide information to teachers and other professionals to assist the teachers and professionals in improving results for children with disabilities.

(d) Application requirements.

Each application for assistance under this section shall identify with specificity the special efforts that the parent organization will undertake —

(1) to ensure that the needs for training and information of underserved parents of children with disabilities in the area to be served are effectively met; and

(2) to work with community based organizations, including community based organizations that work with low-income parents and parents of limited English proficient children.

(e) Distribution of funds.

(1) In general.

The Secretary shall —

(A) make not less than 1 award to a parent organization in each State for a parent training and information center that is designated as the statewide parent training and information center; or

(B) in the case of a large State, make awards to multiple parent training and information centers, but only if the centers demonstrate that coordinated services and supports will occur among the multiple centers.

(2) Selection requirement.

The Secretary shall select among applications submitted by parent organizations in a State in a manner that ensures the most effective assistance to parents, including parents in urban and rural areas, in the State.

(f) Quarterly review.

(1) Meetings.

The board of directors of each parent organization that receives an award under this section shall meet not less than once in each calendar quarter to review the activities for which the award was made.

(2) Continuation award.

When a parent organization requests a continuation award under this section, the board of directors shall submit to the Secretary a written review of the parent training and information program conducted by the parent organization during the preceding fiscal year.

§ 1472. Community parent resource centers.

(a) Program authorized.

(1) In general.

The Secretary may award grants to, and enter into contracts and cooperative agreements with, local parent organizations to support community parent resource centers that will help ensure that underserved parents of children with disabilities, including low income parents, parents of limited English proficient children, and parents with disabilities, have the training and information the parents need to enable the parents to participate effectively in helping their children with disabilities —

(A) to meet developmental and functional goals, and challenging academic achievement goals that have been established for all children; and

(B) to be prepared to lead productive independent adult lives, to the maximum extent possible.

(2) Definition of local parent organization.

In this section, the term "local parent organization" means a parent organization, as defined in section 671(a)(2), that —

(A) has a board of directors the majority of whom are parents of children with disabilities ages birth through 26 from the community to be served; and

(B) has as its mission serving parents of children with disabilities who —

(i) are ages birth through 26; and

(ii) have the full range of disabilities described in section 602(3).

(b) Required activities.

Each community parent resource center assisted under this section shall —

(1) provide training and information that meets the training and information needs of parents of children with disabilities proposed to be served by the grant, contract, or cooperative agreement;

(2) carry out the activities required of parent training and information centers under paragraphs (2) through (9) of section 671(b);

(3) establish cooperative partnerships with the parent training and information centers funded under section 671; and

(4) be designed to meet the specific needs of families who experience significant isolation from available sources of information and support.

§ 1473. Technical assistance for parent training and information centers.

(a) Program authorized.

(1) In general.

The Secretary may, directly or through awards to eligible entities, provide technical assistance for developing, assisting, and coordinating parent training and information programs carried out by parent training and information centers receiving assistance under section 671 and community parent resource centers receiving assistance under section 672.

(2) Definition of eligible entity.

In this section, the term "eligible entity" has the meaning given the term in section 661(b).

(b) Authorized activities.

The Secretary may provide technical assistance to a parent training and information center or a community parent resource center under this section in areas such as —

(1) effective coordination of parent training efforts;

(2) dissemination of scientifically based research and information;

(3) promotion of the use of technology, including assistive technology devices and assistive technology services;

(4) reaching underserved populations, including parents of low-income and limited English proficient children with disabilities;

(5) including children with disabilities in general education programs;

(6) facilitation of transitions from —

(A) early intervention services to preschool;

(B) preschool to elementary school;

(C) elementary school to secondary school; and

(D) secondary school to postsecondary environments; and

(7) promotion of alternative methods of dispute resolution, including mediation.

(c) Collaboration with the resource centers.

Each eligible entity receiving an award under subsection (a) shall develop collaborative agreements with the geographically appropriate regional resource center and, as appropriate, the regional educational laboratory supported under section 174 of the Education Sciences Reform Act of 2002, to further parent and professional collaboration.

§ 1474. Technology development, demonstration, and utilization; media services; and instructional materials.

(a) Program authorized.

(1) In general.

The Secretary, on a competitive basis, shall award grants to, and enter into contracts and cooperative agreements with, eligible entities to support activities described in subsections (b) and (c).

(2) Definition of eligible entity.

In this section, the term "eligible entity" has the meaning given the term in section 661(b).

(b) Technology development, demonstration, and use.

(1) In general.

In carrying out this section, the Secretary shall support activities to promote the development, demonstration, and use of technology.

(2) Authorized activities.

The following activities may be carried out under this subsection:

(A) Conducting research on and promoting the demonstration and use of innovative, emerging, and universally designed technologies for children with disabilities, by improving the transfer of technology from research and development to practice.

(B) Supporting research, development, and dissemination of technology with universal design features, so that the technology is accessible to the broadest range of individuals with disabilities without further modification or adaptation.

(C) Demonstrating the use of systems to provide parents and teachers with information and training concerning early diagnosis of, intervention for, and effective teaching strategies for, young children with reading disabilities.

(D) Supporting the use of Internet-based communications for students with cognitive disabilities in order to maximize their academic and functional skills.

(c) Educational media services.

(1) In general.

In carrying out this section, the Secretary shall support —

(A) educational media activities that are designed to be of educational value in the classroom setting to children with disabilities;

(B) providing video description, open captioning, or closed captioning, that is appropriate for use in the classroom setting, of —

(i) television programs;

(ii) videos;

(iii) other materials, including programs and materials associated with new and emerging technologies, such as CDs, DVDs, video streaming, and other forms of multimedia; or

(iv) news (but only until September 30, 2006);

(C) distributing materials described in subparagraphs (A) and (B) through such mechanisms as a loan service; and

(D) providing free educational materials, including textbooks, in accessible media for visually impaired and print disabled students in elementary schools and secondary schools, postsecondary schools, and graduate schools.

(2) Limitation.

The video description, open captioning, or closed captioning described in paragraph (1)(B) shall be provided only when the description or captioning has not been previously provided by the producer or distributor, or has not been fully funded by other sources.

(d) Applications.

(1) In general.

Any eligible entity that wishes to receive a grant, or enter into a contract or cooperative agreement, under subsection (b) or (c) shall submit an application to the Secretary at such time, in such manner, and containing such information as the Secretary may require.

(2) Special rule.

For the purpose of an application for an

award to carry out activities described in subsection (c)(1)(D), such eligible entity shall —

(A) be a national, nonprofit entity with a proven track record of meeting the needs of students with print disabilities through services described in subsection (c)(1)(D);

(B) have the capacity to produce, maintain, and distribute in a timely fashion, up-to-date textbooks in digital audio formats to qualified students; and

(C) have a demonstrated ability to significantly leverage Federal funds through other public and private contributions, as well as through the expansive use of volunteers.

(e) National instructional materials access center.

(1) In general.

The Secretary shall establish and support, through the American Printing House for the Blind, a center to be known as the "National Instructional Materials Access Center" not later than 1 year after the date of enactment of the Individuals with Disabilities Education Improvement Act of 2004.

(2) Duties.The duties of the National Instructional Materials Access Center are the following:

(A) To receive and maintain a catalog of print instructional materials prepared in the National Instructional Materials Accessibility Standard, as established by the Secretary, made available to such center by the textbook publishing industry, State educational agencies, and local educational agencies.

(B) To provide access to print instructional materials, including textbooks, in accessible media, free of charge, to blind or other persons with print disabilities in elementary schools and secondary schools, in accordance with such terms and procedures as the National Instructional Materials Access Center may prescribe.

(C) To develop, adopt and publish procedures to protect against copyright infringement, with respect to the print instructional materials provided under sections 612(a)(23) and 613(a)(6).

(3) Definitions.

In this subsection:

(A) Blind or other persons with print disabilities.

The term "blind or other persons with print disabilities" means children served under this Act and who may qualify in accordance with the Act entitled "An Act to provide books for the adult blind", approved March 3, 1931 (2 U.S.C. 135a; 46 Stat. 1487) to receive books and other publications produced in specialized formats.

(B) National instructional materials accessibility standard.

The term "National Instructional Materials Accessibility Standard" means the standard established by the Secretary to be used in the preparation of electronic files suitable and used solely for efficient conversion into specialized formats.

(C) Print instructional materials.

The term "print instructional materials" means printed textbooks and related printed core materials that are written and published primarily for use in elementary school and secondary school instruction and are required by a State educational agency or local educational agency for use by students in the classroom.

(D) Specialized formats.

The term "specialized formats" has the meaning given the term in section 121(d)(3) of title 17, United States Code.

(4) Applicability.

This subsection shall apply to print instructional materials published after the date on which the final rule establishing the National Instructional Materials Accessibility Standard was published in the Federal Register.

(5) Liability of the secretary.

Nothing in this subsection shall be construed to establish a private right of action against the Secretary for failure to provide instructional materials directly, or for failure by the National Instructional Materials Access Center to perform the duties of such center, or to otherwise authorize a private right of action related to the performance by such center, including through the application of the rights of children and parents established under this Act.

(6) Inapplicability.

Subsections (a) through (d) shall not apply to this subsection.

§ 1475. Authorization of appropriations.

There are authorized to be appropriated to carry out this subpart such sums as may be necessary for each of the fiscal years 2005 through 2010.

Subpart 4 — General Provisions

Subpart 4 — General Provisions

§ 1481. Comprehensive plan for subparts 2 and 3.

(a) Comprehensive plan.

(1) In general.

After receiving input from interested individuals with relevant expertise, the Secretary shall develop and implement a comprehensive plan for activities carried out under subparts 2 and 3 in order to enhance the provision of early intervention services, educational services, related services, and transitional services to children with disabilities under parts B and C. To the extent practicable, the plan shall be coordinated with the plan developed pursuant to section 178(c) of the Education Sciences Reform Act of 2002 and shall include mechanisms to address early intervention, educational, related service and transitional needs identified by State educational agencies in applications submitted for State personnel development grants under subpart 1 and for grants under subparts 2 and 3.

(2) Public comment.

The Secretary shall provide a public comment period of not less than 45 days on the plan.

(3) Distribution of funds.

In implementing the plan, the Secretary shall, to the extent appropriate, ensure that funds awarded under subparts 2 and 3 are used to carry out activities that benefit, directly or indirectly, children with the full range of disabilities and of all ages.

(4) Reports to congress.

The Secretary shall annually report to Congress on the Secretary's activities under subparts 2 and 3, including an initial report not later than 12 months after the date of enactment of the Individuals with Disabilities Education Improvement Act of 2004.

(b) Assistance authorized.

The Secretary is authorized to award grants

to, or enter into contracts or cooperative agreements with, eligible entities to enable the eligible entities to carry out the purposes of such subparts in accordance with the comprehensive plan described in subsection (a).

(c) Special populations.

(1) Application requirement.

In making an award of a grant, contract, or cooperative agreement under subpart 2 or 3, the Secretary shall, as appropriate, require an eligible entity to demonstrate how the eligible entity will address the needs of children with disabilities from minority backgrounds.

(2) Required outreach and technical assistance.

Notwithstanding any other provision of this title, the Secretary shall reserve not less than 2 percent of the total amount of funds appropriated to carry out subparts 2 and 3 for either or both of the following activities:

(A) Providing outreach and technical assistance to historically Black colleges and universities, and to institutions of higher education with minority enrollments of not less than 25 percent, to promote the participation of such colleges, universities, and institutions in activities under this subpart.

(B) Enabling historically Black colleges and universities, and the institutions described in subparagraph (A), to assist other colleges, universities, institutions, and agencies in improving educational and transitional results for children with disabilities, if the historically Black colleges and universities and the institutions of higher education described in subparagraph (A) meet the criteria established by the Secretary under this subpart.

(d) Priorities.

The Secretary, in making an award of a grant, contract, or cooperative agreement under subpart 2 or 3, may, without regard to the rulemaking procedures under section 553 of title 5, United States Code, limit competitions to, or otherwise give priority to —

(1) projects that address 1 or more —

(A) age ranges;

(B) disabilities;

(C) school grades;

(D) types of educational placements or early intervention environments;

(E) types of services;

(F) content areas, such as reading; or

(G) effective strategies for helping children with disabilities learn appropriate behavior in the school and other community based educational settings;

(2) projects that address the needs of children based on the severity or incidence of their disability;

(3) projects that address the needs of —

(A) low achieving students;

(B) underserved populations;

(C) children from low income families;

(D) limited English proficient children;

(E) unserved and underserved areas;

(F) rural or urban areas;

(G) children whose behavior interferes with their learning and socialization;

(H) children with reading difficulties;

(I) children in public charter schools;

(J) children who are gifted and talented; or

(K) children with disabilities served by local educational agencies that receive payments under title VIII of the Elementary and Secondary Education Act of 1965;

(4) projects to reduce inappropriate identification of children as children with disabilities, particularly among minority children;

(5) projects that are carried out in particular areas of the country, to ensure broad geographic coverage;

(6) projects that promote the development and use of technologies with universal design, assistive technology devices, and assistive technology services to maximize children with disabilities' access to and participation in the general education curriculum; and

(7) any activity that is authorized in subpart 2 or 3.

(e) Eligibility for financial assistance.

No State or local educational agency, or other public institution or agency, may receive a grant or enter into a contract or cooperative agreement under subpart 2 or 3 that relates exclusively to programs, projects, and activities pertaining to children aged 3 through 5, inclusive, unless the State is eligible to receive a grant under section 619(b).

§ 1482. Administrative provisions.

(a) Applicant and recipient responsibilities.

(1) Development and assessment of projects.

The Secretary shall require that an applicant for, and a recipient of, a grant, contract, or cooperative agreement for a project under subpart 2 or 3 —

(A) involve individuals with disabilities or parents of individuals with disabilities ages birth through 26 in planning, implementing, and evaluating the project; and

(B) where appropriate, determine whether the project has any potential for replication and adoption by other entities.

(2) Additional responsibilities.

The Secretary may require a recipient of a grant, contract, or cooperative agreement under subpart 2 or 3 to —

(A) share in the cost of the project;

(B) prepare any findings and products from the project in formats that are useful for specific audiences, including parents, administrators, teachers, early intervention personnel, related services personnel, and individuals with disabilities;

(C) disseminate such findings and products; and

(D) collaborate with other such recipients in carrying out subparagraphs (B) and (C).

(b) Application management.

(1) Standing panel.

(A) In general.

The Secretary shall establish and use a standing panel of experts who are qualified, by virtue of their training, expertise, or experience, to evaluate each application under subpart 2 or 3 that requests more than $75,000 per year in Federal financial assistance.

(B) Membership.

The standing panel shall include, at a minimum —

(i) individuals who are representatives of institutions of higher education that plan, develop, and carry out high quality programs of personnel preparation;

(ii) individuals who design and carry out scientifically based research targeted to the improvement of special education programs and services;

(iii) individuals who have recognized experience and knowledge necessary to integrate and apply scientifically based research findings to improve educational and transitional results for children with disabilities;

(iv) individuals who administer programs at the State or local level in which children with disabilities participate;

(v) individuals who prepare parents of children with disabilities to participate in making decisions about the education of their children;

(vi) individuals who establish policies that affect the delivery of services to children with disabilities;

(vii) individuals who are parents of children with disabilities ages birth through 26 who are benefiting, or have benefited, from coordinated research, personnel preparation, and technical assistance; and

(viii) individuals with disabilities.

(C) Term.

No individual shall serve on the standing panel for more than 3 consecutive years.

(2) Peer-review panels for particular competitions.

(A) Composition.

The Secretary shall ensure that each subpanel selected from the standing panel that reviews an application under subpart 2 or 3 includes —

(i) individuals with knowledge and expertise on the issues addressed by the activities described in the application; and

(ii) to the extent practicable, parents of children with disabilities ages birth through 26, individuals with disabilities, and persons from diverse backgrounds.

(B) Federal employment limitation.

A majority of the individuals on each subpanel that reviews an application under subpart 2 or 3 shall be individuals who are not employees of the Federal Government.

(3) Use of discretionary funds for administrative purposes.

(A) Expenses and fees of non-federal panel members.

The Secretary may use funds available under subpart 2 or 3 to pay the expenses and fees of the panel members who are not officers or employees of the Federal Government.

(B) Administrative support.

The Secretary may use not more than 1 percent of the funds appropriated to carry out subpart 2 or 3 to pay non-Federal entities for administrative support related to management of applications submitted under subpart 2 or 3, respectively.

(c) Program evaluation.

The Secretary may use funds made available to carry out subpart 2 or 3 to evaluate activities carried out under subpart 2 or 3, respectively.

(d) Minimum funding required.

(1) In general.

Subject to paragraph (2), the Secretary shall ensure that, for each fiscal year, not less than the following amounts are provided under subparts 2 and 3 to address the following needs:

(A) $12,832,000 to address the educational, related services, transitional, and early intervention needs of children with deaf-blindness.

(B) $4,000,000 to address the postsecondary, vocational, technical, continuing, and adult education needs of individuals with deafness.

(C) $4,000,000 to address the educational, related services, and transitional needs of children with an emotional disturbance and those who are at risk of developing an emotional disturbance.

(2) Ratable reduction.

If the sum of the amount appropriated to carry out subparts 2 and 3, and part E of the Education Sciences Reform Act of 2002 for any fiscal year is less than $130,000,000, the amounts listed in paragraph (1) shall be ratably reduced for the fiscal year..